Patterns of World History

Patterns of World History

Peter von Sivers
University of Utah

Charles A. Desnoyers
La Salle University

George B. Stow
La Salle University

New York   Oxford
OXFORD UNIVERSITY PRESS

Oxford University Press, Inc., publishes works that further Oxford University's
objective of excellence in research, scholarship, and education.

Oxford   New York
Auckland   Cape Town   Dar es Salaam   Hong Kong   Karachi
Kuala Lumpur   Madrid   Melbourne   Mexico City   Nairobi
New Delhi   Shanghai   Taipei   Toronto

With offices in
Argentina   Austria   Brazil   Chile   Czech Republic   France   Greece
Guatemala   Hungary   Italy   Japan   Poland   Portugal   Singapore
South Korea   Switzerland   Thailand   Turkey   Ukraine   Vietnam

For titles covered by Section 112 of the U.S. Higher Education Opportunity Act, please
visit www.oup.com/us/he for the latest information about pricing and alternate formats.

Published by Oxford University Press, Inc.
198 Madison Avenue, New York, New York, 10016
http://www.oup.com

Library of Congress Cataloging-in-Publication Data
Von Sivers, Peter.
 Patterns of world history / Peter von Sivers, Charles A. Desnoyers, George Stow.
  v. cm.
 Includes bibliographical references and index.
 Contents: v. 1. To 1600 — v. 2. Since 1400 — [v. 3.] Since 1750.
  ISBN 978-0-19-533287-2 (combined v.: acid-free paper) — ISBN 978-0-19-533288-9
(v. 1: acid-free paper) — ISBN 978-0-19-985898-9 (v. 2: acid-free paper) — ISBN 978-
0-19-533334-3 (Since 1750: acid-free paper)   1. World history—Textbooks.   I. Desnoyers,
Charles, 1952–   II. Stow, George B.   III. Title.
 D21.V66 2012
 909—dc23

Printing number: 9 8 7 6 5 4 3 2
Printed in the United States of America
on acid-free paper

Patterns of
World History

PART ONE

From Human Origins to Early Agricultural Centers

PREHISTORY–600 BCE

World history is the discipline that tells us what humans had in common as they evolved both materially and mentally from prehistory to the present. When we study these common patterns, we find that the first period of world history (prehistory–600 BCE) can be subdivided into three wide-ranging phases, which we will discuss very broadly in this part opening essay. We will return to these same patterns as they develop—and discover new, more complex patterns—in Chapters 1–5.

The Origins of Modern Humanity

The first phase (6.5 million years ago–8500 BCE) began with the origins and evolution of humanity in Africa. After about 5.5 million years, around 80,000–70,000 BCE, groups of modern humans left Africa and began carrying their civilization of stone tools, shell jewelry, figurines, carvings, rock paintings, and shamanism across the entire world.

Technologically, the modern humans who left Africa had already acquired the skills to make tools from stone, bone, and wood. Mentally, they were also creating artifacts to which they attributed symbolic meaning, such as seashell necklaces and stone surfaces incised with geometric figures. The tools and artifacts of our earliest ancestors were obviously far less sophisticated than ours today. But they nevertheless defined a fully human civilization which spread across the globe—until the last Ice Age (32,000–12,000 years ago) put a stop to much of their interactions. Separated by impenetrable ice or desert barriers and existing without much contact for thousands of years, modern human groups developed their own distinct regional technologies and cultures.

Wherever our forager forebears were, they organized themselves into larger tribal societies with shared initiation rites and shamans who mediated the material and spiritual worlds. Even the stone tools, jewelry, figurines, and rock images displayed remarkable similarities across this region. In short, African-originated material technology and mental culture dominated the world.

**Origins,
Interactions,
and Adaptations**

7 million years ago
Toumaï, Oldest Possibly
Hominin Fossil to Date

15,500 years ago
Earliest Archaeological Evidence of
Humans in the Americas

200,000 years ago
Homo Sapiens, or Modern
Human, Emerges in East
Africa

11500 BCE
End of Last Ice Age

Coniugi Judithae dilectissimae

      —Peter von Sivers

To all my students over the years, who have taught me at least as much as I've taught them; and most of all to my wife, Jacki, beloved in all things, but especially in her infinite patience and fortitude in seeing me through the writing of this book.

      —Charles A. Desnoyers

For Susan and our children, Meredith and Jonathan.

      —George B. Stow

—*I hear and I forget; I see and I remember; I do and I understand*
(Chinese proverb) 我听见我忘记；我看见我记住；我做我了解

Brief Contents

Part 5 The Origins of Modernity
1750–1900   744

Part 6 From Three Modernities to One
1914–Present   972

Contents

PART ONE

From Human Origins to Early Agricultural Centers

Chapter 1
Prehistory–10,000 BCE

Features:

Patterns Up Close:
Symbolic Thinking   26

Concept Map:
Deep History and
Becoming Human   32

The African Origins of Humanity

Chapter 2
11,500–600 BCE

Features:

Patterns Up Close:
Babylonian Law
Codes   48

Concept Map:
The Creation of
Agrarian–Urban
Society   68

Agrarian-Urban Centers of the Middle East and Eastern Mediterranean

PART TWO

The Age of Empires and Visionaries

Chapter 6
600 BCE–600 CE

Chapter 7
550 BCE–600 CE

Chapter 8
600 BCE–600 CE

Chapter 9
722 BCE–618 CE

PART THREE

The Formation of Religious Civilizations

Chapter 10
600–1300 CE

Islamic Civilization and Byzantium

Features:

Patterns Up Close:
Play Toys for Princes—al-Jazari's Ingenious Mechanical Devices 331

Concept Map:
Islamic and Eastern Christian Civilizations Compared 335

Chapter 11
600–1450 CE

Innovation and Adaptation in the Western Christian World

Features:

Patterns Up Close:
The Gothic Cathedral 366

Concept Map:
Innovation and Adaptation in the Shaping of European Civilization 377

Features:

Patterns Up Close:
Human Sacrifice and
Propaganda   510

Concept Map:
Comparing Patterns of
Innovation in the
Americas and Eurasia,
600–1500 CE   515

**PART
FOUR**

Interactions Across the Globe

1450–1750   518

Chapter 16
1450–1650

The Ottoman-Habsburg Struggle and Western European Overseas Expansion   520

Features:

Patterns Up Close:
Shipbuilding   530

Concept Map:
The Ottomans and
the Habsburgs   556

Chapter 23

1750–1914

Industrialization and Its Discontents   786

Chapter 24

1750–1910

The Challenge of Modernity: East Asia   822

Chapter 25
1683–1908

Adaptation and Resistance: The Ottoman and Russian Empires

Features:

Patterns Up Close:
From Constitutional to
Ethnic Nationalism   870

Concept Map:
Adaptation and
Resistance to the Western
Challenge: The
Ottoman and Russian
Empires   894

Chapter 26
1750–1914

The New Imperialism in the Nineteenth Century

Features:

Patterns Up Close:
Military Transformations
and the New
Imperialism   908

Concept Map:
Patterns of Imperialism
and Colonialism:
Continuity and
Change   932

Chapter 27
1790–1917

Creoles and Caudillos: Latin America and the Caribbean in the Nineteenth Century

PART SIX

From Three Modernities to One

Chapter 28
1900–1945

Chapter 29
1945–1962

Chapter 30
1963–1991

The End of the Cold War, Western Social Transformation, and the Developing World   1060

Chapter 31
1991–2011

A Fragile Capitalist-Democratic World Order   1100

Maps

Studying with Maps and Concept Maps

MAPS

World history cannot be fully understood without a clear comprehension of the chronologies and parameters within which different empires, states, and peoples have changed over time. Maps facilitate this understanding by illuminating the significance of time, space, and geography in shaping the patterns of world history.

Projection

A map *projection* portrays all or part of the earth, which is spherical, on a flat surface. All maps, therefore, include some distortion. The projections in *Patterns of World History* show the earth at global, continental, regional, and local scales.

Topography

Many maps in *Patterns of World History* show *relief*—the contours of the land. Topography is an important element in studying maps because the physical terrain has played a critical role in shaping human history.

Scale Bar

Every map in *Patterns of World History* includes a *scale* that shows distances in both miles and kilometers and, in some instances, in feet as well.

Map Key

Maps use symbols to show the location of features and to convey information. Each symbol is explained in the map *key*.

Global Locator

Many of the maps in *Patterns of World History* include *global locators* that show the area being depicted in a larger context.

The Inca Empire ca. 1525 CE

Inca expansion
- To 1438
- Under Pachacuti, 1438–63
- Under Pachacuti and Tupac Yupanqui, 1463–71
- Under Tupac Yupanqui, 1471–93
- Under Huayna Capac, 1493–1525
- Imperial boundary
- Boundary between the four quarters of the empire
- Inca road
- □ Imperial capital
- ○ Major Inca administrative center
- **PERU** Modern-day country

CONCEPT MAPS

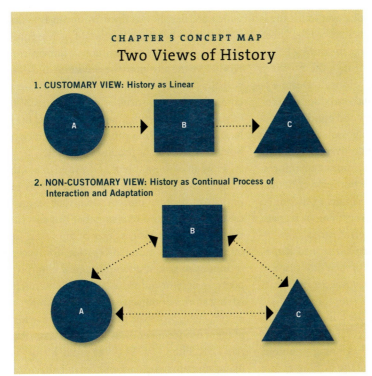

CHAPTER 3 CONCEPT MAP
Two Views of History

1. **CUSTOMARY VIEW: History as Linear**

2. **NON-CUSTOMARY VIEW: History as Continual Process of Interaction and Adaptation**

Ideas and concepts are at the center of *Patterns of World History*. Tackling these ideas and concepts—instead of simply memorizing dates and facts—is what makes history interesting. To help "see" core ideas, *concept maps* at the end of each chapter **use clear, simple, yet provocative graphics to synthesize key take-away points.**

Concept maps **employ simple, universal shapes** to symbolize ideas and processes.

Many concept maps, such as this one, use juxtaposition **to compare and contrast different ways of looking at a topic** or, in the example shown here, to **show change over time**

Clean graphics and clear colors **express big ideas simply and without fuss**—in this case, the changing dynamic between Europe, India, and China between 1500 and 1800.

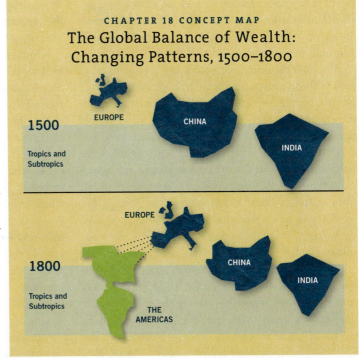

CHAPTER 18 CONCEPT MAP
The Global Balance of Wealth: Changing Patterns, 1500–1800

Preface

It was the most violent earthquake ever to hit the islands in the 150 years during which records had been kept. On March 11, 2011, a quake measuring 8.9 on the 9-point Richter scale ripped through the northern part of the main Japanese island of Honshu. Despite Japan's long experience with earthquakes and some of the most stringent protection measures and building codes on earth, the destruction was on a colossal scale. But the damage itself was almost immediately overshadowed by the destruction wrought by the enormous tsunami generated by the quake, which hit the port city of Sendai and its surrounding vicinity within hours of the initial shocks. A 23-foot wave crushed everything in its path for miles inland and landed even giant cargo ships on the wharves. Oil refinery tanks exploded into flames, children were trapped on the roofs of their schools, and warnings of the tsunami's shockwaves were broadcast around the Pacific Rim.

Amid the vast debris fields and the hundreds of bodies washing up on the beaches, however, the most ominous part of the disaster was only beginning to unfold. The waves in their fury had wrecked the turbine of one nuclear power plant and flooded the entire Fukushima Number 2 nuclear facility to such an extent that the plant had to be shut down—but not before repair crews struggled for weeks to contain the radiation leaks and fallout from a possible meltdown.

The political, economic, social, and even cultural effects of this disaster naturally tell us a great deal about Japan itself; but in some ways they tell us even more about the current state of our modern world. How, for example, has the world come to be globalized to such an extent that an extreme disaster in Japan generates instantaneous international concern? Or, to take things back one historical step, how is it that Japan, once so purposefully isolated from outside influences, has emerged as perhaps the world's most modern society? Indeed, how and why have the vast majority of the world's nations adopted the scientific and industrial systems that have given us the oil refineries and nuclear power plants now so threatened by this epic natural disaster? What are the larger consequences of these systems in possibly altering the balance of life on earth? In another vein, how has the development of electronic "social networking" media—Twitter, YouTube, Facebook, Internet, smart cell phones, and e-mail, all of which are deeply ingrained in our lives—changed the way societies behave in the face of such events? How did human beings cope with natural or human-created disasters before the advent of these systems and devices? And, perhaps the largest question of all, what are the broad currents in human societies over the tens of thousands of years that modern humans have walked the earth that have brought us to our present state in which modernity holds such enormous promise and peril?

How all of these things and a myriad of others came to be is, in a large sense, the theme of this book. One of the hallmarks of our species is that we are historical creatures. We strive to remember the past in innumerable ways for an endless array of purposes: for cultural transmission, for moral instruction, for record keeping, to minimize risk in attempting new enterprises, to improve society or individuals, to tell entertaining or satisfying stories of ourselves. You, your family, your town or city, state, province, or country all have histories, all of them used in an endless variety of ways. As the historian G. R. Elton (1921–1994) put it, history is the only living laboratory we have of human behavior. So how is one to make sense of this bewildering, unending stream of information—especially if, as Elton would have it, the "experiments" in the "laboratory" are running and evaluating themselves?

Our approach in this book is, as the title suggests, to look for patterns in world history. We should say at the outset that we do not mean to select certain categories into which we attempt to stuff the historical events we choose to emphasize; nor do we claim that all world history is reducible to such patterns; nor do we mean to suggest that the nature of the patterns determines the outcome of historical events. We see them instead as broad, flexible, organizational frameworks around which to build the structure of a world history in such a way that the enormous sweep and content of the past can be viewed in a comprehensible narrative, with sound analysis and ample scope for debate and discussion. In this sense, we view them much like the role of armatures in clay sculptures, giving support and structure to the final figure but not necessarily preordaining its ultimate shape.

Take, for example, the role of innovation, in the broadest sense, in world history. The quest for the new and better has always been an animating spirit within the human saga—from the first wheel to the latest smart phone. Certainly, all such innovations, whether they are technological, intellectual, social, political, and so on, are vital to an understanding of human history. Our approach is to highlight the patterns we find in the development of such innovations as a way of taking a step back to make sense of them and the way that they foster change. Take the history of something from our recent past, e-mail, for example: Although electronic technology had advanced to the point in the 1960s where messages could be sent by computer, they could be sent and received only by operators using the same "server," as we would say today. What was needed, therefore, was a new system whereby messages could be sent and received by multiple servers in remote locations. The young engineer Ray Tomlinson (b. 1941), well versed in an early form of computer communication known as "ARPANET," which the American military used to share classified documents, concluded that, given the correct linkage, computers in far-flung locations could "talk" to each other. He worked out the missing piece in the form of the simple "@" sign, which he said "was used to indicate that the user was 'at' some other host rather than being local." Thus, the text message—and the e-mail address format we use today—originated through Tomlinson's interactions with other people and by means of his adapting other technologies available to him; these were then expanded exponentially by millions of others interacting with Tomlinson's breakthrough. This is but one recent example of the unfolding of a pattern of innovation; world history is full of them, and tracing their stories, effects, and implications comprises the heart of this book.

From its origins, human culture grew through interactions and adaptations on all the continents except Antarctica. A voluminous scholarship on all regions of the world has thus been accumulated, which those working in the field have to attempt to master if their explanations and arguments are to sound even remotely persuasive. The sheer volume and complexity of the sources, however, mean that even the knowledge and expertise of the best scholars are going to be incomplete. Moreover, the humility with which all historians must approach their material contains within it the realization that no historical explanation is ever fully satisfactory or final: As a driving force in the historical process, creative human agency moves this process into directions that are never fully predictable.

As we enter the second decade of the twenty-first century, world historians have long since left behind the "West plus the rest" approach that marked the field's early years, together with economic and geographical reductionism, in the search for a new balance between comprehensive cultural and institutional examinations, on the one hand, and those highlighting human agency, on the other. All too often, however, this is reflected in texts that seek broad coverage at the expense of analysis, thus resulting in a kind of "world history-lite." Our aim is therefore to simplify the study of the world—to make it accessible to the student—without making world history itself simplistic.

World History and Patterns of World History

Patterns of World History thus comes to the teaching of world history from the perspective of the relationship between continuity and change. What we advocate in this book is a distinct intellectual framework for this relationship and the role of innovation and historical change through patterns of origins, interactions, and adaptations, or as we like to call it, O-I-A. Each small or large technical or cultural innovation originated in one geographical center or independently in several different centers. As people in the centers interacted with their neighbors, the neighbors adapted to, and in many cases were transformed by, the innovations. By "adaptation" we include the entire spectrum of human responses, ranging from outright rejection to creative borrowing and, at times, forced acceptance.

Small technical innovations often went through the pattern of origin, interaction, and adaptation across the world without arousing much attention, even though they had major consequences. For example, the horse collar, which originated in ninth-century China and allowed for the replacement of oxen with stronger horses, gradually improved the productivity of agriculture in eleventh-century western Europe. More sweeping intellectual–cultural innovations, by contrast, such as the spread of universal religions like Buddhism, Christianity, and Islam and the rise of science, have often had profound consequences—in some cases leading to conflicts lasting centuries—and affect us even today.

Sometimes change was effected by commodities that to us seem rather ordinary. Take sugar, for example:

It originated in southeast Asia and was traded and grown in the Mediterranean, where its cultivation on plantations created the model for expansion into the vast slave system of the Atlantic basin from the fifteenth through the nineteenth centuries, forever altering the histories of four continents. What would our diets look like today without sugar? Its history continues to unfold as we debate its merits and health risks and it supports huge multinational agribusinesses. Or take a more obscure commodity: opium. Opium had been used medicinally for centuries in regions all over the world. But the advent of tobacco traded from the Americas to the Philippines to China created an environment in which the drug would be smoked for the first time. Enterprising rogue British merchants, eager to find a way to crack closed Chinese markets for other goods, began to smuggle it in from India. The market grew, the price went down, addiction spread, and Britain and China ultimately went to war over China's attempts to eliminate the traffic. Here, we have an example of an item generating interactions on a worldwide scale, with impacts on everything from politics to economics, culture, and even the environment. The legacies of the trade still weigh heavily on two of the rising powers of the twenty-first century: China and India. And opium and its derivatives, like morphine and heroin, continue to bring relief and suffering on a colossal scale to hundreds of millions of people.

What, then, do we gain by studying world history through the use of such patterns? First, if we consider innovation to be a driving force of history, it helps to satisfy an intrinsic human curiosity about origins—our own and others. Perhaps more importantly, seeing patterns of various kinds in historical development brings to light connections and linkages among peoples, cultures, and regions—as in the examples—that might not otherwise present themselves.

Second, such patterns can also reveal differences among cultures that other approaches to world history tend to neglect. For example, the differences between the civilizations of the Eastern and Western Hemispheres are generally highlighted in world history texts, but the broad commonalities of human groups creating agriculturally based cities and states in widely separated areas also show deep parallels in their patterns of origins, interactions, and adaptations: Such comparisons are at the center of our approach.

Third, this kind of analysis offers insights into how an individual innovation was subsequently developed and diffused across space and time—that is, the patterns by which the new eventually becomes a necessity in our daily lives. Through all of this we gain a deeper appreciation of the unfolding of global history from its origins in small, isolated areas to the vast networks of global interconnectedness in our present world—that is, how a tsunami in Japan can affect everything from early warning systems in coastal areas of distant countries to fluctuations in international bond and currency markets.

Finally, our use of a broad-based understanding of continuity, change, and innovation allows us to restore culture in all its individual and institutionalized aspects—spiritual, artistic, intellectual, scientific—to its rightful place alongside technology, environment, politics, and socioeconomic conditions. That is, understanding innovation in this way allows this text to help illuminate the full range of human ingenuity over time and space in a comprehensive, evenhanded, and open-ended fashion.

It is widely agreed that world history is more than simply the sum of all national histories. Likewise, *Patterns of World History* is more than an unbroken sequence of dates, battles, rulers, and their activities; and it is more than the study of isolated stories of change over time. Rather, in this textbook we endeavor to present in a clear and engaging way how world history "works." Instead of merely offering a narrative history of the appearance of this or that innovation, we present an analysis of the process by which an innovation in one part of the world is diffused and carried to the rest of the globe. Instead of focusing on the memorization of people, places, and events, we strive to present important facts in context and draw meaningful connections, analyzing whatever patterns we find and drawing conclusions where we can. In short, we seek to examine the interlocking mechanisms and animating forces of world history, without neglecting the human agency behind them.

Patterns of Change and Six Periods of World History

For the convenience of instructors teaching a course over two 15-week semesters, we have limited the book to 31 chapters. For the sake of continuity and to accommodate the many different ways schools divide the midpoint of their world history sequence, Chapters 15–18 overlap in both volumes; in Volume 2, Chapter

15 is given as a "prelude" to Part 4. Those using a trimester system will also find divisions made in convenient places, with Chapter 10 coming at the beginning of Part 3 and Chapter 22 at the beginning of Part 5. Finally, for those schools that offer a modern world history course that begins at approximately 1750, a volume is available that includes only the final two parts of the book.

Similarly, we have attempted to create a text that is adaptable to both chronological and thematic styles of instruction. We divide the history of the world into six major time periods and recognize for each period one or two main patterns of innovation, their spread through interaction, and their adoption by others. Obviously, lesser patterns are identified as well, many of which are of more limited regional interactive and adaptive impact. We wish to stress again that these are broad categories of analysis and that there is nothing reductive or deterministic in our aims or choices. Nevertheless, we believe the patterns we have chosen help to make the historical process more intelligible, providing a series of lenses that can help to focus the otherwise confusing facts and disparate details that comprise world history.

Part 1 (Prehistory–600 BCE): Origins of human civilization—tool making and symbol creating—in Africa as well as the origins of agriculture, urbanism, and state formation in the three agrarian centers of the Middle East, India, and China.

Part 2 (600 BCE–600 CE): Emergence of the axial age thinkers and their visions of a transcendent god or first principle in Eurasia; elevation of these visions to the status of state religions in empires, in the process forming multiethnic and multilinguistic polities.

Part 3 (600–1450): Disintegration of classical empires and formation of religious civilizations in Eurasia, with the emergence of religiously unified regions divided by commonwealths of multiple states.

Part 4 (1450–1750): Rise of new empires; interaction, both hostile and peaceful, among the religious civilizations and new empires across all continents of the world. Origins of the New Science in Europe, based on the use of mathematics for the investigation of nature.

Part 5 (1750–1900): Origins of scientific–industrial "modernity," simultaneous with the emergence of constitutional and ethnic nation-states, in the West (Europe and North America); interaction of the West with Asia and Africa, resulting in complex adaptations, both coerced as well as voluntary, on the part of the latter.

Part 6 (1900–Present): Division of early Western modernity into the three competing visions: communism, fascism, and capitalism. After two horrific world wars and the triumph of nation-state formation across the world, capitalism remains as the last surviving version of modernity. Capitalism is then reinvigorated through the "dot. com revolution," in which increasingly sophisticated software, Internet applications, and electronic communication devices lead to increasing use of social networking media in popularizing both "traditional" religious and cultural ideas and constitutional nationalism in authoritarian states.

Chapter Organization and Structure

Each part of the book addresses the role of change and innovation on a broad scale during a particular time and/ or region, and each chapter contains different levels of exploration to examine the principal features of particular cultural or national areas and how each affects, and is affected by, the patterns of origins, interactions, and adaptations:

- *Geography and the Environment*: As we saw in the opening of this preface, the relationship between human beings and the geography and environment of the places they inhabit is among the most basic factors in understanding human societies. In Japan, for example, earthquakes and tsunamis have always been seen as part of the natural condition of things. Indeed, "tsunami" is a Japanese word with the tragically evocative meaning of "harbor wave." In this chapter segment, therefore, the topics under investigation involve the natural environment of a particular region and the general conditions affecting change and innovation. Climatic conditions, earthquakes, tsunamis, volcanic eruptions, outbreaks of disease, and so forth all have obvious effects on how humans react to the challenge of survival. The initial portions of chapters introducing new regions for study therefore include environmental and geographical overviews, which are revisited and expanded in later chapters as necessary. The larger issues of how decisive the impact of geography on the development of human societies is—as in the commonly asked question "Is geography destiny?"—are also examined here.

- *Political Developments*: In this segment, we ponder such questions as how rulers and their supporters wield political and military power. How do different political traditions develop in different areas? How do states expand, and why? How do different political arrangements attempt to strike a balance between the rulers and the ruled? How and why are political innovations transmitted to other societies? Why do societies accept or reject such innovations from the outside? Are there discernable patterns in the development of kingdoms or empires or nation-states?

- *Economic and Social Developments*: The relationship between economics and the structures and workings of societies has long been regarded as crucial by historians and social scientists. But what, if any, patterns emerge in how these relationships develop and function among different cultures? This segment explores such questions as the following: What role does economics play in the dynamics of change and continuity? What, for example, happens in agrarian societies when merchant classes develop? How does the accumulation of wealth lead to social hierarchy? What forms do these hierarchies take? How do societies formally and informally try to regulate wealth and poverty? How are economic conditions reflected in family life and gender relations? Are there patterns that reflect the varying social positions of men and women that are characteristic of certain economic and social institutions? How are these in turn affected by different cultural practices?

- *Intellectual, Religious, and Cultural Aspects*: Finally, we consider it vital to include an examination dealing in some depth with the way people understood their existence and life during each period. Clearly, intellectual innovation—the generation of new ideas—lies at the heart of the changes we have singled out as pivotal in the patterns of origins, interactions, and adaptations that form the heart of this text. Beyond this, those areas concerned with the search for and construction of meaning—particularly religion, the arts, philosophy, and science—not only reflect shifting perspectives but also, in many cases, play a leading role in determining the course of events within each form of society. For example, the shift to the use of mathematics as a foundation of the "scientific revolution" contributed mightily to the rationalism and empiricism of the Enlightenment—and hence to the development of the modernity that we find ourselves in today. All of these facets of intellectual life are, in turn, manifested in new perspectives and representations in the cultural life of a society.

Features

- **Seeing Patterns/Thinking Through Patterns:** Successful history teachers often employ recursive, even reiterative, techniques in the classroom to help students more clearly perceive patterns. In a similar fashion, "Seeing Patterns" and "Thinking Through Patterns" use a question–discussion format in each chapter to pose several broad questions ("Seeing Patterns") as advance organizers for key themes, which are then matched up with short essays at the end ("Thinking Through Patterns") that examine these same questions in a sophisticated yet student-friendly fashion. Designed to foster discussion, instructors who have class-tested *Patterns of World History* report that "Thinking Through Patterns" also serve as excellent models for writing short essays.

- **Patterns Up Close:** Since students frequently better apprehend macro-level patterns when they see their contours brought into sharper relief, "Patterns Up Close" essays in each chapter highlight a particular innovation that demonstrates origins, interactions, and adaptations in action. Spanning technological, social, political, intellectual, economic, and environmental developments, the "Patterns Up Close" essays combine text, visuals, and graphics to consider everything from the pepper trade to the guillotine to rock and roll.

- **Concept Maps/Putting It All Together:** To further reinforce understanding of the central ideas presented in *Patterns of World History*, each chapter concludes with a "Putting It All Together" section that includes compelling yet simple graphics, called "Concept Maps," that synthesize key take-away points. Carefully designed and field-tested with direct input from world history instructors, Concept Maps can be used to prompt classroom discussion and to help students focus on the big picture. They have been widely praised for the opportunities they offer for visual learning and critical thinking.

- **Voices and Vignettes:** In the end, history is made by people, not anonymous social forces; and while we examine large trends throughout the book, we try never to lose sight of how people in all walks of life originated, interacted, and adapted to the circumstances in which they found themselves or, in some cases, created for themselves. Thus, each chapter includes approximately four "voices"—short excerpts from people from all walks of life whose life experiences shed light on the patterns discussed in each chapter. Additionally, many different people—from contemporary figures like the female Yemeni activist Tawakkol Karman (Chapter 31) to Leo Africanus in the sixteenth century (Chapter 16) and the Chinese sage Mencius in the fourth century BCE (Chapter 9)—are featured in opening vignettes and then woven throughout the chapters to further reinforce the concept of human agency within history.

- **Photo Clusters:** In keeping with the patterns approach of the book, each chapter includes at least one and sometimes as many as three "photo clusters"—assemblages of visual sources, each of which pertains to the same topic, and all sharing a common caption.

- **Marginal Glossary:** To avoid the necessity of having to flip pages back and forth, definitions of words that the reader may not know, as well as definitions of key terms, are set directly in the margin at the point where they are first introduced.

Today, more than ever, students and instructors are confronted by a vast welter of information on every conceivable subject. Beyond the ever-expanding print media, the Internet and the Web have opened hitherto unimaginable amounts of data to us. Despite such unprecedented access, however, all of us are too frequently overwhelmed by this undifferentiated—and all too often indigestible—mass. Nowhere is this more true than in world history, by definition the field within the historical profession with the broadest scope. Therefore, we think that an effort at synthesis—of narrative and analysis structured around a clear, accessible, widely applicable theme—is needed, an effort that seeks to explain critical patterns of the world's past behind the billions of bits of information accessible at the stroke of a key on a computer keyboard. We hope this text, in tracing the lines of transformative ideas and things that left their patterns deeply imprinted into the canvas of world history, will provide such a synthesis.

Additional Learning Resources for *Patterns of World History*

- **Instructor's Resource Manual:** Includes, for each chapter, a detailed chapter outline, suggested lecture topics, learning objectives, map quizzes, geography exercises, classroom activities, "Patterns Up Close" activities, "Seeing Patterns and Making Connections" activities, "Concept Map" exercises, biographical sketches, a correlation guide for the list of assets on the Instructor's Resource DVD, as well as suggested Web resources and digital media files. Also includes, for each chapter, approximately 40 multiple-choice, short-answer, true-or-false, and fill-in-the-blank as well as approximately 10 essay questions.

- **Instructor's Resource DVD:** Includes Power-Point slides and JPEG and PDF files for all the maps and photos in the text, an additional 400 map files from *The Oxford Atlas of World History*, as well as approximately 250 additional PowerPoint-based slides organized by theme and topic. Also includes approximately 1,500 questions that can be customized by the instructor.

- **Sources in Patterns of World History: Volume 1:** *To 1600:* Includes approximately 200 text and visual sources in world history, organized to match the chapter organization of *Patterns of World History*. Each source is accompanied by a headnote and reading questions.

- **Sources in Patterns of World History: Volume 2:** *Since 1400:* Includes approximately 200 text and visual sources in world history, organized by the chapter organization of *Patterns of World History*.

Each source is accompanied by a headnote and reading questions.

- **Mapping Patterns of World History, Volume 1: To 1600:** Includes approximately 50 full-color maps, each accompanied by a brief headnote, as well as Concept Map exercises.
- **Mapping Patterns of World History, Volume 2: Since 1400:** Includes approximately 50 full-color maps, each accompanied by a brief headnote, as well as Concept Map exercises.
- **Companion Web Site (www.oup.com/us/von sivers):** Includes quizzes, flashcards, map exercises, documents, interactive Concept Map exercises, and links to YouTube videos.
- **ClassMate for Patterns of World History:** Includes approximately 800 quizzes (25–30 per chapter) for low- or mid-stakes testing as well as an online gradebook for instructors.
- **E-book for Patterns of World History, Volumes 1 and 2:** An e-book is available for purchase at www.coursesmart.com.

Bundling Options

Patterns of World History can be bundled at a significant discount with any of the titles in the popular Very Short Introductions or Oxford World's Classics series, as well as other titles from the Higher Education division world history catalog (www.oup.com/us/catalog/he). Please contact your OUP representative for details.

Acknowledgments

Throughout the course of writing, revising, and preparing *Patterns of World History* for publication we have benefited from the guidance and professionalism accorded us by all levels of the staff at Oxford University Press. John Challice, vice president and publisher, had faith in the inherent worth of our project from the outset and provided the initial impetus to move forward. In the early stages of the editorial process, Brian Wheel and Frederick Speers provided helpful critiques and advice, saving us from textual infelicities; Meg Botteon later added a final polish. Lauren Aylward carried out the thankless task of assembling the manuscript and did so with generosity and good cheer. Picture researcher Francelle Carapetyan diligently tracked down every photo request despite the sometimes sketchy sources

we provided, Andrew Pachuta copyedited the manuscript with meticulous attention to detail, and Barbara Mathieu steered us through the intricacies of production with the stoicism of a saint.

Most of all, we owe a special debt of gratitude to Charles Cavaliere, our editor. Charles took on the daunting task of directing the literary enterprise at a critical point in the book's career. He pushed this project to its successful completion, accelerated its schedule, and used a combination of flattery and hard-nosed tactics to make sure we stayed the course. His greatest contribution, however, is in the way he refined our original vision for the book with several important adjustments that clarified its latent possibilities. From the maps to the photos to the special features, Charles's high standards and concern for detail are evident on every page.

Developing a book like *Patterns of World History* is an ambitious project, a collaborative venture in which authors and editors benefit from the feedback provided by a team of outside readers and consultants. We gratefully acknowledge the advice that the many reviewers, focus group participants, and class testers (including their students) shared with us along the way. We tried to implement all of the excellent suggestions. Of course, any errors of fact or interpretation that remain are solely our own.

Reviewers

Stephanie Ballenger, Central Washington University

Alan Baumler, Indiana University of Pennsylvania

Robert Blackey, California State University

Robert Bond, San Diego Mesa College

Mauricio Borrero, St. John's University

Linda Bregstein-Scherr, Mercer County Community College

Scott Breuninger, University of South Dakota

Paul Brians, Washington State University

Gayle K. Brunelle, California State University-Fullerton

James De Lorenzi, City University of New York, John Jay College

Jennifer Kolpacoff Deane, University of Minnesota-Morris

Andrew D. Devenney, Grand Valley State University

Francis A. Dutra, University of California, Santa Barbara

Jeffrey Dym, Sacramento State University

Jennifer C. Edwards, Manhattan College

Lisa M. Edwards, University of Massachusetts-Lowell

Charles T. Evans, Northern Virginia Community College

Christopher Ferguson, Auburn University

Scott Fritz, Western New Mexico State University

Arturo Giraldez, University of the Pacific

Candace Gregory-Abbott, California State University-Sacramento

Derek Heng, Ohio State University

Eric Hetherington, New Jersey Institute of Technology

Laura J. Hilton, Muskingum University

Elizabeth J. Houseman, State University of New York-Brockport

Hung-yok Ip, Oregon State University

Geoffrey Jensen, University of Arkansas

Roger E. Kanet, University of Miami

Kelly Kennington, Auburn University

Amelia M. Kiddle, University of Arizona

Frederic Krome, University of Cincinnati-Clermont College

Mark W. Lentz, University of Louisiana, Lafayette

Heather Lucas, Georgia Perimeter College

Susan Mattern, University of Georgia

Susan A. Maurer, Nassau Community College

Jason McCollom, University of Arkansas

Douglas T. McGetchin, Florida Atlantic University

Stephen Morillo, Wabash College

Carolyn Neel, Arkansas Tech University

Kenneth J. Orosz, Buffalo State College

Alice K. Pate, Columbus State University

Patrick M. Patterson, Honolulu Community College

Daniel Pope, University of Oregon

G. David Price, Santa Fe College

Michael Redman, University of Louisville

Leah Renold, Texas State University

Jeremy Rich, Middle Tennessee State University

Jason Ripper, Everett Community College

Chad Ross, East Carolina University

Nana Yaw B. Sapong, Southern Illinois University-Carbondale

Daniel Sarefield, Fitchburg State College

Claire Schen, State University of New York, Buffalo

Robert C. Schwaller, University of North Carolina-Charlotte

George Sochan, Bowie State University

Ramya Sreenivasan, State University of New York, Buffalo

John Stanley, Kutztown University

Vladimir Steffel, Ohio State University

Anthony J. Steinhoff, University of Tennessee-Chattanooga

Micheal Tarver, Arkansas Tech University

Shane Tomashot, Georgia State University

Kate Transchel, California State University-Chico

Melanie Tubbs, Arkansas Tech University

Andrew Wackerfuss, Georgetown University

Evan R. Ward, Brigham Young University

Joseph K. S. Yick, Texas State University-San Marcos

Focus Group Participants
San Diego, California

Robert Bond, San Diego Mesa College

Lisa Marie Edwards, University of Massachusetts-Lowell

Christine Moore, Palomar College

Elizabeth Ann Pollard, San Diego State University

Charles Romney, Whittier College

Tom Sanders, United States Naval Academy

Sharlene Sayegh-Canada, California State University-Long Beach

Micheal Tarver, Arkansas Tech University

Michael G. Vann, California State University-Sacramento

Russellville, Arkansas

Michael Cox, Rich Mountain Community College

Peter Dykema, Arkansas Tech University

Karen Franks, University of the Ozarks

Jan Jenkins, Arkansas Tech University

Alexander Mirkovic, Arkansas Tech University

Carolyn Neel, Arkansas Tech University

Micheal Tarver, Arkansas Tech University

Melanie Tubbs, Arkansas Tech University

Class Testers

Barbara Allen, La Salle University

Robert Bond, San Diego Mesa College

John A. Dempsey, Westfield State University

Candace Gregory-Abbott, California State University-Sacramento

Jeffrey Hamilton, Baylor University

Padhraig Higgins, Mercer County Community College

Lybeth Hodges, Texas Woman's University

John M. Hunt, University of North Florida

Kara Kaufman, Salem State University

Kelly Kennington, Auburn University

Mark Lentz, University of Louisiana, Lafayette

Margaret Markmann, La Salle University

Douglas T. McGetchin, Florida Atlantic University

J. Kent McGaughy, Houston Community College, Northwest

Carolyn Neel, Arkansas Tech University

Patricia O'Neill, Central Oregon Community College

David Peck, Brigham Young University

Walter D. Penrose, San Diego State University

William Pierce, Northern Virginia Community College

G. David Price, Santa Fe College

Michael Redman, University of Louisville

Jason Ripper, Everett Community College

Chad Ross, East Carolina University

Linda Rupert, University of North Carolina-Greensboro

Cliff Stratton, Washington State University-Pullman

Micheal Tarver, Arkansas Tech University

Evan R. Ward, Brigham Young University

Please let us know your experiences with *Patterns of World History* so that we may improve it in future editions. We welcome your comments and suggestions.

Peter von Sivers
pv4910@xmission.com

Charles A. Desnoyers
desnoyer@lasalle.edu

George B. Stow
gbsgeorge@aol.com

Note on Dates and Spellings

In keeping with widespread practice among world historians, we use "BCE" and "CE" to date events and the phrase "years ago" to describe developments from the remote past.

The transliteration of Middle Eastern words has been adjusted as much as possible to the English alphabet. Therefore, long vowels are not emphasized. The consonants specific to Arabic (alif, dhal, ha, sad, dad, ta, za, ayn, ghayn, and qaf) are either not indicated (except for ayn in the middle of words) or rendered with common English letters. A similar procedure is followed for Farsi. Turkish words follow the alphabet reform of 1929, which adds the following letters to the Western alphabet or modifies their pronunciation: c (pronounced "j"), ç(pronounced "tsh"), ğ (not pronounced, lengthening of preceding vowel), ı ("i" without dot, pronunciation close to short e), i/İ ("i" with dot, including in caps), ö (no English equivalent), ş ("sh"), and ü (no English equivalent). The spelling of common Middle Eastern and Islamic terms follows daily press usage (which, however, is not completely uniform). Examples are "al-Qaeda," "Quran," and "sharia."

The system used in rendering the sounds of Mandarin Chinese—the northern Chinese dialect that has become in effect the national spoken language in China and Taiwan—into English in this book is *hanyu pinyin*, usually given as simply *pinyin*. This is the official Romanization system of the People's Republic of China and has also become the standard outside of Taiwan, Republic of China. Most syllables are pronounced as they would be in English, with the exception of the letter *q*, which is given an aspirated "ch" sound; *ch* itself has a less aspirated "ch" sound. *Zh* carries a hard "j" and *j*, a soft, English-style "j." Some syllables also are pronounced—particularly in the regions around Beijing—with a retroflex *r* so that the syllable *shi*, for example, carries a pronunciation closer to "shir." Finally, the letter *r* in the *pinyin* system has no direct English equivalent, but an approximation may be had by combining the sounds of "r" and "j."

Japanese terms have been Romanized according to a modification of the Hepburn system. The letter *g* is always hard; vowels are handled as they are in Italian—*e*, for example, carries a sound like "ay." We have not, however, included diacritical markings to indicate long vowel sounds in *u* or *o*. Where necessary, these have been indicated in the pronunciation guides.

For Korean terms, we have used a variation of the McCune-Reischauer system, which remains the standard Romanization scheme for Korean words used in English academic writing, but eliminated any diacritical markings. Here again, the vowel sounds are pronounced more or less like those of Italian and the consonants, like those of English.

For Vietnamese words, we have used standard renditions based on the modern Quoc Ngu ("national language") system in use in Vietnam today. The system was developed by Jesuit missionaries and is based on the Portuguese alphabet. Once more, we have avoided diacritical marks, and the reader should follow the pronunciation guides for approximations of Vietnamese terms.

Latin American terms (Spanish, Nahua, or Quechua) generally follow local usage, including accents, except where they are Anglicized, per the *Oxford English Dictionary*. Thus, the Spanish-Quechua word "Tiahuanacu" becomes the Anglicized word "Tiwanaku."

We use the terms "Native American" and "Indian" interchangeably to refer to the peoples of the Americas in the pre-Columbian period and "Amerindian" in our coverage of Latin America since independence.

In keeping with widely recognized practice among paleontologists and other scholars of the deep past, we use the term "hominins" in Chapter 1 to emphasize their greater remoteness from apes and proximity to modern humans.

Phonetic spellings often follow the first appearance of a non-English word whose pronunciation may be unclear to the reader. We have followed the rules for capitalization per *The Chicago Manual of Style*.

About the Authors

Peter von Sivers is associate professor of Middle Eastern history at the University of Utah. He has previously taught at UCLA, Northwestern University, the University of Paris VII (Vincennes), and the University of Munich. He has also served as chair, Joint Committee of the Near and Middle East, Social Science Research Council, New York, 1982–1985; editor, *International Journal of Middle East Studies*, 1985–1989; member, Board of Directors, Middle East Studies Association of North America, 1987–1990; and chair, SAT II World History Test Development Committee of the Educational Testing Service, Princeton, NJ, 1991–1994. His publications include *Caliphate, Kingdom, and Decline: The Political Theory of Ibn Khaldun*, several edited books, and three dozen peer-reviewed chapters and articles on Middle Eastern and North African history, as well as world history. He received his Dr. Phil. from the University of Munich.

Charles A. Desnoyers is associate professor of history and director of Asian studies at La Salle University, Philadelphia. He is also past director of the Greater Philadelphia Asian Studies Consortium and president (2011–2012) of the Mid-East Region Association for Asian Studies. His scholarly publications include *A Journey to the East: Li Gui's "A New Account of a Trip Around the Globe"* (University of Michigan Press, 2004) and former coeditor of the World History Association's *Bulletin*.

George B. Stow is professor of history and director of the graduate program in history at La Salle University, Philadelphia. His teaching experience embraces a variety of undergraduate and graduate courses in ancient Greece and Rome, medieval England, and world history; and for excellence in teaching he has been awarded the Lindback Distinguished Teaching Award. Professor Stow is a member of the Medieval Academy of America and a fellow of the Royal Historical Society. He is the recipient of a National Defense Education Act Title IV Fellowship, a Woodrow Wilson Foundation Fellowship, and research grants from the American Philosophical Society and La Salle University. His publications include a critical edition of a fourteenth-century monastic chronicle, *Historia Vitae et Regni Ricardi Secundi* (University of Pennsylvania Press), as well as numerous articles and reviews in scholarly journals including *Speculum*, *The English Historical Review*, the *Journal of Medieval History*, the *American Historical Review*, and several others. He received his PhD from the University of Illinois.

The Origins of Agricultural Centers

The second phase (8500–3300 BCE) began once the global climate normalized, after the "great thaw," when agricultural centers originated in the Middle East, south and east Asia, and the Americas. In the Middle East, foragers resumed their migratory patterns, carrying their languages into regions opened up by receding glaciers and deserts. Between 8500 and 7000 BCE, foragers settled in permanent villages situated below mountain ranges, where seasonal runoff water supported rich forests and meadows. They grew skilled in the collection of plant seeds, which they developed, through selective breeding, into domesticated wheat, barley, rice, millet, and corn. They also captured young animals and domesticated them in their houses for their meat, milk, and hair.

Some of the early hill farmers moved into river valleys and deltas, where they expanded irrigation systems, supporting the rise of cities and kingdoms. The first agrarian-urban centers of the Middle East, India, China, and the Americas originated in irrigated river valleys between 3500 and 2500 BCE. Structured societies emerged in which kings, claiming divine mandates, and administrative and military ruling classes governed craftspeople and farmers.

The Origins of Empires

In the third phase, people outside the Eurasian agrarian centers adapted to agriculture through interaction with the agrarian-urban centers (3300–600 BCE). Steppe peoples, who controlled the mines containing the raw materials for making bronze alloys, used their horses and bronze weapons to migrate to, conquer, or establish new, distant kingdoms. Through their migrations or conquests, the nomadic steppe peoples of Europe and central Asia connected the three agrarian centers of the Middle East, India, and China. A pattern was established whereby the three centers were continuously adapting to each other's technological and cultural achievements, with steppe nomads functioning as their intermediaries.

From 1100 BCE onward the three Asian agrarian centers gradually replaced bronze with a cheaper metal, iron, as the principal material for weapons and tools. As a result, political and military competitiveness among kingdoms escalated dramatically. The first empires—that is, assemblages of conquered kingdoms under a king-of-kings or emperor—appeared, for example, the Neo-Assyrian Empire in the Middle East. Meanwhile, in some regions of the more sparsely populated continents of Africa and the Americas, agrarian centers grew more slowly, from villages to towns and, in a few places, even small kingdoms.

Thinking Like a World Historian

As you read the chapters in this part, consider these questions:

▶ What is the best way to describe the three early phases of world history?

▶ Why and how do we differentiate "modern" humans from earlier ancestors?

▶ What adaptations were necessary to improve agriculture? How did improvements in agriculture affect the development of society?

▶ What adaptations changed the methods of early warfare? How did developments in warfare affect regional interactions among civilizations?

▶ How did regional interactions with agricultural centers give rise to early kingdoms?

9500 BCE
Beginnings of Agriculture in Fertile Crescent

3000 BCE–200 CE
Lapita Cultural Complex in Western Pacific

2500–1700 BCE
Flourishing of Harappan Culture Along Indus River Valley, India

1650 BCE
Hittite Empire; Beginnings of Iron Smelting

ca. 7000 BCE
First Evidence of Rice Cultivation in Yangzi Valley

ca. 2700 BCE
First American City at Caral-Supé in Peru

1766–1122 BCE
Traditional Dates for the Shang Dynasty

750 BCE
City-States in Greece and Ionia

Chapter 1
Prehistory-10,000 BCE

The African Origins of Humanity

SAHARA

AFRICA

Great Rift Valley

☐ Modern rainforest
☐ Ancient rainforest

When Donald Johanson awoke in his tent on the morning of November 30, 1974, he felt that this was the day on which something "terrific" might happen. He and Tom Gray got into their Land Rover and drove for about a half hour to "locality 162" at Hadar in the Afar desert of Ethiopia in northeastern Africa. Once there, the two men walked about, checking the ground carefully for fossils of human predecessors. Members of the expedition had gone over the ground twice before but failed to find anything beyond animal bones.

After 2 hours of fruitless searching, with the temperature now soaring to 110 degrees Fahrenheit, the two took a final glance at a gully the team had

Seeing Patterns

▶ What made it possible for *Homo sapiens* to survive in a dangerous environment? Why is it difficult to imagine life as a prehistoric forager?

▶ Where did humans go when they left Africa, and what kinds of lives did they establish for themselves in the areas where they settled? Which were the most important social patterns that evolved, and how were the humans impacted by the worsening Ice Age?

▶ How did humans express their experience of sharing their life force with animals? How do we know that this experience was important to them?

visited not long before. Amid the heat waves shimmering off of the baking ground, Johanson found himself squinting at something out of place and called out, "That's a bit of a [hominin] arm." With growing excitement, he and Gray began to locate other bones nearby. "An unbelievable, impermissible thought flickered through my mind," Johanson remembered. "Suppose all these fitted together? Could they be parts of a single, extremely primitive skeleton? No such skeleton had ever been found—anywhere." The two raced back to the camp, sharing their excitement with the other scientists and local Afar workers. When night fell and the camp was rocking with joy, a tape recorder was belting out the Beatles' song "Lucy in the Sky with Diamonds"; so fossil Hadar AL 288-1, dated to 3.2 million years ago, became known ever after as "Lucy."

Today, a quarter-century later, Lucy is neither the oldest nor the most significant skeleton ever found. She remains the most famous however. Many of the local people in Afar still think of Lucy as the ancestor of all humankind. Cafés in Ethiopia carry the name "Lossy" in her honor. Her image has appeared on stamps, and her name is a staple in crossword puzzles. For many people Lucy—the petite female buried for 3.2 million years in a

Satellite View Southward Across the African Rift Valley. In the foreground is the southern part of Lake Turkana (much smaller today than 1.6 million years ago). The Rift Valley continues on the right, while the Indian Ocean is on the far left. Mount Kilimanjaro can be seen in the far background to the right. This whole area was at the edge of the rain forest, stretching toward the east (to the right).

sand bank on the edge of a former lake or stream—is all they know about human origins.

This story of Lucy provides our entry into the study of the origins and evolution of humankind. In a slow and ill-understood process of interaction between environment and genetic change, an original lineage of apes in the rain forest split long before Lucy. Like the apes, the new line of hominins, that is, predecessors of humans, continued to live in trees in the rain forest but also adapted to life in the adjacent woodlands and later to the grasslands farther away.

In the course of millions of years of further interactions between cooling climates, more differentiated environments, and genetic changes favoring larger brains, splits among hominin lineages produced early human lines that could fashion at first simple, and later more sophisticated, stone tools. With the help of these first technological breakthroughs, early humans were able to cut meat from animal carcasses. From being vegetarians they turned into *omnivores*, that is, eaters of all types of food. With their more varied diet they could adapt to a host of different environments. Along the way, they also acquired longer legs and bigger brains. The acquisition of all of these attributes eventually enabled one pivotal line of early humans to leave Africa and settle Eurasia.

From among other lineages back in Africa, finally the line of anatomically and intellectually modern humans evolved that fashioned cultural artifacts, such as jewelry, geometrical figures cut into stone, and rock drawings. Once more, humans left Africa and settled the world, not only Eurasia but also Australia and the Americas. For the first time in the history of life on earth, a single species was no longer completely bound to the forces of evolution and its interplay between environment and genetics. These first modern humans had become *cultural beings*, by means of which they had acquired a measure of freedom from evolution: Instead of nature writing their history, they could create their own human history—the world history you are about to enter with this book.

The Origins of Humanity

Becoming human was a long and arduous journey. In the interactions between climate, environment, and genes, every evolutionary step had to build successively on every preceding one so that *anatomically*, as well as *intellectually*, fully evolved modern humans could emerge in Africa about 100,000 years ago. Nothing in this journey was predetermined, but it was also not accidental, given what we know about the genetic architecture of human DNA. It is open-ended, as is the human history which followed the emergence of modern humans. Both evolution and history display recognizable patterns, but these patterns neither were preprogrammed nor occurred by happenstance—they included both predictable and spontaneous occurrences resulting from the constraints and opportunities offered by the interaction of climate, environment, and genes. As we will see throughout this book, however, history equally depends on human agency and its resulting actions. Human prehistory is significant for us today because, thanks to much work done by archaeologists and anthropologists, we are beginning to recognize the complexity of all that had to happen on our evolutionary path to make us fully human: to reach the point where we could become the active creators of our world.

Hominins: No Longer Apes but Not Yet Human

Modern humans are the descendants of long lines of early human-like primates called **hominins**, which in the distant past lived in East Africa. The line of hominins split from that of the apes sometime around 7 million years ago, but the fossil record is still too poor to allow definite conclusions. Equally unclear is the parentage among the twenty or so species of hominins coming thereafter, which *paleoanthropologists* (as the archaeologists and researchers of fossils are called) have discovered so far. The fog begins to lift only around 2 million years ago, with the emergence of *Homo erectus*, the first hominin that left Africa and was adaptable to many new environments in Eurasia. It thus took some 4 million years of dead ends as well as environmentally more adaptable forerunners of humans to pave the way for the human species to emerge.

Hominins: Forerunners of humans after genetically splitting from the chimpanzees.

Many historians view the *pre*history of humans as a field belonging to archaeologists and anthropologists. For these historians, *history* begins only with the rise of the first cities in which scribes created written documents. This view is unfortunate since historians routinely take the findings of scholars in other disciplines, such as archaeology, anthropology, climatology, geography, medicine, and sociology, into consideration when they write histories on topics after about 3500 BCE. Since written records, furthermore, are highly unreliable documents—subject to manipulation by human hand subsequent to their original production—historians

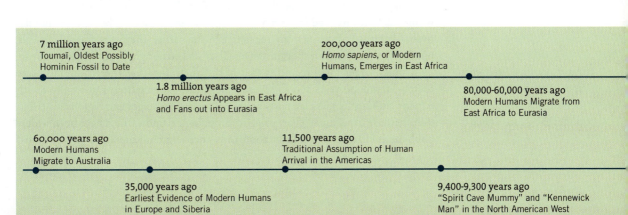

7 million years ago
Toumaï, Oldest Possibly
Hominin Fossil to Date

1.8 million years ago
Homo erectus Appears in East Africa
and Fans out into Eurasia

200,000 years ago
Homo sapiens, or Modern
Humans, Emerges in East Africa

80,000-60,000 years ago
Modern Humans Migrate from
East Africa to Eurasia

60,000 years ago
Modern Humans
Migrate to Australia

35,000 years ago
Earliest Evidence of Modern Humans
in Europe and Siberia

11,500 years ago
Traditional Assumption of Human
Arrival in the Americas

9,400-9,300 years ago
"Spirit Cave Mummy" and "Kennewick
Man" in the North American West

Human Origins. Donald Johanson with Lucy.

regularly take recourse in the more reliable findings of other disciplines wherever they can. Indeed, in the twenty-first century historians with broad visions have pleaded persuasively for eliminating the artificial distinction between prehistory and history. They speak instead—as the medieval cultural historian Daniel Lord Smail does—of the "deep history" of humanity.

Who Are Our Ancestors?   The specific environmental and genetic interactions favorable for the split between the ape and hominin lines are poorly understood. We know that changes in the climate between warm and cool cycles played a part, which were reflected in the African rain forest advancing and retreating. At present, the find of the 6–7 million-year-old skull of Toumaï, discovered in 2001 in Chad, then still covered by rain forest, is the only specimen close to the ape–hominin split. But whether Toumaï is from before or after this split is still hotly debated among scholars. Without additional bones, the solitary Toumaï skull remains tantalizingly ambiguous.

In 2000, a Kenyan–British–French team unearthed a variety of bones of five individuals belonging to the species *Orrorin tugenensis*, dating to 6 million years ago in what was then the edge of a rain forest in western Kenya that had shrunk during a cooling period. Scholars consider the orrorins to be perhaps the first hominins because of their anatomical differences from apes and dental characteristics similar to modern humans. Unfortunately, no skull bones were found to allow any conclusions about brain size. Orrorins lived in trees, where they walked upright on branches with relatively short legs and swung from tree to tree by their arms. They were also able to walk upright on the ground for short distances. They walked upright but only marginally so.

A much larger fossil record is that of the **australopiths**. These hominins date to 3.9–3.0 million years ago and were widespread, ranging from Ethiopia to South Africa (see Map 1.1). We are fairly certain of these date ranges and regional distributions because of a couple of key paleoanthropological finds, which have been widely publicized: (1) a set of fossilized footprints uncovered in Kenya and (2) an almost

Australopiths: Prehuman species that existed before those classed under the genus *Homo*.

MAP **1.1** Early Human Origins to 3 Million Years Ago.

complete skeleton found in Ethiopia, which has become known as "Lucy" (see the vignette at the beginning of the chapter). The footprints reveal how much better the australopiths were as bipedalists but they were still also very much at home in the rain forest. Paleoanthropologists are agreed that the orrorins and australopiths were not related but disagree on everything else, especially on their role as human ancestors. At present, there are many branches but no trunk yet of the hominin tree.

Bipedalism and Environmental Adaptability

Improved **bipedalism** became a key evolutionary advantage to hominins. Walking on two feet is more energy-efficient than knuckle-walking and frees the arms to do something else. Being upright exposes a smaller body surface to the sun, a factor important for venturing out from the rain forest into the woodlands and savanna, that is, the more open forests and the grassland with tree stands. Partaking of the plant resources available in these three natural environments made hominins gradually more flexible than apes, which were limited to their rain forest habitat. On the one hand, the rain forest abounded with fruits and nuts; but on the other hand, the woodlands offered grasses and seeds. From the fossil record, it appears that by around 2.4 million years ago,

Bipedalism: The first human characteristic of hominins, specifically, the ability to walk for short periods or distances on their hind legs, although knuckle-walking and tree climbing continued to be practiced.

Bipedalism

"I believe that our ancestors, pre-Lucy, became upright in the protection of the forests, a familiar environment in which they faced fewer dangers. Then, armed with a new type of locomotion, bipedalism, they were pre-adapted to move onto the savannahs and expand their territory. Once we moved into more open environments, we brought a whole package of advantages with us. Our hands were free to make and use tools, we could walk long distances to collect and carry food (and in doing so benefit from enhanced thermoregulation to prevent overheating), we could look over tall grass if we needed to, and so on."

—Donald Johanson, "How Bipedalism Arose," *Nova*, http://www.pbs.org/wgbh/nova/evolution/what-evidence-suggests.html.

hominins were able to move about in the two environments of the rain forest and savanna.

While all of our hominin ancestors shared basic traits, their lines were about to become much more varied, primarily because of the new and different environments with which each group interacted. In some, brain sizes did not increase much; others reached the volume of half of modern human brains. Indeed, early hominin adaptations to the changing world would later give rise to diverse human cultures; and, as we will see, such different human cultures would, in turn, have a profound effect on our human evolution. This pattern of early human adaptation and cultural diversity is of great importance to historical study because it gives the earliest indications of how humans differentiated themselves—and how they became who we are today.

Oldowan: The earliest stone-carving technique, which consisted of splitting a stone into two, thereby producing sharp edges on both fragments. See also **Acheulian** and **Levallois**.

Paleolithic: Old Stone Age, 2.5 million–11,500 years ago.

On the Threshold of Humanity As they moved more and more easily around in their forest and savanna habitats, about 2.4 million years ago some hominins made another major evolutionary step forward. Improved brainpower enabled one of the new lines, that of *Homo habilis* ("the handy human"), to make simple stone tools: sharp-edged scrapers, called **Oldowan** tools (after the Oldovai region in the Kenyan Rift Valley), with which meat could be removed from the carcasses of animals freshly killed by beasts of prey. *H. habilis* broadened the diet from vegetarian foods to meat. Early humans became omnivores, partaking of the full range of nutrition available in nature.

The making of stone tools marks the beginning of the **Paleolithic**, or Old Stone Age, in prehistory, which lasted until about 11,500 years ago. During this time early humans, and later fully evolved humans, made increasingly varied and refined stone tools. Another cool, dry spell about 1.8 million years ago made mobility even more important. Scientists identify the early humans who adapted to the greater demands of mobility with long legs and comparatively shorter arms as *H. erectus* (Latin, "upright human"; in Africa called *Homo ergaster* ["workman"]). These humans no longer lived in trees, were fully stabilized on their feet, and became regular long-distance walkers adapted to the demands of rain forest, savanna, and now also steppe habitats. They mastered the control of fire, apparently collecting it from lightning-caused wildfires, first in Africa, possibly 1.5–1.4 million years ago, as announced in 2004 on the basis of finds in South Africa and Kenya. Small groups of perhaps two dozen early humans, so scholars assume, huddled around fires in what must have been early camps at cave entrances or rock overhangs. *H. erectus* brain size was about 75 percent of that of the fully evolved *H. sapiens*, and thus, the lines of early humans had become quite distinct from hominins.

The increased mobility and brain volume had their consequences. Soon after 1.8 million years ago, groups of the *H. erectus* line walked across the Suez land passage in the northeast that connected the African continent with southwest Asia.

Once in southwest Asia, these groups quickly scattered in all directions (Map 1.2). The dating of fossils from the country of Georgia in the Caucasus and Java in southeast Asia, as well as stone tools in India, to 1.8–1.6 million years ago demonstrates the relative speed of this dispersion and adaptation to new environments.

Early humans are also well documented in east Asia. The oldest fossil bones, found in 2001 at Nuangjou [New-ahng-JOE] in northern China and in 2010 at Denisova Cave in southern Siberia, point to the presence of early humans in east Asia as early as 1.66 and 1 million years ago, respectively. Fossil finds in Korea and Japan indicate the arrival of *H. erectus* at the southeastern end of Asia around 500,000 years ago. In Spain, the 2007 discovery of a tooth from *H. erectus* documents the presence of this early human from 1.2 million years onward in Europe, the northernmost region it

MAP **1.2** **Human Migration Out of Africa.**

Early Human Toolkit. The preferred materials for Acheulian axes were obsidian, chert, or flint. The stone scraper on the right shows the Levallois technique in which the edges of a stone are trimmed and flaked. Harpoons like the ones shown at the top right were made from reindeer antlers. On the left is a spear thrower from France that dates to about 12,000 BCE. Spear throwers gave hunters the ability to propel their missiles with surer aim. Note the horse-shaped handle.

Acheulian: A technique which consisted of flaking a hard piece of rock (preferably flint, chert, or obsidian) on both sides into a triangle-shaped hand axe, with cutting edges, a hand-held side, and a point.

apparently was able to adapt to. Thus, we have ample documentation that this line of early humans settled in a considerable variety of habitats in Africa and Eurasia.

In addition to being an accomplished walker, *H. erectus* was the creator of vastly improved stone tools. Instead of the simple Oldowan stones with sharp edges, around 1.8–1.6 million years ago, *H. erectus* created the new **Acheulian** [ah-SHOO-lee-yan] stone technology. (This technology appeared first in East Africa, although it was named after St. Acheul, a suburb of Amiens in northern France where finds were made in the nineteenth century.) Acheulian tools were oval or pear-shaped hand axes cut with the help of hammer stones from larger cores, or they were one or more flakes split from cores. When the edges of these hand axes became dull, *H. erectus* split further, smaller flakes away to resharpen the edges. A simple visual examination of Oldowan and Acheulian tools reveals how much the manual skills of early humans advanced in about a million years.

H. erectus showed considerable staying power, thriving in most places until around 350,000 years ago and on the island of Java in southeast Asia until perhaps 27,000 years ago. Strong disagreements exist among scholars whether this early human type spawned intellectually more developed successors, died out, or was absorbed by interbreeding with successor lineages arriving from outside Asia. Therefore, it is unclear how these early humans in Africa and Asia are related to each other.

Flores "Hobbits"   The discovery of *Homo floresiensis* is a startling case of *H. erectus'* longevity. In 2003, an Australian–Indonesian archaeological team unearthed a skull and assorted bones belonging to 13 early humans in a cave on the Indonesian island of Flores. These tiny humans measured only three feet high and had brains no larger than those of chimpanzees or australopiths. Archaeologists dated them to ca. 38,000–12,000 years ago and identified them as descendants of *H. erectus*.

Popularly known as "hobbits"—after the tiny characters in J. R. R. Tolkien's *Lord of the Rings*—these miniature people pose intriguing questions. Were *H. erectus'* descendants capable of crossing the ocean? What caused them to shrink? Did they die out after 12,000 years ago? Hobbits were evidently early builders of rafts since Flores was an island from at least 1 million years ago. Some of their tools were pre-Acheulian, but others were more advanced than the ones of *H. erectus* since the hobbits hunted, using spears and spear points. Isolation might have contributed to their shrinking, like it did to the elephants, also documented through fossils. Other species, such as reptiles, however, developed gigantism; and it is far from clear why the Flores animals and early humans mutated into one or the other genetic variation.

That hobbits continued beyond 12,000 years ago is possible, in view of reports by Indonesian islanders telling visiting Portuguese and Dutch mariners in the 1500s and 1600s about small people in remote rain-forest caves on the slopes of the island's volcano. Gerd van den Bergh, a paleontologist researching fossil plants on the island in the 1990s, reported that he heard stories from islanders about small people with rudimentary language abilities whom they called "the grandmother who eats anything" (*ebu gogo*).

The specific fossils found in 2003 were from hobbits who died in a volcanic eruption, and it is, of course, possible that hobbits in remote parts of the island not affected by the volcano survived. With no immediate answers in sight and the debate concerning these strange early humans continuing, world historians will have to wait for further research to produce more definitive results.

> ## Hobbits
>
> "The ebu gogo were long-haired, potbellied cave dwellers with protruding ears, and long arms and fingers, and they walked with a slightly awkward gait and would climb small trees. The villagers said that the last ebu gogo was seen in the 19th century, when the Dutch settled in central Flores."
>
> —Martin I. Sereno, "Language Origins without the Semantic Urge." *Cognitive Science Online* 3, no. 1 (2005): 1–12.

Human Adaptations: From Africa to Eurasia and Australia

H. ergaster, the African version of *H. erectus*, was the ancestor of *H. sapiens* ("the wise human"), the species of modern humans. Scholars are far from agreed, however, as to how many intermediate lineages can be assumed to have existed between then and now. When *H. sapiens* arrived, however, two characteristics distinguished this human being from its less evolved forerunners: (1) rapidly developing *technical skills* and (2) *cultural creativity*. These two characteristics represent a fundamental transformation of humans that placed them on a path toward liberation from the determinism of nature. The timing and extent of this liberation is still debated by scientists, but world historians generally assume that when *H. sapiens* created a recognizable culture in Africa, it became at least partially the free creator of a new direction in natural history.

The African Origins of Human Culture

H. sapiens appeared around 280,000 years ago in East Africa. (The Latin term "*Homo sapiens*," meaning "wise man," will be used interchangeably with "modern human" in the remainder of this chapter.) The oldest specimen discovered so far is a fossil discovered in 1967 in Ethiopia and dated in 2005 to 195,000 years ago. The archaeological record documenting modern humans is still spotty, but the 17 African sites containing bone and skull remnants of *H. sapiens* as well as a half-dozen sites with human artifacts allow for at least one important conclusion: *H. sapiens*, in a process of gradual development in Africa, became physically and intellectually fully human, endowed with the basics of culture. While humans continued to remain subject to the natural interaction between environment and genes, requiring constant updates in adaptation, culture gave them the freedom to accept and reject—a completely new dimension largely independent from nature.

Livelihood   Early humans, as discussed earlier, did not hunt; they scavenged meat from carcasses with the help of stone scrapers. Early spears made of sharpened sticks for hunting animals are some 400,000 years old, belonging to the elusive post-*H. erectus* lineages. Really effective spears had to await *H. sapiens* as the creator of the much refined new stone-working technique, the **Levallois** [le-val-WAH], derived from the name of a suburb of Paris, France, where in the nineteenth century the first spear points were found. With this technique, a craftsperson chipped off small flakes from the edges of a prepared stone core and then hammered a larger flake—flat on the bottom, domed on the top, and sharpened by the small flakes around the edge—from the center of the core, leaving a more or less deep indentation in the spent core. These center flakes could be as large as hand axes and meat cutters or as small as spear points. The appearance of spear points and increasingly large numbers of animal bones in the archaeological sites was an indicator that *H. sapiens* was emerging as an efficient hunter of animals. The hunt, requiring strength as well as endurance, tended to be the province of males—and remained a prestige occupation for much of human history. But it provided no more than a supplement to *H. sapiens*' nutrition.

The combination of the male-dominated hunt with the communal gathering of vegetal foods defines what is called "forager society." Foraging, sometimes called "hunting and gathering," was the dominant pattern of human history for the longest period, several hundred thousand years. It is also the most spottily documented period, requiring for its understanding a combination of archaeology with the anthropological insights gained from observation of surviving foraging societies in the nineteenth and twentieth centuries. Thus, the descriptions of such societies we offer are unavoidably somewhat speculative.

H. sapiens continued to live in sheltered places provided by cave entrances and rock overhangs, the source of the popular stereotype of the "caveman." But there were also campsites with hut-like shelters made from branches. Clothing consisted of skins and furs acquired through hunting and slung around the body. Hearths, in which *H. sapiens* could build fire at will, served as places for the roasting of meat or the provision of warmth during cold nights. Anthropological studies suggest that extended families congregated around the hearths to groom each other or give each other comfort and companionship. In the vicinity of the campsite, a dozen or so dispersed families were in touch with one another, forming a clan, among which sexual partners were chosen.

Around 120,000 years ago, food gathering and preparation in the camps appear to have become considerably more varied. *H. sapiens* began to include shellfish collected on the beach in their diets. A little later, humans began catching fish on the coasts and in the lakes and rivers of Africa, using tools carved from bone, such as hooks and barbed points mounted on spears. With the help of grindstones, men and women pulverized hard seeds for consumption or storage. Plaster-lined storage pits

Levallois: A stone technique where stone workers first shaped a hard rock into a cylinder or cone.

appeared in the camps, as did separate refuse dumps. And as the settlements became more numerous, trade networks sprang up, providing toolmakers with obsidian mined as far as 200 miles away. *Obsidian* is a glass-like hard rock found near volcanoes and therefore relatively rare, so it was much sought after. We may also see this initial period of trade as marking the beginning of thousands of years of increasing human *interaction*—a process vital to the transferring of cultural and technological innovation among human groups.

Gender Relations   A central element in human culture is the relationship between men and women. Unfortunately, archaeology is unable to reveal anything decisive about this relationship in Paleolithic forager society. Obviously, the roles of men and women were less specialized among foragers than in agrarian–urban society: Males and females spent most of their time collecting and preparing vegetal foods together, and the male-dominated hunt was a supplemental occupation. But how much these occupations furthered a male–female balance or allowed for one of the two genders to become dominant is not easy to determine.

Scholars in the nineteenth century, such as the Swiss anthropologist Johann Jakob Bachofen (1815–1887), speculated that the earliest humans were at first communal, with men and women with no steady partners, followed by a human society in which women were dominant and introduced matriarchal customs. As anthropologists in the twentieth century researched modern forager societies in Australia, Africa, and the Americas more thoroughly, they realized that matriarchal and patriarchal groups were more or less evenly distributed and that gender relations in an even larger number of groups were indeterminate or conflictual. The assumption of an original matriarchy went out of fashion.

With the rise of the feminist movement in the 1970s, scholars revived the idea of an early female-centered society. Marija Gimbutas (1921–1994), a Lithuania-born archaeologist, published several books on what she assumed was a "matristic" society in Russia prior to 4500 BCE. This society, so she asserted, was egalitarian, peaceful, and goddess-oriented. It was by this time agrarian, but by implication matristic culture was assumed to have had deep roots in the preceding forager stage of human life. In her view, aggressive, war-like male dominance came about only with the rise of horseback-riding herders from the southern Russian steppes who were bent on conquest. Other anthropologists, instead, assumed that male dominance began at about the same time that warring kingdoms emerged in the Middle East. War captives became slaves and elaborate hierarchies emerged in which women, in turn, found themselves relegated to inferior positions. However the origins of patriarchy are explained, there is little controversy over its connection with agrarian–urban life. What came before, however, and was prevalent during the Paleolithic forager period of human history is impossible to determine one way or the other. While patriarchy was part and parcel of the agrarian–urban pattern, what we know of the preceding forager society so far does not indicate a prevalence of matriarchy. In African Paleolithic forager society, females and males differed in their functions but not so decisively that the one or the other could easily become dominant.

Creation of Symbols   Parallel to the development of foraging, hunting, and beginning gender roles, there were also first signs of a development of *H. sapiens'* mental life. Activity in the camps expanded from the craftsmanship of tools to that of

The Virgin Goddess

"The Goddess of the Paleolithic and Neolithic is parthenogenetic, creating life out of herself. She is the primeval, self-fertilizing 'Virgin Goddess' who has survived in numerous culture forms to the present day. The Christian Virgin Mary is a demoted version of this original deity. If the role of the father was understood in ancient times, there is no archeological evidence that this was given any importance. From the artifacts it seems clear that woman's ability to give birth and nourish children from her body was deemed sacred and revered as the ultimate metaphor for the divine Creator."

—from Marija Gumbutas, *The Civilization of the Goddess.* New York: Harper Collins, 1991, p. 223.

nonutilitarian objects. This expansion was perhaps the decisive step with which *H. sapiens* left the worlds of animals, hominins, and early humans behind and became truly modern. Around 135,000 years ago, humans in what is today Morocco in northwest Africa took seashells and fragments of ostrich eggshell, perforated them, and strung them on leather strips as pendants and necklaces. The significance of this step cannot be overemphasized. By themselves, seashells and ostrich eggshells are natural objects of no particular distinction, but as jewelry they have the unique meaning of beauty for their wearer: In the form of jewelry they are *symbols*, which are clearly distinct from tools. Jewelry is more than the material it is made of; its beauty gives it its distinction and makes it a symbol of whatever human emotions it is designed to express. *H. sapiens* was the first and only being that did not think only in the concrete, practical terms of tool-making but also in *abstract* symbolic terms by using something to express something else, such as jewelry for feelings. This vital transformation may be seen as the root of the human capacity to conceptualize and, with it, the foundation of art, religion, philosophy, science, and all other intellectual pursuits.

Archaeological examples for the emergence of abstract symbolic thinking in Africa are not yet very numerous. But taken together they powerfully suggest an intellectual modernity emerging to match the anatomical modernity of African *H. sapiens*. From about 90,000 years ago, for example, we begin to see grave sites, an indicator of reflection on the significance of life, death, ancestral dignity, and generational continuity. Humans added jewelry as the preferred grave gift, suggesting the contemplation of an afterlife or spirit world. Another example of symbolic thought may be seen in a rock formation inside a cave, discovered in Botswana in 2006, which had been carved and shaped into the head of a python, complete with scales, an eye, and a mouth, some 77,000 years ago. With this example, we come close to encountering one of the most enduring (religious) symbols, the snake or dragon, signifying water and its power, as well as rejuvenation (shedding and renewing skin). Even more recognizably abstract are the early symbols appearing on a 70,000-year-old small piece of ochre excavated in 1991 from Blombos Cave and on 60,000-year-old ostrich shells excavated in 1996 from Diepkloof Rock Shelter, both in South Africa. They display geometrically arranged engravings, the significance of which is unknown.

Finally, a small stone plaque from Apollo 11 Cave in Namibia discovered in 1969–1972, containing the image of a rhinoceros, is of particular importance for the appreciation of the African origin of *H. sapiens*. The plaque is estimated to be 23,000 years old but, according to some scholars, could date to as many as 59,000 years ago, if measured by the age of strata found on top of the plaque. If the latter age is true, this would be humanity's oldest pictorial representation found to date.

Collectively, these examples can be taken as a confirmation of *H. sapiens* not only as a technically versatile toolmaker but also as the one animal capable of creating symbols that signify something other than the materials from which they were made. Much of what we will see later in this book as the wonderfully varied cultures of the world will ultimately spring from these sources.

Apollo 11 Cave, Namibia. A rhinoceros depicted on a stone slab, from about 59,000–23,000 years ago, making it contemporary with Australian and European rock art. Together with the Blombos Cave ochre, this artwork is evidence of early humans' ability to create symbols.

Migration from Africa   Once the *H. sapiens* lineage was fully equipped with practical skills and the foundations of culture, it was adaptable to almost any environment. Genetic research suggests that the first groups of modern humans left Africa between 80,000 and 60,000 years ago. Many scholars assume that these first groups left Africa for Asia by crossing the straits between Ethiopia and Yemen and between Oman and Iran. The members of this group, so it is thought, drifted like beachcombers along the coast, making their way to India, Malaysia, and Indonesia perhaps about 77,000 years ago. Some of their descendants seemed to have just kept on moving, reaching China about 70,000 years ago, sailing to Australia 60,000 years ago, and crossing from Korea over a then existing land bridge to Japan about 30,000 years ago. Eventually, modern humans from south Asia migrated northwestward to Europe and northeastward to Siberia, where they arrived around 35,000 years ago. The Siberian groups then made their way to Alaska in North America 16,000 years ago, completing the journey around the world in 70,000 years (see Map 1.2).

Migration from South Asia to Australia

The migration of human groups from south Asia to Australia deserves a closer look within the context of foraging society as the basic mode of human social organization. Australia was the only large world region where foraging remained dominant until the modern scientific–industrial age and, therefore, could be studied almost until today. During the geological beginnings of the earth, Australia was part of a vast land mass, called "Sahul." It comprised what is now New Guinea, Australia, and Tasmania and was connected to Antarctica and the Americas. About 100 million years ago Sahul separated and began moving slowly toward Asia. It never connected with Eurasia however, and deep sea channels always kept Sahul separated from the north.

Geography and Migration   About 4–5 million years ago, Sahul had moved far enough northward to encourage the emergence of a variety of geographical zones. In the north (today's New Guinea and far northern Australia), rain forest covered the landscape. In the east (today's eastern Australia), various mixtures of forest, bush, and grassland evolved. The center and most of the west of the continent (today's central and western Australia) developed a mixture of deserts, lakes, steppes, and grassland. The south (today's southeastern Australia and Tasmania) became temperate, with an almost South African or Mediterranean climate. Small pockets of mountain vegetation came into existence only in what are today the central parts of eastern Australia and southern Tasmania. Sahul displayed geological formations and climate zones corresponding to those of Africa south of the Sahara. These geographical environments would become the homes to modern humans, who came originally from Africa and had adapted to life in south Asia.

During an ice age 70,000–60,000 years ago, south Asia and most of the northern islands of Indonesia were connected by land bridges. Farther south, island chains where one could travel by boat without losing sight of land encouraged the idea of further travel. Inevitably, the mariners reached a point where land was no longer visible on the horizon. About 60,000 years ago, the distance from the island of Timor to Australia was 65 miles. Scholars have speculated that smoke rising from lightning-produced brush fires in the south could have suggested to some enterprising mariners that there was land beyond the horizon. Whatever motivated them to take to the sea, they evidently succeeded in crossing it.

Settlement of the Continent   As *H. sapiens* groups arrived on the Australian continent, presumably in the northwest, they fanned out eastward and southward, slowly populating it. The descendants of the original settlers became known in our own time as **Aboriginals**. Bringing their African and south Asian foraging customs with them, the settlers hunted the Australian animals and gathered what was edible of its plant life. Australia's animals, as they are today, were very different from those in Africa and south Asia: On account of the continent's early separation from South America as well as its relatively small size, its game animals were largely marsupials, carrying their newborns in protective pouches during the weaning phase. Unlike in Africa and Eurasia, with their profusion of dangerous animals, there were few marsupial predator species to threaten these first humans. The Aboriginal peoples gradually hunted the large marsupial species to extinction, and by about 16,000 years ago, only small animals were left to hunt.

As elsewhere in foraging societies, men were the hunters. They used spears and *spear throwers*—short sticks with a curve or hook on the end to extend the length of the thrower's arm and give additional power to the flight of the spear—but not bows and arrows, which were introduced in Eurasia and Africa after 60,000 years ago, too late for these settlers to take with them on their journey to Australia. In southern Australia, eel was a major protein staple. Men trapped this fish in rivers and human-made river basins, using nets made of bulrush fiber. In Tasmania the main meat source was the seal. Once the large marsupials were gone, hunting became a highly diversified set of activities for the Aborigines.

Women, and secondarily men, were responsible for gathering vegetal foods. The basic staples were wild millet and rice. The main fruits and vegetables were the solanum [sow-LAH-noom], a tomato-like fruit rich in vitamin C; the yam daisy, a sweet, milky tuber with yellow, daisy-like flowers; and the quandong [KWAN-dong] fruit, also abounding in vitamin C, which was collected from trees and then dried. Women used grindstones to prepare hard seeds and vegetables, such as pine nuts, flax, and acacia seeds, as well as bracken (large fern) and bindweed (family of vines). Yam, taro, and banana, shared with New Guinea until 8,000 years ago when the land bridge was submerged by the sea, thrived only in the northeast. Eucalyptus, a native of Australia found nearly everywhere, served for firewood in the stone-built hearths. People also used fire as a hunting tool and to promote revegetation. Controlled grass and brush fires drove animals in the desired direction where strategically positioned hunting parties could slaughter them. Forest fires were used to synchronize more closely the production and harvest of nuts and fruits on trees, thereby increasing the efficiency of harvests. Over time, the Aborigines developed a keen sense of how to exploit nature efficiently, while consciously setting about preserving it.

Australia was less rich in grasses suitable for grain collection than southwest Asia. For example, Australia had only two types of grain; in southwest Asia, there were around 40 types of grain. The continent did not have the rich concentrations of grains found in the Fertile Crescent of the Middle East, where cereal grain agriculture originated (see Chapter 2). Thus, it should come as no surprise that foraging remained the dominant mode of subsistence, even if people stayed in their

Aboriginals: The original settlers of Australia, who arrived some 60,000 years before European settlers at the end of the eighteenth century CE.

camps for long periods of time before moving them. Only in the south, where eel trapping was the main form of livelihood, did permanent villages appear, similar in many ways to their counterparts in late forager Africa, Europe, North America, and Japan. Aborigines thus remained closely adapted to the basic, relatively modest patterns of forager livelihood until the first English settlers arrived at the end of the eighteenth century CE.

Social Structures and Cultural Expressions   Since modern-day Aborigines have remained faithful to their traditional forms of life, a great deal about their social structures and organization is known. Australian anthropologists have collected a wealth of data, observing forager culture as it existed in the nineteenth and early twentieth centuries. Unfortunately, today foraging is disappearing before our eyes at an accelerated rate. But the existing literature contains much that is rooted in the distant past, even though, of course, the Aborigines changed in the course of world history just like humans on all other continents.

According to this literature, in the traditional Aboriginal society of the nineteenth century or earlier marriages were *monogamous*, that is, they consisted of a husband and wife. Men who not only were successful hunters but also became wealthy through trade could acquire additional wives. Families that camped together and assisted each other in hunting and food gathering formed *clans*, which were units in which all families considered themselves to be descendants of a common ancestor. Groups of clans formed a tribe of between 500 and 1,500 members. Generally, tribes were too large to camp or move about together. They were, rather, loose associations of clans living miles apart but from which they selected their marriage partners. Marriages took place between members of one group of clans and members of another group of clans. Tribes met collectively once a year at one of the sacred places of their land to celebrate shared rituals and ceremonies.

The Dreamtime   Despite this loose social organization, tribal members considered themselves trustees of clearly marked parcels of ancestral land. Typical markers were identifiable features of the landscape, such as rocks, rivers, or trees. Myths and *taboos*—things or practices that were forbidden—surrounded both land and markers. Tribespeople venerated them through rituals, ceremonies, dances, and recounting the myths. Respected elders, who commanded a particularly high degree of regard, presided over the rituals. An elder was venerated when he had a large number of sons, family alliances, and valuable artifacts acquired through trade. The most esteemed elders possessed a deep knowledge of the tribe's past in the **Dreamtime**, the name given to the ancient period in which the tribe's past was embedded.

More specifically, the Dreamtime consisted of the stories, customs, and laws which defined the tribe in its original, perfect state at the time of creation. Elders acquired access to this time through trance states, requiring many years of initiation, training, and practice. Their knowledge of the Dreamtime, it was believed, gave them access to creation's hidden powers, enabling them to read other people's minds, recognize their secret concerns, and heal illnesses. Elders, however, did not possess a monopoly over knowledge of nature's hidden powers. All members of the clan, it was assumed, had access to the tribe's sacred heritage and could use it, to varying degrees, to practice magic, experiment with sorcery, or cast spells.

Dreamtime: In the Australian Dreamtime, the shaman constructs an imaginary reality of the tribe's origins and roots, going back to the imaginary time when the world was created and the creator devised all customs, rituals, and myths.

Aboriginal elders never were able to wield political power through armed force within their own tribes. Since there was no agriculture and, therefore, no agricultural surplus and since trade did not evolve beyond the exchange of obsidian, tools, and weapons, elders could not acquire enough wealth to pay fighters. Only on the continent's northern coast was there a modest trade in local pearls for knives, pottery, cloth, sails, and canoes from Timor; but it too did not make for the rise of powerful chiefdoms. Aboriginal society thus remained "stateless" in the sense of possessing no administrative institutions. Elders in positions of authority used persuasion, not force, to keep the peace.

Australian Rock Art   How much the Dreamtime involved rock paintings, existing in large numbers in Australia, is unfortunately not known. Rock art is the one form of cultural expression where historical change in the otherwise slow-paced Aboriginal culture is evident: Contemporary Aborigines are unable to interpret the meaning of early rock paintings, which archaeologists were able to date. There are many more recent rock paintings, but they are very different in content and style from the earlier ones. Changing climatic conditions leading to different migration patterns are presumably responsible for modern Aboriginals losing their familiarity with the rich culture of ancient Australian rock art.

Archaeologists estimate that examples of early art number in the tens of thousands. A majority of these are located in remote places in the countryside—called the "outback"—of the northwest and have yet to be recorded. There is controversy over the exact age of these images however. Scholars using radiocarbon dating have determined that a red ochre "crayon" found in a rock shelter in northern Australia probably dates to shortly after modern humans arrived about 60,000 years ago. A rock slab painted with red ochre, which fell on a human occupation site in northwestern Australia, dates to 38,000 years ago. It is recognized as the first example of rock art outside Africa, predating that in Europe by some 3,000 years.

Australian Shaman. A Shaman in a trance from a rock carving 40,000–20,000 years ago. This "Bradshaw" figure is usually interpreted as showing movements and communication with the spirits of animate nature.

The best-known Australian rock paintings are the so-called Bradshaw paintings in the Kimberley Region in northwest Australia, which probably date to a period of 30,000–20,000 years ago. Between two ice ages, this region had a fairly even year-round climate with sufficient rainfall to support foraging and, hence, the presence of human groups practicing rock art. At present, scholars work with a classification of the Bradshaw paintings into two major stylistic periods, beginning with (1) indentations, grooves, and animals and followed by (2) elongated human figures with tassels or sashes, fruits and vegetables resembling human figures, as well as clothes pin figures and stick figures.

The two periods are very difficult to date since so far none of the places where they have been found have yielded any material that could be reliably carbon-dated. Only one Bradshaw painting has been dated so far as at least 17,500 years old, thanks to a wasp nest on top of it that contained sand grains suitable for thermoluminescent dating. The painting could be much older, of course, depending on when the wasp settled on it. Scholars generally assume that the proliferation of Bradshaws was roughly contemporary with the efflorescence of European rock art.

The striking parallelism between Australian and European rock art demonstrates that humans did not have to interact to express themselves culturally in similar ways. Similar forager patterns could evolve without mutual contact. It is possible, of course, that symbolic expression of meaning and significance through the painting of animals on rock surfaces existed already before the first groups of *H. sapiens* left Africa, although at present this depends on the definite dating of the Apollo 11 site's rhinoceros. But the fact that a great proliferation of paintings occurred simultaneously in Australia and Europe at a later stage of forager culture leads to the conclusion that none of the human groups migrating away from Africa was privileged over any other. This cultural parity among foragers needs to be kept in mind as we turn to African *H. sapiens* migrating to Europe.

Migration from South Asia to Europe

There was a gap of at least 30,000 years between groups of modern humans leaving Africa (80,000–60,000 years ago) and migrating to Europe (35,000 years ago). Scholars assume that these humans settled first in south Asia before their descendants fanned out to Europe as well as east Asia. Little is known about the migratory path these descendants chose as they walked across the Middle East to Europe. It is generally assumed that they moved from the Black Sea up the valley of the Danube River since the oldest archaeological findings stem from sites near the upper reaches of the river (see Map 1.2).

Two Human Species   When *H. sapiens* arrived in Europe around 35,000 years ago, this region was already settled by another human species, that of the **Neanderthals** [Nay-AN-der-tall, after a valley in northwest Germany where the first specimen was found in the nineteenth century]. This species is assumed to have descended from successors of *H. erectus* in Africa half a million years ago, although the exact line of descent is unclear. Neanderthals are the best-documented Paleolithic fossil humans in Europe and western Asia, with over 600 finds. The fossils range in age from 230,000 to 24,000 years ago and are widely distributed geographically between western Europe, the Altai Mountains in eastern Asia, and the Middle East. *H. sapiens*—or **Cro-Magnon** [Crow-man-YON, after the name of the cave in southwestern France where, in the nineteenth century, European *H. sapiens* bones were first found]—was clearly an intruder in an inhabited, if still sparsely settled, human landscape.

Neanderthals were smaller and more heavily boned than modern humans. In their forager livelihood, the two species were very similar, although Neanderthals buried their dead without the gifts of jewelry and, later, sprinklings of red ochre, a symbol of lifeblood, which modern humans included. The stone and bone toolkits of the two were also alike, but Neanderthals did not leave any artifacts behind, such as carvings, figurines, or paintings carrying symbolic meaning. Paleoanthropologists assume that Neanderthals were able to talk in a rudimentary way but did not yet possess the throat structures of *H. sapiens*. The two species overlapped for about 11,000 years. In 2010, the Swedish-born paleogeneticist Svante Pääbo and his Leipzig, Germany, team completed an analysis of the Neanderthal DNA (through bones from Croatian Neanderthals, from which they first removed microbial contamination)

Mythical Imagery. *Left* Small (two inch) ivory mammoth figurine, 35,000 years old, found 2007 in Vogelherd Cave, southwestern Germany. This figurine is the oldest to date among European artifacts and can be viewed as an example of *Homo sapiens'* curiosity about the surrounding animal world. *Right* Two "lionmen," one apparently dancing, described by the excavator, archaeologist Nicholas Conard, as a "depiction of mythical imagery."

and found that there was interbreeding. Thus, the Neanderthals were absorbed into the modern human genome.

Figurines and Rock Paintings   *H. sapiens'* cultural creativity, which had burst forth in Africa, continued after the migration into Europe. There are some 700 open-air sites with small figurines and caves with rock paintings and engravings. Presently, the oldest known artifact is a small ivory figurine of a mammoth, found in 2007 in Vogelherd Cave in southwestern Germany and dating to the time of *H. sapiens'* arrival in western Europe 35,000 years ago. Two slightly younger, equally small ivory statuettes of humans with lion heads, one of them apparently dancing, were also found in southwestern Germany. The mammoth legs have unpolished holes, leading to the speculation that this artifact was sown to garments. Other figurines might have been worn as pendants.

Several thousand years later, an entire class of female figurines, some thin and delicate and others bulging and coarse, called "Venuses," appeared all over western Europe. These figurines were made of stone or bone and one of them, unearthed in the Czech Republic, was formed of fired clay ca. 26,000 years ago. The creation of the first ceramic pieces was thus a Paleolithic invention, even though the regular production of pottery appeared some 17,000 years later in agrarian society. All figurines were small, fitting comfortably into the palm of a hand, and therefore easily transportable. The bulging Venuses have been interpreted as fertility goddesses, indicating an early matriarchy; but this interpretation is questionable, given the great variety of female and male figurines of the Venus type. Other scholars view these figurines as dolls for children in the camps or as representatives of relatives or ancestors in camp rituals. Hard proof, however, is still outstanding.

The great majority of rock paintings in Europe show animals, alone or in herds, at rest or in motion, either chasing or fleeing other beasts, or locked in conflict with each other. The oldest paintings to date are of animals that humans were familiar with in nature, such as reindeer, horses, cattle, bulls, bison, mammoths, rhinoceroses, lions, and owls. Dating to 30,000 years ago, they were discovered in 1994 in Chauvet [show-VAY] Cave in southern France. One intriguing image in this cave depicts the head and torso of a bison and the legs of a human. A similarly intriguing image from 13,000 years ago, found in the Trois-Frères [Troah-FRAIR] cave in southwestern France, is "the sorcerer," an upright being with human hands and legs but also equipped with reindeer ears and antlers, a bird face, a fox tail, and a phallus. These hybrid beings are rare, however, in comparison to the many types of large mammals on which the painters concentrated.

Hunting scenes and depictions of humans are also rare. The best known, at Lascaux [Las-COE] in southwestern France and dated to 17,000 years ago, is that of an injured bull charging its hunter, who is depicted as a stick figure with a phallus. By contrast, a set of 15,000-year-old engravings on slabs used to cover the floor of La Marche [La-MARSH] Cave in west-central France shows expertly executed, realistic sketches of young and old males and females, dressed in boots, robes, and hats. These sketches could easily be modern cartoons: They demonstrate that there is little that separates contemporary humans from those who lived 15,000 years ago.

Modern chemical analyses have shown that the rock painters knew how to grind and mix minerals to make different colors. They mixed charcoal and manganese dioxide to outline their paintings in black. To add color, they used other ground minerals, such as hematite for red, mixed in various, finely graded proportions. Painters carefully sketched the images before filling them in with paint and shading the figures. They often used protrusions in the rock walls to enhance three-dimensionality and augment the technique of shading. In many images, frontal and lateral views are combined. One image depicts a bison with six legs, evidently simulating its swift motion. Thus, the thematic diversity of images had its complement in technical versatility.

The main places with rock art are halls and domes deep inside the often miles-long caves. The complete darkness was illuminated with torches and grease-filled

Venus Figurine. Excavated at Dolni Vestonice, Czech Republic, in 1986, 25,000 years old. This is the oldest known figurine made of fired clay. Many more broken figurines were found near the kiln. They perhaps represented family members during rituals and, as bearers of their spirits, had to be destroyed at the end of the rituals so as to end their influence.

Chauvet Cave, France. This 33,000 year-old image shows a human, perhaps injured, under attack by a bison.

Animism. The meaning of this cave drawing from Trois-Frères, France—known as the "Sorcerer"—continues to baffle. The figure combines traits of a deer, an owl, a fox, and a human. It could be a hunter stalking prey. The morphing of animal and human qualities characterizes much Ice Age art.

bowls with wicks. Flutes, made of swan bones, and stalagmites, tapped as percussion instruments, testify to the presence not only of painters but also of musicians. To judge by the extant footprints, teenagers as well as adults, men as well as women assembled inside the caves. Modern scholars, such as the South African archaeologist J. David Lewis-Williams, speculate that the caves were places for rituals, perhaps even shamanic assemblies, in which elders, in trance, entered a spiritual world shared with all living beings. Hints of the human mind reflecting on such a shared spiritual world can perhaps be found in the hybrid lionman, bisonman, and sorcerer figurines and rock images mentioned previously. The Australian Bradshaw figures, apparently showing swaying shamans, may similarly point in the direction of such a reflection. It is possible to recognize in the Paleolithic artifacts the roots of *animism*, that is, the idea of a shared life force in the world, which later became prominent in Africa and the Americas. (see "Patterns Up Close" on pp. 26–27)

The Ice Age Crisis and Human Migration to the Americas

In the course of its natural history, the earth has traversed many ice ages. Modern humans experienced two. The first one, 70,000–60,000 years ago, created land bridges that enabled humans to traverse much of the Indonesian archipelago on foot and travel the rest of the distance by boat to Australia. This ice age was comparatively mild and short-lived, in contrast to the last ice age of the world's history, 25,000–13,500 years ago, which severely tested the flora and fauna on all continents. Humans, although suffering through it, exploited it for one major achievement: their migration from Siberia to the Americas.

The Ice Age

Toward its end, the Paleolithic era turned into one of the climatically most inhospitable periods in world history. Large parts of the world either descended into a deep freeze or became bone dry. The northern zone of Eurasia, from England to Siberia, changed into a desolate wasteland, partially covered with gigantic ice sheets. The central zone, from southern France to Mongolia, consisted of tundra (frozen earth) in the winter and semiarid steppe in the summer. The southern zone, from Iberia (today's Spain and Portugal) to southern China, was temperate but semidry, with grasslands and pockets of woodlands. In Africa and Australia, the rain forest was reduced to a few areas in central Africa and the northern tip of Australia, leaving the rest of the continents largely exposed to drought. The northern Sahara and southern Kalahari in Africa as well as the interior of Australia were giant deserts, cutting deep into what were once rich savannas and rain forest. Life for modern humans in Eurasia, Africa, and Australia during this ice age was an arduous struggle for daily survival (see Map 1.3).

Difficult Living Conditions   Signs of stress and even desperation testify to the harsh conditions of the Ice Age. For example, human bone remnants from a number of ancient campsites in modern-day Russia display signs of malnutrition and disease. Because of the difficult conditions, humans abandoned the northern European and Russian plains, which remained uninhabited for 15 millennia. Central European settlements were hemmed in between Scandinavian and Alpine glaciers. In an important development, humans domesticated the dog sometime around 15,000 years ago, probably to help in hunting increasingly rare large animals (mammoth, rhinoceros, and giant deer), which were also suffering under environmental stress. Unfortunately, overhunting became an additional factor in the drastic reduction in the numbers of large animals. Ultimately, most of these huge beasts died out around 6,000–4,000 years ago, forcing humans to go after smaller game.

Although life was not easy, *H. sapiens* possessed the technological and mental resources to survive even the worst climate conditions. The modern humans had at their disposal a great variety of implements for catching fish, snaring birds, and hunting animals, including harpoons, fishhooks, and darts made of bone, fishnets, and bird traps. Boomerangs, invented independently and in parallel with their development in Australia, were also used for hunting larger fowl. Wooden handles attached to large stone axe heads increased the efficiency of cutting meat or wood. In a situation of increasingly disappearing large animals, *H. sapiens* became efficient at hunting larger numbers of small animals.

Human mobility increased substantially. Canoes took the form of dugouts or were constructed of bone and wood frames covered with skins. As a result of innovations like the canoe, the range for trading expanded. Baltic *amber* (fossilized

MAP 1.3 The Ice Age.

Symbolic Thinking

As demonstrated in this chapter, the crucial element that separates *Homo sapiens* from earlier hominins is evidence of what might be called "modern behavior," exemplified by the capacity for symbolic thinking. But what is symbolic thinking? A useful definition offered by archaeologists is the ability to conceptualize images by thinking abstractly; that is, to create symbols out of everyday materials. This unique ability in turn lies at the very foundation of the creation of art, language, and communication. The question is, however, When—and where—did symbolic thinking first appear in the long historical development of humankind?

Until very recently, it was commonplace to point to the stunning cave paintings of southwestern Europe as proof-positive of the earliest expressions of symbolic

The Human Mind. *Top* Ochre from Blombos Cave, 1991, South Africa. *Bottom* Ostrich shell fragments from Diepkloof Rock Shelter, discovered in 1996, South Africa. The ochre and ostrich shell fragments are 70,000 and 60,000 years old, respectively. The incisions are the earliest evidence of geometrical conceptualizations beginning to form in the minds of modern humans, representing culture in the sense of religion, the arts, philosophy, and the sciences.

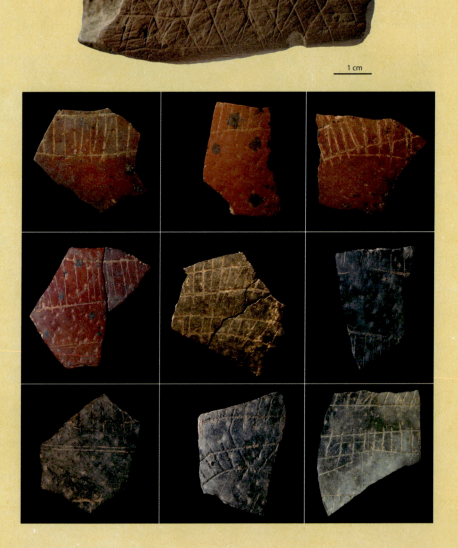

1 cm

thinking. Routinely referred to as a "cultural explosion," it was thought these images represented a sudden creative outburst produced by modern *H. sapiens*, who arrived in Europe around 35,000 years ago. The paintings of Chauvet, for example, dated to 30,000 years ago, depict a wide range of animals including deer, bison, horses, lions, and more exotic creatures like rhinoceroses, leopards, and even an owl. The caves at Lascaux (17,000 years ago) and Altamira (16,500 years ago) present similar images. Taken together, these magnificent cave murals present superb examples of representational art produced by Stone Age artists utilizing sophisticated tools, paints, and techniques such as shadowing and coloration to depict realistic images.

Archaeological discoveries during the 1990s, however, have pushed back the origins of symbolic thinking among *H. sapiens* to a much earlier age—and to a non-European origin. The stunning artifact found at Blombos Cave in southern Africa, dated at around 70,000 years ago, clearly indicates the ability of early *H. sapiens* artists to express thoughts in abstract symbols. According to the Blombos excavation director, Christopher Henshilwood, these intricate designs "could have been interpreted by those people as having meaning that would have been understood by others"; that is, they represent a form of visual communication. Although scholars have debated whether these engravings in fact present clear evidence of symbolic thinking—could they represent mere "doodling" instead?—even more recent discoveries in southern Africa (1999) offer more convincing proof of deliberate attempts at figurative artistic endeavor. At Diepkloof Rock Shelter a team of researchers has dug up several 60,000-year-old, fragmented pieces of carefully inscribed ostrich eggs featuring abstract designs similar to those discovered at Blombos Cave, supporting the notion that these were not mere doodles and that prehistoric African *H. sapiens* possessed a form of symbolic expression.

Taken together, the discoveries at Blombos and Diepkloof Rock suggest that early expressions of symbolic thinking originated in southern Africa 40,000–30,000 years earlier than in Europe. They also attest not only to a quantum leap in the intellectual development of *H. sapiens* over earlier hominins but also to the development of "modern behavior" in *H. sapiens* before this human being migrated out of Africa into Eurasia. In the final analysis, the foundations for the more detailed representational and technically developed cave paintings of France, Spain, and Australia derived from concepts originally conceived in the minds of early African *H. sapiens*.

Questions

- Are there any similarities between the earliest evidence to date of symbolic thinking in Africa and the much later cave paintings in Europe? If so, what does this say about early human culture and society?

- Will it ever be possible to fully comprehend how early humans imagined their world?

resin from fir trees, prized for making jewelry) was found 600 miles away in southern Europe, and Mediterranean shells were carried by traders to the Ukraine, 800 miles away in the northeast. Modern humans dressed themselves warmly, wearing hooded fur coats stitched together with bone needles, using thin leather strips, as evidenced by figurines discovered in Siberia. An imprint left on kiln-fired clay, found in the Czech Republic, indicates that humans also began to weave woolen cloth on looms, another historical first. No doubt, *H. sapiens* groups were decimated by the impact of the Ice Age, but groups of hearty survivors were still tenaciously hanging on when the world warmed up again and became wetter around 14,500 years ago.

The Beringia Land Bridge   During the coldest time in the Ice Age around 19,000 years ago, sea levels dropped by 450 feet, increasing the land mass of the continents by about 100 miles in all directions and exposing land bridges connecting Indonesia to Malaysia, Japan to Korea, and Asia to North America. The land connecting Asia and North America between Siberia and Alaska was Beringia, a large land mass of some half a million square miles.

Most of Siberia was covered with ice, but southern Beringia and Alaska consisted of ice-free tundra. Mammoths and other large, hairy herd animals roamed the land. Whether there was ever a human presence on Beringia is unknown since today the land is submerged by the sea. But there are traces of human presence in both eastern Siberia and Alaska, dating from the Ice Age thawing stage some 16,500–12,500 years ago. In eastern Siberia these traces include the foundations of small houses, hearths, flaked stone points for spear shafts, and a pit containing amber beads and stone pendants for jewelry. In Alaska, archaeologists have found stone tools and spear points. Around 11,500 BCE the warming climate caused the sea to start rising again, covering Beringia with water and cutting off the humans in Alaska from those in Siberia. But by that time, *H. sapiens*, adapting to the changing world of the Ice Age, had successfully migrated from Eurasia to the Americas.

Migration to the Americas

During the coldest time in the Ice Age, a gigantic ice sheet covered North America, preventing the humans in Alaska from migrating south. Around 11,500 BCE, however, it is thought that the glacier split in what is today the Canadian province of Alberta, creating a narrow passageway that made a human pathway from Alaska possible. If there was a migration, it must have occurred soon after the passageway opened. Since many of the thousands of spear points that have been found all over North America south of the ice sheet—the so-called Clovis points (see Chapter 5)—go as far back as 11,000 BCE, there were about 500 years for humans to move from Alaska to North America. Traditionally, scholars have thought it plausible that it was at this time that humans settled the Americas.

Multiple Migrations   In the 1990s and early 2000s, however, a number of spear points and human settlements older than 11,000 BCE were discovered in unanticipated places. Sites at Monte Verde in Chile, Meadowcroft in Pennsylvania, Topper in South Carolina, Cactus Hill in Virginia, Buttermilk Creek in Texas, Taíma Taíma [Ta-EE-ma] in Venezuela, Santana de Riacho [Ree-AT-sho], and Lapa do Boquete [Bo-KE-te] in Brazil have been reliably dated to 16,000–14,000 years ago. The effect of the new research has been that the arrival of humans prior to 11,000 BCE is no longer mere speculation but is fast becoming the scientific consensus (see Map 1.4).

Long-distance ocean travel in ancient times was perhaps less difficult than has been previously assumed. After all, *H. sapiens* had already traveled by boat from Indonesia to Australia 60,000 years ago. Could modern humans have followed the Canadian coastline and sailed down to Washington State about 16,000 years ago? Proof for such a journey would, unfortunately, be difficult to come by since the coastline was some 50 miles farther out in the Pacific than it is today and any settlement traces would now be submerged below sea level. In the absence of underwater archaeology so far, nothing is known about such settlements.

Indeed, a number of small groups could have successfully sailed from Siberia, Japan, or even Sahul at various times prior to the appearance of the Beringian land bridge during the Ice Age or even earlier. Recent linguistic studies, using mathematical models for the development of language families, conclude that the Americas may have been inhabited for as long as 40,000–30,000 years. These models are based on the assumption that the nearly 200 contemporary Native American languages would have required this range of years to diversify, starting from a stock of three or more original languages.

Scientists examining the mitochondrial DNA of contemporary Native Americans have identified four circum-Pacific groups as ancestors migrating as early as 40,000 years ago to the Americas. Mitochondrial DNA relating to a fifth group, discovered in 1997 and found in 3 percent of Native Americans, however, has thrown a curve into this genetic research: It seems to identify a European or Central Asian ancestral group. As we have seen a number of times already, however, in the world of the archaeological, linguistic, and genetic science there is rarely a last word.

By the same token, migrations might have continued after 11,500 BCE. In the 1990s, curators in American museums reexamined their holdings of ancient human fossils, in the wake of an act of the US Congress allowing Native American groups to reclaim these fossils for proper sacred burial. Some 39 specimens—ranging from skulls and full skeletons to single bones—turned out to be much older and ethnically more diverse than previously assumed: They antedated the rise of the so-called Archaic Period of Native Americans after 8000 BCE.

Some 80 skulls, skeletons, and bones unearthed in Brazil during the 1980s and 1990s were similarly discovered to be ethnically diverse. The ages of these fossils, established by radiocarbon dating, ranged between 12,800 and 9,000 years. Moreover, complex measurements of the skulls determined that many of the fossils were more closely related to aboriginal Ainu in Japan, Polynesians on a number of Pacific islands, and Aborigines in Australia than to today's Native Americans. The only conclusion to be drawn from these scientific examinations in North and South America was that isolated communities of early, non-Native American settlers populated the Americas until around 8000 BCE, when these settler groups finally merged into a single Native American population.

Americans Prior to Native Americans   Among these early and surprisingly diverse remains, two North American fossil specimens have attracted special attention. The first is the "Spirit Cave mummy," discovered near Reno, Nevada, in 1940, whose true age of 9,400 years was not determined until 1994. The second set of remains is that of "Kennewick man," discovered accidentally in Washington State in

Human Migration to the Americas

- Extent of ice cover, 19,000 years ago
- Extent of ice cover, 13,500 years ago
- Tundra
- Tundra and coniferous forests
- Land migration route
- Coastal migrations
- Other early habitation sites
- **ALBERTA** Modern state or province
- **CHILE** Modern-day country
- Ancient coastlines

MAP **1.4** **Human Migration to the Americas.**

1996 and dated to 9,300 years ago. On the basis of the anatomical features of both fossils, paleoanthropologists determined that they were of Ainu descent, that is, originating from the first inhabitants of Japan. The Spirit Cave mummy was a man about 45 years old when he died, from fever following dental abscesses. His spine was deformed, and as an adult, he must have lived with considerable back pain. A year before his death, he had suffered skull and wrist fractures, but both were healed when he died. Earlier in his life he was an active forager, but later on he depended on the care of his group, which actually fed him his last meal of fish. The group buried him in a cave, laying him on his side in a flexed position, which was typical also among the foragers in Africa, Australia, and Europe. Dry weather mummified his head and right shoulder and preserved the rest of his bones and clothes, including his moccasins and the bulrush mat in which he was wrapped. No doubt, we will learn much more about him once scholars have carried out a more detailed study.

By contrast, Kennewick man, also resembling the Ainu of Japan, was tall and robust when he died. He was in good health throughout his youth and died also at the age of about 45 years. Similar to the Spirit Cave mummy, however, he suffered several major, even brutal external injuries. His forehead, left elbow, and a number of ribs showed signs of healed-over fractures. His worst wound came from a spear, which had been thrust into his pelvis, leaving a fragment of the spear point in his bone, which produced periodically a festering, debilitating bone wound that might have contributed to his death.

Reconstruction of the Facial Features of Kennewick Man (9,300 Years Ago).

The study of humans of ethnically diverse backgrounds in the Americas both before and after Clovis is still in its infancy, and much will have to be learned before definitive conclusions can be drawn about who migrated when to the Americas. At present, all that can be said is that small groups trickled in at various times, from about 40,000 years ago, and that a uniform Native American population emerged only after 8000 BCE.

Putting It All Together

The time it took from Toumaï to the first modern humans in East Africa was slightly less than 7 million years. Another 100,000 years elapsed before modern humans peopled the earth, down to Clovis and the transition to agriculture in the Fertile Crescent of the Middle East. From there, in another 10,000 years we reached our own time. The proportions are staggering: The history from Clovis and the Fertile Crescent to the present is a mere 0.01 percent of the time from Toumaï to the present and 1 percent from the first *H. sapiens* fossil to the present. Practically the entire time we needed to become genetically human is buried in the "deep history" mentioned at the beginning of this chapter and illustrated in our accompanying Concept Map.

Nearly as deeply buried is the process during which we began to carve out the space for culture, which we possess within the frameworks of our genes and the environment. Realizing how long these genetic and cultural time spans of prehistory are is what matters for us today: The 10,000 years of history from the shift of forager to agrarian–urban and eventually scientific–industrial society represent a breathtakingly short time of development yet one that is so overwhelmingly complex that we have great difficulty understanding it. When we step back from this frenetically paced world history of the past 10,000 years and consider the much

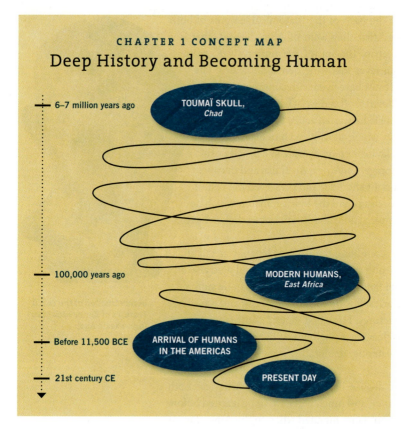

CHAPTER 1 CONCEPT MAP

Deep History and Becoming Human

6–7 million years ago — TOUMAÏ SKULL, *Chad*

100,000 years ago — MODERN HUMANS, *East Africa*

Before 11,500 BCE — ARRIVAL OF HUMANS IN THE AMERICAS

21st century CE — PRESENT DAY

slower deep history of humanity, we become aware that, had it not been for this slow, tortuous, and often dead-end incubation, we would never have been able to sustain the speed of the later history of which we are the current product.

The principal reason for the slow pace of deep history was the conscious effort of foragers to limit population growth as well as the size of their groups. Women as well as men, constantly on the move in search for food, had a strong interest in having few children and weaning them for several years so as to extend birth spacing. Of course, Paleolithic populations grew over the course of the millennia; otherwise, there would not have been a pattern shift from foraging to agrarian–urban life. Thus, even though the culture of foraging sought to inhibit population growth, this culture was not so rigid that people under climatologically and environmentally benign circumstances were not open to material and cultural change. It was under these circumstances at the end of the Ice Age 13,500 years ago that humans in some parts of the world gradually abandoned foraging and began adapting to agriculture.

Review and Respond

1. Define the concept of the "hominin" species and discuss the evolution of these species, from apes to the first early humans.

2. What are the characteristics of a fully evolved anatomical and intellectual humanity?

3. How did forager society develop? Which elements made up the life of foraging groups in prehistory?

4. Who were the Neanderthals? Compare and contrast them with *H. sapiens*.

5. Describe the rock art of *H. sapiens* in Australia and Europe and compare and contrast these two traditions.

6. What characterizes the time depth of prehistory, and why does it matter to us today?

▶ For additional resources, including maps, primary sources, visuals, and quizzes, please go to www.oup.com/us/vonsivers. Please see the Further Resources section at the back of the book for additional readings and suggested websites.

Thinking Through Patterns

▶ **What made it possible for *Homo sapiens* to survive in a dangerous environment? Why is it difficult to imagine life as a prehistoric forager?**

We are twice removed from the world of foragers: After foraging came farming, which is also difficult to understand because today's pattern of life is determined by scientific–industrial civilization. Even those among us who practice wilderness survival still have a lifeline to modern civilization (cell phones, GPS, etc.). *H. sapiens* foragers in prehistory, by contrast, relied on their stone tools, bows and arrows, rock shelters, clan members, and unsurpassed knowledge of animals, berry bushes, fruit and nut trees, mushroom patches, and grass fields to guide them through their daily lives. Collecting vegetal food, catching fish, and killing the occasional animal did not take as much of an effort as farming later did; and foragers had more leisure time than farmers engaged in the annual agricultural cycle.

After modern humans left East Africa, probably in several waves between 80,000 and 60,000 years ago, in all likelihood they first went to northern India, before fanning out in all directions to Australia, Siberia, and Europe. They encountered *H. erectus* and successors, such as Neanderthals, and interbred with the latter. The modern humans who settled in Australia remained foragers because the African flora did not include grasses that could be cultivated through selective breeding into grains. From the complex tribal societies into which they evolved, we can see that forager life could acquire a differentiated culture, expressed in the so-called Dreamtime. However, when the Ice Age hit, forager clans and tribes had to retreat southward and adapt to the harsh environmental conditions. Foremost among the adaptations were the abilities to make protective woolen clothing and build boats with which to travel to more favorable places.

▶ **Where did humans go when they left Africa, and how did they establish themselves in the areas where they settled? How did they adapt to the worsening Ice Age?**

▶ **How did humans express their experience of sharing their life force with animals? How do we know that this experience was important to them?**

The interior lives of early humans are known to us through the figurines and cave paintings which they left behind. These artifacts have given rise to speculations about *H. sapiens'* culture, which are impossible to verify but, at a minimum, demonstrate to us the keen awareness about the difference between the natural world and the companionship that humans and other animals as living beings experienced. Prehistoric humans made a clear distinction between the things seen and unseen, that is, the animals as they are encountered in nature and the life force or motivating spirit which they share with humans.

Chapter 2
11,500-600 BCE
Agrarian-Urban Centers of the Middle East and Eastern Mediterranean

Fertile Crescent

MIDDLE EAST

She was the first writer in world history we know by name. The high priestess Enheduanna [En-hay-doo-AN-nah] lived at the end of the third millennium BCE and was a daughter of Sargon of Akkad, ruler of Mesopotamia's first recorded kingdom. Amazingly, her writings are still available today in translation. Her best-known poem, "The Exaltation of Inanna," was written after a rebel leader had deposed Enheduanna as high

Seeing Patterns

▶ What are the main factors that enabled the transition from foraging to farming?

▶ Where did the pattern of agricultural life first emerge and why?

▶ How did the creation of agrarian–urban society—what we commonly call "civilization"—make for an entirely new pattern of world history?

priestess. In the poem Enheduanna sadly wonders why Inanna (also known as Ishtar), the goddess of love, fertility, and war, has abandoned her: She has fulfilled all rituals and sacrifices, and yet she is exiled from her goddess! Imploring Inanna to take her back into her good graces, Enheduanna marshals all her poetic powers:

> Great queen of queens, issue of a holy womb for righteous divine powers, greater than your own mother, wise and sage, lady of all the foreign lands, life-force of the teeming people: I will recite your holy song! True goddess fit for divine powers, your splendid utterances are magnificent. Deep-hearted, good woman with a radiant heart, I will enumerate your divine powers.

After reciting such prayerful poems night and day, Enheduanna finally succeeded. Inanna accepted her priestess' appeals and the rightful ruler returned Enheduanna to her temple position.

The Standard of Ur. Dating to about 2500 BCE, its function is still unknown. The thin wooden box is inlaid with precious stones and bits of shell. The side shown here—known as the "War" panel—shows one of the earliest representations of a Sumerian army.

Agrarian–urban society: A type of society characterized by intensive agriculture and people living in cities, towns, and villages.

The end of the third millennium BCE, when Enheduanna lived, was a time when **agrarian–urban society**, with its villages and cities, had become well established in several different areas. Foragers had pioneered agriculture and village settlements during a long period of 5,000 years in the Fertile Crescent of the Middle East, a region particularly favored by climate, vegetation, and animal populations. Once these early inhabitants had become farmers, they began interacting with foragers in the marshes of the Mesopotamian river delta, where—with the help of river water conducted via canals to the fields for irrigation—the groups merged. This combined population used the bountiful harvests for the foundation of cities in which craftspeople, priests and priestesses, merchants, kings, and rebels mingled, creating the fundamentals of the urban amenities of contemporary civilization: comfortable houses, places of worship, administrative centers, public archives, taverns, workshops, and markets. Many of these urban achievements are still crucial to our lives today. This chapter will trace the origins of farming, villages, cities, kingdoms, and empires in the Middle East, the first of the agrarian–urban centers in world history.

Agrarian Origins in the Fertile Crescent, ca. 11,500–1500 BCE

The movement from foraging to agriculture—one of the most pivotal patterns in world history—was a slow process covering several millennia. During this time, farmers built villages, in which they worked small garden-like plots and depended on annual rains for the growth of their crops. Farming gathered momentum as people mastered increasingly complex methods of irrigation. Farmers began to settle in the two great river valleys of the Tigris–Euphrates [You-FRAY-teez], in present-day Turkey, Syria, and Iraq, and of the Nile in Egypt. In these valleys, irrigation using river water allowed for larger plots and bigger harvests. Nutrient-rich river silt from the regular floods made the fields even more fertile and provided for often considerable surpluses of grain. These surpluses allowed populations to build cities and states, with ruling institutions composed of kings, advisors, armies, and bureaucracies.

Sedentary Foragers and Foraging Farmers

The region of the Middle East and the eastern Mediterranean stretches over portions of three continents—eastern Europe, southwestern Asia, and northeastern Africa. Historically, this region has always formed a single geographical unit within which there was extensive circulation of goods and ideas, although it did not constitute a single cultural zone. After the rise of the political institution of the empire, from about 1100 BCE, areas in the Middle East and the eastern Mediterranean were often also in competition with each other.

Geography and Environment   To understand how people in the Middle East and eastern Mediterranean adopted farming and settlement, we need to look first at the geography of the region. The western half includes Thrace and Greece in the north, together with numerous islands in the Aegean Sea, a branch of the Mediterranean Sea. The terrain on the mainland as well as the islands is mostly mountainous, covered with forests or brushwood. To the east, adjacent to Thrace and Greece, lies Anatolia, which comprises most of modern Turkey. Anatolia is a peninsula consisting of a central high plain which is ringed by mountain chains and traversed by rivers.

South of Anatolia and lying on the eastern shore of the Mediterranean Sea is the Levant (from French for "rising sun"), encompassing modern Syria, Lebanon, Israel, and Palestine. Along the coastline is a mountain chain reaching from Mount Lebanon in the north to the hill country of Palestine in the south. Mount Lebanon was covered at the time with huge cedars, of which only remnants survive today. The

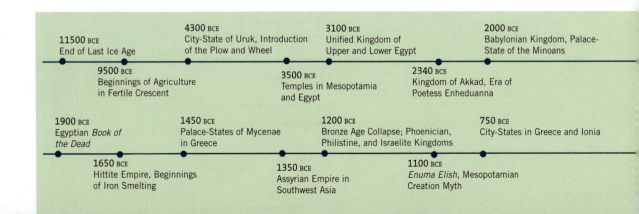

Levant, the Taurus Mountains of southeastern Anatolia, and the Zagros Mountains of southwestern Iran are often referred to as the "Fertile Crescent," to indicate the birthplace of agriculture (Map 2.1).

To the east of the mountain chain extends the Syrian steppe, which gradually gives way to the Arabian Desert. South of the Levant on the African continent are Egypt and Nubia (today's northern Sudan) on both sides of the Nile River. Both are largely covered by desert but bisected by the fertile Nile valley. This valley is wide and swampy in Sudan and narrow in Egypt, except for the Fayyum Depression and the Nile's Mediterranean delta. In the center of the Middle East are three smaller regions:

- Persia (modern-day Iran), stretching from the Caspian Sea southward to the Persian Gulf
- Mesopotamia, "the land between the rivers" of the Euphrates and Tigris in present-day Iraq and Kuwait
- the Arabian Peninsula, modern Saudi Arabia, the United Arab Emirates, Qatar, Oman, and Yemen

Recent historical climate research has established that between the end of the Ice Age (around 11,500 BCE) and 4000 BCE monsoon rain patterns extended farther west than they do today. Monsoon rain currently forms in the summer in South Africa and moves northeastward along East Africa before moving to India and China. When the monsoon still covered the Middle East, from the Mediterranean coast to the Persian Gulf, verdant vegetation covered land that is desert today. At present, only the highlands of Yemen and mountain rings around the central salt desert of

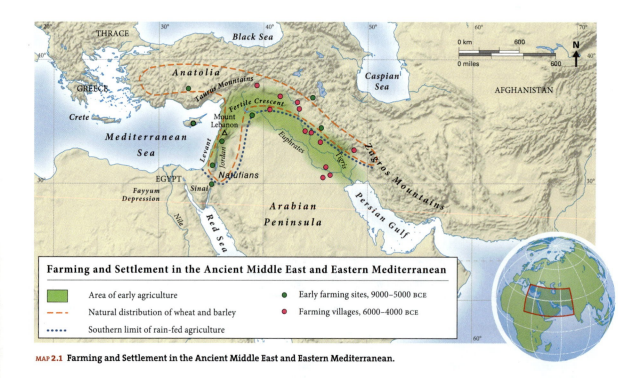

MAP 2.1 Farming and Settlement in the Ancient Middle East and Eastern Mediterranean.

Iran receive enough rain to sustain agriculture. At the eastern end of the Middle East is Afghanistan, a country with steppe plains and high mountains bordering on India—like the Fertile Crescent and Mesopotamia. It was also a center of early **agrarian society**.

The Natufians   The richness of the Fertile Crescent in plants and animals during the early centuries after the end of the Ice Age seems to have encouraged settlement. Foragers found everything they wanted within a radius of a few miles: wild grains, legumes such as lentils and chickpeas, and game. Nature replenished its ample resources year after year. Semipermanent hamlets, forming the Natufian culture (11500–9500 BCE), arose in the Jordan and upper Euphrates valleys.

Each hamlet of the Natufians, consisting of about 60 inhabitants, contained a few semicircular pit houses made up of a stone foundation, posts, thatched walls, and a thatched roof. Sometimes their homes would even become their final resting places—the Natufians buried their dead underneath the floors of abandoned houses or along the edges of settlements. Some graves contained ornaments, and at least two persons have been found buried with their dogs. Later Natufians often removed the skulls of their ancestors—whether before or after the burial of the body is unknown—and venerated them in altar niches in their houses. Thus began an important ancestral cult that spread across the Middle East and lasted for several millennia.

To gather food, the Natufians went out into the woods with baskets and obsidian-bladed sickles. Wild cereal grains had evolved over the millennia so that their seeds scattered easily upon ripening, furthering the growth of new crops. Gatherers carefully tapped plants whose seeds had not yet scattered and collected the grains in baskets. Back in the hamlets, the grain was ground with pestles on grindstones. Storage seems to have been minimal, limited to portable containers, such as baskets. The abundant food supply, however, did not last. A near-glacial cold and dry period from 10900 to 9600 BCE, called the "Younger Dryas" (named after a cold-resistant mountain flower), caused wild cereal stands to wither and game animals to drift away to warmer climes. Most of the sedentary foragers deserted their hamlets and returned to a fully migratory life of foraging. The short-lived, semisettled culture of the Natufians collapsed.

In the few hamlets that survived, people turned to storing grain in plastered pits or stone silos in order to cope with the harsher winters. In spring, they planted some of their stored grain to thicken the sparse wild grain stands. When warmer and more humid weather returned, a new era began, the **Neolithic**, or New Stone Age. Scholars use this designation for the period from about 9600 to 4500 BCE in the Middle East because it was characterized by polished stone implements (spades and sickles), the introduction of agriculture, animal domestication, sun-dried bricks, plaster, and pottery—in short, most of the key elements of agrarian society.

Agrarian society: At a minimum, people engaged in farming cereal grains on rain-fed or irrigated fields and breeding sheep and cattle.

Early Natufian Decorated Skull, from El-Wad. Note the simulation of hair on top of the skull. Eyes were simulated through inlaid semiprecious stones. During 11500–5700 BCE Middle Easterners practiced ancestor cults, with the deceased buried underneath house floors and separated heads often decorated and kept in house niches.

Neolithic Age: Period from ca. 9600 to 4500 BCE when stone tools were adapted to the requirements of agriculture, through the making of sickles and spades.

Selective Breeding of Grain and Domestic Animals   Climatically, the Neolithic Age began with a metaphorical bang. Within just a few generations, summer temperatures increased by an extraordinary 7 degrees. Thereafter, temperatures continued to rise, at a more modest rate, for another 2,000 years. In this balmy climate, both old and newly established hamlets expanded quickly into villages of around 300–500 inhabitants. People continued to collect grain but also began to plant fields. In the early summer, they waited for the moment when the great majority of the grain was still in its ears. Through selective breeding, they gradually weeded out early-ripening varieties and began harvesting fields in which all grain ripened at the same time. The kernels of these first wheat and barley varieties were still small, and it took until about 7000 BCE in the Middle East before farmers had bred the large-grained wheat and barley of today.

Parallel to the selective breeding of grain, farmers also domesticated *pulses*—the edible seeds of pod-bearing plants—beginning with chickpeas and lentils. Pulses had the advantage of helping with the refertilization of the grain fields: Pods, stalks, and roots contain nitrogen needed by all plants to grow. Farmers continued to hunt, but they also captured young wild goats and sheep and through selective breeding accustomed them to live with humans in their houses and pens: the first domestication of livestock. For two millennia, this kind of early farming remained essentially garden farming, with hand-held implements, such as digging sticks, spades, and sickles.

The original agriculture—the cultivation of grain and pulses and the domestication of goats and sheep—relied on annual rains in the Fertile Crescent and became more widespread when farmers tapped creeks for the irrigation of their fields during dry months. Inhabitants of this region discovered the benefits of rotating their crops and driving goats and sheep over the stubble of harvested grain fields, using the animals' droppings for refertilization and leaving the fields fallow for a year. Around 6500 BCE, these peoples added cattle, pigs, donkeys (domesticated first in Nubia), and pottery (clay vessels fired in kilns) to their farms. For the first time in world history, the epic transition from foraging to farming had been completed.

The Origin of Urban Centers in Mesopotamia and Egypt

During the fifth millennium BCE, the climate of the Middle East and eastern Mediterranean changed from monsoon rains falling during the summer to wet winters and dry summers in the west and north and general dryness prevailing in the east and south. Most of the Arabian Peninsula began to dry up. In lower Mesopotamia, drier conditions forced settlers coming from upstream to pay closer attention to irrigation. All of these changes would contribute to the rise of the first agrarian–urban centers founded along rivers—in the Middle East, Egypt, the Indus valley in the Indian subcontinent, and later, the Yellow River valley in China.

FIRST AGRARIAN-URBAN CENTERS

Euphrates and Nile Floods   The Tigris River in eastern Mesopotamia, with its turbulent waters and high banks, did not lend itself early on to the construction of irrigation canals. The Euphrates River in western Mesopotamia, however, flowed more tranquilly and closer to the surface of the land, providing favorable conditions for irrigated farming. At its lower end, in present-day Iraq, the Euphrates united with the Tigris and dispersed out into swampland, lagoons, and marshes, which supported a rich plant and animal life. It was here that the first farmers, coming from central and northern Mesopotamia, settled, establishing the Ubaid culture of villages (6000–4000 BCE).

The annual snowmelt in the mountains of northeastern Anatolia caused the Euphrates and Tigris to carry often devastating deluges of water down into the plain. The floods arrived in early spring just as the first grain was ready for harvest, forcing the farmers into heroic efforts to keep the ripening grain fields from being inundated by water. On the other hand, the spring floods helped prepare the fields for the growing of smaller crops, such as chickpeas, peas, lentils, millet, and animal fodder. The floods also softened hardened soils and sometimes leached them of salt deposits. Thus, in spite of some drawbacks, irrigated farming in lower Mesopotamia, with its more predictable water supplies, was more abundant and reliable than was the more irregular rain-fed agriculture in the Taurus–Zagros–Levant region to the north.

The Egyptian Nile originates in regions of East Africa where the rains hit during the early summer. Much of this rain is collected in Lake Victoria, from where the White Nile flows northward. In the Sudan it unites with the Blue Nile, which carries water and fertile silt from the rains down from the Ethiopian mountains. The Nile usually begins to swell in July, crests in August–September, and recedes during October. For the Neolithic inhabitants of Egypt these late-summer and fall floods created conditions quite different from those of lower Mesopotamia, which depended on the spring floods.

In Egypt, the floods coincided with the growing season of winter barley and wheat. Silt carried by the Nile fertilized the fields every year, instead of every second year, as in Mesopotamia, where ripening fields had to be protected from the floods. Because of the steeper descent in both the long valley and short delta of the Nile, the water table was lower and the danger of salt rising to the surface was less than in Mesopotamia, where over time large areas became infertile. The first agricultural settlements appeared in the Fayyum [Fay-YOOM], a swampy depression off the Nile southwest of modern Cairo, around 5200 BCE. By about 3500 BCE, agriculture had spread south along the Nile and north into the delta.

Early Towns   Between 5500 and 3500 BCE, Eridu and other villages in lower Mesopotamia and Upper Egypt developed into towns. They were composed of a few thousand inhabitants, with markets where farmers exchanged surplus food staples and traders offered goods not produced locally. The Mesopotamian towns administered themselves through local **assemblies**, in Sumerian called *puhrum* [POOH-room]. All male adults came together at these assemblies to decide on communal matters such as mutual help during the planting and harvesting seasons, the digging of canals, punishments for criminal acts by townspeople, and relations with other towns and villages. For nearly two millennia towns in this region regulated their irrigated agriculture through communal cooperation (see Map 2.2).

In Mesopotamian and Egyptian towns an irrigated field produced about twice as much wheat or barley as did a rain-fed field. Indeed, irrigation made it possible for townspeople to accumulate an agricultural surplus that protected them against famines and allowed for population increases. Some people accumulated more grain than others, and the first social distinctions along the lines of wealth appeared. Gradually, wealthy families became owners of land beyond their family properties.

Assembly: Gathering of either all inhabitants or the most influential persons in a town; later, in cities, assemblies and kings made communal decisions on important fiscal or juridical matters.

MAP **2.2** Urban Centers in Mesopotamia and Egypt, 5500–3500 BCE.

Sharecroppers: Farmers who received seed, animals, and tools from landowners in exchange for up to two-thirds of their harvest.

Nomads: People whose livelihood was based on the herding of animals, such as sheep, goats, cattle, horses, and camels; moving with their animals from pasture to pasture according to the seasons, they lived in tent camps.

Sharecroppers who worked these lands were perhaps previously landowners who had fallen into debt and now paid rent (in the form of grain) to the new landowners. Other landless farmers left agriculture altogether and became **nomads**, breeding *onagers* (ancestors of donkeys), sheep, and goats on steppe lands unsuited for agriculture. Wealthy landowners appropriated the places of ritual and sacrifice in the villages and towns and constructed elaborate temples, mansions, workshops, and granaries.

Eventually, the landowning priestly families stopped not only farming their own land but also making tools, pottery, cloth, and leather goods, turning the production of these goods over to specialized craftspeople, such as toolmakers (for stone, bone, or wood tools), potters, weavers, or cobblers and paying them with grain rations. The landowners employed traders who traveled to other areas with crafts (pottery, cloth, leather goods), trading them for raw materials. Mesopotamian merchants traveled with cloth and tools to villages and towns in the Zagros Mountains and returned with timber, stone, obsidian, and copper. Egyptian villagers traded textiles with villagers in the Sinai Peninsula in return for copper and with Nubian villagers in return for gold.

Around 4300 BCE, some mountain people in the region had mastered the crafts of mining and smelting copper. This metal was too soft to replace obsidian, but the many other uses to which it was put have led scholars to mark the middle of the fifth millennium BCE as the moment when the Neolithic, or New Stone, Age of polished stone tools came to an end and the *Chalcolithic*, or *Copper, Age* began.

Temples   In the course of the fifth millennium BCE, wealthy landowners gained control over the communal grain stores and clan shrines and enlarged these into town shrines. In Eridu, the shrine, originally a mud brick structure with an offering table for sacrifices, grew over the millennia through a dozen superimpositions into a monumental temple. Adjacent to the early temples were kilns, granaries, workshops, breweries, and administrative buildings. The wealthy landowners, presiding over the temples as priests, were responsible for the administration of all aspects of cult ritual in the temples, as well as the provision of labor in the temple fields, which included the digging and cleaning of irrigation canals; the planting, harvesting, transporting, and storing of crops; and the pasturing, stabling, and breeding of animals.

The Temple at Eridu. Artist's reconstruction of the temple at Eridu. Note the immense platform supporting the temple and the sacred enclosure, which measured 200 square yards.

In Upper Egypt, landowner-priests presided over the construction of the first temples around 3500 BCE, together with elegantly embellished tombs for themselves. The decorations in both temples and tombs depict boats, animals, and humans. One such painting shows a leader carrying out an expedition on the Nile upstream to Nubia, returning with gold, ebony, and diorite (black rock for statues) to create elaborate ornaments for his temple and tomb. Unfortunately, the sparse archaeological record in Egypt at this point presents few details concerning the transition from village to town.

The World's First Cities

In contrast to a town, a **city** (or **city-state**, if the surrounding villages are included) is defined as a place of more than 5,000 inhabitants, with a number of nonfarming inhabitants, such as craftspeople, merchants, and administrators. The latter lived on the food they received in exchange for their own handiwork, such as pottery, textiles, and traded goods. To keep order in such a large place where many people did not know each other, the dominant landowner-priest created a personal entourage of armed men, wielding police power. The first place in Mesopotamia to fit the definition of a city was Uruk, founded near Eridu around 4300 BCE. Within a millennium, it was a city of 50,000–80,000 inhabitants with a mixture of palaces, multistory administrative buildings, workshops, residences, palace estates, and villages clustered around the city with both large and small individual farms.

City, city-state: A place of more than 5,000 inhabitants with nonfarming inhabitants (craftspeople, merchants, administrators), markets, and a city leader capable of compelling obedience to his decisions by force.

The people of Uruk were important pioneers of technical and intellectual innovations. It was here that the first known plow was found. Mesopotamian plows were sophisticated wooden constructions with seeder funnels on top and pulled by pairs of oxen or donkeys. Plowing and controlled sowing allowed for much larger harvests. Uruk craftspeople introduced the potter's wheel, which accelerated and made more precise the manufacture of earthenware and ceramics. The sizes of jars, pots, and bowls gradually became standardized, simplifying the storage of grain and its distribution in the cities.

At the same time, two- and four-wheeled carts pulled by oxen expedited the transportation of large quantities of grain from the fields to the city. The grain was made into bread, to conveniently feed the populace, and beer, which became the safe, potable, and easily storable drink of choice among urban dwellers. By some

Hymn to Ninkasi, the Goddess of Beer, ca. 1880 BCE

You are the one who waters the malt
set on the ground,
The noble dogs keep away even the potentates,
Ninkasi, you are the one who waters the malt
set on the ground,
The noble dogs keep away even the potentates.

You are the one who soaks the malt in a jar
The waves rise, the waves fall.
Ninkasi, you are the one who soaks
the malt in a jar
The waves rise, the waves fall.

You are the one who spreads the cooked
mash on large reed mats,
Coolness overcomes.
Ninkasi, you are the one who spreads
the cooked mash on large reed mats,
Coolness overcomes ...

When you pour out the filtered beer
of the collector vat,
It is like the onrush of
Tigris and Euphrates.
Ninkasi, you are the one who pours out the
filtered beer of the collector vat,
It is like the onrush of
Tigris and Euphrates.

—Selection adapted from Solomon H. Katz and Fritz Maytag, "Did Beer
Come Before Bread?" Translated by Miguel Civil. *Archaeology* 44, no. 4
(July–August 1991): 24–27.

estimates, more than 40 percent of Mesopotamia's grain was committed to beer production, and archaeologists have unearthed numerous recipes for the brew.

Another particularly serviceable invention was bronze, the world's first *alloy*—that is, a blending of two or more metals in the smelting process. Bronze is an alloy of copper and arsenic or tin, producing a hard, although relatively expensive, metal that could be used in tools and weapons. Bronze became so useful in the Middle East and eastern Mediterranean during the following centuries that it replaced stone and copper implements for all but a few purposes in daily life, leading historians to refer to this as the *Bronze Age* (in the Middle East from 3300 to 1200 BCE). Bronze became one of the hallmarks of agrarian–urban life as its use spread or was independently developed in other places in Eurasia.

Cuneiform Writing The administrators in the bureaucracy, who were responsible for the accounting and distribution of grain, animals, ceramics, textiles, and imported raw materials, greatly simplified their complicated tasks around 3450 BCE by inventing a system of writing. Scribes wrote in cuneiform [Kyoo-NEE-uh-form] (from the Latin, meaning "wedge-shaped") script on clay tablets, using signs denoting objects and sounds from the spoken language. Small stone or clay tokens indicating different types of grain or goods on baskets or containers had been ubiquitous in the Middle East since the late Paleolithic. These tokens with a variety of engraved or imprinted signs might have been precursors of cuneiform writing. Historians are still researching and arguing these points. However the debate is eventually settled, it is obvious that writing was a major expansion of the conceptual horizon of humankind that reached back to the first flaked stones, ornaments, figurines, and cave paintings in the Paleolithic. For the first time, scribes could not only write down the languages they spoke but also clarify for future generations the meaning of the sculpted and painted artifacts which would otherwise have been mute witnesses of history. With the advent of writing, record keeping, communication, increasingly abstract thought, and, for the first time, history could all be recorded.

Kingdoms in Mesopotamia, Egypt, and Crete

With the introduction of the plow and increasing numbers of metal tools, city leaders greatly expanded their landholdings. They employed large groups of laborers to cut canals through riverbanks onto virgin lands. Vast new areas of lowlands, situated at some distance from river-banks, became available for farming. Portions of this land served as overflow basins for floodwaters, to pro-tect the ripening grain fields. Craftspeople invented lifting devices to channel water from the canals into small fields or gardens. As a result of this field and irrigation expansion, the grain surpluses of both temples and villages increased enormously.

Kingship in Mesopotamia A consequence of the expansion of agriculture was the rise of nearly two dozen cities in lower and central Mesopotamia. As cities expanded and multiplied, the uncultivated buffer lands which had formerly separated them dis-appeared. People drew borders, quarreled over access to water, made deals to share it, and both negotiated and fought over the ownership of wandering livestock.

Cuneiform Script.
Scribes impressed the syllables on the wet clay with a scalpel-like writing instrument.

When it became impossible to contain conflicts and wars broke out, city dwellers built walls and recruited military forces from among their young population. The commanders, often of modest origins, used their military positions to acquire wealth and demanded to be recognized as leaders. They disputed authority with the priests, who had been the traditional heads of vil-lages and towns. Depending on circumstances, the Mesopotamian city assemblies chose their leaders from either the self-made or the priestly leaders, calling the former "great man" (*lugal*) and the latter "king" (*en*).

Once in power, a royal leader sought to make his position independent from the assemblies and impose dynastic or family rule on the city. To set himself apart from his assembly colleagues, he claimed divine or sacred sanction for his kingship. The King List of 2125 BCE, in which the reigns of all early kings in lower Mesopotamia were coordinated, begins with "after the kingship descended from heaven, the kingship was in Eridu." In other words, the kings argued that as divinely ordained rulers they no longer needed the consensus of the assemblies for their power or that of their sons and grandsons. The earliest king known by name and attested in the archaeological record was Enmebaragesi [En-me-ba-ra-GAY-see] of Kish, who reigned around 2500 BCE. Later kings are known for all the nearly two dozen cities of Mesopotamia.

Akkadia and Babylonia During the 2000s BCE, these Mesopotamian cities began competing against each other for military supremacy. The first royal dynasty to bring them together in a unified territorial state or kingdom—numbering about 2 million inhabitants—was that of Akkadia (ca. 2340–2150 BCE). Sargon, the first major king (r. 2334–2279 BCE), commanded several thousand foot soldiers armed with bronze helmets, leather coats, spears, and battle-axes. Sargon's grand-son, Naram-Sin, added the Zagros Mountains and Syria to the Akkadian kingdom and claimed to be the "king of the four (world) shores." He considered his state to be an open-ended kingdom stretching in all four directions and limited only by the sea which surrounded the earth. Naram-Sin was the first king to conceive of a grand imperial design which would lead to the unification of the ethnically, linguistically,

Empire: Large multiethnic, multilinguistic, multireligious state consisting of a conquering kingdom and several defeated kingdoms.

and religiously diverse peoples of the Middle East, with or without their consent. However, he did not possess yet the military means to embark on large-scale conquests and **empire** building. The Hittites and Assyrians a millennium and a half later would be the first to reach that milestone (see Map 2.3).

A later major Mesopotamian kingdom was Babylonia. Its best-known king was Hammurabi (1792–1750 BCE), who ordered the engraving of the entire code of Babylonian law onto a 7-foot slab of basalt. Like so many rulers in Mesopotamia and, indeed, in cultures around the world, Hammurabi saw himself as the executor of a stern, divinely sanctioned law that punished evildoers and rewarded the righteous. By today's standards, Hammurabi's laws were harsh, threatening severe punishments for crimes against property, land, and commerce. For example, tavern owners who overcharged customers or who failed to notify the police of the presence of criminals on their property were to be drowned. Priestesses caught in taverns were to be burned to death. The law of Mesopotamia was no longer the customary law of villages and towns but the royal writ, divinely ordained and backed by military force (see "Patterns Up Close" on pp. 48–49).

Patriarchy The pattern of state formation (with the rise of city-states warring against each other for predominance) contained in itself another pattern crucial in the development of society in the Middle East and beyond: the increasingly pronounced patriarchal structure of society. As we have seen in Chapter 1, the archaeological evidence does not allow many conclusions concerning gender functions in Paleolithic society. The Lascaux image of the injured bull charging its hunter, who is depicted as a stick figure with a phallus, is a rare exception. The gathering and preparation of vegetal food was an occupation that required communal cooperation among all and probably more than balanced the special occupation of males in the hunt. The Neolithic rise of agriculture does not seem to have changed much in these largely unstructured gender relations.

The wars among the city-states and kingdoms were important events in the creation of new patterns of gender relations. Large numbers of war captives, providing cheap labor as slaves in temple households and wealthy residences, gave the priestly and self-made kings a decisive edge in beginning the restructuring of agrarian–urban society. A ruling class emerged, composed of dynastic families who collaborated with other landowning and priestly families. One rank below the ruling class were the merchants and craftspeople, who formed a hierarchy among themselves, with merchants and jewelry makers at the top and tanners—because of the unpleasant odor of their manufacturing processes—in the lower ranks. At the bottom of this increasingly structured, hierarchical society were slaves and other marginal urban groups, such as day laborers and prostitutes.

The formation of hierarchical social structures did not stop with the rise of social classes. As we shall see in later

(a)

(b)

MAP **2.3** (a) **The Akkadian Kingdom.** (b) **Kingdom of Babylonia.**

chapters, men assumed legal power over women on all levels of society in nearly every agrarian–urban culture. At first, the patriarchy was still relatively mild. In the ruling classes of Mesopotamia, female members held high positions as priestesses, queen consorts, and in a few cases even queens but only as extensions of male dynastic rule. Enheduanna, in the vignette at the beginning of this chapter, was an example of a highborn woman unhappily dependent on the decisions of the male members of her family.

In New Kingdom Egypt (1550–1070 BCE), princesses had the same rights of divine descent as princes. Sisters and brothers or half-brothers sometimes married each other, reinforcing the concept that their lineage was divine and pure, containing no mortal blood. A famous example is Hatshepsut [Hat-SHEP-soot], who was married to her half-brother. She was a strong-willed woman who became "king" (the title of "queen" did not exist) after the death of her husband, ruling for over two decades (r. ca. 1479–1457 BCE), before a son from one of her former husband's concubines succeeded her.

In later millennia, after empires formed, noble women disappeared from their male-dependent public positions and lived in secluded areas of the palaces. In later chapters we will explore this widespread pattern of how men tightened the law, relegating women to inferior family positions. Patriarchy was thus a product not of agrarian but of urban society in city-states and kingdoms of Mesopotamia and, a little later, Egypt.

Egyptian Kingdoms Villages and towns began developing into cities somewhat later in Egypt than in Mesopotamia, toward the end of the 3000s BCE. The first and largest city was Hierankopolis [Hee-ran-KO-po-lis] on the Upper Nile. Smaller cities dotted the river downstream to the delta. As in Mesopotamia, the rulers of cities began to develop into small-scale kings. Among the first of these we know by name were Menes, Narmer, and Aha. Whoever among these three was the first pharaoh (king, from Egyptian *Pr*, "great house"), he unified all Egyptian lands—stretching from Upper Egypt down the Nile to the delta—and established the first dynasty of Egypt's Early Dynastic Period (ca. 3100–2613 BCE), choosing Memphis, near modern Cairo, as his capital. At first, lesser rulers continued their reigns

Kingdoms of Mesopotamia		
Following the Middle Chronology, calibrated around Hammurabi's reign of 1792–1750 BCE		
Uruk	4300–3100 BCE	Comprising Girsu/Telloh, Umma, Lagash, Eridu, Ur; Hacinebi Tepe, Turkey; Chogha Mish, Iran
Jemdet Nasr Period	3100–2900	Uruk
Early Dynastic Period	2900–2350	Kish, Uruk, Ur, Lagash, Asmar, Mari, Umma, Al-Rawda
Akkadian Dynasty	2340–2150	Agade, Sumer, Lagash, Uruk, Titris Hoyuk
Ur III	2100–2000	Ur, Elam, Tappeh Sialk, Iran
Old Babylonia, Old and Middle Assyria	2000–1000	Mari, Ebla, Babylon, Isin, Larsa, Assur

Patterns Up Close | Babylonian Law Codes

In addition to the invention of cuneiform writing and the use of the wheel, the Babylonians in lower Mesopotamia produced the earliest known collections of written laws. Because of their formal, written nature, these law codes differed from earlier oral and customary law, common to all early cultures. When did these laws originate, how did they develop across time, and what was their influence on later ages?

The origin and evolution of the legal tradition are intertwined with developments associated with the complexity of urban life. In order to sustain sufficient agricultural production, people devised an intricate system of irrigation and drainage canals, along with dikes and dams, to control the often unpredictable flooding of the Tigris and Euphrates Rivers. All of this necessitated not only extensive planning and maintenance but also the allotment of plots of land, some closer and others farther from water sources. In addition, the emergence of complex political, economic, and social relationships—fraught with disputes and inequalities—called for the establishment of a set of centrally administered rules and regulations in order to provide for conflict resolution as well as retribution for wrongdoing.

Across a span of nearly 500 years from the earliest codification of King Urukagina of Lagash in ca. 2350 BCE to the monumental code of Hammurabi in 1750 BCE, law developed through a successive series of increasingly comprehensive and refined legal codes consistent with developing complexities of urban expansion. Consequently, evolving law codes address correspondingly wider audiences, they cover a broader spectrum of social classes, and they present more complex examples of potential infractions as well as more nuanced resolutions. Most legal codes open with a prologue, which is followed by a body of laws, and close with an epilogue. In terms of format, Sumerian laws follow the format of "if this, then that" regarding violations and ensuing punishments, and punishments are meted out with reference to social status. Finally, they pay growing attention to the importance of irrigation, with more and more references to the maintenance of river dikes and irrigation canals, along with harsh consequences for not doing so.

The law code of Hammurabi, king of Babylon (r. 1792–1750 BCE), represents the first complete written and well-organized code of law. An amalgamation of

Stele with Hammurabi's Law.

in the other cities. They even rebelled against the pharaoh from time to time. Therefore, the early policies of the Egyptian kings were focused almost exclusively on the unification of Egypt. Since it was not easy to subjugate the lesser rulers in a country of some 650 miles in length, unification was a protracted process.

The first king claimed divine birth from Egypt's founder god, Horus, the falcon-headed deity. As god on earth, the king upheld the divine order (*ma'at* [Ma-AHT]) of justice and peace for all. For their part, the inhabitants of his kingdom were no more than humble servants whose duty was to provide for the king's earthly and heavenly life by paying him taxes and constructing an opulent palace and tomb for him. Of course, in practice this royal supremacy was far from complete. Even during times of strong centralization there were always some powerful figures—provincial earlier Sumerian precepts, the code exceeds them in its extensions and embellishments; whereas earlier codifications list around 40 laws, those of Hammurabi number fully 282. Like earlier models, the code acknowledges distinctions in social hierarchies along with inequalities among them but goes beyond them in addressing more social classes and grouping the classes according to relative wealth and social standing. Also, like previous collections, the code is broken down into several categories, including issues related to property and family law; but here again it covers many more possible scenarios as ways to close previous loopholes.

Unlike its Sumerian predecessors, however, the code departs significantly when it comes to retribution in that it calls for more extreme punishments according to the principle of *lex talionis* ("an eye for an eye"). Thus, "If a man put out the eye of another man, his eye shall be put out." Further, the importance of maintaining irrigation systems is consistent with earlier themes but in more nuanced terms: "If any one open his ditches to water his crop, but is careless, and the water flood the field of his neighbor, then he shall pay his neighbor [grain] for his loss."

The long-term influence of Sumerian and Babylonian legal codes—particularly Hammurabi's code—extends far beyond ancient Mesopotamia. Many of its concepts and precepts served as predecessors of Hittite, Egyptian, and Assyrian laws. Instances of its influence appear in the development of biblical law, and striking similarities to the notion of *lex talionis* are found in ancient Jewish law. The code was carried westward across the Mediterranean, where many of its principles found their way into Roman law, especially the organized codification of civil cases.

Questions

- What do the first law codes tell us about ancient Sumerian and Babylonian societies?

- Are the legacies of these first law codes still evident in modern Western legal practice today?

landowners and governors, for example—who held title to their properties in their own names and collected rents from the farmers working on these properties. As in Mesopotamia, the claim of the kings to divine sanction or even divinity did not keep rivals from bidding for supreme power.

Hieroglyphs, Bureaucracy, and Pyramids   As with cuneiform in Mesopotamia, the Egyptian kings were greatly aided in the process of unification by the introduction of a system of accounting and writing. Around 3500–3200 BCE, administrators and scribes developed *hieroglyphic* writing in Egypt. In this system, formalized pictures symbolizing objects and syllables were used to represent words. Hieroglyphic writing was limited to royal inscriptions; *hieratic,* a

Egyptian Hieroglyphs, Luxor, Valley of the Kings; Carved into the Wall and Colored.

less elaborate version, was the writing used in bureaucratic documents. The writing material used in Egypt was papyrus, which was more expensive but less cumbersome than the Mesopotamian clay tablets. Papyrus was made from a special kind of Egyptian reed, the core of which was cut into strips, laid out crosswise, and pressed into textured sheets. First documented around 2700 BCE, papyrus became a major export item in the following millennium.

In addition to aiding in communication, writing—as it did in Mesopotamia—lent itself to a larger and more efficient bureaucracy in Egypt. At the beginning of the Old Kingdom (ca. 2613–2160 BCE), heavy Nile flooding enabled the Egyptian kings to expand agriculture on their lands. The royal palace and temple became large, elaborately hierarchical organizations in which everything was minutely regulated, including the food rations distributed to the palace administrators, priests, craftspeople, and laborers. Using arithmetic manuals, scribes calculated the quantities of bread, beer, and meat rations to be distributed; of timber for the shipyards; and of flax for the linen-weaving workshops. For unused fractions of rations a credit system evolved whereby officials traded among themselves what strongly resembled "futures" on a modern commodity market. In its complexity, the Egyptian bureaucratic system of the Old Kingdom easily surpassed that of lower Mesopotamia during the contemporary Akkadian period (see Map 2.4).

The most astounding bureaucratic achievement of the Old Kingdom was Pharaoh Khufu's (r. 2589–2566 BCE) construction of a pyramid near modern Cairo as a funerary monument for himself. (Two smaller pyramids in the vicinity served as tombs for the bodies of later pharaohs.) Under orders of the stern and even cruel Khufu, stone workers quarried local limestone from the cliffs behind the right bank of the Nile for the central portion of each of the pyramids. Finer, less brittle casing stones came from quarries upstream on the Nile. Ramparts of chipped stone and other debris, as well as sledges, rollers, and heavy levers made of timber, helped laborers move the stone blocks into place, as much as 479 feet high. After the completion of the pyramid, the construction machinery was dismantled, and today sand covers what were once the workers' camps.

The workforce, perhaps as many as 10,000 laborers, consisted of farmers who were working off their annual 1-month labor service owed to the king. A special labor office made sure that the withdrawal of groups of laborers from the villages was staggered in such a way that regular field labor was disrupted as little as possible. Foremen administered the groups of laborers. Other officials provided rations for them in their camps. Although the workers were strictly supervised, we know that they also occasionally went on strike. Labor unrest, however, could easily be suppressed by the Egyptian army, which was composed of up to 20,000 soldiers, mostly Nubian archers.

The pharaohs of the Middle Kingdom (ca. 2040–1750 BCE) were more modest builders and focused instead on large-scale agricultural projects, the mining of metals in Sinai, and long-distance trade. During Amenemhet III's long reign (r. ca.

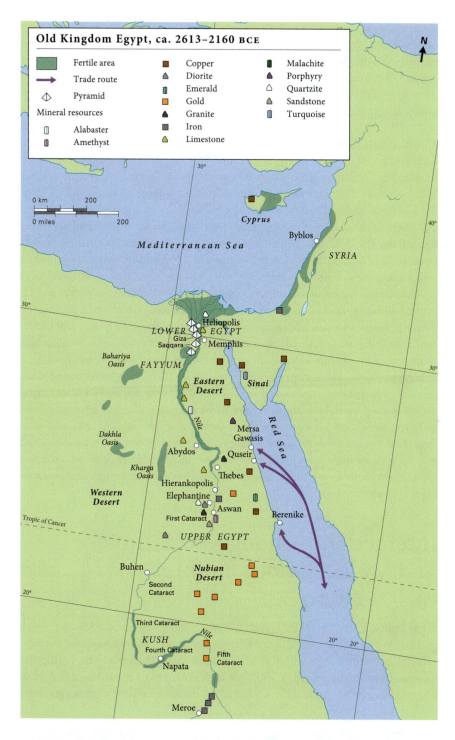

Old Kingdom Egypt, ca. 2613–2160 BCE

- Fertile area
- Trade route
- Pyramid

Mineral resources

- Alabaster
- Amethyst
- Copper
- Diorite
- Emerald
- Gold
- Granite
- Iron
- Limestone
- Malachite
- Porphyry
- Quartzite
- Sandstone
- Turquoise

MAP **2.4** Old Kingdom Egypt, ca. 2613–2160 BCE.

1843–1796 BCE), Egypt reached the peak of its internal development. Workers transferred from Syria drained the Fayyum Depression and created irrigated fields similar to those found around many cities in Mesopotamia. Merchants developed close relations with other merchants in the Levant, from where they imported cedar wood for ships, roofs, and coffins. Egyptian exports consisted of jewelry and art objects made of gold. In the Sinai Peninsula Egyptian miners dug for copper and turquoise. In the desert valleys of Nubia they quarried diorite and mined gold and copper. By the end of Amenemhet's reign, the kingdom numbered about 1 million inhabitants and was a formidable power, even more impressive than the Old Kingdom with its pyramids.

The Minoan Kingdom   After farming had spread from the Levant to Anatolia, seafarers carried the practice westward around 6500 BCE to Greece and the Aegean islands. The first large islands where they settled were Cyprus and Crete. The latter island is about 170 miles long and about 35 miles wide at its widest point. Over the millennia, some of the early villages of Crete grew into towns, and by around 2000 BCE small states with kings, spacious palaces, and surrounding villages were flourishing. The dominant **palace-state** was that of the Minoans (named after its founder, King Minos), a polity with as many as 12,000 inhabitants in the sprawling palace and a few villages outside.

Palace-state: A city or fortified palace with surrounding villages.

The Minoan kingdom was centered on a palace with hundreds of rooms, including vast storage spaces for food and cisterns for the collection of water. Among the palace personnel were scribes who used a pictorial-syllabic script on clay tablets similar to the writing and recording systems of Mesopotamia. Unfortunately, this script, called by scholars *Linear A*, has thus far not been deciphered. In the villages, farmers produced grain, olive oil, wine, and honey. Royal merchants traded these products for obsidian, copper, and tin from Greece, Anatolia, and Cyprus. Craftspeople made pottery, bronze vessels, and jewelry for the palace as well as for export to Egypt, Syria, and Mesopotamia. Minoans were skilled boat builders who constructed oceangoing vessels, some as long as 100 feet, and powered by both sails and rowers. Minoan Crete was closely related to its older neighbors, from whom it had creatively borrowed—but it had also created its own independent trade and seafaring traditions.

Interactions Among Multiethnic and Multireligious Empires, ca. 1500–600 BCE

From around 1700 to 1000 BCE, society in the Middle East and the Mediterranean changed in important ways. Chariot warfare, iron tools, and iron weapons were developed and refined. Agriculture spread from the original core of Syria, Mesopotamia, and Egypt to the periphery in Greece, central Anatolia, central Asia, and Arabia. The peoples in this peripheral area adapted the basic agricultural methods acquired

Minoan Island of Thera, Akrotiri Palace, ca. 1550 BCE. Mural depicting a flotilla of Minoan aristocracy on a visiting tour.

from the core area but also introduced contributions of their own, especially military and transport technologies. On the basis of these contributions, conquerors built large empires in which a small, ethnically defined ruling class ruled over collections of other ethnic groups, speaking a multiplicity of languages and sacrificing to a multiplicity of gods.

The Hittite and Assyrian Empires, 1600–600 BCE

Anatolia (modern-day Turkey) evolved from 7000 to 6000 BCE into the homeland of the so-called Proto-Indo-Europeans. Primarily farmers, Proto-Indo-Europeans migrated in groups over time to eastern and western Europe as well as to central Asia. In these areas they mingled with the local foragers and taught them their languages and farming methods. Groups from one branch, the Indo-Iranians, eventually migrated back to the original agrarian regions of Iran, India, and Mesopotamia. By about 2000–1200 BCE, foragers as far distant as Portugal and Siberia had adopted both Indo-European languages and Middle Eastern farming methods. The only exception was the Basques of modern Spain and France, who became farmers but have preserved their original language to this day.

Horses and Chariots from Central Asia   The spread of agriculture into Europe and central Asia had major consequences for the Middle East and the eastern Mediterranean. Shortly after 3000 BCE, in the region around the Ural Mountains in central Asia, local Indo-European villagers domesticated the horse, using it for its meat and for transporting heavy loads. Around 2000 BCE, after villages in the southern Ural Mountains had been transformed into towns through trade, town leaders emerged who were equipped with horse-drawn chariots, as well as with composite bows, made of a combination of grooved wood and horn carefully glued together. With a length of 4 feet and a range of 150 yards, this bow was much more powerful than the existing simpler and shorter bows dating back to the Paleolithic. A chariot could accommodate two to three warriors, one to guide the horses with leather reins and bronze bits and the others to shoot arrows with the composite bow. Around 1700 BCE, both chariot and composite bow made their entry into the Middle East and eastern Mediterranean region. They contributed to a major transformation of the kingdoms that had hitherto relied solely on foot soldiers.

The Hittite Empire   The first rulers in the Middle East to make use of chariots and composite bows for their military were the Hittites (1650–1182 BCE), who originated in central Anatolia. This area, one of the richest mining regions in the Middle East, had large iron deposits. Iron was a by-product of copper smelting but was initially considered useless since it manifested itself in the form of "bloom iron," a spongy substance with an abundance of ore impurities. Only after prolonged forging, that is, of hammering during which the bloom iron had to be kept red hot, were smiths able to remove the impurities. At the same time, smiths had to add enough carbon from the charcoal in the furnace and allow for exposure to the air to turn the soft metal into hardened iron. By around 1500 BCE, smiths in Anatolia had fully mastered the art of iron making. The Hittites incorporated iron into their chariot armies, in the form of swords, helmets, and protective armor. The combination of these military elements gave the Hittites an early advantage, which they used to become the pioneers of a new type of conquering polity—the multilinguistic, multiethnic, and multireligious empire that was not regionally confined like the kingdom. At its peak, the Hittite Empire stretched from Anatolia to northern Syria, comprising peoples of many languages and religions (see Map 2.5).

To distinguish themselves from ordinary kingdoms, the Hittite kings called themselves "great kings." In their capital, Hattusa, they ruled with an assembly (*panku*) of their principal administrators, recruited from the aristocracy. When they set out on campaign to conquer rival kingdoms, they left the lesser, conquered kings in their positions as provincial rulers. The core of Hittite armies consisted of a nobility of highly trained, disciplined, and mobile chariot warriors. Mercenary foot soldiers, acting as skirmishers, protected the chariots from direct attacks by enemy infantry. These skirmishers were enrolled from among mountaineers, herders, and nomads for the duration of campaigns.

In the conquered lands, the "great kings" placed nobles in strategic garrisons to keep the local, non-Hittite rulers in check. Since the imperial warehouses held limited amounts of foodstuffs, the nobility received land grants, using the rents they extracted from the towns and villages for their livelihood. This Hittite system of

MAP **2.5** The Hittite Empire and Eastern Mediterranean ca. 1500 BCE.

employing both its nobility and local rulers was to become the model of organization for all subsequent Middle Eastern and eastern Mediterranean empires.

The practice of imposing an empire on many regional kingdoms did not make for stable politics. People to the east of the Hittites, the Hurrians in the Zagros Mountains, who also had a king and ruling class equipped with chariots, repeatedly invaded their western neighbors. At one point, in the early sixteenth century BCE, they vied with the Hittites for control of Syria. Their struggle dislodged a Syrian, chariot-equipped people, the Hyksos, who migrated to Egypt, where they established a kingdom in the Nile delta. As a result of losing the delta, the

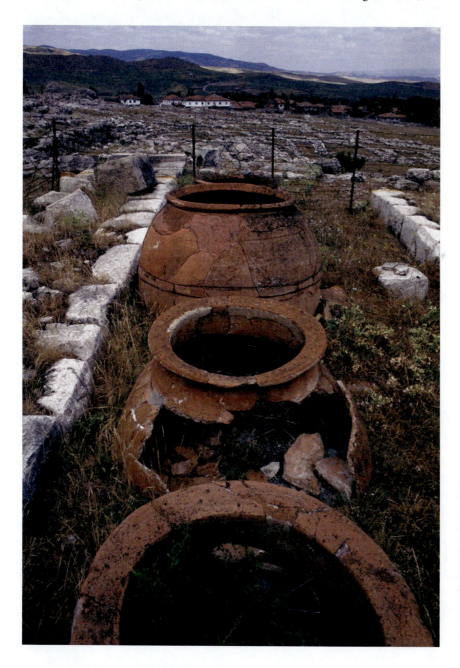

Hattusa, Hittite Empire. The kings of the empire maintained storage centers along the highways of the empire and in the provinces. Troops sent into the provinces supplied themselves from the grain, dried fruits, nuts, arms, and textiles in these storage places. Although transportation by pack animal, cart, or barge was slow and expensive, early empires, like later ones in world history, employed sophisticated logistics to keep functioning.

King Tutankhamen [Tut-an-KHAM-un] (1336–1327 BCE) of Egypt in Full Battle Regalia. The king, accompanied by skirmishers (*lower left*), is aiming at deer in a herd fleeing from his galloping horses

Egyptians adopted chariot warfare and imperialism as well. Under the eighteenth dynasty (ca. 1550–1086 BCE), they inaugurated the New Kingdom, which devoted its military energies to the conquest of Nubia in the south and southern Syria in the north.

Imperial Egypt   During the New Kingdom (1550–1070 BCE), the Egyptians vigorously pushed their border with the Hittites as far north as possible, building garrisons and collecting tributes from a number of coastal cities in southern Syria (modern Palestine). From a rare set of documents, the Amarna Tablets (1386–1335 BCE), found in Egypt in 1887, we receive a glimpse of diplomatic and military interactions among the Middle Eastern empires. Some of these tablets date to the reign of Pharaoh Amenhotep III (r. ca. 1386–1349 BCE), who exchanged lavish gifts with his royal colleagues but, believing himself superior, refused a marriage alliance with the Kassite-Babylonian king Kadashman-Enlil I (r. ca. 1374–1360 BCE).

The Egyptians eventually clashed with the Hittites at Qadesh [KAH-desh] in northern Syria (1274 BCE), where they engaged in the largest chariot battle ever fought in the Middle East. Neither side prevailed, and the two empires decided to curb their imperialism and coexist diplomatically with each other, with Syria divided between them.

A short time later, this coexistence was shattered by invasions of the "Sea People" from the Aegean Sea. Originally a mixture of former foot soldiers, mountaineers, and herders from northern Greece had raided the Mycenaean [My-sen-EE-yan] kingdoms of southern Greece, as we discuss later in this chapter (see The Mycenaeans and Early Greeks). These people, joined by survivors of the collapsing kingdoms, took to the sea (hence their name

A Marriage Proposal

King Kadashman-Enlil I to Amenhotep III: "[Moreove]r, you, my brother, when I wrote [to you] about marrying your daughter . . . [you wrote to me] 'Never has a daughter of the king of Egypt been given to anyone.' Why is [she not given]? . . . [Surely] beautiful women . . . are available. Send me one beautiful woman as if [she were your daughter]! Who would say she is not the king's daughter?"

—Mark William Chavalas, ed. *The Ancient Near East: Historical Sources in Translation.* Translated by Eva von Dassow and Kyle Greenwood, p. 194. Malden, MA: Routledge, 2006.

"Sea People") and sailed to the wealthy kingdoms of the Levant. One group of Sea People, the Ahhiyawa [Ahi-YA-wah], in Greek "Achaians" [A-KAY-ans], presumably remnants of one of the Mycenaean kingdoms, destroyed the Hittite Empire in 1207 BCE, reducing it to a few small fragments. The Egyptian Empire lost southern Syria to another set of seafaring invaders, the Pelesets [PE-le-sets] (Philistines or Palestinians), and retreated to Sinai, abandoning its imperial ambitions.

The invasions by Sea People triggered the so-called **Bronze Age collapse** of ca. 1200 BCE with which the **Iron Age** in the Middle East and eastern Mediterranean began. The collapse is explained as a crisis in which the overextended early empires of the Hittites and Egyptians were unable to sustain the enormous expenses required for chariot warfare. With the decline in the numbers of chariots, large numbers of skirmishers became jobless. Scholars assume that most of the destruction and diminishment of these early kingdoms was due to marauding or migrating skirmishers like the Ahhiyawa and Pelesets who were unemployed.

The Assyrians   Emerging after the Bronze Age collapse, the Assyrians (ca. 1350–607 BCE) founded a new empire, which was also based on rain-fed agriculture, much like the Hittite Empire. Its capital was Assur, a city founded in upper Mesopotamia around 2000 BCE on an island in the Tigris River. Originally, Assur's farming base was too limited to support territorial conquests. Instead, its inhabitants enriched themselves through trade. They built trading outposts as far away as central Anatolia and exchanged textiles for timber, copper, tin, and silver, much of which they sold to the Babylonians in the south. In the fourteenth century BCE, the Assyrian kings began to use Assur's commercial riches to finance their first large-scale conquests.

The Assyrians expanded into both the Zagros Mountains and Syria, reaching the borders of the Hittite Empire and claiming equal status with them. The great king of the Hittites, however, haughtily rejected the upstart's claim: "On what account should I write to you about brotherhood? Were you and I born from the same mother?" Stopped at the Hittite borders, Assyrian troops turned southeastward and expanded into lower Mesopotamia. Here, they occupied Babylon for a short period, humiliating their wealthy neighbors by carrying away the statue of the city god.

After some severe military setbacks, during which Assyria was reduced to its upper Mesopotamian center, ambitious kings renewed Assyrian expansion, creating Neo-Assyria (New Assyria), which lasted from 934 to 607 BCE. They embarked on conquests as had no other kings before them, systematically and ruthlessly conquering the lands around them. The core of the Neo-Assyrian armies consisted of small chariot forces and larger regiments of a new type of warrior—horsemen, chosen from among the nobility. These horsemen rode without stirrup on saddlecloths and fought using bows and arrows. The conquered peoples were forced to contribute soldiers to the Assyrian infantry, thus replenishing and multiplying the ranks of the largest and most expendable forces. Iron swords, iron-tipped lances, full-length scale armor (iron platelets sewn on leather shirts), and iron helmets were now common and helped the Assyrians to become the most formidable empire builders of their day.

In fact, the Assyrians were among the most ruthless campaigners in recorded history. They destroyed temples, razed cities, and forcibly deported the defeated inhabitants of entire provinces to other parts of the empire. Scholars have estimated that hundreds of thousands of deportees, the men among them often in

Bronze Age collapse: Around 1200 BCE, resulting from the collapse of the Hittite Empire and the weakening of the Egyptian New Kingdom; chariot warfare had become unsustainable in these early kingdoms.

Iron Age: Around 1500–1200 BCE, smiths were able to produce sufficiently high temperatures to smelter iron bloom, a mixture of iron and a variety of impurities.

chains, had to walk hundreds of miles through the countryside before being settled in new villages. At the peak of their conquests (745–609 BCE), the Assyrian rulers became the first to unify all of the Middle East, a dream first expressed by King Naram-Sin of Akkad centuries earlier. This same accomplishment would be repeated many more times in years to come (see Map 2.6).

Small Kingdoms on the Imperial Margins, 1600–600 BCE

Syria was a region between the Hittite (or later, Assyrian) Empire in the north and the Egyptian Empire in the south. The dominant form of political organization in these regions was the city-state under a royal dynasty. These city-states were located on the coast and had harbors, a number of surrounding villages, and a larger hinterland of independent villages in the hills and mountains. In northern Syria, the city-states were those of the Phoenicians; in southern Syria, they were those of the Pelesets on the coast and the Israelites in the hills. In the eastern Mediterranean, outside the military reach of the Hittite and Assyrian Empires but in commercial contact with them, were the Mycenaean palace-states and early Greek city-states.

MAP **2.6** The Assyrian Empire.

The Phoenicians The people known in Greek as "Phoenicians" and by the Egyptians as "Canaanites" held the city-states of Byblos (modern Jubeil [Joo-BALE]), Sidon, and Tyre (ca. 1600–300 BCE), each with a population of several tens of thousands. The Phoenicians also controlled the slopes of Mount Lebanon, with its famous cedars. These valuable trees, together with timber from Anatolia, were much sought after in the Middle East and eastern Mediterranean as construction material for buildings and ships. No less important was a species of sea snail collected on the beaches, from which a highly valued purple textile dye was extracted. The surrounding villages produced barley and wheat for the cities as well as olive oil, wine, dried fruits, and nuts for export. Urban craftspeople made ceramics, textiles, leather goods, jewelry, and metalware with distinctive Phoenician designs, destined for sale abroad. More than any other territorial states in the Middle East, the Phoenician city-states were engaged in trade.

Assyrian Transport of Phoenician Timber (Cedar?) from the Levant down the Tigris River.

Phoenicians as traders appear in the historical record from 2500 BCE onward. During ca. 1600–1200 BCE, the Phoenicians and Mycenaeans shared the sea trade of the eastern Mediterranean, transporting their own goods as well as metals, timber, and stone. On land, they preferred paying tribute and occasionally putting their fleets at the service of Hittite or Egyptian imperial overlords. When the Mycenaean kingdoms and Hittite Empire collapsed and the Egyptians withdrew around 1200 BCE under the onslaught of the Sea People, the Phoenicians seized their chance. Systematically expanding their reach in the Mediterranean, they established trade outposts on islands and along the Mediterranean coast as far west as modern Morocco and Spain.

In addition to founding numerous ports and outposts around the Mediterranean (one of which, Carthage, would later become a powerful empire on its own), the Phoenicians acquired world-historical importance through their introduction of the letter alphabet. People in Syria had been familiar with the Mesopotamian cuneiform and Egyptian hieroglyphic writing systems for centuries. Both systems were complicated, however, and required many years of training to learn. From rock inscriptions discovered in 1998 in Egypt it appears that Syrian (or Phoenician) merchants began experimenting around 1900–1800 BCE with a much simplified writing system. In this system letters replaced the traditional signs and syllables, with each letter standing for a spoken consonant. Subsequently, in various parts of Syria, fully developed alphabets with letters for about 30 spoken consonants appeared (the vowels were not written). The Phoenician alphabet of ca. 1200 BCE was the most widely used, becoming the ancestor of all alphabetical scripts.

The Pelesets and Israelites During its imperial phase (ca. 1550–1200 BCE), Egypt controlled the Palestinian towns of Gaza, Ashkelon, Ashdod, Gath, and Ekron. Occasionally, the Egyptian kings aided their governors in these towns by carrying out punitive campaigns. After one such campaign, a defeated people in southern Syria was "stripped bare, wholly lacking seed," as an Egyptian inscription of 1207 BCE recorded. The name used in the inscription for this people was "Israel," the first time this name appeared in the records. "Israel" seems to refer to some sort of tribal alliance among Canaanite villagers and herders in the hills.

When the Pelesets, or Philistines, took over southern Syria and Egypt withdrew a short time later, agriculture and trade quickly recovered from heavy Egyptian taxation. The coastal Philistines established garrisons among the Israelites in order to secure trade routes through the highlands and along the Jordan valley. In response, as is recorded in the Hebrew Bible (the Old Testament in Christian usage), a military leader named Saul and a number of tribal leaders recruited a military force that began a war of liberation against the Philistines. According to this scripture, Saul was killed during the early stages of the war and his successor, David, completed the liberation, establishing himself as king in Jerusalem shortly after 1000 BCE.

According to the Hebrew Bible, Jerusalem was a town on top of a mountain spur in southern Syria. David's son Solomon is said to have greatly enlarged the town, constructing a palace, the famous temple, and administrative buildings. To date, archaeologists have found few traces of Solomon's constructions except a few foundation walls and terraces on the eastern slope of present-day Jerusalem. Moreover, they have not even been able to confirm the rise of Jerusalem from village to city level. For historians, therefore, the biblical account, like that of many ancient texts, is perhaps best understood not as history but as a religious foundation story, demonstrating God's providence.

According to the Hebrew Bible, the two states that emerged after Solomon, Israel in the north (930–722 BCE) and Judah in the south (930–587 BCE), enjoyed only short periods of independence from the coastal Philistines. The empire of Assyria and its successor, Neo-Babylonia (626–539 BCE), conquered the two kingdoms in the sixth century BCE. Thousands of members of the two royal families, priests, scribes, landowners, and craftspeople had to resettle in other parts of Syria or in Mesopotamia. The Philistines, together with people in the Syrian steppes (collectively called "Arabs"), suffered similar fates of defeat and deportation. In their place, Anatolian and Iranian populations settled in Syria. The final wave of Israelite deportations, under the Neo-Babylonians in 597–582 BCE, became the infamous "Babylonian captivity" (*gola*) mourned by several prophets in the Hebrew Bible.

The Mycenaeans and Early Greeks   Parallel to the Phoenicians, Pelesets, and Israelites in Syria, the Mycenaeans arose in Greece and the eastern Mediterranean during the middle of the second millennium BCE. After the adaptation to farming, demand for specialized agricultural products (such as olive oil, wine, dried fruits, and nuts) among the villages had advanced sufficiently to result in the emergence of towns and cities which traded in these goods as well as in copper and bronze wares. Around 1700 BCE, in Attica and the Peloponnesus, two peninsulas with relatively large plains suitable for agriculture, leaders built forts as refuges in times of war for their fellow villagers. The best known among these forts were Mycenae, Tiryns, Pylos, Sparta, and Athens.

Two centuries later, the forts evolved into palaces with warrior lords and kings, as well as administrative offices, surrounded by clusters of villages. In these palace-states, scribes introduced a new, cuneiform-derived script which, contrary to the Linear A of the Minoans, has been deciphered. This *Linear B* script provides us with invaluable sources for understanding early Greek culture. About 1450 BCE, chariot and bronze weapon–equipped Mycenaean warriors sailed to Minoan Crete and conquered the island. For about two and a half centuries the Mycenaeans were the major seafaring power in the eastern Mediterranean, establishing trading outposts in competition with the Phoenicians.

The Mycenaean palace-states were short-lived. When an earthquake hit around 1250 BCE, the walls of many palaces collapsed. Former mercenaries (skirmishers in the chariot armies of the Hittites) joined by herders from northern Greece raided the weakened Mycenaean palace-states. A century later most palaces had disappeared, together with their administrators, scribes, and archives. The descendants of the kings, however, managed to salvage some wealth, as evidenced by their tombs. Iron swords and jewelry found in these tombs were of Phoenician origin and indicate that some sea trade continued even after the destruction of the Mycenaean states.

A general recovery in Greece began during the eighth century BCE. Trade in agricultural goods such as grain, olive oil, and honey was revived in new market outposts in Anatolia, Syria, and Egypt. The Anatolian craft of ironworking spread to Greece. Literacy returned as the Greeks adapted the Phoenician alphabet, adding vowels to the existing consonants to create the Greek alphabet. The population increased, often so quickly that many people were unable to find employment. After 750 BCE, many unemployed or adventurous Greeks seeking new challenges emigrated to the Anatolian west coast or as far as Italy and the Black Sea to colonize the land and establish new cities. As they developed into city-states of their own, the settlements on the Anatolian coast became known collectively as "Ionia."

The distinctive mark of these new cities was the absence of palaces. Instead, a sacred precinct in a city's center served as an open space for general assemblies. Contained within this space were a temple and administrative buildings with porches supported by rows of pillars. The construction techniques and styles for these temples and pillars came from Egypt. Farmers in villages outside the city walls produced grain, vegetables, olive oil, and wine for the urban dwellers. A city with surrounding villages formed a city-state, or *polis*. Each of these new city-states administered its own internal and external affairs, although they also formed alliances or pursued hostilities with each other. That the polis was ideally suited for the Greeks was attested by Aristotle (384–322 BCE).

Initially, kings from among the landowning families were responsible for the administration of the city-states. Their forerunners had been the warrior lords and the landowning families of the post-Mycenaean period and made up what the Greeks called the "aristocracy" of the states. During the period 750–600 BCE, conflict often broke out between the aristocracy and the common folk—merchants, traders, craftspeople, and free farmers—over the distribution of wealth in the growing cities. Some aristocrats exploited these tensions and allied themselves with groups of commoners. Once allied, these aristocrats assumed power as tyrants, who attempted to create family dynasties. Many of the would-be dynasts sponsored festivals, public work projects, and artists; but their popularity rarely lasted beyond the sons who succeeded them.

What Is a Polis?

"Because it is the completion of associations existing by nature, every polis exists by nature, having itself the same quality as the earlier association from which it grew.... From these considerations it is evident that the polis belongs to the class of things that exist by nature, and that man is by nature an animal intended to live in a polis. He who is without a polis, by reason of his own nature and not of some accident, is either a poor sort of being, or a being higher than man: he is like the man of whom Homer wrote in denunciation: 'Clanless and lawless and heartless is he.'"

—Aristotle, *Politics*. Translated by Ernest Barker, bk. 1, chap. 2, sec. 8–9. Oxford: Oxford University Press, 1962.

Other aristocrats opposed the tyrants and agreed to power sharing with the commoners. Through trade, many commoners were becoming wealthier than the aristocrats. Both aristocrats and commoners served as foot soldiers in the city-states' defense forces. These armies relied not on charioteers but on foot soldiers, who were heavily armed with shields, lances, and swords, all made of iron. Their battle order was the *phalanx*, that is, a block of eight or more rows of soldiers marching forward shoulder to shoulder, the shield held in the left hand of each man helping to guard the man to his left, while in his right hand he held a lance or pike.

In the narrow valleys and defiles of Greece and Ionia these bristling "hedgehog" formations were nearly impossible to break with archers, infantry, or cavalry—if each man held his position and the men in the back moved up to take the place of those who fell. In these phalanxes it was not individual aristocratic valor that counted but the courageous willingness of each citizen-soldier to support and protect the other. Thus, as many ordinary city dwellers became the military equals of the aristocracy in the crucible of battle, they quite naturally began to demand an equal share of political power in times of peace.

Political reformers in the sixth century BCE gave commoners their first basic political rights. The best-known reforms were those introduced in Athens and Sparta, the city-states with the largest agricultural territories. In Athens, aristocratic rule was replaced with political rights distributed according to levels of property ownership. The poorest class had the right to participate in the citizen assembly (*ekklesia*), cast votes, and sit on juries; the wealthier classes could run for a variety of leadership and temple offices. A written law code curbed arbitrariness. With these assemblies, the Greek city-states continued the Mesopotamian and Hittite systems of assemblies discussed earlier. Whether the Greeks developed their assemblies independently or adopted them from their predecessors is not known. What can be argued, however, is whether the idea of political participation is deeply rooted in the region of the Middle East and the eastern Mediterranean. In Greece, and later Rome, these traditions would evolve into the ancestral forms of many of the political institutions we live under today, particularly **republican** and **democratic** offices.

Republicanism: A system of government in which, in the place of kings, the people are sovereign, electing representatives to executive and legislative offices.

In Sparta, the traditional rule by two co-equal kings was held in check through the creation of a board of five officers elected annually from among the popular assembly. These officers were responsible for the administration of day-to-day affairs in Sparta. The assembly was made up of all landowners wealthy enough to live in town because of the revenue they collected from their legally indentured (unfree) tenant farmers in the surrounding villages. These political reforms, however, did not prevent new tyrants from rising up in periodic takeover attempts. Thus, in the middle of the first millennium BCE Greeks were still struggling to find a consistent direction for their political development.

Democracy: A system of government in which most or all of the people elect representatives and in some cases decide on important issues themselves.

Religious Experience and Cultural Achievements

By around 5500 BCE, when agriculture had replaced foraging, many human groups began to move from animism to polytheism as their new form of religion. In *animism*, people experience an awe and reverence toward the creatures and forces of the natural world. However, there is no indication in the available archaeological record that people identified these creatures and forces with particular deities. With the rise of cities and the development of writing, these forces received names. *Polytheism* is the general term used to denote religions of personified forces in nature. Artists depicted and sculpted the deities as well as the rulers who derived their mandates from these gods. Writers recorded myths and hymns exploring the relationship between humans and gods. Administrators, responsible for constructing architectural monuments, calculating the calendar, and assessing the taxes laid the foundations of the mathematical and physical sciences. Since many of the religious and cultural achievements were expressed in writing, we can evaluate them today with far better understanding than the culture of the foragers and early farmers.

Toward Polytheism   The creators of the Paleolithic rock paintings in Africa, Europe, and Australia (discussed in Chapter 1) have left us few hints of their spiritual preoccupations in their world full of dangerous animals. The depictions of "lionman," "bisonman," and "sorcerer" are but a few examples where the human and animal worlds are merged, presumably with people in the cave rituals experiencing this merger, with the purpose of influencing the animal world. In the Neolithic transition period from foraging to agriculture, the principal change was the transfer of ritual from caves to aboveground sanctuaries and towns.

An example of the transfer to a sanctuary was Gökbeli Tepe in southern Anatolia, a place where foragers came together for rituals during 9000–6000 BCE. Excavations begun in 1995 are still in progress, but a rich imagery of animals, mostly in the form of reliefs, has already been unearthed. It shows that animism was still in force, even if the venue was no longer a cave. The oldest example documenting the transfer of ritual from the cave to the town is Çatal Hüyük [Tsha-TAL Hoo-YOOK] (7500–5700 BCE) in southern Anatolia, excavated in the 1960s and 1990s. At its height, the town had 5,000 inhabitants, who lived in densely packed houses accessible only from the top with ladders. The inhabitants farmed fields outside of town, using irrigation water from the Taurus Mountains, and hunted extensively. Probably communal rooms in town contained a concentration of artifacts, among which Venus-type figurines and reliefs and wall paintings of animals, especially of *aurochs* (ancestors of bulls), are prominent. The imagery is reminiscent of that of the Paleolithic foragers, but the emergence of urban places of ritual indicates that humans were far along in the transition from nature to civilization.

In Ubaid Mesopotamia (6000–4000 BCE), urban places of ritual evolved into temples. These temples contained figurines of the hybrid human–animal as well as the Venus type of exaggerated female form. Urban dwellers then took the decisive steps of transition from animism to polytheism in the period 3500–2500 BCE when writing developed and kings ruled cities.

This connection between writing, kingship, and gods is crucial for an understanding of polytheism and religion in general: Prior to 3500 BCE, religion was an impersonal and nameless animism; thereafter, it was the polytheism of kings with often colorful personalities, told in myths and epics. Writing made it possible to record the names of individuals, kings viewed themselves as the guarantors of urban life, and gods were the powers that endowed kings with the authority to prevent urban life from slipping back into preurban culture. In the cities, people were no longer in awe of wild animals, as they had been during forager days. But they were still in awe of nature's powers, as they had been during the earlier Neolithic village life, when nature could be benevolent through bounty and fertility as well as wrathful through floods, storms, droughts, or blights.

Polytheism began when kings became individuals—through adopting patron deities—and associated the awe-inspiring natural powers and phenomena with these deities. Perhaps polytheism evolved the other way around: Villagers created rituals to please the awe-inspiring anonymous forces of nature, and after the introduction of writing and kingship, these forces became deities. Either way, the rise of polytheism depended crucially on writing and kingship.

Mesopotamian and Egyptian Literature

Among the earliest writings in the world exploring religious themes are the *Epic of Gilgamesh* and the myth of *Enuma Elish*. These had their origins in third-millennium BCE Mesopotamia but were not recorded for another millennium. The first is the story of Gilgamesh, who was a mythical king in early Sumer. Gilgamesh, according to the epic, ruled Uruk and built its walls. Like the Chinese sage kings we will meet in Chapter 4, he fought many battles and carried out heroic deeds in both this world and the underworld but failed in his ultimate quest to find immortality. In the end, Gilgamesh could not escape the fate of all mortals and had to suffer death as well.

The myth of *Enuma Elish* (named after its first line, which means "when on high...") tells the story of creation when nothing existed but Father Abzu (the Depth or Abyss) and Mother Tiamat (Ocean) and their numerous children, who were the city gods of Mesopotamia. The raucous behavior of his children enraged Abzu. He tried to kill them but was instead murdered by one of them. Tiamat [Tee-ya-MAT] and her second husband continued the violent domestic battle, finally driving the children away. Marduk [MAR-dook], alone among the children, eventually returned and slaughtered both his mother and stepfather. He split Tiamat's body into two halves, which became heaven and earth. From the blood of the stepfather he made humankind, whom he predestined to serve the gods. One senses how the unknown authors of this text struggle with the question of power in nature—at times benevolent and at times violent, always unpredictable, even as one sacrifices to please it.

Egyptian literature similarly had its roots in the third millennium and was written down by the middle of the second millennium. As in Mesopotamia, most Egyptian texts were prayers and songs to the gods. Many were similar to those of Enheduanna, cited in the vignette at the beginning of this chapter. *Epics* (long stories about the exploits of heroes such as Gilgamesh) are absent from Egyptian literature. Instead, Egyptians wrote short tales with serious or humorous, tragic or comical themes, usually involving good or bad kings.

Shrine. Reconstruction of a household shrine from Çatal Hüyük, Turkey, with the ox or bull heads implanted in the walls.

The Egyptian version of the creation myth, like those of the Mesopotamians, also begins with an original ocean. In the Egyptian telling, an island arose from the depth of this ocean. The ruler of this island was the creator god Atum, who contained all the qualities of nature in himself. He created things in pairs, one after the other, beginning with air and water and finishing his handiwork with the male and female of the human race. This Egyptian creation myth is more explicit than its Mesopotamian cousin about the infinity of the original "depth" and "ocean," out of which earth and heaven were created. It is also far less violent, a reflection of the more gradual and harmonious growth of the Egyptian kingdom and empire.

Greek Literature   The earliest Greek literature dates to the eighth century BCE. The period 750–600 BCE was a time of close cultural contact between the rising Greek city-states and Neo-Assyria, which dominated Syria and Anatolia. Not surprisingly, therefore, the Assyrian versions of the Mesopotamian epic and creation myths, *Gilgamesh* and *Enuma Elish*, made their way to the Greeks, where they were incorporated into Greek culture. This incorporation was the work of two gifted writers.

Adapting to Middle Eastern cultural influence, two major figures stand at the beginning of Greek literature, Homer (fl. ca. 730 BCE) and Hesiod (fl. ca. 700 BCE), both from Greek city-states in Anatolia. Homer composed two epics in the form of extended poems, the tragedy *Iliad* and the narrative legend *Odyssey*. The *Iliad* takes place in the camp of the Greeks as they are besieging the Anatolian city of Troy. It describes the jealousies and rivalries among the Greeks as they battle unsuccessfully to take the city. Their luck changed only when the hero Achilles finally came forward and, in a ferocious combat, killed Hector, the prince of Troy. In the *Odyssey*, the hero Odysseus, or Ulysses, was drawn into a lengthy, adventurous sea voyage, beset with many strange hardships, around the Mediterranean. While he was away at sea, his wife, Penelope, was besieged at home by would-be lovers. Ulysses eventually returned and drove the interlopers away, reconciled with Penelope, and restored peace to his kingdom.

Like its Mesopotamian model, Hesiod's *Theogony* begins with "Chaos, the Abyss," out of which the earth, or Gaia, came into being. The rest of the *Theogony* is devoted to telling the stories of some 300 divinities descended from Chaos and Gaia. Three of the first four generations of deities destroyed each other violently. The fourth, the Olympians, became the present pantheon of gods, with Zeus as the patriarch. As we can see from the opening lines, Hesiod, like his Mesopotamian predecessors, goes to great pains to explain how divine, immortal beings could both be responsible for order on earth and act violently through the forces of nature.

As in Mesopotamia and Egypt, seasonal festivals were of great importance in Greece. In contrast to Mesopotamia and Egypt, however, Greek city culture encouraged personal artistic expression. Given the increasing participation of commoners in the state, however, festivals in Greece became occasions for writing songs and poems whose authors were remembered by name. Festivals often had poetry contests, and Hesiod appears as the earliest winner of such a contest. In the following century, a writer who acquired fame outside the poetry contest circuit was Sappho. She was the instructor of female initiation groups in one of the city-states on the island of Lesbos. Her poetry reflects the experience of erotic experimentation among adolescent girls which was part of their preparation for marriage.

Egyptian Statue (*left*) and Early Greek (*right*) Adaptation. The Egyptian influence on the Greek cities is striking. Here, we have a visual example of the pattern of origins, interaction, and adaptation. The Greek example is a creative adaptation of an Egyptian-originated model.

Sculptures and Paintings

Mesopotamian and Egyptian rulers wanted to impress those who observed them as severe, powerful, and pious persons. Early Mesopotamian kings had massive statues made of themselves, showing them posed in prayer. In Egypt, compact, block-like royals stand freely or sit impassively on their thrones. Statues in both regions often have wide, oversized eyes that stare sternly at the viewer. On many half-sculptures carved into stone, larger-than-life-size kings with bulging muscles trample victoriously over diminutive enemies. In all these sculptures the primary objective of the artists was not photographic realism but a clear rendering of the distinctive qualitative differences between gods and kings, on the one hand, and subjects, on the other.

Wall paintings were highly popular among Mesopotamians, Egyptians, and Minoans. Unfortunately, in the humidity of lower Mesopotamia, few such paintings survived. By contrast, in the dry climate of Egypt (except for the delta) a large number still exist. Paintings filled the interior of tombs, illustrating scenes from their owners' lives. The painters' point was not only to show their royal features but also to draw them from all angles: Looking at the images from the perspective of eternal life, the kings should be able to see themselves in all their earthly aspects simultaneously. Accordingly, face, arms, and legs were painted in profile; eyes, shoulders, and upper body appear frontally; and the waist was half frontal but turned to reveal the navel. Later, as more nonroyal people built tombs for themselves, the complex multiangled royal perspective gave way to a simpler, single-angle realism.

The Greek arts began in the Minoan and Mycenaean city-states. Minoan wall paintings, stylistically related to those of the Egyptian New Kingdom (1550–1070 BCE), show realistic scenes with vegetation, birds, dolphins, and bulls. The art of Mycenae is mostly known to us from small sculptures, masks, drinking vessels, and jewelry found in the tombs of royal warriors. Through their close contact with the Assyrians, the Greeks in their growing city-states (during the period ca. 750–600 BCE) learned not only about Mesopotamian literature but also about their arts. Winged and fighting animals, as well as muscular gods and heroes, appear in vase paintings. Egypt was the inspiration for the development of sculptures, which initially were block-like, wide-eyed, and stylized. Gradually, however, with the decline of the aristocracy, stylized representation was replaced by realism. By the 500s BCE, the heavy and stern-looking kings were succeeded by well-proportioned, smoothly muscled, and slightly smiling figures depicted as one would encounter them in the market.

Scientific Beginnings

In both Mesopotamia and Egypt, conceptualization of reality advanced substantially from Old and New Stone Age imagery. For the first time we get glimpses of humans constructing abstract conceptualizations, without recourse to the senses—for example, in mathematics. Mathematical calculations, such as addition and subtraction, began in Mesopotamia even before the first writing system was introduced.

Subsequently, scribes developed tables for multiplication and division, squares, cubes, roots, cube roots, and reciprocal and exponential functions. They calculated numerical approximations for the roots of 2 and 3. Exercise texts from the Old Babylonian period (ca. 2000–1600 BCE) pose such problems as "Beyond the ditch I made a dike, one cubit per cubit is the inclination of this dike. What is the base, the top and the height of it? And what is its circumference?" Babylonian mathematical interests focused primarily on the roots of algebra. Scribes, however, also laid the foundations for geometry and astronomy by devising the system of 60 degrees for arcs, angles, and time—all still in use today. The Babylonians even formulated what would later be called the "Pythagorean theorem"—that is, the sum of the squares of the sides in a right triangle equals the square of the hypotenuse—a millennium before Pythagoras produced it in Greece.

In Egypt, the *Rhind Mathematical Papyrus* (ca. 1550 BCE) is an early handbook of geometrical and algebraic questions typically used by scribes and administrators. It teaches the apprentice scribe how to calculate the volume of rectangles, triangles, and pyramids and how to measure the slopes of angles. Algebraic operations are illustrated through examples such as "[animal] fat [worth] ten gallons [of grain] is issued for one year; what is its share per day?" As in Mesopotamia, Egyptian mathematics implicitly employed important mathematical principles without yet stating them explicitly.

The *Kahun* (ca. 1825 BCE) and *Edwin Smith* (ca. 1534 BCE) *Papyri* are the best-known texts on the applied science of medicine. They cover diagnosis, prescriptions, and surgery. A few examples illustrate ancient Egyptian medical standards. Headache is diagnosed as "half-head," which the Greeks translated as "*hemi-krania*," from which our English word "migraine" is derived. Prescriptions for treating stiffness of limbs, pregnancy, birth complications, and childhood diseases, as well as advice on birth control and abortion, recommend mixtures of homeopathic herbs and elements. Surgeons received advice on how to use copper knives for male and female circumcision and needles for stitching up wounds. During their work, physicians were encouraged to repeat magic healing formulas that encouraged their patients to use their own self-healing powers.

Babylonian Astronomy

"A surviving Babylonian tablet for the year 133/132 BCE calculates where in the zodiac the moon will be at the beginning of consecutive months. The aim is to predict the first appearance of the new moon (important for the calendar since the new moon signified the beginning of a new month.) What makes this a mathematically difficult calculation is the fact that the moon's speed through the zodiac is variable, gradually increasing and decreasing by turns over the course of the year.... On the clay tablet ... the speed assigned to the lunar motion (measured in degrees of the zodiac traversed by month) is assumed to *decrease* by a fixed amount per month for the first three months, to *increase* by a fixed amount per month for the next six months, and finally to *decrease* by a fixed amount per month for the remainder of the year. If graphed ... (something [the Mesopotamians] could not do), the lunar speed over the course of the year appears as a zig-zag function."

—Stephen Toulmin and June Goddfield. *The Fabric of the Heavens: The Development of Astronomy and Dynamics*, p. 50. Chicago: University of Chicago Press, 1999.

Putting It All Together

The beginning of the agrarian age in the Middle East and eastern Mediterranean was marked by agricultural surpluses, especially in irrigated areas. Depending on the size of the surplus, the pattern of state formation became visible along which city-states, kingdoms, and empires emerged in the various areas of the region (see the Concept Map). The central concern of the rulers in these small and large states was establishing and maintaining their authority, which included the use of military force—something not always easy to justify, especially when trade and ruling class cooperation were also important. Therefore, the rulers appealed to gods, that is,

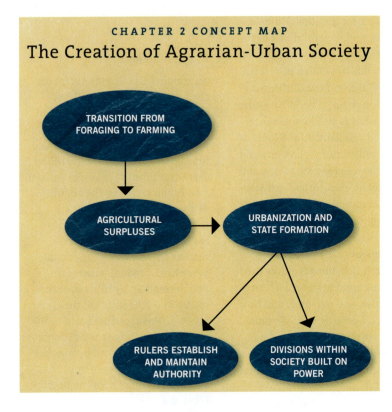

CHAPTER 2 CONCEPT MAP

The Creation of Agrarian-Urban Society

TRANSITION FROM FORAGING TO FARMING

AGRICULTURAL SURPLUSES

URBANIZATION AND STATE FORMATION

RULERS ESTABLISH AND MAINTAIN AUTHORITY

DIVISIONS WITHIN SOCIETY BUILT ON POWER

personalized forces in nature stronger than rulers. The will of these forces, to which even rulers submitted, was conceived as being expressed in the law code of each state. Gods were law-givers, and their law possessed divine authority; thus, rulers became the executers of the god-given law.

Although "divine," the rulers' mandate was never absolute. Popular or aristocratic assemblies from preroyal times of tribal or clan organization survived stubbornly or were revived in the Greek *poleis*. Although the Hittite and Assyrian kings succeeded in marginalizing these assemblies during periods of empire building, the divine mandate was not exclusively theirs and they had to share power, if only to a limited degree. It is important to note that this tradition of assemblies, which we often associate solely with Greece, is widespread in the Middle East. This awareness is necessary to understand the period after 600 BCE when individuals arose with messages of personal salvation and announced that it was not simply fate or misfortune to live and die under these often harsh imperial powers. Instead, they insisted that the destiny of humanity *transcended* these all too human institutions.

Review and Respond

1. Explain and discuss the various steps in the agrarian–urban transformation in the Middle East, from the end of the last Ice Age to the foundation of Eridu.

2. Compare and contrast the early kingdoms of Mesopotamia and Egypt.

3. What were the main characteristics of empires, such as those of the Hittites and Assyrians?

4. Discuss the social structures of Middle Eastern kingdoms and empires. How were gender relations defined?

5. Highlight the major cultural achievements in the Middle East and eastern Mediterranean from the rise of cities and kingdoms to the imperial period and early city-states in Greece.

▶ For additional resources, including maps, primary sources, visuals, and quizzes, please go to www.oup.com/us/vonsivers. Please see the Further Resources section at the back of the book for additional readings and suggested websites.

Thinking Through Patterns

▶ **What are the main factors that enabled the transition from foraging to farming?**

One crucial factor in this pattern was the environment of the Taurus–Zagros–Levant region, the Fertile Crescent. Adequate rainfall, abundant edible plants suitable for domestication, and several animals that proved useful and easy to domesticate characterized the region. But had it not been for human beings mastering irrigation, such a transition might have remained confined to small microclimatic regions. Populations in the great riverine agricultural areas in Mesopotamia and Egypt (and, as we will see in the following chapters, India and China) took as their task the mastery of the fertility of river valleys and the use of reliable river water for irrigation, rather than relying on rainfall. Here was a system adaptable to a variety of climates, as witnessed by the fact that these four early agricultural civilizations arose in dry climates watered by large river systems.

While scholars still debate the absolute origins of the domestication of plants and animals (the Neolithic revolution), most are in agreement that the Fertile Crescent is central to this process. Here, experimentation with local grains, leaf plants, and pulses helped humans develop more reliable and better-yielding crops, which were then traded regionally and, through regional trade, further afield. The climatic zones of Eurasia were especially well suited to this because of the long east–west axis. Animals like sheep, goats, and cattle were similarly found over wide areas and were easy to trade, which led to the sharing of information about raising livestock. Another important factor was that as populations grew from the stability of food production by agriculture, groups split off and started their own communities, carrying the new techniques with them. Thus, by about 5000 BCE, the basic techniques and species of Eurasian and North African domestication were well established.

▶ **Where did the pattern of agrarian life first emerge and why?**

▶ **How did the creation of agrarian–urban society—what we commonly call "civilization"—make for an entirely new pattern of world history?**

The ability of humans to create large food surpluses encouraged a considerable degree of settlement. Such stability enabled the nonproducing part of the population to occupy themselves with creating nonagricultural things—buildings, religious centers, defensive works, dwellings. As these elements of villages and towns grew and became more complex, they allowed the cumulative knowledge and production of human beings to enlarge in these sites. In short, cities created an entirely new kind of society in which elaborate class hierarchies built on power and efficiency increasingly dominated, technology multiplied with growing populations interacting with each other and with society's needs, and rivalries and competition required ever more powerful defenses to protect the people, their wealth, and their trade. From this period, the patterns of urban life and of state formation were established, patterns we readily recognize today as our own.

Chapter 3
3000-600 BCE

Shifting Agrarian Centers in India

ANCIENT INDIA

The objects were beyond curious. They appeared to be ancient seals, but the inscriptions were completely unlike anything General Alexander Cunningham had seen before in India. Many years before, in 1856, British engineers working on an extension of the Indian Railroad near the Ravi River, a tribute of the great Indus system, had found ancient mounds stuffed with uniform, fire-baked bricks. Regarding these sturdy bricks as a godsend for supporting their railroad tracks, they proceeded to loot the mounds of their available building materials. Fortunately, the men noticed that some of the bricks contained these puzzling signs and sent them to Cunningham, who had already built a reputation in archaeological work at

Seeing Patterns

▶ Who were the Harappans? Where did they come from? What evidence exists for their origins?

▶ What explanations have been offered for the collapse of Harappan society? How well do the rival theories hold up, given what scholars and archaeologists have discovered?

▶ How can we know about the newcomers to northern India? What sources exist for historians to examine?

▶ What patterns can we see evolving in the Ganges River states that will mark the subsequent development of Indian civilization?

several north Indian Buddhist sites. Intrigued by their obvious antiquity and aghast at the destruction already visited upon the mounds, he had the sites placed under protection. The tracks of the Indian Railroad, it turned out, were being supported by the remains of one of the world's most ancient cities! Identifying the civilization that created it, however, would prove to be one of archaeology's greatest challenges.

It was well into the next century before scholars really began to understand the place of this "lost city" of Harappa—the center of one of the world's oldest and most mysterious societies. And although a full program of archaeological investigation has been under way at Harappa and dozens of similar sites throughout the Indus valley since the 1920s, some of the most basic questions about this society remain to be answered. For example, how did their writing system—comprised of the symbols carved on the seals first brought to Cunningham—work? Moreover, unlike other early civilizations that endured for thousands of years, Harappan society was relatively short-lived, lasting perhaps 600 years before vanishing almost entirely. Why did it disappear? And while scholars believe the structures of Harappan village life set many of the patterns for later Indian rural society,

The Ruins of Mohenjo-Daro.

exactly how did these structures develop over the intervening generations? Indeed, how and why did urban societies reemerge later along the Ganges River, setting so many of the patterns of south Asian history? In short, what were the fundamental patterns that marked these founding cultures, and how did these patterns change the lives of the peoples in the region and come to be adopted and adapted by them?

As we will see, one important pattern marking the history of northern India, like that of Mesopotamia, lies in regular rhythms of migration and invasion, interchanges of innovation, assimilation of peoples, and the expansion of ideas. In contrast to the long history of political unification in Egypt or China, all of India did not experience rule by a single regime until the nineteenth century CE. Yet, considerable cultural and religious unity had already been created thousands of years earlier under the influence of newly emerging states along the Ganges River. The ability to maintain this cultural continuity while creating social systems with the flexibility to manage innovation from outside has marked India to the present day. Among their most significant achievements, the social, philosophical, and political challenges facing these early Ganges states resulted in some of the world's most important religious movements: Hinduism, Jainism, and the most widespread and influential religious movement in Asia, Buddhism.

The Vanished Origins of Harappa, 3000–1500 BCE

Since the first intensive archaeological work of the 1920s, the sites of the Indus valley have been imbued with all the romance of "lost civilizations." Unlike Egypt (see Chapter 2), where the patterns of society remained remarkably stable for thousands of years, or Mesopotamia, which spawned a succession of states and empires, the cities of the Indus valley flourished for less than 1,000 years—from about 2500–1700 BCE—before vanishing almost without a trace. Anchored by two major cities—Harappa [Hah-RAP-uh] in the north and Mohenjo-Daro [Moe-hen-joe DAH-roe] in the southwest—and extending from the upper Ganges River to the Arabian Sea, a dense network of small cities, towns, and villages marked by a remarkable consistency of architecture and artifact occupied the largest cultural area of the third millennium BCE: twice the size of the Old Kingdom of Egypt and four times that of the empire of Sargon in Mesopotamia. Trade with southwest Asia and Egypt extended Harappan influence even farther.

Yet, this "Harappan" or "Indus valley," culture, as archaeologists have named it, remains by far the most mysterious of the early centers of agriculturally supported urban society. The sophistication and precision of its urban planning, the standardization of weights and measures, and the attention to cleanliness and comfort all suggest an elaborate system of social organization; yet we know virtually nothing of its arrangement. Scholars have labored for nearly a century to unlock the secrets of the Harappan pictographic symbols, yet they remain mostly undeciphered. Most tantalizing of all is the fundamental question: Why, as the new mode of urban society gathered momentum elsewhere, did the inhabitants of this one abandon their cities and slip beneath the surface of the historical record? To look at what we can and do know about these mysterious people, we must start with the geography of the Indus and its region.

The Region and People

Geographers refer to the region encompassed by the modern states of India, Pakistan, and Bangladesh as a *subcontinent*—a large, distinct area of land somewhat smaller than a continent. While the region is attached to the Eurasian landmass, it is almost completely cut off from it by some of the most forbidding physical barriers on earth. The lower two-thirds of India form a vast peninsula surrounded on three sides by the Arabian Sea, the Indian Ocean, and the Bay of Bengal. To the north of the bay, extending from Bangladesh through the Indian province of Assam to the north and east and deep into Myanmar (formerly Burma), are continuous ranges of

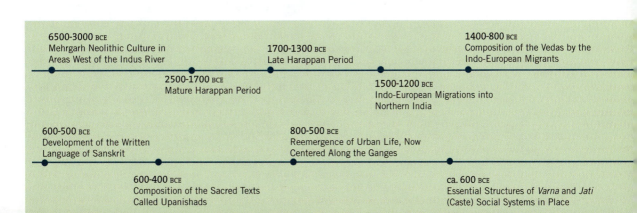

6500-3000 BCE
Mehrgarh Neolithic Culture in Areas West of the Indus River

2500-1700 BCE
Mature Harappan Period

1700-1300 BCE
Late Harappan Period

1500-1200 BCE
Indo-European Migrations into Northern India

1400-800 BCE
Composition of the Vedas by the Indo-European Migrants

600-500 BCE
Development of the Written Language of Sanskrit

600-400 BCE
Composition of the Sacred Texts Called Upanishads

800-500 BCE
Reemergence of Urban Life, Now Centered Along the Ganges

ca. 600 BCE
Essential Structures of *Varna* and *Jati* (Caste) Social Systems in Place

heavily forested mountains. Some of the world's highest annual rainfall totals—over 100 inches—are regularly recorded here.

Forming the northeastern border of the subcontinent above the rain belt is the "roof of the world," the Himalayan Mountains. These meet another set of formidable peaks, the Hindu Kush, which extends into Pakistan and with the Sulaiman and Kirthar ranges marks the northwestern border of the region. Access to the Indian peninsula by land is thus limited to a handful of mountain passes through the Himalayas and the more substantial Khyber and Bolan Passes of the northwest. Historically, these have been the main avenues of trade, migration, and, frequently, invasion (see Map 3.1).

Topography: The physical features—mountains, rivers, deserts, swamps, etc.—of a region.

The Monsoon System   Surrounded by water and framed by high mountains, India's internal **topography** also has a considerable influence on its climate. The Deccan Plateau, Vindhya Range, and other internal highland areas tend to both

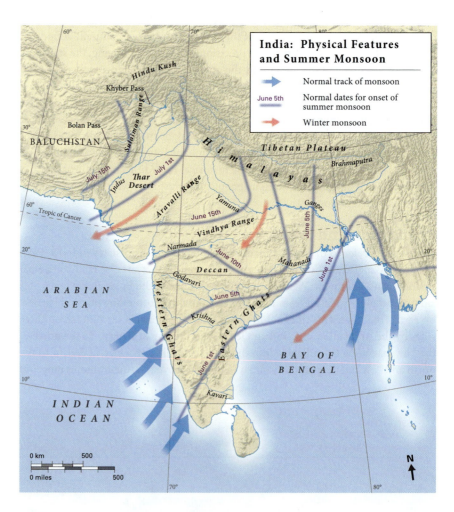

MAP **3.1** India: Physical Features and Summer Monsoon.

trap tropical moisture against the west coast and funnel it toward the region drained by the Ganges River in the northeast. The moisture itself comes from the summer winds of the monsoon system, a term derived from the Arabic word *mausim*, for "season." The winds carry moisture generated from the heat of southern Africa as it flows southwest to the northeast over the Indian Ocean from June through October and govern the climatic cycles of southeastern Asia, Indonesia, and southern China as well as India. In the winter months the winds reverse direction and pull hot, dry air down from central Asia. During this dry season, rainfall is scant or nonexistent over large areas of south Asia.

The extremes of the monsoon cycle, as well as its regularity, exert a powerful influence on Asian agriculture. This is particularly so in India, where the monsoon rainfall amounts differ widely from region to region. Because even minor variations in the timing of the cycle or the volume of rain may spell potential flood or famine, the arrival of the monsoon is even today greeted with nervous anticipation. Generally speaking, the subcontinent becomes drier as one moves farther north and west until one reaches the Thar, or Great Indian, Desert and the plain of Sind, the site of some of the hottest temperatures ever recorded on earth—nearly 130 degrees Fahrenheit. It is this arid region bordered by mountains and watered by the Indus River system that saw the rise of the first Indian cities.

The Indus River   As the Greek historian Herodotus called Egypt "the gift of the Nile," so too, as archaeologists have noted, should Harappan civilization be called the "gift of the Indus." A vast river system composed of seven main branches in ancient times, the Indus' slow, meandering course has for millennia left behind rich deposits of fertile soil, by some estimates twice as much as the Nile. Moreover, like the Yellow River in China, the constant buildup of silt in the riverbed periodically caused the water to overflow its banks and change course—dangerous for those living close by but an effective means of spreading soil over a wide area.

Mehrgarh Culture   Researchers have found a number of Neolithic sites near the river, one of the most productive being Mehrgarh [MARE-gar], located near a strategic mountain pass in Baluchistan. Scholars have dated the Mehrgarh culture to about 6000 BCE, making it perhaps the oldest on the Indian subcontinent. Like the inhabitants of the Fertile Crescent, villagers in Neolithic Baluchistan raised wheat and barley and domesticated sheep, goats, and cattle. As long ago as 5500 BCE pottery was being produced in the area. Also dating from this period are the crafting and trading of fine *lapis lazuli* (an opaque, dark blue gemstone) beadware, or "microbeads," later a coveted item among Harappan luxury goods. Significantly, even the earliest Baluchistani dwellings are made of mud brick, a technique that with greater scope and sophistication became a hallmark of the Harappan cityscape. For all of these reasons, some archaeologists have viewed Mehrgarh culture as a possible precursor to Harappa.

Scholars agree that by about 3000 BCE a culture of villages and towns with elaborate trade networks, sophisticated pottery, and a substantial array of domesticated plants and animals had long been established in the hills of Baluchistan adjacent to the Indus and its western tributaries. Attracted, most likely, by the comparative ease of growing staple crops in the reliably fertile river valleys, the inhabitants of these hill sites extended their settlements eastward sometime before 2600 BCE and began a rapid phase of consolidation, which culminated in the region's first cities.

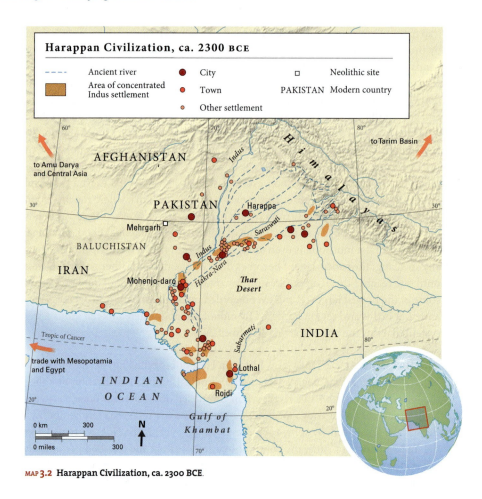

MAP **3.2** Harappan Civilization, ca. 2300 BCE.

Adapting to Urban Life in the Indus Valley

By about 2300 BCE the two major cities of Harappa and Mohenjo-Daro—separated by 350 miles—marked the poles of a system of small cities, towns, and villages sprawled across an area estimated to be between 650,000 and 850,000 square miles (see Map 3.2). At its height, the city of Harappa had a population of over 40,000—comparable to that of the largest Mesopotamian cities of the period—and its defensive walls measured 3.5 miles in circumference. The location of these cities on a floodplain, moreover, dictated that they be built on enormous artificial hills to protect them from damage during times that the rivers overflowed their banks. Mohenjo-Daro, for example, with an estimated 3,000 dwellings and a population of about 41,000, was built on two 40-foot mounds separated by a channel 200 yards wide for easy access to the Indus. More remarkable than the sheer size of these cities, however, are their similarities to each other.

Harappan Uniformity   While all the cities of Mesopotamia and Egypt contained architectural features that make them a recognizable part of their respective cultures, Harappan cities seem almost to have been designed by the same hand. Harappa and Mohenjo-Daro, as well as several smaller cities and numerous towns, are laid out according to a rigorously surveyed and meticulously planned grid, with

The Great Bath at Mohenjo-Daro. This mysterious structure suggests linkages to both the individual Harappan dwellings' inside shower/bath areas and later practices of bathing in rivers such as the Ganges. What conclusions would you draw from its size, structure, and position in the city?

The Sewers of Lothal. The cities of the Indus were drained by what may have been the world's first—and for millennia the most sophisticated—urban sewer systems. Pictured is a sewer main from the seaport city of Lothal. It drained a series of branch lines that were connected in turn to drains from individual dwellings. A system of drops, pits, and wooden screens separated out the solid waste and conducted the liquids to the river.

major thoroughfares running on north/south and east/west axes and squares, public buildings, temples, and markets at regular, convenient locations. The larger streets are paved with brick and remarkably straight. They are laid out according to standard widths, and most have drains and gutters connected to what may be the most elaborate urban sewer system of ancient times (see Map 3.3).

This uniformity appears to have extended into the personal realm as well. Houses of several stories were made of brick and plastered with gypsum, their floor plans strikingly similar even at widely spaced sites. Many had brick-lined indoor wells and primitive toilets emptying into terra-cotta **cesspits** whose overflow connected to the city's drains and sewers. Nearly all dwellings had a bathing room reminiscent of a modern shower stall, complete with a waterproof floor and drain system to direct the water into channels in the street. Inside the dwellings, a staggering array of wheel-turned, mass-produced clay pots, jars, cooking vessels, copper- and bronzeware, and even toys have been found at various sites.

MAP **3.3** Mohenjo-Daro.

The Harappan Diet   The rich alluvial soil of the region supported a wide variety of fruits, vegetables, and grains. Wheat and barley were staple crops, but peas, melons, figs, and sesame were also produced. The recovery of cotton seeds and small patches of cloth and fishing line at Mohenjo-Daro suggests that the Harappans may also have been the first people to raise cotton for use in clothing. Cattle appear to have been the chief domestic animals, and indications of the large herds kept in some areas imply that they were seen as signs of wealth. It is not clear, however, whether they were used principally for food and milk or as work animals, as were water buffaloes. Whatever the case, some scholars see in their importance at this

Cesspits: Deep holes or trenches used to deposit human waste and refuse; in the case of Harappa, they were flushed with water into city sewers and drains ultimately leading to the adjacent river.

The Horned God. The figure on this seal found at Mohenjo-Daro may be a depiction of a Harappan deity. Its cross-legged "lotus" position and multiple faces prompted archaeologist Sir John Marshall to theorize in the 1930s that it was an early version of the Hindu god Shiva. More recently, scholars have moved away from this claim, noting that mention of Shiva does not occur for another 1,000 years during the Vedic years. Above the figure is a typically short sample of the pictographic Harappan script.

early time the origins of the later stereotype of the Indian "sacred cow."

Sheep and pigs were also widespread and appear to have been an important part of the Harappan diet. Seal carvings and figurines suggest that the Harappans were sophisticated dog breeders, with some of the animals wearing what appear to be collars and a variety of different sizes and snout and tail configurations depicted. It is also thought that the chicken was first domesticated here in Neolithic times. Rice, which figures so prominently in later Indian agriculture, may have also been grown but, because of the relatively arid climate, does not appear to have been a staple.

Harappan Identity and Government   But who were they? Even today, evidence concerning the identity of the Harappans is obscure and contradictory. Everyday items and statuary offer few clues. Samples of symbols, most of which are found on what are believed to be merchant seals, were once believed to hold some tenuous links to a "Proto-Dravidian" language group distantly related to that of some modern south Indian peoples. Scholars have also suggested that the Harappans may have been an eastern branch of a people called "Proto-Mediterraneans," who ranged widely across southwest Asia. Complicating the matter further, archaeologists have identified an urban society designated as the "Bactria-Margiana Archaeological Complex" (BMAC) to the northwest of the Indus valley culture that shares some technological features with the Harappans but thus far no other obvious connections beyond some evidence of trade. Such findings are thus intriguing, but the uniqueness of Harappan urban life argues against any theory of simple cultural diffusion.

As with other early urban cultures, there appears to have been a close relationship among the religious, political, and social spheres of Harappan society. Nevertheless, the clues, while suggestive, again yield little that is definitive. For example, the replication of city plans and architecture throughout such a wide area might indicate the kind of strong central authority and bureaucratic control typically found in a kingdom or empire. Yet, we know virtually nothing of how it might have been organized. Moreover, some departures from the otherwise rigorous uniformity of previous sites found in recent work at Rojdi [ROEJ-dee] have led scholars to amend this picture in favor of one of overall unity marked by discernable regional styles. This modified view, along with findings that suggest that a number of pockets of Harappan culture survived the collapse of the cities by many centuries, would, in light of the apparent self-sufficiency of these areas, seem to work against theories of highly centralized control.

Harappan Trade   The ability to mass-produce a vast array of articles implies specialization, regulation, and an occupation-based class system. Moreover, elaborate port facilities suggest the prominence of a merchant class with overseas connections. Mesopotamian records from about 2300 BCE tell of a people called "Meluha" [MUH-loo-hah], now believed to be the Harappans, who carried on extensive seaborne trade and maintained colonies of merchants in several of their cities.

Building Foundations and Street Layout at Lothal. The precision of Indus urban planning and execution is evident in this photograph of a residential area in Lothal.

Harappan seals have been found at Ur in Mesopotamia, and there is evidence of Harappan merchandise being traded as far away as Egypt and central Asia. Because of the apparent occupational specialization of the Harappans, some scholars have theorized that they may have belonged to *guilds*, organizations whose members all pursue the same trade or craft. However, the plainness and uniformity of Harappan dwellings, in contrast to the pervasiveness of their amenities—generous living quarters, indoor plumbing, and so forth—defy any easy generalizations about class structure.

The Harappans appear to have maintained complex trade networks both within their cultural sphere and outside of it. Fortified border settlements, evidently trading posts, extended their influence to the borders of modern Iran and as far north as the Amu Darya, or Oxus River, the region of the BMAC. Curiously, however, we see virtually no evidence of foreign trade goods in the Indus cities, suggesting perhaps tight government control over outside influences. As we have seen, a surprising variety of agricultural products and craft specialties were also created for both internal commerce and overseas export.

In addition to bulk foodstuffs such as grain, the Mesopotamian records of the Meluha note that their merchants dealt in beadwork, lapis lazuli, pearls, rare woods, cotton cloth, and dog and cat figurines. Due in part to our inability to decipher the Harappan symbols, we know much less about their imports, though foodstuffs, oils, and cloth seem to be among them. The network of cities along the Indus also seems to have been pivotal in the long-distance trade of copper from Baluchistan and in the exchange of gold, silver, semiprecious stones, shells, and timber throughout an extensive area north and west into Afghanistan and east to central Asia. Harappan figurines have been found along a broad front of nomadic routes from the Tarim basin west.

Lothal The complexity of these questions of trade and social organization may be seen quite vividly at Lothal [LOW-tall]. Located several miles up the Sabarmati River from the Gulf of Khambat (Cambay), Lothal was a large—perhaps the chief—Harappan seaport. Recent work has shown it to be not only a vital link in Harappan maritime trade in the Arabian Sea and points west but an important manufacturing center of various trade items as well.

Lothal's central structure is an enormous basin, approximately 120 feet long and 70 feet wide, which was once connected to an inlet of the river. Most researchers

---

Harappan Democracy?

"Instead of one social group with absolute control, the rulers included merchants, ritual specialists and individuals who controlled resources such as land, livestock and raw material. Maybe—just maybe—we are seeing an ancient democracy at work."

—Jonathan Mark Kenoyer. *Indus Valley Civilization,* "A Walk Through Lothal" in www .harappa.com.

Dockyard at Lothal. While some scholars maintain that this structure was a holding tank or reservoir, the current consensus is that it was in fact a technologically advanced area for loading and unloading oceangoing ships. A sophisticated system of channels kept it flooded to the proper level, prevented overflow, and, with locks and gates, allowed access to the river and sea.

believe that this was a dock for oceangoing ships, though some contend instead that it was a reservoir for water storage. Nearby are a number of structures believed to have been warehouses, each with numerous cubicles marked with what appear to be the stamps and seals of various merchants.

But Lothal was also a famous regional craft center, with microbeads used for decorative craft items and jewelry as its chief product for internal trade and export. Indeed, scholars theorize that the city's site may have been chosen precisely because of its proximity to convenient sources of precious stones for bead making. The site, with the precise city planning and water systems typical of Harappan cities, is also notable for its numerous specialized pottery kilns and bead "factories," complete with worker housing. Yet, for all this wealth of artifacts, such questions as who the merchants or workers were, how they were organized and governed, what levels of mobility there might have been among different classes, and even precisely what those classes might have been remain elusive.

Harappan Religion   Clues about Harappan religion are equally tantalizing. The swastika, a symbol long associated with the cyclical nature of life in Indian and Buddhist art before its appropriation by the Nazis in the twentieth century, is first found in the cities of the Indus. Moreover, recent scholarship has suggested that the entire Harappan system of symbols, always assumed to be a form of writing, may instead be best understood as a form of religious shorthand for use in the multiethnic and multilingual Indus society. Figurines depicting cows, buffaloes, tigers, crocodiles, elephants, and animals from surrounding regions have also been found. Along with female figurines and **phallic stones**, these perhaps connote a type of fertility religion. Like many Neolithic and agrarian–urban cultures, the Harappans interred their dead with ornaments and pottery, and perhaps food. Such practices have led scholars to speculate that the Harappans may have believed in an afterlife.

The prominence of such combined dualities as male and female or plant and animal may imply a principal deity embodying a unity of opposites, perhaps prefiguring later Indian religious conceptions. Likewise, the central importance of the Indus River and the considerable attention paid to personal bathing are believed to be symbolically linked with a great ritual bath in the center of Mohenjo-Daro, perhaps adding yet another ritual dimension to the picture. Here again, however, the details are obscure and, for the moment, the nature of Harappan religion remains an open question.

The Collapse of the Cities

Around 1900 BCE the major cities of Harappan society appear to have been in decline. Structures of inferior quality seem to have been constructed on top of earlier buildings, suggesting a drop in population with a consequent loss of maintenance and services. By 1700 BCE the great cities appear to have been all but abandoned, their people moving to smaller outlying towns and villages, many returning to farming or becoming herders.

Some recent interpretations of Harappan urban decline attribute it to ecological collapse. The surrounding land—overgrazed, stripped of trees, and reliant upon the river for fertilization—had reached the limits of its capacity to support large cities. Perhaps increased flooding or weather-related problems stretched these limits even further. Some scholars have proposed that increasing salt levels in the Indus played a role, perhaps as the result of diverting too much of its water for irrigation and supplying the cities; one study places part of the blame on earthquakes, which may have partially diverted the river's flow around 1700 BCE. We do know that the Hakra-Nara River was abruptly shunted into the Indus by the early eighteenth century BCE, resulting in a progressive drying up of its old watershed and increased flooding on the lower Indus.

Recent work at sites in the area south of the Indus valley indicate a longer period of survival for some of the smaller late Harappan towns in the region. Nevertheless, by about 1500 BCE it appears that remnants of Indus civilization were to be found only within isolated regional cultures that blended Harappan influences with those of neighboring peoples. The expansion of Harappan village agriculture to the east and south, however, continued. Indeed, the firm base that had made Harappan urban life possible—the cultivation of regionally appropriate staple crops and domesticated animals by people organized in villages—might justly be called the foundation of Indian social history. In that sense, though its cities were long since abandoned, the culture that produced this pattern of world history can hardly be considered "lost." It would be centuries, however, before India again saw the rise of cities.

Interactions in Northern India, 1500–600 BCE

The "villains" of the Harappan collapse were long considered to be Indo-European migrants from the north who called themselves "Aryans" (Sanskrit, "the noble ones")—a term which, through a series of twisted associations and garbled history, Adolph Hitler later identified with Nazi Germany. Aryan tales recount their movement south and east through the Khyber Pass and across the Punjab between 1700 and 1400 BCE. Their accounts of epic battles had formerly been assumed to refer to their conquest of the Harappans. The earliest Aryan religious text, the *Rig-Veda* [Rig VAY-duh], refers to a short, dark-skinned people whom the Aryans contemptuously called *dasas*, or "the others," a term later used to denote servants or slaves. It also mentions conflicts with sedentary phallus-worshipping people living in cities and manning fortifications, which would certainly seem to describe the Harappans.

These works, however, were not written down until centuries after the events may have occurred, and whether their references date from the mid-second millennium BCE or were added later on is still not resolved. Moreover, while battles undoubtedly did occur, long periods of peaceful migration and settlement appear to have taken place as well. Perhaps the most significant problem, however, is that the Harappan cities appear to have been largely abandoned by the time the Aryans arrived on the scene.

In addition, the relative lack of Aryan artifacts; conflicts of interpretation between archaeologists, classical scholars, and linguists; and a growing body of scholarship by Indian researchers have produced in recent years a comprehensive

Phallic stones/phallic: Of or referring to the male sex organ; Indian religions use a host of phallic images, or *lingams*, in shrines, rituals, and festivals to symbolize the male, or active, forces of both natural and supernatural creation.

questioning of the narrative of the role of Aryan migration altogether. Indeed, some scholars have suggested that long-held assumptions about the Aryans grew out of nineteenth-century beliefs of European superiority supported by the British occupation of India. Their contention is that the roots of Vedic society came not with invaders from the north but from peoples already long established in Punjab and, later, along the Ganges River. Since the debate has loomed increasingly large in revisiting broad currents of Indian history and identity, it most likely will remain unresolved for some time to come.

The Vedic World, 1750–800 BCE

Most scholars still assign a prominent, if not predominant, role to the Aryans. Their homeland is unknown, though some scholars believe it to be in the area around the Caspian Sea. Groups of nomadic peoples speaking a set of languages that linguists have designated "Proto-Indo-European" appear to have migrated along a broad front into Asia Minor, the eastern Mediterranean, Iran, and deep into central Asia, as evidenced by the recent find of the Tarim basin mummies. In all these areas they proved to be important catalysts in the diffusion of such technologies as iron working and the horse and chariot.

Indo-European Origins   Their ancestors had already played an extensive role in the spreading of items and ideas throughout Eurasia long before the Aryans arrived in India. Indeed, recent European scholarship has suggested that their presence predated the Neolithic settlement of the continent. More recently, branches are believed to have migrated east and west across the continent from perhaps 4000 to 2500 BCE. In the course of their travels they were active agents in collecting, refining, and spreading a host of Bronze Age technologies. They are believed to have been the people who introduced the domestication of the wild horses of the central Asian steppes on a wide scale, along with such items as bridles and weapons for use on horseback. Similarly, it seems likely that they were instrumental in moving the technology of the chariot along a wide front, ranging from the eastern European steppes to China. As we saw in Chapter 2, around 1000 BCE various Indo-European-descended groups, most prominently the Hittites, brought the techniques of iron making out of Anatolia, ultimately taking them as far as the western reaches of the Yellow River basin.

Scholars have long identified a Proto-Indo-European language these groups are believed to have spoken as the parent tongue of a family of languages that includes Latin, German, Greek, the Slavic languages, Celtic languages such as Gaelic, and what became the Indian literary language, Sanskrit. A number of words with common roots for certain basic objects or concepts may be found among these languages. Examples include *pater* (Latin), *Vater* (German), and *pitar* (Sanskrit) for "father"; *sept* (Latin) and *sapta* (Sanskrit) for "seven"; and the place names "Iran" and "Erin/Eire/Ireland" (from "Aryan"). The identification of the Indo-European family of languages with the peoples of northern Europe in the nineteenth century, particularly the Germans, prompted the Nazi appropriation of the term "Aryan" for those of Germanic ethnicity in the 1930s and 1940s. However, a new group of scholars has argued for a thesis of "Paleolithic continuity theory," in which these groups had already begun to differentiate linguistically by the beginning of the Neolithic period and were not involved in massive "invasions" on the continent from the fifth to the third millennium BCE.

The Vedas   Scholars believe that sometime around 2000 BCE a linguistic group designated "Indo-Aryans" had already split off from the Indo-Iranian subgroup and began moving toward the passes leading to northern India. As noted earlier, however, the confusing written record, the lack of firm archaeological sites, and national politics have made this history extraordinarily difficult to unravel. Some scholars see the Indo-Aryans as emerging from the BMAC culture; others see them as engaging in wars within the BMAC against the indigenous settled inhabitants; still others see them as migrating into the Punjab long after the Harappan cites had been in decline. In this context, they view their accounts of great "battles" and storming "citadels" as in reality cattle raids and attacks on village corrals.

In any case, the migrants appear to have carried with them an oral tradition of epic poetry, hymns, prayers, and heavily allegorical myth and history that would be carefully cultivated and preserved until committed to writing after 600 BCE. The core works, composed from around 1400 to 800 BCE, are the religious hymns known as the Vedas ("knowledge" or "truths"). Like the *Iliad* and *Odyssey* for Homeric Greece, the Vedas are still the principal window through which we can glimpse the world of the Aryans in northern India.

The *Rig-Veda*, the earliest of the Vedas, is currently believed to have been composed between about 1400 and 900 BCE. Some scholars, however, have suggested that some of the references contained in it point to much more ancient indigenous origins for it. Its verses were customarily memorized and passed from generation to generation by Aryan priests and their successors until after 1400 CE. The oldest recorded poetry in any Indo-European language, the *Rig-Veda*'s 1,028 verses provide an idealized and allegorical vision of a society led by hard fighting, lusty warrior chieftains and priests, and composed of herders, cultivators, artisans, and servants. These groups became the prototypes of the four early social divisions, or *varnas*— priests, warriors, merchants, and commoners (see Patterns Up Close). Material wealth and skill in battle were the most valued attributes of Aryan culture. This emphasis on struggle and daring is seen as evidence of a strongly *patriarchal*, or male-led, society with an elaborate hierarchy based on kinship and prowess.

Nearly a quarter of the verses of the *Rig-Veda* celebrate the exploits of the god Indra, who is portrayed as the embodiment of the Aryan heroic ideal. In the accompanying quotation, he battles the serpent demon Vritra and triumphantly releases the rivers it had bottled up.

Early North Indian Society and Economics   Though a nomadic people, the Aryans possessed a high degree of technical skill. Not only had they benefited from the diffusion of earlier Bronze Age crafts, but, as we have seen, they were also important agents in distributing these crafts throughout Eurasia. They were particularly proficient in weaponry, and their bronze spear tips, arrowheads, and blades, in addition to the mobility of their chariots and horseborne warriors, very likely gave them a pronounced advantage over those of the village communities they encountered. After the beginning of the first millennium BCE, they also helped spread the use of iron.

Excellent horsemen, the Aryans made extensive use of horse-drawn wagons and chariots in battle. The earliest Aryan migrants may have introduced the horse to northern India, and it is likely that they first brought the chariot to late Xia or early Shang China. Elaborate equipment such as bridles, yokes, and harnesses and other

Aryan Heroism

"Now I shall proclaim the mighty deeds of Indra, those foremost deeds that he . . . has performed. He smashed the serpent. He released the waters. He split the sides of the mountains. . . . You [Indra] sent forth the seven rivers [i.e., the Indus and its tributaries] to flow. . . . So, as king, he rules over the peoples. As a rim in the spokes of a wheel, he encompasses them."

—from Ainslee T. Embree, ed. *Sources of Indian Tradition*, vol. 1, 2nd ed. New York: Columbia University Press, 1988.

Indra, Aryan God of War. One of the most important of the early Vedic gods, Indra's tales were a key component of the early heroic character of the Rig-Veda. What attributes seem most evident in this depiction of Indra?

items related to the use of horses have been found at a number of sites. The horse was so potent a symbol of power and well-being in Aryan culture and religion that its sacrifice became the most sacred of all ceremonies.

Ranging across vast stretches of grassland, the Aryans carried much of their food supply with them in the form of domestic animals. As for the Harappans, cattle were the chief measure of wealth, thus continuing the centrality of the "sacred cow" to the Indian religious experience. As skilled cultivators as well as herdsmen, the Aryans adapted easily to a wide range of environments. Sheep and goats were also mainstays of their livestock, while milk and butter, particularly the clarified butter called "ghee" [gee, with a hard "g"], occupied a prominent place in their religious symbolism.

As a highly refined product of the cow, ghee came to signify a rain that was at once purifying and fruitful. Even today ghee is used in daily household rituals. In the *Rig-Veda*, it acquired *cosmological* significance. That is, it was seen as something that reveals the underlying meaning and structure of the universe. In the accompanying passage from the *Rig-Veda*, ghee symbolically binds heaven and earth.

As with so many aspects of the deeper Indian past, ghee provides tantalizing clues about ancient practices but still leaves the veil of everyday life tightly drawn.

Aryan Settlement of Northern India   While the Vedas provide a rich literary account of Aryan conceptions of society and religion, the history of the Aryan occupation of northern India is far more obscure. Evidence from assorted sites suggests that there was a prolonged period of migration and settlement in the northwest of the subcontinent marked by a gradual transition of the Aryans from a nomadic and pastoral life to a settled and agricultural one. As early as 1000 BCE, evidence of large towns appears in the area around present-day Delhi. An important catalyst in bringing about the conditions necessary for the reemergence of large cities, however, was the beginning of widespread rice cultivation in the newly opened lands to the east.

First domesticated in Neolithic southeast Asia and south-central China, rice proved well suited to the warm temperatures, monsoon rains, and high fertility of the Ganges basin once the adjoining forests had been cleared. Here, it seems evident that the introduction of iron tools such as plows and axes was instrumental in preparing the land. High yields and a climate warm enough to permit two crops per year helped ensure the surpluses necessary to support an increasingly dense network of villages, towns, and cities, sometimes called by archaeologists India's "second urbanization."

However, the meticulous, intensive labor required at every stage of the rice plant's growth cycle required many hands for its successful cultivation. The plants must be grown in shallow water of a carefully prescribed depth and must be transplanted before the grain is harvested. Hence, the elaborate infrastructure of rice culture—the dikes, drainage ditches, terraces, raised paths, and other items related to water control—demanded a high degree of cooperation and increasingly sophisticated social organization. From roughly 800 BCE, we can trace the development of strong agrarian-based states called *janapadas* [jah-nah-PAH-duhs] ("populated territories" or "clan [*jana*] territories") in northern and northeastern India.

Statecraft and the Ideology of Power, 800–600 BCE

By the sixth century BCE the *janapadas* had encompassed the entire Ganges valley and were leading the way toward a cultural, if not a military, conquest of the subcontinent. Supported by the growing agricultural wealth and trade of the region, their influence was crucial in spreading their increasingly elaborate religion steadily east and south. Sixteen large states, or *mahajanapadas* [MAH-hah-jah-nah-PAH-duhs], now dominated northern India from the Bay of Bengal to the foothills of the Himalayas. The four largest—Avanti, Vatsa, Kosala, and Magadha—grew increasingly powerful, rich, and contentious along the Ganges. Buoyed by large revenues from agricultural and trade taxes and supported by theories that accorded kingship an almost divine status, their respective quests for domination grew as they absorbed their weaker neighbors. In this respect, as we shall see in Chapter 4, these states shared much in common with their contemporaries, the states of Zhou China.

Centralization and Power Among the Ganges States
The growing power and prosperity of the larger states tended to push them toward increasing centralization so that their resources might be used to maximal effect in the struggle for domination and survival. The two wealthiest *mahajanapadas*, Magadha and Kosala, found the route to consolidation through centralized kingdoms supported by the Brahmans, or priests. By the sixth century BCE this combination of state power and religion had produced kings, or *maharajas* [mah-hah-RAH-juhs], who were accorded god-like stature and wielded power that was seen as both secular and divine. For example, a number of kings, with the sanction of the priestly class, conducted increasingly elaborate horse sacrifices. The king's horse, accompanied by soldiers and royal grooms, was first made to wander the kingdom for a year, during which all land within the borders of its travels was claimed by the ruler. Its sacrifice thus became not only a supremely important religious festival but also a reminder of the king's power.

Other large states retained systems of government in which power was more diffuse, often being ruled by councils of various sorts as opposed to kings; scholars sometimes refer to these states as "republics." The most powerful of the republics, the Vajjian Confederacy, was ruled by a chief whose authority was derived from a council made up of heads or representatives of the principal clans. The council members were in turn responsible to local assemblies of clan elders and notables.

Cosmic Milk

"With ghee are covered Heaven and Earth, glorious in ghee, growing in ghee. Wide and broad, these two [heaven and earth] have precedence at the time of the selection of officiating priests. The wise ones invoke these two with a view to asking them for blessings."

—from Ainslee T. Embree, *ed. Sources of Indian Tradition,* vol. 1, 2nd ed. New York: Columbia University Press, 1988.

Even among the republics, the general trend appears to have been that of growing economic prosperity coupled with fierce competition among all the states for domination and survival—requiring ever greater efficiency in collecting revenue and spending for defense—pushing them toward either monarchy or absorption. The Vajjian Confederacy, for example, was eventually absorbed by Magadha during its drive for empire in northern India.

Thus, by the sixth century BCE, these states, like the Greek *poleis* and the states of late Zhou China, found themselves embroiled in continual political crises. Alliances between the states were sought and abandoned as the situation warranted; attempts to create a balance of power repeatedly failed as the largest states relentlessly vied for control. Increasing sophistication in strategy, tactics, and military technology—now including iron weapons, massed cavalry, war elephants, and even giant bows—put a premium on manpower and revenue, thus giving the larger states further advantages. By the late fourth century BCE, when these armies faced the threat of invasion by the forces of Alexander the Great and his successor Seleucus, they would number in the hundreds of thousands of men.

The Ideology of Rulership   Warfare conducted by kings vested with god-like status raised a number of ethical and practical questions about the nature of kingship, the responsibilities of rulers to their subjects, and their role as agents of a universal order. For example, how should a ruler monitor the activities of his subjects? What are the bounds of behavior in terms of diplomacy, espionage, the conduct of conflict, and the long-term welfare of the kingdom? Under what conditions may the rules be broken? In short, how should the ideal ruler comport himself for the good of his kingdom, subjects, and himself in accordance with his divine mission?

The growing size, wealth, and power of the Ganges states made these questions increasingly important as all struggled to expand—or merely survive. By 600 BCE, all the Gangetic rulers were, roughly speaking, in the situation later described by the political strategist Kautilya [Kaw-TEEL-yuh] of Magadha in his grimly realistic, pioneering political treatise, the *Arthashastra* [Arrh-tah-SHAS-truh]. In this constant war of all against all, says Kautilya, the wise ruler understands that those who encircle him on all sides and "prevail in the territory adjacent to his are . . . known as the enemy." On the other hand, those who control the territory "that is separated from the conqueror's territory by one [namely, the enemy's territory] is the constituent known as friend." Hence, one's policy toward neighboring states should be opportunistic: Attack the weak, seek allies against the strong, bide one's time with equals, and practice duplicity wherever and whenever necessary. As we shall see, there are many parallels with late Zhou Chinese treatises such as Sun Zi's *Art of War*. The prime purpose of

---

The Wise Ruler

"A king, with whom it is difficult for the people to have an audience, is made to confuse between right action and wrong action by his close entourage. Thereby he suffers from the disaffection of his own subjects or falls prey to the enemy . . .

"In the happiness of the subjects, lies the happiness of the king. . . . The welfare of the king does not lie in the fulfillment of what is dear to him; whatever is dear to the subjects constitutes his welfare.

"Therefore, ever energetic, a king should act up to the precepts of the science of material gain [i.e., *arthashastra*]. Energetic activity is the source of material gain; its opposite, of downfall."

—Kautilya, *Arthashastra,* translated by R. N. Dandekar in Ainslie T. Embree, ed. *Sources of Indian Tradition,* vol. 1, 2nd ed., pp. 243–244. New York: Columbia University Press, 1988.

such action, however, must always be the welfare of one's subjects by means of the survival and prosperity of the state.

This grim vision of the evolving world of statecraft was tempered somewhat by the themes depicted in the epics, composed during the Vedic period, though committed to writing only in the third century BCE, of which the two most famous are the Mahabharata [Mah-hah-BAH-rah-tuh] and the Ramayana [Rah-muh-YAH-nuh]. Perhaps the world's longest poem—at 100,000 verses in 18 books, it is many times longer than the Bible—the Mahabharata centers on the struggles among the

Illustration from the Mahabharata. The stories of the Mahabharata remain the most popular entertainment in India today. In this 1598 CE painting, Arjuna confronts his relatives on the battlefield.

descendants of the king, Bharata, and especially on the conflicting obligations imposed on the individual by state, society, and religion. The sixth book, Bhagavad Gita [BAH-ghuh-vahd GHEE-tuh] (Song of the Lord), has been called the "Indian gospel" because of its concentration on the tense and intricate combination of ethics and action.

On the eve of a battle in which the enemy includes his relatives and former companions, Arjuna, the protagonist, agonizes over fighting against his family and friends. His charioteer—actually the god Krishna in disguise—reminds him of the need to fulfill his duty according to *dharma* [DAR-mah] (literally "that which is firm"). To act according to dharma means that a person must follow his or her prescribed role according to that individual's place in society and in the natural order. As a warrior and ruler, therefore, Arjuna cannot leave the field of battle because of his personal connections to his opponents. Krishna tells him that the higher law of dharma demands that he put aside his personal reservations and fulfill his larger obligation to fight and win. Hence, Arjuna is urged to perform his duty without attachment as the agent of forces that transcend the immediate ties of friends or family. Thus if Arjuna forces himself to do his duty because it must be done, abandoning his attachment to the result—whatever it may be—then, according to Krishna, he is acting wisely and advancing the course of the universe.

By about 600 BCE, the largest of the northern Indian states, especially Magadha and Kosala, were attempting both to expand southward and to absorb their neighbors along the Ganges. In this volatile political environment, they developed ideologies of kingship and power based on a common understanding of the religious and cultural implications of the Vedas and a realistic appraisal of their respective political environments. At once supported and trapped by the idea of dharma as it relates to kingship, they would struggle for the next several centuries until Magadha incorporated the northern third of the subcontinent (see Map 3.4).

Indian Society, Culture, and Religion, 1500–600 BCE

The first chronicles of Indian history do not make their appearance until well after the beginning of the common era. Because of this, such documentary evidence as we have about social history, especially that of families or village organization, is found in religious and literary texts, law codes, and the collections of folktales and genealogies called the *Puranas* [Poor-AH-nuhs] ("legends"), which date from about 500 BCE.

Society and Family in Ancient India

While part of Indian religious thought was becoming increasingly concerned with the nature of the absolute and ways to connect with it, much of the rest dealt with the arrangement of society, law, and duty; the role of the family and its individual members; and relationships between men and women.

Dharma and Social Class   For example, the Bhagavad Gita contains numerous illustrations of the dilemmas that come from following one's dharma: duty in accordance with one's capabilities and the requirements of one's place in society. Krishna outlines these duties quite succinctly to Arjuna in the Bhagavad Gita in a set of passages that closely echo the structure of the *varnas*: "Tranquility, control, penance, purity, patience, and honesty, knowledge, judgment, and piety are intrinsic to the action of a priest," he notes, while "heroism, fiery energy, resolve, skill, refusal to retreat in battle, charity, and majesty in conduct are intrinsic to the action of the warrior." The activities that support the subsistence of society such as farming, herding cattle, and commerce "are intrinsic to the action of a commoner," while "action that is essentially service is intrinsic to the servant."

The great majority of Indians followed Krishna's last two sets of injunctions. Although one of the distinctive developments in the rise of the Gangetic states had been the rebirth of urban life in India, the village remained the center of the social

MAP **3.4** **Northern India, ca. 650 BCE.**

world for perhaps 80–90 percent of the subcontinent's inhabitants—as it largely does to this day. Tending cattle and water buffalo and raising a variety of crops such as rice, wheat, barley, millet, and, as the southern areas were brought under the sway of the larger northern states, spices, medicinal herbs and barks, and forest products the villages were organized by clan and *jati*, or **caste** (see Patterns Up Close).

Though arranged according to a rigid hierarchy, the social system based on *jati* ("to be born," that is, "born into") functioned in many ways as a kind of extended family, each with its own clans, villages, local dialects, gods, laws, advisory councils, and craft and work specializations. Thus, as the organization of society became more complex—owing to the demands of increased size, trade, population diversity, and urbanization—the ritual importance of the four *varnas* of the nomadic Aryans was slowly giving way to the occupational emphasis of *jati* in the new agrarian–urban order.

As the system expanded south, it incorporated many local leaders, clan elders, and other notables into the higher castes. Sometimes entire villages were accorded their own castes on the basis of lineage or occupational specialty. At its peak, the number of castes and subcastes may have exceeded 3,000. As the various peoples of the subcontinent were brought into the structure, the older ritual and ethnic divisions of the early years of Aryan domination were slowly broken down even further, though their traces remain even to the present.

The all-pervasive force of dharma extended into the personal realm as well as that of politics. Behavior in village society and the family and even the possibilities for religious fulfillment hinged upon understanding and carrying out the demands of dharma. These demands, however, varied greatly according to an individual's social standing, gender, and place in the family.

Gender Roles: Men and Women in Society

The importance of family life in India is readily evident in religious scriptures and the law codes, or *smirti* [SCHMER-tee]. By 600 BCE, *artha* [AHR-tah], the pursuit of gain and subsistence was recognized as a moral course of action necessary to sustain family position and harmony. In addition to tending to the extensive ritual demands of daily life, the male householder of the upper caste was expected to "cast food on the ground for dogs, untouchables [the excluded castes], and crows." Moreover, according to the *smirti*, "Children, married daughters living in the father's house, old relatives, pregnant women, sick persons, and girls, as also guests and servants—only after having fed these should the householder and his wife eat the food that has remained." Thus, the male householder must be willing to habitually sacrifice his own needs for those of his family and dependents.

The position of women in the Indian family and in Indian society is more difficult to determine. At once partner and property, the center of the family, yet burdened with complex restrictions over education and marriage, adult women seem simultaneously to occupy several separated rungs in the hierarchies of family and society. Unswerving loyalty and devotion on the part of wives and daughters was demanded and highly prized. For example, a large part of the epic of the Ramayana, an allegorical account of the conquest of the peoples of the south, centers on the obsessive, though ultimately groundless, suspicion of the hero Rama [RAH-mah] about the faithfulness of his kidnapped wife, Sita. The reciprocal aspect of the demand for loyalty and devotion, as the Code of Manu advises, is that "regarding this as the highest dharma of all four classes, husbands . . . must strive to protect their wives." Thus,

Caste: A system in which people's places in society—how they live, the work they do, and who they marry—are determined by heredity.

The Caste System

More than any other agrarian states, the *janapadas* developed an interlocking social order based on ethnicity and occupation. As the Aryans settled into northern India, the relatively fluid divisions of their nomadic society became more firmly defined according to ritual position and occupational status as the four *varnas* ("colors" or "complexions"): the first three for priests, warriors, and commoners respectively, and a fourth that included both servants and laborers. The origin of the *varnas*, according to the *Rig-Veda*, lay in the seminal sacrifice of the cosmic being Purusha, which gave form to the universe: His mouth became the brahmans or priests; his arms became the kshatriyas [kuh-SHA-tree-yahs] kings and warriors; his two thighs the vaishyas [vy-SHEE-yahs], or merchants; and from his two feet the shudra, or peasants, servants, and laborers.

Brahman

Kshatriya

Vaishya

Shudra

The newcomers' task of establishing and maintaining themselves as an elite class over the indigenous peoples meant that the system had to be expanded to accommodate all but with tight restrictions placed on social mobility. Thus, intermarriage was forbidden between Aryans and *dasas*, the term used for non-Aryans, and the latter were incorporated into the peasant/laborer/servant *varna*. By the sixth century BCE it appears that divisions between Aryans and non-Aryans that might have originally been based on skin color were giving way to ones based on occupation. An elaborate *jati*, or caste system—a term mistakenly derived from the Portuguese word *casta*, for "breed" or "race," later given to these social arrangements—was already developing.

Based on the original divisions of the four *varnas*, each caste was theoretically divisible into an infinite number of subcastes finely graded according to hereditary occupations. A new category of "excluded" castes—the so-called untouchables—was added, comprising people whose occupations were considered ritually unclean: butchers, refuse collectors, privy cleaners, leather workers, and those involved with tending to the dead. The excluded castes also came to include "outcasts," people

a great part of Rama's behavior toward Sita springs from his self-reproach over his failure to fulfill his most basic responsibility of protecting his wife. At the same time, Sita's loyalty to Rama makes her an exemplary model of dharma.

In household matters a wife should be engaged "in the collection and expenditure of . . . (the husband's) wealth, in cleanliness, in dharma, in cooking food for the family, and in looking after the necessities of the household." The position of women in this context, the code says, is "deserving of worship."

Coupled with this ideal of domesticity is a concept of women and women's sexuality as simultaneously compelling and threatening. The idea of kama, as encapsulated in the later *Kama Sutra*, included the enjoyment of a wide variety of sexual who for various offenses had "lost caste" and were therefore placed on the fringes of society. Perhaps a lingering vestige of early Aryan attempts at ethnic segregation, stringent prohibitions were imposed on sexual relations between *shudras* and members of the castes within the first three "twice born" (Aryan) *varnas*—so called because they alone were permitted to undergo the ceremony of the "sacred thread" and be "reborn" as initiates to the mysteries of the Vedic scriptures.

1805 French Lithograph of Indian Funeral (top) and Upper-Caste Dress (bottom).

The evolving *jati* system, with its precarious balance of flexibility and stability, expanded southward as the Ganges River states pushed farther and farther into these areas. Eventually, it incorporated villages, clans, and sometimes even entire tribal groups into their own *jatis.* Though highly restricted in terms of social mobility, these arrangements guaranteed a prescribed place for everyone in society, with at least a minimal degree of mutual support. Moreover, the idea of movement between castes became a vital part of Indian religious traditions through the doctrines of continual rebirth and the transmigration of souls. Thus, the evolving Indian innovation in response to the problem of incorporating a staggering multiplicity of ethnic, linguistic, and religious groups into its expanding culture was to create a space in society for each, while ensuring stability by restricting the social mobility of individuals and encouraging good behavior through the hope of a higher place in the next life. The fact that the system continues today despite its dissolution by the Indian government is testimony to its tenacious cultural roots and long-standing social utility.

Questions

- How is the caste system a cultural adaptation?
- How does the persistence of the caste system today demonstrate its social utility?

pleasures by men and women as part of a balanced social and religious life. Much Indian literature, both sacred and secular, as well as motifs, symbols, and statuary associated with shrines and temples, graphically celebrates the union of male and female as the conduit for the primal creative force of the universe. Female beauty is identified with beneficial natural phenomena, as in the accompanying passage from the *Rig-Veda* celebrating the dawn as a beautiful woman.

Later on, during the period of Classical Hinduism, numerous temples will have carvings depicting men and women in all phases of sexual activity, and even today small local temples feature phallic stones—representing the male member—which worshipers periodically anoint with milk and flowers.

Female Beauty

"The daughter of heaven, facing men, slips down her garments, like a beautiful young woman (before her husband). Opening up all desirable things for him who serves her, the youthful maiden once again, as before, has created her light."

—from Ainslee T. Embree, ed. *Sources of Indian Tradition*, vol. 1, 2nd ed. New York: Columbia University Press, 1988.

In contrast to this concept of truth and purity arising from naked innocence was the idea that the material world in general, and sexuality as its most enticing aspect, could divert a person from fulfilling his or her dharma. As such, it poses a threat to the social and natural order if not properly controlled. The close relationship between society and religion in this regard provided considerable latitude for men to explore ways of going "beyond" the material and sexual world by engaging in solitary, often celibate, religious practices. On the other hand, it also bolstered the idea that a woman without the protection of a husband or family was a danger to herself and a source of temptation to others. For both men and women, independence from the social system of family, clan, or caste—unless channeled into an approved religious or social practice—was subject to severe sanction. But, because of the concept that the family was the foundation of society as a whole and the place of women was at the center of family life, the burdens of supporting the system and the penalties for failing to do so fell far more heavily on women than on men.

Cultural Interactions to 600 BCE

The social system of *varna* and *jati* held together as the religion of the Vedas expanded into the diverse body of beliefs, practices, and philosophy that would later be referred to by outsiders as "Hinduism." The term is derived from the Persian word *hindu*, taken from the Sanskrit *sindu*, or "rivers," in reference to the inhabitants of the Indus valley.

Gods and Priests   Though principally the embodiments or controllers of natural forces, the gods had human personalities as well. Indra, for example, was a swashbuckling warrior with a taste for *soma*, an intoxicating drink used in religious rituals. Varuna was the regulator of cosmic affairs and the lawgiver. Agni encompassed all the forces of light, sun, and fire and was, in a sense, the messenger of the gods, carrying the sacrifices of humans to the other deities.

As the members of the most important and respected *varna*, the prestige of the Brahmans (priests) grew as they monopolized the performance of ever more elaborate rituals and sacrifices. The priests carefully maintained the oral tradition of the Vedas, taking extreme care to pass on the exact formulas of the old rituals, while also creating new, increasingly elaborate ones centered on the needs of a more sedentary, agrarian people. The growing emphasis on the precise details of various rituals, as codified in the Vedic commentaries called Brahmanas, spurred the development of education among the men of the upper castes. By the sixth century BCE, the major works of the Vedic and Brahmanic oral tradition were being committed to writing in Sanskrit, from this time forward the sacred language of Indian scriptures.

Toward New Religious Directions   At the same time, this trend contributed to an increasing *formalism* within the Vedic-Brahmanic tradition: the belief that only the precise observance of all the proper forms of ritual behavior—prayers, sacrifices, daily and seasonal ceremonies—could ensure their effectiveness. Since the formulas for these rituals were for the most part accessible only to the "twice-born" or upper varnas, a small percentage of the population, and considered the special province of the Brahmans, there was considerable social and religious exclusiveness attached to the tradition as well.

A movement away from this restrictive formalism was already apparent by 600 BCE. Instead of appeasing the gods through the precise performance of ritual as a means of ensuring the cosmic order, some in the upper varnas began seeking the forces behind that order and trying to achieve communion with them. Two paths within the Vedic-Brahmanic tradition became discernible in this regard.

One path was *asceticism*, that is, full or partial renunciation of the material world, which, because of its impermanence, was seen as an impediment to a deeper understanding of reality. The Vedic tradition had long held a special reverence for hermits and those who fled society in order to purify themselves. The many schools of ascetic practice held that the multiple distractions of making a living, raising a family, and even the body itself hindered the quest for one's spiritual essence. These schools developed a variety of strategies for uncovering the unchanging, and thus real, "self" removed from a world where everything is impermanent and, hence, illusory.

The practices of certain schools of *yoga* ("discipline"), for example, were based on the belief

Ritual Life of Hinduism. (*a*) Constructing a *Kolam*. The daily routine of ritual life in India is complex and demanding. Women have historically occupied a critical position in Hindu conceptions of well-ordered family life and have therefore carried out a large share of the domestic ceremonial duties. Here, women in southern India create a ritual design of rice flour during a festival season. The design, called a Kolam, will be eaten by insects and symbolizes "feeding the thousands." (*b*) Asceticism. For millennia great respect has been accorded those who withdraw from the lure of the material world and seek the unchanging within. Here, a modern "world renouncer," or *sannyasi*, is shown. (*c*) Bathing in the Ganges at Varanasi. The sacred character of rivers in the Indian religious experience may go back all the way to the Harappans. As the multiple religious traditions we know as Hinduism developed in the Ganges valley, that river assumed a position of central importance in terms of ritual purification. Here, bathers are shown on the *ghats*—steps built on the riverbank—of the city of Varanasi, also known as Benares, site of some of Hinduism's holiest shrines.

Cosmic Essence

"Bring hither a fig from there." "Here it is, sir." "Break it." "It is broken, sir." "What do you see there?" "These extremely fine seeds, sir." "Of those, please break one." "It is broken, sir." "What do you see there?" "Nothing at all, sir." Then he said to Shvetaketu: "Verily, my dear, that subtle essence which you do not perceive—from that very essence, indeed, my dear, does this fig tree thus arise. Believe me . . . this whole world has that essence for its Self; that is the Real (*satya*, truth); that is the Self; that (subtle essence) art thou, Shvetaketu."

—R. N. Dandekar, trans. From "Chandogya Upanishad." In: *Sources of Indian Tradition*, Ainslie T. Emree, ed., vol 1, 2nd ed., pp. 36-7. New York: Columbia University Press, 1988.

that mastery of the body allowed the adept to leave the restrictions of the material world and achieve communion with this inner self. Since the body, as part of the physical world, is subject to constant change, the discipline of postures, breathing, and meditation allows the practitioner to go beyond its limitations and find that which is unchanging within.

The other emerging path to a deeper spiritual reality was scriptural. Between the seventh and fifth centuries—though perhaps from as early as 800 BCE—a diverse group of writings called the Upanishads [Oo-PAHN-ee-shahds] ("secret knowledge") marked a dynamic new direction within the Vedic tradition. The Upanishads represented the Vedanta, "the end," or "fulfillment" of the Vedas, in which the hidden symbolism was revealed, layer by layer, and apparent inconsistencies were reconciled. While different levels of understanding the "true" principles of the Vedas were to be expected of those with limited access to the scriptures, a slavish reliance on the formal aspects of sacrifice was clearly subject to criticism.

The material world was increasingly regarded as extraneous as well. The individual "self" (*atman*) was ultimately to become identified with the cosmic "essence" (*brahman*—note that this usage is different from the same term used to describe the priestly *varna*), as in the accompanying exchange between the student Shvetaketu [Shveh-TA-keh-too] and his teacher.

Karma-Samsara   Though the full impact of these trends would be felt only in succeeding centuries, speculation about the nature of individual and universal "essence" was already beginning to be reflected more broadly in culture and society. The elaboration of the idea of caste and its accompanying obligations carried with it the development of karma-samsara, the transmigration of souls and reincarnation. Though few references to these concepts are found in the Vedas, by the sixth century BCE the two ideas appear to have been widely accepted. The concept of a nonmaterial essence or "soul" carrying with it the residue of one's deeds—*karma*—is coupled with the idea of the rebirth of the soul into a new body—*samsara*. The fidelity with which a person pursues his or her dharma within the context of the caste system ensures an advance in caste in the next life. Ultimately, the doctrine provided for *moksha*—release from the karmic cycle and the achievement of a state of complete understanding in this world—for those who are fully able to grasp the principles of atman–brahman and dharma.

Putting It All Together

In the Indus valley, as we have already seen in Egypt and Mesopotamia, a critical mass of factors required for the transition to agrarian-based cities had come together some time around 2500 BCE. Yet, our inability to decipher the symbols of the Harappans has proven to be a powerful impediment to our understanding of how their society worked and, equally important, why it fell. As we show in the Concept Map, embedded in this problem is a pattern of world history likely to strike one as counterintuitive.

That is, most of us are accustomed to thinking of history as a series of thresholds through which human societies pass in linear, progressive fashion—from forager society to agrarian to urban society, for example—without any substantial backtracking. And yet, there are the Harappans, who, for whatever reason, abandoned their splendid cities for, we must suppose, village agriculture or life in the forest.

Invasion by mobile nomads had formerly been seen as the cause, and this pattern of struggle between the settled and the nomadic will continue in various parts of the world for thousands of years. For the Harappans, however, the coming of the nomadic Indo-Europeans may not actually have had much of an impact, making the questions of interaction and adaptation that much more intriguing.

In India, the interruption in urban life lasted nearly 1,000 years. When cities again arose, they were centered hundreds of miles from the old, now forgotten Harappan sites. Instead of the apparent uniformity of the earlier society, the new one was to be marked by the struggle of individual states for advantage and supremacy. Yet, although these Gangetic states lacked political unity, their cultural and religious similarity remained an important factor throughout Indian history. Their unique innovation of the *jati* system was to act like a great flexible mold within which Indian society was increasingly cast into ever more complex sections.

Not surprisingly, this unsettled period of interaction and adaptation for the Gangetic societies was marked by widespread questioning of social, political, and religious arrangements. In the India of 600 BCE, the beginnings of an important redirection of the Vedic tradition were already under way through the speculations of the earliest Upanishads, which mark a pivotal development in the history of abstract religious and philosophical conceptualization. Moreover, amid the rich diversity of ascetic religious experience, some were shortly to map the direction of entirely new religious paths. One of these, Buddhism, may be seen as perhaps the first avowedly *universal* religious system and, thus, the beginning of a vitally important new pattern of world history.

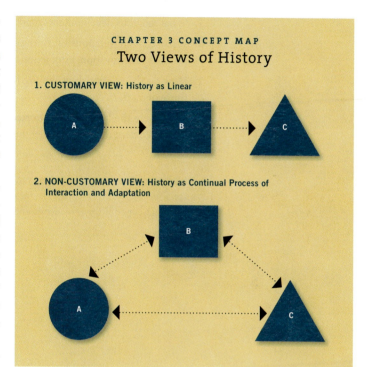

CHAPTER 3 CONCEPT MAP
Two Views of History

1. CUSTOMARY VIEW: History as Linear

2. NON-CUSTOMARY VIEW: History as Continual Process of Interaction and Adaptation

Review and Respond

1. What were some of the most important contributions of the Harappans? Which of these seem most innovative? Why?

2. Why did the Indus valley civilization go into decline? What was its legacy?

3. Why is the history of the early Vedic period so problematic?

4. What were the most important elements of Gangetic social organization?

5. What religious developments marked the period around 600 BCE?

6. What can the relationship between nomadic and settled peoples tell us about patterns of innovation, interaction, and adaptation?

7. How do the relationships among the Gangetic states compare and contrast with those of modern countries?

8. What were the benefits and shortcomings of the caste system for Indian society? To what extent do these parallel the overall position of women in Indian society?

▶ For additional resources, including maps, primary sources, visuals, and quizzes, please go to www.oup.com/us/vonsivers. Please see the Further Resources section at the back of the book for additional readings and suggested websites.

Thinking Through Patterns

▶ **Who were the Harappans? Where did they come from? What evidence exists for their origins?**

The riddle of the origins of the Harappans has been ongoing for close to 100 years. Most scholars believe their ancestors had been in the Indus region or nearby Baluchistan for millennia. Some also see them as perhaps related to extremely ancient peoples inhabiting the region around modern Kerala. Clues for this include archaic chants still practiced in Kerala that contain words that are believed to be so ancient that no one knows their meaning anymore. Carbon-14 dating, linguistic tracking, DNA surveys, and sedimentary analysis of ruins have all enhanced our understanding. One large impediment, however, remains: deciphering Harappan script—or, as we noted in this chapter, even judging whether the symbols the Harappans left behind are in fact a form of writing. Thus, a powerful analytic tool for understanding any civilization, the literary record, remains elusive.

Why do civilizations rise and fall? This is a key question for archaeologists and historians. Collapse can come from predictable causes—war, famine, ecological degradation—or random ones like earthquakes or volcanic eruptions. For the Harappans, the literary record of the Indo-Europeans long suggested that they conquered the Harappans, but it seems in conflict with more recent discoveries about the flooding patterns of the Indus, the sedimentary analysis of building and rebuilding of structures, and salinization levels at various points in the river. As is most often the case, historians generally expect to find no single *sufficient cause*—one that by itself led to the collapse—but rather a number of *necessary causes*—those that contributed but were not capable of causing the collapse all by themselves.

▶ **What explanations have been offered for the collapse of Harappan society? How well do the rival theories hold up, given what scholars and archaeologists have discovered?**

▶ **How can we know about newcomers to northern India? What sources exist for historians to examine?**

Another ongoing debate revolves around the identity and nature of the newcomers into northern India. Here, as noted in the previous discussion, the literary record of the Vedas, particularly the oldest, the *Rig-Veda*, appears in conflict with much of the archaeological evidence. While the Vedas are quite clear about where the newcomers ended up, they are tantalizingly vague about where they originated. Indo-European-speaking peoples ranged widely across Eurasia, which we can tell from the kinds of technologies moving from different regions of the continent that we know are associated with them: horse equipment, chariots, iron. But because they left little in the way of archaeological sites, piecing together their story from their material culture is extremely challenging. For the moment, much of the most productive work is being done through DNA collecting and gene tracing of the area's modern inhabitants, as well as increasingly refined linguistic techniques of *glottochronology*—the tracing of language change over time and space.

Since one of our primary tasks in this text is to help you look for patterns surrounding origins, interactions, and adaptations, the question arises about the nature of patterns we see evolving among the early north Indian states. Not all these states were monarchies, but the religious aura of the monarchs and its relationship to the first stirrings of what will become Hinduism is striking. The permeation of society by religion is certainly a pattern that continues to this day, as is the desire for transcending the bounds of the material world by a variety of ascetic or scholarly methods. The most pervasive pattern lies in the development of the caste system as the basic social structure of society, which tenaciously endures even today in the face of a constitutional ban.

▶ **What patterns can we see evolving in the Ganges River states that will mark the subsequent development of Indian civilization?**

Chapter 4
5000-481 BCE

Agrarian Centers and the Mandate of Heaven in Ancient China

Thousands of miles east of Harappa and several centuries after its decline, the twenty-first Shang king, Wu Ding, prepared to commune with his ancestors in the hope of gaining some insight into the childbearing prospects of his pregnant wife, Fu (Lady) Hao. Fu Hao, his favorite (and most powerful) wife, had come from a noble family outside the Shang capital of Yin, near the modern city of Anyang in northern China. Well educated and highly capable as an administrator, Fu Hao had even on occasion led Shang armies in the field. Now she was entrusted with what Wu Ding and

Seeing Patterns

▶ How did the interplay of environment and climate help to influence the earliest patterns of Chinese civilization? How do historians address the question of whether "geography is destiny" in this case?

▶ What can the remains of Neolithic Chinese settlements tell us about the continuities and disruptions of Chinese history?

▶ How did the Zhou concept of the Mandate of Heaven operate?

his court considered to be the most important duty of all: continuing the line of Shang kings into the future. For the Shang kings believed that the past, present, and future rulers of their line formed an unbroken continuum, with the deceased existing in a spirit realm accessible to the living by ritual divination. Therefore, Wu Ding, whose concern for Fu Hao and her unborn child was paramount, sought the advice of the ancestors about her condition and that of her child to come. Would it be a boy or a girl? Would it be healthy? Would it have the appropriate character for a ruler? Would there be bad luck or danger in the child's future? And so Wu Ding and his chief diviner, Que [Chway], scratched their questions into a cleaned and dried shoulder blade of an ox and held it over heat. The diviner then tapped it carefully with a bronze rod and attempted to read the meaning of the cracks as they appeared in the hot bone.

Like Harappa along the Indus, the Shang state had developed from a process of growth and consolidation among the Late Neolithic settlements along China's Yellow River. Unlike the Indus civilization, however, the form of writing etched in Wu Ding's "oracle bones" here during China's Bronze Age would still be recognizable to Chinese readers thousands of years later.

Skeleton and Shang War Chariot, Anyang, China.

Perhaps even more important, its innovation and versatility would make it not just the first—and, with some modifications, the only—writing system for the Chinese but the first writing system for all of east Asia. With it came an entire world of Chinese culture, ideas, religion, and politics with which peoples of the region interacted and, to a remarkable extent, adapted and adopted.

As for Fu Hao and her child, Que's reading of the cracks was "It is bad; it will be a girl." Although this was considered disappointing for ensuring an heir, Fu Hao remained Wu Ding's most beloved wife until her death. Indeed, after she died, the despondent king frequently sought her advice through the oracle bones on matters of state and private affairs. Fortunately for us, her tomb is one of the most completely preserved from the Shang era. Like the vast caches of oracle bones uncovered over the years, it tells us a great deal about society and gender, economics and trade, and the origins and interactions of Chinese states among themselves and with neighboring peoples. Like the finds at Harappa, such troves of artifacts have gone a long way toward fleshing out the history of early Chinese kingdoms that had formerly been glimpsed only dimly through later literary records.

But the Harappans and the Shang had begun very different paths to the present. Harappa and the other cities of the Indus, as we have seen, all but disappeared, their influence detectable only within the deepest currents of later Indian society. In contrast, the foundations laid by the Shang and subsequent dynasties developing in China's Yellow River valley remained vital into the twenty-first century and profoundly influenced east and southeast Asia. The history of India was one of infusion and synthesis, of cycles of partial political unity punctuated by long stretches of fragmentation. The political and cultural experience of China, however, was marked by relatively little outside influence and thousands of years of centralized rule. Moreover, for the great majority of its history, China would be perhaps the world's greatest exporter of ideas and goods.

The Origins of Yellow River Cultures, 5000–1766 BCE

The sun beyond the mountain glows,
The Yellow River seaward flows,
If you want an even better sight,
Ascend an even greater height.
"Climbing 'Stork Pavilion,'" Wang Zhihuan (648–742 CE)

An observer at the site of the "Stork Pavilion" of poet Wang Zhihuan's reverie could justly claim to have gazed upon the heartland of Chinese history. Situated on a high bluff at Yongji in the south of the modern province of Shanxi, the pavilion marked a celebrated scenic spot commanding a view of the Yellow River as it approaches its great bend to the east. Here, it is joined by the Wei River from the west and rolls across the North China Plain in a leisurely but erratic manner for another 500 miles to the Bohai Gulf, an arm of the Yellow Sea.

Over the centuries, our observer might have witnessed the origins and development of some of China's first Neolithic cultures along the river. Sixty miles up the Wei, he or she could have visited China's most famous Neolithic village at Banpo or one of dozens in between. Even today, on every side of the bend lie burial mounds from a wide selection of China's early village and town cultures. Nearby is the modern city of Xi'an [SHE-Ahn], the capital of no fewer than 13 Chinese regimes during its long history. And here, too, the richest and most famous site of all attracts visitors by the millions: the sprawling tomb complex of China's first emperor, Qin Shi Huangdi [Chin SHUHR Hwang-DEE], packed with thousands of life-sized terracotta soldiers in perfect ranks marching in timeless close-order drill.

Geography and Climate

While China's natural boundaries are perhaps less dramatic than those of India, they have had an equally profound effect on its history and society. As with India, the Himalayas and Pamirs along the southern border of Tibet mark one natural barrier. River systems such as the Amur and Ussuri in the north, the Salween in the southwest, and the Red in Vietnam have also represented past borders, though not impermeable ones. The northern and western deserts—the Gobi, Ordos, and Taklamakan—have also served as natural boundaries that frequently passed in and out of the hands of successive Chinese dynasties as their emperors sought to curb the incursions of nomads or control central Asian trade routes.

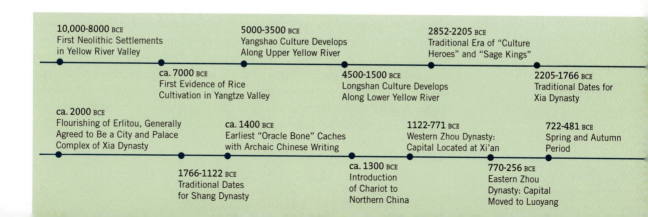

10,000-8000 BCE
First Neolithic Settlements
in Yellow River Valley

5000-3500 BCE
Yangshao Culture Develops
Along Upper Yellow River

2852-2205 BCE
Traditional Era of "Culture
Heroes" and "Sage Kings"

ca. 7000 BCE
First Evidence of Rice
Cultivation in Yangtze Valley

4500-1500 BCE
Longshan Culture Develops
Along Lower Yellow River

2205-1766 BCE
Traditional Dates for
Xia Dynasty

ca. 2000 BCE
Flourishing of Erlitou, Generally
Agreed to Be a City and Palace
Complex of Xia Dynasty

ca. 1400 BCE
Earliest "Oracle Bone" Caches
with Archaic Chinese Writing

1122-771 BCE
Western Zhou Dynasty:
Capital Located at Xi'an

722-481 BCE
Spring and Autumn
Period

1766-1122 BCE
Traditional Dates
for Shang Dynasty

ca. 1300 BCE
Introduction
of Chariot to
Northern China

770-256 BCE
Eastern Zhou
Dynasty: Capital
Moved to Luoyang

The chief effect of these features, however, has been to limit the principal avenues of outside interaction to the narrow corridor running west of Xi'an, south of Mongolia, and north of the modern province of Qinghai, spanning the route of the famous Silk Road. Like the Khyber Pass in India, this route has historically been the main avenue into China; unlike the Khyber, however, it has seldom been an invasion route for outsiders. The result of this has been that, on the one hand, the origins and early development of ancient China were more isolated than those of the other Eurasian centers of civilization. On the other hand, the absence of outside competitors facilitated both cultural and political unification.

While conditioned by many of the same factors found in India, China's climate is more varied. The area south of the Qin [Chin] Mountains marks the northern boundary of the region regulated by the monsoon, with warm temperatures and abundant summer rainfall. During the summer monsoon, rainfall amounts can range from about 40 inches per year in the eastern coastal city of Hangzhou [HAHNG-joe] to over 70 inches in the subtropical south. The suitability of the southern regions for rice cultivation, as with the Gangetic societies of India, resulted in rapid growth and high population density there. Above the monsoon line, temperatures and rainfall amounts are influenced more by the weather systems of the Eurasian interior. Thus, northern China is subject to blistering summers and frigid winters with sparse and unreliable precipitation.

One result of these conditions has been that China's population has historically been concentrated in the plains along the major river valleys and the coast. Three main river systems have remained the primary avenues of agriculture and commerce: the Pearl River (Zhujiang), in the south; the Yangtze [YAHNG-zuh] River (at 3,988 miles, it is the third longest in the world); and the Yellow River (Huanghe), where the most influential early Chinese societies developed (see Map 4.1).

The Yellow River   Rising in the highlands of Gansu and flowing north to the Ordos Desert, the Yellow River then turns south and east out of Inner Mongolia for 500 miles before making its bend to the east and the sea, a total distance of about 3,000 miles. The river gets its name as a result of the *loess*—a light, dry, mineral-rich soil deposited by centuries of strong winds—it picks up as it flows, giving it a yellowish tint. As with the Nile in Egypt, the rich, easily worked soil carried by the river has brought abundant agriculture to arid northern China; but like the Indus, the constant buildup of silt in the riverbed also causes it to overflow its banks, resulting in the devastation of fields and villages in its path through the North China Plain, the vast flatlands lining the river course on its final run to the sea.

"China's Sorrow"   This building up and bursting of natural levees, along with earthquakes and occasional human actions—such as the dynamiting of dikes during World War II to stop the Japanese invasion—have caused the Yellow River to change course 26 times during the last 3,000 years. Its mouth has shifted several times above and below the Shandong Peninsula, assuming its present course to the north following massive floods in 1854–1855. Not surprisingly, efforts to control the river have occupied a prominent place in the mythology, history, and political and social organization of the region from earliest times. For example, Yu, the supposed founder of the Xia dynasty, was said to have labored for decades to control the river's rampages. More recently, some scholars have pointed to the centralized bureaucratic structure

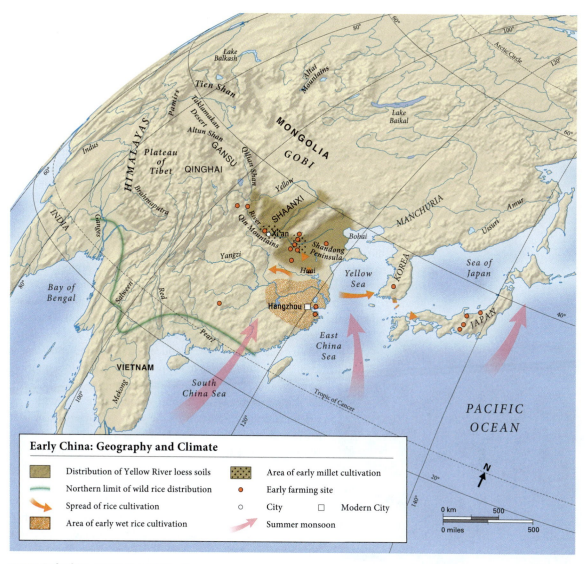

MAP **4.1** Early China: Geography and Climate.

of imperial China and suggested that it was dictated in part by the struggle for mastery of its waterways. Thus, despite its gift of fertility over the course of thousands of years, the Yellow River's unpredictable nature has prompted writers to sometimes refer to it as "China's sorrow."

The Origins of Neolithic Cultures

Between 50,000 and 20,000 years ago modern *Homo sapiens* had become established in eastern Eurasia. Human communities that produced small, refined stone implements such as arrowheads and knives ranged across north and central China from about 30,000 years ago, marking an extensive foraging culture. Within a few millennia of the last glacial retreat, settlements began to appear in northern China containing the first traces in the region of the transition from forager society to an agrarian one, based on agriculture and the domestication of animals (see Map 4.2).

Agriculture developed very quickly in China and included a wide variety of crops and livestock. Sites of rice cultivation in central China are, at 7000 BCE, among the earliest in the world, while several strains of **millet** were already being grown in the north. Recent work suggests that early strains of wheat and barley, perhaps diffused from areas around the Fertile Crescent, may also have been grown. Chickens, pigs, sheep, cattle, and dogs were also widely raised. Areas along the Yellow River contain some of the earliest agricultural villages in China and several *prototypical cultures*—those that pioneered techniques, institutions, or patterns of social organization widely copied in later years—emerged here and along the North China Plain over the next several thousand years.

Millet: A species of grass cultivated for its edible white seeds and as hay for animal feed.

Banpo Village   Perhaps the most studied of the thousands of Neolithic sites across China is Banpo [BAHN-paw] Village, located on the outskirts of Xi'an. Banpo village is representative of Yangshao [YAHNG-shaow], or "painted pottery," culture, which flourished from 5000 to 3500 BCE. Although the potter's wheel had not yet been introduced from western Eurasia, Yangshao communities like Banpo had sophisticated kilns that fired a wide variety of brightly painted storage pots, vases, etc. decorated with animal and geometric designs. The inhabitants of Yangshao villages also produced stone implements such as axes, chisels, and knives to support the community's hunting, farming, and fishing activities.

The perimeter of the Banpo settlement is surrounded by a defensive ditch, rather than the walls characteristic of later towns and cities, with 40 homes arranged around a rectangular central structure believed to be a clan meeting house or religious site. The homes were supported by vertical posts and had thatch roofs that, along with the walls, were plastered with mud and straw. The village contains a number of features that archaeologists believe to be early forms of certain long-standing patterns of rural life in northern China. For example, some of the huts contain raised clay beds with flues laid through them—an early version of the *kang* [kahng], the heated bed still found in older northern Chinese farming homes today. Also, silkworm cocoons and crude needles suggest the early development of silk weaving. Perhaps the most exciting finds, however, are the potsherds bearing stylized pictures of animals and geometric markings that some Chinese scholars have speculated may be ancestral forms of the Chinese written language.

Top: Interior View of Banpo Dwelling. *Bottom:* Circular Foundation Showing Postholes.

Longshan Culture   Settled life in villages and towns appears to have expanded greatly during the Longshan period, from about 4000 to 2000 BCE. Once thought to have grown out of Yangshao culture as it spread east to modern Shandong Province, the dates of the earliest distinct Longshan artifacts have now been pushed as far back as 4500 BCE. A later branch of Longshan culture based in what is now Henan [HEH-nahn] Province is also believed to have arisen around 2000 BCE, lasting until about 1500 BCE, when it was absorbed by the Shang dynasty.

Like their Yangshao counterparts, Longshan potters were highly skilled and pioneered forms and styles still favored by Chinese artisans today. The black-colored pottery associated with Longshan culture is particularly refined. Some of the pieces are so delicate and nearly transparent that they resemble the famous "eggshell porcelain" of later Chinese imperial pottery works. The introduction of the potter's wheel from the west in the mid-third millennium BCE—one of the earliest indications we have of late Neolithic Chinese interactions with other peoples—permitted unprecedented precision, while improved kilns—reaching firing temperatures in excess of 1,800 degrees Fahrenheit—and experimentation with kaolin clays began a long process of ceramic innovation that ultimately resulted in the first porcelain thousands of years later.

Painted Pottery, or Yangshao, Earthenware Basin Found at Banpo Site. Contrast and compare this piece with the one from Longshan below. What similarities and differences can you spot?

After 2000 BCE, the Longshan and other late Neolithic cultures were at a point where a transition to a society marked by large towns and even small cities supported by agriculture was becoming discernable. Towns of several thousand inhabitants have been uncovered, and a number of sites contain elaborate altars. The use of gold, copper, bronze, and jade in jewelry is also increasingly evident. Craft specialization and embryonic social classes are detectable.

Beyond the North China Plain   Given the subtropical environment of the regions below the Yangtze River basin in central China, it would be surprising if archaeologists did not find remains of flourishing cultures there as well. Until recently, however, such artifacts have been marginal and fragmentary. In addition to isolated sites on the western Yangtze River, a few close to modern Shanghai and Hangzhou, and at Dalongtan in Yunnan, the most extensive distinctive culture is that of Dapenkeng [DAH-pen-kehng], which flourished from 5000 to 2500 BCE. Artifacts including potsherds, arrowheads, and polished tools and axes indicate a sophisticated coastal and riverine society along an extensive corridor running from the borders of modern Vietnam along the south China coast to Fujian Province and, most strikingly, across the Taiwan Strait to the western coast of that island.

The vast reach of Dapenkeng culture and the similarity of its relatively sparse artifacts over a wide area suggest extensive interaction with peoples throughout the region. While the origins of this culture may be obscure, they do appear to be quite different from those of the north. Long and patient work by linguists has established this area as part of a Proto-Austronesian culture, one whose parent language is distinct from the Sino-Tibetan language group that contains the various Chinese dialects and that has strong links to the Austronesian speakers on modern Taiwan. This in turn has prompted scholars studying the origins of the Polynesian language family to search for possible links with these people on Taiwan and along the China coast.

Origins of Rice Cultivation   While the staple grain crops of the north included various strains of millet, with wheat and barley not coming into extensive cultivation until the Zhou period, the most far-reaching innovation in the regions

Longshan (Black Pottery) Culture Stemmed Beaker (bei), Shandong, ca. 2000 BCE.

south of the North China Plain was the development of widespread rice cultivation. Two sources have been cited as likely early centers of rice experimentation: southeast Asia and the area extending from China's modern province of Hunan to the coastal reaches of the Yangtze River, where rice grains have been dated to 7000 BCE. While we cannot know with precision which region played the more prominent role in spreading rice cultivation and techniques throughout China, we do know that southeast Asia remained an important source of new rice strains that allowed China's food production to keep pace with its population until well into the nineteenth century CE. Other food sources domesticated elsewhere making their appearance in Neolithic south China include chickens—perhaps obtained from south Asia via southeast Asia—and cattle, especially the water buffalo. Cattle, however, were raised primarily for farm work rather than consumption.

Toward a Chinese Culture With these recent finds, the older view of Chinese civilization being the exclusive product of the Yellow River valley cultures, which then expanded to more distant areas, has undergone considerable modification. Instead, scholars now suggest that the area approximating modern China consisted around 3000 BCE of a collection of agrarian communities that remained distinct in their own right but whose interactions with each other began to contribute common cultural elements that ultimately became identified as "Chinese." Indeed, some scholars have adopted a view of China down through the end of the third millennium BCE as being not so far from the mythical period referred to by ancient writers as *wanguo* [WAHN-gwo]—the "ten thousand states."

Though scholars have filled in much of the picture of these ancient cultures, the precise time and duration of their transition to one marked by cities is still very much open to debate. Chinese chroniclers, however, drawing upon the world's largest and longest literary record, have long given pride of place in this regard to their first three dynasties: the Xia, Shang, and Zhou.

The Age of Myth and the Xia Dynasty, 2852–1766 BCE

The Chinese have been called the most historically minded people on earth. For thousands of years, the use of writing for purposes of record keeping has been of paramount importance and the written word itself was considered to have a kind of inner power. For millennia, the careful study, writing, and rewriting of history have been vital elements of individual self-cultivation as well as key mechanisms for political and social control (see Patterns Up Close).

Among the earliest collections of Chinese writings we have are those of the *Shujing* [SHOO-jeeng]. Also known as the *Book of History* or *Classic of Documents*, the *Shujing* is a detailed compilation of ancient material purportedly from 2357 to 631 BCE. Though heavily encrusted with material of questionable reliability, it remains a principal documentary source for information about the people, places, and events of China's first three dynasties: the Xia [Sheah], Shang [Shahng], and Zhou [Joe]. In a surprising number of cases, its clues have helped to illuminate the archaeological evidence in recent attempts to establish the historical existence of the Xia dynasty.

Moral Leadership

The emperor [Yao] said, "Promote someone who is already illustrious, or raise up someone who is humble and mean." They all said to the emperor: "There is an unmarried man in a low position called Shun of Yu." The emperor said: "Yes, I have heard of him. What is he like?" The Chief [Minister] said, "He is the son of a blind man. His father is stupid, his mother is deceitful, his half-brother . . . is arrogant. Yet he has been able to live in harmony with them and to be splendidly filial. He has controlled himself and has not come to wickedness." The emperor said, "I will try him . . ."

—*The Book of History [Shujing]* in W. T. DeBary, *Sources of Chinese Tradition*, vol. 1, 1st ed. New York: Columbia University Press, 1964, p. 9.

MAP **4.2 Neolithic China.**

Culture Heroes and Sage Kings

According to Chinese legend, mythical culture heroes and sage kings reigned from 2852 to 2205 BCE and introduced many of China's basic elements and institutions. Among the contributions attributed to the first culture hero, Fuxi, were medicine, divination, and, according to some stories, writing. His successor, Shen Nong was credited with developing agriculture. Fire and silkworm cultivation were said to have been introduced during the reign of Huangdi, the "Yellow Emperor," whose reign followed that of Shen Nong. The Yellow Emperor's rule was followed by that of the three sage kings—Yao, Shun, and Yu—who set the example for strong moral leadership and are credited with passing the role of leadership on to the land's most worthy men instead of to their own family members. In the accompanying passage from the *Shujing*, Yao decides to elevate Shun as his successor.

Between Myth and History

The *Shujing* acclaims Yu, the last sage king, as the tamer of the Yellow River. He is also traditionally considered to be the founder of the Xia dynasty in 2205 BCE. Because of the difficulty in establishing a clear archaeological record, however, Yu and his successors have largely remained suspended between myth and history.

Moreover, the character of the *Shujing* as a creation of later Zhou chroniclers—with a specific agenda of justifying Zhou rule—has cast a long shadow over events that allegedly took place over 1,500 years before. More generally, as the sole literary account we have of the period, it has naturally assumed a dominant and, most likely, misleading role as the master narrative of ancient Chinese history. Some scholars have even argued that the Xia were an invention of the Zhou. More recently, some have suggested that their rule was in fact a kind of Shang mythology. On the other hand, some, notably a group of Chinese archaeologists, have noted that the relative accuracy of the dates given in the *Shujing* for events in the Shang dynasty suggests a similar level of reliability for its accounts of the earlier Xia.

Recent archaeological work also has moved somewhat closer to confirming the historical existence of a widespread culture, if not yet a state, corresponding to the literary accounts of the Xia. Excavations at Erlitou [ARH-lee-toe] in southern Shaanxi Province in the 1950s and 1960s revealed that artifacts at the site fall within the traditional dates given for the existence of the Xia. In addition, artifacts, particularly early bronze ritual vessels virtually identical to those at Erlitou, appear widely throughout regions described in the *Shujing* as belonging to the Xia and, in some cases, considerably beyond it.

Xia Society   The small number of purported Xia sites makes it difficult to draw many firm conclusions about their society. Much of what we believe is based on the premise that the Xia was a transitional society, developing and elaborating the material culture of the late Longshan and Yangshao cultural periods. Of particular note in this transition are the growing importance of bronze casting, the increasingly complex symbols on pottery, and the widespread evidence of large-scale communal efforts at flood control, including dams, dikes, levees, and retention ponds.

As we have seen, the Yangshao and Longshan cultures stretched across a continuum from small hunting, fishing, and farming villages to substantial agriculturally supported towns. The Xia, however, though our picture of them is far from complete, appear to have reached the tipping point at which most of the hallmarks of urban society—what we commonly think of as "civilization"—began to appear. For example, the Erlitou excavation, dated to perhaps 2000 BCE, reveals a walled city of moderate size containing what is believed to be the foundation of China's first palace: a stamped-earth terrace extending over 100 yards on each side.

Moreover, the layout of the buildings within walled compounds dating from this time began to resemble that of later official residences. Beams supported by large wooden posts carry the weight of moderately sloped roofs with upturned ends, while "curtain walls"—which bear little or none of the structure's weight—are built between the posts of plastered brick or masonry. Most of the larger buildings are also built along a north–south axis with their courtyards and entrances facing south, an orientation favored even today by Chinese builders.

Literary evidence suggests that Xia leaders exercised a strong family- or clan-based rule, and the archaeological evidence seems to support this to a considerable degree. Evidence indicating the role of the elites as mediators with the spirit world, and particularly with the ancestors of Xia rulers, is also found in abundance at Erlitou. China's first bronze ritual vessels—wine beakers on tripod stands in shapes favored throughout subsequent Chinese history—as well as jade figurines, turquoise jewelry, the world's earliest lacquered wood items, and cowry shells—a medium of exchange monopolized by the Xia rulers—all testify to their leaders' religious and social roles. Moreover, foundations of workers' residences and workshops for copper and bronze casting have also been found. As with a number of Longshan sites, extensive cemeteries outside the city suggest the development of social classes in the number and kind of burial artifacts and the position and richness of elite plots.

Though the boundaries of Chinese history have been pushed back considerably by such work, the Xia remain, like their contemporaries the Harappans, an elusive, if not perhaps a "lost," civilization. Indeed, much of what we believe about them comes from interpretations extended back in time from the period of documented Shang dominance. Unlike the Xia, however, the written records and artifacts of the Shang dynasty offer a much more complete picture of East Asia's first Bronze Age society.

The Interactions of Shang and Zhou History and Politics, 1766–481 BCE

The Shang dynasty represents the first genuine flowering of urban society in east Asia. Though this development occurs somewhat later than in the other core areas of Egypt and the Mediterranean, southwest Asia, and the Indus valley, we nevertheless find here all of the attributes of such cultures elsewhere: a high degree of skill

MAP **4.3 Shang China.**

Social stratification:
Groups or classes within a society arranged in a hierarchy, for example, peasants, merchants, officials, ministers, rulers.

in metallurgy, a large and varied agricultural base, an increasingly centralized political and religious system, growing **social stratification**, a written language, and, of course, cities. In all of these areas the Shang made considerable contributions; in some, such as their spectacular bronzes and especially their system of written characters, they were startlingly original.

The Shang Dynasty, 1766–1122 BCE

Unlike the idealized rule of the sage kings Yao, Shun, and Yu depicted in the *Shujing*, Shang social and political organization was kinship-based, with an emphasis on military power and efficiency of command. As in Mesopotamia, the advent of cities, with their vastly increased populations, now required rulers to wield greater power for defense and internal regulation, while at the same time appealing to an authority beyond human power for legitimacy. Thus, loyalty was pledged to the Shang king and his family. Members of the king's extended family controlled political and religious power, with more distant relatives acting as court officials.

Among the purported 31 Shang kings mentioned in literary records, succession often passed from uncle to nephew, though sometimes from elder brother to younger. Unlike the Aryan system of *varna*, there was no rigidly defined priestly class, though spirit mediums and diviners were widely used by Shang rulers—as we saw with Wu Ding—and exercised considerable influence at court. Local leaders who controlled walled cities and towns and their surrounding lands were employed by the ruling families as regional officials, as were specially designated Shang allies, though the exact nature of these arrangements is not clearly understood.

Shang Armies and Expansion   Though small compared to the forces commanded by their successors, Shang rulers fielded the most powerful armies of east Asia in their day. One expeditionary force of the late thirteenth-century BCE king Wu Ding and his wife Fu Hao numbered more than 13,000 men and included both paid soldiers and local defense forces recruited from the larger walled towns. Excavations reveal that the armies were organized into companies of 100 men who wielded bronze-tipped spears and pikes topped with crescent-shaped axe heads and spear tips (see Map 4.3).

Shang Weapons. A bronze ceremonial axe head with intricate decorative markings, from the 13th -11th centuries BCE (*top*); and a modern-day reconstruction of an ancient Chinese "reflective" composite bow (actually a cross bow), bent back to increase its tensile strength (*bottom*).

The Introduction of the Chariot   Another potent weapon used by the Shang was the chariot, possibly introduced to China through interaction with Indo-Europeans around 1300 to 1200 BCE, when these vehicles first make their appearance in Shang burial sites. Chariots seem to have been shortly preceded by the widespread introduction of the horse from the west, an innovation that had already revolutionized transport and warfare through much of Eurasia. Up to this point, the small

Mongolian ponies native to the northern reaches of Shang lands seem to have attracted little interest, perhaps because of their limitations as transport and draught animals. The larger and faster steeds of central Asia and the western Eurasian steppes, however, were to remain important items of trade for the Chinese for thousands of years and were celebrated in painting, poetry, and song.

Shang chariots were pulled by two horses and generally held three men. Detachable wheels held by linchpins permitted easy storage and repair. Both charioteers and infantry wielded large composite bows—so called because they were made of wood, cattle horn, and sinew. The bows were curved away from the archer in their unstrung state for additional power. As with other ancient peoples, the combination of archers with the chariot gave Shang forces considerable striking power, especially when employed against slower and more unwieldy infantry formations.

Shang Politics and Foreign Relations   Because their prestige depended in large part on their military power and harmony with their ancestors, the Shang rulers constantly mounted campaigns for sacrifice—both material and human. Indeed, the archaeological evidence and oracle bone inscriptions suggest that the greater part of Shang foreign relations with **client states** and allies consisted of setting and enforcing levels of tribute and labor service. Shang kings, especially Wu Ding, continually led expeditions against settled peoples to the west, the most prominent of whom, the Zhou, based around modern Xi'an, were ultimately enlisted as allies and clients. Wu Ding's successors, such as Zu Geng [ZOO-gung] and Di Yin, met with less success however; and over time shifting coalitions of former allies and client states began to encroach on Shang lands. Significantly, even to the end of the Shang period, the interior lands of the state appear to have been considered secure enough to lack walls and other defensive structures around many major towns.

Shang Interactions   Throughout the span of roughly 1,200 years from the traditional beginnings of the Xia to the end of the Shang, interaction between the northern Chinese states and the other Eurasian civilizational cores seems to have

Shang Chariot. Whether used for battle or state functions, Shang era chariots were distinctive in their wide stance, roominess, and portability. The photograph shows a careful reconstruction of a Shang chariot with authentic bronze decorations and lacquered finish. Note the linchpins holding the wheels to the axles. These could be quickly removed for ease in changing wheels or breaking down the chariot in order carry its parts separately.

Client states: States that are dependent on or partially controlled by more powerful ones.

been tenuous at best. The most direct links appear to have been through the trade and migrations of an ethnically and culturally diverse group of nomadic–pastoral peoples who ranged along a broad northern tier of Eurasia from the steppes of modern Ukraine to the area of modern Manchuria in the east. Though they left few traces, and early Chinese accounts use a haphazard collection of names for them, scholars have theorized that these nomads included both speakers of Altaic languages—the distant ancestors of the Mongols, Manchus, Huns, and Turks—and, perhaps more significantly at this point, the Indo-European peoples who played such an important role in spreading a host of ancient technologies throughout Eurasia.

Though direct mention of these nomadic peoples is almost completely absent from Shang records, a number of objects in Shang tombs carry clear signs of their foreign origins. For example, Fu Hao's tomb contains a number of bronze and jade objects—most significantly, bronze mirrors—that only later would come into widespread use in China. For their part, the Shang circulated local and foreign items such as bronze vessels, weapons, and jade throughout the region and beyond.

Many of these foreign items have been found as far south as northern Vietnam, and the peoples of surrounding areas acknowledged Shang predominance in wealth and culture. The picture is complicated somewhat by the recent work on cultures that show a connection to artifacts uncovered at Shang sites, and even at Erlitou, but have distinct—almost exotic—regional variations. The most intriguing example is that of the strange elongated figurines of Sanxingdui [SAN-shing-dway] in Sichuan [SIH-chwan], well out of Shang-dominated territory. On the whole, however, widespread recognition of Shang sophistication marks, with the ascendancy of the Zhou, an important example of a recurring pattern of world history, as well as that of China: conquerors on the cultural periphery interacting with and adapting to the culture of the conquered.

The Mandate of Heaven: The Zhou Dynasty to 481 BCE

Unlike the Xia and Shang dynasties, the nearly nine centuries of Zhou rule are extensively documented in such literary works as the *Zuo Zhuan* [ZWOA-jwan] (*The Commentaries of Mr. Zuo*), the *Chunqiu* [CHWUN-chew] (*Spring and Autumn Chronicles*), and later compilations such as the *Shiji* [SHIH-jee] (*Records of the Historian*) by the second-century BCE historian Sima Qian [Sihma-CHIEN] in addition to the *Shujing*.

Like the *Shujing*, these other Zhou records contain much of questionable value and uncertain origin. Nevertheless, they suggest both an ongoing quest for social, political, and moral order as well as institutional and intellectual experimentation on a grand scale. They also provide us, in the closing date of the *Spring and Autumn Chronicles* (481 BCE), with an important transition point with which to end this chapter. As we will see in Chapter 9, out of the increasingly fierce competition among the Zhou states for expansion and survival in the succeeding Warring States period (formally 403–256 BCE but used to encompass the entire era from 480 down to the creation of the Qin empire in 221 BCE) came China's greatest flowering of philosophical and political theory and ultimate unification into an empire that would last, with brief interruptions, for over 2,000 years.

The Mandate of Heaven   By the twelfth century BCE, it appears through the trend of oracle bone inscriptions that the size of the Shang state had shrunk considerably due to encroachment by peoples to the north and west. The oracle bones also suggest an increased concentration of power in the hands of the last Shang kings, a situation depicted in the literary record as coinciding with their dissolution and corruption. Against this backdrop, the state of Zhou to the west—which, as we have seen, had become a Shang dependency—began to take military action. The *Shujing* tells of the Zhou kings Wen, Wu, and Cheng and Cheng's regent, the Duke of Zhou, systematically pushing their holdings eastward from 1122 BCE, taking much of the Shang territory under their control. Sometime around 1045 BCE, Zhou forces captured and burned the last Shang capital and stronghold near Anyang. In doing so, the Zhou sought to portray their conquest as morally justified after an overlong interlude of Shang decadence.

Unlike the rise and fall of states in other areas, conquest by one of the three dynasties, as depicted in the literary record, did not mean exile, extinction, or enslavement for those defeated. On the contrary, the conquerors were shown as presenting their victories as acts of moral renewal for those they conquered by ridding them of oppressive or degenerate rulers and restoring leadership to the worthy. Although the attitudes of the common people toward such shifts of power remain unknown, the idealized speeches of the new rulers in the *Shujing*, for example, attempt to justify their actions and seek the cooperation of all classes in the new order.

As the compilers of this literary record, the Zhou sought to place themselves firmly within it. While it is unknown whether the practices they recorded had been widespread or newly invented by the conquerors, they provided the backdrop for one of China's most enduring historical and philosophical concepts: the Mandate of Heaven.

According to this idea, a dynasty's right to rule depends on the moral correctness of its rulers. Over time, dynasties grow weaker and tend to become corrupt as individual rulers give in to the temptations of court life or different factions seek to manipulate the throne. Under such conditions, rebellion from within or conquest by outside forces becomes morally justified. The success of such actions is then seen as proof that heaven's approval or "mandate" has been taken from the old rulers and bestowed on the insurgents, who may then legitimately found a new dynasty. Ultimately, however, the new dynasty, too, will decline. Thus, the fall of the Shang dynasty, as described in the *Shujing*, sprang from a loss of virtue, similar to that of the Xia, which had earlier resulted in Shang ascendancy. The idea of such a "dynastic cycle" operating as the driving force of history was later codified by court historians during the Han dynasty (202 BCE–220 CE).

Throughout Chinese history, these concepts not only allowed political renewal to take place internally but framed a remarkably durable system within which the Chinese and outside conquerors could interact and adapt themselves to each other in maintaining governmental and societal continuity.

Western Zhou and Eastern Zhou
By the end of the eleventh century BCE, nearly all of northern China as far south as the Yangtze River had come under Zhou rule. More precisely, a network of over 100 smaller territories was organized under

---

Dynastic Cycles

"We must not presume to suppose that the Xia received the Mandate of Heaven for a fixed period of years. . . . It was because they did not reverently care for their virtue that they early let their Mandate fall. We must not presume to suppose that the Yin [i.e., the Shang] received the Mandate of Heaven for a fixed period of years. . . . It was because they did not reverently care for their virtue that they early let their Mandate fall. Now the king has succeeded them in receiving their Mandate; let us also in regard to the mandate of these two states, continue it with like [good] achievements; then the king will truly now begin to undertake the mandate."

—*The Classic of Documents* [*Book of History*] (*Shujing*) in W. T. DeBary, et al. *Sources of Chinese Tradition*, vol. 1, rev. ed. New York: Columbia University Press, 1999. pp. 36–37.

Feudalism: A system of decentralized government in which rule is held by landowners who owe obligations of loyalty and military service to their superiors and protection to those under them (we will see systems like this in Europe and Japan as well).

MAP **4.4** Zhou China.

Zhou control, marking the beginning of the Western Zhou era, which lasted until 771 BCE. Zhou rulers placed family, distinguished subjects, allies, and even some defeated Shang notables in leadership positions of these territories under a graded system of hereditary ranks. By the eighth century BCE, however, the more powerful of these territories had begun to consolidate their holdings into states of their own. Though the states would continue to pledge their loyalty to the Zhou court, they increasingly worked toward promoting their own interests, which resulted in a weakening of Zhou political power. A half-century of war among court factions for ultimate rule, border struggles with nomadic peoples to the west and north, and a devastating earthquake further weakened Zhou power, resulting in the court being driven from its capital at Xi'an in 771 BCE and relocating to the east in Luoyang. This forced move began the Eastern Zhou period (770–256 BCE).

The Zhou in Decline The Zhou system of decentralized government called *fengjian* [FUNG-jien], usually rendered as **"feudalism,"** gave considerable autonomy to its local rulers and was thus an important reason for the weakening of the Zhou central government and the strengthening of its dependent states. As these dependent states grew in power and their economies flourished, local rulers became less loyal to the Zhou leadership and some rulers even went as far as naming themselves "king" (*wang*) of their own domains.

The prestige of the Zhou court was further weakened after its flight to Luoyang in 770. Continuing border problems with nomadic–pastoral peoples to the north and west around the Zhou home state and the relative isolation of its new capital drastically cut the flow of revenue from the dependent domains. This isolation was especially important since these states were in a period of tremendous economic expansion. Within a few generations of the inauguration of the Eastern Zhou in 770 BCE, Zhou control and power had significantly weakened in absolute as well as relative terms.

Hegemony: A system of state relations in which less powerful states directly or implicitly agree to defer to the lead of the most powerful state, which is, thus, the *hegemon.*

The Zhou decline is graphically described in the *Spring and Autumn Chronicles* and its accompanying work, *The Commentaries of Mr. Zuo*. Compiled in the Zhou state of Lu in the modern province of Shandong, these complementary works detail the maneuverings of states and individuals in northern China from 722 to 481 BCE. The world they depict is one in which repeated attempts at creating a stable political and social order among the 15 major Zhou states are frustrated by constantly shifting power dynamics and especially by the rise of dominant states on the Zhou periphery. In the accompanying passage, we see but one example of the strong-arm tactics of the upstart state of Qin, one day destined to unite China into an empire.

Early on, during the mid-seventh century, the most important of these states was Qi [Chee], which dominated northeast China and much of Shandong. By shrewd diplomacy and careful use of military power, Qi became the first "senior" or *ba* [bah] state in a system of **hegemony** in which the lesser Zhou states deferred to the *ba* state as the protector of the Zhou system. The successive *ba* states mounted alliances against non-Zhou states and attempted to regulate relations among those within the system. They also presided at conferences held from the mid-sixth century BCE aimed at regularizing trade and diplomacy among the states. Qi was succeeded by Jin, which reorganized the *ba* system and, in 579 BCE, sponsored a truce and disarmament conference among the Zhou states.

By the latter part of the sixth century, a rough balance of power among the four leading states of Jin, Chu [Choo] (the premier state of the southern periphery), Qi, and Qin (a rising force in the old Zhou homeland near Xi'an) held sway. While this system functioned for several decades, new powers on the peripheries, expansion into non-Zhou lands, and civil war in Jin ultimately precipitated the partition of Jin in 403 BCE, marking the formal opening of the Warring States period. By its close, Zhou itself had been absorbed by the combatants (in 256 BCE) and Qin would emerge as not just the dominant state but the creator of a unified empire in 221 BCE.

> **Power Politics**
>
> "You have undertaken to relay commands to the other feudal lords, but if you insist that we make hostages of our mothers in order to ensure good faith in our agreements, how can that possibly accord with the commands of the Zhou king? In fact it is a most unfilial order!"
>
> —Burton Watson, trans. The Tso Chuan. *Selections from China's Oldest Narrative History.* New York: Columbia University Press, 1989, pp. 116–117.

Economy, Society, and Family Adaptation in Ancient China

From Neolithic times, the Chinese economy has been based on agriculture. Even today, slightly more than half of the country's people are engaged in some variety of farm work. From early times as well, both the Yellow River states and those in the south of China outside of the control of the Shang and Zhou dynasties relied on a peasant subsistence economy based on family and clan landownership, with much of the local political power diffused to the thousands of villages dotting the landscape. While periodic concentration of landlord power and the problems of land-centered social relationships occupied Chinese rulers over the course of millennia, China, unlike some other agriculturally based societies, never developed an extensive system of slave labor.

Family life played a dominant role among all members of ancient Chinese society. Here, in a way parallel to trends in other agrarian kingdoms, the position of women in power among the elite eroded over time, a process that would be accelerated during the long interval of imperial rule. By the late Zhou period, the hierarchy of patriarchy and the growing influence of notions of *filial piety*—a model of behavior based on relationships among members of a family headed by the father—were on their way to becoming firmly established.

Shang Society

Though Shang leaders, like those of the Xia and Zhou, frequently moved their headquarters for political and military reasons, nearly all of their newly established capitals swiftly grew to proportions comparable to those developing in India and the Mediterranean.

Erligang   The capital city at Erligang [ARRH-lee-gahng] was characteristic of the late Xia or early Shang period. It had a defensive wall 4.5 miles in circumference, enclosing an urban center of about a square mile. The area within the walls was the province of the rulers, related families, diviners, and bronze casters and craftspeople in the direct service of the elites. Merchants and craftspeople involved in the manufacture of items other than bronze, jade, or ritual objects lived outside the city walls, as did peasants and slaves.

The life of the commoners in Erligang centered largely on communal agriculture. They tilled the soil with small plows, stone-tipped hoes, and assorted wooden implements, bronze being considered too valuable for use in agricultural tasks. They grew millet and vegetables as their staples and raised water buffalo, sheep in the more arid areas, chickens, and pigs. The pig, domesticated since at least Yangshao times, continued to be of central importance in the rural diet. Even today, the written character for "family" or "household" (家, *jia*) is represented by a character depicting a pig under a roof.

Social Class and Labor   Within the towns and villages immediately outside the larger cities, a more differentiated social structure was also developing, with artisans of various trades organized according to lineage. Many families and clans tended to pursue the same occupations for generations, and craft guilds and other organizations came to be dominated by family groups—such as potters and ceramics makers—as was the case later in imperial China. The constant warfare of Shang rulers and their increasing interest in monumental projects, for example, flood control along the Yellow River and its tributaries, all boosted the need for labor. Professional soldiers and local militia generally satisfied Shang military needs. Conscript labor, however, constituted an increasingly important part of the work force.

Interactions of Zhou Economy and Society

The large size of the territory claimed by the Zhou dynasty, and the enhanced trade that this expansion entailed, added to the wealth and power of all the rulers of its increasingly autonomous dependencies. The expansion of these dependencies to the Yangtze River basin brought much of east Asia's most productive farmland under some form of Zhou control and stimulated increased interaction with the inhabitants of the region.

Innovation and Adaptation in Agriculture   In the north, the introduction of the soybean from Manchuria, with its high protein content and ability to fix nitrogen in the soil, boosted crop yields and pushed growers to cultivate more marginal lands. The rotation of wheat and different varieties of millet allowed for more intensive farming. The use of more efficient ox-drawn plows and, from the fourth century BCE, iron-tipped tools as well as increasingly elaborate irrigation and water-conservancy efforts pushed yields even further. In the south, the Zhou dependencies, like the *janapadas* of India, developed rapidly as rice cultivation facilitated population growth. With the coming of intensive rice farming, the economic and demographic "center" of China moved steadily southward. By the middle of the sixth century BCE, the Zhou kingdoms taken together constituted the world's most populous, and perhaps richest, agriculturally based urban society.

Zhou Rural Society   The Zhou rulers devised a system of ranks for governing their dependencies based on the size of landholdings:

- *hou* [ho], the title given to rulers of the Zhou dependencies
- *qing* [ching], the chief functionaries of the *hou*
- *shi* [shihr], a general category for lower officials, eventually including talented commoners
- *shuren* [SHOO-ren], the remainder of the commoners

Members of the various ranks of the aristocracy were responsible for collecting taxes from their dependents and the *shuren* and were required to provide military service to those above in return for support and protection. Peasant cultivators worked their own lands, with the lands of the aristocracy often scattered in plots among those of the commoners.

The Well-Field System   In an attempt to untangle the more confusing aspects of this land arrangement, the Zhou were the first among many dynasties to attempt to impose a uniform system of land tenure in China. Later writers, most notably the philosopher Mencius, would look back nostalgically on the idealized *well-field system*—a method of land division said to have been devised by the Duke of Zhou. In this arrangement, each square *li* (one *li* is about one-third of a mile), consisting of 900 *mou* (each *mou* is approximately one-sixth of an acre) was divided into a grid of nine plots. Individual families would each work one of the eight outside plots while the middle one would be farmed in common for the taxes and rents owed the landowner or local officials. The term "well-field" comes from the Chinese character for "[water] well" (井, *jing*) which resembles a grid. Whether the system as idealized by Mencius was ever widely practiced is still a matter of debate among scholars. It did, however, remain the benchmark against which all subsequent attempts at land reform were measured, even into the twentieth century.

By the late 500s BCE, a substantial change had taken place in many of the Zhou states. The needs of individual governments to use the wealth of their states to support their militaries and developing bureaucracies prompted them to institute land taxes based on crop yields and, in some cases, commuting labor obligations to direct taxes payable in kind to the state. Depending on the state and the productivity of the land, these tended to vary from 10 to 20 percent of a family holding's yield. Then, as now, the taxes tended to affect the poor the most.

The New Classes: Merchants and *Shi*   Further evidence for the decline of the Zhou feudal system is the rise of new classes. For the first time, the literary record now includes references to merchants. The growing power of this new class began, among other things, a long-term struggle with various governments for control of such vital commodities as salt and iron. It also marked the beginning of the perception of merchants as *usurpers*—a class with no ties to the land and thus no stake in the values of landholders or peasants—whose drive for profit from trafficking in the goods of others endangered the stability of Zhou social institutions. Accompanying

Tax Burden

Big rat, big rat [i.e., the tax collector]
Do not eat my sprouts
Three years I have served you
But you give me no comfort.
I am going to leave you
And go to those happy fields;
Happy fields, happy fields;
Who there shall long moan?

—from *The Odes*, "Airs of the States," in W. T. DeBary, ed. *Sources of Chinese Tradition*, vol. 1, 1st ed. New York: Columbia University Press, 1964, p. 14.

the rise of a merchant class was the steady advance of a cash economy. The coining of money was becoming widespread by the late Zhou, including the round copper "cash" with the square middle hole—symbolically depicting heaven and earth—which remained almost unchanged for over 2,000 years.

Though often viewed with distaste by the landed aristocracy, merchants, with their wealth and expertise, were increasingly seen as resources to be tapped. Their rapid rise to economic prominence, however, meant that as a group their social position lay outside the traditional structures of agrarian life. Their independence and mobility, along with the steady growth of cities as centers of trade, helped spur political and economic centralization as the rulers of Zhou territories attempted to create more inclusive systems of administration. Direct taxation by the state, uniform law codes, and administrative restructuring were increasingly altering the old arrangement of mutual obligation between aristocratic landowners and dependent peasant farmers. Here, members of the new *shi* class—drawn from the lower aristocracy and wealthier commoners—who, like merchants, were divorced somewhat from the older structures of rural life, took on the role of bureaucrats and advisors. From the ranks of the *shi* would rise many of China's most famous thinkers, starting with Confucius; and the duties and proper conduct of the *shi* would come to occupy a prominent place in their writings from the late sixth century BCE on.

Central Asian Interactions   The growing wealth of north and central China spurred a dramatic increase in trade outside of the Zhou realm as well as among its constituent states, particularly in the south and along well-established routes into central Asia. As one measure of the extent of such interaction, scholars have pointed to silk threads appearing in the bindings of Egyptian mummies dated to 1000 BCE, in Greek gravesites several hundred years later, and even in central and northern European encampments from about 500 BCE. In this interchange, Zhou traders were increasingly helped by the carriers of the central Asian exchange.

By the sixth century BCE, a series of loosely related cultures along this northern front (called *Scythic* because of their broad cultural similarity to the peoples the Greeks called "Scythians") can be clearly discerned. These peoples appear to have taken Zhou goods much farther than originally thought, and scholars are only now beginning to realize the vast extent of their trade relations. What other goods besides silk may have been involved in such exchanges remains unknown, however, until the period of officially sanctioned and better recorded trade along the Silk Road began in the second century BCE.

Artifacts Recovered from the Fu Hao Burial Site.

Gender and the Family

While scholars have long explored the position of women and the family during China's imperial era, notably during the Song and Ming dynasties, serious study of gender roles in ancient China has only recently begun. One obvious reason for this is the relative scarcity of records during earlier times. Another is the development of women's instructional literature from roughly the first century BCE to the first century CE, a phenomenon that has provided modern scholars with an important focal point in charting a shift in perspectives of female "virtue" and proper behavior in the home and in public.

Elite Women of the Shang

In marked contrast to later Chinese court life, with its tightly proscribed etiquette and seclusion of wives and concubines from the avenues of power, elite women of the Shang often participated in political—and even military—affairs. As we saw in the opening of this chapter, one of the most complete Shang burial sites is that of Fu Hao, discovered in 1975. The most prominent of the 64 wives of Wu Ding, Fu Hao's burial artifacts—hundreds of bronzes, jade, and bone ornaments, as well as the sacrificial skeletons of sixteen people and six dogs—help bring to life a woman whose existence, though well established in written records, has otherwise been elusive.

The artifacts also shed light on a number of questions regarding Shang technology and material culture, court life, and especially the position of women among the aristocracy. For example, inscriptions on oracle bones in Fu Hao's tomb indicate that she wielded considerable power and influence even before becoming Wu Ding's principal wife. Prior to coming to court at the Shang capital of Yin sometime in the late thirteenth century BCE, she owned and managed a family estate nearby and was apparently well educated in a number of areas that would serve her well in palace life. She both supervised and conducted religious rituals at court and during military expeditions. As Wu Ding's chief confidant she advised him on political and military strategy and diplomacy. She even conducted her own military campaigns against Shang adversaries. The king apparently considered her so wise and beloved that after her death he frequently appealed to her for guidance through divination with oracle bones.

Women's Status in Transition

Elite women like Fu Hao appear to have shared a comparatively egalitarian status with male rulers, even to the point of leading armies and practicing divination. To the extent that such literature as the *Book of History* and the *Poetry Classic* of the early Zhou era address issues of women and power, women were still depicted as occupying important positions as mentors and advisors. Women's crafts such as spinning and weaving, and especially the different skills demanded in silk production, were highly regarded. In fact, there were government offices supervised and staffed by women to oversee silk and hemp cloth weaving.

The wives and concubines of rulers in many instances had their own sets of records and genealogies as well, an important asset among the powerful in this family-conscious society. Even by the late Zhou period, as one scholar notes, a "model" woman like Lady Ji of the state of Lu was able to instruct her son, the high official Wen Bo (Earl Wen), in the arts of government by comparing the roles of different officials to the proper arrangement of the components of a loom in the process of weaving. In this role of advisor, her virtue was much praised by subsequent thinkers.

Yet it was also true that by this time it was Wen Bo and not Lady Ji who actually held the reins of power. Late Zhou women might be well educated and highly capable, but they seldom ruled in their own right. In fact, the treaties hammered out during the Spring and Autumn period in many cases specifically barred women from involvement in state affairs. The same general trend may be glimpsed at other levels of society as well. The enormously complex web of family, clan, village, and class associations of the Zhou era reflects considerable respect for the wisdom and work of women; but these skills were increasingly seen as best exercised in the home instead of in the public sphere. The later development of state-sponsored Confucianism, with its preponderant emphasis on filial piety, ushered in a markedly secondary role for women.

Interactions of Religion, Culture, and Intellectual Life in Ancient China

In many respects, the evolution of Chinese religion follows a similar pattern to that of other agriculturally based urban societies. That is, like the gods of the early Mesopotamians, the first Chinese gods were local deities that inhabited a spirit world presided over by a ruling god. In China, the rulers' ancestors occupied the highest rungs of the spirit world and worship largely consisted of communication with them by various means. Religion was not separate from everyday life but permeated all aspects of it.

While they creatively adapted and adopted many other aspects of Shang culture, the Zhou era marked a turn toward a more abstract, impersonal, and universal concept of religion. In other words, Shangdi [SHANG-dee], the chief Shang deity—and other beings with superhuman powers but human-like personalities—began to give way to the more distant Zhou concept of "heaven" (*tian* [tien]) as the animating force of the universe. As in other religious traditions, there is a movement to go beyond the invocation of gods through proper sacrifice and divination rituals—*formalism*—in order to seek insight into the forces that control the universe. By the late Zhou era, this concept of heaven as the guiding cosmic force had become central to nearly every major Chinese religious and philosophical tradition.

Oracle Bones and Early Chinese Writing

Scholars agree that samples of Shang characters found on oracle bones are examples of China's earliest known writing, representing an entirely original system. One legend has it that the cultural hero Fuxi discovered writing from symbols etched on the back of a turtle, and indeed, the oracle bones themselves are mostly the undershells of turtles and the shoulder blades of oxen.

Shang Oracle Bone Inscription on Turtle Shell (Plastron).

As we saw with Wu Ding in the opening of this chapter, those seeking guidance would have a diviner incise questions onto the bones. The bones were then heated and tapped with a rod, and the resulting cracks were interpreted as answers. Several thousand distinct symbols have been identified, and many are clearly ancient versions of modern Chinese characters. More importantly, the principles on which these symbols functioned as a form of writing had already moved away from those of other hieroglyphic or pictographic languages. Chinese characters became increasingly stylized and, after the Qin era (221–202 BCE), put into standard forms. But in most cases, these retained enough of their earlier character to be recognizable to later readers. Moreover, the political and religious significance of Shang and Zhou ritual vessels, which, in many cases, contained inscriptions in archaic characters, ensured that some knowledge of them would be preserved.

Shang Bronzes   While it now seems that, like the potter's wheel, some of the early bronze articles and weapons found at late Longshan sites may have come by way of trade routes from western Asia, bronze-casting techniques used in China quite likely diffused northward from southeast Asia at about the same time. The best evidence for this is that the "carved-clay" technique favored by Shang and Zhou casters—in which inner and outer molds of the object are made of clay and molten bronze is poured into the gap between them—is unique to China and radically different from the "lost wax" method of the peoples of western Eurasia. Shang and early Zhou ritual vessels themselves, with their richly stylized *taotie* [TAOW-tea-eh] motifs—fanciful abstract reliefs of real and mythical animals incorporated into the design—are utterly unlike anything outside of east Asia.

Taotie **Design Pattern.**

Shang Religion   The use of bronze vessels with their elaborately stylized *taotie* motifs constituted a central part of Shang religious ceremonies among the elites. Offerings of meats, grains (wheat, millet, and occasionally rice), as well as wine were a regular part of Shang ritual. Except for some limited references in later literature to offerings of wine and millet at local shrines and ancestral graves, we know little about the religious practices of Shang commoners. However, the growing number of artifacts and oracle bones found at the gravesites of elites and at the remains of royal palaces has considerably clarified the belief system of the rulers.

The principal deity, Di or Shangdi, presided over the spirit world and governed both natural and human affairs. Shangdi was joined by the major ancestors of the dynastic line, deities believed to influence or control natural phenomena, and local gods appropriated from various Shang territories. The religious function of the Shang ruler, as it appears to have been for the Xia and would be for subsequent Chinese dynasties, was to act as the intermediary between the world of the spirits and that of humanity. Hence, rituals appear to have consisted largely of sacrifices to ancestors to assure their benevolence toward the living. As we have seen, the Shang sought the guidance of their ancestral spirits through divination on a wide variety of human affairs, such as royal marriages and military campaigns, and on such natural phenomena as droughts, floods, plantings, and harvests. Scholars theorize that many of the animals appearing as designs on ritual vessels represent messengers from the spirit world associated with divination.

Shang Dynasty Bronze Vase, 1300–1100 BCE. Note the stylized animal pattern called *taotie* characteristic of Shang and early Zhou bronzes.

As the Shang state grew more powerful and commanded more and more resources, the size and scope of the sacrifices also increased. Like the Xia, the Shang practiced

The Chinese Writing System

Of all the innovations commonly associated with China—paper, gunpowder, tea, the compass—perhaps the one with the longest-lasting impact was its unique writing system. Like many attempts at symbolic communication, such as those of the Egyptians, the Harappans, and, in the Americas, the Mayans, it was originally a system based on pictures. As with these other systems, the pictures became simplified and to some extent standardized for ease of interpretation. In its earliest form, for example, the Chinese character for the sun is a circle with a dot in the center. In its modern form it is still recognizable as 日.

Even in its archaic form, Chinese contained two basic types of characters: *pictographs*—pictures designating particular objects—and *ideographs*—pictures representing ideas—as well as some purely phonetic characters. Both types became increasingly elaborated and stylized, with the most basic characters acquiring phonetic components and compounds of simple characters formed to represent abstract expressions. For example, compounding the character 女, *nu* [neeu] (female or woman), with 子, *zi* [zuh] (child), created 好, *hao* [how] (good), an abstract expression symbolized quite concretely by a mother and child. Similarly, 女, *nu*, placed under the character for roof yielded the character, 安, *an* [ahhn], meaning peace or contentment. The characters for sun (日) and moon (月) placed together came to mean bright, 明.

The close association of the written language with early Chinese religious practices, court ceremonial functions, and self-cultivation and character development imbued it over the centuries with a kind of spiritual dimension not usually found among the written languages of other peoples. The patience and discipline demanded in learning the thousands of characters necessary for advanced literacy and the artistic possibilities embodied in the brush and ink traditionally used to write them placed calligraphy at the top of Chinese aesthetic preferences. Thus, wherever written Chinese is used, skill at the three interrelated "excellences" of painting, poetry, and calligraphy is esteemed as the highest mode of self-expression.

human sacrifice. Excavations at both the early capital in the Erligang district of the modern city of Zhengzhou and later capitals near Anyang have yielded numerous sites containing headless skeletons. The evidence suggests that the death of a ruler was the occasion to slaughter hundreds of slaves, servants, and war captives, perhaps to serve the deceased in the spirit world.

Adaptations of Zhou Religion, Technology, and Culture

The Zhou, like other conquerors after them, sought to give legitimacy to their reign by adopting many of the forms of art and ritual practiced by the defeated Shang. As before, the ruler maintained his place as mediator between the human and divine worlds. But the Zhou also appear to have followed the trend toward more abstract religious ideas we have observed in other early civilizations.

The Chinese written language had a tremendous impact on the course of Asian history. While it requires extensive memorization compared to the phonetic languages of other cultures, it is remarkably adaptable as a writing system because the meaning of the characters is independent of their pronunciation. Thus, speakers of non-Chinese languages could attach their own pronunciations to the characters and, as long as they understood their structure and grammar, could use them to communicate. This versatility enabled Chinese to serve as the first written language not only for speakers of the Chinese family of dialects and languages on the Asian mainland but also for the Koreans, Japanese, and Vietnamese, whose spoken languages are totally unrelated to Chinese. The pattern of interaction and adaptation prompted by the acquisition of the written language allowed the vast body of Chinese literature, philosophy, religion, history, and political theory to tie the literate elites of these states together within a common cultural sphere. In this respect, it functioned in much the same way as Latin among the educated of Europe. Even today, despite the development of written vernacular languages in all these countries, the ability to read classical Chinese is still considered to be a mark of superior education. Moreover, the cultural heritage transmitted by Chinese characters continues to inform the worldviews of these societies.

Questions

- How would the pattern of interaction and adaptation that characterized the development of the Chinese writing system come to link people together into a common cultural sphere?

- How does the impact of the Chinese writing system compare to the impact other writing systems have had in other parts of the world?

Heaven   They introduced the concept of *tian*, "heaven," as a relatively neutral, impersonal controlling force of the universe, which eventually replaced the more approachable, human-like Shangdi. It was this more abstract heaven whose mandate gave the right to rule to all subsequent Chinese dynasties. Thus, throughout the long history of imperial China, the emperor retained the title of *Tianzi*, "son of heaven," as a symbol of his cosmic filial piety—his obligation to fulfill heaven's mandate as a son serves his father.

Iron Casting   Perhaps the most significant technological innovation introduced during the Zhou period was the use of iron. Late Shang and western Zhou tombs have contained iron objects of foreign origin, probably obtained from Indo-European peoples ranging across central Asia. By the seventh century BCE, basic technologies

Pastoral Scene

In the seventh month the Fire star declines.
In the ninth month we give out the clothes.
Spring days are sunny
And the oriole sings.
The girls take their fine baskets,
And walk down the little paths
To collect the tender mulberry leaves.
Spring days get longer,
In groups they go to pick the artemesia.
A young girl is heartsick,
Waiting to go home with the lord's son.

—from Patricia Buckley Ebrey, ed. *Chinese Civilization: A Sourcebook,* 2nd ed. New York: Free Press, 1993, p. 12.

for mining and working iron are in evidence in western China. Significantly, it appears that the casting techniques of bronze production were adapted to this purpose. When combined with the high-temperature technologies employed by Zhou potters, the Chinese produced the world's earliest cast iron. By the sixth century BCE, cast and wrought iron weapons, tools, and farm implements were in common use; and even some steel objects, including a sword, have been found. As in Gangetic India, they were instrumental in opening up new lands for cultivation and multiplying the deadliness of warfare.

Folk Culture: *The Book of Songs*   As noted in the previous section, we know relatively little about the lives of the common people during the period of the Xia, Shang, and Zhou dynasties. One of the few sources that does provide some clues is the *Shijing*, the *Poetry Classic*, sometimes called *The Book of Odes* or *The Book of Songs*. The subject matter covers a wide range of interest and emotion, from homely observations on the cycles of rural life to protests and cleverly veiled satire. It is believed that, in most cases, the verses were meant to be sung.

As historical source material as well as art, the *Shijing*'s songs and poems of the lives and loves, burdens and laments of peasants and soldiers, young wives and old men are still striking in their immediacy today.

Putting It All Together

The period from the first Neolithic settlements in the Yellow River valley to the birth of Confucius in 551 BCE witnessed the beginning of many of the foundations of the cultures of China and, through interaction with Chinese influences, east and southeast Asia. Like the other agricultural–urban cores in Mesopotamia, along the Nile, and in the Indus valley, the society that emerged in northern China was very much a product of its major river system. As early as 10,000 BCE, the Yellow River basin saw the rise of self-sufficient agricultural villages, marking the transition from forager to agrarian society. It was the early states that developed here that came to dominate the Chinese historical record. With the rise of the Xia dynasty late in the third millennium BCE, the first evidence of Chinese cities and the first people, places, and events traceable through later literary sources all make their appearance.

The Shang conquest of the Xia, traditionally held to be in 1766 BCE, marks the first flowering of China's "bronze age." The centering of political, military, and religious authority in one ruler; the development of a unique and versatile form of writing; the growth of cities; and the widespread use of bronze under the Shang in many ways run parallel to developments in the other early centers of civilization (see Concept Map). In their casting techniques and design motifs of bronze ritual vessels and their system of writing, however, Shang contributions were original and long-lasting.

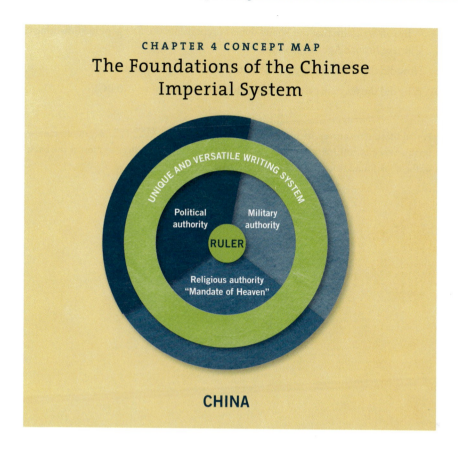

CHAPTER 4 CONCEPT MAP
The Foundations of the Chinese Imperial System

UNIQUE AND VERSATILE WRITING SYSTEM

Political authority

Military authority

RULER

Religious authority "Mandate of Heaven"

CHINA

The theme of moral renewal came with the rise of the Zhou after 1122 BCE and was perhaps made retroactive by them as well. Nearly all of China from the Yangtze River basin north was incorporated into a decentralized governmental system centered on the Zhou court at Xi'an. But, as depicted in the Concept Map, the growing power of the largest Zhou territories eventually eclipsed that of the court; and this began a prolonged era of struggle between the states. The increased wealth and power of rulers, aided by the drive of new social classes such as merchants and the *shi* to share in it, contributed to the breakdown of older feudal social patterns during the Spring and Autumn period from 722 to 481 BCE. Continual warfare stimulated both a drive for political consolidation and a questioning of the foundations of society. With the ideas of Confucius, to whom we turn at the beginning of Chapter 9, a radical direction in conceiving the nature and aims of society would soon take place. His ideas, adopted by a Chinese imperial system that would last over 2,000 years, would profoundly affect hundreds of millions of people inside and outside of China in the centuries to come.

Review and Respond

1. What environmental characteristics of the Yellow River valley encouraged the development of Neolithic settlements there?

2. Why has the Xia dynasty remained shrouded in myth even to the present day?

3. Why can we claim that the Shang dynasty represents the first genuine flowering of Chinese Bronze Age civilization?

4. How did the Zhou concept of the Mandate of Heaven operate?

5. Why did the *fengjian* system of the Zhou break down after 770 BCE?

> For additional resources, including maps, primary sources, visuals, and quizzes, please go to www.oup.com/us/vonsivers. Please see the Further Resources section at the back of the book for additional readings and suggested websites.

Thinking Through Patterns

▶ **How did the interplay of environment and climate help to influence the earliest patterns of Chinese civilization? How do historians address the question of whether "geography is destiny" in this case?**

The relationship of environment to the ways in which a particular culture lives is at once seemingly obvious and quite complex. In the case of northern China, the river both allows a large, reliably fertile area for cultivation to be maintained and restricts the ability to live too close to it because of flooding. Not surprisingly, the collective efforts of the early Chinese states to control the river proved central to the character of these states. But what kinds of larger conclusions can we draw? Some scholars in the past theorized that early civilizations based around rivers developed many similarities in their patterns of governing, such as centralization, bureaucracy, and elaborate labor regulations. But here, the key is in the details: How similar can we say Egypt is to Shang dynasty China? As for the larger question of geography and destiny, most historians would say that it is an important *conditional* factor, among many others, in determining how a civilization develops. But rarely can it be seen as *destiny*—as a *sufficient cause.*

Among other things, these remains can suggest the kinds of plants and animals that were domesticated, the kinds of shelters that housed people, how gender roles were assigned, how they handled their dead, and how they defended themselves. Many of these things are open to debate however. Chinese scholars in the People's Republic, for example, believed that such Neolithic villages were matriarchal and matrilineal; those from outside are less sure of the evidence for this. If true, the later switch to the strong patriarchal tradition represents an important change in the structure of Chinese families.

▶ **What can the remains of Neolithic Chinese settlements tell us about the continuities and disruptions of Chinese history?**

▶ **How did the Zhou concept of the Mandate of Heaven operate?**

The Mandate of Heaven, as we have seen, was at once a way for the Zhou to retrospectively legitimize their conquests and to create a precedent for future moral renewal. As part of a dynastic cycle, it set the fundamental pattern for the way the Chinese tended to view history. The rule of a particular dynasty was expected to advance in reform and expansion in its early stages, reach a comfortable point of harmony in its middle stages, and go into moral and material decline in its final stages. From that point, revolt breaks out and heaven transfers its mandate to a new dynasty—*if it succeeds.* If not, the rebels have committed the worst of crimes. There is a definite closed logic to this system: Heaven approves, so the rebels succeed; the rebels succeed because heaven approves. This pattern of dynastic cycle and heavenly mandate made China's historical experience—conveniently fitted to the theory—not only comprehensible but also predictable. Alert rulers constantly searched for signs that the mandate was in danger; the people themselves often speculated about portents or natural disasters as presaging dynastic change. Even China's modern rulers are heirs to this pattern: During human-made and natural disasters the Communist Party is even more alert to possible signs that the people are expecting a "dynastic" change.

Chapter 5

30,000-600 BCE

Origins Apart: The Americas and Oceania

THE AMERICAS
AND OCEANIA

In a dramatically understated press release from the Chicago Field Museum dated April 26, 2001, anthropological archaeologists Ruth Shady Solis, Jonathan Haas, and Winifred Creamer announced a stunning discovery in the archaeology of the Americas. The scientists had just finished conducting radiocarbon dating tests on plant fibers taken from site excavations of Caral, in the Supé valley in Peru. Though largely ignored for over a century, the site had recently stirred considerable interest because of its immense size (over 200 acres), monumental architecture—pyramids more than 60 feet high and nearly 500 feet square at the base—and evidence of early urban living. The test results, however, now demanded a complete retelling of the main narrative of the history of civilization in the Americas.

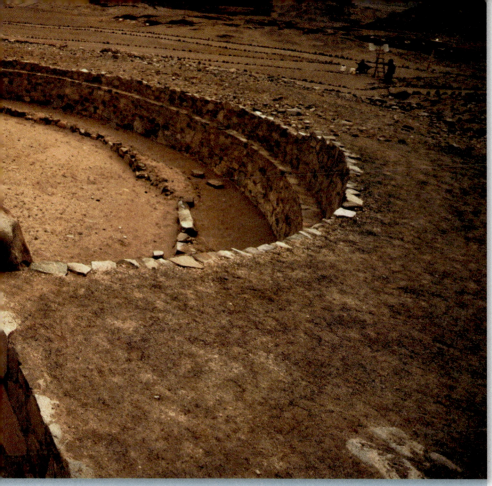

Seeing Patterns

▶ What do historians say about the advantages and disadvantages of the separation of the Americas from the societies of Eurasia and Africa?

▶ The wheel is often cited as the most basic human invention, yet large and sophisticated civilizations were able to flourish without this signal innovation. Why do you think it did not develop in the Americas?

▶ Why did no cities develop on the larger Pacific Islands?

Because earlier evidence pointed toward a relatively late arrival for modern humans in the Americas and given the difficulty of domesticating staple grain plants—corn, for example, it was believed, took at least 1,000 years to breed into a useful food crop—the earliest known American civilizations had been assumed to be much more recent than their earliest Eurasian and African counterparts—until now, that is. For decades, discoveries in North and South America had strongly suggested that humans had migrated much earlier than previously thought, calling into question their puzzlingly swift occupation of the continents.

But the Caral-Supé [Ka-RALL Soo-PAY] results, published in the journal *Science*, put the date of the materials tested at 2627 BCE, making the city as old as the pyramids of Egypt and the most ancient Mesopotamian cities. Indeed, work at nearby sites showed that they had been occupied by substantial villages for far longer, that the entire area was supported by elaborate irrigation works, and that Caral-Supé is only one of 18 similar urban sites in the Supé valley. Clearly, the human urge to create cities, monumental architecture, and religious sites ran deep enough to manifest itself thousands of miles away from other early models.

The Americas, therefore, represent a vital counterpoint to the development of agrarian-based cities and states in Eurasia and Africa, which we

First Andean City Site at Caral-Supé. The first urban site in the Americas to approach the antiquity of those in Eurasia and Africa, Caral-Supé was first brought to light in the 1990s. Dating of artifacts there places them at perhaps 2700 BCE. Moreover, the apparent nature of this as a planned city suggests a power state, perhaps hundreds of years older than any other that may have existed in the region.

129

have discussed in earlier chapters. In some ways, the parallels run very close:

- the development of urban centers as religious and trade centers
- the role of staple food surplus accumulation
- the kinds of buildings—pyramids, for example

Yet some of the differences in the civilizations provide enticing puzzles. For example, Caral-Supé appears to have been thriving long before ceramics turn up in Peru, an innovation that in all cases *predated* cities in Eurasia and Africa. In addition, although there is some evidence of record keeping by *quipú*, the much later system of knotted ropes used by the Incas, there is no writing—again, something the major Eurasian civilizations developed. Finally, as with later American civilizations, there is no evidence of the use of the wheel for transportation or mechanical work. Thus, in our search for patterns of world history, the Americas provide an entirely independent test case for examination and analysis.

- In Chapter 1, we examined the "big bang" of world history: the origins of human society in Africa and the first great pattern of human subsistence: foraging.
- In Chapter 2, we learned about the next great pattern of people moving from foraging to farming societies and some of the consequences that change brought.
- In Chapter 3, we explored how this pattern can be replayed and re-mixed in different ways—in some cases, like that of the Harappans, moving from an urban society back to village farming or foraging.
- In Chapter 4, we learned more about how civilizations become centralized, while at the same time how regional powers can challenge the forces of centralization.

In Chapter 5, we will see examples of all of these patterns but conditioned by the key variable of *separation*. How do we explain these similarities and differences appearing in societies separated by thousands of miles of ocean and with no evidence of contact? A vital part of our examination springs from interactions and adaptations. How did these take place thousands of miles away in the Americas and the islands of the Pacific? How do the critical elements of environment and culture play out in such societies separated from the intense contiguous contact among societies in Eurasia and Africa? How do they alter the patterns we have examined? How much more or less bearing do environment and culture have on the human societies on the thousands of islands of Oceania? How did the peoples interact with each other and adopt or reject certain innovations? Indeed, how "isolated" were they from each other and the societies of Asia, Australia, and the Americas? Finally, given the importance that we place on interaction and adaptation among peoples, what advantages and disadvantages did such separateness bring?

The Americas: Hunters and Foragers, 30,000–600 BCE

The remoteness of human beings on the American continents from the larger and more interconnected societies of Eurasia and Africa raises one of the key questions of world history: What would people do in places far removed from other human communities over long periods of time? The initial great migration out of Africa had equipped human beings with an assortment of tools, practices, and habits that collectively created an effective *foraging*—or hunting and gathering—type of society. As we read in Chapter 1, human foragers spread out to populate the earth in Eurasia and Australia, and the coming of humans to the Americas in many ways represented the final stage of their great migration from Africa.

The advances and retreats of the great ice sheets of the northern polar regions over the last 75,000 years allowed several possible opportunities for humans to migrate from the Eurasian landmass in search of game. Exactly when *Homo sapiens* began to move into these new lands, however, is at present a highly controversial question. Migration might have begun as early as 40,000–30,000 years ago, though only now has enough archaeological evidence accumulated to support dates before about 13,500 years ago. After this date, the number and range of humans multiplied rapidly on the two continents, forming small, highly mobile forager bands.

Yet, even at this stage, the migrants had begun to adapt the technology of spears, bows, and other hunting equipment to the big game of the new continent with astonishing swiftness. And as the success of their hunting began to reduce the populations of their favored game, a question arises for world historians: Would they now follow the same patterns by undergoing a Neolithic revolution and developing practices and institutions similar to those of humans in Eurasia and Africa?

It does indeed appear that they did. During the period from about 6000 to 4000 BCE, in what is today Mesoamerica (Mexico and Central America), and the Andes Mountains in South America in Ecuador and Peru, people began to settle in villages. They domesticated squash, beans, corn, and, somewhat later, potatoes and founded the first forms of agrarian society in the Americas. Separated by thousands of miles and vast bodies of water from the peoples of Eurasia and Africa, they were nevertheless traveling independently along the same crucial early pattern of world history: moving from foraging to farming and to settled life—until, ultimately, they built great cities, states, and empires. As we will see, however, there were also some important differences in their modes of subsistence and technology in the processes involved in the creation of these new societies.

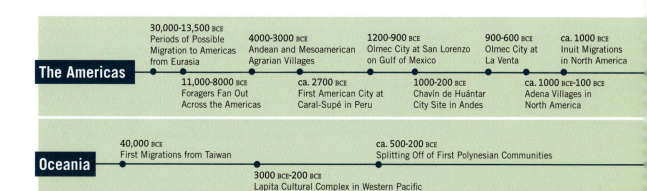

The Americas

30,000-13,500 BCE
Periods of Possible Migration to Americas from Eurasia

4000-3000 BCE
Andean and Mesoamerican Agrarian Villages

1200-900 BCE
Olmec City at San Lorenzo on Gulf of Mexico

900-600 BCE
Olmec City at La Venta

ca. 1000 BCE
Inuit Migrations in North America

11,000-8000 BCE
Foragers Fan Out Across the Americas

ca. 2700 BCE
First American City at Caral-Supé in Peru

1000-200 BCE
Chavín de Huántar City Site in Andes

ca. 1000 BCE-100 BCE
Adena Villages in North America

Oceania

40,000 BCE
First Migrations from Taiwan

ca. 500-200 BCE
Splitting Off of First Polynesian Communities

3000 BCE-200 BCE
Lapita Cultural Complex in Western Pacific

The Environment

Next to Eurasia, the two continents comprising the Americas encompass the largest landmass on earth. From the perspective of Europe, they form the Western Hemisphere, that is, the western "half" of the "sphere" or globe. Located north and south of the equator, the Americas are geographical mirror images of each other, sharing similar types of landscape and climate, though their shapes differ considerably.

Cordilleras: A continuous spine of mountain ranges near or along the entire western coast of the Americas.

The Americas' most prominent geographical feature is a contiguous spine of mountain ranges, or **cordilleras** [cor-dee-YEH-ras], near or along the entire western coast. Known as the Rocky Mountains in the north, these ranges become the Sierra Madre in the center and the Andes in the south. Water from these mountains feeds nearly all river systems, of which there are eight in the north and four in the south. Both continents also share low mountain systems along their eastern coasts. North and South America meet in Mesoamerica near the equator, with North America then reaching northward to the North Pole and South America extending southward almost to Antarctica. Thus, the climatic zones of both South and North America range from extreme cold to subtropical and tropical warmth.

Geographical Regions   North America consists of four main geographical regions:

- The Rocky Mountain region
- The Canadian Shield, which stretches from today's Canada to Greenland
- The Great Plains and central lowlands in the center of today's United States
- The Appalachian Mountains in the east and the broad coastal plain along the Atlantic Ocean

The four regions not only are distinct geographically but also vary considerably in precipitation and temperature. Historically, they have resulted in widely differing modes of subsistence and society among their inhabitants from the time of the first migrants through much of the history of present-day Canada, the United States, and Mexico, as well as among interior regions of all three countries.

Mesoamerica and South America form five distinct geographical regions:

- The Central American mainland and the Caribbean islands
- The Andes Mountain region along the west coast
- The Guyana Shield and Amazon basin in the northeast
- The Brazilian Shield and *Gran Chaco* in the east
- The Patagonian Shield, in the center of the continent's southern tip

Here, the size of the mountains and the extent of the rain forests dictated even greater regional separation than in North America until recent times.

During winters in North America, freezing winds from the Arctic blow south across the Canadian Shield into the central plains, or American Midwest. By contrast, at the southern tip of South America, air currents are predominantly westerly and more moderate and do not push winter frost very far northward. Thus, apart from the southern tip at Cape Horn and Tierra del Fuego—the site of some of the world's most violent seas and frequent storms—snow and frost are mostly limited to the Andes. In North America, winter and summer temperatures vary greatly, except in Florida and southern California, as do precipitation levels, especially in the western half of the continent. Generally, the eastern and midwestern regions of North

America receive regular rainfall throughout the year, while the western regions and lower Pacific coast tend to be drier, with occasional droughts, and intermittently subject to massive forest fires started by lightning strikes.

In Mesoamerica, the Caribbean, and the northern two-thirds of South America, temperatures and humidity levels tend to be relatively high. Large steppe and desert areas cover the western one-third of North America, while in South America deserts and steppes are more limited and mostly found along the northwestern coast and in the interior of the south. Prior to modern times, large forests covered the eastern two-thirds of North America and the northern half of South America.

Ocean Currents, Hurricanes, and El Niño   Like the monsoon system that wields so much influence in the agricultural life of India, China, the Indian Ocean, and western Pacific regions, large-scale weather events governed at least in part by the actions of ocean currents and continental weather systems have played historical roles in the Americas. Unlike the monsoon systems, however, their cycles have only recently come to be understood.

Running roughly parallel to the eastern coasts of northern South America and nearly all of North America, the Gulf Stream current of the Atlantic Ocean moves warm water from the south Atlantic along the Eastern Seaboard of the United States before heading northeast toward the European coast. There, it moderates the climate of northern Europe and the British Isles despite their high latitudes. In the Americas, the Gulf Stream's interactions with changing wind patterns in fall and winter in eastern North America frequently result in large storms called "nor'easters," a phenomenon first studied by the American scientist Benjamin Franklin.

More destructive is the frequency with which the Gulf Stream guides hurricanes into the Caribbean Sea and along the North American coast. The immense "heat pump" of the African interior and Sahara Desert continually spawns tropical disturbances in the eastern Atlantic, which gain strength over the warm waters there and the Caribbean as they move westward. Historically, the east–west winds that drive the tropical disturbances played a vital role in fostering the trans-Atlantic slave trade by making navigation swift and predictable. In the case of hurricanes, however, the storms are often picked up by the Gulf Stream, fed by its warm waters, and directed north from Cuba along the North American coast, where, in modern times, they have caused immense destruction in this heavily populated area.

In the Pacific, the Humboldt and Japan Currents work in a similar fashion, though, in relation to the direction of their waters in the Americas, in reverse. That is, warm waters of the western Pacific and along the Japanese Pacific coast move northward toward the Aleutian Islands and then down the west coast of the Americas. Like the Gulf Stream, this has a considerable moderating effect on climate, particularly from the coast of southern Alaska to northern California, home to much of the world's temperate rain forests. From northern California to Chile, the currents are generally cooler than the surrounding ocean and provide important fish and marine mammal habitats. For millennia, these supplied the peoples of the west coast with sustenance and allowed settled life with a minimum of agriculture.

The Pacific region is also home to the **El Niño** phenomenon, which, though little understood until recently, plays an immense role in global climatology. In cycles that vary from 3 to 8 years, large areas of abnormally warm water appear off the coasts of Peru and Chile (El Niño), which lowers barometric pressures there and raises

El Niño: A periodic reversal of the normal flow of currents in the Pacific, greatly altering weather patterns.

them in the western Pacific. The results tend to vary but usually alter the jet stream patterns and cause abnormal rainfall and storm levels over large areas of the globe, particularly in the Americas. The reverse phenomenon, La Niña, occurs when the oceans in the region have large areas of abnormally cold water.

Human Migrations

As we saw in Chapter 1, one of the most hotly contested debates in modern archaeology is who exactly were the first people to appear in the Americas, and where did they come from? Part of the debate revolves around the authenticity of sites and the accuracy of techniques used to date them; part of it also arises from legal and political issues of who can claim to be the "first" Americans and have rights to the contents of such sites. Generally, however, scholars agree that the earliest period down to 7000 BCE is that of the *Paleoamericans*, whose remains indicate that they are from different areas in Asia, while later arrivals are classified as *Native Americans* (also often called *Amerindians*).

To give some idea of the scope of the problem, some scholars believe that the earliest immigrants might have been people similar to those migrating to Australia. Genetic evidence, however, suggests that later migrants came from southeast and northeast Asia. Complicating the picture even further, as we saw in Chapter 1, Kennewick man, discovered in 1996 on the banks of the Columbia River in Washington State and dated to ca. 9,300 years ago, has been determined to be genetically close to south Asians. Thus, the earliest populations of the Americas may have been far more ethnically diverse than had previously been supposed (see Map 5.1).

When the northeast Asians, the ancestors of the Native Americans of today, arrived is difficult to determine and one of the most contentious problems in American archaeology. Researchers working on Siberian sites have so far been unable to establish connections with the Alaskan sites that are assumed to be the places from which people migrated through the Alberta ice gap into North America around 13,500 years ago. What is known, however, is that these Alaskan immigrants, who formed initially only one group among many others, eventually around 7,000 years ago became the dominant population of "Native Americans."

Early Foragers   One of the ways in which scientists have attempted to track and date the migrations of early Americans is through their hunting technology. The earliest arrivals hunted with *stabbing spears*—weapons meant to be thrust into an animal's body or thrown from a very short distance. During the period from 11,000 to 8000 BCE, such spears were equipped with a stone point that was flat or "fluted" on both sides. These fluted sides allowed the spearhead to be inserted into a groove cut into one end of the spear and fastened there with a leather strip. As in Eurasia and Africa, the size and shape of spearheads and arrowheads provide valuable clues to regional variations in technology and, by tracking these, on migration patterns. In North America, where the spearhead flutes were oval, they are known as "Clovis points," from the town in New Mexico near where scholars identified them for the first time in the 1930s. The pervasiveness of Clovis points in the north and a fishtail style of spear flutes in South America had suggested to scholars until very recently that their users were indeed the first migrants to the continents. It was also widely thought that their close dating and specialized use in big-game hunting indicated that these people had settled both continents within a few years of arriving and had,

The Environment of the Americas

FLORIDA   Modern state or province

CHILE   Modern-day country

▪   Archaeological site

➜   Warm ocean current

➜   Cold ocean current

MAP **5.1** **The Environment of the Americas.**

Big-Game Hunters

"This does not mean that Clovis existed by mammoth alone. Nor does it imply that Clovis peoples only hunted mammoth, bison, and other large animals. There is clear evidence that they did exploit small mammals and reptiles on occasion.

"However . . . Clovis hunter–gatherers often ignored opportunities to harvest smaller game species. Rabbits, rodents, birds, fish, and other small game taxa, however, are not so easily taken since they have evolved sophisticated defense mechanisms to elude numerous predators, and therefore have relatively high handling costs for a relatively small payoff."

—Nicole M. Waguespack and Todd A. Surovell. "Clovis Hunting Strategies, or How to Make Out on Plentiful Resources." *American Antiquity* 68 (2003): 348.

Taxa: The classification of organisms into systems of relationship based on genetic and morphological similarities.

Midden: A refuse pile; archaeologists treasure such piles because a great deal can be learned about the material culture of a society by what the people threw out over long periods of time.

in short order, killed off most of the prehistoric big game such as mammoths, mastodons, ground sloths, and tapirs. The absence of Clovis points in Eurasia, and the presence of less sophisticated points and tools at the newly examined earlier sites (such as Buttermilk Creek in Texas), however, now seem to suggest that the Clovis people had already been here for some time. Indeed, these points might be seen as the first distinctively "American" innovations.

Like their counterparts we examined in Chapters 1 and 2, these early American settlers were hunters and gatherers, or *foragers*. They formed groups of extended families and lived in rock shelters, caves, and huts, moving whenever the food resources in a given territory were exhausted. Once a year, during the summer, extended families met to commemorate a common ancestor by sharing food and performing other rituals. Families held initiation ceremonies for adults, arranged marriages, and exchanged goods such as obsidian, copper, mica (a mineral that flakes off in transparent sheets), and seashells. Most of the time families stayed in their own territory, collecting wild foods such as grass seeds, roots, berries, mushrooms, fruits, and nuts.

As we have seen, the fluted spear points were designed specifically for hunting big game, such as mammoths, moose, and bison. Killing these animals would have required repeated stabbing, for which securely fastened points were necessary. The warming climate, however, favored the expansion of forests but was increasingly unfavorable to the survival of big mammal species. As big game became scarce, hunters shifted to smaller spear points and smaller game, such as antelope, deer, and rabbit. By about 8000 BCE most big mammal species were gone from the Americas.

Toward Settlements As larger game became increasingly scarce, people in coastal areas began relying more on fish and shellfish and those in arid regions increased their collection of wild seeds and nuts. Hunters developed the spear thrower, a device for hurling smaller spears from a greater distance at elusive small animals. Obsidian, recovered from volcanic regions and traded over long distances, became the preferred material for spear points. Following a pattern similar to that of their distant relatives in Eurasia and Africa, humans in the Americas learned to grind, groove, and polish stone to make axes, mortars, pestles, and grindstones. Bone became an important material for spears, fishhooks, awls, needles, combs, and spatulas. Humans continued to live in rock shelters and caves, but now they began to construct huts made of poles and covered with skins or even more permanent wooden structures. These more permanent dwelling places appeared especially along the seacoasts, the Great Lakes, and large rivers, with plentiful resources of fish, shellfish, and waterfowl. The first domesticated animal, the dog, appeared, perhaps descended from the wolves picking through human **middens** or perhaps accompanying hunters migrating to the new continents. As bands of hunters and gatherers acquired more household goods, they became less inclined to move about over large distances. As in Eurasia and Africa, they increasingly tended to stay close to favored long-term food sources and centers of ceremonial life.

Early Ceremonial Life As did their contemporaries in north China, more sedentary foragers began to bury their dead in cemeteries, which soon became territorial centers. Hunter–gatherers in the Americas, like those on the other continents, buried their dead with gifts of ochre, symbolizing the color of life, and tools to help them in the life after death. Leaders of hunter–gatherer bands were often *shamans*, elders with spiritual powers that enabled them to deal with the forces of nature. By donning animal masks, playing music on flutes and drums, and engaging in ritual dance, shamans fell into ecstatic trances. During these trances they experienced themselves merging with powerful animals or other people, charming animals into submission, exorcising evils from humans, or healing afflictions. Leaders worked together with elders, forming councils for the administration of their settlements and hunting grounds.

Shaman-led ceremonies often took place in caves or overhangs, where people painted animals and humans on the rock walls. Probably the oldest paintings are those of Pedra Furada [PAY-drah Foo-RAH-dah] in northeastern Brazil, dating to about 8000 BCE. One of the most distinct paintings in the ceremonial vein is that of the so-called white shaman at Lower Pecos in Texas, dating to 2000 BCE. He is shown in a trance, leaving his body behind. His feet are feline, his arms are feathered, and he is surrounded during his spiritual journey by animals and humans, both dead (upside down) and alive (upright). Hunter–gatherers possessed a complex culture,

The White Shaman, Lower Pecos, Texas, ca. 2000 BCE. The practice of *shamanism*—the belief in the ability of certain individuals to communicate with spirits or inhabit the spirits of people or animals—appears to be a common feature of many widely diverse peoples. Many scholars believe that migrants from Asia carried these religious forms with them to the Americas because of the resemblance to practices among peoples in Siberia and other areas in northern Eurasia.

Pedra Furada, Sao Raimundo Nonato, Piaui, Brazil, ca. 8000 BCE. One of the earliest cave paintings in the Americas, and particularly striking because of its location in Brazil, this artwork perhaps depicts ceremonies related to warfare.

ranging from sophisticated gathering and hunting techniques and settlements ordered by elders to shamanic religious ceremonies.

Agriculture, Villages, and Urban Life

As we have seen in the preceding chapters, far-reaching changes accompanied human societies that made the transition from foraging to agriculture—from hunting and gathering to relying principally on domesticated plants and animals. The first major change we see associated with this momentous pattern is the ability to maintain large populations: to sustain villages, towns, and cities, developing increasingly complex societies with ever more diverse intellectual, cultural, and religious spheres. The second change is the opposite side of the coin: the potential for conflict and destruction on an unprecedented scale. Both of these changes grow from the Neolithic revolution (see Chapter 2). In the Americas, however, this grand pattern of world history appears to have begun somewhat later than in many areas of Eurasia and Africa.

The Neolithic Revolution in the New World

The most noteworthy first steps toward agriculture took place in central and southern Mexico in Mesoamerica and Ecuador and Peru in the Andes. Temperatures in these regions turned warmer after about 4000 BCE. Foragers shortened their annual migrations and extended existing patches of wild bean and *teosinte* [tay-oh-SIN-tay] (believed to be a wild grass precursor of maize) through purposeful planting. Careful harvesting and replanting, probably with obsidian-spiked sickles, led to early domesticated varieties of these plants, increasingly bearing larger kernels. Beans were domesticated first in Peru, and maize/corn followed somewhat later in southern Mexico. By about 3000 BCE, foragers in these regions had completed their transformation into farmers.

Early Domestication of Plants and Animals   Humans in Mesoamerica and the Andes exchanged their domesticated species of beans and corn within their regions and began trading other domesticated staples as well. In Mesoamerica these included squash, manioc (a root), avocado, and chili pepper; in the Andes, quinoa (a seed), amaranth (an herb), potatoes, yams, tomatoes, and cotton. In time, these plants spread via trade throughout both regions wherever the climate and soil would support them.

The domestication of animals in the Americas, however, was more modest than that of plants. Unlike Eurasia and Africa, the majority of large mammals had died out after the last Ice Age, with the result that no draft, pack, or riding animals of sufficient size were left to be domesticated (see Figure 5.1). The Americas thus had no horses or cattle until they were brought by the Spanish in the sixteenth century CE as part of the so-called Columbian exchange of plants, animals, and diseases traveling both directions. The development of the wheel, so intimately connected with draft animals, with its nearly infinite uses on plows, chariots, carts, and other conveyances, never took place in the Americas, though some of the world's best roads were built through the Andes. The only animals suitable for domestication—besides the dog—were the llama, alpaca (both relations of the camel), guinea pig (a rodent), muscovy duck, turkey, and honeybee. The llama, whose capacity is limited to carrying about

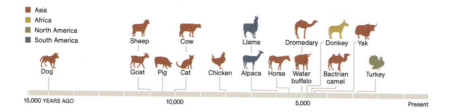

Figure 5.1 Comparative Timeline for Domestication of Animals.

60 pounds for 12 miles per day, was the only animal in pre-Columbian America to provide even modest transportation services. The wool of the alpaca, together with cotton, became an important textile fiber in the Andes. In the relative absence of domesticated animals raised for meat, hunting and fishing remained important methods of obtaining food (see Figure 5.1).

Early Settlements   Early agricultural settlements ranged in size from a few extended families to as many as 1,000 inhabitants. As in Neolithic China, the typical dwelling was a round, dome-shaped, wooden house with a sunken floor, stone foundation, and thatched roof. As in southwest Asia, some early American agrarian peoples mummified their dead by salting or smoking them before burial. Others buried their dead in midden piles on the outskirts of their villages or in the sand dunes along the beaches. Funeral gifts were modest, usually consisting only of the cotton clothes worn during life and a red mat—symbolizing the blood of life—wrapped around the body. In contrast to more transient hunter–gatherer settlements, agrarian villages became settled communities of the living and the dead.

Between 3000 and 2000 BCE, villagers in the lowlands along the Andes coast of Peru built rafts of balsa wood, which enabled them to fish farther from shore. They also pioneered the use of irrigation in the dozens of river deltas along the coast. With crop yields boosted by irrigation, the population of the villages increased to 2,000 or 3,000 inhabitants and the first signs of social stratification and distinctions in wealth appeared. Scholars have speculated that upstream families had more water and, thus, accumulated greater food reserves than downstream families. Under the leadership of upstream elders, inhabitants of several villages pooled their labor and built monumental plazas, platforms, and terraces in central locations in their settlements.

As had other societies making the agrarian transition, Mesoamerican and Andean societies also began producing pottery, which was used in the preparation and preservation of food. The earliest known pottery dates to about 3300–3200 BCE on the northern Andean coast; by 1800 BCE pottery making had spread throughout central and southern Mexico. Cotton textiles dating to about 3000 BCE have been found along the coasts of Ecuador and Peru. Richly colored pieces of cloth served as skirts and overcoats. Condors with outstretched wings, double-headed snakes, felines, and human figures were typical motifs on the textiles.

The Origins of Urban Life

As we saw in the opening vignette to this chapter, in 1994, archaeologists began excavating the ruins of a large, planned city covering over 200 acres at Caral in the Supé River river valley in Peru. Caral-Supé, was one of at least 18 sites of a culture that flourished in the valleys descending from the Andes to the coast. Researchers were stunned at the monumental stone architecture that included what appeared to be

The Origin of Corn

We have no idea who they were nor exactly where they might have lived nor even exactly when the momentous event took place. We do not know whether the idea occurred to a number of people simultaneously or to one lone experimenter. We assume, given the unprepossessing nature of the plant in question, the *teosinte* grass, that it did not suggest itself as a productive food crop, or even as edible, for quite some time. Yet, when these first bold people began to cultivate it, they were unknowingly taking part in one of the most momentous revolutions in world history: a completely independent chapter in the transition from foraging to agriculture and, ultimately, to agrarian-based urban civilization. The ultimate result of their work, maize, or corn, became the staple of the great Mesoamerican civilizations, sustained the early peoples of North America, and ultimately became the world's most versatile and widely grown food crop (see Map 5.2).

The site where we believe the event took place, somewhere in what is now southern Mexico, may have been inhabited by human beings

Various Types of Corn.

for as few as 7,000 or 8,000 years. And it was here, perhaps 6,000–7,000 years ago, that they began the process of cultivating this unpromising grass into the grain that would shortly sustain vast numbers of people. Yet, to this day, plant geneticists are still not in agreement as to how this transition took place.

It was long assumed that *teosinte* was the sole ancestor of corn and that the process was one of painstaking selection and replanting. That is, people would inspect a group of plants and search for the ones with the largest and most numerous kernels and then plant them and repeat the process over many generations, hoping over time to select for those desirable qualities. Given the *teosinte* limit of eight rows of tiny seeds, it was assumed this process would take hundreds, perhaps thousands, of years. Yet, the short time between the known dates of early corn cultivation and the rise of corn-supported societies suggests that the transition

pyramid-shaped temples, plazas, a wide variety of dwellings of different sizes, and, perhaps most intriguing of all, a large amphitheater. As important as the initial survey of the sight turned out to be, its significance grew further in 2001 when carbon dating revealed the artifacts at the site to be from 2627 BCE, making this by far the oldest city in the Americas and contemporary with the early Mesopotamian cities and the Great Pyramid of Egypt. As Jonathan Haas, one of the scientists involved in the dating, noted, "This is a project that comes along once in a generation and offers opportunities rarely glimpsed in the field of archaeology."

was much faster. Because of this, scientists have recently theorized that corn is in fact the result of crossbreeding more than one species of plants.

The most promising results so far were presented by plant geneticist Mary Eubanks in 2004, who attempted to experimentally trace the origins of corn. Her experiments showed convincingly that *teosinte* was, in fact, an ancestor plant of modern corn but that it had at some point been bred with *gamagrass*, which contains key genes for multiplying and enlarging the kernels on each ear. Moreover, her work supported the work of other recent research that suggested that the plant had evolved very rapidly into a usable staple, perhaps in less than a century.

Major Corn-Producing Regions of the World

◼ Major corn-producing regions

MAP **5.2** **Major Corn-Producing Regions of the World.**

We have to assume that this momentous feat was accomplished by plan and experimentation, given its complexity. The result was one that permanently altered the agricultural patterns of world history, particularly over the last 300 years. Corn's versatility allows it to be cultivated on every habitable continent; in dry or moist, hot or cool climates; and often on land too marginal to support any other staple crop. It is widely used as human and animal food and helped to sustain population expansions in North America, Asia, and Europe. It spawned huge industries in such modern foodstuffs as syrup and oil and older ones like whiskey and beer. Most recently, and controversially, it has been touted as a biofuel. In short, this American innovation's uses are still unfolding as we wrestle with the problems of population, land use, and energy consumption.

Questions

- Why is the innovation of corn a "momentous revolution in world history"?

- Does the fact that this example of bioengineering occurred 6,000–7,000 years ago put today's debate on genetically modified foods into a new perspective?

Caral-Supé   Scholars now theorize that this city, like the similarly mysterious sites along the Indus, was part of a fairly large civilization supported by intensive agriculture and fishing, with extensive trading networks and an incipient class system. They have linked the Caral-Supé culture to the ruins at Aspero, on the Peruvian coast, which contain similar pyramids but had been previously covered by centuries of trash heaps. The varied climate, ranging from the coast through lowland plains and river valleys up to mountain highlands, produced pumpkins, squash, yams, corn, chilies, beans, and cotton, while the rivers and sea yielded a variety of edible aquatic life. The agriculture

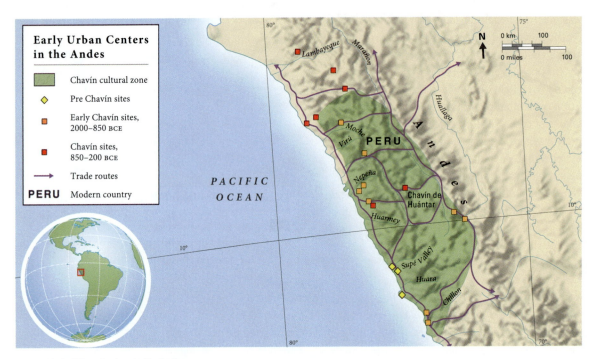

MAP **5.3** **Early Urban Centers in the Andes.**

of the valley was supported by a highly complex and sophisticated irrigation system utilizing mountain runoff and directing water to individual plots (see Map 5.3).

Farmers were the largest social class, with merchants, administrators, and priests also in evidence, though it is not clear at this point exactly what constituted the hierarchy. Widely varying sizes of houses suggest disparities of wealth, and the proximity of some of the houses to pyramids seems to indicate a religious or bureaucratic connection; but the exact nature of these remains the subject of speculation. Similarly, the uses to which the amphitheater was put can only be guessed, though pictures of musicians suggest that they were an important part of festivals held there.

Perhaps the most intriguing artifact of all is an intact *quipú*, a device of elaborate knotted ropes tied together in patterns that form a coded system of communication, a kind of writing system by means of knots. Since the quipú was also used by the Incas over 4,000 years later, it represents not only a direct connection between these two societies but one of the world's first, and oldest, systems of record keeping in continuous use.

Other Andean Cultures   Of smaller scale and a somewhat later period are the structures at El Paraíso, Peru, which date from about 2000 BCE. To construct these monuments, villagers built large rectangles of locally quarried rock and mud mortar. They filled the interior of the rectangle with rock rubble encased in large mesh bags, which may have been used to measure the amount of labor each villager contributed. Multichambered and multistoried buildings made of stone occupied some of the platforms. Steep staircases led from the lower plazas up to these buildings, which were plastered and painted in primary colors. Wooden beams supported the roofs.

Charcoal-filled pits in the building chambers indicate that some form of sacrifice took place there. The chambers were small, allowing access to no more than a few prominent villagers or shamans. The rest of the villagers assembled on upper and lower platforms according to their social status, to participate in religious functions and share communal feasts. Early sculptures dating to 1519 BCE depict ancestral warriors and suggest that villagers might also have come together for military displays.

Farmers in the Andean highlands also built ceremonial centers in their villages. As in the lowlands, these centers contained fire pits for sacrificial offerings. The buildings were, however, much smaller, with only one or two chambers, and stood on modest platforms. Highlanders, in addition to farming, engaged in long-distance trade, exchanging obsidian and cotton from the highlands for lowland pottery. Sometime around 1500 BCE, highlanders developed skills in metallurgy (perhaps including smelting), thus laying the foundation for the development of exquisitely crafted metalwork, including copper, gold, and silver.

Chavín de Huántar   While our understanding of the early Caral-Supé culture is still in its infancy, more extensive work on the later small highland city of Chavín de Huántar [Cha-VIN de Oo-WAN-tar] (ca. 1000–200 BCE) has yielded important insights into Andean cultural patterns. Situated in a valley high in the Andes Mountains on both banks of a tributary to the Marañon River, the modern town was connected by a bridge, which was destroyed in a landslide in 1945. A 3-day journey from both coast and rain forest and at an elevation of 10,000 feet, Chavín carried on an organized long-distance trade, built and graded roads, protected them with retaining walls, and cleared a number of mountain paths to facilitate travel. Residents of Chavín imported obsidian, used in the making of sharp tools, and metals and exported textiles, pottery, and gold and silver artifacts.

Early Chavín was a small place of some 300 inhabitants, most of whom—including priest-rulers and craftspeople—were detached from agriculture. Another 700 full-time farmers and herders lived in outlying hamlets. Farmers grew potatoes, quinoa, and some corn on the slopes and valley floor, supplementing the rainfall with irrigation. Corn was used not only for making bread but also for brewing a type of beer, called *chicha*. On the higher grasslands, herders bred llamas and alpacas. The dried meat and wool of these animals contributed substantially to the village economy, as did the llamas' role as pack animals.

Chavín's ceremonial center consisted of U-shaped ramparts built on a plaza and lined with walls of cut and polished stone. The walls enclosed several partially interconnected underground complexes. Within the U was a round, sunken court accessible via staircase. A cross-shaped, centrally located chamber contained what is assumed to have been the center's main deity, a stone sculpture of a fanged, snarling feline creature, standing upright like a human, with one clawed paw extended upward and the other hanging down. The sculpture might have had a shamanic significance, symbolizing the priest's ability to assume the powers of a wild animal.

Other underground chambers were used for sacrificial offerings. Remnants of pottery once filled with the meat and bones of animals—as well as human bones—found in these chambers suggest animal and human sacrifices. An elaborate system of canals guided water through the underground chambers. Priest-rulers and the assembled villagers used the temple complex to offer sacrifices, observe open-air rituals, celebrate feasts, dance, and perform music.

Chavín de Huántar, New Temple. Chavín is one of the best studied sites and over the years has yielded considerable information about town and small-city life in the ancient Americas.

By around 500 BCE, the population had grown to about 3,000 inhabitants. Artisans living in the town began to specialize in particular crafts. Craftspeople living in one section of town made beads and pendants from seashells, artisans in another section fabricated stone tools, and a third section of the town housed those who made leather goods. Whether these craftspeople had given up agricultural labor completely is not known. Homes for the wealthy were built of stone, while the less well-off lived in houses made of adobe. The rich dined on the meat of young llamas; poorer residents subsisted on the meat of decommissioned pack animals. Around the town, there must have been a number of villages with farmers producing enough food to feed the urban dwellers.

The increased population meant larger assemblies, which in turn required bigger platforms and a larger temple for more sacrifices. Laborers added a square, sunken court, a feature common to many Andean and Mesoamerican cities, and additional underground chambers, mostly for storage. By 400 BCE, Chavín had become the culturally dominant center of the region. Large numbers of travelers, traders, and pilgrims from the coast and rain forest visited the temple. Travelers made offerings of seashells, coca leaves, and textiles to the priests in return for receiving temple blessings, presumably for their health, welfare, and safe return. Residents of Chavín provided services for the visitors, such as lodging and meals. Craftspeople produced clothing, wall hangings, banners, and pottery in what were identifiable Chavín patterns, motifs, and styles. Archaeologists have found Chavín artifacts as far as 350 miles away.

Inhabitants of Chavín pioneered new techniques in the making of textiles and in metallurgy. Textile makers combined the wool from llamas with cotton to create a new blended cloth. They decorated it using new methods of dyeing and painting adapted to wool fibers. Goldsmiths devised new methods of soldering and alloying gold and silver to make large ornamental objects. Small objects, such as golden headbands, ear spools, beads, and pins, signified prestige and wealth. Gold artifacts found in the graves of the wealthy attest to the value residents of Chavín placed on gold.

Chavín came to a gradual end, perhaps declining as other centers began producing equivalent pottery, textiles, and gold jewelry and competing in trade. In any event, sometime after 500 BCE, archaeologists note a decisive trend toward militarization, with the emergence of fortified villages and forts. Possibly, the people of Chavín ultimately fell victim to a military attack. Sometime around 200 BCE, it appears that squatters invaded the largely deserted city, which subsequently fell into ruin.

The First Mesoamerican Settlements

In Mesoamerica, the first permanent villages appear to date from around 1800 BCE. The first ceremonial centers, the collaborative work of farmers from several villages, appeared along the Pacific coast of southern Mexico and Guatemala around 1500 BCE. As in the Andes, the ceremonial centers consisted of plazas, platforms, and terraces. Metallurgy, however, did not develop here for another millennium, and instead, craftspeople used jade for ornaments. (The Spanish believed that this green, translucent gemstone was useful in the treatment of kidney stones, *piedras de hijada*—hence the Anglicized word *jade* for the stone.) By around 1200 BCE, agrarian society throughout the Andes and Mesoamerica was characterized by ceremonial centers centrally located among several villages, monumental structures of plazas and platforms, and an emerging craftsmanship in the production of sacred ornaments.

The Olmec The first important Mesoamerican center was that of the Olmecs at San Lorenzo (1200–900 BCE), located on the Gulf of Mexico in hot, humid, and forested coastal lowlands. The name "Olmec" means "rubber people" in the language of the later Aztecs and refers to the rubber tree farming for which the area was later known. Farmers in these lowlands had to cut down the dense tropical rain forest with stone axes and burn it before they could plant corn. Once the riverbanks had been cleared, the silt deposited by floods during the rainy season and the rich soil created favorable agricultural conditions. As in Mesopotamia, Egypt, India, and China, the rivers here proved marvelously productive. It is estimated that farmers harvested as much as 3,200 pounds of corn per acre from the riverbanks, a yield twice as plentiful as that in the villages of the Mexican valleys and highlands to the west. The high yield allowed for the rise of wealthy ruling families, who assumed a dominant position over small farmers (see Map 5.4).

Pectoral, Chavín de Huántar. The skillful working of gold was practiced by ancient Andean and Mesoamerican peoples, down to the Aztecs and Incas. Shown above is a pectoral—an ornament worn on a person's chest.

The ceremonial center of San Lorenzo was located on a plateau overlooking the surrounding rain forest, villages, and fields. On this plateau, archaeologists have so far unearthed some 60 terraced platforms, 20 ponds, countless basalt-lined drainage troughs, and the foundations of dwellings for 1,000 inhabitants. These dwellings were arranged around small family plazas. Among the household goods found in the dwellings were grindstones for preparing corn and tools for making beads and ear ornaments. The dense concentration of dwellings suggests that San Lorenzo was an urban center, inhabited by priests, administrators, and craftspeople. Based on estimates of crop yields in the area and the number of dwellings at the site, scholars believe that this center was surrounded by some 10,000 small farmers dispersed in outlying villages and hamlets and producing the surplus food needed to feed the urban center.

The priest-rulers of San Lorenzo engaged thousands of farmers as laborers to construct the plateau and its terraced platforms. Laborers quarried blocks of basalt from a mountain range 70 miles to the northwest of San Lorenzo. Large groups of workers shouldered beams from which the basalt blocks, weighing 18 tons on average, hung in slings. They carried these blocks to the coast and shipped them to San Lorenzo on rafts. There, sculptors fashioned the blocks into fierce-looking, helmeted heads, kneeling or sitting figures, and animal statues.

It is unknown whether these figures represented priest-rulers, gods, or divine beings. Olmec priest-rulers also commissioned sculptors to craft figurines and masks of clay. Other craftspeople made figurines from jade and serpentine. One jade figurine is that of a jaguar with a human body representing perhaps the rain god. Like the legendary *werewolf*—a human being who is transformed into a wolf

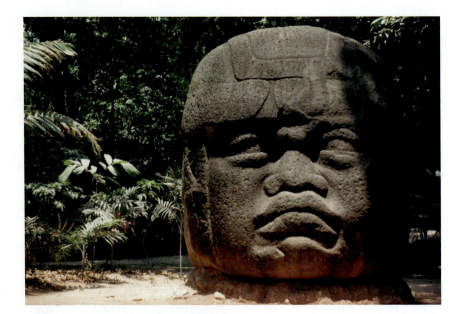

Colossal Olmec Basalt Head. Among the most notable monumental statuary in the Americas are the giant heads sculpted from hard basalt by Olmec craftspeople. The one pictured here is from San Lorenzo, though exactly what its religious significance might be is as yet not known.

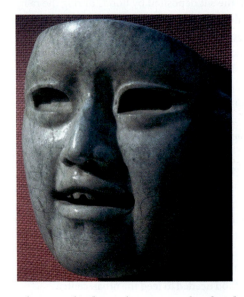

Olmec Jade Mask. Like the Chinese, Mesoamerican peoples appear to have worked jade from very ancient times.

when the moon is full—scholars have speculated that these figures might be *were-jaguars*. That is, the figurine might indicate rituals in which priests possessed shamanic powers shared with jaguars and other wild animals. Since jade and serpentine could be obtained only from areas some 200 miles away, San Lorenzo appears not to have been an isolated urban center with surrounding villages but a place with far-reaching trade connections.

La Venta   Around 900 BCE, a mysterious event took place that destroyed San Lorenzo. Perhaps a religious calendar cycle was completed and a ruler ordered the destruction of the urban center. Perhaps there was an internal uprising, with farmers protesting their oppression by the ruling priests and administrators and then offering ritual atonement. Whatever occurred, the event left San Lorenzo's large stone sculptures mutilated and buried in carefully prepared graves, along with the sculptors' tools used in creating the images.

Following the fall of San Lorenzo, La Venta, 50 miles to the northeast, became the leading Olmec center. The first settlers at La Venta cleared the rain forest from a ridge on a swampy river island in the lowlands and then, like the Harappans on the Indus, graded the ridge to create a plateau. On the plateau they erected terraced platforms and a fluted, 100-foot-high earthen mound to establish an urban center. Burial sites at La Venta contained axes and figurines made of serpentine and jade as well as concave mirrors ground from hematite and other iron-bearing ores. Rulers' regalia included mirrors worn on the chest, but what significance these might have had is unknown.

Three of the burial sites at La Venta contained 485 pieces of serpentine carefully arranged to form a stylized jaguar face. Only two sites contained human remains as the extremely acid soil of La Venta dissolved most human bones. The burial gifts in the site included ochre, figurines, beads, ear ornaments, and awls made of jade. About 600 BCE La Venta ended under circumstances as mysterious as those that destroyed San Lorenzo. The next Olmec center was at Tres Zapotes, a more modest complex 70 miles to the northwest. Tres Zapotes endured from about 500 to 1 BCE, when it was eclipsed by new ceremonial centers in the highlands west of the Olmec lowlands.

MAP **5.4** Olmec Civilization.

Through their long-distance trade, the Olmecs left a strong cultural impact throughout Mesoamerica. Olmec traders, probably accompanied by armed escorts, obtained the obsidian needed for making stone-sculpting tools in Guatemala and jade from mines south of the Valley of Mexico and in Guatemala and Costa Rica. In exchange for these raw materials, the Olmecs exported cacao beans—from which chocolate is obtained—pottery, textiles, and jewelry. Along their trade routes, the Olmecs maintained settler outposts to supply the traders, mostly westward toward the Valley of Mexico, to which they exported their artistic styles.

Olmec Writing   In 2006 an announcement came that, like the work at Caral-Supé, redefined the archaeology of the Americas. Scientists at Cascajal in Veracruz, Mexico, found a large stone with what is currently believed to be Olmec writing on it. Dating to somewhere between 900 and 1100 BCE, it appears to be the oldest writing in the Americas. Moreover, it is unlike any of the later scripts of the Mayas or Aztecs and thus seems to have died out as a system with the decline of the Olmecs.

Like Egyptian hieroglyphics and Chinese Shang era scripts, the Olmec characters contain stylized representations of objects like fish, insects, and plants but also some that seem to have a phonetic component. Unfortunately, the samples contained on the Cascajal stone and a stone roller stamp dating from a few centuries later are simply too small to be deciphered. With the accumulation of other samples in the future it is hoped that the fragments of an Olmec literature may ultimately come to light. In the meantime, like the Linear A script of the Minoans and the seal figures of the Harappans, the Olmec figures present scholars with an important challenge in decoding the past.

Olmec Writing

"It's a tantalizing discovery. I think it could be the beginning of a new era of focus on Olmec civilization. . . . It's telling us that these records probably exist and that many remain to be found. If we can decode their content, these earliest voices of Mesoamerican civilization will speak to us today."

—Stephen Houston, quoted in "Oldest Writing in the New World Discovered in Veracruz, Mexico," Brown University Media Relations, http://www.brown.edu/Administration/News_Bureau/2006-07/06-021.html.

Cascajal Block. Currently the oldest example of writing found in the Americas, this sample dates from the Olmecs of the early first millennium BCE. Notice the stylized renderings of objects and placement horizontally, rather than vertically. What kinds of things do they suggest to you?

Foraging and Farming Societies Outside the Andes and Mesoamerica

After 2000 BCE, many foragers in the forests, deserts, and tundras in North and South America had adopted agriculture as a full or partial mode of subsistence. While most societies in the Andes and Mesoamerica had become fully agrarian by around 2000 BCE, foraging groups in the places already mentioned continued to persist—in some places down to the present. Using stone tools, they hunted in the extreme north, slowly cleared the forests that covered the entire east and midwest of North America, irrigated and farmed arid areas of the southwest, and foraged and farmed in the Amazon basin of South America.

The Inuit   The Inuit [INN-ooh-it] from Siberia arrived in the far northern tundra of North America around 2000 BCE. For a long period the Inuit remained traditional hunter–gatherers, hunting mammals on land and fish in the rivers and sea. Much later, during the first millennium CE, they began hunting whales. As many as 20 sailors with paddles manned a boat built of walrus ribs and skin. In the summer, boats sailed the coastal seas for weeks at a time. When sailors spotted a bowhead whale, they shot a toggling harpoon into the animal. The head of the harpoon detached, burrowing into the skin of the animal. After many more harpoon shots and a long struggle, sailors killed the whale, hauled it ashore, and stored the fat and meat in ice. A whale carcass could feed a hamlet for an entire winter.

The Inuit lived in pit houses framed by whale ribs, covered with walrus skin, and piled over with sod. The entrances were long, dipped tunnels that trapped the cold air below the floor of the house. On winter hunts for seals and walruses, people built snow houses, or *igloos*, from ice blocks. During the summer, the Inuit moved from the often waterlogged pit houses to tents. Women were expert seamstresses, using caribou sinew and seal and caribou pelts to make warm and watertight pants, parkas, and boots. For transportation on snow and ice, the Inuit used dog teams to pull sleds made with bone runners. They traded mammal teeth and carved bone artifacts for timber and earthenware from the south. By 1000 CE the Inuit had expanded from the North American Arctic eastward, eventually reaching Greenland, where the Norse from Scandinavia had established their first settlement in 982 CE.

Adena and Hopewell   Agricultural villages appeared in the cleared forest areas of North America by the first millennium BCE. Village inhabitants planted sunflower, goosefoot, sump weed, and corn. The villagers of the Adena (1000–100 BCE) and Hopewell cultures (200 BCE–500 CE) pooled their labor to build ridges and mounds used in ceremonies and rituals. The phenomenon of mound building, a practice with very ancient roots, seems to have been widespread among peoples living in the east and midwest of North America. A small mound covering a child's grave found in Labrador is estimated to be some 7,500 years old. Others, much larger and more recent (about 4,500 years old), have been found in the lower Mississippi valley; some of these mounds are more than 20 feet high. In the case of the earthworks at Hopewell, large square and circular enclosures contained multiple mounds, tens of feet high, encompassing dozens of acres of land. Research from the mid-1990s suggests that some of the Hopewell settlements were also connected by roads up to 60 miles long, perhaps serving communal purposes of official visits and gift exchanges (see Map 5.5).

Amazonian Peoples   In the flood plains of the Amazonian rain forest in South America, agricultural villages also date to the first millennium BCE. The best-explored culture is that of Marajó, on a large island in the mouth of the Amazon. At its height in ca. 500 BCE, the Marajó built large funeral mounds 30 feet high and 750 feet long. Depending on their social status, the dead were buried with modest grave

Hopewell Artwork. This delicately carved hand, made of mica, was excavated in Ohio. It was likely worn for public display.

Adena and Hopewell Cultures

- Adena site, 1000–100 BCE
- Hopewell area of influence
- Hopewell burial mound site

N   0 km   400
0 miles   400

MAP **5.5** **Adena and Hopewell Cultures.**

gifts or in richly painted, jewelry-filled urns. The cultures of the flood plains in the upper Amazon drainage are still largely unexplored. For example, at an unknown date, the people of the Baures culture in today's Bolivia established a large hydraulic complex of canals, raised fields, moat-enclosed villages with sacred precincts, and causeways connecting the villages. The complexity of this culture left a strong impression on the Spanish missionaries who visited the area in the sixteenth century CE.

The Islands of the Caribbean   The earliest hunter–gatherer settlements in the rain forests of the Caribbean islands date to the fourth millennium BCE, but from where on the mainland these first settlers came is unknown. The first agricultural settlements appeared between 500 BCE and 500 CE, when migrants from the rain forests along the Orinoco River in the northeast of South America colonized the eastern Caribbean as far west as Hispaniola (today's Dominican Republic and Haiti). These people built villages and terraces on which they grew manioc. Their ceramics are in the shape of or painted to display a variety of animals, such as frogs, bats, and turtles, indicative of a shamanic religion. Beginning in eastern Hispaniola around 500 CE, villagers supported the emergence of the Taíno [Ta-EE-no] chieftain society that by ca. 1500 CE comprised nearly the entire Caribbean. Influenced by Mayan culture (see Chapter 6), some Taíno chiefs built ball courts and causeways. In their villages, the chiefs employed specialized craftspeople for the production of ceramics, cotton textiles, as well as stone and woodcarvings. Sailors using canoes traveled extensively to the mainland and among the islands in search of salt, jade, and metals. These travels connected the Taíno chiefdom society with Mesoamerican societies on the mainland.

The Origins of Pacific Island Migrations, 6000–600 BCE

If the early societies of the Americas show how the great patterns of world history can achieve striking variations in separation from other groups, the peopling of the thousands of islands of Oceania may be seen as an extreme case of the interaction of these patterns with culture and an environment apart. In prehistoric times, Asians traveled in multiple waves not only to the Americas but also to the islands of the Pacific and Indian Oceans (see Map 5.6).

The populating of Oceania must rank as one of humankind's greatest feats. Unlike the comparatively short distances involved in establishing human societies on the islands of the Caribbean or Mediterranean, vast amounts of ocean had to be routinely crossed between many of the island groups in the Pacific in order to settle them. Such trips were considered epic voyages as late as the eighteenth century CE. Yet, these early seafaring people settled island after island, traveling restlessly until they had discovered nearly every island of Oceania. As we saw in Chapter 4, their homeland appears to have been Taiwan and the Indonesian-Philippine archipelagos. Using computer-assisted linguistic analysis, modern scholars have now theorized that the people of Oceania are at least partially related to Taiwan's aboriginal population (about half a million members today), mostly concentrated in the central mountains of Taiwan. About 6,000 years ago, the first seafaring people

MAP 5.6 The Colonization of the Pacific.

left Taiwan and, together with subsequent waves of emigrants, spread out in westerly and easterly directions. They settled in the Philippines, Indonesia, and the Malay Peninsula, bestowing their languages and ethnic identities on the aboriginal peoples of these lands.

In later times, descendants of these settlers, all speakers of languages belonging to the Austronesian family, spread farther into the Indian and Pacific Oceans. In the Indian Ocean, they sailed as far west as Madagascar, the island off the east coast of Africa, where they arrived around 200 CE and founded a number of chiefdoms. In the Pacific Ocean, they sailed to the Bismarck Archipelago, off the eastern coast of New Guinea. It was on this archipelago that settlers created the Lapita culture in ca. 1600 BCE, which was the homeland for the colonization of Oceania—that is, the islands of Polynesia, Micronesia, and parts of Melanesia. On the map, Oceania forms a huge triangle encompassing Hawaii, New Zealand, and Easter Island.

Origins of the Polynesians

"If we start with Polynesia and work backwards, the pattern is clearer. Initial settlement of Polynesia by the Lapita culture and lack of evidence for any but Polynesian sub-group languages there would suggest Polynesians, a genetically homogeneous group, are direct descendants of the bearers of Lapita culture. An ultimate origin in Island Southeast Asia for the 'Pre-Polynesians' now seems certain, with some evidence of genetic admixture with populations in northern Island Melanesia."

—Peter Bellwood, James J. Fox, and Darrell Tryon, eds. *The Austronesians: Historical and Comparative Perspectives.* Canberra, Australia: ANU E Press, 1995, p. 131.

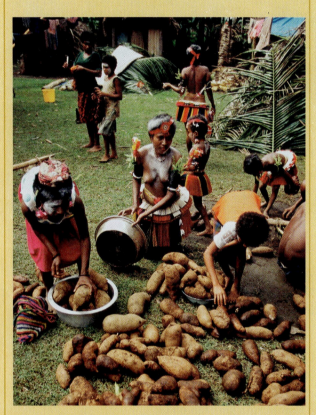

***Bwaimas*, Papua New Guinea.** The earliest known human attempts at agriculture took place in the highlands of Papua New Guinea perhaps 7000–9000 years ago. The introduction of yams several millennia later created an enduring staple crop, and their portability allowed their spread as they sustained seafarers throughout the Pacific.

Lapita and Cultural Origins

By the fourth millennium BCE, a sophisticated system known as the Lapita Cultural Complex had already become well established. Named for a site on the island of New Caledonia, the Lapita culture was a system of kinship-based exchanges among the inhabitants of thousands of islands running from Borneo to the edge of Melanesia in the western Pacific. Of particular importance was obsidian, which, as in the Americas, was highly prized as a material for tools and weapons in the absence of workable metals. Another item in demand was a distinctive kind of pottery decorated with stamped patterns called Lapita Ware, after shards located at that site.

Environment and Long-Distance Navigation

By about 1600 BCE it appears that a number of factors had also come together to allow for decisive innovations in long-distance navigation over hundreds of miles of open sea as well as systematic colonization of otherwise uninhabitable islands. The development of ever larger and more sophisticated sail- and paddle-driven oceangoing canoes, stabilized with outriggers or double hulls, provided reliable craft for such journeys. An extensive, orally transmitted storehouse of navigational information—much of it still retained by Polynesian elders today—enabled sailors to set their courses by the sun and stars, retain elaborate mental maps of islands visited, read winds and currents, and take advantage of seasonal reverses in prevailing wind directions.

Perhaps the most important development centered on supplying such voyages. Here, the cultivation of easily storable root crops, especially yams and taro, proved invaluable in sustaining long voyages. Among other staples circulated about the newly colonized islands were breadfruit, coconuts, and bananas, as well as such domesticated animals as pigs, chickens, and dogs, which entered the trade system from southeast Asia, the Philippines, and Indonesia. Over the centuries from 1600 to 100 BCE, Lapita sailors moved eastward and settled the islands of Vanuatu, Tonga, Fiji, and

Samoa. Archaeologists believe that Fiji may be the ultimate source of the culture that sparked the next outward migration: that of the Polynesians.

Creating Polynesia

As populations grew, the primary mode of governmental and economic organization, the kinship-based chiefdom, became increasingly elaborated. On Tonga, the Society Islands, the Marquesas, and later the Hawaiian Islands, the power of local chiefs extended to nearby island systems. Even here, far removed from outside influences, the inclination of human societies toward centralization and its tension with smaller regional societies that we saw in Chapter 4 is apparent.

Conflict, Interaction, and Expansion   What effect such centralization and the increasingly intensified agriculture of staples in the more productive islands may have had on their inhabitants is uncertain. Up to a point, it may have made these societies more efficient as food producers. But the difficulties we have seen in other societies of sustaining large populations on limited amounts of land were undoubtedly intensified in an island society. Some researchers have theorized, for example, that environmental problems related to overpopulation may have developed in the Cook Islands and the Marquesas around 500 BCE and again in 200 BCE. Political disputes arising from the struggles between centralizing and decentralizing factions may have played a role as well. In any case, there seems to have been a break around 500 CE that resulted in the longest period of migration yet: to Hawaii around 600 CE, Easter Island (Rapa Nui) about 700 CE, and New Zealand by 1200 CE. In the cooler climates of Easter Island and New Zealand the introduction of the South American sweet potato—one of the rare examples of hypothetical Polynesian interaction with continental societies—allowed for a diversity of staple crops to support the population.

Later Interactions   By the time of the first European contact in the early sixteenth century CE, nearly every habitable island had been settled and some, Hawaii and New Zealand perhaps most dramatically, had populations of many hundreds of

Polynesian Sea-Faring Canoe. During the first millennium CE, Polynesian navigators struck out across hundreds and, in some cases, thousands of miles as they colonized far-flung island chains from Tahiti to New Zealand, Easter Island (Rapa Nui), and Hawaii. One reason for their success was an extensive astronomical lore and knowledge of winds and currents that allowed celestial navigation from memory over long distances. Another stemmed from advances in ship design as in the vessel pictured here.

thousands. As we shall see in subsequent chapters, however, this vast achievement of exploration and colonization would soon be threatened by disease and a new breed of conquerors and colonists. Like the Amerindian cultures of the Americas, disease would reduce the populations in some of these islands by perhaps as much as 80 percent. The next three and a half centuries of European exploration of the Pacific would carry with them untold and, all too often, disastrously unforeseen consequences.

Putting It All Together

Though separated from each other by thousands of miles of ocean and spawning radically different cultures, the Americas and Oceania share common patterns with each other as well as with the cultures of Eurasia and Africa. The first pattern that historians can see is that even in such widely separated areas human foraging communities at roughly the same time *independently began a process toward the development of agriculture and animal domestication.* While domestication of the first plants and animals and gathering into more settled village life began shortly after the last retreat of the glaciers in Eurasia, it came somewhat later in the Americas, perhaps because human groups were still rather scattered and few in number and could be sustained by large-game hunting. The many different types of plants available as food—especially legumes— were relatively high in protein, an important feature as large game became increasingly scarce. It is also the case that the plant that ultimately became a chief staple of the American societies, corn, required extensive experimentation before becoming domesticated in anything near its present form. Thus, it is only around 4000 BCE that we see its development and the beginning of its extensive domestication.

The second pattern we can see is *growth and sophistication of social structures and the development of the city and of monumental architecture for religious and political purposes.* Even in Oceania, where the critical population levels for cities were never

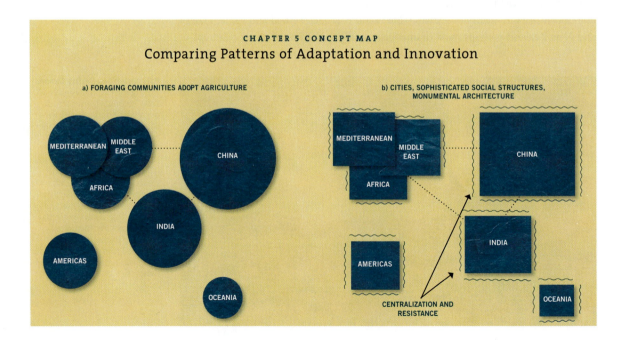

CHAPTER 5 CONCEPT MAP
Comparing Patterns of Adaptation and Innovation

a) FORAGING COMMUNITIES ADOPT AGRICULTURE

MEDITERRANEAN
MIDDLE EAST
CHINA
AFRICA
INDIA
AMERICAS
OCEANIA

b) CITIES, SOPHISTICATED SOCIAL STRUCTURES, MONUMENTAL ARCHITECTURE

MEDITERRANEAN
MIDDLE EAST
CHINA
AFRICA
INDIA
AMERICAS
OCEANIA

CENTRALIZATION AND RESISTANCE

reached, one finds the monoliths of Rapa Nui as evidence of this human pattern. In some cases, the types of structures—pyramids, terraces, and obelisks, for example—seem to follow an almost "universal" pattern, so much so that scholars still struggle to find evidence of contact among widely separated cultures where none appears to have existed.

Recent finds at the Caral-Supé sites show how rapidly the development of astonishingly sophisticated large cities took place once the threshold of plant and animal domestication was crossed. The accomplishments of the society that created Caral and the other sites uncovered so far, like those of the Indus valley, survived in the local practices of Andean peoples long after the cities themselves were abandoned. The settlements of the Olmecs on the southern gulf coast of Mexico, though coming somewhat later, were equally imposing in their architecture, the efficacy of their farming techniques and irrigation practices, the sophistication of their social structures, and, it now appears, their development of writing. Yet, it is also the case that people will not create all the aspects of "civilization" in the same ways and by the same means. One striking example of this is the use of the wheel. Rotation and cyclical motion appear to permeate the ritual lives of people all over the globe, yet the use of the wheel as a conveyance and as a basic concept of technology is not universal. Thus, as with so many human innovations, the intersection of need and opportunity led to a crucial breakthrough. Hence, despite the widespread use of ball courts employing spheres of rubber put through circular hoops as a central political and religious ceremony among Mesoamerican peoples and the enormous cyclical mathematical and time-keeping achievements of later peoples like the Mayas (and even the fact that we have evidence that American societies provided their children with toys that had wheels), the need and means for utilizing heavy-wheeled vehicles never occurred and, thus, never developed as it had in Eurasia and Africa (see Concept Map).

In the case of Oceania, the peopling of the innumerable islands of the Pacific was inseparable from trade and cultural connections. Colonizing uninhabited islands could take place only when the plants and animals required could be brought along and provision could be made to trade for unavailable items. Thus, in terms of square mileage, the Lapita system was one of the world's largest trading spheres, stretching thousands of miles and including thousands of islands. Yet, for a variety of reasons—the necessities traded, the remoteness of the islands from other trade centers, the lack of connections to mainland Asia and the Americas, the unique seafaring skills of the island navigators—the peoples of Oceania remained separated from other such systems. Even here, as in the Americas, Eurasia, and Africa, we see yet another pattern emerging among the political behavior of human societies: *centralization and resistance to it.* As with other fundamental patterns of world history, we will see this one emerge repeatedly in a variety of guises as our story proceeds.

Review and Respond

1. Who were the first humans to arrive in the Americas, and where did they migrate from?

2. What were some of the first crops and animals domesticated in the Americas? How were these different from those of Eurasia and Africa?

3. Where did the first cities appear in the Americas? Why did they appear where they did?

4. Why are the archaeological discoveries at Caral-Supé so significant?

5. How were the first inhabitants of the Pacific Islands able to navigate such long distances without the aid of modern technologies?

▶ For additional resources, including maps, primary sources, visuals, and quizzes, please go to www.oup.com/us/vonsivers. Please see the Further Resources section at the back of the book for additional readings and suggested websites.

Thinking Through Patterns

▶ **What do historians say about the advantages and disadvantages of the separate evolution of the Americas?**

Like the role of geography, this is a question that is often debated. For one thing, we can turn the question around and ask why we should consider the Americas as "isolated," rather than Eurasia and Africa. But it is also true that the societies were not as large or as ethnically diverse as their Eurasian counterparts. Historically, too, scholars still often view the two sets of continents as "old" and "new" and from that perspective view the Americas as "isolated." A big part of how one chooses to look at the question also revolves around how one sees the roles of invasion, infusion of innovation, and cultural competition. Some scholars have argued that the very shape of Eurasia allowed for the brisk dissemination of innovation along broad areas similarly situated in latitude. The Americas, by way of contrast, were more longitudinally oriented, making such diffusion more difficult. Some argue that the separateness of the Americas allowed them to hothouse distinctive cultural traits among their populations. Yet others argue that constant mixing of peoples and ideas accelerates innovation and, hence, "progress." One distinct disadvantage of isolation is that peoples become susceptible to diseases and biological changes suddenly inflicted on them. Thus, from the sixteenth to the early twentieth centuries CE, virulent epidemics of Eurasian and African diseases like smallpox devastated the peoples of the Americas when introduced. Though the Americas in all likelihood introduced syphilis in return, it did not cause nearly the devastation in Eurasia and Africa that the Old World diseases did in the New World.

While the Pacific Islanders had abundant access to food for immediate consumption, the islands themselves were generally too small to prevent the accumulation of enough surplus food to free up the numbers of nonfarmers necessary to build and maintain a city. In addition, the islands themselves contained limited amounts of building materials and freshwater, while their isolation helped guard them against attack. Culturally, the islanders also had grown to *expect* that if their numbers outran the food supply, they could simply find another island to which the excess population could migrate.

▶ **Why did no cities develop on the larger Pacific Islands?**

▶ **The wheel is often cited as the most basic human invention, yet large and sophisticated civilizations were able to flourish without this signal innovation. Why do you think it did not develop in the Americas?**

Historians looking at this question tend to look at it in one of two ways: cultural or practical. Some cultural scholars see a lack of deep-seated affinities for circular motion in the belief systems of the American peoples as helping to prevent them from relating to the motion of the wheel in the way that Eurasian and African peoples did. Yet, American societies had toys with wheels on them, so they were not unaware of the concept of circular motion—indeed, far from it. The scholars favoring a practical or technological approach argue that the environment of the mountains close by seacoasts, rain forests, and dry, hilly regions was not conducive to bulk transport by wheeled vehicles and that the peoples there simply were never forced to look for more efficient means of transport.

PART TWO

The Age of Empires and Visionaries

600 BCE–600 CE

As world history neared the middle of the first millennium BCE, two major transformations changed its course. First, kingdom formation, which had begun earlier in Eurasia, became a near universal pattern in the world, including sub-Saharan Africa and Meso-America. Second, visionaries emerged in Eurasia whose formulations of monotheism and monism laid the foundations of religious civilizations that eventually emerged in the Middle East, India, China, and adjacent regions after 600 CE.

Kingdoms and Empires

Sub-Saharan Africa and the Americas. Around 600 BCE, improvements in agricultural productivity made it possible for some chiefdoms to expand into kingdoms. In sub-Saharan Africa, the kingdoms were Meroë in the steppes of the middle Nile and Aksum in the highlands of Ethiopia; and in Meso-America, the kingdoms were those of the Maya in the Yucatán Peninsula and of Teotihuacán in the Mexican basin.

The Middle East and the Mediterranean. After the Hittites and Neo-Assyrians, around 600 BCE the Persian Achaemenids continued the pattern of empire-building. The Greeks resisted the Persians for a long time with their alternatives of city-states and elective offices. But eventually the Macedonian Greek Alexander the Great, his Hellenist successors, and the republican Romans in the western Mediterranean also adopted the imperial pattern, expanding into the Middle East. The Roman Empire competed with the two Persian successor empires of the Parthians and Sasanid for dominance of the region. The characteristic pattern of the Middle East and Mediterranean was competitive imperialism.

India and China. Intense political–military competition among small states ruled by a military class or royal dynasty led to the elimination of the weakest states and the consolidation of larger kingdoms in both India and China around 600 BCE. In contrast to the Middle East and Mediterranean, the pattern of India and China was that of rising and falling of single empires, followed by long periods of decentralization before the rise of new imperial dynasties that unified much or all of the region.

ca. 800 BCE
Earliest Evidence of Iron-Smelting in Sub-Saharan Africa

551–479 BCE
Traditional Date for Life of Confucius

550–331 BCE
Achaemenid Persia

ca. 427–347 BCE
Plato, Founder of the First Philosophical School, the Academ

Interaction in Eurasia and with Africa. Merchants in the kingdoms and empires of Eurasia and sub-Saharan Africa began to interact during the period 600 BCE–600 CE. They pioneered the sea routes to southern India, China, and eastern Africa and the land routes of the Silk Road through central Asia and the Sahara from northern to western Africa. Exchanges on these routes were not yet regular enough to lead to adaptations, for example, of technological inventions. But the trade whetted the appetites of rulers for luxury goods, such as spices, ointments, silks, and ceramics, stimulating the rise of merchant classes.

Visionaries and the Adoption of State Religions

Visionaries. At the height of the political–military competition among city-states, kingdoms, and empires around 700–500 BCE, individuals arose in Eurasia to proclaim new visions of reality. In the place of the polytheistic universe in which gods and humans mingled, they proclaimed a transcendent God or "first principle" beyond the universe. Their messages were not bound to the particular kingdoms or empires in which the visionaries lived but were addressed to anyone who would listen.

What difference did their new visions of reality make? For the first time in world history, individuals claimed to have discovered standards of truth and justice that were beyond the ever-changing circumstances of kingdoms and empires and their polytheistic pantheons. An unchanging God or first principle, so these individuals argued, was the measure for what was truthful and just on earth.

Empires and the Adoption of State Religions. In the centuries after the visionaries, small groups of followers popularized the messages of monotheism and monism. They formed priestly classes, churches, and/or schools. Interaction among groups of followers led to the adaptation of some monotheisms and monisms to each other. For example, Jews adopted elements from Zoroastrianism and Greek philosophy, Buddhists influenced Confucianism and Daoism, and a group of Jews founded the reform movement of Christianity and merged it with Greek philosophy.

As one might expect, kings and emperors sought to capitalize on the unifying forces they perceived in monotheism and monism. By 600 CE, monotheism or monism had become the dominant religion, philosophy, and/or ethics of the empires and kingdoms in Eurasia and parts of sub-Saharan Africa.

Previous chapters focused on the patterns of social and political formation, from foraging to agricultural villages, as well as towns and cities, and from there to kingdoms and empires. Now—after the adoption of state religions—kings, emperors, and religious officials laid the foundations for the formation of religious civilizations which, after 600 CE, evolved into social and cultural units that were geographically larger and more enduring than kingdoms and empires—lasting, in most cases, right to the present.

Thinking Like a World Historian

▶ What is the connection between food, population density, and patterns of social–political formation in world history, and why were sub-Saharan Africa and the Americas later in the development of these patterns?

▶ Which elements did the visionaries of ca. 700–500 BCE share in common, and what made their visions so decisive in the course of world history?

▶ What is the difference between kingdoms and empires, and how did empires change as a result of the adoption of state religions?

322–185 BCE
Most of India United for the First Time Under Mauryan Empire

196 BCE–284 CE
Early Roman Empire

250–900 CE
Classic Period of Maya Kingdoms

322–550 CE
Much of India Reunited Under Gupta Empire

221–206 BCE
First Chinese Empire Under Qin

100–750 CE
Moche Chiefdom in Northern Peru

300–600 CE
Kingdom of Aksum in Northeastern Sub-Saharan Africa

476 CE
End of Western Roman Empire

Chiefdoms and Early States in Africa and the Americas

A humble stone carving in Oaxaca, southern Mexico, carbon-dated to about 600 BCE, is the earliest documentation for the existence of a 260-day divinatory calendar in Mesoamerica, which later played a central part in Mayan time reckoning and divination. Mexican archaeologists under the leadership of Alfonso Caso excavated the inscription in the 1930s, and an American archaeological team in

llatrix

Orion

Saiph

Sirius

17

16

14

15

Seeing Patterns

▶ How does comparing and contrasting sub-Saharan Africa with the Americas during 600 BCE–600 CE help in understanding the agrarian–urban patterns of social and political development across the world?

▶ Where did chiefdoms, cities, and kingdoms arise in sub-Saharan Africa and why? On which forms of agriculture, urbanization, and trade were they based?

▶ Which areas in the Americas saw the development of a corn- and potato-based agriculture that did not depend on the plow, the wheel, and iron making?

the 1990s discovered perhaps an even earlier version of this calendar in Tabasco to the north of Oaxaca. Amazingly, this calendar system is still in use in southern Mexico, making it among the world's longest-lived methods of reckoning time. Similarly, an astronomical observatory in Kenya, carbon-dated to 300 BCE, is the earliest example of the so-called Borana lunar calendar of 354 days. It is still in use today among the Kushite herders of East Africa. Two American anthropologists, B. M. Lynch and L. H. Robbins, discovered this observatory in Namoratunga [Nah-mow-rah-TOON-ga], Kenya, during fieldwork in 1978. The two calendars not only attest to the cultural prowess of Mesoamerica and sub-Saharan East Africa during the period of 600 BCE–600 CE but, more importantly, are reminders of the diversity and relativity of all calendar systems, including the modern Western one which dominates the world today.

Calendars are based on the time periods of rotations or orbits of celestial bodies (for example, the earth, moon, sun, planets, or other stars and constellations visible in the night sky) depending on the relative position of the observer on the earth. The Western or Gregorian calendar (named for Pope Gregory XIII, who decreed it in 1582) is based on the coordination

Schematic Drawing Showing the Alignments of the Borana Observatory, Kenya. The Namoratunga archaeological site contains the remnants of the Borana Observatory, ca. 300 BCE. A lunar calendar was in use, and basalt pillars were aligned with seven constellations of the night sky and their monthly movements.

Chiefdom: An agricultural village or town of up to 1,000 inhabitants, in which people know each other, requiring a person of authority (an elder or the head of a large family) to keep order as a respected chief.

Kingdom: A city-state or territorial state in which a ruler, claiming a divine mandate and supported by a military force, keeps order and provides for the defense against outside attacks.

of the rotations of the orbits of the earth around the sun and of the moon around the earth, rotations which are easily observed in northern latitudes. Even though they are incommensurable, these rotations are synchronized through the intercalation of shorter and longer months as well as leap years. By contrast, older calendars (like that of the Mesoamericans) tended to be more complex because they also served divinatory purposes.

Interest in time reckoning was not the only similarity between the Americas and sub-Saharan Africa. During the period 600 BCE–600 CE, these regions also resembled each other in terms of patterns of agricultural development, spread of villages, emergence of **chiefdoms**, and early rise of **kingdoms**. These institutions, results of regional interactions and adaptations, evolved more slowly than in the more populated Eurasia, where kingdoms and empires already proliferated prior to 600 BCE–600 CE. Since there was little contact between Eurasia and the Americas and much of sub-Saharan Africa it is all the more remarkable that the patterns of agriculture and life in villages, chiefdoms, and kingdoms were fairly consistent *within* world regions as much as *across* world regions. People did not need to be in contact with each other across the continents to build their cultures in similar ways. All they needed were sufficiently large populations for similar institutions to arise. Nevertheless, as we saw in Chapter 5, the isolated world regions, through their own internal interactions, adapted to a transition from foraging to agriculture. Indeed, as recent scholarship has revealed, urban centers like Caral-Supé appear to be of the same age as some of the earliest Old World sites.

In this chapter, we will see how, through continued internal interactions, sub-Saharan Africans and Americans blazed indigenous trails in pattern formation, from villages to chiefdoms and kingdoms. Sharing a common humanity with the Eurasians, they did not need the direct influence of those peoples to develop strikingly similar social and political patterns. The calendars of these two regions, while strikingly similar to Eurasian models in some respects, also illustrate both the adaptation of the concept to local needs as well as a striking sophistication.

Agriculture and Early African Kingdoms

Largely on account of its relative separation and lower population levels, sub-Saharan Africa (like the Americas and Oceania) transitioned from forager society to agrarian–urban society with its patterns of village, city-state, kingdom, and empire formation somewhat less rapidly or completely than Eurasia. However, north of sub-Saharan Africa inhabitants interacted with the Middle East and adapted to its agrarian patterns early on. They adopted village life, built cities, and created kingdoms (such as Kush and Nubia along the Nile) well before the period of 600 BCE–600 CE. After 600 CE, the kingdoms of Meroë [ME-ro-way] in the Nile valley and Aksum in the Ethiopian highlands flourished, while Africans farther south shifted from foraging to agriculture, villages, and chiefdoms. By 600 CE, urbanism had spread to West Africa and foraging had shrunk to pockets in the center and south of the continent.

Saharan Villages, Towns, and Kingdoms

For many millennia, the Sahara was relatively hospitable, with savannas and steppes, furthering the pattern shift from foraging to agriculture. But when the monsoon rains shifted eastward, ending around 4000 BCE, the desert expanded and savannas and steppes retreated southward. Agrarian life relocated to oases and the Nile River valley. In the northeast, the Kingdom of Meroë, successor of Napata, established its capital by the same name in the middle Nile basin, between the Nile and the western slopes of the northern Ethiopian highlands. The kingdom received its support from a sufficient, although not abundant, agricultural surplus produced with the help of annual Nile floods and irrigation.

Saharan Chiefdoms and Kingdoms   The earliest evidence of Africans shifting from foraging to agriculture comes from the area of the middle Nile around Khartoum, the capital of modern Sudan. Archaeological sites reveal a culture of raising cattle, cultivating sorghum, and shaping distinctive pottery. Sorghum tolerates a climate of less rainfall than wheat and barley, and it is possible that farmers along the middle Nile domesticated it locally, probably after becoming familiar with Middle Eastern farming. By the period between 4000 BCE and the first written records in Egypt in 3100 BCE, a substantial chiefdom of Nilo-Saharan speakers had emerged in northern Sudan, then called "Nubia" (from the Latinized Egyptian word *nebew* for "gold," which was found in a valley off the Nile). This chiefdom was based on farming, livestock raising, and trading of gold as well as rain-forest ivory and timber. Archaeologists have noted that even at this early date tombs in Nubia contained objects rivaling those of the Egyptians, including objects from southwest Asia and beyond. Moreover, Nubian military prowess emerged clearly in Egyptian records, with archers especially sought after as mercenaries. Indeed, the bow and arrow, both African inventions, gave their names to the state which the Egyptians called *Ta-Seti* [Tah-SAY-tee], the "Land of the Bow."

After 2500 BCE, a kingdom grew in wealth and power in Nubia, building a palace, large tombs, temples, and a wall around its capital of Kerma. Kerma was the first city in Africa outside of Egypt, and the kingdom took its name from this city. During 1850–1400 BCE Kerma and Egypt were rivals for the control of Nile trade, with each conquering and ruling the other for periods of time until Egypt eventually destroyed Kerma and colonized Nubia for about half a millennium. Nubia regained autonomy early in the first millennium BCE, centered around the city of Napata, a new capital at some distance upstream on the Nile. Later, the Napatan kings liberated themselves from Egyptian control and even assumed the throne of their northern neighbor as the twenty-fifth dynasty (ca. 780–686 BCE). But when Assyria, the first empire to unify all of the Middle East, conquered Egypt, the defeated king retreated and relocated himself farther upstream at Meroë, south of the Nile bend in the border zone between the southern Sahara and savanna.

The Villages of Tichitt-Oualata

Contemporaneously with the Nubian kingdoms, villages emerged in the southeastern corner of today's Mauretania. As in Nubia, the climate in the western Sahara had changed during 5000–3000 BCE, away from the monsoon regime which since the end of the last Ice Age (12,500 BCE) had supported a steppe and savanna vegetation into what is desert today. As the monsoon patterns moved eastward, foragers retreated to shallow lakes and oases. They left behind a rich collection of cave paintings in the surrounding mountains dating to earlier times when the Sahara was still wet. During 3000–2000 BCE, these foragers—perhaps stimulated by the knowledge of Middle Eastern agriculture—domesticated pearl or bulrush millet, a type of grain requiring less water than wheat or barley to grow.

AFRICA, SHOWING SITES IN MAURITANIA 2000 BCE–600 BCE

Archaeological evidence published by a British team in 2004 points to the emergence of a set of sizeable villages at Dhar Tichitt [Darr-tee-SHEET] and Dhar Oualata [Darr-wah-LAH-tah] in Mauretania around 2000 BCE, which flourished until 600 BCE. There, the team identified centers with large masonry structures. Corrals held large herds of cattle, and granaries held large quantities of millet. Numerous tomb mounds, perhaps for the chiefs in the villages, held beads and copper jewelry. Furnaces contained remnants of charcoal and ore, evidence of craftspeople smelting copper that was mined in the nearby Saharan mountains. While it appears that the social structure was based on wealth in livestock, exactly how society was regulated, what nature of religious order it possessed, and which form of chiefly authority ruled are still unclear. One theory holds that the people eventually retreated farther south, together with the steppe and savanna, as the Sahara continued to dry out. As we shall see in Chapter 14, these migrants might have been the founders of the kingdom of ancient Ghana.

Meroë on the Middle Nile

The kings of Meroë were descendants of the twenty-fifth Nubia-descended dynasty of Egypt, who, under Assyrian pressure, withdrew to the steppes of the middle Nile, about 100 miles north of present-day

Khartoum. Here, they built their capital, Meroë. At that time, the flood plain to the south of the capital still received sufficient monsoon rainfall during the summer to support agriculture. In addition, the kings built large water reservoirs to supply the farmers. The latter grew the African cereals sorghum and millet, but archaeological finds also include barley and wheat, all of which were planted with the plow. Presumably, the kingdom financed itself for the most part from the agricultural surplus.

At its height, from the sixth through fourth centuries BCE, the city of Meroë encompassed 20,000 inhabitants and a substantial population lived in the provincial towns. Although the king was the recognized head of Meroë, the kingdom was largely decentralized. The provinces downstream and upstream along the Nile were largely autonomous, ruled by their own town chiefs who perhaps sent no more than annual presents to the capital. Outside the limited agricultural area, cattle nomads grazed their herds.

The difference in power between the kings and the chiefs was defined by the royal control over trade. Miners in the desert north of the capital produced iron ore and farmers south of the capital grew cotton, both of which were important for the urban crafts. Smiths and weavers in Meroë produced weapons, hoes, utensils, and cloth, both for local consumption and for trade beyond the kingdom. Hunters in the south acquired ivory and feathers from elephants and ostriches hunted in the savanna. Traders carried these goods on donkey and camel caravans on the traditional trade route down the Nile to Egypt or across the Red Sea to Yemen by boat. In return, they brought back olive oil and wine from Egypt and frankincense and myrrh from Yemen (see Map 6.1).

Iron in Sub-Saharan Africa   From the kingdom's inception in the seventh century BCE, people in Meroë mined, smelted, and forged iron; they might have been the first to do so in sub-Saharan Africa. However, how and when the knowledge of smelting and forging iron began in sub-Saharan Africa has been a bone of contention among scholars. As is generally agreed, the craft of iron smelting evolved gradually in Hittite Anatolia during several centuries after 1500 BCE (see Chapter 2). To date, the possible spread of iron-working skills from the Middle East to Africa has not been satisfactorily proved. But the independent origin of iron working in Africa has not been demonstrated conclusively either. Researchers such as Stanley Alpern and Jan Vansina, evaluating the evidence in the early 2000s, came to the conclusion that the earliest reliable carbon date for iron production is 839–782 BCE, in the savanna on the border between today's Central African Republic and Cameroon. If this date is correct, Meroë would have received the impetus for iron production from within sub-Saharan Africa.

What is not disputed, however, is the remarkable inventiveness with which iron workers in African villages adapted iron-making to local village circumstances. Although hot-burning tropical African hardwoods helped furnaces reach the temperatures critical for the production of iron, of greater import was the knowledge of how to forge the *bloom*—the combination of raw iron and slag—into an iron–carbon alloy that was neither too soft nor too brittle. It was this knowledge that made smiths privileged figures in African villages. And it later made Meroë famous as the "Pittsburgh of Africa," to modify a phrase coined by the British archaeologist of the Sudan, A. J. Arkell.

MAP 6.1 The Kingdoms of Meroë and Aksum, ca. 650 BCE–600 CE.

Meroë's Cultural Achievements   In Meroë, the kings adapted their Nubian–Egyptian heritage to the different regional circumstances of the steppe and savanna south of the Sahara. Their monuments acquired a distinct style, as is evidenced by their tombs, pyramids with flat tops, and pyramids with steep angles. Although the main temple and its priesthood remained in the north, the priests added native deities to the pantheon, such as the lion god Apedemek. Meanwhile, Egyptian hieroglyphics seem to have "evolved" into an alphabetic script, visible on many monuments, even though at present this script is still undecipherable.

In spite of its regional orientation, Meroë was well known to the outside world. Mediterranean travelers visited it quite frequently. In the early first century CE the kings of Meroë skirmished with Rome over border issues. And in the third century CE, when Meroë's power was already declining, Heliodorus of Emesa, a Hellenistic-Greek writer, made it the stage for the conclusion of his popular romance novel *Aethiopica*. As much as Meroë provided a physical network for regional travelers, it also provided an intellectual link between Eurasia and Africa; the people of Meroë facilitated this important cultural link through their adaptation.

The Kingdom of Aksum

Meroitic trade with the Red Sea had to cross through the Ethiopian highlands. Exposed to this trade, highlanders gradually acculturated to urbanized Meroë as well as Yemen. Sometime in the early first century CE, a king replaced the chiefdoms of the highlands and established the kingdom of Aksum (300–600 CE). Based on a relatively abundant, plow-driven agriculture, this kingdom assumed control of the trade from Meroë, which declined subsequently. Aksum became the major supplier of African goods to the Roman Empire, from where it accepted Coptic Christianity in the early 300s.

Meroë's Decline and Aksum's Rise

Three factors contributed to Meroë's decline in the third century CE. First, the iron industry devoured immense amounts of charcoal, which is made by burning wood in earth-covered mounds. Once the forests in the east were gone, the iron industry in the capital city was doomed, depriving the kings of a major source of their income. Second, beginning in the late 200s BCE, camel nomads from the deserts east of the Nile raided northern Meroë. Third, the eastern neighbor, Ethiopia, acculturated to Meroë, thanks to the trade that crossed its land. Ethiopian guides and owners of transportation animals became participants in the trade, and then chiefs in the agriculturally rich high plain of Aksum took it over. Aksum was located close to the coast, where the port of Adulis (today Zula) was one of the main transshipment ports in the Red Sea. Thus, a combination of agricultural and commercial wealth enabled the chiefs of Aksum to assume the succession of Meroë.

The agricultural bounty of the Ethiopian highlands southeast of Meroë is due to its plains at 5,000–6,000 feet elevation and surrounding mountains 15,000 feet high. Deep valleys, notably of the Blue Nile and of the Rift Valley, cut into these highlands, which were therefore accessible only over steep ascents. The summer monsoon from the south Atlantic brought sufficient and, in places, abundant rain to the plains and mountains and supported large forests and a productive subtropical agriculture in the lower elevations.

As in the Nile valley, agriculture in the Ethiopian highlands was of considerable age, with evidence—from a rock painting and archaeological finds—of the existence of plow, oxen, barley, and wheat going back several thousand years. In higher elevations where barley and wheat did not prosper, farmers grew teff, a high-yielding grain. Plenty of grasslands supported cattle breeding. The Red Sea coast was dry and hot, with today's Djibouti sporting the highest average temperatures in the world. The coast supported little more than a few ports dependent on their hinterland. Ethiopia was a largely self-contained region in Africa, remaining outside the large population movements and cultural assimilation characteristic of West and East Africa.

Aksum's Splendor

Aksum, founded around 100 CE, came into its own around 300 CE. Its king, Ezana (ca. 303–350 CE), adopted Christianity as the state religion in 333 CE, thereby making Aksum the third Christian kingdom, after Armenia (301 CE) and Georgia (319 CE). Like his Armenian and Georgian counterparts and, somewhat later, the Roman emperor, Ezana replaced tolerance for a multiplicity of polytheistic religions with the requirement of conversion to a single faith (see

Meroë

"Meroë the chief city of Ethiopia is a three-cornered island about which do run navigable rivers, the Nile, and the Astabora and the Asasoba. At the topmost point is the Nile, which there divides itself into two parts; the other two rivers run on both sides one by the other, and then meeting fall into the Nile, and yield their waters and their name. The island is very large and almost imitates the mainland—for it is three hundred three score and fifteen miles long and six score and five broad—and it engenders beasts of wonderful greatness of all kinds and especially elephants. Trees grow there without the work of men, and it brings forth much other fruit. There are palm trees of great height which bear stores of dates, and corn and wheat of such tallness that it will hide a man on horseback and even sometimes though he sits upon a camel. And the reeds that grow there are such as we spake of before."

—Heliodorus, *Aethiopica.* Translated by Thomas Underdowne and F. A. Wright, bk. 10, p. 289. New York: Dutton, 1928. http://www.elfinspell.com/ HeliodorusBk10.html.

Chapter 7). When the Roman emperors, however, embraced what would become the Roman Catholic interpretation of Christianity at the Church Council of Chalcedon (451 CE), Aksum opted for Coptic Christianity, which was dominant in Egypt. In Catholic Christianity Jesus' divinity and humanity are considered to be equal, while in Coptic and Syrian monophysitic Christianity the divinity of Jesus is emphasized over his humanity. The emperors clearly considered the religious unity of the western and eastern halves of the empire as more important than the religious unity with their Middle Eastern provinces. Aksum, on the other hand, embraced union with the Coptic church. Although it did not break with the Roman Empire and even sided with it in the second half of the 500s CE, against the Sasanid Persians, Aksum kept its distance.

Another centralizing policy characteristic for Aksum was the use of a gold-based currency with which the taxation of the market for the import and export of luxury goods was facilitated. The kings of Aksum acquired their gold by sending merchants, protected by accompanying troops, to the southern highlands outside the kingdom, where the gold was mined. The merchants paid with salt, iron, and cattle. Finally, a small central administration of tax collectors, tax farmers, and provincial tribute collectors assured delivery of agricultural surplus to granaries in the towns and the capital. The provinces outside the capital, however, were in reality small kingdoms, federated with Aksum through some kind of tribute system, the details of which are unknown. Even though more centralized than Meroë, Aksum was well below the level of administrative coherence of a typical Middle Eastern or Mediterranean kingdom or empire, such as Ptolemaic Egypt (305–30 BCE) or Antigonid Greece (301–168 BCE).

Even without the support of a bureaucracy, the kings of Aksum engaged in an impressive program of monumental construction. The most characteristic Aksumite monuments are *stelae*, that is, carved and ornamented stone pillars as high as 100 feet erected as markers over royal tombs. Stonemasons cut these stelae in granite quarries near the capital, and workers rolled them on logs to their destination before erecting them with the help of wooden towers and ropes. One particularly massive stela fell over soon after its erection, either due to insufficient anchoring in the ground or as a monument to hubris. Palace precincts included ruling class residences that were up to three stories tall. Other examples of monumental constructions are water reservoirs and agricultural terraces with irrigation in the vicinity of the capital. In contrast to the adobe brick architecture of Meroë, the granite structures of Aksum were much more durable.

Imperialism and Crisis   In the 500s CE, Aksum briefly engaged in imperialism—the only imperialism coming out of sub-Saharan Africa in its entire history. This century was a time of profound crisis in both the Roman and Sasanid Persian Empires, which were under threat by nomadic invaders from the central Asian and Russian steppes (see Chapter 7). Naval trade in the Red Sea declined and the kingdom of Yemen increasingly relied on camel caravan trade along the west coast of Arabia. Perhaps under the influence of Jewish communities at the northern end of the caravan route, a Yemeni usurper who had converted to Judaism seized the throne and persecuted the Christians in his land. In response, and with the encouragement of Rome, the Aksumite king invaded Yemen and defeated the usurper.

Aksumite Stela, pre-400s CE. This is the largest of hundreds of stone monoliths, some with tombs and altars, attesting to the architectural sophistication of the kingdom. Workmen transported them from quarries 3 miles away where they had cut the stelae with iron tools. Some of the stelae, like the one to the right, have false windows and doors, looking like modern art deco buildings.

After a period of political instability, Aksum was able to make Yemen a regular province (543–570 CE).

But Aksum eventually lost this province when the Sasanid Persians invaded by land and sea in 570 CE, to establish their own proxy regime at the commercially important entrance to the Red Sea. The Sasanid had recovered earlier than the Romans from nomadic invasions and were determined to turn the long competition between the two empires (discussed in Chapter 7) to their favor. Seizing control over the entire India and East Africa trade was part of the Sasanid strategy to defeat Rome in the Middle East.

As a kingdom dependent to a considerable degree on transcontinental luxury trade, Aksum eventually became a collateral victim of this new Persian ascendancy. After 570 CE, Aksumite trade in the Red Sea declined precipitously. The capital city shrank to a shadow of itself, and in the following centuries provincial rulers in the highlands farther south rose to prominence. In addition, there were signs of internal problems: Timber resources for Aksum's iron industry in the vicinity of the capital became scarce. Although Ethiopia did not disintegrate, as Meroë had done, after 600 CE it played a much more modest regional role.

The Spread of Villages in Sub-Saharan Africa

By about 600 BCE, agriculture and pastoralism were common not only in East Africa but also in West Africa. Both emerged when a majority of people retreated from the increasingly dry Sahara southward into West Africa. They followed the gradual southward shift of West Africa's three ecological zones, stretching from west to east in the form of more or less broad bands. The first and easternmost zone was the steppe, or **Sahel** (Arabic *sahil*, or "coast" of the "sea" of the Sahara Desert). The second zone was the *savanna*, an expanse of grassland with stands of trees. The third zone was a relatively narrow, up to 150-mile-wide belt of rain forest along the coast from Guinea to Cameroon. Farming villages were dispersed by 600 BCE over all three zones, although they were most numerous in the savanna, where farming was most productive.

Sahel: An area of steppe or semidesert bordering the Sahara.

West African Savanna and Rain-Forest Agriculture

During the period 600 BCE–600 CE the densest village networks were located in the savannas of the inland delta of the Niger and middle Senegal Rivers. The village of Jenné-jeno [Jen-NAY-JEN-no] in the delta developed into a major urban center during 300–900 CE. Indications are that it was a chiefdom with a developing regional trade for raw materials and luxury goods. In the rain forest, the evolution of slash-and-burn agriculture is still largely undocumented by archaeology, although its end result, the so-called Bantu dispersal with its combination of yam and oil palm village agriculture, is well established.

Inland Delta Urbanism   The river Niger originates in the far west of the West African rain forest and flows northeast from the savanna to the Sahel, before turning at a right angle southeastward in the direction of the Atlantic Ocean. Midway along its northeastern leg, it slows and divides into several branches, the 250-mile-long and 50-mile-wide inland delta. In the first millennium BCE, when the climate was still relatively humid, the delta was located entirely in the savanna, forming a huge area of canals, islands, and swamps. Villagers in the delta grew millet and African rice, the latter domesticated around 1500 BCE.

Over time, a dense network of villages developed. After 300 BCE a village division process began, by which some villages, increasing to town size, became the center of satellite villages. This is how Jenné-jeno at the southern end of the delta originated. By 900 CE, so it is estimated, Jenné-jeno was a *city*—that is, a dwelling place for a nonagricultural crafts-based population—of between 5,000 and 13,000 inhabitants. It was surrounded within a circle of half a mile diameter by 25 villages.

Other towns with satellite villages developed farther downstream as well and made the delta the most populated area in West Africa.

Unfortunately, the archaeology of the period under discussion (chiefly by Susan Keech McIntosh and Roderick J. McIntosh) has not revealed much yet about the social stratification and power structures of Jenné-jeno. It is clear that this urban–rural center had a line of chiefs, some basic administrative offices, and craftspeople. The strongest evidence is a gold ring and many objects made of copper and bronze dated to 850–900 CE. Copper and iron ore had to be carried in by donkey or camel from a distance of 30 miles or more from the desert and savanna to be smelted and manufactured in town into weapons and implements. Two chemically analyzed glass beads, dated to the pre-600 CE period, seem to have come from overseas, one from India, southeast Asia, or east Asia and the other from Roman Italy or Egypt. Thus, trans-Saharan trade seems to have been in existence, supporting an incipient urban demand for luxuries.

Rain-Forest Settlements   The earliest evidence for rain-forest agriculture comes from the Kintampo complex of 2250–750 BCE, located in today's Ghana. Here, archaeologists have found traces of wood and mud huts on stone foundations, domesticated cattle and dwarf goats, rats, pottery, terra-cotta figurines, and polished stone implements. The assumption is that the villagers practiced slash-and-burn-farming to grow yams and oil palms. Unfortunately, no archaeological evidence of the cultivation of yams has been found, and the earliest evidence for oil palm cultivation dates to an 800–BCE site in the Atlantic Niger delta. Rain-forest archaeology, burdened by the tendency of the environment to break down the organic matter of artifacts, is lagging behind; and archaeologists have begun producing good data only from the 1990s onwards.

Excavations at Jenné-jeno, showing the walls of a round house (top) and polychrome pottery fragments (bottom).

Slash-and-burn farming consisted of clearing small areas of rain forest for the establishment of villages of up to 500 inhabitants, as well as for yam and oil palm plantations. Virgin rain forest was relatively easy to cut, even with stone tools, prior to the arrival of iron axes in the 800s BCE. Trees between 80 and 125 feet high formed a thick canopy, allowing relatively little light to penetrate and, therefore, not much undergrowth to develop and obstruct the clearing process. Each clearing was large enough for a village of a few hundred farmers, family fields, communal fallow land, and small numbers of cattle and goats.

If a village grew beyond its population capacity, a group had to depart and select a new site in the rain forest for clearing. Yam fields could be cultivated for up to 3 years and had to lay fallow for 10–15 years. During the fallow years, the rain forest grew back, although it now no longer returned to its virgin state. A secondary rain forest developed, with few tall trees and a proliferation of vegetation up to 30 feet high. Given several millennia of slash-and-burn cultivation, over time nearly all virgin African rain forests were replaced by secondary forest. As in so many other places in the world, what we originally conceived as pristine "jungle" here was in fact the creation of human hands, as emphasized by Jan Vansina in his classic on African rain-forest settlement. The transformation of the environment by humans, for better or for worse, is a process that began early on in world history.

Tropical Diseases   The hot and humid environment which farmers encountered in sub-Saharan Africa exposed humans and livestock to health hazards which were different from those in northerly latitudes and required specific adjustments. The most common health threat was malaria, caused by a mosquito-borne parasite in the blood and encountered around stagnant pools of water in swamps and fields, as well as on riverbanks. In the course of time, West Africans developed a protective genetic adaptation, the sickle-cell anemia trait. People with one or two of these genes had malaria-rejecting, sickle-shaped (rather than normal round) red blood cells.

Another tropical parasite carried by an insect, the tsetse fly, abundant along tropical riverbanks, caused sleeping sickness, primarily in animals. In response, West Africans bred disease-resistant dwarf cattle and goats. In East Africa, people either used higher-elevation pastures, as in Ethiopia, where the tsetse fly was absent, or cleared the forests, as in the Great Lakes region, in order to create a drier environment. The Great Lakes region was also one of the breeding grounds of the Black Death, the dreaded bubonic plague, along with Burma in southeast Asia. This disease is caused by a bacterium carried by rodents whose fleas jump over to humans. Further deadly diseases lurking in the rain forest were yellow fever (a viral disease), river blindness (a fly-borne parasite causing blindness), and filariasis (a worm infestation). All were diseases which the majority of Africans and their domestic animals learned to live with but which were lethal to outsiders entering the continent until modern medicine at the end of the nineteenth century developed treatments and eventually cures for them.

The Spread of Village Life to East and South Africa

Groups of yam and oil palm farmers of southeast Nigeria, at the eastern end of the West African rain-forest belt, calling themselves "Bantu" or "the people," exhausted their area for clearings around 2000 BCE. In contrast to their westerly neighbors, they were favored in their search for new spaces to clear because they had the equatorial rain forest of the Congo to the southeast at their disposal. Once there, a northerly group, the Mashariki Bantus, began to disperse around 1500 BCE, this time, however, eastward into the savanna of the Great Lakes in East Africa. On their way, they adapted to the cereal agriculture and iron crafting of the savanna villagers. The Bantu villages of the Great Lakes became the center for one of the great transformation events of history. Under Bantu impact, during 600 BCE–600 CE, nearly all foragers in the southern cone of Africa became either villagers or cattle nomads and adopted Bantu dialects and culture (see Map 6.2).

Inland Villagers and Nomads   At the time of the Mashariki Bantu arrival around 600 BCE, much of the land around the Great Lakes was still heavily forested savanna. As the villagers cleared the forest, the threat of the tsetse fly diminished

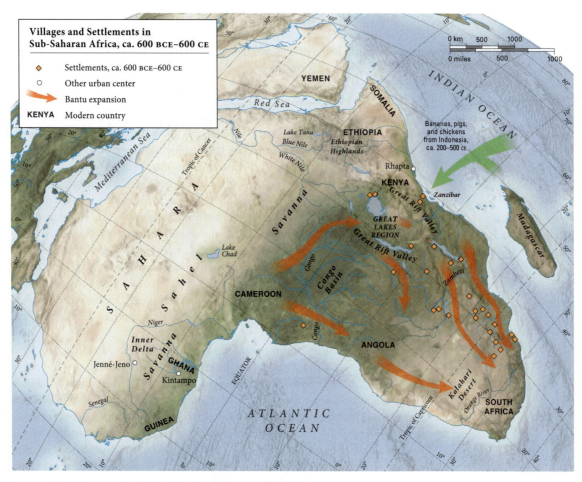

MAP **6.2 Villages and Settlements in Sub-Saharan Africa, 600 BCE–600 CE.**

and nomads from the north were able to expand southward. Many nomads gave up their minimal farming, which they traditionally tended from campsites. As in the Middle East, these nomads entered into a symbiotic relationship with the villagers, from whom they acquired their necessary grain supplements. In the meantime, the descendants of the original Bantu dispersal of 2000 BCE had settled the Congo equatorial rain forest and, under the impact of their eastern cousins, had complemented their yam and oil palm agriculture with millet and sorghum, as well as iron working. Only small pockets of the original Paleolithic foragers of the virgin rain forest, the pygmies, continued their traditional lifestyle, although they eventually adopted Bantu languages.

The conversion of the foragers on the savanna south of the Congo rain forest to farming, from the Great Lakes westward to Angola and southward to the tip of South Africa, was the work of both eastern Great Lakes and western Congo branches of Bantus. The foragers either retreated before the farmers with their iron implements and weapons or adapted voluntarily to farming and speaking a Bantu language. Small numbers of savanna foragers, speaking Khoisan-derived languages, retreated into the Kalahari Desert and steppe in western and central South Africa, hanging on to a precarious hunting-and-gathering survival. As could be expected, the process from Mashariki Bantu origins and Bantu interaction with the nomads and foragers of East and South Africa to the eventual mutual adaptations took time and was still incomplete in 600 CE.

African Traditional Rituals   The results of an analysis of Bantu linguistic roots and of early Iron Age (350–900 CE) sites in South Africa provide a glimpse into African **animism**, summarized by Jan Vansina, a pioneer of Bantu studies. In this animist perception of reality, Bantus distinguished between the daily world of more or less regular cycles of renewal and disintegration in the village (birth, puberty, adulthood, marriage, old age), the fields (rain, plantation, harvest, and dry season), and the calendar movements of heaven (described in the beginning of this chapter). Elaborate rituals, including a scrupulous observance of taboos and omens, had to be followed to keep the village and field cycles in their regular paths. For example, South African sites contain stone cairns marking the space of male circumcision lodges, stone-walled pits for rain-making ceremonies, broken pots symbolizing deflowering in female puberty rites, and ceramic masks used for the representation of ancestors in village feasts. Rituals were the guarantee that the human and field cycles would remain in sync.

Ancestor and nature spirits pervaded the village and fields, and they had to receive their respect through regular sacrifices, lest they disrupt the cycles of renewal and disintegration. Charms, mixed from herbs, protected against unintended insults of the spirits. The worst disruption, however, threatened to come from male or female witches in the villages who, acting out of envy, revenge, or malice, could severely harm or even kill their victims. The only way to avoid death from bewitchment was to seek a diviner or healer (shaman) in the village who, through trances, dreams, oracles, or charms, was able to enter the spirit world, recognize bewitchment, and stop it through **witchcraft**. It appears that in the early African Iron Age the adoption of elaborate rituals involving the human and field cycles—and, in some places, the calendar cycle, as evidenced by the Borana calendar discussed in the vignette at the beginning of this chapter—represented the main changes in the patterns of shamanic conceptualizations dating back to the African origins of humanity.

Indonesian Contacts   Village agriculture received a big boost in 200–500 CE when Indonesian sailors brought the banana, chicken, and pig to East Africa. These sailors were descendants from Austronesian farmers, who had dispersed to the islands of the Pacific, Philippines, and Indonesia, beginning around 2000 BCE. They sailed on large outriggers, the square sails of which were turned at 90 degrees. Historians of technology consider them the forerunners of the lateen sail of ca. 500 CE in the Mediterranean. This canted square sail exposes two triangles to the wind, making it possible to sail a course at an angle from the aft wind. Prevailing wind patterns in the southern Indian Ocean would otherwise have made sailing westward from Indonesia to Africa difficult. Where on the African coast the Indonesians landed is unknown, although they definitely settled the still-uninhabited tropical island of Madagascar, the fourth largest island in the world.

The banana tree yields 10 times more fruit per acre than the yam plant and the fruit is just as nutritious. It was highly adaptable not only to the rain forest, from

Animism: Perception of reality based on the concept of a life force pervading humans, other animals, and, by extension, plants and inanimate objects.

Witchcraft: An animistic belief in which an evil person (male or female) can harm an innocent victim at a distance and cause the victim to become possessed, with attendant illnesses.

Stone Relief of a Large Outrigger Merchant Ship, Buddhist Temple of Borobudur, on the Indonesian Island of Java, ca. 800 CE. This type of ship traveled regularly from Java to East Africa on the Cinnamon trade route, with its merchants exchanging spices for ivory, wild animal skins, and slaves during the early centuries of the first millennium.

where it came, but also to the savanna as well as irrigated orchards in dry climates. In the rain forest it did not require the full clearing that was necessary for the yam and, above all, it demanded far less labor. Chickens, domesticated perhaps in Thailand or India about 5000 BCE, were well represented in the Middle East and Mediterranean from 3000 BCE onward. Curiously, however, the keeping of chickens apparently did not begin in sub-Saharan Africa until the arrival of Indonesian sailors. The practices of cultivating bananas and keeping chickens soon spread all across sub-Saharan Africa, with the rearing of chickens spreading faster than the cultivation of bananas. These two food sources were crucial for the improvement of the meager food supplies in sub-Saharan Africa to a level where dense village networks, towns, and chiefdoms could develop in the period after 600 CE.

Incipient Urbanism on the East Coast

Apart from being the first to improve their agriculture by cultivating bananas and raising chickens, East Africans also benefited from trade with the Middle East. Archaeological evidence points to the inclusion of the northern East African coast into the Yemeni commercial network in the last centuries BCE, which connected Meroë, Ptolemaic and Roman Egypt, Parthian and Sasanid Persia, the Indian west coast, Sri Lanka, and (indirectly) Indonesia and China. Remnants of two camps on the northern coast of Somalia, dating to 150 BCE–500 CE, contain shards of ceramics from all these places. But as impermanent fixtures, these camps do not indicate regular commercial journeys.

The mid-first century CE seems to have been the transition point in the construction of permanent ports. The *Periplus of the Erythraean Sea*, a Greek-Hellenistic source describing for the Romans the monsoon winds for journeys to and from India, mentions Yemenis intermarrying with locals in the town of Rhapta along the Kenyan coast.

Indian Ocean Journeys

"Two days' sail beyond, there lies the very last market-town of the continent of Azania, which is called Rhapta; which has its name from the sewed boats (rhapton ploiarion) already mentioned; in which there is ivory in great quantity, and tortoise-shell. Along this coast live men of piratical habits, very great in stature, and under separate chiefs for each place. The Mapharitic chief governs it under some ancient right that subjects it to the sovereignty of the state that is become first in Arabia. And the people of Muza now hold it under his authority, and send thither many large ships; using Arab captains and agents, who are familiar with the natives and intermarry with them, and who know the whole coast and understand the language."

—H. R. Schoff, trans. *The Periplus of the Erythraean Sea: Travel and Trade in the Indian Ocean by a Merchant of the First Century*, p. 16. New Delhi: Oriental Books, 1912. Reprint, 1974, http://www.ntz.info/gen/n01207.html.

The archaeological remnants of this place have not yet been located, but Roman glass beads and shards found in digs on the island of Zanzibar and the nearby coast suggest regular journeys beginning around 200 CE. The beads and ceramics were presumably intended to be exchanged for ivory, rock crystal, ostrich feathers, and hardwood. If true, the roots of the later Swahili cities antedated the spread of Islam by several centuries—just as they did in the case of Jenné-jero in West Africa before the rise of Islamic Saharan kingdoms.

Patterns of African History, 600 BCE–600 CE

Based on a modestly productive agriculture, sub-Saharan Africa evolved along two basic patterns in the period 600 BCE–600 CE. First, in the northeast Meroë and Aksum adapted themselves to Middle Eastern agriculture, including the plow and irrigation techniques. In addition, both domesticated sorghum and millet—teff as well in Aksum—indigenously. With the help of irrigated farming and long-distance trade, chiefs built kingdoms, which lasted as long as the urban infrastructure could be supported. The exhaustion of timber in the vicinity of the capitals ended the royal pattern of social and political evolution in the sub-Saharan northeast.

Second, in the northwest of sub-Saharan Africa inhabitants pioneered the agricultures of the steppe, savanna, and rain forest on the basis of millet, rice, yam, and the fruit of the oil palm. Millet was productive enough to support the rise of villages. In one steppe region, the inland delta of the Niger, the irrigated farming of millet and rice allowed for the rise of a dense village network, village nucleation, and eventually a city, Jenné-jeno. With its incipient long-distance trade, this city foreshadowed the post-600 rise of Saharan kingdoms. Farther south, in the rain forest, the farming of yam and oil palm supported the emergence of small and widely dispersed villages. The arrival of the banana and the chicken from southeast Asia enriched all African agricultures and the expansion of the Bantus and their culture brought village life as well as iron smelting to all parts of sub-Saharan Africa.

Africa and the Americas

The Americas displayed striking similarities to the internal sub-Saharan interactions and adaptations. The latter, as we have seen, were responsible for patterns of village, city, and kingdom formation. In Mesoamerica as well as the Peruvian Andes mountains, internal processes of interaction and adaptation based on increasingly productive agricultures also supported a pattern of village, city-state, and kingdom development from 600 BCE to 600 CE.

The principal difference, however, was that in sub-Saharan Africa this evolution gradually expanded also to the central and southern regions, whereas in the Americas no such expansion took place until after 600 CE. Social and political formation patterns spread to North America only after 600 CE, as represented by the Pueblo and Cahokia cultures in what are today the US states of Arizona, Utah, New Mexico, and Missouri.

Early States in Mesoamerica: Maya Kingdoms and Teotihuacán

In Chapter 5 we saw that the chiefdoms of Caral-Supé (2600–2000 BCE) and Chavín de Huántar (1000–200 BCE) in the Andes as well as of the Olmecs (1200–600 BCE) in Mesoamerica represent early examples of social progression from agriculture and villages to urbanization, chiefdoms, and kingdoms. In the period 600 BCE–600 CE, in the Yucatán Peninsula of modern southeastern Mexico and the Mexican basin in south-central Mexico, chiefdoms evolved into full-fledged kingdoms. In the Andes, urban centers continued to form under chiefly rule, although in Teotihuacán and Moche the urban culture was nearly as diversified as in the Mesoamerican kingdoms.

The Maya Kingdoms in Southern Mesoamerica

Closeness to the equator and a long rainy season supported a dense rain forest in the central Yucatán Peninsula. By creating clear cuts and heaping up the soil on elevated fields or terraces on hill slopes, Maya villagers built a rich agriculture based on squash, beans, and corn. Around 600 BCE towns evolved into cities, where chieftains transformed themselves into kings. By organizing the labor of the farmers during slack agricultural times in the winter, they created city-states with imposing temple pyramids and palaces, surrounded by outlying villages. Among these city-states, the most powerful during the period 600 BCE–600 CE were Tikal and Kalakmul (see Map 6.3).

Mayaland on the Yucatán Peninsula   The climate of the Yucatán Peninsula is subtropical, with a rainy season extending from May to September. The base of the Yucatán Peninsula consisted of rain-forest lowlands and swamps, traversed by rivers. To the south were rain-forest highlands, sloping from a chain of mountains about 80–110 miles wide, which descended gradually toward the lowlands in the north and abruptly to the Pacific coast in the south. The northern region comprised the tip of the Yucatán and consisted of dry and riverless lowlands. Maya culture began in the center and far south and later radiated into the southern mountains and northern lowlands. Underlying the northern lowland areas was a limestone shelf that provided stone for construction. Here, local *chert* (a fine-grained sedimentary silica rock) and flint deposits provided for the fashioning of tools with which to quarry the limestone. The volcanic south was quarried for its lava stone and was also rich in obsidian and jade. Quetzal birds, whose feathers were used for prestigious ornamentation, inhabited this region as well (see Map 6.3).

The people in the Yucatán, the highlands and lowlands, spoke a variety of Mayan dialects. Even though they were early on exposed to Olmec cultural influence, it does not appear that there was much Olmec immigration as Maya culture formed. As the early Mayas became sedentary in the center of the peninsula and along the Pacific, they cut down the rain forest in order to clear fields, dry out swamps, and build villages on low stone platforms near water sources. Drainage ditches in fields indicate a

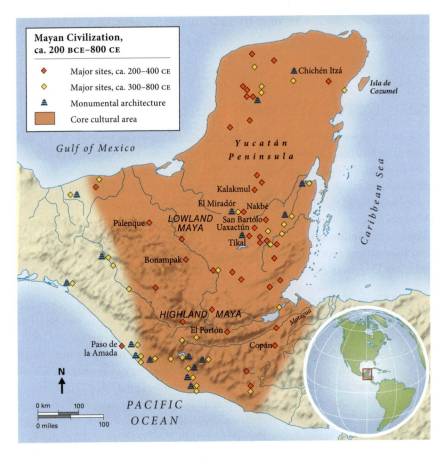

MAP 6.3 Mayan Civilization, ca. 200 BCE–800 CE.

beginning intensification of agriculture. By around 1000 BCE, some villages evolved into towns, dominating village clusters around them. Elite lineages under chieftains resided in the towns and controlled the best lands, while more humble lineages in the surrounding villages were on less productive soils. Although society continued to be organized by familial descent, social stratification by wealth began to differentiate the lineages. This stratification is archaeologically recognizable from rich tomb gifts as well as corrective dentistry: Then as now, the wealthy had enhanced means to beautify themselves.

Early Kingdoms As in the agrarian centers of Eurasia, debt dependence was probably the earliest lever of power in the hands of the Mayan chieftains. Poor farmers, it can be assumed, borrowed seeds from rich farmers and during droughts were often unable to return what they had borrowed. Rich farmers had larger families, built bigger homes, and had more domestic workers producing pottery and textiles. They traded manufactured goods for goods not locally available, such as obsidian and jade. Thus, in the period 1000–600 BCE, these wealthy farmers transformed themselves into chieftains, exerting family rule for more or less extended periods over a central town surrounded by satellite villages.

Beginning in the seventh century BCE, chieftains in some agriculturally rich areas increased their wealth so that they could claim to be kings (Mayan, *ajaw*). Wealthy chieftains were able to surround themselves with military forces through which they made themselves the ultimate arbiters in all town disputes. They began to collect taxes, enlarge their towns into *cities*—that is, centers in which craftspeople and merchants who did not practice agriculture lived—and conquer other villages. During slack times in the agricultural cycle, these kings commanded farmers to construct the first ceremonial monuments—rectangular platforms up to 50 feet in elevation with temples and royal residences on top. Olmec-inspired stone stelae with images of human figures, dressed in Maya-style clothing, were placed around the platforms. Nakbé (700 BCE–150 CE), a city in the north of the central lowlands, was the site of the first temple pyramids on ceremonial platforms. These pyramids were stepped stone structures, as high as 200 feet, with staircases to the temples on top. In those elevated temples, kings conducted their sacrifices in tribute to the gods of the emerging divine pantheon.

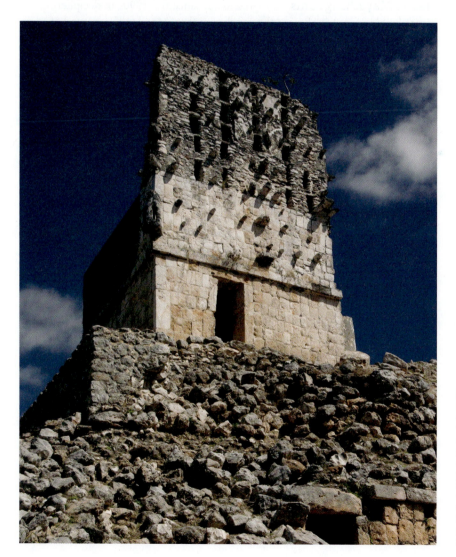

El Miradór, La Danta Temple, 600 BCE–150 CE. By height (230 ft), volume and ground plan, this pyramid was the largest of all Maya sacred structures and one of the largest buildings of the premodern world. At present, the site is only partially excavated and archaeological work is still ongoing. The temple visible atop the pyramid is surmounted by a roosterlike roof comb, once covered by stucco figurines of Maya deities.

A nearby town, El Miradór (600 BCE–150 CE), became a city with surrounding villages about a century after Nakbé. Perhaps favored by better trade connections than Nakbé, El Miradór gradually surpassed its neighbor in size and monumental ambitions. With about 100,000 inhabitants, hundreds of ceremonial and palatial structures on its platforms, and a 216-foot pyramid built around 300 BCE, this Mayan city was the largest early center of what ultimately were more than 4,400 Mayan urban and rural sites. Only the later Tikal (200–600 CE) reached a similar size. El Miradór was explored systematically by archaeologists for the first time only in 1978–1983 and then again beginning in 2003. To their surprise, this site turned out to be as fully Mayan, with its temple pyramids, elite structures, stelae, ball courts, sweat houses, and commoner quarters, as the later and better-known centers of the so-called Early Classic Period (250–600 CE). Maya culture at its peak has to be considered—as is being done in this chapter—under the much longer time horizon that began around 600 BCE.

Classic Maya Kingdoms   Progress made since the 1990s in deciphering the Maya glyphic script has allowed the conclusion that "Mayaland" consisted of some 15–17 fully evolved, dominant kingdoms in the central lowlands during the Early Classic Period, each with a capital and one or more secondary cities, plus countless towns and villages nearby. Marriage alliances among the royal lineages of the capitals and secondary cities served to maintain the cohesion of the kingdom. Rebellions by secondary cities, however, often called the power of the kings into question. Many scholars think that the frequent wars in Mayaland were either intra- kingdom rebellions or wars among secondary cities in different kingdoms. The only exception was the direct military competition between the kingdoms of Tikal and Kalakmul, which endured for many centuries.

Animism and Polytheism   The kings and their royal households lived in palaces adjacent to the temple pyramids. When they ascended the throne, in the tradition of animism, kings often assumed the names of animals or combined them with the names of human-made objects, for example, "Spearthrower Owl," "Shield Jaguar," and "Smoke Squirrel." Heirs to the throne, usually the eldest son, used the same name but with the suffix II, III, etc. On wall paintings, earthenware vessels, and stelae, kings were recognizable through their elaborate headdresses decorated with quetzal feathers, animal masks, and richly embroidered clothing. When sons were still minors, their mothers assumed the roles of regents. Occasionally, women ruled as queens. After death, kings were buried in pyramids or in separate tombs. Dead kings were assumed to have taken their place among the gods, residing in abodes both above and beneath the earth.

Polytheism:
Personification of the forces of nature and performance of rituals and sacrifices to assure the benevolence of the gods and goddesses.

   Polytheism had begun to develop on top of animism after the emergence of the first villages around 2500 BCE. Gods were the embodiments of forces of nature whose favor had to be curried if rich harvests were to result. The Mayan kings considered themselves servants of the many animal, nature, star, and war gods which had come to populate the divine pantheon by the time of the Olmecs in the eleventh century BCE and continued to grow during the Maya period. They fulfilled the demands of these gods for sacrifices during daily rituals in the temples atop the pyramids. The main sacrifice was the gift of blood—a heritage from animism—which Mayan kings drew from their ear lobes, tongues, and penises. During times of war, captured enemies, from kings to commoners, were also sacrificed. Through their blood, the kings nourished nature and supported the human and divine worlds.

The Ruling Classes   Apart from their temple service, kings and leading officials also assembled for the administration of justice, the collection of rents and tributes, commercial exchanges, and diplomatic relations. Many of these functions required expert knowledge of the annual calendar as labor on palaces or pyramids could be required from farmers only during specific times in the agricultural cycle. Other functions, such as military action, required divination so as to discover the most favorable star constellations under which to proceed. The tracking of these units of times required a specialized group of calendar specialists, mathematicians, and astronomers.

The Mayan calendar was an outgrowth of developments that began sometime after 1000 BCE in Olmec-influenced Paso de la Amada. One calendar was the 260-day, or 9-month, divinatory calendar, which scholars interpret as being related to the human gestation period. A second calendar, based on the solar year of 365 days and important for determining the beginnings of the agricultural seasons, was nearly as old. A third calendar was the Mayan Calendar Round, calculated as occurring every 52 years when the divinatory and solar calendars began on the same day. The Mayas believed that this calendar inaugurated cycles of calamitous as well as fortuitous times. The fourth calendar in use among the Mayas was the Long Count Calendar, which counted the days elapsed since the mythical origin of the universe (corresponding to August 11, 3114 BCE, in the Gregorian calendar). A sophisticated mathematics, based on a *vigesimal* system of numbers (twenty-based, in place of our modern decimal system), undergirded the calculations necessary for the coordination of these four calendars.

Other occupations of the royal family and leading courtiers consisted of daily processions and feasts during which copious amounts of cacao, spiced with chili, vanilla, and honey, were consumed. Alternatively, the elite consumed chocolate wafers, forerunners of our modern chocolate bars, which were also used as easily transportable nourishment on journeys. Finally, the court attended ball games in stadiums, which formed part of the temple-palace grounds. As in the kingdoms of Eurasia, but without evidence of any influence, in Maya kingdoms the occupations and functions of the ruling class were ritualized, refined pastimes far beyond the reach of common farmers and craftspeople. A stratified social hierarchy typified the Maya kingdoms (see "Patterns Up Close" on pp. 184–185).

The Commoners   The commoners, whose taxes supported the royal courts, lived in housing compounds of a few thatched huts or clusters of huts erected around courtyards on stone platforms, which allowed them to be above the flood-waters during the rainy season. In these houses, women were in charge of cooking, weaving, pottery making, the growing of garden vegetables and fruits, and the rearing of domestic animals (including dogs, turkeys, and pigeons). Garden fruits included avocado, guava, papaya, vanilla, and pineapple. Within the household, women and men shared the crafts of tool making, fabricating tools from chert, bone, and wood. In larger Maya kingdoms some households seem to have specialized more than others in tool manufacturing and weaving, with both women and men participating.

Mayan Glyphs. Beginning in the 4th century BCE, scribes in the Maya kingdoms developed a written language composed of morphemes (word elements) and syllables, eventually numbering about 800 signs. This language allowed communication among educated people in the different Maya kingdoms who spoke often mutually unintelligible local languages. Because of the double meaning of each glyph as morpheme and syllable, it took most of the 20th century for scholars to decipher the Mayan language. The example shown here is from the Dresden Codex.

Men were in charge of growing corn in fields which were cut into the rain forest through slash-and-burn techniques. Fields near rivers and in swamps were "raised fields" (Spanish *chinampas*), rectangle-shaped islands on which the mud from adjacent canals had been heaped. The main agricultural implement was the digging stick (Mayan *kool* [kohl]) with which farmers loosened the soil and dropped corn kernels into a hole. Slopes along river valleys were terraced in order to retain rain or irrigation water. Cotton, cacao, and tobacco fields formed special plantations because of either special soil preparation or intensive labor needs. Hunting and fishing with bow and arrow, blowguns, and harpoons, skills inherited from forager times, remained important occupations among both royals and commoners.

The hard agricultural labor of the commoners produced an agricultural surplus, which supported ruling dynastic families as well as craftspeople in the cities. Craftspeople worked for the construction and maintenance of royal palaces, creating monuments, wall paintings, pottery, and inscriptions on stone pillars or stelae.

Mayan Writing   Excavations in El Portón and San Bartoló in the early 2000s suggest that Mayan writing might have begun as early as 400–300 BCE. These early texts—although similar in appearance to the fully evolved script of the later centuries—still await decipherment. Their age raised the important question among Maya specialists, whether the notion of the late Olmecs having developed writing first can still be maintained. The Mayas might very likely have been the originators.

Mayan writing is a **glyphic** as well as a syllabic script, numbering some 800 signs. It is structurally similar to Sumerian cuneiform and Egyptian hieroglyphic. The glyphic part consists of *pictograms*, one-word images of the most essential features of what is to be depicted (for example, the glyph for a human being would be a stick figure with body, legs, arms, and a head). Glyphs as syllables consist of one, two, or three signs, which stand for the combination of a consonant and a vowel. Combinations of syllabic glyphs, or *syllabaries*, are pronounced as a series of syllables. Given the mixture of pictograms and syllabaries, which is potentially immense, the complexity of Mayan writing appeared for a long time to be an insuperable obstacle to any effort at deciphering.

A breakthrough came only in the 1960s and 1970s when scholars successfully interpreted a number of stelae monuments to kings recording the dates of their birth, accession to the throne, and death. First, scholars realized that Mayan writing had an important syllabic component; then, the Russian-born American architect and Maya specialist Tatiana Proskouriakoff discovered that the inscriptions on many royal stelae contained information on dynastic dates and events. The final breakthrough came during a conference at the Maya site of Palenque in 1973 when participants recognized the syllables *k'inchi* as referring to the Mayan sun god as well as individual kings. As first in Mesopotamia and then in many other places, kings invoked patron gods that symbolized forces in nature and thereby became founders of polytheism, as mentioned above. In one inspirational afternoon, a working group consisting of the art historian and epigrapher Linda Schele, the linguist Floyd Lounsbury, and the undergraduate Peter Mathews, deciphered the king list of Palenque, containing eight rulers. Since then, scholars have assembled a dictionary of as many as 1,000 words and it has become possible to embark on a systematic chronicling of the dynasties of Maya kingdoms.

Glyphic script: The Maya developed a script of some 800 images. Some are pictograms standing for words, others are syllables to be combined with other syllables to form words.

The Crisis of the Kingdoms Spectacular building activities characterized Mayaland during the Late Classic Period (ca. 400–600 CE). Ruling classes must have grown to considerable sizes, and it is possible that farmers in some kingdoms were no longer willing to produce food staples as well as provide labor for the pyramid temples and palaces. Destruction identified in some archaeological sites could be interpreted as the result of revolts. In other places, overexploitation of the soil, loss of topsoil on terraces, or salinization of lowland fields as the result of neglected drainage might have increased the imbalance between the peasants and ruling classes. Frequent wars among the kings might have reduced the size of the ruling class, but their wars clearly also had negative consequences for the farmers. The interplay between the ruling class, farmers, and the environment produced a crisis beginning in the late 500s CE and extending through the mid-600s CE, leading to the collapse of many older Mayan kingdoms and endangering the survival of the strongest newer ones in the southern lowlands. When the crisis ended, the political weight of Maya power shifted to the northern lowlands of the Yucatán Peninsula.

The Creation Myth of the Maya

"Now it still ripples, it still murmurs, ripples, it still sighs, and it is empty under the sky. Here follow the first words, the first eloquence: There is not yet one person, one animal, bird, fish, crab, tree, rock, hollow, canyon, meadow, forest. Only the sky alone is there; the face of the earth is not clear. Only the sea is pooled under all the sky; there is nothing whatever gathered together. It is at rest; not a single thing stirs. It is held back, kept at rest under the sky. Whatever there is that might be is simply not there…"

—Dennis Tedlock, trans. *Popol Vuh: The Definitive Edition of the Mayan Book of the Dawn of Life and the Glory of Gods and Kings*, p. 64. New York: Touchstone, 1996. Spanish monks recorded the myth in 1701 and it might show traces of their Christian faith.

The Kingdom of Teotihuacán in the Mexican Basin

The subtropical climate of Yucatán extended northward into the highlands, in which the Mexican basin was the largest agricultural region. Although the high elevation did not allow for the full breadth of Maya agriculture, the alluvial soil and water from the surrounding mountains supported a productive agriculture of beans, squash, and corn. The northern part of the basin developed a rich village life later than the south, but its closeness to obsidian quarries gave these villages commercial advantages. Militarily and economically, the town of Teotihuacán in the north caught up to the south around the early 100s CE and developed into a city-state that became politically and culturally dominant across all of Mesoamerica.

The Mexican Basin The Mexican basin is a large, 7,400-foot-high bowl without river outlets in southern Mexico. In the center of the bowl was Lake Texcoco [Tes-CO-co], nourished by rivers flowing down from 15,000-foot-high mountain chains on the eastern and western sides. As in Mayaland, the basin enjoyed a rainy

Patterns Up Close

The Mayan Ball Game

One of the most remarkable features in Mesoamerica was the team ball game. Although it shares its ancient age with similar games in China, the Persian Middle East, and the Greek and Roman Mediterranean, only in Mesoamerica was it a game with formal rules, played in stadiums constructed specifically for this purpose. In Mesoamerica, archaeologists in 1985 discovered the oldest stadium to date, 1400 BCE, in the ruins of Paso de la Amada, a chiefdom town with surrounding villages in the far southeast of today's Mexico. Adjacent to the palace of the chief, this ball court measures 260 by 23 feet, with two 7-foot-high spectator platforms on both long sides. Later on, during the Maya period, these platforms usually rose theater-style on both sides, for better viewing from farther away. Given the proximity of the ball court to the chief's residence, it is possible that other chiefdoms in the area engaged in what we would call today "league tournaments."

The ball was made of solid rubber, from a gum- or latex-producing tree growing in the area of Paso. Mesoamericans traded latex as an expensive luxury good and, apart from making balls, used it for waterproofing ritual clothing and hafting spear tips to arrow shafts. Balls were around 2 feet or more in diameter and weighed 8 pounds. Given these dimensions, players often wore protective gear around their hips and helmets on their heads, as shown in murals and on ceramics.

Under the Maya, who called the game *pitz* and built about 1,500 courts (compared to about 1,000 in existence in all of modern-day Mexico), the rules became more formalized. A basic rule was that the ball had to be hit with the hip only and had to remain aloft. But variations are also known, in which players struck the ball with their forearms, bats, or hand stones. The size of a team extended from one to seven players. The team that lost was the one that dropped the ball most often.

The Ball Court at Chichén Itzá, Yucatán Peninsula. Nearly 200 yards long and 100 yards wide, the ball court at Chichén Itzá is the largest in Mesoamerica. Note the rings on the side walls, through which the rubber balls had to pass.

The Mayan Ball Game. Note the strong body protection around the mid-section of the players as well as the elaborate headdresses, symbolizing animals.

This close-up on the Mayan ball game fits into the larger picture of agrarian–urban society and its chiefdom and kingdom patterns when polytheism with its innumerable rituals and sacrificial practices assumed elaborate proportions. Although the archaeological record is debatable, it appears that ball games took place during chiefly or royal festivities and fertility rituals, perhaps also human sacrifices. The apparent but also disputed role of some players as human sacrifices on a number of murals was a late Mayan phenomenon. Today, in scientific–industrial society, these roots of "games" in past rituals, processions, and reenactments of divine events are largely forgotten. Instead, sports have their own modern rituals, such as flag waving, parading, tailgating, and hooliganism. Whether religious or secular rituals are a permanent fixture and follow their own patterns, parallel to those of society at large.

Questions

- How did the ball game serve as a microcosm for larger patterns in Mayan society?
- What function could the ball game have played in relations among the various Mayan chiefdoms?

season from May to September. River water, channeled through irrigation canals to terraces and the flatlands around the central lake, as well as numerous bays, supported a moderately productive agriculture.

During the period of village expansion (1200–600 BCE), many of the slopes surrounding this bowl were forested. There was plenty of firewood and timber for construction, as well as abundant wildlife for the hunt. Fish in the freshwater bays of the lake was another important food source. Clay deposits in the flatlands and obsidian quarries on the slopes of the still active volcanoes in the northeastern mountains provided resources for the manufacture of ceramics, tools, and weapons. However, the high elevation and temperature differences between winter and summer did not allow for cultivation of the cotton, cacao, vanilla, and tropical fruits which enriched lowland Maya agriculture. These latter products had to be acquired by trade.

The principal plant fiber for the weaving of clothes came from the *maguey* [Ma-GAY] plant, a large, deep-rooted, agave-like cactus that could grow in poor soil and did not need much water. The fiber was gained from scraping the sweet-tasting flesh off the interior of the long, stalk-like leaves. The flesh contained a juice which, in its fermented state, was consumed as an alcoholic drink called *pulque* [Spanish, PULL-kay; Nahuatl, *octli*]. If people wished to manufacture clothes from cotton or acquire cacao, vanilla, jade, or quetzal feathers, they had to trade their obsidian. Commercial exchange was a firm ingredient of the period of village expansion and played a major part in the subsequent pattern of kingdom formation.

Teotihuacán   In a wide valley to the northeast of Lake Texcoco, traversed by the San Juan River and endowed with rich alluvial soil, villagers in the early centuries CE dug a large canal system with raised fields similar to those of the Maya. Around 100 BCE, villages around this canal network began to cluster, eventually forming the city of Teotihuacán. When the transition from chieftains to kings and chiefly dynasties occurred is impossible to determine on the basis of the present archaeological record. The iconic writing system, less developed than that of the Mayas and lacking syllabic elements, does not allow for identification of any rulers or lineages. Teotihuacán was a city-state with an anonymous dynasty, centered in a city and surrounded by villages. In its physical appearance it was even more imposing than most of the Maya kingdoms (see Map 6.4).

In the first century CE, the rulers of Teotihuacán began spectacular building projects that resulted in temple complexes larger than what the Mayan kings built. They laid out an urban grid along a north–south axis, dubbed the "Avenue of the Dead" by archaeologists, which included two densely constructed city quarters of some 2,200 housing units. Each unit housed a patrilineal clan of 60–100 members. Near the central avenue, closely packed and plastered adobe houses were divided by alleyways. Some 600 houses have the appearance of workshops, primarily for the making of tools from the gray and green obsidian mined near Teotihuacán. The workshops indicate a degree of nonagricultural crafts specialization, which one would expect from a city. Farther away, houses and fields were interspersed. Canals, reservoirs, and an extensive drainage system facilitated the transportation of food, the provision of drinking water, and the elimination of waste. By around 300 CE, Teotihuacán had grown to as many as 100,000 inhabitants. It was a metropolis easily comparable to Rome, Ctesiphon, and Alexandria in the Roman Mediterranean and Persian Middle East; Patliputra in Gupta India; and Chang'an in Han China.

Teotihuacán, ca. 300 CE

■ Monumental/ceremonial center

■ Temple complexes/ monumental centers

0 km 1

0 mile 1

Avenue of the Dead

Temples of the Moon and Sun

Rome Ctesiphon Chang'an
Alexandria   Patliputra
Teotihuacán

MAP **6.4** Teotihuacán, ca. 100 CE–500 CE.

An aerial view of Teotihuacán's ruins conveys an idea of the vast scale on which the temple pyramids, palaces, markets, and city quarters were built. The Temples of the Moon and the Sun, built at the northern end of the city, represent the earliest structures. They were ceremonial centers which attracted pilgrims from everywhere in the Mexican basin and beyond. Archaeologists interpret the Temple of the Sun as a construction on top of a cave symbolizing the entrance to the nether world. In the third century CE, the temple of the god of the feathered serpent (Nahuatl *Quetzalcoatl* [Ket-sal-COA]) followed, probably built in honor of the then reigning dynasty. The founding king sacrificed some 260 humans, probably war captives, to garner the good will of the god. After what appears to have been an internal uprising and change in leadership in the 400s CE, the new rulers destroyed the temple's facade and erected an attachment (Spanish *adosada*) in front of it. Colorful wall paintings and pottery, depicting rulers, priests, gods, and mythical figures in processions, rituals, and dances, still survive, attesting to a highly developed aesthetic culture. Today, after a century of intermittent excavations, much has been learned about the city's architecture, but little is yet known about its rulers and inhabitants.

The Decline of the City

As in the case of the Maya kingdoms, the balance among the peasantry, urban inhabitants, dynasties, and construction programs was not always easy to maintain. Hints at an internal upheaval in the 400s CE point to the balance being lost at least once during Teotihuacán's existence. Another such upheaval occurred in the early 500s CE, to judge from fires and destructions along the Avenue of the Dead, possibly in the course of a popular uprising against the rulers. Thereafter, the population of the central city quarters declined rapidly, although the outlying quarters continued to exist, reverting back to the village level as farming communities for centuries to come. The mid-500s CE saw prolonged periods of cooler weather and droughts and were generally a more difficult time for farming in the Americas. As we shall see in Chapter 15, in contrast to the agriculturally richer

Teotihuacán, Temple of the Feathered Serpent God, Quetzacóatl. This sculpture of a serpent's head with its exposed, menacing fangs and the collar made of feathers is one of many along the front wall of this temple. The hybrid deity (green quetzal bird and cóatl snake) bridged the fertile earth and the planet Venus, bringer of rain in the summer.

Maya kingdoms, the less endowed Mexican basin found a return to urbanism and dynastic states more difficult.

At its height, Teotihuacán exerted a commercial, cultural, and perhaps even political influence considerably greater than the Maya kingdoms. Its trade reached deep into Mayaland and beyond, to the Isthmus of Panama. Teotihuacán exchanged its obsidian for cotton, rubber, cacao, jade, and quetzal feathers from the subtropics. Its gods, especially the deity of the feathered serpent, were sacrificed to everywhere in Mesoamerica. Similarly, Teotihuacán was instrumental in spreading the so-called *talud-tablero* architectural style (sets of inward-sloping platforms, surmounted by temples) from the basin of Mexico to the Yucatán Peninsula. In the later 300s CE and throughout the 400s CE, Maya rulers of Tikal, Uaxactún [Wa-sha-TOON], and other kingdoms claimed descent from rulers of Teotihuacán, evidently seeking to benefit from the city's prestige as a ceremonial center.

The Andes: Moche and Nazca

In Andean South America, a pattern of chiefdom formation, wherein chieftains controlled urban ceremonial centers and surrounding villages, evolved between 3000 and 2000 BCE, a millennium earlier than in Mesoamerica. Given the absence of large plains and the enormous differences in elevation within short distances, however, relatively small chiefdoms remained the dominant social formation in the Andes. Still, around 1000–200 BCE, a major ceremonial center like Chavín de Huántar (north of present-day Lima) was a town with fewer than 5,000 inhabitants, even though it was a pilgrimage site for most of the Andes. Chavín's successors, the chiefdoms of Moche and Nazca, although somewhat larger, remained within the chiefdom pattern during the period 600 BCE–600 CE.

The Moche in Northern Peru

The Moche Valley was the place of the two largest ceremonial centers in the Andes, the Temple Pyramids of the Sun and the Moon. The power of its main chiefdom must have been impressive since large numbers of farmers had to be mobilized for the construction of these pyramids. But it remained a federation of village chiefdoms clustered around an urbanized temple center with a dominant chiefly lineage.

Moche Origins The Moche Valley was at the center of nine coastal valleys in what is today northern Peru. It had a subtropical climate south of the equator with moderately wet winters from April to November and dry summers from December to March. It was based on an irrigated agriculture of corn, pulses, cotton, and peanuts; llamas and alpacas from the highlands were domesticated for wool and light transportation. Here, the earliest evidence of the emergence of the Moche chiefdoms (100–750 CE) is the tomb of the "Lord of Sipán," dated to 50 CE. The tomb contained the chief's mummy, clad in warrior clothing and richly decorated with gold and silver necklaces, nose rings, ear rings, helmets, and bracelets. Eight people were buried with him, including his wife, two other women (perhaps concubines), a military officer, a watchman, a banner holder, a child, and a dog. This chieftain was wealthy and powerful indeed.

A Federated Chiefdom Half a century later, Moche chieftains began the construction of the two Temple Pyramids of the Sun and the Moon, huge stepped temple pyramids made of adobe bricks. Markers on the bricks indicate the participation of about 100 village teams in the construction, which lasted intermittently for centuries. The platforms contain the burial places of Moche chieftains and priests and the remains of human sacrifices brought during ceremonies and rituals. At the feet of the two temples was a city that included administrative offices and workshops. Lesser chieftain lineages ruled in the more remote valleys. Altogether the chiefdoms formed a loose federation around a main ceremonial center and pilgrimage place.

None of the participating villages appears to have grown beyond the moderately large spaces at the mouth of valleys, and it seems that they coexisted peacefully for the most part. When the generally cooler and drier climate of the sixth century CE arrived, it had a greater negative impact on the agriculture of the central chiefdom in Moche, closer to the coast and more remote from the river waters, than on the chiefdoms upstream in the adjacent smaller valleys. In the Moche Valley with its two huge temples the balance between chiefly elites and farmers was more difficult to maintain than in the farther valleys with smaller elites and comparatively larger peasantries. Eventually, in the early 600s CE, the Moche elite dissolved, while smaller elites in other valleys carried on and eventually disappeared also, sometime around 750 CE (see Map 6.5).

Moche Terracotta Portrait Vessel with Handle, ca. 100–800 CE. Archaeologists assume that the vessel shows a chief. Other types of Moche vessels show deities, animals, ritual objects, sexual acts (for education?), domestic objects, and crafts activities. Potters often used stone molds for making their wares. Among the Andes people, the Moche potters were among the most imaginative and versatile.

MAP **6.5** **Andean Centers, 750 BCE–750 CE.**

Paracas and the Nazca in Southern Peru

Southern Peru was much drier, and its agrarian population density lagged behind that of the north. The chiefdoms were correspondingly more modest. Nevertheless, Paracas [Pa-RA-cas] represents one of the earliest burial places for mummies in the world, and Nazca offers the most elaborate petroglyphs of the Americas. The two possess, therefore, considerable cultural significance.

Paracas Chiefs   Desert conditions on the southern Peruvian coast and full dependence on runoff water from Andean snowmelt between January and March after the Andes winter required more elaborate irrigation works than on the northern coast. The patterns of social formation from foraging to villages and chiefdoms with ceremonial centers were correspondingly slower and more modest. Shamans and chiefs on the Paracas peninsula and the Ica valley set the pattern in motion when they unified a number of hamlets. Subsequently, other Paracas chiefdoms appeared in neighboring valleys, forming a loose confederation (750 BCE–1 CE). A necropolis on the peninsula contained hundreds of mummies of chieftains, wrapped in the colorful, high-quality wool and cotton mantles still today characteristic of southern Peru. It was primarily through the icons woven into the mantles and painted on pottery that modern scholars identified the Paracas chiefs. These icons included figures—shamanic ancestors or early agricultural, polytheistic deities—holding weapons, plants, or skulls. Other icons were felines, birds, or whales, often with human-like features reminiscent of Paleolithic cave paintings in other parts of the world. Although contemporary with the Maya kingdoms in Mesoamerica, the Paracas chiefdoms in the Andes were culturally still compact.

The Nazca Ceremonial Center

The transition from pottery painted after firing to predecorated or slipware ceramics defines the shift from the Paracas to the Nazca chiefdoms (1–650 CE). Nazca chiefs built ceremonial centers, not the monumental freestanding ones as on the northern Peruvian coast but more modest adobe structures, which actually covered preexisting mounds. Cahuachi [Ca-wooh-WAH-tshee], the main pilgrimage center, contained 40 such structures, assumed to represent the contributing chiefdoms.

During the extended cold weather and drought periods of the sixth century CE, when a number of rivers dried out, Nazca chiefs mobilized the villagers in the valleys for the construction of an extensive tunnel network for irrigation. Workers tapped underground water in the mountains and guided it onto the slopes of the valleys and into reservoirs. These highly sophisticated constructions, with intermittent shafts and manholes for cleaning and repair, were built so sturdily that many of them are still in operation today. Called *puquios* [Quechua, POO-kyos], they are reminiscent of the much later *qanat* [Arabic, Ka-NAHT] structures of Islamic Iran and Morocco. In the agrarian age, chiefdoms could be technologically just as innovative as kingdoms and empires.

The Nazca Geoglyphs

Another Nazca innovation were the so-called Nazca **geoglyphs**, large geometrical and animal figures laid out in the dry highlands and on the valley slopes of the chiefdoms. Villagers constructed straight and zigzag lines, triangles and trapezoids, as well as images of a monkey, spider, whale, and several birds with astounding precision, by removing dark-colored rocks and exposing the lighter sand underneath. These geoglyphs are unique in the Andes, and the closest parallel did not occur

Geoglyphs: Long geometric lines and figures as well as outlines of animals formed in the desert by picking up darker stones and exposing the lighter sand underneath.

Nazca Lines. *Top:* hummingbird; *bottom left:* monkey; *bottom right:* spider. These lines can only be seen from the air—perhaps by a sky god?

until nearly a millennium later when the Incas arranged sacred objects (Quechua, *huacas*) outside their capital, Cuzco, in straight lines.

There are, however, vague parallels with a considerable number of undated later geoglyphs in the Great Basin and other western regions of North America. Native Americans under the leadership of shamans used these geoglyphs during rituals in which they evoked honored figures, animals, and events of the mythical past. Processual archaeologists (archaeologists applying concepts of cultural evolutionism), relate the Nazca symbols to the abstract Paleolithic geometrical cave symbols found in Africa, Europe, and Australia (see Chapter 1). Eventually, the Nazca came under the influence of the highland state of Wari, a later city-state in the Andes (see Chapter 15). This state expanded its political and cultural influence toward the southern Peruvian coast in the first half of the 700s CE and gradually gave the Nazca chiefdoms a new identity.

Putting It All Together

In the period 600 BCE–600 CE, agriculture and life in villages became near universal in the world. Only Australia remained outside this development from foraging to agrarian settlement. Of course, remnants of foraging societies survived, notably in sub-Saharan Africa and even more so in the Americas. But it is nevertheless striking that humans on the latter two continents developed in the same direction as those in Eurasia toward cities, kingdoms, and long-distance luxury trade.

Agrarian-based urban culture, however, was a fragile achievement in Eurasia and even more so in sub-Saharan Africa, Mesoamerica, and the Andes. Irregularities of the weather and, in the latter regions, the slow improvement of food plant productivity (as revealed by plant archaeologists) meant that agriculture was a tenuous enterprise. Corn, especially, evolved only slowly toward a greater cob length and was still quite short during the Maya period. Only by the time of the Aztecs, selective breeding had produced corn of modern proportions. As a rule, dynastic cities regularly outstripped the natural resources of their local environments, as was the case in Meroë, Aksum, the Maya cities, and Teotihuacán. But once the option of urbanization had arrived, it was usually not lost again and sooner or later new city-based states arose.

As we have seen in this chapter, the typical dynastic urban achievements were monumental architecture, sophisticated metal and textile craftsmanship, and, in some cases, forms of intellectual expression. Typical examples covered in this chapter were the remarkably similar monumental temple pyramids and stelae of the kings in northeastern sub-Saharan Africa, Mesoamerica, and the Andes. Metal and textile craftsmanship, of course, had deep village roots on both sides of the Atlantic. Gold, silver, copper, and bronze jewelry was often exquisite; and the iron manufacture in African villages was remarkably developed. But in cities these crafts became the refined products of specialized workers who did not participate in farming.

Similarly, precocious intellectual achievements appeared both in nomadic contexts (complementary to agriculture), as witnessed by the Borana calendar of the Kushite nomads in Kenya, and in small-town agricultural chiefdoms, as seen in the giant geometrical lines and animal outlines created in the desert landscape by the Nazca of Peru. By comparison, the intellectual pursuits in royal cities were on a much larger

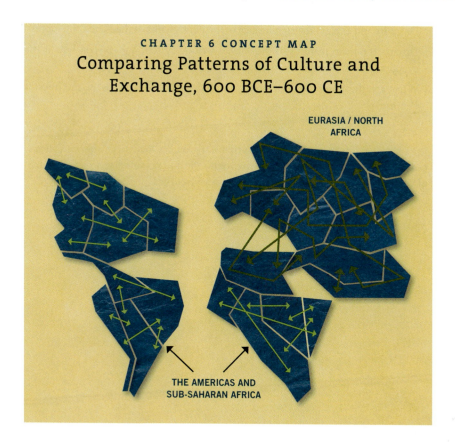

CHAPTER 6 CONCEPT MAP

Comparing Patterns of Culture and Exchange, 600 BCE–600 CE

EURASIA / NORTH AFRICA

THE AMERICAS AND SUB-SAHARAN AFRICA

scale. Here, the Maya took the prize with their complex calendar and script, as well as their elaborate divine pantheon and cosmogony.

Altogether, evolving largely on their own, both sub-Saharan Africa and the Americas made long strides in the period 600 BCE–600 CE toward expressing the same depth of humanity which was already on display in Eurasia. They did not yet have empires or possess the literary breadth that favored the rise of the visionaries of transcendence, hallmarks of the Middle East, India, and China during 600 BCE–600 CE. But their more compact cultures were not lacking in any of the overall patterns that characterized Eurasia, as demonstrated in the accompanying Concept Map.

Review and Respond

1. Describe the distinctive characteristics of the Borana and Maya calendars. In which ways are they different from the Gregorian calendar?

2. Compare and contrast the kingdoms of Meroë and Aksum. What helped them develop into early sub-Saharan African kingdoms?

3. Which geographical features distinguish West Africa, and how did they contribute to the rise of agriculture and villages?

4. Describe and explain the significance of the petroglyphs of the Nazca chiefdoms.

5. Discuss the main features of the Mayan writing system and explain how it was eventually deciphered by modern scholars.

6. What are the common characteristics of the Maya kingdoms in the Yucatán Peninsula?

▶ For additional resources, including maps, primary sources, visuals, and quizzes, please go to www.oup.com/us/vonsivers. Please see the Further Resources section at the back of the book for additional readings and suggested websites.

Thinking Through Patterns

▶ **How does comparing and contrasting sub-Saharan Africa with the Americas during 600 BCE–600 CE help in understanding the agrarian–urban patterns of social and political development across the world?**

Innovations in world history usually originated in one specific place and then radiated outward into new populations through interactions among different peoples. Through adaptation, the new populations incorporated innovations into their own cultures. Adaptation was never slavish imitation; it was always a creative process of shaping something from a different culture to the new culture's needs and circumstances. Sub-Saharan Africa and the Americas were partially or entirely limited to their own internal innovation patterns, given their relative or absolute isolation from Eurasia. Encountering the same experiences and challenges as humans in Eurasia, albeit somewhat later, their responses were remarkably comparable. Thus, the history of the world was not merely the history of peoples coming into more and more intensive contact with each other. It was also the history of peoples experiencing similar challenges without transcontinental interaction.

▶ **Where did chiefdoms, cities, and kingdoms arise in sub-Saharan Africa and why? On which forms of agriculture, urbanization, and trade were they based?**

Agrarian sub-Saharan Africa during 600 BCE–600 CE is an example where interaction with the Middle East—as well as, in some periods, its absence—formed the background for comparable processes of economic, social, and political developments. The middle Nile valley and the highlands of Ethiopia gave rise to the plow-based agrarian kingdoms of Meroë and Aksum, both receiving their original plows and grain from the Middle East and maintaining a lively trade for luxury goods with that region. By contrast, the West African inland Niger delta grew into the urbanized chiefdom of Jenné-jero without recognizable external interactions. Through interaction and adaptation, forms of farming as well as iron smelting (the latter perhaps received from the Middle East) migrated south in sub-Saharan Africa, together with called Bantu expansion.

▶ **Which areas in the Americas saw the development of a corn- and potato-based agriculture that did not depend on the plow, the wheel, and iron making?**

Three regions in the Americas were favorable for the development of densely settled villages, some of which subsequently evolved into cities and kingdoms: Yucatán with its Maya kingdoms, the Mexican basin with the city-state of Teotihuacán, and Peru with the Moche and Nazca chiefdoms. The Maya kingdoms were economically and culturally the most differentiated polities—and the only ones to record the histories of their kings in writing on stelae and other monuments. Highly productive farming took place on riverbanks or hill terraces, with a surplus that supported the construction of elaborate temple pyramids and structures containing painted ceramics and wall paintings.

Chapter 7 | Persia, Greece, and Rome

550 BCE-600 CE

PERSIA, GREECE, AND ROME

Mediterranean Sea

At one of his banquets after vanquishing the Achaemenid [A-KEE-ma-need] Persian Empire in 330 BCE, the world conqueror Alexander the Great (r. 336–323 BCE) had a violent confrontation with one of his leading commanders, Cleitus. Flatterers at the banquet compared Alexander to the gods, and Alexander himself boasted that his conquests were far superior to those of his father, Philip. Cleitus, older than Alexander and an officer in Philip's army who had been engaged in the preparations for the Greek conquest of Persia, angrily interjected. It was the army that was the true victor, he objected, noting that he himself had saved Alexander's life in at least one of the battles against the Persians.

Seeing Patterns

▶ Why should the Middle East and Mediterranean Europe during the period 600 BCE–600 CE be studied as a single unit?

▶ What is transcendence, and why is it important to understand its importance in world history?

▶ Which elements characterize the institutions growing out of the Middle Eastern monotheisms of Judaism and Christianity and the monism of Greek philosophy and science?

The exchange became heated, fueled by copious amounts of wine. At one point, Cleitus loudly complained about Alexander demanding everyone, Greek and Persian, to fall on their knees when entering his presence. As the shouting match continued, Alexander first threw an apple at Cleitus, then reached for his sword—which guards had prudently removed—and finally grabbed a javelin, killing Cleitus with a lightning-like thrust. Almost before the blow had been struck, Alexander regained his senses. Deeply remorseful, he grieved over the death of his companion; according to one source, he abstained from food and drink for several days, bewailing the loss of his veteran commander.

Although the sources that report the incident vary considerably in detail, they agree that the quarrel was about the question of Alexander remaining true to his Macedonian/Greek heritage or becoming a Persian "king of kings." Was he still a first among equals? Was he still bringing liberty to the Greeks of Asia? Or was he becoming a divinely mandated monarch who could command Persians and Greeks alike to obey him on bended knee? Not surprisingly, these questions arose right at the time that Alexander had completed the liberation of the Greeks from Persian rule, destroyed the

Imperial Conflict. This depiction of a battle between Romans and "barbarians," from the Ludovisi sarcophagus from about 175 CE, was influenced by earlier Hellenistic representations of battles between Alexander the Great and the Persians.

Persian Empire, and was about to begin his conquest of India. He was on his way to becoming the exalted single ruler of the then known world, encompassing all nations, languages, and religions on earth, a world similar to that heaven where Zeus ruled all gods and goddesses (or the Libyan god Ammon, from whom Alexander believed he was descended).

The Middle East and Mediterranean during 600 BCE–600 CE was a region that was culturally diverse, as illustrated by Cleitus' contrast between Greek liberties and Achaemenid Persian royal power. It was also an area of intense military rivalry, as we see in Alexander's avenging the Persian dominance of Greece in 386 by his own conquest of Persia in 334. Later on, as we shall learn in this chapter, the successor states of Parthian and Sasanid Persia and Rome continued the rivalry. However, already in the sixth century BCE, Greek, Jewish, and Iranian visionaries introduced very similar *monotheistic* (single personal god) and *monist* (single impersonal principle) forms of thought into the region. Centuries later, in the rivalry between Persia and Rome, the opposing state religions of Christianity and Zoroastrianism also faced off against each other. In short, this chapter focuses on one single region that had evolved from its Mesopotamian and Egyptian agrarian–urban origins and shared such basic patterns as imperialism, monotheism, and monism but was also torn apart by concrete and unbridgeable political and cultural differences. Intense internal interaction and adaptation characterized the Middle East and Mediterranean in the period 600 BCE–600 CE.

Interactions Between Persia and Greece

The Achaemenid Persian conquest of the Middle East, from Anatolia and Egypt in the west to northwestern India in the east, was a relatively easy affair compared to the conquest of Greece, where inhabitants resisted fiercely. Although Persia was able to subjugate the Greek city-states of the Anatolian coast, it proved unable to conquer the Greek mainland. A century and a half later, Alexander the Great unified Greece and led it to victory over Persia, establishing a short-lived Macedonian–Greek Empire. Alexander's generals divided the empire into three successor kingdoms under which politics stabilized until the Persians, under the Parthians and Sasanids, renewed the Persian imperial tradition.

The Origins of the Achaemenid Persian Empire

The Persians originated as agrarian villagers and nomadic horse and sheep breeders during the Bronze Age in central Asia south of the Ural Mountains. Toward the end of the third millennium BCE, groups of nomads migrated from the Urals southward and, by the middle of the second millennium BCE, reached the Aral Sea region. From here, some migrants pushed farther, establishing themselves in Upper Mesopotamia and India around 1200 BCE. The Persians were a branch that migrated sometime before the 800s BCE from the Aral Sea region to the southwestern Iranian province of Fars, from which the name "Persia" is derived.

Persian Conquests   The first Persians to appear in the historical record were the Medes, who presided over a loosely organized kingdom with provincial vassals adjacent to the Assyrian Empire in Fars. The head of one vassal family, Cyrus II the Great (r. ca. 550–530 BCE) of the Achaemenids, assumed the crown of the Persians in 550 BCE and, in contrast to the Medes, embarked on an ambitious imperial program. Cyrus first expanded into Anatolia, where he conquered the kingdom of Lydia [LEE-dee-ya]. The Lydians are notable for having created in 615 BCE the first minted money in world history, coins made of silver and gold and used in trade. Next, Cyrus turned to the neighboring Greek city-states of Ionia on the southwestern Anatolian coast. His generals besieged these cities one by one, until their inhabitants either surrendered or returned to the Greek mainland.

Cyrus himself was busy with the conquest of the Iranian interior and north, as far as Afghanistan. In 540 BCE he began his campaign against Neo-Babylonia in Mesopotamia, capturing the capital of Babylon a year later. The Phoenician city-states in Syria submitted voluntarily in the following years. Within a little more than a decade, Cyrus had defeated the most important powers of the period and had unified all of the Middle East except Egypt, which Persia conquered a little later, in 525 BCE (see Map 7.1).

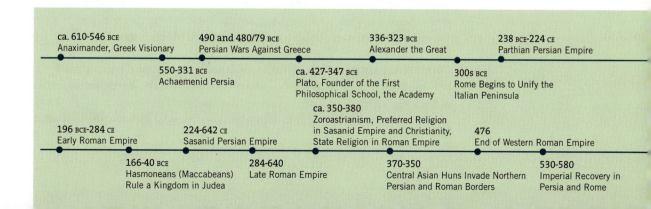

| ca. 610-546 BCE Anaximander, Greek Visionary | 490 and 480/79 BCE Persian Wars Against Greece | 336-323 BCE Alexander the Great | 238 BCE-224 CE Parthian Persian Empire |

550-331 BCE Achaemenid Persia

ca. 427-347 BCE Plato, Founder of the First Philosophical School, the Academy

300s BCE Rome Begins to Unify the Italian Peninsula

ca. 350-380 Zoroastrianism, Preferred Religion in Sasanid Empire and Christianity, State Religion in Roman Empire

196 BCE-284 CE Early Roman Empire

224-642 CE Sasanid Persian Empire

476 End of Western Roman Empire

166-40 BCE Hasmoneans (Maccabeans) Rule a Kingdom in Judea

284-640 Late Roman Empire

370-350 Central Asian Huns Invade Northern Persian and Roman Borders

530-580 Imperial Recovery in Persia and Rome

MAP 7.1 Achaemenid Persian Empire.

Cataphracts: Heavily armed and protected cavalry soldiers.

Persian Arms The Achaemenids achieved their conquests with the help of lightly armed, highly mobile mounted archers as well as heavily armored, slow-moving **cataphracts**—horsemen with protective armor consisting of iron scales sewn on leather shirts. Quilts and iron scales protected the horses. The main Persian steed was a strong, tough central Asian horse called the "Nisaean" or "Turkoman." Armored Indian elephants supplemented the cataphracts. The archers fought with composite bows and the cataphracts, with 5-foot-long, iron-tipped lances for thrusting. Saddles and stirrups had not yet been invented, and hence, the lance—requiring the mounted user to have a firm footing with which to brace himself—was still a relatively short, modest weapon. Infantry soldiers armed with bows, arrows, shields, and javelins provided support for the cavalry, complementing its tank-like thrust.

Hoplites: Greek foot soldiers fighting in closed ranks, called "phalanxes."

Early on, Persian kings supplemented their armies with heavily armored infantry recruited from among the Anatolian Greeks. These foot soldiers, called **hoplites**, fought shoulder to shoulder in ranks, called "phalanxes." They were equipped with 8-foot-long, iron-tipped thrusting spears, short iron swords, large shields held on the left forearm, helmets, and iron-scale protective armor. In close quarters, hoplite phalanxes were nearly invincible. Even in the open, however, phalanxes were difficult to crack, unless attacked by mounted archers on their right, unshielded flank.

The Persian navy comprised as many as 1,200 galleys during its peak in the fifth century BCE. The Ionian and Phoenician provinces of the Persian Empire constructed and staffed these galleys, which were long, narrow ships, approximately 100 feet long and 15 feet wide. Galleys had flat bottoms and removable masts holding sails, bronze ramming devices underneath the waterline at the bow, rowers with oars, and paddles on both sides of the stern for steering. Apart from fighting naval battles against the Greeks, the navy also explored the western Mediterranean and even unsuccessfully attempted the circumnavigation of Africa. Altogether, the Persian military was a formidable fighting machine stationed in garrisons and ports in the various provinces of the Middle East and eastern Mediterranean.

Persian Administration The Achaemenid Persian Empire, encompassing not only the Middle Eastern agrarian centers of Mesopotamia and Egypt but also those of the Indus valley, is estimated to have had some 15 million inhabitants. The kings prided themselves on having at their palace in southwestern Iran containers of water from both the Nile and the Danube, which they served at their banquets to demonstrate their vast power. (King Darius I, the Great [r. 522–486 BCE], campaigned in 514 or 513 BCE against the Scythians in Russia, across the Danube.) The enormous size of the Persian territories demanded creative assimilation of the institutions they inherited. The empire consisted of some 70 ethnic groups, hundreds of temple cults, a small Persian aristocracy, and a limited central bureaucracy. Most kings prayed to the god Ahuramazda of the Zoroastrians, but others selected other deities from the Persian pantheon. Since the Achaemenids granted considerable autonomy to their 30 provinces, many of which retained their native ruling dynasties, temples, and legal systems, a bewildering number of languages, ethnic groups, and religious pantheons coexisted in the empire.

Around 500 BCE, the empire had become integrated enough that the kings could replace indigenous rulers with their own governors from the Persian aristocracy. These provincial governors, or *satraps*, supported by Persian troops in fortresses, were powerful rulers. They administered the Persian law, to which all imperial subjects could appeal from their own legal systems. The satraps also collected tributes and taxes, with which they maintained themselves and their troops, forwarding the remainder to the kings. When called upon by the kings, the governors contributed their provincial troops to the royal army. Officially, the Achaemenid king called himself "king of kings" (*shahinshah* [SHAW-in-shaw]), that is, emperor, in order to make his elevated status clear to all princes and governors of regional and Persian aristocratic origin, as well as the populace.

The venerable, 2,500-year-old Mesopotamian administrative institution, the assembly (*pukhru* [POO-kroo]) of urban citizens (see Chapter 1), remained in place. As in Greece, the members of this assembly were landowners with estates in the villages around the cities, but their formerly unlimited powers were now restricted to judicial matters. Transplanted ethnic groups also administered themselves within their own autonomous communities. This was the case among the Jews and Egyptians in the cities of Babylon, Sippar, and Nippur. Councils of elders in these communities were responsible for distributing water and land, prescribing internal tax assessments, and settling property disputes.

The *shahinshahs* had a number of palaces in Iran and Mesopotamia, among which Persepolis [Per-SAY-pow-lis] is the best known. Here, they maintained the central administration with its treasury and archive. The language used for administrative purposes was imperial Aramaic, a special bureaucratic version of the spoken and alphabetically written Aramaic that had become the predominant language of Mesopotamia and Syria in the previous centuries. Clay tablets continued to be used as writing material, particularly in Mesopotamia; but scribes preferred parchment or papyrus scrolls, which offered them more space. A basic principle of the empire's financial administration was the hoarding of all incoming silver and gold. Trade was not yet fully monetized, and the kings minted only small amounts of coins. As elsewhere in Asia, villagers continued to pay taxes or rents in kind and local markets continued to function primarily on the basis of barter. Enormous quantities of precious metal piled up in the Persian treasuries, with no purpose yet except luxury trade and the giving of presents.

The vast size of the empire dictated that the imperial administration pay close attention to its communication networks. Thus, the Persians created their famous "royal roads," perhaps the first such highways in the world. They consisted mostly of

Persepolis. This relief from the stairs that approach the royal audience hall shows ambassadors from the various lands under the power of the "king of kings" humbly offering tribute.

regularly maintained paths connecting Persia with Anatolia and Mesopotamia as directly as possible. Governors provided the roads with distance markers, constructed inns and depots at regular intervals, and protected them through a chain of police and army posts. The roads were intended primarily for quick troop movements, although traders with carts and pack animals used them as well.

Greek City-States in the Persian Shadow

In the sixth century BCE, while Persia evolved into an empire, hundreds of city-states—cities (singular *polis*; plural *poleis*) with surrounding villages—dotted the landscape in Anatolia, Greece, and Italy. The most populous of these *poleis* were Athens and Sparta. The two competed for dominance; but neither could overcome the other, and their rivalry eventually benefited Persia in its attempt to assume power over Greece.

Oracles: Makers of predictions of the future to petitioners visiting temples situated on the no-man's-land between city-states.

Athens and Sparta   Most of the hundreds of city-states of which Greece was composed ruled themselves independently. The only common bonds, besides language, history, and culture, were a number of so-called **oracles** and the Olympic Games. Greeks went to the oracles to settle disputes or to divine their future. The Olympic Games, in the *polis* of Olympia, brought together the Greek youth for athletic competitions. Athens, with 200,000 inhabitants, and Sparta, with 140,000 inhabitants, were the largest city-states and exerted a certain dominance but ultimately accomplished little in terms of unification (see Map 7.2).

Athens is located on the small peninsula of Attica in southeastern Greece. Its limited agricultural resources forced inhabitants to specialize in the growing of cash crops, such as wine, olive oil, nuts, and dried fruits. They traded these crops, together with woolen textiles and metal goods, for grain and metals from Italy and the Black Sea region. The growing focus on trade helped in the emergence of mercantile interests among the landowning citizenry. Disputes about representation in the ruling council and chronic debt among farmers forced the first among several reforms in 594 BCE

MAP **7.2** Greek City-States in the Sixth Century BCE.

under Solon. In 508 BCE, Cleisthenes, a prominent landowner, forged an alliance between merchant landowners and smallholders to bring about further constitutional reforms, broadening the citizenry to more modest property owners and ending the arbitrary rule of self-appointed strongmen. He expanded the rights among citizens to sit on juries and participate in the legislative assembly, which was enlarged to 500 members. Proposals adopted by the assembly were to be ratified by the citizenry, and executive power was vested in boards of elected magistrates. The reforms of Solon and Cleisthenes are often cited by scholars as the first steps toward the creation of Athenian democracy in the middle of the next century.

Sparta was another major city-state of Greece and Athens' principal rival. It was located on a plain in the Peloponnesus [Pay-lop-pon-NEE-soos] Peninsula southwest of Athens. Unlike the land-poor Athens, Sparta had room to enlarge its agricultural base before eventually turning to maritime trade. Its constitutional organization preceded that of Athens by a century and, therefore, embodies more traditional traits. Citizenship was based on landownership, and Spartan citizens were entitled to stand for participation in the 30-member Council of Elders and the five-member Board of Overseers, the decisions of which were ratified by the assembly of owners of medium-sized properties. Executive power was in the hands of two hereditary kings.

Army service was of crucial importance in Sparta. At age 7, boys left home and entered military camps to train as hoplites. Until the age of 30, married soldiers were not allowed to live with their wives but received extended military leaves in order to create large families. A thoroughgoing code of male citizen discipline dominated

Sparta. Women also received rigorous physical training and were fully imbued with the Spartan military ethic: Wives or mothers seeing their men off to battle customarily handed them their shields with the parting words, "with it or on it."

The village farmers who tilled the land in Athens, Sparta, and the other Greek city-states were noncitizens of unfree status, in contrast to the free farmers in the Middle East. In Athens, they possessed basic rights and, as we have noted, were at the center of early reform efforts. In Sparta, however, the farmers, called *helots*, were the descendants of surrounding peoples conquered by Sparta during its years of expansion and tied to the land in perpetuity. One reason for Sparta's constant military preparedness was fear of rebellion among the helots; thus, magistrates regularly sent informers into the countryside to discover and eliminate suspected plotters against the citizens.

Since, in addition to villagers, women were excluded from political participation, constitutional rule benefited only small minorities in the Greek city-states. This was true even in the mid-fifth century BCE, when the final round of Athenian reforms under Pericles extended voting and office rights to all male citizens. While Athens' "golden age" of democracy was arguably the most open of the ancient world, it was still restricted to no more than one-third of the population at its height. Thus, what has been idealized by people in the modern era as a forerunner of our own institutions was in fact not very different from the urban assemblies in Mesopotamian cities or those of some of the early Indian city-states in the Ganges valley (see Chapter 3). In retrospect, Greece was thus not the only pioneer of constitutional rule: It shared this role with other societies, although each adopted rule by assemblies independently and not as a result of interaction.

Greece and Persia   Their maritime commercial wealth made the Greek city-states irresistible targets of Persian imperialism. When Athens supported a revolt of the southwest Anatolian city-states in 499–494 BCE, the Persian monarchy found its justification to wage war against the Greeks. They suppressed the revolt and organized two large-scale invasions of the Greek mainland in the following years (492–490 and 480–479 BCE). Both invasions were well planned and included vastly superior land and sea forces. Storms took their toll on these forces, however, and long supply lines further compromised Persian military efficiency. To meet the invasion, the Greek city-states on the mainland united under the joint leadership of Athens and Sparta. In two battles, on land at Marathon (490 BCE) and on the sea at Salamis (480 BCE), the united Greeks took advantage of their better knowledge of local conditions and the utility of the phalanx against larger massed forces in narrow areas and repelled both Persian invasions. Greece managed to preserve its liberty and escape Persian imperial dominance. Soon, however, the Greek world was plunged into a long and devastating internal conflict.

After the repulsion of the Persian invasions, Athenian–Spartan unity fell apart. As a substitute, Athens formed a league with as many as 200 *poleis* around the Aegean and Black Seas and for about two decades harassed the Persians in the eastern Mediterranean. When Athens diverted a portion of the league's membership contributions to the reconstruction of its Persian War–damaged citadel, the Acropolis, however, anger against this perceived self-service erupted into the Peloponnesian War (431–404 BCE). During this war, Sparta made itself the champion of liberation from what many Greek cities viewed as an Athenian empire. After depleting Athens' land forces, Sparta—with Persian financial support—built a navy, which won a brilliant victory over Athens, forcing the latter to sue for peace in 404 BCE.

Once involved again in Greek politics, the Achaemenids played their cards carefully, this time stoking fears of Spartan dominance. During yet another round of hostilities, a coalition of city-states led by Athens and backed by Persia defeated Sparta. In the King's Peace of 386 BCE, the Persians granted the Greeks autonomy, or self-rule, according to their city-state constitutions, provided they recognized Persia's overall dominance. Persia held the purse strings, employing some 50,000 Greek hoplite mercenaries who became jobless in Greece after the King's Peace. Persian imperial lordship over Greece had finally become a reality, to last for about half a century.

> **Thucydides (ca. 460–ca. 395 BCE), on the Causes of the Peloponnesian War**
>
> "The real cause I consider to be the one which was formally most kept out of sight. The growth of the power of Athens, and the alarm which this inspired in Lacedaemon [alternative name for Sparta], made war inevitable."
>
> —Thucydides. *History of the Peloponnesian War*, trans. Richard Crawley, Everyman's Library, bk. 1, chap. 1, p. 23. New York: Dutton, 1910.

Alexander's Empire and Its Successor Kingdoms

The one Greek area that remained outside Persian control was Macedonia, on the northern periphery of the Greek city-states. Although the Macedonians spoke a Greek dialect, the city-state Greeks considered them barbarians, that is, people mired in tribal customs and without an urban culture. In the middle of the 300s BCE, however, a king, Philip II (359–336 BCE), unified the country and provided it with a disciplined infantry army. He conquered the Greek city-states to the south, and his son, Alexander, continued the expansion with the conquest of Persia.

Alexander's Conquests   In 337 BCE, Philip employed his greatly enhanced military strength to declare war on the Persian Empire, in revenge for the Persian invasion of Macedonia and Greece a century earlier. He made himself the champion of Greek liberty in Asia, the "liberator" of the city-states in Anatolia. Just as Philip was getting ready to invade Anatolia, he was assassinated in a court intrigue. Philip's 20-year-old son, Alexander, took over both throne and campaign, setting off for Persia in 334 BCE. In three fiercely fought battles (334–330 BCE), Alexander outmaneuvered the Persian defenders with his highly motivated soldiers. The Persian king was the lesser strategist and tactician, but he and the Persian aristocracy resisted tenaciously. The Persian forces retreated slowly into what is today Afghanistan. Alexander occupied the Persian royal towns and confiscated the Persian treasury, including some 7,000 tons of precious metals. During a drunken revelry in the palace town of Persepolis, Alexander had the imperial palace burned down, as a final act of vengeance for the destruction of the Acropolis by the Persians.

After finishing off the Achaemenid forces in Afghanistan and occupying Bactria (modern Uzbekistan) to the northeast, Alexander invaded India. When he reached the Ganges basin, however, persistent monsoon rains and exhausted troops forced him to retreat. As he left, he appointed governors over northwest India. Under these

East Meets West. A turbaned man stands next to a Corinthian capital in the Hellenistic city of Ai-Khanoum founded in what is today northern Afghanistan—ancient Bactria—in the fourth century BCE after Alexander's conquests. Ai-Khanoum was one of the focal points of Hellenism in the East. Archaeological excavations in the 1970s revealed a flourishing city, with a Greek-style theater, a huge palace, a citadel, a gymnasium, and various temples.

governors, Greek culture entered the subcontinent and exerted a palpable influence even beyond 305 BCE when the expanding Maurya Empire conquered India (see Chapter 8). Alexander returned to the Middle East and made plans to trump the Persians by executing their unfulfilled plan to circumnavigate Africa. Before he could depart, however, a fever seized him; and within 10 days, at the age of 33, Alexander was dead (323 BCE). In the stupendously short time of just 11 years, he had turned the mighty Persian Empire into a Macedonian–Greek one (see Map 7.3).

Successor Kingdoms   Not surprisingly, this empire did not hold together. Alexander's one legitimate son was born after his father's death and had no chance to assume the throne. Alexander's generals divided the empire among themselves, founding kingdoms, among which Antigonid Greece (276–167 BCE), Ptolemaic Egypt (305–30 BCE), and Seleucid southwest Asia (305–64 BCE) were the most important. The Antigonid kingdom was the least powerful successor state, suffering

(a)

(b)

MAP **7.3** Alexander's Empire (*a*) and Hellenistic Kingdoms After the Breakup of Alexander's Empire (*b*).

from dynastic instability and frequent challenges by the Greek city-states. Only in the middle of the 200s BCE did the Antigonid kings and the city-states settle into a more or less durable compromise of corule.

Ptolemaic Egypt and Seleucid Syria, Mesopotamia, and Iran were economically more resourceful and politically more stable. The Ptolemies and Seleucids maintained substantial courts and central administrations in their capitals of Alexandria on the Mediterranean coast and Seleucia on the right bank of the Tigris in lower Mesopotamia. The kings ruled their lands through Greek-descended governors and indigenous provincial aristocrats. Some 100 new cities or quarters in existing cities with Greek settlers, some as far away as Bactria, administered themselves under their own officials, even though the kings exercised control over them. Altogether, about 1 million Greeks emigrated during the 200s BCE to the Middle East, assimilating gradually into the local population of some 20 million and imprinting their **Hellenistic** (Greek-influenced) culture on urban life. Thus, even though the Macedonian–Greek Empire failed politically almost immediately, its cultural legacy lasted for centuries, even in far-away central Asia and India.

Hellenistic: Period of Greek history from 323 BCE to 31 BCE.

Interactions Between the Persian and Roman Empires

A century after Alexander's conquests, a resurgent Persia—in the shape of Parthia—appeared on the northeastern border of the Seleucid kingdom. This resurgence coincided with Rome's imperial expansion after the unification of Italy. On the periphery of the successor kingdoms of Alexander's Macedonian–Greek Empire, both Parthia and Rome pressed against the Antigonids, Seleucids, and Ptolemies. After conquering these kingdoms, Rome and Parthia eventually came face to face in Anatolia and Syria in the early second century BCE. Neither, however, succeeded in eliminating the other, as strenuously as they tried in a long series of wars. As a result, the Middle East and the Mediterranean remained politically as divided as they had been in the previous centuries under the successor states of Alexander the Great.

Parthian Persia and Rome

Parthia was originally the name of the northeasternmost province of the Seleucid kingdom. In the 240s BCE, the tribal federation of the Parni, distant relatives of the Achaemenid Persians, migrated from the region east of the Aral Sea in central Asia to Parthia, where they defeated the Seleucid governor. The Seleucids, distracted by conflicts on their western front with Ptolemaic Egypt, were unable to prevent the Parthians from seizing provincial power. Initially, the Parthians recognized Seleucid overlordship, but they also expanded their power and in 141 BCE conquered Iran and Mesopotamia, reducing the Seleucids to a small rump kingdom in northern Syria. In 109 BCE, Mithridates II, the Great (r. ca. 123–88 BCE), formally renewed the Persian Empire in his newly founded capital Ctesiphon, today a suburb of Baghdad, by assuming the title "king of kings" and taking over the traditional Iranian pantheon of gods.

Parthian Diplomacy Parthian Persia was a major power, in large part because of its diplomacy. In 115, Wudi [Woo-DEE] (r. ca. 140–87 BCE), the emperor of Han China, sent a diplomatic mission to Mithridates II, to explore the possibilities of an alliance as well as trade. The mission was part of Wudi's efforts, lasting nearly a quarter of a century, to secure his northern border against Turkic nomadic invaders and find allies among the nomads in Bactria across the Pamir mountains in the northwest of China. Bactria, consisting of the fertile Ferghana [Fer-GAH-nah] valley plain and surrounding mountain chains, had been governed previously by the Achaemenid Persians, Alexander, and Greek generals but had become independent after the end of the Seleucids.

When the first Chinese missions arrived in the valley, many nomads were in the process of settling into agricultural villages and displayed less desire for a military alliance than for trade. The missions then moved westward, where they encountered a militarily strong power in Parthian Persia. No alliance between Persia and China came to pass, however. Instead, this first diplomatic contact opened up the Silk Road, which, for many centuries to come, was the main central Asian trade route over which Chinese silk was exchanged for Nisaean horses. For the Chinese, accustomed to the much smaller Mongolian horses, the Nisaeans were highly desirable prestige objects (see Chapter 9).

At the other end of this empire, on the upper Euphrates River, the Persians established first contacts with Rome, which in 103 BCE had occupied Cilicia, in southeastern Anatolia, and thereby had become Parthian Persia's western neighbor. In a diplomatic meeting, in which the envoy of the small, Persian-descended principality of Pontus in northern Anatolia participated as well, the three sides exchanged vows of friendship. The meeting, however, did not end on a positive note. The Roman governor seated himself in the middle and thereby sought to pull rank on the other two envoys, causing an infuriated Mithridates II to have his ambassador executed for allowing the Roman envoy to claim superiority. Not surprisingly, Rome and Persia soon came to blows.

Roman Republican Origins   The western Mediterranean, adapting to agriculture around 3000 BCE and to the Iron Age after 1000 BCE, became part of the Middle Eastern and eastern Mediterranean agrarian centers in the course of the first millennium BCE. Phoenicians from the eastern Mediterranean established ports along the northern shores of Africa, in Spain, and on the islands of Sicily and Sardinia, attracted by the prospects of rich mineral resources. Their principal port at the entrance to the western Mediterranean, in today's Tunisia, was Carthage. Later on, Greeks established city-states in southern Italy and Sicily. In north-central Italy was the kingdom of the Etruscans, a local people assumed in recent scholarship to be linguistically related to the Hungarians and settled in Italy since ca. 2000 BCE. The kingdom included Rome, founded around 1000 BCE.

Republic: State without a royal dynasty and with an elected executive.

Subsequently, around 500 BCE, the Romans made themselves independent and overthrew their kings. They created a **republic** (from Latin *res publica*, "public matter"), that is, a state without a king, electing leaders and forming a constitutional government. The assembly of the founding tribes, called "Comitia Centuriata," voting in blocks of 100, elected a variety of magistrates, among whom were two executive officers, called "consuls." General assemblies, such as the Senate of aristocratic Romans and later, in addition, the council of commoners, assisted the consuls in their decisions. Around 450 BCE, the Romans adopted the Twelve Tablets, a set of laws covering a variety of legal matters, such as procedure, property, inheritance, constitution, due process, family, and crime. At the same time, the Senate and the council of commoners joined in the legislative process, and by 287 BCE they possessed equal powers. A chief priest was responsible for administering the cult of the patron god, Jupiter, and fixing the calendar. Later on, the Romans sacrificed to hundreds of gods and their polytheistic religious practices acquired a close resemblance to those of the Greeks and Persians. Indeed, the chief gods in the Roman pantheon were taken directly from the Greeks.

Expansion of the Republic In the 300s BCE, when Rome began to unify the peninsula, it organized its citizen army more formally into legions. The heavily armed infantry of **legionaries**, forming the center of each legion, consisted of landed citizens able to pay for their swords, javelins, helmets, shields, and scale armor. Wealthy Romans also manned the light and heavy cavalry, including cataphracts, while small landholders made up the light infantry of skirmishers. With the help of these legionaries, Rome unified Italy and in three wars (246–164 BCE) conquered its strongest rival, Carthage, across the Mediterranean in what is today Tunisia.

Around 200 BCE, during the second war when Carthage was still relatively strong, the North African city-state sought to protect itself against Rome through an alliance with the kingdom of Antigonid Greece. In a first expansion east, the Romans defeated the Antigonids and, in 196 BCE, issued the Isthmus Declaration, according to which the Greeks of Greece, Anatolia, and farther east were to be "free" of Antigonid overlordship and governed by their own laws. In Roman eyes, the Greek cities were now clients. When the Greeks resented this restriction of their laws and rebelled, in the middle of the second century BCE, they were ruthlessly repressed by the Romans, eventually reducing Greece to provincial status. The Isthmus Declaration was Rome's decisive step toward expanding eastward and becoming an empire. It continued its republican institutions for another two centuries and never formally abolished them. Historians usually date the beginning of the Roman Empire to 27 BCE, when the Senate bestowed the title "Augustus" on Octavian; but by that time Rome had been an empire for 200 years in all but name.

In the wake of the imperial expansion of Rome to North Africa, Greece, and Anatolia during the second and first centuries BCE, a new ruling class of wealthy landowners emerged. These consisted of Italian aristocrats who had appropriated the land of smallholders absent for extended periods during their military service as legionaries, turning these lands into large estates called **latifundia**. Ruling-class members also acquired leases of conquered lands overseas, where they established latifundia with enslaved war captives who grew cash crops. Discharged legionaries and dispossessed farmers crowded Rome, while rebellious slaves on latifundia in southern Italy and Sicily rose in massive revolts. The most dangerous revolt was that of Spartacus in 73–71 BCE. Spartacus was an army deserter from Thrace who had been recaptured, enslaved, and trained as a gladiator. The sources describe Spartacus as a skillful tactician who devastated latifundia throughout Italy and held the Roman army in check for 3 years before it succeeded in defeating him.

Efforts by a few social reformers at improving the lot of the poor through food subsidies, land reforms, and public work projects failed against the fierce resistance

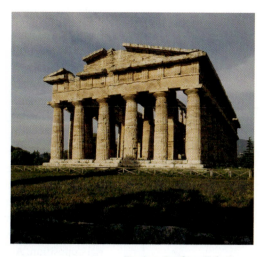

Paestum, Southern Italy. By the sixth century BCE, Greek city-states were flourishing across southern Italy and Sicily, including Paestum, which has some of the best preserved temples outside of Greece, including the Temple of Hera shown here.

Legionaries: Roman foot soldiers fighting in closed ranks.

Latifundia: Large, ruling class–owned estates with tenant farmers or slaves.

of the landowners who controlled the Senate. About the only reform that succeeded was that of Marius, who was senator from 107 to 85 BCE and a successful general in North Africa. He opened the army ranks to the landless, equipped them with arms, and enlisted them for up to 20 years of service. Upon retirement, soldiers received plots of land in conquered provinces. This reform greatly benefited imperial expansion as well as Romanizing conquered provinces through settled veterans. But it also encouraged generals to use the now fully professionalized army for their own ambitions, independent from the Senate.

In the middle of the first century BCE, three ambitious generals were vying for control of the empire. One of them was Julius Caesar (r. 60–44 BCE), from a prominent family of administrators and a successful conqueror of northwestern Europe. Recently returned from triumphant conquests in Gaul (modern France), he defeated his two rivals. When he then assumed several offices traditionally held by separate magistrates, including the title "dictator for life," he provoked much senatorial opposition. An assassin, Marcus Junius Brutus, eventually struck Caesar down; but the Senate failed to regain control over the state's offices. A new "triumvirate" of generals assumed power.

The triumvirate did not last. Civil war broke out, and the ultimate victor was Octavian (r. 31 BCE–14 CE), a distant younger relative of Caesar whose career the latter had furthered. More subtle than Caesar, Octavian gradually created a new constitutional order with himself as leader, always maintaining the pretense of being merely the executive officer of the Senate. In practice he possessed unlimited powers under the title of Augustus ("the Revered One"), which the Senate bestowed on him in 27 BCE and which became his name. Historians officially consider this date as the end of the republican institutions and the beginning of the Roman Empire.

The Augustan Age   To consolidate his power, Augustus limited imperial expansion in the north to France and Germany, west of the rivers Rhine and Danube. He ordered the construction of a wall, called *limes*, linking the two rivers, to keep the Germanic tribes on the other side at bay. In the east, a series of wars with the Persian Parthian Empire (56 BCE–1 CE) over the control of Armenia, Upper Mesopotamia, and Syria ended inconclusively. Egypt, Syria, and Judea came under direct Roman rule, Armenia became a Roman client state, Upper Mesopotamia east of the Euphrates remained Parthian, and peace reigned between Rome and Parthia for two generations. At this time, the Roman Empire had about 55 million inhabitants (see Map 7.4). It was considerably more populous than its Middle Eastern competitor, Parthia, with 10 million, but less so than its territorially smaller contemporary, Han China (202 BCE–220 CE), with 58 million. In addition, the Roman and Parthian Empires were geographically far less compact and had more vulnerable borders than China, disadvantages which hampered political cohesion.

All 44 Roman provinces outside Italy had to pay heavy poll and agricultural taxes in kind and silver coins, primarily to support a standing army, which Augustus reduced by half compared to the earlier civil war armies. Legionaries came from not only Italy but also Gaul and Hispania (modern France and the Iberian Peninsula). In addition, tax money went into the building and upkeep of roads and ports, as well as wheat subsidies and circuses for the inhabitants of Rome and other large cities. In contrast to the huge military, the number of civilian Roman

MAP **7.4** Roman Empire at the Time of Augustus.

administrators in the provinces was small. The Roman Peace (*pax romana*) clearly rested more on the projection of military might than on a civilian administration, as in Han China.

The Roman Peace on the borders was rarely disrupted during the first two centuries following Augustus. Not surprisingly, the disruptions that did occur were on the border with Parthian Persia. Here, the flashpoint was the kingdom of Armenia, which both Parthia and Rome coveted as a client state. Compromise solutions collapsed twice (54–63 CE and 112–117 CE). On the second occasion, Rome came close to destroying Parthia when it succeeded in occupying Mesopotamia for a short time. The subsequent puppet kingdom, however, was unable to maintain itself, and the Parthians returned to independence.

The Sasanid Persian and Late Roman Empires

After renewing its independence, Parthia challenged Rome twice (161–166 CE and 193–198 CE). It lost both times and had to give up the province of Upper Mesopotamia and much of its economic wealth to pay tributes. Divisions in the ruling class of the Parthians began to appear. In the early 200s, the priestly family of a temple to

Anahita, the goddess of water and fertility in the Iranian pantheon in Fars, assumed provincial leadership functions in opposition to the dynasty. Ardashir, a descendant of this priestly family, finally ended Parthian rule in 224 CE and declared himself king of kings of the Sasanid Persian Empire (224–642 CE).

Roman Crisis   Just as Persian imperial power was rejuvenated through a new dynasty, the Roman Empire fell into a political and economic crisis, which lasted half a century (234–285 CE) and profoundly changed its organization. As in all empires, the balance between war booty, tax revenue, and military expenditures was always precarious. Booty acquired in the Parthian wars kept the empire afloat until the 220s, but thereafter emperors had to dilute the silver money paid to the legionaries with cheaper metals. The ensuing inflation angered the soldiers, who supported any claimant to the imperial throne promising higher wages. Some two dozen emperors followed each other in rapid succession on the throne, and for a while the empire even fragmented into three pieces.

In addition to the internal conflicts, Germanic tribes broke through the northern defenses and during 260–276 CE pillaged as far as northern Italy. At the same time, both Rome and Persia were afflicted by what historians of science assume was an outbreak of mass disease along the trade routes in 251–266 CE. It appears that this was among the earliest manifestations of measles in world history, when humans did not yet possess high levels of immunity, foreshadowing the plague of 541 (see Patterns Up Close). The number of deaths was estimated in the hundreds of thousands. At the end of the 200s it appeared as if Rome was at its end.

Emperor Diocletian (r. 285–305 CE), however, salvaged the empire. He divided it into an eastern and a western half, doubled the number of provinces and civil administrators, and created a separate set of military districts. In addition, he ended Italy's tax exemption, regularized tax collection, increased the number of legions by one-third, and created a mobile field army under his command. Civil peace returned to the empire, albeit at the price of an increased militarization.

Adoption of Monotheism   Since the early Sasanids had to consolidate their rule in a large territory, stretching from Upper Mesopotamia to Uzbekistan and northwestern India, they could not exploit the Roman crisis to the fullest. Although they led lightning invasions into Roman territories in Syria and Anatolia, acquired immense booty, received large indemnity payments, and even captured the Roman emperor Valerian in battle in 260 CE, the Romans always in the end regained control over Armenia and Upper Mesopotamia. Diocletian, after his reforms, was even able to push the border eastward to the Tigris River.

In the first half of the 300s, while the inconclusive wars between the two imperial rivals of Rome and Persia continued, both empires took first, halting steps toward a profound internal transformation, that is, a shift away from polytheism and toward the elevation of monotheism to the status of state religion. During the previous polytheist millennia in the Middle East and the Mediterranean, kings and emperors had supported imperial temple priesthoods in their capitals for the justification of their rule. Temples devoted to many other deities existed in their realms, and rulers did not seek their elimination. But when the Romans and Persians suffered their severe internal crises—the former nearly falling apart and the latter changing dynasties—rulers became aware of the need for a unifying single religious bond.

At the beginning of the reign of Emperor Constantine I, the Great (r. 306–337 CE), Christianity's adherents numbered about 10 percent of the Roman population. Christianity had begun three centuries earlier with the preaching of Jesus of Nazareth and Paul of Tarsus. Its growth, despite periodic persecutions, was impressive enough for Constantine to take a first step toward making Christianity the state religion by sponsoring the Nicene Creed in 325 CE as the common doctrinal platform among Christians, as well as granting tax privileges and jurisdictional powers to the Christian Church. Baptized shortly before his death, Constantine can be considered the first Christian Roman emperor.

In Persia, under the sponsorship of Shapur II (r. ca. 307–379), Zoroastrian priests redacted the Avesta, the holy scripture of Zoroastrianism, in its final, written form of Pahlavi Persian. In Rome, several pagan emperors succeeded Constantine, and it was only in 380 that Christianity became the sole state religion. Persia, with its large Jewish and Christian minorities in Mesopotamia, went the different route of making Zoroastrianism the preferential religion in ca. 350, with Christianity and Judaism being accorded a protected status. Thus, both empires sought to strengthen internal unity through the adoption of a single monotheistic faith.

A Description of Constantine

"And now, all rising at the signal which indicated the emperor's entrance, at last he himself proceeded through the midst of the assembly, like some heavenly messenger of God, clothed in raiment which glittered as it were with rays of light, reflecting the glowing radiance of a purple robe, and adorned with the brilliant splendor of gold and precious stones. Such was the external appearance of his person; and with regard to his mind, it was evident that he was distinguished by piety and godly fear. This was indicated by his downcast eyes, the blush on his countenance, and his gait. . . . As soon as he had advanced to the upper end of the seats, at first he remained standing, and when a low chair of wrought gold had been set for him, he waited until the bishops had beckoned to him, and then sat down, and after him the whole assembly did the same."

—Eusebius. *The Life of the Blessed Constantine: From AD 306 to AD 337.* Christian Roman Empire Series, vol. 18, bk. 3, chap. 10. London: Samuel Bagster and Sons, 1845.

Nomadic Invasions The adoption of Christianity and Zoroastrianism to strengthen the cohesion of the Roman and Sasanid Empires came just in time, before the great migration of peoples across Eurasia caused severe disruptions. The migration began in the mid-300s CE when the western branch of the Huns—horse- and sheep-breeding nomads in the steppes between Mongolia north of China and central Asia east of the Ural Mountains—moved westward and southward on the Silk Road. As in the case of the previous migrations out of central Asia in the second millennium BCE, the reasons that the western Huns packed up and journeyed westward remain unclear. One possible factor was the success of the Chinese in driving away nomadic invaders from their Great Wall in the north, resulting in a chain reaction of migrations among neighboring tribes, including the Huns. During their journey westward, the Huns grew into a large federation of nomads, farmers, and town dwellers of mixed ethnic and linguistic composition (Huns, Turks, Mongols, and Iranians).

As the Huns entered the Russian plains, they encountered local Germanic farming populations, whom they defeated. Other Germanic peoples, such as the Visigoths, fled from the Huns and negotiated their entry into the Roman Empire. In the early 400s CE, both Hunnish and Germanic peoples overcame the defenses of the Romans, poured into the western half of the Roman Empire, and eventually ended the western line of emperors, an event remembered as the fall of Rome in 476 CE (see Map 7.5).

Patterns Up Close | The Plague of Justinian

At the end of the 500s, neither the Roman nor the Sasanid Empire was as populous and wealthy as before the nomadic invasions from the north. For the first time, in 541 CE, a mass epidemic, the bubonic plague, hit the world, breaking out first in the Roman Empire and traveling thereafter to Persia and, in cycles of 15 years, by the 600s CE as far as China and England. This plague, recorded as the "Plague of Justinian"—it sickened the emperor himself for several weeks—dramatically reduced population levels everywhere. Scholars have identified three endemic hearths for the bubonic plague bacillus in the world: today's Burma, central Asia, and the lakes region of East Africa. The Plague of Justinian originated either in East Africa or in Burma. It reached the Mediterranean through black rats traveling in ships on the Indian Ocean and Red Sea. The plague's first outbreak was recorded in the Nile delta, and from there it spread east and west along the trade routes, reducing population levels by one-quarter or more.

Portrait of Justinian.

Historians know now that for the plague to spread from fleas and rodents, such as rats, in one of its endemic regions and become a pandemic the region's average temperatures must have declined. Fleas are most active, and most likely to jump from rats to humans, at 59–68 degrees Fahrenheit. Such a temperature decline might have occurred just a few years prior to 541 CE, with the outbreak of the volcano Krakatau in Indonesia in 535 CE, the ashes of which obscured the sun for a number of years around the globe, as we know from contemporary reports. Although the climate returned to normal a few years later, once population centers were infested with the bacillus, recurrent cycles of the plague every decade or two until well into the 700s CE prevented population levels from recovering.

Observers in various cities of the Roman Empire, some afflicted by the plague themselves, have left us vivid accounts. People infected by the plague bacillus typically developed a high fever, followed by swelling of the lymph nodes in the groin, the armpits, and the neck (indicative of the body fighting the fever). In great pain and delirious from fever, most people died quickly after a few days. None of the existing and very detailed handbooks of medicine from this time had anything to say about this mass disease from outside the Middle East and Mediterranean. Although the concept of quarantine was familiar and hospitals kept sick people in isolation, there was no known medicine. Survivors tried folk remedies, to no avail. Many clerical observers at the time were convinced that sinfulness was what had attracted God's wrath. For us modern world-historical observers, the most important lesson of

MAP **7.5** **The Plague of Justinian.**

the Plague of Justinian is the evidence it provides of how interconnected the various parts of Eurasia and Africa were toward the middle of the 500s CE.

The Plague of Justinian shows us patterns of climate and disease behind the patterns of culture discussed in this book. Climate and disease followed their own natural patterns in world history, patterns different from those of the polytheistic and monotheistic city-states, kingdoms, and empires. Climates changed and epidemic plagues struck according to changing tilts in the earth's rotational axis vis-à-vis the sun, more or less intense sunbursts, volcanic eruptions, and warmer/wetter and colder/drier weather conditions. By killing up to one-third of the population and keeping population levels low for at least a century, the Plague of Justinian severely impacted city-state, kingdom, and empire patterns. The reduced population resulted in increased labor costs and food shortages; it also made survivors wealthier, to name only a few initial consequences. On the other hand, since the plagues were equal-opportunity killers, they hit states and societies with the same ferocity. Justinian's plague favored neither Rome nor Persia and, thus, had more quantitative than lasting qualitative effects on the process of world history.

Questions

- What does Justinian's plague tell us about the interconnectedness of Afro-Eurasia at this time?

- How does understanding the impact of disease and climate on human societies add a new dimension to the patterns of world history?

The emperors in the eastern half of the empire withstood the migrants' threat, in part because of Constantinople's strategic location. This city, made the capital by Constantine in 330 CE on the site of an older urban foundation, was relatively close to the endangered northern and eastern borders, allowing for a more rapid deployment of troops than was possible from faraway Rome. The Sasanids initially repelled an attack by another branch of the Huns on their central Asian border in the early 400s CE but succumbed to renewed invasions in 483–485 and were forced to pay tribute for a number of years. A third branch of Huns invaded the Gupta Empire of India toward the end of the 400s CE. In the mid-500s the Sasanids eventually recovered from the invasions, but the Guptas were reduced to small remnants. Further compounding matters, plague struck the Middle East and Europe in 541 BCE (see "Patterns Up Close" on pp. 224–225).

Roman and Persian Recovery   The architect of reconstruction of the Roman Empire was Justinian I, the Great (r. 527–565 CE). Although not a military campaigner himself, Justinian employed talented generals who reconquered most shores of the western Mediterranean from the Germanic invaders, including all of Italy. As the empire stabilized, prosperity returned. With improved tax revenues,

MAP **7.6** Nomadic Invasions and Migrations into the Roman Empire, 375–450 CE.

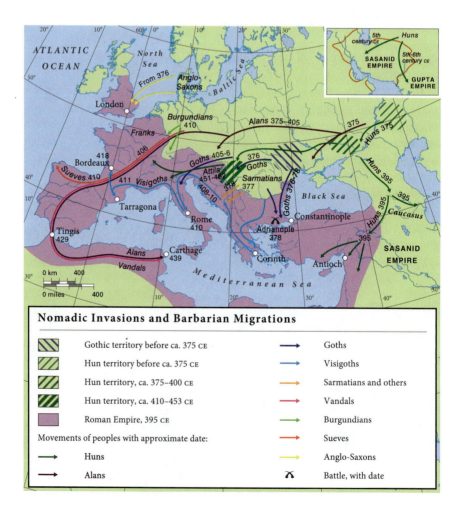

Nomadic Invasions and Barbarian Migrations

Gothic territory before ca. 375 CE	→	Goths
Hun territory before ca. 375 CE	→	Visigoths
Hun territory, ca. 375–400 CE	→	Sarmatians and others
Hun territory, ca. 410–453 CE	→	Vandals
Roman Empire, 395 CE	→	Burgundians
Movements of peoples with approximate date:	→	Sueves
→ Huns	→	Anglo-Saxons
→ Alans	✗	Battle, with date

Justinian was able to finance reform measures. The best known of these reforms was the reorganization of the legal system, based on the codification of the huge body of Roman law that had grown from the initial Twelve Tablets in republican Rome. In addition to the *Codex Justinianus* and *Digests*, he issued an instructional textbook, the *Institutions*, used by law students for centuries after Justinian's death. Originally written in Latin, Justinian's *Codex* was translated later into Greek and became the legal foundation for the Roman Empire's successor, the Byzantine Empire (640–1453 CE), as well as the Islamic empire of the Abbasids (750–1258 CE).

In Persia, it was Khosrow I (r. 531–579) who rebuilt the Sasanid Empire (see Map 7.7). He began his rule in the aftermath of a civil war that pitted Mazdak, a renegade Zoroastrian priest and social reformer, and the dynasty against the Zoroastrian priesthood and the ruling class. In this war, the dynasty confiscated landed estates from the ruling class, opened the latter's granaries to the poor, and distributed its lands to small military landowners (*dihqans*). Khosrow, scion of the dynasty but siding with the ruling class, seized power and had Mazdak executed, ending the social reforms. But he maintained the military reforms in favor of the *dihqans*, thereby distancing himself from the traditional ruling class. After a census of the population, which allowed him to raise taxes and hire bureaucrats, he greatly expanded the central administration at the expense of the ruling class.

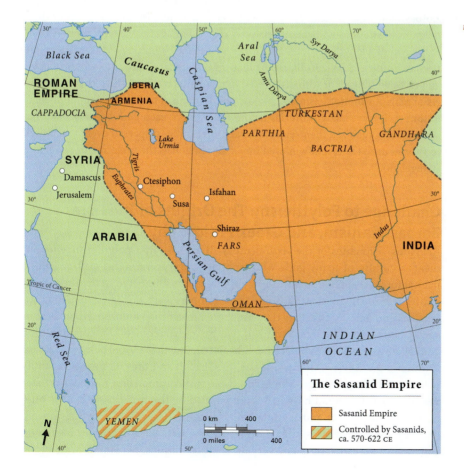

MAP **7.7** The Sasanid Empire.

Like Justinian, Khosrow also pursued military expansion. Acceding to pleas from the Armenians after a revolt against Justinian in 530 CE, Khosrow reopened hostilities against the Romans. Initially, his armies broke through to the Mediterranean and returned with rich loot, but the campaign stalled and the war once more ended in 577 CE with a draw. The Romans agreed to pay a tribute, and Khosrow returned the conquered territories. In the north, Khosrow defeated European and Turkic tribes, expanding the border eastward to Turkistan. A plea from the king of Yemen in southwestern Arabia to aid him in his efforts to repel a Roman-backed Ethiopian invasion brought Khosrow's fleet to southern Arabia in 575–577 CE. On land, Arab vassal kings established Persian control over much of the rest of Arabia. In contrast to Rome, the reach of Persia was much expanded at the end of the sixth century.

Adaptations to Monotheism and Monism in the Middle East

Although demographically weakened by plague, Rome and Sasanid Persia were comparatively strong unitary empires at the end of the 500s CE. Both had regained territories lost to the Asian tribal migrations two centuries earlier and were religiously unified through the adoption of the monotheisms of Christianity and Zoroastrianism as obligatory or preferential state religions. The adoption of these religions, however, had been of relatively recent vintage, as we have seen. It came at the end of a lengthy process that originated at the beginning of the Achaemenid Persian Empire (550–330 BCE). At that time, visionaries arose to whom a single god revealed himself or who discovered fundamental truths. At first, these visionaries of religious monotheism and philosophical monism had only small numbers of followers. It took many centuries before followers of each faith became more numerous and organized themselves in local communities dispersed over the empires' territories until the creeds achieved imperial sanction as the preferred or obligatory state religion.

Challenge to Polytheism: The Origins of Judaism, Zoroastrianism, and Greek Philosophy

Religious visionaries of the sixth century BCE arose in a polytheistic environment, a culture of many gods who embodied overpowering as well as benign natural forces and phenomena. In Egypt these gods numbered in the thousands; in Mesopotamia, Greece, and Rome their numbers were smaller; and among the Persians and ancient Israelites they numbered fewer than a dozen. Regardless of specific numbers, all polytheisms had two basic characteristics in common: The gods all descended from something difficult to name that existed prior to creation (Nothing, the Abyss, Darkness, Waste, or Chaos), and they all formed a family with a common genealogy. Mindful of these two commonalities, sooner or later priests or scribes would have had to be puzzled by the realization that the oneness of the beginning and the totality of all deities in evolved polytheism were logically the same, that is, they both formed unities. But historically, beginning and totality were obviously two very different conditions. Becoming aware of the contradiction between logic and history was at the root of the visionaries breaking away from polytheism and seeking **transcendence**.

Judaism Remarkably, the realization that logic and history were contradictory occurred more or less simultaneously during the 600s BCE in Mesopotamia, Iran, and Anatolia. The historically most influential case was that of an anonymous Jewish visionary, whom scholars dubbed "Deutero-Isaiah" or "Second Isaiah" (fl. ca. 560 BCE) in Mesopotamia. After their deportation by the Neo-Babylonians from Palestine (597–582 BCE), as we saw in Chapter 2, a majority of Israelites lived in Babylonian exile, scattered over areas of Upper and Lower Mesopotamia as well as western Iran and earning their livelihood as scribes, craftspeople, and soldiers. After the establishment of the Achaemenid Persian Empire, these scribes began to compile their Israelite religious traditions from Palestine into larger collections of writings. They became the founders of what is called today "Judaism" and one of them, Deutero-Isaiah, was the first to declare Yahweh [YA-ha-way], or God, to be the only god of the Jews.

In Deutero-Isaiah's words, there are no gods but Yahweh: "Thus says the Lord the king of Israel, and his redeemer the Lord of hosts; I am the first, and I am the last; and beside me there is no other god" (Is. 44:6–8). Yahweh is completely distinct from the traditional gods of polytheism. Yahweh is invisible and cannot be represented by visible images: "Verily you are a God who hides himself, O God of Israel, the Savior" (Is. 45:15). God in Deutero-Isaiah is the single, invisible creator and sustainer of the world. He is beyond our bodily and introspective senses: He is transcendent—he is a conceptual reality beyond the empirical reality of this world.

Some of Deutero-Isaiah's followers inserted revisions in the corpus of early scriptures that the Jews had brought with them into Babylonian exile to emphasize Yahweh's transcendence, particularly in the book of Genesis dealing with creation. (A new element they also introduced in Genesis was the 7-day calendar, an innovation which is today recognized everywhere.) Other followers petitioned the Persian king to allow them to leave for Jerusalem and restore the temple destroyed by the Neo-Babylonians. The Persian king issued the permit in 538 BCE, and a small but determined group of monotheists returned to Jerusalem to construct the Second Temple (completed in 515 BCE). A

Transcendence: A state of being or existence above and beyond the limits of material experience.

When Gods Were Born

Rejoice, daughters of Zeus, and give me a lovely song;
celebrate the holy family of the ever-existing immortals,
who were born of Earth and starry Heaven,
and of dark Night, those whom salty Pontos nourished.
Tell how at first the gods and the earth came into being,
and the rivers and infinite sea, raging with waves,
and the shining stars and wide Heaven up there,
and those who were generated from them, the gods who provide,
and how they divided their resources and how they distributed their honors,
and also how in the beginning they got hold of Olympos of many folds.
Tell me these things, Muses who have Olympian dwellings,
from the beginning, and say what came first of these things.
Surely first of all Choas (Chasm) came into being, and then
Gaia (Earth) of wide bosom, the always-safe sitting place of all
the immortals who hold the peak of snowy Olympos,
and dim Tartaros (Underworld), at the bottom of the earth of wise path,
and Eros (Love), who is fairest among the immortal gods.

—from Hesiod, Theogeny, translated by Carolina Lopez-Ruiz. *When the Gods Were Born: Greek Cosmogonies and the Near East*, 50–51. Cambridge: Harvard University Press, 2010.

new priesthood took up residence in the Temple and, on the basis of new rituals and laws, administered the emerging monotheistic faith of Judaism.

Zoroastrianism   Zoroastrians attribute their origin to Zoroaster (also called Zarathushtra), who, like Moses of the Israelites, is supposed to have lived around 1200 BCE, long before the rise of monotheism. The earliest recorded references to Zoroaster's teachings, however, date only to the rise of the Achaemenid Persian Empire in 550 BCE. These teachings were handed down orally by a priestly class, the magi, until the mid-300s CE, when the Sasanid Persian kings ordered that the Zoroastrian scriptural canon be written down. The main scripture is the Avesta, a body of liturgical texts which the magi used in their religious ceremonies.

The earliest texts form the section called "Yasht" in the Avesta. Zamyad Yasht 19, or "Hymn to the Earth," speaks of the glories of Ahuramazda (God), to whom the priests are bringing sacrifices. The last of his glories, bestowed on humankind at the end of history, is that of the savior (Avestan *saoshyant*):

> He will restore the world "which will [thenceforth] never grow old and never die, never decaying and never rotting, ever living and ever increasing." The end will be a time "when the dead will rise, when life and immortality will come" and "when the creation will grow deathless."   Yasht 15:89–90

Other sections of the Avesta describe in considerable detail an additional period of time just prior to the arrival of the savior, a time of trial and tribulation with horrible calamities and devastations, later called the "apocalypse" (Greek *apocalypsis*, revelation). Both themes—Savior or Messiah and apocalypse—are trademarks of Zoroastrian monotheism. In later centuries they became central in Judaism, Christianity, and Islam. They replaced the polytheistic notion of a shadowy afterlife in the underworld with salvation by the righteous in God's transcendent kingdom.

Unfortunately, the extant sources do not present a clear picture of the evolution of Zoroastrian monotheism after the 500s BCE. It appears, however, that under the Parthians the magi introduced traditional Iranian and Anatolian cults of fire,

Zoroastrian Fire Temple. Consisting of a cube with a superimposed dome, this Zoroastrian temple, one of the best preserved, is located outside Baku, in present-day Azerbaijan. Zoroastrianism was prevalent in the Caucasus region until the arrival of Christianity and Islam.

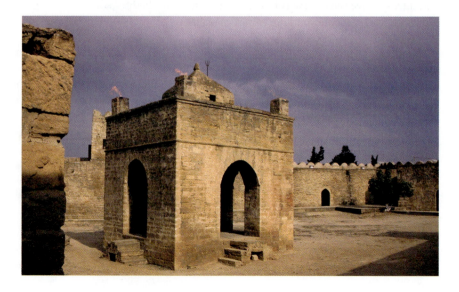

maintained in fire temples, into Zoroastrianism. Similarly, they adopted customs of exposing the dead on rooftops to vultures before burying the bones cleansed of mortal flesh in graves. With the advent of the Sasanids, the magis wrote down the scriptures, outlined the basic doctrines of Zoroastrianism, battled heresies, and supported the building of fire temples across Persia. How far the fire temples evolved into congregational places for priests and laity, however, similar to Jewish synagogues, Christian churches, or Greek philosophical schools, is not known from the available sources.

Greek Philosophy   While the author of Deutero-Isaiah and the Zoroastrian reformers of the 500s BCE are unknown to us today, the first Greek philosophers are known by name: Thales, Heraclitus, and, especially, Thales' pupil, Anaximander, who lived during the first half of the 500s in the city of Miletus on the Anatolian coast. In contrast to Judaism and Zoroastrianism, Anaximander formulated the impersonal, or *monist*, "principle of the infinite" (*apeiron*) as the invisible cause underlying the world (*kosmos*). A lively debate over principles ensued after Anaximander and his successors, also mostly from Anatolia, proposed several other cosmic principles. This debate became the basis for the rise of the mathematical and physical sciences in the subsequent centuries.

The Athenian Plato (ca. 427–347 BCE) was the first systematic thinker who extended the debate from principles in nature to a principle common to all areas of reality, such as politics, ethics, and the arts, calling it Being (*on*, originally coined by his predecessor Parmenides, fl. fifth century BCE). In his thinking, called "philosophy," meaning love of wisdom, and laid out in such works as *Phaedo, Symposium, The Republic, Timaeus, Parmenides*, and *Laws*, Being is embodied in the three transcendent forms (*eidai*) of Truth, Justice, and Beauty. These forms, so Plato argued, represent objective standards against which all earthly assertions about truth, justice, and beauty in daily life are to be measured. Anaximander's monism thus formed the stem from which two major branches, science and philosophy, sprouted.

The Break from Polytheism to Monotheism   The common thread linking the three visions of transcendence is that they all involve transcendent symbols, such as God or Being, which can only be thought but not experienced. By contrast, polytheists both thought of the gods as immortal persons requiring sacrifices and experienced them through the forces of nature. For the Greek, Zoroastrian, and Jewish visionaries, reality consisted of two separate halves, the one that can be comprehended only through abstract thought and the other that can be comprehended concretely by being sensed. Polytheist reality is undivided, with gods and corresponding natural phenomena conjoined. Given this contrast, it is not surprising that monotheism was incompatible with polytheism. Deutero-Isaiah expressed this incompatibility explicitly; in Greek philosophy and Zoroastrianism it was more implicit. Nevertheless, in the long run, polytheism disappeared from the Middle East and Mediterranean, ceding its long reign to monotheism and subsequent religious civilizations.

Toward Religious Communities and Philosophical Schools

The visionaries were founders of small religious communities and philosophical schools amid an initially continuing polytheism in the Greek city-states and the

Persian Empire, both in the Iranian–Mesopotamian imperial center and the Jewish province of Palestine. The small Jewish community that built the Second Temple in Jerusalem grew more rapidly than the Zoroastrian fire temple communities and Greek philosophical schools and led the way to monotheism. It furthermore spawned a Jewish reform movement, Christianity, which in turn changed the Roman Empire from polytheism to monotheism (see Map 7.8).

Judaism in Palestine   The Achaemenid Persian kings allowed the Jews, who had moved from Mesopotamia to Palestine and had founded the Second Temple in Jerusalem, a large degree of autonomy. Under their successors, the Ptolemaic and Seleucid kings in Alexander the Great's successor states, this autonomy declined substantially. These kings introduced Greek-Hellenistic institutions and culture into Palestine, forcing the Jews to allow the *gymnasium* (the basic school which included Olympic sports exercises in the nude) as well as polytheism and philosophy in their midst. A majority resisted the introduction of the gymnasium and Zeus into the temple with fierce and eventually successful rebellions. As a result, the Jews established the autonomous Hasmonean (also called "Maccabean") kingdom (140–37 BCE), which sought to limit the Hellenization of society.

In spite of all Hasmonean attempts to keep Judaism pure, educated Jews learned Greek and read the writings of the Greek philosophers, especially the so-called Cynics who advocated the virtues of natural simplicity far removed from power, wealth, and fame. Scribes translated Jewish scriptures into Greek, and in the second half of the 200s BCE prayer houses, called "**synagogues**," emerged in cities and towns for the study of the scriptures and of the new Jewish law that had evolved since the foundation of the Second Temple. The monotheism of Yahweh continued to be exclusively administered by priests. But preachers in the synagogues, called "pharisees," made this monotheism an increasingly popular faith among ordinary Jews.

In the first century BCE, the Romans and Persian Parthians replaced the Seleucids and the Herodians replaced the Hasmoneans in Palestine. The Jews interacted not only with the culture of Hellenism but also with the culture of the Romans, their new overlords, and the Parthian Persians, their new neighbors to the east. Many Jews adapted to the Roman philosophical school of the Stoics (who, like the Cynics, advocated an ethics in harmony with the laws of nature) and to the Persian Zoroastrian-inspired apocalypse, which predicted God's final war against evil (that is, foreign domination by Rome), the resurrection of the dead, the day of judgment, and salvation in the heavenly kingdom. Elements of philosophy and the apocalypse, coming together in the teachings of the pharisees in the synagogues, found

---

Aristotle, Plato's Student, on the Earliest Philosophers

"Well, of the first philosophers the majority thought that the causes in the form of matter were alone the principles of all things. For that from which all entities come, from which each thing primarily arises and into which it is at the end resolved but the substance remaining but changing as to affections, this they announced to be the element and principle of all entities ... But the number and form of such a principle they do not all proclaim to be the same. Thales, the introducer of this sort of philosophy said that it was water (that is why he declared the earth to be sitting on the water) ... If then this opinion that nature happens to be primordial and ancient is perhaps unclear, yet Thales is said to have made these declarations concerning the primary cause."

—Aristotle, *Metaphysics*, I, 983b-984a; translated by Hugh Lawson-Tancred, London: Penguin, 1998.

Synagogues: Jewish meeting places for prayer and legal consultation.

MAP **7.8** Jewish Communities and Greek Philosophical Schools, ca. 100 CE

widespread followers in the Jewish population. Palestine was a cauldron of cultural influences—some monotheistic, others monist, many clashing with polytheism.

The Origins of Christianity   It was from this cauldron that the Jewish reform movement of Christianity arose in the first century CE. The earliest scriptures of the Christians, contained in the New Testament, describe the founding figure, Jesus of Nazareth, as a preacher in Galilee or northern Palestine, far from Jerusalem. After he was baptized by John, an ascetic preacher on the Jordan River, Jesus is reported to have left the Mosaic as well as the Pharisaic law aside, including the stringent purity laws, and to have preached instead the spirit of the law, which he expressed as the "law of love" (Greek *agape*, Latin *caritas*; Mark 12:29–30). Only if one loved God and one's neighbor as one loved oneself would one acquire the proper understanding of law and be prepared for the apocalypse and salvation in the heavenly kingdom soon to come.

When Jesus is reported to have gone to Jerusalem during Passover, one of three times a year when Jews were enjoined to visit the Temple for sacrifices, he provoked the Temple priests with his ultimate challenge to Jewish law: He overturned the tables of the money changers and sellers of sacrificial birds to Jews who performed the required animal sacrifices. For Jesus, obedience to all these detailed laws and regulations was quite unnecessary in the anticipation of the heavenly

Murals from Dura Europos on the Euphrates. The city, founded in 303 BCE, was home to a sizeable Jewish community whose synagogue was adorned with murals in the Parthian-Hellenistic style. Shown here are scenes from the Bible: (*top*) Exodus; (*middle*) the consecration of the Tabernacle; and (*bottom*) rescuing the infant Moses from the Nile.

kingdom. According to the New Testament, his actions in the Temple initiated the chain of events which ended with the priests turning Jesus over to the Roman governor for death on the cross.

Again according to the New Testament, shortly after Jesus' death, the Pharisee, Roman citizen, and philosophically trained Paul of Tarsus in Anatolia converted to Jesus' law of love. Paul dispensed with another Jewish law, circumcision, and thereby liberated Jesus' message from its last tie to Judaism: Henceforth, anyone could become a follower of Jesus. Paul retained the concept of the apocalypse with its tribulations but also argued that salvation had already begun with Jesus' resurrection from death, ascension to heaven, and imminent return—the Second Coming as the Messiah or Christus, hence Jesus' divine name, "Christ"—and ruler of the heavenly kingdom. According to the letters attributed to his name, Paul traveled widely and preached to numerous small Christian communities, called "churches" (Greek, sing. *ekklesia*), which formed in the Roman Empire during the middle of the first century CE.

The Christian Church   Paul trained the first missionaries, and after him pros-elytizing became a regular feature of the emerging Christian community. The missionaries preached Christianity in the Roman Empire from scriptures which evolved in the first three centuries CE. At this time, the first basic canon of accepted writings, the New Testament, was assembled. A hierarchy of bishops and priests preached from these scriptures to laypeople who congregated in local churches for regular communal services. From an early period, however, Christians were divided on how to understand the New Testament. The philosophically educated tended to interpret it figuratively, that is, by reading their philosophical concepts into scripture. Others, opposed to Greek philosophy, preferred a literal interpretation, even though Paul's Christianity was already philosophically tinged. A long struggle over the integration of scripture and philosophy into a single Christian civilization ensued in the church.

Principal figures in the struggle were bishops, called "church fathers." The earliest among them was Origen of Alexandria (ca. 185–254 CE), who focused not only on the allegorical but also on the ethical interpretation of scripture. His Christian ethics were so severe that he lived a life of perpetual poverty, fasting, and mortification of the flesh, including even self-castration, in preparation for life after death. The intellectually most versatile church father was Augustine (354–430 CE), from what is today Algeria. His two main works are the *Confessions*, in which he describes his conversion to Christianity and reflections on spirituality, and *The City of God*, in which he defends Christianity against the accusation by many Romans that its adoption as the state religion in 380 contributed to the decline of the empire. Although his philosophical training was limited, he was a strong proponent of the allegorical interpretation, which became a principal pillar of church doctrine. Thanks to the church fathers, the church was set on a path of merging monotheism and philosophy, as the basis for the rise of a Christian civilization.

The Beginnings of Science and the Cultures of Kings and Citizens

Monotheism and philosophy entered society early in the Jewish Second Temple kingdom in Palestine, as we have seen. In the Persian and Roman Empires this incorporation, in the form of preferred or state religions, took longer. Greek science, philosophy's older sibling, became important in Ptolemaic Egypt (305–30 BCE). The Ptolemies provided state support for the development of mathematics, physics, astronomy, and the applied science of mechanics as new and independent fields of culture. The other, inherited forms of cultural expression—painting, sculpture, architecture, and literature—remained within traditional polytheistic confines. Nevertheless, in Greece and Rome these cultural forms underwent substantial innovation and differentiation, influenced by Hellenism as well as Parthian and Sasanid Persia.

The Sciences at the Museum of Alexandria

In Athens and other city-states, citizens supported philosophical schools, such as the Academy of Plato or the Lyceum of Aristotle (384–322 BCE), one of Plato's students and tutor of Alexander. These institutions were small if compared with the enormous resources the Ptolemies and their Roman successors poured into a new type of institution of Greek learning, the institute for advanced study, as we would say today. This institute was the Museum of Alexandria (280 BCE–ca. 400 CE), which was devoted primarily to research in the pure and natural sciences. At times, some 100 resident fellows received scholarships from the museum, did research in its library holdings of half a million scrolls, dissected corpses in laboratories, gazed at the stars in the astronomical observatory, strolled through the botanical gardens, and shared meals.

The most developed branch of the sciences at the museum was geometry. Euclid (fl. ca. 300 BCE), one of the founders of the museum, provided geometry with its basic definitions and proofs in his *Elements*, still important today. In addition to geometry, mathematicians laid the foundations for algebra. The pioneer was Diophantus (ca. 214–284 CE), with his exploration of the properties of equations. Hypatia (ca. 360–415 CE), the first known female scientist in world history, is said to have contributed further to the development of algebra; but her work is unfortunately no longer extant. In the absence of a Greek number system, however, algebra remained ultimately stunted in its growth in Alexandria and had to await the Muslims and the Arabic numeral system—originally devised in India—to evolve fully.

Alexandrian geographers and astronomers, trained in geometry, made important calculations of the earth's circumference and tilt and formulated the first heliocentric astronomical theory, according to which the earth spins around the sun. Unfortunately, this theory remained mathematically unsupported, so the opposite theory of the earth at the center of the planetary system became dominant. Claudius Ptolemy (ca. 87–170 CE) devised such a detailed and precise geometric system of the planets' movements that his geocentrism reigned for the next millennium and a half in the astronomies of the Islamic Middle East and western European Christianity, dethroned eventually only by Copernicus in the sixth century.

Apart from astronomy, physics also flourished at the museum. The outstanding physicist was Archimedes (287–212 BCE), who investigated the behavior of floating bodies in the new science of hydrostatics—bold investigations, which had to wait a millennium and a half before being fully appreciated in the works of Galileo Galilei, one of the pioneers of modern physics. Archimedes resided only briefly in Alexandria and introduced most of his inventions, such as a screw in a tube to lift water and an array of mirrors intended to set war galleys aflame, as an applied scientist and engineer in his native Sicily. Versions of his screw are still in wide use, and modern experiments have proven the feasibility of his mirror weapon under ideal conditions.

The museum came to its end under unknown circumstances at the beginning of the 400s CE when the great crisis of the nomadic migrations struck the Roman Empire, engendering a fiscal crisis and depriving the museum of funds. Its legacy, however, was such that later Islamic rulers resumed the tradition of sponsoring institutes for advanced study. Even today, such institutes are important for creative research in the sciences and humanities.

Royal Persian Culture

The Achaemenid Persians arrived in Mesopotamia with their rich Indo-European traditions of divine and heroic myths, which were also characteristic of Aryan migrants to India. These myths told of deities and heroes mingling in a verdant landscape of mountains, rivers, and pastures. Major themes included the protracted, sometimes noble, and occasionally treacherous struggles between the Persians and their tribal rivals in central Asia, whom they called "Turanians." After 600 BCE, monotheistic Zoroastrians reworked the pagan myths in the Avesta so that under the one, invisible God (Ahuramazda) the other deities became lesser beings, such as angels and demons. The myths and epics were handed down orally until the 400s CE, well after the disappearance of the Achaemenids, before they were finally written down.

The Achaemenids adopted and absorbed what they found rather than created their own new traditions. They borrowed freely from Mesopotamian, Egyptian, Syrian, and Anatolian traditions, carefully combining and synthesizing different stylistic elements. For architecture, given the generally ruinous state of the ancient royal palaces such as Persepolis today, we are dependent on educated guesswork. Sculpture, on the other hand, still displays clear evidence not only of stylistic synthesis but also of carefully chosen themes. In contrast to the martial reliefs of their predecessors, the Persians preferred more tranquil reliefs, in which subject peoples stand patiently in long lines bearing tributes and gifts.

As heirs of both Achaemenid Persian and Greek traditions, the Parthians forged a new synthesis between inherited styles and adopted Greek-Hellenistic elements, while maintaining an overall palace-focused culture of their own. For example, courtiers listened to bards who recited the exploits of Hercules and other Greek heroes, thereby laying the foundations for the Rustam story cycle written down several centuries later. Other bards and minstrels traveled among aristocratic families, composing stories of their masters' courtly loves and intrigues or their exploits in battles against nomadic invaders from central Asia. After the Parthians, these stories were handed down orally and grew in both length and complexity. They exist today in a modern Persian version, called the *Book of Kings* (*Shahname* [Sha-ha-na-MAY]), compiled by the poet Firdosi [Feer-dow-SEE] in the eleventh century CE.

Painting and Architecture   The most striking new element in Persian painting was the introduction of the direct gaze of figures at the viewer, an innovation adapted from the Greeks. Representation, however, continued to be symbolical rather than realistic, so statues and murals, while facing the viewer directly, continued to be schematic and allusive, emphasizing the typical royal attributes of sternness, opulence, and remoteness. The style of frontal presentation also traveled eastward to the Parthians' neighbor, the Kushan kingdom in Afghanistan and northern India. Here, painters drew the first frontal images of the Buddha and developed a rich and colorful symbolical pictorial tradition for Buddhist monism (see Chapter 8).

In architecture, the characteristic feature of Sasanid palaces was the monumental dome and barrel vault. Arches, domes, and barrel vaulting had been pioneered in Mesopotamia in the second millennium BCE but only for small structures. These earlier curved constructions consisted of bricks laid and mortared at an angle in the so-called pitched brick style. It is possible that during the Parthian period, when fire temples began to appear among the Zoroastrians, domes topped the cube-shaped chambers of those temples, although the earliest extant domes date to the Sasanids.

Sasanid vaults and domes were massive structures. The central audience hall of the palace in the capital, Ctesiphon, built ca. 250 CE, had a barrel vault 118 feet high. Other palaces had "squinched" domes of up to 45 feet across, covering square audience and banquet halls. *Squinches* were curved triangular transition spaces between the dome and the corners of the halls. In order to contain the outward

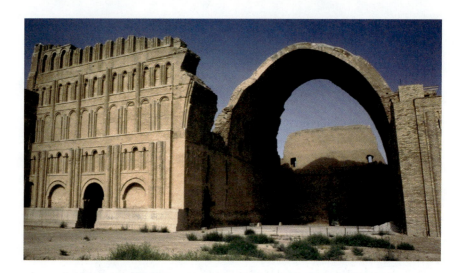

Barrel Vault of the Sasanid
Royal Reception Hall,
Ctseiphon.

thrust of the dome's weight, buttresses supported the walls on the outside. The techniques of both barrel vaulting and the dome were transmitted from Sasanid Persia to Christian Armenia, Rome, and ultimately western Europe, where they appeared in church architecture.

Literature   In literature, the Sasanids were major transmitters of Indian texts to the Middle East and Mediterranean. The most popular text was a translation of animal fables, known in India as *Five Treatises* (*Panchatantra* [Pan-sha-TAN-trah]) and in Arabic as *Kalila wa dimna* [Ka-LEE-lah wa DIM-nah].

In these fables, animals appear in witty, cleverly constructed stories intended to teach lessons to palace courtiers and retainers. Other texts were instruction manuals on chess, a game which made its way to the West during Sasanid times. Also from India came medical texts complete with discussions of anatomy, diseases, and herbs. All these texts, which were both useful and entertaining, played important roles at the Sasanid court.

Greek and Roman Civic Culture

The disappearance of kings and aristocracies in the Greek city-states during the sixth century BCE had momentous consequences for Greek culture. Instead of merely a handful of kings and aristocrats sponsoring the arts, thousands of wealthy citizens began to patronize artists or even create themselves works of literature, sculpture, painting, and architecture. A broad civic artistic creativity arose. Although polytheism, myths, and other ancient traditions remained central for the majority of the citizens and only a minority adapted to the new philosophical and scientific monism, the heritage lost its symbolical, stylized, and generic royal orientation. Instead, Greeks began to experiment with a variety of individual shapes, types, and models, seeking realistic representation in their art.

Greek Literature   Greek literature provides a good case study. The Greek theater emerged around 500–480 BCE out of the stylized traditions and rituals of the Dionysiac cult. Every year in March, during the Dionysiac processions, competitions took place among groups of citizens (later wealthy noncitizens also competed) for the presentation of the best tragedy or comedy. These competing groups, or *choruses*, dressed in sumptuous robes and elaborate masks to perform the chosen dramatic or comic piece through declamation and dance. In the course of time, individual actors emerged from among the chorus members and presented dialogues on which the chorus commented as the plot evolved. Tragedy developed out of Dionysiac myths and comedy from the Dionysiac processions.

Among the most important writers who composed for the early Greek stage were the tragedians Aeschylus, Sophocles, and Euripides, as well as the comedian Aristophanes. At the center of Aeschylus' (ca. 525–456 BCE) plays are characters who commit evil or foolish acts and have to suffer the inescapable and terrible consequences of these acts, as in the best-known group of his plays, the *Oresteia*. Sophocles' (ca. 496–406 BCE) characters suffer even more complicated difficulties. They believe they are acting ethically, but when pain, suffering, and death occur around them, they are forced to recognize how grievously mistaken they are about themselves and/or the divine will, as in the famous *Oedipus Rex*. Euripides (ca. 480–406 BCE) focuses mostly on strong-willed but victimized female characters, as in the play *Medea*. In search of justice, his women become avengers, suffering a brush with madness before their conflicts are resolved. Aristophanes (ca. 448–388 BCE) was famous for his biting satire, which lampooned the rapidly changing customs and values of fifth-century Athens, as exemplified in his play *The Frogs*. All four authors, and many of their successors, continue to exercise a profound influence on the evolution of Western literature today.

Greek Painting and Sculpture

Just as democracy encouraged the exploration of individual character in tragedy and comedy, so it supported the search for character representation in Greek painting and sculpture. Unfortunately, no murals or panels exist today, although a few Roman reproductions survive. Vase painting gives us a good impression of scenes of daily life, even though the medium imposed severe limits of color and composition on artists. Surviving examples of sculptures are plentiful, even if primarily in the form of later Roman copies, which often lack the original Greek refinement.

In the fifth century BCE, sculptors abandoned the last traces of the traditional Middle Eastern symbolic royal style that required figures to be in tranquil repose, projecting dignity and sternness. Instead, sculptors began to explore physical movement and individual emotional states. In terms of themes, poses, and individuality, Greek vase paintings and sculptures achieved a remarkably wide range, from figures exerting themselves in their chosen sports to serene models of human beauty. Greek sculptors and painters abandoned symbolism and, instead, embraced realism as their style of representation (what we would call today "photographic representation").

Roman Literature

Greece influenced Roman culture early on. As early as the middle of the third century BCE, Romans had translated Greek plays and poetry into Latin. Roman playwrights like Plautus (ca. 254–184 BCE) and Terence (ca. 195–159 BCE) were early devotees of Greek forms, introducing them into the

---

An Excerpt from a Story from the *Kalila wa Dimna*

Now it happened that among the lion's attendants were two jackal brothers named Kalila and Dimna who were both very clever and cunning. "I wonder why the lion never leaves his den?" Kalila asked his brother one morning when they were lounging about in the sun.... "If I were you, brother," said Dimna, "I would contain my curiosity on such matters. We are the servants of the lion, and our business is to wait upon him and obey his commands—not to pry into his affairs."

—*Kalila and Dimna: Fables of Friendship and Betrayal*, retold by Ramsay Wood, p. 70. New York: Knopf, 1980.

Greek Realism. The Greeks used decorated stelae to mark the burial places of the dead in much the same way tombstones function today. This intimate relief, from about 450 BCE, memorializes a young girl. The treatment of the child's body is realistic—note the chubby arms—and the way the girl tenderly holds her pet doves transforms the little scene into a touching story.

Roman environment. After the adaptation of Greek poetic metrical patterns to the Latin language, a long line of poets emerged. Prose writings on political and historical themes, also modeled on Greek precursors, appeared in large numbers, particularly by Cicero (106–43 BCE) and Sallust (ca. 85–35 BCE), prominent senators who were engaged in late Republican politics.

Emperor Augustus and his wealthy friend Maecenas, renowned for his sponsorship of the arts, stimulated an outburst of early imperial pride. For example, in his epic poem the *Aeneid*, Virgil (70–19 BCE) played down the influence of Greece by positing the origins of Rome in Troy, the rival of Greece. In his *Odes*, Horace (65–8 BCE) glorified courage, patriotism, piety, justice, and a respect for tradition, which he regarded as uniquely Roman virtues. In his *History of Rome*, Livy (59 BCE–17 CE) celebrated the glories of Rome's past, with lively, although factually dubious, portraits of major historical figures. In his *Transformations*, Ovid (43 BCE–18 CE) Romanized the Greek gods, with all their exploits and follies. All of these writers viewed Rome as the culmination of civilization.

As the empire evolved in the first centuries CE, the newly rich who had benefited from booty and conquered land became the target of biting satire, as in the writings of Juvenal (ca. 50–130). The later shift of power from Rome to the provinces was paralleled by the emergence of provincial Roman arts. The Greek biographer Plutarch (ca. 50–120) is one example of this shift; the North African Apuleius (ca. 125–170), author of the humorous novel *The Golden Ass*, is another. Other provincial writers composed poetry, particularly in the elegant style of *eclogues*—pastoral poems in which shepherds reflect on times of rural simplicity long past.

Roman Sculpture and Painting Roman sculpture followed the Greek civic style closely by emphasizing proportion, perspective, foreshortening, and light and shadow. Among the earliest sculptures were marble busts which aristocratic Romans had made of their patriarchs, cast from wax masks and plaster models. These busts, kept in family shrines, were a central part of aristocratic life in the republic. During the imperial period prior to Christianity as the state religion (31 BCE–380 CE), life-size imitations of Greek and Egyptian statues were commonly found in the households of the wealthy. The statue of Augustus—tall, dignified, with his arm outstretched—became the model for the imperial cult of all subsequent emperors. On columns and triumphal arches, reliefs similar to those of the Persians celebrated military victories. In contrast to the Parthians and Sasanids, civic Romans adorned their cities with numerous monumental structures and, hence, provided their empire with much greater visibility.

Roman pictorial art existed mostly in the form of wood panels, wall paintings, and floor mosaics. In the fifth century CE, the first illustrated book appeared, depicting scenes from Virgil's *Aeneid*. Nearly all panel paintings have perished, but wall paintings have survived in larger numbers, ironically due to their preservation in Pompeii and other cities buried by the eruption of Mt. Vesuvius in 79 CE. The paintings demonstrate Roman art at a remarkably skilled level, with perspective emphasized and executed just as precisely as in Greek art. Outside Italy, in the imperial provinces, a rare second-century CE portrait on the coffin of an Egyptian boy displays superb light and shadow skills. Mosaics excavated in North Africa, Spain, and most recently Anatolia show full adaptation of the provinces to metropolitan Roman artistry.

Rome's architecture was initially closely modeled on the Greek and Etruscan heritage in Italy. In the imperial age, when the desire for monumental architecture developed, the Romans—shortly after the Parthians—adopted the elements of arch and dome for large buildings. An example is the Pantheon in Rome, built in 118–126 CE. This building, a temple dedicated to all the Roman gods, consists of a dome placed on top of a drum and lit by a round open skylight at its apex (diameter and height both 142 feet). The circular foundation wall

Horace, On Dying for One's Country

To suffer hardness with good cheer,
In sternest school of warfare bred,
Our youth should learn; let steed and spear
Make him one day the Parthian's dread;
Cold skies, keen perils, brace his life.
Methinks I see from rampired town
Some battling tyrant's matron wife,
Some maiden, look in terror down,—
'Ah, my dear lord, untrain'd in war!
O tempt not the infuriate mood
Of that fell lion I see! from far
He plunges through a tide of blood!'
What joy, for fatherland to die!
Death's darts e'en flying feet o'ertake,
Nor spare a recreant chivalry,
A back that cowers, or loins that quake.

—Horace. *The Odes*, trans. John Carrington, bk. 3, chap. 2. London: George Bell and Sons, 1882, http://www.perseus.tufts.edu/hopper/text?doc=Perseus%3Atext%3A1999.02.0025%3Abook%3D3%3Apoem%3D2.

Scene from the *Aeneid*. According to Virgil's *Aeneid*, on his journey from Troy, Aeneas landed in North Africa and fell madly in love with Dido, the queen of Carthage. One day, as they were hunting, a storm forced the two to seek shelter in a cave. Destiny, however, demanded that Aeneas travel on to Italy and found Rome. In her disconsolate grief of being without Aeneas, Dido committed suicide. The cave episode is illustrated here in a manuscript of the fifth century CE.

Pompeii, Murals Executed with Careful Attention to Perspective, Light and Shadow, and Foreshortening. An eruption of the Vesuvius volcano buried the city in 79 CE in ash and, thereby, preserved the murals of the city. They provide some of the best evidence we have of life in ancient Rome.

made squinches unnecessary. The courtyard of Emperor Diocletian's palace in Split, Croatia (ca. 300 CE), contains the first example of arches set on pillars, which later acquired crucial importance in Islamic and medieval Christian architectures.

Beginning with the first Christian emperor, Constantine, in the early fourth century CE, there was a return from realistic to symbolical representation in the arts. The rich variety of literature shrank to the one category of religious poetry and hymns. Pagan Greek and Roman realistic artists had emphasized emotional variety in their art, playing with surface detail, perspective, foreshortening, light and shadow, and full and empty space. In contrast, Christian artists began to emphasize what they considered essential. Instead of seeking emotionally diverse forms and expressions, they drew from Middle Eastern models, which retained connections to symbolism. Accordingly, characters and objects became generic and lost their detailed psychological and physical characteristics. Space became two-dimensional and figures were large or small according to their religious importance, not their closeness to or distance from the viewer. What mattered was the paradigmatic saintly comportment of figures, who the believers were supposed to imitate. Religious uniformity came to dominate culture in the Roman and Sasanid Persian Empires, as it dominated their politics in the form of state religion.

Putting It All Together

In 590/591 the Sasanid Empire suffered a war of succession during which one of the rivals, King Khosrow II (r. 590–628), fled to the Romans. Before he arrived in Constantinople, he sent an embassy that pleaded for military support. As Khosrow had hoped, his ambassadors' arguments were persuasive, and he received Roman military support, with which he defeated his rival and regained the Persian throne.

This quote is a fitting conclusion to this chapter on world empires, which began with Alexander's bold quest to unite the Mediterranean, Middle East, and India. For Alexander it was still possible to think in terms of one supreme god in heaven and one empire on earth. But after the introduction of monotheism, the situation changed. For the Persian ambassadors it was impossible for a human empire not only to ever resemble the kingdom of God but also to reign alone on earth. For the Persians and Romans—Theophylactus cites the Persian ambassadors approvingly—the one single God anywhere and nowhere disapproves of all imperial projects on earth and prefers a commonwealth of multiple kingdoms. It is this reevaluation of politics and history which the visionaries can be seen as having contributed to world

> ### One Lord in Heaven, How Many Lords on Earth?
>
> "it is impossible for a single monarchy to embrace the innumerable cares of the organization of the universe . . . it is never possible for the earth to resemble the unity of the divine and primary rule, and to obtain a disposition corresponding to that of the upper order, since it is steered hither and thither towards the breakers by mankind whose nature is unstable and whose judgment most worthless because of its tendency toward evil."
>
> —Theophylactus Simocotta. *The History of Theophylact Simocotta.* Translated by Michael and Mary Whitby, bk. 4, chap. 13, pp. 7–8. New York: Oxford University Press, 1986.

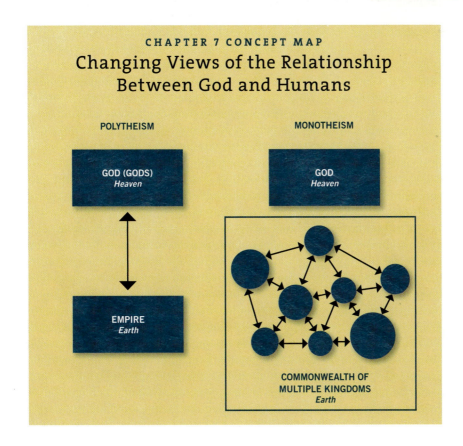

CHAPTER 7 CONCEPT MAP

Changing Views of the Relationship Between God and Humans

POLYTHEISM

GOD (GODS)
Heaven

EMPIRE
Earth

MONOTHEISM

GOD
Heaven

COMMONWEALTH OF
MULTIPLE KINGDOMS
Earth

history, as shown in the accompanying Concept Map. Obviously, many kings and emperors later in history did not accept the idea of the futility of empires. But after monotheism, they had to reckon with forceful critics who would cut their ambitions down to size and remind people of the fundamental difference between the imperfect earthly states and the heavenly kingdom.

Review and Respond

1. Discuss the stages through which Persia and Greece progressed in their complex relationship, from the rise of Achaemenid Persia to the King's Peace.

2. Describe the changes which occurred in Rome during the transition from republic to republican empire.

3. How did the migrating nomadic peoples of the Russian and central Asian plains affect the Persian and Roman Empires? How did these empires recover? Compare and contrast the fates of these empires.

4. What is the significance of the Museum of Alexandria for the evolution of scientific thinking? Discuss select examples of Alexandrian innovations.

▶ For additional resources, including maps, primary sources, visuals, and quizzes, please go to www.oup.com/us/vonsivers. Please see the Further Resources section at the back of the book for additional readings and suggested websites.

Thinking Through Patterns

▶ **Why should the Middle East and Mediterranean Europe during the period 600 BCE–600 CE be studied as a single unit?**

The sharp division between Europe and the Middle East that exists now was the result of the nineteenth-century challenge of European modernity and the Middle East's efforts at adaptation. The opposite was true in the period of late multi-religious and early monotheistic empires, from 600 BCE to 600 CE: Then, the two regions were tightly intertwined. During this period, first the sequence of the multi-religious Persian and Macedonian Empires dominated the Middle East and eastern Mediterranean. After these two, the competition between the subsequent two empires, Rome and Persia, inaugurated a pattern of urbanization, a deepening gulf between the wealthy and poor, and the immigration of tribal people from central Asia.

The experience of transcendence happens constantly, even if it remains for the most part unexpressed and little thought about. In its most common form, it is encountered as the unknown future: You dream of getting a college degree as the entry ticket to your future academic career. After years of toil, sacrifices, and financial cost, the day of graduation arrives. In one moment, as your name is called, the transcendent expectation becomes a reality: As you clutch the diploma, a thrill goes down your spine. Apart from the future, the past as well as space can be thought of as transcendent. The great visionaries of 700–500 BCE abstracted a separate, transcendent God or first principle from the world where there had been, in polytheism, a single cosmos in which heaven with its high god, plus all the other gods and goddesses, intermingled with the world. The visionaries did not merely reflect on gods and humans mixing *in* the world, as in the polytheism of the past. They rather directed their focus on God or the first principle *separate from* the world, thereby creating religious monotheism and philosophical monism. Following the visionaries, thinkers explored new, abstract dimensions of thought in the new intellectual disciplines of science, philosophy, and theology.

▶ **What is transcendence, and why is it important to understand its importance in world history?**

▶ **Which elements characterize the institutions growing out of the Middle Eastern monotheisms of Judaism–Christianity and monism of Greek philosophy-science?**

In the Middle East and eastern Mediterranean, visionaries were the creators of bodies of transcendent thought that evolved into the Zoroastrian and Jewish religions as well as Greek philosophy and science. The visionaries and their early followers created scriptures which expounded in great detail the nature of God or the first principle. Anyone could read or listen to the scriptures and, accordingly, the visionaries and their successors attracted communities of like-minded followers. Zoroastrianism, Judaism, and Christianity were religions of salvation: Firm believers in the power of God's forgiveness would be saved in a transcendent kingdom of heaven. For Zoroastrians, Jews, and Christians—cogs in the giant, brutal, and meaningless multireligious machines of the Persian and Roman Empires—this religious promise of salvation was the only way of making sense out of life. Eventually the emperors themselves converted, making monotheism the state religion.

Chapter 8

600 BCE-600 CE

Empires and Visionaries in India

**INDIA,
800 BCE–800 CE**

It was one of the most intriguing meetings of the ancient world, though no one could have foreseen its ultimate significance at the time. One of the participants, Alexander the Great, as we have seen, had already become by the age of 30 the most successful military leader the world had ever seen. His present interest, however—the conquest of northern India—had so far proved difficult in the face of the huge armies and terrifying ranks of war elephants massed by his opponents. Now, as he prepared to invade the most powerful Indian state, Magadha, Alexander's men were growing anxious about the seemingly insatiable ambition of their commander. Given the opposition within his own ranks and on the battlefield, Alexander had

Seeing Patterns

▶ Think about the reasons for the spread of Buddhism inside and outside of India. How have historians seen the decline of Buddhism in India?

▶ What do you consider to be the most influential patterns in Indian history to this point? Why?

▶ Do you think some of Ashoka's ideas could be implemented by governments today? Why or why not?

retreated to the northern city of Taxila, near the modern capital of Islamabad in Pakistan, to replenish his forces and rethink his situation.

While in Taxila, Alexander met with a man identified by his biographers simply as "Sandrokoptros," who had recently fled the Magadhan court after a failed attempt to overthrow its government. Though we can only speculate about the substance of the talks between the two men, Alexander's use of local politics in his past military campaigns suggests that he sought to take advantage of Sandrokoptros's knowledge of Magadha and its leadership in planning his attack. The intelligence Alexander obtained must have been discouraging, for he soon abandoned his plans to invade India and, facing the possibility of mutiny among his men, withdrew to the safer confines of Persia, where he died in 323 BCE. Following Alexander's death, one of his commanders, Seleucus Nikator [See-LOO-kus Nee-KAY-tor], gained control of the eastern reaches of his empire. By 321 BCE, however, Seleucus Nikator found his territory around the Indus River threatened by a powerful new Indian state created by none other than Alexander's former ally, Sandrokoptros. But it was not until the end of the eighteenth century CE that the shadowy "Sandrokoptros" was identified by English Sanskrit scholars

Sutra of the 1000 Buddhas. Mahayana Buddhism reached Tibet in the seventh century CE. By the end of the eighth century, it was firmly established as the state religion. In the Tibetan Buddhist worldview, time is measured in *kalpas*, vast time spans of millions of years. This seventeenth-century Mahayana Buddhist *sutra*, or canonical scripture, describes the present *kalpas* we live in, in which 1000 Buddhas will appear. Written in gold ink, it includes illustrations showing the future Buddhas, including the one shown in the round circle.

as Chandragupta Maurya [Chahn-drah-GUP-tah MOORY-ah], the founder of India's first and largest empire.

The meeting between Alexander and Chandragupta was significant for many reasons. For one thing, it took place between two men with similar desires for world empire, whose models of leadership inspired a host of imitators. More significant for our purposes, however, was what this meeting symbolized for the future of India: intensifying exchanges of ideas and goods between peoples of vastly different cultures and beliefs. These ranged from the trading of commodities to the exchange of ideas in art, philosophy, science, and religion. In all of these areas, Indian visionaries and innovators made contributions that would have a profound effect on patterns of world history as they made their way throughout Eurasia and North Africa. In turn, India's place as a crossroads of trade and invasion continually replenished the subcontinent with innovation from outside. Many centuries later, the lore of India's wealth and culture would fire the imaginations of Europeans and drive them to seek out the connection first established by the founders of these two model empires so many centuries before.

Patterns of State Formation in India: Republics, Kingdoms, and Empires

When Alexander arrived, the pattern of state formation in India had shifted permanently to the plains and hills of the Punjab and Ganges valley. The shift had begun when tectonic movements in the Himalayas around 1900 BCE caused the drying up of the Sarasvati River in northwest India. People abandoned the agrarian–urban center of the Indus valley and migrated eastward. Much of the land to which they migrated in the Punjab and Ganges valley consisted of rain forest and marshes that required laborious land-clearing. But the settlers drew on their past experience as they built the new agrarian–urban centers of northern India. In contrast to Africa and Mesoamerica where the patterns of state formation from villages and chiefdoms to kingdoms developed slowly, state formation proceeded rapidly. The earliest traces of villages date to about 1200 BCE. Thereafter, polities emerged quickly, in the form of warrior republics and kingdoms. Both flourished in the early first millennium BCE.

A gradual consolidation process set in from about 800 BCE onward, with a few kingdoms emerging as the strongest states while warrior republics disappeared from the scene. At the height of the wars for predominance, around 700–400 BCE, visionaries similar to those appearing at the same time in the Middle East and China offered reforms of the Vedic traditions: the Upanishads, Jainism, and Buddhism. The process of state formation reached a first peak with the Mauryan Empire, which united northern and central India and experimented with Buddhism as a privileged religion. A firm marriage between state and religion, however, occurred with the Hindu Gupta Empire (320–550 CE), which, along with its contemporary, Christian Rome, became the first state in world history to lay the foundation for a religious civilization.

The Road to Empire: The Mauryas

In the early first millennium BCE, the emerging states along the Ganges River valley developed political systems ranging from *gana-sanghas* [GAH-nah SAHN-gahs]—often termed "republics" by scholars—to centralized monarchies whose rulers were accorded god-like status. The agricultural advances made in these formerly forested areas, particularly through the use of iron tools—and the dikes, ponds, flooded fields, and drainage systems necessary for growing rice—resulted in the emergence of wealthy, centralized states led by Magadha and Kosala, along with the lesser kingdoms of Vatsya and Avanti farther west (see Map 8.1).

During the half-century before Alexander attempted to expand his empire into northern India, Mahapadama Nanda [Mah-hah-PAH-dah-mah NAHN-dah], a

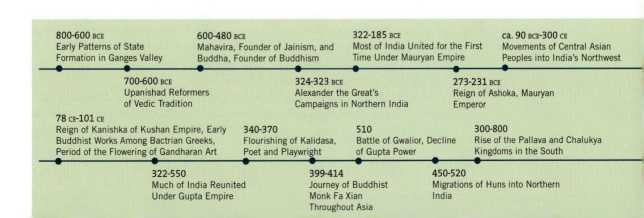

800-600 BCE
Early Patterns of State Formation in Ganges Valley

700-600 BCE
Upanishad Reformers of Vedic Tradition

600-480 BCE
Mahavira, Founder of Jainism, and Buddha, Founder of Buddhism

322-185 BCE
Most of India United for the First Time Under Mauryan Empire

324-323 BCE
Alexander the Great's Campaigns in Northern India

273-231 BCE
Reign of Ashoka, Mauryan Emperor

ca. 90 BCE-300 CE
Movements of Central Asian Peoples into India's Northwest

78 CE-101 CE
Reign of Kanishka of Kushan Empire, Early Buddhist Works Among Bactrian Greeks, Period of the Flowering of Gandharan Art

340-370
Flourishing of Kalidasa, Poet and Playwright

322-550
Much of India Reunited Under Gupta Empire

510
Battle of Gwalior, Decline of Gupta Power

399-414
Journey of Buddhist Monk Fa Xian Throughout Asia

300-800
Rise of the Pallava and Chalukya Kingdoms in the South

450-520
Migrations of Huns into Northern India

Northern India, ca. 400 BCE

☐ Maximum extent of the Nandas, ca. 330 BCE

→ Alexander's invasion of northern India, 327–326 BCE

MAP **8.1** **Northern India, ca. 400 BCE.**

member of the *shudra varna*, seized power in Magadha and embarked on a series of military campaigns against Vatsya and Avanti, both of which he conquered. By the 330s BCE, the Magadhan state stretched across the entire breadth of northern India and the taxes imposed by the Nandas brought unprecedented wealth to their capital of Pataliputra [Pah-tah-lee-POO-trah], the modern city of Patna, on the Ganges. The Nandas, however, were not alone in their aspirations for universal empire.

Chandragupta Maurya   Little is known of Chandragupta's early life. It is believed that at a young age he was put under the care of the philosopher Kautilya, whose *Arthashastra* became the most influential political treatise in Indian history (see Chapter 3). Contemporary accounts of Chandragupta's court and the structure of his government suggest a strong connection to the political practices of the idealized ruler outlined in the *Arthashastra*. At this stage, however, Kautilya was instrumental in the young Chandragupta's first attempt to seize power from the ruling Nandas. Playing on discontent over Nanda taxation and the threat to religious order posed by rulers from the lowest shudra varna, he used his considerable influence to back a palace revolt by the young Chandragupta. When the revolt was unsuccessful, the two fled to Taxila, a dominant trade crossroads strategically located near the Khyber Pass, where they encountered Alexander.

Kautilya and Alexander played important roles in building Chandragupta's empire, though Alexander's role is less obvious. The dislocations in the northwest caused by Alexander's attempted invasions allowed Chandragupta to pursue a patient

MAP **8.2 The Mauryan Empire Under Ashoka, 273–231 BCE.**

strategy of securing the most vulnerable and least contented of the Nandas' client states while methodically surrounding and, ultimately, conquering Magadha. By 321 BCE Chandragupta had secured the capital and embarked on a campaign to enlarge his empire. Following a series of battles with Alexander's successor, Seleucus Nikator, the Greeks surrendered their north Indian and Indus territories to Chandragupta. Though forced from his Indian holdings, Seleucus and his successors maintained cordial relations with the Mauryas and posted the ambassador Megasthenes to the Mauryan capital of Pataliputra. Though little survives of his reports, Megasthenes' accounts of the enormous wealth and population of the capital and the efficiency of Mauryan government formed the basis of much of the classical and medieval European understanding of India.

Although his motivations for doing so are unclear, Chandragupta stepped down from his throne around 297 BCE and joined an ascetic religious order, the Jains, formed on the basis of the teachings of the visionary Mahavira. Legend has it that he ended his life in the Jain monastery at Karnataka, where, in imitation of the order's founder, he refused all food and starved himself to death rather than consume any living thing. Chandragupta's son continued to expand the Mauryan domains to the west and south, but it was his grandson, Ashoka (Ah-SHOW-kah) (r. ca. 273–231 BCE), who emerged as perhaps India's most dominant ruler until the nineteenth century CE.

Ashoka   Born around 304 BCE, Ashoka may have actually seized the throne from his father. Like his predecessors, he soon began a series of military ventures to drive the Mauryan Empire deeper into the south (see Map 8.2). The climax of his efforts was a fierce war he fought with the kingdom of Kalinga, the last adjacent region outside of Mauryan control, on the eastern coast. Though figures given in ancient sources must always be treated with suspicion, by Ashoka's own admission, 100,000 people were killed in the conflict. Yet, it was also here, at the height of his power, that, deeply moved by the carnage in Kalinga, in around 260 BCE he abruptly abandoned the path of conquest, converted to Buddhism, and vowed to rule his kingdom by "right conduct" alone.

Scholars know perhaps more about Ashoka's reign than that of any other ancient Indian monarch. He told much of his own story and outlined his Buddhist-inspired ideas for proper behavior on inscriptions in caves and on rocks and pillars set up in strategic places throughout his empire. Written mostly in Prakrit, the parent tongue of many of the modern north Indian dialects, these inscriptions present a fascinating and human glimpse of the ruler and his personal vision of the idea of dharma (see Chapter 3).

Departing somewhat from the Bhagavad Gita's concept of dharma as duty (see Chapter 3), dharma for Ashoka was simply "that which is good." Among other things, this involved living a life of "kindness, liberality, truthfulness, and purity." Moreover, he believed that following the path of dharma represented the only way one could achieve happiness. One distinctive innovation growing out of Ashoka's support of dharma was his taking up of the Buddhist concept of *ahimsa*, or nonviolence: People should be kind to the weak and disadvantaged and do no harm to any living creature. By way of setting an example, Ashoka declared dozens of animal species to be under his protection, forbade the wholesale burning of forests, and even warned his people not to burn grain husks in order to avoid injuring any creatures living within them. Ashoka's devotion to dharma even extended to sending his sons as Buddhist missionaries to Sri Lanka, where it has remained the principal faith to this day.

Although Ashoka advocated the peaceful principles of dharma, the records of his reign also indicate that his empire was, in many respects, an early kind of police state. He followed many of the political practices suggested in Kautilya's *Arthashastra*, which emphasizes that a monarch must be alert to the moods of his people, on the lookout for enemies, and ready to capitalize on opportunities to exercise power. While allowing the practice of many religions in addition to Buddhism, Ashoka kept a tight rein on his officials and people through a vast network of spies and informers,

---

Ashoka on Right Conduct

"The Beloved of the Gods [Ashoka] . . . is moved to remorse now. For he has felt profound sorrow and regret because the conquest of a people previously unconquered involves slaughter, death, and deportation. But there is a more important reason for the King's remorse . . . all suffer from the injury, slaughter, and deportation inflicted on their loved ones. Even those who escaped calamity themselves are deeply afflicted by the misfortunes suffered by those friends, acquaintances, companions, and relatives for whom they feel an undiminished affection. Thus all men share in the misfortune, and this weighs on King Priyadarsi's [Ashoka's] mind. . . . King Priyadarsi considers moral conquest the most important conquest. He has achieved this moral conquest repeatedly both here and among the peoples living beyond the borders of his kingdom. . . . This edict on Dharma has been inscribed so that my sons and grandsons who may come after me should not think new conquests worth achieving."

—Richard McKeon and N. A. Nikam, eds. and trans. *The Edicts of Ashoka.* Chicago: University of Chicago Press, 1966. pp. 27–28.

a practice begun by his grandfather, Chandragupta. The empire itself was divided into four large regional districts, each with a governor. They and all the officials under them were subject to periodic review by roving special commissioners appointed by the throne, whose chief task was to check on everyone's adherence to dharma. Thus, the entire governmental apparatus was now geared toward uplifting the people's morality and supervising their happiness.

Ashoka also encouraged a unified system of commercial law, standardization of weights and measures, and uniform coinage throughout his realm, innovations that greatly facilitated trade and commerce. A majority of state revenues came from taxes on harvests of wheat, rice, barley, and millet plus those on internal and external trade. Under the Mauryans, India was the major crossroads in the exchange of gold and silver sought by the Hellenistic kingdoms and for the expanding maritime trade accompanying the advance of Buddhism into southeast Asia. In the north, Taxila and the cities and towns along the caravan routes from China to the west grew wealthy from the increasing exchange of silk and other luxury goods.

Within India, the circulation of tropical fruits, medicinal barks, and innumerable other forest products augmented trade still further. Thus, the immense wealth and power flowing into Ashoka's court in Pataliputra made that city of half a million perhaps the richest in the ancient world. The wealth at Ashoka's command and his devotion to dharma allowed the government to spend lavishly in sponsoring public works—palaces, roads, rest stops and hostels for travelers, and parks—as well as temples and shrines for various religious groups.

In all, Ashoka's regime represents a pioneering attempt to construct a workable moral order, a pattern of world history that emerged repeatedly as states seeking to become world empires increasingly turned to religious and philosophical systems that proclaimed universal truths. In India, as in southwest Asia and the Mediterranean, and as we will see in China, these universal truths were proclaimed by visionaries who sensed problems developing in the old order of their respective societies. The ultimate end of this process, which we will explore in detail in Part 3, was the development of religious civilizations.

During the 50 years following the reign of Ashoka, weakness along the Mauryan Empire's northern borders combined with new pressures on a number of nomadic central Asian peoples to spur a series of migrations into northern India. At the same time, the absence of strong leadership during the reigns of Ashoka's successors weakened the empire internally. The last of the Mauryans, Brihadratha [bri-HAD-rah-tah] (d. ca. 181–185 BCE), appears to have been mentally incompetent and was assassinated by his chief military commander. The **successor states**, those of the Shungas and the Kanva, similarly proved unable to stop the loss of the old Mauryan holdings to the new invaders.

The Nomadic Kingdoms of the North
With the end of the Mauryan Empire, northern India was transformed into a series of regional kingdoms run by local rulers. Greek-speaking peoples from Bactria—descendants of troops and colonists who had

Capital of Ashoka Pillar of Sarnath. The triple lion motif atop the *chakravartin* wheel, symbolizing universal kingship, topped one of Ashoka's famous pillars. The one from which this capital was taken had been set up to commemorate the Buddha's first sermon in Sarnath's Deer Park.

Successor states: Political units that take shape in the wake of the breakup of larger states or empires.

come to the area under Alexander the Great—controlled some of these territories. Their most famous ruler, Menander, achieved immortality in Buddhist literature as "King Milinda" by engaging in a debate at court with the philosopher Nagasena. Their talks, as later set down, became an important exposition of Buddhist ideas and purportedly led to Menander's conversion.

By the first years of the Common Era, the Bactrian Greek rulers of northern India confronted new nomadic groups from central Asia, who eventually put an end to Greek rule in the region. These groups had been put into motion by repeated Chinese campaigns against the Xiongnu [SHIUNG-noo] (the Huns) and the Yuezhi [YOO-eh-jih]. As they moved into northern India sometime around 25 CE, the Yuezhi became known as the "Kushans." Under its most famous ruler, Kanishka (r. ca. 78–101 CE), the Kushan Empire expanded into not only northern India but also

Royal Golden Earrings, First Century BCE. These earrings embody a number of designs associated with rulership—an elephant, a winged lion, and triple frond palmettes. Scholars believe the weight of the jewelry probably distended the earlobes of the wearer.

much of modern Pakistan and Afghanistan. Kanishka, like Menander, adopted Buddhism and actively propagated the faith within his growing kingdom and beyond. Through his efforts, the new religion expanded along the caravan routes of central Asia and shortly afterward appears for the first time in Chinese records.

Although the continual arrival of new groups expanded the cultural resources of northern India and greatly aided the spread of Buddhism, it also worked against the development of stable states in the region. With the intensity of the migrations abating by the end of the third century, however, a new and aggressive line of rulers, the Guptas, established power in the Ganges valley and stood poised to reunite the old Mauryan heartland. Under their rule would come India's great classical age.

The Classical Age: The Gupta Empire

The origin of the Gupta line is somewhat obscure, though scholars agree that, like the Mauryans, it originated somewhere near Magadha. The first major ruler of the dynasty was Chandragupta I (ca. 320–335 CE, no relation to the Chandragupta of the Mauryan Empire), whose new state occupied much of the old heartland of Magadha and Kosala. With recognition of the rising power of the Guptas extending

Coins of the Northwest, Second Century BCE and Late First Century CE. The complex history of the area encompassed by modern Afghanistan and Pakistan has been understood principally through the coins minted by the many rulers of frequently shifting territories. The silver coin on the left was minted by a Bactrian Greek king, probably in the second century BCE. The gold coin beside it with the Greek inscription was the product of the reign of the famous Buddhist King Kanishka (78–101 CE) of the Kushans and depicts the king himself.

from Nepal in the north to the Shaka territories in the west, the way lay open for his successor, Samudragupta [Sahm-OO-drah-ghup-tah] (r. ca. 335–380 CE), to expand the borders of the empire even further.

Under Samudragupta, the Gupta sway extended both north and south, securing a swath of territory extending far up the Ganges River to the borders of the Kushans south of Taxila and down the coast deep into the territory of the Pallavas in the south. Like Chandragupta I, he forged ties to regions outside of Gupta control, the people of which in turn pledged their loyalty to him. As was the case of the states of Zhou China, this arrangement has often been characterized as "feudal" in that it resembles the relationships among the states of medieval Europe, though scholars are careful not to push the parallels too far. Samudragupta's son, Chandragupta II (r. ca. 380–413 CE), seized the throne from his elder brother and continued to expand the empire, adding the southern and western Gujarati territories of the Shakas. The cumulative effect of this string of conquests over barely a century was that, once again, the Indian subcontinent stood on the threshold of unity (see Map 8.3).

MOVEMENT OF NOMADIC PEOPLES, 300 BCE–100 CE

Court and Culture   The Gupta era is considered to be the classical age of Indian culture and religion. During the reign of the Guptas, the collection of religious traditions called "**Hinduism**" flourished, becoming the dominant faith of the time. Indeed, the Guptas actively used the gods and practices of Hinduism, particularly in their devotion to Vishnu and Shiva, to extend their legitimacy not just as kings but as universal rulers.

Although the Guptas preferred the king-centered, hierarchical Brahmanic tradition of Hinduism, which they made the privileged religion in the state, they permitted the practice of other faiths, including both Jainism and Buddhism. Under their influence and with their financial support, the first distinctly "Hindu" art is recognizable in the temples and shrines to a variety of deities that were built in staggering profusion. In addition, the era marked a peak of popularity for classical treatises on political and social behavior such as the *Arthashastra* and the *Kama Sutra*, the famous manual of sexual practices and personal deportment, as well as, it is often supposed, the works of the playwright and poet Kalidasa (fl. fifth century CE), sometimes called the "Indian Shakespeare."

Narrative accounts of the world of Chandragupta II can be found in the writings of the Chinese Buddhist monk Fa Xian (see Chapter 9). On a pilgrimage to sacred Buddhist sites in northern India, Fa Xian traveled from Chang'an, the eastern terminus of the Silk Road, to Taxila and Gandhara, and through the old states of Magadha and Kosala before returning home by way of Sri Lanka and Java during the years 399–414 CE. During this arduous journey, Fa Xian found a Buddhist world in which the monks and monasteries were thriving and the people were contented.Government was not intrusive yet the people were well-behaved, there were no restrictions on their movements, and even criminals were treated with admirable leniency: In the most extreme cases, they were only subject to amputation of their right hands.

Hinduism: A convenient, shorthand term for the vast multiplicity of religious practices derived from the Vedic, Brahmanic, Upanishadic, and later traditions in India and those places influenced by Indian culture.

Devotion to Vishnu

"By claiming devotional proximity to Vishnu as the god's supreme devotee ... Chandragupta was claiming a special relationship with the god who had saved the earth and was in ... possession of it. This allowed the king to be called, among other things, the 'Lord of the Earth' ... and to advance the claim that the whole earth belonged to the crown."

—Michael Willis. *The Archaeology of Hindu Ritual: Temples and the Establishment of the Gods*, p. 3. Cambridge: Cambridge University Press, 2009.

The Waning of Gupta Power   Gupta power began to fade under the reigns of Chandragupta II's son and grandson, whose

MAP **8.3** The Gupta Empire.

weakened authority was challenged by groups seeking greater autonomy in the vicinity of Malwa, in central India. By this time, however, a new wave of central Asian nomads, the Hunas, sometimes called the "White Huns," had appeared. By 510 CE, having defeated the Guptas at Gwalior, some 200 miles south of the modern city of New Delhi, the Hunas established themselves as the dominant force in northwest India, and once again the areas along the Ganges were thrust into political disunity. By 515 CE, the eastern tributary states of the Guptas had broken away, while in the west the kingdom of the Rajputanas emerged in Gujarat by mid-century.

The Southern Kingdoms, ca. 300–600 CE

Though their states were constantly contending with each other for wealth, power, and territory, the southern regimes of the so-called "imperial Pallavas," Pandyas,

Cholas and Chalukyas of peninsular India were comparatively stable in cultural terms from the decline of the Guptas until the installation of the Muslim sultanates of the north. One reason for this was the absence of a powerful empire pushing south. Freed from the need to defend themselves from incursion from the north, the southern kingdoms could pursue the pacification of their own realms. Their political and religious systems were also still largely dominated by descendants of northern colonists, so their ruling classes shared to some degree a common culture.

In addition, the development of Hinduism among the Tamils, the region's chief ethnic group, contributed to cultural stability, while its synthesis with local traditions inspired a dramatic flowering of literature and art. These include the rise of **devotional** branches of Hinduism and an outpouring of spectacular religious art rarely equaled in any area of the world. Finally, the power and wealth of the region was enhanced by the promotion of trade, especially with the established "Indianized" enclaves of southeast Asia and the Indonesian archipelago. As a result of these ties, Indian religions, culture, and economics dominated Indian Ocean trade until it was gradually taken over by the Muslims after the fourteenth century CE.

Devotional: In the context of this chapter, dedicating oneself to practices that venerate, honor, or adore a particular god or divinity.

Temple Complexes   The southern kingdoms' most tangible remains are the Hindu temple complexes left behind at a number of sites. The Pallavas, for example, under Mahendra Vikruma Varman I (r. ca. 590–630 CE), constructed the famous Mandapa Temple, carved from solid rock. His descendant, Narasimha Varman II (r. 695–728 CE), sponsored the seven rock pagodas of Mahabali Purana. Perhaps most spectacular of all was the eighth-century CE Rashtakutra complex of Krishna I at Kailasantha again carved from solid rock. The work was so complex, detailed, and painstakingly done that it was said to have moved its master builder to cry, "Oh, how did I do this?"

Regional Struggles   The long process of interaction and adaptation in India had already created a recognizably different society as one moved south from the Ganges. For one thing, the systems of *varna* and *jati* (see Chapter 3) tended to

The Kailasantha Temple. Hewn from a single, solid rock, the Kailasantha Temple, part of an elaborate complex in east-central India, is considered the world's most monumental sculpture. Strongly influenced by south Indian architectural traditions, the temple complex dazzles the visitor with carvings of innumerable deities, mythic figures, and erotic imagery.

revolve more around where one lived than they did in the north. For example, there were major differentiations between those living in the cities and flatland farming communities and the "hill peoples" and "forest peoples," still considered largely uncivilized. A major division also existed between the local leaders, whose families had in many cases emigrated from the north and were members of the upper varnas, and their subjects. Within these divisions, rulers tended to be more predatory in their efforts to enrich themselves and their kingdoms.

The rise of the Chalukya state on the western side of the peninsula in the mid-sixth century CE, along with that of the Vakatakas of the Deccan Plateau and the Rashtakutras in the early eighth century CE, resumed the struggle for wealth and territory among the older southern kingdoms. As we will see in Chapter 13, by the middle of the eighth century CE, the Chalukya state spawned a potent rival when the areas to the north and west broke away from its grasp. The leaders there became known as the "Rashtakutras" and shortly thereafter captured the capital at Badami.

The Vedic Tradition and Its Visionary Reformers

Beginning around 700 BCE, visionaries appeared, seeking to reform a Vedic tradition that they believed had grown overly formalistic and unresponsive to the needs of the people. As we noted in Chapter 3, the first of these men were the thinkers who created the Upanishads, a set of spiritual writings that lay the foundations of *monism*—the belief in a single transcendent first principle—in Hindu thought. In the next two centuries, Mahavira and the Buddha followed, becoming the founding figures, respectively, of Jainism, a small community in today's India, and of Buddhism, today a major religion in southeast Asia, China, and Japan.

Reforming the Vedic Tradition

The Vedas consisted of 10 books of hymns to the gods and goddesses of the Hindu pantheon and described in detail the rituals and sacrifices required to keep the world in harmony with these deities. They thus framed the culture of the period 1200–600 BCE, when the inhabitants of the Indian subcontinent initiated the pattern of Punjab and Ganges valley state formation. As we saw at the beginning of this chapter, several dozen warrior republics and kingdoms competed against each other for wealth and power, similar to the warring states of China that we will explore in Chapter 9. It was against the backdrop of this competition that visionaries critical of the polytheistic Vedic heritage arose and sought to reform it through the formulation of a single first principle. The main figures of these reform efforts were the authors of the Upanishads (ca. 700–300 BCE), Mahavira (trad. 599–527 BCE), and Gautama, the Buddha or Enlightened One (trad. 563–483 BCE).

The Upanishad Visionaries   Many authors of the more than 100 Upanishads are known to us by name. They were Brahmanic priests—and also the daughter of one—whose principal concern was to penetrate beyond the complexities of the tens of thousands of gods (as one of the Upanishads mockingly asserts) to a vision of cosmic unity. This Upanishadic vision, with its opposition to polytheism and the proclamation of monism, was remarkably similar to those propounded in the

Middle East and China during the same time: They proclaimed a transcendent first principle as universal truth, addressed to anyone anywhere.

The Indian visionaries were hermit teachers living in the forests of the Gangetic states to "draw near" to themselves (the meaning of the Sanskrit "Upanishad") disciples who did not want merely to understand the transcendent unity of the universe outside of the individual but also to attain this unity by merging their personal selves (*atman*) into the universal self (*brahman*) and thereby achieve salvation. These visionaries did not develop this theme of the unity of atman–brahman systematically in the form of treatises. Instead, they concentrated on leading their disciples through brief aphorisms, paradoxes, and negations ("not this, nor that") step by step into deep meditation, which they considered as the activity through which salvation could be achieved. As time went on, however, contemplation of the Upanishadic scriptures and their hidden meanings concerning the mysteries of atman–brahman also became a vital part of a new evolving tradition. In the highest state of understanding of atman–brahman, one could attain release from the bounds of the cycles of death and rebirth and thus enter into transcendence, or *moksha*.

Criticism of the Vedic Rituals and Sacrifices

Although they were advocates of monism, or first principle, the authors of the Upanishads remained faithful to the Vedic rituals, sacrifices, and doctrines. Their reforms were limited to creating a meditative supplement to the Vedic religion. However, as strong kingdoms emerged in the 500s BCE and conquered smaller kingdoms and warrior republics, criticism of religious ritual grew. Urbanization and trade created new classes of inhabitants, such as merchants and craftspeople, to whom rituals and sacrifices meant far less than they did to the kings and the priestly class. The merchants and craftspeople viewed the rituals as formalistic and the sacrifices, consisting of burning large quantities of food and killing many animals, as wasteful. For the kings and priests, these religious practices were essential to legitimize their power. The Vedic doctrine that eventually caused the break between the priests and their strongest critics, however, was that of the cycle of karma–samsara (see Chapter 3), death and rebirth.

The Ascetic Break: Jainism

The founder of the Jains, Nigantha Nataputta [Nee-GAN-tah Nah-tah-POO-tah], whose title of Vardhamana Mahavira means "the great hero," was born the son of a warrior chief perhaps around 540 BCE. At the age of 30 he left home and gave up all his worldly possessions to become an ascetic, and after 12 years he found meditative enlightenment. From this point on he was given the title of *jina*, or "conqueror," and from this his followers became known as "Jains." For the next 40 years, he wandered throughout India without clothes or possessions, spreading the new sect's principles and practices. Finally, as the ultimate exemplar of the movement's ideal of not taking the life of any being whatsoever, Mahavira refused all food and performed a ritual fast that led to his death in Pava, near Pataliputra.

While much of the earliest Jain doctrine was lost during its first two centuries of oral transmission, it begins with a universe in which all things possess *jiva*, a kind of "soul" that yearns to be free from the prison of the material world. Jains believe

Statue of the Jain Saint Gomateshwara at Karnataka. The world's largest statue cut from a single stone, this statue was built at the site of the famous Jain monastery, where, it was said, Chandragupta Maurya entered the order and fasted to death, following the example of the sect's founder, Mahavira.

that even inanimate objects, such as stones—as well as plants, human beings, and other animals—possess *jiva*, though at different levels or "senses." These "souls" are governed in turn by the degree to which a thing's past karma stands between it and its release from material bondage. For human beings, karma builds up according to the injuries one does to other beings and objects, intentionally or not. The way to enlightenment is to act in such a way that one acquires as little karma as possible, while performing actions of suffering and self-sacrifice to atone for and reduce the karma one already has. In this sense, karma might be thought of as a kind of weight on the "soul": As karma dissipates, the soul becomes lighter until, finally free, it rises to the very heights of the cosmos and lives for eternity.

Ahimsa   Jain monks take extraordinary pains to prevent injury to any object, especially living things. For example, from the first centuries of the movement there has been a **schism** between those who insist on complete nakedness—to avoid injuring creatures that might be trapped in one's clothing—and those who wear a simple white robe. Other measures include wearing gauze masks to filter out invisible organisms that might be breathed in and carrying brooms to sweep small creatures out of one's path. Monks live by begging food from others—so that they themselves do not have to kill it and add to their karma. Because suffering reduces karma, they frequently undergo extraordinary ordeals, such as allowing themselves to be covered with biting insects or lying on beds of nails. The most dedicated perform the supreme sacrifice and ritually starve themselves to death, which, because of the intense suffering involved and the resolute refusal to harm living things, is seen as the ultimate act of ahimsa, or nonviolence.

> **Schism:** A division; when used in a religious context it usually refers to the splitting of members of a certain religion into two or more camps over matters of doctrine, ritual, etc.

Not surprisingly, the strict practices of the Jains did not appeal to most people. As a result, an extensive laity, especially among the lower castes who identified more with the sacrifices of the monks, grew to support them. The patronage of kings, most famously Chandragupta Maurya, helped ensure the sect's vitality. As a matter of course, Jains would not take up farming, so monastic and lay followers were often involved in business, study, and writing—occupations they still favor today. The religion's most distinctive element is that it is rigorously **atheistic**, choosing not to worship any god but insisting instead on meditatively merging into an eternal, uncreated, indifferent unity that is both universal and transcendent.

> **Atheistic:** Not believing in a god or supreme being.

The Middle Way: Buddhism   The other major movement, Buddhism, began in part as a reaction against such extreme ascetic practices. Siddhartha Gautama, whose title of "Buddha" means "the Enlightened One," is believed to have been born a prince in the Sakya republic in the Himalayan foothills. His traditional birth date is given as 563 BCE, though recent accounts have moved it to at least the mid-400s BCE. Because of his royal pedigree, he is frequently referred to as "Sakyamuni," or prince of the Sakyas. Seeking to shelter him from the evils of the world, Gautama's father secluded him in the palace. At the age of 29, however, Gautama left his world of privilege and followed the paths of various Vedic schools. At one point, following a discipline of extreme asceticism, his path of self-deprivation led him to nearly fast to death.

During his travels, Gautama was exposed to the entire range of human suffering and death from which his father had tried so hard to shelter him. His shock and compassion for the world around him drove him to find a way to understand the endless round of death and rebirth to which all creatures were apparently subject. According to Buddhist accounts, the insight gained from his experiences and a long period of deep meditation sparked his enlightenment one day under a pipal tree in the town of Gaya. Shortly afterward, Gautama went to a deer park in Sarnath, close by the great city of Varanasi (Benares) where he found five former disciples and preached a sermon to them outlining what became known as the Middle Way—the path of moderation.

The Four Noble Truths, the Eightfold Path, and Nirvana

Gautama believed that the fundamental nature of the perceived universe is change. In a constantly changing world, suffering is the common lot of all because they attach themselves to what will ultimately be taken from them. Although they crave permanence, they rely only on their senses, which provide the illusion of stability but actually give a false picture of what is the true, ever-changing nature of things. Pushed into evil deeds in pursuit of whatever they desire, they accumulate karma. Over many lifetimes, the karma they acquire stays with them even after the separation of the material "soul" from the immaterial at death. It builds up with each life and keeps them from breaking free of the cycle of death and rebirth. In that first sermon in Sarnath, Gautama distilled these insights into what he called the Four Noble Truths:

1. that all life is suffering
2. that suffering arises from craving
3. that to stop suffering, one must stop craving
4. that one stops craving by following the Eightfold Path of right views, right resolve, right speech, right conduct, right livelihood, right effort, right mindfulness, and right concentration

Later sermons and vast numbers of commentaries outlined the specifics of the Eightfold Path. Essentially, the path represents a course of life in which one avoids extreme behaviors of any kind, adheres to a code of conduct that favors **altruism** and respects the life of all living beings, and through meditation and "right mindfulness" reaches a state of calm nonattachment with an uncluttered mind able to grasp the universal truth. On reaching this stage during this same lifetime, the karmic traces of past lives are "blown out" like a lamp flame, the literal meaning of the Sanskrit word associated with this final state of enlightenment: *nirvana*, or nothingness. In Buddhism, this nothingness is a more explicit version of the logic of *moksha*—transcendence—first explored in the Upanishads.

Altruism: The practice of acting in an unselfish manner for the good of others.

While the extreme practices of Jainism limited its popularity to India, the moderation and adaptability of Buddhist teachings allowed them to spread outside of the subcontinent. As it began to spread outside of India, the flexibility of Buddhist doctrine in the face of the varied religions with which it interacted and adapted allowed it to take on many of their trappings. Thus, although many scholars do not consider it a "religion" in its earliest stages, by the first centuries of the new millennium, Buddhism had become a new, universal faith.

Even during the Buddha's lifetime his followers had organized into a brotherhood, despite his dying injunction that the true path to enlightenment resided in them as individuals. As in other movements, the void left by the Buddha's death resulted in disputes about the authenticity of certain teachings and questions about how the group should now conduct itself. Over the following two centuries, several

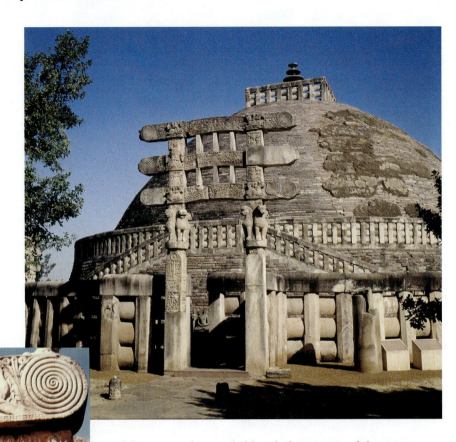

Great Buddhist Stupa at Sanchi. The need for commemorative burial mounds and reliquaries for the Buddha's relics spawned a characteristic structure called a *stupa*, meaning "gathered." Brimming with symbolic motifs representing the stages of enlightenment, the structures changed considerably from this example—built in the first century BCE over an earlier one from the Mauryan period—as they spread through east Asia, where they assumed the shape of the pagoda.

Buddhist councils were held and, during one of these meetings, a division developed, resulting in one group separating from the main body of adherents. The now separate group became known as Theravada [Ter-rah-VAH-dah], "the teachings of the elders." Under Ashoka's influence, Theravada Buddhism became the approved sect, with the first complete surviving texts dating from this time.

Buddhist Texts   The *Pali Canon*, written in Pali, the sacred language of Buddhism, is a collection of texts that forms the foundation of Theravada Buddhism and serves as the fundamental body of scriptures for nearly all Buddhist schools. The collection consists of the *Tripitaka* [Tree-pee-TAH-kuh], or "Three Baskets"; the *Vinaya* [Vee-NAI-yah], treatises on conduct and rules of discipline for monks; the *Sutras* [SOO-truhs], or "discourses," of which there are five groups, with most of them believed to have originated with the Buddha; and the *Abhidhamma* [Ah-bee-DAH-mah], doctrines of philosophy and metaphysics.

As Theravada Buddhism developed and spread in northern India and beyond, a number of developments changed its character, making it more accessible to a larger group of followers. The rich cultural interaction of the many peoples encountering it resulted in a great number of religious ideas and traditions circulating around the region. Questions and problems among Buddhist adherents from these different areas required broader solutions than in earlier times. For example, stories of the Buddha's last days implied that he would save everyone who followed his path, opening the way for the potential enlightenment of all. Coupled with this was a developing tradition of the Buddha as one in a long line of past and future Buddhas, suggesting the potential for a devotional component to the religion. In addition, there was the concept of the *bodhisattva* [boh-dee-SAHT-vuh]—one who, having achieved enlightenment, does not proceed to nirvana but is dedicated instead to helping the suffering achieve their own enlightenment.

Theravada and Mahayana   All of these ideas took shape around the first century CE in what became the largest branch of Buddhism, Mahayana [Mah-hah-YAH-nah], the "greater vehicle." Dismissing Theravada Buddhism as Hinayana [Heen-ah-YAH-nah], or "the lesser vehicle," Mahayana spread along the trade routes into central Asia, into the borderlands of the Parthians, and ultimately to China, Korea, Japan, and Tibet (see Map 8.4). As it spread, its different interpretive schools were, broadly speaking, divided into *esoteric* branches—those seeking enlightenment through scriptural or other kinds of deep knowledge—and devotional branches. Of the devotional schools, that of Amitabha [Ah-mee-TAH-bah], the Heavenly Buddha of the Western Paradise, is today the most popular Buddhist sect in both China and Japan (see Chapters 9 and 13).

As Buddhism was spreading across the greater part of Asia, however, its decline had, in a sense, already begun in the land of its birth. With the revitalization of the older Vedic and Brahmanic traditions into Hinduism, all the schools of Buddhism were to face strong competition for converts and noble patronage.

The Maturity of Hinduism:
From the Abstract to the Devotional

The period from the Mauryans to the rise of the Guptas brought about a number of changes within the orthodox traditions of Indian religion. On the one hand, the continuing push of state formation to the south carried with it the older Vedic and Upanishadic traditions. Along the way, these traditions had incorporated many local deities into their pantheon of gods. Over the next several centuries these southern areas would lead in the rise of devotional cults, especially those of Vishnu and Shiva, culminating in the *bhakti* movements beginning in the seventh century CE.

On the other hand, the growth of new religions like Buddhism and Jainism challenged such cultural mainstays as the caste system, the inevitability of the karmic cycle, and the domination of society and salvation by the traditional ruling classes. As a result of these challenges and through the popularity of the grand epics of the Mahabharata and Ramayana, the spreading of the classical texts of the first and second centuries, and Gupta patronage, a rejuvenated brand of religious experience, Hinduism, is distinctly recognizable by the fourth century CE.

Avatars and Alvars   Among the most consistent Hindu beliefs was the idea that the subcontinent was a land united by faith—*Bharata*—a name used to describe India ever since. Another is the development of a full continuum of religious experience, ranging from the highly abstract to the emotional and mystical, springing from devotion to a particular god. Perhaps due to the egalitarian influence of Buddhism and Jainism, salvation was increasingly seen as accessible to all, according to one's abilities and the restrictions of caste and one's social position.

MAP **8.4** The Spread of Buddhism to 600 CE.

Of the many gods singled out for special attention, the most important were the so-called Indian trinity: Brahma, Vishnu, and Shiva. Of these, the main divisions of devotion emerged between Vishnu, the beneficent preserver, and Shiva, the powerful, fertile giver and destroyer of life, the "Lord of the Dance" of the universe. Both Vishnu and Shiva can manifest themselves through avatars or incarnations, the most popular of which is Krishna, an incarnation of Vishnu, who plays such a central role in the Bhagavad Gita. In addition to guiding that epic's hero, Arjuna, to an understanding of fulfilling his dharma—regardless of the immediate consequences—Krishna reveals to him the true power of devotion to himself as transcending the transitory nature of the material world.

The ability of the new devotional traditions of Hinduism to appeal to all castes made the religion increasingly popular from the time of the Guptas on. Within the all-encompassing character of Hinduism grew the assumption that one could achieve salvation according to one's caste and ability, whether one was a *shudra*, worshiping Shiva with a pure heart, or a highly educated brahman, finding liberation within the most profound texts. By the seventh century CE, religious poets were carrying the message of devotional Hinduism to all believers in vernacular languages. *Alvars* and *nayanars*, singers of praise for Vishnu and Shiva respectively, created some of the most passionate and beautiful religious poetry in any language over the next five centuries and helped bond the people to the orthodox religion as a whole.

Representations of Brahma, Vishnu, and Shiva. From the time of the Guptas, a growing movement within Hinduism was that of devotional practices directed at the trinity of Brahma, the Creator; Vishnu, the Preserver; and Shiva, the Destroyer. The gods are frequently represented with multiple limbs to symbolize their different roles and superhuman functions.

Shakti and Tantra   A related development was that of Shakti, literally "power," sometimes called "tantra." Shakti practitioners often probed the darker edges of the multiple natures of the gods—especially Shiva and his consort Kali, or Durga—associated with death and destruction. Toward this end they purposely violated social norms—by eating meat, having illicit sex (even committing incest), eating human excrement, and, on rare occasions, committing ritual murder. The idea behind such perverse behavior was both to prove one's mastery over attachment to the acts themselves and to push beyond the ordinary dualities of good and evil. Such extreme activities were comparatively rare, though the idea of transcending ordinary norms also passed into Buddhism at about the same time, in the fourth and fifth centuries CE. Here, it was also referred to as "tantra" and often as "the vehicle of the thunderbolt." In this modified form it passed into Nepal and Tibet, where its mysticism and interest in magical practices formed important elements of Tibetan Buddhism.

Stability Amid Disorder: Economics, Family, and Society

Despite India's tumultuous political history, the agrarian-based economy of the subcontinent remained for 2,000 years the richest (along with China) in the world. Its agriculture was enormously productive in its most fertile areas, and the topography and climate allowed an astonishing variety of products, from fragrant woods to pepper and other tropical spices, to be produced for domestic consumption and export. As the economy flourished, society as a whole remained relatively stable. The hierarchical nature of the caste system maintained continuity through times of political turmoil, prescribing set duties and standards of behavior according to social position. Although the newly emerged religions of Buddhism and Jainism did not recognize the caste system, their appearance and spread did not fundamentally alter that system.

The relationships between men and women and among family members outlined in Chapter 3 grew increasingly complex, particularly from the classical age of the Guptas onward. Despite the trend in Buddhism—and, as we shall see in Chapters 10 and 12 in Islam—toward greater equality between men and women, beliefs such as the strictly delineated spheres of husband and wife, the idea of the female as a fundamental force of the universe, and a male vision of women as simultaneously desirable and threatening were considerably enlarged during this time.

Tax and Spend: Economics and Society

By 600 BCE, the inhabitants of the emerging Gangetic states had long since made the transition to being settled agriculturalists. With the vast majority of inhabitants of the new states being peasants from the lowest *shudra varna*, the chief form of revenue was harvest taxes. The average tax levied on the people of these early states appears to have been around one-sixth of their annual harvest.

Accelerating Taxes   With the expansion of Magadha in the fifth and fourth centuries BCE, the agricultural tax increased to one-quarter of the harvest and even higher on royal lands—as much as half the cultivable land in the kingdom. By this time, the accelerating pace of urban life, the explosion of trade, and the increasingly differentiated castes expanded the economy even more, allowing whole new classes of items to be taxed. Thus, the immense wealth wielded by the Mauryans was accumulated through harvest taxes as high as one-half of all the produce raised in the empire, as well as taxes on livestock, internal trade, imports and exports, and such commodities as gold, textiles, salt, horses, and a variety of forest products and spices. Moreover, the increase in trade had led to a growing commercial class expanding beyond the traditional *vaisya* (merchant) *varna*, while the growing need for capital and credit was met by guilds of bankers and traders in precious metals.

Agricultural taxes of about one-quarter to one-third of the harvest continued under the Guptas. The various working guilds, or *sreni* in the major cities were highly organized. As under the Mauryans, bankers and merchants were frequently tapped by rulers for ready cash to fund armies, buy off intruders, or finance other emergency measures. Despite low **tariffs**, the Guptas enjoyed a highly favorable balance of trade. Indeed, the empire's self-sufficiency in nearly all commercial items meant that foreign traders had to pay for their goods in gold or silver. Because of this, the Romans were eventually forced to stop much of their Indian trade because of its drain on their supply of precious metals.

Tariffs: Taxes levied on imports.

Trade and Expansion   By the time of Persia's invasion in the late sixth century BCE, the reputation of the wealth of northern India was already well established among the Greeks. The historian Herodotus (ca. 484–425 BCE), for example, noted that the yearly tribute of gold from the region was several times that of Persian Egypt. Interactions with the expanding Hellenistic world extended the reach of Indian markets and trade through the eastern Mediterranean and, shortly, into the expanding Roman domains.

With the decline of the Mauryans and the adoption of Buddhism by peoples of the northwest, the region around Taxila became the **nexus** of a caravan trade that from the third century BCE to the third century CE, linked nearly all of Eurasia from Roman Britain to Han China and beyond along the famous Silk Road (see Chapter 9). In addition, Buddhist, Jain, and Brahmanic religious elements all spread westward over time to enrich in varying degrees the intellectual climate of the Parthians, Greeks, and Romans.

Nexus: A means of connection, a bond or link; also, a series of connections.

Indians also dominated the region's maritime trade until they were gradually displaced by the Arabs from the ninth to the fifteenth centuries CE and by the Europeans shortly thereafter. The reputations of "Chryse" and "Cheronese," the lands of gold of southeast Asia, were well established among the Romans through Indian trade by the first centuries CE, while Roman and Greek jars and coins could be found as far away as Vietnam, Cambodia, and Java. Colonies of Greek, Roman, Persian, and Arab traders clustered in the western port cities of Broach and Kalliena, trading tin, copper, hides, and **antimony** for the teak, ebony, ivory, spices, and silks available there. A testament to the importance of the trade in the Greco-Roman world was the first-century guide to the Indian Ocean, the *Periplus* (marine atlas) *of the Erythrean Sea* (see "Patterns Up Close: The Global Trade of Indian Pepper").

Antimony: A metal widely used in alloys.

Indian Influence Beyond India   By the first century CE, this expanding trade region had established a network of outposts in southeast Asia and the Indonesian archipelago. Buddhist influence in the area may have come soon after. Though it is unclear whether merchants or missionaries made the first contacts, a series of small settlements of Indians on the Malay Peninsula launched the founding of the first of the Indianized kingdoms in the area, that of Funan in the Mekong delta of southeast Asia by the Brahmin Kaudinya in the second century CE. The spread of both Buddhism and the Indian system of "god-kings" soon reached the nearby Khmers [Khe-MARES] and the state of Champa [KHAM-puh] in modern Cambodia (Kampuchea) and Vietnam. By the seventh and eighth centuries CE, these areas became important trade centers in their own right, connecting the Indian states with Tang China and Heian Japan.

In addition, these countries formed important way stations in the expanding traffic of Buddhist pilgrims. The widespread appeal of Buddhism enhanced the Indian economy by both increasing the volume of trade on the subcontinent and providing a uniform structure for its expansion abroad. The mobility of pilgrims and monks, their role as missionaries, and their aversion to a number of lower-caste occupations made them natural candidates to assist in the increasingly far-flung circulation of goods and ideas. Monasteries served as hostels and way stations along well-traveled routes; larger complexes along branches of the Silk Road often had commercial centers grow up around them, particularly if they were destinations for pilgrims as well. The international character of Buddhism also facilitated contacts among long-distance traders. Perhaps most importantly, it linked India to an emerging cultural sphere that soon spanned Eurasia from the borderlands of the Persian empires to Japan. By the fourth century CE, firm trade ties had been established with the Romans, the Sasanids, the remnant states of Han China, and the Buddhist and Indianizing territories of southeast Asia (see Map 8.5).

Patterns Up Close

The Global Trade of Indian Pepper

As we have seen in previous chapters, the history of humankind is closely interwoven with the history of food. In this context the cultivation of a seemingly humble condiment such as pepper must seem scarcely worth a mention. Yet, its original cul-

Pepper berries drying in the sun. *Piper nigrum*, native to south India, is a vine that twists itself around bushes and small trees. The method of drying freshly picked peppers in the sun for three days, as shown in this photograph, has not changed for millennia.

tivation in south India, diffusion to the rest of the subcontinent, and export throughout Eurasia and parts of Africa made it perhaps the world's most sought-after commodity for thousands of years. Indeed, its primacy among such other rare spices as nutmeg, ginger, cinnamon, and cloves ultimately drove European adventurers and traders to the Americas as they sought a direct all-water route to its source in India.

The pepper plant (*Piper nigrum*) is a vine native to the Malabar Coast of India in the modern state of Kerala. The two main varieties of pepper, white and black, are derived from the same berries: white pepper is the product of crushing the dried seeds (peppercorns), while black pepper comes from soaking and drying the seeds with their fruit coating still attached. As far back as the thirteenth century BCE, Egyptian records show black pepper being used in mummifications, a testament to its early place as a valued import.

By the third century BCE, pepper had become a mainstay of south India's burgeoning Indian Ocean trade, with growing annual cargoes going to China, southeast Asia, and Egypt. The Hellenistic cultural exchange conducted through Ptolemaic Egypt spread the use of pepper throughout the Mediterranean world. By the first century BCE, traders from Egypt, coastal Arabia, and northeast Africa were regularly availing themselves of the monsoon winds to make annual voyages to the Malabar ports for pepper. But it was after the Roman acquisition of Egypt that pepper became a kind of mania throughout their empire. Roman cooks, it seems, added pepper to every conceivable dish, sometimes in amounts that would be unpalatable today. By some estimates, 80% of the dishes recorded in Roman cookbooks called for pepper. Contemporary Romans like Pliny the Elder regularly complained of the huge drain of gold required to keep the empire adequately spiced, and the export of gold to India was ultimately curtailed. Such was the level of "pepper power" that both Alaric the Visigoth and Attila the Hun were said to have demanded great quantities of the spice as part of their ransom demands on the city of Rome in the fifth century.

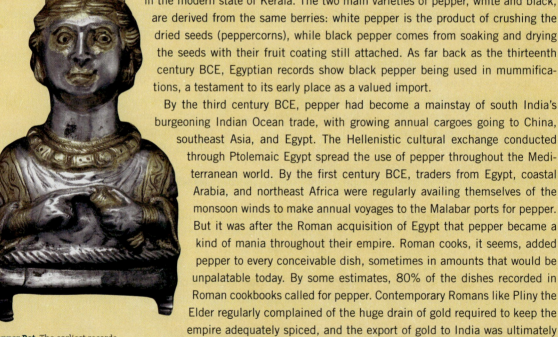

Pepper Pot. The earliest records of pepper being imported into Britain are from the first century. Discovered in 1992, this exquisite pepper pot—a special container intended to keep this expensive spice—is designed in the shape of an "empress" and dates to the fifth century CE. Made of gold and silver, it testifies to the high value placed on such a precious commodity, especially in a remote place like Britain.

How does one account for the huge popularity of a food product that has no nutritive value and burns the tongue? Initially, part of pepper's attraction may have been its exotic quality as a mysterious spice from a faraway land. But it had also long been used for medicinal purposes in India, and from Roman times through the European Middle Ages it was hailed in European and Arab treatises as healthful in a number of ways. Its ability to make one sneeze was seen as helpful in purging

MAP 8.5 Asian Trade Routes, ca. 100 CE.

the body of irritants, its ability to make one perspire was said to help cool the body during a fever, and it was said to settle one's stomach and even calm one's nerves. Most useful of all, perhaps, was its capabilities as a preservative. Long used to preserve fish, meat, and vegetables in tropical south India, pepper was avidly sought throughout Eurasia to treat perishables and enhance their flavors—particularly during the winter months when fresh food was difficult to obtain.

The Arab occupation of the prime transshipment areas of the eastern Mediterranean, the termini of the Silk Road, and, by the fourteenth century, domination of Indian Ocean trade caused the price of Indian commodities to soar in Europe. In the case of pepper, these conditions turned it into a kind of informal currency: In England, for example, one could sometimes pay rents or taxes with it. The urge to break the Islamic monopoly of the spice trade ultimately drove the Portuguese, and Columbus, to set off for India by sailing into the Atlantic, hoping to go directly to the Malabar Coast. When the Portuguese captain Vasco da Gama reached the port of Calicut in 1498, he ended up paying twice the going rate for pepper, cloves, and cinnamon, much of which was later found to be laced with fillers of dirt and bark. Like the meeting between Alexander and "Sandrakoptros" so many years before, there was nothing about this encounter that gave the participants any inkling of what was to come. With the loading of this first unprepossessing cargo by the Portuguese, however, the commercial network built on pepper and other spices was now positioned to drive what would grow into the world's first global trading system.

Questions

- How does the global trade in Indian pepper show the connectedness of Eurasia in this period in world history?

- Use the Origins-Interactions-Adaptation framework to consider the pepper trade more closely. What are the origins of the pepper trade? How did it change over time through interactions? What adaptations, if any, resulted from these interactions?

Caste, Family Life, and Gender

As with the economy, the basic patterns of Indian society were already being forged by the seventh century BCE. The integration of Aryan migrants, the peoples of northwestern India, and the early inhabitants of the Ganges valley had been largely completed. Thereafter, the fusion of Vedic traditions into a distinct form of Hindu culture, drawn heavily from the Brahmanic religious and social practices, proceeded apace. In the Gupta Empire, when Hinduism became the privileged religion of the state and the subcontinent was largely decentralized as regional kingdoms competed with each other, Hinduism evolved into a religious civilization, the form of social organization dominant during the period 600–1450 in world history (see Part 3).

Maturation of the Caste System   Perhaps the most distinctive marker of Hinduism as a religious civilization is the caste (Sanskrit *jati*) system. Scholars are still uncertain as to whether this system originated with the four varnas in the Punjab–Ganges states or whether it evolved later. In any case, varna and caste seem to have merged over time to create a markedly stable, adaptable, yet also repressive system that continues even today, despite being technically unlawful under the Indian constitution. One of the caste system's chief functions was to provide a mechanism for absorbing and acculturating peoples of widely divergent languages, ethnicities, and religious practices into an integrated social whole. Within the framework of caste, all people lived within an interlocking system of reciprocal rights and responsibilities in which even those at the bottom levels had a necessary, if disagreeable, societal function.

Karma–Samsara and Dharma   Although people on every rung of the social ladder had in theory a secure place, there appears to have been more mobility within the system in ancient times. Under certain conditions—for example, financial need—members of the upper castes could take up occupations normally reserved for those below them. A certain amount of flexibility was even allowed the lowest castes in this regard. By the fifth century BCE, the increasing acceptance of the idea of karma–samsara gave a religious foundation to these social structures by holding out the possibility of advancing to a higher caste in the next life. Even most branches of Buddhism and Jainism grudgingly recognized caste as a societal given, according it further legitimacy.

During the Mauryan era, Ashoka's advocacy of dharma also reinforced older notions of duty according to social position, while such treatises on proper behavior as the *Code of Manu* (written down by 200 CE) helped solidify concepts of model conduct among the various classes of society. By the Gupta period, renewed interest in societal stability after nearly five centuries of disorder prompted increased attention to stricter boundaries for acceptable behaviors within the different jati. Along with this, the idea of **ritual pollution** resulting from unsanctioned contact with lower castes—requiring ever more elaborate purification rites to cleanse oneself after such contact—becomes increasingly common. This increasing trend in social segregation led to such things as small closets, nooks, and other places of concealment built into the houses of the upper castes so that their lower-caste servants could instantly hide themselves if their masters suddenly happened upon them.

Ritual pollution: The act of making something or someone "unclean" in terms of their religious taboos or prohibitions.

Yet, such repressive extremes also mask some of the strengths that gave the caste system its vitality and longevity. Like religious organizations and guilds in medieval Europe, jati membership provided a kind of extended family, giving each person a recognized and valued place in society, despised as they might be by their "betters." In some areas, especially in the south, entire villages or clans were incorporated into their own jatis; in others, ethnicity or occupation might be the determining criteria. Although the upper castes dominated the political structure of rural society, social power was in fact more diffuse than is usually appreciated. For example, the members of various caste and guild councils were customarily represented at state functions. In addition, different castes became associated with special feasts and their sponsoring gods or goddesses, giving them a degree of informal power within the larger social structure.

Jainism, Buddhism, and Caste   Jainism and Buddhism had a considerable influence on the caste system as well. Although both religions accepted the theory of karma–samsara, their followers saw their own distinct practices as ways to break out of the cycle of death and rebirth. They thus represented powerful alternative traditions to the acceptance of varna and jati. Moreover, the potential for anyone, regardless of social position, to practice these methods undermined the hierarchical order of the caste system and made Jain and Buddhist practitioners equals in a society of believers. Their alternative institutions such as monasteries for men and women as well as their self-sufficiency, good works, and commercial expertise also gave them considerable material power in the larger community, particularly when patronized by nobles or monarchs.

Family Life and Hindu Culture: Men   Despite the attractiveness for some of monastic or ascetic life, the family remained the primary social unit of Indian society. Norms of proper moral behavior for family life were explicitly outlined in the *Code of Manu* and other legal and religious treatises. Married couples were expected to be monogamous, though in some cases, when they could not have children, it was permissible for a man to take a second wife while remaining married to the first.

A number of texts were devoted to outlining the correct conduct of the "four stages of life" for men: student, householder, hermit, and wanderer. In the first stage, that of the student, boys of the "twice-born" upper castes were to be taken into the household of a *guru*, or teacher, for a minimum of 12 years. During this time, they were expected to study the works of the Vedic–Brahmanic–Upanishadic tradition. Upon entering into the second stage (householder), more mature men with sufficient savings should marry young women of good character and appropriate caste membership. In addition to providing for his household, servants, and relatives, a man should get up before dawn, offer the appropriate sacrifices throughout the day and busy himself studying the Vedas, Puranas [Poor-AHN-ahs] (genealogies and histories), and Itihasas [Ee-tee-HAH-sahs] (legendary histories). As old age approaches, he enters the third stage (hermit) and should retreat to the forest, live on the roots and berries he can gather, and work to master the self in preparation for the end. In the final (wanderer) stage, he moves beyond desire for life or death, wandering without home or possessions. Caring not for anything of this world, he returns good for any evil done him and, ideally, attains moksha or release from the cycle of death and rebirth at his journey's end.

Family Life and Hindu Culture: Women   As we saw in Chapter 3, the role of women both in the family and in Indian society was perhaps more complex than in any other agrarian-based culture. On the one hand, the idea of female "dependence" was central to the Hindu conception of the family. That is, a woman without the support and protection of a web of family relations was cast adrift in society, a kind of "nonperson." Thus, to protect women was to safeguard the family and the social order. It followed from this that obedience and loyalty to senior female and male authority within the hierarchy of the family was the keystone of a woman's dharma, her duty according to her position. This fundamental duty was consistent regardless of her position in the caste system. In some regions, such loyalty found extreme expression in the act of *sati*. This controversial practice of a widow committing suicide by throwing herself on her husband's funeral pyre, however, remained largely confined to northern India and is legally prohibited today.

As in the strict division between men's and women's spheres in Confucian China we will see in Chapter 9, women's education and legal responsibilities in India were considerably narrower than those for men and tended to revolve around maintaining the home. Although in the Tamil areas of the south families remained matrilineal, property rights were limited. Yet, wives customarily exercised the important responsibility of controlling the household accounts and supervising servants and hired help. For the more well-to-do, an appropriate knowledge of poetry, literature, and conversational skills was required, along with other attainments necessary for well-rounded, gracious living. And while men were somewhat less restricted in terms of marrying for love, the vast majority of men and women were united through marriages arranged by their families after careful negotiation and often betrothed before adolescence.

Balancing Male and Female Roles   Although women were, for the most part, treated as subservient members of a patriarchal society, they were also seen by men as complementary opposites, as symbols of harmony and balance, though also as real and imaginary temptations and impediments to their ultimate release (moksha). On the one hand, women in epic and popular literature were often depicted as heroic and resourceful—Draupadi in the Mahabharata, for example, married five brothers in the Pandava family and aided all of them in their battles. Moreover, from the Gupta period on, a bewildering number of goddesses were increasingly appealed to by devotees for a variety of reasons. Fertility, sexuality, and growth, largely associated with femaleness, were all celebrated in Hindu literature, statuary, and religious symbolism. The lush depictions of frank sexuality in Hindu temples are among the most erotically charged artworks produced anywhere in the world. In contrast with this celebration of sexuality, on the other hand, was the perception of women as temptresses who anchored men to the sensual world. This in turn diverted them from the fundamental truth of the material world as transitory, thus potentially delaying their release from the karmic cycle through moksha.

The tensions growing from this duality and the difficulties of controlled enjoyment of the senses for both men and women as part of approved religious practice are graphically illustrated in Vatsyayana's [Vaht-see-ai-AH-nah] famous *Kama Sutra*, or *Aphorisms of Love*, written perhaps sometime in the first or second century CE. Its frank handling of a multiplicity of sexual practices has created an aura of pornography about it for readers outside of India. Within a wider context, however, it should be seen more as a manual on the everyday worship of living. While the more sensational aspects of the arts of sexual love are certainly present, the majority of the text deals with how to become a well-rounded person of taste and culture. For women, no less than 64 separate skills are detailed, including singing, dancing, cooking, chemistry, first aid, metallurgy, architecture, and even driving horses and elephants. Here, at least, the "proper" sphere for women's activities was greatly expanded.

Buddhism and Family Life The impact of Buddhism on family life is difficult to judge. Instructions found in Buddhist works for the conduct of lay followers emphasize kindness and right conduct toward one's family and others, regardless of caste. But the more pronounced impetus toward equality between men and women was found among the members of the orders of monks and nuns. These created a genuine alternative for those who, for whatever reason, sought to escape the strictures of family life. People who had few prospects for financial betterment or risked being committed to a poor marriage often found refuge in the religious orders. Scholars also believe that the Buddhist encouragement of vegetarianism, given a tremendous boost by Ashoka's edicts on ahimsa, had the long-term effect of reducing meat consumption in India, even after Buddhism slipped from favor.

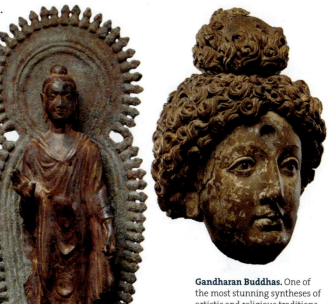

Gandharan Buddhas. One of the most stunning syntheses of artistic and religious traditions occurred in the wake of the decline of the Seleucid states and the invasion of the Kushans. In the area centered around Gandhara (modern Kandahar in Afghanistan) Hellenistic artistic techniques of realistic human representation fused with the developing practices of Mahayana Buddhism to create sculptures like the head pictured here, from the second or third century CE, believed to be that of a bodhisattva, or perhaps of Siddhartha Gautama. A later bronze Buddha from the region, dating from the sixth century, shows a movement away from such early realism toward the more stylized symbolism of the *mandorla*, the halo of flames surrounding the figure. The right hand is raised in the famous gesture inviting the viewer to "banish fear."

Strength in Numbers: Art, Literature, and Science

The vast number of artistic, literary, cultural, and scientific contributions arising from India makes it impossible to do more than hint at their richness here. One area worth noting in terms of its cross-cultural fertilization, however, is that of Gandharan art. During the time of the Kushan Empire, the powerful influences of the old empire of Alexander the Great were meeting the new religious movements arising within Buddhism to create a new "Gandharan" style of art.

Previous representations of the Buddha had not been human but were instead symbols associated with his life and lore: the "wheel of dharma," an empty throne, or a footprint. Around the beginning of the Common Era, perhaps coinciding with the development of Mahayana Buddhism, the distinctly realistic forms of Greek sculpture and the tradition of depicting the Greek gods as human merged with the new Buddhist sensibilities to create the first images of the Buddha, which looked remarkably like the Greek god Apollo. This synthetic Gandharan approach spread

From *The Cloud Messenger*

Thus too, my king, I pray of thee to speak,
Remembering kindness is its own reward;
"Thy lover lives, and from the holy peak
Asks if these absent days good health afford
························ "
Those born to pain must ever use this opening word.

With body worn as thine, with pain as deep,
With tears and ceaseless longings answering thine,
With sighs more burning than the sighs that keep
Thy lips ascorch—doomed far from thee to pine,
He too doth weave the fancies that thy soul entwine.

He used to love, when women friends were near,
To whisper things he might have said aloud
That he might touch thy face and kiss thine ear;
Unheard and even unseen, no longer proud,
He now must send this yearning message by a cloud.

—Verses 38, 39, 40. From www.sacred-texts.com/hin/sha/sha17.htm

Philologist: A specialist in language study, particularly in the history and provenance of important terms.

across northern India, and soon images of the Buddha were being turned out in great profusion. Over time, however, the more familiar, stylized, less realistic, and heavily symbolic representations became standard throughout the Mahayana religious sphere.

The Classical Age   While relatively little art from the Mauryan era has survived, the Gupta period brought an explosion of art and literature from a multitude of artists patronized by the court and the upper classes. The "perfection" of Sanskrit as the medium of the sacred texts of Hinduism under the scholar and grammarian Panini and its systematic study under the **philologist** Patanjali several centuries later solidified the sacred language and caused it to be viewed and preserved as unchanging. As a classical language, Sanskrit was used in a staggering variety of works of poetry, prose, and drama, as well as in the *Puranas*—religious and secular historical genealogies. Other noteworthy works may include the poems and plays of "India's Shakespeare," Kalidasa (though some scholars place his life in the first century CE), such as the poignant romance *Shakuntala* and the poetic yearnings of *The Cloud Messenger*.

In addition to Sanskrit literature, scholarship of all types, including Buddhist works and scientific treatises, was undertaken at the great Buddhist monastery and university of Nalanda in northeastern India, founded in the fourth century CE.

Science and Mathematics   In addition to Buddhism, the most profound intellectual influences from India on the surrounding regions were in science, especially mathematics. Despite the highly sophisticated speculative philosophy of the Upanishads, during the period from the second century BCE until the second century CE India was an importer of scientific and mathematical concepts from the Greco-Roman and Persian spheres. Greek geometry, for example, made its way into northern India during this time. In exchange, however, concepts of Indian health regimens—some involving yoga discipline—along with the vast body of Indian medicine, with its extensive knowledge of herbal remedies, also seem to have moved west. The second century CE medical text *Charaka Samhita* for example, like its counterparts in the Mediterranean and later European world, taught a health regimen based on the balance of humors.

In the area of mathematics and astronomy an important synthesis of ideas took place from the time of the Mauryans through the twelfth and thirteenth centuries CE. Like the early Chinese methods of reckoning time, the first Indian calendars were based on the lunar months, though a year consisted of six seasons and an intercalary period was inserted every 30 months to make up the difference with the solar year. During the Hellenistic period, Indians adopted the calendar of the eastern Mediterranean and southwest Asia, which had a 7-day week, a 24-hour day, and a 365-day solar year—along with the 12 zodiacal signs of the Greco-Roman world.

Indian thinkers refined these imported concepts to levels unsurpassed in the ancient world. The subtleties of some of the philosophical schools had already required intervals of time and numbers that still stagger the imagination today. For example, cycles of time marking eternity in some philosophical schools were measured in intervals larger than current estimates of the age of the universe; the shorter *kalpa*, reckoned at about 4 billion years, is only slightly less than current estimates of the age of the earth. Philosophical discussion on the nature of matter in infinitesimal space among some schools anticipated key arguments of modern physicists regarding the principle of indeterminacy.

The ability to conceive of mathematics on at once such a grand and such a tiny scale seems to have also helped Indian mathematicians and astronomers during the Gupta period to calculate a precise length for the solar year. Like the Chinese, they had already developed a decimal system; however, they now employed the first use of the zero, initially marked by a dot, as a placeholder, and developed a system of positive and negative numbers. Their work with the geometry of the Greeks enabled them to calculate pi to four decimal places as well as develop methods for the solving of certain kinds of algebraic equations. By the eleventh and twelfth centuries CE, the acquisition of these techniques by the Arabs and their transmittal of them to the new universities of Christian Europe gave us the system we still use today, known by the somewhat erroneous name of "Arabic numerals."

Putting It All Together

In roughly a millennium, a number of important patterns of world history emerged in India. The political, cultural, social, religious, and economic systems of the states along the Ganges River were diffused to all parts of the Indian subcontinent, where they were substantially—though by no means completely—received by the surrounding peoples. With the maturing of these patterns came the tendency to see the subcontinent as a unified entity in nearly every way except in politics. Here, despite the accomplishments of the Mauryans and Guptas, unity would prove elusive—in some respects even to the present day. This would prove particularly true, as we will see in later chapters, with the coming of Islam.

In terms of its regional influence and beyond, India's impact was disproportionately large. By at least the time of Ashoka, the population of the subcontinent was second only to that of China. Within it was contained the world's most active source of religious traditions, next to southwest Asia and the Mediterranean. The influence of one of these religions, Hinduism, spread to Indonesia and southeast Asia; that of the other, Buddhism, could lay claim through this period to be the world's largest religious system as well as the first "universal" one.

Paradoxically, many of the factors that allowed for this tremendous richness of religious, cultural, and intellectual traditions also tended to abet the subcontinent's chronic political instability, particularly in the north. Here, continual migrations of outside peoples cross-fertilized the cultural resources of the region but also impeded political unification (see Concept Map).

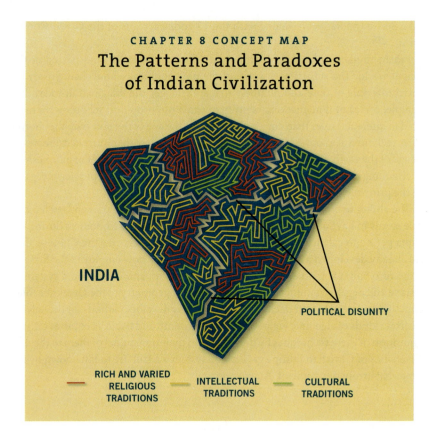

Review and Respond

1. What are the attributes of dharma that Ashoka says his people should aspire to?

2. What are the distinctive features of Jainism and Buddhism?

3. How did the caste system differ in the Gangetic states from the territories in the south?

4. What are some of the reasons that the Gupta period is considered India's "classical age"?

▶ For additional resources, including maps, primary sources, visuals, and quizzes, please go to www.oup.com/us/vonsivers. Please see the Further Resources section at the back of the book for additional readings and suggested websites.

Thinking Through Patterns

▶ **Think about the reasons for the spread of Buddhism inside and outside of India. How have historians seen the decline of Buddhism in India?**

An important historical pattern we examine in this section is that of individuals we call "visionaries"—people who, as the saying goes, "think outside the box" in their own societies. In this chapter, we place the Buddha in this category as a man who sought—and satisfied himself and his followers that he succeeded—to go beyond the Hindu bounds of death and rebirth. Like the other visionaries we examine, however, the Buddha's fundamental message of transcendence and enlightenment can be adapted to any belief system. As his message moves along the trade routes in India, central Asia, and, as we will see in later chapters, China, Korea, Japan, and southeast Asia, it adapts to local customs by borrowing bits of indigenous religious mythology and belief to make it attractive to converts while keeping the fundamental message intact. Local people in turn adapt it to their own beliefs and make it their own. In the case of east Asia, this will receive a large boost by the translation of Buddhist scriptures into literary Chinese and the circulation of Buddhist practitioners, monks, merchants, and pilgrims throughout the Buddhist cultural sphere. Its decline in the place of its birth appears to be due in part to the shift of its cultural center to China and Japan and the official support of the Guptas for Hinduism.

How do historians establish criteria of "importance"? One measure of this is to assess the influence of certain patterns and practices on a culture or society over time. Change over time or the lack of it is an important indicator of the prevalence and kind of innovation taking place in a society. So some influential patterns in Indian history might include the permeation of religion in all aspects of Indian life, the search for transcendence of the material world, the caste system as the social fabric of the subcontinent, and the prominence of India as a trade crossroads astride the trade routes of the Indian Ocean and the great land routes across Eurasia.

▶ **What do you consider to be the most influential patterns in Indian history to this point? Why?**

▶ **Do you think some of Ashoka's concepts could be implemented by governments today? Why or why not?**

Ashoka's ideas seem quite modern in many ways, and his decrees regarding the protection of animals and ecological matters might certainly have some current application. His ideas of not taking life except in extreme circumstances and of giving prisoners time to repent also parallel modern concepts. Yet, it must also be remembered that he is still far removed in time and culture from the modern world. His ideas of dharma as duty might not carry exactly the same import as today. Historians are routinely conscious of the pitfalls of identifying too closely with peoples in very different cultures in the remote past. "The past is a foreign country," it is often said. "They do things differently there."

Chapter 9 | China

722 BCE-618 CE | IMPERIAL UNIFICATION AND PERFECTING THE MORAL ORDER

"**V**enerable sir, since you have not considered a thousand *li* too far to come, may I presume that you bring something that may profit my kingdom?" Even today one can sense the air of challenge, however polite, as the two men begin to take each other's measure. The speaker, King Hui of Liang, had seen his kingdom steadily eroded by the powerful surrounding states of Chu, Jin, and Qin, vying for supremacy at the height of China's Warring States period (403–221 BCE). Given the increasing desperation of his situation, perhaps he can be forgiven his somewhat sharp tone.

The "venerable sir" to whom he addressed his question, however, was in no mood to banter: "Why must Your Majesty use that word 'profit'? I bring

THE FIRST CHINESE EMPIRES

女史司箴敢告庶姬

Seeing Patterns

▶ Was the First Emperor's ruthlessness justified by his accomplishments in his empire?

▶ How would you compare the values expressed by Confucius and Mencius to those of contemporary society?

▶ How have historians viewed the role of women in early imperial China?

only humanity and righteousness," he thundered. Warming to his topic, the Confucian sage Mencius now laid out his rebuttal:

> If Your Majesty says, "How may I profit my kingdom" the great officers will say, "How may we profit our families"; and the lesser officers and common people will say, "how may we profit ourselves." Superiors and inferiors will try to snatch this profit from each other and the kingdom will be endangered. . . . [but] There never has been a humane man who neglected his parents. There never has been a righteous man who made his ruler an afterthought. James Legge, trans. *The Works of Mencius*. New York: Dover Reprint, 1970, pp. 125–126

Chastened by this confrontation, but also intrigued, King Hui now sought Mencius out for advice on a number of fronts. Through it all the sage refused to mince words with him about the extent of his misgovernment. Finally, both Hui and his son and successor, Xiang, said, "I wish quietly to receive your instructions."

This story from the opening pages of the fourth-century BCE *Mengzi*, the *Book of Mencius*, illustrates several important points not only about late Zhou China but also about the role of intellectual innovation, the ultimate

Admonitions of the Instructions to the Court Ladies. The adoption of Confucianism as a state ideology by successive Chinese dynasties led to more restrictive and prescribed model behaviors for everyone, but particularly women. One of the most popular guides for women's behavior was Ban Zhao's (48–116 CE) "Admonitions for Women," a scene of which is depicted in this Tang Dynasty copy of an earlier work by Gu Kaizhi. In this scene, the court instructress is writing down rules for proper decorum for ladies of the court.

direction of Chinese political thought, the way Chinese ideas would influence nearby peoples, and, more generally, the larger pattern of empires and states adopting the ideas of visionary thinkers. As we noted in Chapter 4, the Spring and Autumn and the Warring States periods in China during the final centuries of the Zhou era were socially and politically tumultuous. In spite of, or perhaps because of, this, the period was also the most fertile one in China's long intellectual history. As we shall see, starting with Confucius—from whom Mencius drew his ideas—Chinese thinkers suggested ways of looking at the world, how to behave in it, and how to govern it that ranged from radically abstract to firmly practical, from collective to individualistic, and from an absence of active government to near totalitarianism.

From the time of the Han dynasty (202 BCE–220 CE) until the twentieth century, Confucianism, as interpreted by Mencius and adopted as a means of bureaucratic control, would be the governmental system of China. Moreover, as Chinese is adopted as the first written language by Koreans, Japanese, and Vietnamese, Confucian concepts will be firmly planted in these lands as well. So, in China, as in India, Persia, Rome, and eventually the Islamic world, the legacy of innovators we have identified as "visionaries" will be picked up and adopted by rulers as officially approved thought. As we will emphasize in this and the following chapters, an important pattern of world history emerges by the beginning of the Common Era. Large "world" empires utilize religions and systems of thought that have universal application and appeal.

Visionaries and Empire

The period from the eighth century BCE until the first unification of China under the Qin in 221 BCE is universally regarded as China's most fertile period of intellectual exploration. The foundations of nearly every important school of Chinese philosophy were laid during this era. By the time of the Confucian ethicist and political thinker Mencius in the fourth century BCE, so many competing thought systems had emerged that Chinese chroniclers refer to them as the "hundred schools." Of these various systems, those that are best known and that had the greatest impact were Confucianism, Legalism, and Daoism.

Confucianism, Legalism, and Daoism

Like so many important figures in the world of ideas, the historical Confucius is an elusive figure. Contemporary researchers have widely differing views on his identity and his works. According to traditional accounts, he was born in 551 BCE to a family named Kong. Even today, the Kong family, some of whose members still live in the original family compound at Qufu [CHOO-foo] in modern Shandong Province, maintains what is claimed to be a continuous genealogy of the sage's descendants that are now said to number in the millions.

In Confucian texts he is referred to as "the Master" (*zi* or *fuzi*) or "the Master Kong" (*Kong fuzi*) [Koong-FOO-zuh]. European Roman Catholic missionaries in China during the seventeenth century rendered *Kong fuzi* into Latin, where it became "Confucius." As a member of the growing *shi* class of well-to-do, educated commoners and lower aristocracy (see Chapter 4), Confucius spent much of his early career seeking a position as political adviser to the courts of several of the Zhou states in northern China. Though tradition has him holding a minor position in his native state of Lu, his search for employment was largely unsuccessful. As did the visionaries we saw in the previous chapter in India, he ended up spending most of his life as an itinerant teacher, spreading his ideas about ethics and politics to a growing group of followers. Like the Buddha, however, it would be centuries before his ideas were applied on a large scale by a state.

Confucian Doctrine   Confucius has been called "China's first great moralist." His teachings—as presented in the *Lunyu* or *Analects*, the central Confucian text— have at their core a view of human beings as inclined toward ethical behavior and of human society as a perfectible moral order. According to Confucius, there are certain fundamental patterns that are manifestations of the *Dao* ("the Way") of the universal order.

722-481 BCE Spring and Autumn Period	**604 BCE** Traditional Date for Birth of Laozi	**385-312 BCE?** Life of Mencius, Champion of Confucianism
403-221 BCE Warring States Period	**551-479 BCE** Traditional Date for Life of Confucius	**d. 233 BCE** Han Fei, Philosopher of Legalism
221-206 BCE First Chinese Empire Under Qin	**24-220 CE** Later Han Dynasty	**589-618 CE** Reunification of Empire Under the Sui
202 BCE-8 CE Former Han Dynasty	**220-589 CE** Three Kingdoms, Six Dynasties, North and South Dynasties; Rapid Spread of Buddhism	

One of these fundamental patterns is the relationship between parent and off-spring. A child owes its life and body to its parents. Because of this, a child—even a grownup, who was, after all, once a child—dares not injure him- or herself or others. People develop their moral character to reflect well upon their parents and serve those in higher social or political stations as they serve their own parents. This example of human society as a kind of extended family applies at every level, from the peasant to the ruler—and even beyond: Drawing on the idea of the Mandate of Heaven (see Chapter 4), Confucius makes the ruler himself responsible to heaven for the state of his country. Indeed, emperors in later regimes would habitually refer to themselves as "son of heaven," to emphasize this filial duty.

Reciprocity: Mutual exchange of things, ideas, etc.

Though this view is avowedly hierarchical rather than egalitarian, the mutual obligations present at every level serve as checks for Confucius on the arbitrary exercise of power. Hence, when asked to sum up his thinking in one word, Confucius answered "**reciprocity**": Do not do unto others what you would not have them do unto you. Confucius believed that individuals should strive for the qualities of *ren* (kindness or humaneness toward others) by faithfully following the practices of *li* (the observance of rules of decorum as guides to appropriate behavior toward others). People who did so would not only perfect their own character but also set an example for the rest of society.

Confucian Government

Confucius lived during a time of great social and political disorder, and as a result, many of his teachings center on ways to restore order and make government and society more humane. But because Confucian doctrine places great emphasis on personal responsibility, the structure of government is far less important than the ethical fitness of the ruler and the people. Good government, according to Confucius, begins with educated leaders and officials of strong moral character, like the Zhou kings Wen and Wu and the Duke of Zhou (see Chapter 4), who are often cited in the *Analects* as examples. To describe this ideal of behavior, Confucius introduced the concept of the *junzi* ("the superior man" or "gentleman").

Those able to attain these ideals would comprise for Confucius a kind of aristocracy of merit, while rulers who possessed these qualities would set a sound example for their subjects to follow.

Just as the *junzi* cultivated his personal ethics and morals, a society run by *junzi* would spread these values to society by fostering social institutions that encouraged proper behavior among the people. In the same way that a musician's consistent practice of scales eventually makes playing them correctly second nature, the consistent observance of *li* would help make appropriate behavior routine among ordinary people. Not everyone would necessarily develop the high moral standards of the *junzi*, but at the very least, the majority of people would almost involuntarily develop a sense of right and wrong and thus acquire a stake in the social order. As it is put in the *Analects*,

> Lead the people by laws and regulate them by penalties, and they will obey the laws to avoid being punished, but have no sense of shame. Lead them by rules of decorum (*li*) and they will develop a sense of shame (i.e., a collective sense of proper behavior), and moreover, will become good. William T. DeBary, ed. *Sources of Chinese Tradition*, vol. 1. New York: Columbia University Press, 1964, p. 32

By the time Confucius died in 479 BCE, he had attracted a loyal following of adherents to his teachings. Two later students of Confucian doctrine, Mencius and Xunzi [SHWUN-zuh], continued to spread the teachings of the master, though with their own distinctive contributions. Despite challenges from a number of competing philosophical schools, Confucian ideals ultimately became the standard for Chinese politics and scholarship.

Mencius   By Mencius' time, in the fourth century BCE, the intensity of the competition and continual warfare among the Zhou states had spawned most of the so-called hundred schools of thought as thinkers questioned fundamental assumptions about private and social good. Not surprisingly, given the chaotic times, their answers varied from radical individualism to universal love and altruism, with some, like Sun Zi [Sun Tzu] in *The Art of War* examining the nature and practice of armed struggle.

Mencius (*Mengzi*, or Master Meng; ca. 385–312 BCE), like Confucius, believed that people were fundamentally good and that individuals must continually work to understand and refine this goodness in order to avoid being led astray by negative influences. Mencius used water, the nature of which is to flow downhill, as a familiar metaphor for human nature. It is possible, of course, to force water out of this natural tendency, said Mencius; but once such artificial means are removed, it reverts to its original course. Hence, he concluded, the way to proper behavior is to cultivate the Confucian virtues as a bulwark against forces pushing toward "unnatural" behavior.

Mencius traveled throughout China spreading Confucian ideals, especially as a basis for government practice. The *Mengzi* or *Book of Mencius*, is written in more of a narrative form than the *Analects* and supplemented by stories, parables, and debates with advocates of other schools of thought. Its most powerful sections deal with the obligations of rulers to their subjects. As the center of power and moral authority, in Mencius' view a ruler's primary duty is to maintain the "people's livelihood" and uphold the "righteousness," *yi* (appropriate behavior by and toward all according to social rank), of the state. As an appropriately ideal way to maintain the people's livelihood, for example, Mencius advocated the "well-field" system (see Chapter 4) as a means of ensuring crop surpluses and equality among peasant cultivators.

As for the state, as we saw with King Hui of Liang in the chapter-opening vignette, "I bring only humanity [*ren*]

> ### What Is a Gentleman?
>
> - The gentleman is humane, courteous, kind, and diligent
> - He "loves learning and hates sloth"
> - He "is broadminded and not partisan"
> - He "makes demands on himself rather than on others"
> - He "seeks to help people succeed in what is good but does not help them in what is evil"
>
> —William T. DeBary, ed. *Sources of Chinese Tradition*, vol. 1. New York: Columbia University Press, 1964, pp. 30–33 passim.

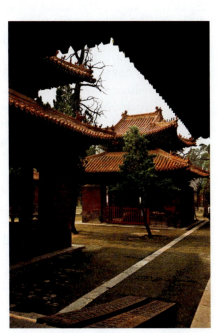

The Kong Family Mansion in Qufu. Though scholars have debated many aspects of the life and activities of the historical Confucius, his descendents have maintained the family line and compound over the centuries at Qufu in modern Shandong province. Since 1055 CE, Chinese emperors have bestowed on the eldest male family member in the direct line from the Sage the title of "Duke Yansheng." The most recent holder of the title, Kung Te-cheng (Kong Dezheng), died in October, 2008 on Taiwan at the age of 89. He was the 77th main-line descendent of Confucius.

and righteousness [*yi*]; why must Your Majesty use that word 'profit'?" Mencius argued that rulers who sought to profit from their states sowed the seeds of their own destruction by encouraging their subjects to profit only themselves. A state ruled by righteousness and humanity, on the other hand, ensured that the people would be prosperous and orderly, which automatically contributed to the "profit" of the ruler. A ruler who abused or neglected his subjects upset the social order and the natural tendency of people toward good. In such a case, the people had not only the right but also the obligation to invoke the Mandate of Heaven and depose him. In the end, said Mencius, anticipating a host of later Chinese thinkers, the people, not the ruler, are the foundation of the state.

Xunzi   As states grew increasingly powerful, their armies larger, and warfare more deadly, Mencius' optimistic view of human nature seemed less and less practical to many thinkers. Like Mencius, Xunzi (trad. ca. 310–219? BCE) was also a student of Confucian philosophy but had a much darker view of human nature. Living during the apogee of the Warring States period, Xunzi came to believe that individuals were self-involved creatures with little interest in society as a whole and capable of regulating themselves only through immense effort. Only by enforcing the restraints of civilization, such as ritual, law, and the example of past model rulers, could individuals approach the Confucian ideals of virtue and humanity. Thus, by the end of the third century BCE, Confucian thinkers had come to radically opposed conclusions about their most fundamental premise: the authentic nature of human beings. In the long run, the more moderate views of Confucius and Mencius won out. Xunzi's more pessimistic view of human nature, however, formed the basis of the Legalist school founded by two of his students, Han Fei and Li Si, that finally restored order and created the first Chinese empire.

Legalism   The Legalist school is the most severe of the three major schools of philosophical thought that emerged during the Warring States period. For Legalists, building a strong state was of utmost importance. Out of Xunzi's view of human beings as inclined toward evil and drawing on the earlier practices of the Qin minister Lord Shang (d. 338 BCE), Han Fei (d. 233 BCE) and Li Si (d. 208 BCE) developed a system of uniform laws and practices based on the absolute will of the ruler. Order in a state, they claimed, could be implemented only through the institution of strict, detailed, and explicit laws diligently enforced on all subjects without regard to rank or class. Since Legalists believed that compliance on small matters led to compliance on larger ones, they imposed harsh punishments—forced labor, mutilation, in some cases death—for even the tiniest infractions.

The Legalists argued that the state was all-important; therefore, all subjects must serve the state through productive activities. Among these activities, agriculture and military service were the highest priorities. Individuals were encouraged to take up farming or military service as their livelihoods; any other occupation was discouraged. Idlers were put to work by force. Since dissent led to disorder, only government-approved history and literature were tolerated.

Although Legalism had many critics, it was its strict practices, not the more moderate ideals of Confucianism or Daoism, that imposed order on China. The price it exacted for doing so, however, was considered by succeeding generations to have been intolerably high.

Daoism While most Chinese philosophical schools accepted the concept of the Dao as the ordering principle of the universe, they varied considerably as to the best means of achieving harmony with it. For Confucians, as we have seen, study and self-cultivation to the point of intuitive understanding put the individual in tune with the Dao. For followers of the Daoist tradition, attributed to Laozi (Lao Tzu) however, the Confucian path prevented genuine understanding of and harmony with the Dao.

The historical Laozi is an even more obscure figure than Confucius. In fact, many scholars believe Laozi to be a mythical figure. Chinese tradition cites his birth date as 604 BCE and his name as Li Er. The honorific title "Laozi" is translated as either "the Old Master" or "the Old Child." The translation "Old Child" captures something of the Daoist belief that only a return to child-like simplicity would lead to union with the *Dao*.

For Daoists, in contrast to the Confucians, the Dao was not the ordering force *within* the universe but the transcendent first principle *beyond* the universe. The Confucian Dao, dealing with the particulars of this world, can be named; the Daoist Dao, like the relationship between atman and Brahman we saw in Chapter 8, transcends all particulars and therefore cannot be named. The Dao is thus beyond all dualities and unifies them in a great oscillating whole.

In fact, the vocabulary Laozi used for this new measure of all phenomena is remarkably similar to that of other Eurasian visionaries during the 600s BCE discussed previously: Deutero-Isaiah, the Zoroastrian reformers, Anaximander, and the Buddha, as well as the Upanishad writers. All were striving in their volatile kingdoms and empires, many of which worshipped large pantheons of gods, for one, single, unchangeable, and all-encompassing standard for morality and understanding.

Since the Dao transcended the world—including all such opposites as "good" and "evil"—no single path of action would lead an individual to union with it. To choose the good, as the Confucians do, is therefore to follow only a limited part of the universal Dao. Instead, the Daoists taught that only through a life of quiet self-reflection and contemplation of opposites and paradoxes might an individual come to know the Dao. A classic tale that expresses this aspect of Daoist thought is the story of the philosopher Zhuang Zhou [JWONG-Joe], who lived in the fourth century BCE and awoke from a dream unsure of whether he had dreamed he was a butterfly or whether he was a butterfly dreaming he was Zhuang Zhou.

Daoism and Government Daoist political theory held that the best government was that which governed least. Here, the key idea is one from the most famous Daoist work, the *Daode Jing* (*The Classic of the Way and Virtue*, often spelled as the *Tao Te Ching*): "By non-action there is nothing that is not done." This is not to say that the ruler literally does nothing; rather, his role is to create the conditions that naturally lead to a society in which everyone spontaneously acts in accordance with the Dao. The ruler should not push specific policies but rather let all things take their natural courses, for even as they run to extremes they will always reverse. The ruler's understanding of the flow of these universal cycles leads to union with the Dao and keeps the world in equilibrium.

Han Fei

"the intelligence of the people is not to be relied upon any more than the mind of a baby . . . if he [the baby] does not have his boil cut open, his illness will go from bad to worse. However, in order to open the boil someone has to hold the baby while the affectionate mother is performing the work, and yet he keeps crying and yelling incessantly. The baby does not understand that suffering a small pain is the way to obtain a great benefit."

—William T. DeBary, ed. *Sources of Chinese Tradition*, vol. 1. New York: Columbia University Press, 1964, p. 129.

These three schools of thought were all to play a role in the development of China's political and cultural life. Confucianism would provide the basis for the bureaucracy of China's empires and ideals of a perfectible moral order; Daoism would provide the mystical dimension of Chinese culture and a profound love and idealization of nature; finally, Legalism would provide the brute muscle of unifying the last of the warring states into a single structure under the Qin [CHIN].

The Qin Dynasty

As the period of the Warring States continued, the Qin state ultimately claimed victory over its opponents and established centralized rule throughout China. At first glance, Qin might seem unpromising as a candidate for empire. It was the smallest and poorest of the Zhou dependencies, located far to the west of most of the other Zhou states. However, Qin had several powerful advantages over its competitors. Its position on the fringe of the Zhou world meant that it was free to expand its economic base by promising land to peasant cultivators as the state seized territory on its western frontier.

Qin and Zhou   The agricultural surplus that resulted from these land grants led to increased prosperity for the small but growing state. Qin's location was also a benefit when it came to military preparedness. Many of the warring states were in close proximity to each other, and the constant battles among them depleted their economic and military resources. Qin, on the other hand, did not have to fight off other states at its borders. Consequently, the Qin participated in limited military campaigns, mostly against nomadic groups, which strengthened their fighting skills but did not upset their economy or weaken their army. By 350 BCE, Qin rulers, particularly the famous Shang Yang, reorganized the state by eliminating the last of the old Zhou institutions and replacing them with a uniform, centralized system that anticipated a number of later Legalist principles. In 256 BCE, the Qin conquered Zhou itself and began the drive for empire in earnest (see Map 9.1).

With its strong economy, expert military, and the Legalist theorists Han Fei and Li Si advising the court, Qin took advantage of the collective exhaustion of the other northern Chinese states and conquered them at a pace reminiscent of Alexander the Great's campaigns of the previous century. With stunning swiftness, Qin armies, now swelling to hundreds of thousands of men, drove south and eliminated the opposition of the many tribal peoples below the state of Yue.

The Qin then continued into the northern part of modern Vietnam—thus beginning a long, and often bitterly contested, relationship with southeast Asia. The Chinese would attempt to rule the area with limited success for over 1,000 years and claim it as a protectorate for nearly another thousand until they were ousted by the French in 1885. In the north and west, Qin armies fought a series of campaigns to drive nomadic peoples, especially the *Xiongnu*, or Huns, from newly established borders and secure the trade routes into central Asia. By the end of the 220s BCE, the Qin had subdued all of the states that would constitute what was about to become the first Chinese empire.

The First Emperor   In 221 BCE, the Qin ruler Cheng (r. 246–221 as Qin ruler; 221–209 BCE as first emperor) proclaimed himself Qin Shi Huangdi, the first emperor of the Qin, and with Li Si as his chief minister instituted the Legalist system

MAP **9.1 The Qin Empire.**

throughout the new empire. As a safeguard against attacks by nomadic peoples in the north, the First Emperor deployed tens of thousands of forced laborers to join together the numerous defensive walls of the old Zhou states. This massive project stretching over 1,400 miles would become the Great Wall of China.

With virtually unlimited resources and the ruthless drive of the Legalists to expand and fortify the state, the First Emperor began a series of projects during his reign of less than a dozen years that are still astonishing today in their scope and ambition. The Chinese writing system was standardized, as were all weights, measures, and coinage. Hundreds of thousands of conscript laborers worked on roads, canals, and a multitude of irrigation and water conservancy projects. The First Emperor also ordered the construction of a tomb for himself, a mammoth complex meant to celebrate his legacy. The discovery of the First Emperor's tomb in 1974 by a peasant digging a well near the modern city of Xi'an unearthed an army of thousands of life-sized terra-cotta warriors marching in orderly ranks, intended to protect Qin Shi Huangdi after his death.

From his palace in Chang'an, the site of modern Xi'an and the ultimate capital of 13 separate dynasties, the First Emperor tightened his control over the state and dealt with opponents with ruthless efficiency. Scholars, particularly Confucians, who objected to government policies were buried alive. Any literature not officially

Terra-cotta Warriors at the First Emperor's Tomb. One of the most important archaeological finds of the twentieth century, the Qin burial complex was discovered in 1974 by local farmers digging a well. Over 5,000 figures have been unearthed so far, all with individualized features. The dig has been enclosed and a museum built on site. Along with the Great Wall, it is one of China's most popular tourist destinations.

sanctioned by the government was destroyed. While it is difficult to assess the extent to which the book burnings actually took place, it is believed that a great many works that existed before the Qin were put to the torch. Writers of the following Han dynasty, emphasizing the horrors of the Qin, have left a number of accounts of mass executions of dissenting scholars.

After a reign of about 12 years as emperor, Qin Shi Huangdi died. His strict laws, severe punishments, and huge construction projects had angered and exhausted the people; and soon after his death the empire erupted in rebellion. Ironically, the government's severe laws and punishments now worked against it as officials attempted to conceal the revolt's severity for fear of torture and execution. At the same time, Minister Li Si provoked additional discontent by conspiring to keep the First Emperor's death a secret in order to rule as regent for the monarch's son. He was captured attempting to flee the rebellion and executed in 208 BCE. In an attempt to make the punishment fit the crime, his captors lashed him to a board and slowly sawed him in half, lengthwise, in accordance with Qin law. After a brief civil war, a general named Liu Bang put an end to the fighting and restored order to the region. He proclaimed himself emperor in 202 BCE and called his new dynasty the Han.

The Han Dynasty

If the Qin constructed the Chinese empire, the Han perfected it. The Han developed over time a centralized political system of rule that blended the administrative structures of the Qin with more moderate Confucian ideals of government as a moral agent. This model of rule endured—with some interruptions and modifications— for over 2,000 years, by having its power tempered by a bureaucracy that saw its role as both carrying out the will of the court and acting as advocates for the people.

Unlike earlier rulers who came from aristocratic families, Liu Bang, who had taken the reign name Gaozu (r. 202–195 BCE), had been a peasant. Perhaps because of this background, he had little interest in restoring the decentralized system of the Zhou, which favored the aristocratic classes. Instead, he left intact the Qin structure of centralized ministries and regional **commanderies**. This structure seemed the only sensible way to keep such a large empire under control. To mollify advocates of returning

Commanderies: Districts under the control of a military commander.

to the old Zhou system, Han rulers offered them token distributions of land. They also reduced taxes and labor obligations and rescinded the most severe punishments imposed under the Qin. Han rulers altered the Qin system of leveling social classes by instituting uniform rules for different segments of society—aristocrats as well as commoners. Under the Han, the upper ranks of society were taxed at lighter rates and exempted from most forms of corporal punishment.

As the Han Empire expanded—reaching a population recorded in 2 CE of just under 60 million—so did its bureaucracy. Within a century of Liu Bang's reign, the number of government officials had swollen to 130,000. Officials were divided into graded ranks ranging from the heads of imperial ministries to district magistrates. Below these officials were clan leaders and village **headmen**. Landowners were to collect and remit the taxes for themselves and their tenants, while the lower officials recorded the rates and amounts, kept track of the labor obligations of the district, and mobilized the people during emergencies.

Wudi, the Martial Emperor

A high point of the Han dynasty came during the rule of the emperor Wudi, whose reign name means the "Martial Emperor" (r. ca. 140–87 BCE). Like both his predecessors and successors, Wudi faced the complex problem of defending the empire's northern and western boundaries from diverse groups of nomadic peoples, especially the Xiongnu. He therefore extended the Great Wall begun by the Qin to provide greater protection. Hoping that a strong Chinese presence would discourage potential invasions, Wudi encouraged people to move to areas along the northern and western borders of the empire (see Map 9.2).

In addition to securing the empire, Wudi had to suppress Xiongnu raids on central Asian trade routes, especially the Silk Road. He made diplomatic efforts, offering the Xiongu food and other necessary supplies; but when those efforts failed, he mounted military campaigns against them. Over the long term, the Han also adopted the practice of "**sinicizing**" the nomadic peoples, a process similar to that pursued by their contemporaries, the Romans, toward the peoples surrounding their empire. The practice of sinicizing involved encouraging nomadic peoples to assimilate themselves to Chinese culture and identity. Once they had been assimilated, the threat of nomadic invasion would be lessened. Wudi drove his armies into central Asia, where he established a lucrative trade with the peoples there, and again into northern Vietnam and Korea, extending Han rule into those areas. Along with the imposition of Han rule came the Chinese writing system and the infusion of Confucian ideology and practices.

Wang Mang and the Red Eyebrow Revolt

Lasting more than 400 years, the Han era has traditionally been divided into the Former or Western Han (202 BCE–8 CE) and the Latter or Eastern Han (24–220 CE). During the brief interval between 8 and 24 CE, Han rule was temporarily interrupted when a relative of the royal family, Wang Mang (45 BCE–23 CE), seized power. Wang Mang attempted to introduce a number of reforms in land distribution in an effort to reduce the huge disparity between rich landowners and peasants, which had been inherited from the Warring States period. Wang Mang's proposed reforms provoked a revolt led by a

Han Dynasty Gilt Bronze Lamp. The sophistication and craftsmanship of Han art can be seen clearly in this bronze oil lamp overlaid with gold—much of which is now missing, revealing the oxidation of the bronze underneath. The three-legged style of the vessel itself goes back at least to the Black Pottery period, while the dragon motif, superficially whimsical in its design, is meant to symbolize strength and is a favorite device of the imperial courts of successive dynasties down to the Qing (1644–1912), who incorporated it into the the first modern Chinese national flag.

Headmen: Local leaders; these are usually chosen by the people of the village, clan, district, etc., rather than appointed by the government.

Sinicize/sinicizing: The pattern by which newcomers to areas dominated by Chinese culture were encouraged to interact and adopt that culture for themselves.

MAP **9.2** The Han Empire.

Daoist secret society called the Red Eyebrows. The rebels killed Wang Mang and sacked the capital of Chang'an. An imperial relative restored the Han dynasty in 24 CE but moved the capital to Luoyang, where the empire continued in somewhat reduced size.

Wang Mang's attempts at land reform and the Red Eyebrow revolt hastened the collapse of the last of the old aristocratic landholdings. Together with the sense of renewal accompanying the restoration of the Han dynasty, these events helped to temporarily mask the empire's growing weakness.

Han Decline By the late second century CE the Han dynasty was showing signs of strain. Ambitious internal improvements ordered by Han emperors were carried out by *corvée* labor—labor required by the government as a form of taxation. These labor obligations made it increasingly difficult for peasants to tend their lands, and as a result, agricultural productivity declined. Furthermore, the loss of some borderland territory reduced the tax base just when the empire required more taxes to maintain the Great Wall and far-flung military outposts also meant to protect the empire from nomadic invasions. Economic crises, however, were not the only threats to the empire. A series of internal battles within the royal family, aggravated by increasing regional power falling into the hands of Han generals and the rise of the Daoist Yellow Turban revolt after 184 CE, finally brought the Han dynasty to an end in 220 CE.

Between Empires   Like the Romans of the late fourth century CE, who saw Germanic migrations as temporary disruptions rather than fatal blows to their empire, the Chinese expected that a new dynasty would shortly emerge after the collapse of the Han. Instead, China experienced its most chaotic postimperial political period. This interlude of turmoil is traditionally divided into the era of the Three Kingdoms (220–280 CE), the overlapping Six Dynasties period (222–589 CE), and the also overlapping period of the North and South Dynasties (317–589 CE).

From the initial Three Kingdoms period through the numerous small, weak, and short-lived "dynasties" that followed, the aim of reconstituting the empire was always present. Many of the factors that had undermined the Han, however—the growing power of landed elites, the increasing weakness of the bureaucracy, the chronic defense problems of the north and west—continued and even multiplied. In the absence of effective centralized administration, the infrastructure fell into disrepair, the enormous internal economy grew more regionalized, external trade declined, and warfare, famine, and banditry haunted the land.

Not until the fifth century CE did the rebuilding process begin, when an eastern Mongolian people known as the Toba established the state of Northern Wei in northern China. Taking advantage of the possibilities of the new military tactics growing from the development of the stirrup, Northern Wei established itself as a dominant power in the region. By the beginning of the sixth century, the Toba had enacted a formal policy of assimilating into Chinese culture—taking Chinese names, marrying into leading families, reviving old imperial rites, and taking on the perennial problem of land reform. In organizing a program of land redistribution to the peasants, they helped pave the way for the return of centralized administration, military service, and tax collection. A Toba general named Yang Jian succeeded in uniting most of the old Han lands in 589 and called the reunified dynasty the "Sui" (see Map 9.3).

MAP **9.3** **China in 589 CE.**

Patterns Up Close | The Stirrup

Given the long list of familiar Chinese pathbreaking technologies such as paper, the compass, the sternpost rudder, printing, the horse collar, and, of course, gunpowder, it may seem strange that we would feature something as simple as the stirrup.

Yet, the stirrup's understated presence has long been recognized by historians as being of major importance. The reason is that it not only completely changed the way humans used horses but ushered in a new type of warfare that altered the structure of societies and dominated military strategy for 1,000 years.

Despite the fact that the horse had occupied a prominent place in Eurasian warfare for over 2,000 years, its utility had been limited to pulling chariots and supporting mounted archers and riders with light spears. The central problem of using horses in pitched battles was that the back of a horse was a precarious perch: It was difficult to mount a horse when one was weighed down with armor and weapons but easy to be knocked from one, especially when one was engaged in close combat and swift maneuvering.

Jin Dynasty Iron Stirrups. Widespread use of the stirrup not only brought the use of cavalry back to the forefront of warfare, but led to a resurgence in power of Eurasian mounted nomadic peoples. The ornate stirrups pictured here helped the nomadic Jurchen people displace the Northern Song Dynasty (see Chapter 12) and set up their own Jin Dynasty that lasted from 1127 to 1234. Their downfall was brought about by another mounted nomadic people—the Mongols—who not only displaced the Jurchens but went on to conquer the Southern Song in 1279 and incorporate their new Yuan Dynasty into the short-lived Mongol super-empire spanning Eurasia in the late thirteenth and early fourteenth centuries.

Around the beginning of the Common Era the first attempts at saddles with straps for supporting a rider's feet began to appear in northern India. But these employed only a simple toe loop, and the saddle concentrated the rider's weight on a small area of the horse's back, tiring and hurting the animal. This basic idea for the stirrup, however, appears to have spread via the Silk Road, and by the early 300s CE a recognizably modern iron stirrup with a flat bottom and semicircular top began to be used in north and central China; the earliest remains discovered so far date to 302 CE. At about the same time, saddles with a rigid frame to distribute the rider's weight more evenly and better padding to cushion its effects on the horse began to be employed.

The effects of these changes were swiftly apparent in a China now dominated by feuding states and marauding nomads in the post-Han era. With his legs secured to his mount and a high saddle back to cushion him in combat, a mounted warrior

The Empire Reclaimed: The Sui Like the Qin before them, the forcefulness with which the Sui pursued empire building—particularly in an ill-conceived invasion of the Korean peninsula after their ascension in 589 CE—prompted unrest among the people. The Sui used forced labor for several elaborate construction projects, including palatial palaces, roads, and, perhaps the most ambitious project of all, the Grand Canal. Linking the Yangzi River with the Yellow River, the Grand Canal facilitated shipment of large quantities of rice and other food crops from the south directly to the refurbished capital at Chang'an. This was to prove a vitally important highway over the coming centuries as northern capitals increasingly depended on food supplies shipped from the south. The Grand Canal, still in operation today, would eventually be extended all the way to the Beihe River, which leads to Beijing.

could use a long lance to charge directly into enemy formations without fear of being immediately unhorsed. Furthermore, he could wear a full complement of armor and armor his horse. The stirrup proved so effective that by the fifth century CE the armies of all the states in China had adopted and refined the technology. In China, it helped pave the way for the Sui reunification in 589.

It was in western Eurasia, however, that the new technology saw its greatest impact after its arrival in the seventh century CE. It has even been argued that the feudal society of Europe was ultimately derived from the stirrup. The ability of a heavy cavalry of armored warriors to break infantry formations and fight effectively at close quarters from horseback placed a premium on refining armor and weapons, training warriors, and breeding bigger, faster, and stronger horses. The politically fractured eras of post-Roman and post-Carolingian Europe meant that local elites and regional strongmen had to mount their own defenses. The stirrup and the military innovations it spawned allowed them to do this without heavily equipped armies, while the expenses necessary to adopt the new technology ensured that it would remain a monopoly of the rich and powerful. Thus the relationships comprising feudalism matured as peasants placed themselves in the service of their mounted protectors. The rough parity and independence of this widely dispersed warrior elite proved a powerful obstacle to the patterns of centralized state formation and empire building. Ironically, it would be another Chinese invention that would ultimately end this way of warfare many centuries later: gunpowder.

Questions

- How does the stirrup show how a technological innovation can lead to cultural and societal adaptations across many regions and across time?

- Which environmental and geographical conditions facilitated the impact of the stirrup across Eurasia in a way that would not have been possible in the Americas?

The outbreak of rebellion following the death of the second Sui emperor, Yangdi, brought the precocious 16-year-old commander Li Shimin to power. Li had the Sui emperor killed, placed his own father on the throne, and announced the founding of the Tang [Tahng] Dynasty in 618 CE. In less than a decade, he forced his father to abdicate and took power in his own right in 627 CE.

As we will see in the next part, the reconstitution of the Chinese empire under the Sui and its expansion and consolidation under the Tang not only marked a dramatic turning point in Chinese political history but also placed China among the world's regions marked by the ascendancy of religious civilizations. Like Christianity in the late Roman Empire, Buddhism made remarkable inroads in China during the period of fragmentation following the collapse of the Han. Indeed, through the work of Chinese monks it had also become firmly established in the Korean kingdoms and the Yamato state in Japan. The Tang would see the completion and high point of this process.

Buddhism and its institutions permeated Tang China to an extent never surpassed or even equaled in later dynasties. For a period in the late seventh and early eight centuries CE it even became the established Chinese state religion, under the remarkable Empress Wu Zetian. In this regard, China became not only part of a giant regional religious and cultural sphere during the Tang but an important part of a new world pattern that would encompass the sway of Islamic civilization, orthodox Christianity in the eastern Roman (Byzantine) Empire and much of eastern Europe, and the Christian civilizations of Roman Catholicism and Protestantism.

The Domestic Economy: Society, Family, and Gender

Throughout Chinese history, various dynasties actively encouraged and supported agriculture as the basis of the domestic economy. Yet, from the Han dynasty on, China exported far more in luxury goods and technology than it imported. Unlike the various regimes in India, which actively sought to foster trade, the Confucian view of the pursuit of profit as corrupting meant that Chinese governments seldom encouraged merchants and generally preferred to adopt a passive, but controlling, role in trade. Although merchants were held in low esteem, the state recognized that trade was indispensable to the financial health of the empire and saw it as an expandable source of tax revenue.

Industry and Commerce

Goods made in and distributed throughout the empire by the time of the Han included some of the best-known items of Chinese production. By the first century CE, Chinese manufacturers were making paper using a suspension of mashed plant fibers filtered through a fine-mesh screen and set aside to dry, a method still considered to produce the highest-quality product for painting or literary work.

Perhaps even more impressive, by this time, too, artisans were producing a kind of "proto-porcelain" that, with increasing refinement, would be known in the succeeding centuries to the outside world as "china." The earthenware produced during the Tang dynasty is among the most coveted in the world today. In other arts, the use of lacquer as a finish, as well as in artwork created by sculpting built-up layers of it, was also well established. By the second century CE, the Chinese had perfected silk production and had become world leaders in textile weaving. Both treadle and water-powered looms were in widespread use, and bolts of silk with standardized designs were produced for export. The Chinese supply of silks could barely keep pace with demand, especially from Persia and Rome. But much of the most important domestic production centered on bulk strategic goods that sparked some of the world's first debates on the government's role in economics.

Iron and Salt   By the Han period, the Chinese were producing cast iron in huge foundries. According to one estimate, by 2 CE, there were no fewer than 48 major ironworks in north China, while the mining industry as a whole may have employed as many as 100,000 people. The foundries, which produced ingots of standardized sizes and weights, used sophisticated systems of forced-air control, including water-powered bellows. Salt mines employed complex gearing for lifting brine from deep wells, systems of bamboo piping for transferring it, and evaporators fired by natural gas for extracting the salt. Because of the enormous productivity of the iron-making and salt-mining industries, the government continually sought ways to regulate and control them.

Despite the increasing importance of industry and commerce to the imperial economy, the Han and succeeding dynasties continued to view merchants as a parasitic class, with no ties to the idealized relationships of agrarian life, trade as a necessary evil. Nevertheless, government programs aimed at improving the empire's infrastructure facilitated commerce. The unpredictable flow of China's rivers required dikes, dredging, reservoirs, and especially canals to ease transportation. Along with roads, canals grew in importance as the empire relied more and more on the produce of the rich lands of the south to supply the capitals of the north. The Han emperor Wudi, as we have seen, began work on the Grand Canal that linked the Yangzi and the Yellow Rivers (see Map 9.4).

Coal Mining. While the miners shore up a tunnel and gather coal into a basket lowered from above, a large bamboo pipe is thrust into the mine to draw off poisonous gases.

Land Reform   By the time of the late Han, China's old aristocracy had largely died out, its place at the top of the social hierarchy assumed by the so-called *scholar-gentry*—the educated large landholders who constituted the Confucian bureaucracy. Despite the elimination of the old aristocracy, landlord holdings continued to expand. Since the upper ranks of the landowners and bureaucrats either were exempt from taxes or paid reduced amounts, the tax burden fell increasingly on tenants and owners of small parcels of land. Poor harvests or bad weather, particularly in the arid north and west, made the situation even worse for those already heavily taxed. Because the north, despite its elaborate irrigation works, was far less productive and more prone to crop failure than the south, it was also proportionally more heavily taxed.

Such problems made land reform and redistribution an ongoing concern. The Tang, for example, continued the policy of land redistribution begun during the brief Sui dynasty by allotting each peasant family a tract of 100 *mou*, one-fifth of which was inheritable, while the remainder reverted to the state for redistribution. Although the Tang land redistribution policy resulted in a relatively high level of prosperity, absentee landlordism, tenancy, and usury also rose again, particularly during times of economic stress. The continual problem of land tenure and attempts at reform and redistribution marked every dynasty and modern government down to the People's Republic—where it is even today a major concern.

Agricultural Productivity   A number of technical and systemic innovations steadily increased agricultural productivity. In addition to such staples as wheat, millet, and barley in the north and rice in the south, a wide variety of semitropical fruits and vegetables were cultivated within the empire. New strains of rice resulted in larger harvests on more marginal land. Trade with central Asia had introduced wine grapes, and fermented grain beverages had become a substantial industry. New

Industry and Commerce Under the Han

- Area of intensive agriculture
- Area of coal mining
- Han Empire 1st century BCE
- Road
- Canal
- Cattle
- Timber
- Paper
- Silk
- Citrus fruit
- Iron working
- Salt mining

MAP **9.4** **Industry and Commerce Under the Han.**

techniques of crop rotation, fertilization, and plowing were gradually introduced, as were the collar for draft animals and the wheelbarrow; oxen-drawn, iron-tipped plows; treadle hammers; undershot, overshot, and other types of waterwheels; the foot-powered "dragon" chain pump for irrigation; and the *fengche*—a hand-cranked winnowing machine with an internal fan to blow the chaff from the grain. With this basic, reliable technology, China led the world in agricultural productivity until the eighteenth century CE.

The Silk Road   The dramatic expansion of maritime and caravan trade from the seventh century CE on, particularly within the huge Buddhist cultural sphere, spread Chinese technology abroad and brought new products into the Chinese empire. During the first millennium and a half of its history, China made numerous connections throughout the world and spread its influence in all directions. Early examples of silk may have reached the Mediterranean and North Africa through a long train of middlemen as early as the first millennium BCE. By the first century BCE, a variety of artifacts clearly identifiable as Chinese had turned up in Egypt; by the fourth and fifth centuries CE, Indian and Persian middlemen extended the Chinese trade to the African empires of Kush and Aksum.

The principal route connecting the Chinese to the various trading centers of central Asia, and ultimately to the Mediterranean and Rome, was known as the **Silk Road**. Along this route, the Chinese would forever be identified with silk; and though they tried to guard the secrets of its production, the demand was so high that many peoples along the caravan routes were soon engaged in making silk themselves. The techniques of raising silkworms and weaving silk reached the eastern

Silk Road: Overland trade routes that connected eastern and western Eurasia, beginning at the end of the fourth century BCE.

Han Era Technology. By the first century CE, Chinese sophistication in crafts and labor-saving devices could be seen in a number of areas. While the illustrations here are from the famous seventeenth-century compendium of technology *Tiangong kaiwu* (*The Works of Nature and Man*), all of them illustrate techniques in use during the Han period. (*a*) Papermaking. (*b*) *Fengche* winnowing machine. (*c*) Undershot waterwheel driving hammers in a pounding mill. (*d*) Horizontal waterwheel driving a chain-bucket "dragon pump" for irrigation.

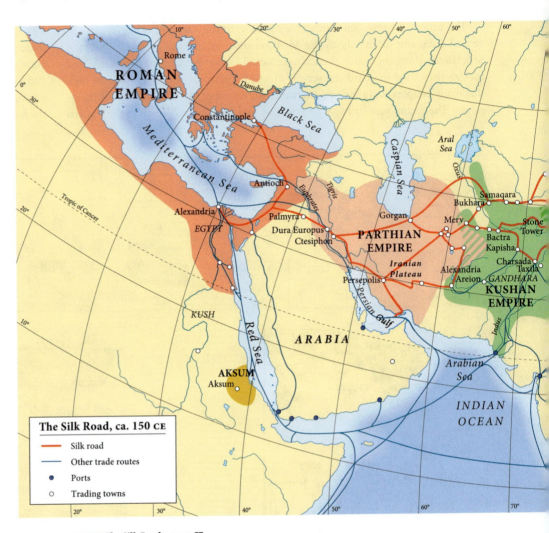

MAP **9.5** The Silk Road, ca. 150 CE.

Mediterranean between the third and fifth centuries CE. Competition among silk producers in western Eurasia became so keen that the Roman emperor Justinian allied with the African kingdom of Aksum in the sixth century CE to try to break the Persian near-monopoly on fine silks. In the process, the Romans created their own monopoly to service the western trade.

Gender Roles

Women in imperial China, as in agrarian-based societies in general, were subordinate to men. Early Confucian works, while emphasizing reciprocal responsibilities within the family, were relatively flexible about the position of women. However, with the rise of the imperial bureaucracy during the Han and the increasing emphasis on filial piety within its new Confucian curriculum, a more rigidly hierarchical, patriarchal model of proper women's behavior gradually developed. At the same time, the emphasis on sons within the extended family as carriers of the ancestral line and their potential to win admission to official state service led to a gradual devaluing of daughters. In times of severe economic stress, when families had difficulty supporting several children, young girls were the first to suffer. Families, especially in rural areas, would sometimes sell their daughters into prostitution or kill female infants. By the Song era (960–1279 CE) problems relating to the treatment of young girls had become so acute that China's first foundling hospitals were opened in 1138 CE.

Although some elite women achieved prominence in intellectual pursuits, like the historian Ban Zhao (48–116 CE), women's education centered primarily on cultivating the domestic virtues of devotion and obedience, as well as mastering crafts such as spinning and weaving. Daughters were "expendable" in the sense that they would marry or be placed with another family through adoption or servitude. Since these last options often brought advantages to the girl's family, daughters were frequently educated in singing, playing instruments, chanting poetry, etc. in order to make them desirable candidates for placement.

From the fifth century CE on, the popularity of monastic Buddhism created attractive alternatives for those fleeing family pressures, especially women. Those women enrolled in Buddhist schools that required extensive scriptural study became highly educated, and the communities themselves, like Christian monasteries in Europe, often owned large tracts of land and wielded considerable local influence. At the same time, the relative strictness of the practices regulating sexual and family life varied, particularly among high officials and the growing urban commercial classes. Foreign influences and fashions also affected behavior, particularly in Chang'an and places engaged in international trade. Tantric Buddhist (see Chapter 8) and Daoist sexual practices, which were used by their followers as a means of spiritual liberation, undoubtedly contributed to a more relaxed approach to relations between men and women during the Tang as well.

Intellectual Trends, Aesthetics, Science, and Technology

As we saw in the opening of this chapter, the period from the sixth century BCE until the first unification of China under the Qin in 221 BCE was marked by a dynamic collision of economic and social forces and is universally regarded as China's most fertile period of intellectual exploration. Long-term contacts with the east Asian Buddhist sphere from the end of the Han through the Tang era resulted in a number of new Buddhist schools being founded and spread throughout east Asia.

Confucianism, Education, and History During the Han

While the first Han rulers tended to favor a philosophical system that combined a more lenient Legalism with aspects of other surviving schools, over time a form of Confucianism became the preferred governmental doctrine. Confucian emphasis on the ethical correctness of officials, caring for the people, filial piety, and the study of history tended to make it a good fit for Han administrators. By the second century CE, the steadily growing popularity of Confucian academies led to their subsidization by the state, in effect placing all official education in the hands of these academies. Since the purpose of such education was state service, it also made knowledge of Confucianism the principal test for entrance into the bureaucracy. This situation, expanded and elaborated over nearly two millennia, would remain in force until the opening years of the twentieth century.

The Han Confucian Synthesis   Although Confucianism served as the foundation for the Han educational curriculum, Confucian doctrine had changed somewhat from the early teachings of Confucius and his disciples. During the Warring States period and the era of Qin rule, much Confucian thought—along with that of other philosophical schools—had been altered to suit the times, while a great many texts had been lost along the way. Thus, the Confucianism that finally received state approval included a number of elements reflecting the new realities of the Han dynasty.

This so-called Han synthesis of Confucian philosophy is evident in the era's chief treatise on government, the *Huainan zi*. In this document, a number of Confucian ideals, all calling for humane, righteous, and filial behavior by the powerful, are linked with Daoist ideas of the ruler as divorced from day-to-day administration and Legalist notions on the role of officials. As the intermediary between heaven, humankind, and earth, the emperor occupied a position of cosmological significance by nourishing the people and holding all in balance. For continuity's sake, a dynasty had to be hereditary—in contradiction to Confucius' ideas. But the idea of dynastic cycles and the Mandate of Heaven became even stronger during this period as they were elaborated by the great Han historians.

Han Historians   As we saw in Chapter 4, while there had been no shortage of history writing in the late Zhou period, much of it was seen even by contemporaries as overly partisan, fanciful, or tied to teaching moral lessons at the expense of accuracy. Mencius, for example, doubted the truthfulness of most of the *Book of History*. By the Han period, with the ideal of empire now encouraging a new sense of cultural unity, a series of court historians attempted to collate historical materials that had survived the Qin purges and to unify and systematize the writing of history.

For these men and women, the purpose of history writing, much as it was for the great Greek historians Herodotus (ca. 484–425 BCE) and Thucydides (ca. 460–ca. 395 BCE), was the accurate transmission of information—often with verbatim copies of important documents—and analysis of the events portrayed in terms of a larger vision of the direction and purpose of human history. For the Han historians, as for Chinese historians throughout the imperial era, history was cyclical: Human events, as manifestations of the great universal cycles of being, are a constant succession of birth, growth, decay, death, and rebirth, in which older ideas of the Mandate of Heaven, dynastic cycles, and yin and yang theory are imbedded. The moral lessons learned are therefore tied to actions taken at various stages of these cycles.

The basic format of long-term history was laid out by the father-and-son team of Sima Tan (d. 110 BCE) and Sima Qian (145–86 BCE). Their *Shiji* (*The Records of the Grand Historian*) attempts the first complete history of the Chinese people from the mythical Yellow Emperor to their own time. One particularly valuable section that became a staple of later histories was a survey of non-Chinese peoples encountered along with their habits, customs, religions, geography, and other significant traits. Hence, the Han records give us our first written accounts of Japan and other places on the Chinese periphery.

Like other Chinese officials, the historians took their role of "conscience" of the government seriously, sometimes at severe peril to themselves. As historian to the powerful Emperor Wudi, for example, Sima Qian offended the ruler by exonerating a general in his writings whom the emperor and court had accused of cowardice. Given the choice between execution and castration, Sima chose the latter; if he were dead, he explained, he could not finish his history, which he believed was his highest duty.

Several generations later, the Ban family comprised another dynasty of Han court historians. Writing after the Wang Mang interval, Ban Biao (3–54 CE) and his son Ban Gu (32–92 CE) pioneered the writing of dynastic history with their *Hanshu* (*The History of the Former Han*), which laid out the format followed by all subsequent dynastic histories. Ban Gu's daughters were also scholars and writers, and as we saw earlier in this chapter, his sister Ban Zhao (48–116 CE) carried on the family tradition of history writing as well as a treatise on proper women's behavior, *Admonitions for Women*. Here, we begin to see a trend toward an increasing restrictiveness on women's activity and a sense that the "inner domain," the home, is the proper sphere for women and girls.

The Inner Domain

"In womanly behavior there are four things [to be considered]: (1) womanly virtue; (2) womanly speech; (3) womanly appearance; and (4) womanly work ... To guard carefully her chastity; to control circumspectly her behavior; in every motion to exhibit modesty; and to model each act on the best usage, this is womanly virtue.

To choose her words with care; to avoid vulgar language; to speak at appropriate times; and not to be offensive to others may be called womanly speech. To wash and scrub dirt and grime; to keep clothes and ornaments fresh and clean; to wash the head and bathe the body regularly, and to keep the person free from disgraceful filth, may be called the characteristics of womanly appearance.

With whole-hearted devotion to sew and to weave; to love not gossip and silly laughter; in cleanliness and order to prepare the wine and food for serving guests, may be called the characteristics of womanly work."

—Ban Zhao. "Nü Jie, or Lessons for Women." In William T. DeBary, ed. *Sources of Chinese Tradition*, 2nd Edition, vol. 1, pp. 823–824. New York: Columbia University Press, 1999.

Interestingly, accounts of the historians' activities themselves may be found in the *Hou Hanshu* (*The History of the Latter Han*), written after the fall of the dynasty by Fan Ye (398–446 CE).

Buddhism in China

The growth of Buddhism as a universal missionary religion came, at least in part, from the adaptability of its doctrines to widely diverse peoples and belief systems. As we saw in Chapter 8, by the mid-first century CE, when it is first mentioned in Chinese accounts, Buddhism had already split into the major divisions of Theravada (Hinayana), which had established itself in southern India and Sri Lanka and was moving into southeast Asia, and Mahayana, which would be established in China, Korea, Vietnam, and Japan.

The introduction of Mahayana Buddhism into China presents a number of interesting parallels with that of Christianity into Rome, though there are important differences as well. Rather than focusing on the problems of practical government, both religions emphasized instead personal enlightenment or salvation. Both, to some extent, were initially seen as "foreign" systems and subjected to periodic persecution before emerging triumphant. Finally, while both challenged existing political and social hierarchies, the institutions of both were also adopted by rulers who wanted to strengthen or expand their power.

Language and Scripture   The incompatibility of the Chinese written language with Sanskrit and Pali scriptures complicated the introduction of Buddhism to China. The earliest Buddhist missionaries had to rely heavily on transliterations, borrow extensively from Daoist terminology, and invent a new and diverse vocabulary of Chinese terms. Over the next several centuries, this eclecticism resulted in a proliferation of sects and a growing need on the part of Chinese and, later, Korean, Japanese, and Vietnamese converts to travel to India for study and guidance. The travel account of the Chinese monk and early pilgrim Fa Xian (see Chapter 8), who journeyed throughout central Asia and India from 399 to 414 CE in search of Pali copies of Buddhist works, contributed greatly to Chinese understanding of the growing Buddhist world. The most famous pilgrim, Xuan Zang (596–664 CE), went to India in 623 CE and brought back the extensive collection of scriptures still housed in the monastery he founded just outside Xi'an. His travels were later immortalized in the popular collection of fabulous tales called *A Journey to the West*.

Buddhist Schools   The period between the dissolution of the Han and the ascendancy of the Tang was also marked by the founding of several of the most important schools of east Asian Buddhism. By the fifth century, the school of popular devotion to Amida, the Buddha of the Pure Land, was spreading rapidly in China. Like the *bhakti* sects in India, no immersion in the texts is necessary for enlightenment for Pure Land followers; merely invoking Amida's name is sufficient for salvation. Even today, it remains the most popular Buddhist sect in both China and Japan. Amida is often pictured with the bodhisattva Guanyin [GWAHN-yin]—*Kannon* in Japan—the Goddess of Mercy who, like the Virgin Mary in Catholicism, is frequently invoked during times of peril.

Another influential Buddhist school was Tiantai, centered on the scripture of the *Lotus Sutra*. Tiantai emphasized contemplation of the sutras as the vehicle to enlightenment and later inspired several schools of esoteric (see Chapter 8) paths to enlightenment. These schools exercised considerable influence over both the Tang and the Japanese court at Heian during the eighth and ninth centuries CE.

Finally, one school that later achieved fame, if not widespread popularity, was Chan Buddhism, better known by the name given it in Japan: Zen. As outlined in its central text, *The Platform of the Sixth Patriarch*, by Hui Neng (638–713 CE), enlightenment is transmitted not through scriptural study or personal devotion to a particular figure but rather through the discipline of meditation and the active example of a master. The intense give and take between master and pupil, the discipline involved in performing humble tasks, and the contemplation of paradoxical questions are all meant ultimately to generate an intuitive flash of enlightenment. While limited in its influence in China, the emphasis on discipline and obedience made Zen the preferred Buddhist school of Japan's warrior aristocracy after the twelfth century CE.

Bodhisattva Guanyin, Sixth Century CE. Originally incorporating aspects of both genders, Guanyin (also Kuanyin) came to be depicted as female as Buddhism became firmly established in China. For Pure Land adherents, she was the bodhisattva invoked in times of extreme peril, and "the miracles of Guanyin" (*Kannon* in Japan) was a favorite theme of both Chinese and Japanese artists.

Intellectual Life

To a considerable degree, Chinese concepts of **aesthetics** developed during the first millennium CE became the founding principles for the arts throughout east Asia. The most important developments during this period were the maturation of three disciplines: poetry, painting, and calligraphy. An important part of a well-rounded education even today, these three disciplines are considered to be closely interrelated and governed by the same overriding principles. Central to each discipline is the idea of spontaneous creation as a reflection of the inner state of the artist. The artist in each of these media seeks to connect with the Dao by indirectly suggesting

Aesthetics (Esthetics): The study of the beautiful; the branches of learning dealing with categorizing and analyzing beauty.

Calligraphy. Detail of calligraphy from Wang Xizhi (303–361). The styles of Chinese characters were standardized for use in formal documents during the Qin and Han eras but have since been endlessly refined as art by master calligraphers. Along with painting and poetry, calligraphy was esteemed as one of the "three excellences" (*sanjue*) of the scholar. Wang Xizhi is, even today, revered as the master of the *xingshu*, or "running script," a cursive form used for private correspondence. This sample is from an early Tang tracing copy of Wang's hand.

Earthquake Detector. One of the more ingenious pieces of high-technology to come out of the Han period was the creation of a working earthquake detector by Zhang Heng (78–139 CE) in 134 CE. In the model illustrated here, carefully balanced balls were placed inside the large, hollow egg-shaped vessel. A tremor coming from a particular direction would jar the ball closest to the direction of the quake loose and send it down a track where it would fly from the mouth of one of the dragons on the outside of the "egg" and fall into the yawning mouth of the frog underneath. Thus, anyone checking the device could tell at a glance that a quake had occurred and from what directions by seeing which frog held a ball.

some aspect of it in the work itself. For example, Chinese landscape paintings often feature misty mountains, lone pines, and tiny human figures, with the action and occasion implied rather than detailed, because too much detail would place limits on the illimitable.

The Sciences   Because the imperial establishment relied on the prediction of comets, eclipses, and other omens to monitor the will of heaven, astronomy and mathematics were especially important disciplines. Chinese mathematicians had long used a decimal system and had worked out formulas and proofs to figure the areas of most standard geometrical forms. They had also calculated pi to four places and were able to solve simultaneous algebraic equations. The astronomers Zhang Heng (78–139 CE) and Wang Chong (27–100) had each championed theories of a universe governed by comprehendible natural forces. Zhang built a water-powered *armillary sphere*—a hollow globe surrounded by bronze bands, representing the paths of the sun, stars, and planets—and, in 134 CE, devised what was perhaps the world's first practical earthquake detector: Small balls were delicately balanced on tracks inside a sculpture faced with frogs, representing the directions of the compass. Even a slight tremor would send one of the balls down the appropriate track and out of the frog's mouth, indicating the direction from which the quake came.

Printing and Proto-Porcelain   One of the signal innovations of Eurasia was printing. Believed to have its origins in the ancient practice of taking rubbings on paper or silk of gravestone inscriptions, by the eighth century CE woodblock prints of popular Buddhist works had become available in major Chinese cities. By the end of the Tang and the beginning of the Song dynasties, presses employing both carved block and movable copper type were in regular use in China, Korea, and Japan. As it would later in Europe, the innovation of printing dramatically raised the literacy rates in all the areas it touched. By the beginning of the Song era, China had some of the highest preindustrial literacy rates achieved in human history—despite the difficulties of the written language.

The techniques involved in generating the extremely high temperatures required for cast iron were also transferable to porcelain production. Though there is debate about when the breakthroughs resulting in true porcelain first occurred, by the Tang period, distinctive brown and green glazed figures, often depicting the vibrant parade of peoples and animals of the caravan trade, were widely exchanged. By the Song, delicate white, cracked glaze and sea-green celadon ware were produced and sought by connoisseurs as the height of aesthetic refinement. Today, such pieces are considered to be among the world's great art treasures.

Putting It All Together

The political and social turmoil of the late Zhou era also marked an enormously innovative period in Chinese intellectual and cultural history. During this era the most important schools of Chinese thought and philosophy developed: Confucianism, Daoism, and Legalism. While Confucianism ultimately triumphed as the ideology of imperial China, it was the Legalist state of Qin that created the empire itself.

When the Qin dynasty fell in 206 BCE, much of the infrastructure of the early empire—including the Great Wall—was in place. The Han dynasty, from 202 BCE to 220 CE, retained the administrative structure of the Qin but softened the harsh laws and punishments of the Legalists. Eventually, the form of Confucianism practiced by the empire's administrators was taught in the imperial schools, becoming in effect the imperial ideology. By the end of the Han, China had created a solid alliance between the state and this all-encompassing ethical and legal system.

Perhaps more important than even the structures themselves, however, was that, like the Egyptians and Romans, the Chinese had become accustomed to what has been called the "habit of empire." As suggested in this chapter, 400 years of unity under the Qin and the Han had conditioned the Chinese to believe that empire was the natural goal of the patterns of political formation in China and that any interruptions in these patterns would be but brief interludes in the dynastic cycle. Thus, Chinese history has been marked by rhythms of inwardness and outwardness, inner renewal and usurpation of rule from the outside. Along with these rhythms came an inherited belief, reinforced by the theories of dynastic historians, that human society and the cosmos were knit together in a moral order, made perfectible by the power of the empire and the dedication of a bureaucracy selected for its understanding of ethics in human affairs (see Concept Map). Throughout the imperial era—and even in our own time—the students and scholars of China have tried to keep faith with this heritage by guiding and remonstrating with those in power.

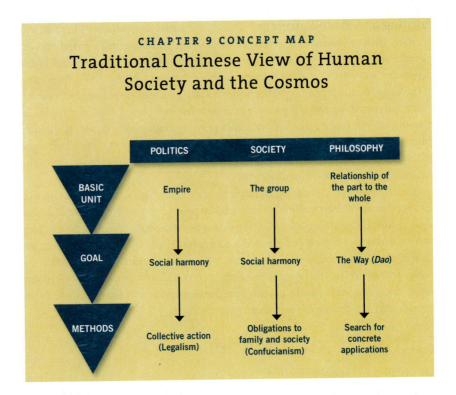

CHAPTER 9 CONCEPT MAP
Traditional Chinese View of Human Society and the Cosmos

	POLITICS	SOCIETY	PHILOSOPHY
BASIC UNIT	Empire	The group	Relationship of the part to the whole
GOAL	Social harmony	Social harmony	The Way (*Dao*)
METHODS	Collective action (Legalism)	Obligations to family and society (Confucianism)	Search for concrete applications

Review and Respond

1. What were China's most important technological contributions during this period?

2. Why did China's First Emperor see Legalism as the best ideology for his new empire?

3. How plausible do you find the Chinese view of how history works? Why?

4. Why, in your view, were the devotional schools of Buddhism more popular than those calling for scriptural study or strict meditation?

5. Like Confucius, if asked to sum up the way of the gentleman and virtuous ruler, what would you say?

▶ For additional resources, including maps, primary sources, visuals, and quizzes, please go to www.oup.com/us/vonsivers. Please see the Further Resources section at the back of the book for additional readings and suggested websites.

Thinking Through Patterns

▶ **Was the First Emperor's ruthlessness justified by his accomplishments in his empire?**

Addressing this question raises a very basic problem: Why do we study history? In ancient times, most people studied history for the moral lessons it offered and to avoid making the same mistakes their ancestors did. As we have also seen, some cultures, like the Chinese, studied it in hopes of grasping its basic patterns so as to understand the present and anticipate the future. Modern historians have generally taken their cue from Leopold von Ranke (1795–1886), who felt that scholars should rise above preconceived ideas and simply seek the past "as it really was." For most of the twentieth century, historians have sought to avoid making moral judgments about the past, to see their job as being "detectives" rather than "judges." By that standard, the historian should empathetically enter the past and seek to understand it; to judge it by the standards of the present is to be "presentist." But how does one deal with such things as genocide, extreme cruelty, or slavery? Thus, one way out of this dilemma might be to weigh the actions of the First Emperor against the standards of morality current in *his* day. Yet here, too, we encounter a problem: There were so many new schools of thought emerging in China then that no single one dominated; moreover, the First Emperor himself created his own system of morality based on Legalism. Perhaps, then, the best that we can do at this point, aside from judging him privately by our personal standards, is to note that he set the fundamental pattern for Chinese imperial government for the next 2,000 years—but at considerable cost.

Perhaps the biggest difference between Confucian society and modern American society is in the way both see the ideal forms of societal relations. Americans see the individual, the rule of law, democracy, and equality as fundamental to a good society. The purpose of government is to allow people to do as they wish but to provide the bounds within which they can do so. Confucian concepts of government and society put a premium on holism, hierarchy, and harmony. People are not seen as mere individuals but as part of larger patterns: family, clan, village, society, state.

▶ **How would you compare the values expressed by Confucius and Mencius to those of contemporary society?**

These are seen as part of a hierarchy that stretches from the poorest peasant to the emperor himself. Reciprocal rights and responsibilities are present at every level for protection of the weak, but equality is not seen as important. The role of government itself is seen in large part as being able to provide a moral example to the people. It if teaches them well through regulations, customs, and ritual, then the people aspire to be good and will police themselves to a great extent.

▶ **How have historians viewed the role of women in early imperial China?**

One of the most unattractive things about imperial China to the majority of us today is that it often appears that women were held in low regard, abused, denied basic human rights, and even tortured for fashion's sake, as with foot binding. The Confucian emphasis on hierarchy within society and the family tends to reinforce this impression. But scholars have in recent years begun to study the role of women at different times and in different regions of China, and the picture now appears much more complex than before. While scholars agree that in some respects, particularly foot binding from the Song period on, women's roles deteriorated, there were also times when the evidence suggests they exercised considerable freedom and influence, such as during the Tang and early Song periods. The pattern of "inner" and "outer" as it governed the traditional Chinese family is still discernable in many Chinese households today: While husbands go off to work, women definitely hold sway within the "inner" realm of the house.

PART THREE

The Formation of Religious Civilizations

600–1450 CE

A vitally important pattern of world history during the period 600–1450 was the emergence and development of what may be called "religious civilizations." By this we mean the formation of religions and cultures in entire world regions, shared by the states and empires in these regions. In all cases, religious, philosophical, and/or ethical traditions based on monotheism or monism helped give legitimacy to the polities that adopted them. They helped link individual states by providing them with a common set of cultural norms and bonds. Six religious civilizations emerged in a relatively short space of time in Eurasia and, to some extent, in Africa during the second half of the first millennium. They were, from west to east, western Christianity (from 476), eastern Christianity (640), Islam (750), Hinduism (550), Buddhism (Korea 550, Japan 594, Vietnam 971), and Neo-Confucianism (China 960, Vietnam 1010). Each occupied a world region.

Uniqueness and Comparability

Uniqueness. The rise of religious civilizations on the continents of Asia, Europe, and Africa is a striking phenomenon that unifies the period 600–1450. In this respect, it may be considered as a continuation of the intellectual and institutional transformations that began with the emphasis on transcendence by the visionaries of the mid-first millennium BCE as a key aspect in understanding the world in which they lived.

Comparability. The religious civilizations were not monolithic and displayed many regional variations. Internal diversity notwithstanding, they shared a number of common characteristics:

- Religious civilizations formed in regions which were larger than any single state within them: They superseded empires as the largest units of human organization. They often consisted of commonwealths of competing states sharing common characteristics and even a common culture.

- The civilizations were *scriptural*, that is, based on bodies of texts inherited in most cases from earlier periods. In each religious civilization, followers were

628–651
Arab Kingdom in Syria; Conquest of Iraq, Egypt, and Iran

1204
Sack of Constantinople by Crusaders

1268
St. Thomas Aquinas' *Summa Theologica*

1453
Constantinople Falls to Ottoman Empire

1336–1564
Dominance of Hindu State of Vijayanagar in Southern India

1238–1492
Muslim Kingdom of Granada

1206–1310
Mongol Conquests of Asia, Eastern Europe, and the Eastern Middle East

1348–1352
Black Death in Middle East and Europe

1206–1526
Muslim Delhi Sultanate at Height of Power

618–960
Tang Dynasty in China

preoccupied with harmonizing the often conflicting texts into one coherent *canon:* a single, official interpretation adhered to by all.

- The guardians of the canon (clergy, scholars, sages) were members of educated elites who taught and interpreted it to laypeople.

- Despite hostilities among religious civilizations, merchants, missionaries, pilgrims, and travelers visited each other's areas in large numbers. They fostered a lively exchange of innovations from one end of Eurasia and Africa to the other.

Origins, Interactions, and Adaptations

The era of religious civilizations provides some striking examples of the processes of origins, interactions, and adaptations that we have emphasized in this book.

Internal Forces. The elements with which people built their religious civilizations came from the intellectual and institutional traditions of empires and kingdoms from the pre-600 period. These elements were for the most part found inside the territories of the evolving religious civilizations. Some exceptions include Korea, Japan, and Vietnam, which adopted Chinese Buddhist civilization more or less ready-made from the outside.

In the majority of religious civilizations, the scriptural canons were completed within two or three centuries. Thereafter, refinement within the confines set by the canons continued for many more centuries, in some cases even beyond 1450. Without outside challenges, however, these refinements slowed. Over time, scholars, thinkers, and artists tended to exhaust the possibilities which their civilizations offered them.

External Challenges. External intellectual challenges contributed to the reshaping of two religious civilizations during the period 600–1450: Neo-Confucian China and western Christianity. China's intellectual foundation from the Han dynasty on was based on Daoism and Confucianism, harmonized with some difficulty during the early centuries of the millennium. Buddhism, coming from India, became a full-blown intellectual and institutional challenge by the 800s. In response, the Chinese reconfigured their canon from the mid-tenth century with the creation of Neo-Confucianism.

In western Christianity, Latin Christians enlarged their canon twice, as a result of adapting to intellectual challenges coming from the outside: first around 1100–1250, after the arrival of Arabic and Greek texts, and second around 1400, after the arrival of another set of Greek and Hellenistic texts.

Thinking Like a World Historian

▶ How were the religious civilizations of the period 600–1450 unique? How were they comparable?

▶ What impact did internal forces and external challenges have on the patterns of development in the religious civilizations of the period 600–1450?

▶ Why do the civilizations of the Americas fall outside the patterns that characterize Eurasian and African civilizations during this period?

960–1127
Neo-Confucian Synthesis in China

794–1185
Heian Period, Japan

1257–1287
Vietnamese Repel Three Attempted Mongol Invasions

1250–1505
Kingdom of Great Zimbabwe in Southern Africa

850–1000
Kingdom of Chichén Itzá in Northern Yucatán Peninsula

1438–1533
Inca Empire in Andes

918–1392
Koryo Kingdom, from which the Name "Korea" Is Derived

ca. 1000
Tale of Genji, perhaps World's First Novel, Japan

ca. 1000–1400
Kingdom of Ife in West African Rain Forest

1240–1645
Empire of Mali in West Africa (Rain Forest, Sahel and Savanna)

1427–1521
Aztec Empire in Meso-America

Chapter 10

600-1300 CE

Islamic Civilization and Byzantium

Byzantium

Islamic Civilization

BYZANTIUM AND THE ISLAMIC WORLD, ca. 1000 CE

O ne cannot help but feel sympathy for Safra, a jilted wife whose husband left her for a more attractive woman in twelfth-century Cairo. Two letters by Safra to her estranged husband Khidr tell of her deep hurt and bitter anguish. She is offended that Khidr denigrates her as unattractive and reveals marriage secrets to his new lover, who is also married. In her words, his "repulsive, shameless talk" causes her deep suffering. Were she not a good Muslim, she says, she would curse him roundly and loudly, both privately and in public.

The letters also reveal that she was independently wealthy, while her husband was not. She freely admits that when they were married 3 years

مبدأ العقد و ابتداء السق الثاني

Seeing Patterns

▶ Why can the period 600–1450 be described as the age of religious civilizations? How do eastern Christian and Islamic civilizations fit this description?

▶ Which cultural traditions combined to form Islamic religious civilization during its formative period? What were the most characteristic patterns?

▶ How did eastern Christian or Byzantine civilization evolve over time? On which institutions was this civilization based, and how did it evolve, wedged between Islamic and western Christian civilizations?

earlier, she did not realize that he was unreliable. Since he could not pay the obligatory portion of the "bride wealth" payable to her at the time of the wedding, she let it stand as a loan. Not only did he not make payments but he did not even feed and clothe her or pay the rent. When he began his affair 2 years earlier, she went to the countryside to find distance and rest. But he tortured her with insistent demands to return, promising her to leave his mistress. The moment she gave in and returned to Cairo, he went back to his lover. Like a ghost, he slipped into Safra's house at night for a few hours of sleep in his room, only to disappear the next morning. During his nightly visits he stole most of the household furnishings so that in the end she found herself in an empty house.

Safra's reflections and actions provide an important glimpse into the legal side of Islamic civilization. Contrary to the widely held opinion in the contemporary West, Islamic law afforded women considerable protections. Safra was a woman of property, holding personal title to possessions as well as to debts payable to her. She could go to court where she had standing as a complainant. She could initiate divorce proceedings, even if a wife's proceedings were more complicated than those of a husband. In short,

Islamic Science. The only treatise on astronomy that survives from classical antiquity is the *Almagest*, composed by the astronomer, mathematician, and Greek-Egyptain geographer Ptolemy in the second century CE. For centuries, however, the best-known and most widely imitated star map of the Greek constellations was the work of not a Greek but rather a Persian scholar writing in Arabic. Abd al-Rahman al-Sufi (903–986) produced his masterwork, *Book of the Fixed Stars*, in Isfahan (Iran) based on close examination of the work of the *Almagest*. Depicted here is a detail of the constellation Aries.

Chapter Outline

Commonwealth: An association of self-governing states sharing similar institutional and cultural traits.

even though Islamic civilization was as patriarchal as the other religious civilizations of the time, women exercised considerably more rights than in the Persian and Roman Empires.

Law formed an important part of the world of Islam in the twelfth century. It was self-sufficient and highly developed, with a court system and extensive juridical literature. Other important elements of Islamic civilization, such as theology, philosophy, science, engineering, and the arts, had also reached high levels of sophistication by that time. Although distinct regional variations existed in the **commonwealth** of states of which Islamic civilization consisted for most of the period 750–1450, the commonalities were even more pronounced. An educated Muslim could feel at home just as easily in Córdoba, Spain, as in Samarkand, Turkestan (now Uzbekistan).

The central patterns of Islamic civilization flowed from an empire that conquering Arabs from northern Arabia built during 628–750. These patterns would then develop across a 5,000-mile swath ranging from Spain to Turkestan. The empire, ultimately ungovernable as a single unit, evolved into a commonwealth of smaller states. From 750 to 950 it underwent a formative period during which its inhabitants adapted to inherited Greco-Roman and Persian cultures. By the mid-tenth century, historians consider the empire "fully developed," meaning that it was subjected to few outside influences that changed it in substantive ways. After this time, Islamic civilization continued to be shaped by its patterns of characteristic religious, political, and cultural traditions and institutions. These patterns remained largely unchanged and unchallenged by new stimuli coming from the outside until well into the modern period. In this respect, Islamic civilization was similar to Byzantine eastern Christian, Hindu Indian, neo-Confucian Chinese, and Confucian–Buddhist Japanese civilizations. All of these, after their formation by the end of the first millennium, developed stimulation more along their established internal patterns than as a result of innovation, interaction, and adaptation coming from the outside.

The Rise of Arab Dominance in the Middle East and Mediterranean

Arab conquests and the rise of the religion of Islam were foundational events during the period 600–900 CE. In the 600s, the Arabs carved out a kingdom for themselves by exploiting the preoccupation of the eastern Roman and Sasanid Persian Empires with their destructive wars of conquest in 610–628. Two Arab dynasties, the Umayyads succeeded by the Abbasids, built a vast empire stretching thousands of miles from east to west. Given the enormous distances, the Abbasids were forced to grant autonomy to many outlying provinces. Their empire thus changed into a commonwealth of many states sharing a single Islamic religion.

From Rome and Persia to the Arab Empire

At the beginning of the 600s, the Sasanid Persian and Roman Empires battled each other in a lengthy and destructive war, which left the Arabs in Syria and Mesopotamia (which the Arabs subsequently called "Iraq") to their own devices. The Arabs had been nomadic inhabitants of the Syrian-Arabian desert since the domestication of the camel around 1200 BCE and were founders of sedentary kingdoms and city-states around the rim of the desert on the Arabian Peninsula in the early centuries CE. In the mid-600s a group of Arabs declared a kingdom in Mesopotamia and Syria, captured Egypt from the eastern Roman Empire, and destroyed the Sasanid Persian Empire. Through further conquests, the Arab kingdom became an empire, stretching by the mid-eighth century from Iberia (Spain and Portugal) in the west to the Indus in the east.

Final Showdown Between Persia and Rome   As we saw at the end of Chapter 7, Khosrow II (r. 590–628) regained the Sasanid Persian throne thanks to Roman help. In gratitude for this help, Khosrow made territorial concessions, ended Roman tribute payments, and terminated the Persian–Roman war inherited from his predecessors. When a mutiny in 602 overthrew his Roman benefactor, however, Khosrow reacted by invading the Roman Empire. By avenging the emperor, Khosrow hoped that he could overcome the stigma of having owed his throne to the Romans. During the first phase of what was to become a new, 26-year-long war, Khosrow succeeded in reconquering Armenia and Upper Mesopotamia.

As the Roman defenses crumbled, a new emperor, Heraclius (r. 610–641) took the throne. To deny the Romans any chance of recovery, Khosrow II initiated the second phase of the war with the conquest of Syria, Palestine, and Egypt (614), as well as the abduction of what was believed to be the "true Cross" (on which

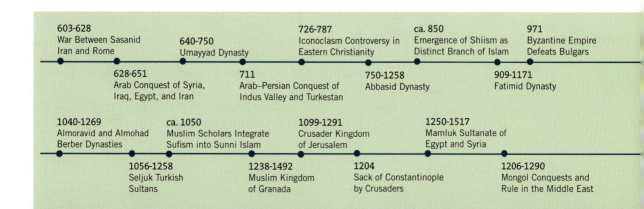

Jesus was supposed to have died) from Jerusalem. In 626, one of Khosrow's generals even fought his way to the Bosporus opposite Constantinople, stopped only by Heraclius' fleet in the Bosporus. The general was to link up with the Avars, an allied tribal federation from the Turkish central Asian steppes, who besieged Constantinople from the European side. A lack of ships, however, prevented the linkup of the two armies.

The Persian failure to cross the Bosporus was the turning point in the war. Within just 2 years, Heraclius was able to push the retreating Persians to the outskirts of their own capital, Ctesiphon, about 20 miles south of modern-day Baghdad. Khosrow fled from his palace and courtiers murdered him in the ensuing anarchy. After reoccupying the provinces lost in the war and restoring the purported "true Cross" to Jerusalem in 628, Heraclius returned to Constantinople in triumph. He left governance of the coastal and interior cities of Palestine and Syria in the hands of bishops supported by a few garrisons and governance of the interior countryside to the Arabs.

Theology and the Origins of Islam   Like scholars seeking the founding histories of many religions or philosophical traditions, modern students of Islam find themselves confronted by a dilemma. On the one hand, they possess a large number of often richly detailed Arabic narratives on the origins of Islam. But the earliest of these narratives date to the early 800s—two centuries *after* 628—and scholars have found it impossible to separate history from theology. In the early 800s, Islamic religious civilization was forming and it was only natural for Muslims at that time to project the tenets of the then evolving Islamic theology and law back into the 600s. On the other hand, narratives by Christians and Jews purportedly from the 600s are brief, lacking in detail, and often confused. Their reliability is frequently questionable, even if they provide seemingly useful information: Later copyists often changed the texts or added details not contained in the original texts. As a result, historians have to be extremely cautious with the available sources.

The theological account of Islamic origins, elaborated during the period 800–950, became the primary narrative of Islamic civilization. Usually referred to as "Islamic tradition," this account includes a number of theological doctrines:

- the revelation of the Quran as the Arab holy scripture
- the role of Muhammad as the Prophet, as told in his biography
- the establishment of a model community in Medina with Muhammad as the lawgiver
- the holy war (**jihad**, also "struggle") of the followers of Muhammad against the paganism (ignorance, or *jahiliyya*) of the Arabs
- the providential Islamic conquest of Sasanid Persia and much of the eastern Roman Empire
- the handing down of reports recording pronouncements and decisions of Muhammad and his companions in the early community, collectively called "tradition"

Jihad: According to Islamic tradition, war against unbelievers or pagans.

In short, Islamic tradition is the theology of Islam as the completion of the previous revelations of Christianity and Judaism and its mission to bring the world under God's rule.

More specifically, Islamic tradition begins with Muhammad's birth during the "year of the elephant." It was in this year, assumed to be 570 or 571, that Aksum's vice-regent in Yemen led an unsuccessful expedition (with elephants in his war train) against the western Arabian trading and pilgrimage city of Mecca. He laid siege to Mecca either in the name of the king of Aksum (in today's Ethiopia) or as a rebel seeking to consolidate his own rule but was beaten back by a flock of birds that supposedly dropped deadly rocks on the besiegers. Muhammad is described as a descendant of a prominent Meccan family of guardians of the sanctuary but also as an early childhood orphan who had to struggle for recognition. As a mature man, Muhammad received Allah's (God's) calling as a prophet of the Last Judgment, soon to arrive. The Meccans not only rejected his message but forced Muhammad and his small band of followers into an emigration (*hijra*) northward in 622, which became the first year of the Islamic calendar.

**Circling the Ka`ba.** Muslims on pilgrimage perform a number of rituals, among which is the sevenfold counterclockwise circumambulation of the Ka`ba, the sanctuary at the heart of Mecca. A large black cloth, called the kiswa, covers the sanctuary and is renewed annually. According to tradition, Abraham was the founder of the Ka`ba.

Muhammad resettled with his small band of followers in Yathrib, an oasis city farther north where he had ancestors on his mother's side. Local notables hired him as an arbiter among warring factions, including pagan Arab and Jewish tribes. In this city, renamed "Medina" (city [of the Prophet]), he molded a nascent community (*umma*) of Muslims by eliminating polytheism and expelling the Jewish tribes. Muhammad continued to receive divine revelations, and he undertook military campaigns against the Meccans, who persisted in their hostility. After 8 years of warfare and damage to their trade, the Meccans capitulated, agreeing to give up their paganism and convert to Islam.

According to the traditional account, the Prophet briefly returned to Mecca to rededicate the pilgrimage sanctuary of the city to monotheism. Called the Ka`ba [KAH-bah], this sanctuary was said to date back to Abraham, the father of both Israelites and Arabs in the Hebrew Bible. Two years later, in 632, Muhammad died in Medina, survived by several wives and daughters but no son. The first four successors in the leadership of the community—early converts and companions of the Prophet—kept the Muslims from dividing into warring factions and guided the early conquests of Syria, Iran, and Egypt. Paganism in Arabia ended, and Muslims established their own imperial rule over the Zoroastrians, Christians, and Jews of the Middle East.

As is clear from this summary of the tradition, Islam is not only a monotheistic religion opposed to paganism but also a faith that united a community of converts from paganism, which Muhammad governed through God's commands and laws of revelation. The Quran, the holy scripture that contains God's commandments and laws, speaks about a chain of preachers of monotheism, including biblical figures such as Joseph, Moses, and Jesus as well as Arab figures. Islamic tradition depicts Muhammad as the final prophet who laid the base for the moral and legal code, the **Shari`a**, which functioned as the blueprint for the perfect community that was Medina. In sum, this theology, created during 800–950 and projected back into western Arabia in the early 600s, is that of a communally organized Islam, destined to rule the world as the final revealed religion.

Shari`a: The entirety of Islamic morality and law, revealed in the Quran and the tradition.

From the Arab Empire to Islamic Civilization

While the theology of a fully evolved Islamic community in Medina in the early 600s is a vital topic for religious scholars to discuss, historians working with verified documents can say only that from 628 to 651, in the wake of the Roman–Sasanid

Islamic Conquests to 750 CE

▮ to 632	——	Boundary of Byzantine Empire, ca. 630
▮ 632–634	——	Boundary of Sasanid Empire, ca. 630
▮ 634–644	→	Main routes of advance of Muslim armies
▮ 644–661	✗	Battle with date
▮ 661–750	⊠	Military settlement or camp
TURKS Name of people	◆	Unsuccessful sieges of Constantinople

MAP **10.1** Islamic Conquests to 750.

war, Arabs from the north of the Arabian Peninsula conquered Sasanid Persia and assumed power in Roman Syria. In the course of the following century, Arabs established an empire extending to the Iberian Peninsula in the west and central Asia and northwestern India in the east. In this empire, they interacted with conquered Romans, Persians, North African Berbers, Iberian Visigoths, and central Asian Turks, incorporating them into their administration and adopting the cultural heritage of both Rome and Iran. Toward the end of the 700s the Arabs began to shape an emerging Islamic religious civilization patterned by influences from Christian theology, Roman and Jewish law, Greek philosophy and science, as well as Persian and Indian literature and science (see Map 10.1).

The Arab Empire   The Umayyads were the ruling dynasty of the early Arab empire (640–750), with their capital in Damascus. After establishing a kingdom in Syria and conquering Iran as well as the agriculturally rich Roman province of Egypt, the Umayyads led several campaigns by land and sea as far as Constantinople. The conquering Arab armies were increasingly composed of cavalry forces which had adopted the Chinese innovation of saddle frames and stirrups (see Chapter 9). This innovation was first recorded toward the end of the sixth century in an eastern Roman war manual. In both Roman and Persian armies, saddle frames and stirrups

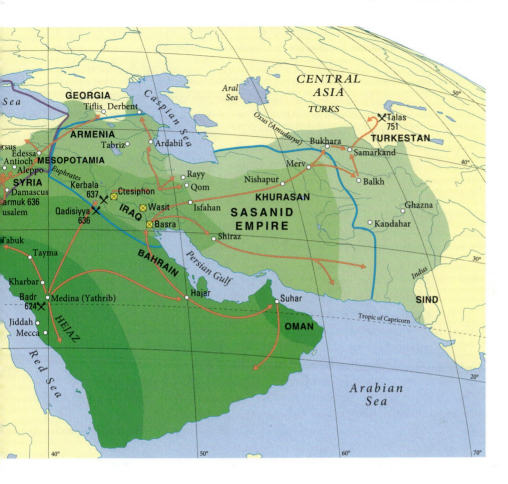

allowed for the riding of horses over long distances without injury to the horses' backs. They anchored riders firmly on their steeds, enabling them to fight not only with bow and arrow in quick maneuvers but also in frontal attacks with heavy armor and long lances. With their new form of cavalry, the Arabs inaugurated the cavalry age, which lasted in Eurasia until the 1400s when firearms became sufficiently effective to swing the advantage back toward infantries.

Under the reign of Abd al-Malik (685–705), the first signs of a religious orientation in the Arab Empire became visible. Earlier coins minted in the empire made no religious pronouncements, although the rulers were depicted with Christian crosses. By contrast, on a coin of 687, Abd al-Malik inscribed the formula "in the name of God, *Muhammad* the servant of God." The meaning of the Arabic word is ambiguous, for it can be read either as the name of the prophet called "Muhammad" or as the invocation "praise be." Accordingly, the inscription would read either as "Muhammad is the servant of God" or as "praise be to the servant of God." In the context of the inscription, this servant is Jesus.

Gold Coin of Abd al-Malik, ca. 696 CE. The coin displays the characteristics of what were to become Islamic coins; that is, the avoidance of images and the use of religious phrases.

Caliph: Representative of God, later of Muhammad, on earth.

The discussion among historians on how to read the word has barely begun and is still marred by polemics. However this discussion will be settled, one conclusion can definitely be drawn: Abd al-Malik had a strong interest in shaping religious doctrine for the empire. Since Arab coins from the 690s show Christ with either a flaming halo or a sword, indicative of his second coming, we can furthermore conclude that Abd al-Malik saw himself as the last **caliph** (from Arabic *khalifa*, or representative of God) before the end of time who would turn over his Islamic or Christian caliphate to God or Christ at the Last Judgment.

Abd al-Malik's view of the end of time led him to renew Arab efforts to take over Byzantium. (According to convention in recent scholarship, the Roman Empire after 640 is called "Byzantium.") Umayyad armies composed of Arabs and Berbers conquered Byzantine North Africa in 686–698, reducing Byzantium to Anatolia, the Balkans, and parts of Italy. Once North Africa was conquered, Abd al-Malik's successors became entangled in western Christian politics. In 711, dissident Visigothic nobles called Berber and Arab troops into the Iberian Peninsula to help them in their bid to oust the dominant Visigothic king. After destroying the Visigothic kingdom, the Berbers, Arabs, and Visigothic allies divided Iberia among themselves.

Two decades later, the Iberian Berbers and Arabs pushed into France. One of these raids is commemorated in western Christianity as the Battle of Tours and Poitiers in central France (732 or 733). Here, the founder of the western Christian Carolingian Empire, Charles Martel (r. 714–741), beat back the invading raiders. Similarly, Arab campaigns in the Caucasus to take the Russian steppes failed around 740. By contrast, in the east of the Arab Empire, Persian and Arab troops advanced to the lower Indus valley, as well as Turkestan in central Asia, at the western end of the Silk Road from China. In 751, a Persian-Arab army defeated Chinese and Uighur forces and turned the Silk Road into an Arab caravan route.

Arabs disappointed in the setbacks of the Umayyad conquests, however, turned to a radical movement that renewed Abd al-Malik's preaching of the end of time. In 750 they succeeded in overthrowing the Umayyad dynasty. The movement began in the distant province of Khurasan with local Persian military lords and Arab settlers, stirring them to arise under the banner of a "rightly guided" leader (*Mahdi*, or Messiah) and establish a realm of justice on earth at the end of time. The beneficiary of the overthrow was the new dynasty of the Abbasids, who derived legitimacy from their claim to belong to the "family of Muhammad" from which the Mahdi would rise. In order to distinguish themselves from the Umayyads, the Abbasid caliphs moved the capital from Damascus to the newly founded city of Baghdad in the center of Iraq, an agriculturally highly productive province since Sasanid times (see Map 10.2).

The Mahdi, however, did not arrive and the Abbasids quickly squashed all end-of-time expectations. They also realized that the far-flung Arab Empire could be governed only if

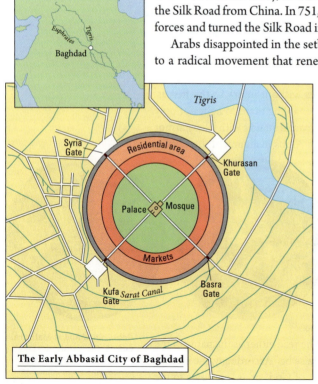

The Early Abbasid City of Baghdad

MAP **10.2** **The Early Abbasid City of Baghdad.**

they bestowed autonomy to the provinces of Iberia, North Africa, Egypt, Iran, and central Asia. Emirates (from Arabic *amir*, or "leader") under provincial leaders developed their own administrative and fiscal offices and pursued conquests of their own. The Abbasids themselves maintained an active military front against the Byzantines in Anatolia. In the early 800s, the Abbasids' emphasis shifted from territorial expansion to consolidation, focusing on the development of the new civilization of Islam. A world region emerged that was no longer ruled by a single emperor but was instead a commonwealth of states in which Islamic religious civilization formed.

The Beginnings of Islamic Civilization   At the center of the emerging new Islamic civilization, Baghdad became a magnet for the bright and ambitious in the Middle East and Mediterranean. Christians, Jews, and Zoroastrians settled with their intellectual, literary, and artistic heritages in this metropolis of several hundred thousand inhabitants. The Abbasid caliphs established an institute for advanced study (*dar al-hikma*, "house of wisdom," 813–833), to which they invited scholars from across the Islamic world as well as Byzantium. At this institute and elsewhere during the 800s and early 900s, teams of scholars translated large numbers of legal, philosophical, scientific, and literary works from Syro-Aramaic, Greek, Pahlavi, and Sanskrit into Arabic. By interacting with the cultural heritages of the conquered provinces, Muslims engaged in a selective adaptation to these heritages for the purpose of creating a unified religious civilization. Thus, influences from many sources contributed to the shaping of Islamic civilization.

On the basis of translated Roman law handbooks, the caliphs had legal scholars devise a new, universal legal codex to replace the diverse legal systems inherited in the provinces from pre-Islamic times. The court jurist Muhammad al-Shaybani (d. 805) used Roman law to arrange caliphal case law in the same way as Roman jurists did but in addition provided it with a religious grounding. He declared the individual laws to be based on pronouncements of Muhammad, called *hadiths*. These pronouncements, taken together, became subsequently known as the **Sunna**, that is, the "path" of Muhammad to be emulated by each Muslim.

The Separation of State and Religion   The caliph's claim for divinely based legislative authority did not go unopposed in the first half of the 800s. At this time, a debate developed between the government lawyers and theologians, on one hand, and critics in the population at large, on the other. The latter claimed that all doctrines and laws of Islam had been revealed to the Prophet Muhammad and that the caliphs had no right to add any new ones. The critics busily collected traditions far more numerous than those employed by Shaybani, provoking the government to denounce them as forgers who invented hadiths for their own political purposes. Other traditionalists gained popular support with their literalist doctrine of the Quran as the eternal word of God, while the government theologians rejected this doctrine as incompatible with the notion of God's transcendence. In a more general sense, the debate between the caliphal government and the traditionalist opposition

> **The House of Wisdom**
>
> "Our share of wisdom would have been much reduced, and our means of acquiring knowledge weakened, had the ancients [the Greeks] not preserved for us their wonderful wisdom, and their various ways of life, in writings which have revealed what was hidden from us and opened what was closed to us, thereby allowing us to add their plenty to the little that we have, and to attain what we could not reach without them."
>
> —from al-Jahithi (ca. 776–869 CE), *The Book of Animals* (ca. 850 CE), as excerpted in Jim Al-Khalili, *The House of Wisdom*. New York: Penguin, 2011.

Sunna: The way of life prescribed as normative for Muslims on the basis of the traditions about the teachings and practices of Muhammad and his interpretations of the Quran.

Abbasid Glory. Little is left of the Abbasid splendor during the 800s since Iraq suffered several invasions in later history, in which palaces, mosques, and other structures were destroyed. The picture on the top left shows the eighth-century Abbasid palace of Ukahidhir, south of Baghdad. The palace included gardens, baths, residential suites, courtyards, and audience halls with frescoes, like the one on the right, depicting female dancers with wine flasks. The fresco shows Byzantine and Iranian influences.

pitted the proponents of a figurative interpretation of scripture (Quran and Sunna) against the proponents of a literal interpretation.

In order to break the opposition of the traditionalists, the caliph decreed in 833 that all religious scholars and jurists occupying government positions had to swear a loyalty oath (*mihna*) in support of caliphal legislation. Supported by a reported groundswell of popular support in Baghdad, however, a minority of traditionalists refused to give the oath, even going to jail for their conviction. Unnerved, in 849 the government ended the enforcement of its decree.

Although the caliphs continued to rely on religious advisors to their liking, they gradually gave up their legislative powers. Around 950, the two sides reached a compromise, in which the caliphs gave up any further legislation in return for the religious scholars recognizing the caliphs' executive power. Caliphs and opposition agreed to share in the administration of scripture: The religious scholars were to be the interpreters of the Quran and Sunna, while the caliphs were the only authorities to apply law and theology. The compromise resulted in an early instance of separation between state and religion. This separation became the basic characteristic of Sunni Islam, the branch to which the vast majority of Muslims subsequently adhered and still adhere today.

Sunnism: Majority faith in Islamic civilization, based on the separation of religion and state.

Shiism: Minority faith in Islamic civilization, based on the figure of the Hidden Imam, who is expected at the end of time to establish a realm of justice in which state and religion are one.

Sunni Islam   At its core, **Sunnism** consists of five basic ritual obligations, the so-called Five Pillars: the profession of faith, prayer, fasting, alms giving, and pilgrimage to Mecca. The profession of faith is summed up in the formula "There is no God but God and Muhammad is his messenger." The five-times daily prayer requires the washing of hands and feet for ritual cleanliness and the performance of a sequence of bodily motions and prayers. On Fridays the noon prayer is to be performed in the congregational mosque. Fasting means a month-long abstinence from food, drink, and sex during the daylight hours. Alms giving is a small (2.5 percent) donation or tax to the poor, and the pilgrimage is a journey made at least once in one's life to Mecca. The adherents of minority **Shiism** observe the Five Pillars with the key addition of an additional prayer formula in praise of Ali, Muhammad's relative, who is considered by the followers of this minority branch of Islam, the Shiites, to have been the true successor of the Prophet. According to Muslim doctrine, fulfillment of these basic religious obligations defines a "good" Muslim in the eyes of God.

The Abbasid Crisis   During the second half of the 800s—around the same time that religion and state were beginning to separate—there was a fiscal crisis in the caliphal administration in Iraq. The Sasanid Persian expansion of agriculture between the Euphrates and Tigris Rivers, continued by the Abbasids, reached the limits of its potential in the mid-800s. The soil became too salty due to poor drainage in the fields in the flat terrain of lower Iraq. Crop yields declined and agricultural tax revenue shrank. As a result, the administration found it increasingly difficult to pay the military, causing its officers to take over still fertile tax districts directly as personal assignments.

At the same time, there was a generational shift in ethnic composition in the ruling class from Arabs and Persians to Turks from central Asia. Muslim slave raiding parties had captured non-Muslim boys and girls during campaigns into Turkish central Asia. Merchants sold these youths to the caliphs in Baghdad, where they were trained in the palace and converted to Islam. From 861 to 945, Turks seized power over the Abbasid caliphs in Baghdad while retaining the caliphs as titular heads of the government. The main function of the Turkish generals was the control of political affairs in Iraq. But they also provided important military services. Like their Umayyad predecessors, the Abbasids devoted themselves to the completion of the jihad against the eastern Christian empire of Byzantium in order to fulfill the original dream of uniting the Sasanid and Byzantine Empires into one single Islamic Empire—the last one before the end of time, to be handed over to God at the Last Judgment.

Byzantium: Survival and Recovery

Under siege by the Umayyads and Abbasids, the old eastern Roman Empire, now "Byzantium," had retreated to Anatolia and parts of the Balkans. It survived because its emperors reconstituted the state on a new military and religious basis: locally organized border defense and redefinition of Christian doctrine. Fortunately, its capital, Constantinople, was situated at a significant distance from the Muslims and was protected by thick walls on a nearly impregnable peninsula on the European side of the Bosporus, astride the entrance to the Black Sea. Under difficult circumstances, Byzantine emperors overcame outside attacks by Muslims and Norsemen and the loss of the Balkans to the Slavs and Bulgars, as well as internal religious conflicts. When the principality of Kiev in modern-day Ukraine adopted Christianity, Byzantium eventually changed into a commonwealth of eastern Christianity similar to the Islamic one of the Abbasids.

Survival Strategies   Under constant Arab pressure in eastern Anatolia and northern Africa (636–863), the Byzantine Empire shrank to a small Anatolian–Balkan realm. Both the Umayyad and Abbasid caliphs either led or sent invasion forces a total of seven times between 653 and 838 by land and sea to attack Constantinople. The empire survived the onslaught only by completely reorganizing its armed forces. Emperors after Heraclius restructured the mobile field armies into four stationary cavalry and auxiliary infantry regiments settled in Anatolia along the border with the

Arab Empire. To reinforce these regiments, the emperors withdrew troops from the Balkans, which they abandoned to recently arrived Slavic tribes.

A nucleus of Slavs probably originated in the large lowland area extending from Poland eastward across modern Belarus and northern Ukraine into northwestern Russia. They, together with people of other ethnic backgrounds, migrated in the 500s from there southward into the Balkans, the Ukraine, and eastern Russia. Although linguistically related, in the Balkans the Slavs became a composite ethnic population, incorporating speakers of other languages, such as Turkish-speaking groups of Bulgars from eastern Russia. These Bulgars migrated in the 500s to the Byzantine lower Danube, where they were influenced by Slavic culture and asserted their independence from the empire in 681. As the Byzantines were fighting for survival against the Arabs in Anatolia, the Bulgars became a major power in the Balkans.

External and Internal Threats

The Anatolian regiments of Byzantium were known as "themes" (Greek *themata*). New research has demonstrated that the central administration in Constantinople recruited the themes from among volunteers in the interior Byzantine provinces. It paid them in cash and food provisions, which were collected as taxes from estates and free farmers. Since the 25,000 cavalry troops making up the Anatolian themes were only half the number of their Muslim opponents, cunning had to substitute initially for brute force. The themes' main task was to shadow and harass their mightier Arab rivals, waiting for a lucky moment to strike back. One effect of these tactics was an impoverishment of the Anatolian interior, which suffered deeply from constant Muslim raids. Provincial life in Anatolia became increasingly hard for its Christian inhabitants, and even Constantinople declined in wealth.

Throughout this difficult period the Byzantine emperors continued to be active in the shaping of religious doctrine and law. One of the most important religious disputes to wrack the empire was the **iconoclasm** controversy (726–787 and 814–842). Christians of all theological directions had been embroiled for centuries in controversies over the visual depiction of Jesus and Mary. By the eighth century proponents argued for a total ban on holy pictures and statues, based on the biblical injunction against "graven images." In 726 the emperor Leo III (r. 717–741) decided to reform Christian theology by imposing a ban on all such art (*ikons*). He ordered the destruction of religious art, hence the term *iconoclasm*—smashing the icons. The reform pitted the emperor and his clerical advisors against the imperial church hierarchy, including the papacy in Rome, which defended what it considered the legitimate tradition of Christian imagery. As in the case of the Islamic traditionalists insisting on the literal reading of the Quran, eastern Christian traditionalists sided with church practices which were widely shared by ordinary believers.

Iconoclasm: Removal of all religious images from churches and monasteries during a period in the Byzantine Empire, under orders of the emperors and patriarchs of Constantinople.

Even though belief in God *and* divine images violated strict interpretations of monotheism—as with the doctrine of God's transcendence in Islam—for ordinary believers such imagery was seen as a tangible link to the divine. Pressured by popular demand, in 842 the Byzantine emperor, like the Abbasid caliph a few years later, ended his control over religion and law. Although the emperors did not become figureheads like the caliphs, their authority nevertheless was considerably diminished vis-à -vis an invigorated church hierarchy. As we will see shortly, similar disengagement between politics and religion occurred in western Christianity during the investiture conflict two centuries later. In this respect, the religious civilizations of Islam, Byzantium, and western Christianity followed similar patterns of development.

Transformation into a Commonwealth   As the internal doctrinal quarrel over iconoclasm was being settled in the mid-800s, the strategy of using themes to harass and carry out counterstrikes against the Muslims in Anatolia finally paid off. By exploiting the fiscal crisis of the Abbasids, theme commanders were able to go on the offensive and raid Arab settlements in eastern Anatolia and northern Iraq. A century later, in 965, Byzantium regained all of Anatolia and the emperors were able to turn their attention to the Balkans. Here, the Bulgars had converted to eastern Christianity in 864 and, under their own emperors, had forced Byzantium to pay tributes in the early 900s. But in 971, the Byzantines crushed the Bulgars and reintegrated their realm into the empire. Toward the middle of the eleventh century, Byzantium encompassed again a respectably large territory, extending from Belgrade across the Balkans some 1,100 miles southeast to Antioch in northern Syria (see Map 10.3).

MAP **10.3** The Byzantine Empire, ca. 1025 CE

The Byzantine Commonwealth. Characteristic of eastern Christianity are the many churches dedicated to Hagia Sophia, "holy wisdom," which can be found throughout the Byzantine commonwealth, from the Balkans to the Caucasus. Though each region developed its own architectural style, they all organized sacred space in similar ways. A masterpiece of design and engineering based in part on the theories of the third-century BCE mathematician Archimedes, the Church of Hagia Sophia in Constantinople was dedicated in 537 by the emperor Justinian on the foundations of an earlier structure (*a*). Its massive dome was often compared to the great dome of heaven itself, and the church would become the prototype for many others throughout the commonwealth in subsequent centuries, including the Cathedral of Saint Sophia in Kiev, whose foundations were laid early in the eleventh century (*b*). While it exhibits a distinctly Kievan style of church architecture, including over a dozen cupolas, the cathedral nonetheless embodies an unmistakable Byzantine tradition whose roots extend deep into the past.

The settlement of the iconoclasm controversy and recovery of imperial power formed the background for the transformation of Byzantium into a commonwealth of Christianity in eastern Europe. In the late 700s, Kiev in the Ukraine had emerged as a western outpost of the large, ethnically Turkish, and religiously mixed Jewish, Christian, and Muslim Khazar realm in southern Russia. The traders in Kiev were "Rus" (from which the name "Russia" is derived), of Scandinavian Norsemen (Viking or Varengian) origin. By the 800s, most had intermarried with Slavs and become culturally Slavic. The Rus traded furs from Scandinavia and the Urals and wine from western Europe for Indian spices and Chinese silk, traveling on the Dnieper and Volga Rivers and the Baltic Sea between the Abbasid and Carolingian Empires. In addition to trading, the Rus repeatedly raided Byzantium, thereby adding to the difficulties of the empire during the 800s and early 900s. By the mid-900s, Rus trading and raiding had made Kiev a regional power.

In 988, Grand Prince Vladimir I of Kiev (r. 980–1015) decreed the conversion of his subjects to Christianity. According to legend, Vladimir rejected "joyless" Islam (no pork and no alcohol) and "unimpressive" Judaism (because it had lost Jerusalem to Rome) for eastern Christianity after envoys had given him enthusiastic reports about the magnificence of its church services. The more prosaic Islamic sources report that the conversion was part of a deal whereby Vladimir would convert and receive a Byzantine princess for marriage if he would assist the emperor Constantine VII with Kievan troops against internal rebels. With this conversion of the Ukraine, eastern Christianity expanded beyond the Byzantine Empire into the much larger region of Russia. Thus, a commonwealth of states emerged in this region similar to that of Islam.

Islamic Civilization in the Commonwealth of Dynastic States, 900–1300

In the Islamic commonwealth in the early 900s, the Fatimid caliphate challenged the rule of the Abbasids as well as the Umayyads of Iberia. (In 756, an Umayyad refugee prince had declared an independent emirate in Iberia.) In a parallel development, Islamic civilization took root among non-Arabs on the margins of the commonwealth, among such peoples as the Berbers in North Africa and the Turks in central Asia. These newly converted people migrated into the Islamic heartland, establishing new states which assumed leadership in the commonwealth. But this leadership was short-lived since western Christians (such as the Spanish kings and the European crusaders) as well as central Asian Mongols similarly established themselves through conquest. For about two centuries, from 1100 to 1300, political instability reigned until the Egyptian Mamluks defeated the crusaders and Mongols. When the Mongols converted to Islam, Islamic civilization returned to its previous condition of competitive politics in a commonwealth of states.

The Fatimid Challenge The Abbasid fiscal difficulties and declining power encouraged the formation of a new group of oppositional Muslims, the party (*shi`a*) of Ali. Islamic tradition projects the origins of the Shi`a to an early period of the Arab Empire (656–685), but the Shiites, as the followers of this minority branch of Islam are called, emerged as identifiable believers only in the second half of the 800s. At that time, their leaders claimed to be descendants of Muhammad via a different line from that of the Abbasids: Instead of an uncle of the Prophet, they claimed the Prophet's daughter Fatima and her husband Ali (in Islamic tradition also the cousin of Muhammad) as their ancestors. The eldest male in each generation since the 600s was held to have been infallible, possessing knowledge of the "inner" or figurative meaning of the Quran. He, therefore, was empowered to issue new doctrines and laws, in contrast to the Sunni caliph. He was also entitled to be the leader (imam) of the Islamic community. However, since the Abbasids were the reigning titular rulers in the commonwealth, Shiite leadership remained purely theoretical. In contrast to the Sunni religious scholars who had wrested the power to control doctrine and law away from the Abbasids, the Shiites acknowledged leaders who claimed full powers over doctrine and law, even though in practice these leaders were private persons keeping a low profile to protect themselves from the Abbasid police.

According to Shiite tradition, the line of firstborn males descended from Fatima and Ali died out in 874. This event was at the root of the belief that the last childless imam went into hiding and would return at the end of time as the Mahdi, or "rightly guided one." As the Savior or Messiah, he would establish a realm of justice. Since the last imam was the twelfth in descent, beginning with Ali, the followers became known as Imami or "Twelver" Shiites. There was, however, a minority of so-called Sevener Shiites forming at the end of the 800s, who claimed that the line of descendants had actually ended well before 874, with the seventh imam, who was the one to return as the Mahdi. Followers of this doctrine of the seventh descendant revived the belief in the apocalypse, suppressed earlier by the Abbasids, and expected the Mahdi's return and the establishment of the realm of justice to occur prior to the year 300 AH (after hijra, i.e., 912 CE). They engaged in underground preaching and agitation against the Abbasid regime. Followers of the idea of the twelfth descendant were quietists, waiting for his arrival without calculating the date and willing to endure Abbasid rule.

Propagandists among the Sevener Shiites or Fatimids chose the faraway province of eastern Algeria in the early 900s to preach their revolutionary cause to remote mountain Berbers, who probably were not yet Muslims. After coming to power, the first Fatimid imam claimed to be the Mahdi at the end of time, who would conquer the Abbasids and bring justice to the world. At the head of Berber armies, the imam's successors created a powerful empire in North Africa, Egypt, Syria, and western Arabia (909–1171). But the revolutionary zeal gradually died down, and by the eleventh century it was clear that the Fatimid countercaliphate was unable to expand from Syria to Iraq and replace the Abbasids.

A similar initial effort of the Fatimids to conquer Iberia fizzled early. Here, the governing Umayyad caliphs, descendants from a refugee of the defeat in 750 at the hands of the Abbasids, arrested a Fatimid advance party sent to probe the weak spots in the Iberian emirate. In response, the Umayyads elevated the peninsula in 929 into a caliphate in its own right, in competition with both the Fatimids and Abbasids. Meanwhile, in 945 there was a change of leadership in Baghdad. In the place of the military regime of Turkish generals, the new military regime of Persian Buwayhids from the Caspian Sea confined the Abbasids to their palace. The Buwayhid generals were Twelver Shiites opposed to revolutionary beliefs and with no interest in making common cause with the Fatimid Seveners. Like their Turkish predecessors, the Buwayhids retained the Abbasids as figureheads, even though they disagreed with the latter's Sunnism. By the mid-900s, a commonwealth of three competing caliphates and numerous provincial dynasties in Arabia, Iran, and Turkmenistan had emerged within Islamic civilization (see Map 10.4).

The Umayyads in Iberia   The westernmost competing state, the caliphate of the Iberian Umayyads, covered three-quarters of the peninsula at its height. Visigothic refugees, who in the late 700s had survived precariously in their small mountain refuge in the northwest of the Iberian Peninsula, improved their livelihood in the 800s through raids against the Umayyads and founded a number of small Christian kingdoms. The kings took the apostle James, said to have converted Iberia to Christianity, as their patron saint for the proclamation of the reconquest (Spanish *reconquista*) of Iberia and parts of North Africa, once ruled by the Visigoths, from the Muslims.

In the 900s, however, the Umayyads checked the Christian military advances. The caliphate prospered, thanks to an expanding long-distance trade through the

The Great Mosque of Córdoba. This congregational mosque, called *Mezquita* in Spanish, was built in the years following 784 and was enlarged twice until it reached its final dimensons in 987. To heighten the ceiling, the architects topped the short marble pillars taken from Roman ruins with brick pillars and double arches, covered in white and red plaster. Light entered through three domes above the wall facing Mecca.

MAP **10.4** The Islamic Commonwealth, ca. 1022 CE.

Moroccan Sahara for West African gold. The caliphs and their administrators spent lavish sums on monuments, libraries, court physicians, poets, musicians, and scholars. Umayyad Córdoba became the political and cultural center of the Islamic west, or Maghreb. Perhaps 90,000 inhabitants called the city their home, more than in any other European city except Constantinople. The Córdobans were a cosmopolitan mix of Arab- and Berber-descended Muslims, Islamized Iberians, Arabic-speaking Christian Iberians, and Sephardic Jews, that is, Jews who had migrated from Palestine to Spain during Roman times. By about 1000, Muslims were a majority in the Umayyad caliphate.

The military of the caliphate became increasingly diverse in the early 1000s, with regiments composed of Arabs, Berbers, Christian mercenaries from the north, and military slaves called *saqaliba* [Sa-KAH-lee-bah] from the Balkans. The caliphs bought the *saqaliba* from Christian merchants in Venice and Prague, who acquired them from raiding parties roaming in the then not yet fully Christianized parts of eastern Europe. In spite of their wealth, the caliphs lost control over the army, just like their Abbasid colleagues had a century earlier. In 1031, the caliphate disintegrated altogether, leaving a collection of provincial emirates in its wake.

Emboldened, the Christian kings demanded tributes in gold from the Islamic emirates. The emirs had no choice but to pay, given the same problem of heterogeneous troops as in the preceding caliphate. In 1085, the kings grew even bolder and conquered the emirate of Toledo in the center of the peninsula. This conquest was a pivotal event in western Christianity: Thanks to Toledo's collections of Arabic manuscripts containing the Greek heritage, Europe experienced its second cultural stimulus (after the first stemming from Rome after 476). The far-reaching consequences of this stimulus for the growth pattern of western Christianity as a religious civilization are discussed in Chapter 11.

To block Christian advances in central Iberia, the remaining Muslim emirates in 1086 turned to the newly Islamized Berber dynasty of the Almoravids (1086–1147) for military support. Astride the Saharan trade route for gold from West Africa, the Almoravids had converted to Islam in the mid-1000s. They and their successors, the Almohads (1147–1269) from the southern Moroccan mountains, held power among the Iberian Muslims and stopped the Christian *reconquista* for nearly two centuries. Under the Almohads, who sponsored theology, law, philosophy, medicine, and architecture, Islamic civilization in the west experienced its most active period.

Almohad dominance, however, did not last long. Both Almoravids and Almohads were handicapped by the economic weakness of their North African base. The central Moroccan plains were too small to support numerous villages and large cities. The two dynasties did not dispose of sufficient manpower and tax resources to stabilize their initial conquests and recruit new troops in North Africa. The Christian kings succeeded in 1212 at inflicting a crushing defeat on the Almohads, forcing them to retreat back to North Africa. Only the well-protected Muslim mountain kingdom of Granada in southern Iberia, with its rich silk, cotton, and sugar cane production and flourishing Mediterranean trade, remained under Muslim rule for several more centuries (1238–1492).

The Seljuk Turks and Byzantium   Similar to the conversion of the pagan Berbers to Islam under the Almoravids and Almohads in Morocco, there was a contemporaneous Islamization process among the Turks in the steppes of eastern Russia and western central Asia around the Ural Mountains. Turkish rulers astride the Volga trade route to the Baltic Sea had initiated this process in the early 900s and a century later Turks east of the Ural Mountains converted to Islam. Among the converts was a Turkish confederation led by the Seljuks [Sel-JOOKS], a dynasty of rulers that conquered the steppes from Turkmenistan to Iran and Iraq. In 1055–1059, these rulers ended the Buwayhid regime in Baghdad and assumed power under the title "sultan" (from the Arabic for "power"). As newcomers to Islam, the Seljuk sultans made themselves champions of campaigns against Christians and heretical Muslims, among whom they counted the Fatimids. In eastern Anatolia they defeated the Byzantines at Manzikert in 1071, and in Syria they conquered Damascus from the Fatimids in 1079. By the early 1080s, the Seljuks had become rulers of a large sultanate comprising nearly all of the Middle East, except Egypt (see Map 10.5).

The Seljuk Empire in 1092 CE

▉ Territory directly administered by Seljuk sultans	▨ Tributary state
▨ Territory ruled by branches of Seljuk family	✕ Battle

MAP **10.5** The Seljuk Empire in 1092 CE.

The Seljuk defeat of the Byzantines was possible because of a change of policies that had taken place in Constantinople during the 900s and early 1000s. After the theme commanders had regained eastern Anatolia and northern Syria from the Muslims, the emperors—concerned about the rising power of these commanders—had systematically expanded their palace regiments stationed in Constantinople, avoiding recourse to the themes. Included among the palace regiments were contingents of Norman mercenaries from France. Altogether, these regiments, however, were not large enough without theme reinforcements to halt the Seljuks. After a resounding victory at the battle of Manzikert in Armenia 1071, the Seljuks advanced across Anatolia to Nicaea, which they took in 1087, bringing them within 100 miles of Constantinople.

By this time, Emperor Alexios I (r. 1081–1118) was thoroughly alarmed. He was wary of his Norman mercenaries in the palace guards who had developed ambitions of their own, conquering Sicily from the Muslims as well as invading Byzantine Greece. In spring 1095, the emperor requested military aid from Pope Urban II (r. 1088–1099), in the hope that he would receive western European soldiers more reliable than the Normans to reinforce his palace troops and beat back the Seljuks.

The Crusader Kingdom of Jerusalem   As we will see in Chapter 11, Urban II granted Alexios' request, taking into consideration a number of his own religious and political ambitions vis-à-vis the European kings. The pope and his clergy preached what was later called the Christian "Crusade" to an enthusiastic nobility chafing under efforts by the French and English kings at political centralization. On their way during 1096–1099 from western Europe to the Middle East, the crusaders returned Nicaea to Byzantium and captured Jerusalem. They overcame extremes of hot and cold weather, disease, and the determined resistance of the Seljuks as well as the Fatimids (who had reconquered Jerusalem from the Seljuks in 1098); but in all likelihood the Crusade probably would have failed had it not been for the timely disintegration of the unified Seljuk realm after the death of its sultan in 1092.

By the mid-1100s, the crusader kingdom centered on Jerusalem had evolved into a strategically placed, well-organized, 300-mile-long state along the Syrian and Palestinian coast (see Map 10.6). It possessed fortified seaports and a string of defensive castles on the edge of the desert east of the Jordan River. Two further Crusades and newly founded military orders which recruited unmarried knights in Europe provided a minimum of cavalry forces to defend the kingdom. Traumatized at first by the unanticipated appearance of the crusaders, who they considered to be barbarian cousins of the Byzantines, the Seljukids (successors of the Seljuks) recovered gradually and, in the middle of the twelfth century, regained the initiative.

Saladin [Arabic Salah al-Din] (r. 1174–1193), the Kurdish successor of the Fatimids in Egypt and Seljukids in Syria, nearly ended the crusader kingdom in 1187. He trapped and destroyed almost the entire military forces of the kingdom in the Battle of Hattin near the Sea of Galilee and reconquered Jerusalem. But a remnant of these forces was able to reconstitute a small kingdom limited to the coast, with Acre as its capital. This state survived for another century, until 1291, because Venice and Genoa made it a commercially viable transit zone for Indian spices and Chinese silk via the Gulf of

MAP **10.6** The Crusader Kingdoms, ca. 1140 CE.

The Crusaders: A Muslim View

"The Franks are without any vestige of a sense of honor and jealousy. If one of them goes along the street with his wife and meets a friend, this man will take the woman's hand and lead her aside to talk, while the husband stands by waiting until she has finished her conversation. If she takes too long about it he leaves her with the other man and goes on his way."

—Francesco Gabrieli, partial trans. "Usama Ibn Munqidh (1095–1188)." In: *Book of Instruction: Arab Historians of the Crusades*, p. 7. Berkeley: University of California Press, 1969.

Aqaba. Since the Muslims profited from this trade as well, they tolerated the small crusader state.

Beginning in the mid-1200s, however, it was only a question of time before the crusader kingdom would become the victim of new and powerful political forces arising in the Middle East. In 1250 the Mamluks—Turkish military slaves from the Russian steppes and dominant in the armies of Saladin's successors—established their own regime in Egypt (1250–1517). Barely in power, in 1260 the Mamluks had to face the Mongols, who had emerged in the previous half-century under Genghis Khan (r. 1206–1227) and his descendants as a major power (see Chapter 13). The Mongols were conquerors of a giant but loosely organized cavalry-borne empire in central Asia, China, eastern Europe, and the eastern Middle East—so they were tough competition for the Mamluks.

The Mongols stormed into the Middle East in 1255, conquering Iran and Iraq, ending what had remained of the Abbasid caliphate in Baghdad in 1258 and advancing into Syria. After conquering Baghdad, they tolerated the weak crusader kingdom since their main target was the Mamluk sultanate as the last remaining Islamic power in the Middle East. The Mamluks, however, defeated the Mongols in several battles between 1260 and 1281, thanks to their much heavier cavalry, and pushed them from Syria back into Iraq and Iran. Under the name of "Ilkhanids," the Mongols converted to Islam and became linguistically and ethnically Persian. Finally free of the Mongol threat, the Mamluks terminated the crusader state in 1291 with the conquest of Acre. The commonwealth of Islamic dynastic states thus returned to self-determination.

A Shrinking Byzantium   The Crusades had initially helped the Byzantines to halt the losses of imperial territory. Energetic emperors extended eastern Christian sovereignty across western Anatolia and into northern Syria in the middle of the 1100s, where they gained control over the crusader principality of Antioch. But the Fourth Crusade of 1204 reversed these gains. The knights and foot soldiers of the Fourth Crusade were the compliant instruments of a conquest scheme hatched by Venice, the German Hohenstaufen emperor, and a refugee claimant of the Byzantine throne at the Hohenstaufen court, with the compliance of the pope. As a result, western Christians conquered Constantinople from the Byzantines and established a Latin empire.

But what was behind this conquest? First, there was the split of the church into feuding western and eastern, or Catholic and Orthodox, branches in 1054. The two branches split over irreconcilable jurisdictional and doctrinal differences, dividing the pope in Rome and the patriarch in Constantinople: The pope demanded subordination from the patriarch, and the patriarch rejected the Catholic innovation of elevating Jesus to a position of equality with God in the definition of Trinity (the so-called filioque doctrine, dating to 1014). Second, Venice had long played a dominant commercial role in Byzantium's long-distance trade, but its competitor, Genoa, was still entrenched in Constantinople as well. The audacious scheme of taking over

The Siege of Baghdad. In the 1200s and early 1300s, the caliphs in Baghdad had struggled free from the overlordship of the Seljuks and rebuilt a modest regional realm. The pagan Mongols interrupted this rebuilding and, with their victory in the siege of 1258, ended the 500-year-old caliphate. The image is a miniature in Rashid al-Din's *World History* of ca. 1325. It shows the besiegers on the bottom, with a siege engine, and the defenders on both sides of the Tigris.

Byzantium was a golden opportunity for Venice to become the dominant commercial power in the Mediterranean.

After the crusaders stormed Constantinople, Venice plundered the city of its riches and the pope appointed a Catholic archbishop. But the supply of manpower from western Europe did not flow any better to Byzantium than to the kingdom of Jerusalem. By 1261 the emperor of the Byzantine successor state of Nicaea had been able to drive the western Christians from Constantinople. Subsequently, Byzantium regained a semblance of power but within a much smaller territory, limited to western Anatolia and the eastern end of the Balkans.

Islamic and Eastern Christian Civilizations at Their Height

While the western Christians lost the crusader kingdom and Byzantium in the Middle East, they gained the Muslim emirates of Iberia (except for Granada) in western Europe. By 1300, the borders between western and eastern Christianity and Islam were again clearly drawn. At this time, the Mamluk sultanate, victorious against the crusaders and the Mongols, was the richest and most powerful state in the region, enduring for nearly three centuries (1250–1517). It represented Middle Eastern Islamic civilization at its peak, eventually succeeded only by the Ottoman Empire, which then shifted the center of Islamic civilization from Egypt northward to Anatolia and the Balkans.

State and Society in Mamluk Egypt

The Mamluk sultanate, centered in agriculturally rich Egypt, completed the rise of the Turks to dominance in the Arab Middle East. Its ruling class consisted of Islamized Turkish-born slaves from the Russian steppes, called Mamluks, who formed a tightly knit military regime. (After 1377, the Mamluk sultans were ethnic

THE MAMLUK EMPIRE, ca. 1300

Caucasians.) Few in this ruling class spoke Arabic or intermarried with the indigenous population of their realm in Egypt and Syria. The indigenous population in turn possessed its own autonomous institutions, which provided for most of its needs. Although the Mamluks provided military protection, the indigenous population had to pay for it dearly with high taxes and often arbitrary rule.

The Mamluk State   At the top of the Mamluk ruling class was the sultan, who controlled the annual purchases of slaves and commanded the largest cavalry regiment. Raiding parties in the Mongol state of the Golden Horde (1241–1502) on the Russian steppes captured boys and girls from nomadic tribes and sold them to Genoese merchants, who shipped the slaves to Alexandria. The popes protested against the slave trade but to no avail.

The Mamluk sultan governed in consultation with a group of a dozen or so emirs, stationed in the provincial cities of Egypt and Syria and each commanding a cavalry regiment of his own. Additional auxiliary troops, both infantry and light cavalry, consisted of sons of Mamluks, tribal nomadic contingents, and freeborn Turks. The sultans maintained a lavish court, which included a splendid kitchen and some of the finest cooks of their time. A large civilian bureaucracy in Cairo, composed of Muslim, Coptic Christian, and Jewish scribes and accountants, staffed the three main ministries—correspondence and archives, tax collection, and army administration. Other officials oversaw the construction and/or administration of granaries, oil presses, the mint, hospitals, the postal service (including pigeon courier), water supplies, sanitation, stud farms, horse stables, and the hippodrome (for polo games).

Mamluk power was based on a large, state-centered economy. The Mamluks owned buildings and collected rents from residences, mills, ovens, workshops, inns, public baths, and bazaars. They hired large labor forces for the construction or repair of mosques, city walls, fortresses, and waterworks. Sultans and emirs even built entire city quarters. They usually paid regular wages to their workers but occasionally also used forced labor. The sultans had their own permanent labor force, which included prisoners and slaves; and they occasionally rented laborers to emirs for large construction projects. From time to time, the sultans sent craftspeople and laborers

Mamluk Cavalry. Mamluk horsemen engaged in military exercises, wielding swords and protected by chainmail armor. Stationed in barracks on Nile islands near Cairo, the pagan, Asian-born but Muslim-educated Mamluks formed a standing army of a dozen regiments that trained daily and could be mobilized within a short time. Their children were not slaves but freeborn Muslims, who were admitted only to auxiliary military units.

to Medina and Mecca to keep the pilgrimage sanctuaries in good repair. The importation of timber and metals was a state monopoly, providing the raw material for the shipyards. As consumers of all manner of crafts products, for both military needs and extravagant luxuries, the Mamluks by far outpaced the wealthy urban merchant class. Their military campaigns were occasions for large numbers of craftspeople, traders, storytellers, entertainers, prostitutes, and other hangers-on to find additional employment.

The Religious System   On the intermediate level of authority were the Muslim religious scholars. They were of indigenous Arab origin and often came from a merchant or craftspeople background. If they could afford it, they pursued their scholarship independently. But many depended on appointments by the sultan's administration to positions at courts, mosques, colleges, lodges, orphanages, and hospitals. Although dependent for their personnel on state appointments, these institutions were financially autonomous since they were supported by fees as well as endowments, that is, revenue accruing from urban property or rural farmland originally deeded by pious individuals.

Divorce Court. Husband and wife arguing about a divorce before a judge; scene from al-Hariri, *Maqamat* (ms. dated 1222). Hariri's stories, among the most popular during the classical period, involve a poor but eloquent storyteller traveling from town to town in changing disguises but being recognized each time by the fictional author. The stories include occurrences of everyday life, like this divorce.

At the head of the juridical system were the chief judges of the four legal traditions in Islamic civilization. These traditions, distinguished by their broader or narrower interpretations of law, were Hanafism (today central Asia, Turkey, Syria, and Iraq), Shafiism (Yemen, East Africa, and Indonesia), Malikism (northern and West Africa), and Hanbalism (Saudi Arabia). In larger cities all four traditions were usually represented. Lower-level judges staffed the courts in towns and large villages. They could decide cases only if an aggrieved party sought relief, as exemplified by the story of Safra at the beginning of this chapter. In preparation for their decisions, judges employed one or two investigators to establish the facts of the legal cases brought before them. In addition to their juridical functions, judges were responsible for the appointment and supervision of the mosque officials (preachers, scripture reciters, and prayer callers). They were also responsible for the office of the market inspector and his deputies. The market inspector was a religious official who prosecuted and punished violations of the public order on markets and thoroughfares, thus cooperating with the Mamluk ruling class for police functions.

Similar to the juridical system, the educational system was based on a combination of state appointments and endowment finances. Primary schools, attached to mosques, taught children to read and write using the Quran and quranic recitation. Colleges (*madrasas*) provided basic instruction in logic, mathematics, and astronomy but focused on a mostly religious curriculum of prophetic traditions, law, and theology. The professors taught courses from specific books assigned to each class, reading and commenting as they went along. Colleges often had substantial libraries, dormitories, and kitchens and provided scholarships to their students. For graduation, a college required a certain number of books to be read and the contents thereof to be mastered. Wealthy urban families sent both boys and girls to primary schools and colleges, and a small number of professors were women. Since education was not compulsory, however, literacy was largely limited to the religious, mercantile, and crafts elites of the urban centers.

Gender Relations   Islamic civilization followed the traditional Middle Eastern patriarchal family system. Within this system, as we saw at the beginning of the chapter, married women had definite rights and were no longer the chattel they were in the Assyrian Empire. But we also saw how shocked Usama Ibn Munqidh was when he observed the behavior of the men and women in the crusader kingdom: Husbands allowed their wives in public to walk around alone and shake hands and converse with men to whom they were not married. The patriarchal order in Islamic civilization was clearly stricter than that in western Christianity, and Ibn Munqidh had only contempt for crusaders who had such a low sense of honor that they even went home alone when their wives wished to continue their chats (perhaps even flirtations) with other men. Evidently, a significant cultural difference existed between western Christianity and Islamic civilization.

The Urban Working Population   Below the Mamluk ruling class and the intermediate urban elite were craftspeople, laborers, domestics, and farmers. Urban laborers lived in city quarters, which were organized according to religious (Christian, Jewish), ethnic (Arab, Kurdish, Iranian), and, in the case of the Sunni majority, clan ties. The city quarters were not closed communities, however, and always contained minorities.

City quarters, crafts clusters, and neighborhood mosques and lodges were autonomous structures in urban life. Although overseen by appointees of the market inspectors, the residents often engaged in acts of resistance and rebellion against the Mamluks in times of famine, overtaxation, or arbitrary rule. In addition, Syrian cities, such as Damascus and Aleppo, had a long tradition of rebellious youth gangs fomenting unrest in suburbs and adjacent villages outside the city walls. The gang members wore distinctive hairstyles and cloaks and found their recruits mostly from among ditch diggers, canal dredgers, and brick layers as well as from among the occasional discontented cooks, traders, spinners, and carpenters. During times of peace these gangs collected protection money from owners of workshops and market stalls, inevitably coming into conflict with the market inspectors and their deputies whose turf they invaded. At times of economic or political distress they linked forces across city quarters and transformed themselves into formidable militias, holding down entire Mamluk regiments for days or weeks. Given the relatively slight state–society relations, the gangs provided a degree of protection for society from the state.

Commercial Relations from the Atlantic to the South China Sea

The Persians and Romans had pioneered the trade of gold and silver for subtropical and tropical luxuries during the period 600 BCE–600 CE, as we discussed in

Chapter 7. An enormous leap forward in this trade occurred during the rise and flourishing of Islamic civilization in Mamluk Egypt. The Islamic imperial unification of most of the Middle East and the Mediterranean, the urbanization process exploding in its wake, and the western Christian recovery after ca. 1050 all contributed to this leap. In short, an Afro-Eurasian world commercial system, extending from West Africa to China and regularly connected by seasonal travel, emerged where there had been none before. The accounts that the Moroccan-born scholar Ibn Battuta (1304–1369) left of his 30 years of journeying along the trade routes from West Africa to China provide an invaluable source of information about the cultures and peoples that were connected by this vast network (see Map 10.7).

Trade Routes and Commerce   To understand the West Africa–China world trade, we begin with West Africa. Villagers mined gold in the rain forest on the upper Niger and Senegal Rivers and traded with African merchants from Islamic kingdoms located along the middle Niger. The kings sent raiding parties to other regions in the rain forest to capture slaves. Merchants and kings then sold the gold and surplus of slaves not employed in the kingdoms to visiting Muslims from North Africa and Iberia.

The visitors from the north paid with North African and Iberian manufactures and with salt from mines in the Sahara. In the Mediterranean basin, Muslims, Jews, and western and eastern Christians shared the trade of West African gold (minted

MAP **10.7** The Afro-Eurasian World Commercial System, ca. 1300.

Maritime Trade. This image, an illustration in Hariri's *Maqamat* (ms. dated 1236), depicts an oceangoing sailboat between Arabia and India. It has a black crew, stern rudder, movable sail (perhaps a lateen sail), iron anchor, and traveling merchants in below-deck quarters or cabins. The image contains all critical technological elements of Indian Ocean sailing.

Tax farming: A system for collecting taxes and rents from the population, where the state grants the right of collection to private individuals.

into coins) and European timber for Indian and Indonesian spices, dye stuffs, ointments, and cottons as well as Chinese silks, porcelain, and lacquerware. The Mamluks did not allow Christians to travel beyond the Mediterranean, and thus, Muslims, Jews, and Indians were the only ethnic groups who participated in the Indian Ocean and Chinese Sea trade of gold for luxuries.

In addition to these main routes, there were three secondary trade routes. First, there was the overland Silk Road with its gold-for-luxuries trade that connected Iran with China via central Asia. Second, there was the maritime East African trade route, where merchants exchanged manufactures for ivory, gold, and slaves. The latter route connected Egypt and Iraq with the Swahili coastal Muslim city-states along the African coast and the gold mines of Zimbabwe (see Chapter 14). And third, there was the Volga route, where Norman merchants traded gold, silver, spices, ivory, silk, wine, and fur, connecting the Middle East with western Europe. The Mamluk military was a major consumer of the goods that flowed down from the Volga trade route, using Russian and Scandinavian furs for the designation of its ranks. Both primary and secondary trade routes yielded immense supplementary tax revenues, which added to the basic and highly dependable agricultural tax income of the Mamluks.

Islamic and Jewish merchants in the Egyptian center of this network were for the most part wholesalers for whom the import and distribution of eastern luxuries formed only a part of their overall commercial activities. They also organized the regional production and distribution of raw materials, such as textile fibers (wool, flax, cotton, and silk), chemicals for dyeing and tanning, metal ingots for making utensils and jewelry, and pitch for caulking ships' planks. They contracted with craftspeople for the production of soap, glassware, candles, and perfume. Tailors, cobblers, and sugar mill owners delivered robes, slippers, and bags of refined sugar to the merchants. To provide their accountants, scribes, porters, and guards with daily food, these merchants had caterers deliver lunches and dinners to their residences and warehouses. Merchants who were also **tax farmers** maintained grain stores, with employees responsible for collecting, shipping, brokering, and marketing the grain. Others "farmed" the taxes from ports or public auction houses. Diversification was the preferred path to consistent profitability in the merchant class.

The Black Death   Extensive travel, however, yielded not only profits but also unforeseen horrors. The more densely people lived together in cities and the more frequently they traveled, the more often they incurred the risk of spreading terrifying and lethal diseases hitherto confined to small, isolated regions of the world. The Black Death of 1346 was the second time that an outbreak of this ghastly plague occurred in world history (the first was the Plague of Justinian in 541, see Chapter 7). Scholars, such as William McNeill and Stuart J. Borsch, agree that the Mongol invasion of Vietnam set off the spread of this horrific mid-fourteenth-century pandemic. The Mongols acquired the bubonic plague bacillus in southeast Asia, one of its permanent breeding grounds, from rodent fleas and dispersed it via China and the Silk Road to the Black Sea area. From here, Genoese merchants carried the virulent disease to the Mediterranean and northwest Europe (see Chapter 11 for a more detailed discussion of ravages of the bubonic plague).

Egyptian sources vividly recount the devastation which the plague wrought on the population. The plague was both sinister and incomprehensible to people at the time who had never experienced it, possessed no effective medical resources, and thus, found themselves powerless to fight it. Similarly difficult to fathom was the recurrence of the plague every generation or so for another century and a half, hitting rulers and subjects; rich and poor; men, women, and children with equally appalling force. Not until the 1500s did Middle Eastern population levels recover to pre-1346 levels.

Religion, Sciences, and the Arts in Two Religious Civilizations

Despite the impact of the Black Death, Mamluk Egypt and reconstituted Byzantium during the 1300s and 1400s were highly active cultural centers. Although they received little further cultural stimuli from outside their civilizations, scholars and artists developed their respective cultures further within traditional boundaries. In Islamic civilization, the most important new cultural phenomenon was mystical Islam, and in eastern Christianity it was a revival of Platonism.

Islamic Culture: Intellectual and Scientific Expressions

Like a number of other religions we have examined, Islam developed a devotional mystical tradition of its own. Mystical Islam, or **Sufism**, was an outgrowth of meditative thought and practices developed from the Christian, Zoroastrian, and Greek philosophical heritages interacting within the Muslim world. Around 1050 Muslim scholars integrated Sufism into the Sunni-dominated Islamic civilization, and around 1200 Sunni mystics adapted Sufism to Islamic civilization in the form of popular brotherhoods. Educated Muslims, in addition, were conversant in philosophy or the sciences, both of which experienced an important flowering in the period 1050–1300.

Sunni–Sufi Islam
The pioneer of Sufism was the Persian Mansur al-Hallaj (858–922), who was a popular preacher in Iraq when Sunnism was not yet fully formed. The proponents of Sunnism accused Hallaj of heresy for claiming identity with God in his moment of ecstasy. They persuaded the political authorities to execute him but were unable to halt the growth of Sufism's popularity. A century and a half later, Sunnis and Sufis agreed to a compromise. The major mystics representing this compromise were the Persian Abd al-Hamid al-Ghazali

Sufism: Meditative devotion to faith, expressed in the form of prayer, ecstasy, chanting, or dancing.

Execution of Mansur al-Hallaj. This miniature shows the gruesome last moments of the mystic. Hallaj's sermons included the bold proclamation "I am the Truth," which alluded to one of God's 99 names in Islam. Sunni scholars interpreted this proclamation as blasphemy, hence the trial, condemnation, and execution. Sufis, of course, wrestle with the difficult problem of having to express the simultaneity of God as in the world (present in one's consciousness) and transcendent (utterly other)— this is how "I am the Truth" has to be understood. But it is also easily misunderstood, as the Sunni scholars did.

(1058–1111) and the Iberian Muhyi al-Din Ibn Arabi (1165–1240). Ghazali acquired fame as a figure who succeeded in expanding Islam from the highly technical Sunnism focusing on law to the personal commitment to God. Ibn Arabi provided Muslims with perhaps the most sophisticated conceptualization of God, both in transcendence and in the world. Ghazali and Ibn Arabi struggled with the problem that absolute transcendence can be thought but not experienced unambiguously (see the discussion in Chapter 7). Ghazali introduced a persuasive metaphor to overcome this problem with his wine glass example: Believers, looking at a glass of red wine from a distance, are unable to decide whether they are not instead seeing an empty red glass. God, being both beyond and in the world, can only be "seen" like one sees the one or the other aspect of the glass but never both simultaneously.

Through meditative practice, however, so Ghazali and Ibn Arabi taught, Muslims can reduce the ambiguity in thinking/experiencing God. The more Muslims removed themselves, step by step, from the distractions of daily life and focused only on their inner self through meditation, the more they would be able to approach God. In the 1200s, mystics—often revered as saints—founded lodges in which they provided instruction and training in meditative practice for Muslims. With time, these lodges branched out, with hundreds of sublodges organized along the specific practices of its founder saints. The lodges represented widely dispersed brotherhoods in Islam, located in urban centers as well as in rural areas, and even difficult-to-organize nomadic areas. Sunni Muslims of all walks of life joined, from legal scholars and judges to craftspeople, farmers, and nomads. By around 1450, Islamic civilization was a commonwealth not only of competing states but also of competing Sufi brotherhoods. The Sunni–Sufi compromise dominated in Islamic civilization until 1900.

Philosophy and Sciences   As in the case of Sufism, philosophers also encountered opposition from among the proponents of early Sunnism and did so for the same reason of violating the transcendence doctrine. Greek philosophical writings were accessible in translation since the 800s and had attracted Muslim thinkers well before the emergence of Sunnism. Among the more prominent of these were the Arab Abu Yusuf al-Kindi (801–873) and the Turk Muhammad al-Farabi (Latin Abunaser, ca. 870–950). Once Sunnism was established, figures such as Abu Ali al-Husayn Ibn Sina (Latin Avicenna, 980–1037), Abu al-Walid Muhammad Ibn Rushd (Latin Averroës, 1126–1198), and Abd al-Rahman Ibn Khaldun (1332–1406) wrote in favor of the integration of Sunnism and philosophy. All four commented voluminously on the entire range of Greek philosophy.

The first two philosophers emphasized Platonic thought, following the precedent set by the thinkers in the Christian Roman Empire. Ibn Rushd and Ibn Khaldun reconciled Aristotle with Islam. Ibn Rushd wrote no fewer than three sets of commentaries on Aristotle's works. In Latin translation, his commentaries greatly stimulated the adaptation of western Christian civilization to Aristotelianism in the 1200s. Ibn Khaldun, chief Maliki judge in Mamluk Egypt, developed an innovative analysis of the four Aristotelian causes operative in the rise and decline of states in Islamic civilization. All four philosophers argued that faith, if interpreted figuratively, is in full harmony with reason.

As in philosophy, scientific texts were also available in translation from around 800 onward. Islamic scientists made major contributions early on, pushing beyond the discoveries of the Greeks. The Greeks had excelled in developing geometry into a mathematical science, but in the absence of a numbering system—they used letters as numbers—they had left algebra undeveloped until the Alexandrian period of Hellenism. The Persian Muhammad Ibn Musa al-Khwarizmi (ca. 780–850) laid the foundations for the conversion of algebra into a science. In his textbooks, computation is based on a decimal system of "Arabic" numerals, from 0 to 9. He borrowed this system from India (where it had been developed 150 years earlier) and introduced algebraic equations for the determination of unknown quantities, expressed through letters, as is still done today.

The proponents of Sunnism in the tenth century left the scientists largely alone, in contrast to Sufis and philosophers. The sciences were useful for the determination of the month of fasting, the direction of prayer toward Mecca, and astrological predictions. After 950, mathematicians developed decimal fractions, raised numbers to high powers, extracted roots from large numbers, and investigated the properties of complex equations with roots and higher-degree powers. Other scientists used applied mathematics in engineering, such as the Arab, al-Jazari (see "Patterns Up Close"). The Arab astronomer Ahmad Ibn al-Shatir (1304-1375) simplified the work of the Hellenistic astronomer Ptolemy (d. ca. 168), whose trigonometry was based on an awkward geometric plurality of world centers. One physicist, the Persian Abu al-Fath al-Khazini (fl. ca. 1115-1130), elaborated on Archimedes' investigations into the physics of balances and weights. Another, the Iberian Abu Bakr Ibn Bajja (Latin Avempace, 1095–1138), developed the impetus theory of motion (force applied to thrown objects) adopted in western Christian physics and dominant there until the time of Galileo in the 1500s.

In medicine, the physician Abu Ali al-Hasan Ibn al-Haytham (Latin Alhazen, ca. 965–1039), an accomplished ophthalmologist, advanced the theory of light being emitted from objects rather than from the eye, as Aristotle maintained. The philosopher Ibn Sina, mentioned earlier, was the author of a comprehensive handbook on medicine, which contains chapters on anatomy, bodily fluids or "humors," diseases, diagnosis, surgery, therapy, and drugs. Specialized medical fields included ophthalmology (the treatment of eye diseases); obstetrics and pediatrics (which also dealt with sexual hygiene, birth, breast-feeding, childhood, and related diseases); and pharmacology, with descriptions of medicinal plants. Abu al-Hasan Ali Ibn al-Nafis (1213–1288), a physician at the main hospital in Cairo, discovered the pulmonary circulation system of the body, a historic first.

Artistic Expressions in Islamic Civilization

During the formative period of Islamic civilization (800–950), secular poetry and prose flourished. As Sunni–Sufi Islam fully evolved (950–1200), religion was interwoven with the telling of stories, the painting of miniatures, and the building of mosques and palaces. Persian artistic traditions reemerged from pre-Islamic times, and Turkish central Asian steppe traditions entered Islamic culture. In the eastern Christian civilization of Byzantium, the arts suffered greatly during the defensive period against the Arabs, Slavs, Bulgars, and Rus of Kiev. They rebounded after 950, and the painting of icons experienced a veritable explosion, making icons the distinctive feature of eastern Christian art.

Islamic Literature The first extant poems in Arabic were odes celebrating the tribal ethos of courage, trust, generosity, and hospitality in pagan Arabia. They

Patterns Up Close | Play Toys for Princes—al-Jazari's Ingenious Mechanical Devices

Many Islamic courts employed engineers for entertainment as well as military tasks. One of these engineers was Abu al-Izz al-Jazari (1136–1206) at the court of the Artukid beys (1092–1409) in what is today Diyarbakir, southeastern Turkey. Jazari was a gifted engineer in the Greek and Hellenistic tradition as well as a fine painter of miniatures in the Syrian–Iraqi style. He left us a work entitled *The Book of Knowledge of Ingenious Mechanical Devices* (1206), with descriptions of the devices he built, together with rich illustrations of their functions. It contains chapters on water clocks, drinking machines, music boxes, fountains, water lifting devices, and locks. Many of the devices were driven by water or air and their power was transmitted by pipes, valves, gears, pistons, and crankshafts (the latter a first in history). Precision was achieved through laminating the wooden pieces and sand-grinding the gears and pistons. Unfortunately, we know nothing about Jazari's life, except that his patron commissioned the book.

Mechanical devices also enjoyed wide distribution in the other religious civilizations of the age. Elaborate Chinese water clocks, employing floats, wheels, gears, and chains, were used during the same time period for the determination not only of daily time but also of the imperial Chinese astronomical and astrological calendars. In Europe, monks used simpler water clocks during the medieval period in monasteries for their prayer hours. The privilege of inventing the first mechanical, weight-driven clock goes to Norwich, England, where the citizens could watch the lapse of time beginning in 1325 on their cathedral tower.

Perhaps the most elaborate device was Jazari's 6-foot-high elephant clock, which contained a water basin with a perforated float inside the elephant. Included in the actions were a phoenix, chirping on top; a scribe in the middle, marking the hours on a dial; and a driver, exhorting the elephant. The hourly mechanism functioned—verified through a modern reconstruction—by a perforated float in the interior of the elephant, slowly filling with water. When full, the float activated a lever connected to a trap, which released a ball on top of the clock. When this ball fell into the mouth of a Chinese dragon (causing the dragon to pivot) it rolled into a container connected to a cymbal and struck the hour. A chain attached to the pivoting dragon's tail lifted the float inside the elephant out of the water. After being

Donkey Clock.

Phoenix

Chinese dragon

Scribe

Elephant driver

Water basin with perforated float

Elephant Clock.

drained of the water, the float repeated the mechanical action and did so as long as there were balls in a container on top to drop. What a conversation piece this clock must have been, in the middle of the table around which the bey and his visitors were feasting!

Questions

- How do Jazari's mechanical devices show the many ways classical learning was expressed and adapted in the postclassical era?

- Which specific features of Jazari's clock show the wide diffusion of varied cultural influences across Eurasia during this time?

follow the quest theme common to many folktales and myths, with its three distinct stages of loss, marginality, and reintegration that the hero has to experience to find peace. New forms of literature evolved in the cosmopolitan culture of Baghdad, which brought together highly literate secretaries and officials from a variety of non-Arab ethnic backgrounds. Poetry with urban themes, such as the pleasures of sensual abandonment, seduction, and homosexual love, appeared under the pen of the Iranian Abu Nuwas (ca. 756–815), among others. Cosmopolitan Córdoba in Iberia was famous for its sensual *muwashshah* [moo-WASH-ah] poetry, which was composed in Arabic but also contained Romance language verses and was influential in the development of medieval troubadour lyrics in western Europe.

Essays expressing refined taste, elegance, and wit also circulated widely in the Baghdad of the 800s. The best-known representative of this genre was the East Africa–descended Amr Ibn Bahr al-Jahiz (781–868), author of such essays as "The Art of Keeping One's Mouth Shut," "Against Civil Servants," "Arab Food," "In Praise of Merchants," and "Levity and Seriousness." The most popular collection of short stories was the *Maqamat* about an impersonator telling tall stories to gullible listeners, collecting money for his tales, and traveling from city to city in ever-new disguises.

Another collection of stories is the *Arabian Nights*, narrated by the concubine of a brutal ruler who had the habit of executing each virgin after he had spent the night with her, to prevent her from becoming unfaithful to him. One of the virgins, named Scheherazade, outwitted him by telling him every night such captivating stories that the ruler could not wait to hear the conclusion. *Arabian Nights* includes Indian and Greek materials, refers to the cosmopolitan period of Baghdad, and was first written down in Mamluk Damascus during the 1300s. Even today, one admires the refined taste, elegance, and wit which people of cosmopolitan Islamic urbanity possessed.

Persian and Turkish Muslims preserved their pre-Islamic pasts in epics celebrating the heroic deeds of their ancestral leaders in central Asia. In the case of the Iranians, the poet Firdosi (940–1020) spent a lifetime collecting the traditions of the Persians and rendering them into the 60,000 verses of the *Book of Kings* (*Shahnameh*). The anonymous epic *Dede Korkut* originated among the central Asian Turks at the time of the Arab conquests and was written down in the 1300s. Both ethnic groups also produced outstanding poets, among whom the Persian Hafiz (1325–1390) is the best known. Mystical poetry, which appeared among the Arabs first in the work of the female poet Rabi`a al-Adawiyya (717–801), found its most universal expression in the Afghanistan-born Jalal al-Din Rumi (1207–1273), still popular today across the entire world.

Painting and Architecture in Islam

In the visual arts, Arabs and early Muslims embraced the eastern Roman-Sasanid symbolic style which Christians, Jews, and Zoroastrians preferred over the realistic style of the Greeks and Romans. In this style, artists sought to capture the inner essence of their subjects, rather than draw them according to their surface. The distinction was not always rigid however, and Islamic artists sometimes applied subtle techniques of shading and modeling, with which they approached realism.

Moreover, since Islamic law contains prohibitions against painting and sculpting, similar to Byzantine iconoclasm, the visual arts disappeared entirely from public spaces and retreated to the domestic sphere of the households of rulers. The Umayyad and early Abbasid caliphs loved frescoes with hunting, drinking, and

A Game of Chess. Although Islamic theology is iconoclastic, similar to eastern Christian theology (730–842) and the doctrines of some Protestant denominations, Islamic civilization possessed developed pictorial traditions such as this painting from Islamic Iberia, showing a game of chess.

dancing scenes but confined them to the chambers of their palaces. The rulers of Granada in the 1400s enjoyed scenes of courtly love in their royal chambers. The Seljuk and Ilkhanid rulers were lavish sponsors of miniature painters, as we have seen in the case of Jazari and his book on mechanical devices. They delighted in richly illustrated biographies and histories, which played the role in their libraries of what we would consider today coffee-table books.

By contrast, the architecture of mosques and palaces was intended for public use, often in commemoration of their state sponsors. Mosques followed the architectural style of the Arab open courtyard and covered prayer hall or Persian open courtyard with surrounding half domes and galleries, both with roots in the pre-Islamic past of the Middle East. Among the surviving palaces, the best preserved is the Alhambra of Granada (ca. 1350–1450), with its exquisite honeycomb-style decorations. Religious and palace architectures were perhaps the most direct forms in which the identity of Islamic culture was expressed. They are still admired today for their variation and richness.

Intellect and the Arts in Byzantium

In contrast to Islamic civilization, the eastern Christianity of Byzantium was a fully formed religious civilization from its beginning in 640, even if it underwent major doctrinal changes thereafter. During its difficult struggle for survival against the Arabs, Slavs, Bulgars, and Rus, Constantinople declined in both wealth and sponsorship of knowledge and the arts. The teaching of the liberal arts inherited from the earlier Roman period barely survived. The liberal arts included the preparatory *trivium* (grammar, rhetoric, and dialectics), advanced *quadrivium* (arithmetic, geometry, music, and astronomy), and philosophy as the capstone. The Hagia Sophia, for centuries the largest church in the Christian world and seat of the patriarch, the highest eastern Christian official, was about the only place where eastern Christians could pursue the study of the liberal arts, theology, philosophy, and science.

The outstanding figure of Christian learning during this early period was John of Damascus (ca. 675–749). He was, however, a Monophysite Christian opposed to the eastern Christianity of Byzantium and lived under the Umayyad caliphs, never setting foot in the empire. (Monophysites believed that Jesus was wholly divine, not both divine and human, as in eastern and western Christianity.) His theological writings are of great importance for the understanding of early Islam, which he still considered, at the time of Abd al-Malik's successors, to be a variant form of Christianity and not yet as Islam.

The improvement in Byzantium's military fortunes in the mid-900s encouraged a cultural revival, which extended up to the Fourth Crusade (1204). Memories of the difficult defense of the empire during the 700s and early 800s gave rise to a remarkable cycle of semihistorical epic episodes, entitled *Deeds of Basileios Digenis Akritis*. This epic glorifies the military and amorous exploits of a Byzantine nobleman of half-Arab descent on the Anatolian frontier. It was probably recited during banquets and other gala events at the residences of the great theme commanders in Anatolia before it was written down during the 1100s.

The Veroli Casket. We tend to associate Byzantium with religious art, but secular works, such as this tenth century trinket box decorated with scenes from antiquity, provide a different glimpse into Byzantine daily life. The casket's panels depict scenes from Classical mythology. On the left is the hero Bellerophon with the winged horse Pegasus, and on the right is Iphigenia who, according to Euripides, was willing to sacrifice herself so that the Greeks could sail to Troy. The Byzantines consciously cultivated their Greek roots.

In the arts, Byzantine iconoclasm during the 700s and 800s caused the destruction of innumerable and irreplaceable icons and mosaics. It also disrupted the transmission of artistic techniques from masters to subsequent generations of artists. When the public display and veneration of images became the officially sanctioned doctrine again in the mid-800s, it took a while for the arts to recover. As artists were relearning their craft, they engaged in much initial experimentation. The subsequent mature period of ca. 950–1200 saw a veritable explosion in the production of icons, mosaics, and frescoes as well as the building of new churches and monasteries. Byzantine mosaic craftspeople and painters were also much sought after by the caliphs in Córdoba, who avoided hiring artists from their Abbasid and Fatimid rivals. Byzantine craftspeople were also popular with the princes of Kiev, who after their conversion carried the Byzantine arts into the commonwealth of eastern Christian states.

The Latin disruption of 1204–1261 saw again a tremendous loss of Byzantine art as well as manuscripts, this time to Venetian pillage after the Fourth Crusade. When Byzantium recovered, Plato scholars initiated a strong philosophical recovery, which resulted in a return of western Christians, this time peacefully, to that city in search of Platonic writings. The Academy of Florence invited Byzantine Plato scholars, and further scholars emigrated to Italy after the fall of Constantinople to the Ottomans in 1453. Thus, western Christianity renewed its adaptation to stimuli from a neighboring civilization, in contrast to eastern Christianity and Islamic civilization, which continued within their existing traditions.

Putting It All Together

Both Islamic civilizations and eastern Christian civilization were based on a synthesis of religious revelation and Greek philosophy and science, as shown in the accompanying Concept Map. This synthesis had begun in the Roman and Sasanid Persian Empires. Muslims accomplished their cultural synthesis after the period of Arab conquest, roughly during 800–950. Eastern Christians completed their synthesis in the period 950–1050, after their recovery from the Arab, Slav, Bulgar, and Rus onslaughts. Both refined their internal civilizational achievements to a high degree well into the 1400s. Thereafter, they did not absorb substantial new cultural stimuli from the outside until about 1700 when the Muslim Ottoman sultans and the Russian czar Peter the Great invited western Europeans to reform their respective empires (see Concept Map).

Islamic civilization was an outgrowth of the Arab conquests in the Middle East, central Asia, northern Africa, and Europe in the 600s and early 700s. It emerged as an adaptation of the Arabs to the heritages of the Jews, Christians, Greeks, Romans,

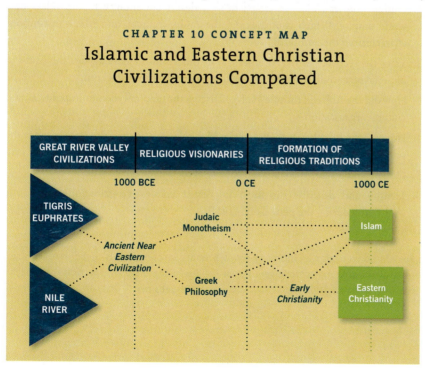

and Persians. Its core was the monotheism of Allah, and its cultural adaptations were to Greek philosophy and science, Roman law, Persian statecraft, as well as a variety of artistic and architectural traditions of the Middle East and Mediterranean. At its height, during 950–1450, a commonwealth of competing Islamic states represented Islamic civilization. This ethnically diverse commonwealth with Arab, Turkish, Persian, and Berber rulers and states shared a number of common characteristics, among which were the same canon of scriptures (the Quran and the Sunna), laws and moral norms (Shari`a), and religious institutions (separate state and religious authorities as well as Sunni–Sufi brotherhoods). These characteristics endured to 1450.

The Byzantine Empire succeeded the Roman Empire around 640 when the emperors, under attack by the Arabs, reorganized their military forces and redefined the inherited Christian theology. This Christianity acquired its specific eastern identity by becoming clearly separate from the other Christianities outside the Byzantine Empire, such as Catholic western European, Syrian and Egyptian Monophysitic, and Asian Nestorian Christianities. Byzantium recovered politically and culturally in the mid-900s, and the empire changed into a commonwealth when Russian Kiev converted to eastern Christianity. Unfortunately, the recovery lasted only a century. The Seljuk Muslim Turks conquered most Anatolian provinces of Byzantium (1071–1176), and the Venetians conquered Constantinople in the Fourth Crusade (1204–1261). Byzantium recovered thereafter for another two and a half centuries and even flourished culturally, but after 1453 the center of eastern Christian civilization would shift northward to Russia.

Review and Respond

1. Outline the transition of Arabs from a desert community to the rulers of a world empire. Which countries did the Arabs conquer, and which institutions characterized their empire?

2. Trace the recovery of Byzantium from its precarious defense against the Arabs to imperial recentralization during the first half of the eleventh century.

3. How did the Abbasid Empire evolve? Discuss the empire's economic, political, and cultural organization.

4. How did the Mamluk victory over the Mongols and the crusader states change the power balance in the Middle East?

5. Outline and discuss the state and society of the Mamluk sultanate.

6. Identify and describe the most important cultural contributions of Islamic civilization during the period 600–1450.

▶ For additional resources, including maps, primary sources, visuals, and quizzes, please go to www.oup.com/us/vonsivers. Please see the Further Resources section at the back of the book for additional readings and suggested websites.

Thinking Through Patterns

▶ **Why can the period 600–1450 be described as the age of religious civilizations? How do eastern Christian and Islamic civilizations fit this description?**

The adoption of Christianity and Zoroastrianism as state or privileged monotheistic religions in the Roman and Sasanid Empires was late and ultimately did not prevent these empires from reaching the end of their existence. But they helped in launching the period of religious civilizations. New empires arose in this period, beginning around 600. Byzantium was Christian from the start. The Arab Empire adopted Islam early on, initially under the Umayyads and fully in the Abbasid-led commonwealth of states. Eastern Christian and Islamic civilizations fit the age of religious civilizations insofar as both were patterned by basic religious scriptures, a form of separation of state and religion, and the adaptation to inherited cultural traditions.

Specifically, the evolution of Islamic civilization was patterned by revealed scriptures, a religiously interpreted history, the separation of state and religion, the fusion of revealed religion and Greek philosophy, and the adaptation to the scientific and artistic heritage from Rome and Persia. The pattern was completed early, by about 950 with the emergence of Sunni Islam, but continued to evolve internally, without further outside stimuli, through Sufi Islam and a myriad of Sufi brotherhood lodges. The result was an Islamic civilization around 1450 which was composed of many states and even more autonomous religious congregations existing alongside the mosques.

▶ **Which cultural traditions combined to form Islamic religious civilization? What were the most characteristic patterns?**

▶ **How did eastern Christian or Byzantine civilization evolve over time? On which institutions was this civilization based, and how did it evolve, wedged between Islamic and western Christian civilizations?**

The late Roman Empire achieved a close integration of Christianity, Greek-Hellenistic philosophy and science, as well as Roman law; but it was hard-pressed for survival by the conquering Arabs. When the eastern Roman, or Byzantine, Empire recovered, it elevated eastern Greek Orthodox Christianity to a supreme position. A powerful recentralization effort strengthened the empire, especially in the Balkans. But in the wake of the Seljuk invasions and Western Christian Crusades, the empire weakened again, surviving in a much diminished form until it was conquered by the Ottoman Muslims in 1453. Eastern Christianity survived in Russia.

Chapter 11

600-1450 CE

Innovation and Adaptation in the Western Christian World

Latin Christendom, ca. 700

Canterbury
Paris
Rome

Area converted to Latin Christianity ca.1000

LATIN CHRISTENDOM, ca. 700–1000

Around 575 CE a casual encounter took place in Rome that had enormous implications for the future of western Europe. While strolling through the Forum, a young monk from the monastery of St. Andrew came upon several boys for sale in the slave market. Struck by their fair skin and light hair, he asked about their ethnic origin. He was informed that the youths were from the far-off island of Britain and were called "Angles." The monk replied that because of their angelic appearance they should instead

▶ How did the Merovingians and Carolingians construct a new Christian European civilization during the seventh and eighth centuries?

▶ What were key factors in the political, economic, and social recovery of Europe during the eleventh and twelfth centuries?

▶ What were some of the cultural and intellectual developments during the "twelfth-century renaissance," and how did they contribute to medieval civilization?

▶ How did the church influence political developments in Europe during the twelfth and thirteenth centuries?

▶ What events made fourteenth-century Europe so dismal? How did these combine to spell the gradual demise of medieval institutions and perspectives?

be called "angels." He then asked whether the inhabitants of this far-off land were Christians. When told that they still clung to pagan beliefs and practices, he sighed and remarked that it was a pity that such beautiful young persons were not blessed with Christian worship.

A few years later the young monk, now elevated to the papacy as Pope Gregory I (r. 590–604), followed through on his earlier determination to convert the peoples of Britain from paganism to Christianity. In 596 Pope Gregory dispatched a group of monks to Britain, led by Augustine (later named the first archbishop of Canterbury), to mount an aggressive missionary campaign of conversion among the Anglo-Saxons of southern England. Throughout the seventh century Roman Christianity slowly spread northward into Anglo-Saxon England (formerly the Roman province of Britain, overrun by the Germanic Angles and Saxons in the fifth and sixth centuries), where it challenged and eventually overcame the already established Celtic form of the faith brought over from Ireland in the fifth century. During the first half of the eighth century English missionary monks carried Christianity to the continent. Most notable among them was St. Boniface (ca. 680–754),

Detail from _The Effects of Good Government on Town and Country_, Ambrogio Lorenzetti (ca. 1290–1348). Part of a series of panels in the Palazzo Pubblico in Siena, Italy, this fresco provides a realistic glimpse into the bustling world of medieval cities, including shops, a school, and countryfolk bringing livestock and produce to market.

Latin Christendom:
Those countries professing Christian beliefs under the primacy of the pope.

whose conversion of Germans beyond the Rhine followed by his reforms of the Frankish church, brought both regions into close alignment with Rome.

The papal reign of Gregory I represented the dawn of a new era in the history of western Europe as it was the start of an emerging European Christian civilization. By encouraging the conversion of Germanic kings to Christianity in return for the sanction of the church and by studiously advancing the role of the papacy in both ecclesiastical and secular affairs throughout Europe, Gregory was responsible for making the Roman papacy a significant power in the West. In the process, Gregory inaugurated new links between Rome and northwest Europe that went a long way toward the emergence of a new civilization distant from the Mediterranean. In addition, Gregory's efforts led to the assertion of the independence of **Latin Christendom** from the Eastern Greek Church at Constantinople. Moreover, Gregory established an effective institutional structure and organized a hierarchy that provided the framework for a unified and well-regulated Christian civilization in emerging Europe that would endure until around 1450, when the Renaissance ushered in a new phase in European history.

The Formation of Christian Europe, 600–1000

During the fifth century, Roman provincial rule in the West collapsed and a new post-Roman period of cross-cultural interactions began, which included not only Greco-Roman traditions but also Germanic contributions, as well as Christian spiritual and educational values. Gradually, these various ways of living coalesced to form the foundation of a distinctively Christian European civilization. An important feature of this new civilization was the overarching importance of the church, whose alliance with Frankish kings—particularly Charlemagne during the eighth century—initiated a new church–state relationship in the West. This civilization nearly dissolved during the internal civil wars among Charlemagne's successors and the ninth-century invasions by non-Christians (Norsemen, Muslims, and Magyars). During the tenth century, however, the slow process of restoring order was under way in post-Carolingian Europe. Despite the turbulence of the ninth and tenth centuries, a new cultural and religious cohesiveness—realized in the age of Charlemagne—provided a new sense of forward-looking optimism; Latin Christendom had survived. In this section we will trace the series of successive interactions and adaptations from ca. 600 to 1000 that resulted in the transformation of western Europe from several pagan Germanic kingdoms to a unified Christian civilization.

Frankish Gaul and Latin Christianity

Amid the chaos and confusion caused by Germanic invasions and the breakdown of Roman rule during the fifth century, the first attempt to restore a semblance of political order appeared in Frankish Gaul. Merovingian kings relied on brute force to begin the slow process of assembling a unified kingdom. Significantly, however, they also recognized the importance of the church and its leaders as a unifying force. After an interim period of political confusion a new line of Frankish kings, the Carolingians, emerged during the eighth century. At the same time, the Christian Church played an integral role in the shaping of Frankish Gaul and, in a larger sense, early medieval European civilization. Two developments were forthcoming as a result. First, it was during the eighth century that subjects of the extensive Carolingian Empire began to sense that they shared a common identity, which later came to be called "European." Second, it was during this period that the concept of *Christendom* as a common identity through the practice of western Christianity began to crystallize.

The Merovingians   Unlike other Germanic tribes, the Franks did not invade the western Roman Empire but, rather, expanded from within the confines of its

590-604
Papacy of Gregory I
("The Great")

987-1325
Capetian Kings of France

1095-1204
Crusades to the Holy Land

1215
Magna Carta, England

768-814
Reign of Charlemagne

1066-1327
Norman and Angevin
Kings of England

1200
Foundation Charter of
University of Paris

1268
St. Thomas Aquinas' *Summa Theologica*

1337-1453
Hundred Years' War

1415-1417
Council of Constance

1305-1378
The "Babylonian Captivity"

1348-1352
Black Death

1453
Constantinople Falls to Ottoman Turks

borders. Again, unlike most other Germans, the Franks became western Christians, rather than Aryan Christians. As a result, they were not rejected as heretics by native Gallo-Romans. For these reasons, Frankish Gaul was ideally suited to lay the foundation for the emergence of a Christian state in post-Roman Europe.

The first Frankish dynasty, the Merovingians [Mer-oh-VIN-gee-anz] was firmly established by the Frankish king Clovis (r. 481–511), who succeeded in unifying a number of northern Frankish tribes and defeating neighboring Germanic states. At some point in his reign, perhaps in 498, Clovis adopted Christianity, which gave him the backing of Christian bishops in Gaul. As a result, Clovis had powerful allies in his attempt to solidify his control over a unified Christian kingdom. However, because of the Merovingian practice of dividing inheritances among surviving heirs, soon after his death Clovis' kingdom was split up into Austrasia in the east, Neustria in the west, and Burgundy in the southeast (see Map 11.1).

MAP **11.1** The Frankish Kingdoms.

The Frankish Kingdoms

- - - - Frankish Kingdom in 511 CE

Lands gained by Clovis's sons 511–536 CE

The Carolingians During the eighth century one aristocratic family, the Carolingians, gradually rose to power in Austrasia and eventually took control of all of the Frankish lands. Although their official title was "mayor of the palace," the Carolingians—and not the royal successors of Clovis—exercised real authority in Frankish Gaul, while the Merovingian kings grew weaker and weaker. The power of the Carolingians was greatly enhanced during the eighth century by two outstanding leaders. Charles Martel, "The Hammer"—so called because of his military prowess (ca. 714–741)—increased the authority of the Carolingians in two ways. First, Martel encouraged the expansion of Christianity by supporting Christian missionaries, who in turn converted thousands to Christianity while at the same time establishing administrative centers and monasteries. Martel also actively promoted his ties with the church, as attested by his affiliation with the abbey church of St. Denis near Paris. Then, as a result of his defeat of advancing Muslim armies at the Battle of Tours in 732, he emerged as not only the most powerful man in Frankland but also the leader of the most powerful force in Latin Christendom.

Martel's son, Pepin III ("The Short") (751–768), succeeded his father as mayor of the palace in 741, and enhanced ties with the church in two ways. First, in 751 he was crowned by the reigning pope as the king of the Franks, thereby replacing the former Merovingian line of kings with a new Carolingian dynasty. Second, the coronation established a new Franco-papal alliance. One consequence of this was the establishment of a closer affinity between Rome and Frankish Gaul, an important factor in allowing Europe to develop independently of the Byzantine Empire in the East. In addition, in the **coronation** of Pepin, the pope included the ceremony of **unction** (used earlier by the Visigoths), in which the newly crowned person was anointed with holy oil. Historians have seen in this practice the introduction into

Coronation: The act or ceremony of crowning a sovereign.

Unction: The act of anointing with oil as a rite of consecration.

western European history of the concept of sacred kingship, whereby kings now began to call themselves "kings by the grace of God."

The Early Medieval Church   The church contributed greatly to the development of a new era in Western history during the early medieval period. The *secular clergy* (from the Latin *saeculum* [CY-cu-lum] or "world") included bishops—among them bishops of Rome, who later became popes—and priests in the cities. The *regular clergy* (from the Latin *regula*, or "rule") were monks who adopted a particular monastic rule and who lived in rural monasteries. Each of these monasteries made distinctive contributions to early medieval culture.

The model for monastic living and organization was established by St. Benedict (ca. 480–543), who provided a set of guidelines, known as Benedict's *Holy Rule*, governing such matters as the times for rising, praying, eating, and retiring, all supervised by an *abbot*, or head of the monastery. The daily lives of Benedictine monks were devoted to prayer and work and were regulated by a series of "offices," or times of the day given over to communal prayer and to manual labor around the monastery.

In economic terms, Benedictine monasteries helped to revitalize rural agricultural production because of their emphases upon economic self-sufficiency and manual labor as a form of prayer. Most monasteries had a watermill and a forge (for wrought iron implements), and the large landholdings of monasteries produced significant quantities of grain, along with wine from vineyards. In addition, Benedictine monks expanded arable lands within their regions by draining swamps and clearing forests. Benedictine monasteries also stood as havens of security and civility amid the social and economic turbulence of the post-Roman, Germanic West.

Above all else, monasteries preserved classical and early Christian culture in the midst of a mostly illiterate Germanic population. The limited education available during the early medieval period took place mostly in monasteries and emphasized not only studying the Bible and church doctrine but also the "seven liberal arts"—consisting of the *trivium* (grammar, rhetoric, logic) and the *quadrivium* (arithmetic, geometry, music, astronomy). Monks copied and studied the works of the church fathers (Augustine, Jerome, and Ambrose), along with texts from the Bible and scattered papal decrees, thus laying the foundation for a new, Christian civilization for medieval Europe.

The Papacy   While monks lived and worked in isolated monasteries in rural areas, bishops of the church resided in urban centers. Although major cities throughout the Roman Empire had bishops, the bishop of Rome emerged as spiritual head of the Christian Church in western Europe. The most important of the early medieval popes, and indeed the pope usually credited with the foundation of the medieval papacy, was Gregory I.

One of Gregory's contributions to medieval civilization was the close cooperation between the monastic and papal arms of the church in civilizing the society of the West. In addition, Gregory popularized the theology of St. Augustine and spread the appeal of Benedictine monasticism. Another of Gregory's works, *Pastoral Care*, instructed bishops on proper procedures of administration. In a more particular sense, Gregory composed Christian hymns, and he added music as an accompaniment to the Mass, known as **Gregorian chant**.

Gregorian chant:
An unaccompanied, monophonic liturgical chant.

In a wider sense, however, Gregory was
responsible for making the Roman papacy a
power in the West and for establishing the independence of Latin Christendom from the Eastern Greek Church at Constantinople. Gregory
clearly understood that by 600 the Latin west
was emerging as a distinct civilization, and he
recognized that an alliance with the Frankish
kings would benefit both parties. Gregory's letters to Childebert II (r. 575–595), king of the
Franks, laid the foundation for the Franco-papal alliance that came to fruition in the eighth
century. Gregory also enhanced the prestige of
the Roman papacy in Italy, which laid the foundation for the Papal States in Italy, separating
the Roman from the Byzantine Church.

The Age of Charlemagne   Following the
death of Pepin III in 768, his son Charlemagne
("Charles the Great") (r. 768–814) inherited
the Frankish crown. In his personal preferences and in his official policies, Charlemagne
represents the first full synthesis of Roman,
Germanic, and Christian elements to forge a
unified Christian empire. Charlemagne also established what many consider the
"first Europe." By creating a distinctive Western cultural identity and by raising the
status of western Europe to rival the civilizations of Byzantium and Islam, the Mediterranean was no longer the center of civilization in the West.

Charlemagne's Throne.
Charlemagne frequently
traveled throughout his realm,
and one place where he stopped
several times was Ravenna
on the Adriatic coast of Italy,
where he would admire the
magnificent sixth-century
church of San Vitale. Inspired by
its harmonious proportions and
stunning mosaics, Charlemagne
determined to build a replica at
Aachen. The Palatine Chapel, the
only surviving component of his
palace, combines Byzantine and
Carolingian architectural styles.

Charlemagne was a command-
ing figure. At above 6 feet, 3 inches
tall he towered over other men,
whose average height was around
5 feet, 5 inches. He was known
for boundless energy and athletic
prowess. Even more remarkable
were his intellectual interests.

Through a combination of extensive military campaigns and attention to effective rule, Charlemagne
constructed and administered the
largest empire in Europe since the
collapse of Roman rule in 476 (see
Map 11.2). An important step was
the creation of a magnificent palace
complex at Aachen [AH-ken] (Aix-
la-Chapelle in French). Although
most of its buildings have long
since been destroyed, its Palatine

MAP **11.2** **The Empire of Charlemagne.**

chapel housed Charlemagne's throne—and both have survived to this day. From here Charlemagne ruled over a highly centralized empire, that is, a polity comprised of many different ethnic and linguistic groups. Charlemagne also reformed legal practices by instituting the Frankish inquest, a forerunner of the jury system, which was carried to England at the time of the Norman Conquest.

The Carolingian Renaissance   Charlemagne's reign also resulted in significant intellectual contributions to medieval Europe. Scholars have debated whether or not the new intellectual climate at his court was indeed solely owing to Charlemagne's personal influence. Nevertheless, in an attempt to both revive and reform learning, especially among the aristocracy and the clergy, Charlemagne orchestrated and oversaw a program of educational reform throughout his vast empire. Key to this effort was the appointment of Alcuin of York (ca. 735–804), the leading intellect of his age, as master of the palace school. Monks in several monastic schools were instructed to engage in the laborious process of copying both Roman manuscripts and a wide range of Christian texts, including the Bible and the *Rule* of St. Benedict. Moreover, Carolingian monks introduced a new, more legible script known as "Carolingian minuscule," and they compiled manuscripts in expensive and ornate bindings and covers. Through this painstaking process, which continued throughout the ninth century, around 50,000 books were produced, including many classical authors and texts, which were preserved and passed on to Western culture.

The Coronation of Charlemagne   Like his forebears, Charlemagne also took an active interest in affairs of the church. Not only did he promote the interests of Christianity throughout his kingdom, but he also intervened in papal affairs in Rome. In 774 Charlemagne journeyed to Rome to offer protection against the Lombards, and in 800 he gave assistance to Pope Leo III (r. 795–816), who was attacked by rivals. While attending mass at St. Peter's on Christmas day, Charlemagne was suddenly crowned "emperor of the Romans" by a grateful Leo III.

The creation of a new Roman emperor in the West announced the new independence of western Europe from the Byzantine east, and it signaled a shift in the center of power away from the Mediterranean and toward Europe north of the Alps. Charlemagne's new imperial status was recognized (reluctantly) not only by the Byzantine court but also by the Abbasid caliph in Baghdad, Harun al-Rashid (r. 786–809). In recognition of Charlemagne's status as the most powerful ruler in the West, Harun al-Rashid sent Charlemagne silken robes, a tent of linen, perfumes, an elaborate water clock (doubtless borrowed from contacts with China), and an elephant named Abul Abbas. In return, Charlemagne sent Harun-al-Rashid Spanish horses, mules, hunting dogs, and woolen cloaks.

Post-Carolingian Europe   Charlemagne's empire did not long survive his death in 814. Soon after his passing it was torn apart by a series of internal wars and divisions. Charlemagne's eldest son, Louis the Pious (r. 814–840), followed the old Frankish custom of dividing the empire among his three sons, who then proceeded to squabble over their respective shares. By the terms of the Treaty of Verdun in 843 the empire was divided into eastern, western, and central portions. At the same time, a series of devastating raids from outside Europe further disturbed the situation. From the north came the Norsemen, or Vikings, motivated by the quest for land and treasure. They sailed from Scandinavia into West Frankland and England in shallow-draft "long ships," causing terror and destruction wherever they landed along Europe's rivers. From the south, marauding bands of Muslim pirates created fear and destruction along the French coast of the Mediterranean and even penetrated inland as far as the Alps and into Rome itself in 846. Magyar horsemen from the plains of Hungary terrorized East Frankland in the same period, although they were more inclined to settle onto farmlands than to merely plunder (see Map 11.2).

Feudalism: An arrangement in which vassals were protected and maintained by their lords, usually through the granting of fiefs, and required to serve under them in war.

The Feudal Age   The name traditionally given to the form of governance that arose in West Frankland during the ninth through the eleventh centuries is **feudalism**. But what, precisely, was feudalism? Historians have never fully agreed on a precise definition of the term, and some have suggested abandoning it altogether as essentially meaningless. Complicating the picture further for world historians, the term is often used to describe similar arrangements that arose, in different periods, in Zhou China and Tokugawa Japan. It is true that feudalism was not a system per se; it was based on no theory, and it was nowhere uniform or consistent. Yet, amid the growing chaos and confusion of the ninth and tenth centuries, feudalism provided security at the local level in the absence of central government.

Essentially, feudalism represented a new form of governance at the regional and local levels instead of from a centralized royal court. Feudalism consisted of powerful landed aristocrats (lords) who gathered together small private armies consisting of dependents (vassals) in order to meet the military emergencies posed by the Norsemen, Muslims, and Magyars. Since wealth and power were now measured in terms of landholdings, vassals were rewarded for their services with grants of land, known as *fiefs* [feefs]. The Latin word for *fief* is *feudum*, thus the term "feudalism." It is important to remember that feudalism was a French, western German, and English phenomenon not shared by southern Europe. This difference would have important repercussions later.

Lord–vassal relationships and institutions marked a turning point in European history in that they laid the foundation for the later formation of centralized kingdoms. Most important was the concept of honor and loyalty to someone higher in the feudal hierarchy. Even though in practice the local aristocratic lords were sometimes stronger than royal figures, in theory all land and power were possessed by kings, who stood at the apex of the feudal hierarchy. By using these and other elements of feudal relationships to his advantage, a royal figure could convert the feudal relationships to royal control in his realm.

Whereas feudalism refers to the political and governmental aspects of life in the ninth and tenth centuries, **manorialism** refers to social and economic affairs of the

Manorialism: The medieval European system of self-sustaining agricultural estates.

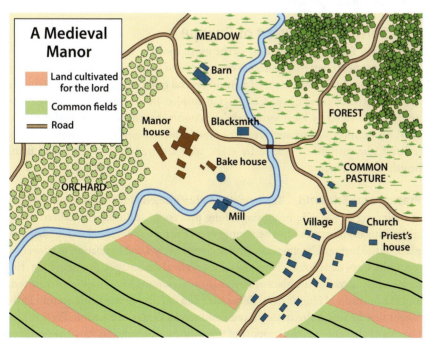

Figure 11.1 A Medieval Manor. This illustration shows the layout of a typical manor, with the manor and its satellite buildings next to a village surrounded by fields for planting and common (waste) land.

time. Large manorial estates were established in rural areas and constituted self-sustaining agricultural communities. In appearance, the manorial estate consisted of several prominent buildings: the castle or manor house, the church, the barn, and the mill (see Figure 11.1).

Peasants lived in small cottages or huts in a confined area of the estate. The typical cottage was constructed of mud and straw, with an earthen floor and without windows. A small stone hearth was used for cooking, with a hole in the roof to allow smoke to escape the interior. Interiors were without light of any kind, and privacy was nonexistent. Surrounding all this were fields for agricultural production, a large wooded area for timber and fuel, and a fish pond. The fields were arranged into long, narrow strips, some farmed by peasant families and others owned by the lord of the manor, on which the peasants had to provide free labor, called "boon work." The physical pattern of such manors may still be seen in many areas of France even today.

Recovery, Reform, and Innovation, 1000–1300

From about 1000 to 1300 medieval Europe experienced a period of revitalization, expansion, and cultural creativity and innovation. The period began with the appearance of several competing, politically centralizing kingdoms and with advancements in agriculture, commerce, and trade. Reforms in the church provided an overarching framework that defined a unified western European Christian religious civilization, culminating in papal supremacy over Europe around the beginning of the thirteenth century. During the so-called twelfth-century renaissance, extending from ca. 1050 to 1250, a cultural revolution in universities produced new philosophical and scientific perspectives that, along with interaction with the Islamic world, came to distinguish western Europe from other world civilizations.

The Political Recovery of Europe

If we survey Europe in the middle of the ninth century, we find chaos and confusion everywhere, caused by internal civil wars and external invasions from nearly all directions. As we have seen, all signs of central government had disappeared as a result of the collapse of the Carolingian empire. In this turbulent setting most people were ruled by local lords—dukes, counts, barons, or other regional officials. By around 1300, however, each of these areas was governed by well-run centralized administrations headed by kings, who restored both political and fiscal health to their realms.

France and England   The French nobility elected Hugh Capet (r. 987–996) as their king in 987 CE, beginning a long process of restoring centralized monarchy. This event marked the beginning of a new royal dynasty, the Capetians, in place of the former Carolingians. Although relatively weak in relation to powerful lords, the Capetians could claim several theoretical advantages. For one thing, the king's court served as the place where all disputes among his vassals were resolved, and the location of Hugh's royal **demesne** [deh-MAIN] in the lands around Paris meant that he was at the strategic and commercial center of events in France. The Capetians also enjoyed the support of the church. Not only did they have control

Demesne: All territories within France controlled directly by the king.

over dozens of bishoprics and monasteries but they alone were anointed with holy oil as a part of the coronation ceremony, making their persons sacrosanct and safe from bodily injury.

Over the next 300 years, Capetian kings extended royal control in France. Success in petty wars against the nobles and arranged marriages between Capetian heirs and members of the nobility helped extend the domain and enhance Capetian power. Determined to make France the most powerful country in Europe, Philip IV (r. 1285–1314) established a representative assembly in France, the **Estates-General**, in order to raise needed revenues. Comprised of the three social "estates" in France—the clergy, the nobility, and the townspeople—this body played an important role in later events leading up to the French Revolution.

Compared to the long and slow process of building a centralized monarchy in Capetian France, the establishment of centralized rule in England took place over a much shorter period of time. After the Norman duke William the Conqueror defeated an Anglo-Saxon army at the Battle of Hastings in 1066, he was proclaimed king of England as King William I (r. 1066–1087). William then proceeded to seize control of all lands in the realm, to distribute them to his followers, and to secure his claim to the throne by building castles throughout the country.

William's successors continued his practice of centralizing authority. Henry II (r. 1154–1189), the first of the **Plantagenet** kings of England, reformed the judicial system by making royal courts the final courts of appeal, particularly in disputes over land, thereby overriding the authority of baronial courts. Moreover, Henry established a uniform code of justice (known as English common law) throughout the realm, which replaced the complex and frequently contradictory jurisdictions of baronial and local courts. Even more effective was Henry's reliance upon roving royal justices and the use of royal **writs** and the jury system, which provided justice for all disputants.

Henry's son John (r. 1199–1216), however, alienated the baronage of England, who forced the king to sign Magna Carta ("The Great Charter") in 1215. Magna Carta established several important principles: the king must rule in accordance with established feudal practices; he must consult with the barons before levying taxes; and all free men have the right to trial by jury if charged with a crime. Many of these concepts also contributed to the appearance of a new institution known as **Parliament**.

Across the thirteenth century the English Parliament increased its power and scope. It also established certain principles that would be contested periodically by English monarchs over the next five centuries. In order to raise money for an anticipated French attack against England, Edward I (r. 1272–1307) found it expedient to convene in 1295 the so-called Model Parliament, comprised of an upper house of nobles and a lower house of "knights of the shires and burgesses of the towns." This precedent established the origin of Parliament's House of Lords and House of Commons, which continues today.

Germany   Events in East Frankland, or Germany, took a different turn. One setback to centralized rule was the division of the eastern portion of Charlemagne's realm into five regional groupings, or *duchies*, each under the control of a powerful duke. The result was that successive kings were chosen by the five regional princes, making it difficult for kings to centralize royal authority.

Estates-General: The French representative assembly, comprised of the three social "estates" in France, first convened by Philip IV.

Plantagenet: Royal dynasty that ruled England from 1216 to 1399.

Writ: A written order issued by a court, commanding the party to whom it is addressed to perform or cease performing a specified act.

Parliament: A representative assembly in England that, by the fourteenth century, was composed of great lords (both lay and ecclesiastical) and representatives from two other groups: shire knights and town burgesses.

Christ Receiving Magdeburg Cathedral from Otto I. Otto ordered the construction of the cathedral as evidence of his political power even before his coronation as emperor. The cathedral was completely rebuilt in the thirteenth century in the Gothic style.

Furthermore, imperial involvement in papal affairs in Italy provided another impediment to centralization. When Otto I of Saxony (r. 936–973) took power as king of the Germans, he extended Germanic influence in Italy in order to reestablish Charlemagne's protection of the papacy. In 962, Otto put down political disturbances and protests against the church. In gratitude, Pope John XII (r. 955–964) proclaimed Otto "emperor of the Romans," forming the basis of what has been termed the "Holy Roman Empire." Otto's successors continued the policy of interfering in papal affairs, with momentous results for both church and state.

The Economic and Social Recovery of Europe

Yet another area of recovery for Europe around the year 1000 was in economics. In the year of the millennium there was little manufacturing and commerce in Europe, agriculture was still the mainstay of its economy, there were few cities (and even these were underpopulated), and society was broken up into only three classes: those who work, those who fight, and those who pray. By 1300, however, the map of Europe was crisscrossed by scores of trade routes, trade and commerce were important features, urban life was humming, and a new social class of businesspeople had emerged in cities (see Map 11.3). How are we to explain this remarkable economic resurgence?

The Agricultural Revolution   We can begin to account for Europe's economic revival by studying developments in agriculture. The first step in this direction was land reclamation. During the tenth and eleventh centuries the cessation of internal wars and outside invasions provided the freedom to undertake the arduous work of reclaiming land for increased cultivation—primarily clearing forests and draining swamps. In addition, many areas of northern Europe, particularly France, enjoyed deep deposits of topsoil rich in nutrients, which, combined with a climatic warming trend, provided a perfect environment to grow new crops.

An important factor in the agricultural revolution was the heavy-wheeled plow, fitted with an iron blade and a *moldboard* (a curved iron blade to cut through the heavy sod of the region and lift and turn the newly dug soil). The use of new fertilizers and the transition from a two-field to a three-field system also provided a 33 percent increase in crop production. In the three-field system, one field was planted in the spring for a fall harvest, another was planted in the winter for a spring harvest, and the third remained fallow to enable its soil to regenerate nutrients. The three-field system resulted from the introduction of pulses (beans, peas, lentils, etc.), which added nitrogen as the new fertilizer.

Apart from European contributions, however, it is important to note that the agricultural revolution was in large part the result of innovations that originated elsewhere in Eurasia (perhaps in China), which were transmitted to Europe through

MAP **11.3** The Urban Population of Europe, ca. 1300.

cross-cultural interactions, mostly via trade across the Silk Road network. Among these innovations were the the use of horses with collar harness (instead of slower-moving oxen), which provided a fivefold increase in traction, not to mention less injury to the animal; the use of iron horseshoes; the use of the tandem harness, allowing horses to work in pairs and further increasing production; the vertical water-wheel; and the single-wheeled barrow.

Moreover, new forms of mechanical energy—also of Asian origin—were introduced to Europe through interactions and contacts with the Islamic world. As early as 1050 watermills were in wide use; and although some historians attribute the water-mill to Roman origin, its design—particularly the incorporation of the trip-hammer—indicates an Asian origin. Windmills were subsequently borrowed from Islamic Iran during the twelfth century. The circular motion of the wheel, driven by either water or wind, was then converted by a series of cranks, gears, and camshafts into pounding and grinding motions, thereby greatly increasing the production of cloth goods, beer, and especially grain products, which in turn led to an increase in food production. Even the first deep-drilled water well, introduced in the twelfth century, was of Chinese origin. Finally, through Muslim Spain the Europeans benefited from several Islamic advances in agriculture, such as the new crops of rice, sugarcane, watermelons, bananas, and improvements in techniques of irrigation and drainage.

Man Plowing with Oxen. The place and origin of the heavy-wheeled plow are still uncertain, but certainly by the year 1000 it was having a dramatic impact on agriculture, allowing for new lands to come under cultivation. Its use required several oxen or other draft animals and, thus, complemented the cooperative nature of the manorial system.

These new techniques meant an increase not only in the quantity of agricultural production but also, more importantly, in the quality of new foods. Before the agricultural revolution, European diets were based mainly on grains and, thus, were rich in carbohydrates but low in protein. Peas and beans provided much needed proteins, which when combined with chicken, fish, and eggs resulted in a more balanced and nutritious diet. Improvements to the European diet resulted in an increase in Europe's population: in 1000, the population stood at about 36 million; by 1100 it had jumped to 44 million and by 1200, to 58 million. By 1300 the European population reached about 80 million.

Commerce and Trade   The revolution in agricultural production sparked in turn a rejuvenation of commerce and trade that spread throughout and beyond medieval Europe. As Europe's population grew, so did the demand for all manner of consumer goods, ranging from agricultural implements to household utensils, clothing and shoes, and numerous other commodities. The expansion of mercantile elites in thriving urban centers also provoked a brisk demand for luxury goods from beyond Europe, including silks, spices, and sugar.

One focal point of the revival of trade and commerce developed in northern Europe. Cloth goods, especially woolen products, had been a staple item in Flanders (modern-day Belgium) along the coast of the North Sea in northeastern France, even before the Carolingian era. After the cessation of Viking raids, Flemish weavers began a flourishing exchange with wool-producing centers in England, particularly with monasteries in the north of the island, in the twelfth century. Another very productive source of the commercial trade revival in northern Europe was the importation of French wines into England beginning in the later eleventh century, occasioned by the Norman Conquest in 1066. German merchants established trade routes to London in the west and to Russian cities like Riga and Novgorod in the east. These were ultimately linked together in a system of trading ports called the Hanseatic League.

Far more vital, however, was the remarkable revival of European commerce and trade across the Mediterranean. When Umayyad rulers were displaced by the Abbasids, who ruled from 750 to 1258, maritime contacts between Islamic and Christian merchants resumed. At around the same time, the Byzantine Empire turned its attention to extending its power into the Balkans and northeastward toward Russia. As a consequence, its military interests lay more in developing landed, rather than naval, forces, thereby ceding involvement in the Mediterranean to European traders. In addition, the Norman conquest of southern Italy and Sicily (1046–1091) afforded the northern Italian maritime cities of Pisa, Genoa, and Venice the opportunity to collaborate with Islamic merchants in Alexandria and the Levant. By the end of the eleventh century, Italian traders had established commercial ties with Constantinople, Syria, and Cairo and had begun the exchange of all manner of goods between Europe and Asia.

The most momentous change in European trade and commerce took place near the close of the thirteenth century. Around 1275, first Genoese and then Venetian maritime traders sailed westward across the Mediterranean, through the Strait of Gibraltar, and then out into the Atlantic. Then, Fernando IV (r. 1295–1312) claimed control of Gibraltar from the Muslims in 1309, ensuring full access to the waters of the Atlantic. Not only did this open the Atlantic to Italian maritime traders but it also established profitable trading relations between the woolen markets of England and the Netherlands as well as Mediterranean port cities. Yet another consequence was that European merchants were able to achieve something of a balance in trading contacts with the East. Before these developments, trading patterns were primarily of a one-way nature: European merchants imported modest quantities of goods like *alum* (a mineral essential for dyeing cloth), spices, and silks from China and India. Thanks to economic advances in the West, however, European merchants now had products to export to the East: wool and tin from England, finished French and Flemish cloth goods, and manufactured items like iron agricultural and household implements (see Map 11.4).

Navigational Innovations Cross-Mediterranean trade and commerce were facilitated by several innovations, some of which were assimilated as a result of interactions with Islamic and Byzantine merchants, while others were of independent origin.

Navigation was tremendously improved by advances in European ship design. Among the most important was the incorporation of the sternpost rudder. This concept was familiar to Chinese and Muslim sailors, but the European version—in use on ships of the Hanseatic League as early as 1180—was unique in its design and function in that it used hinged iron plates firmly mounted to the ship's stern. The principal advantage of the stern-mounted rudder was that it allowed for the construction

MAP **11.4** **Mediterranean Trade in the Twelfth and Thirteenth Centuries.**

of larger ships, which in turn greatly increased the volume of transported goods. Another improvement was provided by the adoption from Muslim sailors of the *lateen sail*, a front-mounted triangular sail that allowed for tacking into the wind. It was largely owing to this navigational device that Italian ships were able to sail into the westerly winds that had previously prevented their sailing through the Strait of Gibraltar into the Atlantic. Most important was the introduction of the magnetic compass. Whether of independent invention or derived from China, where it was used on Chinese ships as early as around 1090, the magnetic (or mariner's) compass first appeared in Europe in 1190. Use of the compass greatly facilitated maritime travel beyond the sight of land, particularly across the Mediterranean.

Early Capitalism and a Cash Economy

This renewed trans-Mediterranean commercial activity resulted in several innovations in commerce and monetary exchange that laid the foundation for the development of European **capitalism**. Increasing commercial transactions prompted a need for coined money—mostly in the form of silver coins—in order to arrange easy payment for exchanged goods and products. Meanwhile, medieval fairs gradually created new business procedures like record keeping and accounting practices, along with bills of exchange (the forerunner of the modern bank check) to replace transport of large amounts of coins. These transactions were facilitated by the use of paper, invented in China during the Han dynasty (see Chapter 9), then adopted by Islamic merchants, and subsequently transmitted to Europe in the eleventh century through Muslim Spain.

Several innovative financial and legal instruments were also devised to facilitate long-distance trade. Among these was the commenda, first in use by Venetian traders in the eleventh century and borrowed from interactions with their Byzantine and Islamic counterparts. Essentially, the *commenda* was a legally binding partnership

Capitalism: An economic system characterized by private or corporate ownership of capital goods, by investments that are determined by private decision, and by prices, production, and the distribution of goods that are determined mainly by competition in a free market.

Marco Polo's Departure from Venice. From at least the ninth century, Venice's political and economic fortunes were linked inextricably to the East; and by the fifteenth century it had gained undisputed supremacy over its rivals, Genoa and Pisa, in the trade with the Levant. Overseas commercial ventures, such as the famous journey of Marco Polo to Asia in the late thirteenth century, involved a great degree of risk; but the prospect of lucrative profits was irresistible.

in which one partner provided the funds to initiate a seagoing venture, and the other carried out the voyage; upon a successful conclusion, both partners shared an agreed-upon portion of the profits.

Urban Growth   The revitalization of trade and commerce contributed to the rejuvenation of urban life in eleventh-century Europe. Many Roman towns survived the tribulations of the early medieval period, although most resembled underpopulated ghost towns. The repopulation of these existing urban sites plus the creation of new cities attests to the influence of the economic revival of the eleventh century. Artisans and merchants were drawn to these vibrant urban centers, along with craftspeople and laborers, many of whom fled rural manors in order to begin new lives in cities. These cities were small in comparison with today's standards. Most numbered around 5,000 people, although cities like London and Bruges held about 40,000 inhabitants, while cities like Venice and Genoa in northern Italy boasted populations of around 100,000. Churches and castles were the most prominent physical sites in cities, and most urban areas were enclosed within stone walls outside of which were surrounding agricultural fields.

Social Patterns   Social patterns within the revitalized urban centers of the eleventh and twelfth centuries underwent change for several reasons. Of primary importance was the return of a money economy, which not only spelled the demise of feudalism—in that kings and nobles could now pay for armies with cash rather than with grants of land—but also resulted in the appearance of a new social class: the military. The effects of a new cash economy were noticeable especially in cities, which benefited from the cash contributions of wealthy businessmen in order to build cathedrals and large town halls. Finally, cities produced a new class of people, the **bourgeoisie**. Comprised of merchants and artisans who lived in "burghs" (or cities) the bourgeoisie made their livings from producing and selling goods for commercial exchange. This new, "middle class" of people was destined to exert an enormous influence on the development of medieval representative governments, primarily because their access to liquid cash made them attractive to European rulers.

Bourgeoisie: The urban-based middle class between the wealthy aristocracy and the working class.

Urban Women   Urban women worked in a variety of occupations, especially craft industries. Among these crafts we find women employed as butchers, candlemakers, metal crafters, silk weavers, and bookbinders. Nevertheless, working women were not always welcomed by their male counterparts, primarily because they were considered competitors for jobs. Moreover, women were rarely admitted as full members to craft guilds, and even in the silk industry—the one area where women did predominate—there is no evidence of a guild. For the great majority of working women, better opportunities were available in what were known as "bye industries," or home-based enterprises, like spinning cloth and brewing ale. In some cases widows took over their late husband's trade and worked as single women.

Jews in Medieval Europe   Jews occupied a distinct position in medieval towns and cities during the early years of the urban revival in the eleventh century. Comprising a small but distinct minority of the European population,

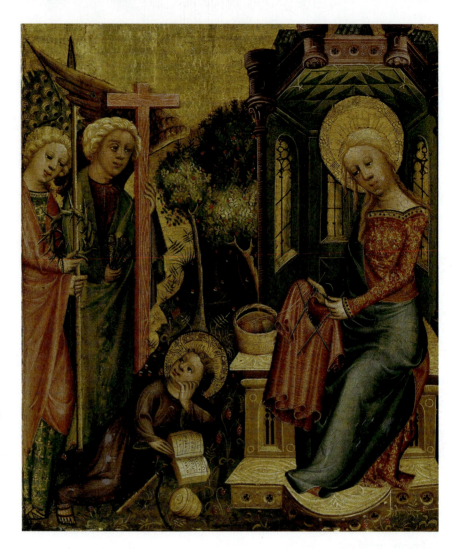

The Virgin Mary Knitting. This fourteenth-century drawing of the Virgin Mary knitting a garment for her unborn child is the earliest known representation of knitting, a medieval innovation. Knitwear was unknown in the ancient Mediterranean but was essential in the cold, damp climate of northern Europe.

communities of Jews were spread around the Mediterranean world. Through their travels and interactions with a wide variety of peoples, Jews developed both wide geographical knowledge and the command of multiple languages. For these reasons they sometimes served as diplomats, and they engaged in money lending and banking.

As the eleventh century unfolded, however, tolerance toward Jews began to wane. Jews were increasingly vilified as murderers of Christ, a sentiment sparked by the First Crusade in 1096. It became increasingly common for Jews to be restricted to separate quarters in towns, and during the early twelfth century Christians began to murder Jewish populations of many towns in Germany. In 1144 a full-scale assault against Jews was unleashed in the English town of Norwich. In many cases Jews were forced to live together in walled-off, gated ghettos in towns, which frequently held charters of liberty separate from those of the towns. Ghettos appeared as early as the thirteenth century in Spain, Portugal, Germany, and elsewhere. Several countries expelled Jews—England in 1290, France in 1306, and a number of continental cities in the early 1400s—resulting in their dispersal throughout eastern Europe. The tension between the Christian populace of the towns, frequently aroused by demagogues to virulent hatred of Jews, and the need of rulers for their cash and financial expertise made their position a precarious one in Europe for centuries to come.

Consecration of the Church at Cluny. Surrounded by his retinue, Pope Urban II on the left consecrates the high altar of the new church of the abbey of Cluny on October 25, 1095, while on the right, the abbot and his monks arrange themselves on the other side.

Religious Reform and Expansion

During the period from 1000 to 1300 the clerical establishment of medieval Europe underwent dramatic reform as the church struggled to recover from nearly two centuries of decentralization and decline of learning. The reform movement in the church began in monasteries, then spread to the ecclesiastical hierarchy in cities, and eventually resulted in a new age of religious enthusiasm throughout Europe.

Monastic Reform   The effort at monastic reform began in France in a monastery founded at Cluny in 910 by Duke William I (875–918) of Aquitaine. Cluny was established as a monastery totally free of obligations to either feudal lord or local ecclesiastical control, being subordinated only to papal control. Another objective of the Cluniac reform movement was strict adherence to the Benedictine rule, which laid down strict guidelines for the monastic life. The number of reformed monasteries increased across the eleventh and twelfth centuries. The most successful of new monastic orders was the Cistercians, founded in 1098 in a remote area of France at Citeaux. At its inception the order numbered only a handful of monastic houses, but by 1200 nearly 500 Cistercian monasteries were active throughout France. The appeal of the Cistercian order lay in its simple and austere way of life; Cistercian monasteries were founded in remote areas of wasteland, and their interiors were bare and stripped of expensive adornments. They were enjoined to work and live in poverty and to devote their total beings to "God's work" (*opus Dei*).

Papal Reform and the Investiture Controversy   As the monastic reform movement progressed, a similar reform effort took place in the papacy. One of the major concerns of the church was to establish its independence from secular influence, particularly the practice by which lay rulers appointed clergy, including the pope, to their offices. Popes, however, believed it was the exclusive right of the clergy to make such appointments. After Pope Leo IX (r. 1049–1054) created the College of Cardinals Pope Nicholas II (r. 1059–1061) proclaimed the Papal Election Decree in 1059, which began the practice whereby only the College of Cardinals is empowered to elect the pontiff of the Holy Catholic Church. The result was the elimination of the role of the Holy Roman (German) emperor in the appointment of popes.

This conflict came to a head in what is known as the "investiture controversy." Pope Gregory VII (r. 1073–1085), a staunch advocate of papal reform, insisted that appointment of the clergy was in future to be controlled solely by the church. When the German emperor Henry IV (1056–1106) openly challenged Gregory's proclamation, the pope excommunicated him. The struggle between popes and emperors dragged on for more than 40 years, until 1122 when an agreement known as the Concordat of Worms (named for the German city where the agreement was made) was reached. This agreement stipulated that German bishops must be elected by church officials.

The investiture controversy produced mixed results. On the one hand, Gregory's actions represented the enhanced power of the church and proved that popes could force emperors to acknowledge papal authority. Henry had famously traveled to the papal residence at Canossa and waited barefoot in the snow for Gregory to lift the ban of excommunication on him. On the other hand, Henry IV's struggle with the church proved disastrous for his successors. Later German emperors never fully recovered from this policy of attempting to control matters in both Germany and Italy. Even such otherwise strong figures as Frederick I (r. 1152–1190) and Frederick II (r. 1215–1250), known to his contemporaries as *stupor mundi* ("the wonder of the world"), were unable to establish centralized rule in Germany. Moreover, efforts by German emperors to exert political influence over northern Italy also kept that region divided between partisans of the emperor and those of the pope for centuries to come. After Frederick's death, the five Germanic principalities reasserted their independence from royal control, and Germany remained disunited until the later nineteenth century.

Popular Piety and a Religious Society

As early as the eleventh century Europe experienced a dramatic increase in popular piety, when ordinary people took a more active interest in religion and religious issues. This movement was caused by several factors. One was the reform movement in the church, which resulted in both higher standards of conduct among regular and secular clergy and the increased visibility and temporal authority of the pope following the investiture controversy. Another factor was the construction of numerous shrines dedicated to Christian saints, whose *relics* (venerated items connected with their lives) were considered powerful aids in the quest for personal salvation.

Additional factors responsible for generating a wave of renewed enthusiasm for religion concerned new depictions of Jesus and Mary, the mother of Jesus. Whereas in the earliest years of the church in the fifth century CE the Crucifixion of Jesus was rarely shown—and, if at all, in a stylized and unemotional manner—by the tenth century Christ was depicted as a compassionate figure, whose tragic death on the Cross was portrayed as a reminder of his sacrifice for the redemption of humanity's sins.

During the early years of the church and throughout the early Middle Ages, only scattered references were made to the Virgin Mary. Thanks largely, however, to the efforts of St. Bernard to present the church as more accessible to the faithful and more receptive to personal redemption, the Virgin was cast as a merciful intercessor between humankind and God. Mary's image touched the emotions of all Christians in the West, and at this time the prayer Ave Maria (Hail Mary) became popular. Also, statues of Mary adorned every church, and sanctuaries in her name sprang up all over Europe, as exemplified by Notre Dame (Our Lady) in Paris. Interestingly, the rise of the veneration of Mary coincides with that of the bodhisattva Guanyin (or Kannon), another female figure of mercy, among Buddhists in China and Japan,

(a)

(b)

as the center of a popular devotional movement. Here, the pattern of a need for devotional dimensions of religion takes on strikingly similar forms, actions, and beliefs about the central figure.

Measurement of Time   An important contribution of the popularization of Christian piety is evident in the introduction of new concepts of time. One concept derives from the book of Genesis in the Bible, where the creation of the earth took 6 days, leaving the seventh day as a day of rest, set aside for Sunday. Moreover, the numbering of years in accordance with the Christian era was introduced in 532 by Dionysius Exiguus (ca. 470–544), a Roman monk. For Dionysius historical time really began with the birth of Christ, hence his designation of *Anno Domini* ("in the year of the Lord") to denote a new dating system. The new system was used by the eighth-century Anglo-Saxon scholar Bede (ca. 673–735) in his *Ecclesiastical History of the English People* and then popularized in Europe by Alcuin of York during the reign of Charlemagne.

These and other associations with Christianity carried with them several implications that altered the lives of Europeans. For one thing, two crucial Christian feast days now became standard: the birth of Christ was celebrated on December 25 (Christmas) and his resurrection on a movable date called **Easter**. For another, saints' days, set aside for reflection and celebration, constituted major events around which Europeans' lives centered. Finally, the ringing of church and monastery bells announced the hours of the day, which provided for regulation of daily routines. Mechanical clocks, introduced into Europe in the early fourteenth century—and most likely derived from earlier Chinese models—provided for more precise measurement of the daily hours.

New Religious Orders   Another aspect of popular piety was an alarming trend toward the appearance of heretical movements within the church. Criticisms of church practice and doctrines, especially over the church's growing worldliness and political maneuvering, began to arise, particularly in the cities and towns of southern France. In an effort to channel the devotion of the faithful, particularly in cities, Pope Innocent III (r. 1198–1216) licensed two new religious orders of friars ("brothers"), the Franciscans and the Dominicans.

Changing Views of Christ. The Crucifixion scene from the door of the basilica of Santa Sabina, Rome, ca. 430, is formal and stylized: Christ is remote. *(a)* In contrast, the Crucifixion commissioned by the archbishop of Cologne, Germany, just before 1000 shows a suffering Christ—a human being in agony and sorrow, hanging from a cross *(b)*.

Easter: Christian celebration of the Resurrection of Christ; celebrated on the Sunday following the first full moon after the vernal equinox.

Founded by St. Francis of Assisi (1181/82–1226), a prosperous Italian merchant who willingly disposed of his family wealth in order to live a life of poverty and charity, the Francisan order inspired a new dedication to Christianity by living simply among the people, preaching repentance for sins and aiding the poor and the sick. The Dominicans, founded by St. Dominic (1170–1221) in 1216, also lived among the people; but they were more interested in preaching and teaching, believing that the best way to combat heresy was to teach the doctrines of the church. The Dominican order included many famous medieval theologians in its ranks, such as St. Thomas Aquinas (ca. 1225–1274).

The Crusades   A movement that reflects both the growing appeal and power of the church as well as the renewed energy of a revitalized Europe centers on the Crusades. Like the reform movement of the church, the Crusades were in part inspired by the new wave of religious enthusiasm sweeping Europe during the period of recovery from the horrors of the ninth and tenth centuries. But there were other causal factors as well. One of the most fundamental causes was the so-called *Reconquista*, or reconquest, of formerly Christian lands that had been taken over by Muslims.

Until the year 1000 Spanish Christians were forced to retreat into the far northwestern section of the peninsula, while the Muslims controlled most of the lands from their capital in Córdoba. In 1031, however, internal squabbling among Muslim factions led to a loosening of Muslim control over all of Spain, which in turn prompted two kings of Christian territories to launch an offensive in order to reclaim land from the Muslims. The real breakthrough occurred in 1085 when Toledo was liberated from Muslim control, resulting in almost half of Spain returning to Christian control.

A similar effort to retake Christian territory from Muslim control took place in southern Italy and Sicily. Beginning in 1061, a group of Norman knights began wresting Sicily from Muslim control. Across the twelfth century their successors established a strongly centralized Norman kingdom in Sicily. The Norman kings of Sicily allied themselves with the papacy, and in return for their protection of the papacy, they were given the status of permanent papal legates, which in turn gave them total control over all the higher clergy in their realm.

These spectacular successes against the Muslims in the western Mediterranean occurred simultaneously with alarming developments in the eastern Mediterranean. After the death of the eastern Roman emperor Basil II in 1025, a series of weak successors was unable to maintain effective centralized administration, resulting in the appearance of feudal-like conditions in the Byzantine state. At the same time, a new menace appeared from the east, the fearsome Seljuk Turks. After their conversion to Islam, the Seljuks launched a series of raids against the Byzantines; and at the Battle of Manzikert in 1071 they routed their Christian opponents, resulting in the loss of all Christian lands in Asia. In 1076 the Turks overran Jerusalem itself. Fearing for the survival of the Byzantine state, the Byzantine emperor Michael VII (r. 1071–1078) sent an appeal for aid to the Roman pope, Gregory VII. As we have seen, Gregory was preoccupied with the investiture controversy, so he declined to intervene in the east.

But when the next emperor, Alexius Comnenus (r. 1081–1118) followed up with another request to Gregory's successor Urban II, the latter felt it was time to intervene against a total Muslim takeover in the eastern Mediterranean. Inspired by recent victories over Muslims in the western Mediterranean, Urban II was driven by any number of possible motives: he wanted to liberate the Holy Land in order to guarantee the safety of Christian pilgrims anxious to view the holiest Christian sites in Syria and Palestine; he was anxious to enhance papal prestige in the contest with the German emperor; he wanted to siphon off some of the destructive energy of feudal knights and to follow up on the church's programs of the Peace of God (to limit the violence of private warfare) and the Truce of God (to ban warfare on certain days of the week and on holy days); and he may have wanted to heal the schism between the western and eastern churches occasioned by the split in 1054.

Accordingly, on November 27, 1095, Pope Urban II called for the launching of a crusade to the Holy Land during the Council of Clermont in France. Urban called particularly on the great barons of Europe to gather together their feudal armies and march to the east to liberate Jerusalem from Muslim control. For their part, although they may have been partially driven by religious enthusiasm, Europe's feudal nobility most likely saw in this expedition the promise of new lands and a chance to use their military training in a good cause. In the summer of the following year the main force, consisting of approximately 7,000 mounted knights along with around 35,000 infantry and augmented by thousands of attendants, suppliers, and prostitutes, gathered for the journey eastward. When the eastern emperor realized the size and potential unruliness of the approaching crusader army, he is supposed to have said, "I asked for rain and have been given a flood." Eventually, the entire army crossed over into Asia Minor and in 1097 took Nicaea from the Turks; and two years later, in the summer of 1099, Jerusalem was finally freed from Islamic control at a terrific cost in human life. As a result of the crusaders' victory, new "crusader states" were established along the eastern Mediterranean and papal authority gained new respect among western secular rulers (see Map 11.5).

MAP **11.5** The First Crusade, 1095–1099.

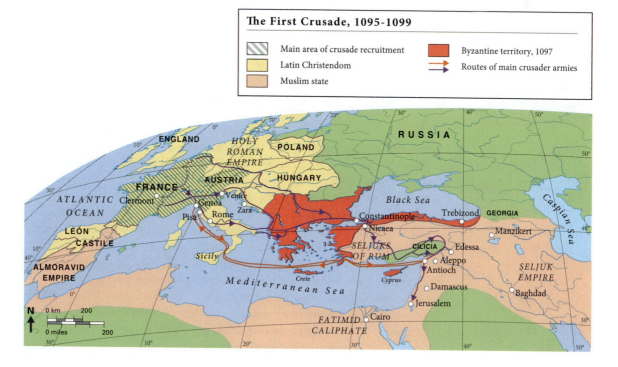

The Sack of Constantinople

"How shall I begin to tell of the deeds wrought by these nefarious men! Alas, the images, which ought to have been adored, were trodden under foot! Alas, the relics of the holy martyrs were thrown into unclean places! . . . Nor can the violation of the Great Church [the Hagia Sophia] be listened to with equanimity. For the sacred altar, formed of all kinds of precious materials and admired by the whole world, was broken into bits and distributed among the soldiers, as was all the other sacred wealth of so great and infinite splendor. . . . When the sacred vases and utensils of unsurpassable art and grace and rare material, and the fine silver, wrought with gold, which encircled the screen of the tribunal and the ambo, of admirable workmanship, and the door and many other ornaments, were to be borne away as booty, mules and saddled horses were led to the very sanctuary of the temple. Some of these which were unable to keep their footing on the splendid and slippery pavement, were stabbed when they fell, so that the sacred pavement was polluted with blood and filth. . . . No one was without a share in the grief. In the alleys, in the streets, in the temples, complaints, weeping, lamentations, grief, the groaning of men, the shrieks of women, wounds, rape, captivity, the separation of those most closely united. . . . Oh, immortal God, how great the afflictions of the men, how great the distress!"

—Nicetas Choniates. *The Sack of Constantinople*. Translated by D. C. Munro. *Translations and Reprints from the Original Sources of European History*, series 1, vol. 3, pp. 15–16 (rev. ed.). Philadelphia: University of Pennsylvania Press, 1912.

Other crusades followed throughout the twelfth century. In 1144 the fall of the crusader state of Edessa (in present-day Syria) to a resurgence of Islamic militancy caused renewed interest in a second crusade. Called for in a sermon by Bernard of Clairveaux, the crusade was led by King Louis VII of France and Conrad III, Holy Roman emperor. The two leaders failed to coordinate their movements once they reached the east, and the result was the failure of the expedition to reach Jerusalem. A surge of renewed interest in the crusading movement occurred in 1187, when Jerusalem was overrun by the renowned Muslim leader Saladin. Known as the "Crusade of the Three Kings," the army was led by Frederick I of Germany, Philip II of France, and Richard I of England. The accidental drowning death of Frederick I removed the German contingent from the force, but the combined English and French forces managed to capture Acre from the Muslims in 1191. At that point, however, dissension between Philip I and Richard I resulted in Philip's hasty return to France, where he engaged in stirring up trouble against the English monarch. Although Richard stayed on for a while in Palestine, he eventually withdrew without securing significant military victories and while traveling through Austria on the way home was captured and held for ransom, one of the causes of the later baronial revolt against his brother and successor, King John.

Yet another crusading effort, the Fourth Crusade, instigated by the leader of Venice, was launched in 1201. Consisting mainly of French knights, the crusading army desired to travel to the Holy Land by sea instead of taking the usual landed route. When they reached Venice, the Crusade's leaders contracted with the Venetians for passage by ship to the east. The crafty Venetians were quick to realize the advantage of transporting a crusading army and, after leaving port attacked the Adriatic port city of Zara, their commercial rival. Outraged by an attack on a Christian city, Innocent III excommunicated the crusaders, who blithely ignored the papal ban. From Zara the Venetians transported the army to Constantinople in 1204, where they plundered the city. Nicetas Choniates (ca. 1155–1215), a Byzantine historian, provides a gruesome eyewitness account of the crusaders' rampage.

Although the crusading movement ultimately failed to liberate Jerusalem from Muslim hands and although the cumulative casualty estimates run into the millions, the Crusades produced some positive achievements for Europeans. The ability of Western popes to organize European knights into armies and to send them far afield in service of the church enhanced their prestige in both the west and the east. The Crusades also helped to establish western Christian dominance of sea traffic in the Mediterranean. Finally, the retaking of Christian territories in southern Italy, Sicily, and Spain—an effort that began in local areas before the First Crusade—provided European scholars access to new sources of Greco-Arabic scientific advances, known collectively as the "New Logic."

Intellectual and Cultural Developments

Closely associated with the religious recovery of Europe during the High Middle Ages (ca. 1000–1300) was a series of important new directions

A Medieval Italian Classroom. As the master recites passages from a text, some students copy verbatim what is read aloud, while others either listen attentively or even sleep.

and institutions reflective of the intellectual and cultural expressions of western Christian religious civilization. Perhaps the two most visible symbols of this civilization—the Gothic cathedral and the university—were produced during the "twelfth-century renaissance" (see Patterns Up Close). It was in the university that the study of Aristotle provoked a renewed interest in science and the natural world.

Universities   As a result of the urban revolution of the eleventh century, monastic schools in rural areas began to lose ground to cathedral schools in urban centers, which offered more relevant instruction in reading and writing, mathematical reckoning, and logical reasoning—skills needed for success in the commercial world of the twelfth century. The most creative thinkers were now attracted to cathedral schools in the larger cities of Europe, where they in turn began to attract eager young students. In time, larger groups of students and teachers formed the first universities at Salerno, Bologna, and Paris.

Particularly in Paris, the university curriculum began to focus on the philosophy of Aristotle, who had been all but ignored during the early Middle Ages. In large part this was owing to the efforts of Gerbert of Aurillac (ca. 946–1003), known by his contemporaries as "the most learned man of his century" and later named Pope Sylvester II (r. 999–1003). As a young man Gerbert had studied in Islamic Spain, where he acquired an interest in mathematics and astronomy, along with a fascination with Aristotelian logic. Later, as deacon of the cathedral school at Reims, Gerbert introduced both the sciences and Aristotelian logic to his students, many of whom in turn helped spread the new learning throughout cathedral schools in Europe.

During the eleventh and twelfth centuries, two important developments in universities resulted from the growing popularity of Aristotelian logic. One of these was the emergence of a new method of pursuing philosophical and theological truth by use of Aristotelian logic, known as **scholasticism**. Adherents of this new methodology began to subject long-held doctrines of the church to rigorous scrutiny. The problem was that Aristotle posed a serious threat to church authority since a better understanding of his ideas revealed just how incompatible his thinking was

Scholasticism: A medieval method of determining theological and philosophical truth by using Aristotelian logic.

The Castration of Abelard

"When her uncle and his kinsmen heard of this, they were convinced that now I had completely played them false and had rid myself forever of Heloise by forcing her to become a nun. Violently incensed, they laid a plot against me, and one night while I all unsuspecting was asleep in a secret room in my lodgings, they broke in with the help of one of my servants whom they had bribed. There they had vengeance on me with a most cruel and most shameful punishment, such as astounded the whole world; for they cut off those parts of my body with which I had done that which was the cause of their sorrow. This done, straightway they fled, but two of them were captured and suffered the loss of their eyes and their genital organs. One of these two was the aforesaid servant, who even while he was still in my service, had been led by his avarice to betray me."

—Peter Abelard, *The Story of My Misfortunes*, trans. Henry Adams Bellows (Glencoe, Illinois: Free Press, 1958), pp. 29-30.

---

with religious doctrine. For example, Aristotle denied the creation of the world in favor of the world's eternity, and he denied the immortality of the soul.

What emerged was a fundamental disagreement between those who placed the truths of *faith* before the truths of *reason* in attempting to gain knowledge of God's existence and those who held the opposite view.

The most famous advocates of these opposing schools of thought were St. Anselm (ca. 1034–1109) and Peter Abelard (1079–1142). Anselm argued that faith must precede reason ("I believe in order that I might understand"). He further argued that proof of God's existence could be deduced by first accepting church doctrine on the basis of faith and then proceeding to support these notions by reasoned argument. Abelard, the most popular teacher at the cathedral school of Notre Dame in Paris during these years, disagreed, arguing that "I understand in order that I might believe." Abelard's apparent favoring of reason over faith tipped the balance in favor of those who were inclined to question traditional Christian doctrine. And what made Abelard's position all the more popular was his fame and notoriety among twelfth-century scholars, the result of a sensational and tragic love affair that resulted in the pregnancy of his student Heloise, niece of the canon of the cathedral school of Notre Dame. The most sensational portion of Abelard's *Historia Calamitatum* (*The Story of My Misfortunes*) concerns his description of how Heloise's uncle took revenge upon discovering that after their secret marriage Abelard sent Heloise off to a nunnery.

So alarmingly popular was Aristotle by the middle of the thirteenth century that in addition to the earlier division between those who advocated either the truths of faith or reason, a third perspective was offered by those who took a middle path. It was from the latter camp that St. Thomas Aquinas (ca. 1224–1274) originated. In his famous *Summa Theologica*, Aquinas argued that, instead of considering the truths of reason as being totally irreconcilable from the truths of faith, it was possible to consider a compromise, or a synthesis of the two, that would in the end lead to a knowledge of God's existence and, thus, to personal salvation. According to this construct, one could begin an upward journey to an understanding of God by first relying upon the truths of reason; but at a certain point one would have to abandon pure reason for the more enlightened approach afforded by faith, which would then allow an understanding of the mysteries of Christian doctrine and, thus, of God. Aquinas put it this way: "Grace (faith) does not destroy nature (reason)—it perfects her."

Law and Medicine Consistent with the necessity of providing the requisite skills for advancement in the new urban and cosmopolitan ambience of twelfth-century urban life, universities began to offer training in law and medicine. By the early years of the twelfth century scholars at Bologna discovered the Roman legal tradition preserved in Justinian's celebrated *Corpus Iuris Civilis*. It was at Bologna around 1140 that the *Corpus* inspired a monk named Gratian to compile a comprehensive compendium of ecclesiastical law known as the *Decretum*. Gratian's student Peter Lombard's *Book of Sentences*, produced in 1150, served along with the *Decretum* as the foundation for the development of **canon law**, utilized by the papacy in its struggles to contest secular power.

Canon law: The law of the church.

Medical studies were taught at Salerno in the late eleventh century. Thanks to its location in Sicily, Salerno was able to assimilate Islamic and Byzantine medical advances. Serving as the nucleus of medical studies at Salerno were the works of the Roman physician Galen and the *Canon of Medicine* compiled by the Islamic scholar Ibn Sina (or Avicenna, 980–1037). These works formed the foundation of medical studies throughout medieval European universities.

Medieval Science   Another consequence of the appeal of Aristotle was a corresponding fascination with scientific texts of the ancient Greeks. The initial impulse in this direction was provided not only by Gerbert of Aurillac but also by Christian advances into Spain and southern Italy during the waning years of the eleventh century. The Christian conquest of Toledo in 1085, followed by the retaking of Sicily in 1091, provided opportunities for so-called wandering scholars from all over Europe to gain access to Islamic treasure troves of scientific learning. Adelard of Bath (ca. 1080–1152) was one of the forerunners of twelfth-century Western scholars who translated Greek scientific texts from Arabic into Latin. As such, Adelard served as an important bridge, or conduit, between the Islamic and western Christian worlds; and it was largely owing to his efforts that a new awareness and sense of curiosity about the mysteries of natural science began to circulate in Western intellectual circles. Adelard's most important work is his *Natural Questions*, written around 1116. In the accompanying exchange, Adelard attempts to convince his nephew of the superiority of Arabic scientific reasoning as opposed to traditional western European approaches.

Adelard contributed to what is often referred to as the age of Latin translators. The most prolific of these translators was Gerard of Cremona (ca. 1114–1187), who provided Latin translations of over 70 Greek scientific texts, including Ptolemy's *Almagest* and most of Aristotle's works on physics, along with numerous mathematical treatises such as Euclid's *Elements* and al-Khwarizmi's *Algebra* and several medical treatises such as Galen's text and Avicenna's *Canon of Medicine*.

Perhaps the most important of Adelard's successors in England was Robert Grosseteste (ca. 1175–1253). Grosseteste represented a rare combination of

The Superiority of Arabic Scientific Reasoning

"ADELARD: You perhaps take a little more on you than you ought; but as this arrangement will be profitable not only to you but to many others, I will pardon your forwardness, making however this one stipulation, that when I adduce something unfamiliar, people are to think not that I am putting forward an idea of my own, but am giving the views of the Arabs. . . . I, with reason for my guide, have learned one thing from my Arab teachers, you, something different; dazzled by the outward show of authority you wear a head-stall. . . . We must first search after reason, and when it has been found, and not until then, authority if added to it, may be received. Authority by itself can inspire no confidence in the philosopher, nor ought it to be used for such a purpose. Hence logicians have agreed in treating the argument from authority not as necessary, but probable only. If, therefore, you want to bear anything from me, you must both give and take reason."

—H. Gollancz, ed. and trans. "Adelard of Bath." In *Dodi Ve-Nechdi*, pp. 91–92, 98–99. London: Oxford University Press, 1920.

Patterns Up Close | The Gothic Cathedral

Of all the contributions of medieval Europe, the best-known and most readily recognizable is the Gothic cathedral. But the origins and evolution of this iconic symbol of medieval European Christianity are less familiar.

The origin of the cathedral can be traced back ultimately to late imperial Rome. Following Constantine's Edict of Milan in 313, Christians were no longer forced to worship in secret locations, and church leaders began the quest to identify a type of public building that could accommodate larger and larger congregations. Roman temples were ready to hand, but they were deemed unsuitable not only because of their pagan associations but also because pagan rituals took place outside temple walls; the interiors were reserved for statues and images of the gods.

St. Denis Cathedral—Nave.

Many features of the Roman *basilica*, a civic hall traditionally used for business transactions, legal affairs, and other public functions, rendered it ideally suited to the needs of early Christian worship. Its design was therefore assimilated by the early church and transformed from pagan to Christian usage. The basilica style featured a long central aisle (or nave), roofed over with timber, ending with an intersecting transept and an arched passage into a semicircular *apse* (or sanctuary) with a raised platform where the presiding magistrate sat in judgment. The first adaptation of the pagan basilica plan to Christian usage appeared in several churches constructed during Constantine's reign. The first of these, known as St. John Lateran Basilica, was begun in 314 CE and is often referred to as the "Mother Church" since it served as the basic model for later Christian churches in the West. Constantine then ordered the construction of three more churches with this architectural design. One of these, known as Old Saint Peter's Rome, was completed by 333 and was the precursor to the modern church of St. Peter in the Vatican. Among its unique features were the first incorporation of a transept at the end of the nave, coincidentally forming a cruciform design, symbolizing the cult of the Cross, and the substitution of an altar for the magistrate's throne in the apse.

Several factors combined during the post-Roman, early medieval period to produce the assimilation of some earlier Roman and Christian architectural styles with evolving European circumstances. The result was the Romanesque style of church architecture, which appeared in different guises across the period ca. 800–1000. An early example is provided by Charlemagne's Palatine Chapel, consecrated in 805, which combined elements of Byzantine architecture borrowed from the church of San Vitale in Ravenna, completed in 548. Most important, however, was the incorporation of several features associated with Romanesque architecture: the replacement of the basilica's low timber roofs with heavy stone barrel vaults, which spanned the space over the nave and in turn required massive stone piers and exterior walls to support the weight, and the resulting gloomy interiors. In addition, the apse was expanded beyond the transept by the addition of a circular walkway (the ambulatory) to allow crowds of pilgrims to view Christian relics; and the focal point of the exterior was now the western facade, flanked by two towers, with a tympanum featuring scenes like the Last Judgment. The spread of Benedictine monasteries as well as the emergence of powerful German emperors during the tenth and eleventh centuries provoked additional changes in Romanesque churches. Among these were the enlargement of interiors, the increased height of the nave—utilizing vaulting and groin arches—and the addition of a clerestory with rounded arches above the nave to admit more light into the interior, as in Speyer Cathedral.

The revitalization of urban life in the eleventh and twelfth centuries, along with a marked increase in lay piety, prompted architects to assimilate some features of the Romanesque into a new design more in keeping with changing tastes and practices. The first attempt to open up gloomy Romanesque interiors—and to lay the foundations for what emerged as the new Gothic style—was made at the abbey church of St. Denis in Paris under the direction of its abbot, the famous Suger (1085–1151). In his rebuilding of the abbey church of St. Denis near Paris in 1144, Suger's intention was to enlarge the interior spaces of Romanesque churches, to provide more light, and at the same time to increase the upward reach of their exteriors. Among the innovations at St. Denis was the incorporation of stained glass panels in the outer walls, which provided dazzling arrays of color in the interior and presented stories from the Bible. Thus, Suger writes, "the whole [church] would shine with the wonderful and uninterrupted light of most sacred windows, pervading the interior beauty."

Speyer Cathedral—Interior.

Three subsequent architectural inventions of the twelfth century enabled architects to expand on Suger's original contributions: the ribbed vault, the pointed arch, and the flying buttress. The ribbed vault allowed for thinner outer walls, with the result that they could be opened up to contain large glass windows that allowed more light. Pointed arches, copied from earlier Islamic architecture through cultural interactions in Sicily and Spain, allowed for higher vertical thrusts in weight distribution, resulting in soaring naves, many well over 100 feet in height. Flying buttresses—perhaps the most innovative feature of the Gothic style—were then used to support the thinner outer walls, distributing the thrust of the ribbed vaults and pointed arches away from the outer wall and down toward the ground.

From 1170 to 1270, 80 Gothic cathedrals (including Chartres and Notre Dame in Paris) and nearly 500 churches were built throughout France. From France the Gothic style spread throughout Europe; in 1175 the cathedral at Canterbury, England, was rebuilt in the Gothic style. That these monuments of Christian devotion and medieval architectural ingenuity continue to inspire awe is a testament to the cultural contributions of medieval European civilization.

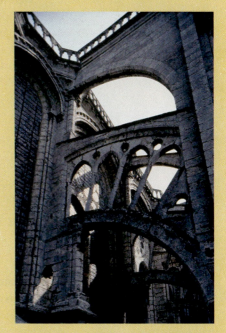

St. Denis Cathedral—Flying Buttress.

Questions

- How does the Gothic cathedral demonstrate the origins-interactions-adaptations process in action?

- What types of cultural adaptations are evident in houses of worship built today?

ecclesiastical and secular interests; he was for a time bishop of Lincoln but also a dabbler in the new scientific studies of natural phenomena. All sorts of curiosities and problems in the world of nature caught Grosseteste's eye: the motions of the tides, the causes of earthquakes and volcanic eruptions, the properties and transmission of light rays (leading to his grinding of lenses and to the invention of reading glasses). Grosseteste made a distinctively important contribution to the advancement of science in that he recognized the value of mathematics, and he was among the earliest scholastics to question the scientific authority of Aristotle, particularly Aristotle's theory of the formation of rainbows.

Grosseteste's arguments were absorbed and carried forward by his student Roger Bacon (ca. 1214–1294). Although Bacon dabbled in all sorts of scientifically related fields like alchemy and foresaw flying machines and underwater vessels, his principal contribution to the development of Western science was to emphasize the role of induction and experimentation. Bacon was especially interested in the science of optics, for which he relied heavily on earlier Islamic scientists; and he incorporated elements of geometry into his research.

The advances made by Grosseteste at Oxford were carried across the Channel to Paris, where scholars like Jean Buridan (ca. 1300–1370) and Nicole Oresme (1323–1382) continued the assault on Aristotle's credibility. Through a series of commonsense experiments, Buridan disproved Aristotle's theory of motion, which erroneously argued that objects remain in motion only through the continuous application of an external force. Rather, Buridan demonstrated that some sort of inner force, imparted to an object at the moment it was set in motion, was the agent. Buridan used the term *impetus* to describe this impressed force; this was an important first step toward the modern theory of inertia. Buridan also conducted experiments on falling bodies, which contributed to later theories of their acceleration. Like Buridan, Oresme also took issue with many of Aristotle's scientific propositions, particularly the idea that the earth is immobile at the center of the cosmos. Instead, Oresme proposed several explanations—mostly philosophical—in favor of the earth's daily axial rotation, including the notion that it would be far easier for the earth to rotate at a slower speed than the whole of the heavenly orbs, which have to whirl around at speeds "far beyond belief and estimation."

Church Architecture   The economic recovery of Europe, combined with the increase in popular piety in the eleventh century, led to the construction of magnificent churches all over Europe. Whereas eleventh-century churches were built in the Romanesque style, around the middle of the twelfth century a new architectural style, later called "**Gothic**," began to appear in Europe.

Gothic: Architectural style that began in the twelfth century and that featured new design elements, including ribbed vaults, pointed arches, flying buttresses, and stained glass.

Crisis and Creativity, 1300–1415

The fourteenth century marks the final phase of European Christian civilization and is often considered an age of transition to the European Renaissance. The early part of the century witnessed a series of economic reversals. Near mid-century a devastating plague originating in southeast Asia ravaged Europe, killing as much as one-third of its population and generating further social upheaval. Centralized kingdoms developed a sense of national identity and consolidation; one result was a long, drawn-out period of war between England and France that began in 1337 and ended in 1453. In addition, the authority of the papacy was challenged from without by powerful European secular rulers and weakened from within by a series of internal problems and philosophical disputes. As bleak as things were, however, the fourteenth century can be considered a time of transition from medieval institutions and perspectives to early Renaissance ideals. Signs of new creative forces arising from the ashes of the fourteenth century appeared as early as the middle of the century.

The Calamitous Fourteenth Century

Fourteenth-century Europe experienced all manner of dearth, disease, death, and dissolution. The early part of the century witnessed a series of reversals in the economic and social realms, brought on initially by a dramatic climatic change in the year 1315 that resulted in a prolonged period of poor harvests followed by famine. Near mid-century a disastrous plague added to the misery of daily life.

Famine   During the early years of the fourteenth century Europe was hit by a disastrous combination of factors that produced a prolonged period of famine. One factor was a sudden disparity between an expanding population and its available food supply. From ca. 1000 to 1300 Europe's population had nearly doubled to a total of around 80 million, thanks to advances in agricultural technology. By 1300, however, no new advances were forthcoming. In addition, after centuries of expansion and clearing of lands, Europe suddenly ran out of new frontiers, resulting in a shortage of land available for increased agricultural production. To make matters worse, the average annual temperature dropped during this period, which shortened the summer growing season. At the same time, an unusually prolonged series of rainy seasons in the spring and summer planting seasons, followed by a succession of harsh winters, resulted in a famine that extended from 1315 to 1322.

Plague   Near mid-century, Europe's already weakened populations suffered a horrific outbreak of bubonic plague. The disease originated in Cambodia, Burma, and Vietnam; it was then transmitted across Asia in goods and wares transported by Mongol traders in the 1330s. From there it spread westward along trade routes to the Black Sea. The plague was introduced to the West when grain-carrying Genoese merchant ships, infested with diseased rats, sailed from the Crimea to ports in Sicily and northern Italy in 1346–1347. Within a year, the plague had spread into northern Europe via trade routes, carried by infected rats and fleas, fanning out across Europe north of the Alps.

The disease took its name "Black Death" from the appearance of blackened body sores, called "*buboes*" (hence the name "bubonic plague"), especially in the lymph nodes, that announced the arrival of the disease. Once the dreaded black sores appeared, infected people suffered horribly with high fevers, swollen lymph nodes, and painfully aching joints and usually had only 3 days to live. The plague ran unchecked throughout Europe from 1348 to 1352 and returned sporadically in the 1360s, 1370s, and 1390s. The highly contagious disease was next to impossible to contain for a variety of reasons. For one thing Europe's population was weakened and ravaged as a consequence of the great famine. For another, overcrowded European cities, with their lack of sanitation, created ideal breeding conditions for the rapid spread of the disease. Mortality figures are difficult to establish with certainty. Nevertheless, it has been estimated that England alone may have lost nearly 1 million from a total population of around 4 million. Urban areas were the hardest hit; Florence suffered losses amounting to around 50,000 out of a total population of 85,000. A reasonable estimate of the number of people who died throughout Europe as a result of the first wave of the plague puts the total loss at about one-third of the entire population (see Map 11.6).

A series of economic and social consequences of the Black Death resounded throughout Europe. The falling off of Europe's population resulted, in urban areas, in less demand for goods and manufactured items, causing a downturn in commerce and trade, and, in rural areas, in a similar decline in demand for grain products. Another result of the overall decline in Europe's population was the reduction in the number of agricultural workers, whose labor was suddenly more sought after than before the plague. The result of these increasing tensions between the well off and those less well off was a series of social uprisings throughout Europe. In Paris a disturbance known as the "Jacquerie" broke out in 1358, and in Florence the Ciompi

MAP **11.6** The Spread of the Black Death in Europe.

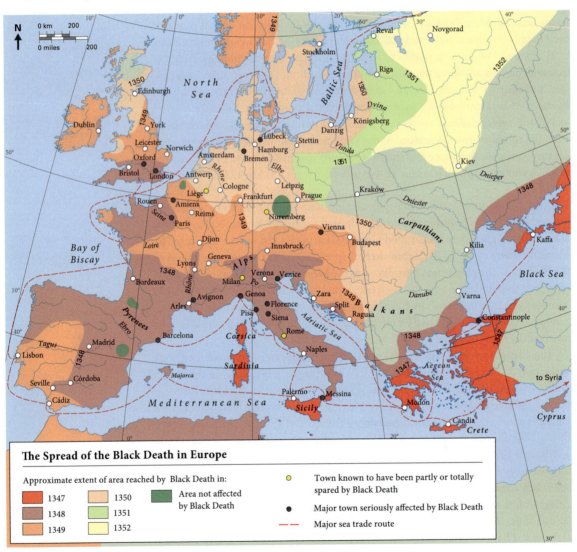

The Spread of the Black Death in Europe

Approximate extent of area reached by Black Death in:

1347	1350	Area not affected by Black Death
1348	1351	
1349	1352	

○ Town known to have been partly or totally spared by Black Death

● Major town seriously affected by Black Death

---- Major sea trade route

rebellion flared up in 1378. The most serious social revolt occurred in London in 1381. Known as "The Peasants' Revolt," the uprising was more broadly based and included wealthy country residents as well as participants from the ranks of the urban working classes.

The Hundred Years' War   From the mid-fourteenth to the mid-fifteenth century, Europe was embroiled in a disastrous conflict, coined the "Hundred Years' War" by nineteenth-century historians. At issue was a long-simmering dispute over English landholdings in France, the result of the Norman Conquest. More immediately, when the English king Edward III (r. 1327–1377) laid claim to the vacant French throne in 1328, his claim was rejected in favor of Charles IV (r. 1322–1328), the first of the Valois rulers. These issues came to a head in 1337 when Philip VI (r. 1328–1350) seized control of Gascony and fighting erupted in earnest between the two countries.

The conflict was fought in three phases. Early on, English forces racked up significant victories at the Battle of Crécy in 1346 and then again at the Battle of Poitiers in 1356, where English longbowmen handed smashing defeats to the mounted French knights. The same thing occurred later at the Battle of Agincourt in 1415, where Henry V (r. 1413–1422) led vastly outnumbered English forces (only 6,000 as opposed to 20,000) to score a surprising victory while suffering relatively few casualties. Suddenly, however, when it seemed that English forces were on the verge of declaring victory, a 17-year-old peasant girl, Joan of Arc (ca. 1412–1431) encouraged the uncrowned Charles VII (r. 1422–1461) to relieve the siege of Orleans in 1429, where English forces were routed. The victory at Orleans inspired the French to one success after another. The conflict finally came to an end in 1453, when the English conceded a French victory in terms agreed to in the Treaty of Paris, leaving the English in possession of only the port of Calais (see Map 11.7).

Consequences of the Hundred Years' War   The Hundred Years' War affected almost every aspect of European life. The long, drawn-out conflict added to the misery of the fourteenth century, a period already suffering from famine and plague. Like the plague, the war was a constant reminder of the omnipresence of death. The economic consequences of the war were equally serious. The war—fought entirely on French soil—destroyed both crops and small farms. In both England and France, financing the war meant new and increased taxes—and further woes for the peasantry, who bore the brunt of these increased financial obligations. The war even affected the religious realm. It prevented the resolution of the **Great Schism** as rival popes sought the support of contending French and English kings and their subjects.

Over 100 years of war brought about a number of innovations in weaponry, military tactics, and strategy. The English use of foot soldiers armed with longbows resulted in the dominance of the infantry over the cavalry of armored, mounted knights. Important advances in warfare resulted from the first extensive

Burial of Plague Victims. With up to 50 percent of the people in some places in Europe dying of the plague, burial scenes, such as this one depicted in a Flemish manuscript, were common throughout the middle and late fourteenth century.

Great Schism: The period 1378–1417 marked by divided papal allegiances in Latin Christendom.

The Hundred Years' War, 1337-1453

⚔ Site of major battle   ▨ Lands held by England in 1360

▨ Area recognizing Plantagenet kingship, 1428

MAP **11.7** **The Hundred Years'**
War, 1337–1453.

European use of various sorts of firearms, invented in China and transmitted to the West by Muslims. In the final phases of the war, for example, French soldiers using artillery and handguns defeated English archers at the battles of Formigny (1450) and Castillon (1453). Giant wrought iron cannons called "bombards" fired stone balls weighing around 220 pounds to a range of around 240 yards. By the war's end French soldiers were using handheld matchlock guns that fired lead bullets.

Crises in the Church   Troubles began during the papacy of Pope Boniface VIII (r. 1294–1303), whose stubborn personality clashed with the ambitious national interests of Philip IV (r. 1285–1314) of France. Philip, desperate for money in order to consolidate royal power, levied a tax on the French clergy. In response, Boniface excommunicated Philip; he retaliated by ordering the imprisonment of the pope in 1303, who subsequently died from the shock of this rude treatment. Boniface's successor, Clement V (r. 1305–1314), left Rome and took up residence in a splendid palace at Avignon, on the French border. Clement appointed a number of French clergymen to the College of Cardinals. From 1305 to 1378 successive French popes continued to reside at Avignon, a period known as the *Avignon Papacy*.

The Great Schism   In 1378 Pope Gregory XI (r. 1370–1378) returned to Rome, but he died shortly after his arrival there. Acting, as they later said, under pressure of a Roman mob to elect "a Roman, or at least an Italian" as the next pope, the predominantly French College of Cardinals elected an Italian archbishop, Urban VI (r. 1378–1389). Urban badly mistreated the cardinals and insisted on a series of outlandish reforms. The cardinals, regretting their selection of Urban, returned to Avignon and promptly elected a Frenchman as the new pope, Clement VII (r. 1378–1394). An attempt of the Council of Pisa in 1409 to resolve the conflict merely intensified the embarrassment. The council deposed both reigning popes and named a new one, Alexander V (r. 1409–1410). However, the two reigning popes refused to step down, with the result that the church had not one or two but *three* popes.

Adding to the church's problems were several outspoken critics of its doctrine. One of the earliest of these critics was John Wycliffe (ca. 1330–1384), an Oxford theologian. Wycliffe railed against the wealth and abuses of the higher clergy, denied the power of priests to act as intermediaries between believers and God, and disputed the validity of many **sacraments**, including the most central of Christian dogmas, the sacrament of the Eucharist (sometimes referred to as Communion or the Lord's Supper), which holds that Christ's presence is revealed in consecrated bread and wine. Wycliffe also oversaw the translation of the Bible into Middle

Sacrament: An outward and physical sign of an inward and spiritual grace.

English. Wycliffe's teachings reached Bohemia in eastern Europe when the English king Richard II (r. 1377–1399) married the princess Anne of Bohemia. John Huss (1370–1415), a radical religious reformer and preacher at Prague, enthusiastically supported Wycliffe's ideas, especially the English theologian's argument for the primacy of scripture as the basis for all Christian doctrine (see Map 11.8).

Signs of a New Era in the Fifteenth Century

All of the instances of doom and gloom we have mentioned signaled the waning of earlier medieval values, perspectives, and institutions. Yet, at the same time, dire situations in the fourteenth century prompted adaptations and subsequent transformations in the succeeding century that prefigured the transition to the Renaissance. We can observe these adjustments in political, economic, and cultural aspects of fifteenth-century Europe.

Political Reorganization in France and England

Out of the ashes of the Hundred Years' War arose new conceptions of royal authority in both England and France that in many ways set the stage for the appearance of the "new monarchies" in the second half of the fifteenth century. In France, for example, fifteenth-century rulers utilized the demands and pressures of warfare as rationales to centralize their authority. One expedient was to overhaul the royal bureaucracy in order to enhance its efficiency and power. Another, more profitable tack was the raising of new taxes without consulting the Estates-General. In 1343 Philip VI established a new tax on salt, highly valued as a preservative of meats. Later, in 1439, Charles VII converted a temporary tax on land paid by all subjects of the realm into a permanent tax in order to build up the first professional standing army in western Europe, consisting of nearly 10,000 cavalry forces. An ancillary boost to royal power was the result of the Pragmatic Sanction of Bourges (1438), by which the church ceded control of its French assets to the government.

The state of politics in England was similarly affected by the course of the Hundred Years' War. Across the course of the war English monarchs were repeatedly forced to convene Parliament in order to gain quick access to much needed funds to prosecute the war effort. Before granting monies to the crown, however, the House of Commons, consisting of merchants and lesser nobility, insisted on "redress of grievances before consent to taxation." As a result, the House of Commons eventually gained the right to introduce all important tax legislation in Parliament, it was granted its first speaker in 1376, and it was given the right to impeach irresponsible members of the king's government.

The Great Schism, 1378–1417

▨ Center of Hussite activity	▨ Areas recognizing Rome-based pope
▨ Area most affected by teachings of John Wycliffe	▨ Areas recognizing Avignon-based pope

MAP **11.8** The Great Schism, 1378–1417.

European Commerce and Trade

Europe's fifteenth-century economic recovery was even more pronounced in commerce. When France regained control of Flanders during the course of the Hundred Years' War, England—currently at war with the French—was forced to abandon its profitable wool trade with Flemish merchants. As a result, England developed a far more lucrative trade in manufactured cloth products, of which by 1500 it had become a leading exporter. Flemish towns changed practices as well, switching from the sale of expensive finished garments to trade in cheaper cloths that were sold to wider markets.

When the Hundred Years' War disrupted trade in France, new lanes of commerce opened up across Europe. Germanic towns in northern Europe had formed a trading alliance, known as the **Hanseatic League** (from *hansa*, meaning "company") as early as the thirteenth century. The league reached the peak of its influence during the later fourteenth and fifteenth centuries, with trading links from London in the west to Novgorod in eastern Europe. A new commercial axis extended from the cities of the Hanseatic League in the north southward to the northern Italian cities of Venice and Genoa. Crossing the Alps, this new trade route stretched through the German states to the northern reaches of Europe.

Hanseatic League: A trade network of allied ports along the North Sea and Baltic coasts, founded in 1256.

Of crucial importance for the future of European trade was the collapse of the so-called Pax Mongolica in 1368. Following the expansion of the Mongol Empire during the thirteenth and fourteenth centuries, travel and trade networks flourished between China and the West across the Silk Road. Thus, the Mongols facilitated the transfer of significant technological innovations from China to Europe, including gunpowder and mechanical clocks. When, however, Mongol rule in China dissolved and was replaced by the Ming dynasty, less interested in ties with the West, travel on the Silk Road was no longer safe or profitable. Faced with the necessity of reaching the riches of the East by alternate means, European merchants were forced to resort to southern maritime routes, in use from the 750s onward.

Innovations in Business Techniques

A combination of innovative economic practices contributed to a revitalization of Europe's economy during the fifteenth century. Smaller markets, caused by the economic crises of the fourteenth century, brought on increased competition among merchants, who sought ever more creative business methods in order to remain solvent. New accounting procedures, such as double-entry bookkeeping, increased the efficiency of record keeping. In addition, the introduction of maritime insurance, which protected investments in risky seaborne trade, fueled an increase in trans-Mediterranean trade and commerce, while at the same time increasing profits for individual investors.

New banking procedures also facilitated the expansion of Europe's economy by providing loans to merchants and manufacturers and by establishing bills of exchange (a form of credit, or payment by checks, drawn on funds on deposit in banks), which greatly eased long-distance financial translations. Florence emerged across the fifteenth century as the center of huge banking partnerships, like the Bardi, Peruzzi, and Medici; and although the Bardi and Peruzzi eventually collapsed, the Medici family went on to dominate Florentine civic affairs by 1500.

Developments in the Church

As a consequence of the disintegration of papal leadership during the fourteenth century, the church was controlled by councils of bishops in the early fifteenth century. The movement that emerged from the decisions made by the Council of Constance was known as *conciliarism*. In order to resolve the crises of the fourteenth century, the Council of Constance (1414–1417) was convened by the Holy Roman emperor. Its first order of business was to depose the three reigning popes and to restore papal authority to a single pontiff, who took the name Martin V (r. 1417–1431). Second, to put an end to heretical movements, principally the followers of John Wycliffe, the council convicted John Huss of heresy and burned him at the stake. The execution of Huss had momentous implications for the future of the church, especially in Germany.

Bankers. A Florentine banker and his assistant seated on their *bancum* (bench) in which they kept their *conti* (accounts).

Huss's region of Bohemia emerged as a hotbed of heresy, and these anticlerical sentiments helped fuel Martin Luther's Protestant Reformation, which began in neighboring Saxony in the next century. Finally, to improve the management of the church, the council declared that henceforth councils of bishops would meet frequently in order to place popes under their strict control.

The conciliar movement was an attempt by the bishops to wrest control of the church from popes and to manage church affairs on their own through a succession of councils. The popes resisted the conciliar movement but had to make concessions to secular rulers to gain their support. In 1438, for example, the Pragmatic Sanction of Bourges granted the French king control over church affairs in France. The Pragmatic Sanction of Mainz, issued the following year, conceded control over church matters to the Holy Roman emperor. The result of these concessions was the further weakening of the Roman Church and the creation of national churches, independent of control from Rome.

Literature   Equally as dramatic as new directions in religion were significant and widespread changes in literary expression. Most basic was the growing popularity of cultural expression in the vernacular instead of Latin. Although the vernacular first made its appearance in France in the later 1100s, education in the vernacular was especially popular in the city-states of northern Italy, where the emphasis was on educating students for productive careers in the secular world, rather than training them to become priests. In Florence, for example, classes were increasingly conducted in the vernacular Italian (not in Latin, the language of the church) and students learned the basics of reading, writing, and accounting in their native language.

Consistent with the increase in vernacular literacy, particularly in Florence, a number of Italian authors chose to write in the vernacular rather than in Latin. A particularly noteworthy example is the poet Dante Alighieri (1265–1321), author of *The Divine Comedy*, a long epic poem written in Italian and completed in 1321. The theme of Dante's *Divine Comedy* is the author's journey from the pit of hell, through the torments of purgatory, and into the blessings of paradise. In terms of political thought, too, Dante moves beyond medieval conceptions. In his *On Monarchy*, completed in 1313, Dante anticipates Marsilius of Padua (ca. 1275–1342) in placing kings and emperors over popes: "… it is agreed that the whole of mankind is ordered to one goal, ... there must therefore be one person who directs and rules mankind, and he is properly called 'Monarch,' or 'Emperor.'"

Two Italian authors of the next generation continued Dante's legacy. Francesco Petrarch (1304–1374), known as "the father of Renaissance humanism," turned to Roman authors and classical texts, whose values more closely resembled the secular, materialistic world of everyday life in Florence. Petrarch also wrote a series of love sonnets to his beloved Laura, in Tuscan Italian. In Giovanni Boccaccio (1313–1375) also we move even further from the medieval toward the Renaissance. Boccaccio's *Decameron*, written between 1352 and 1353, is a collection of bawdy stories and erotic themes on such topics as adultery and fornication. The *Decameron* represents a further drift away from medieval literary conventions—and toward the Roman classical past—in that it draws its inspiration from the first-century Roman author Petronius and his scandalous *Satyricon*.

English and French writers of the fourteenth century also began to produce works in their native languages. *Piers Plowman*, composed in Middle English by William Langland (ca. 1332–1400), presents a series of complaints and laments about current abuses in late fourteenth-century England, especially among the aristocracy and the clergy. Geoffrey Chaucer (ca. 1340–1400), a friend and contemporary of Langland's, also wrote in Middle English. Like Langland, Chaucer satirized abuses in contemporary society. His *Canterbury Tales* are a series of stories told by travelers making their annual pilgrimage from London to the shrine of St. Thomas Becket in Canterbury. Christine de Pizan (ca. 1364–1430) of France composed both poetry and prose; she was primarily concerned with advancing the status of women and for her criticisms of male behaviors is often considered the first feminist writer. In her *Epistle to the God of Love*, for example, she criticizes the Roman poet Ovid for attributing to women:

> "... nasty ways,
> Repulsive, sordid, filled with wickedness.
> That women have such vices I deny;
> I take my arms up in defense of them..."

Philosophy   Running parallel with new dimensions in literature were bold departures in philosophy that challenged basic medieval theological beliefs. In place of St. Thomas Aquinas' attempt to reconcile differences between the truths of faith and reason, the intellectual world of fourteenth-century Europe turned decidedly toward the latter, especially toward Aristotle. The earliest philosopher to take this approach was the Oxford Franciscan John Duns Scotus (ca. 1266–1308). Critical of Aquinas, Scotus argued for the strict separation of reason from theology. William of Ockham (ca. 1285–1349), another Oxford Franciscan, carried the assault on the Aquinas synthesis even further. He argued for extreme nominalism, arguing that only the truths of reason, vested in individual things, could be known for certain. Therefore, no metaphysical knowledge is possible; and from this, it is impossible to have any sure knowledge of the existence of God. That being the case, only a personal, mystical association with God was available to the believer.

Putting It All Together

Following the collapse of the united Mediterranean Roman Empire, a new postclassical, Christian religious civilization gradually developed in western Europe during the period ca. 600–1400. The Germanic invasions that brought down Roman rule in the western provinces destroyed imperial unity in the West and created in Europe a series of smaller political entities. After a brief period of centralized imperial rule during the reign of Charlemagne in the later eighth century, medieval Europe fell back in the ninth and tenth centuries into a pattern of decentralized political entities that provided for law and order at the local, instead of an empire-wide, level. Feudalism, as this arrangement is known, prevented the reassertion of a centralized European empire and prepared Europe for the appearance of several highly centralized, competing kingdoms. One advantage of this "political pluralism" was the appearance of competition among the states of Europe, which in turn created a sense of vitality and progress in the West.

In terms of cultural developments, the Germanic invasions and subsequent destruction of Roman rule in the West were far more disruptive than anywhere else on the globe and forced the formation of a new, distinctly European, postclassical culture. Whereas other civilizations experienced similar periods of chaos, these were often mere interruptions, to be followed by the reappearance of slightly altered pre-existing cultural patterns. In Europe, however, a brand new culture began to emerge from the rubble of the disintegration of the Greco-Roman classical civilization,

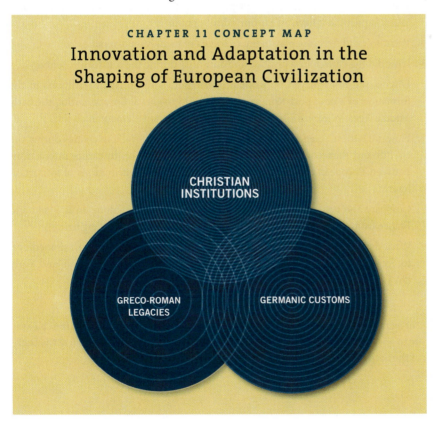

CHAPTER 11 CONCEPT MAP
Innovation and Adaptation in the Shaping of European Civilization

CHRISTIAN INSTITUTIONS

GRECO-ROMAN LEGACIES

GERMANIC CUSTOMS

formed from a blending of three elements that had formerly been antagonistic to each other: Roman legacies, Germanic customs, and Christian institutions (see Concept Map). Of these, the role of the Christian Church would prove the most important in the long run in shaping a new European religious civilization. In much the same way that Buddhism, Hinduism, Confucianism, and Islam undergirded civilizations in Asia and Africa, Christianity served as the basic unifying force that held together the new European civilization.

During the fourteenth century Europe experienced several transforming events. The horrors of famine and plague, accompanied by over a century of warfare between England and France, cast a pall of gloom over European society, which in turn called into question traditional medieval values and perspectives. In addition, a series of internal problems in the church resulted in a lessening of its authority and prestige. At the same time, however, several developments—particularly in the cultural arts—prepared Europe for the transition to Renaissance secularism and humanism.

Review and Respond

1. What were Charlemagne's most important contributions to the development of medieval Europe?

2. Discuss at least three key factors in the development of the agricultural revolution in Europe during the eleventh century.

3. When and where did the Black Plague originate? Where and how did it spread? What impact did it have on Europe's development?

4. What role did Aristotle play in the curricula of medieval universities?

5. How did the church lose prestige and authority during the fourteenth century?

6. Discuss the roles played by Roman, Germanic, and Christian traditions in the formation of a new, post-Roman civilization in medieval Europe during the early Middle Ages. Why was Christianity such an important element in all this?

7. How did natural science originate and develop in medieval universities during the twelfth and thirteenth centuries? Pay particular attention to earlier interactions between European and Islamic scholars. Discuss the contributions of important figures.

8. Compare and contrast the development of centralized kingdoms in England and France from ca. 1000 to 1300. Refer to the contributions of leading figures.

9. What developments would you identify as signaling the transition from medieval to Renaissance institutions and perspectives during the fourteenth and early fifteenth centuries? Cite specific examples in support of your answer.

> For additional resources, including maps, primary sources, visuals, and quizzes, please go to www.oup.com/us/vonsivers. Please see the Further Resources section at the back of the book for additional readings and suggested websites.

Thinking Through Patterns

▶ **How did the Merovingians and Carolingians construct a new Christian European civilization during the seventh and eighth centuries CE?**

The Merovingians and Carolingians constructed a new Christian European civilization during the seventh and eighth centuries by utilizing the support of the Christian Church. Through their conversion to Christianity, as well as their support and encouragement of monastic expansion, they earned the support of bishops, priests, and monks in all regions of their kingdom. In addition, the creation of the Franco-papal alliance during the eighth century, followed by Charlemagne's personal involvement in church affairs, ensured the emergence of a new Christian foundation for Europe.

Some key factors in the political, economic, and social recovery of Europe during the eleventh and twelfth centuries included the emergence of centralized kingdoms in France and England, which replaced the decentralized cells of political authority during the ninth and tenth centuries. The expansion of agricultural advances and the development of commerce and trade produced a population surge, which in turn resulted in urbanization and the emergence of a new bourgeois middle class of merchants and traders.

▶ **What were key factors in the political, economic, and social recovery of Europe during the eleventh and twelfth centuries?**

▶ **What were some cultural and intellectual developments during the "twelfth-century renaissance," and how did they contribute to medieval civilization?**

During the "twelfth-century renaissance" urban-centered cathedral schools developed into universities in Europe. In order to serve the needs of an expanding urban and commercial economy, more practical disciplines like law and medicine were developed in revised curricula. The influx of Aristotelian logic and science, assimilated from contacts in Spain and Sicily between Latin scholars—known as the Latin translators—and their Islamic counterparts, resulted in a prolonged debate between the truths of reason and the truths of faith. Although temporarily resolved by Aquinas in the later thirteenth century, Aristotelian nominalism dominated philosophy and theology in the fourteenth century. Another result of the fascination with Aristotle was the development of natural science at Oxford and Paris, which during the later thirteenth and early fourteenth centuries began to uncover flaws in Aristotelian celestial and terrestrial scientific conceptions.

As a result of a series of ecclesiastical reforms in both the monastic and episcopal arms of the church, a series of increasingly powerful popes began to assert papal primacy over secular rulers and, indeed, over all European institutions. Pope Gregory VII humbled the German emperor Henry IV in the eleventh century, and Pope Innocent III did the same with King John of England in the beginning of the thirteenth century.

▶ **How did the church influence political developments in Europe during the twelfth and thirteenth centuries?**

▶ **What events made fourteenth-century Europe so dismal? How did these combine to spell the gradual demise of medieval institutions and perspectives?**

The "calamitous fourteenth century" witnessed several unprecedented setbacks that, taken together, signaled the end of the medieval era and the early stages of the Renaissance era. Among these events were the Black Death, the Hundred Years' War, and the Avignon papacy followed by the Great Schism, which produced not one, not two, but eventually three popes. At the same time men of letters, philosophers, as well as theologians began to challenge earlier assertions of papal authority, resulting in the Council of Constance in (1414–1417), which ultimately replaced papal control of the church with councils of bishops during the fifteenth century.

Chapter 12
600-1600 CE
Contrasting Patterns in India and China

CHINA

INDIA

While Arab armies had worked their way through Sasanid Persia by the middle of the seventh century CE, their first reports on northwest India were not terribly encouraging. The land was described as desert waste, with few resources and a hostile populace. They made at least 10 attempts to invade the northwest Indian region of Sind, and all 10 times they were defeated by local rulers. According to the *Chachnama* (the history of the campaign written hundreds of years later, in the thirteenth century), following these failed attempts a more ambitious invasion was mounted by Muhammad Ibn Qasim, a cousin of the governor of Iraq who was responsible for the conquest of eastern lands.

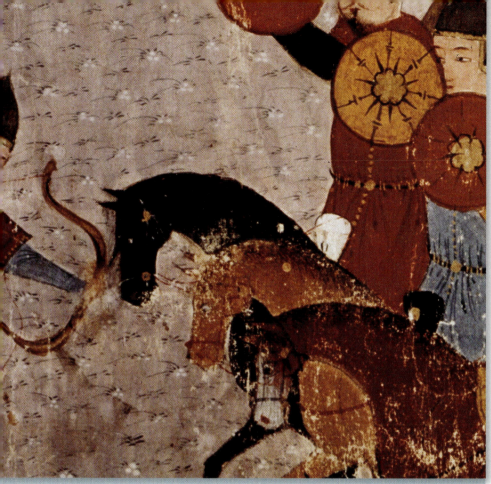

Seeing Patterns

▶ How did interactions between Muslims and Hindus in India lead to religious syncretism?

▶ What steps were taken by Hindus and Muslims to lessen the conflicts between the two rival religious traditions?

▶ How was the Tang dynasty in China different from its predecessors and successors?

▶ How effectively did the religious and philosophical traditions of Buddhism, Confucianism, and Daoism blend together in creating Neo-Confucianism? Where did they clash?

Ibn Qasim's army pursued the move into India with brutal efficiency. Wearing coats of chain mail armor and equipped with siege machinery for hurling projectiles and battering down walls, they decimated the major cities, executed most of the defenders, and extracted plunder and slaves before moving in to completely occupy the area in 711 CE. Though Ibn Qasim's rule in the wake of his violent conquest was considered relatively moderate, the *Chachnama* claims that he met his death through a spectacular episode of duplicity concocted by his new subjects.

When the daughters of Dihar, the ruler of the conquered city of Dehal (Karachi in modern Pakistan), were taken back to the governor of Iraq as tribute, they accused Ibn Qasim of making sexual advances toward them. The governor immediately ordered his cousin Ibn Qasim to be sewn up in a stifling raw leather sheath and transported home. This torturous mode of transport was meant to inflict maximal suffering, and indeed, the heat and lack of room for breathing soon did their work. Ibn Qasim died 2 days into the journey, and when his putrefied body was shown to the women who had accused him, they proudly confessed their deception and revenge on their conqueror.

Fearsome Warriors. Mongol archers, from a fourteenth-century illustration, rain arrows on their enemies. Mongol horsemanship and composite bows were used with devastating effect in battle. One favorite tactic was to advance within range of the enemy and fire rounds of arrows into its midst, inflicting high casualties, and then suddenly retreat before the opposing army had the chance to counterattack. For nearly 90 years the Mongols ruled China, and though they never conquered India, another fierce warrior from central Asia, Timur-leng, sacked Delhi in 1398.

Though the reliability of the account is questionable, it has come to symbolize the dramatic clash of cultural and religious outlooks that have marked the history of the Indian subcontinent ever since. In this contested area between radically different religious civilizations, the Hindu vision of Islam has remained one of ruthless conquest and purposeful disregard for long-established religious traditions. Muslims, on the other hand, have tended to view Hindus as despised infidels for whom no act of treachery is out of bounds. Such competing visions, despite periodic efforts to find common ground, have created over the centuries the pattern of *syncretic* social and political formation (a pattern in which two different traditions evolve with little or no common ground). In this case, the two cultures actually coexist with considerable hostility toward one another. Despite extensive interaction, neither side has adopted much from the other; in fact, the dominant pattern has been that each has used the differences of the other to define its own religious civilization more consciously and distinctly.

The case of China provides a useful contrast. Here, despite a pervasive belief among officials and scholars of the Song dynasty (960–1279) that the fall of the previous dynasty, the Tang, had come about in large part because of the influence of the "foreign" religion of Buddhism, there were no mass persecutions or forced conversions. While Song Confucian scholars tended to lecture their audiences about "unseemly" Buddhist "superstitions," they also borrowed from Buddhist cosmological perspectives and Daoist beliefs to create a pattern of *synthetic* social and political formation (a pattern in which the most durable opposing elements merge together into a compatible whole). The result was a coherent Chinese religious civilization for the next 1,000 years, based on Neo-Confucianism, the fused body of Daoist and Buddhist religious traditions, and Confucian ethics.

India: The Clash of Cultures

As we saw in Chapter 8, the early centuries of the Common Era marked the maturing of two large divisions among the multiple varieties of religious and cultural experience of India. The first was the rise and spread of Buddhism out of northern India into central Asia via the Silk Road and on to China and ultimately to Korea, Japan, and Vietnam. Along the way, the main branches of the various Buddhist schools were created—Theravada and Mahayana—and their scriptural foundations solidified.

More important for the long term of Indian history, however, was that the efforts of the Guptas during India's "golden age" from the fourth to the sixth centuries CE helped in the maturation of the vast variety of religious practices that we know as "Hinduism." For it was Hinduism, rather than Buddhism, that would dominate Indian cultural and religious life until Islam ultimately established itself in the north. In the south and some areas of the north, however, Hinduism remained the dominant religious tradition down to the present day. Hence, India was transformed from a Hindu religious civilization into a frontier between the competing religious civilizations of Islam and Hinduism.

India After the Guptas

By the 500s CE, the last Gupta monarchs were under increasing pressure from a branch of the central Asian Huns pressing on their borders. Following the old invasion routes through the Khyber Pass into northern India, the Huns established themselves in the Punjab and adjacent regions and soon settled in to create new states as the Gupta lands shrank and finally dissolved.

Harsha Vardhana   One relatively stable regime that achieved a certain degree of power in the north following the Guptas was that of Thanesar [TAHN-uh-sar] under its ruler Harsha Vardhana (r. 606–647). Like Ashoka of the Mauryans, Harsha is one of the few Indian monarchs about whom we know a good deal. The *Harshacarita* or *Life of Harsha*, by the poet Bana and the account of the famous Chinese Buddhist pilgrim Xuan Zang (see Chapter 9), who traveled throughout India from 630 to 644, offer a number of insights into Harsha's reign.

When Xuan Zang met Harsha in his capital at Kanauj on the Ganges River, he discovered that the ruler was a devout Buddhist. Xuan Zang's account notes the degree to which Buddhism had once permeated the land, despite the favoritism shown by the Guptas earlier toward Hinduism. It was also clear, however, that many Buddhist monasteries were now abandoned or in disrepair. Bolstered by the new devotional

Harsha's Empire, ca. 645 CE

MAP **12.1** Harsha's Empire, ca. 645 CE.

strains of Hinduism, the decline of Buddhism on the subcontinent as a whole was well advanced.

Still, Xuan Zang found Harsha's kingdom well run, wealthy, justly administered, and in many ways a model state. The state, however, barely outlived its ruler. The middle years of Harsha's reign saw the new power of the Arabs probing the borders of Sind, the arid plain to the east of the Indus River, in advance of their full conquest in 711. Meanwhile, following Harsha's reign, northern India was once again divided into regional kingdoms (see Map 12.1).

In the interim, the political center of the subcontinent had shifted south. By the latter part of the ninth century, a Chola [KO-luh] state based in Tanjore [Tan-JO-ray] had concluded its long and bitter contest with the Pallavis. In 897 they captured Kanchipuram [Kan-chih-POOR-um], advanced into the Pandya kingdom in the southern tip of the peninsula, and captured their capital at Madurai. In the next century, the Cholas conquered Kerala, invaded Sri Lanka, and launched campaigns aimed at expanding their control of the trade with southeast Asia. The Cholas then advanced northward, allying themselves with the eastern Chalukyas in 1030. In the west, however, the revived western Chalukyas absorbed the Rashtakutras in 970 and repeatedly fought the Cholas to a standstill.

In the meantime, the development of the clove trade of the Moluccas (in what is now Indonesia) vastly increased the strategic value of the area, which the Indian-influenced

(*a*) **Rajarajeshwara Temple, Tanjore India.** This early eleventh-century Hindu temple is the largest in all of India and one of the most beautiful. It was richly endowed with spoils taken from Chola conquests.

(*b*) **Temple of Narasimba-Varman II Near Madras.** This early eighth-century temple of the Pallava king Narasimba-Varman II was built on the shore at Mamallapuram along the southeast coast of peninsular India. It represents one of the first examples of the new Hindu temple architecture spreading through the south from the seventh century on.

Sumatran state of Srivijaya attempted to exploit in the tenth and eleventh centuries. In response to the exorbitant rates and threats of piracy Srivijaya posed, the Cholas sent a maritime expedition in 1025 that smashed its major ports and reduced its power for a time. In this context, the coming of the Arabs to India resulted in a broadening of the subcontinent's position in world trade. Along the western ports of India, Arab merchants continued to ply their trade much as before. Despite the newfound religious antagonisms, caravan traffic also continued much as before and India became the bottom leg of a triangle of trade that spanned Eurasia (see Map 12.2).

Vijayanagar   After several centuries of expansion southward by Muslim sultanates in north and central India, a new Hindu state emerged in 1336 with the founding of the city of Vijayanagar ("City of Victory"). The last in the two-millennium pattern of rule by god-kings, the new state was deemed fabulously wealthy by visitors to its capital, including the first Portuguese traders in the sixteenth century. From the City of Victory, the rulers presided over an arrangement that, like the Gupta Empire, some scholars have described as feudal as it absorbed the remnants of the older southern kingdoms. For example, local leaders called *nayaks* collected taxes and provided men and provisions for the army, while retaining considerable autonomy within their own realms.

For more than 200 years the state of Vijayanagar withstood penetration by the various Islamic sultanates of the north. In fact, following the destruction of the Tugh-Lug line of Muslim rulers in Delhi in 1398, Vijayanagar and its associated Hindu

MAP 12.2 Eurasian Trade Routes, ca. 1000 CE.

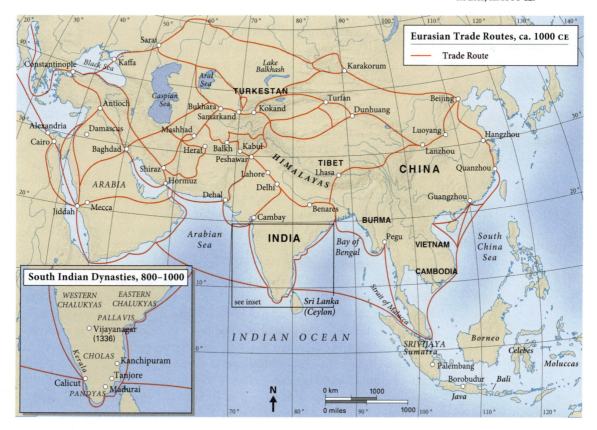

nayaks expanded their control to nearly the entire southern third of India. In 1564, however, their huge armies were decimated by a regional coalition of northern sultanates whose forces were equipped with the newest technologies—cannon and small arms. The city of Vijayanagar was abandoned, and for the next several centuries various *nayaks* ruled independently in different areas of the peninsula. By this time, however, Hindu India was already centuries into an ideological, political, and military struggle that continues in many respects to this day. For despite their cultural domination, the power of the Hindu southern states was being eclipsed by the most potent outside force the region had yet faced: Islamic religious civilization.

Islam in India, 711–1398

As we have seen, conquering Arabs incorporated much of modern Afghanistan, Pakistan, and some parts of northwest India into their empire during the early 700s. But for several centuries the rest of India experienced the religion of Islam, which arose in the wake of the Arab conquests, more peacefully through maritime trade conducted by Muslim merchants. In central Asia, Arab armies moving eastward along the caravan routes advanced through conquest, settling in the cities of Turkestan and raiding into the territories of Turkic nomadic tribes. During 700–1000, first Arab governors and later Persian autonomous rulers supported a profitable slave trade.

The Career of Mahmud of Ghazna   The Persian rulers in Iran and central Asia enrolled these slaves in their palace guards and converted them to Islam. The son of one of these slave officers was Sultan Mahmud of Ghazna, who declared himself independent of his Persian overlord and conquered the city of Ghazna in Afghanistan. In 997 Mahmud embarked on a career of expansion lasting three decades, until his death in 1030. His tactical brilliance and utter ruthlessness have left his name both revered and reviled in Muslim and Hindu circles ever since.

Early in his career, Mahmud conquered an immense territory comprising part of Iran as well as Afghanistan and Turkestan. The wealth he extracted from this empire turned Ghazna into an opulent city and left the door open for the next round of expeditions into the old Ganges River states (see Map 12.3).

A New Style of Warfare   For those encountering Mahmud and his successors for the first time, the scope and ferocity of these raids were especially unsettling. Warfare among the Hindu states had been the exclusive domain of the military castes. With casualties largely limited to the combatants and the various opponents sharing the same religious and cultural traditions, society as a whole generally suffered a minimum of disruption. The Muslims, however, tended to practice warfare on a much wider scale and saw their role of spreading the rule of Islam as central. Consequently, in addition to the destruction involved in the conquest and looting of an area, they frequently attempted widespread changes involving the destruction of temples; the establishment of shari`a, or quranic law, in occupied areas; and the imposition of the head tax (*jizya*) on non-Muslims—though practical rulers learned over time to go about this judiciously.

The Northern Sultanates Mahmud and his successors, the Ghaznavids, ruled for nearly two centuries. The provinces of their empire, however, were too disparate—ranging from the central Asian desert to the rain forests of northern India—to cohere. A Persian ruler subject to the Ghaznavids, Muhammad of Ghur, declared his independence and conquered most Ghaznavid lands. In 1192, he defeated the Rajputs, considered Hindu India's most ferocious warriors, allegedly killing 100,000 soldiers. Striking deep into northern India, Muhammad set up a Muslim state at Delhi. He subsequently lost his territories in the north, but the Indian state he had set up endured (1181–1526) under the name of the "Sultanate of Delhi." The founders of this state were, like many state builders we have seen in Islamic history, Turkic generals of slave origin who seized power after the death of Muhammad. Their successors were Turkic and Afghan dynasties who ruled until the invasion of Babur, the Mongol-descended founder of the Mughal Empire of India in 1526 (see Map 12.4).

MAP **12.3** **The Empire of Mahmud of Ghazna.**

The Delhi Sultanate successfully weathered an attempted invasion by Genghis Khan in 1222, whose military campaigns had so devastated the lands of southwest Asia and central Europe. Among the more colorful rulers of the Delhi Sultanate was the female sultan Raziya, who ruled from 1236 to 1240. Raziya seized the throne from her dissolute brother and, in an even more provocative move, dispensed with the veil required of Muslim women and wore male attire on the battlefield. During her short reign, she pressed south and east to Bengal and settled Muslim refugees from Mongol-controlled lands within her own domains. A scandal involving her liaison with an Ethiopian adviser soon sparked a conspiracy against her. Captured while suppressing one of the accompanying revolts,

Qutb Minaret, Delhi. The sense of the northern Indian sultanates being a sanctuary for Muslims from other locales translated into efforts on the part of rulers to outperform their counterparts. The wealth of the area allowed them the resources with which to build a number of spectacular structures. The Qutb Minar, built next to Delhi's first mosque, is said to still be the world's largest minaret, requiring the efforts of two rulers before being finished by the Tugh-Lug sultan Feroz Shah (d. 1388).

India Under the Sultanate of Delhi

- Sultanate of Delhi, 1236
- Area subject to influence of Sultanate of Delhi, 1335
- Hindu areas not under Muslim control
- Timur-leng's invasion and sack of Delhi, 1398–1399

MAP **12.4** **India Under the Sultanate of Delhi.**

she won over and actually married one of the conspirators. Defeated in an attempt to retake Delhi, Raziya and her new husband were ultimately killed as they tried to escape.

The renewed Mongol expansion which led to the sack of Baghdad and the destruction of the Abbasid caliphate in 1258 was accompanied by raids along the Delhi Sultanate's borders. Out of this unsettled period came the long reign of Balban, who exercised power informally in Delhi for 20 years before ruling in his own right from 1266 through 1287. Balban's iron hand in suppressing potential rivals resulted in a succession struggle at his death, and a new set of sultans, the Khalijis, came to power in 1290. Like nearly all of their predecessors, the Khalijis soon expanded into southern India, where they acquired loot and established a short-lived overlordship. The court politics of the sultanates were always ripe with intrigue because of the vulnerability of the relatives of the heir apparent. On accession to the throne, a sultan's family members were routinely executed to prevent succession battles. Frequently, they secured the loyalty of ambitious allies on the outside in order to forestall their own deaths. Slaves were largely insulated from these intrigues and, thus, constituted a favorite group of potential supporters; indeed, it was possible for an ambitious slave to seize power in his own right.

A product of this situation was Ala-ud-din, who gained the sultanate by assassinating his predecessor. On his death in 1316, a short period of uncertainty prevailed until the 1320 accession of the Tugh-Lug rulers, who held power until 1413. Perhaps the most controversial ruler of the line was Muhammad Ibn Tugh-Lug (d. 1351), named by his detractors "Muhammad the Bloody." Discontent over high taxes, debased coinage, famine, and ruthless atrocities against his enemies was prevalent during his reign. Such acts, however, seemed to contradict his considerably more peaceful personal attainments. By all accounts he was highly educated, a renowned poet and calligrapher, and humble and chaste in his behavior at court. Regardless of the ultimate effects of his rule, by the time of his death at mid-century, powerful forces were once again gathering to the north. Within a few decades they would bring about the end of Tugh-Lug rule and alter the region's politics for generations to come.

Toward the Mughal Era, 1398–1450

In 1398, one of the last great invasions of central Asian nomads, that of Timur—also Timur-leng or Tamerlane, "Timur the Lame" (r. 1370-1405) on account of a riding accident—descended on northern India and southwest Asia. Though

Tughluqabad Fort. Anxious to preserve their rule as a minority surrounded by a restive Hindu population and ringed by potentially hostile states, the sultans of the north took considerable pains to erect defensive works. This example is Tughluqabad Fort in Delhi, built by the first Tugh-Lug sultan, Ghiyas-ud-din, between 1321 and 1325.

himself a Muslim, Timur did not spare the Muslim capital of Delhi. He went on in 1402 to defeat the Ottoman Empire in the Middle East, but his giant empire did not survive his death in 1405. Nevertheless, though the wave of violence accompanying his conquests quickly subsided, his invasion had broken the power of the ruling Tugh-Lugs. Two smaller sultanates, those of the Sayyids (1414–1451) and the Lodis (1451–1526), held the area around Delhi. Once again, northern India had moved into a period of political disorder.

Meanwhile, the Mongol Empire put together by Genghis Khan and his successors had long since broken into various feuding regional states, a number of which had converted to Islam. In Ferghana, a small central Asian state astride the Silk Road—famous for centuries for its Turkoman or Nisean horses—a fifth-generation descendant of Timur, Zahir-ud-din-Muhammad, was born in 1484. Early on, he adopted the name of "Babur," the Tiger. The dynasty he would found, that of the Mughals, was destined to be India's last empire.

Economics in Islamic India   India's rich economy generated repeated political problems. It continually attracted invasions by outsiders eager to take advantage of its wealth. While scholars have long debated whether the first Arab and Turkic incursions into India were motivated primarily by religious or economic reasons or a combination of the two, the vast wealth accumulated as a result provided ample justification for continuing them. Like the constantly feuding southern states of the subcontinent, the turnover of goods acquired through raids and warfare helped finance the economies of the emerging northern Muslim sultanates. Even after these states became financially stable, the attraction of the wealth of the southern states resulted in frequent expeditions against them for financial gain.

The northern sultanates also supported their economies through heavy taxation. In addition to the *jizya* tax on nonbelievers, Ala-ud-din of the Tugh-Lugs, for example, instituted a 50 percent land tax, taxes on the ownership of milk cows, and a household tax. Beyond this, he embarked on an ambitious campaign to institute wage and price controls on a dizzying array of occupations and commodities in order to keep food prices low and urban granaries full. In this, Ala-ud-din was surpassed in zeal by the notorious Muhammad "The Bloody" Tugh-Lug, who had one tax offender flayed alive, his skin stuffed and mounted, and his remains served as a meal to his unfortunate relatives.

Muhammad also instituted price controls and attempted to stabilize the currency by minting new gold coins, debasing silver ones, and manufacturing bronze tokens for use as temporary currency, measures ultimately abandoned as disruptive to the economy. Despite the sultans' constant need for money, however, Muslim prohibitions against **usury** kept banking and capital firmly in the hands of Hindus, Buddhists, and *Parsees* (descendants of Zoroastrian emigrants from Persia).

Usury: For Christians, the sin of lending money at high rates of interest; for Muslims, charging any interest at all on money loaned.

Muslims and Caste   The role of Islam in calling the faithful together as equals tended to appeal to those most discontented with the caste system. Islam's minority status in India, however, meant that it was never possible to carve out an Islamic state within the sultanates in the same fashion as had been the case in other parts of the Muslim sphere.

Over time, a certain amount of cross-cultural compromise was reluctantly granted on both sides. Nearly all Hindu and Muslim sects were eventually allowed to practice to some degree, with the dress and markings distinguishing different castes allowed to continue. Muslim repugnance toward Hindu nakedness—as in the case of devotees of certain gods and the working attire of some of the lower castes—as well as discomfort with Hindu concepts of religious sexuality, gradually became less overt. At the same time, Hindus in some areas adopted the Muslim practice of veiling women.

By the time it established itself as a dominant presence in northern India, Islam had developed a complete package of law and customs centered on the Quran and tradition in which the place of women and that of the family were sharply defined. The family was central in a social order defined by Allah through revelations to Muhammad and governed by sharia, that is, the complete body of Islamic moral and legal precepts. Unlike the strict monogamy of the Hindus, a Muslim man could have up to four wives, and divorce, while permissible in Islam, was far easier for men than women.

The Sikhs   Despite their profoundly different worldviews, traditions, and practices, by the fifteenth century the unique position of the Muslim sultanates of northern India as havens for refugees from the ravages of the Mongols, as well as for Sufis (practitioners of Islamic mysticism) and Muslim dissidents, provided a rare opportunity for interchange between Muslim and Hindu sects. Starting with the poet Kabir (1440–1518), the commonalities of the ecstatic, mystical experience of communion with the absolute shared alike by Hindu and Muslim devotional sects was the subject of repeated attempts to find common ground between their two faiths.

The climax of this movement came with the guru ("teacher") Nanak (1469–1539), who founded the faith of **Sikhism**, *sikh* meaning "disciple," which also emphasized a direct emotional experience with the divine. Combining elements of Hinduism and Islam, the Sikhs, due to religious persecution in the seventeenth century, eventually became more of a fighting faith, a stance that, even to the present, has served to continually place them at odds with various Indian governments.

Sikhism: Indian religion founded by Nanak Guru that combines elements of Hindu and Muslim traditions.

While Sikhism at first appeared to be a step toward reconciliation between Islam and Hinduism, it in fact became the exception that proved the rule of their competition. Indeed, both Hindus and Muslims opposed the Sikhs and they were persecuted a number of times under the Mughals. India thus remained a syncretic religious and cultural society among the world's religious civilizations. The experience of China, on the other hand, would be far less traumatic.

Interactions and Adaptations: From Buddhism to Neo-Confucian Synthesis in China

The Tang dynasty (618–907) marked the completion of the reconstitution of the Chinese empire begun under the Sui. At its height, the influence of Buddhism at the imperial court, especially with the famous Empress Wu, made China a Buddhist empire. Since the Han, China's ideology had been based on the ethics of Confucianism combined with the imperial structure inherited from the Qin (see Chapter 9). By the mid-600s this ideology of statehood had fused with Mahayana Buddhism to give China for the first time an overtly religious civilization. China thus dramatically joined the ranks of Hindu India (soon to be split by Islam), the growing spread of the Islamic caliphates, the Christian eastern Roman Empire, and the developing states of western Christian Europe as states dominated by a universal religion. Such states would dominate world history until the European Enlightenment and Industrial Revolution created an entirely new type of society.

But the Tang, with their connections to the larger Buddhist cultural sphere, ultimately fell. The dynasty of their successors, the Song (960–1279), has often been seen as the beginning of China's early modern period, supported by the world's largest and most productive agrarian state. The political system that marked China from this period until the twentieth century, however, was in part derived from a departure from Buddhism, which was blamed for the downfall of the Tang. Instead, the new synthesis of official beliefs blended the ideas of three ethical-religious schools—Confucianism, Daoism, and Buddhism—to create a system called "Neo-Confucianism." Unlike India's competing religions, Neo-Confucianism in China had no real religious competitors inside or outside the empire and its debates centered instead on interpretations and approaches to understanding its core teachings—not on the teachings themselves.

Creating a Religious Civilization Under the Tang

As we saw at the end of Chapter 9, the installation by Li Shimin of his father on the throne in 618 saw the founding of the Tang. His dismissal of his father in 627 saw it begin in earnest. For the next 150 years, the dynasty expanded its reach deep into central Asia and made incursions into Korea and Vietnam until its shape resembled a dumbbell, bulging at both ends connected with the narrow territory adjacent to the Silk Road.

Expansion and Consolidation   Determined to complete the consolidation begun under the Sui and expand the empire, the Tang led military expeditions into central Asia. By the end of the seventh century, they had expelled the major nomadic

Nestorian Christianity: Christian sect that was condemned as heretical by Orthodox Christians and Catholics but which spread across central Asia along the Silk Road.

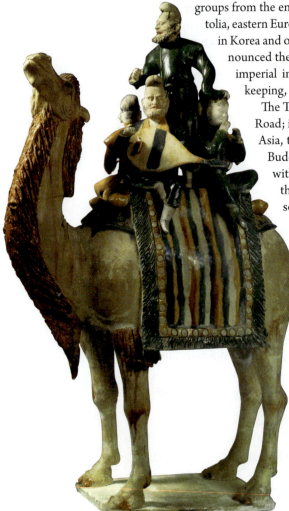

Camel with Musicians. Music played an important role in Tang China and was enjoyed privately as well as on public occasions. This brightly colored glazed earthenware sculpture, dated to 723 CE, shows three musicians riding a Bactrian (two-humped) camel. Their long coats, facial hair, and hats indicate that they are from central Asia; indeed, the lute held by one of the figures is an instrument that was introduced to China from central Asia in the second century CE.

groups from the empire's western borderlands, pushing them west to Anatolia, eastern Europe, and the Mediterranean. The Tang reestablished rule in Korea and opened diplomatic relations with Japan, which in 645 announced the *Taika* (Great Reform)—a wholesale adoption of Tang imperial institutions, Buddhism, Confucian bureaucracy, record keeping, and even architecture.

The Tang Empire's position as the eastern terminus of the Silk Road; its enhanced maritime trade with India, Japan, southeast Asia, the Middle East, and even Africa; and its integration of Buddhist culture led to China's first extensive encounter with the major agrarian–urban societies to the west. During the seventh century, the Umayyad–Abbasid conquests in southwest Asia brought China into contact with the rapidly expanding Arab Empire. In 674, members of the Sasanian Persian royal house fled the advancing Arabs to the Tang capital at Chang'an, bringing in their wake communities of merchants who established a taste among the Tang elites for Arab, Persian, and central Asian musical forms (China's first real orchestral music), dance, silver artwork, and a host of other items.

China's major cities now had quarters set aside for foreign traders, which by the end of the Tang era included Jews, **Nestorian Christians**, Zoroastrians, members of the major Indian traditions, and the beginnings of what would one day be a substantial Muslim minority. Indeed, the modern Chinese city of Xi'an (old Chang'an) even today has a large historic Muslim market area. Arab and Indian intermediaries extended trade from China all the way to the East African coast.

With the Tang Empire expanding, trade booming, and the bureaucracy well staffed and run, the Tang capital of Chang'an grew into perhaps the largest city in the world, with its core comparable in size to Baghdad or Constantinople in the same era and as many as 2 million people living in its metropolitan area. Its streets, official buildings and residences, and south-facing imperial palace dominating the center became the model for urban planning throughout eastern Asia (see Map 12.5).

The Examination System   The Tang refined the bureaucratic structure pioneered by the Han into a form that, with only minor alterations, survived into the twentieth century. The most noteworthy aspect of the Tang bureaucratic structure was the introduction of an examination system for entry into government service. The initial entry-level tests, based on knowledge of the Confucian classics and, for most of the Tang era, Buddhist and Daoist texts, were open to men of all classes except merchants, artisans, and convicted criminals. The few who passed the initial, district-level tests could sit for provincial exams and, if successful, would be eligible for minor posts. Individuals who passed the metropolitan tests, usually held every 3 years in the capital, were eligible for national service. Other reforms undertaken by the Tang included the

East and Central Asia, 618–960

- Tang Empire, 618–960
- Chinese cultural region outside empire
- Area under Tang control, 645–763
- Tang military protectorate, 659–665
- Eastern boundary of the Abbasid caliphate, ca. 750

Jurchens People

✕ Battle

— Silk Road

CHANG'AN

- imperial park
- imperial palace
- imperial city
- west market
- east market
- Great South Gate

PACIFIC OCEAN

Tropic of Cancer

JAPAN

Sea of Japan

KOREA

Yellow Sea

East China Sea

Khitan

Jurchens

Hangzhou

MANCHURIA

Yellow

Luoyang

CHINA

Uighurs

Chang'an

MONGOLIA

Guangzhou

South China Sea

Dunhuang

Yangzi

Beshbaliq 791 ✕

Turfan

YUNNAN

Dali 751 ✕

VIETNAM

Mekong

TURKESTAN

Taklamakan Desert

Talas River 751 ✕

Tashkent

FERGHANA

TIBET

Pamirs

Khotan

HIMALAYAS

Samarkand

Ganges

Caspian Sea

ABBASID CALIPHATE

Indus

INDIA

Bay of Bengal

INDIAN OCEAN

Arabian Sea

Tropic of Cancer

0 km 500

0 miles 500

MAP 12.5 East and Central Asia, 618–960.

creation of a board of censors to check arbitrary behavior among officials, the obligation of lower officials to report the infractions of those above them, and the practice of rotating official posts to prevent individuals from developing local power bases.

The Confucian educational system had a huge impact on Chinese history. Until the twentieth century, it was the only sure route to both wealth and power. Because the exams were open to a relatively large portion of the male population, the goal of state service ensured a degree of social mobility based on merit rather than birth. Schools and academies educated and socialized large groups of people in the Confucian canon, not only in China but also in areas subject to Chinese influence.

At different times, the Vietnamese, Koreans, Manchus, and Japanese all had some variation of a Confucian civil service. The examination system spurred a devotion to education that remains exceptionally strong to this day. Chinese history is replete with tales of family fortunes rising and falling with the progress of a son's studies; of merchants purchasing coveted official degrees; of students taking the tests over and over into their seventies and receiving honorary degrees from the emperor for their lifelong dedication. For all of this lore, however, it should be remembered that only a tiny fraction of the applicants ever passed even the initial round of tests.

Prosperity and Its Discontents   As the prosperity of the Tang dynasty expanded, many of the problems of uneven growth that had plagued the Han dynasty began to reassert themselves. For example, as the center of population continued to move south, the northern regions languished in relative poverty, while the capital grew economically isolated. The agriculturally productive subtropical areas south of the Yangzi now yielded about 90 percent of the empire's taxed grain and contained as much as 70 percent of the population. Moreover, as maritime trade grew and ports increased in size and number, the connecting infrastructure of roads, courier stations, and especially canals required ever more investment and attention. This was a particularly acute problem in the case of communication with the capital. As an administrative center and trade crossroads, the capital city of Chang'an had ballooned to a size that was now unsustainable without constant grain shipments from the south, while its isolation made it particularly vulnerable to attack. Thus, even before the Tang, work on the Grand Canal, connecting the Yangzi and Yellow Rivers, had been pushed forward to enhance water-based transport in the north. Since the capitals of succeeding dynasties tended to be in the old northern heartland as well, this problem of maintaining communication with and provisioning them remained a chronic one throughout the imperial era.

Tang efforts to control military outposts along the Silk Road, with its lucrative trade and Buddhist shrines, brought the empire into conflict with Arab expansion by the early eighth century. Despite some early successes, Tang armies suffered a decisive defeat by the Arabs at the Battle of Talas in 751. This loss followed a series of setbacks at the hands of the Tibetans from 745 to 750 and simultaneous uprisings in the border areas of Manchuria, Korea, and the southern province of Yunnan. From 755 to 762 a general revolt initiated by the Tang commander An Lushan (703–757) devastated large sections of the empire and resulted in heavy land taxes after its suppression. As with the later Han, the dynasty was now in a downward spiral, from which recovery would prove increasingly difficult.

For the next century and a half some economic and political recovery did in fact occur, but the problems of rebuilding and revenue loss persisted, accompanied by a questioning of a number of the premises of the regime, particularly by the

Confucians. For example, Confucians criticized Buddhism for being patronized and subsidized by the Tang court. They were particularly critical of its "foreign" ideas and practices, such as monasticism, celibacy, and personal enlightenment, which contradicted the Confucian standards of filial piety, family life, and public service. At the same time, Buddhist monasteries, which paid no taxes, were tempting targets for an increasingly cash-strapped government. In 845, despite Tang sponsorship of Buddhism, the government forcibly seized all Buddhist holdings, although followers were allowed to continue their religious practices. Even with renewed campaigns against border peoples and other attempts at reinvigorating the empire, sporadic civil war continued for the remainder of the century, leading to the collapse of the Tang dynasty in 906. Following this collapse, China again entered a period of disunity as regional states battled for ultimate control. None of these states would be victorious until the emergence of the Song in 960.

Cosmopolitan Commerce   From the capital in Chang'an, merchants, monks, pilgrims, diplomats, and travelers made their way along the Silk Road, while Chinese, Indian, and Arab ships plied the seas as far away as Africa. The compass, invented by Chinese fortunetellers and adapted for use in keeping to a constant direction at sea, now guided ships throughout the Indian Ocean and southeast Asia. In the Chinese versions of this instrument, however, the needle was considered to point due south—the preferred direction of good fortune and architectural orientation. Spurred by lucrative opportunities, colonies of Chinese merchants could be found throughout the Indian Ocean and southeast Asia; colonies of foreign merchants, including East Africans, Arabs, Persians, Indians, Jews, and Nestorian Christians, all had their own quarters in China's larger port cities, at trade crossroads, and most prominently in the capital.

Among the export items most coveted by foreign merchants were tea and silk. Initially brought to China from southeast Asia, tea quickly established itself as the beverage of choice during the Tang and vied with silk for supremacy as a cash crop during the Song. Tea had a profound effect on the overall health of the population in China, Vietnam, Korea, Japan, and central Asia. Middle Easterners, however, did not adopt it until early modern times. The simple act of boiling water renders tea potable, while the tea itself contains a number of healthful, even medicinal, properties. In addition, its caffeine makes it desirable for those who need to keep alert, such as monks in meditation. Tea production, particularly in the region near the city of Hangzhou, became a major industry and for hundreds of years remained China's most lucrative export item.

The influence of foreigners in art and artifact, fashion, taste, music, and dance marks a radical departure in many respects from the more demure Chinese styles that came before and after. For example, the Persian-influenced costumes of Tang dancers—with their daring and distinctive bare midriffs and transparent tops and trousers—were celebrated at the court in Chang'an but scandalized the more modest sensibilities of later centuries. Indeed, the period saw a number of controversial trends regarding the role and deportment of women.

Empress Wu   The most noted exemplar of these contradictory trends toward both greater restrictiveness and wider latitude in personal behavior was the Tang ruler Wu Zetian, or Empress Wu (r. 690–705). The daughter of a public works official, she spent a brief period at court as a servant to the empress. Disillusioned at life in the capital and drawn to the austerities of Buddhism, she joined a women's monastery, only to return to the palace when her beauty piqued the interest of an imperial prince. Seeing the opportunities this opening presented, she exploited them ably and ruthlessly.

Like Cleopatra in Egypt, hostile chroniclers in subsequent dynasties attributed much of her success to her sexual exploits, though the records also note that she was well educated, shrewd in her dealings with ministers, and a polished hand at employing imperial spectacle. In 684, after the death of her husband, who had become the emperor, she ruled as **empress dowager** and as regent for her son. In reality, however, she held all the real power. A devout Buddhist, she declared Buddhism the state religion. She intrigued and maneuvered to rule in her own right, and in 690, she inaugurated a new Zhou Dynasty. The final step came in 693, when she took the Buddhist title "Divine Empress Who Rules the Universe." Though an able ruler according to the Tang official histories, the act of creating her own dynasty and new titles for herself was considered usurpation by many of her subjects and a resistance soon followed. Unlike many other Chinese rulers, she was able to put the revolt down and preserve the continuity of the dynasty, only succumbing to natural causes in 705. Following the Confucian backlash of the Song era, no woman in imperial China would wield this kind of power again until the reign of the Empress Dowager Cixi in the late nineteenth and early twentieth centuries. Even today, however, she is widely celebrated in China as an early feminist role model.

Empress dowager: In monarchical or imperial systems in which succession is normally through the male line, the widow of the ruler.

Tang Poetry   Tang poetry, especially the compressed "regulated verse" of eight five-character lines and the terse four-line "cut-off line" poems, attempts to do the same thing: suggest powerful emotions or themes in minimalist fashion. For example, the deep Confucian sensibilities of the Tang poet Du Fu (ca. 721–770) are often detectable in his emotionally charged poems such as "Mourning Chen Tao." Li Bai (or Li Bo, 701–762), his friend, was in many ways his opposite in both the way he lived his life and the emotions he sought to stir. Carefree, witty, a lover of wine and women—according to legend, Li Bai drowned after a drunken challenge to "embrace the moon" reflected in the water—his poetry evokes happier moments but frequently conveys them as fleeting and bittersweet. Wang Wei (ca. 699–759) was a third renowned Tang poet. Of him, it was later said that "in every one of his poems is a painting, and in every painting a poem."

Powerful Emotions, Minimally Expressed
(Chinese lines read vertically, right to left)

复	返	但	空	Empty mountains sees no one,
照	景	闻	山	Yet is that a voice I hear?
青	入	人	不	Where the sunlight enters the deep grove,
苔	深	语	见	And shines back on the verdant moss?
上	林	响	人	

—Wang Wei. "Deer Park." In *19 Ways of Looking at Wang Wei.* Edited by Eliot Weinberger and Octavio Paz. Hubbardston, MA: Asphodel Press, 1995.

For all the accomplishments of the Tang, however, the role of Buddhism as a privileged religion left the dynasty open to severe criticism. With the coming of the Song, China would become a religious civilization in which its people reemphasized the indigenous traditions of Confucianism and Daoism, with elements of Buddhism on a more reduced level.

The Song and Yuan Dynasties, 960–1368

During the Song dynasty, China achieved in many ways its greatest degree of sophistication in terms of material culture, technology, ideas, economics, and the amenities of urban living. Its short-lived incorporation into the huge empire of the Mongols opened the country to renewed influence from neighboring peoples and helped to spread Chinese influence westward, most famously through the accounts of the travelers Marco Polo and Ibn Battuta. Finally, the new synthesis of Neo-Confucianism would carry China as a religious civilization into the twentieth century.

Reforms of Wang Anshi
Like the Tang, the Song instituted a strong central government based on merit rather than heredity. The Song, however, broadened the eligibility of those seeking to take the civil service exams; and with increased opportunities to join the government service, a huge bureaucratic system emerged. This unwieldy system placed an enormous financial burden on the state, which, to secure revenue, placed heavy taxes on individuals outside the bureaucracy. The constant demand for revenue by the state would ultimately lead to rebellion.

The need for administrative reform spurred the official Wang Anshi (1021–1086) to propose a series of initiatives designed to increase state control over the economy and reduce the power of local interests. Wang proposed state licensing of both agricultural and commercial enterprises, the abolition of forced labor, and the creation of a system of government pawnshops to loan money at reduced rates, in order to break the power of usurers and middlemen. He also urged greatly reducing the number of bureaucratic positions in order to lessen the power of local officials and clan heads.

Opposition to his proposed reforms forced Wang from office in 1076. The question of government involvement in commerce and the economy has been the subject of vigorous debate throughout the history of imperial China, particularly during times of internal crisis.

In addition to internal problems, such as the financial strain of maintaining a huge bureaucracy, the Song faced external problems. Because the Tang had lost much of northern China, including the Silk Road, to nomadic groups, Song lands from the start were substantially smaller than those of the Tang. Although the Song spent a great deal of treasure and energy to maintain a professional army of more than 1.5 million as well as a formidable navy, this massive but ponderous force ultimately proved ineffective against the expert militaries of invading nomadic groups using swiftness to their advantage. The Song also tried careful diplomacy and bribery to maintain China's dominance. Such efforts, however, were unable to keep the

> **Bureaucratic Reform**
>
> "When we consider the men selected through 'understanding of the classics,' however, it is still those who memorize, recite, and have some knowledge of literary composition who are able to pass the examination, while those who can apply them [the classics] to the government of the empire are not always brought in through this kind of selection."
>
> —From *Linchuan xiansheng wenji, 39:1a–19a* in W. B. DeBary, et al. *Sources of Chinese Tradition,* vol. 1, p. 616.

Song Cityscape. The northern Song capital of Kaifeng was one of the world's largest and busiest cities. Situated on the Grand Canal near the major artery of the Yellow River, it was a crossroads of internal and international trade. This painting, by Zhang Ziduan (Chang Tse-tuan), is from a scroll titled "Life Along the River During the Qingming Festival."

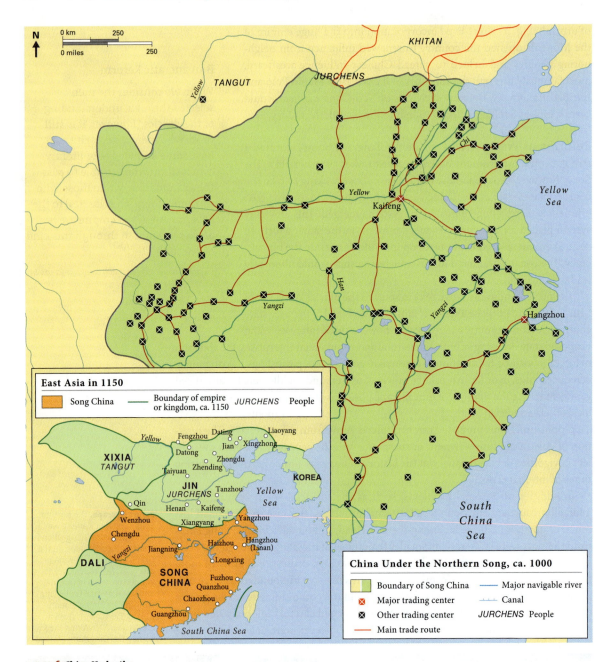

MAP 12.6 China Under the Northern Song, ca. 1000.

northern part of the empire from falling to the nomadic Jurchens in 1127. Forced to abandon their capital at Kaifeng on the Grand Canal just south of the Yellow River, the Song created a new capital at Linan, the modern city of Hangzhou.

The decreased size of the Song Empire resulted in a more southern-oriented and urbanized economy. The new capital at Hangzhou, described by Marco Polo as the most beautiful city in the world, may also have been the largest, with a population estimated at 1.5 million. Despite the bureaucracy's disdain for the merchant and artisan classes, the state had always recognized the potential of commerce to generate revenue through import, export, tariffs, and taxes. Thus, while attempting to bring the largest enterprises under state control, the government pursued measures to facilitate trade, such as printing the world's first paper notes, minting coins, and restraining usury. These practices, combined with an excellent system of roads and canals, fostered the development of an internal Chinese market (see Map 12.6). The Song conducted a lively overseas trade, and Chinese merchants established colonies in major ports throughout southeast Asia and the Indian Ocean.

The Mongol Conquest   Commercial success, however, could not save the Song from invasion by neighboring nomadic peoples. For centuries, disparate groups of nomadic Mongols had lived in tribes and clans in eastern central Asia. There was no real push to unite these groups until the rise to power of the Mongol leader Temujin (ca. 1162–1227). Combining military prowess with diplomatic strategy, Temujin united the various Mongol groups into one confederation in 1206. Temujin gave himself the title "Genghis Khan" ("Universal Ruler") of the united Mongol confederation.

Following confederation, the Mongols launched a half-century of steady encroachment on northern China. The Mongols had several enormous advantages over the infantry-based armies of their opponents:

- their skill at horsemanship and archery
- their unsurpassed ability to fire arrows at pursuers while galloping away from them at full speed
- their repeatedly successful tactics of feigned retreat

Genghis Khan's grandson Khubilai Khan (1215–1294) resumed the Mongol offensive in southern China after the Song unwisely attempted to enlist Mongol aid against the Jurchens. In 1267 he moved his capital from Karakorum to Khanbaligh, called by the Chinese "Dadu"—the future city of Beijing—and steadily ground down the Song remnant. Hangzhou fell to the Mongols in 1276; the death of the young Song emperor in 1279 as he attempted to flee by sea brought the dynasty to an end.

The Yuan Dynasty   In 1280 Khubilai Khan proclaimed the Yuan dynasty. This short-lived dynasty pulled China into an empire spanning all of Eurasia from Korea to the interior of Poland and probing as far as Hungary, Java, and Japan. Like their predecessors in the Northern Wei and Sui dynasties, however, the Mongols found themselves adapting to Chinese culture in order to administer the densely populated and complex society they had wrested from the Song. Thus, while some senior Song bureaucrats resigned in protest from the new Mongol government, most carried on with their posts, and the examination system begun under the Han dynasty was finally reinstated in 1315.

Now that China was part of a much larger empire, its culture was widely diffused throughout Eurasia. In addition, China was open to a variety of foreign goods, ideas, and travelers. Paper money, gunpowder, coal, the compass, and dozens of other important Chinese innovations circulated more widely than ever, while emissaries and missionaries from the developing states of Europe traveled east to the Chinese capital city of Khanbaligh. Rabban Sauma, a Turkish Nestorian Christian who had been

Khubilai Khan as the First Yuan Emperor, Shizu (Shih-tzu).

Gunpowder

If fine porcelain, lacquerware, landscape painting, poetry, and calligraphy marked the refined side of Song life, the most momentous invention to emerge from the era was gunpowder. As far back as the second century BCE, the Han emperor Wudi, a patron of Daoism, had encouraged the experiments of Daoist adepts in developing elixirs of longevity. Out of their initial attempts came the concept of heating saltpeter and sulfur together. By the Tang period, alchemists had begun to add charcoal to the mix. The substance was originally used as a medicine for skin irritations until its propensity to burn rapidly was established. The early Chinese term for gunpowder, *huoyao* (火药) "fire medicine," preserves this sense of its use.

Though long packed into bamboo tubes to create fireworks ignited during religious festivals, it is unclear when the first weapons employing gunpowder were used. By the Southern Song, however, the Chinese army and navy had a wide array of weapons that utilized gunpowder either as a propellant or as an explosive. The use of "fire arrows"—rockets mounted to arrow shafts—was recorded during a battle with the Mongols in 1232. The Song navy launched missiles and even employed ships with detachable sections filled with explosives with which to ram other ships. By the end of the century, primitive cannon were also employed as well as gunpowder satchels to blow open city gates and fortifications.

The widespread use of gunpowder weapons by the Song against the Mongols was a powerful inducement to the invaders to adopt them for themselves. Indeed, toward the end of the war, the Mongols increasingly employed explosives in their siege operations against Chinese walled cities. They also used them in the 1270s and 1290s during their failed invasions of Japan. The need for these weapons pushed their dispersion throughout the Mongol holdings and beyond. Their rapid spread through India and the Arab world has suggested to some scholars the possibility of a simultaneous development for them. By the late thirteenth century, the mention of gunpowder in the writings of the English Franciscan monk Roger Bacon marked its full diffusion throughout Eurasia.

From this point, it is difficult to overestimate the importance of gunpowder in human affairs. The next round of empires, the Ottomans, Safavids, and Mughals, made its use in warfare so central to their efforts that historians often refer to them as "the gunpowder empires." Its use in sixteenth-century Japan was so important in battle that the Tokugawa Shogunate banned it for two centuries once peace had been established. But it was among the states of Europe that these weapons achieved their highest levels of development over the following centuries. Incessant

Song Naval Technology. The Song maintained a powerful fleet and were perhaps the first to use gunpowder weapons at sea. In 1161 they defeated a far larger Jin naval force by means of rockets, catapult-launched bombs, mines, and vessels of the type pictured here. The boat was rowed into position near an enemy ship, and its explosive-laden bow was then detached with the fuses lit, detonating the charge when the stern had moved off a safe distance.

Korean Rocket Launcher.
Adapting Mongol and Chinese military technology, the Koreans repelled a Japanese invasion in 1592 with *hwacha*, mobile rocket launchers that were used with great effect against both enemy land forces and ships.

warfare among the European states and against the Ottomans fueled the development of bigger and deadlier cannon and lighter and more accurate small arms. The use of these weapons helped speed the decline of the heavily armed and armored mounted knight and brought on the age of the infantry armed with muskets as "the queen of battles." By the end of the eighteenth century, even though muskets and artillery were technologically more or less the same the world over, a high degree of drill among bayonet-equipped grenadiers gave European armies an edge against the Ottomans, Mughals, and Africans. With the coming of the Industrial Revolution in the following century, the huge array of ever deadlier weapons and new explosives propelled a new age of empire and world war. By the twenty-first century, the descendants of the "fire-arrows" of the Song visited other planets and propelled the first human creations beyond our solar system.

Questions

- How do gunpowder's origins as an elixir and a medicine complicate the way we typically view technological and cultural adaptations?

- What would have been the consequence for world history if the military uses of gunpowder had never been discovered?

Huang Gongwang's (Huang Kung-wang's) Dwelling in the Fu-ch'un Mountains (1350). Like the era immediately after the Han, the turbulent political situation of the Yuan dynasty forced many of the educated elite to withdraw from the bureaucracy and cultivate aesthetic pursuits. The period thus saw some of the most expressive examples of Chinese monochrome ink landscape painting. In this section from Huang's scroll, the artist has encoded subtle messages to the knowledgeable viewer. Among these is that the site itself was famous as the retreat of a first-century Daoist hermit who chose to live in seclusion rather than serve the government.

born in China, traveled from Khanbaligh to Paris and Rome, even celebrating a mass with the pope in 1278. The two most famous travel accounts of the era, those of the Venetian Marco Polo (1254–1324) and Ibn Battuta of Tangier (1304–1369), who lived and traveled throughout the Mongol Empire, are testament to the powerful impact of Mongol rule on facilitating travel over such a vast area. Indeed, it was during the brief rule of the Mongols that the European image of China as a fairyland of exotica, fabulous wealth, and wondrous inventions was firmly set (see Map 12.7).

For Chinese historians, however, the Yuan period is almost universally regarded as one of imperial China's darkest times. Although the Mongols quickly restored order, administered the empire effectively, and allowed a relative tolerance of religious practice and expression, the Yuan period was seen as an oppressive time of large standing armies, withdrawal from service of many Chinese officials, forced labor, and heavy taxes. Compounding the intensity of these conditions was perhaps the single worst disaster of the fourteenth century, the bubonic plague, as we saw in Chapter 11. While scholars have only recently begun to examine Chinese mortality rates resulting from the plague, Chinese accounts suggest that they were in all likelihood similar to those of Europe in some areas, with perhaps one-third of the population of about 100 million dying from the 1340s until the end of the century.

By mid-century, all of these factors contributed to outbreaks of rebellion in China. Moreover, the Mongol Empire spanning Eurasia had now begun to dissolve into a series of increasingly squabbling regional states. By 1368, a coalition led by the soldier-Buddhist monk Zhu Yuanzhang (1328–1398) had driven the Mongols from the capital at Khanbaligh and proclaimed a new dynastic line, the Ming. A final measure of revenge came when the last Mongol pretender to the throne was driven into the sea—just as the last Song emperor had been by the Mongols.

MAP **12.7** The Mongol Empire.

The Ming to 1450: The Quest for Stability

The "Pig Emperor," as Zhu was sometimes derisively called because of his ungainly features, took the reign name of "Hongwu" and spent much of his rule driving the remaining Mongols out of his empire. Under Hongwu's leadership, Chinese politics and customs were restored and a powerful centralized government was put into place. This new imperial state that Hongwu and his successors created would, with minor modifications, see China into the twentieth century.

During the 88 years of the Yuan dynasty, Chinese political and cultural traditions had been compromised in a number of ways. Mongol overlords relied on their own administrative practices and even placed foreign administrators from Persia and other countries in official positions. Marco Polo, for example, claimed to have worked as an official in China. In doing so, the Confucian educational and examination system that had been a mainstay in China since the Han dynasty had been considerably devalued by having outsiders placed in key positions at the top. Ming emperors, however, reinstated a number of Chinese institutions and renewed the primacy of the Confucian bureaucracy.

The Grand Secretariat   Hongwu sought to streamline this newly reconstituted bureaucracy by concentrating power and governmental functions around the emperor, a practice that had been common during the Qin, Han, and Tang dynasties. Thus, one of his first steps in reshaping the government was to create the Grand Secretariat in 1382. This was a select group of senior officials who served as an advisory board to the emperor on all imperial matters. The Grand Secretariat became the highest level of the bureaucracy and the most powerful level of government after the emperor. Although military needs eventually moved much of its power to the Grand Council set up by the Qing in the mid-1700s, the secretariat remained at the apex of imperial Chinese power into the twentieth century. With a powerful, centralized government in place, Ming emperors now had a base from which to take measures to protect the empire from incursions by Mongols and other nomadic groups in the north. One step to protect against invasion was taken in 1421, when the capital of the empire was moved from Nanjing in the south to the old site of Kambaligh, now renamed "Beijing" (northern capital) so that a strong Chinese presence in the region would discourage invasion. Further safeguards against invasion included the upgrading of the fortifications along the Great Wall.

Population Recovery   While the country fortified its borders and reinstated political systems that had been dismantled by the Mongols, it also had to contend with a sharp drop in population due to warfare and the lingering effects of the bubonic plague that ravaged the country in the 1340s. The population rebound, however, did not assume significant proportions until it was aided by the introduction of a number of new food crops in the sixteenth and seventeenth centuries, which boosted agricultural productivity.

With the coming of new food and cash crops from the Americas by way of Spanish and Portuguese merchants, including potatoes, sweet potatoes, maize (corn), peanuts, and tobacco, the country's population grew from a low of perhaps 60 million at the end of the Yuan period to an estimated 150 million in 1600. The efficiency of Chinese agriculture and the consequent growth of the empire's immense internal trade contributed to another doubling of the population to perhaps 300 million by 1800.

The Interlude of Naval Power   Thanks to the foundation laid by Hongwu, the dynasty's third emperor, Yongle, inherited a state in 1403 that was already on its way to recovering its economic dynamism. Taking advantage of this increasing prosperity and fearful of potential usurpers, he ordered China's first and last great naval expeditions. These voyages, sent out from 1405 to 1433 under the command of his childhood friend and imperial eunuch, Zheng He (1371–1435), were perhaps the most remarkable feats of their day.

The story of Zheng He himself is equally remarkable. Born to a Muslim family in the southern province of Yunnan in 1371, Zheng was taken captive when Ming armies conquered Yunnan in the bloody war to recover the last Mongol strongholds in the region. Ten-year-old Zheng's quick wit impressed a Ming general, who spared the boy's life and placed him as a servant in the household of the future Yongle emperor.

Although Zheng's life was not taken, he suffered the fate of all captured males in the region: castration. His genitalia were claimed at the stroke of a knife, and his traumatized urethra was capped with a wooden plug. Unlike many of his fellow captives, however, Zheng survived the aftereffects of his castration and grew into a physically imposing man, with his boyish face and high-pitched voice being the only outward signs of his ordeal. His condition also allowed him a privileged place in the inner precincts of the imperial household. Emperors often placed considerable trust and power in the hands of their court eunuchs because they could not produce heirs and, thus, were unable to build a power base that could challenge imperial authority. Zheng He's steadfast loyalty won him particular favor when Yongle ascended the throne.

The vast fleets that Zheng now commanded were the largest amphibious forces the world would see until the twentieth century. With a length of over 400 feet, the largest of Zheng's "treasure ships," as they were called, were more than four times the length of Columbus' *Santa Maria* and many times its bulk and were accompanied by a diverse array of smaller vessels that carried cargo, supplies, and troops. There were even tankers that carried fresh water for the fleet, while the larger ships grew fresh fruits and vegetables on their aft decks. Zheng's ships also carried a formidable arsenal of cannon, bombs, rockets, and other weaponry and a force of nearly 30,000 men. In addition, they featured such technological innovations as watertight compartments, sternpost rudders, magnetic compasses, and paper maps.

Chinese Treasure Ship Compared to Columbus's *Santa Maria*. Over 400 feet in length, the largest of Zheng He's treasure ships was nearly five times as long as the ships Columbus used to sail across the Atlantic.

The first voyages were expeditionary forces aimed largely at overawing any nearby foreign powers that might be harboring pretenders to Yongle's throne. As the realization set in that these foreign threats were nonexistent, the voyages became focused on trade and exploration and ranged farther and farther afield, ultimately covering the Indian Ocean, the Persian Gulf, and the East African coast. Along the way they planted or reestablished contact with Chinese merchants in south and southeast Asia. Of particular interest were the first direct Chinese contacts with the Swahili-speaking states of East Africa. In one famous exchange of gifts, the king of Malindi (modern Kenya) sent Yongle a giraffe, which found the emperor among the awestruck admirers of the creature at the imperial court. Even today one can still see the stone markers left by the Chinese along the East African coast where their ships landed (see Map 12.8).

MAP **12.8** Voyages of Zheng He, 1405–1433.

The End of Maritime Power   Although Zheng He's explorations firmly established Chinese predominance in naval technology and power, Yongle's successors put an end to the expeditions. The reasons for this abrupt turnabout were both political and strategic. By the 1430s the Mongols, having regrouped from their defeats, were again threatening the northern frontiers. The huge expense of the voyages and the realization that there were no significant naval rivals were convincing arguments to discontinue them in the face of the Mongol threat. In addition, the Confucian officials, always suspicious of the profit motive, argued that maritime trade was not useful to the overall welfare of the empire.

With maritime travel ended, China's only contact with the outside world came through so-called tribute missions in which representatives from other countries would visit the imperial court. As a result of these ceremonial visits, the emperor would usually allow those countries' merchants to trade in China for a set period of time. While a more secure China was the ultimate goal of the ban on maritime travel and the system worked reasonably well until the nineteenth century, this decision would have far-reaching consequences when China faced the new naval technologies of the industrializing West.

Toward the Ming Decline   The activist style of Hongwu and Yongle proved to be the exception rather than the rule during the nearly three centuries of Ming rule. As had so often been the case in Chinese history, a degree of weakness at the center of power encouraged probes of the frontier by nomadic peoples on the empire's periphery, a condition neatly summarized by the Chinese proverb "disorder within, disaster without." A disconcerting foretaste of this occurred in 1449, when the emperor was taken prisoner by the Mongols following the defeat of his expeditionary force. Through most of the sixteenth century, a succession of weak emperors would erode the stability of the reformed Ming imperial system, which had been based on enhancing the emperor's power. To compensate for the chronic weakness at the center, power was increasingly diffused throughout the system. Over time, much of it was acquired by the grand secretaries and provincial governors, while at the village level magistrates and village headmen assumed the bulk of power and responsibility.

Society, Family, and Gender

With the refinement of the examination system and the elaboration of the bureaucracy during the Song, which was renewed during the Ming, the key point of intersection between the people and the government was the district magistrate. While magistrates occupied the lowest official rung of the bureaucracy, they wielded considerable power at the local level and constituted the entry-level position for the majority of those called to service. Some experience at the magistrate's level was considered essential for ambitious officials, and the wide-ranging skills developed during one's district tenure often proved indispensable for advancement to the higher levels of the bureaucracy.

"Father and Mother to the People"   The position of magistrate brought with it enormous responsibility. Even in rural areas, the magistrate might have charge of

100,000 people—and in urban areas perhaps 250,000. Assisted by a small group of clerks and secretaries, messengers, and constables, he supervised all aspects of local government: collecting taxes, policing and security, investigating and prosecuting crimes, settling legal disputes, sentencing and overseeing punishments—including executions—presiding over all official ceremonies, conducting the local Confucian examinations, and setting an exemplary moral example for his constituents. He was constantly on the move, traveling around his district and discharging his duties. When disaster struck, it was the magistrate who had charge of organizing local relief efforts; if floods, disturbances, or famines were the result of negligence, it was he who would be punished—in especially serious cases, by death or banishment. The magistrate's responsibilities and powers were so all-encompassing that he was referred to as "father and mother to the people."

With so much responsibility vested in such a low position in the civil service, a number of safeguards were built into the system to prevent abuses. Magistrates were required to write extensive reports on all activities of any consequence. Their staff was encouraged to report any improprieties to the magistrate's immediate superiors. By the Ming period, a rule of avoidance had been instituted. This measure prevented officials from serving in their home districts and required them to be reassigned every 3 years in order to discourage corruption and influence peddling.

Despite the hectic schedule of the magistrate, he remained a remote figure for the vast majority of the people in his district. "Heaven is high and the emperor is far away" was a Chinese proverb that seems to have been equally applicable to the local officials. For most people, the main figures of authority remained the leading families of the village, their own clan leaders, and the headmen in the *lijia* and *baojia* systems of village organization.

The Scholar-Gentry and Rural Society   While China boasted some of the world's largest cities, more than 85 percent of the country remained rural during the period from the Song to the Ming. At the top of the local structures of power and influence were the *scholar-gentry*. As a class, they were by definition the educated and included all ranks of degree holders, whether in or out of office, and their families. By imperial edict and custom, they were expected to exercise leadership over the classes of peasants, artisans, and merchants and, along with the district magistrate, to take the initiative during times of trouble in safeguarding the lives and property of the community. Like the magistrate, they were expected to set a high Confucian moral tone for their villages and districts.

Scholar-gentry membership was in theory open to most males and their families, though in practice it seldom exceeded 1–2 percent of the population in most areas of the empire. The chief qualification was attainment of at least the lowest official degree, *shengyuan*, which enabled the bearer to attend a government-sponsored academy for further study and draw a small stipend. The demands of memorizing the classical canon and learning to write in the rigid essay format required for the exams, however, were such that the wealthy had a distinct advantage in their leisure time, access to tutors, and the connections required to pass the exams. Still, there were enough poor boys who succeeded by hard work and the sacrifices of their families and neighbors to provide a surprising degree of mobility within the system.

Since prestige within the scholar-gentry derived from education even more than wealth, it was not uncommon for individuals to purchase degrees, though technically they were barred from doing so in the upper three categories. Thus, there was

Sumptuary laws:
Regulations mandating or restricting the wearing of certain clothes or insignia among different classes of people.

considerable snobbery among the upper gentry of advanced degree holders and officials toward the lower gentry. This was reinforced by an array of **sumptuary laws** and a court-directed protocol of buttons worn on the hats of officials signifying to which of the nine official grades—each with an upper and a lower rank—they belonged. Individuals could also attain honorary ranks, awarded by the emperor, for meritorious service in the military, outstanding ability during times of emergency, decades of diligent study unaccompanied by success in the exams, and even living to a ripe old age. Commoners reaching the ages of 80, 90, and 100 were awarded official ranks of the ninth, eighth, and seventh grades, respectively, and given the honorary title of "Elder."

In keeping with their role as the informal administrative apparatus of the magistrate, the scholar-gentry enjoyed a number of privileges as well as responsibilities. At the same time, their position as community leaders and their grounding in Confucian ethics frequently placed them in tension with the official bureaucracy, especially when local interests appeared at odds with regional or imperial ones. For example, the general reverence for education ensured that the scholar-gentry were exempted from the labor tax of the Ming, as well as from judicial torture and corporal punishment. If convicted of felonies or capital crimes, elaborate procedures had to be followed to strip gentry of their degrees before the sentence could be carried out. By a variety of stratagems available only to the wealthy, the scholar-gentry were frequently able to conceal the amount of taxable land they possessed and generally paid lower rates than the commoners. Along with the district magistrate, they presided over all ceremonies at temples, and those holding the highest ranks led all clan ceremonies. In addition, the scholar-gentry mingled with the official authorities more or less as social equals; in the case of those in between appointments to high office, they frequently outranked the local magistrate.

Song Women Weaving Silk on a Draw Loom. Increased commercialization and the demand for silk in the national and international markets made sericulture and weaving two of Song China's largest industries. Women played a predominant role in the industry as well as in the production of cotton and hemp textiles. The illustration on the top is taken from a thirteenth-century copy of a Song text on silk manufacture; the diagram on the botom of the workings of the draw loom—a device dating from the Former Han used for weaving intricate designs—is from the *Tiangong Kaiwu*.

Their privilege and wealth, however, also meant that they were expected to function as community leaders. As with all those in positions of power in imperial China, it was assumed that the scholar-gentry would live up to the moral authority invested in them as teachers and exemplars. They were expected to engage regularly in philanthropic activities, such as raising subscriptions for schools, temples, public works, and other local needs. In times of famine, they raised funds for relief; during times of unrest, they organized militia and paid for and supervised defensive works. As local leaders, they settled small disputes and lawsuits. They also wrote the local histories of their districts—even today, among the most important primary sources for Chinese social history.

Local government relied to an extraordinary degree on the cooperation of the gentry and people with the magistrates, subprefects, and prefects in order to function. Because the presiding officials were moved so frequently, the gentry represented a consistent network of people to carry out the day-to-day work of government. They took very seriously the Confucian injunction to remonstrate with officials, especially when their complaints coincided with local interests. Thus, they could—and did—rally the people to subvert the policies of unpopular magistrates. Moreover, as influential men themselves—and often officials with national connections—they could force the resignation of officials and sometimes even bring about changes in regional or imperial policy.

Village and Family Life

The tendency toward greater centralization under the Ming also reverberated within the structures of Chinese village life. While much of local custom and social relations among the peasants still revolved around family, clan, and lineage—with the scholar-gentry setting the pace—new institutions perfected under the Ming had a lasting impact into the twentieth century.

Originally conceived during the Song dynasty, the *baojia* system of village organization called for families to register all members and be grouped into clusters of 10. One family in each cluster was then assigned responsibility for the others. Each group of responsible families would then be grouped into 10, and a member would be selected from them to be responsible for the group of 100 households, and so on up to the 1,000-household level. The *baojia* headmen at each level were to be chosen by the families in the group, though they received their office from the magistrate. They were to report to the magistrate on the doings of their respective groups and were held accountable for the group's behavior. The system was especially important in that it allowed the authorities to bypass potential gentry resistance to government directives and guaranteed a network of informers at all levels of rural life.

Peasant Women's Lives

Despite China's technological prowess and the introduction of new rice strains during the Song period that propelled a surge in population, the patterns of work and the overall rhythms of peasant life changed little from the Song through the Ming. The tools available to the vast majority of cultivators, as later depicted in the seventeenth-century technology manual *Tiangong Kaiwu* (*The Works of Nature and Man*), had remained fundamentally unchanged from their prototypes of the preceding centuries. The very simplicity and efficiency of such tools in such a labor-rich environment encouraged their continued use.

Tensions in the older patterns of village life tended to be magnified during times of stress in the lives of women and girls. On the one hand, the education of upper-class women tended increasingly toward those areas aimed at making them more marriageable. Study of proper Confucian etiquette (as outlined in Ban Zhao's *Admonitions for Women*, discussed in Chapter 9), light verse, and a heavy dose of filial piety occupied a large portion of their curriculum. For example, women were expected to be chaste, loyal, and obedient; and marriage and property laws functioned to reinforce these qualities. In addition to the premium placed on mourning by both sexes, widows were expected to remain single out of duty and loyalty to their departed husbands. Indeed, widows who remarried forfeited all inherited property to their husband's closest male relative—including what remained of the dowry they had originally brought with them. The custom of painful **foot binding** originated during the Song, gained ground during the Ming, and continued until it was banned by the People's Republic of China after 1949. **Female infanticide** also rose markedly in rural areas during times of famine or other social stress. As in previous periods, rural girls were frequently sold into servitude or prostitution by financially pressed families.

Foot binding: The practice of tightly wrapping the feet of young girls in order to break the bones and reset them in such a way that the feet are compressed to about one-third of their normal size; this was generally done by mothers to their daughters to make them more marriageable since tiny feet were considered the epitome of female beauty.

Female infanticide: The killing of girl babies.

Perceptions of Perfection: Intellectual, Scientific, and Cultural Life

The period from the Tang to the Ming was marked by unsurpassed technological prowess. Indeed, according to the leading scholar of China's record of innovation, Joseph Needham, China remained the world's leading producer of new inventions until roughly 1500. So striking is this record, and so suddenly does it subside after this time, that historians sometimes refer to the problem of why it took place as "the Needham question." One possible answer may be simply that the Chinese considered that they had achieved a degree of perfection in so many areas that, like their great naval expeditions, there was simply no pressing need to advance them further. Within a few hundred years, however, the momentum of technological innovation had shifted decisively to the small, feuding states of Europe.

The Neo-Confucian Synthesis   The long period of the intermingling of Confucianism with Buddhist, Daoist, and other traditions of thought forced an extensive reformulation of its core concepts by the Song period. During the twelfth century, this reformulation matured into Neo-Confucianism, which combined the moral core of Confucian ethics with a new emphasis on speculative philosophy borrowed from Buddhist and Daoist thinkers.

Neo-Confucianism holds that one cannot sit passively and wait for enlightenment, as the Buddhists do, but must actively "seek truth through facts" in order to understand correctly the relationships of form (*li*) and substance (*qi*) as they govern the constitution of the totality of the universe, or "supreme ultimate" (*taiji*). As self-cultivation of the Confucian virtues is the means of discovering one's true *li*, so investigation of the physical world is a means of discovering one's place in the larger *li* of the supreme ultimate. Hence, knowledge is a cumulative, unified whole, with the moral dimension of knowledge taking precedence over mere observation.

One experiences the ethical and epistemological strands of this exploration holistically in a manner beyond mere analytical reason and more akin to a Buddhist flash of enlightenment. Exploration of the physical universe undertaken in this spirit is thus the ultimate act of Confucian self-cultivation in that one apprehends the Way (*Dao*) on every level. This vision of Neo-Confucianism was propounded by the Cheng brothers, Hao (1032–1085) and Yi (1033–1107), and perfected by Zhu Xi (ca. 1129–1200), generally recognized as the leading Neo-Confucian thinker. Not surprisingly, these ideas came to prominence during the Song period, riding a wave of anti-Buddhist reaction in the wake of the fall of the Tang. The incorporation of Buddhist approaches to cosmology made the philosophy attractive to those who were intrigued by inquiries into the nature of the universe while retaining the Chinese ethical precepts of family relationships and behavior.

Zhu Xi's speculative Neo-Confucianism lost favor somewhat during a Buddhist revival of sorts during the Ming, in favor of the more direct ethical action favored by Wang Yangming (1472–1529). For Wang, as for Zhu Xi, truth, whether in terms of epistemology or ethics, was unitary. He believed that all people carry within them an "original mind" in which rests an intuitive sense of the fundamental order of the universe. It is out of this instinct toward the right that one investigates the physical and moral universe in order to refine one's conclusions.

Bound Foot. One of the Song practices that would have long-term repercussions for Chinese women was the fashion of foot binding. These so-called lily buds represented the height of male eroticism well into the twentieth century and were the result of years of careful, painful wrapping of the feet of young girls until they assumed the misshapen form depicted here.

Wang, however, departed from Zhu Xi's emphasis on a rigorous "investigation of things" as the necessary route to understanding the nature of the world. Instead, he insisted that such investigation merely hones one's existing instincts in these areas to a higher degree. For example, the innate feelings one has toward one's parents naturally lead one to see filial piety as a fundamental condition of the universe; further investigation allows one to grasp its subtleties.

Wang's other area of emphasis, nurtured by a long study of Buddhism—especially *Chan* (*Zen*)—and Daoism, was the unity of knowledge and action. While everyone has the spark of intuition, he argued, true understanding is inseparable from active pursuit and cultivation of that spark. Moreover, the sage must act in the world as his knowledge becomes increasingly refined, both to be a moral example to others and to complete his own self-cultivation.

The end point comes when, like Confucius at age 70, one can "follow one's heart without transgressing what is right." Thus, for Wang, "knowledge is the beginning of action, and action is the completion of knowledge." While Wang's school remained a popular one, especially because of its implicit critique of some of the more speculative areas of Zhu Xi's Neo-Confucianism, Zhu Xi's school remained the orthodox one and, with later support from the Qing, continued to be so until the last years of the imperial era.

Technological Peaks   In many respects, the notion of perfectibility woven through Song and Ming philosophy presented itself in the scientific and technical realms as well. A number of previous innovations were refined and, in some cases, brought to highly developed states. In a great many other cases, however, high points were achieved early on and continued substantially unchanged. For example, Zheng He's ships, with their dazzling array of innovative features in the fifteenth century, remained unsurpassed triumphs of Chinese naval architecture until the mid-nineteenth century, when the empire's first steamships were launched from Western-style dockyards. While new firearms were introduced in the seventeenth and eighteenth centuries, they came in part by way of Jesuit missionaries from Europe and remained essentially unchanged until the 1840s—yet another revealing pattern of core innovation (gunpowder weapons) reintroduced in improved form from the periphery.

From the Tang through the Southern Song, China was the site of an unprecedented number of technological innovations that would have a profound effect inside and outside the empire. The horse collar, moldboard plow, wheelbarrow, advanced iron casting, compass, gunpowder, porcelain, and paper diffused widely throughout Eurasia and the Indian Ocean basin. By the height of the Song period, tea, sugar, silk, porcelain, paper, and cotton cloth had all become major industries and China dominated—in some cases, monopolized—production and distribution of all of them. An increasingly sophisticated infrastructure of commercial credit, printed paper money, and insurance for merchant houses and their agents supported and secured China's vast network of industry and trade.

Porcelain and Literature   As we can see, many of the technical advances that took place revolved around luxury items. Most notable in this regard was the development of true porcelain. Following centuries of experimentation with kaolin clays, glazing mixes, and extremely high firing temperatures, Song craftspeople hit

Song Porcelain. Porcelain reached its full maturity during the Song Dynasty and objects from that period are even today highly coveted. On the left is a white-glazed ding jar from the Northern Song (960–1127). On the right is a water jar in green-glazed celadon with a floral design, believed to be from either the late Northern Song or early Southern Song (1127–1279) period.

upon the formula for creating the world's most celebrated ceramics. Elegant white and celadon (a shade of green) porcelain vessels were manufactured in great numbers, and the surviving examples of Song wares today are among the world's most precious art treasures. Techniques for using distinctive blue cobalt oxide pigments were originally introduced from Iraq in the ninth century and were being utilized by Song and Ming potters to brighten their porcelain ware. Government-sponsored and -run kilns, notably at the Jingdezhen works in Jiangxi Province, allowed for unprecedented volume and quality control.

The growing wealth, leisure, and literacy of the scholar-gentry and urban classes also created an increased demand for popular literature. The novel as a literary genre first made its appearance in China during the Yuan period but emerged as a form of mass entertainment only in the sixteenth century. Written in a rapidly evolving combination of classical and colloquial language, the swashbuckling adventures of the multiauthored *Water Margin* (or *All Men Are Brothers*) and the tale of family intrigue and woe of Cao Xueqin's *The Dream of the Red Chamber* captured the imaginations of seventeenth- and eighteenth-century readers.

Putting It All Together

The experiences of India and China during the period from the seventh through the fifteenth centuries provide us with several important areas of comparison. The first is in the realm of political continuity. India was subject to a succession of governments set up by invaders from the north and west, while the kingdoms to the south jockeyed for power among themselves and for power over the Indian-influenced states of southeast Asia. While there was considerable cultural and religious continuity in the south, the north was alternately dominated by the Hinduism of the late Gupta period, the revived Buddhism of the seventh century, and ultimately by Islam. In the end, none of these claimed full dominance, though Islam remained the religion of the rulers after the twelfth century.

In the case of China, despite the Mongol invasion and political domination of China during the fourteenth century, the basic political structure changed relatively little and reemerged with greater centralization than ever during the Ming dynasty. Culturally, the Mongols' influence on China was negligible; moreover, the Mongols increasingly were compelled to make themselves culturally "Chinese" in order to rule, despite their concerted efforts to maintain their ethnic autonomy. Through it all, not only did Chinese leadership in technical innovation in so many fields keep up its former pace but the brief incorporation into the Mongol Empire helped to greatly facilitate other cultures' interaction with and adaptation to Chinese advances.

The most dramatic difference, however, came in the realm of interaction with and adaptation to religion. India, from the time of Mahmud of Ghazna, never completely adapted itself to Islam—a situation that continues to the present day. Thus, northern India became a *syncretic* area—an area in which the worldviews of rival religious civilizations confronted each other but were not significantly adopted or adapted by the other. Instead, Hindus and Muslims attempted to coexist with each other. Even notable attempts to bridge the gulf between Hindus and Muslims, such as the Sikhs, were not successful in attaining widespread acceptance.

In China, however, the dominant political structures of empire and the cultural assumptions of Confucianism not only resisted Mongol attempts to circumvent them but in the end were largely adopted by the conquerors. Unlike the Muslim conquerors in India, the Mongols did not adhere to a powerfully articulated universal religion. In fact, they proved receptive to several of the religious traditions they encountered in their conquests: Islam, Buddhism, and Nestorian Christianity all gained Mongol adherents. Even before this, however, in marked contrast to India's encounter with Islam, the very real tensions between Buddhism and Confucianism in China resulted not in persecution of the Buddhists but in Confucian thinkers borrowing their approaches to speculative philosophy and creating an expanded synthetic ideology, Neo-Confucianism (see Concept Map).

CHAPTER 12 CONCEPT MAP
Religious Civilizations in India and China Compared

ISLAM

SIKHISM

BUDDHISM

HINDUISM

Daoism

Confucianism

NEO-CONFUCIANISM

Buddhism

INDIA = SYNCRETISM

CHINA = SYNTHESIS

Thus, until the nineteenth century, these religious and cultural trends would continue: India, dominated by the Muslim Mughals in the north and increasingly by the British from the eighteenth century on, would struggle to reconcile and balance the tensions of syncretism. The British, quick to sense these tensions, increasingly exploited them in their strategy of "divide and rule." The Chinese, firm in the belief that all outsiders could ultimately "become Chinese" continued to pursue this policy through the same period. Ultimately, both empires would be reduced by the British and their fellow European powers, whose centuries-long rise was shortly to begin.

Review and Respond

1. What do we mean when we say India is a "syncretic" society? What do we mean when we say China is a "synthetic" society?

2. How did the approaches of Muslims to India differ in the north and in the south? What reasons would you give to explain this difference?

3. What advantages did the Mongols bring to the battlefield?

4. What measures did the Ming take to restore China after the Mongol era?

5. Why is Mahmud of Ghazna considered such a controversial character? What implications can you draw about his character and motivations from the differing views of him among Muslim chroniclers? What can you infer about the motivations of the chroniclers themselves?

6. Why has it been so challenging to reconcile Hindu and Muslim beliefs and culture in India? What measures do you think rulers could have taken to encourage this process?

7. Why do you think the Chinese have believed for so long in their ability to "sinicize" invaders? Would they have been as successful, do you think, at sinicizing invaders like the Muslims in northern India?

8. China is widely agreed to be the world's preeminent technology developer in the centuries up to roughly 1500. Why was this so? What reasons can you suggest for this preeminence and its later decline?

▶ For additional resources, including maps, primary sources, visuals, and quizzes, please go to www.oup.com/us/vonsivers. Please see the Further Resources section at the back of the book for additional readings and suggested websites.

Thinking Through Patterns

▶ **How did interactions between Muslims and Hindus in India lead to religious syncretism?**

In contemplating this question, we must consider what the fundamental beliefs of these two religious traditions were and what kinds of changes take place as religions move from one place to another and interact with other long-established beliefs. For Hindus, this is somewhat difficult because Hinduism encompasses many different religious assumptions. Moreover, it has a long tradition of trying to fit newly arrived belief systems into its own traditions. This is where the clash with Islam is most evident. Islam teaches that there is no God but God (Allah); Hinduism would place Allah next to its other gods, which Muslims find intolerable. This fundamental clash of views makes any compromise difficult. But Muslim leaders find that they simply cannot coerce their Hindu subjects, who vastly outnumber them, to accept the new religion by force. They must therefore find ways to lessen its impact while holding true to the strictures of Islam. Thus, some leniency must be given, or rule becomes impossible; but each side keeps its distance from the other for fear of giving up core values. Thus, they coexist, albeit very uneasily.

Some compromises were made along the way to lessen conflict between the major traditions. Muslim rulers routinely had to suspend their insistence on governing by strict Islamic law and let the Hindu majority govern itself according to their own traditions. In some cases, Hindu women even adopted the veil, like their Muslim counterparts. The most spectacular steps were the founding of new religious traditions incorporating both Hindu and Muslim elements—the Sikhs, for example, and, as we will see in chapter 19, the Mughal ruler Akbar's attempt at a synthetic religion.

▶ **What steps were taken by Hindus and Muslims to lessen the conflicts between the two rival religious traditions?**

▶ **How was the Tang dynasty in China different from its predecessors and successors?**

As we saw, the Tang was China's most cosmopolitan dynasty, and this alone made it quite different from its predecessors. But why was it so cosmopolitan? Here, a large part of the answer must be seen in the widespread practice of Buddhism. China was now integrated in a Buddhist cultural sphere that allowed a greatly enhanced circulation of ideas and goods. Thus, China's rulers knew a good deal more about their neighbors than ever before and through Buddhism shared a community of religious interest with them. The reaction to Buddhism as a "foreign" faith in the Song period made China turn more inward; consequently, its larger ties with the Buddhist world deteriorated, never to reach Tang-level connections again.

The longevity and diversity of Neo-Confucianism over time suggest that the blending was quite effective. It represented a synthesis in which ethics and epistemology—Confucian, humanist-based morality coupled with the speculative ventures of Daoists and Buddhists—created a complete, self-sustaining system. In this, it parallels attempts by contemporary Christian and Muslim thinkers to marry faith and reason into an all-encompassing system designed to provide a means to answer both concrete and speculative questions.

▶ **How effectively did the religious and philosophical traditions of Buddhism, Confucianism, and Daoism blend together in creating Neo-Confucianism? Where did they clash?**

Chapter 13

550-1500 CE

Religious Civilizations Interacting

KOREA, JAPAN, AND VIETNAM

The brushstrokes flowed across the fine rice paper, as they had thousands of times since she began carefully practicing them as a young girl. For Murasaki Shikibu (ca. 973–1025), the daughter of a minor noble in the court at Heian-Kyo in central Japan, the words that now came so effortlessly had become her refuge from the rigid routine of palace life, where a woman's every move was carefully prescribed. The court women of Heian Japan (794–1185 CE), in their thick, stiff winter kimonos, their teeth blackened and faces powdered white to enhance their beauty, were

Seeing Patterns

▶ How was the history of Korea affected by its relations with China? With Japan?

▶ Which important elements of Chinese culture were adapted by the Japanese for their own purposes? What advantages did Japan have over Korea and Vietnam in this regard?

▶ Which Japanese adaptations of Chinese institutions did not work well in Japan? Why?

▶ In what ways was the experience of Vietnam similar to that of Japan and Korea? How was it different?

carefully monitored by palace chamberlains and commented on by court gossips. Some of the women, like Murasaki's older contemporary, Sei Shonagon, responded to this restricted life with savage wit and scathing commentary, skewering its pretentions in her scandalous *Pillow Book*.

Murasaki's literary interests, however, took a somewhat different turn. Though trained in *kanji*, the literary Chinese that functioned as Japan's first written language, her private writings, as were those of the handful of other literate Japanese women, were written in the simpler *kana* script based on a **syllabary** of sounds in the Japanese spoken language. Like Sei's, her work also centered on court life. But her subject was the adventures, loves, trials, and triumphs of a fictional prince named Genji. When it was finished, she had created in her *Genji Monagatori*, the *Tale of Genji* (ca. 1000), what scholars have since recognized as the world's first novel. It remains even today Japan's most popular work of fiction and one of the world's great literary masterpieces.

The story of Murasaki, the court women of Heian-Kyo—the city we know today as Kyoto—and eleventh-century Japan more generally all help to

Syllabary: A system of written characters representing the sounds of syllables, rather than individual sounds.

The Tale of Genji. The story of courtly intrigues and complex love affairs of the imperial palace at Heian-Kyo, a scene from which is depicted here in this twelfth-century scroll, has endured for over a millennium.

illustrate the patterns of world history featured in this book. In the case of Japan, Chinese writing, culture, thought, and Buddhism had arrived simultaneously in the sixth century CE and were swiftly adopted by the ambitious Japanese state of Yamato. Sensing that power and prestige would grow from adapting China's centralized imperial institutions to Japanese conditions, Yamato leaders thoroughly remade their state along these lines over the next two centuries. But in many ways, as we shall see, the suitability of these institutions to Japan's clan-based society was at best uneven. The tensions in state formation, both large and small, created by this situation were already noticeable by Murasaki's time.

The situation in Korea and Vietnam, also in the process of interaction and adaptation to Chinese institutions, would result in similar tensions. Like the Japanese, the Koreans and Vietnamese would go on to create their own writing systems while retaining Chinese as a literary language. They would also struggle, like the Japanese and Chinese, to balance the differing traditions of Buddhism with the practical elements of Confucian government. The dynamism within these tensions would allow each to ultimately make Chinese imported culture their own as they followed their own distinct courses of state formation: Korea and Vietnam, often struggling under China's political shadow, and Japan, clinging fiercely to its independence and protected by the intervening Sea of Japan.

Korea to 1450: Innovation from Above

Like the influence of the Greek-Hellenistic and Roman worlds, that of imperial China became widespread throughout east, northeast, and southeast Asia. Chinese writing, literature, law, government, and thought, as well as imported religions such as Buddhism, came to overlay local social, cultural, and religious customs and practices. But as these imports were often imposed from the top down, they met frequent resistance at the village and clan levels. Thus, tensions between elites and locals continually played out in the assorted Korean kingdoms against a backdrop of invasion and collaboration. From the beginning these societies asserted their political independence from the Chinese. However, their position on or near the Chinese border, the role of the Korean kingdoms as havens for refugees, and the continual pressures of possible invasion provided a conduit for the spread of Chinese innovations—even to the islands of Japan. For the Koreans themselves, shifting relations with China provided both unity and disarray in the struggles of different kingdoms for dominance.

People and Place: The Korean Environment

The terrain of the Korean peninsula resembles in many ways that of the adjacent region of Manchuria. The north is mountainous, marked by the Nangnim and Hamyong ranges running northeast to southwest, with the Taebaek chain running north and south along the coast facing the Sea of Japan. The Amnokkang, better known as the Yalu River, and Kangnam Mountains form the present dividing line with Manchuria; but Korean kingdoms have at times extended far beyond them into modern China's northeast. The areas south of the modern city of Seoul are somewhat flatter; but the entire peninsula is generally hilly, and agriculture has historically been concentrated in the river floodplains and coastal alluvial flats.

Climate and Agriculture   The climate of Korea is continental in the north but influenced by the monsoon system in the south. As in northern China, summer and winter temperatures tend to be extreme, with distinct rainy (summer) and dry (winter) seasons. Because of the configuration of the mountains and the peninsula's position along the northern perimeter of the monsoon, annual rainfall amounts differ

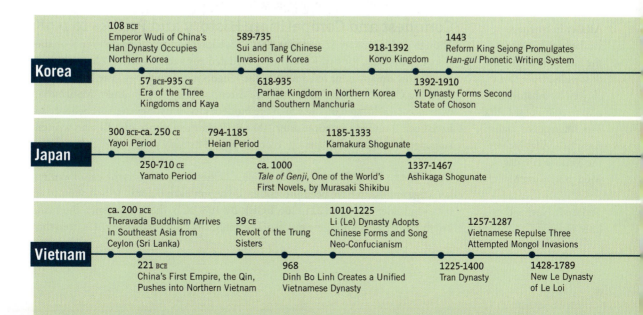

Korea

108 BCE
Emperor Wudi of China's Han Dynasty Occupies Northern Korea

57 BCE-935 CE
Era of the Three Kingdoms and Kaya

589-735
Sui and Tang Chinese Invasions of Korea

618-935
Parhae Kingdom in Northern Korea and Southern Manchuria

918-1392
Koryo Kingdom

1443
Reform King Sejong Promulgates Han-gul Phonetic Writing System

1392-1910
Yi Dynasty Forms Second State of Choson

Japan

300 BCE-ca. 250 CE
Yayoi Period

250-710 CE
Yamato Period

794-1185
Heian Period

ca. 1000
Tale of Genji, One of the World's First Novels, by Murasaki Shikibu

1185-1333
Kamakura Shogunate

1337-1467
Ashikaga Shogunate

Vietnam

ca. 200 BCE
Theravada Buddhism Arrives in Southeast Asia from Ceylon (Sri Lanka)

221 BCE
China's First Empire, the Qin, Pushes into Northern Vietnam

39 CE
Revolt of the Trung Sisters

968
Dinh Bo Linh Creates a Unified Vietnamese Dynasty

1010-1225
Li (Le) Dynasty Adopts Chinese Forms and Song Neo-Confucianism

1225-1400
Tran Dynasty

1257-1287
Vietnamese Repulse Three Attempted Mongol Invasions

1428-1789
New Le Dynasty of Le Loi

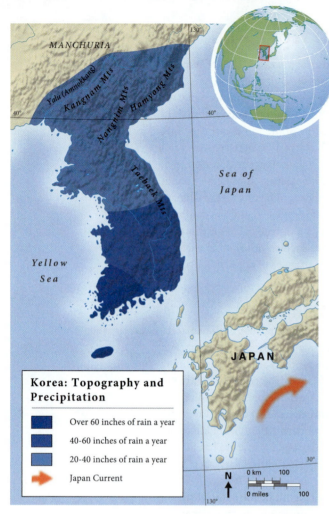

Korea: Topography and Precipitation

- Over 60 inches of rain a year
- 40-60 inches of rain a year
- 20-40 inches of rain a year
- Japan Current

MAP 13.1 **Korea: Topography and Precipitation.**

widely: from average lows of 30 inches in the northeast to 60–70 inches in the southwest. Like the western side of the Japanese islands, however, Korea is largely blocked by Japanese mountain ranges from the moderating effects of the Japan Current.

The difficulties of the terrain and the ever-present possibility of drought have rendered the challenges of the region similar to those facing agriculturalists in northern China, with crops such as millet and wheat dominating and rice farming catching on only much later in the south, where rainfall and the terracing of hillsides made it feasible. Scholars have noted similarities to archaic Greece, where geography fostered the development of isolated, independent communities and worked against political unification, though early on a degree of cultural unity appears to have prevailed (see Map 13.1).

Ethnic Origins   The ethnic origins of the Koreans are still obscure, though the slim archaeological and linguistic evidence seems to point to a central Asian homeland and links to the **Altaic**-speaking peoples. In this sense, the modern Korean language may be distantly related to such languages as Mongolian, Manchu, and possibly Japanese. East and northeast Asia, as we have seen, was home to some of the world's first pottery, though the potter's wheel did not arrive in the area for millennia. In the case of the Korean peninsula, potsherds dating from 4000 BCE have been uncovered in **striated** styles not unlike the Jomon wares of Japan, which some scholars have suggested points to an early period of interaction or perhaps even a common ancestry.

Altaic: In language studies, referring to the family of languages descended from that spoken by inhabitants of the region of the Altai Mountains in central Asia. Examples include the Turkish languages, Mongolian, and Manchu.

Striated: Having thin lines or bands.

Conquest and Competition: History and Politics to 1598

Though developments in northern China have long had a bearing on events on the Korean peninsula, the first Korean state predated any such influence. Zhou Chinese annals contain apparent references to the kingdom of Choson—"The Land of the Morning Calm." Choson seems to have extended deep into southern Manchuria, with its capital located on the site of the modern city of Pyongyang. It is believed to have been founded sometime after 1000 BCE. In the absence of a Korean written language, however, no indigenous records exist of its early years.

The "Three Kingdoms"   Such Chinese cultural influences as the use of written language appear to have been present in the region even before the first attempt at invasion under the Qin (221–206 BCE). By 108 BCE, their successors, the Han, briefly succeeded in bringing much of the peninsula under their sway. It is from this period that the first written records of exchanges with such outlying peoples as the Koreans, Japanese, and Vietnamese find their way into Han histories. Long before this, however, Chinese agricultural techniques and implements, methods of bronze and iron smelting, and a wide variety of other technologies found their way to Choson and beyond. Early contacts between Choson and the Zhou Chinese states from the ninth century BCE on saw the arrival of bronze tools, coins, and weapons. By the fifth century BCE, the technology of iron smelting was also firmly established on the Korean peninsula.

Following the Han conquests, a more systematic Chinese transformation was attempted. The Han incorporated approximately two-thirds of the peninsula into their empire and took over Pyongyang as their regional capital. They also encouraged Chinese settlement in the newly acquired territories in order to help ensure loyalty. One of the indirect effects of the conquest was a steady stream of refugees into the unoccupied regions of the south and to the small tribal societies of Japan. This constant traffic back and forth across the narrow, 100-mile strait separating the Japanese islands from the mainland created a transient population of colonists in both places and greatly facilitated cultural exchanges. Koreans became established as important factors in early Japanese history, and with the founding of the small Japanese holding of *Kaya* [Gaya] in 42 CE, Japanese territorial claims were established on the peninsula.

At the same time, the foundations had been laid for the so-called Three Kingdoms of Korea: *Koguryo* [Go-GUR-yo] (37 BCE–668 CE), *Paekche* [BAAK-chih] (18 BCE–660 CE), and *Silla* [SEE-lah] (57 BCE–935 CE). By the fourth century CE, the dissolution of the Han Empire encouraged the Koreans to push the Chinese out of the peninsula. In the wake of their retreat, the three rival kingdoms began a process of intrigue and intermittent war among themselves for dominance. Koguryo, in the extreme north, formed the largest state as the Chinese evacuated, moving into southern Manchuria in the absence of any strong rivals. In the south, the areas that had never been under Chinese control had a history of close ties to the developing Japanese clan powers and, consequently, tended to be more outward-looking (see Map 13.2).

In 372 the Chinese state of Jin began sending Buddhist missionaries to Koguryo. With them came Chinese writing and literature—and, significantly, ethics and political thought. Within a few decades, as the elites of Koguryo sensed the power of these tools to enhance their statecraft, a Confucian academy was established in the kingdom. In 427, Koguryo remade itself along Chinese lines. From Pyongyang a central Confucian bureaucracy was set up, examinations were instituted, and a reconstituted land tax and conscription system were installed.

Meanwhile, the two southern kingdoms fought continually to stave off domination by their northern rival. Paekche's maritime contacts with south China aided the spread of Buddhism there, as did, to some degree, its wars with Koguryo from 364 to 371. Buddhism had also come to Silla, but Chinese political institutions did

---

Founding of Pyongyang

"In the year of Kyongin, the fiftieth year of the reign of the Yao king ... Wanggom moved the capital to Pyongyang and ... named the country Choson. The place is also called Kummidal, as well as Kungholsan, according to the region. He ruled the land for 1500 years. In the Kimyo year, when King Wu of Chou (Zhou Dynasty in China) enfeoffed Kija with Choson, Tangun moved to Chandan'gyong. However, he returned later and hid at Asadal as the mountain god. He was said to be 1908 years old."

—*Remnants of the Three Kingdoms* [1285]. In: David Richard McCann. *Early Korean Literature*, pp. 16–17. New York: Columbia University Press, 2000.

MANCHURIA

Songhua Jiang

CHINA

KOGURYO

Yalu (Amnokkang)

Pyongyang

Sea of Japan

Seoul

SILLA

Kyongju

Yellow Sea

PAEKCHE

KAYA

JAPAN

Korea, ca. 500 CE

——— Boundary of kingdom, 500 CE

0 km 200
0 miles 200

N

MAP **13.2** **Korea, ca. 500 CE.**

not take the same form there as elsewhere. A clan-based, autocratic monarchy, Silla adopted a Chinese-style bureaucracy but retained its system of hereditary ranks, leaving power largely in the hands of warrior aristocrats.

The power struggle among the peninsular states was long and bitter and from time to time also involved China. In 550, Silla allied with Paekche against the renewed expansionist aims of Koguryo, in the course of which Kaya was eliminated in 562. The reunification of China under the short-lived Sui dynasty in 589 soon resulted in another invasion of the north. The strains of Sui expansion into Koguryo, however, spelled the end of the Sui dynasty, ushering in the Tang in 618. Once again, Tang consolidation in China was followed by renewed attempts to subdue Koguryo. After several Tang campaigns were repulsed, the Chinese decided on a new strategy and concluded an alliance with Silla in 660, spelling the immediate end of Paekche. Threatened along two fronts, Koguryo itself finally submitted in 668. Following decades of resistance against the Tang, Silla was recognized by the Chinese as controlling all of Korea south of Pyongyang in 735. Although politically free of the Chinese, Silla remained a client state of the Tang and shared with them incorporation into an east Asian Buddhist cultural sphere, which now included Japan as well. Meanwhile, remnant forces of Koguryo moved north and set up a state called Parhae [BAHR-hay] in northern Korea and Manchuria that lasted until 926, when it was overrun by the Qitans [Khitans] (see Chapter 12).

The dislocations of the sixth and seventh centuries had a profound impact on northeast Asia. In Silla, the expansion of Mahayana Buddhism and the proliferation of its schools as they spread throughout the region encouraged the dominance of literary Chinese as a medium of expression. In both Korea and Japan it became the first written language, with far-reaching consequences for the cultural development of both places. Japan, as we noted in the opening to this chapter, would eventually supplement the use of literary Chinese with the *kana* phonetic system. In Korea, however, a similar end would be pursued several steps further, resulting in the creation of a government-instituted phonetic system, *han-gul,* in the fifteenth century. Yet, in both places, even today, knowledge of literary Chinese is still considered an important mark of cultural and aesthetic refinement. From the seventh through much of the twentieth centuries it provided a common culture for the elites of China, Korea, Vietnam, and Japan in much the same way as did Latin in western Europe.

Korea to the Mid-Fifteenth Century   By the middle of the eighth century, Silla was in decline. In 780 the king was assassinated, and revolts led by various

Pulguksa Temple. Buddhism put down strong roots in Silla after its introduction in the fourth century. The Pulguksa temple was first built in Kyongjiu, the Silla capital, in 535 as part of the state Buddhist school. The stone pagodas were built in the ninth century under the auspices of the new Son school, better known by its Japanese name, Zen.

pretenders threatened to leave the country unstable for some time to come. Among the most restive members of Silla society were the merchants who, like their counterparts in China, were aware of their growing economic power, though sensitive to the fear and contempt in which they were held by the Confucian-influenced aristocracy and bureaucrats.

One such merchant, Wong Kon (d. 943), subdued the crumbling kingdom and reconstituted it as Koryo—from which comes the name "Korea." The Chinese imperial model of state formation proved attractive to Wong, who, after the practice of Chinese emperors, was accorded a posthumous reign name, Taejo. He moved the capital to Kaesong, where he laid out a city in the grid pattern of the Tang capital of Chang'an and adopted Chinese-style bureaucratic and tax systems, with military and labor conscription. Koryo even built its own version of the Great Wall near the Yalu River as a barrier to the nomadic peoples of the north (see Map 13.3).

By the middle of the thirteenth century, Koryo, like much of the rest of Asia, had begun to feel the power of Mongol expansion. In 1231, with rockets, bombs, and assorted other new military items acquired from their victories over the Chinese, Mongol forces laid siege to Kaesong. The fall of the city inaugurated four decades of irregular warfare against the occupiers and forced the withdrawal of the government to the south. The Mongols' imperial ambitions prompted the deportation of perhaps 250,000 Koreans as slave

MAP 13.3 Korea Under the Koryo, 936–1392.

Korea Under the Koryo, 936–1392 CE

⎯⎯	Boundary of administrative district
●	Capital cities
●	District administrative headquarters
⌐_⌐	Defensive wall

laborers to other parts of the Mongol Empire, beginning in 1254. The Koryo court finally capitulated in 1259, following which, as they had in other areas, the Mongols intermarried and assimilated to Korean culture. As in most of the occupied areas of Eurasia, the advantages wrought by Mongol unity in terms of easier travel and transport and increased public works were eclipsed in Korea by the cruelty of the conquest itself, the widespread perception of misrule, and oppressive taxation.

In 1368, the Mongol Yuan dynasty in China was overthrown by the forces of the soldier monk Zhu Yuanzhi, who inaugurated the Ming dynasty (1368–1644). As had nearly every previous dynasty, the Ming laid plans to invade Korea. In 1388 the Korean leader Yi Song-gye made the strategic decision not to resist the Ming but moved against the Korean court instead, founding the Yi dynasty in 1392 and resurrecting the name of Choson for the new state. The Yi proved to be Korea's final imperial dynasty, ruling until the peninsula was annexed by Japan in 1910. The Yi concluded an agreement with China that formed the heart of what is often, though somewhat erroneously, referred to as the Ming "tribute system" (see Chapter 12). Diplomacy with the surrounding states was conducted by the Chinese on the basis of their perceived place at the top of a Confucian hierarchy of relationships. Regular ceremonial visits by delegations of Korean, Okinawan, Vietnamese, Japanese, and various central Asian representatives to the Chinese court were rewarded with smooth diplomatic relations and favorable trade conditions.

Meanwhile, the Yi polity once again adapted to Chinese-style institutions. The highly centralized governmental structure of the Ming was echoed in Choson, and the adoption of Neo-Confucianism slowly began to drive out older local customs. A new capital was set up on the site of present-day Seoul, and the state was divided into eight provinces. Within each of these, the Chinese model of prefectures and districts was followed. A uniform law code was later promulgated in 1485, calling for, among other things, a permanent hereditary class structure. The Confucian exam structure was also broadened to include a two-tiered official class, the *yongban* and *chongin*.

Yet, for all the advantages created by the new class structure, old cleavages in many cases remained and new unanticipated ones soon developed. As a means of stabilizing the *yongban* class (and, so it was assumed, society as a whole), the Yi rulers made large land grants to the great officials of the kingdom. These landholders, however, tended to use such grants to amass more and more local power. Unlike Chinese officials, who were moved from place to place for just this reason, they tended to remain in their own territories, where they could use a host of informal controls to resist attempts from the throne to rein in their excesses. Over time, many became like regional rulers.

Economy, Society, and Family

Like their counterparts in China, rulers and government officials in the various Korean kingdoms tended to be preoccupied with recurrent problems of landlordism and tenancy, land reform, and maintenance of local infrastructures—especially in wet rice-producing areas—and alleviating want during times of shortage.

Land Reform At various times, therefore, those under Chinese influence proposed schemes of land redistribution based on the Chinese "well-field" model (see Chapter 4). More ambitious was the *chongjon* system of Silla, begun in 722. Following a combination of Buddhist and Confucian precepts and with an eye to local custom, the *chongjon* system mandated a government-sponsored distribution of land, with taxes paid in kind. Additionally, peasants were instructed to develop specialized cash crops or engage in small-craft manufacture. A prime example was the planting of mulberry trees as food for silkworms and the development of **sericulture**.

Sericulture: Raising silkworms in order to obtain raw silk.

Under the Yi dynasty of Choson, the implanting of Neo-Confucian values in the countryside as well as among elites became a prime consideration. Edicts were handed down about proper deportment of family members, inheritance practices, and relations between men and women, as well as land policy. Here, a new system of land tenure was made part of a more general stabilizing of all classes. Peasant rents were fixed at half the crop and a hierarchy of village headmen, bureaucrats, and magistrates similar to the Chinese system was set up to collect taxes, settle disputes, and dispense justice.

As noted previously, the institution of Chinese systems in Korea tended to attract the elites more than the peasant and artisan classes. Their spotty success in taking root tended in many ways to aggravate societal tensions, despite the governmental efficiencies they created. One factor in this was a repeated attempt on the part of the bureaucracy to enhance its power at the expense of the merchant and artisan classes. In the countryside, power remained in the hands of the landholder aristocracy, which tended to ensure that the peasants would be bound to them in a fashion not unlike the serfdom of their European contemporaries.

Neo-Confucian Influence   Particularly in the cities, the high level of Song Chinese-influenced material culture was increasingly evident. Interregional trade was brisk, and luxury items like silk, porcelain, and lacquerware were widely available. Korea's position at the center of the east Asian Buddhist world tended to make it a trade and pilgrimage crossroads, and its artisans became highly proficient in the new technologies of porcelain making and book printing. Many of the oldest Chinese, Korean, and Japanese works extant were printed by Korean publishers.

Under the Yi, the Confucian exams became more open, though the new arrangement called for two official classes, the *yongban*, or scholar-gentry, drawn from high civil and military officials, and the *chungin*, or minor officials. Below these were the *yangmin*, commoners of different professions as well as peasants and serfs, while the lowest group, the *chonmin*, consisted of bond slaves, laborers, and prostitutes.

Though approximating the class structure in China, the new system was more like the composite one created in Heian Japan. As in Japan, it proved a troublesome fit, particularly in remote rural areas. Though the Confucian exams theoretically allowed for some degree of social mobility, they tended to be monopolized by the *yongban*. The institution of hereditary classes, intended to create a stable and harmonious social structure, instead concentrated wealth in the hands of the rural gentry, who often lacked a proper Confucian sense of the official responsibilities of their positions. In many places, the older patterns of aristocratic local power simply continued with only cosmetic changes. Thus, by the sixteenth century, the divide between the wealthy, educated, sophisticated capital and large provincial cities and the tradition-bound countryside was steadily increasing.

Women and Society   Until the arrival of Confucian institutions in the Korean countryside, local village life, as in Vietnam and Japan, tended toward more egalitarian structures, especially between men and women, than would later be the case. In Korea, this egalitarianism retained a remarkable vitality in the face of Neo-Confucian precepts. Even today, there is far less of the traditional emphasis on filial piety and patriarchal custom than in China. Until the sixteenth and seventeenth centuries, for example, bilateral and **matrilocal** marriage patterns tended to be the norm. As in Japan and Vietnam, the communal nature of rice agriculture, and its emphasis on meticulous, intensive cultivation, tended to lessen the division between "male" and "female" work roles and made women and girls more equal partners in local rural society. Women's property and inheritance rights, far more expansive than in Confucian China, also reflected this.

Matrilocal: Living with the family of the bride.

Under the Neo-Confucian reforms of the Yi, however, some of these practices began to change. The idea of strictly delineated gender roles, of men dominating in the "outer" world and women being preeminent in the "inner" world of the home—long a staple among the urban elites and official classes—now became a cornerstone of moral training in rural academies and in the home.

Religion, Culture, and Intellectual Life

As with many peoples of north and central Asia, early Korean religion appears to have been animistic. One could appeal to the spirits through shamans or animals believed to have certain powers. Like Shinto in Japan, these beliefs continued at the local level for many hundreds of years after the introduction of more formalized systems. The invasion of the Han brought the Chinese concepts of heaven, earth, and humankind along with the imperial rituals associated with them. Of more long-term importance, however, was the introduction of Buddhism to the Three Kingdoms during the fourth century CE.

Impact of Buddhism   All the Korean kings seized to varying degrees on the combination of Buddhism, Han Confucian political and moral philosophy, and their supporting institutions as ways to enhance their own state formation. In Silla, for example, the court pursued a course of striving for Buddhist "perfection." It patronized a popular Buddhist-Confucian society, Hwarang—the "Flower of Youth Corps"—that helped to build the 210-foot Hwang Nyonsu temple in 645. Others sponsored mammoth publication projects of Buddhist works: Koryo produced a version of the *Tripitaka* printed on 80,000 hand-carved wood blocks as an act of piety and supplication during the war with the Mongols. Indeed, the relatively high level of functional literacy in written Chinese among Korean elites was greatly aided by the immense popularity of the many schools of Buddhism—Tiantai, Amida (Pure Land), and, by the 1100s, Zen. As a result, twelfth-century Korea developed into one of the world's handful of centers of printing and publishing due in large part to the demand for Buddhist works. By the 1100s as well, publishers were employing what may have been the world's first movable, cast metallic type (see "Patterns Up Close: Printing").

Korea's leading role in world literacy in the preindustrial era received a further boost during the reign of King Sejong (r. 1418–1450). Here, the development of the Korean phonetic script *han-gul*, like the use of *kana* in Japan, made the introduction of writing much simpler and closer to the vernacular than literary Chinese. Like the *kana* system in Japan, *han-gul* helped the spread of literacy in a far more efficient manner than had been the case with literary Chinese. Yet, like *kana* in Japan, it also tended to create a two-tiered system of literacy: Chinese tended to remain the written medium of choice among the highly educated and largely male elites, while *han-gul* became the language of the commoners and, increasingly, women. One of the best examples of this is the anonymous, autobiographical *Memoirs of Lady Hyegong*, written in the eighteenth century. Such divisions notwithstanding, however, the explosion of vernacular literature—satires on *yongban* manners, social criticism, fiction, advice manuals for a variety of tasks—all contributed to Korea attaining, with Japan, some of the highest levels of functional literacy in the preindustrial world.

Vowels Consonants	ㅏ [a]	ㅑ [ya]	ㅓ [ŏ]	ㅕ [yŏ]	ㅗ [o]	ㅛ [yo]	ㅜ [u]	ㅠ [yu]	ㅡ [ŭ]	ㅣ [i]
ㄱ [k,g]	가	갸	거	겨	고	교	구	규	그	기
ㄴ [n]	나	냐	너	녀	노	뇨	누	뉴	느	니
ㄷ [t,d]	다	댜	더	뎌	도	됴	두	듀	드	디
ㄹ [r,l]	라	랴	러	려	로	료	루	류	르	리
ㅁ [m]	마	먀	머	며	모	묘	무	뮤	므	미
ㅂ [p,b]	바	뱌	버	벼	보	뵤	부	뷰	브	비
ㅅ [s,sh]	사	샤	서	셔	소	쇼	수	슈	스	시
ㅇ²	아	야	어	여	오	요	우	유	으	이
ㅈ [ch,j]	자	쟈	저	져	조	죠	주	쥬	즈	지
ㅊ [ch']	차	챠	처	쳐	초	쵸	추	츄	츠	치
ㅋ [k']	카	캬	커	켜	코	쿄	쿠	큐	크	키
ㅌ [t']	타	탸	터	텨	토	툐	투	튜	트	티
ㅍ [p']	파	퍄	퍼	펴	포	표	푸	퓨	프	피
ㅎ [h]	하	햐	허	혀	호	효	후	휴	흐	히

The Conventions and Alphabet of Han-gul. As originally given by King Sejong in his 1446 *Hunmin chong-um* ("Proper Sounds to Instruct the People"), *han-gul* contained 28 syllables. These have now been reduced to 24, with five double consonants and the additional vowels shown. The ease of learning the system is such that Korea has one of the highest levels of literacy in the world.

Japan to 1450: Selective Interaction and Adaptation

Of all the places we have examined in east and south Asia thus far, Japan raises the most exciting questions about the effects of relative isolation. Like Britain in its "splendid isolation," Japan's geographical position allowed it to selectively interact with and adapt to continental innovations, experimenting, refining, and occasionally abandoning them as needed. Indeed, having never experienced a successful invasion, Japan's acculturation was almost completely voluntary, a position unique among the societies of Eurasia.

The Island Refuge

Japan's four main islands, Honshu, Hokkaido, Kyushu, and Shikoku, contain a varied set of climatic conditions. The northernmost island of Hokkaido has cold, snowy winters and relatively cool summers; the central island of Honshu, bisected roughly north to south by substantial mountain ranges, has a temperate to subtropical climate on the eastern side—where it is moderated by the Japan Current—and a colder, more continental climate to the west of the mountains on the side facing Korea and northeastern China. The small southern island of Shikoku and the southernmost island of Kyushu have an abundance of warm, moist weather and are largely governed by the Pacific monsoon system (see Map 13.4).

The Limitations of the Land   The formation of Japan's islands from volcanic activity means that only about one-fifth of the territory has historically been arable. In the narrow plains and valleys, however, the majority of which are on the temperate Pacific side of the mountains, the soil is mineral-rich and the rainfall abundant. But the islanders from early on have also had to face the limitations of the land in supporting a steadily growing population. Like the Korean peninsula, the ruggedness of the land tended to force its people to live in politically isolated, culturally united communities. Thus, communication by water was often the most convenient method, both among the Japanese home islands and across the hundred-mile strait to southern Korea.

Adaptation at Arm's Length: History and Politics

Like the first peoples to inhabit the Korean peninsula, the origins of the Japanese are obscure. Two distinct groups appear to have migrated to the islands from the

Patterns Up Close | Printing

While the invention of the printing press and movable type is widely recognized as having revolutionized the intellectual life of early modern Europe, it is equally true that these developments seven centuries before in east Asia had a similar effect. Yet, in many respects, the consequences of these innovations were different because of the requirements of the languages used and the technical media with which printers in China, Korea, Japan, and Vietnam worked. As in other places, the cultural patterns of handwriting and calligraphy as artistic skills necessary for elites to cultivate in order to complete their moral development also hampered the spread of printing to some degree. Yet, for all these differences, by the fourteenth century, the societies of east Asia still achieved the highest preindustrial literacy rates in the world. These would be unmatched in Europe until centuries after the use of printing had become widespread there. Indeed, with the introduction of the *han-gul* syllabary in Korea a decade before Gutenberg's first work, Korea became the world leader in minimal functional literacy, with rates estimated by some scholars at close to 40 percent.

The Korean Printing Industry. Because of its position as the northern crossroads of the Buddhist and Chinese literary world, Korea was a major center of printing. Printing with carved wooden blocks had been developed during the eighth century, and large publishers and academies kept great numbers of them on hand. The most famous was this storehouse, which still preserves the 80,000 blocks of the *Tripitaka*, carved between 1237–1257. The book page is from a Buddhist work dated 1377 and may be the world's oldest extant piece printed on movable metal type.

The origins of east Asian printing are obscure, but possible clues remain even today in cultural patterns and practices. In China, for example, one still sees people doing stone-rubbing art, which involves taking a sheet of fine paper or silk, placing it against a low-relief stone carving of a text, and rubbing it with charcoal or a pencil to get an image of the carving. Scholars believe this may have first been done during the Han period, in part because of the popularity of low-relief carvings then and in part because the introduction of papermaking and commercial silk production made it practical. The increased prominence of stone inscriptions in approved, standardized Chinese characters may also have popularized this method for dissemination of decrees, laws, advertisements, and so on.

By the fall of the Han dynasty in 220 CE, we have the earliest remnant examples of woodblock printing. Instead of bulky, heavy stone carvings being used as the original to be copied, printers carved single- or double-page blocks of text on book-sized boards, inked them, and pressed the cloth or paper pages on them to get their copies. The boards could then be shaved down and carved again as needed. By the eighth century the Chinese had also begun to experiment with copper movable type inserted vertically into standardized rows in a system very much like the one Gutenberg devised centuries later. But, ironically, these presses remained more curiosities than practical devices for printing a variety of documents. Here, the chief problem was the nature of the Chinese written language—and at this time, the written languages of Korea, Japan, and Vietnam as well. Unlike the English alphabet with its 26 letters, literary Chinese has thousands of different characters. It was simply impractical for typesetters to cast adequate supplies of even the most common characters, organize them, and sort through them to compose the text to be copied. It was far less work to just carve the text blocks from scratch, especially of popular works that would be widely copied and circulated.

In this case, one of the chief catalysts for printing was the growing popularity of Buddhism throughout east Asia. The earliest complete printed book in the world, now in the British Museum, is a text of the Diamond Sutra bearing the date of May 11, 868. As would be the case centuries later with the spread of religious tracts during the Protestant Reformation, the desire of Buddhists to read scriptures and the openness of the various schools to all classes proved a stimulus to literacy, though in practical terms only those with considerable leisure could master the literary Chinese of the scriptures. Still, by the fourteenth century, the pattern of woodblock printing as a major industry in east Asia, with printing centers in the major cities of China, Japan, and Korea, has been seen by a variety of scholars as one of the hallmarks of early modernity centuries before that term is applied to Europe.

Questions

- How did the innovation of woodblock printing facilitate the spread of Buddhism throughout east Asia?

- What does the use of *han-gul* script in Korea say about the relationship between literacy and state formation?

MAP **13.4** Japan: Topography and Climate.

Asian mainland via Ice Age land bridges, perhaps 10,000–20,000 years ago. Their descendants, the Utari are today regarded as Japan's aboriginal peoples and referred to by the Japanese as *Ainu* the "hairy ones," or in early imperial times as *Emishi*. Their physical features, tribal hunting society, and language mark them as distinct from the later arrivals. Details of their religious practices have led some anthropologists to link them to the peoples of central Asia, Siberia, and the Americas.

The later inhabitants may have originally come from the peoples who migrated into southeast Asia, Indonesia, and eventually the central Pacific. They may also have been descended from later Polynesian travelers and later migrants from the Asian mainland. Linguistic evidence suggests a very tenuous connection to Korean and even to the Altaic language family. Japan's long linguistic isolation, however, renders its ultimate origins obscure at the present time.

Phallic: Of, relating to, or resembling a penis.

Microlith: A very small blade made of flaked stone and used as a tool, especially in the Mesolithic era.

Jomon and Yayoi   Japan's prehistory, which lasted from ca. 10,000 BCE down to 300 BCE, has been designated by archaeologists as the Jomon period. The most distinctive artifacts from the era are lightly fired clay vessels marked with a unique horizontal herringbone pattern and often fanciful decorations, clay female figurines called *dogu*, and **phallic** symbols called *bo*. Others include a wide assortment of **microlith** items: arrowheads, spear points, tools made of bone and antler, and nets and fishhooks. **Matriarchal** and **matrilineal** clans appear to have dominated society, clustered mostly near the sea or slightly inland. Because game was increasingly limited on the islands, fishing and harvesting seaweed were the major forms of subsistence. As among the American peoples of the Pacific Northwest, the bounty of the sea and forests enabled substantial settled village life to develop in the absence of an early agricultural revolution.

During the final half-millennium before the Common Era, increased intercommunication among Japanese, Koreans, and some members of the Late Zhou Chinese coastal states laid the groundwork not only for the introduction of agriculture to the Japanese islands but for an almost simultaneous Bronze Age as well. During the last centuries of the Jomon period, it appears that some of the grain crops of northern Asia (such as millet) found their way to the islands. During a 600-year period designated Yayoi (300 BCE–300 CE), imported and domestically manufactured bronze and iron articles made their appearance. The fertile plains of southern Honshu and Kyushu also saw the cultivation of northern Eurasian vegetables and fruits and, most significantly, rice. The swiftness of these changes came in part because of the dislocations resulting from the creation of China's first empire in 221 BCE and the influx of Korean refugees in the wake of the initial Chinese invasion of Korea.

As it had in other areas of Asia, the rice revolution not only allowed the development of larger populations in Japan but also demanded them for efficient cultivation. The movement away from fishing and gathering combined with the efficiency of metal tools and weapons also fostered state formation among the larger and more powerful clans, or *uji*. The role of the new technologies is witnessed by the items included even now in the imperial regalia at the Shrine of Ise in southern Honshu: a jewel, a bronze mirror, and an iron sword, all of which date from about 260 CE. Thus, sometime after 250 CE, Japan's first fully evolved state, Yamato, centered on the Kanto Plain near modern Tokyo, emerged and quickly expanded, absorbing its weaker rivals on Honshu. Japan's first monumental architecture, enormous burial mounds called *kofun* date from this period.

Matriarchal: A social system in which the mother is head of the family.

Matrilineal: Relating to, based on, or tracing ancestral descent through the maternal line.

Jomon Jar and Yamato Sharinseki Disk. The distinctive herringbone pattern and flared top mark this pottery as Middle Jomon, perhaps 5,000–6,000 years old. The disk made of finely worked steatite was taken from a third-century CE *kofun* burial mound in central Japan. It may be related as a religious object to similar kinds of ornaments found in China.

Toward the Imperial Order

While the nature of rulership in Yamato is still clouded by myth, the earliest written records describing the state, composed by Chinese chroniclers in 297 CE, attest to the increased notice it had achieved—though, characteristically, the writers considered their subjects scarcely civilized.

Although there had been steady diplomatic and cultural contact back and forth across the Sea of Japan from the first century CE, a particularly high level was reached during the later sixth century CE. In 552, tradition has it that Buddhism was introduced to the islands from Paekche. With it came the Chinese writing system and written works of every description. A decade later, in 562, the Korean kingdom of Silla eliminated the Japanese colony of Kaya on the peninsula, precipitating a new flow of refugees to Japan. As we have seen, the years from 589 into the early seventh century saw the rise of the Sui and Tang dynasties in China, resulting in yet more Chinese attempts to dominate the Korean kingdoms, and pushing the level of emigration to new levels.

The impact of these events on Yamato cannot be overstated. The growing power of China and Silla helped prompt the Soga *uji*'s Empress Suiko (r. 592–628) and her nephew, Prince Shotoku (ca. 573–621), to connect Yamato more firmly to the mainland and its conceptions of politics, culture, literature, and, ultimately, the imperial system itself. A few signposts along the way include the adoption of Buddhism as a state religion (594), the adoption of the Chinese lunar calendar for state record keeping (604), and the adoption of the prince's 17-article constitution modeled on Confucian and Buddhist precepts (604). But perhaps the most far-reaching changes came later in the century, with the *Taika*, or Great Reform, of 645.

The systematic remaking of the Yamato regime along Chinese lines in the wake of the *Taika* marks the beginning of the imperial Japanese state, that is, of a kingdom bent on expansion over multiple political groups and clans. Among other things, Soga clan control of the court was overturned and Fujiwara No-Kamatari, who emerged as adviser to the new emperor, Tenchi, ushered in a connection between his family and the imperial court that continued into the twentieth century. In less than a century the first Chinese-style imperial histories, the *Kojiki* (712) and *Nihongi* (720), were composed; the concept of the "Mandate of Heaven" was adopted to justify the overthrow of the Sogas; the emperor as the center of a hierarchical system of government run through a rigorously selected bureaucracy was institutionalized; and a census, uniform taxation on land and produce, and systems of conscription and labor service were enacted. The edicts mandating these changes were promulgated as the Taiho Code of 702, which remained the basis of Japanese law until the late nineteenth century. The accompanying quotation gives a description of the highest state official under the Taiho Code (notice the Confucian phraseology).

Yamato's spiritual roots in Shinto, with its connection to the rhythms of nature and renewal, had dictated that the seat of the state be frequently moved. Even today, the sacred shrine at Ise is disassembled and rebuilt every 20 years. Because of the requirements of a far larger and more sophisticated system of government, however, it was decided that a permanent capital be built. The first site selected, at Nara, saw the creation in 710 of a close replica of the Tang capital at Chang'an, down to the axial boulevards, grids of streets, and propitious placement of temples and government buildings. In 794, a larger capital was completed nearby along the same lines called Heian-kyo, the future city of Kyoto. The era of imperial rule from this capital, which lasted until 1185, is thus often referred to as the "Heian" period (see Map 13.5).

MAP 13.5 Heian Japan.

Heian Japan

○   Capital
■   Buddhist temple
●   Shinto shrine
—   Provincial border, ca. 800

Heian Japan   As the imperial order penetrated all the Japanese home islands except Hokkaido and the widespread adoption of Buddhist culture plugged Japan into an enormous, interconnected economic and cultural Asian sphere, Heian Japan increasingly became a land of contrasts, with local rumblings of discontent never far below the surface. For the elites of the capital and provincial administrative centers, life was not unlike that of their counterparts in Korea, Vietnam, or even China itself. The spread of literacy at the top and the common currency of Confucianism, Chinese literature, and the various Buddhist schools helped these elites see themselves as part of a cosmopolitan world, as did frequent travel for trade and pilgrimage. The latest fashions in poetry, literature, fine arts, calligraphy, music, and (to a lesser extent) clothing all found their way to court and beyond.

For the members of the new classes into which the vast majority of Japan's people had now been placed (peasants, artisans, and merchants—with Buddhist monks occupying an increasingly significant position in the hierarchy), many of the changes had been disruptive at best. Perhaps most tellingly, power, and soon military strength, was diffusing from the court and capital out into the countryside. This was particularly true in more remote regions where the most aggressive *uji* had assembled forces in support of their battles with the *Emeshi*. The bureaucracy, a tenuous institution at best during the Heian period, became weaker as the local *uji* began to reassert power. This was given a considerable push in the wake of a virulent smallpox epidemic (735–737), during which the population may have been reduced by as much as one-third.

Despite court attempts to create a Chinese-style "well-field system," tenancy became a chronic problem. In many cases, the *shoen*, or clan estates, were given tax-exempt status because of their military contributions. The estates of Buddhist monasteries were similarly exempt and provided social services and refuge for outcasts, in effect becoming shadow societies of their own. By the late eleventh century, perhaps half of the land in the empire had become exempt from taxes. As the

Confucian Ideals

"The Chancellor ... shall be a leader and pattern, setting an example to the Four Seas. He must order the State and deliberate upon the Way.... He must harmonize *yin* and *yang*. If there is no suitable person, there shall be no appointment made."

—David John Lu. *A Documentary History of Japan*, vol. 1, p. 31. Armonk, NY: M. E. Sharpe, 2005.

Plan of the Capital at Heian-kyo (Kyoto). The desire to copy the grandeur of Tang institutions extended even to city planning for the eighth-century Japanese court. The capital city at Heian was a faithful copy of the plan of the Tang capital of Chang'an, at the time one of the world's largest cities. The city grid was strictly laid out on a north–south axis, with the most important structures like the imperial palace placed in the northern section and their courtyards and main gates all facing south, the most propitious direction, indicated by the Chinese character highlighted in red at the bottom of the page, meaning "south." The placement of gardens and outlying structures was also carefully calculated according to Chinese notions of *feng shui* geomancy regarding trees, hills, and water.

countryside became more self-sufficient, the capital became more isolated—and more reliant on local military cooperation.

In addition, the court itself was often divided by factional disputes, spurred by the practice of emperors abdicating but staying on as regents or advisers. Three decades of civil war between factions supporting the claims of the Taira clan and those pledged to the Minamoto, or Genji, finally ended in 1185 with the defeat of the Taira. Shortly thereafter, Minamoto Yoritomo was given the title Sei-i-tai **Shogun** (the "Great Barbarian-Suppressing General") and the period of the **Shogunates** was inaugurated, lasting until 1867.

Shogun: The chief military official of Japan. The office later becomes hereditary under the Tokugawa family from 1603 till 1867.

Shogunate: The government, rule, or office of a shogun.

Japan Under the Shoguns   Though the emperor at Kyoto theoretically remained in charge with the shogun as his deputy, the arrangement in fact hastened the drain of power from the capital. Because of its parallels to the political and social order in Europe at the time, the term "feudal" has sometimes been applied to this period. As we saw in Zhou China, however, such similarities should not be pushed too far. In order to restore order in the hotbed of Taira opposition, Yoritomo set up his headquarters at Kamakura, several hundred miles from Kyoto, beginning an interval known as the "Kamakura Shogunate," 1185–1333. The court itself remained the center of religious and ceremonial life as well as a forum for intrigue, but the real center of power now resided at the shogun's headquarters. Meanwhile, in 1274, the Mongols launched the first of two major attempts to invade Japan. Their first armada was defeated handily, while in 1281 a much larger second fleet was smashed by a typhoon, known ever after by the Japanese as *kamikaze*, "the divine wind." Though the country was briefly roused to common action in the face of this threat, the dissipation of imperial power for the most part continued unabated.

Court life became even more stilted and formalized, while emperors very occasionally led unsuccessful attempts to reassert power for themselves. The most ambitious of these, though ultimately unsuccessful, was the revolt by Emperor Go-Daigo in 1333. Securing the support of the powerful leader Ashikaga Takauji [Ah-shee-KAH-gah Tah-kah-OO-jee], Go-Daigo's faction was crippled when the opportunistic Ashikaga switched sides twice during the conflict. Ashikaga finally placed his own candidate on the throne, drove the old emperor into exile, and moved his headquarters to the Muromachi [Moo-roe-MA-chee] district in northern Kyoto. For the first time in nearly 200 years, the seats of political and cultural influence were reunited in the same city (see Map 13.6). Even more important for the future of Japanese aesthetics and cultural institutions, the refinements of court life were now available to the warrior classes. There thus was born the union of *bu* and *bun*, the "dual way" of the sword and writing brush. The patronage of the *daimyo*, or regional lords, and their retainers, the **samurai**, ensured steady development of the Chinese-inspired arts

MAP **13.6** Japan, ca. 1350.

of painting, poetry, and calligraphy, while the introduction of Zen and tea in the twelfth century forged an armature of discipline in both the martial and courtly arts that helped to foster the preservation of both for centuries to come.

While the aesthetic refinement of the warrior classes proceeded, the size and scope of warfare itself grew larger and ever more deadly. Like the codes of chivalry current in Europe at this time, *daimyo* and samurai prided themselves on acting according to a strict system of loyalty and honor, *bushido*, "the Way of the Warrior." A samurai was expected to be not just expert with sword and writing brush but unswervingly loyal to his *daimyo* to the point of death. Indeed, the tradition of *seppuku*, or *hara kiri*—ritual suicide—developed originally as a way to show one's "sincerity" and disdain for death and capture on the battlefield. One was also expected to show honor and respect to one's opponents, and tales abound from the period of warriors perfuming their helmets and decorating themselves so that whoever killed them would have a tolerable aesthetic experience amidst the gore of the battlefield.

By the fifteenth century, however, these personal touches were giving way to armies increasingly dominated by massed ranks of infantry, in some cases ballooning into the hundreds of thousands of men. By the middle of the following century, the adoption of firearms and accompanying advances in fortification made Japan perhaps the most heavily armed country on earth. The fluidity of the military situation had major social consequences as well, and by the middle of the sixteenth century it was increasingly possible for commoners to rise through the ranks and become commanders and even *daimyo*.

One important reason for these conditions was the chronic instability of the Ashikaga Shogunate. The position was never intended to be hereditary and was always the subject of *daimyo* intrigue both in Kyoto, where manipulation of the emperor was vital in order to achieve favor, and in the countryside, where power had become increasingly concentrated. In 1467, factional struggles would finally erupt into all-out war for 10 years, the effects of which would last more than a century.

Economy, Society, and Family

The real beginning of the diversification of Japan's economy came with the Yayoi period, beginning around 300 BCE. As the early Japanese communities adopted wet rice and vegetable agriculture they gained the ability to sustain a sedentary population, which would prove crucial for assimilating new technologies and allowing the concentration of power for state formation. The limited amount of arable land also meant that the populations of the few large open areas like the Kanto Plain were in an advantageous position to subdue their less numerous neighbors. In addition, they were better able to adopt technologies like bronze and iron making, silk weaving, and so forth that required an increasingly complex infrastructure. By the high point of the Yamato period, therefore, one finds Chinese accounts describing an economy that seems to resemble that of the Chinese or Korean countryside, with the majority of inhabitants engaged in agriculture and identifiable merchant and artisan classes coming into view.

The New Economy
The introduction of Chinese writing, concepts of law, and Buddhism during the sixth century allows historians to view in far greater detail the workings of Japanese economics. By this point, nearly every appropriate domesticated plant and animal from the mainland had been introduced to Japan; and the

Samurai: A Japanese warrior who was a member of the feudal military aristocracy.

Japanese *Daimyo* Armor. This extraordinarily well-preserved torso armor and helmet is believed to date from the fourteenth century and may have belonged to the Shogun Ashikaga Takauji (r. 1338–1358). The helmet is bronzed iron, while the cuirass is made of thousands of overlapping iron and lacquered leather scales held together in horizontal rows by means of rivets. The combination made for effective protection against swords and arrows while allowing considerable freedom of movement.

efficiency of the island's agriculture would soon approach levels comparable to those in China and Korea. Like its counterparts on the mainland, the Yamato court and its successors at Nara and Heian-kyo attempted to regulate economic activity in the form of land and produce taxes, taxes on trade, monopolies on strategic commodities, and requisitions of labor for infrastructural projects.

Yet almost from the beginning, as we noted earlier, these efforts at centralization were only partially effective. The larger *uji*, whose power had theoretically been cut by the creation of a state bureaucracy, got around the problem by supplying many of the officials for the new body. They took advantage of government incentives to reclaim land from the wilderness and the Ainu. By such means the large *shoen* and monastery estates with their tax exemptions tended to acquire regional political and military power.

Such multiple centers also produced an increase in and decentralization of trade. The period from 1250 to 1450 saw cycles of expansion in overseas commerce, with colonies of Japanese merchants—and often, Japanese pirates—operating in the Philippines, Java, and Malacca as well as Korea and China. Through their wares, the *daimyo* and samurai became increasingly sophisticated connoisseurs of luxury goods such as silks, jade, porcelain, lacquerware, rare woods, and books and paper. As the early ports, market towns, regional capitals, and, by the sixteenth century, castle towns, grew, Japanese craftspeople became adept at imitating and refining Chinese crafts, in some cases surpassing the quality of the originals. Moreover, a growing and increasingly diverse middle class of merchants, artisans, actors, dancers, **sake** brewers, ship builders, and others organized into trade guilds (*za*) all partook of such luxury items. The increased demand for capital among them spurred a monetization of the economy and the beginnings of banking and credit systems.

Sake: Traditional alcoholic drink brewed from rice.

Advances in Agriculture

Most of this would not have been possible without dramatic increases in food production. The period from 1250 to 1600 saw a vast increase in both intensive cultivation of Japan's limited arable land and the introduction of a host of new crops to multiply its productivity. As it had throughout east Asia, the widespread use of fast-ripening Champa rice strains from southeast Asia in southern Honshu, Kyushu, and Shikoku vastly enhanced stocks of this staple. In Kyushu it allowed three crops a year; in other areas, the wet paddy fields it required allowed dry raised beds for vegetables to be made from the soil taken out of the paddies. At the same time the introduction of the Chinese "dragon wheel pump" (see Chapter 9) allowed for easy, small-scale irrigation. Finally, a triple-cropping system consisting of buckwheat in winter, wheat in spring, and rice during the monsoon, with vegetables grown on the raised beds in between fields, allowed an average family to sustain itself on only a few acres of land.

If one factors in the use of terracing and dry rice cultivation in more marginal areas, and the introduction of oranges, grapes, and tea, the leaps in population seem almost inevitable. From an estimated population of about 5 million in 1100 a doubling occurred, perhaps as early as 1300; by 1450 it was on its way to doubling again.

Family Structure

As in Korea, the earliest social structures of Japan appear to have been matrilocal and, most likely, matriarchal. *Uji* before the sixth century were organized around female lineages, and the first Chinese accounts mention semi-mythical figures such as "Queen Pimiko." With the coming of Chinese institutions, however, this changed radically at the uppermost levels and more gradually below. As we have seen, during the early importation of Chinese influences in the sixth and seventh centuries, women at the top could still wield considerable political power, as witnessed by Empress Suiko of the Soga clan. By the height of the power of the Heian court, Confucian patriarchal institutions had made a great deal of headway in Japan but were moderated somewhat by the pervasive influence of Buddhism and Shinto. Thus, aristocratic women controlled property, though they increasingly tended to wield political power through men. They were sequestered at court and forced into a highly refined and regulated ritual life, yet they created their own highly influential cultural world. Women like Murasaki Shikibu and Sei Shonagon (ca. 965–1025) defined the guidelines for literary and aesthetic appreciation for generations to come in the *Tale of Genji* and *The Pillow Book*, respectively.

Outside the court, the moderating institution for commoners, and particularly women, was the Buddhist monastery. As in China and Korea, the monasteries provided havens for women and men who did not marry or had fled bad marriages. They provided enough education to read the **sutras**, thus helping to increase literacy. They also provided important avenues of political power as large landholders, innkeepers, peacekeepers, and advisers. A famous example was the monastery at Mt. Hiei above Kyoto, whose monks provided guidance to the court for centuries.

As in China and Korea, however, the family life of commoners was mostly governed by a mix of Confucian filial piety, local clan relations, and the desire to improve the family's position through marriage. As in China, girls came to be considered "expendable" because they would move in with their husband's family. Arranged marriages were the norm, and by way of forcing such issues, rape, kidnapping, and family vendettas were all too common. A woman who would not consent to such a marriage, for example, could evade it only if she fled to a monastery before the groom's relatives caught up with her. Failure to escape could result in a beating or even murder. Such informal sanctions eventually gave way under the Tokugawa Shogunate to strictly regulated Neo-Confucian family codes enforced by the shogun's local officials.

> **Sutras:** In Buddhism, a collection of aphorisms relating to some aspect of the conduct of life.

Religion, Culture, and Intellectual Life

The foundations of Japan's original religion, Shinto, go far back into remote antiquity. Some scholars have used the word "vitalism"—akin to animism in Africa and shamanism in Siberia and the Americas—to describe its common features: a deep-seated belief in the power of *kami*—spirits of divinities, beings living and departed, nature as a whole, and even inanimate objects like mountains and streams. Reverence for these forces extended early on to fertility and earthly vitality. Even today Shinto priests commonly wear a stiff black hat that has a phallic figure rising prominently from it.

The importance of ritual vitality was reinforced by a tremendous emphasis on ritual purity—as Chinese observers recorded nearly 2,000 years ago, the Japanese seemed to bathe constantly—and waterfalls were enormously popular as places of ritual ablution and even miracle working. On the other hand, death and corruption were things to be separated from as much as possible—hence the practice of distancing shrines from burial mounds.

The Way of the Gods   Shinto means "the way of the gods," and Japanese mythology recognized a staggering array of deities. Chief among these were Izanagi and

Izanami, whose initial sexual act created the Japanese home islands, as well as Amaterasu, the sun goddess, considered the ancestor of Japan's emperors, purportedly starting with Jimmu in 660 BCE. Until the emperor Hirohito officially renounced his divinity at the end of World War II, every Japanese emperor has been considered a god in the Shinto pantheon by believers.

Although it had undoubtedly arrived some time before, the customary dating of the introduction of Buddhism to Japan is 552 CE, when the king of Paekche sent a collection of Buddhist scriptures as a present to Yamato. Under the missionary Kwalluk, the new religion soon became well established among Japanese elites. As we have seen, after four decades of struggle with the Shinto establishment at court, Buddhism had become the state religion of Yamato in 594. Both religious traditions, however, were ultimately able to coexist and, to some extent, fuse. The ability of Buddhism to adapt the cosmologies of other traditions to its core beliefs, its reverence for nature, emphasis on the transcendental, and lack of a priestly hierarchy made it an easy fit for Shinto. For their part, Shinto believers could add the bodhisattvas and other Buddhist entities to the list of *kami*. Coupled with an already great admiration for things Chinese in Japan, such accommodations made the spread of the religion relatively easy.

Most of the schools of Buddhism established in Japan had first become popular in China. With the exception of the earliest variants, all of them were Mahayana schools. The first to establish itself at Nara was the Hosso school, based on the newly recovered texts brought back by the Chinese monk Xuan Zang from India. This was shortly displaced by the highly influential Tendai (from the Chinese Tiantai) school of Saicho (767–822) and the Shingon sect of Kukai (774–835), which dominated the imperial court for most of the Heian period.

As noted in Chapter 12, for Tendai followers, the most important scripture was the Lotus Sutra. This sutra includes the key revelation that all beings possess a "Buddha nature" and, hence, the potential for salvation. Esoteric Buddhism, on the other hand, placed more emphasis on scriptural study and aesthetics. For both, the degree to which one can grasp the central truth varies according to the capacity of the individual to study and contemplate it but that central truth is in theory open to all at some level. The popular devotional schools of Buddhism also came to Japan during the eighth and ninth centuries. Their simplicity and optimism—simply bowing repeatedly and calling on Amida Buddha with a sincere heart in order to be saved (*nembutsu*)—and the hope for a place in the Pure Land, or Western Paradise, ensured widespread adherence. Even today, it remains the most popular of the Japanese Buddhist schools.

Though neither achieved widespread popularity, two other Buddhist schools deserve mention because of their influence. The first is a wholly Japanese development. Nichiren (1222–1282) advocated a Japan-centered, patriotic form of Buddhism. Japan, he believed, because of its unique history and centrality in the Buddhist world, had become the repository of "true" Buddhism in the present decadent age and must be defended at all cost, a view that he believed was confirmed by the miraculous Japanese deliverance from the Mongols.

Perhaps more influential was the practice of Zen. Again, the Chinese origins of this movement, known as *chan*, were introduced in Chapter 12. Arriving in Japan in the twelfth century, its popularity spread among the *daimyo* and samurai, who had the discipline to pursue its rigors. Zen seeks to achieve *satori*, a flash of enlightenment signaling the recovery of one's Buddha nature. Everyone's path to this is different, so one must follow the instructions of an experienced master rather than engage in prolonged scriptural study. Zen practitioners seek to open themselves to enlightenment by humble, repetitive tasks, contemplating paradoxes (*koans*) and, in some schools, sitting in meditation (*zazen*).

All of these practices can be useful to a warrior. Endless drilling with bow and arrow or sword to the point that the use of each weapon becomes instinctive certainly refines one's martial talents. Such an approach is equally useful in painting, poetry, and calligraphy, where a distinct Zen style of spontaneous, minimalist art suggesting the true inner nature of subject and artist is still a vital area of Japanese aesthetics today.

One final area in which Zen permeated the life of the warrior classes was in the use of tea. Introduced from China by the Zen monk Eisai (1141–1215), tea drinking in Japan became widely adopted as an aid to discipline and meditation among monks in the twelfth century. Soon, however, it became quite popular among the upper classes, and its presentation was ultimately refined into the ritual of the tea ceremony. Here, inside the teahouse where all were equal, under the movements prescribed by the sixteenth-century tea master Sen-no Rikyu (1522–1591), host and guest were to approach their encounter as if they were sharing their last moments together on earth. Since the ceremony was a popular preparation for battle among *daimyo* and samurai, this was often the case.

The Miracles of Kannon.
Amida Buddhism was the most popular school throughout east Asia, and the most popular figure of the many bodhisattvas was Kannon (Guanyin in China). On this long hand scroll dated to 1257, Kannon saves her followers from assorted tribulations: Here, she appears to two men set upon by soldiers or brigands.

The Storyteller's Craft

"But I have a theory of my own about what this art of the novel is, and how it came into being. To begin with, it does not simply consist in the author's telling a story about the adventures of some other person. On the contrary, it happens because the storyteller's own experience of men and things, whether for good or ill—not only what he has passed through himself, but even events which he has only witnessed or been told of—has moved him to an emotion so passionate that he can no longer keep it shut up in his heart . . .

"Clearly then, it is no part of the storyteller's craft to describe only what is good or beautiful. Sometimes, of course, virtue will be his theme, and he may then make such play with it as he will. But he is just as likely to have been struck by numerous examples of vice and folly in the world around him, and about them he has exactly the same feelings as about the pre-eminently good deeds which he encounters: they are more important and must all be garnered in. Thus anything whatsoever may become the subject of a novel, provided only that it happens in this mundane life and not in some fairyland beyond our human ken."

—*The Tale of Genji*. In: W. T. De Bary, ed. *Sources of Japanese Tradition*, vol. 1, pp. 177–178. New York: Columbia University Press, 1964.

Forging a Japanese Culture   With the importation of Chinese political theory to Japan came an understanding of the importance of histories and record keeping. Thus, the first Chinese-influenced Japanese histories, the *Nihongi* (*Chronicles of Japan*) and *Kojiki* (*Records of Ancient Matters*), made their appearance during the early eighth century. At about the same time, the first collection of Japanese poetry published in Chinese, the *Man'yoshu* (*The Ten Thousand Leaves' Collection*) appeared in 760. This work, however, also illustrated the problems inherent in using Chinese as a method of rendering Japanese sounds.

The *Man'yoshu* uses one-syllable Chinese characters picked for their similarity to Japanese sounds and strings them together into Japanese words. If one can follow the *sounds* of the words, one can grasp the meaning of the poems; if, however, one attempts to read them based on the *meaning* of the characters, they become gibberish. This fundamental problem was solved by devising the *kana syllabary*, a system of 50 sounds that form the building blocks of Japanese words. By the late ninth century, a kind of social divide had arisen—as it did later with *han-gul* in Korea—between predominantly male, Buddhist, elite users of literary Chinese and literate women and members of the lower elites who favored the convenience of the *kana* system. As in China and Korea, the technology of printing greatly spurred the circulation of these works and over the centuries helped push functional literacy to some of the highest premodern levels in the world.

In addition to the development of the 31-syllable *tanka* poetry form, perhaps the most important literary developments to come from the use of *kana* were the novel and the prose diary. The former, as we have seen, is credited to Murasaki Shikibu, whose *Tale of Genji* is often considered the world's first novel. A skilled diarist as well, Murasaki was a tutor to the powerful courtier Fujiwara Michinaga, and she put all of her acute observations of the subtleties of court life into *Genji*. Seclusion for court women fostered a considerable amount of self-analysis, and one sees in Murasaki's writing a tension between Buddhist ideas and the requirements of place, name, reputation, and hierarchy at court. Enduring aesthetic guidelines that emerge in the work include the concept of *aware* (a-WAHR-ei), an intensity of feeling with elements of sadness, melancholy, fragility, and the fleetingness of life, often symbolized by cherry blossoms; *okashi*, an ability to make light of the tragic; *en*, an appreciation for visible beauty; and *miyabi*, courtliness and refinement. Similarly, her older contemporary, Sei Shonagon, in her *Pillow Book*, sets an almost modern tone in her astute, funny, and sometimes spiteful categories of likes and dislikes at court.

Chinese artistic genres also strongly influenced Japanese practitioners of the "three excellences" (painting, poetry, and calligraphy). But Japanese sensibilities often took a slightly different direction from their Chinese counterparts. Where Chinese artists tended to strive for symmetry in design in their pursuit of the natural, Japanese craftspeople in pottery, interior design, and visual arts frequently sought "purposeful imperfection." Hence, the *raku* ware of the potter Chojiro, purposely "primitive" in shape, had glazes spontaneously applied and fired; teahouses would have an asymmetrical placement of windows and a rough-cut tree trunk placed off center as a support. Yet while designers created interiors with Spartan simplicity and almost no ornamentation, those pursuing decorative arts often went in for bold, even garish colors and washes of gold and silver. Prime examples of such techniques come from the sixteenth- and seventeenth-century studios of the Kano family, whose screens decorated the castle interiors of Japan's leading *daimyos*.

Vietnam: Human Agency and State Building

For much of the twentieth century, the history of southeast Asia was written according to the cultural divisions separating the areas influenced by China from those influenced by India. In the 1960s, however, this concept of a derivative "Indo-Chinese" history was challenged by scholars, who emphasized the similarities of the lived experience of the common people on both sides of the cultural divide. Of equal importance in this new approach was the *agency* of the people in question: their taking of the initiative in deciding matters of acculturation, political systems, and so forth. Our focus on the interactions and adaptations here is to explore the agency of people in their acceptance and rejection of certain influences and innovations. As with Korea and Japan, therefore, it is crucial to remember that the history of Vietnam and southeast Asia is by no means simply an imitation of Chinese or Indian patterns but the cumulative result of innumerable conscious decisions by millions of people over thousands of years.

The Setting and Neolithic Cultures

The topography of southeast Asia as a whole is similar from the borders of Assam in India to the Mekong delta in the south of what is now Vietnam. Divided by several major river systems—the Irawaddy, Salween, and Mekong—running roughly north to south, and by the Red River, running northwest to southeast through Hanoi and meeting the Gulf of Tonkin at Haiphong, their watersheds are separated by low to medium mountain ranges running generally parallel to them. Even today much of the region is heavily forested, with abundant rainfall supplied by the summer monsoon, which acts as the region's principal climatic regulator. The river valleys and coastal plains are believed to have supplied the wild ancestors of the first rice plants, as well as some of the world's first domesticated fowl sometime after 8000 BCE (see Map 13.7).

The Neolithic revolution appears to have taken place in southeast Asia at about the same time as it did in southwest Asia. This Hoabinhian culture was characterized by the cultivation of root crops, millet, and rice and by about 6000 BCE saw the domestication of pigs and chickens. By 4500 BCE, the famous Dongsan cultures had come on to the scene, marked shortly after by some of humankind's earliest bronze artifacts. The origins of these peoples are still obscure, with contemporary speculation centering on a homeland perhaps in southern China, like the Thai, Laotians,

MAP **13.7** **Southeast Asia: The Physical Setting.**

Burmese, and Cambodians. Out of the fertile, subtropical and tropical regions in which they settled, it is believed that the basics of wet rice agriculture and the domestication of chickens and pigs may well have diffused north into China and perhaps west to northern India.

Village Society and Buddhism

The earliest records of the peoples and states in the region are likewise fragmentary. Late Zhou Chinese references frequently mention the state of Yue, but its southern borders appear to have been fluid and probably included parts of the modern provinces of Guangdong and Guangxi and perhaps the northern part of Vietnam. Once more, the social structure suggests a village-based agricultural system in which women enjoyed far more equality than would later be the case. Villages and clans were often bilateral or matrilineal and matrilocal. Men paid a **bride price** to the families of their wives, and divorce for either spouse appears to have been relatively easy. As in other places in east Asia during the first millennium BCE, women occupied roles as officials, diplomats, merchants, and small-business operators. The area also became one of the first outposts of Theravada Buddhism outside India through the efforts of missionaries from Ceylon (Sri Lanka) in the second century BCE. It would come to be the majority religion in the region for the next 2,000 years.

The "Far South": History and Politics to 1450

With the unification of China under the Qin in 221 BCE, Yue was incorporated into the First Emperor's new state. Thus began a prolonged period of Chinese occupation and local resistance in the area, ultimately lasting over 1,000 years. As in Korea, the occupation brought with

Bride price: Amount negotiated between the family of the groom and the family of the bride to be paid by the former to the latter in some marriage traditions, as compensation for the loss of her labor.

it a cultural invasion, including the full spectrum of Chinese writing, political ideas, and cultural preferences. Like their counterparts in Korea and Japan as well, the new Vietnamese literate elites were incorporated into the increasingly far-flung world of Chinese civilization and the Buddhist cultural and religious sphere. Southeast Asia's geographical position in the center of the maritime portion of this economic and cultural sphere encouraged a considerable openness to outside influences.

Sinification and Resistance   On the other hand, the repeated invasions from the north also went far to cement a Vietnamese ethnic identity. The collapse of the Qin in the period 206–202 BCE encouraged a rebellion against the local Chinese officials of "Nam Viet"—the Vietnamese name for the Chinese *Nanyue* ("Far South"), as the Qin had called their new southern province." The Han emperor Wudi reoccupied northern Vietnam in 111 BCE, however, and swiftly reimposed Chinese institutions on the region.

Han attempts at sinification raised tensions between the new Chinese-influenced elites and those who thus far had managed to retain their cultural independence. The situation was sufficiently volatile that in 39 BCE another rebellion began that to this day is commemorated as helping to form the modern Vietnamese national identity. Trung Trac, the widow of a local leader executed by the Chinese, and her sister Trung Nhi (both ca. 12–43), led their local militia and defeated the Han garrison, sparking a general revolt. The Chinese shortly regrouped, however, and overpowered the forces of the Trung sisters, who drowned themselves rather than be taken alive. For the next millennium, northern Vietnam would be firmly within the imperial Chinese orbit.

In the three and a half centuries following the breakup of the Han Empire in 220 CE, the region was able to gain a degree of political autonomy, but the power of Vietnam's sinified elites continued to ensure their cultural loyalty to China. The growing regional power of the north allowed it to expand into the more Indian-influenced Buddhist kingdoms to the south. With the reunification of China under the Sui and Tang, the drive for Chinese political control of the region was taken up again and the north was soon fully reincorporated into imperial China. During the political chaos following the fall of the Tang, however, the long-awaited opportunity for independence arrived again.

Independence   Dinh Bo Linh, the first emperor of Vietnam, solidified his control of the region in 968. Though politically independent of China, Vietnam's new Li dynasty (1010–1225), long immersed in Chinese notions of Confucianism and statecraft, swiftly instituted Song-style institutions and created its own bureaucracy. Continuing what by now was a long-established pattern of expansion, the Li systematically pushed south during their two centuries of control.

With the fall of the Li dynasty, the Tran dynasty (1225–1400) soon faced the potent threat of the Mongols, who in 1280 would subdue the southern Song in China and form the Yuan dynasty. The first Mongol attempt at invasion, in 1257, was mounted as the Mongols were busily reducing the last strongholds of the southern Song. Once this was accomplished, the attempt was renewed in 1285 and again in 1287. The unsuitability of Mongol strategy and tactics and the stubborn resistance of the Vietnamese ultimately prevented further Mongol expansion and allowed the Tran to keep the dynasty intact.

Vietnam, ca. 1428 CE

Approximate extent of major kingdoms in the early 15th century

→ Trade routes

Khmers Peoples

CHINA

DA VIET

Gulf of Tonkin

Hainan

LAOS

Khmers

CHAMPA

FUNAN

Gulf of Thailand

N

0 km 200

0 miles 200

MAP 13.8 Vietnam, ca. 1428.

Cultural and Political Conflict Even during the height of the Mongol threat, the Tran continued to push southward. Much of this drive was aimed at the state of Champa—the site of the fast-growing rice strains that would do so much to increase east Asian populations. Champa itself had ambitions to achieve regional dominance. Centuries before, in the complex interplay of political and cultural rivalries marking the region, the Vietnamese had expanded at the expense of Champa. Champa and the Khmers, heavily influenced by India, had briefly united to subdue another Indian-influenced state, the trading kingdom of Funan, in the 600s. Now a reconstituted Champa represented not just a strong political threat but, as a Sanskrit, Hindu, and Theravada Buddhist state, a cultural rival as well. In the resulting war, the new Le dynasty of Dai Viet ("Great Viet"), founded in 1428 by Le Loi, decisively broke the power of the Chams in 1471. The remnants of their state were incorporated into Vietnam in 1720 (see Map 13.8).

Economy, Society, and Family

Since the Neolithic domestication of rice, Vietnam has been one of the world centers of wet rice cultivation. Perhaps 300 strains of rice were cultivated in northern Vietnam by the mid-fifteenth century, with yields running as high as 25 bushels per acre (seed-to-harvest ratio of 1:25, compared to the much smaller ratio of 1:5 in wheat-growing Europe at the same time). Roughly 90 percent of the people were engaged in agriculture, a figure consistent with other east Asian agrarian-based societies. Like them, too, the rhythms of the agricultural year were governed by the monsoon cycle. During the long rainy season of the summer, rice, vegetables, and commercial crops such as hemp would be cultivated. The area was the first to use the famous Champa strain of rice, and from the twelfth century on it allowed two crops per year in the southern areas of the country. The dry season was a time for holiday feasting and mending the dikes, retaining ponds, and other structures and tools involved in farming.

As in southern China and Japan, families could be sustained on relatively small amounts of land and required few complex tools beyond the treadle-powered "dragon pump" or a hand-cranked winnowing machine (see Chapter 9). Along with draft animals like water buffalo, these would often be held communally by clans within the *xa*, or village. Villages commonly consisted of raised, thatch-roofed dwellings, surrounded by a bamboo fence and centered on the shrine to the ancestral spirits.

Politics, Labor, and Trade Two key political institutions kept order and acted as checks upon each other. The village headman, the *xa troung*, was elected but had to be approved by the imperial court, which, like its Chinese counterpart, ruled through a Confucian bureaucracy of provincial governors, prefects, and magistrates.

The magistrate and his staff were the last official layer above the *xa troung*, so the headman had considerable power and responsibility at the local level. He collected the taxes and dues and sat with a council of notables. His powers, however, were checked by the council itself, which consisted of members of a scholar-gentry class much like that in China and who had to share in all major decisions, especially those regarding the use of communal land, about 20 percent of the total by the end of the sixteenth century. Thus, there was a balanced tension between the power of the central government and local interests. As in both China and Korea, however, the power of the local council often resulted in periods of increased landlordism and tenancy.

One legacy of the long period of Chinese occupation was the use of conscription and **corvée** labor by Vietnamese dynasties. Peasants were required to serve in the army 4 months per year—indefinitely during national emergencies. They could also be sentenced to slave labor for various offenses. In many cases, they would be sent to open up virgin land for agriculture, which was theirs to keep upon the expiration of their sentences.

Corvée: Labor exacted by a local authority for little or no pay or instead of taxes.

The position of Vietnam and southeast Asia as a whole made it a vital trade crossroads as well as a cultural frontier. This was particularly true as the southern areas were taken from Champa. Nearly all the goods of China, India, and all of their surrounding trade regions passed through the area. In addition, commercialization for regional and statewide markets grew rapidly from the fifteenth century on. Competition among villages supplying different commodities or maintaining craft monopolies was fierce. In some areas, women were forbidden to marry outside the village for fear they would take craft secrets with them.

Changing Position of Women   One pattern of history the Vietnamese shared with the other societies we have examined in this chapter is that of changes in the status of women over time. The nature of the agricultural work undertaken was communal, and men and women tended to work in the fields together. As in Korea and Japan, kinship lines were bilateral—traced through either spouse—or matrilineal. Here again, the long period of Chinese influence and Neo-Confucian emphasis on filial piety, hierarchy, and sharply separate roles for men and women eroded this equality somewhat, though much less markedly than in Korea or Japan. In the villages, or in the ports and market cities, women commonly exercised prominent roles as merchants, entrepreneurs, and craftspeople. This was reinforced by the prominence of the different Mahayana schools of Buddhism. Once more, as in China, Korea, and Japan, the role of the monastery for both men and women allowed a place for and gave an education to those who for whatever reason were on society's fringes. Buddhist nuns and abbesses thus wielded considerable power, though their positions were often at odds with the Confucian precepts of the elites. Still, women's rights to divorce and property ownership were upheld in the Neo-Confucian law code of 1460.

Religion, Culture, and Intellectual Life

Just as the Vietnamese struggled to maintain their political independence, they continually labored to develop their own cultural distinctiveness. While the porous border region with southern China and geographical and ethnic ties to other southeast Asian peoples assured a constant flow of influences, not all were readily absorbed and some were played against each other.

Temple of Literature, Hanoi. The independent Vietnamese states, beginning with Dai Viet in 939, instituted Chinese-style examinations for their civil service. The Temple of Literature was the first national academy for Confucian training, founded in 1076. This building was the examination hall for those testing for the equivalent of the Chinese *jinshi*, or metropolitan degrees. The large Chinese characters, read right to left, carry the motto "A Pattern for Emulation Through the Ages."

Mahayana Buddhism Among the most important of these influences was that of religion. Whether the practice of ancestor veneration arrived with the Chinese or whether it was present before is as yet unsettled. Nearly all villages even into the twentieth century, however, had a shrine for a founding ancestor or famous headman where periodic ceremonies honoring him would take place. As in Korea, the coming of the Han emperor Wudi's armies in the second century BCE brought the imperial system of the Son of Heaven as intermediary between heaven and earth. At about the same time, however, Theravada was being established in the Indianized ports of southeast Asia and became the first branch of Buddhism to be established there. Thus, as the Han retreat from the north allowed some political breathing space, the barest beginnings of Mahayana began to come into the area as well. For several hundred years, though, Indian-influenced Theravada dominated the religious and cultural life of Vietnam. Buddhist stupas were erected and the austere, mendicant, saffron-robed monks held sway in northern Vietnam, as they still do in much of southeast Asia.

The Tang occupation brought a large infusion of Mahayana influence with its vibrant art motifs, temples, and monasteries as well as the entire spectrum of Confucian and Daoist ideas. While Mahayana became the dominant division from this time on, the Vietnamese at the local level tended to pursue a synthesis of all of these systems in their beliefs. As in China, this collection was often referred to as *tam giao*, after the Chinese *san jiao*—"the three religions."

Similarly, the Vietnamese court sought to reconcile the differences among the systems by promulgating edicts on their compatibility. Indeed, some emperors sought to take a leading role in developing a unique strain of Vietnamese Buddhism. The later emperor Minh Mang (r. 1820–1841), for example, advocated combining the opposites of "abstention" from the world and "participation" in it.

Chu Nom During the fifteenth-century consolidation of Dai Viet, the Le dynasty undertook a thoroughgoing sinification of the country, in much the same way as under the Yi in Korea. Chinese law codes and even dress was adopted. As in Korea and Japan, Chinese-style histories were also compiled and court-sponsored literary projects of various sorts commissioned. Yet here again, the literary language favored by the court for such projects continued to be the Chinese of the elites who had the time and means to undertake its study. As in Korea and Japan, an attempt was made to develop a vernacular writing system, in this case sometime during the tenth century. Called *chu nom* ("southern characters"), the new script combined existing Chinese characters picked for the similarity of their sounds to Vietnamese words with newly invented Chinese-style characters for meaning. It was similar in this respect to the formation of many complex Chinese characters but would in theory be easier to use as a tool for literacy. Poets like Nguyen Thuyen and his contemporary Ho Quy Ly in the fourteenth century used this system, translating Chinese works into the script. However, it never had the widespread circulation of *han-gul* or *kana* in Korea or Japan.

Putting It All Together

While there are a great many commonalities among the patterns of state formation and religious interaction among the states along the outer ring of Chinese influence, each responded to that influence in its own way (see Concept Map). From the beginning, each state sought to maintain its political independence, though all acculturated to some degree to Chinese models. Yet, here it should be stressed that the relative attractiveness of those models was largely related to their usefulness in state building. That is, while the Koreans and Vietnamese struggled to throw off the Chinese political yoke, the systems and values of the invaders also gave powerful tools to the invaded, allowing them to organize their new regimes after they had won independence. In a sense, the invaders had provided a ready-made package of laws, moral codes, and social organization for the new states but also came with moderating institutions like Mahayana Buddhism. They were therefore equipped with a wide range of options to adopt or discard as the situation demanded. In that sense, the cultural intrusion was far more successful than the political one.

In the case of Japan, since the early Yamato state did not have Chinese traditions imposed on it from the outside, its leaders could afford to be more selective in what to adopt. However, the wholesale adoption of Chinese institutions proceeded even more quickly in Japan than on the mainland. Part of this may be attributed to the

饒融情英媕。
良心吧勤沛對處貝
特造化頒朱理智吧
吧權利吧。每喌智調
自由吧平等術人調品
畢奇每趴生翽調特

Chu nom **Script.** Like *han-gul* in Korea and the *kana* syllabaries in Japan, *chu nom* ("southern characters") represents an attempt by the Vietnamese to create a workable vernacular writing system. Unlike the other two systems, however, the Chinese characters are not simplified or put into an alphabetical arrangement. While useful in rendering Vietnamese sounds, it still required considerable memorization of the characters themselves, which remained something of an impediment to widespread literacy.

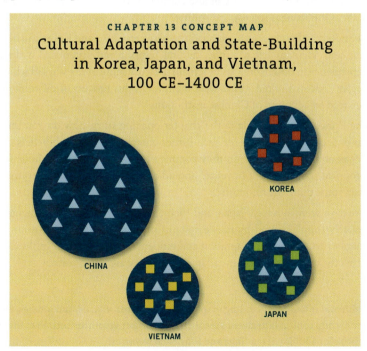

CHAPTER 13 CONCEPT MAP
Cultural Adaptation and State-Building in Korea, Japan, and Vietnam, 100 CE–1400 CE

KOREA

CHINA

JAPAN

VIETNAM

growing sense of the power that such institutions could provide to a government; part of it may also have been a growing sense on the part of the Japanese that states on the mainland based on these institutions were a potential threat. In essence, they felt they had to "join them" before they were beaten by them.

By the end of the fifteenth century, all three of these states were in the process of consolidating civilizations based to varying degrees on Chinese models and prominently included Neo-Confucianism and Buddhism among their governing traditions. They may therefore be considered part of the dominant trend toward the formation of religious civilizations, a pattern we have emphasized in Part 3 of this volume. However, given the specific adaptations to local conditions, the three states were quite different from each other and from China. Even at the most signified level of governmental organization, the Japanese role of *daimyo* as feudal lords and samurai as retainers, to cite just one example, would have been unthinkable in China, Vietnam, or Korea. Yet all four of these countries, faced with varying degrees of dislocation, foreign intrusion, or rebellion, would seek similar solutions to solve these problems.

Review and Respond

1. What were the most important innovations brought by the Chinese to Korea?

2. Which of these innovations were, in your view, the best fit for the early Korean states? Why?

3. What were the most important advantages of Japan's geographical position with regard to the Asian mainland? What were the most important disadvantages?

4. How was the situation of Japan with regard to receiving innovation from the mainland different from that of Korea or Vietnam?

5. What were the advantages of Chinese culture for the elite of Vietnam? How did this affect Vietnamese society and culture?

6. As we noted in this chapter, the interaction between China and Korea and between China and Vietnam left a strong cultural imprint and stimulated a drive for independence in both Korea and Vietnam. Discuss some of the ways in which this complex process worked. What were the roles in this process of different groups influenced by adoption of Chinese institutions?

7. Using Prince Genji's criteria in the chapter-opening story, how do you think his ideas of acceptable material for such stories compare to Buddhist beliefs current in Japan at the time? How do they compare to your own beliefs about what is appropriate material for a novelist? Should novelists write about everything, or should some things be off-limits?

8. As we have seen, in Korea, Japan, and Vietnam, the Chinese literary language was ultimately supplemented by native systems of writing. What other examples of cultural or technological adaptation and refinement can you trace in these areas? Discuss the importance of these adaptations on the areas in question.

▶ For additional resources, including maps, primary sources, visuals, and quizzes, please go to www.oup.com/us/vonsivers. Please see the Further Resources section at the back of the book for additional readings and suggested websites.

Thinking Through Patterns

▶ **How was the history of Korea affected by its relations with China? With Japan?**

The most obvious and dramatic way the various Korean kingdoms were affected by China was through conquest. Chinese culture and institutions were firmly planted in Korea during the Qin, Han, Sui, and Tang eras. In many respects this also prompted the Korean kingdoms to assert their political independence and to be discriminating about which Chinese institutions to adopt. Thus, Neo-Confucianism was adopted because of its use as a state-supporting ideology. Chinese writing, though quite useful as the means of acquiring the literature of China, ultimately yielded to the *han-gul* system as more convenient and user-friendly.

In the case of Japan, Korea's situation was as a cultural intermediary and as a mainland target for conquest. Thus, during certain periods, Korea's status as a buffer between the two regional powers made its position precarious.

In addition to the Bronze Age elements of wet rice cultivation and bronze implements—which moved Japan ultimately toward agrarian–urban society—the cultural elements, beginning with the Chinese writing system, were the most influential. With the writing system came ideas of government, ethics, philosophy, literature, and, of course, Buddhism. Unlike Korea and Vietnam, Japan acquired all of these more or less voluntarily and had the leisure to adopt them according to its own needs, rather than have them imposed by conquest.

▶ **Which important elements of Chinese culture were adapted by the Japanese for their own purposes? What advantages did Vietnam have over Korea and Japan in this regard?**

▶ **Which Japanese adaptations of Chinese institutions did not work well in Japan? Why?**

While the Chinese writing system gave Japan a ready-made literature, the language itself was not well suited to the Japanese vernacular. Thus, by the 800–900s it had to be supplemented with the *kana* systems. But more serious was the less than perfect fit of the Chinese government structures on Japan's still clan-based society. Here, the cleavages developing during the Heian period would cause the social breakdown that resulted in the era of the shoguns, lasting until 1867.

Like Japan and Korea, much of Vietnam was influenced by the importation of Chinese culture, including Buddhism, the imperial system, and Confucianism. Like Korea, and unlike Japan, Vietnam suffered centuries of Chinese invasion and occupation. But Vietnam, positioned on the border with the Indianized states of southeast Asia, also was influenced by Indian culture in its southern and western areas, causing interactions and adaptations that did not take place in the other states inside the Chinese sphere of cultural and political influence.

▶ **In what ways was the experience of Vietnam similar to that of Japan and Korea? How was it different?**

Chapter 14 | Patterns of State Formation in Africa

600-1450 CE

AFRICA

According to local tradition, the founder of the gold-trading kingdom of ancient Ghana (ca. 400–1200) in West Africa was Dinga. He was a descendant of Bilal, the Ethiopian who was chosen by the Prophet Muhammad as the first *muezzin*, or crier who calls the Muslim faithful to prayer. When Dinga arrived from Arabia in the Sahel, the east–west belt of steppe south of the Sahara Desert in West Africa, he asked a many-headed snake at a well for water. The snake refused, and Dinga subdued her through magic to receive his drink. After marrying the snake's three daughters, he fathered three sons, the eldest of whom was a half-human, half-serpent

Seeing Patterns

▶ What patterns of adaptation did the Christian kingdoms of northeast Africa demonstrate in their interactions with the civilizations of the Middle East and eastern Mediterranean?

▶ What were the responses of Africans to Muslim merchants who connected them with the trading zone of the Indian Ocean and Mediterranean? As these Africans adapted to Islam, which forms of political organization did they adopt?

▶ In what ways did the economic and political transformations on the east African coast and West Africa affect developments in the interior?

being who went to live underground. The two younger sons were still growing when their father left to return to Arabia.

The second son grew into a man with little consideration for others. He mistreated his father's old servant by wiping his hands on the servant's head after finishing his meals. The third son turned into a much kinder person, giving the same servant his leftovers. Years later, Dinga, nearly blind, felt his end coming and summoned the two sons to his side, to give them their respective heritages. The elderly servant, who had never forgotten the kindness of the younger son, persuaded the youngest son to go first, in the guise of his older brother, to receive the lion's share of Dinga's estate. Indeed, the father bestowed his power of magic as well as the kingdom on the youngest son, while the older son received the more modest power of rain making.

Back in the kingdom, the two sons struck a deal whereby Ghana would receive enough rain and gold as long as the people of the kingdom would sacrifice every year a virgin and a colt. After many years of human and animal sacrifices, a Wagadu man and admirer of a virgin about to be sacrificed slew the snake brother. As he was dying, the snake brother cursed the

Mansa Musa, King of Mali.
Detail from the *Catalan Atlas* (1375), showing Mansa Musa, the fabulously rich king of Mali, seated on a throne and holding a gold nugget—the source of his wealth. The European-style crown and beard reveal the mapmaker's ignorance of Africa, though reports of his wealth fired people's imaginations far and wide.

451

Animism: The experience of and/or belief in the presence of a life substance or spirit shared by all living beings and things in nature.

people of Wagadu, which lost its abundance of rain and gold. A parched and impoverished Ghana fell to its enemies.

This story gives us a glimpse of the main pattern underlying the history of sub-Saharan Africa between 600 and 1450. In this period, rulers converted to Islam and incorporated its beliefs and practices into their traditional African spirituality of **animism**. For example, we learn that Dinga was a descendant of a companion of the Prophet Muhammad. The account of the aging father and the heritage for his two sons is obviously an adaptation from the Hebrew Bible and its story of Isaac, Esau, and Jacob. The appearance of creatures with many heads—as a symbol for the invincibility of a dragon—has Sumerian origins and resurfaces in the Hebrew and Christian Bibles as well as in popular Islam. Indeed, in his traditional biography, the Prophet Muhammad is said to have slain several dragons. Traditional African spirituality is prominent in the ambiguous figure of the serpent, which controls the water and demands sacrifices in order to remain benevolent, and in the king, who is endowed with the power of magic. Thus, this foundation myth shows the complexity and creativity of these interacting indigenous and adopted cultural heritages.

While the Eurasian and North African pattern during 600–1450 was that of the formation of religious civilizations that contained commonwealths of states, the pattern of sub-Saharan Africa in the same period was that of religious kingdom and empire formation. In the northeast of sub-Saharan Africa, kingdoms had already adapted to Christianity prior to 600, and the new kingdoms of Nubia and Ethiopia continued the Christian heritage. In West Africa, Mali, the successor of ancient Ghana, adapted to Islamic imperial traditions and became the only multilinguistic, multiethnic, and multireligious empire of sub-Saharan Africa during 600–1450. On Africa's east coast, a set of small Islamic merchant states emerged, the Swahili port cities, under either kings or councils of notables. Finally, in the interior of central and southern Africa, indigenous kingdoms rose on the basis of the African tradition of magic-empowered authority, descended from the animist heritage.

Christians and Muslims in the Northeast

During 600–1250, Nubia was a Christian kingdom along the middle Nile in the Sahara and sub-Saharan steppe, built on agriculture and trade between tropical Africa and the Middle East. Ethiopia, Nubia's neighbor in the highlands to the southeast, was similarly Christian but, unlike Nubia, was initially a collection of decentralized chiefdoms. When one of the chiefs eventually centralized rule in 1137, the new kingdom of Ethiopia unified the highlands, sent missionaries to the southern provinces to convert non-Christian Africans, and battled the Muslims in the lowlands on the Red Sea coast in the name of a Christian Crusade. Both Nubia and Ethiopia were fascinating cases of sub-Saharan polities adopting patterns of state formation from the Middle East into their African heritage: They adapted to Middle Eastern plow agriculture and Christianity, while long retaining African traditions of decentralization.

Nubia in the Middle Nile Valley

About a century after the end of the kingdom of Meroë, sometime around 350 (see Chapter 6), small Nubian successor states dominated the middle Nile valley from north to south. In the course of the mid-500s, these states converted to Coptic Christianity and subsequently united into a single kingdom. Open to trade with the then rising empire of the Arab Umayyads, Nubia experienced a gradual ascendancy of Arab merchants to dominance in Nubian commerce. Eventually, the enhanced position of these merchants led to Muslim political control: In 1276, the Egyptian Mamluks defeated the Christian king of Nubia and installed a puppet regime. By around 1450 Christianity in Nubia had largely given way to Islam.

The Rise of Christian Kingdoms in Nubia   Meroë's power ended as a result of deforestation near the capital and nomadic attacks against its northern provinces. The nomads had adapted to the use of the camel in the early centuries of the Common Era, which allowed them to carry out swift long-distance raids over vast tracts of inhospitable territory. Indeed, the use of the camel created a transportation revolution in the Sahara in general and opened up new routes for commerce and invasion. One immediate result of this was that a new ruling class of Nubians arose in the middle Nile valley during the 400s. Nubian chiefs and their followers established three small kingdoms along the middle Nile that prospered in large part as the result of the rapid spread of the animal-driven waterwheel (*saqiya* [SAH-qee-ya]) invented in Egypt in the first century CE. Water could now be lifted into channels all year round, even at some distance from the river, for the purpose of planting two

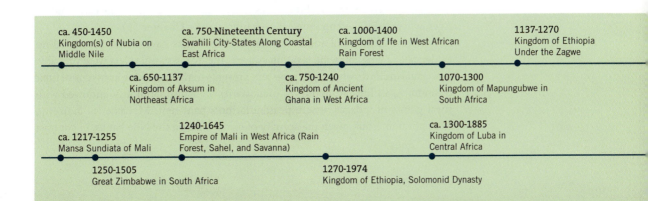

ca. 450-1450
Kingdom(s) of Nubia on Middle Nile

ca. 750-Nineteenth Century
Swahili City-States Along Coastal East Africa

ca. 1000-1400
Kingdom of Ife in West African Rain Forest

1137-1270
Kingdom of Ethiopia Under the Zagwe

ca. 650-1137
Kingdom of Aksum in Northeast Africa

ca. 750-1240
Kingdom of Ancient Ghana in West Africa

1070-1300
Kingdom of Mapungubwe in South Africa

1240-1645
Empire of Mali in West Africa (Rain Forest, Sahel, and Savanna)

ca. 1300-1885
Kingdom of Luba in Central Africa

ca. 1217-1255
Mansa Sundiata of Mali

1250-1505
Great Zimbabwe in South Africa

1270-1974
Kingdom of Ethiopia, Solomonid Dynasty

annual grain crops. Archaeological evidence points to a substantial increase in the number of villages in the region as a result of this innovation.

In the 500s, Egyptian missionaries converted the Nubians to Christianity. Pagan temples became churches, and new churches and monasteries were built, ultimately in nearly every village. Kings and members of the ruling class sponsored these Christian institutions, providing them with rich wall paintings, crosses, *reliquaries* (containers for saints' relics), *censers* (incense burners), baptismal spoons (to pour holy oil on infants), *chalices* (wine cups for the Eucharist), and bowls. As did their contemporaries in the Mediterranean and Middle East, the Nubian rulers appreciated the unifying effect of a single state religion over the multiplicity of local temple cults.

Barely Christianized, Nubia now had to withstand an invasion of Arabs from Egypt. After the establishment of the Arab caliphate of Syria, Iraq, and Egypt (see Chapter 10), the new governors in Egypt organized military campaigns into neighboring countries. In 652, one of these campaigns penetrated deep into Nubia. The Arab military used siege engines and caused considerable damage to one of the Nubian capitals. But an army of Nubian archers, long famous for their skill with bow and arrow, defeated the Arabs, forcing them to retreat. In a subsequent agreement, the two sides formally recognized each other, made a pact, and drew up a schedule of future friendly exchanges among their respective rulers. Later Muslim historians reinterpreted this pact, ignoring the defeat and presenting it as a treaty of submission to Islamic hegemony. Such differing interpretations notwithstanding, the pact endured and blocked the advance of Islam into East Africa for 600 years.

Royal Power and Governance

At of the turn of the 700s, a "great king" emerged who unified the three Nubian kingdoms. Power remained largely decentralized, however, with a dozen vassal rulers and an appointed—later hereditary—official called an "eparch." This official governed the northern subkingdom and was responsible for its defense against Egypt. The distinctive features of the great kings were a crown and rich Byzantine-inspired robes, indicative of the Nubian sense of the divine character of Christian rulership. There were half a dozen central administrators, bearing Greek titles; but their functions are unknown. The Coptic patriarch of Alexandria appointed the bishops, who, therefore, were independent from the kings, in marked contrast to Ethiopia as well as Catholic Europe in the early Middle Ages, where the kings appointed church officials (see Chapter 11).

In terms of financial administration, archaeologists have so far discovered no evidence of a kingdomwide taxation system. The dozen vassal rulers were probably powerful landlords who might have sent presents to the great king as tokens of their position. As in Europe, abbots of monasteries were also landlords, endowed with royal grants of villages, where peasant-farmers paid rent. Monasteries, however, were not numerous, given the scarcity of fertile land on the Nile banks, in contrast

---

A Tenth-Century Muslim View of the Nubian Kingdoms

"Some of the [people of the] Sudan who live nearer to [the well-known kingdoms of the Middle East], do resort to religious beliefs and practices and law, approaching in this respect the people of these kingdoms. Such is the case with the Nuba [Nubians] and Habasha [Ethiopians], because they are Christians, following the religious tenets of the Rum [Byzantines]. Prior to the rise of Islam they were in neighbourly contact with the Byzantine Empire because the land of the Nuba borders on Egypt and the Habasha live on the Sea of Qulzum [Red Sea]."

—Abu Ishaq al-Istakhri (d. ca. 950), *Kitab masalik wa al-mamalik.* In N. Levtzion and J. F. P. Hopkins, eds. *Corpus of Early Arabic Sources for West African History*, pp. 40–41. Princeton, NJ: Markus Wiener, 2000.

to Ethiopia, western Europe, and Byzantium. Most likely, in the vicinity of the great king's residence some basic fiscal mechanisms existed whereby village headmen delivered taxes in kind. Another, perhaps even the principal, source of income for the kings and eparchs was long-distance trade, which they controlled. In this respect, the Christian great kings of Nubia were similar to their Islamic counterparts in eastern and western Africa.

Agriculture   The farmland of the Nubian villages consisted of small strips of arable land on the up to 2-mile-wide fertile banks of the Nile. The annual summer floods between June and September inundated these strips, leaving them covered with rich sediment. In a few places, a wider valley or low-level islands in the river allowed for the farming of additional fields. Palm orchards helped to anchor the silt, and stone walls and jetties built into the Nile captured additional amounts of alluvial soil. As the floods receded in fall, villagers grew sorghum, millet, barley, wheat, and cotton with the help of plows pulled by oxen.

Timeless Technology. This early-twentieth century photograph shows an animal-driven *saqiya*, the construction of which has remained virtually unchanged for nearly two millennia. The vertical wheel in the well carries earthenware pots that scoop up water and empty it into an elevated irrigation channel (not visible in this image).

Higher fields away from the banks, which required waterwheels for irrigation, were planted during the winter with pulses, okra, melons, and other garden crops for spring harvesting. In the spring, farmers planted second crops on both the banks and higher elevations. Vineyards became more important as the kingdoms evolved, and wine was consumed by villagers in taverns as well as by priests and monks in daily religious services. Farmers also planted limited amounts of alfalfa for the feeding of cattle and donkeys. Sheep and goats fed on the stubble of grain fields and on scrubland, while pigs ate household remnants. Arabic written sources report the necessity of occasional food transports during local famines on the Nile, but generally the Nubian villages were self-supporting.

Long-Distance Trade   The pact of 652 between the Arabs and Nubia included clauses concerning the trade of Egyptian cloth, pottery, iron utensils, leather goods, and wine for ivory and slaves. The latter two items came from the tropical territories on the White Nile, though nothing is known about how Nubian merchants and slave raiding troops operated in these territories. Whatever the specifics of the Nubian activities along the White Nile, the kings taxed the merchant caravans at various resting places along the way.

In the period between 800 and 1200, the long-distance trade attracted Muslim merchants and craftspeople from beyond Aswan to the northern province of the Nubian kingdom, where they settled in a number of villages and possibly built mosques. A ruling in the mid-800s by an Egyptian Muslim judge recognized by Nubia allowed the Muslims in Nubia to acquire private property. A money economy then emerged, based on Islamic gold dinars. Muslim merchants also settled along the Red Sea coast, especially once the North African Fatimid caliphs had conquered Egypt in 969. To compete with the Iraqi Abbasid caliphs on the Persian Gulf, the Fatimids developed maritime trade with India through the Red Sea. Both of these trade avenues would bolster the commerce of the entire Mediterranean region and even reach to far-off western Europe (see Map 14.1).

MAP **14.1** Long-Distance Trade in Northeast Africa and the Middle East, 800–1200.

From Christian to Islamic Nubia   In the mid-1000s, to secure their hold on the Red Sea, Egyptian rulers resettled nomadic tribes from Arabia to Upper Egypt. Unfortunately for Nubia, these tribes and their neighbors began raiding the kingdom in the 1100s. The local rulers in northern Nubia, principal defenders against the raids, gained in power vis-à-vis the Nubian kings. Perhaps as a consequence, dynastic rivalries broke out; and in the 1200s both usurpers and pretenders to the throne appealed to Egypt for support. The Mamluks, who governed Egypt at this time (1250–1517), responded to the appeals with enthusiasm, adding Nubia to their anti-Christian holy war effort. They propagated the reinterpretation of the pact of 652 as a treaty requiring regular tributes, particularly the delivery of slaves, from Nubia. In 1276, they conquered Nubia, installed a Christian vassal king, and levied the head tax, which non-Muslims in Islamic lands had to pay. In due time, the Christian dynasty gave way to Muslim rulers; and in 1365, after a new wave of Arab nomadic incursions, the Nubian kingdom ceased to exist altogether.

Viewed in retrospect, through interaction with the Roman Empire Nubia adapted itself to the Christian institutions of sacred kingship. A specifically Nubian pattern of political formation emerged that resembled the feudal practices (see Chapter 11) of many other places around the world, in which kings acted as representatives of God on earth but lacked the resources to govern with the help of centralized institutions. Instead, they relied on the support of federated chiefs, who functioned much like vassals. The kings were also not strong enough to incorporate the clerical hierarchy into their states, so the patriarch of Alexandria never lost control over the appointment of Nubian bishops—unlike the pope in his struggles with the Holy Roman emperors over lay investiture. Nubian churches were outposts of the Egyptian **Coptic** Church rather than indigenous institutions with their own hierarchy intertwined with the Nubian royal dynasty. Had the Nubian Church been a "national church" like those we will examine in Europe (see Chapter17), it might have been in a better position to resist Islamization once Muslim rulers took over.

Ethiopia in the Eastern Highlands

After the Christian kingdom of Aksum had lost Yemen to the Sasanid Persians in 570 and had exhausted the timber resources around its capital in the 600s, it shriveled to a chiefdom. However, in cooperation with the Coptic Church, Aksum continued to represent the church's mission to convert the southern highland Africans. Eventually, new dynasties arose and renewed the mission, among which the Solomonids and their Christian Crusades were the most successful. In Ethiopia, the adaptation to Christianity was more thorough than in Nubia. The Ethiopians embarked on a pattern of forming an African Christian civilization, including the Judeo-Christian symbolism of Zion and Christian law.

Coptic Christianity: A branch of Christianity centered in Egypt that affirms the sole divine nature of Jesus, in contrast to Catholic western and Orthodox eastern Christianities, in which the combined divine and human nature of Jesus is proclaimed.

Christianity in the Highlands   The kings of Aksum and the patriarch of the Coptic Church abandoned the capital perhaps as early as the mid-600s and reestablished themselves in a modest chiefdom with better agrarian resources farther south. They continued to trade ivory, ostrich feathers, musk, and myrrh for linen and cotton textiles as well as spices on the Red Sea but no longer issued coins. When Muslim rulers in Egypt in the late 800s occupied ports on the west coast of the Red Sea and expanded trade with India and East Africa, Aksum became a partner in this trade. In addition to these goods, it sold slaves captured in raids in the lowlands to the south. The main effort of the small Aksum kings was directed toward campaigning southward, taking priests and settlers with them to convert and pacify the defeated highland Africans. A monastery, founded in the late 800s some 200 miles southwest of Aksum, became the main center for sending out missionaries to the south. Reduced as it was, Aksum continued to be a factor in highland politics.

Quite dramatically, however, in the 970s the Africans subjected to conversion struck back. A mysterious queen, Gudit or Judith, led several destructive campaigns in which churches and monasteries were burned, towns destroyed, and thousands of people killed or enslaved. The situation was so chaotic that the patriarch of Alexandria refused to appoint the customary metropolitan bishop from Egypt to the country. Scholars, scouring the scant evidence to identify the area of this queen's origin, have determined that she might have been from the recently Christianized parts of the highlands. After her regime of terror of allegedly 40 years, a remnant of the Aksumite kingdom recovered and survived modestly for another century; but little is known about its kings and nothing about the extent of their rule.

State and Church Under the Zagwe Kings   Political stability eventually returned to the highlands with the foundation of the Zagwe dynasty (1137–1270), centered on a Christianized province some 300 miles south of Aksum. To its neighbors, the Zagwe kingdom was "Ethiopia" or "Abyssinia," names rooted in the Hebrew and Christian Bibles. The Zagwe kings laid the foundation for a return to dominant

Church of St. George, Lalibela, Ethiopia. Stone masons cut this church and its interior from the surrounding rock formation. This and 11 other churches, built in the early 1200s, are part of a pilgrimage center created in the image of the Holy Land in Palestine.

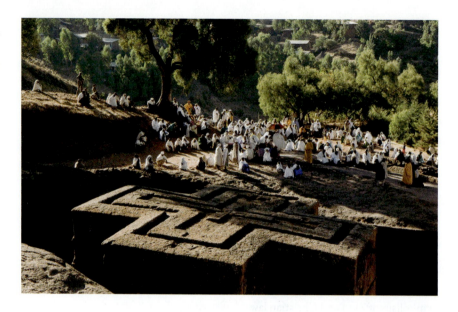

royal power and continued the Aksumite tradition of church sponsorship and missionary work in the south.

A first step toward reunification was the request of an early king in the mid-twelfth century to his metropolitan bishop to appoint seven additional bishops. The idea was that this nucleus of an Ethiopian episcopate would later grow to the 10 members required for a vote of independence from the patriarch of Alexandria. The king, however, did not get far with his attempt to create an independent Ethiopian Church. After lengthy negotiations with the patriarchs of Egypt and Syria and the Muslim ruler of Egypt, the latter refused the split. The Muslims were not about to relinquish the indirect leverage they possessed in Ethiopia through their political control over the patriarchs in Egypt. Had Ethiopia succeeded, the interesting development of a "national church" would have occurred: just the opposite of the situation in Europe at that time, where the pope wrested control of the church from the kings during the investiture controversy.

Church sponsorship expressed itself in the construction of 11 remarkably innovative structures carved out from subterranean rock during the early 1200s, called the Lalibela churches. The kings arranged the churches in two groups, separated by a stream named Yordanos, named after the biblical Jordan River. The policy of the Zagwe dynasty was the recreation of Zion, perhaps in succession of Jerusalem, which the Muslims reconquered in 1187 from the western European crusaders. Accordingly, the dynasty used these churches for elaborate annual masses and processions during Passion Week. The Lalibela monoliths are unique in the history of Christian church construction and have no parallels elsewhere.

Administrative Organization   Under the Zagwe kings, the conversion of the peoples in the central and southern highlands to Christianity resumed. In addition, the kings encouraged the colonization of the land with Christian settlers from the north. These settlers introduced the plow and cereal agriculture, replacing the previous hoe and tuber crops (ensete, taro, and yam). The central and southern highlands were geographically much larger than the north and offered ample opportunities for the establishment of new villages, fields, and pastures. With its fertile volcanic soil, southern Ethiopia became one of the most productive agricultural regions of sub-Saharan Africa.

The political system that emerged in the center and south was an extension of what Aksum had pioneered in the north. Under a king ruling by divine right, Ethiopia was a confederation of provincial lords, some of whom also used royal titles. These lords lived in villages among their farmers and collected rents, consisting of grain, pulses, and cattle. Each farming household had a hut or house, wooden scratch plow, six or more cattle (enough to reproduce one or two oxen needed for pulling the plow), seed, and storage space. Since none of these items represented a heavy investment, households were not tied to particular properties in the village. Plots were constantly divided and reconstituted as a result of deaths, marriages, or divorces. Since both daughters and sons inherited land equally, plots circulated among the villagers more frequently than in Muslim countries, which favored male inheritance and excluded females from farmland inheritance. Legally, ownership of the land was vested in families and had the status of inalienable property, even if the lords had the right to collect rents.

The Solomonid Dynasty Once Christians from the north had settled as farmers in the central highlands and had converted the locals to Christianity, they shifted the focus of their missionary efforts southward. In 1270, a new dynasty of kings, the Solomonids, emerged some 300 miles south of Aksum, in the region of today's capital of Ethiopia, Addis Ababa. These new kings claimed descent from the Aksumite kings and sponsored the composition of an elaborate foundation narrative, the *Kebra Negast*, which legitimized the Solomonid dynasty until its fall in 1974. According to this narrative, the kings of Aksum were not only the descendants of a union between the queen of Sheba and the Israelite king Solomon but also the heirs to the Israelite Ark of the Covenant after the destruction of the First Temple by the Neo-Babylonians. The Ethiopians thus appropriated the biblical heritage more thoroughly than any eastern or western European Christian peoples did. The religious heritage of the Solomonids still lives on in Ethiopia. Outside Africa, this heritage has been embraced by the *Rastafarians*—Afrocentric Christians who form a small minority in Jamaica and have found many admirers, some perhaps more because of the popular reggae music of Bob Marley (1945–1981) than its doctrines.

Ethiopian Christians and Coastal Muslims During the 1300s and most of the 1400s, Ethiopia was a powerful kingdom. The kings continued to depend on the collaboration of their provincial lords, but they also commanded a sizeable mercenary army of their own. With this army, they extended their authority over small principalities of Christians, animists, and Muslims in the southern highlands and

---

The Ethiopian Christian Crusade

"Have we not conquered through the power of God, killed (our enemies), and taken prisoner the survivors, great and small, including their rulers? Now be not afraid in face of the rebels; be not divided, for God is fighting for us. And if they come against you with the bow and the spear, you (also) have the bow and the spear. Have you not heard what these Muslim rebels who know not Christ say against the anointed of God: 'When the Christians kill us we become martyrs, and when we kill the Christians we gain paradise'? Thus do the rebel Muslims speak, who have no hope of salvation and are (yet) eager to die. Why, then do you fear the rebels, you who know the Father, the Son, and the Holy Spirit, who are baptized in His name, and are sanctified by the Blood? For long you have made yourselves ready to fight for me; now be ready to fight for Christ, as it is said in the Book of Canons, 'Slay the infidels and renegades with the sword of iron, and draw the sword in behalf of the perfect faith.' Gird on then your swords, make ready your hearts, and be not fearful in spirit, but be valiant and put your trust in God."

—G. W. B. Huntingford, trans. *The Glorious Victories of Amda Seyon, King of Ethiopia*, p. 69. Oxford: Clarendon Press, 1965.

Rift Valley, as well as Muslim sultanates along the Red Sea coast. This extension began with the conquests of King Amda Seyon (r. 1314–1344), who in effect doubled the kingdom's territory. An unknown priest accompanied the king on his campaigns, which he related to posterity in vivid prose and with great detail in *The Glorious Victories of Amda Seyon*, one of the earliest written histories in sub-Saharan Africa. A century after the Mamluks had eradicated the crusader kingdom of Jerusalem in the Middle East (1291), Solomonid Ethiopia was carrying on the Christian holy war in sub-Saharan Africa (see Map 14.2).

Foremost among the Muslim sultanates along the Red Sea coast, which came under Ethiopian authority, were Ifat (1285–1415) and its successor state Adal (1415–1555) on the west coast of the Red Sea, at the entrance from the Indian Ocean. Both relied principally on trade, linking East Africa via the Rift Valley with the India–Mediterranean sea lane. Only the sultanate of Zayla, near modern Djibouti, and a few other places along the coast had sufficient water from wells to allow for a modest garden agriculture. The steppe lowlands farther away from the coast were too dry to support more than widely dispersed populations of camel nomads, who supplied animals and guides to the trade caravans and soldiers to the wars of the sultans against Ethiopia. Urban dwellers, nomads, and pastoralists astride the trade route through the Rift Valley had converted to Islam gradually in the centuries after

MAP **14.2** The Ethiopian Highlands, ca. 1450.

800 when autonomous Muslim rulers in Egypt began the expansion of trade via the Red Sea with India and East Africa.

The Law of the Kings   The Ethiopian kings were ruthless in their efforts to subdue the sultans. But the kings' crusading image notwithstanding, they were also pragmatic enough to exempt Muslim merchants and pastoralists from the church's missionary efforts in the south of the kingdoms. Similarly, the kings had little choice but to tolerate the sultans of Ifat and Adal as Muslim vassals. Ethiopia became de facto a multiethnic, multilinguistic, and multireligious state in which the kings limited the church's conversion efforts.

Legally, however, the kings continued to emphasize their Christian identity, adopting in the mid-1400s a Christianized version of Roman law, *The Law of the Kings* (*Fetha Nagast*), from the Egyptian Copts. The law trailed behind it an intriguing history. According to Islamic law, Christians in Islamic civilization were entitled to self-rule; and for this purpose, the Coptic Church in Egypt adopted portions of Justinian's code and resolutions of church councils for its governance. In the mid-1300s, an Egyptian Copt compiled these law books and resolutions into a single codex governing church affairs, civil law, and criminal law, translated from Greek into Arabic. The Ethiopian translator added a section on kingship, and as such, *The Law of the Kings* remained the law of the land until 1930, when the Ethiopian emperor Haile Selassie issued the first modern constitution.

Contacts with Western Christianity   The reinvigorated Ethiopian kingdom of the Solomonids was keenly interested in establishing contacts with western Christianity, wishing especially for the dispatch of craftspeople (and receiving a few). A first embassy of 30 members traveled in 1297–1312 to visit the popes. A churchman in Genoa reported on these visitors, identifying their king for the first time with the mythical Prester John, a great Christian ruler in the "east" expected to come to the aid of the crusaders in recovering Jerusalem and the Holy Land. Previously, Prester John had been considered to be an Indian priest-king, commander of a huge army; but now after the loss of the Holy Land in 1291, Ethiopia appeared as a better hope for an ally than the more distant India.

The yearning for the recovery of Jerusalem led to the exchange of a dozen or so further letters and embassies between the Ethiopian and European sides during the 1300s and 1400s. But the obstacles against assembling an army in Europe and shipping it through the Mediterranean, let alone coordinating it with Ethiopia, were insurmountable and ultimately resulted in nothing. On the other hand, the improved knowledge of each other was a major factor playing into the eventual Portuguese project of circumnavigating Africa, linking up with the Ethiopian "Prester John," and recovering Jerusalem.

Adaptation to Islam: City-States and Kingdoms in East and South Africa

During the period 600–1450, the Swahili people emerged as an indigenous African population of Muslims. They formed a society with common features but were divided into dozens of city-states along a 2,000-mile stretch of the African east coast, from today's Somalia in the north to Mozambique in the south. The Swahilis' most common feature was their function as merchant middlemen between the interior of East Africa and the Middle East as well as India. In the interior, increasing agricultural resources and trade with the Swahili encouraged the expansion of chiefdoms but not yet the rise of kingdoms, except in the far south, in the middle Limpopo valley and on the Zimbabwean plateau where local people mined gold. Here, beginning around 1075, towns, cities, and kingdoms arose, the best known of which was Great Zimbabwe (ca. 1250–1505).

The Swahili City-States on the East African Coast

Dissenting Arabs, driven by the centralizing caliphs to the margins of the Arab Empire in the Middle East, were the first to establish trade contacts in the 700s with Bantu-speaking villagers in coastal East Africa. In the following centuries, these villagers adapted themselves to long-distance trade and Islamic civilization. They evolved into an urban society of kings, **patricians**, religious scholars, sailors, fishermen, and farmers based in small port cities. The kings and patricians were consumers of luxury goods brought to them by Middle Eastern and Indian merchants. As sellers of goods manufactured in their cities to the populations of the interior, the patricians acquired goods from the interior, which the Muslim merchants from overseas took back home. Thus, the Swahili were brokers in a complex system of exchanges among the people around the Indian Ocean.

Patrician: Term used in this chapter to denote Muslims in Swahili society claiming Middle Eastern descent and, by virtue of profiting from long-distance trade with the countries around the Indian Ocean, either ascended to the throne of their cities as kings or governed their cities in councils, together with other patricians.

Swahili Beginnings   The East African coast follows a fairly straight line from the northeast to the southwest, with few bays and natural harbors. For the most part, the coast is low, in most places rising only gradually. Many small rivers open into the Indian Ocean, and their estuaries provide some room for anchorage. Only the Zambezi River in the south was large enough to allow longer-range water traffic and the building of inland towns. Islands, reefs, and mangrove swamps were numerous and limited the construction and use of large vessels among the Swahilis. Under the influence of the monsoons blowing from the northeast from April to September, the northern half of the East African coast—from today's northern Tanzania to southern Somalia—receives most of its annual rain during the summer. These monsoon winds supported sailing with the wind to the Middle East and India. The opposite direction of the winter monsoons facilitated the return voyages. The southern half of the coast, from northern Tanzania to Mozambique, has rainy winters and no reliable seasonal winds, making sailing conditions less predictable. Accordingly, the southern half was less settled than the northern part.

The main ethnic group in the interior of sub-Saharan Africa was the Bantu, who had migrated to central, eastern, and southern Africa from roughly 600 BCE to 600 CE (see Chapter 6). The Bantus possessed a diversified agriculture and a wide variety of iron implements. In the mid-700s CE, a cultural differentiation between the Bantu of the interior and the east coast began to emerge. Archaeological remnants from Shanga, near today's Somali–Kenyan border, indicate the existence of a small wooden Islamic congregation hall, holding perhaps 25 people, and Muslim burials with an orientation toward Mecca. Small silver coins with Islamic inscriptions similar to Yemeni coins of the same period but minted in Shanga have also been found. The coastal population thus adapted to Islam, while the hinterland remained wedded to traditional animist spirituality.

The earliest Muslim merchants in East Africa were Khariji dissidents from the Middle East. These Muslims were sectarians who opposed the emergence of a centralized empire, the caliphs of which were actively shaping the emergent Islamic state religion. The caliphs pursued them relentlessly, pushing them into political insignificance in far-away provinces, such as Oman at the mouth of the Persian Gulf and oases in the North African Sahara. Given the agricultural limits in these regions, the Kharijis took to trade, in both East and West Africa.

Early on, the Kharijis were mostly interested in slaves, who were in great demand in the Islamic empire. Merchants in Basra, the main port for the Indian Ocean trade, invested their profits in the purchase of marshland around the mouth of the Tigris River and in the acquisition of slaves from East Africa to clear this land for the planting of rice and sugarcane. From 868 to 883, a revolt among these slaves disrupted the Abbasid Empire's entire trade through the Persian Gulf with India, East Africa, and China. When the caliphs finally succeeded in suppressing the revolt, large-scale agricultural slavery in the region ended. Black slave imports from East as well as West Africa continued on a smaller scale, however, primarily for domestic purposes.

Adapting to Islam   After the Kharijis lost their edge in the trade, mainstream Muslim merchants from the heartland of the Islamic empire traveled with textiles, glazed pottery, and glassware to East Africa to purchase luxury goods, such as ivory, hardwoods, and skins. One of the heartland cities was Shiraz, the capital of the Shiite dynasty of the Buyids (945–1055) in Iran. Their prestige appears to have surpassed that of the Kharijis since wealthy Swahili merchant families associated themselves with them, claiming Shirazi descent. Members of these families migrated from the northern Swahili city of Shanga southward and founded new trading centers as far away as the Comoros Islands. After 1055, mainstream Islam, with its mixture of Sunnism and mysticism, rose in prestige. *Sharifian* descent, that is, the possession of a genealogy going back to the Prophet Muhammad, began to rival Shirazi descent among the coastal elites. Leading Islamic families claiming Shirazi or Sharifian descent thus assumed a dominant position in the Swahili cities, from Mogadishu in the north to Chibuene (in Mozambique) in the south.

Urbanism   Swahili urbanism along the East African coast encompassed several hundred towns and about two dozen city-states of up to 10,000 inhabitants, either on the mainland or on islands off the coast (see Map 14.3). The mark of many cities was the central open space containing the Friday mosque for the congregational noon prayer, the main city well, and tombs of Islamic saints. Around the mosque and usually facing the sea were the densely built inner cities of the patricians. In the less densely settled outskirts, nonpatricians from overseas or the interior and manumitted slaves earned their living as craftspeople. On the perimeter were cemeteries, pastures, brushland, and mangrove swamps. Separate commoner towns housed fishermen, boat builders, and sailors. Their families grew vegetables and fruits in their gardens and sold the surplus in the nearby patrician cities. Further inland lived various non-Muslim client populations who traded meat and food staples, primarily sorghum, to the cities. Cities, towns, and inland people thus formed loosely organized city-states under the leadership of the patricians.

In the early centuries, the patrician dwellings were built with mangrove timber and, later, with coral, clay, and plaster. From about 1320, the typical patrician

MAP **14.3** Swahili City-States, ca. 1400.

residences were one- or two-story houses built of coral and lime, while nonpatricians continued to live in the older housing type. The architecture of the rectangular patrician houses displayed the Middle Eastern trait of inward orientation, with no more than a few small windows to the outside, but was otherwise uniquely Swahili. One entered through a porch to an open courtyard, which on its opposite side led to two to six rows of rooms for living, sleeping, and storing, plus a washing room and pit latrine. Each room was as wide as the house but only 2.6 yards deep, corresponding to the length of the mangrove poles which supported a flat coral roof. Wells in the courtyards tapped into the fresh groundwater atop the heavier seawater. Nonpatrician houses had a central hallway with rooms on both sides and a thatched roof. A system of drains along the alleyways took the waste water to the sea. Swahili cities were spatially well organized, even when they outgrew their original plans.

Governance

In the period 600–1450, the Swahili city-states were governed by kings and/or councils of patrician elders. Mainland cities, such as Mogadishu, Gede, and Malindi, were more vulnerable to occasionally hostile hinterland people and, therefore, more dependent on inland alliances than cities located on islands, such as Lamu, Paté, Pemba, or Zanzibar. Both hinterland and inland populations were trade partners whom the Swahili patrician merchants or their agents—usually slaves— visited but where they did not settle. The merchants did not establish mosques in the interior, and the interior population did not convert to Islam. Nor did holy men venture into non-Islamic territories to establish retreats or pilgrimage centers. In the absence of Islam as a common bond, the office of chieftainship as the traditional African institution binding tribal federations together served to express the communality of the cities and surrounding rural peoples. The mainland kings were Muslims from leading Shirazi or Sharifian patrician families, but in the dealings with their non-Muslim allies they acted more like traditional chiefs. By contrast, the patrician councils in the island cities—often clusters of several cities, commoner towns, and villages—had no inland allies and at times even dispensed with kings.

The Swahili city- or port-states were considerably smaller than the Christian or Islamic kingdoms of Nubia, Ethiopia, and southern, central, and western Africa. Nevertheless, the patricians' regalia clearly expressed the same royal aspirations. The Moroccan Muslim traveler Ibn Battuta (1304–1369) visited Mogadishu in 1331 and left a detailed description of the animist and Islamic royal customs as displayed by Sheikh Abu Bakr, who claimed Yemeni Sharifian descent. Every Friday, so Ibn Battuta writes, the king attended the noon prayer in his enclosed space in the mosque. Afterward, in a procession led by royal musicians (playing large drums, trumpets, and wind instruments), the king, judge, officials, and military commanders walked through town to the audience hall of the palace. Only the king, lavishly dressed and turbaned, wore sandals. He was shielded by four silken canopies, each topped by a golden bird. Large drums, wind instruments— probably including the *siwa* horn, made of a cattle horn and played sideways—sandals, and canopies were all traditional African regalia. Mosques with separate royal enclosures, Fridays as days of royal power displays, and audiences for royal judgments were elements of caliphal power adopted from the Middle East. The most important royal prerogative was the minting of coins, made of copper or gold. Given, however, that power on the Swahili coast was based on commercial, and not landed, wealth from which to collect taxes, in administrative practice the kings were never more than firsts among equals in the patriciate.

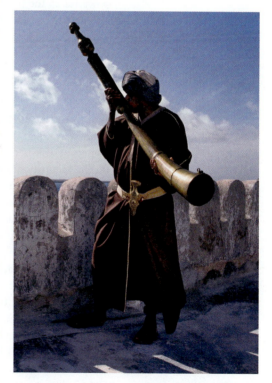

Musician, in Traditional Garb, Blowing the Siwa Horn. Magnificent horns such as this were part of the royal music repertoire of the mainland city-state kingdoms of the Swahili coast. This musician is from Lamu, in today's Kenya.

The Hinterland   Archaeological finds in the East African interior of Middle Eastern glass beads and glazed pottery shards document a network of exchanges, beginning around 800 and reaching as far as Lake Albert and the Zimbabwean plateau, up to 600 miles inland. The farmers, herders, and foragers in the hinterland, of course, engaged in trade among themselves, mostly for iron, copper, and salt. Farmers also produced grain, textiles, and pottery in return for animal products from herders. But the rising demand on the coast for ivory, skins, hardwoods, and rock crystal from the interior encouraged chiefs to develop a taste for Swahili cloth and overseas glass beads, glazed pottery, and the occasional Chinese dish. In both volume and value, the trade between coast and hinterland was minimal and should not be taken as a decisive factor for chieftain enrichment in the interior of Africa. Rather, this trade was part and parcel of increasing wealth in farming and cattle herding.

Traditional Kingdoms in Southern and Central Africa

The first region in the interior where a pattern of increasing wealth and population density became visible during the period 600–1505 was southern Africa, on and around the Zimbabwean plateau. Here, the original foragers of the vast grasslands were in the process of adapting to the Bantu culture arriving from the north, which included the influx of herders and farmers discussed in Chapter 6. Chiefs became powerful on the basis of large herds of cattle. Later, by trading first ivory and then also gold to coastal Swahili merchants, the chiefs initiated a pattern of political formation, building cities and kingdoms, such as Mapungubwe and Great Zimbabwe. Adapting their new economic power to indigenous traditions, these kings assumed the same exalted status which we encountered in the cases of Christian Nubia and Ethiopia.

Ivory and Gold in Southern Africa   Cattle herding, supplemented by sorghum and millet farming, was the source of early social differentiation since the owners of large herds, by loaning their animals to poorer relatives or parleying them for the acquisition of wives, could build powerful chiefdoms. Farming was initially limited to small, protected pockets, given the danger from elephants roaming the grasslands. In spite of the danger, hunting for elephant meat was a major occupation among the herders and farmers. In the course of the 700s, however, hunters increasingly went after elephants for their ivory. Khariji Swahili merchants from the north had founded the coastal town of Chibuene for the purpose of buying ivory, in return for textiles, glass beads, glazed pottery, and glass bottles. These items, being storable goods (in contrast to cattle), added to the wealth accumulated by chiefs. Thus, the ivory trade marked the beginning of the south African hinterland being incorporated into Swahili long-distance trade.

When chiefs acquired cattle and imported goods from the coast, the first towns arose in the interior, beginning with Schroda, 350 miles upstream on the middle Limpopo River, which flourished from 850 to about 1000. Schroda, a place of 300–500 inhabitants, yielded a number of yellow, blue, and green glass beads and glazed pottery shards of Shiraz origin from archaeological excavations. Larger towns nearby with around 1,500 inhabitants followed during the next few centuries, culminating with Mapungubwe [Mah-poon-GOOB-way], the capital of the first full-fledged kingdom (1070–1300), with some 5,000 inhabitants. In the early 900s, villagers to the north, on the Zimbabwean plateau, began to mine gold, which for the next four centuries was the major export item from Swahili cities to the Middle East and India. Workshops for the manufacture of ivory and gold figurines in the Limpopo towns testify to the emergence of an indigenous demand for the products of specialized craftspeople. When Mapungubwe arose as an urban-centered kingdom, the southern African interior not only was integrated into the Swahili Indian Ocean trade but also possessed the crucial urban and royal mark of an urban craftspeople class who did not practice agriculture and cattle herding.

The Kingdom of Mapungubwe   Excavations in Mapungubwe and ethnographic studies have yielded important insights into the institution of southern African kingship. The king resided on what had been previously a hill for chiefly rain-making ceremonies. He was in ritual seclusion from the commoners, who lived in the town at the foot of the hill. Stone walls had their origin in early southern African settlements for the enclosure of cattle. On the Mapungubwe hill, stone walls enclosed a platform with huts for the king's audience room and residence, the chief messenger, senior sister, diviner, sanctuary, and storage room for the royal drum and gold scepter. The hill also contained residences for a few senior wives. The remainder of the wives resided in villages outside Mapungubwe, where they were married to allies and clients of the kings. The graves of the royal cemetery contained large numbers of gold and glass beads, a bowl made of gold leaf, as well as shards of Chinese dishes. Seclusion and an elaborate set of regalia thus marked the king of Mapungubwe.

Court rituals also emphasized the exalted position of the king. Visitors had to first see the royal messenger, who accompanied them to the diviner. After the diviner had figured out the visitors' intentions, the messenger led the visitors into the audience hut, where all nonroyals had to kneel and address the king through an intermediary. Singers and musicians, perhaps playing *mbiras* (a stringed instrument) and xylophones, performed at the audiences and processions; soldiers guarded the walled precinct. The king was in charge of rain-making ceremonies and harvest feasts, but the actual rituals were conducted by the diviner. Of forager descent and often itinerant, diviners were experts in spirituality, experienced in handling the realm of the benevolent and evil spirits. Although royal power was associated with spiritual authority, there was an institutional division between the king's power over life and death and the diviner's authority to summon the spirits. Thus, African kingship shared the pattern of rulership development encountered also in Eurasia and the Americas: Royal power was legitimate only if combined with spiritual or divine authority.

The city on the bottom of the hill was the abode of dignitaries as well as commoners, that is, craftspeople, farmers, and herders. The dignitaries, close to the hill, were royal relatives, living in residences that were stone-walled, albeit with roughly cut rocks. The commoner quarters, without stone walls except around the perimeter, were more densely settled. A younger brother of the king was responsible for communicating between the king and the commoners. On the borders among the neighborhoods of the dignitaries and commoners, this intermediary resided with

Golden Rhinoceros. This golden rhinoceros was found among the items of the royal dynasty of Mapungubwe, signifying the power and magic of the kings. The kingdom was organized around the mining and trading of gold with the Swahili cities and, from there, with the Islamic Middle East.

his family in a hut atop a walled platform, next to the commoner court, where messengers summoned the people for trials. Headmen and elders wielded considerable authority in the neighborhoods, but royal justice—administered through the king's brother—was the final word.

The Kingdom of Great Zimbabwe The kingdom of Great Zimbabwe (1250–1505) ("the great house built of stone boulders" [Shona, *ziimba remabwe* or *ziimba rebwe*]) represents the culmination of the southern African kingdoms (see Map 14.4). Initially a tributary state of Mapungubwe, Great Zimbabwe emerged as a kingdom in its own right when the cooling and drying trend in the climate, which in Eurasia signaled the end of the early medieval agricultural expansion, made agriculture in the relatively dry Limpopo valley more difficult. Inhabitants abandoned Mapungubwe in the second half of the 1200s, with evidence of some royalty migrating north to Great Zimbabwe, which was more humid.

The capital city was located at the southern end of the arc of rock surfaces on the Zimbabwean plateau where gold was found. Granite for the construction of stone walls could be quarried easily, using heat from fires to split off layers of rock. Regular building blocks could be dressed with less effort from these layers than in Mapungubwe. At its height, the capital encompassed 18,000 inhabitants and was the seat of a kingdom extending northward across the Zimbabwean plateau. Most settlements

MAP **14.4** Great Zimbabwe, ca. 1450.

in the kingdom were dedicated to gold mining and trading, but a few practiced different trades, such as iron mining and salt panning. The primary sources of income, however, were cattle and grain.

Today, three main archaeological complexes remain of the capital. The first is a hill with a walled palace, accessible through a staircase. Two other complexes at a distance of half a mile to the south are the Western and Central Valley Walled Enclosures. The best-known structure is the so-called Great Enclosure within the Western Enclosure complex, an imposing 36-feet-high circular wall built of closely fitting blocks of granite. The royal palace precinct contained buildings similar to those in Mapungubwe. In the enclosures, some of the better-preserved ruins indicate that they once were buildings with solid stone walls, with plastered and perhaps even painted surfaces inside. Some residences were connected with walls which formed courtyards or narrow passageways. All enclosures were once densely packed with houses, presumably occupied by the kings and/or the ruling classes. Commoners lived perhaps in simple thatched huts built with timber and plastered with clay in the space between the hill and around the two enclosures.

Scholars still disagree concerning the relationship between the hill and the enclosures. Currently, the most accepted theory assumes a development from a city with a hill palace and residences directly underneath to one of two royal enclosures, either at the same time or sequentially. If this theory is correct, the kings and court would have moved at some time from the hill palace to the Great Enclosure, though why they would have done so is unknown.

The kingdom of Great Zimbabwe ended around 1505 when Swahili merchants replaced the initial southern Limpopo trade route with the shorter northern Zambezi route. A Chinese porcelain dish bearing this date was found in a burned and collapsed structure in the compound, though it appears that portions of Great Zimbabwe were still inhabited for some time. Thus, there was some overlap between the decline of Zimbabwe and the rise of the new trade route.

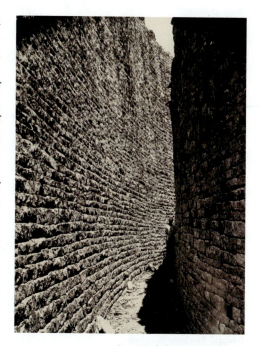

Great Zimbabwe, Passageway. The boy, visible at the end of the curve, provides an idea of the massive urban structures erected under the kings. The stone masons were highly specialized craftspeople, who constructed walls that have outlasted the demise of the Zimbabwe kingdom in the middle of the fifteenth century.

Central African Chiefdoms and Kingdoms

The central African rain forest and savanna, although more sparsely settled than the other parts of Africa during 600–1450, nevertheless participated in the general pattern of increased agricultural production and population expansion. In a number of places, especially the Congo Basin, favorable agricultural conditions supported the formation of chiefdoms which evolved into kingdoms. One savanna site, the Lake Upemba depression in the south of today's Democratic Republic of the Congo, was the home of the Luba people, who founded a kingdom based on a diversified agriculture and regional trade sometime in the period between 1000 and 1300 (see Map 14.5).

Luba Origins   Archaeologists dated the earliest evidence for the existence of permanent agricultural and fishing settlements around Lake Upemba to the period around 800. They found these settlements between the lakes, marshes, and rivers of one of the tributaries of the Congo River. Apart from fish, the villagers also relied

The Luba Kingdom, ca. 1400 CE

Rainforest	••••• Luba cultural zone
Luba Peoples	➤ Trade flows

MAP **14.5** **The Luba Kingdom, ca. 1400.**

on sorghum, millet, chickens, goats, and sheep for their livelihood. Locally produced iron and salt added to the resources. Hunting groups cut across the village lineages and formed the nucleus, around 1000, for the emergence of chiefs who were recognizable in their graves through copper ornaments. Copper had to be acquired through regional trade with the west, and its value made it into the metal preferred for jewelry, as in many other parts of Africa.

Luba Kingship   Luba oral tradition reaches back to the period between 1000 and 1300. It tells of a mythical first king known widely for his cruelty. A hunter arrived at the king's compound and decided that he would teach the king civility. The hunter, however, was not only a teacher but also a lover. After he had impregnated two sisters of the king, the hunter and the king had a falling out, resulting in the hurried departure of the hunter. The king relapsed into cruelty after the two sisters each bore a son: Fearful of losing his throne, he sought to kill his nephews. One of them, however, escaped to his hunter father, who gave him an army with which to return. The nephew defeated and killed the tyrant and became king of the Luba kingdom, ruling with justice and benevolence.

The founding myth appears to refer to a process whereby two chiefs, each claiming his own source of legitimacy, were competing for the unification of the villages. As in many other African foundation stories, the true founder is conceived of as a suffering, disadvantaged hero who has to endure trials before becoming a successful founder king. In the traditions of Africa, as in those of many other parts of the world, exalted kingship was acceptable only if rooted in humble beginnings.

As in Zimbabwe, Luba kings possessed magic powers, which entitled only descendants from his bloodline to succeed to the throne. The chieftains of other clans, although holding court offices and meeting in council to assist in the administration, were excluded from the succession. The royal clan maintained a small military force, sufficient to collect tributes from outlying villages but not large enough to destroy any of the chieftainships. A stable balance was established between the king and the chieftains, making Luba the model for subsequent kingdoms in the savanna of central Africa. The Luba kingdom itself survived until the arrival of Belgian colonialism at the end of the nineteenth century.

Cultural Encounters: West African Traditions and Islam

A pattern of regional trade, urbanization, and chiefdom formation was also characteristic for the Sahel and savanna of West Africa from the middle of the first millennium CE onward. Around 600, chiefs became kings when they unified their clans, conquered some neighbors from whom they collected tributes, and arranged alliances with others. Like their later African colleagues in the eastern half of Africa, they claimed to possess magic powers and adopted royal customs of seclusion. Two kingdoms, ancient Ghana and Mali, followed each other in the period 600–1450. Their royal–military ruling clans benefited from trans-Saharan trade with Islamic civilization and gradually converted to Islam, while the general population of herders, farmers, miners, smiths, and other craftspeople remained faithful to their animist traditions.

The Kingdom of Ancient Ghana

Ancient Ghana emerged in the 600s as the strongest group of chiefdoms in the Sahel and savanna between the Niger inland delta in the east and the Senegal valley in the west. It advanced to the status of a kingdom after 750, when it became the center for trade across the Sahara with the North African Islamic states. Thanks to this trade, the kingdom was dominant in the Sahel for half a millennium. In the 1100s, however, drought and provincial unrest   weakened Ghana. The kingdom gave way in 1240 to Mali, an empire which began its rise in the upper Niger rain forest and savanna.

Formation of Ancient Ghana   As discussed in Chapter 6, a long period of progressive desertification (2500–300 BCE) had   driven   the inhabitants of the southern Sahara southward into what became the Sahel, a belt of steppe, grassland, and marginal agriculture. They had domesticated millet and bred cattle herds in Saharan villages shortly before the desiccation began. During the period 600 BCE–600 CE, the climate stabilized and millet agriculture, cattle herding, and village formation expanded across the Sahel and northern savanna from the Senegal valley in the west to Lake Chad in the east. In some places, as in the inland delta of the Niger, where irrigation was possible, villages were clustering. Jenné-jeno emerged around 300 as a city surrounded by a collection of villages. The city was a center of regional trade for iron and gold from the upper Niger and Senegal valleys and copper from the Sahara, in return for urban manufactures, such as textiles, leather goods, metal implements, and utensils. The people who populated the Sahel were ethnically Soninke, speaking a Bantu language, like the majority of West Africans.

After 300, the regional trade became a long-distance trade. Thanks to the arrival of the Arabian camel among the Berbers of North Africa and the northern Sahara, it became possible to travel through the desert. Long-distance merchants from the cities of Roman North Africa made contact with Soninke merchants in the Sahel, some 3 months away by camel caravan. They exchanged Roman manufactures, such as glassware, cloth, and ceramics, plus Saharan copper and salt for gold. Berber miners in the central Sahara quarried salt from deposits left by dried-up prehistoric lakes. Cowrie shells, imported by Rome from the Indian Ocean and exported to West Africa, document trade connections even farther than the Mediterranean.

It took some time, however, for the initially infrequent trans-Saharan exchanges to intensify and become regular. Only after the loss of their gold mines in northwestern Iberia to Germanic tribal migrants did the Romans regularize the trans-Saharan trade, beginning in the mid-500s. The regularization had a profound effect in the

Luba Mask and Axe. The Luba developed a specific style of masks and utensils in central Africa. The mask on the left, with its cattle horns, is indicative of royal magical power. Its wearer would have been the embodiment of the benevolent ancestral spirit of a dynasty of rulers during enthronement ceremonies. The axe on the right combines hardwood with a skillfully forged blade.

Sahel. In the 600s, Soninke chiefs on the western outskirts of the inland Niger delta, enriched by the profits from the Saharan trade, equipped their followers with arms, such as swords and lances. Riding on small West African horses immune to the diseases carried by the tsetse fly, they subjugated more distantly related Soninke groups in the Sahel between the Niger and Senegal valleys. In the mid–700s, one of the chiefs proclaimed himself king in Wagadu, a city in the Sahel northwest of the inland delta, and founded the kingdom of ancient Ghana (as distinguished from the modern state of Ghana).

As told in the founding myth at the beginning of this chapter, Dinga was the first mythical king. His kingdom, so it was foretold, was destined to rule the Sahel, dominate the gold trade, and benefit from abundant rain as long as its subjects sacrificed a virgin and a colt every year to its well-dwelling patron snake. Modern scholars would say that ancient Ghana lasted through the wet period of the first millennium (300–1100) and eventually succumbed to its successor Mali when it could not adapt in the Sahel to the emerging dry period (1100–1500).

From Roman to Islamic Trade

Ancient Ghana received its gold from Bambuk, a region in the rain forest at the western edge of the kingdom. Villagers on a left-bank tributary of the middle Senegal River panned and mined the metal during the dry season, and Soninke merchants transported it by donkey and bullock some 500 miles east to Wagadu. The Bambuk gold fields occupied a no-man's-land between the kingdom of ancient Ghana and the chiefdom of Takrur on the lower Senegal. The two polities left the villagers to their own devices since neither possessed the technical and administrative means to organize or even control the panning and mining operations. Soninke merchants went no farther than nearby towns, from where they conducted their trading activities with the villagers.

Romanized Berbers gave way to Islamized Berbers in the trans-Saharan trade after about 750. As was the case in Swahili East Africa, Khariji merchants pushed by the emerging Islamic empire into the outer provinces were the first Muslims to travel to the African interior. According to an eleventh-century Arabic source, Wagadu was a twin city, with its merchant and royal halves several miles apart. If Wagadu can be identified with the partially excavated ruins of Koumbi-Saleh on the southern border of today's Mauritania—an identification still disputed among scholars—the merchant city had a dozen mosques, a market place, and residences.

The royal city consisted of a domed palace and other domed buildings, including a courthouse and the homes of the king's treasurer, translator, and other ministers. A grove surrounded the palace area, containing the royal prison and the dwellings of the priests and diviners, as well as the tombs of ancestral kings. In contrast to their Swahili colleagues, the kings of Ghana avoided a combination of traditional kingship with Islam. Even though they benefited from including Muslims in their administration, they were not about to surrender their exalted, magical royal authority over life and death to the supremacy of Islamic law.

From Animism to Islam in the Ruling Class

Abu Ubayd al-Bakri also provides insight into the type of authority claimed by the kings of Ghana. Audiences were announced with the royal drum, and the king sat in judgment or received ambassadors and petitioners with great pomp, which included an entourage of 10 horses with soldiers as well as the sons of the vassal chiefs, evidently residing as hostages at the court, all richly bedecked with gold embroidery or jewelry. Arabic sources referring to other West African kingdoms report that the kings either were believed to magically need no food, could not be seen eating, or were to be honored during their dinner time by a complete cessation of activities in town.

While the kings of Ghana had reasons to hold on to traditional African animist spirituality, the Soninke merchants gradually converted to Islam. Business with the North African and Middle Eastern merchants was easier to transact if everyone adhered to the same ethics and laws. By the early 1000s, the merchants in the trading towns near the Bambuk villages were Muslims, and the adjacent state of Takrur had also become Islamic. The sectarian Khariji Islam gave way to mainstream Sunnism, which rose to dominance in the Islamic world after 950. In North Africa, the proponents of Sunnism were the Almoravids, southern Moroccan Berbers who spearheaded a movement that evolved into a short-lived empire in Morocco, the western Sahara, and Islamic Spain (see Chapter 10).

Perhaps under pressure of the Almoravids, in the early 1100s the kings of Ghana followed their merchants by also converting to Islam. The Sahel and savanna villagers, however, remained wedded to their African spirituality. As a result, Ghana now resembled the states on the Swahili coast and their hinterlands, where only the rulers and merchants were Islamic. In addition to the villagers, a number of allied Soninke chiefs remained faithful to traditional spirituality; and during the second half of the 1100s the cohesion of the kingdom began to soften. In 1180, the founding clan of ancient Ghana ceded power to another clan, which established a new dynasty in Wagadu and adopted a policy of conquest of the southern savanna. For the next half-century Ghana was an imperial power, trading gold not only from the Senegal River in the west but also from newly developed fields in the rain forest on the upper Niger and Black Volta Rivers (see Map 14.6).

The Empire of Mali

The opening of new gold fields in the rain forest exposed hitherto marginal peoples to the influence of long-distance trade, royal rule, and Islam. One of these peoples, the Malinke, followed the by now familiar pattern of rallying around an inspiring chief who, as a conqueror, built the foundations for an expanding polity. By uniting both savanna and Sahel peoples, the Malinke built the empire of Mali, a polity of many ethnic, linguistic, and religious groups. At its height, Mali stretched from the Atlantic to the Niger bend and from the Sahara to the rain forest.

Sundiata, Founder King   Mali was the beneficiary of a significantly increased demand for gold in Islamic civilization on the other side of the Sahara. In addition to the existing Islamic mints, Christian mints began to stamp gold coins. The king of Castile in Spain was the first, in 1173; and by the mid-1200s Italian city-states had followed suit. In response to this increased demand, merchants encouraged the opening of new gold fields in the rain forest. The people in the savanna of the upper

> ### Abu Ubayd al-Bakri (d. 1094) on the Gold Trade
>
> "On every donkey-load of salt when it is brought into the country their king levies one golden dinar and two dinars when it is sent out.... The best gold is found in his land comes from the town of Ghiyaru, which is eighteen days' traveling distance from the king's town over a country inhabited by tribes of the Sudan whose dwellings are continuous."
>
> —N. Levtzion and J. F. P. Hopkins, eds. *Corpus of Early Arabic Sources for West African History*, p. 80. Princeton, NJ: Markus Wiener, 2000.

MAP 14.6 West African States, 600–1450.

West African States, 600–1450 CE

——	Approximate extent of empire of Ghana, ca. 1050	▨	Source of gold	▨	Desert
——	Approximate extent of empire of Mali	△	Source of salt		Semi-desert (Sahel)
→	Direction of trade	*Soninke*	Peoples		Savanna
--→	Trade route	**MOROCCO**	Modern country		Lowland rainforest

Niger and its tributaries were Malinke villagers who spoke a language related to that of the Soninke but who were ethnically distinct. In the course of the 1000s, these villagers had acculturated to ancient Ghana, which they recognized as overlord. Although composed of dozens of chiefdoms, the Malinke also encompassed hunter associations, which cut across the chiefdoms and formed the basis for ambitious leaders seeking to unify the Malinke. When the new dynasty of Ghana conquered much of the Malinke lands at the end of the 1100s, resistance led by the hunters against the new rulers rose quickly. In a rebellion in 1230–1235, the Malinke not only liberated themselves but went on to conquer ancient Ghana.

The leader of the conquest was the inspiring hero Sundiata (also spelled Sunjata or Sundjata, ca. 1217–1255). He and his adventures were at the center of an **oral tradition**, with traveling bards telling stories which they handed down from generation to generation and told and retold publicly in villages. In the nineteenth and twentieth centuries, anthropologists recorded these traditions and made them available in translation.

> **Oral traditions:** Myths, tales, stories (e.g., the foundation myth of Wagadu) handed down from generation to generation.

As was the case with so many other oral traditions or epics across the world, Sundiata was conceived as having been of high birth but marginal status. On the one hand, Sundiata's father, a chief of the leading Malinke clan, was assumed to have been of illustrious early Islamic descent (from Bilal, Muhammad's prayer caller, mentioned at the beginning of this chapter). On the other hand, the story makes Sundiata's mother a hunchback and Sundiata himself a cripple, unable in his youth to walk. Furthermore, we are told that when a younger brother succeeded the father in the chiefdom Sundiata was forced into exile. In the story, he returned only when the brother could not stop the Ghanaian invasion mentioned earlier in this chapter. At the head of a cavalry force borrowed from a chiefdom in the Sahel, Sundiata defeated ancient Ghana in 1235 and founded the empire of Mali, with its capital, Niani, on an upper Niger tributary in modern Guinea.

The Malian Empire

Mali was the first enduring empire in sub-Saharan Africa, lasting officially for over four centuries (1235–1645). At its height in the early 1300s, Mali encompassed most of the West African Sahel, large parts of the savanna, and the gold fields in the rain forest—a territory surpassed only by that of the contemporary Mongol Empire. At the core of the empire were privileged Malinke clans whose kings and chiefs formed an alliance and met in an assembly (Malinike *gbara*), under the emperors who assumed the title of *mansa*. We do not know how frequently or long this assembly met. Oral tradition records the laws, customs, and traditions of which it was the guardian and according to which the empire was governed. As in Mesopotamia, Vedic India, Greece, and Rome, Mali preserved traditions of chiefly assemblies from preroyal forms of social organization.

Similar to ancient Ghana, Mali's power rested on a large, horseborne army recruited from the Soninke clans that could move swiftly and overwhelm its opponents with surprise attacks. From the 1300s onward Mali began to import tall Middle Eastern and North African horses in larger numbers and to form cavalry units equipped with chain mail, lances, and swords. But this cavalry was probably not numerous enough to become the elite force characteristic of the Middle East and Europe prior to the introduction of firearms. Infantry, using bow and arrow and moving about on small horses, continued to form the backbone of the military.

> **Sundiata's Rise**
>
> "Sunjata is at first unable to defeat Sumanguru [the Ghanaian conqueror of Mali] and is defeated in a series of battles. Things look very bad for the hero. Clearly, Sumanguru's control of *nyama*, occult power, is greater than his own, and unless he can learn Sumanguru's secret he will never succeed. His [Sunjata's] sister, Sogolon Kulankan, comes to the rescue. She goes to Sumanguru and offers herself to him and as their intimacy progresses she lures him into revealing his secret . . . : he can be killed only by an arrow tipped with the spur of a white cock. . . . She comes to her brother with the information and the battle is won."
>
> —Stephen Belcher. *Epic Traditions of Africa*, pp. 103–104. Bloomington: Indiana University Press, 1999.

Also like their royal predecessors in ancient Ghana, the Malian emperors relied on a small central administration primarily concerned with finances and justice and run by Muslims as well as by slaves. The empire financed itself by tributes from vassal kingdoms in the Sahel and river chiefdoms with villagers and fishermen, as well as taxes on the commerce of gold, iron, copper, salt, textiles (both local and foreign), leather goods, and other manufactures. Since the new gold fields and the capital of Niani were located on a tributary of the Niger, the rulers relied on water transport down river to the cities of Jenné-jeno, Timbuktu (founded in 1100), and Gao. In the mid-1300s, these three cities replaced Wagadu as the main transshipment centers of goods for the Saharan caravans. Thus, with the rise of Mali, the trans-Saharan trade shifted eastward.

The City of Timbuktu   In 1324, the most famous ruler of Mali, Mansa Musa (r. ca. 1312–1337), annexed the city of Timbuktu from its Touareg Berber founders. The *mansas*, or kings, had been Muslims from the beginning but stressed their Islamic allegiance only from 1270 onward, when the first emperor went on his pilgrimage to Mecca. Mansa Musa displayed his piety even more strongly by not only traveling to Mecca and dispensing lavish quantities of gold coins along the way but also by endowing Timbuktu with three well-appointed mosques. He commissioned an Iberian architect with the construction of these mosques, which therefore display some Western Islamic stylistic elements, especially in the tiered minarets. But with their characteristic mud brick and protruding timber construction, these first mosques set the pace for a pronounced West African Islamic style that is still extant today.

Mansa Musa also founded a college (Arabic *madrasa*) and library, part of the Sankoré Mosque. Timbuktu became a center of learning, focused on Islamic law but also offering geometry, algebra, geography, and astronomy as ancillary fields of study, which judges and independent scholars were required to know. The independent scholars were often well-off members of merchant families. Many kept private libraries in their residences, where they and their descendants accumulated masses

The Sankoré Mosque, of Timbuktu, Mali. The mosque evolved in the fourteenth century into a large university with a library housing hundreds of thousands of manuscripts. A preservation program under United Nations' auspices seeks to restore and preserve these manuscripts today.

of manuscripts over the centuries, estimated today to number in the hundreds of thousands. In the mid-1400s, with some 100,000 inhabitants, the commercial and scholarly hub of Timbuktu was one of the larger cities in the world.

The Decline of Mali   Timbuktu flourished even while its imperial overlord, Mali, declined in the later 1300s. Weak rulers arrived on the throne and dynastic disputes broke out. Outside groups that had adapted to Mali influences—rain-forest groups with newly acquired horses and Touareg nomads from the desert—attacked from the south and north. As a result, some of the subjugated provinces in the Sahel began to break away and establish independent kingdoms. More generally, even though Mali had exploited the weakening of ancient Ghana at the onset of the dry period after 1100, the deepening of the drought conditions eventually caught up with Mali as well. By 1450, Mali had shrunk to the size of a kingdom in the savanna.

Rain-Forest Kingdoms

As discussed in earlier chapters, the West African rain forest was a 200-mile-wide strip of tropical vegetation stretching from modern Guinea above the southwestern corner of West Africa to Cameroon on the bend to central Africa, where it transits to the Congo rain forest. In the earlier period of 600 BCE to 600 CE, savanna peoples with iron implements had entered the rain forest and founded villages in clearings, farming yam and oil palm kernels. The banana, arriving from East Africa around 800, was an important addition, helping in the increase of agricultural productivity. As elsewhere in Africa, the result was a pattern of political formation which included village clusters, chiefdoms, and kingdoms with urban centers and sophisticated crafts, such as bronze casting in Nigeria.

The Kingdom of Ife   The earliest village cluster to urbanize was that of Ife [EE-fay], west of the Niger delta in 500 CE, the spiritual center of the Yoruba ethnic group and its oral traditions. By 1000 it was a kingdom with a walled capital, which enclosed a palace, groves, shrines, stone-built residences, and craft workshops for pottery, textiles, and glassware (especially beads). Courtyards and passageways in the city were terra-cotta-paved, to remain passable during the rainy season. One highly developed art was sculpting, in terra-cotta, copper, or bronze.

Sungbo's Eredo   Ife set the example for several further chiefdoms to advance to the threshold of kingdoms between 1000 and 1450. One of them toward the north was Oyo, which (thanks to the adoption of a cavalry force) expanded from the rain forest northward toward the edge of the savanna. It arose as a trade center for the exchange of palm oil kernels and kola nuts (a mild narcotic containing caffeine) in return for Mediterranean manufactures and Sahel horses, through first Ghanaian and then Malian merchants. In the other chiefdoms, leaders mobilized villagers for the construction of earthworks, which astound even today by their size and scope. One of these chiefdoms, Ijebu, encompassed a capital and villages on a territory of 22 square miles, surrounded by a moat and rampart combination up to 70 feet deep/high and 100 miles long. In nearby Benin, smaller earthworks around villages collectively added up to 10,000 miles and became the nucleus for an important kingdom in 1440. In both Ijebu and Benin, the moats and ramparts cut through the hard,

Patterns Up Close | The Sculptures of Ife

Sculptures, figures, and figurines in Africa followed a pattern that was shared early on with Eurasia and, during the periods of 600 BCE–600 CE and 600–1450 CE, also with Australia, the Pacific, and parts of the Americas. Broadly speaking, forager, village, and pastoral societies developing in the direction of chiefdoms, but not yet kingdoms, preserved traditional ancestor cults within their animist spirituality. Ancestor cults were concerned with preserving the memory of the forebears, usually including that of the founder of the lineage, the grandparents, the father, and the mother.

As lineages evolved, the growing generations between founder and the grandparents blurred so that these in-between ancestors became an anonymous collective. The spirits of the ancestors in the invisible world, therefore, were conceived as being collectively present, to be consulted, nourished through sacrifices, cajoled, etc. One could "trap" them in sculptures, figures, and figurines, which emphasized the head, believed to be the seat of the spirit, at the expense of the torso and limbs, which were indicated in rudimentary fashion. Even the heads were generally fashioned in abstract, geometrically simplified ways, corresponding to the collective nature of the ancestors. These artifacts, therefore, were not "primitive," even though they are still today often described as such. Their style was generic because the collective of the ancestors was generic.

When societies reached levels of wealth and complexity that led to the emergence of kingdoms, kings became exceptional persons, endowed with ancestral magical (in Africa) or a transcendent divine mandate (in Eurasia) to exercise power, not merely chiefly authority. As wielders of power, they typically conquered and demanded that their conquests be remembered as their personal accomplishments. Generic ancestor "traps" would not do: Artists had to apply the techniques of naturalistic representation so that the kings would recognize themselves in them. Of course, after a while sculptures turned into generic likenesses again, as they did in Mesopotamia and Egypt, since kingship became an ordinary institution with undistinguished kings not worth remembering (a).

The Ife terra-cotta, copper, and bronze royal heads as well as the unique bronze figure of a seated male stem (b) from that short, experimental, and highly innovative time period of about 200 years (1100–1300) when kingship was new in Ife. The naturalism of these figures is striking, especially when one takes into consideration that western European figurative art during the same period was still "primitive," in the sense of being iconic. (It typically

(a) Guardian Figure, Bakota Area, Gabon, Nineteenth–Twentieth Century. The abstract Bakota figure, above, with its generic geometrical elements, represents the collective chiefly spirit; the much more realistic Nigerian figures represent royalty who wished to be remembered individually.

(b) Seated Copper Figure from the Village of Tada, Nigeria, ca. 1300.

(*c*) Ife Shrine Head, Terra-Cotta, Nigeria, ca. 1200.

(*d*) Obalufon Bronze Mask, Ife, ca. 1300 CE.

represented standardized ideas about how biblical figures should look so that their God-pleasing nature was immediately recognizable.) The stripes on the faces of some Ife figures (*c*) are believed to represent *scarifications*, or scars marking the passage from youth to adulthood or distinguishing one lineage from another, as practiced in parts of Africa. The holes on others (*d*) are assumed to be remnants of the "entrapping" feature, into which the hair strains of the portrayed king were placed. Thus, as naturalistic as these sculptures are, they remain unmistakably rooted in their African traditional spirituality of animism.

Questions

- How does the history of African sculpture, such as those from Ife, provide evidence for studying the patterns of state building in this period?

- Why does material culture play such an important dimension in understanding the African past?

iron-saturated soil, rivers, and swamps, requiring centuries of hard labor with nothing more than iron shovels.

Scholars are still undecided over the purpose of these constructions: Did they protect against enemies and elephants, were they boundary markers for ancestral lands and their spirits, or did they facilitate the collection of tolls? Perhaps they were intended for all three. Equally difficult is the explanation for the phenomenon of collective labor: How were chiefs able to motivate workers to contribute their voluntary efforts? Evidently they were, as they were also in the Americas and Pacific, where followers built huge temples or rolled heavy stone sculptures across distances. Authority without power, buttressed by ancestral pedigree and spirituality, can thus be seen as a powerful motivator to take on great tasks and validate the institutions it represents.

Today, the structure around Ijebu is called "Sungbo's Eredo" ("moat-rampart"), a name which refers to Bilikisu Sungbo, a priestess-queen in ancient times who is credited in local tradition with commanding its construction and whose shrine is an important local pilgrimage place. She is identified with the queen of Sheba, who, according to Islamic tradition, worshiped the sun but was converted to faith in God after visiting King Solomon of Israel. Edo tradition has the queen of Sheba traveling from Israel to Ijebu, thereby making her the female counterpart of Bilal, the Muslim ancestor of the dynasties of ancient Ghana and Mali whom we met at the beginning of the chapter. The oral literature of the rain forest thus reflects the same adaptation to Islam as that of the Sahel and savanna.

Putting It All Together

Africa in the period 600–1450 displayed patterns of political and cultural development that included creative adaptation of animism to the monotheisms of Christianity and Islam and indigenous kingdom formation. Depending on regional conditions and the degree of integration into Eurasian long-distance trade, peoples in the different parts of sub-Saharan Africa mixed the two cultural heritages of Christianity and Islam in a variety of ways. The Nile valley and northeastern highlands, long adapted to the Mediterranean prior to 600, incorporated Christianity into their local traditions. They adopted the Christian institutional division between kingship and church, in which kingship was a sacred office but subject to law and Christian ethics. The church, for its part, was an autonomous, hierarchical body. As in post-1000 Christian western Europe, the Nubian and Ethiopian churches were subject to a distant religious authority.

Coastal East and West Africa adopted Islam, which arrived through merchants, not missionaries. In eastern Africa, Islam took root among the coastal people and did not penetrate inland. In western Africa, only merchants and kings converted but did so across the interior. Thus, Africans adapted to Christianity and Islam during 600–1450 in very different ways.

In the same period, African kingship was a new institution with roots in the traditions of chieftainship in villages and village clusters. The kings emphasized their royal powers over life and death but also continued to claim the traditional chiefly powers of spirituality and magic. As Christians or Muslims, they at least paid lip service to the divine laws to which they were subject. In southern and central Africa, kingship arose from its African context without modification by

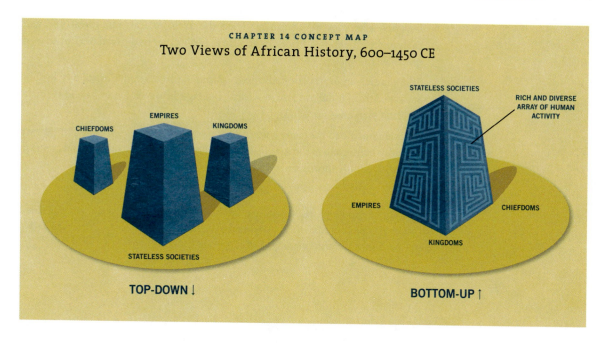

CHAPTER 14 CONCEPT MAP
Two Views of African History, 600–1450 CE

Christian or Islamic law, and it is important to emphasize that Africa needed nei-ther Christianity nor Islam to embark on its own distinctive pattern of kingdom formation.

During 600–1450, however, this pattern clearly remained an exception amid the sub-Saharan population, the majority of which remained "stateless," to use an ex-pression in common use among historians of Africa. This population, organized in farming villages or pastoral camps, possessed chiefs and hunting or youth societies cutting across village and camp boundaries but did not unite into larger polities or trade farther away than regionally for locally unavailable metals and salt. It had spe-cialized craftspeople, such as smiths and miners, who, were also farmers. The unique position of this silent majority of stateless Africans should always be kept in mind, alongside the kingdoms and empires, in seeking to understand Africa's significance in world history during this period. In this regard, a "bottom up" view of African history, though impeded by a lack of sources, can provide as much insight as a "top down" perspective (see Concept Map).

Review and Respond

1. Compare and contrast a monotheistic and an animist African kingdom. What are the salient features of each? In which ways are the patterns of their development significant in a global context? How does the story of Dinga in the chapter opener illustrate some of the underlying patterns of how these traditions interacted?

2. Discuss Africa's role in Eurasia's maritime long-distance trade network. Comment on trade routes, goods traded, and the mechanics of trade within sub-Saharan Africa.

3. How were the Swahili states and societies organized? What made the coastal and island states different from each other?

4. Describe examples of African art from the West African rain-forest belt and analyze their meanings. Place this art into the context of traditional African animist spirituality.

5. Ethiopia was an example of advanced adaptation to eastern Christianity in sub-Saharan Africa. It did not lose its African heritage, however. Describe and evaluate the Ethiopian example of adaptation.

6. Mali demonstrated the same pattern of empire formation as witnessed in Eurasia centuries before and in the Americas at about the same time. Compare and contrast Mali with empire formation on the other continents.

For additional resources, including maps, primary sources, visuals, and quizzes, please go to www.oup.com/us/vonsivers. Please see the Further Resources section at the back of the book for additional readings and suggested websites.

Thinking Through Patterns

▶ **What patterns of adaptation did the Christian kingdoms of northeast Africa demonstrate in their interactions with the civilizations of the Middle East and eastern Mediterranean?**

In the period 600–1450, the northeast of sub-Saharan Africa was firmly drawn into the orbit of eastern Christian and Islamic civilizations, without, however, fully adapting their formative patterns. Perhaps the closest adaptation occurred in the sphere of trade, where the Christian kingdoms became the providers of luxury goods, such as ivory, skins, and hardwoods from tropical Africa to the Middle East and eastern Mediterranean, in return for manufactures, Indian spices, and Chinese silks. Beginning in 1250 in the Nilotic kingdom of Nubia, the expansionist regime of the Muslim Mamluks in Egypt put the African Christians on the defensive. By 1450 the middle Nile region was Islamized. In contrast, an expansionist Christian Ethiopia put Muslims on the coast of the Red Sea on the defensive and Christianized the pagan southern highlands.

The inclusion of the East African coast and sub-Saharan West Africa into the orbit of Muslim Indian Ocean and Mediterranean trading zone resulted in the rise of small coastal Swahili states and two large West African polities: the kingdom of ancient Ghana and the empire of Mali. Muslim mariners and merchants interacted with Islamized local African rulers and merchants to exchange Middle Eastern textiles, leather goods, and metal wares for ivory, gold, slaves, skins, and hardwoods. African rulers and merchants obtained their African goods from pagan miners and hunters in the African interior outside their states. Adaptation to Islamic religious civilization was a phenomenon limited to the ruling classes and associated merchant circles.

▶ **What were the responses of Africans to Muslim merchants who connected them with the trading zone of the Indian Ocean and Mediterranean? As these Africans adapted to Islam, which forms of political organization did they adopt?**

▶ **In what ways did the economic and political transformations on the east African coast and West Africa affect developments in the interior?**

The adaptation of coastal East Africa to Islamic religious civilization had an indirect effect on the interior in the region of southern Africa. Here, chiefs in Zimbabwe attached themselves to the Swahili trade network and used the wealth from this trade for the transformation of their chiefdoms into kingdoms. Impressive masonry constructions serving as centers for incipient administrative structures testify to the ability of kings to transform chiefly authority into royal military power. The East and West African expansion of trade under the impact of Islam may have also indirectly led to a population increase in the interior of Africa. Such an increase became noticeable toward the 1300s, especially in the Congo basin, where the Luba kingdom was the first to emerge.

Chapter 15

600-1550 CE

The Rise of Empires in the Americas

Just outside Lima, in a sandy and dry ravine 3 miles to the east, is the shantytown of Túpac Amaru, named after the last Inca ruler, who died in 1572. People fleeing the Maoist-Marxist "Shining Path" guerillas in the highlands southeast of Lima settled here during the 1980s. Archaeologists had known for years that the site was an ancient burial place called "Puruchuco" (in Quechua "Feathered Helmet") but could not prevent the influx of settlers. By the late 1990s, the temporary shantytown had become an established settlement with masonry houses, streets, and a school. Dwellers were anxious to acquire title to their properties, introduce urban services and utilities, and clean up ground contaminated in many places

Seeing Patterns

▶ Within the patterns of state formation basic to the Americas, which types of states emerged in Mesoamerica and the Andes during the period 600–1550? What characterized these states?

▶ Why did the Tiwanaku and Wari states have ruling classes but no dynasties and central bureaucracies? How were these patterns expressed in the territorial organization of these states?

▶ What patterns of urban life characterized the cities of Tenochtitlán and Cuzco, the capitals of the Aztec and Inca Empires? In which ways were these cities similar to those of Eurasia and Africa?

by raw sewage. However, residents realized that archaeologists had to be called in before the shantytown could be officially recognized. Túpac Amaru was facing an increasingly familiar dilemma in the developing world, pitting modern needs against the wish to know the past through discovering and (if possible) preserving its last traces.

During emergency excavations from 1999 to 2001, the archaeologist Guillermo Cock, together with Túpac Amaru residents hired as field assistants, unearthed one of the most astounding treasures in the history of American archaeology. The team discovered some 2,200 mummies, most of them bundled up in blankets and perfectly preserved with their hair, skin, eyes, and genitals intact. Many bundles also contained rich burial gifts, including jewelry, corn, potatoes, peanuts, peppers, and coca leaves. Forty bundles had false heads made of cotton cloth, some topped with wigs, making the bundles look like oversized persons.

One bundle, stuffed with over 300 pounds of cotton, contained the mummies of a child and a man of about 40, dubbed the "cotton king" because of his many sumptuous burial gifts. In 2004, during renewed excavations, Cock discovered the remains of 72 hastily buried bodies that had not

Excavations in Tupac Amaru in 1999–2001. During excavations in Túpac Amaru, a slum in Lima, Peru, in 1999–2001, archaeologists unearthed some 2,200 mummies. They dated them to the Inca period (1438–1533). Many mummies were surrounded by rich grave gifts of food and jewelry.

been mummified, many of which bore traces of violence. One skeleton with a hole in the skull was declared to have been the first victim of a gunshot in the Americas, fired by a Spanish conquistador in 1536 during an Inca uprising in Lima. Altogether, Cock was able to excavate about 40 percent of Puruchuco, collecting mummies, skeletons, and artifacts in numbers not previously seen in Peru.

The cemetery was once part of a larger complex, excavated in 1956, that also included what was perhaps an Inca administrative center and colony or a provincial ruler's palace. Scholars hope that in a few years, when all of the mummies will be unwrapped, answers can be given as to the social characteristics of the buried people. Were they members of an Inca colony planted into one of the empire's provinces? Or were they locals under their own lord, recognizing Inca overlordship? Were they specialized laborers, such as weavers, who produced cloth tributes for the Incas? Were children and women sacrificed to accompany the cotton king in his journey to the afterlife? Had assimilation between the conquerors and conquered begun? These questions are difficult to answer as so much about the Inca Empire that ruled the Andes from 1438 to 1533 remains unknown. Yet, the questions are exciting precisely because they could not have been posed prior to the discovery of these mummies.

The Inca Empire and its contemporary, the Aztec Empire (1427–1521), both grew out of political, economic, and cultural patterns that began to form around 600 CE in Mesoamerica and the Andes (see Chapter 5). At that time, kingdoms had emerged out of chiefdoms in two small areas of Mesoamerica, the southern Yucatán Peninsula and the Valley of Mexico. After 600, kingdom formation became more general across Mesoamerica and arose for the first time in the Andes. These kingdoms were states with military ruling classes that used new types of weapons and could conquer larger territories than was possible prior to the 600s. Military competition prepared the way for the origin of empires—multireligious, multilinguistic, and multiethnic states encompassing many thousands of miles. Even though empires arrived later in the Americas than in Eurasia, they demonstrate that humans, once they had adopted agriculture, evolved in remarkably similar patterns of social and political formation across the world.

The Legacy of Teotihuacán and the Toltecs in Mesoamerica

As discussed in Chapter 5, the city-state of Teotihuacán had dominated northern Mesoamerica from 200 BCE to the late 500s CE. It fell into ruin probably as the result of an internal uprising against an overbearing ruling class. After its collapse, the surrounding towns and villages, as well as half a dozen other cities in and around the Valley of Mexico, perpetuated the cultural legacy of Teotihuacán for centuries. Employing this legacy, the conquering state of the Toltecs unified a major part of the region for a short period from 900 to 1180. At the same time, after an internal crisis, the southern Maya kingdoms on the Yucatán Peninsula reached their late flowering, together with the northern state of Chichén Itzá.

Militarism in the Valley of Mexico

After the ruling class of Teotihuacán disintegrated at the end of the sixth century, the newly independent local lords and their supporters in the small successor states of Mesoamerica continued Teotihuacán's cultural heritage. This heritage was defined by Teotihuacán's temple style, ceramics, textiles, and religious customs, especially the cult of the feathered serpent god Quetzalcoatl [Ketz-al-CO-wa]. The Toltecs, migrants from the north, militarized the Teotihuacán legacy and transformed it into a program of conquest.

Ceremonial Centers and Chiefdoms
In the three centuries after the end of the city-state of Teotihuacán, the local population declined from some 200,000 to about 30,000. Although largely ruined, the ceremonial center continued to attract pilgrims, but other places around the Valley of Mexico and beyond rose in importance. The semiarid region to the northwest of the valley had an extensive mining industry, with many mine shafts extending a mile or more into the mountains. It produced gemstones, such as greenstone, turquoise, hematite, and cinnabar. Independent after 600, inhabitants built ceremonial centers and small states of their own, trading their gemstones to their neighbors in all directions.

To the north were the Pueblo cultures in today's southwestern United States. These cultures were based on sophisticated irrigated farming systems and are known for their distinctive painted pottery styles. They flourished between 700 and 1500 in the canyons of what are today the states of New Mexico, Arizona, southwestern Colorado, and southeastern Utah. In turn, these cultures might have been in contact with the Mississippi cultures, among which the ceremonial center and city of Cahokia (650–1400) near modern St. Louis is the best known. An obsidian scraper from the Pachuco region north of the Valley of Mexico found in Spiro Mounds, Oklahoma, attests to at least occasional contacts between Mesoamerica and the Mississippi culture (see Map 15.1).

In western Mesoamerica, ceremonial centers and chiefdoms flourished on the basis of metallurgy, which arrived through Ecuadoran seaborne merchants

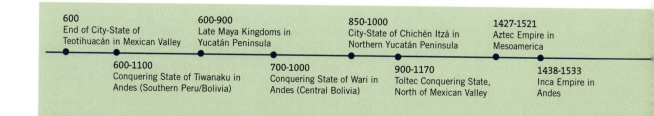

600		600-900		850-1000		1427-1521
End of City-State of Teotihuacán in Mexican Valley		Late Maya Kingdoms in Yucatán Peninsula		City-State of Chichén Itzá in Northern Yucatán Peninsula		Aztec Empire in Mesoamerica

	600-1100		700-1000		900-1170		1438-1533
	Conquering State of Tiwanaku in Andes (Southern Peru/Bolivia)		Conquering State of Wari in Andes (Central Bolivia)		Toltec Conquering State, North of Mexican Valley		Inca Empire in Andes

A Tearful Departure

"1. At Tula there stood the house of beams, there yet stands the house of plumed serpents left by Nacxitl Tolpitzin; going forth weeping, our nobles went to where he was to perish, down there at Tlapallan [mythical place on the Gulf of Mexico] . . .

"4. With the falling down of mountains I wept, with the lifting up of sands I was wretched that my lord had gone.

"5. At Tlapallan he was waited for, it was commanded that there he should sleep, thus being alone."

—Daniel Brinton, ed. and trans. *Ancient Nahuatl Poetry*, New York: AMS Press, 1969, p. 105 . Originally published 1887.

ca. 600–800. The Ecuadorans received their copper from Peru, in return for seashells found in the warm waters off their coast as well as farther north. Copper, too soft for agricultural implements or military weapons, served mostly in households and as jewelry for the rich. Smiths fashioned domestic articles such as needles and tweezers, as well as ornaments and bells, from the metal. Members of the ruling classes typically used copper earrings, pendants, and strings of bells around their ankles as markers of their elevated rank.

In the south, a number of small, fortified hilltop states flourished in the post-Teotihuacán period. Their inhabitants built moats and ramparts to protect these states. More than in other Mesoamerican states, the southern ruling classes were embroiled in fierce wars during 600–900, images of which are depicted in the stone reliefs of gruesome battle scenes. In one such relief, "bird men" and "jaguar men" are shown pitted against each other, amid flowing blood, severed heads, and disemboweled bodies. One of these groups of antagonists was possibly a band of mercenary troops, dislodged from a defeated state and seeking employment or even dominance elsewhere in the south.

The Toltec Conquering State   Early after the collapse of Teotihuacán, craftspeople and farmers migrated some 60 miles north to Tula, a place on a ridge in the highlands watered by two tributaries of a river flowing into the Gulf of Mexico. They founded a small ceremonial center and town with workshops known for the high quality of the scrapers, knives, and spear points fabricated from the local Pachuca obsidian. Around 900, new migrants arrived from northwest Mexico as well as the Gulf coast. The northerners spoke Nahuatl [Na-hua], the language of the later Aztecs, who considered Tula their ancestral city.

The integration of the new arrivals was apparently not peaceful since it resulted in the abandonment of the temple and the departure of a defeated party of Tulans. This abandonment may well have been enshrined in the myth of Tolpiltzin, a priest-king of the feathered serpent god Quetzalcoatl, who after his departure to the east would one day return to restore the cult to its rightful center. The myth later played a fateful part in the establishment of Spanish rule in the Americas.

The new Tula of 900 developed quickly into a large city with a new temple, 60,000 urban dwellers, and perhaps another 60,000 farmers on surrounding lands. It was the first city-centered state to give prominence to the sacrifice of captured warriors. The captives were apparently slaughtered on a skull altar so that the gods would be properly served with blood, the life-giving substance of humankind. As it evolved, Tula became the capital of the conquering state of the Toltecs, which imprinted its warrior culture on large parts of Mesoamerica from around 900 to 1180 (see Map 15.1).

Militarism   The Toltec innovation of a military state with a warrior class is extensively documented by sculptures. Toltec warriors, probably recruited from among

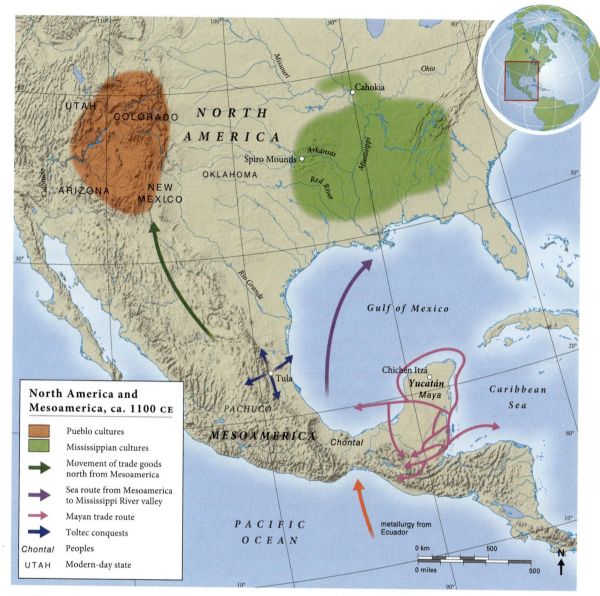

MAP **15.1** **North America and Mesoamerica, ca. 1100.**

newly arriving immigrants from northwest Mexico, were organized into regiments identified by totem animals, such as the coyote, jaguar, and eagle. Standard-bearers, displaying the totems, rallied the warriors around their officers. Wooden butterfly breastplates, worn over thick cotton shirts, also displayed totems. Helmets made of layers of cotton and festooned with bird feathers protected the heads. Shields were worn for the protection of the back. Not all warriors wore full armor, but those who did were clearly well protected.

The Toltecs introduced two innovations in weaponry that improved the effectiveness of hand-to-hand combat. First, there was the new weapon of the short (1.5-foot) sword made of hardwood with inlaid obsidian edges, which could slash as well as crush, in contrast to the obsidian-spiked clubs that had been primary weapons in earlier times. Second, warriors wore obsidian daggers with wooden handles inside a band on the left arm, replacing simpler obsidian blades, which were difficult to use as they had no handles. Traditional dart throwers and slings for stone projectiles completed the offensive armament of the warriors. Soldiers of lower rank were largely without protective armor and wore simple loincloths, their weapons limited to sticks for striking and fending off opponents. Some officers depicted in the sculptures wear nose rings or nose/ear plugs, indicating their noble status. Coming from a military culture in which status depended on performance, these officers appear to have been adopted into the lineages of the ruling elite as a result of their successes in war.

The Toltec army of 13,000–26,000 soldiers was sufficiently large to engage in battles of conquest within an area of 4 days' march (roughly 40 miles) away from Tula. Any target beyond this range was beyond their capabilities at this point, given the logistics of armor, weapons, food rations, narrow dirt roads, and uneven terrain—and, of course, Toltecs did not have the benefit of wheeled vehicles. Thus, the only way of projecting power beyond the range of 40 miles was to establish colonies and to have troops accompany traders, each of which could then supply himself by foraging or through trade along the way. As a result, the Toltec state projected its power by the prestige of its large military, rather than through a full-scale imperial program with the imposition of governors, tributes, and taxes.

Trade   Apart from demonstrating military might, the Toltecs pursued the establishment of a large trade network. Merchants parlayed Tula's obsidian production into a trade network that radiated southward into the cacao, vanilla, and bird feather production centers of Chiapas and Guatemala; to the north into gemstone mining regions; and westward into centers of metal mining. Metallurgy advanced around 1200 with the development of the technology of bronze casting. Bronze axes were stronger and more useful for working with wood than copper axes. Bronze bells produced a greater variety of sounds than those of copper. As ornamental objects, both were trade goods highly prized by the elites in Tula.

The Late Toltec Era   Toltec military power declined in the course of the twelfth century when the taxable grain yield diminished, because of either prolonged droughts or a depletion of the topsoil on the terraces, or a combination of the two. Sometime around 1180, a new wave of foraging peoples from the northwest invaded, attacking with bows and arrows and using hit-and-run tactics against Toltec communication lines. The disruptions caused an internal revolt, which brought down the ceremonial center and its palaces. By 1200, Tula was a city with a burned-out center, like Teotihuacán six centuries earlier; and Mesoamerica relapsed into a period of small-state coexistence characteristic of the pre-600 period.

Late Maya States in Yucatán

Teotihuacán's demise at the end of the sixth century was paralleled by a realignment of the balance of power among the Maya kingdoms in the southern Yucatán lowlands of Mesoamerica. This realignment, accompanied by extensive warfare, was resolved by around 650. A period of late flowering spanned the next two centuries, followed by a shift of power from the southern to the northern part of the peninsula.

The Southern Kingdoms   At its height during the fourth and fifth centuries, Teotihuacán in the Valley of Mexico had interjected itself into the delicate balance of power existing among the Maya kingdoms of southern Yucatán. Alliances among the states shifted, and prolonged wars of conquest racked the lowlands, destroying several older states. A dozen new kingdoms emerged and established a new balance of power among themselves. After a lengthy hiatus, Maya culture entered its final period (650–900).

The most striking phenomenon of the final period in the southern, rain forest–covered lowlands and adjacent highlands were massive new programs of agricultural expansion and ceremonial monument construction. Agriculture was expanded again through cutting down the rain forest on hillsides and terracing the hills for soil retention. The largest kingdoms grew to 50,000–60,000 inhabitants and reached astounding rural population densities of about 1,000 persons per square mile. (In comparison, England's most densely populated counties just prior to its agricultural expansion after 1700 were Middlesex and Surrey, with 221 and 207 persons per square mile, respectively.) Although the late Maya states were geographically small, they were administratively the most centralized polities ever created in indigenous American history.

The late Maya states did not last long. In spite of all efforts, the usually torrential downpours of the rainy season gradually washed the topsoil from the newly built hillside terraces. The topsoil, accumulating as alluvium in the flatlands, was initially quite fertile; but from around 800 onward it became more and more depleted of nutrients. In addition, in many wetlands, farmers found it difficult to prevent clay from forming over the alluvium and hardening in the process. Malnutrition resulting from the receding agricultural surface began to reduce the labor force. Ruling classes had to make do with fewer workers and smaller agricultural surpluses. In the end, even the ruling classes suffered, with members killing each other for what remained of these surpluses. By about 900, the Maya kingdoms in southern Yucatán had shriveled to the size of chiefdoms with small towns and villages.

Chichén Itzá in the North   A few small Maya states on the periphery survived. The most prominent among them was Chichén Itzá [Chee-CHEN Eat-SA] in the northern lowlands, which flourished from about 850 to 1000. At first glance the region would appear to be less than hospitable for a successful state. The climate in the north was much drier than that in the south. The surface was rocky or covered with thin topsoil, supporting mostly grass, scrub vegetation, and isolated forests. In many places, where the soil was too saline, agriculture was impossible and the production of salt was the only source of income. There were no rivers, but many sinkholes in the porous limestone underneath the soil held water. Countless cisterns to hold additional amounts of water for year-round use were cut into the limestone and plastered to prevent seepage. This water, carried in jars to the surface, supported an intensive garden agriculture, productive enough to sustain entire towns and city-states.

Chichén Itzá was founded during the phase of renewed urbanization in 650. It was built near two major sinkholes and several salt flats. The population was composed of local Maya as well as the Maya-speaking Chontal from the Gulf coast farther west. Groups among these people engaged in long-distance trade, both overland and in boats along the coast. Since trade in the most lucrative goods (such as cacao, vanilla, jade, copper, bronze, turquoise, and obsidian) required contact with

Chichén Itzá, El Caracol ("The Snail") Observatory. This domed building was aligned with the northern extreme of the path of Venus. Here, astronomers made the lengthy and systematic observations necessary to coordinate the three different calendars in use in Mesoamerica from about 500 BCE (see Chapter 6).

people well outside even the farthest political reach of either Teotihuacán or Tula, merchants (*pochtecas* [potsh-TAY-cas]) traveled in armed caravans. These merchant groups enjoyed considerable freedom and even sponsorship by the ruling classes of the states of Mesoamerica. Such was their importance that they occupied positions of high honor in ceremonies and festivities.

Chontal traders adopted Toltec culture, and when they based themselves in Chichén Itzá around 850 they superimposed their adopted culture over that of the original Maya. How the city was ruled is only vaguely understood, but there is some evidence that there were two partially integrated ruling factions, possibly descended from the Chontal and local Maya, sharing in the governance of the city. At the very end of the period of Teotihuacán, Maya, and Toltec cultural expansion, the three cultural traditions finally merged on the Yucatán Peninsula in only one geographically marginal region. This merger, however, did not last long; already at around 1000 the ruling-class factions left the city-state for unknown reasons. As a result, the city-state diminished in size and power to town level.

The Legacy of Tiwanaku and Wari in the Andes

Mesoamerica and the Andes, from the time of chiefdom formation in 2500 BCE in Caral-Supé onward, shared the tradition of regional temple pilgrimages. In the Andes, the chiefdoms remained mostly coastal, with some inland extensions along valleys of the Andes. Around 600 CE, the two conquering states of Tiwanaku in the highlands of what are today southern Peru and Bolivia, and Wari, in central Peru, emerged. Both states encompassed several tens of thousands of inhabitants and represented a major step in the formation of larger, militarily organized polities.

The Conquering State of Tiwanaku

Tiwanaku was a political and cultural power center in the south-central Andes during the period 600–1100. It began as a ceremonial center with surrounding villages and gradually developed into a state dominating the region around Lake Titicaca. At its apogee it was an expanding state, planting colonies in regions far from the lake and conveying its culture through trade to peoples even beyond the colonies.

Agriculture on the High Plain The Andes consist of two parallel mountain chains stretching along the west coast of South America. For the most part, these chains are close together, divided by small plains, valleys, and lower mountains. In southeastern Peru and western Bolivia an intermountain plain, 12,500 feet above sea level, extends as wide as 125 miles. At its northern end lies Lake Titicaca, subdivided into a larger and deeper northern valley and a smaller, shallower, swampy, and reed-covered southern valley. Five major and 20 smaller rivers coming from the eastern

Andes chain feed the lake, which has one outlet at its southern end, a river flowing into Lake Poopó [Po-POH], a salt lake 150 miles south. The Lake Titicaca region, located above the tree line, receives winter rains sufficient for agriculture and pasture, whereas the southern plain around Lake Poopó is too dry to sustain more than steppes.

In spite of its elevation, the region around Lake Titicaca offered everything necessary for an advanced urbanization process. The lake's freshwater supported fish and resources such as reeds from the swamps, which served for the construction of boats and roofs. Corn flourished only in the lower elevations of the Andes and had to be imported, together with the corn-derived *chicha*, a beer-like drink. Instead of corn, food staples were potatoes and quinoa. Potatoes were preserved for the harsh winter months through drying. The grasslands of the upper hills served as pastures for llama and alpaca herds. Llamas were used as transportation animals, and alpacas provided wool. The meat of both animals—preserved for winter through drying—was a major protein source. Although frost was an ever-present danger in Tiwanaku, nutrition was quite diversified.

Tiwanaku, Kalassaya Gate. Within the Temple of the Sun, this gate is aligned with the sun's equinoxes and was used for festive rituals. Note the precise stone work, which the Incas later developed further.

Farmers grew their crops on hillside terraces, where runoff water could be channeled, or on raised fields close to the lake. The raised-field system, which farmers had adopted through interaction with the peoples of the Maya lowlands, consisted of a grid of narrow strips of earth, separated from each other by channels. Mud from the channels, heaped onto the strips, replenished their fertility. A wooden foot plow with perhaps a bronze blade seems to have been the main farming implement, although hard archaeological proof is still elusive. By 500, the combined sustenance from fishing, hunting, farming, and herding supported dozens of villages and, by 700, the city of Tiwanaku and its 20,000 inhabitants.

The ceremonial center of Tiwanaku consisted of a sunken courtyard dating to the pre-600 period and several temples on platforms or sets of platforms constructed later. The most sumptuous residential quarters were next to the new temples. There, elite family lineages lived in walled compounds with houses built around courtyards. Underground drainage canals with manholes at regular intervals for cleaning took care of the removal of waste. Farther away from the centers were poorer residential areas with communal kitchens, which probably served for the preparation of foods consumed at ceremonial feasts.

Coordinated with the calendar as well as life-cycle events (such as initiation rituals), ceremonial feasts brought together elite lineages and clients, or ordinary craftspeople and villagers. Elites and clients cohered through **reciprocity**, that is, communal labor for the construction of the ceremonial centers and elaborate feasting, in which elite wealth was expended for the ceremonial leveling of status differences. Until shortly before the end of the state it does not appear that this reciprocity gave way to more forcible ways of allocating labor through conscription or taxation.

Reciprocity: In its basic form, an informal agreement among people according to which a gift or an invitation has to be returned after a reasonable amount of time; in the pre-Columbian Americas, an arrangement of feasts versus taxes between ruling classes and subjects in a state.

Expansion and Conquest

Like Tiwanaku, the core region around the southern arm of Lake Titicaca housed a set of related but competing elite–client hierarchies. Ruling clans with intermediate leaders and ordinary farmers in the villages comprised a state capable of imposing military power beyond the center. But counterbalancing clans at the head of similar hierarchies prevented the rise of dynasties that would command permanent, unified central administrations and military forces. The projection of power over the northern lake, therefore, was not primarily of a military nature. Whatever the military expeditions by ruling clans outside the city, the primary form of Tiwanaku authority was the unrivaled prestige of its ceremonial center. This center attracted pilgrims not merely from the northern lake but also from more distant regions. Pilgrims partaking in Tiwanaku feasting ceremonies can be considered as extensions of the reciprocity and clientage system of the ruling classes and, hence, of Tiwanaku power.

More direct expressions of Tiwanaku influence beyond Lake Titicaca were armed trading caravans and the foundation of colonies in the western valleys of the Andes. Merchants accompanied by warriors and llama drivers crossed multiple polities in order to exchange textiles and ceramics for basalt cores in the south, metal ingots and obsidian cores in the north, and coca leaves and other psychotropic substances in the east, often hundreds of miles away. Colonies were more tangible forms of power projection, especially those established in the Moquegua [Mow-KAY-gah] valley 200 miles or 10–12 days of walking to the west. Here, at some 2,800 feet above sea level, Tiwanaku emigrants established villages, which sent their corn or beer to the capital in return for salt, as well as stone and obsidian tools. Although overall less militarily inclined than the Mesoamerican states of the same time period, Tiwanaku wielded a visible influence over southern Peru (see Map 15.2).

The Expanding City-State of Wari

Little is known about early settlements in central Peru, some 450 miles or 3–4 weeks of foot travel north from Tiwanaku. The state of Wari emerged around 600 from a number of small polities organized around ceremonial centers. Expansion to the south put Wari into direct contact with Tiwanaku. The two states came to some form of mutual accommodation, and it appears that neither embarked on an outright conquest of the other. Their military postures remained limited to their regional spheres of influence.

Origins and Expansion   Wari was centered on the Ayacucho valley, a narrow plain in the highlands of northern Peru. Here, the land between the two chains of the Andes is mountainous, interspersed with valleys and rivers flowing to the Pacific or the Amazon. The elevation of 8,000 feet in the Ayacucho valley allowed for the cultivation of potatoes as well as corn and cotton. In the course of the seventh century, Wari grew into a city of 30,000 inhabitants and brought a number of neighboring cities under its control. It also pushed for an enlargement of the agricultural base through the expansion of terrace farming for the growing of corn, fruits, peppers, and coca. Like Tiwanaku, Wari eventually became the center of a developed urbanism and a diversified agriculture.

Some local traditions that continued under the Wari elite deserve comment. One city specialized in rituals that included the smashing of heads taken as trophies from killed war captives, marking a parallel to the militarism of some of the Mesoamerican polities. Another town had tombs in which high-status women were buried with copper jewelry, ceramic vessels, and weaving tools, illustrating the function

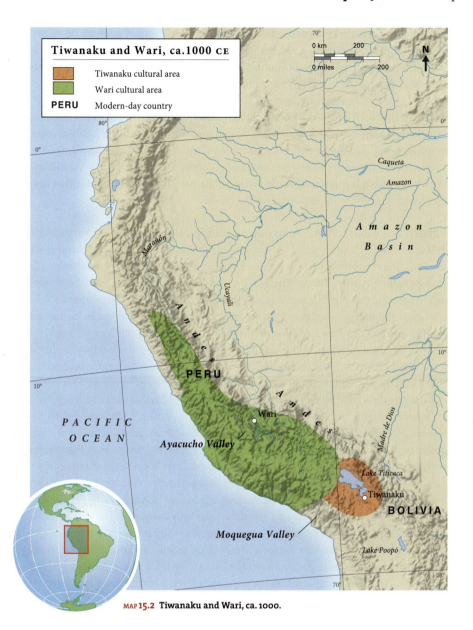

MAP **15.2** Tiwanaku and Wari, ca. 1000.

of women as weavers and brewers in their own right in elite society. Although American agrarian society was nearly as patriarchal as that in Eurasia, it apparently also relaxed its gender segregation for elite women.

In addition to maintaining control over the cities in its vicinity, Wari employed architects who constructed new towns. These planned centers included plazas, housing for laborers, and halls for feasting. Outside the core area, Wari elites established colonies, some of which appeared—even if only briefly around 800—in northern Peru as far as 450 miles away. It appears that Wari exercised much stronger political control over the elites of its core region than Tiwanaku and was more active in founding colonies.

The Wari–Tiwanaku Frontier   Early on, Wari established a colony upstream in the Moquegua valley on southern Peru's west coast, some 100 miles away. The settlers built extensive terraces and canals together with protective walls and settlements on mountain peaks. This building activity coincided with the Tiwanaku establishment of downstream farming colonies. It is possible that there was considerable tension with Tiwanaku during the initial period (650–800) over the division of water between the two colonies. But during 800–1000 the two agricultural communities developed closer ties, with indications that the two local elites engaged in a peaceful sharing of the water resources and common feasting activities. Very likely, the Moquegua valley was politically so far on the periphery of both states that neither had the means to impose itself on the other.

Return to Coexistence   At its origins, Wari was an expanding state very similar to Tiwanaku. Both were governed by elite clans under leaders who derived their strength from reciprocal patron–client organizations binding leaders to farmers and craftspeople. Extensive feasts strengthened the bond. Something must have happened to erode this bond, however, since there is evidence of increased internal tension after 950 in the two states. Groups arose which defaced sculptures, destroyed portals, and burned down edifices. Somehow, crowds previously happy to uphold elite control in return for participation in the lavish feasts (provided by the elites) must have become angry at these elites, their ceremonies, and the temple sculptures. Scholars have argued that it was perhaps the fragility of power based on an increasingly unequal reciprocity that caused the rift between elites and subjects.

Janusek's argument, however, provokes a deeper question: Why would elites allow reciprocity to be weakened to such a degree that it became a sham? Previous generations of scholars argued that climatic change deprived the elites of the wherewithal to throw large feasts. In the case of Tiwanaku there is evidence that a drought hit the high plain beginning in 1040, but this date is clearly a century too late for an explanation. A more convincing explanation suggests environmental degradation as the result of agricultural expansion. Land that was only marginally suitable for agriculture was exhausted and could no longer sustain a vastly increased population, as with the late Maya kingdoms. Unfortunately, there is still too little evidence to extend the environmental argument from the Maya kingdoms to the Andes highland and sierra. An ultimate explanation for the disintegration of the expanding states of Tiwanaku and Wari thus remains elusive.

American Empires: Aztec and Inca Origins and Dominance

Expanding and conquering states in the Andes and Mesoamerica gave way in the early fifteenth century to empires. At this time, demographic growth and the evolution of militarism in the Americas reached a point of transition to the pattern of imperial political formation. Conquering states had been cities with ceremonial centers, which dominated agricultural hinterlands and projected their prestige or power across regions. By contrast, the Aztec (1427–1521) and Inca (1438–1533) Empires in Mesoamerica and the Andes were states with capitals and ceremonial centers, vastly larger tributary hinterlands, and armies capable of engaging in campaigns at distances twice (or more) as far away than previous states. As in Eurasia, they were centralized multireligious, multiethnic, and multilinguistic polities: empires in every sense of the word.

The Aztec Empire of Mesoamerica

Hailing from the mountainous semidesert regions of northwest Mexico, the ancestors of the Aztecs entered history as migrants in search of a better life. They found this life as conquerors of the Valley of Mexico, the site of today's Mexico City (after the drainage of most of the valley). In the course of the fifteenth century they conquered an empire that eventually encompassed Mesoamerica from the Pacific to the Gulf of Mexico and from the middle of modern northern Mexico to the Isthmus of Panama.

Settlement in the Mexican Valley   The Aztecs traced their origins back to a founding myth. According to this myth, the first Aztec was one of seven brothers born on an island in a lake or in a mountain cave, "150 leagues" (450 miles) northwest of the Valley of Mexico. The distance, recorded by Spaniards in the sixteenth century, can be interpreted as corresponding to a mountain in the modern state of Guanajuato [Goo-wa-na-hoo-WA-to]. This Aztec ancestor and his descendants left their mythical homeland as foragers dressed in skins and lacking agriculture and urban civilization. Their hunter–warrior patron god Huitzilpochtli [Hoo-it-zil-POSHT-lee] promised to guide them to a promised land of plenty.

After settling for a while in Tula (claimed later as a place of heritage), their god urged the foragers to move on to the Valley of Mexico. Here, an eagle perched on a cactus commanded the Aztecs to settle and build a temple to their god. In this temple, they were to nourish him with the sacrificial blood of humans captured in war. Like many peoples in Eurasia as well as the contemporary Incas, the Aztecs contrasted their later empire and its glory with a myth of humble beginnings and long periods of wandering toward an eventual promised land.

The historical record in the Valley of Mexico becomes clearer in the fourteenth century. In the course of this period, the Aztecs appeared as clients of two Toltec-descended overlords in states on the southwestern shore. Here, they created the two islands of Tenochtitlán [Te-notsh-tit-LAN] and Tlatelolco [Tla-te-LOL-co], founded a city with a ceremonial center on Tenochtitlán, engaged in farming, and rendered military service to their overlords. Thanks to successes on the battlefield, Aztec leaders were able to marry into the elites of the neighboring city-states and gained the right to have their own ruler ("speaker," *tlatloani* [Tla-tlo-AH-nee]) presiding over a council of leading members of the elite and priests. Toward the end of the fourteenth century, an emerging Aztec elite was firmly integrated with the ruling classes of many of the two dozen or so city-states in and around the valley.

The Rise of the Empire   After a successful rebellion in 1428 of a triple alliance among the Aztec city-state of Tenochtitlán and two other vassal states against the reigning city-state in the Valley of Mexico, the Aztec leader Itzcóatl [Its-CO-aw] (r. 1428–1440) emerged as the dominant figure. Itzcóatl and his three successors, together with the rulers of the two allied states, expanded their city-states on the two islands and the shore through conquests into a full-fledged empire. Tenochtitlán, on one of the islands, became the capital, growing into an empire that consisted of a set of six "inner provinces" in the Valley of Mexico. Local elites were left in place, but they were required to attend ceremonies in Tenochtitlán, bring and receive gifts, leave their sons as hostages, and intermarry with the elites of the triple alliance. Commoner farmers outside the cities had to provide tributes in the form of foodstuffs and labor services, making the imperial core self-sufficient.

After the middle of the fifteenth century, the triple alliance conquered a set of 55 city-states outside the valley as "outer provinces." It created an imperial polity from the Pacific to the Gulf, from Tarasco, 200 miles to the northwest, to Oaxaca, over 500 miles to the south (see Map 15.3). This state was now far more centralized than the preceding Teotihuacán and Toltec city-states. In this empire, local ruling families with their ceremonial centers and gods were generally left in place, but commoners had to produce tributes in the form of raw materials, such as obsidian, gold, silver, copper, bronze, gemstones, cotton, and cacao, or lightweight processed and manufactured goods, such as dried peppers and fruits, feathers, rubber balls, incense, textiles, basketry, ropes, and live birds.

In some provinces, Aztec governors replaced the rulers; in most others, Aztec tribute collectors (supported by troops) held local rulers in check and supervised the transportation of the tributes by porters to the valley. Reciprocity, once of central importance in Mesoamerica, continued on a grand scale but was now clearly subordinate to military considerations.

List of Tributes Owed to the Aztecs. The list includes quantities of cotton and wool textiles, clothes, headgear with feathers, and basketry. The Aztecs did not continue the complex syllabic script of the Maya but used instead images, including persons with speech bubbles, for communication. Spanish administrators and monks who copied the Aztec manuscripts added their own explanations to keep track of Native American tributes.

Imperial Policies   The resulting multiethnic, multireligious, and multilinguistic empire of eventually some 19 million inhabitants was still a work in progress in the early sixteenth century when the Spanish arrived. Right in the middle of the empire, just 50 miles east of the Valley of Mexico, the large state of Tlaxcala [Tlash-KAH-lah], Nahuatl-speaking like the Aztecs, held out in opposition, together with multiple enemy states on the periphery. Although the ruling elites of the triple alliance did everything to expand, including even inviting enemy rulers to their festivities in order to secure their loyalty through gestures of reciprocity, pockets of anti-Aztec states survived and eventually became crucial allies of the Spanish, providing the latter's tiny military forces with a critical mass of fighters.

Some outer provinces possessed strategic importance, with Aztec colonies implanted to prepare for eventual conquest of remaining enemies outside the empire. The most relentlessly pursued policy of continued expansion of Aztec central control was the threat of warfare, for the purpose of capturing rebels or enemies as prisoners of war to be sacrificed to the gods in the ceremonial centers. Death on the battlefield was bad enough, but to have one's heart ripped out on top of the Tenochtitlán pyramid must have been outright horrifying to the enemies of the

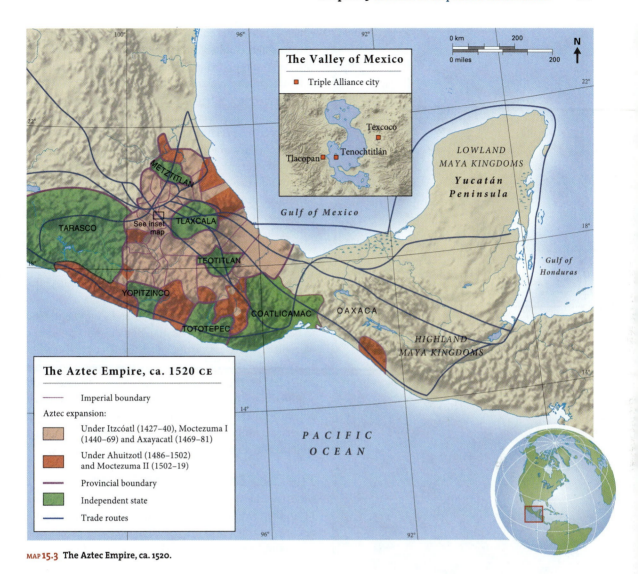

The Valley of Mexico

■ Triple Alliance city

Texcoco

Tlacopan   Tenochtitlán

Gulf of Mexico

0 km   200
0 miles   200

N

LOWLAND
MAYA KINGDOMS
*Yucatán
Peninsula*

METZTITLAN

TARASCO

See inset
map   TLAXCALA

TEOTITLAN

YOPITZINCO

COATLICAMAC   OAXACA

TOTOTEPEC

*Gulf of
Honduras*

HIGHLAND
MAYA KINGDOMS

The Aztec Empire, ca. 1520 CE

——— Imperial boundary

Aztec expansion:

▢ Under Itzcóatl (1427–40), Moctezuma I
(1440–69) and Axayacatl (1469–81)

▢ Under Ahuitzotl (1486–1502)
and Moctezuma II (1502–19)

——— Provincial boundary

▢ Independent state

——— Trade routes

*PACIFIC
OCEAN*

MAP 15.3 **The Aztec Empire, ca. 1520.**

Aztecs—as it was later to the Spanish. This fear-inducing tactic—or "power propaganda"—was an integral innovation in the imperialism of the Aztecs.

The Military Forces   The triple alliance ruled a Nahuatl-speaking population of some 1.5 million inhabitants in the core provinces of the Valley of Mexico. This number yielded a maximum of a quarter of a million potential soldiers, taking into consideration that most soldiers were farmers with agricultural obligations. From this large number of adult males, the Aztecs assembled units of 8,000 troops each, which they increased as the need arose. Initially, the army was recruited from among the elite of the Aztecs and their allies. But toward the middle of the fifteenth century, Aztec rulers set up a military school system for the sons of the elite plus those commoners who were to become priests. A parallel school system for the sons of commoners, aged 15–20 years, also included military training. After graduation, recruits began as porters, carrying supplies for the combat troops—an Aztec innovation

Aztec Weapons. Aztec weapons were well-crafted hardwood implements with serrated obsidian edges, capable of cutting through metal, including iron. As slashing weapons they were highly effective in close combat.

which considerably enlarged the marching range of armies on campaign. Soldiers rose in the army hierarchy on the basis of merit, particularly their success in the capture of enemies for future sacrifice. After four captures, a soldier was considered a veteran; additional captures yielded the ranks of captain, general, and commander in chief. Elite sons served in special regiments, identified by emblems of coyotes, jaguars, or eagles on their uniforms.

The Aztecs inherited the weaponry and armor of the Toltecs but also made some important innovations. The bow and arrow, which arrived from northwest Mexico at the end of Toltec rule, became a standard weapon in Aztec armies. In addition, perhaps as late as the fifteenth century, the Aztecs developed the three-foot obsidian-spiked broadsword, derived from the Toltec short sword, in order to enhance the latter's slashing force. As a result, clubs, maces, and axes declined in importance in the Aztec arsenal. Thrusting spears, dart throwers, and slings continued to be used as standard weapons. Body armor, consisting of quilted, sleeveless cotton shirts, thick cotton helmets, and round wooden or cane shields, was adopted from the Toltecs. With the arrival of the Aztecs, the Americas had acquired the heaviest infantry weaponry in their history, reflective of the intensity of militarism reached in their society—a militarism which was also typical of the earlier empires of the beginning Iron Age in the Middle East.

The Inca Empire of the Andes

After the disintegration of Tiwanaku and Wari around 1100, the central Andes returned to the traditional politics of local chiefdoms in small city-states with ceremonial centers and agricultural hinterlands. The best-known city-state was Chimú on the Peruvian coast, with its capital of Chan Chan numbering 30,000 inhabitants. Tiwanaku cultural traditions, however, remained dominant and were expressed in religious ceremonies, textile motifs, and ceramic styles.

Given the fierce competition among the pilgrimage centers, insecurity was rampant during the period 1100–1400, with particular influence granted to charismatic military leaders who could project military force and pacify the land. After a gestation period during the fourteenth century, the southern Peruvian city-state of Cuzco with its Inca elite emerged in the early fifteenth century at the head of a highly militaristic, conquering polity. Within another century, the Incas had established an empire, called "Tawantinsuyu" [Ta-wan-tin-SOO-yuh] (Quechua, "Four Regions"), symbolizing its geographical expanse. It stretched from Ecuador in the north to central Chile in the south, with extensions into the tropical upper Amazon region and western Argentinean steppes (see Map 15.4).

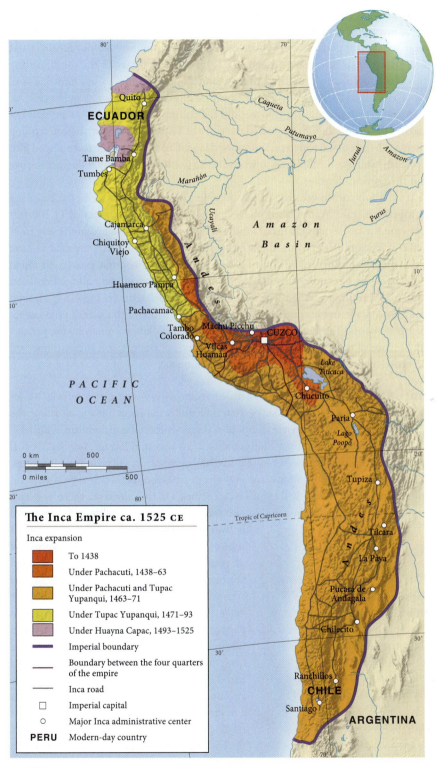

The Inca Empire ca. 1525 CE

Inca expansion

- To 1438
- Under Pachacuti, 1438–63
- Under Pachacuti and Tupac Yupanqui, 1463–71
- Under Tupac Yupanqui, 1471–93
- Under Huayna Capac, 1493–1525
- Imperial boundary
- Boundary between the four quarters of the empire
- Inca road
- □ Imperial capital
- ○ Major Inca administrative center
- **PERU** Modern-day country

MAP **15.4** The Inca Empire, ca. 1525.

From Myth to History   As in the case of the Aztecs, the founding myth of the Incas involves a cave, an island, and a promised land of rich agriculture. In one version, the creator god Viracocha [Vee-rah-KOT-shah] summoned four brothers and four sisters from caves "seven leagues" (21 miles) from Cuzco to the south, pairing them as couples and promising them a land of plenty. They would find this land when a golden rod, to be used on their wanderings, would get stuck in the soil. Alternatively, the sun god Inti [IN-tee] did the pairing of the couples on an island in Lake Titicaca and thereby bestowed the glory of Tiwanaku on them, before sending them with the golden rod to their promised land. Cuzco, where the rod plunged into the fertile soil, was settled land however; and a war ensued in which the Incas drove out the previous farmers.

In the fourteenth century, Cuzco became a serious contender in the city-state competition. Like Wari, Cuzco was located at a highland elevation of 11,300 feet between the two Andes chains of southern Peru, roughly one-third of the way from Lake Titicaca north to Wari. Eight rulers (*curacas* [koo-RA-kas]) are said to have succeeded each other in the consolidation of Cuzco as a regional power. Although their names are recorded, events are hazy and dates are missing altogether. Firm historical terrain is reached with the ninth ruler, Pachacuti (r. 1438–1471), who overthrew his father and might have appropriated some of the latter's political accomplishments. The history of the Incas after 1438 is known much better, primarily because of the memories of the grandchildren of the original Inca conquerors, recorded by the Spanish who defeated them in turn.

Imperial Expansion   The system of reciprocity which characterized earlier Mesoamerican and Andean history continued under the Incas but was also, as in the case of Aztecs, decisively cast in the mold of power-enforced unilateralism. *Ayllu* [AY-yoo], the Quechua term for a household with an ancestral lineage, implied mutual obligations among groups of households, neighborhoods, villages, and city-states. To negotiate these obligations, society—from households to city-states—was divided into halves with roughly equal reciprocities. On the elite level, there were two sets of reciprocities, the first within two main branches of the elite and the second between the two branches of the elite and the subjects. The most important social expression of reciprocity remained the feast—extended celebrations with common meals and the consumption of beer fermented from corn or *molle* [MOI-yee] berries (from the Peruvian pepper tree, *molli* in Quechua). In the Incan Empire, the state collected considerably more from the subject *ayllus* than Tiwanaku and Wari had done, but whether it returned comparable amounts through feasts and celebrations was a matter of contention, often leading to armed rebellion.

The earliest conquests under Pachacuti were toward the near south around Lake Titicaca, as well as the agriculturally rich lands north of the former Wari state. Thereafter, in

---

From the Ordinances of the Inca

"We order that everyone bury their deceased in a chamber [*pucullo*], stone tomb, that the dead not be buried in their houses and that the deceased's spindle, dining service, food, drink and garments be buried with them.... We order that the children obey their parents, elders, grandees, and elder sons throughout the kingdom. For the first disobedience the child will be given a whipping; for the second the child will be banished to the silver and gold mines."

—Felipe Guaman Poma de Ayala. *The First New History and Chronicle of Good Government*. Translated by Roland Hamilton, p. 143. Austin: University of Texas Press, 2009.

the later fifteenth century, the Incas expanded 1,300 miles northward to southern Ecuador and 1,500 miles southward to Chile. The final provinces, added in the early sixteenth century, were in northern Ecuador as well as on the eastern slopes of the Andes, from the upper Amazon to western Argentina. The capital, Cuzco, which counted some 100,000 inhabitants in the early sixteenth century, was laid out in a cross-shaped grid of four streets leading out into the suburbs. Symbolically, the capital reached out to the four regions of the empire—coast, north, south, and Amazon rain forest.

Administration   Ethnic Inca governors administered the four regions, which were subdivided into a total of some 80 provinces, each again with an Inca sub-governor. Most provinces were composites of former city-states, which remained under their local elites but had to accept a unique decimal system of population organization imposed by the Inca rulers. According to this system, members of the local elites commanded 10,000, 1,000, 100, and 10 household or *ayllu* heads for the purpose of recruiting the manpower responsible for the *mit'a* [MIT-ah] ("to take a turn," in reference to service obligations rotating among the subjects). The services,

Inca Roads. Inca roads were paths reserved for runners and the military. They were built on beds of rocks and rubble and connected strategic points in the most direct line possible. They included staircases and suspension bridges, often over very steep and alpine terrain.

which subjects owed the empire as equivalents of taxes, were in farming, herding, manufacturing, military service, and portage. In its structure it was not unlike the Ming and Qing Chinese systems of local organization called *baojia*.

The mit'a was perhaps the single most important innovation the Incas contributed to the history of the Americas. In contrast to the Aztecs, who shipped taxes in kind to their capital by boat, the Incas had no efficient means of transportation for long distances. The only way to make use of the taxes in kind was to store them locally as provisions for visiting administrators and soldiers, apart from the traditional feasting in the villages. The Incas built tens of thousands of storehouses everywhere in their empire, requiring subjects to deliver a portion of their harvests, animal products, and domestically produced goods under mit'a obligations to the nearest storehouse in their vicinity.

The architecturally standardized storehouses, often grouped in multiples along the roads but also around cities and on state farms, contained supplies of durable food staples—corn, beer, dried potatoes, quinoa, beans, coca leaves, and dried meat called *charqui* [TSHAR-kee], from which the English term "jerky" is derived and which could last for years. Storehouses also contained raw cotton, wool, textiles, ceramics, ropes, and weapons. These supplies were available to officials and troops and enabled the Incas to conduct military campaigns far from Cuzco without the need for foraging among local farmers. In addition, it was through the mit'a that quotas of laborers were raised for the construction of inns, roads, ceremonial centers, palaces, terraces, and irrigation canals, often far away from the urban center. Finally, mit'a provided laborers for mines, quarries, state and temple farms, and colonies. No form of labor or service went untaxed.

To keep track of mit'a obligations, officials passed bundles of knotted cord (*khipu* [KEE-poo]) upward from level to level in the imperial administration. The numbers of knots on each cord in the bundles contained information on population figures and service obligations. As discussed in Chapter 5, the use of khipus was widespread in the Andes long before the Inca and can be considered as the Andean equivalent of a communication system. The only innovation contributed by the Incas seems to have been the massive scale on which these cord bundles were generated and employed. Unfortunately, all modern attempts to decipher them have so far failed, and thus, it is impossible to accurately outline the full picture of Inca service allocations.

Military Organization   Perhaps the most important mit'a obligation which subject households owed to the Inca in the conquest phase of the empire was the service of young, able-bodied men in the military. Married men 25–30 years old were foot soldiers, often accompanied by wives and children; unmarried men 18–25 years of age served as porters or messengers. As in the Aztec Empire, administrators made sure that enough laborers remained in the villages to take care of their other obligations of farming, herding, transporting, and manufacturing. Sources report armies in the range of 35,000–140,000. Intermediate commanders came from the local and regional elites, and the top commanders were members of the upper and lower Inca ruling elites, as we saw at the beginning of this chapter.

Inca weaponry was comparable to that of the Aztecs, consisting of bows and arrows, dart throwers, slings, clubs with spiked bronze heads, wooden broadswords, bronze axes, and bronze-tipped javelins. Using Bolivian tin, Inca smiths were able to make a much harder and more widely useful bronze than was possible with earlier techniques. The Incas lacked the Aztec obsidian-serrated swords but used a snare (which the Aztecs did not possess) with attached stone or bronze weights to entangle the enemy's legs. Protective armor consisted of quilted cotton shirts, copper breastplates, cane helmets, and shields. These types of weapons and armor were widely found among the Incas and their enemies. The advantage enjoyed by the Incas resulted from the sheer massiveness of their weapons and supplies, procured from craftspeople through the mit'a and stored in strategically located armories.

During the second half of the fifteenth century the Incas turned from conquest to consolidation. Faced at that time with a number of rebellions, they deemphasized the decimal draft and recruited longer-serving troops from among a smaller number of select, trusted peoples. These troops garrisoned the forts distributed throughout the empire. They also were part of the settler colonies implanted in rebellious provinces and in border regions. The fiercest resistance came from the people of the former Tiwanaku state and from the northeast Peruvian provinces, areas with long state traditions of their own. Since elite infighting also became more pronounced toward the end of the fifteenth century, personal guards recruited from non-Inca populations and numbering up to 7,000 soldiers accompanied many leading ruling-class members. The professionalization of the Inca army, however, lagged behind that of the Aztecs since the Incas did not have military academies open to subjects.

Communications   Although they lacked the military professionalization of the Aztecs, the Incas created an imperial communication and logistics structure that was unparalleled in the Americas. Early on, the Incas systematically improved on the road network which they inherited from Tiwanaku, Wari, and other states. Two parallel trunk roads extended from Cuzco nearly the entire length of the empire in both southerly and northerly directions. One followed the coast and western slopes of the western Andes chain; the other led through the mountain lands, valleys, and high plains between the western and eastern Andes chain. In numerous places, additional highways connected the two trunk roads. Suspension bridges made of thick ropes crossed gorges, while rafts were used for crossing rivers. The roads, 3–12 feet wide, crossed the terrain as directly as possible, often requiring extensive grounding, paving, staircasing, and tunneling. In many places, the 25,000-mile road network still exists today, attesting to the engineering prowess of the Incas.

The roads were reserved for troops, officials, and runners carrying messages. For their convenience, every 15 miles, or at the end of a slow 1-day journey, an inn provided accommodation. Larger armies stopped at barracks-like constructions or pitched tents on select campgrounds. Like the Romans, and despite the fact that they did not have wheeled transport, the Incas were well aware how crucial paved and well-supplied roads were for infantry soldiers.

Imperial Society and Culture

As Mesoamerica and the Andes entered their imperial age, cosmopolitan capitals with monumental ceremonial centers and palaces emerged. The sizes of both capitals and monuments were visual expressions of the exalted power which the rulers claimed. Almost daily ceremonies and rituals, accompanied by feasts, further underscore the power claims of rulers. These ceremonies and rituals expressed the shamanic and polytheistic heritage but were modified to impress on enemies and subjects alike the irresistible might of the empires.

Imperial Capitals: Tenochtitlán and Cuzco

In the fifteenth century, the Aztec and Inca capitals were among the largest cities of the world, encompassing between 100,000 and 200,000 inhabitants. Both cities maintained their high degree of urbanism through a complex command system of labor, services, and goods. Although their monumental architecture followed different artistic traditions, both emphasized platforms and sanctuaries atop large pyramid-like structures as symbols of elevated power as well as closeness to the astral gods, especially those associated with the sun and Venus.

Tenochtitlán as an Urban Metropolis   More than half of the approximately 1.5 million people living during the fifteenth century in the Valley of Mexico were urban dwellers, including elites, priests, administrators, military officers, merchants, traders, craftspeople, messengers, servants, and laborers. Tenochtitlán was among the 10 largest world cities of the fifteenth century. Such an extraordinary concentration of urban citizens was unique in the agrarian world prior to the industrialization of Europe (beginning around 1800), when cities usually held no more than 10 percent of the total population (see Map 15.5).

The center of Tenochtitlán, on the southern island, was a large platform where the Aztec settlers had driven pilings into marshy ground and heaped rocks and rubble. In an enclosure on this platform were the main pyramid, with temples to the Aztec gods on top, and a series of smaller ceremonial centers. Adjacent to this on the platform were a food market and a series of palaces of the ruling elite, which included guest quarters, administrative offices, storage facilities for tributes, kitchens, the high court for the elite and the court of appeals for commoners, the low court for civil cases, workshops for craftspeople, the prison, and councils for teachers and the military. Large numbers of Aztecs and visitors assembled each day to pay respect to the ruler and to trade in the market in preparation for assemblies and feasts.

Aqueduct from the Western Hills to Tenochtitlán. This aqueduct, still standing today, provided fresh water to the palace and mansions of the center of the island, to be used as drinking water and for washing.

In 1473, the southern island was merged with the northern island, to form a single unit. At the center of the northern island was a platform that contained the principal market of the combined islands. This daily market attracted as many as 40,000 farmers, craftspeople, traders, porters, and laborers on the main market day. Traders sold raw materials such as clay, basalt, obsidian, timber, lime, cotton, or silver to craftspeople, many of whom maintained workshops in the market where they made pottery, knives, wooden implements, or jewelry. Goods were exchanged through either barter or the use of cacao beans and copper and bronze ornaments as payment. The market also had bars, restaurants, and hotels. Itinerant hucksters dispensed water or juices, and day laborers lined up in a corner to wait for employment. Government officials saw to the observance of standardized measures and weights. Policemen hauled thieves to a courthouse at the center of the market. The sophistication of the market was comparable to that of any market in Eurasia during the fifteenth century.

A number of causeways crossed the capital and linked it with the lakeshore. People also traveled inside the city on a number of main and branch canals. Dikes with sluices on the east side regulated both the water level and the salinity of the lake water around the islands. The runoff during the summer rainy season from the southwestern mountains provided freshwater to lighten the lake's salinity, and the eastern dikes kept out salt water from the rest of the lake. Potable water arrived from the shore via an aqueduct on one of the western causeways. This aqueduct served mostly the ceremonial center and palace precinct, but branches brought potable water to a number of elite residences nearby as well. Professional water carriers took freshwater to commoners in the various quarters of the city; professional waste removers collected human waste from urban residences and took it to farmers for fertilizer. In short, Tenochtitlán possessed a fully developed urban infrastructure comparable to the best amenities found elsewhere in the world at that time.

The two city centers—the pyramid and palaces in the south and the market in the north—were surrounded by dozens of residential city quarters. Built on a layer of firm ground, many of these quarters were inhabited by craftspeople of a shared profession, such as merchants, feather workers, mat makers, and gold- and silversmiths, who practiced their crafts in their residences. As discussed earlier in this chapter, merchants occupied a privileged position between the elite and the commoners. As militarily trained organizers of large caravans of porters, the merchants also provided the Aztec capital with luxury goods. Depending on their social rank, craftspeople occupied residences of larger or smaller size, usually grouped

MAP 15.5 Tenochtitlán and the Valley of Mexico.

into compounds of related families. The rooms of the houses surrounded a central patio on which most of the household activities took place—an architectural preference common to Mesoamerica and the Andes, as well as the Middle East and Mediterranean.

Farming in the Suburbs   Residents of quarters farther away from the center were farmers. In these quarters, making up nearly two-thirds of Tenochtitlán's surface, families not only produced household basics, such as pottery and textiles, but also engaged in intensive farming, which approached horticulture in its precision and complexity. Here, a grid of canals encased small, rectangular islands devoted to housing compounds and/or farming. People moved within these barrios by boat. Since the Valley of Mexico received year-round rains that were often insufficient for dry farming, a raised-field system prevailed, whereby farmers dredged the canals, heaped the fertile mud on top of the rectangular islands, and added waste from their households or brought by boat from the urban neighborhoods. In contrast to the luxurious palaces of the elite, housing for farmers consisted of plastered huts made of cane, wood, and reeds. As in all agrarian societies, farmers—subject to high taxes or rents—were among the poorest folk.

On the surface of the raised beds, or *chinampas*, farmers grew corn, beans, squash, amaranth, and peppers. These seed plants were supplemented by

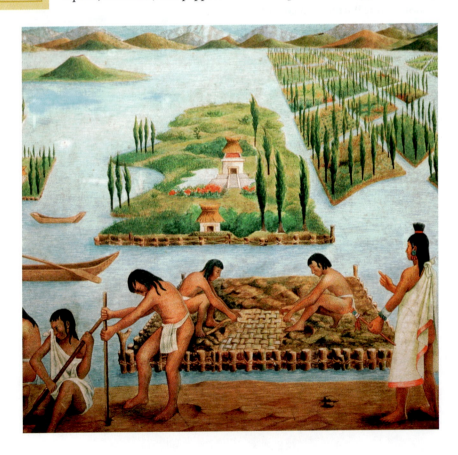

The *Chinampa*. The raised field (*chinampa*) was either a square or a rectangular strip of soil surrounded by irrigation channels. The water and mud from the channels kept the soil moist and fertile. Villagers harvested rich crops from these fields.

Cuzco Stone Masonry. Inspired by the masonry of the people of Tiwanaku, the Inca built imposing structures with much larger blocks of limestone or granite. To cut the blocks, masons used copper and bronze chisels, making use of natural fissures in the stone.

maguey [mag-AY], a large cactus related to the agave. This evergreen plant grew in poor soils; had a large root system, which helped in stabilizing the ground; and produced fiber useful for weaving and pulp useful for making *pulque* [POOL-key], a fermented drink. To plant these crops in the soft soil, a digging stick, slightly broadened at one end, was sufficient. Regular watering made multicropping of seed plants possible. Trees, planted at the edges, firmed up the islands against water erosion.

Ownership of the *chinampas* was vested in clans, which, under neighborhood leaders, were responsible for the adjudication of land allocations and disputes as well as the payment of taxes in kind to the elite. But there were also members of the elite who, as absentee owners, possessed estates and employed managers to collect rents from the farmers. Whether there was a trend from taxes to rents (that is, a central tax system to a decentralized landowner class) is unknown. Given the high productivity of raised-field farming, which was similar to that of the Eurasian agrarian–urban centers, such a trend would not have been surprising.

Cuzco as a Ceremonial-Administrative City
The site of the Inca city of Cuzco was an elongated triangle formed by the confluence of two rivers. At one end, opposite the confluence, was a hill with a number of structures, including the imperial armory, and a temple dedicated to the sun god. Enormous, zigzagging walls followed the contours of the hill. The walls were built with stone blocks weighing up to 100 tons and cut so precisely that no mortar was needed, a technique which the Incas adopted from Tiwanaku. Inside the walls today can be seen the ruins, dating from the Spanish siege in 1536, of multiple buildings which might have served religious and/or administrative purposes. No agreement exists on who resided on the hill or what the function of the heavy stone works was.

Below, on the plain leading to the confluence, the city was laid out in a grid pattern. The residents of the city, all belonging to the upper and lower Inca ruling class,

Patterns Up Close | Human Sacrifice and Propaganda

Archaeologists disagree over the extent to which Paleolithic hominins or humans engaged in human sacrifices. Atapuerca in northeastern Spain is a Paleolithic site from 850,000–750,000 years ago where bone fragments suggestive of violent deaths have been found. How the victims got into the pit at the site, however, and under which circumstances, remain so far a mystery. During the Bronze Age, in Mesopotamia and in other places in Eurasia (3000–1300 BCE), children, servants, retainers, and soldiers were buried together with the kings whom they followed in death. By contrast, in the Iron Age beginning around 1000 BCE, human sacrifices declined almost everywhere in Eurasia. With the concept of transcendence emerging in the seventh century BCE, that is, of a single, invisible God or principle of truth and justice, human sacrifice was essentially abandoned.

Tolland Man. Discovered in a bog in Denmark in 1950, this nearly perfectly preserved man, killed by hanging around 750 BCE, was clearly not a criminal; he was given a dignified burial after his death. Most likely, he was sacrificed to the gods.

In the first millennium CE, Mesoamerica and the Andes evolved broadly along patterns similar to those in Eurasia, from shamanic animism to polytheism, but without the conceptualization of transcendence. The animist heritage, however,

Royal Bloodletting. Mayan kings and queens communicated with gods or ancestors through ritual bloodletting. In this example, from an early eighth-century stone relief from southern Mexico, the queen draws a spiked rope through her tongue while her husband holds a large torch above her head.

remained a strong undercurrent. Both American regions engaged in human as well as animal and agricultural sacrifices. Rulers appeased the gods also through self-sacrifice, that is, the piercing of tongue and penis, as was the case among the Olmecs (1400–400 BCE) and Mayas (600 BCE–900 CE). The feathered serpent god Quetzalcoatl was the Mesoamerican deity of self-sacrifice, revered in the city-states of Teotihuacán (200 BCE–570 CE) and Tula (ca. 900 CE). Under the Toltecs and the Aztecs, this god receded into the background, in favor of warrior gods such as Tezcatlipoca and Huitzilpochtli. The survival of animist blood rituals within polytheism was a pattern that distinguished the early American empires from their Eurasian counterparts.

Whether human sacrifices were prolific under Aztec and Inca imperialism is questionable. About the same number of human victims were excavated at the Feathered Serpent Temple of Teotihuacán and at the Templo Mayor of Tenochtitlán: 137 versus 126. These numbers are minuscule in comparison to the impression created by the Spanish conquerors and encourage doubts about the magnitude of human sacrifices in temple ceremonies. It appears that even though the Aztec and Inca ruling classes were focused on war, the ritual of human sacrifice was not as pervasive as has been widely assumed.

Could it be that there was no significant increase in human sacrifice under the Aztecs and Incas, as the self-serving Spanish conquerors alleged? Were there perhaps, instead, imperial propaganda machines in the Aztec and Inca Empires, employed in the service of conquest and consolidation—similar to those of the Assyrians and Mongols in Eurasia who sought to intimidate their enemies? In this case, the Aztec and Inca Empires would not be exceptional barbaric aberrations in world history but two typical examples of the general world-historical pattern of competitive militaristic states during the early agrarian era, using propaganda to further their imperial power.

52.

Human Sacrifice. Human sacrifice among the pre-Columbian Mesoamericans and Andeans was based on the animist concept of a shared life spirit or mind, symbolized by the life substance of blood. In the American animist-polytheistic conceptualization, the gods sacrificed their blood, or themselves altogether, during creation; rulers pierced their earlobes, tongues, or penises for blood sacrifices; and war captives lost their lives when their hearts were sacrificed.

Questions

- In examining the question of whether empires such as the Inca and the Aztec employed human sacrifice for propaganda purposes, can this practice be considered an adaptation that evolved out of earlier rituals, such as royal bloodletting?

- If the Aztec and the Inca did indeed employ human sacrifice for propaganda purposes, what does this say about the ability of these two empires to use cultural and religious practices to consolidate their power?

Fortress of
Sacsayhuamán

Cuzco

Huatanay

to
Chinchaysuyu

to Antisuyu

N

Haucaypata
Plaza

Cusipata
Plaza

to
Collasuyu

Acllawasi, "convent" for
chosen women of the Sun

Coricancha,
Temple of the Sun

Tullumayo

to Cuntisuyu

0 yds   400

0 meters   400

Chunchul

Cuzco

Upper Cuzco		Assembly hall	
Lower Cuzco		Temple	
Surviving Inca stone wall		School for nobles	
Road		Palace	

MAP **15.6** **Cuzco.**

lived in adobe houses arranged in a block and courtyard pattern similar to that of
Wari. Several squares and temples within the city served as ceremonial centers. One
plaza contained a platform, with the imperial throne and a pillar, placed symbolically atop what the Incas considered the earth's center or navel. The Coricancha
[Co-ri-CAN-tsha], the city's main temple, stood near the confluence of the rivers.
This temple was a walled compound comprised of six buildings set around a courtyard. Chambers in these buildings contained the Inca gods and goddesses as well as
the divine statues or sacred objects confiscated from the provinces. Each year priests
of the empire's ceremonial centers sent one such sacred object to the Coricancha, to
document their obedience to the central Inca temple (see Map 15.6).

Across the rivers, in separate suburbs, were settlements for commoners with
markets and storehouses. They were surrounded by fields, terraces, and irrigation
canals. In the fields, interspersed stone pillars and shrines were aligned on sight
lines radiating from the Coricancha, tying the countryside closely to the urban
center. These alignments were reminiscent of the Nazca lines drawn half a millennium earlier in southern Peru (Chapter 9). Farther away were imperial estates

with unfree laborers from outside the *mit'a* system and its feasting reciprocities. In contrast to the Aztec elite, which allowed meritorious generals to rise in the hierarchy, the Inca elite remained exclusionary, allowing no commoners to reside in Cuzco.

Power and Its Cultural Expressions

Ruling elites, as repeatedly emphasized in this chapter, put a strong emphasis on the display of their power during the period 600–1500. This was particularly true with the Aztecs and Incas during the fifteenth century. Among these displays were human sacrifices, mausoleums, and mummy burials. Although all three involved changes in social relations, these changes were accommodated in the existing overall religious culture.

Inca Ruling Class Gender Relations

The ruling classes in the Inca Empire displayed their power in several ways. Among the examples were the "Houses of Chosen Women" in Cuzco and provincial colonies. The greatest honor for Inca girls was to enter, at age 10–12, into the service of these houses. An inspector from Cuzco made regular visits to the villages of the empire to select attractive young girls for the service. The girls were marched to the capital or the colonies, where they were divided according to beauty, skills, and social standing. These houses had female instructors who provided the girls with a 4-year education in cooking, beer making, weaving, and officiating in the rituals and ceremonies of the Inca religion. After their graduation, the young women became virgin temple priestesses, were given in marriage to non-Incas honored for service to the ruler, or became palace servants, musicians, or concubines of the Inca elite. The collection of the girl tribute was separate from the reciprocity system. As such, it was an act of assigning gender roles in an emerging social hierarchy defined by power inequalities.

Traditionally, gender roles were less strictly divided than in Eurasia. The horticultural form of agriculture in Mesoamerica and the Andes gave males fewer opportunities to accumulate wealth and power than plow agriculture did in Eurasia. Hoes and foot plows distinguished men and women less from each other than plows and teams of oxen or horses did. Nevertheless, it comes as no surprise that the gradual agrarian–urban diversification of society, even if it was slower in the Americas than in Eurasia, proceeded along similar paths of increasing male power concentration in villages, ceremonial centers, temple cities, conquering states, and empires. Emphasizing gender differences, therefore, should be viewed as a characteristic phenomenon arising in imperial contexts.

Inca Mummy Veneration

Other houses in Cuzco were ghostly residences in which scores of attendants and servants catered to what were perceived as the earthly needs of deceased, mummified Inca emperors and their principal wives. During the mummification process attendants removed the cadaver's internal organs, placed them in special containers, and desiccated the bodies until they were completely mummified. Servants dressed the mummies (*mallquis* [MAY-kees]) in their finest clothing and placed them back into their residences amid their possessions, as if they had never died. The mummies received daily meals, and their retinues carried them around for visits to their mummified relatives. On special occasions, mummies were lined up according to rank on Cuzco's main plaza to participate in ceremonies and processions. In this way, they remained fully integrated in the daily life of the elite.

"Ghost residences" with mummies can be considered an outgrowth of the old Andean custom of mummification. This custom was widely practiced among the elites of the ceremonial centers, who, however, generally placed their ancestors in temple tombs, shrines, or caves. Mummies were also buried in cemeteries, sometimes collectively in bundles with "false heads" made of cotton, as we discussed in the vignette at the beginning of this chapter. Preserving the living spaces of the deceased obviously required considerable wealth—wealth provided only by imperial regimes.

As a general phenomenon in Andean society, of course, mummies were a crucial ingredient in the religious heritage, in which strong shamanic elements survived underneath the polytheistic overlay of astral gods. In the shamanic tradition, body and spirit cohabit more or less loosely. In a trance, a shaman's mind can travel, enter the minds of other people and animals, or make room for other people's minds. Similarly, in death a person's spirit, while no longer in the body, remains nearby and therefore still needs daily nourishment in order not to be driven away. Hence, even though non-Incan Andean societies removed the dead from their daily living spaces, descendants had to visit tombs regularly with food and beer or provide buried mummies with ample victuals.

The expenses for the upkeep of the mummy households were the responsibility of the deceased emperor's bloodline, headed by a surviving brother. As heirs of the emperor's estate, the members of the bloodline formed a powerful clan within the ruling class. The new emperor was excluded from this estate and had to acquire his own new one in the course of his rule, a mechanism evidently designed to intensify his imperial ambitions for conquest. In the early sixteenth century, however, when it became logistically difficult to expand much beyond the enormous territory already accumulated in the Andes, this ingenious mechanism of keeping the upper and lower rungs of the ruling class united became counterproductive. Emperors lacking resources had to contend with brothers richly endowed with inherited wealth and ready to engage in dynastic warfare—as actually occurred shortly before the arrival of the Spanish (1529–1532).

Putting It All Together

During the short time of their existence, the Aztec and Inca Empires unleashed extraordinary creative energies. Sculptors, painters, and (after the arrival of the Spanish) writers recorded the traditions as well as the innovations of the fifteenth century. Aztec painters produced codices, or illustrated manuscripts, that present the divine pantheons, myths, calendars, ceremonial activities, chants, poetry, and administrative activities of their societies in exquisite and colorful detail. They fashioned these codices, using bark paper, smoothing it with plaster, and connecting the pages accordion-style. Today, only a handful of these codices survive, preserved in Mexican and European libraries.

The most invaluable surviving work informing our understanding of Incan culture is a 1,200-page text with nearly 400 drawings that dates to 1600–1615, nearly a century

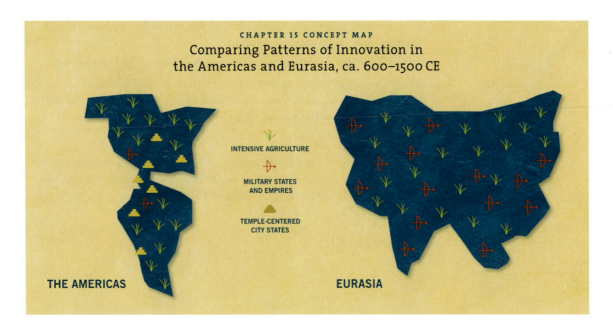

after the Spanish conquest. Its author, Guamán Poma (ca. 1550–1616), intended this work to be a petition to the Spanish, demanding reforms in the administration, although the Spanish king never received it. The drawings are superb illustrations of life in the Inca Empire. These cultural creations make one wonder how the empires would have evolved, had they not been cut short by the Spanish conquests.

However, even if they were short-lived, the Aztec and Inca Empires were polities that illustrate how humans not in contact with the rest of the world and living within an environment that was different from Eurasia and Africa many respects developed patterns of innovation that were remarkably similar. On the basis of an agriculture that eventually produced ample surpluses, humans made the same choices as their cousins in Eurasia and Africa. Specifically, in the period 600–1500, they created temple-centered city-states, just like their Sumerian and Hindu counterparts. Their military states were not unlike the Chinese warring states. And, finally, their empires—although just beginning to flourish in the Bronze Age—were comparable to those of the New Kingdom Egyptians or Assyrians. The Americas had their own unique variations of these larger historical patterns, to be sure; but they nevertheless displayed the same humanity as found elsewhere.

Review and Respond

1. Discuss the evolution of the ruling classes in Mesoamerica and the Andes in the period 600–1100. How did militarism express itself in the states of the period 600–1100?

2. Compare indigenous American imperialism with that of Eurasia. What were the similarities? In which ways did it differ?

3. Discuss the process of militarization in Mesoamerica. Which weapons were used?

4. Describe and analyze life in the cities of Tenochtitlán and Cuzco. How were farming, trade, and crafts organized?

5. How did the Incas assure communications and supplies in their vast empire?

6. Human sacrifices were a common phenomenon in early kingdoms in Eurasia (Sumer, pharaonic Egypt, Crete, Vedic India, Ancient China, Celtic Europe), as well as the polities of the Americas. How do you explain this phenomenon?

> ▶ For additional resources, including maps, primary sources, visuals, and quizzes, please go to www.oup.com/us/vonsivers. Please see the Further Resources section at the back of the book for additional readings and suggested websites.

Thinking Through Patterns

▶ **Within the patterns of states formation basic to the Americas, which types of states emerged in Meso-america and the Andes during the period 600–1550? What characterized these states?**

The basic pattern of state formation in the Americas was similar to that of Eurasia and Africa. Historically, it began with the transition from foraging to agriculture and settled village life. As the population increased, villages under elders became chiefdoms, which in turn became city-states with temples. As in Eurasia and Africa, American city-states often became conquering states, beginning with the Maya kingdoms and Teotihuacán. Both, however, remained small. Military states, in which ruling classes sought to expand regions, such as Tula and, to a lesser degree, Tiwanaku and Wari, were characteristic for the early part of the period 600–1550. The successors of these—the Aztec and Inca Empires—were multiethnic, multilinguistic, and multireligious polities that dominated Mesoamerica and the Andes for about a century, before the Spanish conquest brought them to a premature end.

The states of Tiwanaku and Wari had more or less cohesive ruling classes but no dynasties of rulers and centralized bureaucracies. These ruling classes and their subjects—corn and potato farmers—were integrated with each other through systems of reciprocity, that is, military protection in return for foodstuffs. They customarily rejuvenated the bonds of reciprocity in common feasts. After one or two centuries, however, tensions arose, either between stronger and weaker branches of the ruling classes or between rulers and subjects over questions of obligations and justice. When these tensions erupted into internal warfare, the states disintegrated, often in conjunction with environmental degradation and climate change.

▶ **Why did the Tiwanaku and Wari states have ruling classes but no dynasties and central bureaucracies? How were these patterns expressed in the territorial organization of these states?**

▶ **What patterns of urban life characterized the cities of Tenochtitlán and Cuzco, the capitals of the Aztec and Inca Empires? In which ways were these cities similar to those of Eurasia and Africa?**

Tenochtitlán and Cuzco, the capitals of the Aztec and Inca Empires, were two urban centers organized around temples and associated residences of the ruling dynasties and their priestly classes. They also contained large city quarters inhabited by craftspeople, specializing in the production of woven textiles, pottery, leather goods, and weapons. Large central markets provided for the exchange of foodstuffs, crafts, and imported luxury goods. Armed caravans of merchants and porters transported the luxury goods, such as cacao, feathers, obsidian, and turquoise, across hundreds of miles. Tenochtitlán had an aqueduct for the supply of drinking water, and Cuzco was traversed by a river. Both capitals had agricultural suburbs in which farmers used irrigation for the production of the basic food staples.

PART FOUR

Interactions Across the Globe

1450–1750

Starting around 1450, important changes can be detected in the patterns of world history. The religious civilizations that emerged in the period after 600 CE continued to evolve, but the competing states that constituted these civilizations began to give way to new empires, such as the Mughals, the Ottomans, the Safavids, and the Habsburgs. China, historically an empire, had already reconstituted itself under the Ming after the collapse of the Mongol superempire that had straddled Eurasia. Finally, on the Atlantic coast, smaller European countries, such as Portugal, Spain, the Netherlands, England, and France, were creating the first global seaborne empires. Large or small, land-based or maritime, however, all of these empires employed the vitally important innovation of firearms. In addition, many reorganized themselves as *fiscal–military states* based on money economies, centralizing bureaucracies, and professional armies. Locked into far-flung competition for resources, markets, and ideological influence, they interacted with each other with increasing intensity.

While this renewal of the drive for empire among these civilizations was a significant turning point in world history, two new phenomena appeared during the three centuries in question that would have far-reaching implications. Indeed, they would ultimately provide the basis on which our modern society would be built: the New Science (or Scientific Revolution) and the Enlightenment. Attempts to found an understanding of the universe on mathematics and experimentation would lead to the primacy of science as the chief mode of interpreting the physical realm. Attempts to apply the principles of science to understanding and improving human societies would lead to the concepts of individual rights, natural law, and popular sovereignty that would become the modern legacy of the Enlightenment. The combination of these two trends would create the foundations of the *scientific–industrial society* that now dominates our modern global culture.

The process by which this took place was, of course, extremely complex, and it is impossible for us to do more than suggest some of the larger components of it here. Moreover, because of the long-standing argument in Western historiography for European "exceptionalism"—that there was something unique in the European historical experience that preordained it to rise to dominance—we must be careful to explore the various aspects of this process without sliding into easy assumptions

1440–1897
Benin Kingdom, West Africa

1453
Ottoman Capture of Constantinople

1492
Spanish Conquest of Granada, Expulsion of Jews, and Discovery of the Americas

1498
Vasco da Gama's Circumnavigation of Africa and Journey to India

ca. 1500
Beginning of Columbian Exchange

1511
First African Slaves Land in Hispaniola

1514
Nicolaus Copernicus Formulates the Heliocentric System

1517
Beginning of Martin Luther's Reformation

about their inevitability. For example, one question that suggests itself is, To what extent did the societies of western Europe (what we have termed the "religious civilization" of western Christianity) part ways with the other religious civilizations of the world? Here, the aspects of the question are tantalizingly complex and, thus, have recently been the subject of considerable debate:

- On the one hand, there appears to have been no movement comparable to that of the European Renaissance or Reformation arising during this time in the other parts of the world to create a new culture similar to that of Europe. The Middle East, India, and China for the most part continued ongoing cultural patterns, although often on considerably higher levels of refinement and sophistication. Recent scholarship on neglected cultural developments in these areas from 1450 to 1750 has provided ample proof for the continuing vitality of Islamic, Hindu, Buddhist, Confucian, and Daoist cultural traditions. Thus, former assumptions of stagnation or decline no longer seem supportable.

- On the other hand, Europe, like much of the rest of the world, remained rooted in agrarian–urban patterns until the effects of the Industrial Revolution began to be felt some time after 1800. The centuries-old patterns in which the majority of the population being in agriculture in support of cities continued unchanged. Furthermore, through nearly this entire period, China and India were more populous and at least as wealthy and diversified in their economies and social structures as their European counterparts. The "great divergence," as scholars currently refer to it, happened only *after* the Western constitutional and industrial revolutions. Nonetheless, the overall wealth of European countries involved in the conquest and exploitation of the resources of the Americas and the development of global trading systems advanced immensely—as did knowledge of the globe as a whole. Thus, while India and China had possessed these resources partially or completely already for a long time, European countries were now utilizing them at an accelerating rate. This wealth and the patterns of its acquisition and distribution would soon have far-reaching consequences.

It is important to emphasize that these developments we deem crucial today were not immediately apparent to the people living at the time. Indeed, for the great majority of people, even in 1750, much seemed to go on as before. Everywhere in the world empires continued to grow and decline, religious tensions continued to erupt into warfare, and rulers continued to ground their authority not in their peoples but in the divine. Thus, for a full understanding of world history during 1450–1750 one has to carefully balance cultural, political, social, and economic factors and constantly keep in mind that although change was certainly occurring, it was often too imperceptible for contemporaries to detect.

Thinking Like a World Historian

▶ What new and different patterns characterized the development of states and empires in the period 1450–1750?

▶ How did the emergence of fiscal–military states lead to more intensive and frequent interactions among empires in the period 1450–1750? What were the consequences of this far-flung competition for new resources and markets?

▶ How did the New Science and the Enlightenment lay the foundation for the scientific–industrial society that dominates our global culture today?

▶ To what extent did the societies of western Europe part ways with the other civilizations of the world in the period 1450–1750? Why is the notion of "exceptionalism" a problematic way to examine this question?

Chapter 16

1450–1650

The Ottoman–Habsburg Struggle and Western European Overseas Expansion

Al-Hasan Ibn Muhammad al-Wazzan (ca. 1494–1550) was born into a family of bureaucrats in Muslim Granada soon after the Christian conquest of this kingdom in southern Iberia in 1492. Unwilling to convert to Christianity, Hasan's family emigrated to Muslim Morocco around 1499–1500 and settled in the city of Fez. Here, Hasan received a good education in religion,

Seeing Patterns

▶ What patterns characterized Christian and Muslim competition in the period 1300–1600? Which elements distinguished them from each other, and which elements were similar? How did the pattern change over time?

▶ How did the fiscal–military state in the Middle East and Europe function in the period 1450–1600? How did economics, military power, and imperial objectives interact to create the fiscal-military state?

▶ Which patterns did cultural expressions follow in the Habsburg and Ottoman Empires? Why did the ruling classes of these empires sponsor these expressions?

law, logic, and the sciences. After completing his studies, he took a position as secretary at the insane asylum of Fez but found this first job less than fulfilling. His ambition was for a more exciting life. He wanted to become a diplomat, travel, go on pilgrimage, and engage in trade. After entering the administration of the Moroccan sultan, Hasan was soon entrusted with a diplomatic mission to rulers in sub-Saharan Africa. From there, he traveled to the Middle East and performed his pilgrimage to Mecca. Along the way he traded for a variety of goods, to pay for his extended journey.

In 1517, as he was returning home from a mission to Istanbul, Christian **corsairs** kidnapped him from his ship. Like their Muslim counterparts, these corsairs roamed the Mediterranean to capture unsuspecting travelers, whom they then held for ransom or sold into slavery. For a handsome sum of money, they turned the cultivated Hasan over to Pope Leo X (1513–1521) in Rome. A member of the famed Florentine Medici family and a luxury-loving patron of the arts, architecture, and literature, Leo was delighted to add a learned Muslim world traveler to his stable of luminaries.

Leo ordered Hasan to convert to Christianity and baptized him with his own family name, Giovanni Leone di Medici. Hasan became known in

Buying Captives Their Freedom. An imperial officer in the army of Charles V places some coins in the hands of the Muslim captor of two Christian women, one of whom is accompanied by a young boy. This detail, from a tapestry, which was part of a series commissioned to celebrate the Habsburg capture of Tunis in 1535, documents the way in which individuals such as Leo Africanus became entangled in the zones of contest between empires—in this case, the Ottoman and Habsburg struggle for supremacy in the Mediterranean.

Corsairs: In the context of this chapter, Muslim and Christian pirates who boarded ships, confiscated the cargoes, and held the crews and travelers for ransom; nominally under the authority of the Ottoman sultan or the pope in Rome, but they operated independently.

Rome as Leo Africanus ("Leo the African"), in reference to his travels in sub-Saharan Africa. He stayed for 10 years in Italy, initially at the papal court, later as an independent scholar in Rome. During this time, he taught Arabic to Roman clergymen, compiled an Arabic–Hebrew–Latin dictionary, and wrote an essay on famous Arabs. His most memorable and enduring work was a travelogue, first composed in Arabic and later translated into Italian, *Description of Africa*, which was for many years the sole source of information about sub-Saharan Africa in the western Christian world.

After 1527, however, life became difficult in Rome. In this year, Charles V (r. 1516–1558), king of Spain and emperor of the Holy Roman Empire of Germany, invaded Italy and sacked the city. Hasan survived the sack of Rome but departed for Tunis sometime after 1531, seeking a better life in Muslim North Africa. Unfortunately, all traces of Hasan after his departure from Rome are lost. It is possible that he perished in 1535 when Charles V attacked and occupied Tunis (1535-1574), although it is generally assumed that he lived there until around 1550.

The world in which Hasan lived and traveled was a Muslim–Christian world composed of the Middle East, North Africa, and Europe. Muslims on the Iberian Peninsula and in the Balkans formed a bracket around this world, with the western Christians in the center. Although Muslims and Christians traveled in much of this world more or less freely—as merchants, mapmakers, adventurers, mercenaries, or corsairs—the two religious civilizations were locked in a pattern of fierce competition. For the Muslims, *jihad*, or holy war, against Christianity defined this pattern. For the western Christians the competition was twofold. On the Iberian Peninsula it expressed itself in the Reconquista (Spanish for "reconquest"), a euphemism for the conquest of the Muslim lands of Iberia and North Africa that had once been Christian. And in the Middle East this competition was defined by the Crusade for the liberation of Jerusalem from the Muslims. As much as Christians and Muslims benefited from peaceful commercial and cultural exchanges, they also suffered from immense destruction inflicted on each other in the name of their religious civilizations.

By the fifteenth century, the missions of the Reconquista and the Crusades were largely identical in the mind of the Iberian Christians, who saw the liberation of Iberia and North Africa from Muslim rule and circumventing the Muslims in the Mediterranean as stepping stones toward rebuilding the crusader kingdom of Jerusalem, which had been lost to the Muslims in 1291. Searching for a route that would take them around Africa, they hoped to defeat the Muslims in Jerusalem with an attack from the east. Driven at least in part by this search, the Christians discovered the continents of the Americas. For their part, the Muslims sought to conquer eastern and central Europe (the Balkans, Hungary, and Austria), while simultaneously shoring up their defense of North Africa and seeking to drive the Portuguese out of the Indian Ocean. After a hiatus of several centuries—when commonwealths of states characterized western Christian and Islamic civilizations—imperial polities reemerged, in the form of the Ottoman and Habsburg Empires vying for world rule.

During the climax of their battles in the sixteenth century, the Ottoman and Habsburg Empires poured gigantic resources into their military struggle, beginning a pattern of **fiscal–military state** formation by monetizing their taxation system through the use of a silver coinage. They used the money to pay professional infantry soldiers and equip them with firearms—momentous innovations that vastly enhanced state power. In this part we will see several other states—the Safavids in Persia, the Mughals in India, as well as the Ming and Qing dynasties in China—moving in a parallel direction. In the long run, however, neither the Habsburgs nor the Ottomans could sustain this gigantic war effort. The two found themselves forced to cease hostilities around 1600. Although nominally still under the rule of the two imperial dynasties, Middle Eastern Islam and western Christianity returned to competitive commonwealth politics.

The great wealth at the disposal of the two empires during their heyday also allowed for a pattern of projecting glory and cultural splendor to friend and foe alike. Rulers built palaces and embellished cities with buildings and residences, even as their battles raged. A class of wealthy aristocrats (Habsburg Empire) and administrators (Ottoman Empire) emerged who sponsored writers, painters, and architects. The sixteenth century was thus also a time of great cultural expression in the two empires, and we admire many of the literary, pictorial, and architectural achievements of the period to this day.

Fiscal–military state: Early modern conquering polity, such as the Ottoman, Habsburg, and Safavid Empires and the French, English, and Swedish kingdoms, in which the rulers raised their revenues in the form of cash and employed firearm-equipped foot soldiers for pay.

EURASIAN LAND EMPIRES, ca. 1600

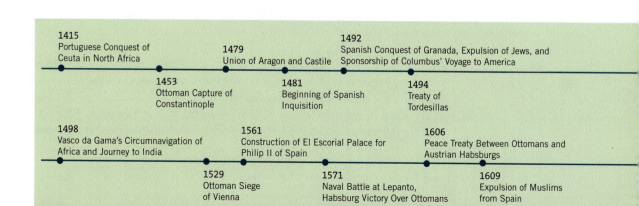

1415
Portuguese Conquest of Ceuta in North Africa

1453
Ottoman Capture of Constantinople

1479
Union of Aragon and Castile

1481
Beginning of Spanish Inquisition

1492
Spanish Conquest of Granada, Expulsion of Jews, and Sponsorship of Columbus' Voyage to America

1494
Treaty of Tordesillas

1498
Vasco da Gama's Circumnavigation of Africa and Journey to India

1529
Ottoman Siege of Vienna

1561
Construction of El Escorial Palace for Philip II of Spain

1571
Naval Battle at Lepanto, Habsburg Victory Over Ottomans

1606
Peace Treaty Between Ottomans and Austrian Habsburgs

1609
Expulsion of Muslims from Spain

The Muslim–Christian Competition in the East and West, 1450–1600

After a long period during which the Christian kings in Iberia found tributes by the Muslim emirs more profitable than war, in the second half of the fifteenth century the kings resumed the Reconquista. During the same time period, the small principality of the Ottomans took advantage of Mongol and Byzantine weakness to conquer lands in both Anatolia and the Balkans. After the Muslim conquest of Constantinople in 1453 and the western Christian conquest of Granada in 1492, the path was open for the emergence of the Ottoman and Habsburg Empires.

Iberian Christian Expansion, 1415–1498

During a revival of anti-Muslim Crusade passions in the course of the fourteenth century, Portugal resumed its Reconquista policies by expanding to North Africa in 1415. Looking for a way to circumvent the Muslims, collect West African gold along the way, and reach the Indian spice coast, Portuguese sailors and traders established fortified harbors along the African coastline. Castile and Aragon, not to be left behind, conquered Granada in 1492, occupied ports in North Africa, and sent Columbus on his way to discover an alternate route to what the Portuguese were seeking. Columbus' discovery of America did not yield Indian spices but delivered a new continent to the rulers of Castile and Aragon (see Map 16.1).

Maritime Explorations   Portugal's resumption of the Reconquista had its roots in its mastery of Atlantic seafaring. In 1277–1281, mariners of the Italian city-state of Genoa pioneered commerce by sea between the Mediterranean and northwestern Europe. One port on the route was Lisbon, where Portuguese shipwrights and their Genoese teachers teamed up to develop new ships suited for the stormy Atlantic seas. In the course of the early fifteenth century, they developed the *caravel*, a small ship with high, upward-extending fore and aft boards; a stern rudder; and square as well as triangular lateen sails. With their new ships, the Portuguese became important traders between England and the Mediterranean countries.

The sea trade now stimulated an exploration of the eastern Atlantic. By the early fifteenth century, the Portuguese had discovered the uninhabited islands of the Azores and Madeira, while the Castilians, building their own caravels, began a century-long conquest of the Canary Islands. Here, the indigenous, still Neolithic Berber inhabitants, the Guanches, put up a fierce resistance. But settlers, with the backing of Venetian investors, carved out colonies on conquered parcels of land, on which they enslaved the Guanches to work in sugarcane plantations. They thus adopted the slave labor and sugarcane plantation system from the eastern Mediterranean, where it had Byzantine and Crusader roots on the island of Cyprus, as discussed in greater detail in Chapter 18.

Apocalyptic Expectations   Parallel with the Atlantic explorations, Iberian Christians began to rethink their relationship with the Muslims on the peninsula. The loss of the crusader kingdom in Palestine to the Muslim Mamluks in 1291 was an event that stirred deep feelings of guilt among the western Christians. Efforts to organize military expeditions to reconquer Jerusalem failed to get off the ground,

Military orders: Ever since the early 1100s, the papacy encouraged the formation of monastic fighting orders, such as the Hospitalers and Templars, to combat the Muslims in the crusader kingdom of Jerusalem; similar Reconquista orders, such as the Order of Santiago and the Order of Christ, emerged in Iberia to eliminate Muslim rule.

Apocalypse: In Greek, "revelation," that is, unveiling the events at the end of history, before God's judgment; during the 1400s, expectation of the imminence of Christ's Second Coming, with precursors paving the way.

MAP **16.1** Africa and the Mediterranean, 1415–1498.

however, mostly because rulers in Europe were now more interested in warring against each other for territorial gain. The failure did not dampen spiritual revivals, however, especially among the monks of the Franciscan and **military orders** of Iberia. These monks, often well connected with the Iberian royal courts as confessors, preachers, and educators, were believers in revelation (Greek *apocalypsis*), that is, the imminent end of the world and the Second Coming of Christ.

According to the **Apocalypse**, Christ's return could happen only in Jerusalem, which, therefore, made it urgent for the Christians to reconquer the city immediately. They widely believed that they would be aided by Prester John, an alleged Christian ruler at the head of an immense army from Ethiopia or India. In the context of the intense religious fervor of the period, Christians as well as Muslims saw

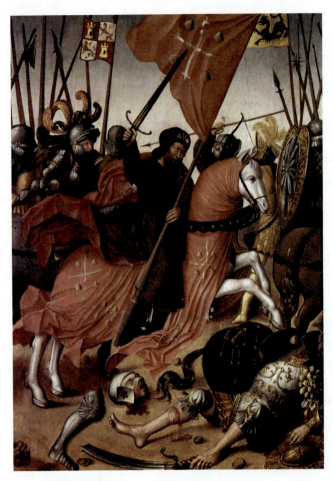

St. James the Moor-Slayer.
As the twin impulses of Reconquista and crusade surged in fifteenth-century Spain and Portugal, devotion to warrior cults increased among the Christian faithful. The cult of St. James the Moor-Slayer gained particular prominence among crusading knights during this time as the saint's miraculous appearance was believed to have helped a vastly outnumbered Christian army defeat Muslim forces in 844. Devotion to the saint (*Santiago Matatmoros*) remains high in Spain today. In 2004, authorities reversed an earlier decision to relocate an enormous statue of St. James the Moor-Slayer from the cathedral of Santiago de Compostela in northwest Spain after a storm of protest.

no contradiction between religion and military conquest. A providential God, so they believed, justified the conquest of lands and the enslavement of the conquered. The religious justification of military action, therefore, was not a pretext for more base material interests (though these would be a likely effect of such conquests) but a proud declaration by believers that God was on their side to help them convert and conquer the non-Christian world. Even today such ideas still can be found in many religious traditions; that they were very real in the minds of the Portuguese and Spanish conquistadores of the period between 1400 and 1500 is well documented as a motive for political and military action.

In Portugal, political claims in the guise of apocalyptic expectations guided the military orders in "reconquering" Ceuta, a northern port city of the Moroccan sultans. The orders argued that prior to the Berber–Arab conquest of the early eighth century CE, Ceuta had been Christian and that it was therefore lawful to undertake its Reconquista. Accordingly, a fleet under Henry the Navigator (1394–1460) succeeded in taking Ceuta in 1415, capturing there a huge stock of West African gold ready to be minted as money. Henry, a brother of the ruling Portuguese king, saw himself as a precursor in the unfolding of apocalyptic events and invested huge resources into the search for the *Rio de oro*, the West African "river of gold" thought to be the place where Muslims obtained their gold. He also instructed the explorers to look for a sea bay alleged to be in the middle of Africa that would give them access to Christian Ethiopia and Prester John. By the middle of the fifteenth century, Portuguese mariners had reached the "gold coast" of West Africa (today's Ghana), where local rulers imported gold from the interior Akan fields, near a tributary of the Niger River—the "gold river" of the Muslim merchants. The sea bay turned out to be a figment of the imagination.

Reforms in Castile   The Portuguese renewal of the Reconquista stimulated a similar revival in Castile. For a century and a half, Castile had collected tributes from Granada instead of completing the reconquest of the peninsula. The revival occurred after the dynastic union of Castile and Aragon–Catalonia under their respective monarchs Queen Isabella (r. 1474–1504) and King Ferdinand II (r. 1479–1516). The two monarchs, now joined by marriage, embarked on a political and religious reform program designed to strengthen their central administrations and used the reconquest ideology as a convenient vehicle to speed up the reforms.

Among the political reforms was the recruitment of urban militias and judges, both under royal supervision, to check the military and judicial powers of the aristocracy. Religious reform focused on improved education for the clergy and stricter enforcement of Christian doctrine in the population at large. The new institution entrusted with the enforcement of doctrine was the Spanish Inquisition, a body of clergy first appointed by Isabella and Ferdinand in 1481 to ferret out any beliefs and practices among people that were deemed to violate Christian theology and church law. With their religious innovations, the monarchs regained the initiative from the popes and laid the foundations for increased state power.

The Conquest of Granada   The Reconquista culminated in a 10-year campaign (1482–1492), now fought on both sides with cannons—the military innovation also employed half a century earlier at Constantinople to batter down walls. In the end, Granada fell into Christian hands because the Ottomans, still consolidating their power in the Balkans, sent only a naval commander who stationed himself in North Africa and harassed Iberian ships. The Mamluks of Egypt, less powerful than the Ottomans, sent an embassy to Granada that merely made a feeble threat of retribution against Christians in Egypt and Syria. Abandoned by the Muslim powers, the last emir of Granada negotiated terms for an honorable surrender. According to these terms, Muslims who chose to stay as subjects of the Castilian crown were permitted to do so, practicing their faith in their own mosques.

The treaty did not apply to the Jews of Granada, however, who were forced either to convert to Christianity or to emigrate. In the 1300s, anti-Jewish preaching by the Catholic clergy and riots by Christians against Jews in Seville had substantially reduced the Jewish population of some 300,000 at its peak ca. 1050 to a mere 80,000 in 1492. Of this remainder, a majority emigrated in 1492 to North Africa and the Ottoman Empire, strengthening the urban population of the Muslims with their commercial and crafts skills. Thus, the nearly millennium and a half–long Jewish presence in "Sefarad," as Spain was called in Hebrew, ended, with an expulsion designed to strengthen the Christian unity of Iberia.

After the expulsion of the Jews, it did not take long for the Christians to violate the Muslim treaty of surrender. The church engaged in forced conversions, the burning of Arabic books, and transformations of mosques into churches, triggering an uprising of Muslims in Granada (1499–1500). Christian troops crushed the rising, and Isabella and Ferdinand took it as an excuse to abrogate the treaty of surrender. In one province after another during the early sixteenth century, Muslims were forced to either convert or emigrate. Like the family of al-Hasan al-Wazzan described at the beginning of this chapter, thousands of Muslims left for North Africa rather than convert to Christianity. The number of remaining Muslims, however, exceeded the ability of the Inquisition to enforce the conversion process. In practical terms, baptized Muslims—called *moriscos* ("Moor-like")—continued to practice Islam, even if discreetly, for another half-century.

Columbus' Journey to the Caribbean   At the peak of their royal power in early 1492, Isabella and Ferdinand seized a golden opportunity to catch up quickly with the Portuguese in the Atlantic. They authorized the seasoned mariner

---

The Sorrows of Exile

"Time with his pointed shafts has hit my heart and split my gut, laid open my entrails, landed me a blow that will not heal, knocked me down, left me in lasting pain. Time wounded me, wasted away my flesh . . . used up my blood and fat in suffering, ground my bones to meal, and rampaged, leapt, attacked me like a lion in his rage . . ."

—Scheindlin, Raymond P., trans. "Judah Abravanel to His Sons." *Judaism* 41 (Spring 1992): 190–199. Judah Abravanel, refugee from Granada, official convert (*marrano*) to Christianity and physician to the Spanish viceroy in Naples, Italy, in a letter to his son Isaac, a *marrano* in Portugal, in 1503.

Christopher Columbus (1451–1506), the son of a Genoese wool weaver, to build two caravels and a larger carrack and sail westward across the Atlantic. Columbus promised to reach India ahead of the Portuguese, who were attempting to find a route to India by sailing around Africa. The two monarchs pledged him money for the construction of ships from Castilian and Aragonese Crusade levies collected against the Ottomans. In September, Columbus and his mariners departed from the Castilian Canary Islands, catching the favorable south Atlantic easterlies. After a voyage of a little over a month, Columbus landed on one of the Bahaman islands. From there he explored a number of Caribbean islands, mistakenly assuming that he was close to the Indian subcontinent. After a stay of 3 months, he left a small colony of settlers behind and returned to Iberia with seven captured Caribbean islanders and a small quantity of gold.

Columbus was a self-educated explorer. Through voracious but indiscriminate reading, he had accumulated substantial knowledge of such diverse subjects as geography, cartography, the Crusades, and the Apocalypse. On the basis of this reading (and his own faulty calculations), he insisted that the ocean stretching between western Europe and eastern Asia was relatively narrow. Furthermore, he fervently believed that God had made him the forerunner of an Iberian apocalyptic world ruler who would recapture Jerusalem from the Muslims just prior to the Second Coming of Christ. For many years, Columbus had peddled his idea about reaching Jerusalem from the east at the Portuguese court. The Portuguese, however, while sharing Columbus' apocalyptic fervor, dismissed his Atlantic Ocean calculations as fantasies. Even in Castile, where Columbus went after his rejection in Portugal, it took many years and the victory over Granada before Queen Isabella finally listened to him. Significantly, it was at the height of their success at Granada in 1492 that Isabella and Ferdinand seized their chance to beat the Portuguese to Asia.

Although disappointed by the meager returns of Columbus' first and subsequent voyages, Isabella and Ferdinand were delighted to have acquired new islands in the Caribbean, in addition to those of the Canaries. In one blow they had drawn even with Portugal. To secure their territorial gains, Castile–Aragon had the Castilian-born pope Alexander VI draw a line at some distance west of Portuguese Cape Verde, allocating all territories beyond this line to Castile. Since the Portuguese had to sail far out into the middle of the Atlantic in order to catch the winds blowing toward South Africa, they demanded a correction. In a revision concluded in 1506, the Iberian monarchs agreed to move the line farther westward. Thereby, Portugal gained the entire Atlantic and, as it turned out, much of Brazil; in return, Castile gained what became their colonies in the Americas.

Vasco da Gama's Journey to India

Portugal redoubled its efforts after 1492 to discover the way to India around Africa. In 1498, the king appointed an important court official and member of the crusading Order of Santiago, Vasco da Gama (ca. 1469–1524), to command four caravels for the journey to India. Da Gama, an experienced mariner, made good use of the accumulated Portuguese knowledge of seafaring in the Atlantic and guidance by Arab sailors in the Indian Ocean. After a journey of 6 months, the ships arrived in Calicut, the main spice trade center on the Indian west coast.

The first Portuguese sent ashore in Calicut encountered two Iberian Muslims, who addressed him in Castilian Spanish and Italian: "The Devil take you! What

Admiral of the Sea. As a reward for his discoveries, in 1493 the Spanish crown rewarded Columbus with a coat of arms, which satisfied his obsession with status and privilege. The coat of arms depicted above reflects the modifications he made to the original crest, including a continent with islands in the bottom left quarter and golden anchors, meant to symbolize his title as "Admiral of the Sea," set in the bottom right quadrant.

brought you here?" The Portuguese replied: "We came to seek Christians and spices." When da Gama went inland to see the ruler of Calicut, he was optimistic that he had indeed found what he had come for. Ignorant of Hinduism, he mistook the Indian religion for the Christianity of Prester John. Similarly ignorant of the conventions of the India trade, he offered woolen textiles and metal goods in exchange for pepper, cinnamon, and cloves. The Muslim and Hindu merchants were uninterested in these goods designed for the African market and demanded gold or silver, which the Portuguese had only in small amounts. Rumors spread about the Muslims plotting with the Hindus against the apparently penniless Christian intruders. Prudently, da Gama lifted anchor and returned home with small quantities of spices.

After these modest beginnings, however, within a short time Portugal had mastered the India trade. The Portuguese crown organized regular journeys around Africa, and when Portuguese mariners on one such journey discovered northeast Brazil—located on their side of the Tordesillas line—they claimed it for their expanding commercial network. During the early sixteenth century, the Portuguese India fleets brought considerable amounts of spices from India back to Portugal, threatening the profits of the Egyptian and Venetian merchants who had hitherto dominated the trade. Prester John, of course, was never found; and the project of retaking Jerusalem receded into the background.

Rise of the Ottomans and Struggle with the Habsburgs for Dominance, 1300–1609

While Muslim rule disappeared in the late fifteenth century from the Iberian Peninsula, the opposite happened in the Balkans. Here, the Ottoman Turks spearheaded the expansion of Islamic rule, initially over Eastern Orthodox Christians, and eventually over western Christians. By the late sixteenth century, when the east–west conflict between the Habsburgs and Ottomans reached its peak, entire generations of Croats, Germans, and Italians lived in mortal fear of the "terrible Turk" who might conquer all of Christian Europe.

Late Byzantium and Ottoman Origins
The rise of the Ottomans was closely related to the decline of Byzantium. The emperors of Byzantium had been able to reclaim their "empire" in 1261 from its Latin rulers and Venetian troops by allying themselves with the Genoese. This empire, which during the early fourteenth century included Greece and a few domains in western Anatolia, was no more than a mid-size kingdom with modest agricultural resources. But it was still a valuable trading hub, thanks to Constantinople's strategic position as a market linking the Mediterranean with Slavic kingdoms in the Balkans and the Ukrainian–Russian principality of Kiev. Thanks to its commercial wealth, Byzantium experienced a cultural revival, which at its height featured the lively scholarly debate over Plato and Aristotle that exerted a profound influence on the western Renaissance in Italy.

Inevitably, however, both Balkan Slavs and Anatolian Turks appropriated Byzantine provinces in the late thirteenth century, further reducing the empire. One of the lost provinces was Bithynia, across the Bosporus in Anatolia. Here, in 1299, the Turkish warlord Osman (1299–1326) gathered his clan as well as a motley assembly of Islamic holy warriors (Turkish *ghazis*), including a local saint and his followers, and declared himself an independent ruler. Osman and a number of other Turkish lords in the region were nominally subject to the Seljuks, the Turkish dynasty which

Patterns Up Close | Shipbuilding

Patterns of Shipbuilding. From top: (a) Hellenistic-Roman roundship, (b) Chinese junk, (c) Indian Ocean dhow.

Early humans undoubtedly traveled by sea in their migrations out of Africa nearly 100,000 years ago, though no evidence of their seafaring has survived. These sea voyages, which hugged coastlines and traveled across relatively modest expanses of water, were likely made in rafts. It is not until the Bronze Age (ca. 3000–1300 BCE) that we encounter the earliest evidence of planked ships. We have records of shipwrights in Egypt constructing ships plank by plank, tying the planks together internally with ropes and cross bars. In addition, they used various types of pegs to join the planks. Side oars served for steering and square linen sails for propulsion. This "sewed" shipbuilding pattern allowed for the construction of seaworthy, flexible, relatively small boats that could be dragged through surf and pulled up on rocky shores. The pattern appeared across most of the world, either through independent invention in multiple places or by interaction and adaptation from Middle Eastern origins. The latter was certainly possible, given the diffusion of other discoveries and inventions from Mesopotamia and Egypt to India and China during the Bronze Age.

With the appearance of empires during the subsequent Iron Age, builders replaced the original sewed shipbuilding pattern with new regional traditions. Four regional but interconnected traditions—Mediterranean, Indian Ocean, Chinese Sea, and North Sea—emerged. In addition, the Pacific outrigger tradition as well as Andean and Arctic raft- and canoe-building patterns evolved separately.

In the Mediterranean, around 500 BCE, shipwrights shifted from sewed to nailed planks for their war galleys as well as cargo transports around 500 BCE, as evidenced by shipwrecks of the period. In the Roman Empire (ca. 200 BCE–500 CE), nailed planking allowed the development of the roundship (photo a), a large transport of 120 feet length and 400 tons of cargo transporting grain from Egypt to Italy. The roundship and its variations had double planking, multiple masts, and multiple square sails. After 100 BCE, the triangular ("lateen") sail allowed for zigzagging ("tacking") against the wind, greatly expanding shipping during a summer sailing season.

The Celtic North Sea tradition adapted to the Mediterranean patterns of the Romans. When the Roman Empire receded during the 300s CE, shipwrights in Celtic regions continued with their own innovations, shifting to frame-first construction for small boats in the 300s, three centuries before Byzantium in the Mediterranean. At the same time Norsemen, or Vikings, innovated by introducing overlapping ("clinkered") plank joining for their elegant and eminently seagoing boats. The North Sea innovations, arriving as they did at the end of the western Roman Empire, remained local for nearly half a millennium.

The evolution of China into an empire resulted in major Chinese contributions to ship construction. In the Han period (206 BCE–220 CE) there is evidence from clay models of riverboats for the transition from sewed to nailed planks. One model, dating to the first century CE, shows a central steering rudder at the end of the boat. At the same time, similar stern rudders appeared in the Roman Empire. Who adapted to whom, if at all, is still an unanswered question.

Shipbuilding innovations continued after 600 CE. In Tang China, junks, with multiple watertight compartments ("bulkheads") and multiple layers of planks appeared. The average junk was 140 feet long, had a cargo capacity of 600 tons, and could carry on its three or four decks several hundred mariners and passengers (see photo *b*). Admiral Zheng He's junk in the early 1400s, which guided Chinese fleets to southeast Asia and eastern Africa, was double the average junk size. Junks had multiple masts and trapezoid ("lug") and square sails made of matted fibers and strengthened ("battened") with poles sewed to the surface. The less innovative Middle Eastern, eastern African, and Indian *dhow* was built with sewed or nailed planks and sailed with lateen and square sails, traveling as far as southern China. It also came in many varieties, and the largest type could be as large as a small junk (see photo *c*).

In western Europe, the patterns of Mediterranean and North Sea shipbuilding merged during the thirteenth century. At that time, northern shipwrights developed the cog as the main transport for Baltic grain to ports around the North Sea. The cog was a ship of some 60 feet in length and 30 tons in cargo capacity, with square sails, flush-planking below, and clinkered planking above the water line. Northern European Crusaders traveled during 1150–1300 on cogs via the Atlantic to the Mediterranean. Builders adapted the cog's clinker technique to the roundship tradition that Muslims as well as eastern and western Christians had modified in the previous centuries. Genoese clinkered roundships pioneered the Mediterranean–North Sea trade in the early fourteenth century (see photo *d*).

Patterns of Shipbuilding. From top: (*d*) Baltic cog, and (*e*) Iberian caravel. These ships illustrate the varieties of shipbuilding traditions that developed over thousands of years.

Lisbon shipwrights in Portugal, learning from Genoese masters, borrowed from local shipbuilding traditions and Genoese roundship construction patterns for the development of the caravel around 1430. The caravel was a small and slender 60-foot-long ship with a 50-ton freight capacity, a stern rudder, square and lateen sails, and a magnetic compass (of Chinese origin). The caravel and, after 1500, the similarly built but much larger galleon were the main vessels the Portuguese, Spanish, Dutch, and English used during their oceanic voyages from the mid-fifteenth to mid-eighteenth centuries (see photo *e*).

Questions

- How does the history of shipbuilding demonstrate the ways in which innovations spread from one place to another?

- Do the adaptations in shipbuilding that flowed between cultures that were nominally in conflict with each other provide a different perspective on the way these cultures interacted?

Power Politics

"You stupid Greeks, I have known your cunning ways for long enough. The late sultan was a lenient and conscientious friend of yours. The present Sultan Mehmet is not of the same mind. If Constantinople eludes his bold and impetuous grasp it will only be because God overlooks your devious and wicked schemes."

—Doukas, Michael, *Decline and Fall of Byzantium to the Ottoman Turks: An Annotated Tranlsation of the 'Historia Byzantina-Turca.'* Trans. Harry J. Magoulias, p. 289. Detroit: Wayne State University Press, 1975. Ottoman minister (vizier) Halil Pasha addressing himself to Byzantine diplomats seeking to deflect the Ottoman threat of conquest.

had conquered Anatolia from the Byzantines two centuries earlier but by the early 1300s had disintegrated.

During the first half of the fourteenth century, Osman and his successors emerged as the most powerful emirs by conquering further Anatolian provinces from Byzantium. The Moroccan Abu Abdallah Ibn Battuta (1304–1369), famous for his journey through the Islamic world, Africa, and China, passed through western Anatolia and Constantinople during the 1330s, visiting several Turkish principalities. He was duly impressed by the rising power of the Ottomans, noting approvingly that they manned nearly 100 forts and castles and maintained pressure on the eastern Christian infidels. In 1354, the Ottomans gained their first European foothold on a peninsula about 100 miles southwest of Constantinople. Thereafter, it seemed only a question of time before the Ottomans would conquer Constantinople.

Through a skillful mixture of military defense, tribute payments, and dynastic marriages of princesses with Osman's descendants, however, the Byzantine emperors extended their rule for another century. They were also helped by Timur the Great (r. 1370–1405), a Turkish-descended ruler from central Asia who sought to rebuild the Mongol Empire. He surprised the Ottomans, who were distracted by their ongoing conquests in the Balkans, and defeated them decisively in 1402. Timur and his successors were unsuccessful with their dream of neo-Mongol world rule, but the Ottomans needed nearly two decades (1402–1421) to recover from their collapse and reconstitute their empire in the Balkans and Anatolia. Under Mehmet II, the Conqueror (r. 1451–1481), they finally assembled all their resources to lay siege to the Byzantine capital.

From Istanbul to the Adriatic Sea

Similar to Isabella and Ferdinand's siege of Granada, Mehmet's siege and conquest of Constantinople (April 5–May 29, 1453) was one of the stirring events of world history. The Byzantines were severely undermanned and short of gunpowder, unable to defend the full length of the imposing land walls that protected the city. Although they had some help from Genoese, papal, and Aragonese forces, it was not nearly enough to make a difference. With a superiority of 11 to 1 in manpower, the Ottomans besieged and bombarded Constantinople's walls with heavy cannons. The weakest part of the Byzantine defenses was the central section of the western walls where it was relatively easy to tunnel into the soil underneath. Here, Mehmet stationed his heaviest guns to bombard the masonry and have his sappers undermine the foundations of the walls.

Another weak section was on the north side, along the harbor in the Golden Horn, where the walls were low. Here, the Byzantines had blocked off the entrance to the Golden Horn with a huge chain. In a brilliant tactical move, Mehmet circumvented the chain. He had troops drag ships on rollers over a hillside into the

Siege of Constantinople, 1453. Note the soldiers on the left pulling boats on rollers and wheels over the Galata hillside. With this maneuver, Sultan Mehmet II was able to circumvent the chain spanned across the entrance to the Golden Horn (in place of the anachronistic bridge in the image). This allowed him to speed up his conquest of Constantinople by forcing the defenders to spread their forces thinly over the entire length of the walls.

harbor. The soldiers massed on these ships were ready to disembark and assault the walls with the help of ladders. On the first sign of cracks in the northern walls, the Ottoman besiegers stormed the city. The last Byzantine emperor, Constantine XI, perished in the general massacre and pillage which followed the Ottoman occupation of the city.

Mehmet quickly repopulated Constantinople ("Istanbul" in Turkish, from Gr. "to the city," *istin polin*) and appointed a new patriarch at the head of the eastern Christians, to whom he promised full protection as his subjects. In quick succession, he ordered the construction of the Topkapı Palace (1459), the transfer of the administration from Edirne (which had been the capital since 1365) to Istanbul, and the resumption of expansion in the Balkans, where he succeeded in forcing the majority of rulers into submitting to vassal status (even though almost constant campaigning was necessary). One of the Balkan lords resisting the sultan was Vlad III Dracul of Wallachia, who in 1461–1462 impaled a contingent of Ottoman troops sent against him on sharpened tree trunks. Mehmet replaced Dracul with his more compliant brother, but the memory of the impalements lived on to inspire vampire folktales and, eventually, in 1897, the famous Gothic horror novel *Dracula*.

Mehmet's ongoing conquests eventually brought him to the Adriatic Sea, where one of his generals occupied Otranto on the heel of the Italian peninsula. The Ottomans were poised to launch from Otranto a full-scale invasion of Italy, when the sultan died unexpectedly. His successor evacuated Otranto, preferring to consolidate the Ottoman Empire in the Middle East, North Africa, and the Balkans before reconsidering an invasion of central and western Europe.

Vlad Dracul in a Wall Painting (*left*) and next to Impaled Ottoman Soldiers (*right*). The woodcut depicts the alleged impalement of 1,000 Ottoman soldiers sent against Vlad Dracul, prior to Sultan Mehmet II leading a victorious campaign into Wallachia and removing Dracul from power.

Imperial Apogee   Between 1500 and 1600 the Ottoman sultans succeeded magnificently in the consolidation of their empire. In 1514, with superior cavalry and infantry forces, cannons, and muskets, the Ottomans defeated the Persian Safavids in Iran, who had risen in 1501 to form a rival Shiite empire in opposition to the Sunnite Ottomans. In the southern Middle East, intermittent tensions between the Ottomans and the Mamluk Turks in Egypt, Syria, and eastern Arabia gave way to open war in 1517. The Ottomans, again due to superior firepower, defeated the Mamluks and took control of western Arabia, including the holy

MAP **16.2** The Ottoman Empire, 1307–1683.

pilgrimage city of Mecca. A year later, in 1518, Sultan Süleyman I, the Magnificent
(r. 1520–1566), appointed a naval commander to drive the Spanish from a series of
fortifications and cities in North Africa, which the latter had conquered in the name
of the Reconquista in the 1490s and early 1500s.

In the Balkans, the Ottomans completed their conquests of Serbia and Hungary
with the annexation of Belgrade and Buda (of Budapest) as well as a brief siege of Vienna in 1529, begun too late in the year and eventually stopped by the approaching
winter. By the second half of the sixteenth century, when the submission of most of
Hungary had been secured, the Ottoman Empire was a vast multiethnic and multireligious state of some 15 million inhabitants extending from Algeria in the Maghreb
to Yemen in Arabia and from Upper Egypt to the Balkans and the northern shores of
the Black Sea (see Map 16.2).

Morocco and Persia

In the early modern period 1450–1600, the two large empires of the Ottomans and Indian Mughals dominated Islamic civilization. Two smaller and more short-lived realms existed in Morocco and Persia, ruled by the Saadian (1509–1659) and Safavid (1501–1722) dynasties, respectively. The Saadian sultans defended themselves successfully against the Ottoman expansion and liberated themselves from the Portuguese occupation of Morocco's Atlantic ports which had followed the conquest of Ceuta in 1415. In 1591, after their liberation, the Saadians sent a firearm-equipped army to West Africa in order to revive the gold trade, which had dwindled to a trickle after the Portuguese arrival in Ghana. The army succeeded in destroying the West African empire of Songhay but failed to revive the gold trade. Moroccan army officers assumed power in Timbuktu, and their descendants, the Ruma, became provincial lords independent of Morocco.

Safavid Warrior's Tunic. It was customary in the Muslim world for soldiers to go into combat wearing talismanic undershirts designed to protect them from harm and to guarantee victory on the battlefield. This Safavid battle tunic, from about 1600, is embroidered with verses from the Quran that exhort the faithful to victory.

The Saadians, unable to improve their finances, split into provincial realms. The still-reigning Alaouite dynasty of Moroccan kings replaced them in 1659.

The Safavids grew in the mid-1400s from a Turkish mystical brotherhood in northwestern Iran into a Shiite *ghazi* organization (similar to the Sunni one participating in the early Ottoman expansion) that carried out raids against Christians in the Caucasus. In 1501, the leadership of the brotherhood put forward the 14-year-old Ismail as the Hidden Twelfth Imam. According to Shiite doctrine, the Hidden Imam, or Messiah, was expected to arrive and establish a Muslim apocalyptic realm of justice at the end of time, before God's Last Judgment. This realm would replace the "unjust" Sunnite Ottoman Empire. The Ottomans countered the Safavid challenge in 1514 with the Battle of Chaldiran, where they crushed the underprepared Safavids with their superior cannon and musket firepower. After his humiliating defeat, Ismail dropped his claim to apocalyptic status and his successors assumed the more modest title of "king" (Persian *shah*) as the head of state, quite similar in many respects to that of the Ottomans.

Learning from their defeat, the Safavids recruited a standing firearm-equipped army from among young Christians on lands conquered in the Caucasus. They held fast to Shiism, thereby continuing their opposition to the Sunni Ottomans, and supported the formation of a clerical hierarchy, which made this form of Islam dominant in Iran. As sponsors of construction projects, the Safavids greatly improved urbanism in the country. After moving the capital from Tabriz to the centrally located Isfahan in 1590, they built an imposing palace, administration, and mosque complex in the city. In a suburb they settled a large colony of Armenians, who held the monopoly in the production of Caspian Sea silk, a high-quality export product which the Dutch—successors of the Portuguese in the Indian Ocean trade—distributed in Europe.

As patrons of the arts, the shahs revived the ancient traditions of Persian culture to such heights that even the archrival Ottomans felt compelled to adopt Persian manners, literature, and architectural styles. Persian royal culture similarly radiated to the Mughals in India. Not everyone accepted Shiism, however. An attempt to force the religion on the Afghanis backfired badly when enraged Sunni tribes formed a coalition, defeated the Safavids, and ended their regime in 1722.

Rise of the Habsburgs   Parallel to the rise and development of the Safavid state, Castile–Aragon on the Iberian Peninsula evolved into the center of a vast empire of its own. A daughter of Isabella and Ferdinand married a member of the Habsburg dynastic family, which ruled Flanders, Burgundy, Naples, Sicily, and Austria, as well as Germany (the "Holy Roman Empire of the German Nation," as this collection of principalities was called). Their son, Charles V (r. 1516–1558), not only inherited Castile–Aragon, now merged and called "Spain," and the Habsburg territories but also became the ruler of the Aztec and Inca Empires in the Americas, which Spanish adventurers had conquered in his name between 1521 and 1536. In both Austria and the western Mediterranean the Habsburgs were direct neighbors of the Ottomans (see Map 16.3).

After a victorious battle against France in 1519, Charles V also won the title of emperor, which made him the overlord of all German principalities and supreme among the monarchs of western Christianity. Although this title did not mean much in terms of power and financial gain in either the German principalities or western Christianity as a whole, it made him the titular political head of western Christianity and thereby the direct counterpart of Sultan Süleyman in the struggle for dominance

MAP 16.3 Europe and the Mediterranean, ca. 1560.

Europe and the Mediterranean, ca. 1560

- Boundary of the Holy Roman Empire
- Austrian Habsburg territories
- Spanish Habsburg territories
- Ottoman Empire
- Tributary to the Ottoman Empire
- Venetian territories

How to Win Against the "Terrible Turk"

"My advice, then, is that we not insufficiently arm ourselves and send our poor Germans off to be slaughtered. If we are not going to make an adequate, honest resistance that will have some reserve power, it would be much better not to begin a war, but to yield lands and people to the Turk in time, without useless bloodshed, rather than have him win anyhow in an easy battle and with shameful bloodshed, as happened in Hungary with King Louis [in the Battle of Mohacs, 1526]. Fighting against the Turk is not like fighting against the king of France, or the Venetians, or the pope; he is a different kind of warrior. The Turk has people and money in abundance; he defeated the Sultan [of the Mamluks, 1516–1517] twice in succession, and that took people! Why, dear sir, his people are always under arms so that he can quickly muster three or four hundred thousand men. If we were to cut down a hundred thousand, he would soon be back again with as many men as before. He has reserve power."

—Martin Luther. *Selected Writings, 1529–1546.* Edited by Theodore G. Tappert, pp. 49–50. Minneapolis, MN: Fortress Press, 1967.

in the Christian–Muslim world of Europe, the Middle East and northern Africa. Both the Habsburgs and the Ottomans renewed the traditional Arab/Islamic–Christian imperialism which had characterized the period 600–950 and which had given way to the Muslim and Christian commonwealths of 950–1450.

Habsburg Distractions   Charles V faced a daunting task in his effort to prevent the Ottomans from advancing against the Christians in the Balkans and Mediterranean. Multiple problems in his European territories diverted his attention and forced him to spend far less time than he wanted on what Christians in most parts of Europe perceived as a pervasive Ottoman–Muslim threat. During the first three decades of the sixteenth century, revolts in Iberia, the Protestant Reformation in the German states, and renewed war with France for control of Burgundy and Italy commanded Charles' attention.

The emperor's distractions increased further in 1534 when, in an attempt to drive the Habsburgs out of Italy, France forged an alliance with the Ottomans. This alliance horrified western Europe. It demonstrated, however, that the Ottomans, on account of their military advances against the Christians in eastern Europe and the western Mediterranean, had become a crucial player in European politics. As fierce as the struggle between Muslims and Christians for dominance was, when the French king found himself squeezed on both sides of his kingdom by his archrival Charles V, the Ottomans became his natural allies.

Habsburg and Ottoman Losses   All these diversions seriously strained Habsburg resources against the Ottomans, who pressed relentlessly ahead on the two fronts of the Balkans and North Africa. Although Charles V deputized his younger brother Ferdinand I to the duchy of Austria in 1521 to shore up the Balkan defenses, he was able to send him significant troops only once. After a series of dramatic defeats, Austria had to pay the Ottomans tribute and, eventually, even sign a humiliating truce (1562). On the western Mediterranean front, the Habsburgs did not do well either. Even though Charles V campaigned several times in person, most garrisons on the coast of Algeria, Tunisia, and Tripoli were too exposed to withstand the Ottoman onslaught by sea and by land. In 1556, at the end of Charles V's reign, only two of eight Habsburg garrisons had survived.

A third frontier of the Muslim–Christian struggle for dominance was the Indian Ocean. After Vasco da Gama had returned from India in 1498, the Portuguese kings invested major resources into breaking into the Muslim-dominated Indian Ocean trade. In response, the Ottomans made major efforts to protect existing Muslim commercial interests in the Indian Ocean. They blocked Portuguese military support for

Ethiopia and strengthened their ally and main pepper producer the sultan of Aceh on the Indonesian island of Sumatra, by providing him with troops and weapons. War on land and on sea, directly and by proxy, raged in the Indian Ocean through most of the sixteenth century. In the long run, the Portuguese were successful at destroying the Ottoman fleets sent against them, but smaller convoys of Ottoman galleys continued to harass Portuguese shipping interests. As new research on the Ottoman "age of exploration" in the Indian Ocean has demonstrated, by 1570 the Muslims traded again as much via the Red Sea route to the Mediterranean as the Portuguese did by circumventing Africa. In addition, the Ottomans benefited from the trade of a new commodity—coffee, produced in Ethiopia and Yemen. Portugal (under Spanish rule 1580–1640) reduced its unsustainably large military presence in the Indian Ocean, followed by the Ottomans, which allowed the Netherlands in the early seventeenth century to overtake both Portugal and the Ottoman Empire in the Indian Ocean spice trade (see Map 16.4).

Habsburg–Ottoman Balance   In the 1550s, Charles V despaired of his ability to ever master the many challenges posed by the Ottomans as well as by France and the Protestants. He decided that the only way to ensure the continuation of Habsburg power would be a division of his western and eastern territories. Accordingly, he bestowed Spain, Naples, the Netherlands, and the Americas on his

MAP **16.4** Ottoman-Portuguese Competition in the Indian Ocean, 1536-1580.

Ottoman-Portuguese Competition in the Indian Ocean, 1536-1580

- 🟧 Portuguese trading posts and claimed possessions, ca. 1580
- — Portuguese trade routes
- ⚔ Battles between Ottoman and Portuguese forces, 1536–1580
- 🟩 Ottoman Empire, ca. 1580

Paolo Veronese, The Battle of Lepanto (ca. 1572), altar painting with four saints beseeching the Virgin Mary to grant victory to the Christians. In the sixteenth century, the entire Mediterranean, from Gibraltar to Cyprus, was a naval battleground between Christians and Muslims. The Battle of Lepanto was the first major sea battle in world history to be decided by firepower: Even though Christian forces had slightly fewer ships, they had more and heavier artillery pieces. At the end of the battle "the sea was entirely covered, not just with masts, spars, oars, and broken wood, but with an innumerable quantity of blood that turned the water as red as blood."

son Philip II (r. 1556–1598). Further, Charles V had his brother Ferdinand I (r. 1558–1564) crowned Holy Roman Emperor by the pope, thereby making him overlord of the German principalities as well as ruler of the direct Habsburg possessions of Austria, Bohemia, and the remnant of Hungary not lost to the Ottomans. Together, Charles hoped, his son and his brother would cooperate and help each other militarily against the Ottomans.

When Philip took over the Spanish throne, he realized, to his concern, that most of the Habsburg military was stationed outside Spain, leaving that country vulnerable to attack. As the Ottomans had recently conquered most Spanish strongholds in North Africa, a Muslim invasion of Spain was a distinct possibility. Fearful of morisco support for an Ottoman invasion of Spain, Philip's administration and the Inquisition renewed their decrees of conversion which had lain dormant for half a century. This sparked a massive revolt among the moriscos of Granada in 1568–1570, supported by Ottoman soldiers and Moroccan arms. Philip was able to suppress the revolt only after recourse to troops and firearms from Italy. To break up the dangerously large concentrations of Granadan moriscos in the south of Spain, Philip ordered them to be dispersed throughout the peninsula. At the same time, to alleviate the Ottoman naval threat, Philip, the pope, Venice, and Genoa formed the Holy Christian League. Its task was the construction of a fleet which was to destroy Ottoman sea power in the eastern Mediterranean. The fleet succeeded in 1571 in bottling up the entire Ottoman navy at Lepanto, in Ottoman Greece, destroying it in the ensuing firefight.

The Ottomans, however, had enough resources not only to rebuild their navy but also to capture the strategic port city of Tunis in 1574 from the Spaniards. With this evening of the scores, the two sides decided to end their unsustainable naval war in the Mediterranean. The Ottomans turned their attention eastward, to the rival Safavid Empire, where they exploited a period of dynastic instability for the conquest of territories in the Caucasus (1578–1590). The staunch Catholic Philip II, on his part, was faced with the Protestant war of independence in the Netherlands. This war was so expensive that, in a desperate effort to straighten out his state finances, Philip II had to declare bankruptcy (1575) and sue for peace with the Ottomans (1580).

The Limits of Ottoman Power   After their victory over the Safavids, the Ottomans looked again to the west. While the peace with Spain was too recent to be broken, a long peace with Ferdinand I in Austria (since 1562) was ready to collapse. A series of raids and counterraids at the Austrian and Transylvanian borders had inflamed tempers, and in 1593 the Ottomans went on the attack. Austria, however, was no longer the weak state it had been a generation earlier. Had it not been for a lack of support from the Transylvanian and Hungarian Protestants, who preferred the sultan to the Catholic emperor as overlord, the Austrians might have actually prevailed over the Ottomans. However, thanks to the Protestants' support, the Ottomans drew even on the battlefield with the Austrians. In 1606, the Ottomans and Austrian Habsburgs made peace again. With minor modifications in favor of the Austrians, the two sides returned to their earlier borders. The Austrians made one more tribute payment and then let their obligation lapse. Officially, the Ottomans conceded nothing, but in practical terms Austria was no longer a vassal state.

Expulsion of the Moriscos   In the western Mediterranean, the peace between the Ottomans and Spanish Habsburgs held. But Philip and his successors remained aware of the possibility of renewed Ottoman aid to the moriscos. Even though they had been scattered after 1570, the moriscos continued to resist conversion. Among Castilians, an intense debate began about the apparent impossibility of assimilating them to Catholicism in order to create a religiously unified state. The church advocated the expulsion of the moriscos, arguing that the allegedly high Muslim birth rate in a population of 7.5 million (mostly rural) Spaniards was a serious threat. Fierce resistance against the proposed expulsion, however, rose among the Christian landowners in the southeastern province of Valencia. These landowners benefited greatly from the farming skills of the estimated 250,000 morisco tenant farmers who worked their irrigated rice and sugarcane estates. Weighing the potential Ottoman threat against the possibility of economic damage, the government decided in 1580 in favor of expulsion. Clearly, they valued Christian unity against the Ottomans more than the prosperity of a few hundred landowners in Valencia.

It took until 1609, however, before a compensation deal with the landowners in Valencia was worked out. In the following 5 years, some 300,000 moriscos were forcibly expelled from Spain, under often appalling circumstances: They had to leave all their possessions behind, including money and jewelry, taking only whatever clothes and household utensils they could carry. As in the case of the Jews a century earlier, Spain's loss was the Ottoman Empire's gain, this time mostly in the form of skilled irrigation farmers.

Fiscal-Military State: Origins and Interactions

The major technological change that occurred in the Middle East and Europe during 1250–1350 was the growing use of firearms. It took until the mid-1400s, however, before cannons and muskets were technically effective and reliable enough to make a difference in warfare. At this time, a pattern emerged whereby rulers created centralized, fiscal–military states to finance their strategic shift to firearm-bearing

Shining Fragment of a Vanished World. The expulsion of the Moriscos from Spain in 1609 marks the final demise of a culture that fused Muslim, Christian, and Jewish traditions into a brilliant synthesis. Lusterware—the process by which pottery is fired with a metallic glaze to produce an iridescent effect—was introduced into Spain from the Middle East as early as the tenth century. The region of Andalusia, in particular the city of Málaga, was the center of lusterware production in Spain, and the fame of "Málaga-ware" was so great that this luxury craft was sought after by wealthy buyers throughout all of Europe. One fifteenth-century observer commented that "the Pope himself and the cardinals and princes of the world all covet it, and are amazed that anything so amazing and noble could be made from common clay." The example shown here, from ca. 1470, is a wing-shaped vase, most likely intended to hold a bouquet of flowers, and was commissioned by one of the wealthiest and most discerning patrons of the era, Lorenzo de Medici ("the Magnificent") of Florence.

infantries. They resumed the policy of imperialism, which had lain dormant during the preceding period, when the religious civilizations of Islam and Christianity had evolved into commonwealths of many competing realms. Both the Ottomans and the Habsburgs raised immense amounts of cash in silver and gold to spend on cannons, muskets, and ships for achieving world rule.

State Transformation, Money, and Firearms

In the early stages of their realms, the kings of Iberia (1150–1400) and the Ottoman sultans (1300–1400), with little cash on hand, compensated military commanders for their service in battle with parcels of conquered land, or *land grants*. That land, farmed by villagers, generated rental income for the officers. Once the Iberian and Ottoman rulers had conquered cities and gained control over long-distance trade, however, patterns changed. Rulers began collecting taxes in cash, with which they paid regiments of personal guards to supplement the army of land-grant officers and their retainers. They created the fiscal–military state, forerunner of the absolutist state of the early seventeenth century.

The Land-Grant System

When the Ottoman *beys*, or chieftains, embarked on their conquests in the early 1300s, they created personal domains on the choice lands they had conquered. Here, they took rents in kind from the resident villagers to finance their small dynastic households. Their comrades in arms, such as members of their clan or adherents (many of whom were holy warriors and/or adventurers), received other conquered lands, from which they also collected rents. As the Ottomans conquered Byzantine cities, first in Anatolia and, in the second half of the 1300s, in the Balkans, they gained access to the **money economy**. They collected taxes in coins from the markets and tollbooths at city gates where foods and crafts goods were exchanged, as well as from the Christians and Jews responsible for the head tax (Turkish *cizye*). The taxes helped in adding luxuries to the household of the Ottoman emirs, which became a palace.

Money economy: Form of economic organization in which mutual obligations are settled in the form of monetary exchanges; in contrast, a system of land grants obliges the holders themselves to provide military service to the grantee (sultan or king).

As a consequence of the full conquest of the southern Balkans by the Ottoman Empire in the fifteenth and sixteenth centuries, both the land-grant system and the money economy expanded exponentially. An entire military ruling class of grant holders emerged, forming the backbone of the early Ottoman army and administration. The grant holders were cavalrymen who lived with their households of retainers in the villages and towns of the interior of Anatolia and the Balkans. Most of the time, they were away on campaign with the sultans, leaving managers in charge of the collection of rents from the villagers on their lands.

The main purpose of the rents was to support the grant holders as well as finance the additional numbers of horsemen (as well as their horses, infantry retainers, and baggage carriers). The grant holders were also responsible for supplying their own arms (bow and arrow, lance, and sword), armor, and foodstuffs during campaigns. At the conclusion of the rapid growth period of the Ottoman Empire toward the end of the fifteenth century, the landed ruling class of cavalrymen numbered some 80,000, constituting a vast reserve of warriors for the mobilization of troops each summer.

Janissaries: Centrally paid infantry soldiers recruited through the *devshirme*, or levy of boys, among the Christian population of the Ottoman Empire.

The Janissaries

An early indicator of the significance of the money economy in the Ottoman Empire was the military institution of the **Janissaries**—troops which received salaries from the central treasury. This institution probably appeared during the second half of the fourteenth century and is first documented for 1395. It was based on a practice (called **_devşirme_**) of conscripting young boys, which palace officers carried out irregularly every few years among the empire's Christian population. For this purpose, the palace officers traveled to Christian villages, towns, and cities in the Balkans, Greece, and Anatolia. At each occasion, they selected hundreds of boys between the ages of 6 and 16 and marched them off to Istanbul, where they were converted to Islam and trained as future soldiers and administrators. The boys and young men then entered the central system of "palace slaves" under the direct orders of the sultan and his viziers or ministers.

During the time of its existence as a levy of Christian boys (c. 1380–1648), the devshirme was mostly administered in the poor, remote villages of the Adriatic mountains (opposite Italy), which could least resist it. Christian cities either negotiated their exemption or successfully resisted the levy until the administration gave up. Other communities bribed the recruiters or, occasionally, liberated child transports. During the height of the levy's administration, therefore, the great majority of Janissaries originated from a relatively small number of regions, mostly in Albania and Bosnia.

In fact, the devşirme contradicted Islamic law, which forbade the enslavement of "peoples of the Book" (Jews, Christians, and Zoroastrians). Its existence, therefore, documents the extent to which the sultans reasserted the Roman–Sasanian–Arab imperial traditions of the ruler making doctrine and law. Ruling by divine grace, the Ottomans were makers of their own law, called _kanun_ (from Greek _kanon_). Muslim religious scholars, who had assumed the role of guardians of law and doctrine during the preceding commonwealth period of Islamic civilization (950–1300), had no choice but to accept sultanic imperialism and seek to adapt it to the Shari`a as best they could.

Toward the first half of the fifteenth century, the sultans equipped their Janissaries with cannons and matchlock muskets. According to reports in Arabic chronicles, firearms first appeared around 1250 in the Middle East, probably coming from China. When the Janissaries received them, firearms had therefore undergone some 150 years of experimentation and development in the Middle East and North Africa. Even though the cannons and muskets were still far from being decisive in battle, they had become sophisticated enough to make a difference. By the mid-1400s, gigantic siege cannons and slow but reliable matchlock muskets were the standard equipment of Ottoman and other armies. The sultans relied on large numbers of indigenous, rather than European, gunsmiths, as new research in Ottoman archives has revealed.

Boy Levy (_devşirme_) in a Christian Village. This miniature graphically depicts the trauma of conscription, including the wailing of the village women and the assembly of boys waiting to be taken away by implacable representatives of the sultan.

Devşirme: The levy on boys in the Ottoman Empire; that is, the obligation of the Christian population to contribute adolescent males to the military and administrative classes.

Ottoman Siege of a Christian Fortress. By the middle of the fifteenth century, cannons had revolutionized warfare. Niccolò Machiavelli, ever attuned to new developments, noted in 1519 that "no wall exists, however thick, that artillery cannot destroy in a few days." Machiavelli could have been commenting on the Ottomans, who were masters of siege warfare. Sultan Mehmet II, the conqueror of Constantinople in 1453, founded the Imperial Cannon Foundry shortly thereafter; and it would go on to make some of the biggest cannons of the period.

Revenues and Money   The maintenance of a salaried standing army of infantry soldiers and a central administration to provide the fiscal foundation would have been impossible without precious metals. Therefore, the Ottoman imperial expansion was guided by the need to acquire mineral deposits. During the fifteenth century the Ottomans captured the rich silver, lead, and iron mines of Serbia and Bosnia. Together with Anatolian copper, iron, and silver mines occupied earlier, the Balkan mines made the Ottomans the owners of the largest precious metal production centers prior to the Habsburg acquisition of the Mexican and Andean mines in the mid-1500s.

The sultans left the mining and smelting operations in the hands of preconquest Christian entrepreneurs from the autonomous Adriatic coastal city-states of Ragusa and Dubrovnik. These entrepreneurs were integrated into the Ottoman imperial money economy as tax farmers obliged to buy their right of operation from the government in return for reimbursing themselves from the mining and smelting profits. **Tax-farming** was the preferred method of producing cash revenues for the central administration. The holders of tax farms delivered the profits from the production of metals, salt, saltpeter, and other minerals to the state, minus the commission they were entitled to subtract for themselves. They also collected the head tax—payable in money—from the Jews and Christians and the profits from the sale of the agricultural dues from state domains. Thus, tax farmers were crucial members of the ruling class, responsible for the cash flow in the fiscal–military state.

The right to mint silver into the basic coin of the empire, the *akçe* [ak-TSHAY], was similarly part of the tax-farm regime, as were the market, city gate, and port duties. The tax-farm regime, of course, was crucially dependent on a strong sultan or chief minister, the grand vizier. Without close supervision, this regime could easily deteriorate into a state of decentralization, something which indeed eventually happened in the Ottoman Empire on a large scale, although not before the eighteenth century.

Süleyman's Central State   The centralized fiscal–military state of the Ottomans reached its apogee under Sultan Süleyman I, the Magnificent. At the beginning of the sultan's reign, the amount of money available for expenditures was twice that of half a century earlier. By the end of his reign, this amount had again doubled. With this money, the sultan financed a massive expansion of the military and bureaucracy. Palace, military, and bureaucracy formed a centralized state, the purpose of which was to project power and cultural splendor toward its predominantly rural subjects in the interior as well as Christian enemies outside the empire.

The bureaucrats were recruited from two population groups. Most top ministers and officers in the fifteenth and sixteenth centuries came from the devşirme among the Christians. The conscripted boys learned Turkish, received an Islamic education, and underwent intensive horsemanship or firearm training, in preparation for salaried service in the Janissary army or administration. The empire's other recruits came from colleges in Istanbul and provincial cities to which the Muslim population of the empire had access. Colleges were institutions through which ambitious villagers far from major urban centers could gain upward mobility. Graduates with law degrees found employment as clerical employees in the bureaucracy or as judges in the villages, towns, and cities. Only the judges in the upper ranks of jurisdiction, however, such as the chief judges of Anatolia and the Balkans and the supreme judge of the empire, occupied positions of influence in the administration. Muslims of Christian parentage made up the top layer of the elite, while Muslims of Islamic descent occupied the middle ranks.

Tax-farming:
Governmental auction of the right to collect taxes in a district. The tax farmer advanced these taxes to the treasury and retained a commission.

Under Süleyman, the Janissaries comprised about 18,000 soldiers, divided into 11,000 musket-equipped troopers, a cavalry of 5,000, and 2,000 gunners who formed the artillery regiments. Most were stationed in barracks in and near the Topkapı Palace in Istanbul, ready to go on campaign at the sultan's command. Other Janissaries provided service in provincial cities and border fortresses. For his campaigns, the sultan added levies from among the cavalry troops in the towns and villages of the empire. Typical campaigns involved 70,000 soldiers and required sophisticated logistics. All wages, gunpowder, and weapons and the majority of the foodstuffs were carried on wagons and barges since soldiers were not permitted to provision themselves from the belongings of the villagers, whether friend or foe. Although the fiscal–military state collected heavy taxes, it had a strong interest in not destroying the productivity of the villagers.

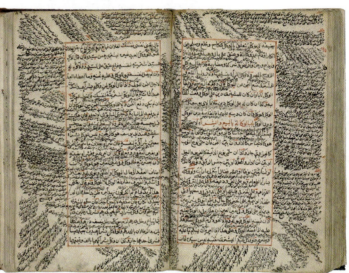

Ottoman Law Book. Covering the entire range of human activity—from spiritual matters, family relations, inheritance, business transactions, and crimes—the *Multaka al Abbur (The Confluence of the Currents)* was completed in 1517 and remained for hundreds of years the authoritative source for many of the laws in the Ottoman Empire. Written in Arabic script by the legal scholar Ibrahim Al-Halabi, later commentators added annotations in the margins and within the body of the text itself.

Charles V's Central State   The fiscal–military state began in Iberia with the political and fiscal reforms of Isabella and Ferdinand and reached the mature phase of centralization under Charles V. From the late fifteenth century onward, Castile and Aragon shared many fiscal characteristics with those of the Ottomans. The Spanish monarchs derived cash advances from tax farmers, who organized the production and sale of minerals and salt. From other tax farmers, they received advances on the taxes collected in money from the movement of goods in and out of ports, cities, and markets, as well as on taxes collected in kind from independent farmers and converted through sale on urban markets. In addition, Jews and Muslims paid head taxes in cash. Most of the money taxes were also enforced in Flanders, Burgundy, Naples, Sicily, and Austria, after Iberia's incorporation into the Habsburg domain in 1516. Together, these taxes were more substantial than those of Spain, especially in the highly urbanized Flanders, where the percentage of the urban population was about twice that of Spain.

From 1521 to 1536, the Spanish crown enlarged its money income by the one-fifth share to which it was entitled from looted Aztec and Inca gold and silver treasures. Charles V used these treasures to finance his expedition against Tunis. Thereafter, it collected a one-quarter share from the silver mines in the Americas that were brought into production beginning in 1545. Full production in the mines did not set in until the second half of the sixteenth century, but already under Charles V Habsburg imperial revenues doubled, reaching about the same level as those of the Ottomans. Thus, at the height of their struggle for dominance in the Muslim–Christian world, the Habsburgs and the Ottomans expended roughly the same amounts of resources to hurl against each other in the form of troops, cannons, muskets, and war galleys.

In one significant respect, however, the two empires differed. The cavalry ruling class of the Ottoman Empire was nonhereditary. Although land-grant holdings went in practice from father to son and then grandson, their holders had no recourse to the law if the sultans decided to replace them. By contrast, ever since the first half of the thirteenth century, when the Iberian kings were still lacking appreciable monetary resources, their landholders possessed a legal right to inheritance. The landholders met more or less regularly in parliaments (Spanish *cortes*), where they could enforce their property rights against the kings through majority decisions. When Isabella and Ferdinand embarked on state centralization, they had to wrestle with a powerful, landed aristocracy that had taken over royal jurisdiction and tax prerogatives (especially market taxes) on their often vast lands, including cities as well as towns and villages. The two monarchs took back much of the jurisdiction but were unable to do much about the taxes, thus failing in one crucial respect with their centralization effort. Although Habsburg Spain was a fully evolved fiscal–military state, it was in the end less centralized than that of the Ottomans.

The Habsburgs sought to overcome their lack of power over the aristocracy and the weakness of their Spanish tax base by squeezing as much as they could out of the Italian and Flemish cities and the American colonies. But in the long run their finances remained precarious, plentiful in some years but sparse in others. Relatively few Spanish aristocrats bothered to fulfill their traditional obligation to unpaid military service, and if they did, they forced the kings to pay them like mercenaries. As a result, in the administration and especially in the military, the kings hired as many Italians, Flemings, and Germans as possible. At times, they even had to deploy them to Spain in order to maintain peace there. Most of these foreigners were foot soldiers, equipped with muskets.

The Ottoman and Habsburg patterns of fiscal–military state formation bore similarities to patterns in the Roman and Arab Empires half a millennium earlier. At that time, however, the scale was more modest, given that the precious metals from West Africa and the Americas were not yet part of the trade network. In addition, earlier empires did not yet possess firearms, requiring an expensive infrastructure of charcoal and metal production, gunsmithing, saltpeter mining, and gunpowder manufacture. Thanks to firearms, the fiscal–military states of the period after 1450 were much more potent enterprises. They were established states, evolving into absolutist and eventually national states.

Imperial Courts, Urban Festivities, and the Arts

Habsburg kings and Ottoman sultans set aside a portion of revenues to project the splendor and glory of their states to subjects at home as well as enemies abroad. They commissioned the building of palaces, mosques, and churches and sponsored public festivities. Since the administrators, nobility, tax farmers, and merchants had considerable funds, they also patronized writers, artists, and architects. Although Christian and Muslim artists and artisans belonged to different religious and cultural traditions and expressed themselves through different media, their artistic achievements were inspired by the same impulse: to glorify their states through religious expression.

The Spanish Habsburg Empire: Popular Festivities and the Arts

The centrality of Catholicism gave the culture of the Habsburg Empire a strongly religious coloration. Both state-sponsored spectacles and popular festivities displayed devotion to the Catholic faith. More secular tendencies, however, began to appear as well, if only because new forms of literature and theater emerged outside the religious sphere as a result of the Renaissance. Originating in Italy and the Netherlands, Renaissance aesthetics emphasized pre-Christian Greek and Roman heritages, which had not been available to medieval Christian artists.

Capital and Palace   The Habsburgs focused relatively late on the typical symbols of state power and splendor, that is, a capital city and a palace. Most Spaniards lived in the northern third and along the southern and eastern rims of the Iberian Peninsula, leaving the inhospitable central high plateau, the Meseta, thinly inhabited. Catholicism was the majority religion by the sixteenth century and a powerful unifying force, but there were strong linguistic differences among the provinces of the Iberian Peninsula. Charles V resided for a while in a palace in Granada next door to the formerly Muslim Alhambra palace. Built in an Italian Renaissance-derived style and appearing overwhelming and bombastic in comparison to the outwardly unprepossessing Alhambra, Granada was too Moorish and, geographically, too far away in the south for more than a few Spanish subjects to be properly awed.

Only a few places in the river valleys traversing the Meseta were suited for the location of a central palace and administration. Philip II eventually found such a place near the city of Madrid (built on Roman-Visigothic foundations) which in the early sixteenth century had some 12,000 inhabitants. There, he had his royal architect in chief and sculptor Juan Bautista de Toledo (ca. 1515–1567), a student of Michelangelo, build the imposing Renaissance-styled palace and monastery complex of El Escorial (1563–1584). As a result, Madrid became the seat of the administration and later of the court. A large central square and broad avenue were cut across the narrow alleys of the old city, which had once been a Muslim provincial capital. People of all classes gathered in the square and avenue, to participate in public festivities and learn the latest news "about the intentions of the Grand Turk, revolutions in the

The Escorial Palace of King Philip II. Note the austere façade and the long horizontal lines of this building, representative of the Renaissance interpretation of the classical Greek-Roman architectural heritage.

Passion play: Dramatic representation of the trial, suffering, and death of Jesus Christ; passion plays are still an integral part of Holy Week in many Catholic countries today.

Netherlands, the state of things in Italy, and the latest discoveries made in the Indies."

Like its Italian paradigm, architecture of the Spanish Renaissance emphasized the Roman imperial style—itself derived from the Greeks—with long friezes, round arches, freestanding columns, and rotunda-based domes. With this style, Spanish architects departed from the preceding Gothic, stressing horizontal extension rather than height and plain rather than relief or ornament-filled surfaces. Interestingly, however, some Spanish architects incorporated the inherited traditions of the richly ornamental Gothic and Islamic styles into their Renaissance-style buildings, where these traditions appear in the so-called plateresque façades of buildings. This type of façade continued in the later Baroque style and was also transferred to the Americas (the oldest example being the monastery of San Agostín Acolman, 1560, in the outskirts of Mexico City) as well as the United States (one example, the entrance to the Hearst Castle, 1919). Plateresco is a uniquely Hispanic contribution to the architectural styles of the world.

Christian State Festivities   Given the close association between the state and the church, the Spanish crown expressed its glory through the observance of feast days of the Christian calendar. Christmas, Easter, Pentecost, Trinity Sunday, Corpus Christi, and the birthdays of numerous saints were the occasion for processions and/or **passion plays**, during which urban residents affirmed the purity of their Catholic faith. Throngs lined the streets or marched in procession, praying, singing, weeping, and exclaiming. During Holy Week preceding Easter, Catholics—wearing white robes, tall white or black pointed hats, and veils over their faces—marched through the streets, carrying heavy crosses or shouldering large floats with statues of Jesus and Mary. A variety of religious lay groups or confraternities competed to build the most elaborately decorated floats. Members of flagellant confraternities whipped themselves. The physical rigors of the Holy Week processions were collective reenactments of Jesus' suffering on the Cross.

By contrast, the Corpus Christi (Latin, meaning "body of Christ") processions that took place on the Sunday after Trinity Sunday (several weeks after Easter) were joyous celebrations. Central to these processions was a float with a canopy covering the consecrated host (bread believed to have been transfigured into the body of Jesus). Marchers dressed as giants, serpents, dragons, devils, angels, patriarchs, and saints participated in jostling and pushing contests. Others wore masks, played music, performed dances, and enacted scenes from the Bible. Being part of the crowd in the Corpus Christi processions meant partaking in a joyful anticipation of salvation.

The Auto-da-Fé   The investigation or proceeding of faith (Portuguese *auto-da-fé,* "act of faith") was a show trial in which the state, through the Spanish Inquisition, judged a person's commitment to Catholicism. Inquisitional trials were intended to display the all-important unity and purity of Counter-Reformation Catholicism.

Auto-da-Fé, Madrid. This detail from a painting showing a huge assembly in Plaza Mayor, Madrid, in 1683, captures the drama and spectacle of the auto-da-fé. In the center, below a raised platform, the accused stand in the docket waiting for their convictions to be pronounced; ecclesiastical and civil authorities follow the proceedings from huge grandstands set up for the event. On the left, an outdoor altar is visible—the celebration of mass was a common feature of the auto-da-fé, which would often last for several hours.

The Inquisition employed thousands of state-appointed church officials to investigate anonymous denunciations of individuals failing to conform to the prescribed doctrines and liturgy of the Catholic faith.

Suspected offenders, such as Jewish or Muslim converts to Catholicism or perceived deviants from Catholicism, had to appear before one of the 15 tribunals distributed over the country. In secret trials, officials determined the degree of the offense and the appropriate punishment. These trials often employed torture, such as stretching the accused on the rack, suspending them with weights, crushing hands and feet in an apparatus called "the boot," and burning them with firebrands. In contrast to the wide perception of the Inquisition as marked by pervasive cruelties, however, scholarship has emphasized that in the great majority of cases the punishments were minor or investigations did not lead to convictions.

On the other hand, whenever conviction entailed major penalties, the sentencing was a public spectacle. On the appointed day of punishment, to the accompaniment of trumpets and drums, the convicts were marched to a stage on the city square, dressed in yellow tunics and pointed fools' caps. After long sermons and solemn affirmations of Catholic doctrines, officials read the sentence. These sentences ranged from the wearing of the yellow tunic (the color of shame and the dress of Judas, who in the Christian gospels betrayed Jesus) in public for stipulated amounts of time to condemnation to hard labor as rowers on war galleys to execution. Offenders condemned to death were turned over to executioners on the outskirts of the city, who burned them at the stake. Autos-da-fé were usually scheduled to coincide with important dynastic events, such as royal accessions, weddings, and births, or to celebrate military victories, thus emphasizing the overwhelming power of the state.

Popular Festivities *Jousts* (mock combats between contestants mounted on horseback) were secular, primarily aristocratic events, also frequently connected with dynastic occurrences. The contestants, colorfully costumed as "Muslims," "Turks," and Christians, rode their horses into the city square accompanied by trumpets and drums and led their Arabian thoroughbreds or Lusitanian warmbloods through a precise and complex series of movements. At the height of the spectacle, contestants divided into groups of three or four at each end of the square. At a signal, they galloped at full speed past each other, hurling their javelins at one another while protecting themselves with their shields. The joust evolved eventually into exhibitions of dressage ("training"), cultivated by the Austrian Habsburgs, who in 1572 founded the Spanish Court Riding School in Vienna.

Bullfights, also fought on horseback, often followed the jousts. Fighting wild animals, including bulls, in spectacles was originally a Roman custom that had evolved from older bovine sacrifices in temples around the Mediterranean. During the Middle Ages, bullfights were aristocratic occupations that drew spectators from local estates. Bullfighters, armed with detachable metal points on 3-foot-long spears, tackled several bulls in a town square, together with footmen who sought to distract the bulls by waving red capes at them. The bullfighter who stuck the largest number of points into the shoulders of the bull was the winner. The bullfight remained an encounter between mounted man and animal in Portugal. In the expanding cities of eighteenth-century Spain, slaughterhouse workers popularized the modern version of the bullfight, in which a rapier-wielding matador on foot engages in a deadly fight with a bull bred to kill.

Theater and Literature   The dramatic enactments of biblical scenes in the passion plays and Corpus Christi processions were the origin of a new phenomenon in Spain, the secular theater. During earlier centuries, traveling troupes had often performed on wagons after processions. Stationary theaters with stages, main floors, balconies, and boxes appeared in the main cities of Spain during the sixteenth century. A performance typically began with a musical prelude and a prologue describing the piece, followed by the three acts of a drama or comedy. Brief sketches, humorous or earnest, filled the breaks. Plays dealt with betrayed or unrequited love, honor, justice, or peasant–nobility conflicts. Many were hugely successful, enjoying the attendance or even sponsorship of courtiers, magistrates, and merchants.

The outstanding Spanish dramatist of the second half of the sixteenth century was Félix Lope de Vega (1562–1635). His father, an embroidery shop owner, sent him to college, although he left without graduating. Lope de Vega's works, of which nearly 500 are extant, use plots, themes, and dramatic devices designed to appeal to a mass urban audience. Many of his dramas reflect his own adventurous life, which included military campaigns, countless love affairs, abductions, and several marriages. He also wrote historical plays dramatizing national events and heroic pieces based on Spanish legends. For many years, Lope de Vega lived from hand to mouth, finding aristocratic patrons only toward his later life. At the time of his death, Lope de Vega was a celebrated poet laureate of Spanish literature.

Another important writer of the period was Miguel de Cervantes (1547–1616), who wrote his masterpiece, *Don Quixote*, in the new literary form of the novel. *Don Quixote* describes the adventures of a poverty-stricken knight and his attendant, the peasant Sancho Panza, as they wander around Spain searching for the life of bygone Reconquista chivalry. Their journey includes many hilarious escapades during which they run into the reality of the early modern fiscal–military state dominated by monetary concerns. Cervantes confronts the vanished virtues of knighthood with the novel values of the life with money.

Cervantes' personal life was full of struggle. The son of a poor surgeon, he received a literary education before enlisting in the military. In the battle of Lepanto in 1571, an injury incapacitated his left arm. In 1575, Muslim corsairs from North Africa captured and imprisoned him in Algiers. Like Leo Africanus, discussed in the vignette at the beginning of this chapter, he was one of tens of thousands of kidnap victims on both the Christian and Muslim sides during the 1500s. Cervantes regained his freedom 5 years later when a Catholic religious order seeking release for captives in North Africa paid his ransom. Cervantes' early publications attracted little attention, and several times he was imprisoned for unpaid debts. Not until late in life did he receive recognition for his literary works.

Painters   The outstanding painter of Spain during Philip II's reign was El Greco (Domenikos Theotokopoulos, ca. 1546–1614), a native of the island of Crete. After early training in Crete as a painter of eastern Christian icons, El Greco went to Venice for further studies. In 1577, the Catholic hierarchy hired him to paint the altarpieces of a church in Toledo, the city in central Spain which was one of the residences of the kings prior to the construction of El Escorial in Madrid. El Greco's works reflect the spirit of Spanish Catholicism, with its emphasis on strict obedience to traditional faith and fervent personal piety. His characteristic style features elongated, pale figures surrounded by vibrant colors and represents a variation of the so-called mannerist style (with its perspective exaggerations), which succeeded the Renaissance style in Venice during the later sixteenth century.

King Philip II was not very fond of El Greco's paintings. While he approved of the latter's engagement in religion, he had more conventional Renaissance ideas about how personal piety should be represented in paintings. He preferred Titian (ca. 1490–1576), the more accessible and much sought-after Italian portraitist and painter of allegorical themes who, despite being lavished with favors by the king, never came to Spain. El Greco, nevertheless, found enough clerical patrons who supported his Toledo workshop until the end of his life.

El Greco, *View of Toledo*, ca. 1610–1614. The painting, now in the Metropolitan Museum, New York, illustrates El Greco's predilection for color contrasts and dramatic motion. Baroque and Mannerist painters rarely depicted landscapes and this particular landscape is represented in eerie green, gray, and blue colors giving the impression of a city enveloped in a mysterious natural or perhaps spiritual force.

The Ottoman Empire: Palaces, Festivities, and the Arts

Similar to the Habsburgs, the Ottomans built palaces and celebrated public feasts to demonstrate their imperial power and wealth. In Ottoman Islamic civilization, however, there were no traditions of official public art. The exception was architecture, where a veritable explosion of mosque construction occurred during the sixteenth century. High-quality pictorial artistry, in the form of portraits, book illustrations and miniatures, was found only inside the privacy of the Ottoman palace and wealthy administrative households. As in Habsburg Spain, theater and music enjoyed much support on the popular level, in defiance of official religious restrictions against these forms of entertainment.

The Topkapı Palace   When the Ottoman sultans conquered the Byzantine capital Constantinople in 1453, they took over one of the great cities of the world. Although richly endowed with Roman monuments and churches, it was dilapidated and depopulated when the Ottomans took over. The sultans initiated large construction projects, such as covered markets, and populated them with craftspeople and traders drawn from both Asian and European sides of their empire. By 1600 Istanbul was again an imposing metropolis with close to half a million inhabitants, easily the largest city in Europe at that time.

One of the construction projects was a new palace for the sultans, the Topkapı Saray or "Palace of the Gun Gate," begun in 1463. This palace is one of the world's most sumptuous urban dynastic residences, like the Forbidden City in Beijing or the Louvre in Paris. By design or circumstance, its sprawling size, with its many recesses, hidden rooms, and dark alleyways, made it an object of fear and fascination among the sultan's subjects. The Topkapı was a veritable minicity, with three courtyards, formal gardens, and forested hunting grounds. It also included the main administrative school for the training of imperial bureaucrats, barracks for the standing troops of the Janissaries, an armory, a hospital, and—most importantly—the living quarters, or harem, for the ruling family. Subjects were permitted access only through the first courtyard—reserved for imperial festivities—to submit their petitions to the sultan's council of ministers.

Imperial Hall, Topkapı Palace.
The Ottomans never forgot their nomadic roots. Topkapı Palace, completed in 1479 and expanded and redecorated several times, resembles in many ways a vast encampment, with a series of enclosed courtyards. At the center of the palace complex were the harem and the private apartments of the sultan, which included the Imperial Hall where the sultan would receive members of his family and closest advisors.

The institution of the harem rose to prominence toward the end of the reign of Süleyman. At that time, sultans no longer pursued marriage alliances with neighboring Islamic rulers. Instead, they chose slave concubines for the procreation of children, preferably boys. Concubines were usually from the Caucasus or other frontier regions, often Christian, and, since they were slaves, deprived of family attachments. A concubine who bore a son to the reigning sultan acquired privileges, such as influence on decisions taken by the central administration. The head eunuch of the harem guard evolved into a powerful intermediary for all manner of small and large diplomatic and military decisions between a sultan's mother, who was confined to the harem, and the ministers or generals she sought to influence. In addition, the sultan's mother arranged marriages of her daughters to members of the council of ministers and other high-ranking officials. In the strong patriarchal order of the Ottoman Empire, it might come as a surprise to see women exercise such power, but this power evidently had its roots in the tutelage exercised by mothers over sons who were potential future sultans.

Public Festivities   As in Habsburg Spain, feasts and celebrations were events which displayed the state's largesse and benevolence. Typical festivities were the Feast of Breaking the Fast, which came at the end of the fasting month of Ramadan, and the Feast of Sacrifice, which took place a month and a half later at the end of the Meccan pilgrimage. Festive processions and fairs welcomed the return of the Meccan pilgrimage caravan. Other feasts were connected with the birthday of the Prophet Muhammad and his journey to heaven and hell. Muslims believed that the Prophet's birth was accompanied by miracles and that the angel Gabriel accompanied him on his journey, showing him the joys of heaven and the horrors of hell. Processions with banners, music, and communal meals commemorated the birthdays of local Muslim saints in many cities and towns. As in Christian Spain, these feasts attracted large crowds.

The circumcision of a prince was an occasion for joyous public celebrations in the city. The sultan and his administrators rode out from the palace to the Hippodrome, the stadium for public festivities left over from Roman–Byzantine days. There, they tossed fistfuls of coins to the crowds. From stands in the stadium, they watched lengthy processions of the crafts guilds. Members of the guilds pulled floats on which colleagues demonstrated their skills. Bakers made bread in real ovens, cooks roasted meats, florists created flower arrangements, and glassblowers made bottles. Fishermen pulled a boat on wheels, architects carried the model of a mosque, and gardeners carried an artificial hill, complete with sheep and gazelles. The Janissaries rolled along atop a wheeled tower, firing their muskets in mock volleys against the "Christians," who marched beside them. Other Janissaries paraded with giants and monsters made of papier-mâché. Costumed and masked dancers, accompanied by musicians, waltzed along. The guild of street sweepers concluded the procession, parading as they were cleaning up the mess left by their preceding colleagues.

Wrestlers, ram handlers, and horsemen performed in the Hippodrome. Elimination matches in wrestling determined the eventual champion. Ram handlers spurred their animals to gore one another with their horns. Horsemen stood upright on horses, galloping toward a mound, which they had to hit with a javelin. At the harbor of the Golden Horn, tightrope artists stood high above the water, balancing themselves on cables stretched between the masts of ships, as they performed juggling feats. Fireworks—producing a variety of effects, noises, and colors—completed the circumcision festival in the evening. Court painters recorded the procession and performance scenes in picture albums. The sultans incorporated these albums into their libraries, together with history books recording in word and image their battle victories against the Habsburgs.

Popular Theater   The evenings of the fasting month of Ramadan were filled with festive meals and a special form of entertainment, the Karagöz ("Blackeye") shadow theater. This form of theater came from Egypt, although it probably had Javanese–Chinese roots. The actors in the Karagöz theater used figures cut from thin, transparent leather, painted in primary colors, and fashioned with movable jaws and limbs. With brightly burning lamps behind them, actors manipulated the

---

A Glimpse Inside the Harem

"The number of women reached 4,000, including those in his [the Sultan's] mother's service, as well as his lover's. Although the plague often devastated such a multitude, their numbers never fell below 2,000, owing to the careful and continuous recruitment of replacements.... They wore the most expensive clothes, belts, and fasteners studded with gems, earrings, and several strings of pearls. Each mistress of the sultan had the power to free and give in marriage any slave girls who were in her service or who aroused her jealousy."

—from the diary of Thomas Dallam, an English visitor to the Turkish court in 1599, from *Early Voyages and Travels in the Levant*. London: Hakluyt Society, 1893.

Ottoman Festivities, 1720. The sultan watches from a kiosk on the shore of the Golden Horn as artists perform high-wire acts, musicians and dancers perform from rowboats offshore, and high officials and foreign dignitaries view the festivities from a galleon.

figures against a cloth screen. The audience was seated on the other side of the screen, following the plays with rapt attention (or not).

The actors played burlesques, usually in four acts, narrating the slapstick encounters between Karagöz, the streetwise simpleton, and Hacivat [Ha-jee-VAT], his educated, conceited, but innocent counterpart. Other figures in the stories included a drunkard, an opium addict, a dwarf, a spendthrift, a woman of loose morals, assorted ethnic figures, monsters, and animals. The stories played on social contrasts and stereotypes, often containing political undertones. Theater companies toured the cities of the empire. Karagöz presentations by resident theaters also took place in taverns and coffeehouses. Like the Spanish theater with its dramas and comedies, the Ottoman Karagöz theater was a secular form of urban entertainment outside the religious circuit.

Among boys, a performance of the Karagöz theater accompanied the ritual of circumcision, a rite of passage from the ancient Near East adopted in Islamic civilization. It called for boys between the ages of 6 and 12 to be circumcised. Circumcision signified the passage from the nurturing care of the mother to the educational discipline of the father. Groups of newly circumcised boys were placed in beds from which they watched the antics of Karagöz and Hacivat. Supposedly, these churls distracted them from their pain.

Mosque Architecture   During the sixteenth century, the extraordinarily prolific architect Sinan (ca. 1492–1588) filled Istanbul and the earlier Ottoman capital Edirne with a number of imperial mosques, defined by their characteristic slender minarets. According to his autobiography, Sinan designed more than 300 religious and secular buildings, from mosques, colleges, and hospitals to aqueducts and bridges. Sultan Süleyman, wealthy officials, and private donors provided the funds. Sinan was able to hire as many as 25,000 laborers, enabling him to build most of his mosques in six years or less.

Sinan was a Christian-born Janissary from a Greek village in northwestern Anatolia. He entered the palace school at the comparatively late age of 19, and it was only after many years of service in the army corps of engineers before he received his first commission for a mosque in 1538. Sinan himself describes the Shehzade and Süleymaniye mosques in Istanbul and the Selimiye mosque in Edirne as his apprentice, journeyman, and master achievements. All three followed the central dome-over-a-square concept of the Hagia Sophia, which in turn is built in the tradition of Persian and Roman dome architecture. His primary, and most original, contribution to the history of architecture was the replacement of the highly visible and massive four exterior buttresses, which marked the square ground plan of the Hagia Sophia, with up to eight slender pillars as hidden internal supports of the dome. His intention with

Selimiye and Hagia Sophia. The architect Sinan elegantly melded the eight, comparatively thin columns inside the mosque (*a*) with the surrounding walls and allows for a maximum of light to enter the building. In addition, light enters through the dome (*b*). Compare this mosque with the much more heavily built, late Roman-founded Hagia Sophia (*c*).

each of these mosques was not massive monumentality but elegant spaciousness, giving the skylines of Istanbul and Edirne their unmistakable identity.

Putting It All Together

The Ottoman–Habsburg struggle can be seen as another chapter in the long history of competition that began when the Achaemenid Persian Empire expanded into the Mediterranean and was resisted by the Greeks in the middle of the first millennium BCE. Although India and China were frequently subjected to incursions from central Asia, neither of the two had to compete for long with any of its neighbors. Sooner or later the central Asians either retreated or were absorbed by their victims. The Ottomans' brief experience with Timur was on the same order. But the Middle East and Europe were always connected, and this chapter, once more, draws attention to this connectedness.

There were obvious religious and cultural differences between the Islamic and western Christian civilizations as they encountered each other during the Ottoman–Habsburg period. But their commonalities are equally, if not more, interesting. Most importantly, both Ottomans and Habsburgs were representatives of the return to imperialism, and in the pursuit of their imperial goals, both adopted the fiscal–military state with its firearm infantries and pervasive urban money economy. Both found it crucial to their existence to project their glory to the population at large and to sponsor artistic expression. In the long run, however, the imperial ambitions of the Ottomans and Habsburgs exceeded their ability to raise cash. Although firearms and a monetized urban economy made them different from previous empires, they were as unstable as all their imperial predecessors. Eventually, around 1600, they reached the limits of their conquests.

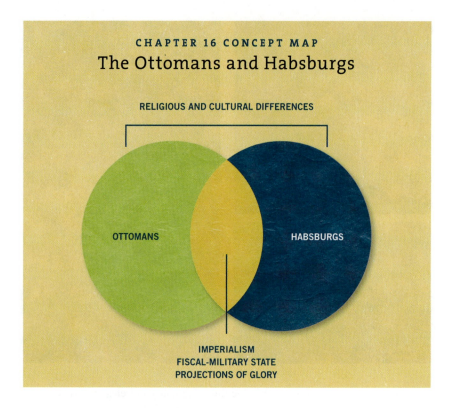

Review and Respond

1. Sketch the evolution of the Christian–Muslim struggle in Iberia. How did Portuguese and Spanish overseas explorations shape this struggle?

2. Provide an outline of the Ottoman–Habsburg struggle for dominance in Europe and the Mediterranean. What were the main theaters and stages of the struggle on land and at sea? How does the career of Leo Africanus display many of the themes that characterized this competition?

3. How were the Ottoman and Habsburg states organized? What were their economic bases? What were their social structures?

4. Who were the Janissaries, and how does the institution of the *devşirme* fit into their recruitment?

5. What was the Spanish Inquisition? What role did it play in Spanish society?

6. What were the principal cultural expressions of the Ottoman and Habsburg empires? In which ways were they similar, and in which ways were they different?

> ▶ For additional resources, including maps, primary sources, visuals, and quizzes, please go to www.oup.com/us/vonsivers. Please see the Further Resources section at the back of the book for additional readings and suggested websites.

Thinking Through Patterns

▶ **What patterns characterized the Christian and Muslim imperial competition in the period 1300–1600? Which elements distinguished them from each other, and which elements were similar? How did the pattern change over time?**

In 1300, the Ottomans renewed the Arab-Islamic tradition of jihad against the eastern Christian empire of Byzantium, conquering the Balkans and eventually defeating the empire with the conquest of Constantinople 1453. They also carried the war into the western Mediterranean and Indian Ocean. In western Christian Iberia, the rekindling of the reconquest after the lull of the thirteenth and fourteenth centuries was more successful. Invigorated by a merging of the concepts of the Crusade and the Reconquista, the Iberians expanded overseas to circumvent the Muslims and trade Indian spices directly. The so-called Age of Exploration, during which western Christians traveled to and settled in overseas lands, is deeply rooted in the Western traditions of war against Islamic civilization.

In the mid-1400s, the Middle East and Europe returned to the pattern of imperial state formation after a lull of several centuries, during which states had competed against each other within their respective commonwealths. The element which fueled this return was gunpowder weaponry. The use of cannons and handheld firearms became widespread during this time but required major financial outlays on the part of the states. The Ottomans and Habsburgs were the states with the most resources, and the Ottomans even built the first standing armies. To pay the musket-equipped soldiers, huge amounts of silver were necessary. The two empires became centralized fiscal–military states based on a money economy: Bureaucracies maintained centralized departments that regulated the collection of taxes and the payroll of soldiers.

▶ **How did the fiscal–military state in the Middle East and Europe function in the period 1450–1600? How did economics, military power, and imperial objectives interact to create the fiscal-military state?**

▶ **Which patterns did cultural expressions follow in the Habsburg and Ottoman Empires? Why did the ruling classes of these empires sponsor these expressions?**

The rulers of these empires were concerned to portray themselves, their military, and their bureaucracies as highly successful and just. The state had to be as visible and benevolent as possible. Rulers, therefore, were builders of palaces, churches, or mosques. They celebrated religious and secular festivities with great pomp and encouraged ministers and the nobility to do likewise. In the imperial capitals, they patronized architects, artists, and writers, resulting in a veritable explosion of intellectual and artistic creativity. In this regard, the Ottomans and the Habsburgs followed similar patterns of cultural expression.

Chapter **17**

1450-1750

Renaissance, Reformation, and the New Science in Europe

**URBAN POPULATION
OF EUROPE IN 1700**

London · · Amsterdam
Paris ·
Naples ·

- Over 30%
- 25-30%
- 10-15%
- 5-10%
- 1-5%
- 0-1%
· city with population
  over 200,000

Though less celebrated than her male contemporaries, one of the most remarkable scientific minds of the seventeenth century was that of Maria Cunitz (ca. 1607–1664). Under the tutorship of her father, a physician, she became accomplished in six languages (Hebrew, Greek, Latin, Italian, French, and Polish), the humanities, and the sciences. For a number of years while the Thirty Years' War (1618–1648) raged in Germany and her home province of Silesia, Cunitz and her Protestant family sought refuge in a Cistercian monastery in neighboring Catholic Poland. There,

Seeing Patterns

▶ What were the patterns of fiscal–military state formation and transformation in the period 1450–1750? How did the Protestant Reformation and religious wars modify these patterns?

▶ What are the reasons for the cultural change that began in Europe around 1750? In which ways were the patterns of cultural change during 1450–1750 different from those in the other religious civilizations of Eurasia?

▶ When and how did the New Science begin, and how did it gain popularity in northwestern Europe? Why is the popularization of the New Science important for understanding the period 1450–1750?

under difficult living conditions, she wrote *Urania propitia* (*Companion to Urania*), in praise of the Greek muse and patron of astronomy. When the family returned to Silesia after the war, Cunitz lost her scientific papers and instruments to a fire; but she continued to devote her life to the New Science through her careful astronomical observations.

Cunitz's book is a popularization of the astronomical tables of Johannes Kepler (1571–1630), the major scientific innovator remembered today for his discovery of the elliptical trajectories of the planets. Cunitz's book makes corrections in Kepler's tables and offers simplified calculations of star positions. Written in both Latin and German, she published it privately in 1650. It was generally well received, although there were a few detractors who found it hard to believe that a woman could succeed in the sciences. Whatever injustice was done to her during her lifetime, today the scientific community has made amends. A crater on Venus has been named after her, and a statue of her stands in her Silesian hometown.

Cunitz lived in a time when western Christianity had entered the age of early global interaction, from 1450 until 1750. During most of this time, Europe remained institutionally similar to the other parts of the world,

Renaissance Perspective. This 1525 print by the great German Renaissance artist Albrecht Durer is from his *Four Books on Measurement* and shows an artist and his assistant working with a *camera lucida, an* apparatus used to help convert three-dimensional objects into two-dimensional drawings, in this case, a lute. Durer was the first northern European to treat problems of perspective in a mathematical and scientific way.

especially the Middle East, India, China, and Japan. Rulers throughout Eurasia governed by divine grace. All large states followed patterns of fiscal–military organization. Their urban populations were nowhere more than 20 percent, and their economies depended on the prosperity of agriculture. As research on China, the Middle East, and India during 1450–1750 has shown, the "great divergence" in the patterns of political organization, social formation, and economic production between western Christianity and the other religious civilizations, whatever the characteristics that made each unique in other ways, did not take place until around 1800.

Culturally, however, northwestern Europe began to move in a different direction from Islamic, Hindu, Neo-Confucian, and Buddhist civilizations. The New Science and the Enlightenment of England, France, the Netherlands, and parts of Germany initiated new cultural patterns for which there was no equivalent in the other parts of Eurasia, including southern Europe. As significant as these patterns were, for almost the entire three centuries of 1450–1750 the New Science and the Enlightenment remained limited to a few hundred and later to a few thousand educated persons, largely outside the ruling classes. Their ideas and outlooks diverged substantially from those represented by the Catholic and Protestant ruling classes and resulted frequently in tensions or, in a few cases, even repression of New Scientists by the authorities. The new scientific and intellectual culture broadened into a mass movement only after 1750. The subsequent Industrial Revolution was rooted in this movement.

This chapter begins with a focus on the political pattern of fiscal–military state formation which coincided with the Protestant Reformation. The combustible mix of large armies of firearm-bearing mercenaries and fiery anti- and pro-Catholic polemics exploded in a series of religious wars lasting for a century and a half. When the religious fervor eventually died down, Europe separated into Catholic and Protestant fiscal–military states, now called "absolutist," which struggled with the challenges of economic viability. Accompanying the political–religious struggle was a pattern of rapid cultural transformations, explored in the second half of this chapter. The European Renaissance, Baroque, and New Science formed a sequence that was discontinuous with the western Christian Middle Ages and signified the search for a new cultural consensus. Cultural discontinuity, a rapid succession of different styles of cultural expression, and the absence of a consensus typified western Christianity, in contrast to the Middle East, India, and China, where cultural continuity reigned until the 1800s.

Fiscal–Military States and Religious Upheavals

The pattern of the fiscal–military state transforming the institutional structures of society was a characteristic not only in the Ottoman and Habsburg Empires during 1450–1750 but also in other countries of Europe, the Middle East, and India. The financial requirements for sustaining a fiscal–military state required everywhere a reorganization of the relationship between rulers, ruling classes, and regional as well as local forces. The Protestant Reformation and religious wars slowed the pattern of fiscal–military state formation, but once the religious fervor was spent, two types of states emerged: the French, Russian, and Prussian landed fiscal–military state and the Dutch and English naval fiscal–military state.

The Rise of Fiscal–Military Kingdoms

The shift from feudal mounted and armored knights to firearm-equipped professional infantries led to the emergence of the fiscal–military state. Rulers sought to centralize state power, collect higher taxes to subsidize their infantries, and curb the decentralizing forces of the nobility, cities, and other local institutions. Not all autonomous units (such as city-states, city-leagues, and religious orders dating to the previous period, 600–1450) were able to survive the military challenges of the rulers. A winnowing process occurred during 1450–1550, which left a few territorially coherent fiscal–military kingdoms in control of European politics.

The Demographic Curve Following the demographic disaster of the Black Death in 1348 and its many subsequent cycles, the population of Europe expanded again after 1470. It reached its pre-1348 levels around 1550, with some 85 million inhabitants (not counting the Spanish Habsburg and Ottoman Empires). The population continued to grow until about 1600 (90 million), when it entered a half-century of stagnation during the coldest and wettest period in recorded history, the "Little Ice Age" (1550–1750).

During 1650–1750, the population rose slowly at a moderate rate from 105 to 140 million (see Figure 17.1). In 1750, France (28 million) and Russia (21 million) were the most populous countries, followed by Germany (18 million), Italy (15 million), Poland (13 million), England (7 million), and the Netherlands and Sweden (2 million each). While the population figures of the individual countries for the most part bore little resemblance to their political importance during 1450–1750, as we shall see, the overall figures for Europe demonstrate that western Christianity had risen by 1750 to a status of demographic comparability vis-à-vis the other two major religious civilizations of India (155 million) and China (225 million).

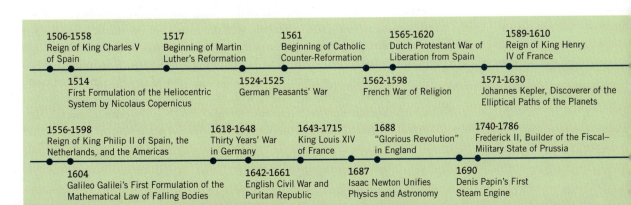

1506-1558 Reign of King Charles V of Spain	1517 Beginning of Martin Luther's Reformation	1561 Beginning of Catholic Counter-Reformation	1565-1620 Dutch Protestant War of Liberation from Spain	1589-1610 Reign of King Henry IV of France

1514 First Formulation of the Heliocentric System by Nicolaus Copernicus	1524-1525 German Peasants' War	1562-1598 French War of Religion	1571-1630 Johannes Kepler, Discoverer of the Elliptical Paths of the Planets

1556-1598 Reign of King Philip II of Spain, the Netherlands, and the Americas	1618-1648 Thirty Years' War in Germany	1643-1715 King Louis XIV of France	1688 "Glorious Revolution" in England	1740-1786 Frederick II, Builder of the Fiscal–Military State of Prussia

1604 Galileo Galilei's First Formulation of the Mathematical Law of Falling Bodies	1642-1661 English Civil War and Puritan Republic	1687 Isaac Newton Unifies Physics and Astronomy	1690 Denis Papin's First Steam Engine

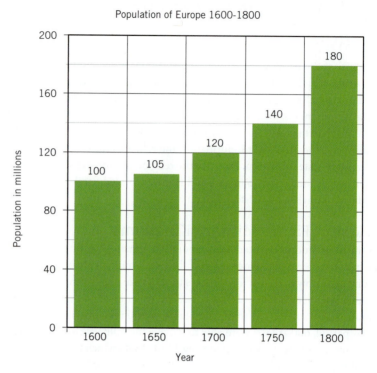

Figure 17.1 Population of Europe 1600–1800

Political Realignments   Bracketed between the two empires of the Ottomans and Habsburgs at either geographical end, western Christian Europe during the second half of the fifteenth century was a quilt of numerous independent or autonomous units, including the nascent fiscal–military kingdoms of France and England, the Hanseatic League of trading cities, the Catholic crusading order of Teutonic knights, and the small kingdoms of Denmark, Sweden, Norway, Poland–Lithuania, Bohemia, and Hungary. It furthermore comprised the principalities and cities of Germany, the duchy of Burgundy, the Alpine republic of Switzerland, and the city-states of Italy. At the northeastern periphery was the Grand Duchy of Moscow, representing eastern Christianity after the fall of Byzantium to the Ottomans in 1453. In this quilt, the majority of units competed vigorously with each other, seeking either to exploit the new possibilities which armies of mercenaries with firearms gave them or to survive as best as possible with just a handful.

By the first half of the sixteenth century, the competition had produced a number of winners and losers. Burgundy's dream for an independent kingdom came to an end with its defeat by and incorporation into France in 1477. France's further territorial expansion at the expense of the Italian city-states, beginning with Milan and Naples in 1499–1501, initially looked promising but eventually failed against Spain's similar aims. By the middle of the 1500s only Venice remained independent from Spain. The biggest winner was the Habsburg King Charles V of Spain (r. 1516–1558), who ended the imperial ambitions of King Francis I (r. 1515–1547) of France when the pope, handsomely bribed with Habsburg loans, bestowed the crown of the Holy Roman Empire (Germany, Austria, and the Netherlands) on Charles. Habsburg rounded off its territories in 1526 with the acquisition of Bohemia and the non-Ottoman portion of Hungary. But its lack of territorial cohesion limited its fiscal–military effectiveness.

In northern and eastern Europe, a similar sorting out occurred. England lost Calais, its last toehold on the European continent, to France in 1558. Militarily uninvolved on the Continent and with no need for a standing army, it fell behind in its evolution toward a fiscal–military state. The rising territorial kingdom of Poland–Lithuania (an elective kingdom after 1569) assumed control over a number of Baltic cities of the Hanseatic League and absorbed the lands of the Teutonic Order in 1525 as the duchy of Prussia. When united with Brandenburg in 1618, Prussia evolved into a potent fiscal–military kingdom independent from Poland. On the other side of the Baltic Sea, the union of the Scandinavian countries broke apart when Sweden, with the invasion of Danish Stockholm in 1526, declared its fiscal–military ambitions. On the eastern periphery, the Russian ruler Ivan IV, the Terrible (r. 1533–1584), took the title of emperor (*tsar*, from Latin for "caesar") in 1547 and embarked on a program of conquest which later made Russia a full-fledged fiscal–military rival of the Ottoman Empire.

Military and Administrative Capacities

The fiscal–military kingdoms which arose in the sixteenth century remained at the forefront of military innovation. In the course of the century, some kingdoms turned their mercenary troops into standing armies and stationed them in star-shaped forts, a fifteenth-century Italian innovation that made walls more resistant to artillery fire and trapped attackers in cross fires. Sweden introduced the line infantry in the mid-seventeenth century. In this strategy, three-deep lines of musketeers advanced on a broad front toward the enemy, with the front line firing, stepping back to reload, and making room for the next two lines to step forward and repeat the action. These forces underwent extensive peacetime drills and maneuvers. They wore uniforms and soon fired bayonet-equipped flintlock muskets, both introduced in the late seventeenth century in France. Pikemen, equipped with thrusting spears-cum-battle-axes for the protection of musketeers in hand-to-hand combat, were phased out with the appearance of the bayonet. By 1750, armies in the larger European countries were both more uniform and more numerous, increasing from a few thousand to hundreds of thousands of soldiers (see Map 17.1).

Musketeers. These pictures from an English illustrated drill manual demonstrate the steps by which a 17th-century musketeer "makes ready" his weapon, typically in less than 30 seconds. In battle, a sergeant would stand alongside each company of musketeers, organizing its movements and volley fire. Once a rank of musketeers had discharged its weapons it would move out of the way for another rank to fire. If combat was joined at close quarters, the musketeers would use their rifle butts as clubs.

MAP **17.1** European Warfare, 1450–1750.

The military forces devoured copious amounts of tax money. Accordingly, taxes expanded substantially during the period 1450–1550. But rulers could not raise land, head, and commerce taxes without the formal (in assemblies) or informal (based on customs and traditions) assent of the ruling classes and cities. Similarly, villagers voted with their feet when taxes became too oppressive. The taxation limits were reached in most European countries in the mid-sixteenth century, and for the next two centuries rulers could raise additional finances only to the detriment of their previously acquired central powers, such as by borrowing from merchants and selling offices. The Netherlands was an exception. Only there did the urban population rise from 10 to 20 percent, willing to pay higher taxes on expanded urban manufactures and commercial suburban farming. The Dutch government also derived substantial revenues from charters granted to armed overseas trading companies. Given the severe limits on revenue-raising measures in most of Europe, the eighteenth century saw a general deterioration of state finances, which eventually became a major contributing factor to the American and French Revolutions.

The Protestant Reformation, State Churches, and Independent Congregations

Parallel to the growing centralism of the kings, the popes restored the central role of the Vatican in the church hierarchy, after the devastating Great Schism of competing papal lines (1305–1415). Outwardly, the popes displayed this restoration through expensive Vatican construction projects that aroused considerable criticism outside Rome, especially in Germany where the leading clergy under a weak emperor was more strongly identified with Rome than elsewhere. Growing literacy and lay religiosity helped in the growth of a profound theological dissatisfaction which exploded in the **Protestant Reformation**. The Reformation began as an antipapal movement of reform in the early sixteenth century that demanded a return to the simplicity of early Christianity. The movement quickly engulfed the fiscal–military kingdoms and divided their ruling classes and populations alike. Vicious religious wars were the consequence. Although these wars eventually subsided, the divisions were never healed completely and mark the culture of many areas in Europe even today.

Background to the Reformation   Several religious and political changes in the fifteenth century led to the Protestant Reformation. One important religious shift was the growth of popular religiosity, a consequence of the introduction of the printing press (1454/55) and the distribution of printed materials. A flood of devotional tracts catered to the spiritual interests of ordinary people. Many Christians attended mass daily, confessed, and did penance for their sins. Wealthy Christians endowed saint cults, charitable institutions, or confraternities devoted to the organization of processions and passion plays. Poor people formed lay groups or studied scripture on their own and devoted themselves to the simple life of the early Christians. More Europeans than in previous centuries had a basic, though mostly literal, understanding of Christianity.

An important political change in the fifteenth century was an increasing inability for the popes, powerful in Rome, to appoint archbishops and bishops outside Italy. The kings of France, Spain, England, and Sweden were busy transforming their kingdoms into centralized fiscal–military states, in which they reduced the influence of the popes. Only in Germany, where the powers of the emperor and the rulers in the various principalities canceled each other out, was the influence of the popes still strong. What remained to the popes was the right to collect a variety of dues in the kingdoms of Europe. They used these dues to finance their expensive and, in the eyes of many, luxuriously worldly administration and court in Rome, from which they engaged in European politics. One of the dues was the sale of **indulgences**, which, in popular understanding, were tickets to heaven. Many contemporary observers found the discrepancy between declining papal power and the remaining financial privileges disturbing and demanded reforms.

Luther's Reformation   One such observer was Martin Luther (1483–1546), an Augustinian monk, ordained priest, and New Testament professor in northeastern Germany. Luther was imbued with deep personal piety and confessed his sins daily, doing extensive penance. After a particularly egregious sale of indulgences in his area, in 1517 he wrote his archbishop a letter with 95 theses in which he branded the indulgences and other matters as contrary to scripture. Friends translated the theses from Latin into German and made them public. What was to become the Protestant Reformation had begun.

Protestant Reformation: Broad movement to reform the Roman Catholic Church, the beginnings of which are usually associated with Martin Luther.

Indulgence: Partial remission of sins after payment of a fine. The payment would mean the forgiveness of sins by the church, but the sinner still remained responsible for his or her sins before God.

Anti-Catholic Propaganda.
This anonymous woodcut of 1520 by a German satirist depicts the devil (complete with wings and clawed feet) sitting on a letter of indulgence and holding a money collection box. The devil's mouth is filled with sinners who presumably bought letters of indulgence in good faith, thinking they had been absolved from their sins.

News of Luther's public protest traveled quickly across Europe. Sales of indulgences fell off sharply. In a series of writings, Luther spelled out the details of the church reform he envisaged. One reform proposal was the elevation of original New Testament scripture over tradition, that is, over canon law and papal decisions. Salvation was to be by faith alone; good works were irrelevant. Another reform was the declaration of the priesthood of all Christians, doing away with the privileged position of the clergy as mediators between God and believers who could forgive sins. A third reform was a call to German princes to begin church reform in their own lands through their power over clerical appointments, even if the Habsburg emperor was opposed. Finally, by translating the Bible into German, Luther made the full sacred text available to all who, by reading or listening, wanted to rely solely on scripture as the source of their faith. Luther's Bible was a monument of the emerging literary German language. A forceful and clear writer in his translation and own publications, Luther fully explicated the basics of Protestantism.

Reaction to Luther's Demands Both emperor and pope failed in their efforts to arrest Luther and suppress his call for church reform. The duke of Saxony was successful in protecting the reformer from seizure. Emperor Charles V, a devout Catholic, considered Castile's successful church reform of half a century earlier to be fully sufficient. In his mind, Luther's demands for church reform were to be resisted. Two other pressing concerns, however, diverted the emperor's attention. First, the Ottoman-led Islamic threat, in eastern Europe and the western Mediterranean, had to be met with decisive action. Second, his rivalry with the French king precluded the formation of a common Catholic front against Luther. Enthusiastic villagers and townspeople in Germany exploited Charles' divided attention and abandoned both Catholicism and secular obedience. A savage civil war, called the "Peasants' War," engulfed Germany from 1524 to 1525, killing perhaps as many as 100,000 people.

Luther and other prominent reformers were horrified by the carnage. They drew up church ordinances that regulated preaching, church services, administrative councils, education, charity, and consistories for handling disciplinary matters. In Saxony, the duke endorsed this order in 1528. He thereby created the model of Lutheran Protestantism as a state religion, in which the rulers were protectors and supervisors of the churches in their territories. A decade later, Saxony was fully Lutheran.

A minority of about half a dozen German princes and the kings of Denmark and Sweden followed suit. In England, Protestants gained strength in the wake of Henry VIII's (r. 1509–1547) break with Rome and assumption of church leadership in his kingdom (1534). Although remaining Catholic, he surrounded himself with religious reformers and proclaimed an Anglican state church whose creed and rites combined elements of Catholicism and Protestantism. A similar pattern was followed in other states in northern Europe (except for France), where upon breaking with Catholicism they established state churches (see Map 17.2).

MAP **17.2** The Protestant Reformation, ca. 1580.

Calvinism in France

In France, as in England, the king controlled all church appointments. King Francis I, however, did not take the final step toward the creation of an independent state church. Since he competed with Charles V for dominance over the papacy in Italy, he had to appear especially loyal and devout. When a few Protestants in France went public with their demands for church reform, Francis I gave them the stark choice of exile or burning at the stake. One reformer who chose exile was the French lawyer John Calvin (1509–1564, Fr. Jean Cauvin). Calvin went to republican Switzerland, where, in the absence of a central state authority, magistrates implemented the Protestant Reformation in a number of cities.

In Geneva, the magistrates called on Calvin to help them devise a strict Protestant moral code, which they introduced in 1541. The city was under the nominal rule of the duke of Savoy (himself under the nominal rule of the Habsburgs) and not yet part of Switzerland. As expressed in Calvin's central work, *Institutes of the Christian Religion* (1536), and numerous other writings, a crucial doctrine of Calvin's was *predestination*. According to this doctrine, God has "predestined"

> ### Ignatius of Loyola on Free Will and Good Works
>
> "...[W]e ought not to speak so lengthily and emphatically about grace that we generate a poison harmful to freedom of the will. Hence one may speak about faith and grace as much as possible, with God's help, for the greater praise of his Divine Majesty; but not in such ways or manners, especially in times as dangerous as our own, that works and free will are impaired or thought worthless."
>
> —Ignatius of Loyola, *Spiritual Exercises and Selected Works*, p. 213. Translated by George E. Ganss. New York: Paulist Press, 1991.

each human prior to birth for heaven or hell. Believers could only hope, through faith alone, that sometime during a life of moral living they would receive a glimpse of their fate. In contrast to Luther, however, Calvin made the enforcement of morality through a formal moral code, administered by local authorities, part of his version of Protestantism. Calvin died in his Genevan exile, but Geneva-trained Calvinist preachers went to France and the Netherlands in the mid-1500s. Under the protection of local magistrates, they organized the first clandestine independent Calvinist congregations. Calvinist religious self-organization by independent congregations thus became a viable alternative to Lutheran state religion.

The Counter-Reformation The rivalry between Spain and France made it initially difficult for the popes to tackle the problem of Catholic reforms in order to meet the Protestant challenge. When they finally called together the Council of Trent (1545–1563), they abolished payment for indulgences and phased out other church practices considered to be corrupt. These actions launched the **Counter-Reformation**, an effort to gain back lapsed Catholics. Supported by the kings of Spain and France, however, the popes reaffirmed the doctrines of faith together with good works, priestly mediation between believer and God, and monasticism. They even tightened church control through the revival of the papal Inquisition and a new Index of Prohibited Books. To counterbalance these punitive institutions, the popes furthered the work of the Basque priest Ignatius Loyola (1491–1556). At the head of the new order of the Society of Jesus, or "Jesuits," Loyola devoted himself tirelessly to the education of the clergy, establishment of a network of Catholic schools and colleges, and conversion of Protestants as well as non-Christians by missionaries to the Americas and eastern Asia. Thanks to Jesuit discipline, Catholics regained a semblance of self-assurance.

Counter-Reformation: Reaffirmation of the Catholic papal supremacy and the doctrine of faith together with works as preparatory to salvation; such practices as absenteeism (bishops in Rome instead of their bishoprics) and pluralism (bishops and abbots holding multiple appointments) were abolished.

Religious Wars and Political Restoration

The growth of Calvinism led to a civil war in France and to a war of liberation from Spanish Catholic rule in the Netherlands in the later sixteenth century. In England, the slow pace of reform in the Anglican Church, with which neither Calvinists nor Catholics could identify, erupted in the early seventeenth century into a civil war. In Germany, the Catholic–Protestant struggle turned into the devastating Thirty Years' War (1618–1648), which France and Sweden won at the expense of the Habsburgs. On the religious level, western Christians grudgingly accepted denominational toleration; on the political level, the fiscal–military states evolved into polities based on a combination between absolutist and decentralized administrative practices.

Civil War in France During the mid-1500s, Calvinism in France grew to about 1,200 congregations, mostly in the western cities of the kingdom, where literate merchants and craftspeople catering to trade overseas were receptive to Protestant publications. Calvinism was essentially an urban denomination, and peasants did not join in large numbers. Some 2 million, or 10 percent of the total population of

18.5 million, were "Huguenots," as the Protestants were called in France. They continued to be persecuted, but given their numbers, it was impossible for the government to imprison and execute them all. In 1571, they even met in a kingdom-wide synod, where they ratified their congregational church order. They posed a formidable challenge to French Catholicism.

In many cities, relations between Huguenots and Catholics were uneasy. From time to time, groups of agitators crashed each other's church services. The arrival of a child king to the French throne in 1560 was an open invitation to escalate hostilities. In vain, the queen mother, Catherine de' Medici (1519–1589), who acted as the king's regent, offered a compromise. She issued a decree that legitimized Huguenot church services, provided they took place outside cities. In defiance of this decree, in 1562 a band of Catholics under the leadership of the duke of Lorraine of the Guise family slaughtered 74 Huguenots during a church service in the small town of Vassy in northeastern France. This massacre, crying out for revenge, was the first round in a cycle of destructive religious warfare in France that lasted for over a generation, from 1562 to 1598.

As in the case of the Peasants' War in Germany (1524–1525), the French war of religion was a vicious affair in which each party claimed to have God on its side. Aristocracy and commoners showed no mercy in their religious frenzy, often mutilating the bodies of massacred men, women, and children alike. The first three rounds of war ended with the victorious Huguenots achieving full freedom of religious practice and self-government in four western cities. Given this situation, Catherine de' Medici renewed her attempts at compromise. She arranged in 1572 for the marriage of her daughter to King Henry III of Navarre (later King Henry IV of France, 1589–1610), a Protestant of the Bourbon family in southwestern France. Henry had risen to the leadership of the Huguenots a few years earlier, but he detested the fanaticism that surrounded him.

The prospect of a Huguenot king drove the Catholic aristocracy into a renewed frenzy of religious persecution. On St. Bartholomew's Day (August 24, 1572), just 6 days after the wedding of the future Henry IV, they perpetrated a wholesale slaughter of thousands of Huguenots. This massacre, in response to the assassination of a French admiral, occurred with the apparent connivance of the queen. For over

Wars of Religion. The massacre of 74 Huguenots (as the Calvinists were called in France) in the town of Vassy east of Paris in 1562 was the opening salvo in the French wars of religion. The Huguenots held religious services in a barn when followers of Francis, duke of Guise, fell into a quarrel with the unarmed Calvinists and the duke was hit by a stone, inciting a bloody revenge.

a decade and a half, civil war raged, in which Spain aided the Catholics and Henry enrolled German and Swiss Protestant mercenaries.

A turning point came only in 1589 when Henry of Navarre became King Henry IV. Surviving nearly three dozen plots against his life, the new king needed 9 years and two conversions to Catholicism—"Paris is well worth a Mass," he is supposed to have quipped—before he was able to calm the religious fanaticism among the majority of French people. With the Edict of Nantes in 1598, he decreed freedom of religion for Protestants. A number of staunch Catholic adherents were deeply offended by the edict as well as the alleged antipapal policies of Henry IV. The king fell victim to an assassin in 1610. Catholic resentment continued until 1685, when King Louis XIV revoked the edict and triggered a large-scale emigration of Huguenots to the Netherlands, Germany, and England. At last, France was Catholic again.

Dutch War of Independence   In the Netherlands, the Counter-Reformation Spanish overlords were even more determined to keep the country Catholic than the French monarchs prior to Henry IV. When Charles V resigned in 1556 (effective 1558), his son Philip II (r. 1556–1598) became king of Spain and the Netherlands, consisting of the French-speaking regions of Wallonia in the south and the Dutch-speaking regions of Flanders and Holland in the north. Like his father, Philip was a staunch supporter of the Counter-Reformation. He asked the Jesuits and the Inquisition to aggressively persecute the Calvinists. For better effect, Philip subdivided the bishoprics into smaller units and recruited clergymen in place of members of the nobility. In response, in 1565 the nobility and Calvinist congregations rose in revolt. They dismantled the bishoprics and cleansed the churches of images and sculptures, thereby triggering what was to become a Protestant war of Dutch liberation from Catholic Spanish overlordship (1565–1620). Philip retaliated by sending in an army that succeeded in suppressing the liberation movement, reimposing Catholicism, and executing thousands of rebels, many of them members of the Dutch aristocracy.

Remnants of the rebellion struggled on and, in 1579, renewed the war of liberation in three of the 17 northern provinces making up the Netherlands. Later joined by four more provinces, the people in these breakaway regions called themselves members of the "United Provinces of the Dutch Republic." Spain refused to recognize the republic and kept fighting until acute Spanish financial difficulties prompted the truce of 1609–1621. But the truce collapsed at the outbreak of the Thirty Years' War, and the Netherlands were drawn into the European conflagration. Spain eventually relinquished its claims only in 1648, when the European powers ended the Thirty Years' War with the peace settlement of Westphalia.

At the head of the Dutch republic was a governor (*stadhouder*) from the House of Orange-Nassau, one of the leading aristocratic families of the Netherlands. The representative body, with which the stadhouder governed, was the States-General and the privileged religious body was the Calvinist Dutch Reformed Church. In the Netherlands, about 20 percent of the population of 1 million was Calvinist, double the percentage in France and England. But there were also sizeable groups of Catholics and other Protestants. Among the latter, the Anabaptists and Mennonites (characterized by the doctrines of adult baptism and pacifism, respectively) were prominent. The Netherlands was also a haven for Jews, who had originally arrived there after their expulsion from Spain and Portugal in 1492–1498. Gradually, the

Dutch accepted each other's doctrinal differences and the Netherlands became a model of religious tolerance.

Civil War in England

As in the Netherlands, the dominant form of Protestantism in England was Calvinism. During the sixteenth century, the Calvinists numbered about 10 percent in a kingdom in which the Anglican Church encompassed the majority of subjects in a total population of 6 million. English Catholics, who refused to recognize the king as the head of the Anglican Church, numbered 3 percent. The percentage of Calvinists was the same as in France, but the partially reformed Anglican Church was able to hold them in check. The Calvinists were, furthermore, a fractious group, encompassing moderate and radical tendencies which neutralized each other. Among the radicals were the Puritans, who demanded the abolition of the Anglican clerical hierarchy and a new church order of independent congregations. Other radicals, such as the Diggers, demanded distribution of land from the commons. In the early seventeenth century, when Anglican Church reform slowed under the Catholic successors of Elizabeth I (r. 1558–1603), the Puritan cause began to acquire traction. Realizing that these Stuart successors and their bishops were immovable, some Puritans emigrated to North America rather than continue to chafe under the Anglican yoke. Other Puritans began to agitate openly.

Along with their efforts to restrain would-be reformers, the Stuart kings were busy building their version of the fiscal–military state. They collected taxes without the approval of Parliament. Many members resented being bypassed since Parliament was the constitutional cosovereign of the kingdom. A slight majority in the House of Commons was Puritan, and the stalled church reform added to their resentment. Eventually, when all tax resources were exhausted, the king, Charles I (r. 1625–1649), had to call Parliament back together. Mutual resentment was so deep, however, that the two sides were unable to make any decisions on either financial or religious matters. The standoff erupted into civil war, which cost the king his life and ended the monarchy.

Despite the brutal fate of Charles I, the English civil war of 1642–1651 was generally less vicious than that in France. Nevertheless, because of widespread pillage and destruction of crops and houses, the indirect effects of the war were severe for the population of thousands of villages. The New Model Army, a professional body of 22,000 troops raised by the Puritan-dominated Parliament against the king, caused further upheavals by cleansing villages of their "frivolous" seasonal festivals,

Religious Toleration in the Netherlands

"The great care of this state has ever been, to favour no particular or curious Inquisition into the faith or religious principles of any peaceable man, who came to live under the protection of their laws, and to suffer no violence or oppression upon any man's conscience.... It is hardly to be imagined how all the violence and sharpness which accompanies the difference of Religion in other countries, seems to be appeased or softened here, by the general freedom which all men enjoy ..."

—Sir William Temple. *Observations upon the United Provinces of the Netherlands*, ed. Sir George Clark, pp. 103 and 106. Oxford: Oxford University Press, 1972.

Frivolous Pagan Customs. During the English Civil War, Oliver Cromwell and the New Model Army espoused many Puritan doctrines, including the need to fight "frivolous" pagan customs deeply entrenched in village culture. In this woodcut from 1653, Father Christmas finds himself caught between the two opposing sides.

deeply rooted in local pagan traditions and featuring pranks, games, dances, drunkenness, and free-wheeling behavior. A republican theocracy emerged, with preachers enforcing Calvinist morality in the population.

Republic, Restoration, and Revolution

The ruler of this theocracy, Oliver Cromwell (r. 1649–1658), was a Puritan member of the lower nobility (the gentry) and a commander in the New Model Army. After dissolving Parliament, Cromwell handpicked a new parliament but ruled for the most part without its consent. Since both Scotland and Ireland had opposed the Puritans in the civil war, Cromwell waged a brutal war of submission against the Scottish Presbyterians (Calvinists organized in a state church) and Irish Catholics. The Dutch and Spanish, also opponents of the Puritans in the civil war, were defeated in naval wars that substantially improved English shipping power in the Atlantic. But the rising fear among the gentry in Parliament of a permanent fiscal–military state led Cromwell's parliament to refuse further funds. After Cromwell's death in 1658, it took just 3 years for the restoration of the Stuart monarchy and the Anglican state church to their previous places.

The recalled kings in the Restoration of 1661–1688 resumed the policies of fiscal–military centralism and Catholicism. As before, the kings called Parliament together only sparingly and raised funds without its authorization. Their standing army of 30,000, partially stationed near London, was intended more to intimidate the parliamentarians than to actually wage war. In the "Glorious Revolution" of 1688 the defiant Parliament, dominated since the Restoration by mostly Anglican gentry, deposed the Catholic king, James II (r. 1685–1688). It feared that the recent birth of a royal son threatened the succession of the king's daughter by his first marriage, Mary, a Protestant married to William of Nassau-Orange, the *stadhouder* of the Netherlands. It offered the throne to William and Mary as joint monarchs, and the Stuarts went into exile in France.

Outbreak of the Thirty Years' War

As religious tensions were mounting in England during the early seventeenth century, they erupted into a full-blown war in Germany, the second such conflagration in a century. As we saw earlier, Lutheran Protestantism had become the state religion in a majority of the two dozen largest and most powerful princely German states. Lutheran minorities were generally free to practice their religion in the Catholic German states. Not all rulers, however, were satisfied with the status quo among the princes. One of these rulers was the Jesuit-educated Ferdinand II (r. 1619–1637), ruler of the Holy Roman Empire, who resented the century-old religious freedoms enjoyed in Bohemia by Protestants. As newly elected king of Bohemia (and before becoming emperor), he began to exclude members of the Protestant aristocracy from administrative offices in re-Catholicized cities of the Bohemian kingdom. In response, Protestant leaders in 1618 unceremoniously threw two Habsburg emissaries out of a window of the Prague castle (the "Defenestration of Prague") and made the Calvinist prince of Palatinate in the Rhineland their new king. With these events in Bohemia, open hostilities between religious groups began in Germany.

Ferdinand and the Catholic princes suppressed the Bohemian rebellion in 1619, confiscated the properties of the Protestant aristocracy, and officially converted the kingdom to Catholicism. An imperial army of over 100,000 men chased the Calvinist prince not only from Prague but also from Palatinate and advanced toward northern Germany, capturing further territories for reconversion to Catholicism. When the Danish king intervened in favor of Lutheranism, he was crushed and the Protestant cause seemed to be doomed.

Outside Powers and the Peace of Westphalia
In 1630, however, the Lutheran king Gustavus II Adolphus (r. 1611–1632) of Sweden decided to intervene. The king's main goal was the completion of a Swedish-Lutheran fiscal–military state around the Baltic Sea, a project begun before the Thirty Years' War. By aiding the German Lutherans, he hoped to consolidate or even enlarge his predominance in the region. Louis XIII (r. 1610–1643) of France granted Sweden financial subsidies since he was concerned that Ferdinand's victories would further strengthen the Habsburg Spanish–Flemish–Austrian–German–Italian grip around France. For the French, the fact that Gustavus Aldolphus was a Protestant was secondary to the intra-Catholic rivalry between the Habsburgs and France. With the politically motivated alliance between Sweden and France, the German Catholic-Protestant war turned into a war for state dominance in Europe.

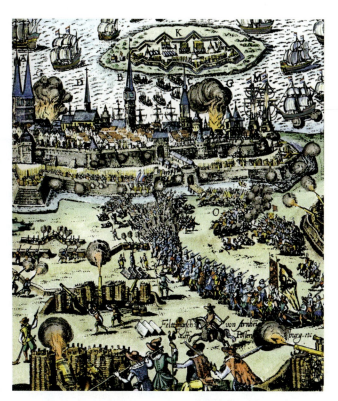

Fiscal–Military States at War. German imperial troops besiege Swedish troops in the northern German city of Stralsund in 1628. The etching shows typical features of the fiscal–military state, from top to bottom: galleon-style warships (successors of the caravel); a star-shaped fort (an Italian innovation) designed to withstand artillery barrages; the medieval walls of the city; musket-equipped infantry troops; field cannons; and the colorful Baroque uniforms worn by the musketeers of the period.

At first, Swedish troops turned the situation in favor of the Protestants. Gustavus Adolphus advanced victoriously as far as Bavaria in the south. On the verge of a final victory, however, the king fell in battle and the Swedes withdrew to northern Germany. In a position of renewed strength but fearful of a French entry into the war, Ferdinand II decided to compromise with the Protestant princes of Germany. In the peace of 1635, the two sides agreed to a return to the prewar territorial division between Catholic and Protestant princes in northern Germany.

Since the French were determined to break the Habsburg grip, they now entered the war. During the next 13 years, French armies sought to cut the Habsburg supply lines from Italy to the Netherlands by occupying Habsburg Alsace. Swedish armies, exploiting the French successes against the Habsburgs, fought their way back into Germany. In the end, the Austrian–German Habsburgs, pressured on two sides, agreed in October 1648 to the Peace of Westphalia. They allowed religious freedom in Germany and ceded territories in Alsace to France and the southern side of the Baltic Sea to Sweden. The Spanish Habsburgs, however, continued their war against France until 1659, when they also bowed to superior French strength, giving up parts of Flanders and northeastern Spain. France now emerged as the strongest power in Europe (see Map 17.3).

Absolutism in France?
During its period of greatest political dominance, France came under the rule of its longest reigning monarch, King Louis XIV (1643–1715). He was of small stature—for which he compensated with high-heeled

MAP **17.3** Europe in 1648.

shoes—but his hardy constitution and strong self-discipline helped him to dominate even the most grueling meetings with his advisors. He enjoyed pomp and
circumstance and built Versailles—his gigantic palace and gardens near Paris, populated with 10,000 courtiers, attendants, and servants—into a site of almost continuous feasting, entertainment, and intrigue. It was here that Louis, the "Sun King,"
beamed benevolently with his "absolute" divine mandate upon his aristocracy and
commoners alike. Versailles played an important role in Louis's efforts to undercut
the power of the nobility. Anyone with any aspirations of attracting the king's attention had to come to the palace to attend him. By keeping both friends and potential
enemies close by and forcing them to spend lavishly to stay abreast of the fashions
inspired by the king and vie for his attention, he was able, like the Tokugawa shoguns
in Edo, Japan, to bypass them administratively and rule through central bureaucratic
institutions.

Absolutism: Theory
of the state in which
the unlimited power of
the king under God is
emphasized.

    In practice, the French **absolutism** of Louis XIV and his eighteenth-century suc-
cessors, as well as practitioners in other European countries, was a complex mixture
of centralized and decentralized forces. On the one hand, after the end of the religious wars in 1648, mercenary armies under autonomous dukes and counts disappeared from the European scene, replaced by permanent armies or navies under the
central command of fiscal–military royal or princely dynasties. The kings also no

longer called their respective assemblies of nobles and notables together to have new taxes approved (in France from 1614 to 1789), and thus, many of the nobility's tax privileges disappeared.

On the other hand, the kings of the seventeenth century were acutely aware that true absolutism was possible only if centrally salaried employees collected taxes. It was physically impossible to transport tax revenues, in the form of silver money and grain, from the provinces to the capital, pay the central bureaucrats, and then cart the remaining revenues back to the provinces to pay salaried tax collectors there. A centrally paid bureaucracy would have required a central bank with provincial branches, using paper money. The failed experiment with such a bank in Paris from 1714 to 1720 demonstrates one such effort to find a solution to the central salary problem. But the bank's short life demonstrates that absolute central control was beyond the powers of the kings and princes.

Instead, the kings had to rely on subcontracting most offices and the collection of most taxes out to the highest bidders, who then helped themselves to the collection of their incomes. Under Louis XIV, a total of 46,000 administrative jobs were available for purchase in Paris and the provinces. Anyone who had money, or borrowed it from financiers, was encouraged to buy an office—from the old aristocracy of the "sword," receiving rents from the farmers on their rural estates, to ordinary merchant sons with law degrees, borrowing money from their fathers. Once in office, the government often forced these officers to grant additional loans to the crown. To retain their loyalty,

Versailles. Built between 1676 and 1708 on the outskirts of Paris, Versailles emphatically demonstrated the new centralized power of the French monarchy. The main building is a former hunting lodge that Louis XIV decorated with mythological scenes that showed him as the "Sun King." The outer wings housed government offices. Behind the palace, elaborate entertainments were held in the gardens.

the government rewarded them with first picks for retaining their offices within the family, buying landed estates, or acquiring titles of nobility to the secondary (and less prestigious) tier of the "nobility of the robe" (as opposed to the first-tier "nobility of the sword," which by the seventeenth century was demilitarized).

About the only way for Louis XIV to keep the semblance of a watchful eye on the honesty of the officeholders was to send salaried, itinerant *intendants* around the provinces to ensure that collecting taxes, rendering justice, and policing functioned properly within the allowable limits of "the venality of office," as the subcontracting system was called. Louis XIV had roughly one intendant for each province. About half of the provinces had *parlements*—appointed assemblies for the ratification of decrees from Paris—whose officeholders, drawn from the local noble, clerical, and commoner classes, frequently resisted the intendants. The Paris *parlement* even refused to accept royal writs carried by the intendants. In later years, when Louis XIV was less successful in his many wars against the rival Habsburgs and Protestant Dutch, the crown overspent and had to borrow heavily with little regard for the future. Louis's successors in the first half of the eighteenth century were saddled with crippling debts. French-inspired European "absolutism" was thus in practice a careful (or not so careful) balancing act between the forces of centralization and decentralization in the fiscal–military states of Europe.

The Rise of Russia   Although France's absolutism was more theory than practice, its glorious ideological embodiment by the Versailles of Louis XIV spawned adaptations across Europe. These adaptations were most visible in eastern Europe, which was populated more thinly and had far fewer towns and cities. Since rulers in those areas did not have a large reservoir of urban commoners to aid them as administrators in adopting the fiscal–military state, they had to make do with the landowning aristocracy. As a result, the villagers who in agrarian society bore the brunt of taxation were more exposed to the absolutist aspirations of the rulers and their administrators than in western Europe.

In Russia, Tsar Peter I, the Great (r. 1682–1725), of the eastern Christian Romanov dynasty, was a towering figure who singlehandedly sought to establish the

A World Turned Upside Down. In this popular satirical woodcut of 1766, based on a similar woodcut from the early 1700s, the mice are capturing and burying the cat: In other words, Peter the Great has turned the world upside down with his reforms.

fiscal–military state during his lifetime. At nearly 7 feet tall, Peter was an imposing, energetic ruler, controllable only by his second wife (and former mistress) Catherine, a warmhearted woman and beloved tsarina. Peter invited western European soldiers, mariners, administrators, craftspeople, scholars, and artists into his service and succeeded within just a few years in building a disciplined army and imposing navy. He built ports on the Baltic Sea and established the new capital of St. Petersburg, distinguished by many very beautiful palaces and official buildings. A typical example among thousands invited to Russia by the tsar was Peter von Sivers, a Danish mariner (and ancestor of one of the coauthors of the book) who rose to the position of vice admiral in the Baltic fleet that broke Swedish dominance in northern Europe. Since the tsar was not able to pay these advisors salaries (any more than Louis XIV could pay salaries to advisors to the French court), he gave many western guests estates with serfs in the Baltic provinces and Finland, conquered from Sweden, and made them aristocrats in his retinue.

The Russian military was completely reorganized by the tsar. After a rebellion early on, Peter savagely decimated the inherited firearm regiments and made them part of a new army recruited from the traditional Russian landed nobility. Both classes of soldiers received education at military schools and academies and were required to provide lifelong service. In order to make his soldiers look more urban, Peter decreed that they shave their traditional beards and wear European uniforms or clothes. Every twentieth peasant household had to deliver one foot soldier to conscription. A census was taken to facilitate the shift from the inherited household tax on the villagers to a new capitation tax collected by military officers. In the process, many free farmers outside the estate system of the aristocracy found themselves classified and taxed as serfs, unfree to leave their villages. The result of Peter's reforms was a powerful, expansionary fiscal–military state that played an increasingly important role among European kingdoms during the eighteenth century (see Map 17.4).

The Rise of Prussia

Similar to Russia, the principality of Prussia-Brandenburg was underurbanized. It had furthermore suffered destruction and depopulation during the Thirty Years' War. When the Lutheran Hohenzollern dynasty embarked on the construction of a fiscal–military state in the later seventeenth century, they first broke the tax privileges of the landowning aristocracy in the estates-general and raised taxes themselves. As in Russia, farmers who worked on estates held by landlords were serfs. Since there were few urban middle-class merchants and professionals, the kings enrolled members of the landlord aristocracy in the army and civilian administration.

Elevated by the Habsburg Holy Roman emperor to the status of kings in 1701, the Hohenzollern rulers systematically enlarged the army, employing it during peacetime for drainage and canal projects as well as palace construction in Berlin, the capital. Under

Prussian Military Discipline. The Prussian line infantry made full use in the mid-1700s of flintlock muskets, bayonets, and drilling. Most of the drilling concerned the rotation of the front line with the rear lines after salvos, for the purpose of reloading. The introduction of the bayonet made pikemen—infantry with long thrusting spears employed to protect the musketeers from hand-to-hand combat—obsolete.

The Expansion of Russia, 1462–1795

- Russian territory, 1462
- Acquisitions, 1462–1533
- Acquisitions, 1533–98
- Acquisitions, 1598–1619
- Acquisitions, 1619–89
- Occupied by Russia, 1644–89
- Acquisitions, 1689–1795
- Main trading post/fortress with date of foundation
- Extent of Empire, 1795

MAP **17.4** **The Expansion of Russia, 1462–1795.**

Frederick II, the Great (1740–1786), Prussia pursued an aggressive foreign policy, capturing Silesia from the Habsburgs in a military campaign. Frederick also expended major efforts into attracting immigrants, intensifying agriculture, and establishing manufacturing enterprises. Prussia emerged as a serious competitor of the Habsburgs in the Holy Roman Empire of Germany.

English Constitutionalism   In contrast to Prussia, France, Spain, Austria, and other European states, England had since 1450 a political system ruled by a king or a queen, with a parliament composed of the aristocracy as well as representatives of towns and cities. Only in England did the interests of the nobility and the urban merchants gradually converge. Rulers on the European continent financed their early fiscal–military states through raising indirect taxes on sales, commerce, imports, and exports, affecting cities more than noble estates. In England, the cities allied with the aristocracy in resisting indirect tax increases and forcing the throne to use the less ample revenues of its royal estates to pay soldiers. Efforts of the Stuart kings to create a fiscal–military state based on firearm infantries failed. Instead, the ruling class preferred to build a naval fiscal–military state. After the Glorious Revolution of 1688, this state achieved dominance on the world's oceans.

After its victory over the Stuart kings, Parliament consolidated its fiscal–military powers through the creation of the Bank of England in 1694, two decades before a similar but ill-fated attempt in France. When first Mary and then William died without children, England continued in 1701 with a distantly related dynasty from the principality of Hannover in Germany. Under a new monarch, England and Scotland united in 1707, creating the "United Kingdom." Parliament collected higher taxes than France and, through its bank, was able to keep its debt service low. The navy grew twice as large as that of France and was staffed by a well-salaried, disciplined military, while the few land troops, deemed superfluous, were mostly low-paid Hessian-German mercenaries. A rudimentary two-party system of two aristocracy–merchant alliances came into being. The two parties were known as the Whigs and the Tories, the former more parliamentarian and the latter more royalist, with the Whigs in power for most of the first half of the eighteenth century.

Cultural Transformations: Renaissance, New Science, and Early Enlightenment

The rise of the fiscal–military state coincided with the **Renaissance**, a period of cultural formation which in the fifteenth century followed the scholastic Middle Ages in western Christianity. With state profits, rulers, courts, and merchants sponsored much of the arts and sciences that flourished during the Renaissance. In many ways, the Renaissance was an outgrowth of scholasticism, but its thinkers and artists saw themselves as people who had broken away from its precepts. They considered their period as a time of "rebirth" (which is the literal meaning of "renaissance" in French), during which they were powerfully influenced by the writings of Greek and Hellenistic-Roman authors who had been unknown during the scholastic age. In the sixteenth century, the Renaissance gave way to the Baroque in the arts and the **New Science** in astronomy and physics, which in turn produced the Enlightenment. Thus, the Renaissance was just the first of further periods of cultural formation following each other in rapid succession.

Renaissance: "Rebirth" of culture in its full sense, based on large-scale publications and translations of Greek, Hellenistic, and Roman authors whose writings were previously unknown in the West.

The Renaissance and Baroque Arts

Beginning around 1400 in Italy and spreading later through northwestern Europe, an outpouring of learning, scholarship, and art came from theologians, philosophers, writers, painters, architects, and musical composers. These thinkers and artists benefited from Greek and Hellenistic-Roman texts which scholars had discovered recently in mostly eastern Christian archives in Byzantium. In addition, in the early fifteenth century Byzantine scholars from Constantinople arrived in Italy with new texts, which exerted a profound impact. The emerging cultures of the Renaissance and Baroque were creative adaptations of those Greek and Hellenistic-Roman writings to the cultural heritage of western Christianity. Out of this vibrant mixture arose the overarching concept of **humanism**.

New Science: Changes in the practice of science inherited from the Middle Ages; the discovery of the Americas inspired Copernicus to abandon the Aristotelian theory of elements and adopt heliocentrism; Galileo then replaced Aristotelian descriptive science with mathematized science, through the law of falling bodies.

New Manuscripts and Printing Byzantium experienced a cultural revival between its recovery in 1261 from the Latin interlude and its collapse in 1453 when the Ottomans conquered Constantinople. During this revival, for example, scholars engaged in a vigorous debate about the compatibility of Plato and Aristotle with each other. The debate made Italian scholars fully aware of how much of Greek literature was still absent from western Christianity; at the time, they possessed just two of Plato's 44 dialogues. Italians invited about a dozen eastern scholars, who brought manuscripts to Florence, Rome, and Venice to translate and to teach. Their students

Humanism: Intellectual movement focusing on human culture, in such fields as philosophy, philology, and literature, as based on the corpus of Greek and Roman texts.

Bookseller. By 1600, the increase in literacy levels combined with widespread printing of books, pamphlets, and tracts had made images like this itinerant bookseller in Italy a commonplace sight throughout much of Europe.

became fluent in Greek and translated Hesiod and Homer, the Greek tragedies and comedies, Plato and the Neo-Platonists, the remaining works of Aristotle, Hellenistic scientific texts, and the Greek church fathers. Western Christianity had finally absorbed the ancient heritage (see Table 17.1).

The work of translation was helped by the development of a more rounded, simplified Latin script, which replaced the angled, dense Gothic script used since the 1150s. In addition, the costly vellum (scraped leather) writing material on which many manuscripts had been laboriously written was replaced by cheaper paper, introduced from Islamic Spain in the early twelfth century and common in the rest of Europe by 1400, which allowed for more space on each page. Experimentation in the 1430s with movable metal typeface, arranged in frames and combined with traditional wooden presses for grape or olive crushing, resulted in the innovation of the printing press. The best known among the experimenters was the German Johannes Gutenberg (1398–1468), who printed the first Bible, still in Gothic script and with many copies in vellum, in 1454 or 1455. A half-century later, with more than 1,000 printers all over Europe and more than 8 million books in the hands of readers, a veritable printing revolution had taken place in Europe.

Table 17.1

First Appearance of Selected Ancient Greek Texts in Italy

1400	Homer, *Odyssey*; Plutarch, *Lives*; Thucydides, *History*
1402	Aristotle, *On the Soul*
1405	Plato, *Gorgias, Cratylus, Phaedo*; Ptolemy, *Geography*
1407	Aristotle, *Physics*
1415	Aristotle, *On the Parts of Animals, On the Heavens*
1416	Aristotle, *Nicomachean Ethics*
1417	Lucretius, *On the Nature of Things*
1418	Plato, *Protagoras*
1419	Aristotle (ascribed author), *Economics*
1421	Herodotus, *Histories*
1423	Plato, *Apology, Crito, Phaedrus*
1424	Plato, *The Republic*
1425	Aristotle, *Rhetoric*
1438	Aristotle, *Politics*
1440	Ptolemy, *On Astronomy*
1454	Plato, *Symposium*
1455	Aristotle, *Logic*; Euclid, *Geometry* (corrected retranslation)
1468	Archimedes, *Different Geometric Operations*; Euclid, *Elements*; Strabo, *Geography*

Philology and Political Theory   The flood of new manuscripts and the re-newed examination of existing manuscripts in libraries encouraged the study of Greek, Latin, and Hebrew philology. Scholars trained in these languages edited definitive texts based on multiple manuscripts and exposed inauthentic texts. The best known among these philologists was the Dutchman Desiderius Erasmus (1466–1536), who published an edition of the Greek and Latin New Testaments in 1516. The most infamous fake text to be exposed was the so-called Donation of Constantine, which the Italian Lorenzo Valla (1407–1457) proved through textual criticism to have been a self-serving forgery favoring the papal claims to supreme authority in the Middle Ages. Critical textual research, which became central to all subsequent scholarship, can trace its foundations to the Renaissance.

Biting criticism also emerged as a central element in political thought. In *The Prince*, Niccolò Machiavelli (1469–1527) reflected on the ruthless political competition among the princes of Europe for dominance over his hopelessly disunited native Italy. What Italy needed, Machiavelli argued, was a unifier who practiced what Aristotle enumerated in Book 5 of his *Politics*, that is, an intuitive ability to take proper action when survival in power was at stake. He called this ability *virtù*, by which he meant the power instinct of a ruler to take any appropriate measure, forceful or subtle, in order to remain in control of the vicissitudes—or, in his words, the *fortuna*—of politics. The New Scientists rejected Aristotle and the majority of humanists preferred Plato over Aristotle, but Machiavelli remained faithful to Aristotle, the superior political realist—an Aristotle held in high esteem centuries later by the American founding fathers.

The Renaissance Arts   In Italy, the reception of the new texts of the fifteenth century was paralleled by a new artistic way of looking at the Roman past and the natural world. The first to adopt this perspective were the sculptor Donatello (ca. 1386–1466) and the architect Filippo Brunelleschi (1377–1446), who received their inspiration from Roman imperial statues and ruins. Donatello created the sculpture of the Apostle St. Mark (1411–1413), a freestanding, classically relaxed sculpture in a niche on the outside of the dome of Florence. In 1421, Brunelleschi began the construction of the classically and humanly dimensioned Church of San Lorenzo in Florence. Both Donatello and Brunelleschi inspired a legion of Italian artists in the fifteenth and sixteenth centuries.

The artistic triumvirate of the high Italian Renaissance included Leonardo da Vinci (1452–1519), Michelangelo (1475–1564), and Raphael (1483–1520), renowned for their paintings *The Last Supper, Mona Lisa, The Creation of Adam, The Last Judgment, Madonna del Granduca,* and *The School of Athens.* Michelangelo excelled also in sculpture, as evinced by his great *David* and the *Pietà,* as well as architecture, with the dome of St. Peter's. Inspired by the Italian creative outburst, the Renaissance flourished also in Germany, the Netherlands, and France, with such artists as Hieronymus Bosch (ca. 1450–1516), Albrecht Dürer (1471–1528), Hans Holbein the Younger (ca. 1497–1543), and Pieter Bruegel the Elder (ca. 1525–1569). With a bit of exaggeration one could conclude that sponsorship of the arts by the ruling classes became almost as competitive as victory in battle.

The earliest musical composers of the Renaissance in the first half of the fifteenth century were Platonists, who considered music a part of a well-rounded education. The difficulty, however, was that the music of the Greeks or Romans was completely unknown. A partial solution for this difficulty was found through emphasizing the

Renaissance Art. Brunelleschi's cupola for the cathedral of Florence, completed in 1436, was one of the greatest achievements of the early Renaissance (*a*). Raphael's *School of Athens* (1509–1510) depicts some 50 philosophers and scientists, with Plato (in red tunic) and Aristotle (blue) in the center of the painting (*b*). Peter Bruegel's *The Harvesters* (1565) shows peasants taking a lunch break (*c*).

relationship between the word—that is, rhetoric—and music, which coincided in the sixteenth century with the Protestant and Catholic demand for liturgical music. During this century, a huge output of hymns and masses in church music and *madrigals* (verses sung by unaccompanied voices) in secular music attests to this emphasis. The works of the Italian composer Giovanni Pierluigi da Palestrina (ca. 1525–1594) represent Renaissance music at its most exquisite. The two main characteristics of Palestrina's music were the consonant third and the development of counterpoint, that is, the development of divergent but harmonic parallel melodies—compositional elements which became foundations for the development of Western music.

The theater was a relatively late expression of the Renaissance. The popular mystery, passion, and morality plays from the centuries prior to 1400 continued in Catholic countries. In Italy, in the course of the fifteenth century, a secular popular theater, the *commedia dell'arte* emerged, often using masks and staging plays of forbidden love, jealousy, and adultery. In England during the sixteenth century the popular traveling theater troupes became stationary and professional, attracting playwrights who composed more elaborate plays. Sponsored by the aristocracy and the Elizabethan court, playwrights wrote hundreds of scripts—some 600 are still extant—beginning in the 1580s. The best known among these playwrights was William Shakespeare (1564–1616), who also acted in his tragedies and comedies. One of Shakespeare's innovations was the history play, which explored tragic flaws in rulers. Greek tragedy and comedy as well as the Italian commedia dell'arte were the English Renaissance's models, although with entirely new plots and characters suited to audiences of their own times.

The Baroque Arts   The Renaissance gave way around 1600 to the Baroque, which dominated the arts until about 1750. Two factors influenced its emergence.

First, the Protestant Reformation, Catholic Counter-Reformation, and religious wars changed the nature of patronage, on which architects, painters, and musicians depended. Many Protestant churches, opposed to imagery as incompatible with their view of early Christianity, did not sponsor artists for the adornment of their buildings with religious art. Wealthy urban merchants, often Protestant, stepped into the breach but avoided paintings with religious themes, preferring instead secular portraits, still lives, village scenes, and landscapes. The best-known representatives of these themes were Frans Hals (ca. 1580–1666), Rembrandt van Rijn (1606–1669), and Jan Vermeer (1632–1675). These painters were too creative to restrict themselves to secular themes, but they nevertheless were responsible for the rise of a nonreligious Baroque sensibility.

Second, the predilection for Renaissance measurement, balance, and restraint gave way in both Catholic and Protestant regions to greater spontaneity and dramatic effect, as visible in the paintings of the Catholics Peter Paul Rubens (1577–1640) and Diego Velázquez (1599–1660) and the Protestant Rembrandt. Even more pronounced was the parallel shift in church and palace architecture to a "baroque" voluptuousness of forms and decorations, exemplified by Bavarian and Austrian Catholic churches, the Versailles Palace, and St. Paul's Cathedral in London, all completed between 1670 and 1750. Baroque music, benefitting from ample church and palace patronage, experienced a veritable explosion of unrestrained exploration. New instruments, new forms (opera, cantata, oratorio, and concerto), and new melodic complexities characterized the Baroque style, culminating with Georg Philip Telemann (1681–1767), George Frederic Handel (1685–1759), and Johann Sebastian Bach (1685–1750). Prolific artistic creativity coincided with a tumultuous political period in Europe.

The Pioneers of the New Science

Eastern Christian scholars invited from Byzantium to Florence in Italy during the first half of the fifteenth century brought with them full sets of Platonic manuscripts, which stirred much interest among western Christian scholars. It did not take long for these scholars to realize that Plato was not fully compatible with Aristotle, whose writings had dominated the debates since the thirteenth century. Scholars also began to pay attention to other Greek authors outside the Aristotelian tradition, such as the scientist Archimedes. Eventually, three great scientific pioneers—Copernicus, Galileo, and Newton—overturned the *descriptive* science of Aristotle in the sixteenth and seventeenth centuries and replaced it with the *mathematical* New Science, which many centuries later became the basis of modern scientific–industrial society.

Copernicus Questions Aristotle According to the scholastic heritage, based on Aristotle's physics, all objects in nature were composed of the four elements (in ascending order of lightness) of earth, water, fire, and air. In astronomy, based on Aristotle and Ptolemy, earth was in the center of the planetary universe, with planets composed of the fifth element of ether traveling around the earth in concentric circles. Both of these theories collapsed during the Renaissance, when a chorus of critics of Aristotle arose. One of the critics was Nicolaus Copernicus (1473–1543) from Torun, a German-founded city which had come under Polish rule a few years before his birth. Copernicus began his studies at the University of Kraków, the only eastern European school to offer courses in astronomy. During the years 1495–1504, he continued his studies—of canon law, medicine, astronomy, and astrology—at Italian universities. In 1500 he briefly taught mathematics in Rome and perhaps read Greek astronomical texts translated from Arabic in the library of the Vatican. Eventually, Copernicus graduated with a degree in canon law and took up an administrative position at the cathedral of Torun, which allowed him time to pursue astronomical research.

Sometime between 1507 and 1514 Copernicus became aware of the scientific significance of Columbus's discovery of the Americas. Spanish and Portuguese mariners sailing north and south from the Caribbean a few years after 1492 had realized that the Americas, with their long coastlines, were not at all islands off the coast of India, as Columbus had thought. As a result, in 1507 the German cartographer Martin Waldseemüller (ca. 1470–1520) published an early map and an accompanying updated version of Ptolemy's geography, both showing the east coast of the Americas. He was, thus, the first to describe the Americas as continents in their own right.

Copernicus saw the map soon after its publication and realized that, rather than a deep ocean, the Americas on the other side of the globe formed an entire "inhabited world" (Gr. *oikumene*). With this realization it became impossible for Copernicus to think that earth was the heaviest element: Too much earth in the form of continents was protruding from the oceans. Consequently, Copernicus rejected Aristotle's descriptive science of five elements and with it the idea that the earth was in the center of the planetary universe. He exchanged the places of the earth and sun, which described similar circles in the Ptolemaic system, and concluded that nothing much needed to be modified in the trigonometry of this system to accommodate that exchange. A century later, Johannes Kepler corrected the circles into concentric ellipses.

Waldseemüller's 1507 World Map. Although most of its features would have appeared on any Ptolemaic map of the era, this influential map is notable for one major mistake. The German map maker, Martin Waldseemüller (1470–1520), lacked any first-hand knowledge of the places he depicted on his map and he was unable to access the newly developed nautical charts of the world. Instead, he relied upon secondhand sources, including the misleading accounts of the Italian navigator, Amerigo Vespucci (1454–1512) who claimed that he, not the Portuguese, discovered the Atlantic seaboard of Brazil. As a result, instead of putting the original Portuguese name on the coast (Land of the True Cross), he placed the name of Amerigo (America). Waldseemüller soon realized his mistake, for the name America never reappeared on any of his subsequent maps.

Galileo's Mathematical Physics   During the near-century between the births of Copernicus and Galileo Galilei (1564–1642), mathematics—with its two branches of Greek geometry and Arabic algebra—improved considerably. Euclid's *Elements*, badly translated from Arabic in the late twelfth century with a garbled definition of proportions, was retranslated correctly from the Greek in 1543. In physics, the new translation in 1544 of a text on floating and sinking bodies by the Hellenistic thinker Archimedes (287–212 BCE) attracted enthusiastic attention. The text, unknown to the Arabs, had been translated from the Greek already in the thirteenth century but subsequently remained unappreciated, on account of its incompatibility with the then-prevailing Aristotelianism. All that was needed was for an anti-Aristotelian genius to bring together geometry, algebra, and Archimedian physics. In 1604, that genius came forward in the person of Galileo, who formulated his mathematical law of descending bodies (see Concept Map).

Running Afoul of the Church   Galileo was also a first-rate astronomer, one of the first to use a telescope, which had been recently invented in Flanders. On the basis of his astronomical discoveries, in 1610 he received a richly endowed appointment as chief mathematician and philosopher at the court of the Medici, rulers of Florence. But his increasing fame also attracted the enmity of the Catholic Church. As a proponent of Copernican heliocentrism, Galileo seemed to contradict the passage in the Hebrew Bible where God stopped the motion of the sun for a day, to allow the Israelites to win a battle (Joshua 10:12–13). In contrast to the more tolerant pope at the time of Copernicus, the Counter-Reformation Inquisition favored a strictly literal interpretation of this passage, which implied that the sun moves unless halted by God. In 1632 Galileo found himself condemned to house arrest and forced to make a public repudiation of heliocentrism.

The condemnation of Galileo had a chilling effect on scientists in the southern European countries where the Catholic Counter-Reformation reigned. Wealthy patrons reduced their stipends to scientists, and scientific research declined. During the seventeenth century, interest in the New Science shifted increasingly to France, Germany, the Netherlands, and England. There, no single church authority dominated, of either the Catholic or the Protestant variety, to enforce the literal understanding of scripture, as much as each would have wanted. These countries produced numerous mathematicians, physicists, and inventors, both Catholics as well as Protestants. The New Scientists in northern Europe had a certain liberty which their southern colleagues lacked. It was this intellectual freedom, not any great sympathy on the part of religious authorities for the New Science, which allowed the latter to flourish, especially in the Netherlands and England.

Isaac Newton's Mechanics   In the middle of the English dispute over the dominance of Protestant or Catholic authority, Isaac Newton (1643–1727) completed the New

> ### Copernicus Rejecting Aristotle
>
> "We should not listen to certain Peripatetics [Aristotelians] who . . . say that land has emerged for a certain distance [the length of Eurasia and Africa] because, having hollow spaces inside, it does not balance everywhere with respect to weight and so the center of gravity is different from the center of magnitude. But they fall into error through the ignorance of geometry; for they do not know that there cannot be seven times more water and some parts of the land still remain dry unless the land abandon its center of gravity [the earth as center of the planetary universe] and give place to the waters as being heavier."
>
> —Nicolaus Copernicus. *On the Revolutions of the Heavenly Spheres.* Translated by Charles Glen Wallis, pp. 9–10. Philadelphia: Running Press, 2002.

The Mathematization of Science, 1500–Present

According to Archimedes (and contrary to Aristotle), stones sink in water at the same speed, regardless of their weight. Galileo was able to prove that Archimedes was correct and that bodies descend with the same acceleration if one disregards the medium. To create the experiment, he had a craftsperson build him a 6.5-foot inclined, grooved beam, propped up at an angle, down which brass balls could be rolled. For timing, Galileo used the swings of a pendulum. After many experiments and false starts, he decided to divide the time of the ball's accelerating descent down the beam into eight equal segments. For the passing of each time segment he placed markers on the incline and carefully measured the resulting unequal distances.

As he compared these distances, he realized that their increasing lengths roughly followed the progression of the odd integers 1, 3, 5, 7, 9, 11, 13, 15, etc. On the basis of Euclid's mathematics of ratios, Galileo concluded that these distances, added together, corresponded to squares of time ($1 + 3 = 2^2$, $1 + 3 + 5 = 3^2$, $1 + 3 + 5 + 7 = 4^2$, and so forth). (Today, this lengthy number sequence is expressed in the short equation $s = t^2$, where s is distance and t is time.) Galileo concluded that, contrary to Aristotle, earthly motion—such as the accelerating motion of a body rolling down in the groove of a beam or falling from a tower—could be mathematized.

Acceleration Experiment. This nineteenth-century reconstruction of Galileo's inclined plane is located in the Museum for the History of Science in Florence, Italy. The metal gates, spaced along the grooved inclines according to Galileo's ratio of uneven integers, held bells, which helped him to measure the elapsed time segments as the balls passed through.

Galileo's math of ratios strikes us today as elementary. Several New Scientists after him, such as Descartes, Pascal, Leibniz, and Newton, created new fields of higher mathematics that enabled Newton to unify Copernican–Keplerian astronomy and Galilean physics into a single theory of a fully determined mechanical universe. Newton's concepts of atoms, forces, and planetary bodies dominated the sciences from the early eighteenth century to the early twentieth century. They became such impressively powerful tools that mathematically untrained philosophers like Auguste Comte (1798–1857) and Karl Marx (1818–1883) drew the conclusion that not only nature but also history were mechanically determined and that one could predict the future of social developments in the same way scientists predicted ballistic trajectories or astronomical constellations.

In the early twentieth century, Albert Einstein (1879–1955) formulated the theory of relativity as a replacement of Newtonianism. At the speed of light and across vast distances, space and time are no longer absolute but relative to each other, forming a single curved space–time, which in turn can be related to mass, energy, and momentum with the help of Einsteinian field equations. Newtonian planetary motions are for Einstein straight movements that appear curved because of space–time. While Newtonian mechanics can still be imagined and, therefore, mistaken as applicable to society and history, the theory of relativity is so abstract that words fail to render it comprehensible.

Between 1920 and 1930, scientists such as Nils Bohr (1885–1962) pushed scientific abstraction even further and developed quantum theory. Here, in the very small, subatomic realm of physics, as opposed to Einstein's very large space physics, scientists discovered that energy waves and subatomic particles form an indivisible duality. Paradoxical phenomena are the result: A single particle goes simultaneously through two slits, and particles at a distance from each other act instantaneously in tandem, without evidence of them being in contact, even at the speed of light. Quantum theorists assume an invisible subatomic continuum of particle waves that underlies the Einsteinian universe of space–time where relativity theory applies. The mathematics of particle waves, however, have withstood so far all efforts of unification with the mathematics of space–time, and scientists in the twenty-first century are still on the elusive hunt for what they call a "theory of everything."

Questions

- How do Galileo's experiments with falling bodies demonstrate the shift away from descriptive science to mathematical science?
- Why did the New Science lead to conflicts between thinkers like Galileo and the church?

Science of Copernicus and Galileo. As a professor at the University of Cambridge, he worked in the fields of mathematics, optics, astronomy, physics, alchemy, and theology. His main early contribution to the New Science was calculus, a new field in mathematics, which he developed at the same time as the German philosopher Gottfried Wilhelm Leibniz (1646–1716). Later in his career, Newton unified the fields of physics and astronomy, establishing the so-called Newtonian synthesis. His *Mathematical Principles of Natural Philosophy*, published in 1687, one year before the English settled their religious and constitutional disputes with the compromise of the Glorious Revolution, was the towering achievement of the New Science. It established a deterministic universe following mathematical rules and formed the basis of science until the early twentieth century.

The New Science and Its Social Impact

Scientists in the seventeenth century were in close communication with each other. They met in scientific societies or residential salons. Popularizers introduced an increasingly large public to the New Science. Scientists carried out experiments with constantly improved scientific instruments, such as telescopes, microscopes, thermometers, and barometers. Experience with barometers led technically versatile scientists and engineers to experiment with vacuum chambers and cylinders operating with condensing steam. Experimentation culminated with the invention of the steam engine in England in 1712.

New Science Societies   When the Counter-Reformation drove the New Science to northwestern Europe, the Italian-style academies gave way to chartered scientific societies, such as the Royal Society of London (1662) and the Paris Academy of Sciences (1666). Other countries, like Prussia, Russia, and Sweden, soon followed. These societies employed staffs of administrators, co-opted scientists as fellows, held regular discussion meetings, challenged their fellows to answer scientific questions, awarded prizes, and organized field trips and expeditions. They also published transactions, correspondences, and manuscripts. Many societies attracted thousands of members—famous pioneers, obscure amateurs, technically proficient tinkerers, theoretical mathematicians, daring experimenters, and flighty dreamers—representing an important cross section of the upper strata of seventeenth-century urban society in northwest Europe (see Map 17.5).

Other popularizers were textbook authors and itinerant lecturers who addressed audiences of middle-class amateurs, instrument makers, and specialized craftspeople, especially in England and the Netherlands. Many lecturers toured coffeehouses, urban residences, country estates, and provincial schools. Coffeehouses allowed the literate urban public to meet, read the daily newspapers (first published in the early seventeenth century), and exchange ideas. Coffee, introduced from Ethiopia and Yemen via the Ottoman Empire in the sixteenth century, was the preferred nonalcoholic social drink before the arrival of tea in the later eighteenth century. Male urban literacy is estimated to have exceeded 50 percent in England and the Netherlands during this period, although it remained considerably lower in France, Germany, and Italy.

Some lecturers were veritable entrepreneurs of the speaking circuit, teaching a kind of "Newtonianism-lite" for ladies and gentlemen with little time or patience for serious study. Other lecturers set up subscriptions for month-long courses. Wealthy

MAP 17.5 Centers of Learning in Europe, 1500–1770.

businessmen endowed public lectures and supported increasingly elaborate experiments and expensive laboratory equipment. In the first half of the eighteenth century, the New Science triumphed in northwestern Europe among a large, scientifically and technically interested public of experimenters, engineers, instrument makers, artisans, business people, and lay folk.

Women and the New Science   Women formed a significant part of this public. In the fields of mathematics and astronomy, Sophie Brahe (1556–1643), sister of the Danish astronomer Tycho Brahe (1546–1601), and Maria Cunitz (see chapter-opening vignette) were the first to make contributions to the new astronomy of Copernicus and Kepler. According to estimates, in the second half of the seventeenth century some 14 percent of German astronomers were women. A dozen particularly prominent female astronomers practiced their science privately in Germany, Poland, the Netherlands, France, and England.

New Scientist. Maria Cunitz is honored today with a sculpture in Ratusz, Poland. Crater Cunitz is one of the larger craters (30 miles across) on the planet Venus which were named in the twentieth century to honor female scientists like Cunitz.

One later woman not content with private practice and intent on breaking into the male-dominated world of the university was the Italian Laura Bassi (1711–1778). Her father, a lawyer in Bologna in northern Italy, provided her with an early education in mathematics and physics. As a young scholar, Bassi became a member of the Academy of the Bologna Institute of Sciences and, in 1732, earned her doctorate at the city's university, the first woman to receive a doctorate in the New Science.

Bassi's lectures on Newtonian physics attracted large audiences, although the university senate refused to grant a position as a chair (a permanent member of the faculty) to a woman. Undaunted, Bassi pursued her career as a lecturer and experimenter in the new field of electricity, earning a salary higher than that of the Bologna Academy's president. She continued her scientific activities even after marrying a fellow physicist and rearing eight children. The period was a time of scholarly opportunity for a fair number of women scientists, even in Counter-Reformation Italy.

Social Salons   Another institution which helped in the popularization of the New Science was the salon. As the well-furnished, elegant living room of an urban residence, the salon was both a domestic chamber and a semipublic meeting place for the urban social elite to engage in conversations, presentations, and experiments. The culture of the salon emerged first in Paris sometime after the closure of the court-centered Palace Academy in the 1580s. Since the Catholic French universities remained committed to Aristotelianism, the emerging stratum of educated urban aristocrats and middle-class professionals turned to the salons as places to inform themselves about new scientific developments. Furthermore, French universities as well as scientific academies refused to admit women, in contrast to Italian and German institutions. The French salon, therefore, became a bastion of well-placed and respected female scholars.

One outstanding example of French salon science was Gabrielle-Emilie du Châtelet (1706–1749). In her youth, Châtelet fulfilled her marital duties to her husband, the Marquis of Châtelet. She had three children before turning to the sciences. In one of the Paris salons she met François Marie Arouet, known as Voltaire (1694–1778), the eighteenth-century Enlightenment writer, skeptic, satirist, and amateur Newtonian. Châtelet and Voltaire became intimate companions under the benevolent eyes of the Marquis at the family estate in Lorraine in northwestern France.

Voltaire had fled Paris after the publication of his Anglophile *Philosophical Letters* (1733), which angered the anti-English French court. The Châtelets offered him a refuge in exchange for Emilie being introduced to, and tutored by, the leading scientists and friends of Voltaire in Paris. The estate became a veritable intellectual center, equipped not only with a salon and laboratory but also with a theater, where Emilie Châtelet acted in plays written by Voltaire. His best known work today, however, is his satirical novel, *Candide* (1759), that mocks Leibniz' idea of theodicy, that is, the notion that history progresses and everything happens for an ultimately beneficial purpose. Voltaire uses the example of the devastating earthquake of 1750 that leveled Lisbon to argue that there is no theodicy. Humanity, in the absence of divine providence, has to remain satisfied with events as they occur. Although Voltaire published prolifically, Châtelet eventually outstripped him both in research and scientific understanding. Her lasting achievement was the translation of Newton's *Principles* into French, published in 1759.

Discovery of the Vacuum   Among the important scientific instruments of the day were telescopes, microscopes, and thermometers. It was the barometer, however, that was the crucial instrument for the exploration of the properties of the vacuum and condensing steam, eventually leading to the invention of the steam engine. The scientist laying the groundwork for the construction of this instrument was Evangelista Torricelli (1608–1647), mathematician and assistant of Galileo. In collaboration with Florentine engineers, he experimented with mercury-filled glass tubes, demonstrating the existence of atmospheric pressure in the air and of vacuums in the tubes.

Four years later, the French mathematician and philosopher Blaise Pascal (1623–1662) had his brother-in-law haul a mercury barometer up a mountain to experiment with demonstrations of lower air pressures at higher altitudes. Soon thereafter, scientists discovered the connection between changing atmospheric pressures and the weather, laying the foundations for weather forecasting. The discovery of the vacuum, the existence of which Aristotle had held to be impossible, made a deep impression on the scientific community in the seventeenth century and was an important step toward the practical application of the New Science to mechanical engineering in the eighteenth century.

Another important step in the transition from New Science to mechanics was the development of precision machining. Scientists wanted to experiment with precision instruments and gadgetry, such as air pumps and sealed vacuum chambers. The first to build a workable pump and chamber was the German Otto von Guericke (1602–1686). In the 1650s and 1660s Guericke carried out experiments with two hollow and conjoined copper hemispheres. Sealed tightly and emptied of their inside air with the help of pumps, these hemispheres held together so firmly that a team of workhorses was unable to pull them apart. Guericke and the Englishman Robert Boyle (1627–1691) were also early experimenters with electricity, which

Vacuum Power. In 1672, the New Scientist and mayor of Magdeburg, Otto von Guericke, demonstrated the experiment that made him a pioneer in the understanding of the physical properties of the vacuum. In the presence of German emperor Ferdinand III, two teams of horses were unable to pull the two sealed hemispheres apart. Guericke had created a vacuum by pumping out the air from the two sealed copper spheres.

they produced by rubbing balls of sulfur with their hands. Metal workshops in Paris and Leiden began producing air pumps, and vacuum chambers became standard equipment in laboratories.

The Steam Engine   The French Huguenot scientist and engineer Denis Papin (ca. 1647–1712) took the first crucial step from the vacuum chamber to the steam engine. Papin began his career as an assistant in English scientific laboratories, where he familiarized himself with the phenomenon of steam contracting its volume when cooled in a chamber, creating a vacuum in the process. In 1690, when he was a court engineer and professor in Germany, Papin constructed a cylinder with a piston. Weights, via a cord and two pulleys, held the piston at the top of the cylinder. When heated, water in the bottom of the cylinder turned into steam. When subsequently cooled through the injection of water, the steam condensed, forcing the piston down and lifting the weights up. Papin spent his last years (1707–1712) in London where the Royal Society of London held discussions of his papers, thereby alerting engineers, craftspeople, and entrepreneurs in England to the steam engine as a labor-saving machine. In 1712, the mechanic Thomas Newcomen built the first steam engine to pump water from coal mine shafts.

Altogether, it took a little over a century, from 1604 to 1712, for Europeans to apply the New Science to the development of the steam engine. Had it not been for the New Science, this engine—based on contracting steam—would not have been invented. (Hero of Alexandria, who invented steam-driven machines in the first century CE, made use of the expanding force of steam.) Prior to 1600, mechanical inventions—such as the wheel, the compass, the stern rudder, and the firearm—were constructed by anonymous tinkerers with a good commonsense understanding of nature. With the arrival of the New Science, Aristotelian common sense was no longer a virtue. It became a hindrance for the building of mechanical machinery. In 1700, engineers had to have at least a basic understanding of mathematics and such abstract physical phenomena as inertia, gravity, vacuums, and condensing steam if they wanted to build a steam engine or other complex machinery.

The Early Enlightenment in Northwestern Europe

The New Science engendered a pattern of radically new intellectual and religious thinking, which evolved in the course of the seventeenth and early eighteenth centuries. This thought, called the "Enlightenment," was deemed to be incompatible with the inherited medieval scholasticism. It eventually evolved into a powerful instrument of critique of Christian doctrine and the constitutional order of the fiscal–military states. Initially, the Enlightenment was confined to a few thinkers, but with the Glorious Revolution of 1688 in England it became a potent social force.

Descartes and Bacon   After the replacement of descriptive physics with mathematical physics, brought about by Galileo with his law of descending bodies, the question arose whether Aristotelian philosophy and Catholic theology were still adequate for the understanding of reality. New Scientists perceived the need to start philosophizing and theologizing from scratch. The first major New Scientist who, in his own judgment, started a radical reconsideration of philosophy from the ground up was the Frenchman René Descartes (1596–1650). He earned a degree in law, traveling widely after graduation. In the service of the Dutch and Bavarian courts, he bore witness to the beginning of the Thirty Years' War and its atrocities committed in the name of religious doctrines. During the war, he spent two decades in the Netherlands, studying and teaching the New Sciences. His principal innovation in mathematics was the discovery that geometry could be converted through algebra into analytic geometry.

Descartes was shocked by the condemnation of Galileo and decided to abandon all traditional propositions and doctrines of the church as well as Aristotelianism. Realizing that his common sense (that is, the five senses of seeing, hearing, touching, smelling, and tasting) were unreliable, he determined that the only reliable body of knowledge was thought, especially mathematical thought. As a person capable of thought, he concluded—bypassing his unreliable senses—that he existed: "I think, therefore I am" (*cogito ergo sum*). A further conclusion from this argument was that he was composed of two radically different substances, a material substance consisting of his senses and another immaterial substance consisting of thought. According to Descartes, body and mind, although joined through consciousness, belong to two different realms of reality.

While *Cartesian* (from Descartes) rationalism represented one road to understanding reality within the New Science, the *empirical* path of Francis Bacon (1561–1626), emphasized direct study and experimentation. In his *Novum Organum* (*New Instrument*), published in 1620, Bacon criticized current approaches to knowledge as being influenced by various kinds of common human error—"idols," as he characterized them—and argued instead for *inductive reasoning*: the close study of specific examples of phenomena from which their general principles are then *induced*. This forms the basis of what we call today the "scientific method": forming hypotheses,

A Mechanical Universe.
Descartes was also a physicist, and in *Principia philosophiae* (1644) he outlined his "mechanical universe theory" in which he described the universe as a continuously operating machine that God had set in motion. Composed of "subtle matter," it swirled in whirlpools, or vortices. In this illustration, the vortices move the planets around the Sun.

Mathematics: The New Divine of Science

"I say that the human intellect does understand some of them [propositions] perfectly, and thus in these it has as much absolute certainty as nature itself has. Of such are pure mathematics; that is, geometry and arithmetic in which Divine intellect indeed knows infinitely more propositions, since it knows all. But with regard to those [propositions] which the human intellect does understand, I believe that its knowledge equals the Divine in objective certainty."

—Galileo. *Dialogue Concerning the Two Chief World Systems.* Translated by Stillman Drake, 2nd ed., p. 103. Berkeley: University of California Press, 1967.

testing them through experimentation, and revising them accordingly. Thus, Bacon's "inductive method" along with Descartes' "deductive method"—reasoning from the general to the specific—have remained the twin pillars from which subsequent scientific research has proceeded.

The Philosophy of the New Science Descartes's distinctions between body, mind, and consciousness stimulated a lively debate not only among the New Scientists but also among the growing circle of philosophers of the New Science. The Englishmen Thomas Hobbes (1588–1679) and John Locke (1632–1704) were among the latter. Hobbes, interested in the New Science since his student days, described himself as a philosopher. Locke had a basic medical education but made his contributions to the field of philosophy. Both applied Descartes's New Science philosophy to constitutional theory, making crucial contributions to the formation of constitutional nationalism in the United States, France, and Haiti at the end of the 1700s. Constitutional nationalism and its later rival, ethnic nationalism, are today the main political forces driving the patterns of world politics.

Thomas Hobbes As a nonscientist outside the field of mathematics, astronomy, and physics—the most advanced mathematical sciences in the seventeenth and eighteenth centuries—Hobbes had little interest in Galileo's and Descartes's concept of the mind as pure mathematical thought. Therefore, it escaped him that for Descartes (as also, before him, Plato and Galileo) mathematics was the new divine: God was equivalent to mathematics; and the Mind, insofar as it could conceive of mathematics, was pure, transcendent thought.

The nonmathematician Hobbes paid attention only to consciousness; that is, the personal mind in a living body, subject to the law of motion. And since bodies are made up of corpuscles (later scientists and philosophers would speak of atoms), so, Hobbes concluded, reality is entirely material and determined by the law of motion. With Hobbes, the philosophy of materialism was born, according to which nothing but matter exists and anything mathematical, intellectual, or spiritual is dependent on matter.

Once Hobbes decided that materialism was the only possible new philosophy, the extension of materialism to political philosophy followed easily. If people are nothing but bodies, they are equal to each other with their basic bodily functions, such as their emotions and passions. Foremost among the passions, so Hobbes concluded, is selfishness. Therefore, in the natural state of humanity, which is defined as millions of atoms in motion, clashing with each other, there is "war of every man against every man."

In this general war, fear of death—another major passion—drives humans to give up their sovereignty, their "absolute" personal liberty to wage war. They do so either because they are forced by a single sovereign to do so or because they transfer their sovereignty voluntarily to a sovereign or a collective representative assembly that possesses sovereignty. Hobbes, well aware of the horrors of the recent English religious wars, preferred the alternative of the single sovereign. Thus, we can conclude that it is on the grounds of materialist philosophical thinking that Hobbes arrived at the principles of equality, rule by law, and the constitutional state. It was from the philosophy of the New Science, and specifically the concept of mathematical equality, that the theory of democracy arrived on the world historical scene.

John Locke   Locke also outlined a philosophy derived from the New Science that makes the conscious mind rigorously dependent on matter. According to Locke, the mind is a blank slate at birth on which sense perception impresses all categories of thought and reflection. Matter, in the form of atoms, impresses itself on the mind and creates consciousness. Through trial and error we overcome what Descartes considered to be the deception by the senses. Locke, in the Anglo-American philosophical tradition, became the principal figure of Enlightenment materialism.

The early Enlightenment was a curious mixture of a flawed philosophy of base human passions and an eventually highly successful political theory of democracy. Forgetting that Descartes held fast to the Platonic–Galilean notion of the divine as mathematics and the mind as pure mathematical thought, they developed a philosophy of consciousness as the concrete individual mind in a moving body determined by passions. A split occurred between the New Science, in which mathematics functioned as the new equivalent of religion, and the Enlightenment philosophy of materialism, in which no religion was needed, even if philosophers remained nominally Christian. This division is still unhealed today, with both scientists and the general public unaware that the equivalent of the divine in the modern age is the **transcendence** of mathematics.

In the political realm, Locke also took the passions as his starting point. But, for him, the basic passion was the desire of ownership—of oneself, one's labor, and property—which he considered to be inalienable rights. Self-possession excluded slavery, ownership of one's labor meant self-employment, and ownership of property included land and portable wealth. When this passion could no longer be satisfied, war would break out. But once the passions of war subsided, reason would lead humans to the establishment of a peaceful or civil government. In so doing, however, humans would not give up their liberty, as argued by Hobbes. They would merely empower the government to protect private property. Therefore, also in contrast to Hobbes, citizens retained the right to rise against an unjust government. Ironically, by default, Locke allowed for the kind of general war to which Hobbes was opposed.

The Social Contract. Hobbes believed that the "war of all against all" could only be avoided when human beings entered into a contract in which they agreed to be ruled by an absolute sovereign. The title page from his most famous work, *Leviathan,* depicts the ruler as an absolute monarch, but one whose body incorporates the many individuals of society who have consented to live in a commonwealth under his authority.

Transcendence: Realm in reality that is as real as matter; the transcendent realm is both separate and mingled with the realm of matter; the difficulty of thinking of the two as both separate and mingled has caused much confusion, beginning with Hobbes and Locke.

Putting It All Together

Prior to 1500, all religious civilizations possessed sophisticated mathematics and practiced variations of descriptive science, such as astronomy, astrology, geography, alchemy, and medicine. Only after 1550 did astronomy and physics in western

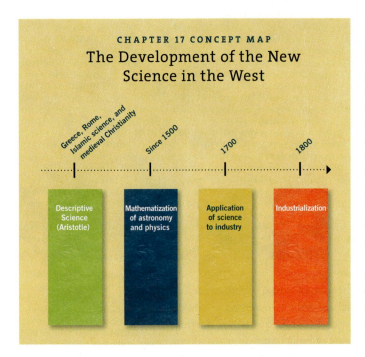

CHAPTER 17 CONCEPT MAP

The Development of the New Science in the West

Greece, Rome, Islamic science, and medieval Christianity

Since 1500

1700

1800

Descriptive Science (Aristotle)

Mathematization of astronomy and physics

Application of science to industry

Industrialization

Christianity transform themselves into mathematical science. This transformation, however, had no practical consequences prior to the invention of the steam engine in the 1700s and the subsequent industrialization of England in the 1800s. Furthermore, the mathematization of astronomy and physics did little to influence the continued prevalence of description as the chief underlying pattern of the other sciences. Astrology, alchemy, and medicine continued with what we regard today as mistaken descriptive theories well into the nineteenth century.

Most importantly, the rise of the New Science and Enlightenment should not be confused with the vast political, social, economic, and cultural changes, called "modernity" after 1750, which propelled the West on its trajectory of world dominance. Although the West began to acquire its specific scientific and philosophical identity with the introduction of mathematical science in the one hundred-year span between Copernicus and Galileo, its impact on the world became felt only after it applied science to industry. Once this process got underway, in the nineteenth century, Asia and Africa had no choice but to adapt to modern science and industrialization (see Concept Map).

Review and Respond

1. How did the Protestant Reformation originate, and who were its main representatives?

2. What were the key political and religious differences between France, Russia, Prussia, and England during the period 1450–1750?

3. What was humanism, and what role did it play in the Renaissance?

4. What are the differences between descriptive and mathematical science, and who pioneered the latter? What impact did women scientists such as Maria Cunitz have on the popularization of the New Science?

5. Discuss three inventions that illustrate the popularization of the New Science during 1450–1750.

Thinking Through Patterns

▶ **What were the patterns of fiscal–military state formation and transformation in the period 1450–1750? How did the Protestant Reformation and religious wars modify these patterns?**

European kingdoms, such as France, Sweden, and Prussia, expanded their powers of taxation to the detriment of the nobility. With the accumulated funds, they hired and salaried mercenary infantries equipped with firearms, using them to conquer land from their neighbors. The religious wars of the 1500s and 1600s strengthened centralization efforts and hastened the demise of the nobility as obstacles to the fiscal–military state. In England, Parliament blocked the Stuart kings from building an infantry fiscal–military state and instead pursued the construction of a naval state, which succeeded a similar one built by the Netherlands in 1688.

Located far from the traditional agrarian-urban centers of Eurasia, western Christianity repeatedly adapted its culture (particularly theological, philosophical, scientific, and artistic forms of expression) in response to outside stimuli coming from Islamic and eastern Christian civilizations. Without these stimuli, the Renaissance, Baroque, New Science, and Enlightenment would not have developed. In contrast, the Middle East, Byzantium, India, and China, originating firmly within the traditional agrarian-urban centers, received far fewer outside stimuli prior to the scientific–industrial age.

▶ **What are the reasons for the cultural change that began in Europe around 1750? In which ways were the patterns of cultural changes during 1450–1750 different from those in the other religious civilizations of Eurasia?**

▶ **When and how did the New Science begin, and how did it gain popularity in northwestern European society? Why is the popularization of the New Science important for understanding the period 1450–1750?**

The discovery of the two new continents of the Americas prompted Nicolaus Copernicus to reject Aristotle's astronomical theory of spheres and to posit a sun-centered planetary system. It continued with Galileo Galilei's discovery of the mathematical law of falling bodies in physics and was completed with Isaac Newton unifying physics and astronomy. The New Science became popular among educated urban circles in northwestern Europe, where Catholic and Protestant church authorities were largely divided. In southern Europe, where the Catholic Counter-Reformation was powerful and rejected the New Science, no such popularization occurred. The New Science possessed practical applicability: After discovering the properties of the vacuum and condensing steam, scientists began experimenting with steam engines, which served as the principal catalyst for the launching of the scientific–industrial age.

Chapter 18

1500-1800

New Patterns in New Worlds

COLONIALISM AND INDIGENOUS RESPONSES IN THE AMERICAS

THE AMERICAS IN 1750
- Spanish
- Portuguese
- British
- French
- Dutch

ATLANTIC OCEAN

PACIFIC OCEAN

Alonso Ortíz was a deadbeat. He fled from his creditors in Zafra, Estremadura, in southwestern Spain, in the early 1770s to find a new life in the Americas. In Mexico City, with the help of borrowed money, he set up shop as a tanner. His business flourished and, with a partner, Ortíz expanded into two rented buildings. Eight Native American employees, whom he had trained, did the actual labor of stomping the hides in the vats filled with tanning acids. A black slave, belonging to his partner, was the

Seeing Patterns

▶ What is the significance of western Europeans acquiring the Americas as a warm-weather extension of their northern continent?

▶ What was the main pattern of social development in colonial America during the period 1500–1800?

▶ Why and how did European settlers in South and North America strive for self-government, and how successful were they in achieving their goals?

supervisor. Happy that he no longer had to take his shoes off to work, Ortíz concentrated on giving instructions and hustling up business.

Ortíz's situation in Mexico City was not entirely legal however. He had left his wife, Eleanor González, and children alone in Zafra, though the law required that families should be united. The authorities rarely enforced this law, but that was no guarantee for Ortíz. Furthermore, he had not yet sent his family any remittances, leaving Eleanor to rely on the largesse of her two brothers back home for survival. And then, there was still the debt. Ortíz had reasons to be afraid of the law.

To avoid prosecution, Ortíz wrote a letter to Eleanor. In this letter, he proudly described the comfortable position he had achieved. He announced that his kind business partner was sending her a sum of money sufficient to begin preparations for her departure from Spain. To his creditors, Ortíz promised to send 100 tanned hides within a year. "Your arrival would bring me great joy," he wrote to Eleanor, reneging on an original promise to be already back home in Spain. Evidently aware of her reluctance to join him in Mexico, Ortíz closed his letter with a request to grant him 4 more years

The Meeting of Moctezuma and Cortés. Antonio de Solís (1610–1686) served as the official historian of the Indies for the Spanish monarchy. In this capacity he produced his monumental work, *The History of the Conquest of Mexico by the Spaniards*. Removed by more than 150 years from the events, de Solís relied heavily on the work of previous chroniclers of the Conquest, such as Bernal Diaz del Castillo, and Cortés himself. With its artful writing style, de Solis's book was a bestseller, helping to solidify a heroic view of the Conquest that persists to this day. Shown here is the frontispiece to de Solis's book; much of what is depicted is fanciful or imaginary: Tenochtitlán is portrayed as a European-style city, and the dress of the Aztecs bears little resemblance to what they actually wore.

abroad and to do so with a notarized document from her hand. Unfortunately, we do not know her answer.

The Ortíz family drama gives a human face to European emigration and colonialism from Europe to the Americas. Like Alonso Ortíz, some 300,000 other Spaniards emigrated between 1500 and 1800. They came alone or with family, temporarily or for good, and either failed or succeeded in their new lives. A few hundred letters by emigrants exist, giving us glimpses of their lives in Mexico, Peru, and other parts of the Americas conquered by the Spanish and Portuguese in the sixteenth century. As these relatively privileged immigrants settled, they hoped to build successful enterprises using the labor of Native Americans as well as black slaves imported from Africa. As the example of Ortíz documents, even in the socially not very prestigious craft of tanning a man could achieve a measure of comfort by having people of even lower status working for him.

The Americas became an extension of Europe. European settlers extracted mineral and agricultural resources from these new lands. In Europe these resources had become increasingly expensive and impractical to produce (if they could be produced at all). A pattern emerged in which gold and silver, as well as agricultural products that could not be grown in Europe's cooler climate—such as brazilwood, sugar, tobacco, rice, cacao, indigo, and cochineal—were intensively exploited. In their role as supplementary subtropical and tropical extensions of Europe, the Americas became a crucial factor for Europe's changing position in the world. First, Europe acquired large quantities of precious metals, which its two largest competitors, India and China, lacked. Second, with its new access to warm-weather agricultural products, Europe rose to a position of agrarian autonomy similar to that of India and China. In terms of resources, compared with the principal religious civilizations of India and China, Europe grew between 1550 and 1800 from a position of inferiority to one of near parity.

The Colonial Americas: Europe's Warm-Weather Extension

The European extension into the subtropical and tropical Americas followed Columbus's pursuit of a sea route to India and its spices that would circumvent the Mediterranean and its dominance by Muslim traders. The Spaniards justified the conquest of these new continents and their Native American inhabitants with Christ's command to convert the heathen in the Spanish Habsburg world empire, the glorious final empire before Christ's return. They financed their imperial expansion as well as their wars against Ottoman and European rivals with American gold and silver, leaving little for domestic investment in productive enterprises. A pattern evolved in which Iberian settlers transformed the Americas into mineral-extracting and agrarian colonies based on either cheap or forced labor.

The Conquest of Mexico and Peru

The Spanish conquerors of the Aztec and Inca Empires, although small in number, succeeded by exploiting internal weaknesses in the empires. They swiftly eliminated the top of the power structures, paralyzing the decision-making apparatuses long enough for their conquests to succeed. Soon after the conquests, the Old World disease of smallpox—to which New World inhabitants had never been exposed and, therefore, had never developed immunity—ravaged the Native American population and dramatically reduced the indigenous labor force. To make up for this reduction, colonial authorities imported black slaves from Africa for employment in mines and in agriculture. Black Africans, who had long been in contact with Eurasia, were, similar to Europeans, less susceptible to smallpox. A three-tiered society of European immigrants, Native Americans, and black slaves emerged in the Spanish and Portuguese Americas.

From Trade Posts to Conquest Columbus had discovered the Caribbean islands under a royal commission, which entitled him to build fortified posts and to trade with the indigenous Taínos. The Portuguese had pioneered the use of fortified trade posts in their explorations along the costs of West Africa. Friendly trade relations with the Taínos, however, quickly deteriorated into outright exploitation, with the Spaniards usurping the traditional entitlements of the Taíno chiefs to the labor of their tribesmen, who panned gold in rivers or mined it in shallow shafts. With the help of **land-labor grants** (Spanish *encomiendas*), the Spanish took over from the Taíno chiefs and, through forced labor, amassed sizeable quantities of gold. What had begun as trade post settlement turned into full-blown conquest.

Land-labor grant (*encomienda*): Land grant by the government to an entrepreneur entitling him to use forced indigenous or imported slave labor on this land for the exploitation of agricultural and mineral resources.

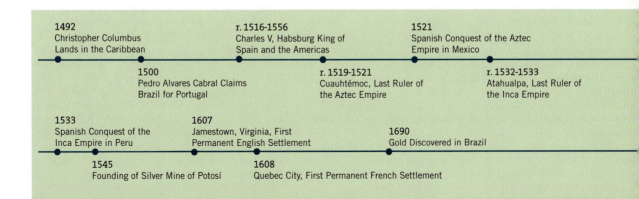

1492
Christopher Columbus
Lands in the Caribbean

r. 1516-1556
Charles V, Habsburg King of
Spain and the Americas

1521
Spanish Conquest of the Aztec
Empire in Mexico

1500
Pedro Alvares Cabral Claims
Brazil for Portugal

r. 1519-1521
Cuauhtémoc, Last Ruler of
the Aztec Empire

r. 1532-1533
Atahualpa, Last Ruler of
the Inca Empire

1533
Spanish Conquest of the
Inca Empire in Peru

1607
Jamestown, Virginia, First
Permanent English Settlement

1690
Gold Discovered in Brazil

1545
Founding of Silver Mine of Potosí

1608
Quebec City, First Permanent French Settlement

The Fourth Part of the World. "Now these [three] parts of the Earth have been extensively explored," the German cartographer Martin Waldseemüller wrote in 1507 (see Chapter 17), "but now a fourth part has been discovered by Amerigo Vespucci." This "fourth part"— America, both North and South—fired European imaginations. Drawn in 1562 by Diego Gutiérrez, the map shown here catalogs the wonders of America, as viewed through Spanish eyes. After just four decades of European exploration, the continent is already filled with place names. The course of the Amazon is accurately shown, and parrots, monkeys, cannibals, giants, and an erupting volcano speak to the riches that bedazzled the settlers. In the North Atlantic, Charles V, ruler of Spain's vast New World empire, glides across in a chariot to claim his possessions.

The Spaniards conquered the Caribbean islands not only through force. Much more severe in its consequences was the indirect conquest through disease. The Old World disease of smallpox quickly wiped out the estimated 250,000 to 1 million Taínos (estimates vary widely) on the larger northern islands as well as the less numerous Caribs on the smaller southern Caribbean islands. Isolated for more than 10,000 years from the rest of humankind, Native Americans possessed no immunity against smallpox and were similarly ravaged by other introduced diseases such as measles, diphtheria, mumps, plague, influenza, typhoid, malaria, and yellow fever.

Protests, mostly among members of the clergy, arose against both the brutal labor exploitation by the conquerors and the helplessness of the Taínos dying of disease. Unfortunately, the protesters remained a small minority, even within the clergy. The best-known among several was Bartolomé de las Casas (1474–1566), from a family of merchants in Seville. Las Casas had practiced law before emigrating to Hispaniola, where he received an *encomienda*. After becoming a priest in 1510 and later a Dominican monk, however, he became a bitter opponent of the labor grant system. He demanded nothing less than the end of this institution, something that did not come until after 1542 with the introduction of the *repartimiento* system.

First Mainland Conquests

Another early settler on Hispaniola was Hernán Cortés (1485–1547). His father was a lower-level nobleman in Estremadura, a rough, formerly Islamic frontier region in southwestern Iberia. Chosen by his parents for a career in law, Cortés learned Latin but left the university before graduation. After his arrival in the New World in 1504, he advanced quickly from governmental scribe in Hispaniola to mayor of Santiago in Cuba. Thanks to several labor grants, he became rich. When the Cuban governor asked him in the fall of 1518 to equip and lead a small preparatory expedition for trade and exploration to the Yucatán Peninsula in southeastern Mexico, Cortés enthusiastically agreed. Within a month he assembled 300 men, considerably exceeding his contract. The governor tried to stop him, but Cortés departed quickly for the American mainland.

As the Cuban governor had feared, Cortés did not bother with trade posts in Yucatán. The Spanish had previously learned of the existence of the Aztec Empire, with its immense silver and gold treasures. In a first encounter,

Cultural Intermediary. The Tabascans gave Malinche, or Dona Marina, to Hernán Cortés as a form of tribute after they were defeated by the Spanish. Malinche served Cortés as a translator and mistress, filling a central role in Cortés's eventual victory over the Aztecs. She was in many respects the principal face of the Spanish and is always depicted center stage in Native American visual accounts of the conquest.

Cortés's motley force—numbering by now about 530 Spanish men—defeated a vastly superior indigenous force at Tabasco, mostly thanks to the Spaniards' pikes, swords, daggers, plate armor, and a few matchlock muskets and horses. Their steel weapons and armor proved superior in hand-to-hand combat to the obsidian-spiked lances, wooden swords, and quilted cotton vests of the defenders. Among the gifts of submission presented by the defeated Native Americans in Tabasco was Malinche, a Nahuatl [NA-hu-wah]-speaking woman whose father, an Aztec lord, had given her as a teenager to the Tabascans. Malinche quickly learned Spanish and became the consort of Cortés, teaching him about the subtleties of Aztec culture. In her role as translator, Malinche was nearly as decisive as Cortés in shaping events. Indeed, Aztecs often used the name of Malinche when addressing Cortés, forgetting that her voice was not that of Cortés. With Tabasco conquered, Cortés quickly moved on; he was afraid that the Cuban governor, who was in pursuit, would otherwise force him to return to Cuba.

Conquest of the Aztec Empire   On the southeast coast of Mexico, Cortés founded the city of Veracruz as a base from which to move inland. In the city, he had his followers elect a town council, which made Cortés their head and chief justice, allowing Cortés to claim legitimacy for his march inland. To prevent opponents in his camp from notifying the Cuban governor of his usurpation of authority, Cortés had all ships stripped of their gear and the hulls sunk. Marching inland, the Spaniards ran into resistance from indigenous people, suffering their first losses of horses and men. Although bloodied, they continued their march with thousands of Native American allies, most notably the Tlaxcalans, traditional enemies of the Aztecs. The support from these indigenous peoples made a crucial difference when Cortés and his army reached the court of the Aztecs.

Tlaxcalan Support for Cortés

"Xicotenga [Shee-co-TEN-ga, the ruler of Tlaxcala] made many complaints about Montezuma [Moctezuma] and his allies, for they were all enemies of the Tlaxcalans and made war on them. However, they had defended themselves very well, and had meant to do the same against us. But although they had gathered against us with all their warriors three times, this had not been possible because we were invincible. Having discovered this they wished to become friends with us and vassals of our lord the Emperor for they felt certain that in our company, their wives, and their children would be guarded and protected, and freed from the danger of surprise attacks by the treacherous Mexicans [Aztecs]. Xicotenga said much else besides, and placed his people and his city at our disposal."

—Bernal Díaz del Castillo, *The Conquest of New Spain*. Translated by J. M. Cohen, pp. 167–168. London: Penguin, 1963.

When Cortés arrived at the city of Tenochtitlán on November 2, 1519, the Emperor Moctezuma II (r. 1502–1519) was in a quandary over how to deal with these invaders whose depredations neither his tributaries nor his enemies had been able to stop. To gain some time for deliberating about how to deal with Cortés, Moctezuma greeted the Spaniard in person on one of the causeways leading to the city and invited him to his palace. Cortés and his company, now numbering some 600 Spaniards, took up quarters in the palace precincts. After a week of gradually deteriorating discussions, Cortés suddenly put the incredulous emperor under house arrest and made him swear allegiance to Charles V.

Before being able to contemplate his next move, however, Cortés was diverted by the need to march back east, where troops from Cuba had arrived to arrest him. After defeating those troops, he enrolled the straggling Cuban soldiers into his own service and marched back to Tenochtitlán. During his absence, the Spaniards who had remained in Mocte-zuma's palace had massacred a number of unarmed Aztec nobles participating in a religious ceremony. An infuriated crowd of Tenochtitlán's inhabitants invaded the palace. In the melee, Moctezuma and some 200 Spaniards died. The rest of the Spanish fled for their lives, retreating east to their Tlaxcalan allies, who, fortunately, remained loyal. Here, after his return, the indomitable Cortés devised a new plan for capturing Tenochtitlán.

After 10 months of preparations, the Spaniards returned to the Aztec capital. Numbering now about 2,000 Spanish soldiers and assisted by some 50,000 Native American troops, Cortés laid siege to the city, bombarding it from ships he had built in the lake and razing buildings during forays onto land. After nearly 3 months, much of the city was in ruins, fresh water and food became scarce, and smallpox began to decimate the population of some 3–4 million inhabitants in the Valley of Mexico and 25 million in the Aztec Empire. On August 21, 1521, the Spaniards and their al-lies stormed the city and looted its gold treasury. They captured the fiercely resisting last emperor, Cuauhtémoc [Cu-aw-TAY-moc], a few days later and executed him in captivity in 1525, thus ending the Aztec Empire (see Map 18.1).

Conquest of the Inca Empire   At about the same time, a relative of Cortés, Francisco Pizarro (ca. 1475–1541), conceived a plan to conquer the Andean empire of the Incas (which, in 1492, comprised some 9–12 million inhabitants). Pizarro, like Cortés born in Estremadura, was an illegitimate son of an infantry captain from the lower nobility. Illiterate and without education, he had come to Hispaniola as part of an expedition in 1513 that discovered Panama and the Pacific. He became mayor of Panama City, acquired some wealth, and began to hear rumors about an empire of gold and silver to the south. After a failed initial expedition, he and 13 fol-lowers captured some precious metal from an oceangoing Inca sailing raft. Since the governor of Panama opposed a new expedition, Pizarro traveled to Spain to receive direct authorization for a trade post from Charles V. He returned with his permit, four brothers, and other relatives to Panama City and, in late December 1530, de-parted south with a host of 183 men.

In a grimly fortuitous bit of luck for Pizarro, smallpox had preceded him in his ex-pedition. In the later 1520s, the disease had ravaged the Inca Empire, killing the em-peror and his heir apparent. A brutal and protracted war of succession between two surviving sons broke out. Atahualpa, in the north, sent his army south to the capital, Cuzco, where it defeated his half-brother, Huascar. When Pizarro entered the Inca Empire, Atahualpa was encamped with an army of 40,000 men near the northern town of Cajamarca, on his way south to Cuzco to install himself as emperor. Arriving at Cajamarca, Pizarro succeeded in arranging an unarmed audience with Atahualpa in the town square. On the fateful day of November 16, 1532, Atahualpa came to this audience, surrounded by several thousand unarmed retainers, while Pizarro hid his soldiers in and behind the buildings around the square. At a signal, these sol-diers rushed into the square, horses neighing, guns blazing, and swords unsheathed. Some soldiers captured Atahualpa to hold him hostage, while others charged the retainers. A bloodbath ensued, with some 1,500 panic-stricken and fleeing Inca re-tainers killed or trampled to death. When survivors reached the Inca camp, most of the encamped army panicked as well, scattering in all directions. Not one Spanish soldier was killed, and the whole massacre was over in less than an hour.

European Exploration of the Americas, 1519–1542

Central and North America, 1519–1550

→ Cortés, 1519–21
⇢ Cortés, 1524–25
→ Narváez and de Vaca, 1528–36
→ De Soto, 1539–43
→ Alarcón, 1540
→ Coronado, 1540–42

Cortés's Expedition to Tenochtitlán

→ Cortés's route to Tenochtitlán, 1519
⇢ Forced march, 1520
⇢ Retreat and return, 1520–21

South America, 1526–1542

→ Cabot, 1526
→ Francisco Pizarro, 1531–33
→ Amalgro, 1535–37
→ Federmann, 1537–39
→ Benalcazar, 1538–39
→ Orrellana, 1540
→ Gonzalo Pizarro, 1540–42
→ Valdivia, 1540–47
→ Quesada, 1542

MAP **18.1** The European Exploration of the Americas, 1519–1542.

With his ambush, Pizarro succeeded in paralyzing the empire at the very top. Without their emperor Atahualpa, none of the generals in Cuzco dared to seize the initiative. Instead of ordering his captors to liberate him, Atahualpa sought to pacify their greed with a room full of gold and silver as ransom. In the following 2 months, Inca administrators delivered immense quantities of precious metals to Pizarro.

Inevitably, resentment arose among the Spaniards over the distribution of the loot. When the time came to march on Cuzco, those Spaniards who felt shortchanged by the unequal distribution of loot cooled their anger by instigating the execution of the hapless Atahualpa on July 26, 1533.

The Spaniards took Cuzco 3 months later. They did so against minimal resistance, massacring the inhabitants and stripping the city of its immense gold and silver treasures. Pizarro did not stay long in the now worthless, isolated capital in the Andes. Leaving the emperor in Cuzco, in 1535 Pizarro founded a new capital, Lima, which was more conveniently located on the coast and about halfway between Cajamarca and Cuzco. As the immensity of their defeat began to sink in, the hitherto paralyzed Inca generals finally bestirred themselves. Learning from past mistakes, they avoided mass battles, focused on deadly guerilla strikes, and rebuilt a kingdom that held out until 1572. It was only then that the Spanish gained full control of the Inca Empire.

Conquest by Surprise. The Spanish conqueror Francisco Pizarro captured Emperor Atahualpa (top left) in an ambush (top middle). Atahualpa promised a roomful of gold in return for his release, but the Spaniards collected the gold (top right) and murdered Atahualpa (right) before generals of the Inca army could organize an armed resistance.

The Portuguese Conquest of Brazil

The Portuguese were not far behind the Spaniards in their pursuit of conquest. Navigators of three fleets, two Spanish and one Portuguese, sighted the Brazilian coast in 1499/1500. The Portuguese commander Pedro Alvares Cabral, on his way to India, immediately notified his king of his discovery so that the latter could claim the land as lying within the Portuguese, not Spanish, sphere of interest (see Chapter 16). Brazil's indigenous population at that time is estimated to have amounted to nearly 5 million. The great majority were tribally organized and lived in temporary or permanent villages based on agriculture, fishing, and hunting. Only a small minority in remote areas of the Amazon were pure foragers.

The Portuguese were interested initially in trade with the tribes, mostly for a type of hardwood called "brazilwood," which was ground into sawdust and used as a red dye. When French traders showed up, ignoring the Portuguese commercial treaties with the tribes, the Portuguese crown shifted from simple trade agreements to trade post settlements. This involved giving land grants to commoners and lower noblemen with the obligation to build fortified coastal villages for settlers and to engage in agriculture and friendly trade. By the mid-sixteenth century, a handful of these villages became successful, their inhabitants intermarrying with the surrounding indigenous chieftain families and establishing sugarcane plantations.

Explanations for the Spanish Success

The slow progression of the Portuguese in tribal Brazil is readily understood. But the stupendous victories of handfuls of Spaniards over huge empires with millions of inhabitants and large cities defy easy explanation. Five factors invite consideration.

First, and most importantly, the conquistadors went straight to the top of the imperial pyramid. The emperors and their courts expected diplomatic deference by inferiors, among whom they included the minuscule band of Spaniards. Confronted, instead, with a calculated combination of arrogance and brutality, the Spaniards threw the emperors and courts off balance. Exploiting their opportunity, the conquistadors struck with deadly determination. Most importantly, as the emperors were removed from the top level, their administration immediately below fell into paralysis, unable to seize the initiative and respond in a timely fashion. There are parallels in world history for this phenomenon of administrative paralysis after the defeat of a ruler. Alexander the Great's victory over Darius III in the invasion of Achaemenid Persia in 331 BCE, Tariq ibn Ziyad's victory over Roderic in the Berber-Arab invasion of Visigothic Iberia in 711 CE, and William the Conqueror's victory over Harold Godwinson in the Norman invasion of England in 1066 come to mind as examples.

Second, both the Aztec and Inca Empires were relatively recent creations in which there were individuals and groups who contested the hierarchical power structure. The conquistadors either found allies among the subject populations or encountered a divided leadership. In either case, they were able to exploit divisions in the empires.

Third, European-introduced diseases, traveling faster than the conquerors, took a devastating toll. In both empires, smallpox hit at critical moments during or right before the Spanish invasions, causing major disruptions.

Fourth, thanks to horses and superior European steel weapons and armor, primarily pikes, swords, and breast plates, small numbers of Spaniards were able to hold large numbers of attacking Aztecs and Incas at bay in hand-to-hand combat. Contrary to widespread belief, cannons and matchlock muskets were less important since they were useless in close encounters. Firearms were still too slow and inaccurate to be decisive.

In contrast to a popular view, a fifth factor, indigenous religion, was probably of least significance. According to this interpretation, Moctezuma was immobilized by his belief in the prophecy of having to relinquish his power to the savior Quetzalcoatl returning from his mythical city of Tlapallan on the east coast (see Chapter 15). Modern scholarship provides convincing reasons, however, to declare this prophecy a postconquest legend, circulated by Cortés both to flatter Charles V and to aggrandize himself as a savior.

Spanish Steel. The Lienzo de Tlaxcala, from the middle part of the sixteenth century, is our best visual source for the conquest of Mexico. In this scene, Malinche, protected by a shield, directs the battle on the causeway leading to Tenochtitlán. The two Spanish soldiers behind her, one fully armored, brandish steel swords, which were more effective than the obsidian blades carried by the Aztec defenders (one of whom is dressed in leopard skins), shown on the left.

The Establishment of Colonial Institutions

The Spanish crown established administrative hierarchies in the Americas, similar to those of the Aztecs and Incas, with governors at the top of the hierarchy and descending through lower ranks of functionaries. A small degree of settler autonomy was permitted through town and city councils, but the crown was determined to make the Americas a territorial extension of the European pattern of fiscal–military state formation. Several hundred thousand settlers (including Alonso Ortíz) found a new life in the Americas, mostly as urban craftspeople, administrators, and professionals. By the early seventeenth century, a powerful elite of Spanish who had been born in America, called **Creoles** (Spanish *criollos*, Portuguese *crioules*, natives) was in place, first to assist and later to replace most of the administrators sent from Spain in the governance of the Americas (see Map 18.2).

Creoles: American-born descendants of European, primarily Iberian, immigrants.

From Conquest to Colonialism The unimaginable riches of Cortés and Pizarro inspired numerous further expeditions. Adventurers struck out with small bands of followers into Central and North America, Chile, and the Amazon. Their expeditions, however, yielded only modest amounts of gold and earned more from selling captured Native Americans into slavery. One of the best-known and most infamous adventurers was Lope de Aguirre, whose exploits in the Amazon were made famous by the 1972 movie *Aguirre, the Wrath of God*. Only the fortified village chiefdoms of the 1 million Muisca, in what is today Colombia, yielded significant quantities of gold to their conquerors, in 1537. In the north, expeditions penetrated as far as Arizona, New Mexico, Texas, Oklahoma, Kansas, and Florida but encountered only villagers and the relatively poor Pueblo towns. No new golden kingdoms (the mythical El Dorado, or "golden city") beyond the Aztec and Inca Empires were discovered in the Americas.

In the mid-sixteenth century, easy looting was replaced by a search for the mines from where the precious metals came. In northern Mexico, Native Americans led a group of soldiers and missionaries in 1547 to a number of rich silver mines. In addition, explorers discovered silver in Bolivia (1545) and northern Mexico (1556), gold in Chile (1552), and mercury in Peru (1563). The conquistadors shifted from looting to the exploitation of Native American labor in mines and in agriculture.

Bureaucratic Efficiency During the first two generations after the conquest, Spain maintained an efficient colonial administration, which delivered between 50 and 60 percent of the colonies' revenues to Spain. These revenues contributed as much as one-quarter to the Spanish crown budget. In addition, the viceroyalty of New Spain in Mexico remitted another 25 percent of its revenues to the Philippines, the Pacific province for which it was administratively responsible from 1571 onward. As in Spain, settlers in New Spain had to pay up to 40 different taxes and dues, levied on imports and exports, internal trade, mining, and sales. The only income tax was the tithe to the church, which the administration collected and, at times, used for its own budgetary purposes. Altogether, however, for the settlers the tax level was lower in the New World than in Spain, and the same was true for the English and French colonies in North America.

In the 1540s the government introduced rotating **labor assignments** (*repartimientos*) to phase out the encomiendas which powerful owners sought to perpetuate within their families. This institution of rotating labor assignments was a

Labor assignment (*repartimiento*): Obligation by villagers to send stipulated numbers of people as laborers to a contractor, who had the right to exploit a mine or other labor-intensive enterprise; the contractors paid the laborers minimal wages and bound them through debt peonage to their businesses.

continuation of the mit'a system, which the Incas had devised as a form of taxation, in the absence of money and easy transportation of crops in their empire (see Chapter 15). Rotating labor assignments meant that for fixed times a certain percentage of villagers had to provide labor to the state at low pay for road building, drainage, transportation, and mining. Private entrepreneurs could also contract for indigenous labor assignments, especially in mining regions.

In Mexico the repartimiento fell out of use in the first half of the seventeenth century as a result of the continuing Native American population decline due to recurring smallpox epidemics. It is estimated that the indigenous population in the Americas, from a height of 54 million in 1550, declined to 10 million by 1700 before recovering again. The replacement for the lost workers was wage labor. In highland Peru, where the indigenous population was less densely settled and the effects of smallpox less ravaging, the assignment system lasted to the end of the colonial period. Wage labor expanded there as well. Wages for Native Americans and blacks remained everywhere lower than for those for Creoles.

The Rise of the Creoles   Administrative and fiscal efficiency, however, did not last very long. The wars of the Spanish Habsburg Empire cost more than the crown was able to collect in revenues. King Philip II (r. 1556–1598) had to declare bankruptcy four times between 1557 and 1596. In order to make up the financial deficit, the crown began to sell offices in the Americas to the highest bidders. The first offices put on the block were elective positions in the municipal councils. By the end of the century, Creoles had purchased life appointments in city councils as well as positions as scribes, local judges, police chiefs, directors of processions and festivities, and other sinecures. In these positions, they collected fees and rents for their services. Local oligarchies emerged, effectively ending whatever elective, participatory politics existed in Spanish colonial America.

Over the course of the seventeenth century a majority of administrative positions became available for purchase. As might be imagined, the effects of the change from recruitment by merit to recruitment by wealth on the functioning of the bureaucracy were far-reaching. Creoles advanced on a broad front in the administrative positions, while fewer Spaniards found it attractive to buy their American positions from overseas. The only opportunities which European Spaniards still found enticing were the nearly 300 positions of governors and inspectors since these jobs gave their owners the right to subject the Native Americans to forced purchases of goods, yielding huge profits. For the most part, wealthy Spanish merchants delegated junior partners into these highly lucrative activities. By 1700, the consequences of the Spanish crown selling most of its American administrative offices were a decline in the competence of office holders, the emergence of a Creole elite able to bend the Spanish administration increasingly to its will, and a decentralization of the decision-making processes.

Northwest European Interference   As Spain's administrative grip on the Americas weakened during the seventeenth century, the need to defend the continents militarily against European interlopers arose. At the beginning, there were European privateers, holding royal charters, who harassed Spanish silver shipments and ports in the Caribbean. In the early seventeenth century, the French, English, and Dutch governments sent ships to occupy the smaller Caribbean islands not claimed by Spain. Privateer and contraband traders stationed on these islands engaged in further raiding and pillaging, severely damaging Spain's monopoly of shipping between Europe and the Caribbean.

Conquests of Spanish islands followed in the second half of the century. England captured Jamaica in 1655, and France colonized western Hispaniola in 1665, making it one of their most profitable sugar-producing colonies. Along the Pacific coast, depredations continued into the middle of the eighteenth century. Here, the galleons of the annual Acapulco–Manila fleet carrying silver from Mexico to China and returning with Chinese silks, porcelain, and lacquerware were the targets of English privateers. Over the course of the seventeenth century, Spain allocated one-half to two-thirds of its American revenues to the defense of its annual treasure fleets and Caribbean possessions, which continued despite limited losses to pirates and storms. Only the defense of the many islands eventually proved too difficult for the thinly stretched Spanish forces to maintain.

Bourbon Reforms   The last of the Spanish Habsburg rulers produced no heirs, and after the demise of the dynasty in 1700, the new French-descended dynasty of the Bourbons made major efforts to regain control over their American possessions. They had to begin from a discouragingly weak position as nearly 90 percent of all goods traded from Europe to the Americas were of non-Spanish origin. Fortunately, population increases among the settlers as well as the Native Americans (after having overcome their horrific losses to the epidemics) offered opportunities to Spanish manufacturers and merchants. After several false starts, in the middle of the eighteenth century the Bourbon reform program began to show results.

The reforms aimed at improved naval connections and administrative control between the mother country and the colonies. The monopolistic annual armed silver fleet was greatly reduced. Instead, the government authorized more frequent single sailings at different times of the year. Newly formed Spanish companies, receiving exclusive rights at specific ports, succeeded in reducing contraband trade. Elections took place again for municipal councils. Spanish-born salaried officials replaced scores of Creole tax and office farmers. The original two viceroyalties were subdivided into four, to improve administrative control. The sale of tobacco and brandy became state monopolies. Silver mining and cotton textile manufacturing were expanded. By the second half of the eighteenth century, Spain had regained a measure of control over its colonies.

As a result, tax receipts rose substantially. Government revenues increased more than twofold, even taking into account the inflation of the late eighteenth century. In the end, however, the reforms remained incomplete. Since the Spanish economy was not also reformed, in terms of expanding crafts production and urbanization, the changes did not diminish the English and French dominance of the import market by much. Spain failed to produce textiles, metalwares, and household goods at competitive prices for the colonies; and as a result, English and French exports to the Americas remained high.

Early Portuguese Colonialism   In contrast to the Spanish Americas, the Portuguese overseas province of Brazil remained initially confined to a broad coastal strip, which developed only slowly during the sixteenth century. The first governor-general, whose rank was equivalent to a Spanish viceroy, arrived in 1549. He and

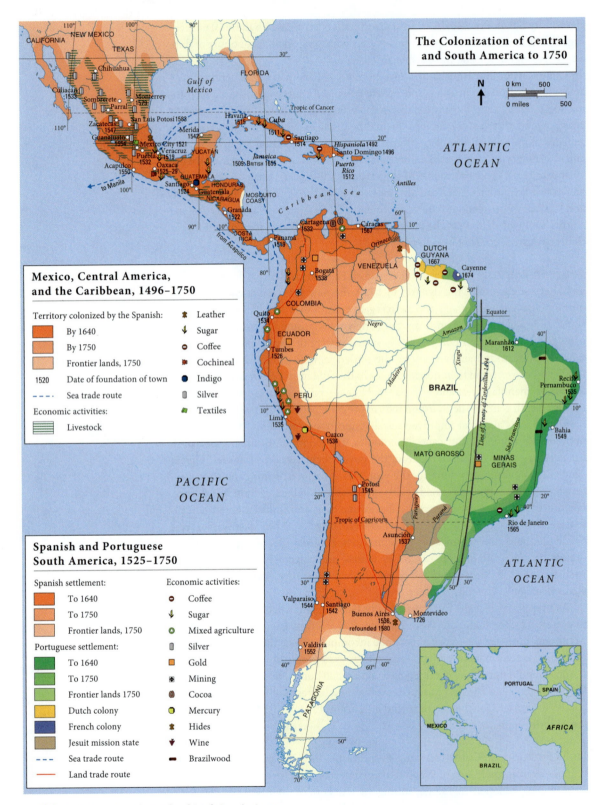

The Colonization of Central
and South America to 1750

N

0 km   500

0 miles   500

**Mexico, Central America,
and the Caribbean, 1496–1750**

Territory colonized by the Spanish:

▮	By 1640	🦌 Leather
▮	By 1750	↓ Sugar
▮	Frontier lands, 1750	⊖ Coffee
1520	Date of foundation of town	✴ Cochineal
- - -	Sea trade route	● Indigo
		▯ Silver
Economic activities:		◿ Textiles
▤ Livestock		

**Spanish and Portuguese
South America, 1525–1750**

Spanish settlement: Economic activities:

▮	To 1640	⊖	Coffee
▮	To 1750	↓	Sugar
▮	Frontier lands, 1750	◉	Mixed agriculture
Portuguese settlement:		▯	Silver
▮	To 1640	▪	Gold
▮	To 1750	⊕	Mining
▮	Frontier lands 1750	◉	Cocoa
▮	Dutch colony	◉	Mercury
▮	French colony	✶	Hides
▮	Jesuit mission state	♥	Wine
- - -	Sea trade route	▬	Brazilwood
——	Land trade route		

MAP **18.2** The Colonization of Central and South America to 1750.

his successors were members of the high aristocracy, but their positions were salaried and subject to term limits. As the colony grew, the crown created a council in the capital of Lisbon for all Brazilian appointments and established a high court for all judicial affairs in Bahia, northern Brazil. Commoners with law degrees from the Portuguese university of Coimbra filled the nonmilitary colonial positions. In the early seventeenth century, however, offices became as open to purchase as in the Spanish colonies, although not on the city council level, where a complex indirect electoral process survived.

Jesuits converted the Native Americans, whom they transported to villages that the Jesuits administered. Colonial cities and Jesuits repeatedly clashed over the slave raids of the "pioneers" (*bandeirantes*) in village territories. The bandeirantes came mostly from São Paulo in the south and roamed the interior in search of human prey. Native American slaves were in demand on the wheat farms and cattle ranches of São Paulo as well as the sugar plantations of the northeast. Although the Portuguese crown and church had, like the Spanish, forbidden the enslavement of Native Americans, the bandei-

Mine Workers. The discovery of gold and diamonds in Minas Gerais led to a boom, but did little to contribute to the long-term health of the Brazilian economy. With the Native American population decimated by disease, African slaves performed the back-breaking work.

rantes exploited a loophole. The law was interpreted as allowing the enslavement of Native Americans who resisted conversion to Christianity. For a long time, Lisbon and the Jesuits were powerless against this flagrantly self-interested interpretation.

Expansion into the Interior   In the middle of the seventeenth century, the Jesuits and Native Americans finally succeeded in pushing many bandeirantes west and north, where they switched from slave raiding to prospecting for gold. In the far north, however, the raids continued until 1680, when the Portuguese administration finally prevailed and imposed an end to Native American slavery, almost a century and a half after Spain. Ironically, it was mostly thanks to the "pioneer" raids for slaves that Brazil expanded westward, well beyond the demarcation line of Tordesillas agreed to with Spain, to assume the borders it has today.

As a result of gold discoveries in Minas Gerais in 1690 by bandeirantes, the European immigrant population increased rapidly, from 1 to 2 million during the 1700s. Minas Gerais, located north of Rio de Janeiro, was the first inland region of the colony to attract settlers. By contrast, as a result of smallpox epidemics beginning in the 1650s in the Brazilian interior, the Native American population declined massively, not to expand again until the end of the eighteenth century. To replace the loss of labor, Brazilians imported slaves from Africa, at first to work in the sugar plantations and, after 1690, in the mines, where their numbers increased to two-thirds of the labor force. In contrast to Spanish mines, Brazilian mines were surface operations requiring only minimal equipment outlays. Most blacks worked with pickaxes and shovels. The peak of the gold boom came in the 1750s, when the importance of gold was second only to that of sugar on the list of Brazilian exports to Europe.

Early in the gold boom, the crown created a new Ministry of the Navy and Overseas Territories, which greatly expanded the administrative structure in Brazil. It established 14 regions and a second high court in Rio de Janeiro, which replaced Bahia as the capital in 1736. The ministry in Lisbon ended the sale of offices, increased the efficiency of tax collection, and encouraged Brazilian textile manufacturing to render the province more independent from English imports. By the mid-1700s, Brazil was a flourishing overseas colony of Portugal, producing brazilwood, sugar, gold, tobacco, cacao, and vanilla for export.

North American Settlements   Efforts at settlement in the less hospitable North America in the sixteenth century were unsuccessful. Only in the early part of the seventeenth century did French, English, and Dutch merchant investors succeed on the northeastern coast in establishing small communities of settlers, who grew their own food on land purchased from the local Native American villagers. These settlements were Jamestown (founded in 1607 in today's Virginia), Quebec (1608, Canada), Plymouth and Boston (1620 and 1630, respectively, New England), and New Amsterdam (1625, New York). Subsistence agriculture and fur, however, were meager ingredients for the settlements to prosper. The northerly settlements struggled through the seventeenth century, sustained either by Catholic missionary efforts or by the Protestant enthusiasm of the Puritans who had escaped persecution in England. Southern places like Jamestown survived because they adopted tobacco, a warm-weather crop, as a cash crop for export to Europe. In contrast to Mexico and Peru, the North American settlements were not followed—at least not at first—by territorial conquests (see Map 18.3).

Native Americans   Once they had settled down and established themselves agriculturally, the European arrivals in North America began supplementing agriculture with trade. They exchanged metal and glass wares, beads and seashells for furs, especially beaver pelts, with the Native American tribal groups of the interior. The more these tribal groups came into contact with the European traders, however, the more dramatic the demographic impact of the trade on them was: Smallpox, already a menace during the 1500s in North America, became devastating as contacts intensified. In New England, for example, of the ca. 144,000 estimated Native Americans in 1600, fewer than 15,000 remained in 1620. The introduction of guns contributed an additional lethal factor to trading arrangements: English, French, and Dutch traders provided their favorite Native American trading partners with flintlocks, in order to increase the yield of furs. As a result, in the course of the 1600s the Iroquois in the northeast were able to organize themselves into a heavily armed and independent-minded federation, capable of inflicting heavy losses on rival groups as well as on European traders and settlers.

Further south, in Virginia, the Jamestown settlers encountered the Powhatan confederacy. These Native Americans, living in some 200 well fortified, palisaded villages, dominated the region between the Chesapeake Bay and the Appalachian Mountains. Initially, the Powhatan supplied Jamestown with foodstuffs and sought to integrate the settlement into their confederation. When this invitation to integration failed, however, benevolence turned to hostility and the confederacy raided

The Colonization of North America to 1763

British settlement:
- To 1640
- To 1750
- Frontier lands in 1750

Spanish settlement:
- To 1750
- Frontier lands in 1750

French settlement:
- To 1750
- Frontier lands in 1750

Huron Native American people

→ Trade route

Economic activity, ca. 1750:
- Mixed agriculture
- Fishing
- Fur trapping
- Cattle
- Grain
- Tobacco
- Rice
- Indigo
- Timber
- Shipbuilding
- Ironworks

MAP 18.3 The Colonization of North America to 1763.

Jamestown twice in an attempt to rid their region of foreign settlers. But the latter were able to turn the tables and defeat the Powhatan in 1646, thereafter occupying their lands and reducing them to small scattered remnants. (Pocahontas, daughter of the Powhatan chief at the time of the foundation of Jamestown, was captured during one of the raids, converted to Christianity, and lived in England as the wife of a returning settler for a number of years. Her life has been the subject of many books, fireside stories, two Hollywood movies, and a video game.) The decline of the Powhatan in the later 1600s opened the way for English settlers to move westward, in contrast to New England where the Iroquois, although allied with the English against the French, de facto blocked any western expansion.

The Iroquois were fiercely determined to maintain their dominance of the fur trade and wrought havoc among the Native American groups living between New England and the Great Lakes. In the course of the second half of the 1600s they drove many smaller tribal groups westward into the Great Lakes region and Mississippi plains. Here, these groups settled as refugees. French officials and Jesuit missionaries sought to create some sort of alliance with the refugee tribes, to counterbalance the powerful Iroquois to the east. Many Native Americans converted to Christianity, creating for themselves a Creole Christianity similar to that of the Africans of Kongo and the Mexicans after the Spanish conquest of the Aztecs.

Major population movements also occurred further west on the Great Plains, where the Apaches arrived from the southwest on horses. They had captured horses which had escaped during the Pueblo uprising of 1680–1695 against Spain. The Comanches, who also arrived on horses at the same time from the Great Basin in the Rockies, had, in addition, acquired firearms. The Sioux from the northern forests and the Cheyenne from the Great Basin added to the mix of tribal federations on the Great Plains in the early 1700s. At this time, the great transformation of the Native Americans in the center of North America into horse breeders and horsemen warriors began. Smallpox epidemics did not reach the Plains until the mid 1700s while in the east the ravages of this epidemic had weakened the Iroquois so much that they concluded a peace with the French in 1701.

Land Sale. Signatures of the Iroquois federation leaders to a treaty with Thomas and Richard Penn in 1736. By the terms of this treaty the Iroquois sold land to the founders of the English colony of Pennsylvania. The leaders of the six nations that made up the Iroquois federation (Mohawk, Oneida, Onondaga, Cayuga, Seneca, and Tuscarora) signed with their pictograms. The names were added later.

French Canada   The involvement of the French in the Great Lakes region with refugees fleeing from the Iroquois was part and parcel of an expansion program into the center of North America, begun in 1663. The governor of Quebec had dispatched explorers, fur traders, and missionaries not only into the Great Lakes region but also the Mississippi valley and the Mississippi delta. The French government then sent farmers, craftspeople, and young single women from France with government-issued agricultural implements and livestock to establish settlements. The most successful settlement was in the subtropical district of the delta, called "La Louisianie," where some 300 settlers with 4,000 African slaves founded sugar plantations. Immigration was restricted to French subjects and excluded Protestants. Given these restrictions, Louisiana received only some 30,000 settlers by 1750, in contrast to English North America, with nearly 1.2 million settlers by the same time.

From English to British Colonies

As immigration to New England picked up, the merchant companies in Europe, which had financed the journeys of the settlers, were initially responsible for the administration of about a dozen settlement colonies. The first settlers to demand participation in the colonial administration were Virginian tobacco growers with interests in the European trade. In 1619 they deputized delegates from their villages to meet as the House of Burgesses. They thereby created an early popular assembly in North America, assisting their governor in running the colony. Using this example of self-administration as a model, the other English colonies soon followed suit, with the creation of their own assemblies. In contrast to Spain and Portugal, England—wracked by its internal Anglican–Puritan conflict—was initially uninvolved in the governance of the overseas territories.

When England eventually stepped in and took the governance of the colonies away from the charter merchants and companies in the second half of the seventeenth century, it faced entrenched settler assemblies, especially in New England. Only in New Amsterdam, conquered from the Dutch in 1664–1674 and renamed "New York," did the governor initially rule without an assembly. Many governors were deputies of wealthy aristocrats who never traveled to America but stayed in London. They were powerless to prevent the assemblies from appropriating rights to levy taxes and making appointments. The assemblies thus modeled themselves after Parliament in London. As in England, these assemblies were highly select bodies that excluded poorer settlers, who did not meet the property requirements to vote or stand for elections.

Steady immigration, also from the European mainland, encouraged land speculators in the British colonies to cast their sights beyond the Appalachian Mountains. (According to historical convention, the English are called "British" after the English–Scottish union in 1707.) In 1749, the Ohio Company of Virginia received a royal permit to develop land, together with a protective fort, south of the Ohio River. The French, however, also claimed the Ohio valley, considering it a part of their Canada–Mississippi–Louisiana territory. A few years later, tensions over the valley erupted into open hostility. Initially, the local encounters went badly for the Virginian militia and British army. In 1755, however, the British and French broadened their clash into a worldwide war for dominance in the colonies and Europe, the Seven Years' War of 1756–1763.

The Seven Years' War

Both France and Great Britain borrowed heavily to pour resources into the war. England had the superior navy and France, the superior army. Since the British navy succeeded in choking off French supplies to its increasingly isolated land troops, Britain won the war overseas. In Europe, Britain's failure to supply the troops of its ally Prussia against the Austrian–French alliance caused the war on that front to end in a draw. Overseas, the British gained most of the French holdings in India, several islands in the Caribbean, all of Canada, and all the land east of the Mississippi. The war costs and land swaps, however, proved to be unmanageable for both the vanquished and the victor. The unpaid debts became the root cause of the American, French, and Haitian constitutional revolutions that began 13 years later. Those revolutions, along with the emerging industrialization of Great Britain, signaled the beginning of the modern scientific–industrial age in world history.

The Making of American Societies: Origins and Transformations

The pattern of transforming the Americas into an extension of Europe evolved unevenly. The exploitation of both mineral resources and tropical agricultural resources, powered largely by the forced labor of Native American and black slaves, developed along different lines in the Spanish, Portuguese, French, and English colonies. Before we examine these differences, it is worth pausing for a moment to consider that the creation of new societies and economies in the Americas was made possible by the **Columbian Exchange**. The transfer of plants, animals, and diseases from the Old Word to the New and from the New World to the Old marks a major turning point in human history. Without this exchange of biota the European exploitation of the Americas cannot be fully appreciated (see Patterns Up Close).

Columbian Exchange:
Exchange of plants, animals, and diseases between the Americas and the rest of the world.

Spanish exploitation of the Americas emphasized mineral extraction and focused on plantation agricultural production only at a later stage, while the Portuguese proceeded in the reverse direction. France and England, initially unable to develop either mineral or agricultural exploitation in the cold northeast, expanded southward, where they could develop plantations. Since European settlers acquired their mineral and agricultural wealth through forced labor, a social hierarchy evolved which prevented Native Americans and African slaves from rising in rebellion. Western Europe was linguistically deeply divided but ethnically relatively homogeneous. By contrast, the American colonies were linguistically largely uniform (in the upper strata) but ethnically deeply divided. In the long run, this contrast in social divisions contributed to widely divergent political paths along which Europe and the Americas embarked.

Exploitation of Mineral and Tropical Resources

The pattern of European expansion into subtropical and tropical lands began with the Spanish colonization of the Caribbean islands. When the Spanish crown ran out of gold in the Caribbean, it exported silver from Mexico and Peru in great quantities to finance a fiscal–military state that could compete with the Ottomans and European kings. By contrast, Portugal's colony of Brazil did not at first mine for precious metals, and consequently, the Portuguese crown pioneered the growing of sugar on plantations. Mining would be developed later. The North American colonies of England and France had, in comparison, little native industry at first. By moving farther south, however, they adopted the plantation system for indigo and rice and, thus, joined their Spanish and Portuguese predecessors in exploiting the subtropical–tropical agricultural potential of the Americas.

Silver Mines   When the interest of the Spaniards turned from looting to the exploitation of mineral resources, two main mining centers emerged: Potosí in southeastern Peru (today Bolivia) and Zacatecas and Guanajuato in northern Mexico. For the first 200 years after its founding in 1545, Potosí produced over half of the silver of Spanish America. In the eighteenth century, Zacatecas and Guanajuato jumped ahead of Potosí, churning out almost three times more of the precious metal. During the same century, gold-mining in Colombia and Chile rose to importance as well, making the mining of precious metals the most important economic activity in the Americas.

Innovations, such as the "patio" method, which facilitated the extraction process through the use of mercury, and the unrestrained exploitation of indigenous labor, made American silver highly competitive in the world market. Conditions among the Native Americans and blacks employed as labor were truly abominable. Entrepreneurs paid by daily quota, not by day as the law demanded. The annual rest weeks were fewer than prescribed. Loads were heavier than permitted. Day and night shifts followed each other with less rest than required. Workers had to do cleaning work overtime and use children for additional tasks, such as help in carrying loads, providing messenger services, spinning cotton, and making candles from cattle tallow. Entrepreneurs who rented the general store to mining supervisors combined the fines for labor infractions with the debts the workers owed for their purchases of coca leaves and alcohol, throwing them into permanent debt dependence. Lung diseases and mercury poisoning were endemic. Few laborers lasted through more than two forced recruitment (*repartimiento*) cycles before they were incapacitated or dead.

Given gaps in bookkeeping and high degrees of smuggling, scholars have found it extremely difficult to estimate the total production of the American mines from 1550 to 1750. The best current estimate is that Spanish America produced 150,000 tons of silver (including gold converted into silver weight). This quantity corresponded to roughly 85 percent of world production. The figures underline the extraordinary role of American silver for the money economies of Spain, Europe, the Middle East, and Asia, especially China.

The Silver Mountain of Potosí. Note the patios in the left foreground and the water-driven crushing mill in the center, which ground the silver-bearing ore into a fine sand that then was moistened, caked, and eventually amalgamated with mercury. The mine workers' insect-like shapes reinforce the dehumanizing effects of their labor.

Since the exploitation of the mines was of such central importance, for the first century and a half of New World colonization the Spanish crown organized its other provinces around the needs of the mining centers. Hispaniola and Cuba in the Caribbean were islands which had produced foodstuffs, sugar, and tobacco from the time of Columbus but only in small quantities. Their main function was to feed and protect Havana, the collection point for the Mexican and Peruvian silver and the port from where the annual Spanish fleet shipped the American silver across the Atlantic.

A second region, Argentina and Paraguay, was colonized as a bulwark to prevent the Portuguese and Dutch from cutting across the southern end of the continent and to access Peruvian silver. Once established, the two colonies produced wheat, cattle, mules, horses, cotton, textiles, and tallow to feed and supply the miners in Potosí. The subtropical crop of cotton, produced by small farmers, played a role in Europe's extension into warm-weather agriculture only toward the end of the colonial period.

Patterns Up Close | The Columbian Exchange

Few of us can imagine an Italian kitchen without tomatoes or an Irish meal without potatoes or Chinese or Indian cuisine without the piquant presence of chilies, but until fairly recently each of these foods was unknown to the Old World. Likewise, the expression, "as American as apple pie" obscures the fact that for millennia apples, as well as many other frequently consumed fruits, such as peaches, pears, plums, cherries, bananas, oranges, and lemons, were absent from the New World. It was not until the sixteenth century, when plants, animals, and microbes began to flow from one end of the planet to another, that new patterns of ecology and biology changed the course of millions of years of divergent evolution.

Smallpox Victims. The protracted isolation of the peoples of the Americas from the rest of the world made them vulnerable to a battery of diseases European colonists brought with them: the "breath of a Spaniard" was said to be sufficient enough to kill. These sixteenth-century illustrations, drawn by a native Mexican artist, depict smallpox victims. In the upper left panel a doctor attempts to treat his patient—undoubtedly he failed.

While the Columbian Exchange was the largest and most consequential transfer of life-forms in human history, it certainly was not the first. By 500 CE, Indonesian sailors had brought the banana to the east coast of Africa. A few hundred years later, Muslim traders facilitated the transmission of rice, oranges, lemons, sugarcane, eggplant, and cotton—all of which are indigenous to south and southeast Asia—throughout the Mediterranean and eventually to western Europe, transforming both diets and economies. Plagues, such as the Black Death of 1348–1350, also periodically swept across one end of Eurasia to another, with devastating results. Still, these intrahemispheric transfers pale in comparison to the exchange of diseases, plants, and animals between previously disconnected continents that was set in motion after 1500 (see Map 18.4).

When historians catalog the long list of life-forms that moved across the oceans in the Columbian Exchange, pride of place is usually reserved for the bigger, better-known migrants like cattle, sheep, pigs, and horses. However, as the historian Alfred Crosby pointed out in his pioneering work from over 30 years ago, the impact of European weeds and grasses on American grasslands, which made it possible for the North American prairie and the South American pampas to support livestock, should not be overlooked. By binding the soil together with their long, tough roots, these "empires of the dandelion" provided the conditions for the grazing of sheep, cattle, and horses, as well as the planting of crops like wheat.

A Beverage Fit for Kings. By 1720, when this painting was made, drinking chocolate—in a fashion similar to the manner in which the Aztecs consumed it—was a widespread habit among European elites, including King João V of Portugal, who is shown expertly pouring the luxury beverage in front of an approving audience.

The other, silent invader that accompanied the conquistadors was, of course, disease. Thousands of years of mutual isolation between the Americas and Afro-Eurasia rendered the immune systems of Native Americans vulnerable to the scourges that European colonists unwittingly brought with them. Smallpox, influenza, diphtheria, whooping cough, typhoid, chicken pox, measles, and meningitis wiped out millions of Native Americans—by some estimates, the Indian populations of Mesoamerica and the Andes plummeted by 90 percent in the period 1500–1700. In comparison, the contagion the New World was able to reciprocate upon the Old World—syphilis and tuberculosis—did not unleash nearly the same virulence, and the New World origin of these diseases is still debated.

From Eurasia to the Americas

almonds	measles
apples	meningitis
bananas	onions
cattle	oranges
cherries	peaches
chicken pox	pears
chickens	pigs
coconuts	plums
coffee	rice
dandelions	sheep
diphtheria	smallpox
grapes	sugar
horses	typhoid
influenza	wheat
lemons	whooping cough

From the Americas to Africa and Eurasia

beans
cacao
cassava (manioc)
chillies
maize
peanuts
pineapples
potatoes
squash
sweet potatoes
syphilis
tobacco
tomatoes
tuberculosis
turkeys
vanilla

From Africa to the Americas

African rice
collard greens
okra
palm oil
yams

The Columbian Exchange

MAP **18.4** **The Columbian Exchange.**

It is therefore obvious that the big winner in the Columbian Exchange was western Europe, though the effects of the New World bounty took centuries to be fully discerned. While Asia and Africa also benefited from the Columbian Exchange in the forms of new foods that enriched diets, the Europeans got a continent endowed with a warm climate in which they could create new and improved versions of their homelands—what Alfred Crosby calls "Neo-Europes." Undoubtedly, Native Americans were the biggest losers: They were nearly wiped out by disease, their lands appropriated, and the survivors either enslaved or marginalized. Africans were losers as well. The precipitous drop in the population of Native Americans, combined with the tropical and semitropical climate of much of the Americas, created the necessary conditions for the Atlantic slave trade. Even though the introduction of corn and manioc from the Americas fueled population growth across Africa and more than offset population loss from slaving, overall, the traffic in slaves negatively affected African societies.

Because of the profound changes it wrought on so many societies and cultures across so many continents, few events can match the Columbian Exchange for the size and scope of its impact on the patterns of world history—something to chew on the next time you order takeout from your local pizza joint.

Questions

• Can the Columbian Exchange be considered one of the origins of the modern world? How? Why? How does the Columbian Exchange demonstrate the origins, interactions, and adaptations model that is used throughout this book?

• Weigh the positive and negative outcomes of the Columbian Exchange. Is it possible to determine whether the effects of the Columbian Exchange on human society and the natural environment were for the better or for the worse?

A third colonial region, Venezuela, began as a grain and cattle supply base for Cartagena, the port for the shipment of Colombian gold, and Panama and Porto-belo, ports for the transshipment of Peruvian silver from the Pacific to Havana. Its cocoa and tobacco exports flourished only after the Dutch established themselves in 1624 in the southern Caribbean and provided the shipping. Thus, three major regions of the Spanish overseas empire in the Americas were mostly peripheral as agricultural producers during the sixteenth century. Only after the middle of the century did they begin to specialize in tropical agricultural goods, and they were exporters only in the eighteenth century. By that time, the Dutch and English provided more and more shipping in the place of the Spanish.

Wheat Farming and Cattle Ranching   To support the mining centers and administrative cities, the Spanish colonial government encouraged the development of agricultural estates (*haciendas*). These estates first emerged when conquistadors used their *encomienda* rights to round up Native American labor to produce subsistence crops. Native American tenant farmers were forced to grow wheat and raise cattle, pigs, sheep, and goats for the conquerors, who were now agricultural entrepreneurs. In the latter part of the sixteenth century, the land grants gave way to rotating forced labor as well as wage labor. Owners established their residences and built dwellings for tenant farmers on their estates. A landowner class emerged.

Like the conquistadors before, a majority of landowners produced wheat and animals for sale to urban and mining centers. Cities purchased wheat and maintained granaries in order to provide for urban dwellers in times of harvest failure. Entrepreneurs received commissions to provide slaughterhouses with regular supplies of animals. As the Native American population declined in the seventeenth century and the church helped in consolidating the remaining population in large villages, additional land became available for the establishment of estates. From 1631 onward, authorities granted Spanish settler families the right to maintain their estates undivided from generation to generation. Through donations, the church also acquired considerable agricultural lands. Secular and clerical land-owning interests supported a powerful upper social stratum of Creoles from the eighteenth century onward.

Plantations and Gold Mining in Brazil   Brazil's agricultural industry began with brazilwood, followed by sugar plantations, before gold mining rose to prominence in the eighteenth century. A crisis hit sugar production in 1680–1700, mostly as a result of the Dutch beginning production of sugar in the Antilles. It was at that time that the gold of Minas Gerais, in the interior of Brazil, were discovered.

Gold-mining operations in Brazil during the eighteenth century were considerably less capital-intensive than the silver mines in Spanish America. Most miners were relatively small operators with sieves, pickaxes, and a few black slaves as unskilled laborers. Many entrepreneurs were indebted for their slaves to absentee capitalists, with whom they shared the profits. Since prospecting took place on the land of Native Americans, bloody encounters were frequent. Most entrepreneurs were ruthless frontiersmen who exploited their slaves and took no chances with the indigenous people. Brazil produced about 100,000 tons of gold in the eighteenth century, a welcome bonanza for Portugal at a time of low agricultural prices. Overall, minerals were just as valuable for the Portuguese as they were for the Spanish.

Plantations in Spanish and English America   The expansion of plantation farming in the Spanish colonies was a result of the Bourbon reforms. Although sugar, tobacco, and rice had been introduced early into the Caribbean and southern Mexico, it was only in the expanded plantation system of the eighteenth century that these crops (plus cactuses for cochineal, and indigo, and cacao) were produced on a large scale for export to Europe. The owners of plantations did not need expensive machinery and invested instead in African slave labor, with the result that the slave trade hit its full stride, beginning around 1750.

English North American settlements in Virginia and Carolina exported tobacco and rice beginning in the 1660s. Georgia was the thirteenth British colony, beginning in 1733 as a bulwark against Spanish Florida and a haven for poor Europeans. In 1750 it joined southern Carolina as a major plantation colony and rice and indigo producer. In the eighteenth century, even New England finally had its own export crop, in the form of timber for shipbuilding and charcoal production in Great Britain, at the amazing rate of 250 million board feet from about 1 million acres per year by the start of the nineteenth century. These timber exports illustrate an important new factor appearing in the Americas in the eighteenth century. Apart from the cheap production of precious metals and warm-weather crops, the American extension of Europe became increasingly important as a replacement for dwindling fuel resources across much of northern Europe. Altogether, it was thanks to the Americas that cold and rainy Europe rose successfully into the ranks of the wealthy, climatically balanced, and populated Indian and Chinese empires.

Shades of Skin Color: Social Strata, Castes, and Ethnic Groups

The population of settlers in the New World consisted entirely of Europeans who came from a continent that had barely emerged from its population losses to the Black Death. Although population numbers were rising again in the sixteenth century, Europe did not have masses of emigrants to the Americas to spare. Given the small settler population of the Americas, the temptation to develop a system of forced labor in agriculture and mining was irresistible. Since the Native Americans and African slaves pressed into labor were ethnically so completely different from the Europeans, however, a social system evolved in which the latter two not only were economically underprivileged but also populated the ethnically nonintegrated lowest rungs of the social ladder. A pattern of legal and customary discrimination evolved which, even though partially vitiated by the rise of ethnically mixed groups, prevented the integration of American ethnicities into settler society.

> **1543 Petition by Native Americans in Mexico to Raise Silk (from Tejupan in Southern Mexico)**
>
> "And now the Indians of that town appeared before me and reported that the time of the contract [with three Spaniards] was finished and that they wished to raise silk on their own for the profit and usefulness that (the industry) would bring them.... You are to allow them and to permit them to raise silk and not stop them nor allow any obstacle whatever nor that [the three Spaniards] raise silk in the said town since the contract and agreement made with the Indians of the town has expired."
>
> —Richard Boyer and Geoffrey Spurling, *eds. Colonial Lives: Documents on Latin American History, 1550–1850*, p. 9. New York: Oxford University Press, 2000.

The Social Elite   The heirs of the Spanish conquistadors and estate owners—mixed farmers, ranchers, and planters—maintained city residences and employed managers on their agricultural properties. In Brazil, cities emerged more slowly, and for a long time estate owners maintained their manor houses as small urban islands. Estate owners mixed with the Madrid- and Lisbon-appointed administrators and, during the seventeenth century, intermarried with them, creating the top tier of settler society known as Creoles. This tier, the "respectable people" (Spanish *gentes decentes*), encompassed about 4 percent of the total population. In a wider sense, the tier included also merchants, professionals, clerks, militia officers, and the clergy. They formed a relatively closed society in which descent, intermarriage, landed property, and a government position counted more than money and education.

The great majority of estate owners were mixed farmers and ranchers. In the seventeenth and eighteenth centuries, they farmed predominantly with Native American forced labor. The estates produced grain and/or cattle, legumes, cattle, sheep, and pigs for local urban markets or mining towns. In contrast to the black slave plantation estates of the Caribbean and coastal regions of Spanish and Portuguese America, the mixed farming estates did not export their goods to Europe. Madrid and Lisbon, furthermore, discouraged these mixed estates from producing olive oil, wine, or silk, to protect their home production. Nevertheless, there were Mexicans who produced silk in the second half of the sixteenth century and Peruvian and Chilean vintners who produced wine by the seventeenth century and brandy by the following century, albeit for American consumption only.

As local producers with little competition, mixed farming and ranching estate owners did not feel market pressures. Since for the most part they lived in the cities, they exploited their estates with minimal investments and usually drew profits of less than 5 percent of annual revenues. They were often heavily indebted, and as a result, there was often more glitter than substance among the *gentes decentes*.

Lower Creoles   The second tier of Creole society consisted of people like Alonzo Ortíz, the tanner introduced at the beginning of this chapter. Even though of second

Textile Production. Immigrants from Spain, like Alonso Ortíz discussed at the start of the chapter, established workshops (*obrajes*) as tanners, weavers, carpenters, or wheelwrights. As craftspeople producing simple but affordable goods for the poor, they remained competitive throughout the colonial period, in spite of increasingly large textile, utensil, and furniture imports from Europe. At the same time, indigenous textile production by native women continued as in the preconquest period, albeit under the constraints of labor services imposed by officials or clergy, as shown in these examples.

rank, these "popular people" (*gentes de pueblo*) were privileged European settlers who, as craftspeople and traders, theoretically worked with their hands. In practice, many of them were owner-operators who employed Native Americans and/or black slaves as apprentices and journeymen. Many invested in small plots of land in the vicinity of their cities. As in Spain, they were organized in guilds, which controlled prices and quality standards.

Wealthy weavers ran textile manufactures (*obrajes*), mostly concentrated in the cities of Mexico, Peru, Paraguay, and Argentina. In some of these manufactures, up to 300 Native American and black workers produced cheap, coarse woolens and a variety of cottons on dozens of looms. Men were the weavers and women, the spinners—in contrast to the pre-Columbian period, when textile manufacture was entirely a woman's job. These textiles were alternatives to the higher-quality European imports, unaffordable to most. On a smaller scale, manufactures also existed for pottery and leather goods. On the whole, the urban manufacturing activities of the popular people, serving local markets, remained vibrant until well into the nineteenth century, in spite of massive European imports.

Race, Class, and Gender in Colonial Mexico. An outraged mulatta defends herself against an aggressive Creole, with a fearful child clinging to the woman's skirt.

Mestizos and Mulattoes The mixed European–Native American and European–African population had the collective name of "caste" (*casta*), or ethnic group. The term originated in the desire of the Iberian and Creole settlers to draw distinctions among degrees of mixture in order to counterbalance as much as possible the masses of Native Americans and Africans, especially from the eighteenth century onward. The two most important castes were the *mestizos* (Spanish) or *mestiços* (Portuguese), who had Iberian fathers and Native American mothers, and *mulatos*, who had Iberian fathers and black mothers. By 1800 the castas formed the third largest population category in Latin America as a whole (20 percent), after Native Americans (40 percent) and Creoles (30 percent). In Brazil, mulattoes and black freedmen were even with Creoles (28 percent each), after black slaves (38 percent) and before Native Americans (6 percent in the settled provinces outside Amazonia). In both Spanish and Portuguese America, there was also a small percentage of people descended from Native American and black unions. Thus, most of the intermediate population groups were sizeable, playing important neutralizing roles in colonial society, as they had one foot each in the Creole and subordinate social strata (see Figure 18.1).

As such neutralizing elements, mestizos and mulattoes filled lower levels of the bureaucracy and the lay hierarchy in the church. They held skilled and supervisory positions in mines and on estates. In addition, in the armed forces mulattoes dominated the ranks of enlisted men; in the defense militias, they even held officer ranks. In Brazil, many mulattoes and black freedmen were farmers. Much of the craft production was in their hands. A wide array of laws existed to keep mestizos and mulattoes in their peculiarly intermediate social and political positions.

- American Indian
- Mestizo
- Creole
- Mulatto
- African

Figure 18.1 Ethnic Composition of Latin America, ca. 1800.

Women   The roles played by women depended strongly on their social position. Well-appointed elite Creole households followed the Mediterranean tradition of secluding women from men. In separate women's quarters, married women had servants for all their needs. On average, elite Creole women married three years younger than women in Spain. When they went out—seldom to anything but mass, religious festivals, or family visits—they had chaperones for protection. The public mixing of genders had to be avoided at all costs.

Within their confines of the household, elite women were persons of means and influence. They were the owners of substantial dowries and legally stipulated grooms' gifts. Often, they actively managed the investment of their assets. Outside their confines, however, even elite women lost all protection. Crimes of passion, committed by honor-obsessed fathers or husbands, went unpunished. Husbands and fathers who did not resort to violence nevertheless did not need witnesses to obtain court judgments to banish daughters or wives to convents for alleged lapses in chastity. Thus, even elite women obeyed definite limits set by a patriarchal society.

On the lower rungs of society, be it popular Creole, mestizo, mulatto, or Native American, gender separation was much less prevalent. After all, everyone in the family had to work in order to make ends meet. Men, women, and children shared labor in the fields and workshops. Girls or wives took in clothes to wash or went out to work as domestics in wealthy households. Older women dominated retail in market stalls. As in elite society, wives tended to outlive husbands. In addition, working families with few assets suffered abandonment by males. Women headed one-third of all households in Mexico City, according to an 1811 census. Among black slaves in the region of São Paulo, 70 percent of women were without formal ties to the men who

Illustration from an Indian Land Record. The Spaniards almost completely wiped out the Aztec archives after the conquest of Mexico; surviving examples of Indian manuscripts are thus extremely rare. Although the example shown here, made from the bark of a fig tree, claims to date from the early 1500s, it is part of the so-called "Techialoyan" land records created in the seventeenth century to substantiate native land claims. These *"titulos primodiales,"* as they were called, were essentially municipal histories that documented in text and pictures local accounts of important events and territorial boundaries.

fathered their children. Thus, the most pronounced division in colonial society was that of a patriarchy among the Creoles and a slave society dominated by women, with frequently absent men—an unbridgeable division that persists today.

Native Americans In the immediate aftermath of the conquest, Native Americans could be found at all levels of the social scale. Some were completely marginalized in remote corners of the American continents. Others acculturated into the ranks of the working poor in the silver mines or textile manufactures. A few even formed an educated Aztec or Inca propertied upper class, exercising administrative functions in Spanish civil service. Social distinctions, however, disappeared rapidly during the first 150 years of Spanish colonialism. Smallpox reduced the Native American population by nearly 80 percent. Diseases were more virulent in humid, tropical parts of the continent than in deserts; and the epidemics took a far greater toll on dense, settled populations than they did on dispersed forager bands in dry regions. In the Caribbean and on the Brazilian coast, Native Americans disappeared altogether; in central and southern Mexico, their population shrank by two-thirds. It was only in the twentieth century that population figures reached the preconquest level again in most parts of Latin America.

> **Yellow Fever Arriving from Africa in 1521**
>
> "Great was the stench of the dead. After our fathers and grandfathers succumbed, half the people fled to the fields. The dogs and vultures devoured the bodies. The mortality was terrible. Your grandfathers died, and with them died the son of the king and his brothers and kinsmen. So it was that we became orphans, oh, my sons! So we became when we were young. All of us were thus. We were born to die!"
>
> —Arana Xajilá, Francisco Hernández, and Francisco Díaz Gebuto Quej. *The Annals of the Cakchiquels.* Edited and translated by Adrián Recinos and Delia Goetz, pp. 115–116. Norman: University of Oklahoma Press, 1953.

Apart from European diseases, the native forager and agrarian Native Americans in the Amazon, Orinoco, and Meracaíbo rain forests were the least affected by European colonials during the period 1500–1800. Not only were their lands economically least promising, but they also defended those lands successfully with blowguns, poison darts, and bow and arrow. In many cold and hot arid or semiarid regions, such as Patagonia, southern Chile, the Argentine grasslands (*pampas*), the Paraguayan salt marshes and deserts, and northern Mexican mountains and steppes, the situation was similar. In many of these lands, the seminomadic Native Americans quickly adopted the European horse and became highly mobile warrior people in defense of their mostly independent territories. Ironically, their successful assimilation of this European import allowed them to delay their ultimate full surrender (and adaptation) to the European colonizers.

The villagers of Mexico, Yucatán, Guatemala, Colombia, Ecuador, and Peru had fewer choices. When smallpox reduced their numbers in the second half of the sixteenth century, state and church authorities razed many villages and concentrated the survivors in *pueblos de indios*. Initially, the Native Americans put up strong resistance against these resettlements, by repeatedly returning to their destroyed old settlements. From the middle of the seventeenth century, however, the pueblos were fully functional, self-administering units, with councils (*cabildos*), churches, schools, communal lands, and family parcels.

The councils were important institutions of legal training and social mobility for ordinary Native Americans. Initially, the traditional, "noble" chiefly families descending from the preconquest Aztec and Inca ruling classes were in control as administrators. The many village functions, however, for which the *cabildos* were responsible, allowed commoners to move up into auxiliary roles. In some of these roles, they had opportunities to learn the system and acquire modest wealth. Settlers constantly complained about insubordinate Native Americans pursuing lawsuits in the courts. Native American villages were closed to settlers, and the only outsiders admitted were Catholic priests. Contact with the Spanish world remained minimal, and acculturation went little beyond official conversion to Catholicism. Village notaries and scribes were instrumental in preserving the native Nahuatl in Mexico and Quechua in Peru, making them into functional, written languages. Thus, even in the heartlands of Spanish America, Native American adaptation to the rulers remained limited.

Unfortunately, however, tremendous demographic losses made the Native Americans in the pueblos vulnerable to the loss of their land. Estate owners expanded their holdings, legally and illegally, in spite of the heroic litigation efforts of the villages opposed to this expansion. When the population rebounded, many estates had grown to immense sizes. Villages began to run out of land for their inhabitants. Increasing numbers of Native Americans had to rent land from estate owners or find work on estates as farmhands. They became estranged from their villages, fell into debt peonage, and entered the ranks of the working poor in countryside or city, bearing the full brunt of colonial inequities.

In the southwestern United States, the pueblo Native Americans remained in their traditional farming villages, but estate owners subjected them first to the *encomienda* and later the *repartimiento* on their ranches. Estate farming and Native American conversion to Catholicism proceeded more slowly in this sparsely populated part of the Spanish colony. Among the indigenous people, the adaptation process to Spanish culture reached a critical point in the 1660s when priests outlawed the local masked *kachina* dances and sought to destroy masks. Tensions over these measures built, with public hangings and whippings of Native Americans convicted of sorcery. During 1680–1695, the indigenous villagers were in full revolt, killing priests, burning churches, and chasing estate owners from their lands. Spanish forces eventually suppressed this extraordinary Native American rebellion in their American colonies but ended the repartimiento system as a measure of pacification.

New England Society   For a long time in the early modern period, the small family farm where everyone had to work to eke out a precarious living remained the norm for the majority of New England's population. Family members specializing in construction, carpentry, spinning, weaving, or iron works continued to be restricted to small perimeters around their villages and towns. An acute lack of money and cheap means of transportation hampered the development of market networks in the interior well into the 1770s. The situation was better in the agriculturally more favored colonies in the Mid-Atlantic, especially in Pennsylvania. Here, farmers were able to produce marketable quantities of wheat and legumes for urban markets. The number of plantations in the south rose steadily, demanding increasing numbers of slaves (from 28,000 to 575,000 in 1700–1776), although world market fluctuations left planters vulnerable. Except for boom periods in the plantation sector, the rural areas remained largely poor.

Real changes occurred during the early eighteenth century in the urban regions. Large port cities emerged which shipped in textiles and ironwares from Europe in return for timber at relatively cheap rates. The most important were Philadelphia

(28,000 inhabitants), New York (25,000), Boston (16,000), and Newport, Rhode Island (11,000). A wealthy merchant class formed, spawning urban service strata of professionals (such as lawyers, teachers, and newspaper journalists). Primary school education was provided by municipal public schools as well as some churches, and evening schools for craftspeople existed in some measure. By the middle of the eighteenth century a majority of men could read and write, although female literacy was minimal. Finally, in contrast to Latin America, social ranks in New England were less elaborate.

The Adaptation of the Americas to European Culture

European settlers brought two distinct cultures to the Americas. In the Mid-Atlantic, Caribbean, and Central and South America, they brought with them the Counter-Reformation Catholicism of southern Europe, a culture and perspective that resisted the New Science of Galileo and the Enlightenment thought of Locke until the late eighteenth century. In the northeast, colonists implanted dissident Protestantism as well as the Anglicanism of Great Britain. The rising number of adherents of the New Science and Enlightenment in northwestern Europe had also a parallel in North America. Settlers and their locally born offspring were proud of their respective cultures, which, even though provincial, were dominant in what they prejudicially viewed as a less civilized, if not barbaric, Native American environment.

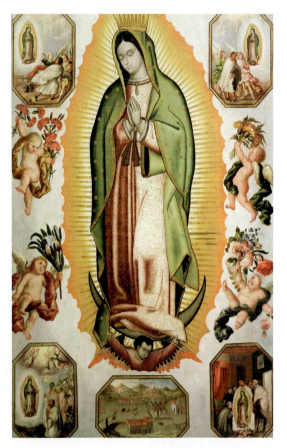

Virgin of Guadalupe. There is perhaps no more potent symbol of the new patterns of religious belief that emerged out of the Spanish conquest of Mexico than the Virgin of Guadalupe. Missionary sources, written years after the fact, tell of an indigenous inhabitant of Mexico City, Juan Diego, who in 1531 had visions of the Virgin Mary on the hill of Tepeyac, which Aztec traditions associated with the mother goddess Tonantzin. By the eighteenth century, the hill attracted pilgrims throughout Mexico and the Church created books, images, and organizations devoted to her cult. To this day, the Virgin of Guadalupe remains one of the most powerful and revered symbols of Mexico.

Catholic Missionary Work   From the beginning, Spanish and Portuguese monarchs relied heavily on the Catholic Church for their rule in the new American provinces. The pope granted them patronage over the organization and all appointments on the new continents. A strong motive driving many in the church as well as society at large was the belief in the imminent Second Coming of Jesus. This belief was one inspiration for the original Atlantic expansion (see Chapter 16). When the Aztec and Inca Empires fell, members of the Franciscan order, the main proponents of the belief in the imminence of the return, reinterpreted its meaning as imposing the urgent duty to convert the Native Americans to Christianity. If Jesus' kingdom was soon to come, according to this interpretation, all humans in the Americas should be Christians.

Thousands of Franciscan, Dominican, and other preaching monks, later followed by the Jesuits, fanned out among the Native Americans. They baptized them, introduced the sacraments (Eucharist, baptism, confession, confirmation, marriage, last rites, and priesthood), and taught them basic theological concepts of Christianity. The missionaries learned native languages, translated the catechism and New Testament into those languages, and taught the children of the ruling native families how to read and write. Thanks to their genuine efforts to understand the Native

Americans on their own terms, a good deal of preconquest Native American culture was recorded without too much distortion.

The role and function of saints as mediators between humans and God formed one element of Catholic Christianity to which Native Americans acculturated early. Good works as God-pleasing human efforts to gain salvation in the afterlife formed another. The veneration of images of the Virgin Mary and pilgrimages to the chapels and churches where they were kept constituted a third element. The best-known example of the last element is Our Lady of Guadalupe, near Mexico City, who in 1531 appeared in a vision to a Native American in the place where the native goddess Tonantzin used to be venerated. On the other hand, the Spanish Inquisition also operated in the Spanish and Portuguese colonies, seeking to limit the degree to which Catholicism, animism, and polytheism mingled. The church tread a fine line between enforcement of doctrine and leniency toward what it determined were lax or heretical believers.

Education   The Counter-Reformation expressed itself also in the organization of education. The Franciscans and Dominicans had offered general education to the children of settlers early on and, in colleges, trained graduates for missionary work. The first New World universities, such as Santo Domingo (1538), Mexico City, and Lima (both 1553) taught theology, church law, and Indian languages. Under the impact of the Jesuits, universities broadened the curriculum, offering degrees also in secular law, Aristotelian philosophy, the natural sciences, and medicine. In the seventeenth and eighteenth centuries, the number of universities grew to 26. By contrast, Brazil did not offer higher education prior to 1800. In spite of this greater breadth, however, the Counter-Reformation universities did not admit the New Sciences and Enlightenment of northwestern Europe into their curriculum prior to the independence of the colonies.

"How an Animal Is Taken from the Poor Old Man to Pay for the Tribute." Felipe Guamán Poma de Ayala, a Peruvian claiming noble Inca descent, was a colonial administrator, well educated, and an ardent Christian. He is remembered today as a biting critic of the colonial administration and the clergy, whom he accused of neglecting their duty to protect the Andean population.

Recording and Writing   As mentioned earlier, missionary monks collected and recorded Native American manuscripts and oral traditions, such as the Aztec *Anales de Tula* and the Maya *Popol Vuh*. Others wrote histories and ethnographies of the Taíno, Aztec, Maya, Inca, and Tupí peoples. Bartolomé de las Casas, Toribio Motolonía de Benavente, Bernardino de Sahagún, Diego de Landa, Bernabé Cobo, and Manoel de Nóbrega are merely a handful of noteworthy authors who wrote about the Native Americans. Many labored for years, worked with legions of informers, and produced monumental tomes.

A number of Native American and mestizo chroniclers, historians, and commentators on the early modern state and society are similarly noteworthy. Muñoz Camargo was a Tlazcaltecan; Fernando de Alva Ixtlixóchitl and Fernando Alvarado Tezózomoc were Mexican mestizos; and Juan de Santa Cruz Pachacuti Yamqui and Felipe Inca Garcilaso de la Vega were Peruvian mestizos, all writing on their native regions. Felipe Guamán Poma de Ayala (ca. 1535–1616), a native Peruvian, is of particular interest. He accompanied his 800-page manuscript, entitled *The First New Chronicle and Good Government*, with some 400 drawings of daily-life activities in the Peruvian villages. These drawings provide us with invaluable cultural details, which would be difficult to render in writing. Unfortunately, King

Philip II of Spain, a relentless proponent of the Counter-Reformation, took a dim view of authors writing on Native American society and history. In 1577 he forbade the publication of all manuscripts dealing with what he called idolatry and superstition. Many manuscripts lay hidden in archives and did not see the light of day until modern times.

Contemporary or later Creole historians wrote their own histories. They celebrated the heroic conquest and settlement of their provinces by their Spanish ancestors, the attractiveness of their cities or regions, and the moral superiority of their cities. Much of this literature is undistinguished, but it laid the foundations for the emergence of a distinct American patriotism among the Creoles by the eighteenth century. One exceptional example is Bartolomé Arzáns de Orsúa y Vela (1676–1736), whose *Tales of Potosí* are still enjoyable to read today. His chronicle of the mining city purports to be factual, although it is better described as historical fiction. It tells colorful stories of wondrous or scandalous alleged events as collected from local informants or observed personally. Arzáns is not a Cervantes, but his stories are nonetheless entertaining illustrations of Creole life in the provinces.

Theater   Stage pieces and music in Creole society were either borrowed from Iberia or composed locally in the prevalent Baroque style. On the popular level, Creole versions of religious processions, presentations, masquerades, and dances emerged. Among Native Americans and mestizos, theater had its roots in short morality plays or recreations of biblical scenes in the Catholic missions, interspersed with dances and music on indigenous instruments. Blacks appropriated this form of theater as well, and mulattoes developed it further with secular themes. Actors and musicians often came from the membership of lay religious brotherhoods responsible for processions on Christian holidays, the only institutions through which Native Americans and blacks could legitimately organize themselves in cities and towns. Thus, even though Counter-Reformation Catholicism was the religious expression of a dominant culture, variations of it became appropriated by the dominated ethnic groups.

Protestantism in New England   From the start, religious diversity was a defining cultural trait of English settlements in North America. The spectrum of Christian denominations ranged from a host of English and continental European versions of Protestantism to Anglicanism and a minority of Catholics. As if this spectrum had not been sufficiently broad, dissenters frequently split from the existing denominations, moved into new territory, and founded new settlements. Religiosity was a major characteristic of the early settlers.

An early example for religious splintering was the rise of an antinomian ("anti-law") group within Puritan-dominated Massachusetts. The Puritans dominant in this colony generally recognized the authority of the Anglican Church but strove to move it toward Protestantism from within. The preachers and settlers represented in the General Court, as their assembly was called, were committed to the Calvinist balance between "inner" personal grace obtained from God and "outer" works according to the law. The antinomian group, however, digging deep into early traditions in Christianity, advocated an exclusive commitment to inner grace through spiritual perfection. Their leader was Anne Hutchinson, an early and tireless proponent of women's rights and an inspiring preacher. She was accused of arguing that she could recognize those believers in Calvinist Protestantism who were predestined for salvation and that these believers would be saved even if they had sinned. After a power struggle with the deeply misogynistic magistrates opposed to influential women, the General Court prevailed and forced the Antinomians to move to Rhode Island in 1636.

The example is noteworthy because it led to the founding of Harvard College in 1626 by the General Court. Harvard was the first institution of higher learning in North America, devoted to teaching the "correct" balanced Calvinist Protestantism. A few years later, the college became a university and functioned as the main center for training the colony's ministers in Puritan theology and morality. In spite of its primary function as a seminary, however, Harvard did not remain closed to the New Science of Copernicus and Galileo. Copernicus's new heliocentric astronomy was part of the curriculum by 1659 at the latest. The university installed the first telescope in North America in 1672. Soon thereafter, some of Harvard's first professors published papers on astronomical subjects which caught the attention of Isaac Newton (1643–1727) at the University of Cambridge; Newton was then at work on his unification of Copernican astronomy and Galilean physics. Although Harvard was clearly provincial, it became an early outpost of the New Science.

Harvard College. The General Court of Boston founded Harvard College in 1636 as a seminary to teach "correct" Calvinism, in the face of dissenting preachers and their followers. In the second half of the 1600s, it incorporated the teaching of the New Science into its curriculum and became an important, if provincial, outpost of Copernican, Galilean, and Newtonian astronomy and physics. This engraving of 1767 is by Paul Revere.

New Science Research   As discussed in Chapter 17, the New Science had found its most hospitable home in northwestern Europe by default. The rivalry between Protestantism and Catholicism had left enough of an authority-free space for the New Science to flourish. Under similar circumstances—intense rivalry among denominations—English North America also proved hospitable to the New Science. An early practitioner was Benjamin Franklin (1706–1790), who began his career as a printer, journalist, and newspaper editor. Franklin founded the University

A Westerly View of The Colledges in Cambridge New England
A Harvard Hall   B Stoughton   C Massachusett   D Hollis   E Holden Chapel

of Pennsylvania (1740), the first secular university in North America, and the American Philosophical Society (1743), the first scientific society. This hospitality to the New Science in North America was quite in contrast to Latin America, where a uniform Catholic Counter-Reformation prevented its rise. Here, the earliest stirrings of the New Science date to the mid-eighteenth century and did not include a recognition of Galileo. Thus, a multiform Protestantism of competitive denominations allowed for a space in which the New Scientists devoted to the pursuit of secular knowledge could assemble and carry out their experiments.

The New Science in the New World. This painting by Samuel Collings, *The Magnetic Dispensary* (1790), shows how men and women, of lay background, participated in scientific experiments in the English colonies of North America, similar to educated middle-class people in western Europe at the same time.

Under the impact of the New Science, seventeenth-century northern European philosophers had begun the task of replacing Aristotelianism, the dominant medieval form of philosophy, with new forms of thought. Among the early New Science–influenced philosophers in England were James Harrington (1611–1677) and John Locke (1632–1704). Both wrote constitutional treatises influenced by the experience of the New World. Harrington's *Oceanea* (1656) and Locke's political thought, later published as *Two Treatises on Civil Government* (1690), inspired the founders of Carolina (1664) and Pennsylvania (1681) in their experiments of colonialism. Thus, the tradition of American secular intellectual as well as political constitutionalism was born and evolved parallel to the traditions of Protestant political self-organization in the colonies.

Secular American constitutionalism, as represented later by the founding fathers, relied on Harrington's innovative concept of a **civil theology**. The myriad religious denominations competing in English North America, so secular constitutionalists argued, had in common a basic set of essential theological agreements about God, providence, and the moral order on which society is built. Hence, any commonwealth based on the will of the people was a polity in which everyone had to agree on a minimum of religious doctrines but was otherwise free to add his or her own specific religious obligations in the congregations to which he or she belonged. Today, of course, civil theology is understood to be the notion of a political order that relies on neither the acceptance of God nor providence but on a universal moral order that is shared by the members of all religious civilizations and formulated concretely in the Preamble of the United Nations Charter.

Civil theology: Form of thought according to which the state supports basic religious principles, without espousing a particular denomination.

Witch Hunts and Revivalism

The level of religious competitiveness and intensity remained high throughout the seventeenth century. In the last decade of the century, religious fervor was at the root of a witchcraft frenzy which seized New England. The belief in witchcraft was a survival of the animist concept of a shared mind or spirit which allows initiates to influence other people, either positively or negatively. Witches, male and female, were persons exerting a negative influence, or black magic, on their victims. Legislation against black magic and sorcery is as ancient as

Hammurabi's law in the Middle East (1700 BCE) and continued in religious civilizations from India to China. In animist Africa, as discussed in the example of Dona Beatriz's early training in Angola (see Chapter 19), the distinction between benevolent and evil magic was fundamental, as it was in Native American society.

But why was there an outburst of witchcraft hysteria in Europe between 1550 and 1800? Systematic scholarship on the phenomenon of the witch craze in both Catholic and Protestant Europe during the past two decades has arrived at the consensus that it was the result of a combination of factors coming together with a rare force. In brief, Europe (and the northern hemisphere) entered the Little Ice Age of 1550–1750, a period in which temperatures fell and agriculture became more precarious. A majority of witchcraft persecutions involved villages and towns where peasants who relied on subsistence agriculture had fallen on hard times. Women, as the embodiments of fertility, were particularly vulnerable in these persecutions. At the same time, populations, increasing again after the Black Death, put pressure on the food supply. The emerging centralized states, especially the fiscal–military ones, weakened local autonomies. And finally, religious wars tore the social and economic fabric of many European countries apart. For the world historian looking at broad patterns, it is quite understandable that this combination of natural and human-made factors could persuade literal-minded or fundamentalist believers untrained in theology that evil forces were at work.

In colonial Catholic and Protestant America, not surprisingly, the fear of witches was as widespread as in Europe. The one case where it erupted into hysteria and which therefore has attracted most attention was that of Salem, Massachusetts. Here, the excitement began in 1692 with Tituba, a Native American slave from Barbados who worked in the household of a pastor. Tituba practiced voodoo, the central African–originated, part-African and part-Christian religious practice found on some Caribbean islands. A cornerstone of voodoo belief is that evil can be removed from a person and transferred somewhere else through the administration of charms (see Chapter 19). When a young daughter and niece in the pastor's household suffered from convulsions, the hysteria erupted. In a snowballing effect, 140 persons, most of them women, were accused of being witches and 20 were even executed. A new governor finally calmed the hysteria, emptied the jails, and pardoned the accused. The problem in Salem was evidently the clash between two sets of religious practices, voodoo and literal or fundamentalist Protestantism—exhibit A for the plea to set aside practice and focus on the more basic theological commonalities of civil theology.

A literal understanding of Protestantism was also central in the "Great Awakening" of the 1730s and 1740s. The main impulse for this revivalist movement came from the brothers John and Charles Wesley, two Methodist preachers in England who toured Georgia in 1735. Preachers from other denominations joined, all exhorting Protestants to literally "start anew" in their relationship with God. Fire-and-brimstone sermons rained down on the pews, reminding the faithful of the absolute sovereignty of God,

Witch Trial. In the course of the 1600s, in the relatively autonomous English colonies of North America more witches were accused, tried, and convicted than anywhere else. Of the 140 persons coming to trial between 1620 and 1725, 86 percent were women. Three witch panics are recorded: Bermuda, 1651; Hartford, Connecticut, 1652–1665; and Salem, Massachusetts, 1692–1693. This anonymous American woodcut of the early 1600s shows one method to try someone for witchcraft: swim if innocent, or sink if guilty.

the depravity of humans, predestination to hell and heaven, the inner experience of election, and salvation by God's grace alone. Thus, revivalism, recurring with great regularity to the present, became a potent force in Protestant America, at opposing purposes with the civil theology of founding father constitutionalism. Even today, the United States is torn between religious commitment, with its emotional engagement for the specifics of religious practice, and the more detached view of civil theology, with its much more universal principles of faith and morality.

Putting It All Together

During the period 1500–1800 the contours of a new pattern in which the Americas formed a resource-rich and warm-weather extension of Europe took shape. During this time, China and India continued to be the most populous and wealthiest agrarian–urban regions of the world. Scholars have estimated China's share of the world economy during this period as comprising 40 percent. India probably did not lag much behind. In 1500, Europe was barely an upstart, forced to defend itself against the push of the Ottoman Empire into eastern Europe and the western Mediterranean. But its successful conquest of Iberia from the Muslims led to the discovery of the Americas. Possession of the Americas made Europe similar to China and India in that it now encompassed, in addition to its northerly cold climates, subtropical and tropical regions which produced rich cash crops as well as precious metals. Over the course of 300 years with the help of its American extension, Europe narrowed the gap between itself and China and India, although it was only after the beginning of industrialization, around 1800, that it eventually was able to close this gap (see Concept Map).

Narrowing the gap, of course, was not a conscious policy in Europe. Quite the contrary, because of fierce competition both with the Ottoman Empire and within itself, much of the wealth Europe gained in the Americas, especially silver, was wasted on warfare. The fiscal–military state, created in part to support war, ran into insurmountable budgetary barriers, which forced Spain into several state bankruptcies. Even mercantilism, a logical extension of the fiscal–military state, had limited effects. Its centerpiece, state support for the export of manufactures to the American colonies through shipping monopolies in return for primary goods (minerals and warm-weather cash crops), functioned unevenly. The Spanish and Portuguese governments, with weak urban infrastructures and low manufacturing capabilities, especially in textiles, were unable to enforce this state-supported trade until the eighteenth century and even then only in very limited ways. France and especially England practiced mercantilism more successfully but were able to do so in the Americas only from the late seventeenth century onward, when their plantation systems began to take shape. Although the American

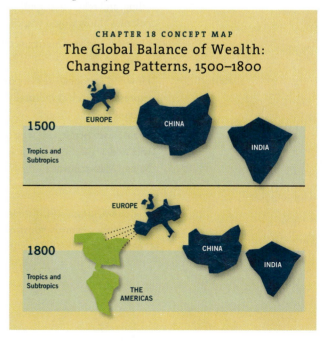

CHAPTER 18 CONCEPT MAP
The Global Balance of Wealth:
Changing Patterns, 1500–1800

1500 — EUROPE, CHINA, INDIA; Tropics and Subtropics

1800 — EUROPE, CHINA, INDIA, THE AMERICAS; Tropics and Subtropics extension of Europe had the potential of making Europe self-sufficient, this potential was realized only partially during the colonial period.

A fierce debate has raged over the question of the degree of wealth the Americas added to that of Europe. On the one hand, considerable quantitative research has established that the British slave trade for sugar plantations added at best 1 percent to the British gross domestic product (GDP). The profits from the production of sugar on the English island of Jamaica may have added another 4 percent to the British GDP. Without doubt, individual slave-trading and sugar-producing enterprises were at times immensely profitable to individuals and groups, not to mention the mining of silver through forced labor. In the larger picture, however, these profits were considerably smaller if one takes into account the immense waste of revenues on military ventures—hence, the doubts raised by scholars today about large gains made by Europe through its American colonial acquisitions.

On the other hand, the European extension to the Americas was clearly a momentous event in world history. It might have produced dubious profits for Europe, but it definitely encouraged the parting of ways between Europe and Asia and Africa, once a new scientific–industrial society began to emerge around 1800.

Review and Respond

1. How did the colonial administration of the Spanish and Portuguese colonies evolve, and how do they compare with that of the English in the Americas?

2. Compare the extraction of minerals and the production of cash crops in the Americas. Which mining and agricultural enterprises did specific colonizing countries undertake? Which timelines did these economic activities follow in the various parts of the Americas?

3. American colonial societies were multitiered and complex. What were the various ethnic and religious population groups in the Latin American, English, and French colonies? How would you characterize the relations among these diverse groups?

4. How did Native Americans adapt to the new social and economic patterns of the colonies?

5. How did European settlers in the Latin American and North American colonies express themselves culturally? What were the differences between the two types of expression?

6. What is witchcraft, and why do people's concerns with its allegedly harmful effects wax and wane throughout history? Why did hysteria about witchcraft erupt in Salem, Massachusetts?

For additional resources, including maps, primary sources, visuals, and quizzes, please go to www.oup.com/us/vonsivers. Please see the Further Resources section at the back of the book for additional readings and suggested websites.

Thinking Through Patterns

▶ **What is the significance of western Europeans acquiring the Americas as a warm-weather extension of their northern continent?**

In their role as supplementary subtropical and tropical extensions of Europe, the Americas became a crucial factor for Europe's changing position in the world. First, Europe acquired large quantities of precious metals, which its two largest competitors, India and China, lacked. Second, with its new access to warm-weather agricultural products, Europe rose to a position of agrarian autonomy similar to that of India and China. In terms of resources, compared with the principal religious civilizations of India and China, Europe grew between 1550 and 1800 from a position of inferiority to one of near parity.

Because the numbers of Europeans who emigrated to the Americas was low for most of the colonial period—just 300,000 Spaniards left for the New World between 1500–1800—they never exceeded the numbers of Native Americans or African slaves. The result was a highly privileged settler society that held superior positions on the top rung of the social hierarchy. In principle, given an initially large indigenous population, labor was cheap and should have become more expensive as diseases reduced the Native Americans. In fact, labor always remained cheap, in part because of the politically supported institution of forced labor and in part because of racial prejudice.

▶ **What was the main pattern of social development in colonial America during the period 1500–1800?**

▶ **Why and how did European settlers in South and North America strive for self-government, and how successful were they in achieving their goals?**

Two contrasting patterns characterized the way in which European colonies were governed. The Spanish and Portuguese crowns, primarily interested in extracting minerals and warm-weather products from the colonies, had a strong interest in exercising as much centralized control over their possessions in the Americas as they could. In contrast, the British crown granted self-government to the North American colonies from the start, in part because the colonies were initially economically far less important and in part because of a long tradition of self-rule at home. Nevertheless, even though Latin American settlers achieved only partial self-rule in their towns and cities, they destroyed central rule indirectly through the purchase of offices. After financial reforms, Spain and Portugal reestablished a degree of central rule through the appointment of officers from the home countries.

Chapter 19

1450-1800

African Kingdoms, the Atlantic Slave Trade, and the Origins of Black America

THE ATLANTIC WORLD, 1500–1800

The Capuchin Catholic monks of the kingdom of Kongo had just denounced as a heretical abomination the claim of Dona Beatriz Vita Kimpa (1684–1706) to have died and been reborn as St. Anthony of Padua. For many subjects of the kingdom, however, this claim was perfectly reasonable as part of an African Christian spirituality in which a gifted person

Seeing Patterns

▶ What was the pattern of kingdom and empire formation in Africa during the period 1500–1800?

▶ How did patterns of plantation slavery evolve in the Atlantic and the Americas?

▶ What are the historic origins of modern racism?

could enter other people's minds and assume their identity. But the monks prevailed. One of the claimants to the throne of the kingdom of Kongo had Dona Beatriz condemned after a trial and burned at the stake.

Dona Beatriz was intellectually precocious. In her childhood, her family had her initiated in a *Kimpasi* enclosure as a *nganga marinda* (Kikongo word derived from "knowledge" or "skill"). Such enclosures at the edges of towns and cities contained altars with crosses and censers (for burning incense). Other paraphernalia included statues believed to be capable of recognizing evildoers, animal claws to grab them, horns to mark the line between the worlds of nature and the spirit, and animal tails symbolizing power. In a ceremony, the head woman of the enclosure put Dona Beatriz into a trance that enabled her to recognize and repel all the troubling forces that disturbed a person or the community. People in Kongo were very much aware, however, that not all *ngangas* were benevolent. Some *ngangas* were thought to misuse their spiritual powers for witchcraft. Missionary Capuchin monks, preaching orthodox Counter-Reformation Catholicism, made every effort to denounce all *ngangas* as witches. Whether the young

New Patterns in Africa. In the wake of the Portuguese arrival in the kingdom of Kongo in 1483, Capuchin monks converted the royal dynasty as well as large numbers of subjects to Catholicism. Since the church did not have enough monks and clergy, it commissioned lay assistants to convert the populace and appointed schoolmasters for instruction in reading, writing, and the Catholic faith. Here, a Capuchin monk and lay assistants are moving in procession. The watercolor was drawn by the Capuchin monk Antonio Cavazzi, who served in Kongo and Angola in the second half of the 1600s.

Dona Beatriz was intimidated by these denunciations or not, she renounced her initiation, married, and pursued the domestic life of any other young woman in Kongo society.

But the spirit did not cease to move Dona Beatriz. In 1704, she had again deep spiritual experiences in which she died, only to be reborn as St. Anthony of Padua (1195–1231). St. Anthony, a Portuguese Franciscan monk, is one of the patron saints of Portugal. Devotees of the saint believe he blesses marriages and helps people find lost items. With her new saintly and male identity, more powerful than her earlier one as an *nganga*, Dona Beatriz preached a novel and inspiring vision: She was God's providential figure, arrived to restore the Catholic faith and reunify the kingdom, both of which she saw as having been torn asunder during nearly half a century of dynastic disunity and civil war (1665–1709).

After her supposed rebirth, Dona Beatriz immediately went to Pedro IV, king of Kongo (r. 1695–1718), and his Capuchin ally, the chief missionary Bernardo da Gallo, accusing them of being laggards in their efforts to restore the faith and unity of Kongo. Pedro temporized in his response, but Bernardo subjected Dona Beatriz to an angry interrogation about her faith and "possession." Beatriz countered with a remarkable attack on the Catholic cornerstone of sacraments. Intention or faith alone, she argued, not the sacraments of the church (such as baptism or confession), would bring salvation. Unlike the Protestant reformer Martin Luther, however, Dona Beatriz did not derive her theological convictions from the letters of St. Paul in the New Testament but from her *nganga* initiation: It was good intentions which distinguished the inspired preacher from the witch.

Initially unable to conceive of a concerted plan of action, the king and Bernardo let Beatriz go. In a journey reminiscent of that of Joan of Arc, Beatriz led a growing crowd of followers to the ruined capital of Kongo, M'banza (São Salvador). There, she trained "little Anthonies" as missionaries to convert the Kongolese to her Antonian-African Christianity. Under the protection of a rival of the king, Beatriz was at the pinnacle of her spiritual power when everything unraveled. As already at the time she was a married woman, in between her two lives as *nganga* and St. Anthony, the flesh reasserted itself. She gave birth to a child, conceived with one of her followers. She did so secretly at her ancestral home in Pedro's territory, evidently in a deep crisis about her spiritual mission. Allies of the king discovered the lovers by accident and arrested them. They brought them before Pedro, who, in the meantime, had decided to reject Beatriz's challenge and silence her. After a state trial—the church stayed out of the proceedings—Beatriz, her companion, and the baby were executed by burning at the stake.

This moving story illustrates a major pattern discussed in this chapter: the process by which Africans adapted their indigenous heritage to the western Christian challenge. Europeans arrived on the western coast of Africa in the fifteenth century as both missionaries and slave traders (at times also as slave raiders). Africans responded with their own adaptive forms of Christianity, as well as efforts—as in Kongo, Angola, and Benin—to limit the slave trade in accordance with their own existing political interests. Elsewhere, however, African kings and chiefs exploited the traditional indigenous system of household, agricultural, administrative, and military slavery to reap voluminous profits. As is now well recognized by scholars, the unprecedented, massive transfer of African slaves to the plantations and mines of the Americas brought to the new continents not only animist tribal Africans but also diverse peoples with complex and sophisticated Creole (mixed) cultures of their own, cultures that survived in the Americas under extraordinarily difficult circumstances.

Creolization can be understood as a cultural process parallel to the patterns of state formation in Africa and European colonization in the Americas during the period 1500–1800. While Islamic and Christian kingdoms continued to dominate the northern parts of sub-Saharan Africa in this period, population increases in the center and south of the region contributed to an acceleration of the transition from chiefdoms to kingdoms. In the Americas, the agricultural pattern of warm-weather cash crop production on plantations that relied on African slavery formed the basis upon which Europeans maintained political control of these continents.

African States and the Slave Trade

In the north of sub-Saharan Africa the pattern of Islamic and Christian dynastic state formation that had been ongoing for centuries continued to dominate herder and village societies in the period 1500–1800. An invasion by Muslim forces from Morocco during the sixteenth century, however, ended the trend toward empire building and strengthened the forces of decentralization. By contrast, in the savanna and Great Lakes regions of central Africa, improved agricultural wealth and intensified regional trade helped perpetuate the kingdom formation already under way. An

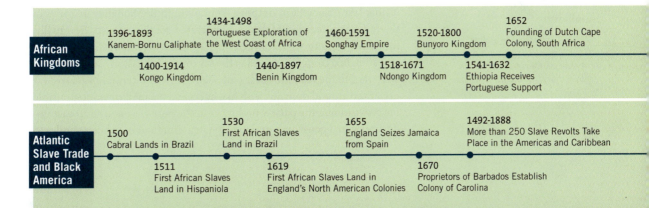

African Kingdoms

1396-1893 Kanem-Bornu Caliphate

1400-1914 Kongo Kingdom

1434-1498 Portuguese Exploration of the West Coast of Africa

1440-1897 Benin Kingdom

1460-1591 Songhay Empire

1518-1671 Ndongo Kingdom

1520-1800 Bunyoro Kingdom

1541-1632 Ethiopia Receives Portuguese Support

1652 Founding of Dutch Cape Colony, South Africa

Atlantic Slave Trade and Black America

1500 Cabral Lands in Brazil

1511 First African Slaves Land in Hispaniola

1530 First African Slaves Land in Brazil

1619 First African Slaves Land in England's North American Colonies

1655 England Seizes Jamaica from Spain

1670 Proprietors of Barbados Establish Colony of Carolina

1492-1888 More than 250 Slave Revolts Take Place in the Americas and Caribbean important institution in the chiefdoms and states of Africa was slavery. When the Europeans inserted themselves into this institution, they profoundly altered it to benefit their own interests in the production of warm-weather cash crops on American plantations. Some African kings resisted the sale of slaves to the Europeans, while other kings and chiefs enriched themselves through slave raiding and selling.

The End of Empires in the North and the Rise of States in the Center

The Eurasian empires of the premodern world united peoples of many different religions, languages, and ethnic affiliations. Mali (1240–1460) was the first African empire that was similar to the old empires of Eurasia. Mali's successor state, the focus of this section, was the even larger Songhay Empire (1460–1591). It did not last long however.

Origins of the Songhay   Songhay was initially a tributary state of Mali. It was centered on the city of Gao downstream on the River Niger from the agricultural center of Jenné-jeno and the commercial and scholarly center of Timbuktu. Gao's origins dated to 850, when it emerged as the end point of the eastern trans-Saharan route from Tunisia and Algeria, parallel to the more heavily traveled western route from Morocco. Gao was located at the northern end of the Songhay Empire, near the Niger Bend, and was inhabited by the Songhay, an ethnic grouping composed of herders, villagers, and fishermen.

The Songhay were ethnically distinct from the Soninke of the Kingdom of Ancient Ghana and the Malinke of the Mali Empire further west. Their homeland was located to the east and southeast of the Niger Bend. At the end of the eleventh century, the leading clans of the Songhay, profiting from the trans-Saharan trade, converted to Islam. Two centuries later the warriors among them assumed positions of leadership as vassals of the *mansa*, or emperor, of Mali. By this time, tall Barbary warhorses, bred from North African stock, had become common in the steppe and savanna of West Africa, the semiarid pasture lands near the Sahara and the semiforested grasslands suitable for agriculture farther south. However, the tsetse fly, which transmits a parasite deadly to livestock, limited the range of these horses. Periodic purchases from North Africa were necessary for the Songhay to maintain their fighting strength.

A Ruthless Conqueror and Harsh Ruler

"As for the great oppressor and notorious evil-doer, Sunni Ali [the founder of the Songhay Empire, 1464–1492] . . . he was a man of great strength and colossal energy, a tyrant, a miscreant, an aggressor, a despot . . . and a butcher who killed so many human beings that only God Most High could count them. He tyrannized the scholars and holymen, killing them, insulting them, and humiliating them."

—Abd al-Rahman al-Saadi. *Timbuktu and the Songhay Empire: Al-Sa'di's Tarikh al-Sudan down to 1613 and Other Contemporary Documents.* Translated by John O. Hunwick, p. 91. Leiden, the Netherlands: Brill, 2003.

The Songhay Empire   The Songhay began their imperial expansion in the mid-1400s, toward the end of the dry period in West Africa (1100–1500), during which control of the steppe region was sometimes difficult to maintain. Mali, which had its center in the much wetter savanna, lost its northern outpost, Timbuktu, to the Songhay in 1469. In the following decades, Mali slowly retreated southwestward. Eventually, it became a minor vassal of the Songhay. At its height, the Songhay Empire stretched from Hausaland in the savanna southeast of Gao all the way westward to the Atlantic coast (see Map 19.1). The central province was organized around domains with managers and tenant farmers responsible for provisioning the palace, provinces in the near west and southeast under appointed governors, and vassal states with their own kings similar to

MAP 19.1 Peoples and Kingdoms in Sub-Saharan Africa, 1450–1750.

Mali. The provinces and vassal states had to provide taxes in kind, auxiliary troops, hostages, gifts, or marriage alliances, depending on the shifting abilities of Songhay rulers to enforce their authority.

As in the previous centuries under ancient Ghana and Mali, the decisive difference which elevated the Songhay emperors (*askiyas*) above their vassals was their taxation of the gold trade. The gold fields of the Upper Niger, Senegal, and Black Volta Rivers in the southern rain forest were outside the empire; but merchant clans, often accompanied by troop detachments, transported the gold to Timbuktu and Gao. Here, North African merchants exchanged their Mediterranean manufactures and salt for gold, slaves, and kola nuts. Agents of the *askiyas* in these cities collected market taxes in the form of gold, which they used for the maintenance of their central administration and troops, the production of arms and armor, and the construction of palaces and mosques. Agricultural taxes and tributes supported kingdoms; long-distance trade was needed in addition for an empire to come into being.

Songhay's Sudden End   After the initial, ruthless conquests, the Songhay Empire had little time to overcome its violent origins and consolidate on a more peaceful footing. After only a little over a century of dominance, the Songhay Empire came to a sudden end in 1591 when a Moroccan force invaded from the north. The commander was an Iberian Muslim general whose troops, consisting of a black slave infantry, were equipped with muskets and cannons. They defeated the Songhay cavalry and infantry, which fought with lances, sabers, and bows and arrows. The Moroccan sultans had successfully driven Portugal from their Atlantic coast but followed with concern the flourishing Portuguese trade for gold on the West African coast. They decided to find and occupy the West African gold fields in the rain forest, thereby depriving the Portuguese of the precious metal.

However, after defeating Songhay, they were unable to march any farther, lacking necessary logistic support from Morocco through the Sahara. Although the officers turned the Niger delta and Bend initially into a Moroccan province, within a generation they assimilated into the West African royal clans. As a result, imperial politics in West Africa disintegrated, together with much of the trans-Saharan gold trade, which was siphoned off by the Portuguese on the African Gold Coast (modern Ghana).

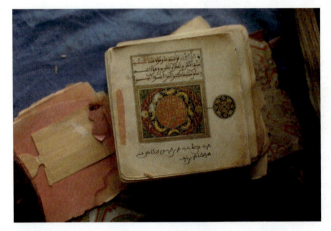

Arabic Manuscript, Timbuktu. Though undergirded by its strategic position on the caravan routes and its proximity to the gold fields, Timbuktu's key role was cultural. From the middle of the fifteenth century to the end of the eighteenth, Timbuktu was the preeminent center of Islamic learning in West Africa, with hundreds of schools, impressive mosques, and renowned libraries filled with rare manuscripts assiduously copied by hand.

The Eastern Sahel and Savanna   The steppe peoples between Songhay in the west and Ethiopia in the northeastern highlands near the Red Sea also possessed Islamic regimes governing moderate to large territories. Kanem-Bornu (1396–1893) was a long-lived Islamic realm, calling itself a "caliphate," with a majority of animist African subjects. Located in both the steppe and savanna, it was based on a slave and ivory trade with the Mediterranean and on agriculture and fishing for its internal organization on the south side of Lake Chad. Kanem-Bornu's imperial frontier was in the southwest, where it waged long, intermittent wars with the savanna kingdoms of Hausaland.

The Hausa kingdoms, numbering about half a dozen, had formed during the height of the Mali-dominated trans-Saharan trade as southeastern extensions of this trade into rain-forest Africa. Although they were under frequent attack by Songhay and Kanem-Bornu during the period 1500–1800, the Hausa kingdoms enjoyed periods of independence during which many of the ruling clans converted to Islam. Like their northern neighbors, they maintained cavalry forces, which—apart from military purposes—served to protect the caravans of the traders. In addition to taxing these traders, the Hausa kings collected dues from the villagers, who bred cattle and grew millet, sorghum, kola nuts, and cotton. Craftspeople in the capitals and some villages produced pottery, iron implements and utensils, cotton cloth, basketry, leather goods, and iron weapons. In other villages, miners and smiths smelted and forged copper, iron, and steel. Although more agricultural in orientation, the Hausa kingdoms closely resembled their northern neighbors in the steppe.

Farther east, in the steppe between Lake Chad and the Nile, the Fur and the Funj, cattle-breeding tribal federations, converted fully to Islam, from the royal clans down to the commoner clans. In contrast, in West Africa only the dynasties and merchants became Muslim. Their leaders adopted the title "sultan" and became Arabized in the period 1500–1800, while Christianity along the Nile disappeared completely.

Islamization and Arabization, however, reached a southern limit beyond which the two were not to penetrate until recently. This limit was located along a west–east line separating the steppe, with its cattle herders, from the savanna, which was suitable to the farming of millet, sorghum, and cotton. Most of the savanna villagers were animists who farmed and formed chiefdoms. Others also kept cattle and participated in regional trade for salt, slaves, iron, hardwood, and exotic animal skins, supporting small kingdoms with dynasties of kings as well as queens, such as the Shilluk people (*Chollo* in their own language), regionally powerful during the second half of the seventeenth and early eighteenth centuries.

South Central Africa   Most of the steppe and savanna in the northern half of sub-Saharan Africa interacted with Mediterranean Islamic civilization to some degree. They remained largely outside the sphere of the European slave trade during the period 1500–1800. On the southern side of the rain forest, the eastern part of the southern savanna and the Great Lakes area in central Africa remained similarly outside the reach of the slave trade. As a result, their population continued to grow. Large numbers of farmer and cattle herder groups, organized in chiefdoms, inhabited these regions. In the eastern savanna, the kingdom of Luba emerged precociously before 1500; and others followed at various intervals thereafter.

A steady increase in regional trade for copper, iron, salt, dried fish, beads, cloth, and palm oil enabled chieftain clans to consolidate their rule and enlarge their holdings into kingdoms. Living in enclosures and surrounded by "courts," or dense ruling-class settlements, kings maintained agricultural domains worked by slaves. Villages nearby delivered tribute in the form of foodstuffs. From the mid-seventeenth century onward, the American staples corn and cassava broadened the food supply. Tributaries at some distance delivered prestige goods, especially copper and ironware, as well as beads. At times, the kings mobilized thousands of workers to build moats and earthworks around their courts, which became centers of incipient urbanization processes.

The Great Lakes region, to the north and south of Lake Victoria, was a highly fertile eastward extension of the southern savanna with two annual crops of sorghum and sesame, as well as banana groves and herds of cattle. Traders distributed salt, iron, and dried fish in a lively regional trade. Agriculture, cattle breeding, and trade supported intense political competition in the lakes region. Small agricultural–mercantile kingdoms shared the region, but sometime in the sixteenth century cattle breeders—the Luo, relatives of the Shilluk—arrived from southern Sudan and shook up the existing political and social structures. Pronounced disparities in cattle ownership emerged on the rich pasture lands. Cattle-owning warlords rose as competitors of the kings.

North of Lake Victoria, the Bunyoro kingdom, based on agriculture and regional trade, held the cattle lords at bay, while on the south side of the lake the cattle lords created new small kingdoms. After a while cattle breeders and farmers settled into more or less unequal relations of mutual dependence. Under the colonial system in the nineteenth century, these unequal relations froze into a caste system in which the minority Tutsi cattle breeders faced off against the majority Hutu farmers. Eventually, this volatile arrangement led to the genocide committed by the Hutus against the Tutsis in 1993-1994. Farther south the pre-1500 tradition of gold-mining kingdoms, such as Great Zimbabwe, continued. But here the interaction of Africa with Portugal, to be discussed next, set the kingdoms on a different historical trajectory.

Portugal's Explorations Along the African Coast and Contacts with Ethiopia

The Portuguese expansion into North Africa and the exploration of the African coast were outgrowths of both the *Reconquista* and crusading impulses. Mixed in with these religious impulses, yet without any contradiction (as opposed to our modern views), was the practical necessity of financing the journeys of exploration through profits from trade. The combination of the two guided Portugal within one century around the African continent to India. Along the coast, the Portuguese established forts as points of protection for their merchants. In Ethiopia they supported the Christian kingdom with military aid, providing protection against the Ottomans in Yemen, just across the Red Sea.

Chartered Explorations in West Africa   Henry the Navigator (1394–1460), brother of the ruling king, a principal figure of the Portuguese *Reconquista*, and chief embodiment of the crusading zeal, occupied the Moroccan port of Ceuta in 1415. He claimed that Ceuta had been Christian, prior to the Berber-Arab conquest and subsequent Islamization of Iberia. He also wished to renew crusading for the reconquest of Jerusalem, lost to the Muslims in 1291. But the merchant wing of the Lisbon court was wary of the military expenditures. During the fifteenth century, campaigns for the military occupation of other cities of Morocco, mostly along the Atlantic coast, alternated with voyages financed by Portuguese groups of merchants and aristocrats for commerce along the West African coast.

In 1434, mariners discovered that ships could overcome adverse currents and winds and return from the West African coast by sailing out into the Atlantic, setting course for the islands of the newly discovered Canaries, Madeira, and Azores, before turning east toward Lisbon. It was the impossibility of returning along the coast from the southern part of West Africa that had doomed all previous efforts. Sailors either had to return by land, via the Sahara to the Mediterranean, or they disappeared without a trace. Thus, sailing south in the Atlantic and developing a route by which to return was a decisive step toward circumnavigating the continent.

Between 1434 and 1472, through a combination of royally chartered, private merchant–financiered as well as public state-organized expeditions, Portuguese mariners explored the coast as far east as the Bight of Benin. Trade items included European woolens and linens, in exchange for gold, cottons, and Guinea pepper (also called "malagueta pepper," not to be confused with malagueta chili pepper from South America). Small numbers of black slaves were included early on as trade items, mostly through purchases from chieftains and kings. Several uninhabited tropical islands off the coast were discovered during this time, and the Portuguese used slaves for the establishment of sugar plantations on these islands. They shipped other slaves to Europe for domestic employment, adding to the long-standing Mediterranean and trans-Saharan practice of household slavery.

Portugal and Ethiopia   By the second half of the fifteenth century, private merchant interests focused on West Africa provided few incentives for further explorations. It required the military wing of the Portuguese court to revive crusading. From 1483 through 1486 the king organized state expeditions for further expansion from the Bight of Benin south to the Congo River. Here, mariners sailed upstream in hopes of linking up with Prester John (see Chapter 16), a mythical king believed to live in Ethiopia or India. He was supposedly at the head of huge Christian armies, ready to help Portugal in the reconquest of Jerusalem. Instead of Prester John, the Portuguese mariners encountered the ruler of the powerful kingdom of Kongo, who converted to Christianity and established close relations with Portugal.

Prester John. The legend of Prester John, a Christian ruler whose lost kingdom in northeast Africa, surrounded by Muslims and pagans, captivated the European imagination from the twelfth through the seventeenth centuries. Purportedly a descendant of one of the Three Magi, Prester John (or Presbyter John) presided over a realm full of riches and fabulous creatures, and it was supposed to border the earthly paradise.

A few years later, after Christopher Columbus had discovered the Americas for Castile-Aragon in 1492, the Portuguese crown continued the search for a way to Ethiopia or India, a route presumed to lie around the southern tip of Africa. Eventually, Vasco da Gama circumnavigated the southern tip, established trade outposts in Swahili city-states of East Africa, and reached India in 1498. But Prester John was never found, and the idea of crusading receded as the Portuguese development of the Indian spice trade grew in importance.

In fact, as the Portuguese discovered in the early sixteenth century, not only did a mythically powerful king not rule Ethiopia but the kingdom was extremely weak in the face of the aggressive Muslim sultanate of Adal, on the Red Sea to the east. Until the end of the fifteenth century, Ethiopia had been a powerful Coptic Christian kingdom in the highlands of northeastern Africa. Its people practiced a productive plow-based agriculture for wheat and teff (a local cereal), and its kings controlled a rich trade of gold, ivory, animal skins, and slaves from the southern Sudan through the Rift Valley to the Red Sea. Possession of a Red Sea port for this trade, however, was a bone of contention between Ethiopia and Adal during the first half of the sixteenth century.

A Christian incursion into Muslim territory in 1529 triggered a response by Adal in the form of a furiously destructive Muslim holy war. Ethiopia would have been destroyed in this war had it not been for the timely arrival in 1541 of a Portuguese fleet with artillery and musketeers. For its part, Adal received Ottoman Muslim artillery and musketeer support from Yemen, but 2 years later, after several fierce battles, the Christians prevailed.

Ethiopia paid a high price for its victory. Adal Muslim power was destroyed, but in its place, the Ottomans took over the entire west coast of the Red Sea, mostly in order to keep out Portugal. Animist cattle breeders from the southwest occupied the Rift Valley, which separated the northern from the southern Ethiopian highlands and had been depopulated during the Christian–Muslim wars. Christians in the southern highlands were left to their own devices, surviving in small states. Small numbers of Portuguese stayed inside Ethiopia, with Jesuit missionaries threatening to dominate the Ethiopian church as well as the kings. In 1632 the Ethiopian king expelled the Jesuits and consolidated the kingdom as a shrunken power within much smaller borders.

Initially, Ethiopia continued to be culturally active under a strong court, expressed mostly through theological writings and iconic paintings. But from about 1700 Ethiopia decentralized into provincial lordships with little interest in their cultural heritage. Only in the mid-nineteenth century, in response to the Western challenge, did the kings take back their power from the provincial lords.

Coastal Africa and the Atlantic Slave Trade

After Portuguese mariners had circumnavigated Africa, they initially focused on developing their spice trade with India. Gradually, however, they also built their Atlantic slave trade, which took off in the early seventeenth century, to be followed by mariner-merchants from other European countries. To understand the pattern underlying the slave trade from 1500 to 1800 it is crucial to be aware of the importance of slavery within the African historical context. African slavery was a traditional African institution that existed in the place of landownership. The more slaves a household, chief, or king owned, to work at home or in the fields, the wealthier he was. **Household slavery**, as African slavery may also be called, existed everywhere in Africa.

Household slavery: African chiefs and kings maintained large households of retainers, such as administrators, soldiers, domestics, craftspeople, and farmers; many among these were slaves, acquired through raids and wars but also as a result of punishments for infractions of royal, chiefly, or tribal law.

Trade Forts   Early on, in the 1440s, Portuguese mariners raided the West African coast in the region defined by the Senegal and Gambia Rivers—Senegambia—for slaves. But they suffered losses in the process since their muskets were not yet superior to the precisely aimed poisoned arrows of the Africans. Furthermore, dwelling in a rain forest with its many rivers opening to the coast, West Africans possessed a well-developed tradition of boat-building and coastal navigation. Boats hollowed out from tree trunks could hold as many as 50 warriors. These warriors paddled swiftly through the estuaries and mangrove swamps along the coast and picked off the mariners from their caravels if they approached the coast too closely in a hostile manner. The Portuguese thus learned to approach the coast in a less threatening way and began what developed into a lucrative coastal fort trade in a variety of items, including slaves.

(a) **Elmina as It Appeared in a European Etching from 1562.**

(b) **Entrances to Slave Holding Cells.**

Through treaties with local African leaders, Portugal acquired the right to build posts or forts from which to trade. Africans involved in trade in these regions produced a variety of items that were soon in demand in Europe. They wove colorful cotton cloth and wore it by the yard. A particular kind of bark or leaf cloth from central West Africa was at times highly sought in Portugal and the Caribbean. For a long time, Senegambian mats were preferred as bedcovers in Europe. In many places, Africans smelted iron and forged steel that was of higher quality than that of iron-poor Portugal. Africans paid with a currency—seashells—that resembled more closely our modern idea of abstract paper money than the silver and gold coins used by the Europeans. For adornment and celebration Africans wore bead necklaces and drank alcoholic beverages (beer from millet or sorghum, palm wine from sap, and fermented drinks from honey). Africans possessed the basic goods for a civilized and even sophisticated life on their continent.

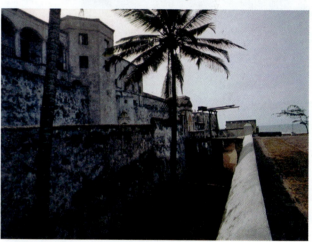

(c) **Outer Defensive Walls.**

Elmina, in present-day Ghana, was, along with the village of São Jorge da Mina, the first Portuguese fortified trading post on the African coast, from 1482 until it passed to the Dutch in 1637. Merchants used it for storing the goods they traded and for protection in case of conflicts with Africans. It was staffed by a governor and 20–60 soldiers, a priest, surgeon, apothecary, and a variety of craftspeople. Throughout the first half of the sixteenth century Elmina was the center of Portuguese slaving activities.

Trade, as in most other parts in the world during the period 1500–1800, was for expensive luxury goods, not ordinary articles of daily life. Merchants had to be able to achieve high profits, while carrying comparatively little to weigh them down. African rulers purchased luxuries in order to engage in conspicuous consumption, fashion display, and lavish gift giving—all ways to enhance their status and cement power relations. They sold slaves to the Europeans, in a similar fashion, as luxuries in return for luxuries. Thus, scarcity raised demand on both sides in their respective quest for luxury items.

African Slavery

Sub-Saharan Africa—with its extended distances and few long rivers—was the one continent with the greatest hurdles to a shift in patterns from self-sufficiency to exchange agriculture and urbanization. Exchanges of food for manufactured goods over distances greater than 20 miles were prohibitively

Portuguese Traders. This brass plaque, from about the middle of the sixteenth century, decorated the palace of the Benin Obo and shows two Portuguese traders. The fact they are holding hands suggests that they could be father and son.

expensive. Human portage or donkey transport, the only available forms of moving goods, were limited to highly valuable merchandise, such as salt, copper, and iron. Everything else was manufactured within self-sufficient households, such as pottery, textiles, mats, basketry, utensils, implements, leather goods, and weapons, alongside a full range of agricultural goods.

Self-sufficiency required large households. In villages with limited outside trade, the polygamous household with the largest number of males and females employed at home and in the fields was the wealthiest. To increase his wealth further, a household master often raided neighboring villages and acquired captives, to be enslaved and put to work inside and outside the household. Not surprisingly, therefore, slave raiding and household slavery were general features in sub-Saharan African societies. The more stratified such societies were—with chiefly or royal institutions such as central administrations, armies, and juridical and fiscal offices—the more slaves rose into positions of responsibility and, frequently, autonomy. Thus, African slavery was a highly flexible institution.

Of course, slaves could always run away. In sub-Saharan Africa, they could return to freedom in their native villages, although this was difficult if these villages were still weak or destroyed altogether from the most recent raid. Running away would have been much easier if there had been walled towns or cities nearby where runaways could have sought employment in a craft. Since the urban alternative did not exist to any large degree in the interior of sub-Saharan Africa—in contrast to an urbanizing western Europe, where unfree labor in agriculture disappeared gradually after 1350—slavery, in the flexible household pattern, continued during the period 1500–1800 largely unchanged.

Limited Slave Trade from Benin   When Portugal began the slave trade for sugar plantations on West African off-coast islands, African chiefs and kings had to evaluate the comparative value of slaves for their households or for sale. The kingdom of Benin in the rain-forest region west of the Niger delta was an early example of this calculation. The ruler Ewuare (r. 1440–1473) was the first to rise to dominance over chiefs (*azuma*) and assume the title of king (*obo*). Through conquests in all directions, Ewuare acquired large numbers of slaves. A kingdom emerged on the basis of slaves employed in the army and for the construction of extensive earthworks protecting the capital, Benin City.

Early trade contacts between Portuguese mariners and Benin intensified when the successor of Ewuare granted permission to build a fort on the coast in 1487. But the king kept the exchange of palm oil, ivory, woolens, beads, malagueta pepper, and slaves for guns, powder, metalware, salt, and cottons under close control. A generation later, when the kings prohibited the sale of male slaves, the Portuguese promptly abandoned their fort. Later, a compromise was reached whereby a limited number of slaves was traded, perhaps some 30 percent of the total trade volume between Portugal and Benin, in return for firearms. The kingdom admitted missionaries and members of the dynasty acculturated to the Portuguese, making Benin an economically diversified and culturally complex African Atlantic state.

Slave exports remained restricted during the following two centuries, when Benin was a strong, centralized state. Under subsequent weak kings, decentralization set in. Provincial chiefs began to compete with each other, requiring increased numbers of firearms. To buy more weapons, toward the end of the seventeenth century a weak Benin palace lifted the restrictions on the slave trade. Even more weapons were purchased and slaves were sold during a civil war in the first half of the eighteenth century. But the kingdom reunified and the palace never lost complete control over Benin's trade with the Portuguese and, from the mid-seventeenth century onward, Dutch and British mariners and merchants. From the mid-eighteenth century, the kings even encouraged indigenous gunsmiths to make muskets to help render the country independent from imports, although apparently nothing came of this encouragement. Compared to the slave trade farther west on the West African coast, the large centralized kingdom of Benin with its high internal demand for slave labor remained a modest exporter of slaves.

The Kingdom of Kongo

Farther south, on the central West African coast, the Portuguese established trade relations with several coastal kingdoms, among which Kongo and Ndongo were the most important. These kingdoms were located south of the Congo River, with rain forest to the north and savanna to the south. Kongo, the oldest and most centralized kingdom in the region, emerged about 1400, or a century before the arrival of the Portuguese. Its capital, M'banza (São Salvador), was 20 miles inland in the fertile highlands. With 60,000 inhabitants in the sixteenth century it contained a large palace population and a royal domain, where slaves farmed sorghum, millet, and corn.

Within a radius of some 20 miles, the kings governed a region of about 300,000 independent villagers directly. To defend their rule, they relied on a standing army of 5,000 troops, including 500 musketeers, in the sixteenth century. They appointed members of the royal family as governors, who were entitled to rents but were also obliged to deliver taxes in kind to the palace. In addition, the kings collected a head tax in the form of cowrie shells, an indication that farmers engaged in a limited form of trading their agricultural surplus on markets in the capital to provide themselves with the shells for the tax. This region of direct rule was marked by a unified law and administration. Royal representatives traveled around to represent the royal writ. Farther away, vassal kings, called "dukes" (Portuguese *duque*), governed and sent tributes or gifts to the capital. They sometimes rebelled and broke away; thus, the territory of Kongo, similar to that of Songhay, shifted constantly in size.

The kings of Kongo converted to Christianity early and sent members of the ruling family to Portugal for their education. Portuguese missionaries converted the court and a number of provincial chiefs. In the ruling class, many read and wrote Portuguese and Latin fluently, impressing European aristocrats with their comportment whenever they went on missions. Muslim ethnic stereotypes against "reddish" Christians and Christian stereotypes and patronizing attitudes against dark Muslims, called "*moros*," and, by extension, blacks from sub-Saharan Africa had existed for a long time in Iberia and expressed themselves in Portugal's dealings with Kongo.

Kongolese Cross of St. Anthony. Considered an emblem of spiritual authority and power, the Christian cross was integrated into Kongo ancestral cults and burial rituals and was believed to contain magical protective properties. In Antonianism, the religious reform movement launched by Dona Beatriz, or Kimpa Vita, in 1704, St. Anthony of Padua, a thirteenth-century Portuguese-born saint, became known as Toni Malau, or "Anthony of Good Fortune," and was the patron of the movement. His image was widely incorporated into religious objects and personal items, such as this cross.

Kongolese royalty wore Portuguese dress, listened to church music and hymns, and drank wine imported from the Canaries. Lay assistants converted many urban and villager commoners to Catholicism, and schoolmasters instructed children at churches and chapels. The result was an African Creole culture, in which the animist veneration of territorial and ancestral spirits was combined with Catholicism. As the story of Dona Beatriz Kimpa Vita demonstrates, this Creole culture should not be viewed as a simple facsimile of European culture. Instead, it was a creative adaptation of Portuguese Catholicism to the indigenous African heritage, in the same way that East and West Africa adapted to Coptic Christianity or Islam and represented genuine variations of African culture.

Kongo began to sell slaves to Portuguese traders as early as 1502 for labor on the sugar plantations of the island of São Tomé. By the mid-1500s, the kings permitted the export of a few thousand slaves a year. But Portugal wanted more slaves, and in 1571 the crusader King Sebastião I (r. 1557–1578), who renewed Henry the Navigator's devotion to territorial conquest, chartered a member of the aristocracy with creating a colony in the adjacent kingdom of Ndongo for the mining of salt and silver by slaves. At first, this holder of the charter assisted the king of Ndongo in defeating rebels; but when his colonial aims became clear, the king turned against him and a full-scale Portuguese war of conquest and for slaves erupted.

In this war, which lasted with short interruptions from 1579 to 1657, the Portuguese allied themselves with Ibangala bands. The Ibangala were a large group of loosely organized, fierce warriors from the eastern outreaches of Kongo and Ndongo into central Africa who raided in both kingdoms for slaves. Their propaganda as well as their swift campaigns threw the population into fear and turmoil. Tales of cannibalism and the forcible recruitment of child soldiers spread by word of mouth. The Ibangala consumed large quantities of palm wine and imported Portuguese wine from the Canaries, the latter received from traders in payment for slaves. Together, a few hundred Portuguese musketeers and tens of thousands of Ibangalas raided the kingdoms of Ndongo and Kongo for slaves, often as many as 15,000 a year.

The war reduced the resourceful Queen Nzinga (r. 1624–1663) of Ndongo to a guerilla fighter. In the end, thanks to an alliance with some Ibangalas, she recreated a kingdom, greatly reduced in size, that also engaged in the slave trade. The widening conflict also spilled over into Kongo, where Portuguese and allied Ibangala troops exploited a long civil war (1665–1709) and enslaved even Catholic and Antonian Christians. The war expanded further when new entrants onto the scene, the Dutch West India Company, mistakenly assumed that the small numbers of Portuguese troops would be no match for a quick conquest of the coastal forts. Thanks to Brazilian help, however, Portugal was able to drive out the Dutch. The latter decided to return to a more peaceful trade for slaves from other fortified strongholds on the African west coast.

The Dutch in South Africa

In 1652, the Dutch built a fort on the South African coast to supply fresh water and food to ships traveling around the Cape of Good Hope. Employees of the company, working on time contracts, grew wheat on small lots and bought cattle from the Khoi, local cattle breeders. A few

---

African Christianity

"Even slaves dress up as if great lords, with a great escort they go to church where they hear Mass, take communion, and contract marriage according to the form of the Roman Church, then go back with great escort."

—Giovanni Francesco da Roma. *Breve relazione . . .* (1648). Excerpt translated in Linda M. Heywood and John K. Thornton, *Central Africans, Atlantic Creoles, and the Foundation of the Americas, 1585–1660*, p. 174. Cambridge: Cambridge University Press, 2007.

Queen Nzinga. In this contemporary engraving, Queen Nzinga is shown conducting negotiations with the Portuguese in 1622. She sits on a slave's back to avoid having to stand in the presence of a person beneath her rank.

wealthy landowners imported the first black slaves in 1658, from Dahomey, on the West African coast, to convert the original Dutch smallholdings into larger wheat and grape plantations. Gradually, a culturally Dutch settler society emerged, which included Protestants fleeing religious persecution in France and Germany.

The majority of these settlers were urban craftspeople and traders, while most of the actual farmers employed slaves from Mozambique, the island of Madagascar, and even as far away as Indonesia, the epicenter of Dutch colonial ambitions in the East Indies. Around 1750, there were about 10,000 *Boers* (Dutch for "farmer" [rhymes with "boars"]) in the Cape Colony, easily outnumbered by slaves. Through relentless land expansion into the interior, ranchers destroyed the Khoi, forcing their absorption into other local groups. The Boers governed themselves, following the model of Dutch representative institutions. Their descendants would one day fight the Zulu for land and the British for independence and create the system of apartheid in South Africa as they became "Afrikaaners"—as they called themselves. Today, they share political power and a troubled political legacy with their black African countrymen.

American Plantation Slavery and Atlantic Mercantilism

The pattern of African slavery was different from the pattern of American plantation slavery. While European slave traders exploited an existing African slave system, the American plantation slave system had its roots in the eastern Christian religious civilization of Byzantium. There, the Roman institution of agricultural estate slavery survived, in both law and practice. Imperial estates on the warm southern Mediterranean islands of Cyprus and Crete employed Muslim prisoners as well as captives from the Russian steppes as slaves for the expansion of such labor-intensive crops as wine and

The Spread of Sugar Cultivation, 600 BCE–1900 CE

0 km   2500   5000
0 miles   2500   5000

MAP **19.2** The Spread of Sugar Cultivation, 600 BCE–1900 CE.

olive oil. After 1191, when crusaders conquered Cyprus from Byzantium, crusader landlords and Venetian and Genoese merchants expanded into sugar production, which had been introduced in the eastern Mediterranean by Arabs in the period 800–1000. Two and a half centuries later, Venetians, Spaniards, and Portuguese established slave-based sugarcane plantations on the islands of Madeira, the Canaries, and São Tomé off the West African coast. Thus, through Byzantine, crusader, Venetian, Arab, and Iberian interaction and adaptation over the course of hundreds of years, the massive system of Atlantic–American plantation slavery came into being around 1500. About 80 percent of all slaves brought from Africa to the Americas were taken to work on sugar plantations (see Map 19.2).

The Special Case of Plantation Slavery in the Americas

In examining the rise and perpetuation for more than three centuries of the patterns of American **plantation slavery**, a number of questions arise: How many Africans were forcibly taken from Africa to the Americas? Who were they, and who were the people who exploited their labor? What institutions were created to capture, transport, supply, and work slaves? What did the labor of the African slaves help to build? And, perhaps most of all, why did this system develop the way it did—and last so long?

Plantation slavery: Economic system in which slave labor was used to grow crops such as sugar, tobacco, and cotton on large estates.

Numbers   The enslavement of Africans for labor in the Western Hemisphere constituted the largest human migration—voluntary or involuntary—in world history before the later nineteenth century. Though it is estimated that millions of Africans had earlier been taken into servitude in the Muslim world from the eighth to the fourteenth century, their numbers are dwarfed by those shipped across the Atlantic from the fifteenth through the early nineteenth century.

While the figures have been hotly debated by scholars and activists over recent decades, the latest estimates put the numbers of Africans shipped out of Africa at around 12.5 million—more than twice the number taken in the so-called Oriental slave trade to the Middle East and Indian Ocean basin during the period 700–1400. Nearly half of these slaves, 5.8 million, went to Brazil. While historical demographers and other scholars are trying to amass figures to determine how many slaves died in the process of being transferred to the African coast after their initial capture and how many more perished at sea, their conclusions are at present only tentative. However, most estimates place the numbers of slaves lost during these transfers at another 1.4 million, or 12 percent, with a total of 11 million reaching the American shores. These figures, it should be noted, exclude the numbers killed in the African slave raids and wars themselves, which will probably never be precisely known (see Map 19.3).

Chattel: Literally, an item of moveable personal property; chattel slavery is the reduction of the status of the slave to an item of personal property of the owner, to dispose of as he or she sees fit.

Chattel Slavery   By the mid-eighteenth century African slaves everywhere in the New World had been reduced to the status of **chattel**. That is, they were legally considered to be (and, in practice, were treated as) the property of their owners and

MAP **19.3** Regions from which Captured Africans Were Brought to the Americas, 1501–1867.

held the same status as farm animals or agricultural implements. The perfect expression of this condition may be found in the famous Dred Scott decision, handed down by the US Supreme Court a century later, in 1857. In the court's opinion, the Chief Justice, Roger B. Taney, forcefully stated that black African slaves "had no rights which a white man was bound to respect."

Within this statement we see another qualitatively different element from earlier kinds of slavery: what came to be known as the "color line." While color was sometimes not the determining factor in the early years of American slavery, it had very much come to be so by the eighteenth century. The equation of blackness with slavery prompted assumptions over time of African inferiority and created the basis for the modern expression of the phenomenon of racism, a problem that has plagued nearly all societies touched by the institutions of African slavery to this day.

The Problem of Presentism

One of the most difficult tasks historians face is to objectively determine the origins of long-term developments given the fact that they benefit from their knowledge of how things will turn out later. The progress of events becomes all too easily inevitable and can block a historian's vision from the alternatives that the people at the time might have considered. This is particularly true where the developments in question are vitally important but repugnant to our sensibilities and beliefs today. For example, how could otherwise "moral" people have deliberately created a system of slavery destined to harm or kill millions of fellow human beings? Shouldn't they have seen where their actions were ultimately leading?

Historians have long debated the role of present-day sensibilities and issues in the study of the past. The practice of looking at the past through the lens of the present is called **presentism**. Of course, everyone brings his or her own views and biases along when studying history. Historians, however, consciously try to distance themselves from these while attempting to empathetically enter the past. Nowhere is this problem more evident than in looking for the origins of the plantation system and African slavery. Here, the origins are certainly modest and distant in time and present many alternatives. But, above all, what those origins led to remains repellant to our present sensibilities.

> **Presentism:** A bias toward present-day attitudes, especially in the interpretation of history.

Caribbean Plantations

Soon after the discovery of the Americas and the establishment of the first Spanish settlements in the Caribbean, the indigenous population of Taínos and Caribs disappeared, decimated by the European smallpox against which the native peoples were helpless. Beginning in the sixteenth century, Native Americans on the mainland were similarly decimated by smallpox. To replenish the labor force, as early as 1511, the Spanish crown authorized the importation of 50 African slaves for gold mining on the island of Hispaniola. In the following decades thousands more followed for work on newly established sugar plantations. The Africans, at this point primarily from Senegambia, shared a similar pool of disease immunities with the Europeans. They were acclimated to tropical temperatures and conditions and had no home base in the American islands to which to flee. For their European overlords, this made them ideal workers. Indeed, by the late sixteenth century African slaves outnumbered Europeans in the Spanish-controlled islands and in Mexico and Peru, where they were primarily involved in mining.

Apart from mining, plantation work for sugar is among the most arduous forms of labor. Sugar cane leaves have sharp edges and the mature stalks must be cut down with *machetes*—long, heavy knives. The stalks are then bundled, loaded into a cart, and carried to a mill. The early mills utilized horizontal rotating millstones (later versions used stone or metal rollers) turned by human, animal, or water power. Once the stalks were crushed and their juice extracted, the waste was used for animal or occasionally for slave food. The refining process involved boiling successive batches of juice, itself a hot and taxing process. The charred animal bones added to the refining were often supplemented by those of deceased slaves, thus contributing a particularly sinister element to the process.

In all, the average slave field hand on a sugar plantation was estimated to live just 5 or 6 years. Early on, the slave workforce was largely male, which meant that there were relatively few children to replenish the slave population. With the price of slaves low and the mortality rate high, it was economically more desirable to literally work slaves to death and buy more than to make the extra investments necessary to cultivate families. Not surprisingly, revolts, work slowdowns, and sabotage of equipment and cargoes were frequent, with punishments being severe and public. Slaves were flogged and branded for minor infractions and maimed, castrated, hanged, burned, and sometimes dismembered for more severe crimes.

Grinding Sugarcane. The steps in the making of refined sugar were elaborate and backbreaking. In the center, a wagon brings the harvested cane in from the fields, while slaves in the foreground sort the stalks under the watchful eyes of an overseer. The wind-powered mill uses rollers to crush the cane and extract its juice for boiling.

Mercantilism in Action in the Caribbean   With the decline of Spanish power and the rise of the North Atlantic maritime states during the seventeenth century, a profound shift of the political balance in the Caribbean took place. Portugal, Spain, the Netherlands, Great Britain, and France all followed a similar path to enrichment that came to be known as "**mercantilism**"—that is, when the wealth of the state depends on having the maximum amount of gold and silver in its treasury. Thus, states should keep their economies blocked off from competitors and import as little and export as much as possible. Colonies were seen as vital to this economic system because they supplied raw materials to the European homeland and provided safe markets for manufactured goods from the homeland.

It followed that one way to enhance your riches was to capture those of your rivals. Thus, from the late sixteenth through the early eighteenth centuries, the navies of the Dutch, English, French, Spanish, and Portuguese all attacked each others' shipping interests and maritime colonies. The Spanish, with their lucrative treasure fleets to Acapulco and through the Caribbean along the "Spanish Main," were the favorite targets of all. Moreover, all of these governments issued "letters of marque" allowing warships owned by individuals or companies called **privateers** to prey on the shipping of rival powers for a share in the prize money they obtained. Not surprisingly, a number of individuals also went into this business for themselves as pirates. Long before the motion pictures of the same name, there were a great many wildly diverse "pirates of the Caribbean."

The growing trade in plantation commodities from the Caribbean compelled Spain's European competitors to oust the Spanish from their valuable sugar islands. Thus, the rising naval power of England seized Jamaica from Spain in 1655. Jamaica's sugar production grew so valuable that the annual worth of its commodities was greater than that of all of England's North American colonies combined. The French, by the mid-seventeenth century the premier continental European power, followed a decade later in seizing the western part of Hispaniola, which came to be called Saint-Domingue.

This process was accompanied by two developments that enhanced the mercantilist economics of both powers. First, English, French, as well as Dutch merchants

Mercantilism: Political theory, according to which the wealth derived from the mining of silver and gold and the production of agricultural commodities should be restricted to each country's market, with as little as possible expended on imports from another country.

Privateers: Individuals or ships granted permission to attack enemy shipping and to keep a percentage of the prize money the captured ships brought at auction; in practice, privateers were often indistinguishable from pirates.

became involved in the African slave trade, usurping the Portuguese from their near-monopoly of the traffic. The second was that the growing demand for molasses (a syrup by-product of sugar refining) and the even greater popularity of its fermented and distilled end product, rum, pushed both sugar planting and slavery to heights that would not reach their peak until after 1750. As we will see in more detail, sugar, slaves, molasses, and rum form the vital legs of the famous triangular trade that sustained the Atlantic economic system.

The human toll, however, was appalling. Barbados, for example, was settled initially in 1627 by English planters, who grew tobacco, cotton, indigo, and ginger, employing English and Irish **indentured laborers**. In 1640, however, planters switched to the more profitable sugarcane. English and Irish indentured laborers now proved so unwilling to leave their home countries for Barbados that law courts in the home ports resorted to convicting them on trumped- up charges and sentencing them to "transportation." In addition, so many were tricked or seized by press gangs and sent there that being "barbadosed" quickly became a popular slang term for kidnapping. So great was the mortality of their African counterparts that they had to be shipped to the sugar islands at a rate of two to one in order to keep the population from declining. Thus, the pioneer of modern economics, Adam Smith (1723–1790), would note that "the profits of a sugar plantation in any of our West Indian colonies are generally much greater than those of any other cultivation that is now either in Europe or America. Yet for the slave it is, 'a more dreadful apprehension . . . than we can have of hell.'" It was a hell that they apprehended even before being led off the ship.

Indentured laborers: Poor workers enrolled in European states with the obligation to work in the Americas for 5–7 years, in return for their prepaid passage across the Atlantic.

A Vision of Hell

"The Negroes are so wilful and loth to leave their own country, that they have often leap'd out of the canoes, boat and ship, into the sea, and kept under water until they were drowned, to avoid being taken up and saved by our boats, which pursued them; they having a more dreadful apprehension of Barbadoes than we can have of hell . . ."

—Thomas Phillips. "The Voyage of the Ship *Hannibal* of London, in 1693." In: *Ships and Slaving*, ed. George Francis Dow, pp. 31–71, quote from pp. 62–63. Salem, MA: Marine Research Society, 1927. Reprint Mineola, NY: Dover, 2002.

The Sugar Empire: Brazil   The Portuguese first planted sugarcane as a crop in Brazil in the 1530s, well before Caribbean planters began to grow it and a generation after the original trade in brazilwood (a red dye) was established. Portuguese colonists turned to the production of sugar because, unlike their counterparts in the Caribbean, Mexico, and Peru, they did not find any gold or silver. Like the Spanish, the Portuguese crown repeatedly issued edicts to the colonists to refrain from enslaving indigenous people for work on the sugar plantations; these edicts were widely ignored. In addition, in the 1530s, the Portuguese trading network on the West African coast began to supply the colony with African slaves. By the end of the century, a dramatic rise in demand for sugar in Europe increased the importation of black slaves, of which the Portuguese carefully cultivated their carrying monopoly. In the next century, the insatiable demand of the sugar industry for slaves received a further boost in 1680 when enslavement of Indians was finally abolished; and in 1690 the discovery of gold in Minas Gerais, in the interior, led to a gold boom and increased demand for labor even more. Brazil ultimately became the final destination of nearly half of all the slaves transported to the Americas. Indeed, Brazil went on to be the largest slave state in the world, with about two-fifths of its entire population consisting of blacks. In the end, it was the last country in the Americas to give up the institution, in 1888 (see Map 19.4).

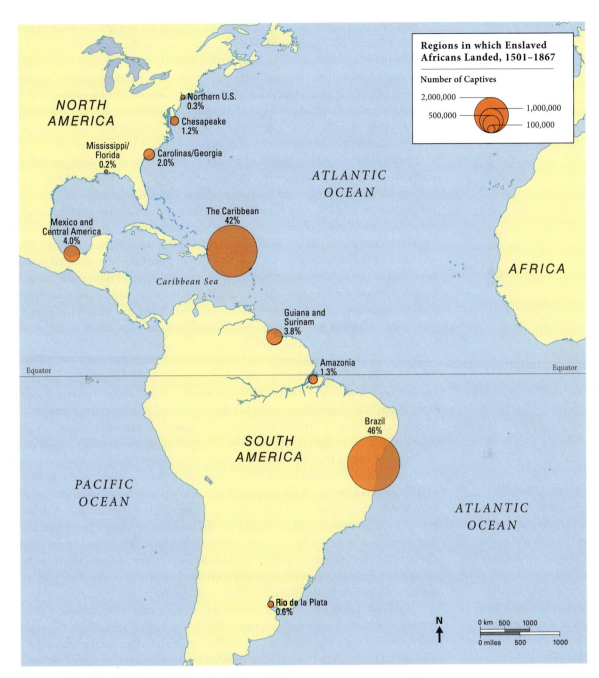

MAP **19.4** Regions in which Enslaved Africans Landed, 1501–1867.

The "Peculiar Institution" in British North America

In the 1850s a number of writers and politicians in the southern United States waxed enthusiastically about the possibility of "filibustering" expeditions to Central America, Cuba, and even Brazil to win these lands for the United States. Later, during the American Civil War, some leaders of the Confederate States even called for a great

Confederate "tropical empire," extending from Virginia in the north to the southern border of Brazil. The reason for this enthusiasm was that these men recognized a phenomenon that historians have only lately come to reexamine: that these territories, regardless of their national boundaries, shared a common economic system based on plantation agriculture producing valuable commodities for export; relied on imported manufactured goods; shared a common aristocratic culture; and relied almost totally on what was quaintly referred to in the American southern states as "the peculiar institution" of slavery to support it.

Modern historians have identified a plantation zone which, in 1750, extended unbroken from the Chesapeake Bay in England's American colonies to Brazil, embracing the entire Caribbean in the process. Such a zone represented a pattern unprecedented in world history. No system of cash cropping had ever been this large, extended over so much territory, or brought so much profit to its owners and investors. It created the largest demand for human labor yet seen, which after 1700 was satisfied almost exclusively through the African slave trade. As we noted in the beginning of this section, this in turn created a nearly immutable color line that defined a permanent underclass and identified blackness with slavery and inferiority. Though it was eventually destined to die out in the northernmost British and French possessions as well as the northern United States, legal slavery at one time extended far beyond the plantation zone into what is now Canada.

The "Sot Weed" Enterprise

As we saw in preceding chapters, the first permanent English settlements in the Americas were the for-profit enterprise at Jamestown in 1607 and the religious "errand in the wilderness" of the initial settlements in Massachusetts from 1620 on. Both would soon count Africans among them, though their descendants in Jamestown would be by far the more economically important. In August of 1619 a Dutch privateer surprised a Portuguese slaver en route to Vera Cruz, Mexico, and relieved her of 60 of her *piezas de India*—"pieces of the Indies," or African slaves. By the end of the month, the ship put in at Jamestown, which had been barely hanging on as an enterprise, and disembarked "twenty and odd Negroes," some of whom were Christians from the kingdom of Kongo. These were the first slaves sold in the English colonies of North America. They would be far from the last. Though only about 3–5 percent of the slaves shipped from Africa ended up in North America, through procreation on the continent their numbers grew to more than 4 million by the eve of the American Civil War.

Their labor, along with that of increasing numbers of indentured workers from Europe, was needed for a new enterprise that, it was hoped, would save the colonial enterprise from failure: tobacco. The Powhatan and other local peoples grew tobacco for themselves, but it was considered by the increasing numbers of European smokers to be inferior to the varieties grown in the Caribbean. The English, however, had acquired some of the Caribbean plants and begun intensive cultivation in the Chesapeake Bay region of this "sot weed," as it came to be called. Indentured labor was widely used, but those workers were bound to stay only until they had worked off the cost of their passage, usually 5–7 years. After that, they worked for wages or acquired their own land. Under these conditions, slaves came to be the preferred labor source in the colony of Virginia.

Though a surprising number of Africans earned **manumission** from their owners, gaining their freedom, acquiring land, and on occasion even starting their own

Manumission: The process by which slaves are legally given freedom; in the days of Atlantic slavery, this was most commonly done by slaves saving enough to buy themselves from their owners, by outsiders buying them and setting them free, or by owners simply granting them freedom; during the nineteenth century, abolitionists often collected money to buy the freedom of slaves or bring them north by the famous Underground Railroad.

plantations with their own slaves during the seventeenth century, the colonial authorities eventually passed laws firmly fixing the slave underclass as one based on color. For example, as if anticipating Justice Taney's ruling of 1857, the colony of Carolina's Lords Proprietors stated as early as 1669 that "freemen" were to have "absolute power and authority," over their "[N]egro slaves." Throughout the eighteenth century, slave-based tobacco-raising remained the dominant plantation activity in the upper south.

Sugar, Rice, and Indigo in the Lower South

The colony of Carolina came under the purview of the Lords Proprietors in Barbados, who began sending settlers in 1670 as a way to transport religious dissenters and to form a bulwark against the Spanish in Florida. As part of a vast pine forest running from southern Virginia to northern Florida, its position as a provider of naval stores—pitch, tar, rosin, and turpentine—as well as tall, straight tree trunks for ships' masts, was vital in the age of wooden vessels. Even today, there is a sizeable town in North Carolina named Tarboro, and the state's nickname is "The Tarheel State." Although indentured laborers and slaves were involved in these enterprises, plantation crops were destined to see the largest demand for their labor.

In the seventeenth and early eighteenth centuries, the settlers ran what was by far the most successful attempt ever to enslave Native Americans in the Carolinas. As many as 50,000 slaves labored here by the early eighteenth century. Native resistance to slaving resulted in war between the settlers and a Native American alliance in 1715–1717 that almost lost the colony for the Lords Proprietors. The settlers, angry with what they considered the mismanagement of the Lords Proprietors, appealed to the crown; and South Carolina was split off in 1719 and set up as a royal colony shortly thereafter. Deprived of Native Americans for slaves, the colonies began to import large numbers of West African slaves as the Dutch dominance of the trade gave way to the British. This initial wave of slave immigration ultimately grew to a point that made South Carolina the only North American colony, and later state, in which African Americans outnumbered Europeans.

In addition, South Carolina produced many of the same plantation commodities as Brazil and the Caribbean, along with one vitally important new addition. Sugarcane and molasses, for example, were produced in the southern lowlands and tidewater regions. Carolina rice became a vital food source and one whose production was taken up throughout the flatlands of the Deep South. Many West Africans brought with them the skills and knowledge of long-grain rice cultivation ideal for the lowlands. It was indigo, however, that was destined to become the colony's most important cash crop until the cotton boom of the nineteenth century.

The dark blue dye produced from the tropical plant *Indigofera tinctoria* had been grown

Advertisement for a Slave Auction. In this notice from 1766, potential slave buyers in Charleston, South Carolina, are informed of the time and place for the sale of a "choice cargo" of recently arrived Africans. As Charleston was undergoing a smallpox epidemic at the time, potential customers are reassured that the captives are healthy and likely to be immune to the disease.

extensively throughout Asia, the ancient Mediterranean, and North and West Africa. A similar American species, *Indigofera suffruticosa*, had long been in use in Mexico and Central America. Maritime countries with Indian and East Asian connections imported vast quantities of it into Europe, while the Spanish began to cultivate the American variety. Sales in northern Europe were initially hampered because there indigo competed with the local production of dyes made from the woad plant. Restrictions on imports were gradually lifted, and South Carolina entered an indigo boom starting in the 1740s. The burgeoning need for labor in planting, stripping the leaves, fermenting, cleaning, draining, scraping, and molding the residue into balls or blocks—all accompanied by a considerable stench—drove the slave trade even further.

The final English possession in southern North America prior to 1750 was Georgia. The southern regions of what was to become the colony of Georgia had been claimed by the Spanish as early as 1526 as part of their exploration of Florida and the Gulf Coast. Attempts by the French to found a colony near Port Royal, South Carolina, and Fort Caroline (near present-day Jacksonville) in the 1560s were ultimately undone. With the expansion of the English presence in the seventeenth century and the French concentrating on their vast claims in Canada and the Mississippi valley, the territory between Carolina and the Spanish fort at St. Augustine became increasingly disputed.

Into this situation stepped James Oglethorpe (1696–1785), the only founder of an English colony in North America who lived to see it become part of the United States. Oglethorpe's vision was to set up a colony for England's poor, debtors (who would otherwise be imprisoned), and dispossessed. He obtained a royal charter for his idea and in 1733 landed with his first band of settlers at the site of the modern city of Savannah. After buying land from the local Native Americans, he began to develop the colony as a free area in which slavery was banned. The Spanish attempted to claim Georgia in 1742 but were repulsed. Pressed by settlers bringing their slaves in from South Carolina, Georgia's ban on slave labor was soon rescinded. By the end of Oglethorpe's life, which he spent in retirement in England, Georgia had developed its own slave-based plantation economy, producing rice, sugar, indigo, and, on the Sea Islands along the coast, a fine, long-fiber variety of cotton, which proved to be a harbinger of the commodity that would ensure slavery's survival in the United States until 1865.

The Fatal Triangle: The Economic Patterns of the Atlantic Slave Trade

As mentioned, the European countries that successively dominated the transportation of slaves from the West African coast moved steadily northward in a pattern that paralleled their naval and merchant marine power. That is, during the fifteenth and sixteenth centuries, Portugal had an effective monopoly on the trade from outposts in Senegambia, Elmina, and Ndongo. The success of Dutch and English privateers encouraged more concerted economic warfare and, with it, the seizure by the Dutch of Elmina in 1637. Now it was the Dutch who became the principal slave carriers, part of a pattern of aggressive colonizing that made the Netherlands the world's richest country in per capita terms through much of the seventeenth century. The rise of England's naval power at the expense of the Dutch and the fading of the Spanish and Portuguese naval presence allowed the English—and, to a lesser extent, the French—to dominate the slaving trade. By the mid-eighteenth century, as the trade approached its height, it had become the base upon which the world's most lucrative economic triangle was constructed (see Map 19.5).

Rum, Guns, and Slaves

As we have seen, England's colonies in the Americas, especially those in the Caribbean, were by the eighteenth century producing valuable crops, including sugar, tobacco, cotton, and indigo, for export to the Old World. Tobacco was raised mainly in England's North American colonies, along with some cotton for export to England, though at this point England still imported most of its cotton from India. So profitable were these exports that, in keeping with the policy of mercantilism, the crown passed a series of acts in 1651 and 1660 that produced even greater profits for merchants in the motherland. The Navigation Acts required that all goods imported to England from American colonies had to be transported only in English ships, thereby guaranteeing a virtual monopoly on trans-Atlantic trade.

British merchants acquired enormous profits from their colonial trading practices, particularly with the Atlantic colonies. We are afforded a good example of how this worked through an analysis of the Atlantic system, or the "triangular trade." In

MAP **19.5** The North Atlantic System, ca. 1750.

Atlantic system:
Economic system in which European ships would exchange goods for slaves in West Africa and slaves would then be brought to America and exchanged for goods that would be carried back to the home port.

general terms, British ships would leave home ports in either their North American colonies or Britain with goods of various kinds, then travel to ports along the western coast of Africa, where these goods would be exchanged for African slaves; these ships would then sail across the Atlantic, where slaves would be exchanged for goods produced in western Atlantic colonies; and finally, these goods would be carried back to the home port.

A particular pattern consisted of the following: An English ship loaded with New England rum would sail from Europe to the western coast of Africa, where the rum would be exchanged for a cargo of slaves; laden with slaves, the ship would then sail westward across the Atlantic to sugar colonies in the Caribbean, where the slaves would be exchanged for a cargo of molasses; the ship would sail to New England, where the molasses would be processed into rum. A variant pattern was the following: A British ship would leave its home port—increasingly Liverpool, the port that benefited most dramatically from the slave trade—loaded with manufactured goods, such as guns, knives, textiles, and assorted household wares. It would sail to the western coast of Africa, where these goods would be exchanged for a cargo of slaves; the ship would then sail westward across the Atlantic to the British colony of Virginia, where its human cargo would be exchanged for tobacco; the ship would then sail eastward across the Atlantic to its home port in Britain, where the tobacco would be unloaded and then sold to British and European merchants.

To a large extent, the **Atlantic system** depended upon the import of ever-increasing numbers of slaves from Africa. Beginning in the early eighteenth century, the numbers skyrocketed as the English and French imported slaves for their colonies in the Caribbean and in North America. The numbers were pushed further by the demise of Native American slavery in the Carolinas after 1719. Thus, at its height in the eighteenth century, more than half of the nearly 12 million Africans estimated to have been transported to the Americas were landed.

Bristol Docks and Quay in 1760. Up until 1750, Bristol was the largest slave-trading port in England. It supplied the majority of slaves sent to Jamaica to work in the island's booming sugar plantations. However, its small and congested harbor caused it to fall behind Liverpool as the leading British port in the Atlantic slave trade.

The Middle Passage Following capture in Africa, prisoners were usually marched to slave markets and embarkation ports roped, chained, or ganged together by forked tree trunks. Slave lots were then wholesaled to middlemen or auctioned directly to foreign factors. From this point they would be imprisoned in fortified slave pens called "barracoons" until the next ship bound for their sale destination arrived. But it was on the voyage from Africa to the Americas, the infamous "Middle Passage," that the full horror of the slave's condition was most fully demonstrated.

Because the profits involved in transportation were so high for captains, officers, and even crewmen, they constantly experimented with ways to pack the maximum number of human beings into the holds of their ships. Because a certain percentage of mortality was expected during a voyage that lasted from a few weeks to nearly 2 months, some ship captains favored "tight packing"—deliberate overcrowding on the assumption that a few more might survive than normal. On the other hand, some captains favored the "loose pack" method, with the assumption that a higher percentage would survive if given marginally more room than normal. In either case, conditions were abominable.

Due to well-founded fears of slave mutiny, the holds of slave ships were locked and barred and the hatchways and vents covered with iron gratings. The slaves were chained to tiny bunks arranged in tiers configured to maximize the space of the hold. Food was minimal, usually corn mush, and sanitation

> ### The Middle Passage
>
> "But when a vessel arrived to conduct us away to the ship, it was a most horrible scene; there was nothing to be heard but rattling chains, smacking of whips, and the groans and cries of our fellow-men. Some would not stir from the ground, when they were lashed and beat in the most horrible manner."
>
> —Excerpt from Quobna Ottobah Cugoano, *Thoughts and Sentiments on the Evil and Wicked Traffic of the Slavery and Commerce of the Human Species*, ed. Vincent Caretta, p. 15. New York: Penguin, 1999.

Plan of a Slave Ship, 1789. This image, based on the *Brooks*, a Liverpool slave ship, was one of the first to document the horrors of the slave trade. It shows the captives laid like sardines beneath deck. In such conditions slaves perished at the rate of 10–30 percent during the Middle Passage. The engraving was widely distributed by British abolitionists, who eventually succeeded in banning the trade in 1807.

nonexistent. Small groups of captives would be brought up on deck on a rotating basis to be haphazardly washed of their vomit and feces with buckets of frigid ocean water thrown at them by the crew. They would then be "danced" for minimal exercise and sent back down, and the next group would be brought up. The dead, sick, and resistant would simply be thrown overboard. The ship and crew were also well armed to fight off attacks by competitors or pirates. On landing at their destination, the slaves were again "barracooned," cleaned up, and given better meals pending their auction to individual buyers. In the process somewhere between 5 and 20 percent of them died en route.

Culture and Identity in the African Diaspora

The original meaning of the term "diaspora" referred to the dispersal of the Jews around the Roman Empire after their revolt of the first century CE was put down. Scholars now use the term more generally for the wide dispersal by forced or voluntary migration of any large group. In the case of the **African diaspora**, in which Africans moved to nearly all parts of the Americas primarily through the slave trade, the story is far too varied and complex for us to do more than note some general patterns related to culture and identity.

African diaspora:
Dispersal of African peoples throughout the world, particularly the Americas, as part of the transatlantic slave trade.

A New Society: Creolization of the Early Atlantic World

As discussed earlier in this chapter, one of the effects of the Portuguese implantation on African coasts through trade forts and colonies was the adaptation of coastal African societies to western Christianity and Portuguese culture. These societies were highly diverse. Some were tribal and peaceful, others tribal and militarily oriented; still others had transformed themselves into kingdoms, cooperating intermittently or permanently with the Portuguese and later with the Dutch, English, and French. Depending on the type or intensity of interaction, African Creole cultures emerged, that is, cultures in which an adaptation to Catholicism occurred and in which Africans appropriated cultural elements into their own heritage.

In earlier scholarship this creolization was often described as resulting in certain elements of an alien, colonizing culture uneasily grafted onto "genuine" Africanness. As in the case of Dona Beatriz and the rise of a Kongolese Catholicism, however, Creole culture has to be seen as a phenomenon in its own right. This is similarly true for black Creole cultures in the Americas. Blacks arrived either as animists with very localized animist heritages or as enslaved Creole Christians and Muslims since foreign and indigenous slave raiders penetrating inland Africa made no distinctions among their victims. Either way, African slaves adapted to their plantation life through creolization or, as African Christian or Muslim Creoles, through further creolization, a process that expressed itself in distinct languages or dialects as well as synthetic (or hybrid) religious customs. Adaptation was not imitation but a creative transformation of cultural elements to fit the conditions of life.

Recent scholarship suggests that a key formative element in the development of culture and identity of Africans in the Americas lay in the influence of the central African Creoles from Kongo and Ndongo (today's Congo and Angola) up to the middle of the seventeenth century. The Christianity of some believers and its later variants helped to nurture this religion among Africans in the new lands, especially when it was reinforced by the religious practices of the slave owners. The mix of language and terms for a multitude of objects similarly gave the early arrivals a certain degree of agency and skill in navigating the institutions of slavery as they were being established.

An example of a Creole language that has survived for centuries is Gullah, used by the somewhat isolated slaves along the coastal islands of South Carolina and Georgia and still spoken by their descendants today. In Haiti, Creole (*krayòl*) is not only the daily spoken language but also used in the media and in literary works. French is recognized as the other national language, especially in law and official pronouncements. Creole cultures typically involve not only the phenomenon of adaptation but also multiple identities—in language, religion, and culture.

Music and Food It can justifiably be said that the roots of nearly all popular music in the Americas may be found in Africa. Regardless of where they came from in Africa, slaves brought with them a wide variety of musical instruments, songs, and chants, all of which contributed to shaping the musical tastes of their owners and society at large. The widespread use of rhythmic drumming and dance in African celebrations, funerals, and even coded communications has come down to us today as the basis for music as diverse as Brazilian samba, Cuban and Dominican rumba and meringue, New Orleans jazz funerals, and American blues, rock-and-roll, soul, and hip-hop. It is difficult to imagine American country and western music, or bluegrass, without the modern descendant of a West African stringed instrument we know today as the banjo. The chants of field hands, rhyming contests, and gospel music contributed mightily to many of these genres.

Like music, cuisine passed easily across institutional barriers. Here, the dishes that most Americans consider "southern" have in many cases deep African roots. As mentioned earlier, the earliest rice brought to the Carolinas was a variety native to the Niger inland delta in West Africa. Africans brought with them the knowledge of setting up and running an entire rice-based food system, which was established in the Carolina lowlands and Gulf Coast. The yam, the staple of West African diets, also made its way to the Americas. The heart of Louisiana Creole cooking, including rich and spicy gumbos, "dirty rice," jambalaya, and other dishes, comes from the use of the African vegetable okra and a heady mixture of African, American, and Asian spices along with rice.

Plantation Life and Resistance Although nineteenth-century apologists for slavery frequently portrayed life under it as tranquil—"a positive good," in the words

> ### The Lord's Prayer in Gullah
>
> We fada wa dey een heaen,
> Leh ebrybody hona ya nyame.
> We pray dat soon ya gwine rule oba de wol.
> Wasoneba ting ya wahn,
> Leh um be so een dis wol
> Same like e da dey een heaben.
> Gii we de food wa we need
> Dis day yah an ebry day.
> Fagibe we fa we sin
> Same lik we fagibe dem people
> Wa do bad ta we.
> Leh we dohn hab haad test
> Wen Satan try we.
> Keep we fom ebil.
>
> —Wilbur Cross. *Gullah Culture in America*, p. 99. Westport, CT: Praeger, 2008.

Slave Culture. This ca. 1790 painting from Beaufort, South Carolina, shows the vibrancy of African American culture in the face of great hardship. Note the banjo, whose origins lie in West Africa and which would have a great impact on the development of American music.

Patterns Up Close | Voodoo and Other New World Slave Religions

Altar and Shrine from the Interior of the Historic Voodoo Museum in New Orleans.

One prominent pattern of world history that we have seen a number of times already is the way indigenous elements work to shape the identity of imported religions as they are taken up by their new believers. Buddhism in China and Japan, for example, adopted elements from Daoism and Chinese folk beliefs as well as spirits and demons from Shinto. Christianity added Roman and Germanic elements to its calendar of holidays, architecture, and cult of saints. Islam in Iran and India and Christianity in Africa underwent similar processes. In Kongo, for example, the African Christian cult of St. Anthony merged Portuguese Catholic and Kongolese animist spiritual traditions into a new church. This trend of interaction continues today, where we find the African Christian churches among the fastest growing in the world and increasingly sending clergy and missionaries to Europe and the United States.

In the Americas three main strains of this kind of interaction and adaptation of imported and indigenous traditions developed over time and are still widely practiced today: Santeria is found primarily in Cuba and among the Spanish-speaking Africans of the Caribbean but is now also in the larger cities of North America with communities of Caribbean immigrants; vodoun, usually written as "voodoo," developed in Haiti and old St. Domingue and is widely practiced among

of South Carolina's John C. Calhoun—for slave and master alike, the system was in fact one of constant real and implied violence. Most slaves reconciled themselves to their condition and navigated it as best they could, but the reminders of their status were constantly around them. Obviously, those who endured the Middle Passage had violence thrust upon them immediately upon capture. Even those born into slavery, however, lived in squalid shacks or cabins; ate inadequate rations, perhaps supplemented with vegetables they were allowed to grow themselves; and spent most of their waking hours at labor.

Those working as house servants had a somewhat easier life than field hands. In some cases, they were the primary guardians, midwives, wet nurses, and even confidants of their masters' families. Often, there was considerable expressed affection between the household slaves and the masters' family. But more often, this was tempered by the knowledge that one or one's family could be sold at any time, that infractions would be severely punished, and that one would be treated as a kind of unruly, temperamental child at best.

As we saw earlier, field hands led a far harder and shorter life. The price of slavery for the master was eternal vigilance; his nightmare was slave revolt. Over the

African-descended French speakers around the Caribbean and in areas of Louisiana; as well as Candomblé, whose adherents are mostly confined to Brazil.

All three are syncretic religions composed of elements that appear disconnected to outsiders but which practitioners see as part of an integrated whole. They intermingle Roman Catholic saints with West African natural and ancestral spirits and gods, see spiritual power as resident in natural things, incorporate images of objects to represent a person or thing whose power the believer wants to tap or disperse (as in the use of so-called voodoo dolls), and hold that proper ritual and sacrifices by priests and priestesses can tune into the spirits of the natural world. In some cases, they see these practices as curing sicknesses and raising the dead—the source of the famous "zombie" legends. Such innovations allowed the slaves to create a religious and cultural space in which they carried out autonomy from their masters—indeed, in which they *were* the masters. They also provided a kind of alternate set of beliefs which could be invoked alongside more mainstream Christian practices. In a real sense, they provided a precious degree of freedom for people who had almost no other form of it.

Mami Wata. Both a protector and a seducer, Mami Wata is an important spirit figure throughout much of Africa and the African Atlantic. She is usually portrayed as a mermaid, a snake charmer, or a combination of both. She embodies the essential, sacred nature of water, upon whose waves so many African Americans traveled across in their diaspora.

Questions

- How do black Christianity and voodoo religion show the new patterns of origins, interaction, and adoption that emerged after 1500?

- Can you think of more recent examples of syncretic religions? If so, which ones? Why are they syncretic?

years a variety of methods were developed to keep slaves in line and at their work. Overseers ran the work schedules and supervised punishments; drivers kept slaves at their work with a long bullwhip in hand to beat the slow or hesitant. Slaves leaving plantations on errands had to carry passes, and elaborate precautions were taken to discourage escape or even unauthorized visits to neighboring plantations. In the Carolinas, for example, owners spread tar on fence rails so that slaves attempting to climb or vault them would be marked for easy detection. Runaways were pursued with relentless determination by trackers with bloodhounds and flogged, branded, maimed, or castrated when returned.

Given these conditions, slave behaviors designed to try to manage their work on their own terms or to get back at their owners were frequent. Slaves would constantly stage work slowdowns, feign illnesses, engage in sabotage of tools and equipment, or pretend not to understand how to perform certain tasks. Kitchen slaves would sometimes spit or urinate into soups or gravies. Despite the risks involved, runaways were quite common. Later, in the United States in the 1850s, enforcement of the Fugitive Slave Act would be a prime factor driving the country toward civil war.

Punishing Slave Revolts. John Gabriel Stedman (1744–1797) was a British–Dutch soldier and writer whose years in Surinam, on the northern coast of South America, were recorded in his *The Narrative of a Five Year Expedition against the Revolted Negroes of Surinam* (1796). With its graphic depictions of slavery it became an important tract in the abolitionist cause. In this illustration, *A Negro Hung Alive by the Ribs to a Gallows,* engraved by the famous artist and romantic poet William Blake (1757–1827), Stedman shows a rebel who was hung by his ribs for two days as punishment for his crimes. Masters routinely cut off the noses of their slaves, burnt them alive, and whipped them to death with impunity.

Despite all their precautions, slave owners throughout the Americas constantly faced the prospect of slave insurrection. By some estimates, there were more than 250 slave uprisings involving 10 or more slaves during the four centuries of Atlantic slavery. In some cases, these rebellions were successful enough for the slaves to create their own isolated settlements where they could, for a time, live in freedom. These escapees were called *Maroons,* and three of the more famous instances of Maroon settlements existed in Jamaica, Columbia, and Surinam. In Brazil, slaves developed their own system of weaponless martial arts called *capoeira,* in which fighters walk on their hands and use their legs to strike. Map 19.6 lists some of the larger slave insurrections from 1500 to 1850.

Putting It All Together

Portugal, the Netherlands, England, France, and Spain built up a fully evolved pattern of trading for plantation slaves on the Atlantic coast of Africa in the course of the sixteenth and seventeenth centuries. The trade took off toward the end of the sixteenth century, with 28,000 slaves annually, and by 1700 had reached 80,000 annually, where it stayed until the early nineteenth century, when the slave trade was abolished. As for the patterns of state formation in Africa, on the whole, the more powerful a kingdom was, the fewer slaves it sold, given its own labor requirements. Conversely, the more conducive the circumstances were for the collapse of chiefly or royal rule and the emergence of raider societies such as the Imbangala, Ashante, or Dahomey, the more damaging the impact was on a given population. Thus, no global judgment is possible. Undoubtedly, in some regions of West and central Africa the effects were grave, while in

Maroon Leader and His Sons. The maroon kingdom of Esmeraldas, in present-day Colombia, remained virtually independent from the late sixteenth century until the early nineteenth century. Its leader, Don Francisco Arrove, and his two sons were painted in 1599 to commemorate a peace treaty with the Spanish. The sumptuous clothing and ornamentation of the maroons blends Spanish, Native American, and African styles.

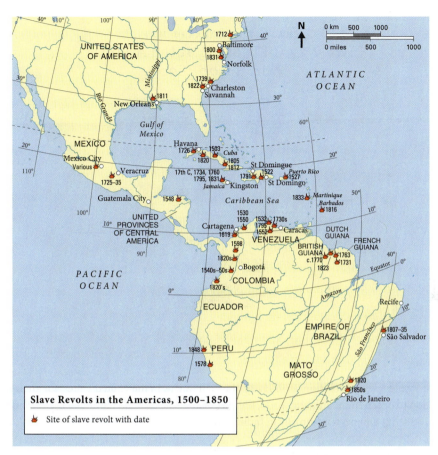

MAP 19.6 Slave Revolts in the Americas, 1500–1850.

others, often directly adjacent, the impact was less decisive. Nonetheless, the period marked a profound transformation, with many areas depopulated by the slave trade, some enhanced through the trade and the introduction of new food crops like maize and cassava, and others undergoing creolization to some degree.

The interaction and adaptation patterns of Europeans and Africans in Africa and Europeans, Africans, and Native Americans in the Caribbean and Americas over the course of three centuries (1500–1800) created not just a new, two-hemisphere world system of trade but a new kind of society as well (see Concept Map). The Atlantic slave trade was the foundation on which the mass production of cash crops and commodities, the first world pattern of its kind, was brought into being. This economic sphere was by far the richest of its kind in the world, but with it came the creation of an enduring social underclass and the foundation of modern racism.

Yet even in the 1750s, one finds the origins of the abolition movement—the international movement to end first the slave trade and ultimately slavery itself. Among the leaders of Europe's Enlightenment, thinkers were already calling for the end of the trade and institution. Within a few decades, works like the memoirs of the former slave and abolitionist Olaudah Equiano (ca. 1745–1797) would push the movement forward, as would the work of England's William Wilberforce (1759–1833), who actually lived to see the outlawing of the trade and of English slavery itself. Elsewhere,

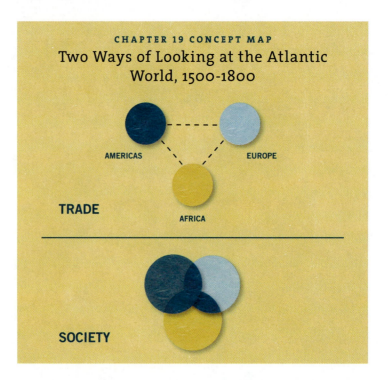

it would take a revolution, as in Haiti, or a civil war, as in the United States, for abolition to occur. In the Atlantic world, the "peculiar institution" finally ended in Brazil in 1888. But it persists informally in India, Africa, and the Middle East even today.

Review and Respond

1. What is the significance of the Songhay Empire for West African history? How did it originate, and how did it fall?

2. What impact did the Portuguese have on Ethiopia? How did this country evolve during the period 1500–1800?

3. How did the Portuguese arrive and progress along the West African coast? Describe their role and impact.

4. How was the kingdom of Kongo organized, and what role did Catholicism play in its society?

5. How did the Middle Passage function, and what role did it play within the triangular trade in the Atlantic?

6. What is Creole culture, and what forms did creolization take?

7. How did plantation slavery evolve in North America? What were the origins of African American culture, and how did that culture evolve through interaction and adaptation?

> For additional resources, including maps, primary sources, visuals, and quizzes, please go to www.oup.com/us/vonsivers. Please see the Further Resources section at the back of the book for additional readings and suggested websites.

Thinking Through Patterns

▶ **On what was the pattern of kingdom and empire formation in Africa based during the period 1500–1800?**

What is remarkable about Africa during these 300 years is that it continued its pattern of kingdom and empire formation and actually did so on an accelerated pace, on the basis of increased intra-African trade. The half-dozen examples analyzed in this chapter could be applied to another dozen states. In the interior of Africa the pattern continued in spite of the demographic effects (whatever they were in specific regions) of the Atlantic slave trade.

The pattern of plantation production evolved over several centuries before it was transplanted to the islands of the Atlantic and the Caribbean as well as the Americas. It was above all a system for growing labor-intensive cash crops—indigo, sugar, tobacco—that relied increasingly on African slave labor. By 1800, the demand for plantation commodities by Europeans and the guns, textiles, rum, and other manufactured goods that Africans took in trade for slaves pushed the system to huge proportions. In turn, the mercantilist economics of Western Europe regulated the trade within an efficient, tightly controlled, triangular system.

▶ **How did the patterns of slave trade and plantation slavery evolve in the Atlantic and the Americas?**

▶ **What are the historic roots from which modern racism evolved?**

The gradual domination of African slavery in the Americas and Caribbean over other kinds of servitude created a pattern of racism, in which blackness was permanently associated with slavery. As the economics of slavery became entrenched, the participants in the system answered the criticism of slavery on moral grounds by claiming that black Africans were inherently inferior and thus deserved to be enslaved. The argument was essentially circular: They were enslaved because they were inferior, and they were inferior because they were slaves.

In North America, long after slavery was abolished, these attitudes were preserved in law and custom in many places and reinforced during the colonization of Africa in the nineteenth century and in the practice of segregation in the United States. In Latin America—although racism is no less pervasive—racial views are more subtle. People describing themselves as *mulato*, *sambo*, or *pardo* have a better chance to be recognized as members of their own distinct ethnic groups than in the United States, where the Census classifies people simply as either black or Caucasian.

Chapter 20 | The Mughal Empire:

1400-1750 | MUSLIM RULERS AND HINDU SUBJECTS

June 17, 1631, could hardly have been a less auspicious day for the family of the Mughal emperor Shah Jahan. Though he ruled over the most powerful empire in India's history and commanded unprecedented wealth, the emperor's beloved wife, Mumtaz Mahal, had just died in giving birth to their fourteenth child. The royal family was naturally plunged into mourning, a grief conveyed by the following lines read at the announcement of her death:

> The world is a paradise full of delights,
> Yet also a rose bush filled with thorns;

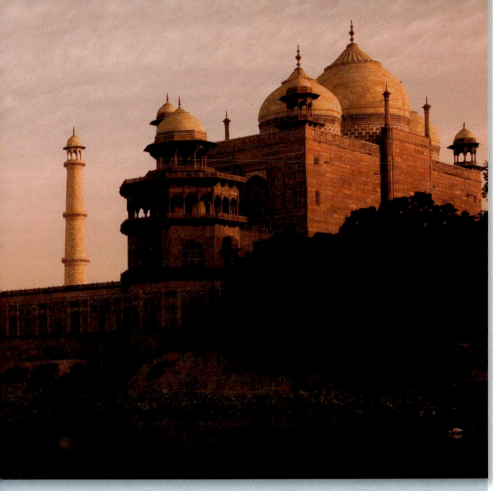

Seeing Patterns

▶ What were the strengths and weaknesses of Mughal rule?

▶ What was the Mughal policy toward religious accommodation? How did it change over time?

▶ What influences shaped culture and the arts during the Mughal era?

▶ What factors account for the Mughal decline during the eighteenth century?

▶ How did the Hindu majority adapt to Mughal rule?

He who picks the rose of happiness
Has his heart pierced by a thorn . . .

Shah Jahan himself, however, plumbed far greater depths of depression. His beard turned gray, and it was said that he wept for nearly 2 years afterward. Indeed, his eyes grew so weak from his tears that he needed to wear glasses to read his daily correspondence. Inconsolable for months on end, he finally resolved to build a magnificent tomb complex for Mumtaz Mahal over her burial site along the Jumna (or Yamuna) River near the giant fortress at Agra. At a time when monumental building projects were the order of the day for Mughal rulers, this tomb, with its balance of deceptively simple lines, harmony of proportion, and technical skill, would become the most recognized symbol of India throughout the world: the Taj Mahal.

Beyond its architectural elegance, however, the Taj Mahal also conveys a great deal of information about the circumstances of Mughal rule in India, particularly about the syncretism of Muslim rulers and Hindu subjects we first saw in Chapter 12. Like their predecessors, the Mughals discovered the difficulties of being an ethnic and religious minority ruling a huge and

The Taj Mahal. Along with the Eiffel Tower and the Great Wall of China, the Taj Mahal is perhaps the most recognizable structure in the world. Its clean lines and understated elegance mark it as the high point of an architectural synthesis of both Hindu and Muslim Indian influences and Persian classicism. It remains even today a rare symbolic triumph over the difficult history of interaction and adaptation marking India's early modern history.

Allegory: A literary, poetic, dramatic, pictorial, or architectural device in which the parts have symbolic value in depicting the meaning of the whole.

diverse population. By Shah Jahan's time, moreover, religious revival was sweeping Islamic India and past Mughal rulers were subject to criticism about their laxity in ruling according to Islamic law and the accommodations they had made with India's other religious communities. Shah Jahan therefore devoted himself anew to a study of the Quran and resolved to rule insofar as possible according to Islamic precepts. Over the coming decades, such policy changes would raise tensions between Hindus and Muslims.

For the moment, however, Shah Jahan's renewed faith found its highest expression in the design and details of the Taj. Its gleaming white stone dome and minarets are, of course, instantly identifiable as the form of a mosque. But this building is only the centerpiece of a much larger complex that is, in fact, a vision of the entrance to paradise recreated on earth. From its four large water channels, central tank, and wide main entrance down to its smallest details, like the strategic placement of appropriate quranic verses, the complex is, as one scholar put it, a vast **allegory** of Allah's judgment in paradise on the day of the resurrection.

In the end, Mughal ambition to create an empire as the earthly expression of this vision lent itself to that empire's ultimate decline. The constant drive to bring the remaining independent Indian states under Mughal control continually strained imperial resources. Dynastic succession almost always resulted in internal wars fought by rival claimants to the Mughal mantle. By the eighteenth century, prolonged rebellion and the growing power of the East India companies of the European powers would conspire to put the dynasty into a downward spiral from which it never recovered. But its most visible symbol, the Taj Mahal—literally the "Crown Palace"— remains more than ever the emblem of India's peak as a syncretic religious civilization in the modern period.

History and Political Life of the Mughals

Though we have noted previously that relations between Muslims and India's other religions were *syncretic*—that they coexisted, sometimes on difficult or hostile terms, but remained largely separate—the political and social systems created by the Mughals were in many respects a successful *synthesis*. That is, the Mughals brought with them a tradition that blended the practices of what social scientists call an "extraction state"—one that supplies itself by conquest and plunder—with several centuries of ruling more settled areas. This legacy would guide them as they struggled with a set of problems similar to those faced by rulers in other areas in creating an empire centered on one religion. Aided in their conquests by the new military technologies of cannon and small firearms, the Mughals created a flexible bureaucracy with a strict hierarchy of ranks and sophisticated separation of powers but with ultimate power concentrated in the hands of the emperors. Like those of the Chinese and Ottomans, the system was easily expanded into newly conquered areas, gave considerable scope to the ambitious, and weathered all the major political storms it encountered until its decline during the eighteenth century.

From Samarkand to Hindustan

As we have seen in earlier chapters, the rise to prominence of the Turkic-speaking members of the larger Altaic language group had taken place over the course of many centuries. From at least the time of the peoples called by the Chinese *Xiongnu*, known in western Eurasia as the Huns, these groups regularly coalesced into potent raiding and fighting forces, often putting together short-lived states such as those of the Toba in fifth- and sixth-century China, the Uighurs in the eighth and ninth centuries, and, most importantly, the Mongols in the twelfth and thirteenth centuries. But the Mongol Empire, the largest in world history, soon fell apart; and in its wake the central Asian heartland of the Turkic peoples—roughly speaking, from the Sea of Azov to the western reaches of present-day Mongolia—evolved into a patchwork of smaller states, many of whose rulers claimed descent from Genghis Khan. With the ousting of the Mongol Yuan dynasty from China in 1368, the eastern regions of this vast territory were thrown into further disarray, which set the stage for another movement toward consolidation.

The Empire of Timur Aided by the ease of travel within the Mongol Empire, Islam had by the fourteenth century become the dominant religion among the central Asian Turkic peoples. By this time some of the Turkic groups, like the Seljuks and the Ottomans, had long since moved into the eastern Mediterranean region and Anatolia. In the interior of central Asia, however, the memory of the accomplishments of the Mongol Empire among the inhabitants of Chaghatay—the area given to Genghis Khan's son of that name—was still fresh. Their desire for a new Mongol Empire, now coupled with Islam, created opportunities for military action to unite

1336-1405	1542-1605	1618-1707	1739
Timur (Tamerlane), Founder of Timurid Line of Rulers	Akbar, Most Innovative of Mughal Rulers	Aurangzeb, Last Powerful Mughal Ruler	Invasion by Persians, Looting of Delhi, Taking of Peacock Throne

1483-1530	1627-1657	1707-1858
Babur, Founder of Timurid Line in India—the Mughals	Shah Jahan, Builder of Taj Mahal	Ebbing of Mughal Power in India, Rise of British Influence

MAP **20.1** **Area Subjugated by Timur-i-lang, 1360–1405.**

Bayazid Caged at Timur's Court. Though accounts conflict regarding Bayazid's treatment as a prisoner of Timur, his imprisonment in an iron cage was routinely depicted in popular lore. In this 1680 gouache painting, the unhappy sultan languishes in his perch before his conqueror and entourage while appearing to urinate on a careless onlooker. One tradition holds that Bayazid killed himself by bashing his head against his bars, another that he took poison concealed in his ring.

the settled and nomadic tribes of Chaghatay. The result by the end of the fourteenth century was the stunning rise of Temur Gurgan (r. 1370–1405), more widely known by a variation of the Persian rendering of his name, Timur-i lang, as Timur the Lame, or Tamerlane.

What little is known about Timur's early years has been clouded by the mystique he cultivated as a ruler, which continued to grow long after his death. Though he came close to matching the conquests of Genghis Khan, his forebearers were not direct descendants of the conqueror. He therefore devised genealogies connecting him to the dominant Mongol lines to give him legitimacy as a ruler, and he even found a direct descendant of Genghis Khan to use as a figurehead for his regime. He also portrayed himself as a man whose destiny was guided by God from humble beginnings to world domination.

From 1382, when he secured the region of his homeland around the capital, the Silk Road trading center of Samarkand, until his death in 1405, Timur ranged widely through western central Asia, Afghanistan, northern India, Iran, Anatolia, and the eastern Mediterranean lands (see Map 20.1). Like his model, Genghis Khan, he proved surprisingly liberal in his treatment of certain cities that surrendered peacefully, sometimes displaying his intellectual prowess in debates with local scholars after occupation. Many more times, however, he reduced besieged cities to rubble, slaughtered the inhabitants without mercy, and erected pyramids of skulls as blunt propaganda warning others to submit. "Your sins must be great indeed for God to send me to punish you," he would tell his unfortunate opponents.

On at least one celebrated occasion, public humiliation was considered the most appropriate penalty for a conquered leader. Buoyed by his stunning victory over the cream of European knighthood at Nicopolis in 1396, the Ottoman sultan Bayazid unwisely battled Timur near Ankara in modern Turkey in 1402. After capturing Bayazid alive, Timur was said to have kept him in a small cage atop a pedestal at court for his entourage to enjoy.

At the time of his death in 1405, Timur was contemplating the invasion of Ming China. This, however, never came to pass; and Timur's empire, like that of Genghis Khan, did not long outlast him. As it fell apart, the various Chaghatay peoples largely resumed their local feuds, once again leaving the way open for a strong military force to impose order.

Babur and the Timurid Line in India

By the beginning of the sixteenth century, the region from Samarkand south into the Punjab in northern India had largely become the province of feuding Turkic tribes and clans of Afghan fighters, many of whom had migrated south to serve with the Lodi sultans of India. Into this volatile environment was born Zahir Ud-din Muhammad Babur, more commonly known as simply "Babur" (though the Turkic "Babur" means "lion," Zahir's nickname was from the Persian "Babr" for "leopard" or "tiger") in 1483. Babur's (1483–1530, r. 1526–1530) claims to legitimate rule were considerable: His father was a direct descendant of Timur, while his mother claimed the lineage of Genghis Khan. We know a considerable amount about Babur—though much of it must be seen through a lens of self-justification—through his autobiography, the *Baburnama*.

Babur's autobiography was perhaps the first by a sitting ruler. In this he set a precedent for self-chronicling that would be carried out by many of his Mughal successors. His military career began at a tender age: In the *Baburnama* he claims to have ruled over the central Asian region of Ferghana—the area of modern Uzbekistan, Tajikistan, and Kyrgystan, for centuries a fabled source of fine horses—at the age of 12.

At 14, he took Samarkand, though he was soon forced out by a competing tribe. Like Timur and Genghis Khan, his accomplishments as a youthful prodigy led him to believe that God had provided him with a special destiny to fulfill. This tended to sustain him during the next several years when, out of favor with certain powerful relatives, he roamed the border regions seeking an opportunity to return to power.

In 1504, accompanied on a campaign by his strong-willed mother, Yunus Khan, Babur moved into Afghanistan, captured Kabul, and went on to raid points farther south over the following decade. By 1519, he stepped up his raids into northern India with a view to subjugating and ruling it. As a measure of his seriousness in this endeavor, he named his son born that year "Hindal," or "Take India!" After 7 more years of campaigning, this goal was achieved in the north. In 1526, Babur's highly mobile army of approximately 12,000 met the forces of Sultan Ibrahim Lodi, whose army boasted perhaps 100,000 men and 1,000 elephants, at Panipat, near Delhi. Though the sultan enjoyed such vast numerical superiority, Babur's forces employed the new technologies of matchlock muskets and field cannon to devastating effect. In the end, the Lodi sultan was killed along with many of the Afghan tribal chiefs whose forces made up the bulk of his army, and Babur's way was now clear to consolidate his new Indian territories.

Victory at Panipat was swiftly followed by conquest of the Lodi capital of Agra and further success over the Hindu Rajputs in 1528. On the eve of his death in December 1530, Babur controlled an enormous swath of territory extending from Samarkand in the north to Gwalior in India in the south (see Map 20.2). For Babur and his successors, their ruling family would always be "The House of Timur," prompting historians to sometimes refer to the line as the "Timurids." Because of their claims to the legacy of Genghis Khan, however, they would be better known to the world as the "Mughals" (from "Mongols").

> **Babur Reflects on His Conquests (after taking and losing Samarkand, Babur paused at a mountain spring and reflected)**
>
> Many men like us have taken breath at this spring,
> And have passed away in the twinkling of an eye;
> We took the world by courage and might,
> But we could not take it with us to the grave.
>
> —*Baburnama*. Translated by Wheeler M. Thackston. New York: Oxford University Press, 1996.

Portrait of Babur. This imagined portrait of Babur was done about sixty years after his death. He is shown receiving representatives of the Uzbeks of central Asia and the Rajputs of India in an audience dated December 18, 1528.

MAP **20.2** The Conquests of Babur.

Loss and Recovery of Empire   As had been the case so many times in the past with other newly conquered empires, the House of Timur's new rulers were now faced with the problem of consolidating, organizing, and administering Babur's vast domain. Like Timur before him, Babur had given comparatively little thought to the arts of peace. Now it fell upon his son Humayun (r. 1530–1556) to create a state. Unfortunately, Humayun's interests were geared more toward Islamic **Sufi** mysticism, poetry, astrology, and at times wine and opium than they were toward responsible leadership. Though chroniclers have generally been critical of him for losing much of Babur's legacy, he tapped a considerable reservoir of courage and determination to ultimately win it back.

A chronic problem for the long-term health of the dynasty was the **institutionalization** of traditional nomadic succession practices among the Mughal rulers. Though only one son was designated as the ruler's successor, the others were given substantial territories to govern within the empire, a situation that frequently led to conflict. In addition to such ongoing family difficulties, Humayun faced various hostile military forces still active in unconquered areas of northern India and Afghanistan. An Afghan leader named Sher Khan Sur managed to unite many of these forces and invaded the extreme eastern region of Bengal. Twice routed, Humayun fled to Persia in 1540, where, utterly humiliated, he was forced to convert to Shia Islam in a desperate bid to court the favor of the Safavid ruler, Shah Tahmasp. As distasteful as this was for him as a Sunni Muslim, he now at least had Persian backing and proceeded to move into Afghanistan and, ultimately, to Delhi. By 1555, after 15 years of exile and fighting, the dynasty was restored. For Humayun, however, the peace brought only a brief respite. In a final irony for this bookish man, he fell from the roof terrace of his palace library and died in January 1556.

Sufi: Any one of various mystical branches of Islam; Sufis have often been instrumental in spreading Islam, but they have also been viewed suspiciously by Muslim authorities.

Institutionalization: The creation of a regular system for previously improvised or ad hoc activities or things, for example, law codes to replace local customs.

Consolidation and Expansion   Because of the difficulties involved in Humayun's own accession to the throne, his death was kept secret for several weeks, while the court worked out plans for a **regency** for the emperor's son, 14-year-old Jalal Ud-Din Akbar (r. 1556–1605). The man chosen for this task, Bairam Khan, was able and attentive; and Akbar proved in many ways to be an apt pupil. His military education began quickly as Humayun's old enemy, Sher Khan Sur, sent an army to attack Delhi in 1557. In a close fight, Mughal forces finally carried the day. Over the next year and a half, they secured the eastern, southern, and western flanks of their lands, bringing them conclusively into the Mughal fold and again anchoring Islam in the former areas of its influence—"Hindustan."

Upon finally taking power in a palace coup, Akbar plunged into renewed campaigning in quest of more territory. Along the way, he seemed at once determined to master all India by any military means necessary but intolerant of cruelties practiced by his subordinates in his name. Confronting one of his commanders who had executed the surrendered garrison at Malwa, for example, an enraged Akbar threw the man from an upstairs window. On seeing he survived the fall, Akbar dragged him back upstairs and threw him out the window again, finally killing him. Despite this violent streak—or perhaps because of it—Akbar abhorred religious violence of any kind and spent much of his rule attempting to reconcile the different religious traditions of his empire. In the end his attempts, though remarkably farsighted, would prove futile and earn him the enmity of many of his fellow Muslims, who felt he had become an unbeliever.

Humayun Being Received by the Persian Shah Tahmasp. This gouache rendering of a pivotal moment in Mughal dynastic history is from a painting on a wall at Chel Soloun in Isfahan. Although all seems cordial between the two men and Humayun was treated well by the Shah, a number of accounts claim that he was threatened with execution if he did not covert to Shia Islam.

Visions of Akbar. Two very different depictions of Akbar, from 1600 (*left*) and ca. 1630 (*right*). On the left is a sketch of the emperor from life, perhaps as a preliminary drawing for a portrait painting. On the right he is depicted in all of his religious glory: surrounded by a luminous halo, surmounted by angels glorifying him and holding his crown, and graced with the holiness to make the lion lie down with the heifer.

Regency: The setting up of a guardian for an underage or incapacitated monarch to rule in his or her stead.

As a warrior Akbar was far more successful. Through the 1560s, aided by capable military advisors, Mughal armies continued to push the boundaries of the empire west, south, and east. In 1562 they subdued Malwa and in 1564, Gondwana; in 1568, the great Rajput fortress of Chitor fell. This string of victories continued into the next decade, with the long-sought conquest of Gujarat taking place in 1573. Turning eastward, Akbar set his sights on Bengal, which, along with the neighboring regions of Bihar and Orissa, fell to the Mughals by the mid-1570s. They remained, however, volatile and hostile to Mughal occupation. Both Muslim and Hindu princes in the region continued their campaigns of resistance into the following decades (see Map 20.3).

In the meantime, resistance and rebellion periodically plagued other areas of the empire. In central Asia, as early as 1564, a rebellion of Mughal Uzbek allies required a skilled combination of warfare and diplomacy to defuse. At the same time, revolts in Malwa and Gujarat required reconquest of those territories. In order to keep the old Islamic heartland of northern India—Hindustan—under firm Mughal control, the Mughals built fortresses at strategic points throughout their inner domains as well as along the frontier. Among the most important of these were Allahabad, Lahore (in modern Pakistan), Ajmer, and the largest at Agra, in its ultimate state the famous Red Fort. These remained important strong points for the remainder of the Mughal era and even during the height of British power in India.

The New City   In addition to fielding large armies—one European observer estimated that the army he accompanied on one of Akbar's campaigns surpassed

MAP **20.3** Mughal India Under Akbar.

100,000—and huge, expensive forts, the immense revenues of the Mughal lands allowed other monumental projects to be undertaken. In an effort to show solidarity with his non-Muslim subjects, Akbar had married a Hindu Rajput princess named Manmati. Manmati had twins, who tragically died; and a distraught Akbar sought advice from a famous **Sufi** holy man named Salim Chishti. Salim told Akbar that he would ultimately have a son. When that son—named "Salim" in honor of the holy man—was born, Akbar began to build a city on the site of Salim Chishti's village of Sikri. Fatehpur Sikri, as the new city was known when it was completed in 1571, was built from the same red sandstone as the great fort at Agra, 26 miles away. As a man of many enthusiasms, Akbar's instincts for design and dynastic propaganda were everywhere evident within it. At its center was the mosque, which now housed the tomb of Salim Chishti and swiftly became an object of veneration and pilgrimage for Indian Sufis. Among the architectural innovations of Akbar's urban palace was a kind of early air-conditioning system: Reflecting pools were strategically placed to catch prevailing breezes and vent the cool moist air into the sleeping chambers of

Salim Chishti's Tomb at Fatehpur Sikri. The tomb of Sufi mystic Salim Chishti shows the sense of restrained flamboyance that marks the mature Mughal architectural style. The Chishtis had long been revered by India's Sufis and Salim's simple, elegant tomb, with its domed sarcophagus, multihued marble, and quranic inscriptions, quickly became a favorite pilgrimage site. Surrounding it is one of the red sandstone courtyards of Akbar's Fatehpur Sikri.

Akbar's Attempt at Religious Synthesis

اوزای بودیا درے ریزلف ازولنٹوران نصاری بنهم وفطرت ٹنان کنجانبی دانست دران بزمکنی کنجه علراز

Akbar Presiding Over a Religious Debate. Akbar's distaste for religious orthodoxy manifested itself most dramatically in his conducting regularly scheduled debates among theologians from many of India's faiths. Here, a discussion is taking place with two Jesuit missionaries, Fathers Rudolph Aquaviva and Francis Henriquez (dressed in black) in 1578. Interestingly, the priests had unfettered access to Akbar, were free to preach, and even gave instruction to members of Akbar's family at his request.

Like their predecessors, the Mughals as Muslim rulers in India were faced with an immense array of diverse, and sometimes antagonistic, religious and cultural traditions. Amid this "religious syncretism," as we have termed it, Akbar's innovation within the world-historical pattern of religious civilizations was to create a new religion that would encompass these traditions and bind his followers directly to him as emperor and religious leader: to create an Indian "religious synthesis."

Already graced with a larger-than-life reputation for charisma and openness, he was also resistant to the strictures of Sunni Islam or any other organized religion. As a boy, he was condemned by his tutors as uneducable because he remained unable to read or write. Some scholars have suggested that he was dyslexic. Perhaps because of this, he developed an extraordinary memory for literature and poetry. Some have also suggested that his illiteracy was in emulation of the stories of the early prophets, who found illumination directly from God. In any case, his tastes within Islam centered on Sufi mysticism, which had a long tradition of tolerance and eclecticism. This openness encouraged him to study the mystical traditions of the Hindus, Parsis (Zoroastrian immigrants from Persia), and Christians. After establishing himself at Fatehpur Sikri, he sponsored regular Thursday night theological debates, mostly among Muslim scholars but gradually including Hindus, Parsis, and in 1578 Catholic missionaries. He honored many of the cultural traditions of India's various religions as well: He wore his hair long under his turban like the Hindus, coined emblems of the sun to honor the Parsis, and kept paintings of the Virgin Mary as a nod to the Christians.

During one particularly lavish and bloody hunting party in 1578, he had a sudden, intense mystical experience. Like Ashoka so long before him—of whom Akbar was completely unaware—he was now appalled by the destruction and waste in which he had participated. Out of this experience and his religious consultations, he gradually developed a personal philosophy he called *sulh-i kull*—"at peace with all." While this did not end his military campaigns, which he saw as ordained by God, it did push him to develop a new religion he called *din-i ilahi* (divine faith). Akbar shrewdly directed the movement at key courtiers, nobles, and those aspiring to gain favor from the regime. He devised elaborate rituals in which adherents swore loyalty to himself not only as emperor but as the enlightened religious master of the new sect. Borrowing heavily from Sufi mysticism, Persian court protocols, Zoroastrian sun and fire veneration, and even Muslim- and Christian-influenced **Neo-platonic** spiritualism, he sought to at once limit the power of Sunni Islamic clerics and draw followers of other religions to what he taught was a "higher" realm, one that embraced all religions and provided the elect with secret insights into their ultimate truths.

In the end, however, despite its creative merging of the needs of state and religion to overcome what had been considered deep religious and cultural divisions, Akbar's attempt must be counted as a failure. While some Hindu and Muslim courtiers embraced *din-i ilahi* enthusiastically for its perceived religious truths, many did so for opportunistic reasons and it was roundly condemned by most Sunni theologians. And while Akbar's personal magnetism was able to hold the sect together during his lifetime, his successors not only repudiated it but swung increasingly in the direction of stricter Sunni Islam.

The Virgin Mary and the Christ Child. The role of Jesus as a precursor to Muhammad is an important one in Islam, as is that of Mary as His mother. Renderings of the Madonna and Christ Child were a common theme in Mughal art, particularly during the time of Akbar. Here, Mary is portrayed in an honored position and—like some Renaissance European depictions of her—as wealthy, leisured, and sophisticated (as indicated by the open book on the pillow), as she nurses the infant Jesus.

Questions

- How does Akbar's attempt at religious syncretism demonstrate the pattern of origins–innovations–adaptations that informs the approach of this book?

- Why was Akbar's attempt to create a new divine faith doomed to failure?

Neo-Platonic/Neo-Platonism: A movement among European scholars in the fifteenth century that revived the idealist philosophy of Plato, especially the idea of an unseen reality beyond the material world.

the structure. Despite such amenities, however, the city was untenable in the long run and ultimately abandoned because there was simply not enough available water to sustain the population.

The Summer and Autumn of Empire

In a way, the saga of Fatehpur Sikri runs parallel to Mughal fortunes over the next century. The military accomplishments of the dynasty are in many ways spectacular, but they were eventually worn down by internal rebellion and succession struggles; the immense fortunes of the rulers were ultimately squeezed by the needs of defense and of ostentation to demonstrate power; and new economic and, ultimately, military competitors arrived on the scene with the coming of the Europeans.

The Revolt of the Sons   In 1585, Akbar left Fatehpur Sikri with his army for Lahore, which he would make his temporary capital for most of the rest of his life. Once again, the Afghan princes were chafing under Mughal domination and intriguing with the Uzbeks and Safavid Persians to wrest local control for themselves. For Akbar, as for his predecessors, it was vital to maintain control over these areas because of their historical connection to the Chaghatay and the need to keep control of the essential Silk Road trade. Now the key city of Kandahar, in modern Afghanistan, was in Safavid hands, disrupting Mughal control of the trade. For the next 13 years, Akbar and his generals fought a long, stubborn war to subdue the Afghans and roll back the Safavids. Though his forces were defeated on several occasions, in the end the Mughals acquired Sind and Kashmir, subdued for a time the region of Swat, and, with the defection of a Safavid commander, occupied Kandahar. By 1598, the regions in question were secure enough for Akbar to move back to Agra.

In 1600, Akbar embarked on his last great campaign against the remaining free Muslim sultanates of central India. These were reduced within a year, but Akbar was now faced with a domestic crisis. His son Salim launched a coup and occupied the fort at Agra. Salim declared himself emperor, raised his own army, and even had coins struck with his name on them. In the end, one of Akbar's wives and a group of court women were able to reconcile Akbar and Salim. Salim was confined within the palace amid intrigues that threatened to bypass him as heir in favor of his own son, Khusrau. In the end, however, he retained his position; and upon Akbar's death on October 25, 1605, Salim acceded to the throne as Jahangir (r. 1605–1627).

Renewed Expansion of the "War State"   As if to underscore the dynasty's continual problems with orderly succession, Jahangir's son, Khusrau, left the palace, quickly put a small army together, and marched on Lahore. When negotiations with his son went nowhere, Jahangir's forces swiftly defeated the insurgents. To invest his son with a special horror in what he had done, Khusrau was made to watch his comrades put to death by impalement—a punishment also used by the Ottomans and the famous Vlad "The Impaler" Dracul (Chapter 16). Sharpened posts were driven through their midsections and planted in the ground so that they would die slow, agonizing deaths suspended in the air. The doomed soldiers were made to salute Khusrau, who was forced to ride among them in a macabre military review. Undeterred, Khusrau rebelled again; and on failing this time, he was blinded and imprisoned for his efforts.

As one scholar writes, "Under Jahangir the empire continued to be a war state attuned to aggressive conquest and territorial expansion." This now meant pushing south into the Deccan and periodically resecuring Afghanistan and its adjacent regions. A move into Bengal, however, foreshadowed a major clash with a very different kind of enemy: the Shan people of southeast Asia called the "Ahoms." Southeast Asia was where the expanding cultural and political influence of China met that of Hindu and Buddhist India. In the case of the Ahoms, the territory in question was in the vicinity of Assam, along the Brahmaputra River to the north of Burma and Thailand. Though they had recently converted to Hinduism, the Ahoms had no caste system and drew upon a legacy of self-confident expansion that the Mughals had not encountered before in their opponents. With little fixed territory to defend because of their mobility, the Ahoms proved the most stubborn enemies the empire had yet encountered. Year after year, Jahangir's armies labored to secure the northeastern territories only to have the Ahoms bounce back and mount fresh offensives against them. Though both sides employed troops armed with matchlocks and cannon, neither side could obtain a clear tactical edge and their wars dragged on for decades.

More culturally and psychologically threatening to the Mughals was their relationship with the empire to their west, Safavid Persia. Both sides constantly jockeyed for position against each other and periodically went to war. There was also intense religious rivalry, with the predominantly Sunni Mughals and Shiite Safavid Persians each denouncing the other as heretical unbelievers. For the Mughals, moreover, it was particularly galling that they owed the survival of their dynasty in part to the Persian Shah Tahmasp, who had given aid to Humayun—forcing him to convert to Shiism to do so. In addition, there was a sizeable number of Persians and Shiites among the Mughal elites. Moreover, there was a pronounced feeling among these elites that Persian culture, language, and literature were superior to those of the Turks and Muslim India as a whole. In some respects, both Persians and "Persianized" Indians saw Muslim India as a kind of cultural colonial outpost, in much the same way that Chinese sophisticates viewed the high cultures of Japan, Korea, and Vietnam. This made for a highly complex set of relations between the two empires, with both vying for power in religious and cultural terms as much as in the political and military realm.

New Directions in Religious Politics   In October 1627 Jahangir died of a fever, after which his oldest son, Khurram, outmaneuvered his younger brother for the throne and reigned as Shah Jahan (r. 1627–1657). His rule coincided with perhaps the high point of Mughal cultural power and prestige, as reflected in its iconic building, the Taj Mahal. His record is less spectacular in political and military terms however. In this case, the Mughal obsession with controlling the northern trade routes coincided with the need to take back the long-contested great fort at Kandahar, Afghanistan, once again in Persian hands. Thus, Shah Jahan spent much of his reign on the ultimately fruitless drive to finally subdue the northwest. As the Mughal historian Sadiq bluntly put it, "Nothing resulted from this expedition except the shedding of blood, the killing of thirty to forty thousand people, and the expenditure of thirty-five million rupees."

As we noted earlier, the reign of Akbar and, to a considerable extent, that of Jahangir had marked a time of extraordinary religious tolerance. The attraction of both men to the Sufi school of Salim Chishti, with its mystical leanings and parallels with similar Hindu movements, created a favorable emotional community for religious pluralism. It also made Muslims for whom strict adherence to Sunni doctrine was necessary to guard against undue Persian Shia influence, apprehensive. Others, noting the ability of Hindus to incorporate the gods and beliefs of other faiths into their own, feared that the ruling Muslim minority might ultimately be assimilated to the Hindu majority.

With Shah Jahan, however, we see a definite turn toward a more legalistic tradition. Under the influence of this trend among leading Sunni theologians, Shah Jahan began to block construction and repair of non-Muslim religious buildings, instituted more direct state support for Islamic festivals, and furnished lavish subsidies for Muslim pilgrims to Mecca. The old ideal of a unified Muslim world governed by quranic law steadily gained ground at the Mughal court and would see its greatest champion in Shah Jahan's son, Aurangzeb. In the meantime, the trend lent itself to the creation of a new capital, Shajahanabad Delhi, just south of Delhi, complete with the largest mosque, college (*madrasa*), and hospital complex in India—and, of course, one of the most recognizable and beautiful buildings in the world, the Taj Mahal.

The Pinnacle of Power   The ascendancy of Aurangzeb (r. 1658–1707) was marked yet again by the now all-too-familiar pattern of princely infighting. In this case it was brought on by the extended illness of Shah Jahan in 1657. A four-way struggle broke out among the sons of Shah Jahan and his beloved Mumtaz Mahal. Although Shah Jahan soon recovered, he returned to Agra broken and depressed, while his sons fought bitterly for control. Aurangzeb outmaneuvered his older brother, surrounded the fort at Agra, and placed his father, Shah Jahan, under arrest. From this point he held the strongest position, though his brothers fought on. By 1661 they had each been defeated and assassinated, leaving Aurangzeb in control of the empire. Shah Jahan lived on in captivity until 1666.

Aurangzeb's long rule, despite its disruptive introduction, seemed to begin auspiciously enough. Renewing the Mughal bid to expand into the northeastern areas controlled by the Ahoms, his armies fought them to a standstill in the early 1660s and made them Mughal clients. When Mughal control of the area around Kabul and the Khyber Pass was threatened by a revolt of Pathan tribesmen, Aurangzeb fought several stubborn campaigns to retain control of the region and bought off other potentially troublesome groups with lavish gifts (see Map 20.4).

With these campaigns, the political power of the Mughals reached perhaps its greatest extent. But the period also marked a watershed in at least two respects: First, it saw the opening of decades-long wars with the Hindu Marathas, a federation of fiercely independent clans in west central India who speak the Mahrathi language, in which the empire's cohesion was steadily eroded. In addition, the various trading companies of the British, French, and Dutch expanded their own fortified outposts in Indian ports outside Mughal domains. As Mughal power was sapped by the revolts of the eighteenth century, the companies' armed forces became important players in regional politics.

The other watershed was Aurangzeb's bid for a more effective "Islamification" of Mughal India. As a member of the Sunni Hanafi school of Islamic law, Aurangzeb's vision for the empire was to rule by Islamic sharia law. As an Islamic state, connected to the larger commonwealth of Islamic states, he believed that Mughal rule should be primarily for the benefit of Muslims. This was an almost complete repudiation of his great-grandfather Akbar's vision of religious transcendence. While Aurangzeb stopped short of forcible conversion, he did offer multiple inducements to bring unbelievers into the faith. Elites who converted to Islam were given lavish gifts and preferential assignments, while those who did not convert found themselves isolated from the seat of power. Discriminatory tax rates were also levied on unbelievers, including a new tax on Hindu pilgrims. Zealous Muslim judges in various cities prompted protests from Hindus regarding their rulings. Moving a step beyond the actions of Shah Jahan, Aurangzeb ordered the demolition of dozens of Hindu temples that had not been constructed or repaired according to state-approved provisions. The most unpopular measure, however, was the reimposition of the hated *jiziya*, a graduated head tax on unbelievers that had been abolished by Akbar. When this was announced in 1679, massive Hindu protests broke out in several major Indian cities. In Delhi, a great crowd attempted to appeal to the emperor, who, along with his entourage, was riding an

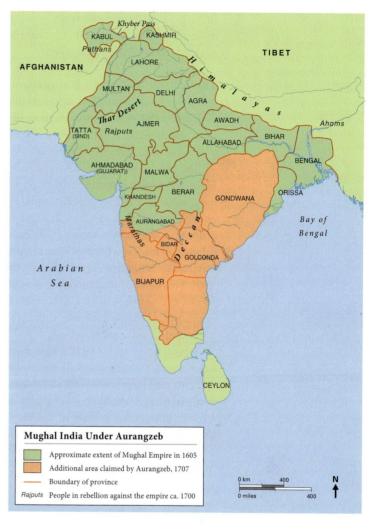

MAP 20.4 **Mughal India Under Aurangzeb.**

elephant on his way to Friday prayers. After a brief standoff, Aurangzeb ordered the elephants forward and a number of people were crushed in the chaos to clear the way. Although the intensity of the protests ultimately died down, the tax remained a sore point, even prompting some conversions simply to avoid the extra tax burden.

The new religious policies also created problems in dealing with self-governing, non-Muslim groups within the empire. The legacy of distrust of the Mughals among the Sikhs, who blended Hindu and Muslim traditions, was enhanced by Aurangzeb's heavy-handed attempts to intervene in the selection of a new Sikh guru, or religious leader, and by the destruction of some Sikh temples. When the Sikhs did not choose the candidate Aurangzeb favored, the emperor arrested the other candidate for allegedly converting Muslims and had him executed. His son and successor, Gobind Singh, would later lead a full-blown Sikh revolt. Similarly, the mostly Hindu Rajputs, who had been guaranteed representation among the nobility under previous emperors, found their position rapidly eroding under Aurangzeb's policies. Intervening in a succession struggle among the Rajputs, the emperor's attempts to put a Muslim candidate on the Rajput throne sparked yet another revolt, which, though largely suppressed by 1680, prompted continual tension among the Rajputs. Indeed, the following year, Rajput emissaries approached Aurangzeb's son to lead a palace revolt against his father. The revolt ultimately failed and, as with the Sikhs, left a legacy of mistrust toward the Mughal regime.

The Maratha Revolt   Notwithstanding these internal problems, Aurangzeb's military prowess netted him key areas that had long eluded Mughal efforts: Bijapur, Golconda, and much of the Maratha lands of the Deccan region of south central India. Yet, even here, the seeds were being cast for the rebellion that would eat away at the vitals of the empire for generations (see Map 20.4).

The Hindu Marathas, like the inhabitants of many regions bordering Mughal India, had evolved working relationships with the old Muslim sultanates that, over time, were annexed by the Timurids. For the earlier Mughal rulers, it was often enough for these small states to remit tribute and, on occasion, supply troops in order to retain their autonomy. For Aurangzeb, however, commitment to a more robust and legalistic Islam also meant political expansion of the Mughal state. This was justified on religious grounds in that the sultanates to the south had drifted from correct observance of quranic law, the lands of unbelievers were permissible to confiscate, and unbelievers would more likely convert if guided by proper Muslim rulers. Hence, Aurangzeb spent much of the last two decades of his life campaigning to bring central India under his sway.

Despite the tenacity of Maratha resistance, Aurangzeb's "carrot and stick" strategy—supporting pro-Mughal factions among the Maratha leaders, lavishing money and gifts on Maratha converts and deserters, and fielding several large armies to invest Maratha fortifications—bore fruit. In the early 1690s 11 Maratha strongholds fell to his forces. Yet prolonged fighting, with the emperor staying in the field year after year, also led to problems at court and in the interior of the empire.

The demands of constant campaigning reduced the flow of money and goods from south to north and east to west across central India. Moreover, by the early eighteenth century, the Maratha frontier, far from being steadily worn down, was actually expanding into Mughal areas. The Marathas had set up their own administrative system with its own forts and tax base and encouraged raids on Mughal caravans and pack trains. By Aurangzeb's death in 1707, the Marathas were noticeably expanding their sway at Mughal expense. With the weakening of the Mughal interior, the old enemy, Persia, took the opportunity to settle scores. The Persians sent an expeditionary force that sacked Delhi in 1739 and carried off Shah Jahan's fabled Peacock Throne—from this time forward associated with the monarchs of Persia and Iran, rather than with India and the Mughals.

The East India Companies   Within a dozen years of Vasco da Gama's first voyage to India in 1498, armed Portuguese merchant ships seized the port of Goa in 1510. Portugal's pioneering efforts in capturing the spice trade and setting up fortified bases from which to conduct business were swiftly imitated by other European maritime countries. For the English, Dutch, and French, these enterprises were conducted by royally chartered companies, which were given a monopoly over their country's trade within a certain region. Because these companies were operating thousands of miles from home in areas that were often politically chaotic, they acted much like independent states. They maintained fortified warehouses, their armed merchant ships functioned as naval forces, and they assembled their own mercenary armies.

Throughout the seventeenth century English, French, and Dutch enterprises largely supplanted Portuguese influence in the region, while the location of their trading ports outside Mughal lands allowed them considerable freedom. European naval prowess had by this time also surpassed that of any of the Indian states, and European ships controlled the sea-lanes to Indian ports. Thus, the companies grew richer and more powerful and increasingly found themselves involved in local politics. For the English, the acquisition of Bombay (Mumbai) from Portugal in the 1660s gave the company a superb harbor. In 1690, after unwisely becoming involved in a struggle with Aurangzeb, British traders were pushed down the Hugli (also Hoogli or Hooghly) River in Bengal and began building a new trading station called "Calcutta" (not to be confused with the port of Calicut, on the west coast of India). For their competitors, the French and Dutch, the ongoing Mughal wars in the Deccan were a windfall. The French station at Pondicherry, for example, supplied both Aurangzeb and the Marathas with money, goods, and even guns and gunners, while providing a haven for refugees from the war-torn interior. Aurangzeb's relations with these autonomous European enclaves remained strained however. European piracy, practiced against each other as well as on unarmed Indian merchant ships, proved a major irritant. Pirates also preyed upon vessels of pilgrims bound for Mecca, increasing religious tensions. While the companies usually paid damages to the Mughals when pressed, they continually upgraded their defenses, making it increasingly difficult for Mughal armies to successfully coerce them. By 1750, the power of the Dutch in India had been eclipsed by that of the British and French East India Companies. With the victory of the British East India Company commander, Robert Clive, at Plassey over the French forces in 1757 came British domination of Bengal and, by century's end, much of northern India.

The Dutch Trading Post at Hugli, 1665. The mid-seventeenth century was the high point of Dutch influence and trade in Asia, and the Dutch East India Company was one of the most powerful entities in the region. This fortified outpost on the Hugli River was typical of European trading establishments in the region during the late sixteenth and most of the seventeenth centuries. By the end of the century, however, the Dutch would be supplanted on the Hugli by their archrivals, the English, who would establish their own base that would swiftly grow into the great trading center of Calcutta.

Administration, Society, and Economics

One of the large patterns characteristic of the period under consideration in this section is a pronounced trend toward centralization. In a way, this phenomenon is not surprising since the creation of states and empires requires power at the center to hold the state together, assure consistent governance, provide for revenues, and maintain defense. What is noteworthy, however, is that in widely separate regions throughout Eurasia a variety of states concurrently reached a point where their governments, with armies now aided by firearms, made concerted efforts to focus more power than ever at the center. As part of this trend toward the development of fiscal–military states, some form of enforcement of approved religion or belief system legitimating the rulers was also present. As we saw in the Ottoman and Habsburg

Empires in Chapter 16 and in seventeenth-century France and other European countries in Chapter 17, the trend was toward what came to be called "absolutism," with vast powers concentrated in the person of the monarch. In China and Japan, as we will see in Chapter 21, it meant additional powers concentrated in the hands of the emperor (China) and shogun (Japan). For Mughal India, the system that attempted to coordinate and balance so many disparate and often hostile elements of society is sometimes called "autocratic centralism." While never as effective as the Chinese bureaucratic system or as tightly regulated as absolutist France, its policies and demands stretched into the lives of its inhabitants in often unexpected ways.

Mansabdars and Bureaucracy

As we mentioned earlier in this chapter, Babur and his successors found themselves forced to govern a largely settled, farming and city-dwelling society, whose traditions, habits, and (for the majority) religious affiliations were different from their own. While not unfamiliar with settled societies, the nomadic Timurids initially felt more comfortable in adapting their own institutions to their new situation and then grafting them onto the existing political and social structures. The result was a series of hybrid institutions that, given the tensions within Indian society, worked remarkably well when the empire was guided by relatively tolerant rulers but became increasingly problematic under more dogmatic ones.

Political Structure   The main early challenge faced by the Timurids was how to create a uniform administrative structure that did not rely on the unusual gifts of a particular ruler to perpetuate. It was the problem of moving from what social scientists call "charismatic leadership" (in which loyalty is invested in a leader because of his personal qualities) to "rational-legal" leadership (in which the institution itself commands primary respect and loyalty). Thus, Akbar created four principal ministries: one for army and military matters; one for taxation and revenue; one for legal and religious affairs; and one for the royal household. All of these ministries had wide latitude in their powers. The household ministry, for example, also controlled the building and maintenance of the empire's infrastructure. These primary ministries were directly responsible to the court, and the emperor reserved the right to take on responsibilities that were not directly spelled out in their respective mandates. In a departure from the practice in other Islamic states, the Mughal emperor also took direct control of the foreign affairs and diplomacy of his lands.

Below the broad central powers of these ministries, things functioned much the same on the provincial and local levels. The provincial governors held political and military power and were responsible directly to the emperor. In order to prevent their having too much power, however, the fiscal responsibility for both the civil and military affairs of the provinces were in the hands of officers who reported to the finance minister. Thus, arbitrary or rebellious behavior could, in theory at least, be checked by the separation of financial control.

Administrative Personnel   One key problem faced by the Mughals was similar to that confronting the French king Louis XIV and the Tokugawa shoguns in Japan during the following century—that is, how to impose a centralized administrative system on a state whose nobles were used to wielding power for themselves, or, in effect, acting as "emperors" in their own regions. In all three cases, the

Dealing with the Nobles

"In order to prevent the great nobles becoming insolent through the unchallenged enjoyment of power, the King [*sic*] summons them to court . . . and gives them many imperious commands, as though they were his slaves—commands, moreover, obedience to which ill suits their exalted rank and dignity."

—From Antonio Monserrate *Commentary*, quoted in Richards, *The Mughal Empire*, p. 65

solutions were remarkably similar. For the Mughals, India's vast diversity of peoples and patchwork of small states offered a large pool of potential noble recruits, and the competition among the ambitious for imperial favor was intense. The Timurid rulers were careful to avoid overt favoritism toward particular ethnic, or even religious, groups; and though most of their recruited nobility were Sunni Muslims, Hindus and even Shiite Muslims were also represented.

The primary criteria—as one would expect in a fiscal–military state—were military and administrative skills. An elaborate, graded system of official ranks was created in which the recipients, called *mansabdars*, were awarded grants of land and the revenues those working the land generated. In turn the mansabdars were responsible for remitting the correct taxes and, above a certain rank, for furnishing men and materiel for the army. Standards for horses, weapons, and physical qualities for soldiers, to which recruiters were expected to adhere, were established by the central government. The positions in the provincial governments and state ministries were filled by candidates from this new mansabdar elite chosen by the court. Thus, although the nobles retained considerable power in their own regions, they owed their positions to the court and had no hope of political advancement if they did not get court preferment.

The Mughals and Early Modern Economics

Mughal India had a vigorous trade and manufacturing economy, though, as with all agrarian-based societies, land issues and agriculture occupied the greatest part of the population. Unlike the societies of China, Japan, Korea, and Vietnam, which were influenced to a greater or lesser degree by Neo-Confucian ideas that regarded commerce as vaguely disreputable, Hindu, Muslim, Buddhist, and Jain traditions reserved an honored place for commerce and those who conducted it. Thus, Mughal economic interests routinely revolved around keeping the flow of goods moving around the empire, maintaining a vigorous import and export trade, and, as we have seen, safeguarding access to the Silk Road routes.

Imperial Reception of Dignitaries and Diplomats. Mughal rulers held regular *durbars*—public audiences. Here, in an illustration from Akbar's biography *Akbarnama*, he receives diplomats from Badakshan at a durbar in 1561.

Agriculture and Rural Life
The basic administrative unit of rural India at the time of the Mughals was the *pargana*, a unit comprising an area usually containing a town and from a dozen to about 100 villages. It was in the pargana that the lowest levels of officialdom had met the network of clan and caste leaders of the villages under both the Hindu rajas and the Muslim sultans before the Timurids, and this pattern continued over the coming centuries. But because the earliest years of the Mughals were marked by conquest and plunder, and later by an administrative apparatus that contented itself with taxation and defense at the local level, life in the villages tended to go on much as it had before the conquest. Thus, the chief duties of the *zamindars*, as the local chiefs and headmen were called, was to channel the expansive and competitive energies among local clans, castes, and ethnic and religious groups into activities the Mughals considered productive. In border areas especially, this frequently involved clearing forests for farmland, harvesting tropical woods and products for market, and often driving off bands of foragers from the forests and hills.

A Merchants' Dispute. In this whimsical gouache miniature, dated 1640, confusion ensues as a young boy attempts to undersell a group of water merchants who then come after him and attempt to drive him off. While artists generally concentrated on depicting the elites who sustained them, genre paintings of social activities, markets, and holy sites were also popular. This piece was part of a manuscript once belonging to a daughter of Emperor Aurangzeb.

Agricultural expansion went hand in hand with systematic integration of the rural and town and city economies. One enormous obstacle facing the Mughals, as it had faced previous regimes, was efficiency and equity in rural taxation. Grain and other agricultural commodities provided the bulk of Indian tax revenues, but vast differences in regional soil conditions, climate, and productivity made uniform tax rates extremely difficult to enforce. During Akbar's reign, therefore, massive surveys of local conditions were conducted to monitor harvests and grain prices over 10-year periods. These were then compiled into data tables used by local officials to calculate expected harvests and tax obligations. Imperial and local officials would sign agreements as to grain amounts to meet tax obligations over a set period. These obligations, like the Chinese "single-whip" system (see Chapter 21), would then be paid in silver or copper coin in four installments. Peasants needing loans to carry them to harvest season could obtain them from government-approved moneylenders, and the remission of vast amounts of grain and agricultural commodities at regular intervals to towns and cities contributed to their economic integration with the countryside. The system worked well through the sixteenth and seventeenth centuries, with tax rates on grain usually about one-third of the annual harvest and perhaps one-quarter of that of other agricultural commodities. Transport of bulk cargoes was eased by the excellent road system maintained by the Mughals.

The net effect of rural economic expansion was that Mughal India's growth kept pace, roughly speaking, with that of China from the mid-sixteenth century to the beginning of the nineteenth. Expansion in Bengal and northeast India of wet rice cultivation and the introduction of American crops such as maize and potatoes in dryer areas allowed for a population increase from about 150 million in 1600 to 200 million in 1800. Moreover, acreage under cultivation increased by perhaps as much as one-third over this same period. Preferential tax rates on tobacco, indigo, sugarcane, cotton, pepper, ginger, and opium ensured that supplies of these coveted trade items would be secure. India began a burgeoning silk industry during this time as well. Thus, revenues more than doubled between Akbar's and Aurangzeb's reigns, to about 333.5 million rupees a year, while the increase in population meant that the per capita tax burden actually went down.

International Trade India had been the center of Indian Ocean trade for nearly two millennia before the rise of the Mughals, but the advent of the world trading systems being created by the Atlantic maritime states added a vastly expanded dimension to this commerce. The intense and growing competition among the English, Dutch, and French East India Companies meant that Indian commodities were now being shipped globally, while imports of American silver and food and cash crops were growing by the year. By the mid-seventeenth century, the Dutch and British dominated maritime trade in Indian spices. Between 1621 and 1670, for example, Indian exports of pepper to Europe doubled to 13.5 million pounds. An often added bonus was Indian saltpeter, a vital component of gunpowder, used as ships' ballast (see Map 20.5).

Perhaps of even more long-term importance, however, was the growth of India's textile trade. Here, French access to Bengali silk contributed immensely to French leadership in European silk products, while Indian indigo supplied European needs for this dye until slave production of it in the Americas lowered its cost still further. Most momentous of all, though, was the rapid rise of Indian cotton exports. Lighter and more comfortable than wool or linen, Indian cotton *calicoes* (named for Indian port of Calicut) proved immensely popular for underwear and summer clothing. Indeed, the familiar term "pajamas" comes from the Hindi word *pyjama*, the lightweight summer garments worn in India and popularized as sleepwear in Europe. The immense popularity of cotton can be seen by the imports of the British East India Company, which, in the 20 years from 1664 to 1684, saw its imports of Indian cotton cloth rise sevenfold to 27 million square meters. The low price and huge popularity of Indian textiles would play a central role in both the British effort to develop machine spun and woven cotton goods to compete with the Indian product and the colossal expansion of slavery in the American South to grow cotton during the first part of the nineteenth century.

Society, Family, and Gender

Though the majority of the material in this chapter describes the activities of the Muslim Timurids in Indian history and society, it must be kept in mind that the vast majority of people in all areas of India were Hindus rather than Muslims. Thus, although the laws and customs of the areas controlled by the Mughals had a considerable effect on all members of Indian society, most of the everyday living of Indians at the pargana, village, clan, and family levels went on much as it had before the arrival of the Mughals—or, for that matter, before the arrival of Islam.

Caste, Clan, and Village
As we saw in earlier chapters, the ties of family, clan, and caste were the most important for the majority of Indians (most of whom were Hindu), particularly in rural society, which comprised perhaps 90 percent of the subcontinent's population. Even after the reimposition of the tax on unbelievers by Aurangzeb and the restrictions on the building and rehabilitating of Hindu temples, Hindu life at the local level went on much as it had before. Indeed, many new converts to Islam kept up their caste and clan affiliations much as before, especially in areas in which caste affiliation was determined by language, village designation, or profession.

Attempts by the Mughals to create a uniform system of taxation and military obligation ran up against a familiar problem of minority rulers: How does one persuade the people to go along with new systems that have not grown organically out of their own institutions? In the case of local rural life in India, perhaps the most important obstacle was the clan council, whose network of village headmen connected by real or adopted blood relations conducted most of the business of the pargana. One vital source of early modern Indian social history is the archives of clan councils, and the records of their deliberations and voting provide researchers with a vital counterpoint to the carrying out of Mughal official policy. Much like their counterparts in rural Chinese society, Indian clan councils organized militias for defense, collected donations for disaster relief, and arbitrated disputes. Unlike rural Chinese society, however, there was nearly always a degree of tension between these bodies and the Mughal hierarchy of zamindars and mansabdars. While Chinese clan leaders and village headmen frequently had disagreements with individual Confucian magistrates and both Ming and Qing dynasties attempted to bypass the power of local elites with alternative schemes of village organization, there was still fundamental agreement with the system as a whole.

European Trading Posts in India and Southeast Asia, ca. 1690

- ● Dutch possessions
- ● Portugese possessions
- ● Spanish possessions
- ● British possessions
- ● Danish possessions
- ● French possessions

1616   Year of acquisition

Principal Trade Commodities in India, ca. 1650

- Silk
- Cotton textiles
- Spices

MAP **20.5** **European Trading Ports in India and Southeast Asia, ca. 1690.**

For rural Indian society, however, even in areas under Muslim control for centuries, religious and cultural tensions as well as local friction with central authority were present. Thus, during the reign of Akbar, whose tolerant rule eased tensions somewhat, clan archives are relatively quiet; to the contrary, during Aurangzeb's long rule and during periods of internal conflict, these same archives bristle with militia drives and petitions for redress of assorted grievances. In areas only marginally under Mughal control, clan councils offered resources for potential rebels.

Family and Gender   For the Indian elites outside the areas of Mughal control, family life of the higher castes went on largely as it had from the time of the Guptas. The "twice-born" Hindus of the brahman varna went through lengthy training and apprenticeship in the household of a trusted guru in preparation for their roles as religious and societal leaders through their various stages of life. Women, who in the pursuit of dharma it was said are "worthy of worship," nevertheless spent most of their lives in seclusion. Whether among the highest castes or the lowest, their primary duties still included the running of the household and childrearing. Among the elites, where education in literature, poetry, and basic mathematics was also available to certain women, maintaining the household accounts, supervising servants, as well as education in the arts of living and loving as depicted in the *Kama*

Sutra were also considered part of a wife's proper knowledge. In all cases, however, as in China, the "inner" world of the household and the "outer" world of business, politics, warfare, and so on were clearly defined by gender. In rural areas, the lives and work of peasant families, though generally guided by traditional gender roles, were more flexible in that large collective tasks such as planting and harvesting required the participation of both men and women.

The conquests of the Mughals brought with them a somewhat different temperament among their elites. The nomadic Turkic peoples of the Asian steppes, with their reliance on mobility and herding and organization around small groups of fiercely independent families and clans, had not developed the elaborate class, caste, and gender hierarchies of their settled neighbors. Women could, and often did, exercise a far greater degree of power and influence than even among the Hindu, Sikh, or Muslim elites in India.

Even after the conversion of these nomadic peoples to Islam, this tradition of female independence continued among the Timurids. As we saw earlier, for example, Babur's mother played a vital role in his rise to power, and emperors' wives, like Mumtaz Mahal, exercised a considerable degree of control in the imperial household. Moreover, since marriages played a vital role in cementing diplomatic and internal relations, women exercised a good deal of influence in terms of the extension of imperial power. Nur Jahan (d. 1645), the striking Persian princess married to Jahangir, played a leading role in court politics and in mediation during the succession wars at the end of Jahangir's reign. Indeed, Jahangir turned the running of the empire over to her on several occasions, stating that he felt quite secure that it was in her capable hands.

Jahangir's Influential Wife, the Former Persian Princess Nur Jahan, in Her Silk Gauze Inner Court Dress.

As the Mughals assimilated local Muslim elites, the court quickly set up the harem as an institution of seclusion and protection for court women. Yet, within the harem, women enjoyed considerable freedom, constructed their own hierarchies among the imperial wives and their attendants, and celebrated their own holidays and ceremonies surrounding marriages, births, and deaths largely insulated from the influence of men. It was in many respects a kind of alternative women's society, in which a distinct system of values was instilled in daughters and, crucially, newcomers by marriage. For women newly married into the household, navigating the harem's social relationships was of supreme importance since the inner harmony of the court—and sometimes lives—depended on it.

Science, Religion, and the Arts

While science and technology in Mughal India did not enjoy the same pace of advancement that was being set during the scientific revolution in western Europe, there were nonetheless several noteworthy developments in weaponry, mathematics, and astronomy. In terms of religion, as we have seen, the great theological differences between Hindus and Muslims persisted—and with the reign of Aurangzeb increased. Again, however, the tendency of Hinduism to assimilate other traditions and the relative compatibility of Islamic Sufi practices with other mystical traditions did sometimes decrease tensions. This, of course, was most dramatically seen with Akbar's efforts at bridging the religious gaps of his empire.

Finally, one could say that where attempts at reconciling religions failed, language, literature, art, and architecture often succeeded and left a brilliant legacy of cultural synthesis.

Science and Technology

As they had done for centuries already, Muslim scholars in India drew upon the rich scientific history of the subcontinent and merged it with their efforts at preservation, commentary on, and transmittal of the Greco-Roman and Persian achievements of the ancients. Among the most important developments in this regard, as we have seen in other chapters, was the spreading of the Indian decimal number system and the use of zero as a placeholder in mathematical computations. This had already had a profound effect on the development of European science, which forever after referred to that system as "Arabic numerals." Among the developments that directly fostered the rise of Muslim empires, none was more important than the rapid development of gunpowder weapons.

New Directions in Firearms in the Gunpowder Empires

The spread of firearms from China and the shift in emphasis among weapons developers from rockets to tubular weapons firing projectiles is an extraordinarily complex subject and one littered with claims and counterclaims for the ultimate sources of particular innovations. We can say, however, that by the beginning of the sixteenth century, the armies of the major European kingdoms, Ming China, Ottoman Turkey, and Persia had all become accustomed to employing cannons and explosive charges for besieging fortresses, were developing more convenient and effective small arms for their infantries, and were beginning to employ lighter, more portable cannons as field guns for pitched battles. The use of these weapons became so pervasive and the changes that accompanied them so important that scholars often refer to the states of the Mughals, Persians, and Ottomans as the **gunpowder empires**.

Gunpowder empires: Muslim-ruled empires of the Ottomans, Safavids, and Mughals that used cannons and small arms in their military campaigns, 1450–1750.

Given the desire on the part of all armies to expand their firepower, it is not surprising that a gifted engineer, astronomer, and philosopher named Fathullah Shirazi (ca. 1580) came up with a concept for a multibarreled gun—similar in design to that of Leonardo da Vinci—for Akbar's armies. In this case, 12–16 light cannons were mounted side by side on a gun carriage and fired by the operator in quick succession. Two other ingenious military devices sprang from Fathullah's mind as well: a large revolving "tree" apparatus powered by an ox that was designed to clean powder residue from 16 gun barrels at a time, and field and siege cannons whose barrels could be dismantled section by section for ease of transport. For his part, Akbar designed prefabricated quarters and movable buildings to support his continual campaigning.

Mathematics and Astronomy

India's long history of mathematical innovation merged with Muslim work on astronomical observation to make impressive advances in celestial calculation. A century before Akbar, Indian mathematicians had pushed their calculations of the value of pi to nine decimal places and expanded their facility with the geometric relationships surrounding sine, cosine, and tangent to the point where some of the fundamental concepts of infinite series and calculus had been worked out.

By the sixteenth century, astronomical observation was a popular activity among elites—all the Mughal emperors had observatories, and the dynamic empress Nur

Jahan had planned one for herself—and one that entailed practical utility as well. Like other agrarian peoples reliant on an accurate calendar for the yearly agricultural and ceremonial cycle, Mughal rulers had a vital interest in knowing when unusual celestial phenomena such as comets, eclipses, and meteor showers were due and in having explanations for them ready to hand. Using extremely fine calculations and careful observation, the astronomers of the Kerala school, active from the fourteenth to the sixteenth centuries, had calculated elliptical orbits for the visible planets a century in advance of Johannes Kepler and suggested systems of planetary orbits similar to those of both Tycho Brahe and Copernicus (Chapter 17).

Perhaps the most spectacular scientific and technical development of the Mughal era was the construction of 21 seamless celestial globes during the sixteenth and seventeenth centuries. Ali Kashmirir ibn Luqman of Lahore is believed to have devised a variation of the ancient "lost-wax" casting technique for these unique devices in 1589. In addition to their utility as global star maps, it was believed into the twentieth century that casting seamless globes was a technological impossibility. The rediscovery of these instruments in the 1980s added an entirely new dimension to our understanding of the technological capabilities of the Mughal period.

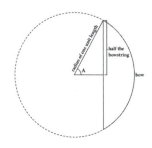

Origins of the Trigonometric Sine of an Angle as Described by Indian Mathematicians. Indian mathematicians did pioneering work in all of the fields of mathematics, particularly arithmetic and geometry. Hindu geometers knew of the trigonometric sine of an angle from at least the eighth century CE, if not earlier. In the early ninth century, the great Arabic mathematician al-Khwarizmi described the sine of an angle in his treatise on "Hindu" numbers, which was subsequently translated into Latin in the twelfth century. Through a series of mistranslations from one language to another, the original Sanskrit word for sine, *jya-ardha* ("half the bowstring") ended up being rendered as "sine" in Latin and other western European languages.

Religion: In Search of Balance

As scholars have often noted, Indian Islam has gone through relatively open, inclusive, and Sufi-oriented cycles—most notably in this chapter during the reigns of Babur, Humayun, and Akbar—and phases in which a more rigorous attention to orthodox Sunni practices and the desire to connect with Muslim communities beyond India prevail, such as during the reigns of Jahangir, Shah Jahan, and especially Aurangzeb. These periods, as we have already seen, had a profound effect on the relations of minority Muslim rulers with non-Muslim subjects. But they also played an important role in mandating which forms of Islam would be most influential in Mughal India and the relations of the Mughals with the Muslims of other regions.

The Position of Non-Muslims in Mughal India   As we have seen in earlier

chapters, despite profound theological differences between the monotheism of Islam and the profuse polytheism of popular Hindu religious traditions, there was a degree of attraction between the adherents of one and the other. As was the case with mystical and devotional sects of both, they saw a commonality in their ways of encountering the profound mysteries of faith. Thus, as we saw with Akbar, his grounding in Islamic Sufi mysticism made him interested in and receptive to Hindu mystical traditions. For their part, in addition to the mystical elements of Islam—in any case accessible only to a relative few—far more Hindus of the lower castes were attracted to the equality before God of all Islamic believers. Thus, like Buddhism before it, Islam promised emancipation from the restrictions of the caste system and a shared brotherhood of believers without regard for ethnicity, race, job, or social position.

More generally, however, the religious divisions remained difficult to reconcile. From the time of the first territories occupied by Muslim armies in the seventh century, nonbelievers had been granted the legal status of "protected peoples" (Chapter 10). That is, they were allowed to worship as they pleased and govern according to their own religious laws. There were also inducements and penalties aimed at conversion to Islam. Unbelievers were subject to the jiziya and pilgrimage taxes, and they suffered job discrimination in official circles, all of which did not apply once they converted. For their part, Hindus considered Muslims to be ritually "unclean" (*mleccha*), and upper-caste members underwent elaborate purification rites after coming into contact with them.

Yet the presence of a vastly larger Hindu population also meant that considerable accommodations had to be made by the rulers in order to run the empire effectively and even more to maintain order at the local level. Akbar, as we noted earlier, banned the discriminatory taxes on unbelievers. In addition, the financial skills of Hindus and Jains were increasingly sought by the court, and their status rose further when Akbar made a Hindu his finance minister and employed Hindu court astrologers. Perhaps of even more symbolic and political importance was the habit of Mughal rulers of occasionally marrying Hindu women. In order to cement good relations with the Rajputs, for example, Akbar married several Rajput princesses, including Manmati, who became the mother of the next emperor, Jahangir.

Seeing himself as emperor of all the people, Akbar also took part in Hindu festivals. The festival of *holi*, for example, in which the revelers squirt each other with red-colored water, was popular at the Mughal court; and a number of paintings depict men and women merrily engaged in it. At the same time, like his fellow monarchs, he was taken by the impulse to reform practices among both Muslims and unbelievers that he found disquieting. Like the British in the eighteenth and nineteenth centuries, he sought to ban the compulsory practice of *sati* (suttee), in which newly widowed women committed suicide by throwing themselves on the deceased's funeral pyre.

The position of Christians was similar. They, along with Jews, were considered "people of the Book" and, therefore, "protected" but still subject to the same taxes and impediments before the reign of Akbar. While the position of Christian missionaries in Mughal lands was often precarious, the reverence with which Muslims regarded the biblical prophets and Jesus also helped to smooth diplomatic relations at court. Akbar invited Jesuits to his debates, and paintings of Christian religious figures, especially the Virgin Mary, can be found in Mughal depictions of court life.

Yet this period of relative openness toward religion peaked with Akbar, and the pendulum soon shifted and picked up speed. Mughal receptiveness toward Islamic mysticism and other religions, as most dramatically displayed by Akbar's new din-i-ilahi religion, offended more orthodox Sunni Muslims. Their influence was felt at court during the reign of Jahangir and especially during that of Shah Jahan, whose love and piety came together in the form of the Taj Mahal. It reached its zenith during Aurangzeb's reign. As Mughal lands stretched to their farthest point, the austere Aurangzeb reimposed the taxes on unbelievers and purged many Hindus from his court.

One group greatly affected by all of these changes was neither Hindu nor Muslim. The Sikhs had grown during the sixteenth century into a movement seeking to transcend the religious differences between Hindus and Muslims. Though awarded the city of Amritsar, the Golden Temple of which became their religious center, Mughal repression of the Sikhs provoked a prolonged rebellion, which turned them into a fierce fighting faith. Sikh men are distinctive even today for their uncut hair piled within tall turbans, large beards, the carrying of daggers, and the adoption by many of the surname "Singh" (meaning "lion"). They established control of most of the Punjab region during the eighteenth-century decline of the Mughals. During the days of British control, the reputation of the Sikhs as fierce fighters prompted the British to employ them as colonial troops and policemen throughout their empire.

Islamic Developments   While the vast majority of India's Muslims remained adherents of the Sunni branch and Hanafi school of interpretation of Islamic law, there were also several noteworthy developments in other areas. First, as we have noted several times already, there was an influential Shiite presence in India. For centuries, Shiites had migrated into Hindu areas of southern India, where, despite being a notable minority, they generally escaped discrimination from Sunnis characteristic of the north. In addition, Mughal relations with Safavid Persia, where Shia Islam was the official state religion, meant a certain influence on the Mughal court was unavoidable. Hence, Akbar studied mystical elements of Shiism, while Jahangir married the Safavid princess Nur Jahan, probably the most powerful woman of the Mughal period.

One branch of Shiism that attained considerable influence despite its small numbers was the Ismailis. Like a number of Muslim mystical brotherhoods, the Ismailis, originally refugees from the fall of the Fatimid caliphate, blended Shiite mysticism with practices borrowed from the devotional (*bakti*) cults of Hinduism. During Aurangzeb's reign they were suppressed as part of his general drive to make Indian Islam more in accordance with Islamic law. They survived and later prospered however, and in the twentieth century, their leader, the Aga Khan, was one of the world's wealthiest men.

Of the many Sufi branches of both Sunni and Shia Islam, the one most favored during much of the Mughal era was that of Chishtis. The voluntary poverty, mystical personae, and deep piety of the Chishtis had, as we have seen, a profound effect on Humayun and Akbar and influenced the latter's ideas of religious tolerance. Some Sufi groups sought a mystical encounter with the divine through strict contemplation of the Quran and demanded absolute obedience to religious law. Other groups that developed outside the mainstream of Sunni Islam included the Maddawis, who preached the arrival of the Mahdi ("the rightly guided one"), a savior who would lead an Islamic renewal and reunite all the Islamic lands. The Maddawis preached poverty and devotion to God and the Mahdi and were severely persecuted. One final movement worth mentioning is that of the Nuqtawis. This was a heretical sect that mixed Sufi mysticism with the belief that Muhammad was not the final prophet and preached the unity of all creation. One practitioner found his way to Akbar's court in 1576 and may have influenced the emperor's insistence on "peace with all."

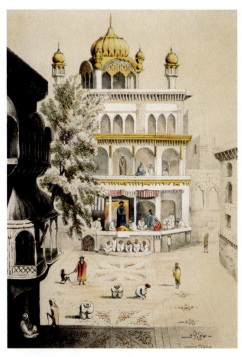

The Golden Temple at Amritsar. Sikhism, founded in part as an attempt to reconcile differences between Hindus and Muslims, ended up being persecuted by both by the seventeenth century, and ultimately was transformed into a faith that aggressively defended itself. In the accompanying illustration of the most sacred Sikh shrine, the Golden Temple at Amritsar, one can see the faithful in typical postures of worship, their hair uncut and wound up under their turbans, and their beards mandated to grow untrimmed.

Literature and Art

The Mughal period was one of India's most prolific in terms of its profusion of literary genres. Moreover, literature, art, and architecture were the areas in which India's rich multicultural environment produced its most arrestingly synthetic works. In translation projects, classical Persian works, poetry in nearly all of India's languages, even treatises on law and theology, Indian writers borrowed freely and frequently from each other. In painting, realistic portraits of personages and dramatic contemporary and historical scenes were recorded; and of course, the great buildings of the era, many of which are currently on the United Nations Educational, Scientific,

Life's Tragedy

Not only the laughing buds
Are always fleeing from me;
No, even the desert thorns
Draw their pricks away from me . . .
Life's tragedy lasts but two days.
I'll tell you what these two are for:
One day, to attach the heart to this and that;
One day, to detach it again.

—Abu Talib Kalim, Diwan in Annemarie Schimmel, *The Empire of the Great Mughals.* (London: Reaktion Books, 2004), p. 248

and Cultural Organization (UNESCO) register of world landmarks, remain for many the "authentic" symbols of India.

New Literary Directions   As they had been for centuries in Islamic India, Arabic and Persian remained the principal literary languages. The use of both, however, was considerably enlivened by the introduction of the latest wave of Turkic terms by the Chaghatay–Turkic Mughals. Chaghatay itself remained in use among the elites until the nineteenth century, while many of its loan words, along with a considerable Persian and Arabic vocabulary, were grafted onto the base of Sanskrit grammar to form the modern languages of Hindi and Urdu. Regional languages, such as Kashmiri and Bengali, also rose to prominence for both literary and general use.

Ironically, one of the catalysts for the explosion of literary work from the mid-sixteenth to the mid-seventeenth centuries came from the Mughals' most humiliating period. The exile of Humayun to Persia in the 1540s coincided with the Persian Shah Tahmasp embarking on a program of self-denial and abstinence in response to criticism about the worldliness of his court. Writers, painters, and poets who suddenly found themselves out of favor at the Persian court attached themselves to Humayun. They followed him to India, where their talents enlivened the arts already developing there. Their classical Arab and Persian verse forms were ultimately adopted into Urdu, as seen in the classical verse forms of *qasida* and *mathnavi*. By the following century, these forms had matured with the verses of Qudsi and Abu Talib Kalim (d. 1602).

Sanskrit and Hindi poets also continued verse forms pioneered by Chandra Lor in the 1300s, and the Mughal rulers up to Aurangzeb all had Hindi court poets—in some cases, members of the same family over several generations. Perhaps of more importance in terms of cultural synthesis, however, were the efforts pioneered by Akbar and Jahangir at translations of the great works of non-Muslim Indian literature into Persian. It was here that the émigrés who traveled with Humayun made their greatest contributions. Despite the objections of the more orthodox members of his court, Akbar commissioned a complete translation of the Mahabharata, followed shortly by the Ramayana. These he had read to him, and he had the members of his cult study them as well.

Though Sunni scholarship languished somewhat under Akbar, Sufi works proliferated, many borrowing concepts and terminology from non-Islamic sources. The most famous of these was Muhammad Ghauth Gwaliori's "The Five Jewels," which tapped sources from Hindu and Muslim astrology and Jewish Kabbala traditions, as well as Sufi mysticism. By Aurangzeb's reign, the pendulum had swung back to the more "Mecca-centered, prophetic, and exclusive" strain in Indian Islam. Thus, the works tended to be more geared toward treatises on Islamic law, interpretation of *hadith*—the traditions of the Prophet—and Sunni works on science and philosophy.

Art and Painting   One of the more interesting aspects of Islam as practiced by the Mughals—as well as the Safavid Persians and Ottomans—is that, like prohibitions on wine and other intoxicants, the injunctions against depicting human beings in art were often widely ignored in the inner chambers and private rooms of the court. Of course, during Aurangzeb's long reign, there was a marked drop in artistic output because of his much more strict interpretation of proper Islamic behavior. Nonetheless, the accompanying pronouncement of Akbar might be seen as more typical of the Timurids in general.

Not surprisingly, Akbar had a direct hand in the creation of what is considered to be the first painting in the "Mughal style"—a combination of the extreme delicacy of Persian miniature work with the vibrant colors and taste for bold themes of Hindu painters. Akbar inherited two of the master painters who accompanied Humayun from Persia, and the contact they acquired with Hindu works under Akbar's patronage resulted in the first of hundreds of Mughal **gouache** works: 250 miniature illustrations of the *Tutinama* and the colossal illustrated *Hamzanama* of 1570. The Persian tradition of miniature painting flourished under the Mughals, as did larger works on a variety of backings. Charcoal sketches and especially gouache were the preferred artistic media. Illustrations of Muslim and Hindu religious themes and epics were perennial favorites, as were numerous depictions of imperial *durbars*— receptions requiring noble attendance at court. These usually included authentic portraits of key individuals and provide scholars with important clues as to the identities of courtiers and dignitaries. Mughal artists often passed their skills on within their families over generations and represented an important subset of members at the imperial court and among the entourages of regional elites.

By the end of the sixteenth century, a new influence was moving into Mughal art: Europeans. The realistic approach of European artists and their use of vanishing point perspective began to be felt at the courts of Akbar and Jahangir. One prominent female artist, Nadira Banu, specialized in producing Flemish-style works. Some took European paintings and added "Mughal" touches—flatter backgrounds, gold leaf, and mosques in the distance. The period of Akbar's religious experiments also prompted an unparalleled interest among Mughal painters in Christian religious figures. Depictions of Christ from the gospels and from Muslim tales were popular fare, as were angels; even more so was the figure of the Virgin, a picture of whom even appears in a portrait of Jahangir. It was perhaps the most dramatic meeting of cultural influences since the era of the Gandharan Buddhas that were fashioned in the style of the Greek god Apollo.

Gouache: Watercolors with a gum base.

Architecture

Nowhere was the Mughal style more in evidence than in the construction of tombs and mausoleums. The most prominent of these, the Taj Mahal, was introduced in the opening to this chapter and needs little additional discussion. The ethereal lightness of so colossal a construction and the perfection of its layout make it the most distinctive construction of its kind. Europeans sometimes assumed that its architects were influenced by French or Italian artistic trends, though this remains a subject of debate. The chief architect, Ustad Ahmad Lahori (d. 1649), also designed the famous Red Fort of Shah Jahan's city, Shahjahanabad.

The Taj Mahal is scarcely the only noteworthy mausoleum of the Mughal period. All of the emperors commissioned massive tomb complexes for themselves and loved ones. Most of these survive in some form today, though many have been stripped at various times for their marble and other valuable building materials. Two of the more noteworthy tombs include Humayun's complex near Delhi and

Akbar on Painting

"There are many that hate painting; but such men I dislike. It appears to me, as if a painter had quite peculiar means of recognizing God, for a painter in sketching anything that has life ... must come to feel that he cannot bestow personality on his work, and is thus forced to think of God, the giver of life, and this increases his knowledge."

—Akbar, (unattributed) quoted in Schimmel, page 270.

Durbar of Jahangir. The tradition of the durbar—lavish imperial receptions for nobles and dignitaries, including foreign ambassadors and leading merchants—lasted throughout the Mughal era and was continued by the British into the twentieth century. In this portrayal of a durbar held by Jahangir (r. 1605–1627), the realism of the faces of the participants, many of whom are identifiable to scholars, is apparent. The emperor himself sits under the pillared canopy in the top center of the painting; on the lower left one can see a black-robed Jesuit priest among the attendees.

Akbar's tomb in Sikandra, near Agra. Though neither is as elaborate as the Taj, both include most of the same elements of mausoleum, mosque, and gardens.

A less benign way of demonstrating the power of the empire was the building of forts throughout the realm. While fortifications on the frontier were fairly austere and utilitarian compared to their counterparts in the capital and major cities, their watchtowers, crenellations, and central bastions all have a kind of artistic flair and lightness to them that belie the structures' primary belligerent purpose. While highly effective against the siege techniques of the day, they seem ironically in many ways more like the tomb complexes of their sponsors. The most famous of these structures was the Red Fort at Agra. Built up over centuries from the local red sandstone, the fort housed the palaces of Babur, Humayun, Akbar, Jahangir, and Shah Jahan. Shah Jahan made it the centerpiece of his new city, Shajahanabad, and expanded it into its present size and configuration. It is said that he died in one of its towers gazing at his wife's resting place, the Taj Mahal, a mile and a half distant.

During the high point of Mughal wealth and power, several Mughal emperors built entire cities. By far the most famous of these, as we have previously seen, was Akbar's Fatehpur Sikri. Indeed, as an idealized tribute to the inclusive Sufi master Salim Chishti, with architectural influences from Hindu and Muslim sources, materials from all over India, and a quote from Jesus, as handed down in Islamic lore, over its gateway—"The world is but a bridge; cross over it but build no house upon it"—it does indeed reflect Akbar's vision of what his realm should be. Not to be outdone, of course, Shah Jahan created his own city complex at Delhi, Shahjahanabad.

As one would expect, just as they were integral to the tomb complexes of the Mughals, mosques would be among the empire's most important constructions. Many were built as shrines at holy sites or to mark significant events in the lives of holy men or martyrs. Once again, a distinctive style emerged in which the basic form of the dome symbolically covering the world and the slender arrow of the minaret pointing heavenward interacted with central Asian, Persian, and even Hindu architectural influences. The largest Mughal mosques, like the Friday Delhi Mosque in Shahjahanabad and Aurangzeb's huge Badshahi Mosque in Lahore, contain immense courtyards, surrounded by cloisters leading to small rooms for intimate gatherings, domed areas for men and women, and distinctive minarets with fluted columns and bell-shaped roofs. One mosque in Burhanpur built by Shah Jahan even has quranic verses translated into Sanskrit in it. As scholars have noted, the location of many of the largest mosques, like that of some European cathedrals, is adjacent to government buildings and forts in order to demonstrate the seamless connections of these religious civilizations.

Putting It All Together

The rise of the Turkic central Asian peoples to prominence and power in a variety of areas, from the borders of successive Chinese dynasties to Anatolia and the domains of the Ottomans, and with the Timurids or Mughals in India, is one of the most dramatic sagas of world history. In India, this latest group of outside conquerors faced what might be called the "great question" of the subcontinent: how to create a viable state out of so many long-standing religious traditions, many of which are in direct opposition to each other. Even before the coming of Islam, rulers such as Ashoka felt the need to use transcendent concepts, such as dharma, to try to bridge cultural and religious gaps. The Guptas, for their part, tried to use state-supported Hinduism. With the coming of Islam, a new religion that stood in opposition to the older Hindu pattern of assimilation of gods and favored instead the conquest and conversion of opponents, a divide was created, which persists to this day. It should be remembered that, as recent scholarship has shown, even within these dramatically opposed religious traditions, much more accommodation than previously supposed had taken place. The later development of Sikhism, as another attempt to bridge India's religious syncretism, both added to attempts at greater tolerance and at times contributed to religious tensions.

Against this backdrop the accomplishmentss of the Mughals must be weighed as significant in terms of statecraft and artistic and cultural achievement, and perhaps less so in religious areas. At its height, Mughal India was the most populous, wealthy, politically powerful, and economically vibrant empire in the world next to China. It thus allowed the Mughal rulers unprecedented wealth and financed the proliferation of monumental architecture that became forever identified with India: the Red Fort, Fatehpur Sikri, and, above all, the Taj Mahal.

Yet, for all its wealth and power, the Mughal dynasty was plagued by problems that ultimately proved insoluble. The old nomadic succession practices of the Timurids repeatedly led to palace revolts by potential heirs. These wars in turn encouraged conflict with internal and external enemies who sensed weakness at the core of the regime. Protracted conflicts in Afghanistan, with Safavid Persia, and in Bengal also bled this fiscal–military state of resources. Finally, the Maratha wars slowly wore down even the semblance of unity among the rulers following Aurangzeb.

But perhaps an equally important factor in the ultimate dissolution of the empire was that of Hindu–Muslim syncretism. Here, we have two of the world's great religions interacting with each other in prolonged and profound ways, with the added complication of Muslim rulers and Muslims in general being a small minority among the subcontinent's people. Despite the flexibility of the early rulers in trying to deemphasize the more oppressive elements of Islamic rule in Hindu India—most dramatically, Akbar through his effort to create an entirely new religion—the attempt at a stricter orthodoxy under Aurangzeb hardened Hindu–Muslim and Sikh divisions for centuries to come (see Concept Map).

Throughout the period, one other factor loomed on the horizon but became larger day by day as the dynasty went into decline. The well-financed and well-armed trading companies of the Europeans, increasingly adept at reading Indian politics, gradually moved into positions of regional power. By 1750, they were on the cusp of changing the political situation completely. Indeed, the seeds that had been planted by 1750 would soon be reaped as the first great clash of mature religious civilizations with the new industrially based societies. By 1920, all of these religious civilizations would be gone.

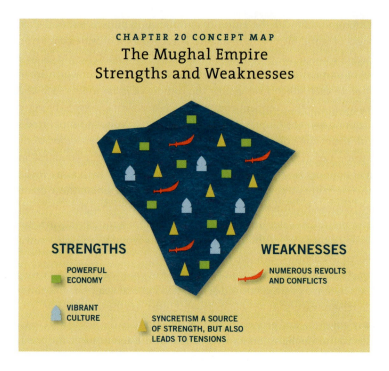

Review and Respond

1. What do you see as the greatest strengths of the individual Mughal rulers? Their greatest weaknesses?

2. What, in your view, provides a state with more stability: unity of religion or plurality of religion? Why? How did religious differences affect the Mughals?

3. Although the Mughals often struggled with the religious aspects of their empire, they seem to have been wonderfully successful on the cultural and artistic front. Why was this so?

For additional resources, including maps, primary sources, visuals, and quizzes, please go to www.oup.com/us/vonsivers. Please see the Further Resources section at the back of the book for additional readings and suggested websites.

Thinking Through Patterns

▶ **What were the strengths and weaknesses of Mughal rule?**

The weaknesses are probably more obvious than the strengths at first glance. Two things are immediately apparent: first, the position of the Mughals as an ethnic and religious minority ruling a vastly larger majority population and, second, the conflict-prone succession practices of the older central Asian Turkic leaders. The minority position of the Mughals aggravated long-existing tensions between Muslim rulers and Hindu subjects in India, of which the Mughals were to be the last line. In an age of religious civilizations, where some kind of unity of religion was the ideal, this put considerable strains on the Mughals as rulers—as it did the Ottomans in predominantly Christian lands and Catholics and Protestants in Europe. Central Asian Turkic succession practices almost always guaranteed conflict when it was time for a new ruler to accede the throne. Nearly every Mughal successor during this period ended up having to fight factions and family to gain the empire.

In some respects the strengths of Mughal rule were in reaction to these problems. Babur and Akbar, in particular, were extraordinarily tolerant rulers in terms of religion. When later rulers like Aurangzeb returned to strict Sunni Islamic policies, it prompted resistance, especially among Hindus. Also, while Mughal rulers were never able to completely free themselves from succession struggles, they succeeded in setting up a well-run fiscal–military state with the mansabdar system, largely undercutting old local and regional loyalties and tying the new loyalty to the state. Like France, the Ottomans, and the Confucian states of eastern Asia, the development of bureaucratic forms was an important earmark of the early modern era.

As we noted, Mughal rulers faced the problem confronted by nearly all "religious civilizations": Religious orthodoxy was seen, in theory, as a vital element of loyalty to the state. But for the Mughals, as for previous Muslim rulers in India, the desire for strict adherence to Muslim law was always tempered by the problem of Islam being a minority religion in India. Here, as we saw, the early Mughal rulers— Babur, Humayun, Akbar—were far less tied to strict Sunni Islam than their successors. Thus, their way of ruling was to uphold Sunni Islam as the approved state religion but to scrupulously refrain from forcing Muslim practices on other religious groups. Akbar went so far as to create a new religion and held Thursday night discussions with leaders of other religions to find ways to satisfy the desires of all. With Shah Jahan, however, the reaction building among reform-minded Sunni Muslims to this liberalization turned to enforcing more strict practices, which peaked during the long reign of Aurangzeb. By the end of Aurangzeb's reign the Sikhs were near revolt and the long Hindu Maratha revolt was in full swing. But even during this period, local religious customs remained largely intact and, indeed, often thrived.

▶ **What was the Mughal policy toward religious accommodation? How did it change?**

▶ **What factors account for the Mughal decline during the eighteenth century?**

At the beginning and for much of the eighteenth century, Mughal India was the second richest and most prosperous empire in the world, after China. But by 1750 it was already in pronounced decline. A large part of this was due to rebellions by the Sikhs, Rajputs, and especially the Marathas that raged off and on through the century. By the 1750s as well, the European trading companies with their small but well-trained armies were becoming locally powerful. Here, the great milestone would take place during the Seven Years' War (1756–1763), when the British East India Company eliminated its French competitors and in essence took over the rule of Bengal from its headquarters in Calcutta. Within 100 years it would take over all of India.

Chapter 21

1500-1800

Regulating the "Inner" and "Outer" Domains

CHINA AND JAPAN

The time seemed right for a letter home. In only 2 weeks the Japanese invasion force had captured the Korean capital of Seoul, and the skill and firepower of the Japanese warriors seemed to brush their opponents aside at will. The Japanese commander, Toyotomi Hideyoshi, was a battle-hardened commoner who had risen through the ranks of his patron, Oda Nobunaga, as Oda fought to unite Japan before his assassination in 1582. Now, a decade later, Hideyoshi, as he was still known (as a commoner he had no surname and had only been given the family name "Toyotomi" by

Seeing Patterns

▶ Why did late Ming and early Qing China look inward after such a successful period of overseas exploration?

▶ How do the goals of social stability drive the policies of agrarian states? How does the history of China and Japan in this period show these policies in action?

▶ In what ways did contact with the maritime states of Europe alter the patterns of trade and politics in eastern Asia?

▶ How did Neo-Confucianism in China differ from that of Tokugawa Japan?

the imperial court in 1586) had embarked on an audacious campaign to extend his power to the Asian mainland. Six years before, he had written his mother that he contemplated nothing less than the conquest of China. Now seemed like a good time to inform her that his goal was at last within his grasp.

As if in an eerie foreshadowing of another Korean conflict to come centuries later, however, the Japanese soon faced a massive Chinese and Korean counterattack and became mired in a bloody stalemate, their guns and tactics barely enough to compensate for the determination and numbers of their enemies. After 4 more years of negotiation punctuated by bitter fighting, Hideyoshi finally withdrew to Japan. One final invasion attempt of Korea in 1597 collapsed when his death the following year set off a bloody struggle for succession, which ultimately placed in power the Tokugawa family, who would go on to rule Japan for more than 250 years.

Hideyoshi's dream of conquering China was, in a sense, a quest to claim the wellsprings of Japanese civilization as well. The episode brought together the politics, cultures, and fortunes of three of the four fiercely independent realms that together wove the primary strands of an east Asian

The Floating World. Perhaps the most popular painting style for mass consumption in Japan during the Tokugawa Shogunate was the ukiyo-e wood block print. An artist often considered the founder of the style, Hishikawa Mononobu (ca. 1625–1694), painted a variety of subjects but was especially renowned for his renderings of Japan's "floating world" (a literal translation of ukiyo-e) of the pursuit of pleasure. In this picture featuring the "blown-out" perspective of seeing behind the walls, a brothel in the capital of Edo's Yoshiwara quarter—even today the modern capital of Tokyo's most famous red light district—is depicted in which men are engaged in a variety of enjoyable pursuits with the women of the house. In the central room they talk with the proprietor [in black] in front of a screen with the kanji (Chinese) character doku—here, meaning "sole" or "alone"— and suggesting the private pleasures to be had within ...

pattern of history. The fourth, Vietnam, while not involved in this particular struggle, had been subject to similar pressures of Chinese cultural and political diffusion for eighteen centuries. As we have seen in other areas, such as the Mediterranean and the expanding kingdoms of Europe, the rise of Japanese power represents a vitally important pattern of world history: A state on the periphery absorbs innovation from a cultural center, in this case China, and then becomes a vital center itself. And like the other states in the region, Japan had absorbed the structures of "religious civilizations," as we have termed them—in this case, the philosophical system of Neo-Confucianism.

Of equal importance, Hideyoshi's invasion was made possible in part by the arrival of a new factor: the appearance of the first Europeans in the region. While their arrival in the sixteenth century provided only the barest inkling of the reversals of fortune to come, by the middle of the nineteenth century their presence would create a crisis of power and acculturation for all of east Asia. For Japan, the industrializing West would then become a new center from which to draw innovation. For the present, however, European intrusions provided powerful incentives for both China and Japan to turn inward to safeguard their own security and stability.

Late Ming and Qing China to 1750

Proclaimed as a new dynasty in 1368, the Ming in its early years appears to have followed the familiar pattern of the "dynastic cycle" of previous dynasties. Having driven out the Mongol remnant, the Hongwu emperor and his immediate successors consolidated their rule, elevated the Confucian bureaucracy to its former place, and set up an administrative structure more focused on the person of the emperor than in previous dynasties. In 1382, the Grand Secretariat was created as the top governmental board below the emperor. Under the Grand Secretariat were the six boards, the governors and governors-general of the provinces, and various degrees of lower-level officials down to the district magistrate.

In this section we will also examine the question of China's greatest maritime expansion—and sudden withdrawal to concentrate on domestic matters. Why such an abrupt change in policy? What factors led to the ultimate decline of the Ming dynasty and the rise to power of the Manchus, a bordering nomadic people who drove out the Ming and created China's last imperial dynasty, the Qing [CHING]? By what means did the Manchus create a state in which, despite being a tiny ruling minority, they held their grip on power into the twentieth century? Finally, what faint hints of the dynasty's problems appeared during its time of greatest power in the mid-eighteenth century?

From Expansion to Exclusion

During the late fourteenth and early fifteenth centuries, while China was rebuilding from the war to drive out the Mongols, the more pressing problems of land distribution and tenancy had abated somewhat. As in Europe, the depopulation of some areas from fighting and banditry and the lingering effects of the Black Death (which had reduced China's population from perhaps 100 million to about 60 million) had raised the value of labor, depressed the price of land, and increased the proportional amount of money in circulation. While the problems of land tenure would recur, another period of relief from their full effects soon came, albeit indirectly, from the creation of overseas empires by the Portuguese and the Spanish in the sixteenth century. The resulting Columbian Exchange saw the circulation of a number of new food crops on a global scale that had a substantial impact on the world's agricultural productivity (see Chapter 18).

New Food Crops   In addition to new, higher-yielding rice strains coming out of southeast Asia (as they had a number of times in the past), the Chinese began to cultivate sugarcane, indigo, potatoes, sweet potatoes, maize (corn), peanuts, and tobacco that came from Africa and the Americas by way of the Spanish in the Philippines and the Portuguese at Macao. Corn and potatoes, versatile crops suitable

China				
1368-1398 Founding of Ming Dynasty	**1405-1433** Voyages of Zheng He to Southeast Asia, India, Arabia, and Africa	**1577** Matteo Ricci, First Jesuit Missionary in China	**1664-1722** Reign of Kangxi Emperor	
	1382 The Grand Secretariat Is Formed	**1540s–1580s** "Single Whip" Tax Edicts Instituted	**1644** Qing Dynasty Proclaimed	**1736-1795** Reign of Qianlong Emperor, China's High Point of Wealth and Power

Japan			
		1720 Japan's Population Reaches Approximately 33 Million, Edo Becomes World's Largest City	
1603 Establishment of Tokugawa Shogunate			
	1637 Shimabara Rebellion Against the Shogunate		**1653-1724** Life of Chikamatsu Monzaemon, Japan's Leading Playwright

for cultivation in a variety of marginal environments, accounted for a considerable increase in the arable land within China. Peanuts, sugarcane, indigo, and tobacco quickly established themselves as important cash crops. Even today, cigars and to-bacco products sometimes carry the characters *lusong* a transliteration of "Luzon," the island in the Philippines from which they were first obtained from the Spanish. Cotton, first cultivated in China for its fiber during the Song period, had also now become a major part of what had grown into the world's largest textile industry.

Aided by the productivity of these new crops, China's population grew from its low of perhaps 60 million at the beginning of the Ming period to an estimated 150 million by 1600. There was also a marked growth in urbanism as market towns and regional transshipment points multiplied. The efficiency of Chinese agriculture, the continued incorporation of marginal and border lands into production, and the refinement of the empire's immense internal trade all contributed to another doubling of the population to perhaps 300 million by 1800. This accelerating growth began China's movement toward what some historical demographers have called a *high-level equilibrium trap*—a condition in which the land has reached its maximum potential for feeding an increasing population; that population then (barring radical improvements in crops or technology) becomes slowly squeezed into impoverishment (see Map 21.1).

MAP 21.1 China in 1600.

China and the World Commercial Revolution   China's rapid recovery, particularly as the sixteenth century brought new crops from the Americas, placed the late Ming and Qing Empires in the center of an increasingly extensive and complex worldwide commercial revolution (see "Patterns Up Close: The China Trade"). The competition for markets among the emerging maritime Atlantic states of Europe pushed them to develop ever-widening trade networks in the Indian Ocean, the Pacific, along the African coast, and in the Americas. In all of these regions (except the Americas) they faced stiff competition from local traders long involved in regional networks, particularly in the Indian Ocean, among the many ports of what is now Indonesia.

Among the European states, commercial, political, and religious competition resulted in policies of mercantilism (see Chapters 17 and 18), in which countries strove to control sources of raw materials and markets. Similarly, China and Japan (by the early seventeenth century) sought to tightly control imports, regulate the export trade, and keep potentially subversive foreign influences at bay. China's immense production of luxury goods, the seclusion policies of Japan and Korea, and the huge and growing demand for porcelain, tea, silk, paper, and cotton textiles made the Chinese empire the world's dominant economic engine until the productive capacity of the Industrial Revolution vaulted Great Britain into that position in the nineteenth century. Indeed, recent work by world historians has shown how extensively China's economy powered that of Eurasia and much of the world before what Kenneth Pomeranz has called "the great divergence" of Western economic ascendancy (see Map 21.2).

MAP **21.2** **World Trade Networks, ca. 1770.**

World Trade Networks, ca. 1770

——— Trade networks

PACIFIC OCEAN

AUSTRALIA

NORTH AMERICA

ASIA

INDIAN OCEAN

EUROPE

SOUTH AMERICA

AFRICA

ATLANTIC OCEAN

Patterns Up Close

The "China" Trade

Ming and Qing China may be said to be at the heart of two innovations of enormous importance to the patterns of world history. The first is one that we have tracked through all of the chapters in this book pertaining to China: the technical and aesthetic development of ceramics culminating in the creation of true porcelain during the Song period (960–1279). The early Ming period saw the elaboration of the use of kaolin white clays with what are called "flux" materials—minerals, metals, and compounds—that can fuse with the clay under extremely high temperatures to form durable glazes and striking artistic features. Thus, the Song and Yuan periods were characterized by pure white and green celadon wares, some with a purposely created "crackled" glaze on them, while by the Ming period, highly distinctive blue and white ware—the result of employing pigments with cobalt oxide imported from the areas around modern Iran and Iraq—set the world standard for elegance.

The artistic excellence of Chinese porcelain, like earlier styles of Chinese ceramics, spawned imitators throughout the Chinese periphery. By 1500, porcelain works in Korea, Japan, and Vietnam supplied a burgeoning market both at home and throughout east and southeast Asia. While these regional manufacturers for the most part followed the designs of the Chinese imperial works at Jingdezhen, some, especially the Japanese ceramicist Chojiro, preferred highly rustic, rough-hewn earthenware designs with glazes that formed spontaneous designs as the pieces were fired—the famous raku ware. Thus, there was already a highly developed regional market for what was, at the time, arguably the world's most highly developed technology.

The period from 1500 to the mid-nineteenth century brings us to the second great innovation in which China was the driving force: the world market for porcelain.

Porcelain Vase, Ming Period.
Porcelain ware of the Song and Ming periods are among the most coveted Chinese art objects even today. Here we have a Ming vase showing characteristically vibrant colors and a degree of technical perfection indicative of the best Chinese pottery works, such as Jingdezhen. The motif of the grass carp on the vase is symbolic of endurance and perseverance, and thus associated with the god of literature and scholarship.

MAP 21.3 **Silver Flows and Centers of Porcelain Production.**

China's wares had found customers for centuries in nearly every corner of Eurasia and North and East Africa. Shipwrecks have been found in the Straits of Malacca laden with Ming porcelain; traders in the Swahili cities along the East African coast were avid collectors, while Africans farther inland decorated their graves with Chinese bowls. All stops on the Silk Road had their precious supplies of porcelain, while the Ottoman Turks did their best to copy the blue and white Ming wares in their own factories at Izmir.

Before the sixteenth century, a trickle of Ming porcelain also made its way to Europe. With the establishment of the first European trade empires, however, the demand for porcelain skyrocketed. Portuguese, Spanish, and later Dutch, French, English, and (after 1784) American merchants all sought porcelain in ever-increasing amounts. From 1500 to 1800 it was arguably the single most important commodity in the unfolding world commercial revolution. While estimates vary, economic historians have suggested that between one-third to one-half of all the silver produced in the Americas during this time went to pay for porcelain. Incoming ships often used the bulk cargoes of porcelain as ballast, and foreign merchants sent custom orders to their Chinese counterparts for Chinese-style wares designed for use at Western tables. Such was the prominence of this "export porcelain" in the furnishings of period homes that scarcely any family of means was without it (see Map 21.3).

With the prominence of mercantilist theory and protectionism toward home markets during the seventeenth and eighteenth centuries, it is not surprising that foreign manufacturers sought to break the Chinese monopoly. During Tokugawa times, the Japanese, for example, forced a group of Korean potters to work at the famous Arita works to turn out Sino–Korean designs; the Dutch marketed "delftware" as an attempt to copy Chinese "blue willow" porcelain. It was not until German experimenters in Saxony happened upon a workable formula for hard-paste porcelain—after years of trial and error, even melting down Chinese wares for analysis—that their facility at Meissen began to produce true porcelain in 1710. Josiah Wedgwood set up his own porcelain factory in 1759 in England. But Chinese manufacturers would still drive the market until the end of the nineteenth century. And fine porcelain would forever carry the generic name of "china" regardless of its origins.

Porcelain Candlestick for the Export Market, Qing Period. By the early 1700s, luxury exports from China such as porcelain, lacquerware, and, of course, tea had become important staples of European maritime trade. Export porcelain—items either made to order by Chinese porcelain works for overseas buyers, or generic ones made to suit European and colonial tastes—had become such a big business that cheaper pieces were sometimes actually used as ship's ballast on the homeward voyages. Shown here is a candlestick for use in a European home with Chinese motifs of vessels at the top. The cobalt blue color is characteristic of the Ming and Qing designs.

Questions

• How does the development of porcelain serve as an example of Chinese leadership in technical innovations during the premodern and early modern periods?

• How did the emergence of a global trading network after 1500 affect both the demand for porcelain and its impact on consumer tastes?

In the midst of this growth, the government took steps to simplify the system of land taxation. As in previous regimes, land was assessed and classified according to its use and relative productivity. Land taxes were then combined into a single bill, payable in silver by installments over the course of the year: the so-called single-whip tax system. The installment plan allowed peasants to remain relatively solvent during planting season when their resources were depleted, thus reducing the need to borrow at high rates from moneylenders at crucial times of the yearly cycle. Significantly, the requirement that the payment be in silver also played a crucial role in the increasing monetization of the economy. *Corvée* labor—the contribution of labor as a form of tax—was effectively abolished as well.

Regulating the Outer Barbarians

By the late fifteenth century, Ming China had made considerable progress toward the goals of peace and stability long sought by Chinese regimes. In addition to the practical requirements of defending the historic avenues of invasion in China's remote interior, the view of the empire cultivated by China's elites placed it at the center of a world order defined by Neo-Confucian philosophy and supported by a host of Chinese cultural assumptions. As we will see in the following sections, like the Tokugawa shogunate in Japan in the seventeenth century, the Ming, and later the Qing, had come to view foreign influence as less "civilized" and far too often injurious to established social order. Hence, successive rulers placed severe restrictions on maritime trade and conceived of diplomatic relations primarily in commercial terms. "All the world is one family," imperial proclamations routinely claimed, and the emperor was conceived as the father, in Confucian terms, of this world-family system. "Tribute missions," a term sometimes (though somewhat misleadingly) applied to this diplomatic–commercial relationship, were sent from Korea, Vietnam, the Ryukyu Islands, and occasionally Japan to pay periodic ceremonial visits to the emperor, who then bestowed presents on the envoys and granted them permission to trade in China. This arrangement worked reasonably well within the long-standing hierarchy of the Confucian cultural sphere. By the late eighteenth century, however, it came into direct conflict with the more egalitarian system of international trade and diplomacy that had evolved in the West.

Tribute Mission. This illustration, from a popular English travel account first published in 1745, shows the retinue of the Siamese (Thailand) ambassador being escorted to an audience with the emperor inside the Forbidden City. For the Qing, these annual tribute missions had as much symbolic importance as anything diplomatic. As the "Son of Heaven," the emperor's supreme cultural authority over the lands in his "inner" domains was to be acknowledged through elaborate gift-giving and the performing of the kowtow by the ambassador—a deep bow in which one's head touches the ground.

The Ming in Decline   Despite the increased attention directed at the Mongol resurgence of the 1440s, periodic rebellions in the north and northwest punctuated the late fifteenth and sixteenth centuries. The huge commitment of Chinese troops in Korea against the forces of the Japanese leader Hideyoshi during his attempted invasion of Korea and China from 1592 to 1598 weakened the dynasty further during a crucial period that saw the rise of another regional power: the Manchus. By the turn of the seventeenth century, under the leadership of Nurhachi (r.1616–1626) and Abahai (r.1636–1643), the Manchus, an Altaic-speaking nomadic people inhabiting the northeastern section of the Ming domain, had become the prime military force of the area and dissident Chinese sought them as allies. In 1642, the Chinese general Wu Sangui invited the Manchu leader Dorgon to cross the Great Wall where it approaches the sea at Shanhaiguan. For the Chinese, this event would come to carry the same sense of finality as Caesar's crossing of the Rubicon: The Manchus soon captured Beijing and declared the founding of a new regime, the Qing, or "pure," dynasty. Like the defeated remnant of the Nationalist regime in 1949, some Ming loyalists fled to the island of Taiwan, where they expelled the Dutch (who had established a trading base there) and held on until succumbing to Qing forces in 1683.

Banner system: The organizational system of the Manchus for military and taxation purposes; there were eight banners under which all military houses were arranged, and each was further divided into blocks of families required to furnish units of 300 soldiers to the Manchu government.

The Spring and Summer of Power: The Qing to 1750

Like the Toba and Mongols before them, the Manchus now found themselves in the position of having to "dismount and rule." A good deal of preparation for this had already taken place within the borderland state they had created for themselves—for a time, successfully isolated by the Ming—on the Liaodong Peninsula of south Manchuria. Long exposure to Chinese culture and Confucian administrative practices provided models that soon proved adaptable by Manchu leaders within the larger environment of China proper.

The Banner System   The **banner system**, under which the Manchus were organized for military and tax purposes, was also expanded under the Qing to provide for segregated Manchu elites and garrisons in major cities and towns. Under the banner system, the Manchu state had been divided into eight major military and ethnic (Manchu, Han Chinese, and Mongolian) divisions, each represented by a distinctive banner. Within each division, companies were formed of 300 fighters recruited from families represented by that banner. Originally organized for a mobile warrior people, the system eventually became the chief administrative tool of the Manchu leadership. It was now introduced into China in such a way as to constitute the Manchus as a hereditary warrior class occupying its own sections of major Chinese cities. The Han, or ethnic Chinese, forces were organized into their own "Armies of the Green Standard," so named for the color of the flags they carried.

Manchu Bannermen, Canton, ca. 1872. Until the twentieth century, the Qing maintained garrisons of Manchu soldiers organized under the old "banner system" in all of China's major cities. The bannermen lived in their own quarter, often in reduced circumstances, as a check on the local Chinese population. Significantly, in terms of China's difficulties with Western imperialism in the later nineteenth century, the group pictured here was part of the guard of the British consul.

Minority Rule   Always conscious of their position as a ruling minority in China, with their numbers comprising only about 2 percent of the population, the Manchus, like the Mongols before them, sought to walk a fine line between administrative and cultural adaptation and the kind of complete assimilation that had characterized

Dyarchy: A system of administration consisting of two equal or parallel parts.

previous invaders. Thus, under what is sometimes termed the Sino–Manchu **dyarchy**, Chinese and Manchus were scrupulously recruited in equal numbers for high administrative posts; Manchu quotas in the examination system were instituted; edicts and memorials were issued in both Chinese and the Manchu written language; Qing emperors sought to control the empire's high culture; and, of course, Manchu "bannermen" of the various garrisons were kept in their own special quarters in the towns and cities. In addition, the Manchu conqueror Dorgon instituted the infamous "queue [pronounced like the letter Q] edict" in 1645: All males, regardless of ethnicity, were required on pain of death to adopt the Manchu hairstyle of shaved forehead and long pigtail in the back—the *queue*—as the outward sign of loyalty to the new order. This hairstyle can be seen in early photographs taken of Chinese men until the Qing dynasty fell in 1912. As it was put with a kind of sinister whimsy, "Keep the hair, lose the head; keep the head, lose the hair."

The results, however, were bloody and long-lasting. The queue edict provoked revolts in several cities, and the casualties caused by its suppression may have numbered in the hundreds of thousands. For the remainder of the Qing era, rebels and protestors routinely cut their queues as the first order of business; during China's Taiping Rebellion (1851–1864), perhaps the bloodiest civil war in human history, insurgents were known as "the long-haired rebels" for their immediate abandonment of the Qing hair style.

As a number of scholars have suggested, the situation of the Qing represents a curious relationship between a cultural core and its periphery, in which the conquest of the core by the periphery brings the core temporary renewal but the interests of stability loom so large for the newcomers that they become the ones who cling most tenaciously to the forms of the old order. In this view, by the end of the Qing period, when the empire was faced with foreign pressure and domestic agitation for reform, the Manchu court and nobility were willing to risk the collapse of the empire to preserve the power of their dynasty and position.

Creating the New Order

Though the Qing kept the centralized imperial system of the Ming largely intact, while importing the banner system as a kind of Manchu parallel administrative apparatus, they also made one significant addition to the uppermost level of the bureaucracy. While retaining the Ming Grand Secretariat, the emperor Kangxi's successor, Yongzheng, set up an ad hoc inner advisory body called the "Grand Council" in 1733. Over the succeeding decades the Grand Council became the supreme "inner" advisory group to the emperor, while the Grand Secretariat was relegated to handling less crucial "outer" matters of policy making and implementation.

For much of the seventeenth century, however, the pacification of the empire remained the primary task. Under the able leadership of Nurhachi's great-grandson, the Kangxi emperor (r. 1661–1722), the difficult subjugation of the south was concluded, the Revolt of the Three Feudatories (1673–1681) ultimately crushed, and the naval stronghold of the Ming pretender called "Koxinga" by the Dutch captured on Taiwan in 1683.

As had been the case in past dynasties, the Qing sought to safeguard the borders of the empire by bringing peoples on the periphery into the imperial system through a judicious application of the carrot and the stick, or, as it was known to generations of Chinese strategists, the "loose rein" and "using barbarians to check barbarians."

In practical terms, this meant a final reckoning with the Mongols in the 1720s by means of improved cannon and small arms, along with bribes and presents to friendly chieftains, and the intervention of the Qing in religious disputes regarding Tibetan Buddhism, which had also been adopted by a number of the Mongol groups. Toward this end, the Qing established a protectorate over Tibet in 1727, with the Dalai Lama ruling as the approved temporal and religious leader. To cement the relationship further, the emperor built a replica of a Tibetan stupa just outside the Manchu quarter in Beijing and a model of the Dalai Lama's Potala Palace at the emperor's summer retreat in Jehol [Yeh-hole].

The Qianlong Emperor

With the traditional threats from the borders now quashed, the reign of the Qianlong [Chien-LUNG] emperor, from 1736 to 1795, marked both the high point and the beginning of the decline of the Qing dynasty—and of imperial China itself. The period witnessed China's expansion to its greatest size during the imperial era. This was accompanied by a doubling of its population to perhaps 300 million by 1800. By almost any measure, its internal economy dwarfed that of any other country and equaled or surpassed that of Europe as a whole until the Industrial Revolution was well under way.

Tibetan Stupa and Temple, Beijing. This marble *chorten*, the Tibetan version of the Buddhist stupa, or reliquary, was built by the Qianlong emperor for the visit of the Panchen Lama in 1779, in part to cement the new Sino–Tibetan relationship growing from the establishment of a Qing protectorate over Tibet.

The Qing army, though perhaps already eclipsed in terms of efficiency and weaponry by the leading nations of Europe, was still many times larger than that of any potential competitor. Moreover, Qianlong wielded this power successfully a number of times during his reign, with expeditions against pirates and rebels on Taiwan and in punitive campaigns against Vietnam, Nepal, and Burma between 1766 and 1792 (see Map 21.4). During his long life, he also tried, with limited success, to take up the writing brush of a scholar and connoisseur, creating the collection of art that is today the core of the National Palace Museum's holdings on Taiwan. Under his direction, the state sponsored monumental literary enterprises on a scale still awesome to contemplate today. Based on the small but steady stream of information on the Qing empire circulating around Europe, it seemed to some that the Chinese had solved a number of the problems of good government and might provide practical models of statecraft for Europeans to emulate.

Early European Contacts

Ironically, it was precisely at the time that China abandoned its oceanic expeditions that tiny Portugal on the Atlantic coast surmounted its first big hurdle in pursuit of what would become a worldwide maritime trade empire (see Chapters 16, 18, 19) By the 1440s, Portuguese navigators had

MAP 21.4 China During the Reign of Qianlong.

rounded the bulge of West Africa and opened commercial relations with the coastal kingdoms there. Scarcely a decade after Vasco da Gama arrived in Calicut in 1498, the first Portuguese ships appeared in Chinese waters. By 1557, these *Folangqi*—the Chinese transliteration of "Franks," a generic term for Europeans transmitted by the Arabs to Malacca, where it was transformed into *Ferenghi* [Fa-REN-gee]—had wrested the first European colony from the Chinese at Macao. It was destined to be the longest-lived European colony as well, remaining under Portuguese control until 1999. From this point on, through merchants and missionaries, the contacts would frequently be profitable—and, sometimes, disastrous. Ultimately, they provided some of the most far-reaching interactions of world history.

The first Portuguese and Spanish traders were less than impressive to the Chinese officials charged with handling commercial affairs. Confucian tradition had long maintained that merchants were generally a disreputable, if necessary, class. The outlandish appearance, disagreeable smell—from months aboard ship with primitive sanitary facilities—and aggressive behavior of these "men of the Western Ocean" only solidified this impression. Additionally, trade restrictions imposed by the Ming had only partially reduced the network of Chinese merchants long established in the ports of southeast Asia, Malaya, and the Moluccas. In these areas they often traded in contraband goods and competed for markets with Arab, Malayan, and Japanese merchants and pirates. In short, the Europeans had now entered a region of trade where the lines were quite fluid between legitimate and illegitimate enterprises, and both they and the Chinese authorities reacted accordingly.

Missionaries The arrival of the first European merchants in east Asia was followed shortly by that of the first Catholic missionaries. Although the crusading impulse was still very much alive in Christian dealings with Muslim merchants in the Indies, Christian missionaries (at first from Franciscan and Dominican orders and later from the Jesuits) were quick to realize the vast potential for faith conversions in China and Japan. The various missionary orders set up headquarters in Malacca, and in 1549 the Fran-

Matteo Ricci and Li Paul. The cross-cultural possibilities of sixteenth- and seventeenth-century Sino–Western contact were perhaps best exemplified by the activities of the Jesuit Matteo Ricci (1552–1610). Ricci predicated his mission in China on a respectful study of the language and classical canon of the empire coupled with a thorough knowledge of the new mathematics and astronomy of the West. Here, he is pictured with one of his most prominent converts, a literatus and veteran of the war against the Japanese in Korea, Li Yingshi. Upon his conversion in 1602, Li took the Christian name of Paul.

ciscan Francis Xavier landed in Japan. The endemic conflict among the *daimyo* (regional warlords) of Japan helped create a demand for Western goods, especially firearms; and the association of these with Christianity allowed considerable progress to be made in gaining conversions. China, however, required a vastly different strategy.

Wary of potentially disruptive foreign influences, the Ming at first refused entry to missionaries. Once admitted, the Franciscans and Dominicans, with their limited training in Chinese language and culture, made little headway. Additionally, their efforts were largely aimed at seeking conversions among the poor, which won them scant respect or influence among China's elite. The Jesuits, however, tried a different tack. Led by Matteo Ricci (1552–1610) and his successors Adam Schall Von Bell (1591–1666) and Ferdinand Verbiest (1623–1688), they immersed themselves in the classical language and high culture of the empire and gained recognition through their expertise in mathematics, astronomy, military science, and other European skills sought by the imperial court. Jesuit advisors served the last Ming emperors as court astronomers and military engineers and successfully made the transition to the new dynasty. The high point of their influence was reached during the reign of the Qing Kangxi emperor. With Schall as the official court astronomer and mathematician and an entire European-style observatory set up in Beijing, Kangxi actively considered conversion to Catholicism.

The papacy, however, had long considered Jesuit liturgical and doctrinal adaptations to local sensibilities problematic. In China, the Jesuits' use of tea and rice during the Eucharist instead of bread and wine set off the "rites controversy." The liturgical substitution proved unacceptable to Rome, as did Jesuit tolerance of their converts' veneration of Confucius and maintenance of ancestral shrines. After several decades of intermittent discussion, Kangxi's successor, Yongzheng, banned the order's activities in China in 1724. Christianity and missionary activity were driven underground, though the Qing would retain a Jesuit court astronomer into the nineteenth century.

China and the European Enlightenment   While the European intellectual influence on China was limited to a small circle at court, the reports of the Jesuits and other foreign observers from the empire had a considerable effect on several of the important figures of the Enlightenment and on creating an overall image of China in the West. For the *philosophes* (e.g. Voltaire, Liebnitz, Diderot, and Montesquieu) the vision of a vast, wealthy, and powerful empire governed by a highly developed bureaucracy according to a pragmatic and secular system of ethics provided much ammunition for their critiques of European regimes. A Chinese Christian convert, Hoange [HO-ahn-guh], who secured a minor position in the French government as a cataloguer of its Chinese works, provided a wealth of information to the young Montesquieu, who incorporated it into his satire of French life, *The Persian Letters*. The emphasis placed on the importance of land by Chinese officials was also reflected in the economic arguments of the physiocrats, whose chief exponent, Francois Quesnay, was sometimes called "the Confucius of Europe." Philology was also greatly enhanced by the production of the first Chinese dictionaries for use with European languages. Finally, the growing trade in luxury goods spurred both a fashion for *chinoiserie* (items manufactured in Chinese styles, real or imagined) among the elite and a desire among European manufacturers to develop domestic industries in such items as silk and porcelain. While viable silk industries were created in both France and Italy, the manufacture of true porcelain in Europe would not be seen until the innovations of Meissen and Wedgwood (see Patterns Up Close).

The Canton Trade   While China's commerce with the maritime Atlantic states grew rapidly in the eighteenth century, the Europeans had not yet been fully incorporated into the Qing diplomatic system. A century before, the expansion of Russia into Siberia and the region around the Amur River had prompted the Qing to negotiate the Treaty of Nerchinsk in 1689. Under its terms, negotiated with Kangxi's Jesuit advisors acting as interpreters and go-betweens, the Russians agreed to abandon their last forts along the Amur and were given rights to continue their lucrative caravan trade in the interior. Formal borders were established in Manchuria, and the first attempts at settling claims to the central Asian regions of Ili and Kuldjia were made. Significantly, Russian envoys were also permitted to reside in Beijing but in a residence like those used by the temporary envoys of tribute missions.

The situation among the European traders attempting to enter Chinese seaports, however, was quite different. The British East India Company, having established its base at Calcutta in 1690, soon sought to expand its operations to China. At the same time, the Qing, fresh from capturing the last Ming bastion on Taiwan and worried about Ming loyalists in other areas, sought to control contact with foreign and overseas Chinese traders as much as possible, while keeping their lucrative export trade at a sustainable level. Their solution, implemented in 1699, was to permit overseas trade only at the southern port of Guangzhou [GWANG-joe], more widely known as Canton. The local merchants' guild, or *cohong*, was granted a monopoly on the trade and was supervised by a special official from the imperial Board of Revenue. Much like the Tokugawa in seventeenth-century Japan, the Qing permitted only a small number of foreigners, mostly traders from the English, French, and Dutch East India Companies, to reside at the port. They were confined to a small compound of foreign "**factories**," were not permitted inside the city walls, and could not bring their wives or families along. Even small violations of the regulations could result in a suspension of trading privileges, and all infractions and disputes were judged according to Chinese law. Finally, since foreign affairs under these circumstances were considered a dimension of trade, all diplomatic issues were settled by local officials in Canton.

The eighteenth century proved to be a boom time for all involved in trade, and the British in particular increasingly viewed it as a valuable part of their growing commercial power. While the spread of tea drinking through Europe and its colonies meant that tea rapidly grew to challenge porcelain for trade supremacy, silk also grew in importance, as well as lacquerware, wicker and rattan furniture, and dozens of other local specialties increasingly targeted at the export market. After 1784, the United States joined the trade; but despite the growing American presence, it was the British East India Company that dominated the Canton factories. Both the cohong and foreign chartered companies carefully guarded their respective

Factory: In the sense used in this chapter, the place where various "factors" (merchants, agents, etc.) gathered to conduct business.

Canton Factories, ca. 1800. Under the "Canton system" begun in 1699, all maritime trade with the Europeans was tightly controlled and conducted through the single port of Canton, or Guangzhou. Foreign merchants were not allowed to reside within the walled city, so they constructed their own facilities along the Pearl River waterfront. Though it kept profits high for the concerned parties, the restrictiveness of the system caused nineteenth-century merchants and diplomats to push the Chinese to open more ports to trade, which proved to be a major sticking point in Sino–Western relations.

monopolies, and the system worked reasonably well in keeping competition low and profits high on all sides.

Village and Family Life

Just as the effort toward greater control and centralization was visible in the government and economy of China during the Ming and Qing, it also reverberated within the structures of Chinese village life. While much of local custom and social relations among the peasants still revolved around family, clan, and lineage—with the scholar-gentry setting the pace—new institutions perfected under the Ming and Qing had a lasting impact into the twentieth century.

Organizing the Countryside   During the sixteenth century, the administrative restructuring related to the consolidation of the tax system into the "single-whip" arrangement led to the creation of the *lijia* system. All families were placed into officially designated *li*, or "villages," for tax purposes; 10 households made up a *jia*, and 100 households comprised a *li*, whose headmen, appointed by the magistrate, were responsible for keeping tax records and labor dues.

While the lijia system was geared primarily toward more efficient tax collection and record keeping, the *baojia* (Chapter 12) system functioned as a more far-reaching arrangement of government surveillance and control. The baojia system required families to register all members and be organized into units of 10 families, with one family in each unit assuming responsibility for the other nine. Each of these responsible families were arranged in groups of 10, and a member of each was selected to be responsible for that group of 100 households, and so on up to the *bao*, or 1,000-household level. Baojia representatives at each level were to be chosen by the families in the group. These representatives were to report to the magistrate on the doings of their respective groups and held accountable for the group's behavior. The system was especially important during the Qing, when it allowed authorities to bypass potential local gentry resistance to government directives and guaranteed a network of informers at all levels of rural life. During the White Lotus Rebellion at the end of the eighteenth century and the Taiping Rebellion of the 1850s and 1860s, the government relied on this mode of organization extensively.

Glimpses of Rural Life   As with other agrarian–urban empires, much of what little we know about Chinese peasant life comes through literary sources. Most of these were compiled by the scholar-gentry, though starting in the seventeenth century a small but influential number of chronicles were also produced by Westerners traveling in China. The local histories and gazetteers, with their reliance on unusual events—famines, revolts, riots, spectacular feats, and exemplary wives—generally fit peasant experiences, when they are addressed at all, into the mold of history as Confucian morality. More authentic, though still fragmentary, pictures of village life emerge from the works of popular writers like Pu Songling in his rich depictions of folk myth and religious syncretism. Even with these limitations, however, some generalizations can still be made about rural and family life in Ming and Qing times.

First, while the introduction of new crops during the period had brought more marginal land under cultivation, allowed for a huge increase in the population, and helped lend momentum to the trend toward more commercialization of agriculture, the work, technology, and overall rhythms of peasant life had changed little over the centuries.

Second, as with gathering political tensions, some early signs of economic stress were already present toward the end of Qianlong's reign. Chief among these was the problem of absentee landlordism. This would grow increasingly acute as the vitality of the commercial networks and market towns of central and southern China increased and the gentry were drawn away from the countryside by urban opportunities and amenities. In addition, successful tea, cotton, silk, and luxury goods traders frequently retained their compounds in the cities while buying land and degrees and becoming scholar-gentry, further increasing the incidence of absenteeism in the countryside. During the next century, with the dislocations of the Opium Wars, the Taiping Rebellion, and the foreign treaty ports, the problem of absentee landlordism greatly accelerated.

Third, as we have seen before, pressures on patterns of village life tended to be magnified in the lives of women and girls. Elite women were routinely educated to be as marriageable as possible. Study of proper Confucian decorum, writing model essays, chanting poetry, and a firm grasp of the *Xiaojing* (*Classic of Filial Piety*) were central to their lessons. As noted earlier, women were expected to be modest and obedient and were usually separated from and subordinate to men. In addition, marriage and property laws were set up to reinforce these qualities. In addition to the emphasis placed on mourning by both sexes, widows were expected to remain single and be subordinate to their oldest sons. As also noted previously, the custom of foot binding had long since become institutionalized, though in some areas—among south China's Hakka minority, for example—it never caught on. The sale of infant girls and, in extreme cases, female infanticide rose markedly in rural areas during times of war, famine, or other social stresses. It should be remembered, however, that, as in previous Chinese dynasties, the dominance of women over the "inner realm" of the family remained largely complete.

Science, Culture, and Intellectual Life

As we saw in Chapter 12, the Ming dynasty in many ways marked the high point as well as the beginning of the decline of China's preeminent place as a world technological innovator. One area in which this became painfully evident by the eighteenth and nineteenth centuries was in military matters.

Superpower   The Ming at their height have been described by some Chinese scholars as a military superpower. Perhaps most important in this regard was that

Chinese Commercial Enterprises. The growing volume and profits of the export trade encouraged further development and specialization of long-standing Chinese domestic industries during the eighteenth and nineteenth centuries. The men in the first photograph are *shroffs*, moneychangers involved in testing the quality of silver taken from foreign concerns in exchange for Chinese goods. The second picture depicts a worker and overseer running a silk reeling machine. The third illustrates women sorting tea while a foreman looks on. The packing chests for the tea are stacked in back of the sorters. The hairstyle of the men in the photos—shaved forehead with long braid called a *queue*—was mandatory for all Chinese males as a sign of submission to the Qing.

the ascendancy of the Ming in 1368 marked the beginning of what one historian has called a "military revolution" in the use of firearms. The first use of metal gun barrels in the late thirteenth century spurred the rapid development of both cannon and small arms—so much so that by the mid-fifteenth century the Ming arsenal at Junqiju [JWUN-chee-joo]was producing thousands of cannon, handguns, and "firelances" every year. By one estimate, in 1450 over half of the Ming frontier military units had cannon and one-third of all troops carried firearms. As early as the 1390s large shipborne cannon were already being installed in naval vessels. Indeed, court historians of the late Ming credited nearly all the military successes of the dynasty to the superiority of their firearms.

By the Qing period, however, following the pacification of the realm, the need for constant improvement of arms was seen as increasingly costly and unnecessary. While marginal improvements were made in the **matchlock** firing mechanisms of Chinese small arms, such improvements as were made in larger guns were largely directed by European missionary advisors to the throne.

Matchlock: An early type of gun in which the gunpowder charge is ignited by a burning taper (the "match") attached to the trigger mechanism.

Science and Literature   In geography, mathematics, and astronomy a fruitful exchange was inaugurated between European Jesuit missionaries in the seventeenth and eighteenth centuries and a small but influential group of Chinese officials. The most lasting legacy of this meeting was the European-style observatory in Beijing and a number of new maps of the world based on sixteenth- and seventeenth-century explorations. Unfortunately, by the nineteenth century these were all but forgotten, and the inadequacy of the geographical knowledge of Chinese officials in policy-making positions was soon all too apparent.

As in seventeenth-century France, the centralizing tendency of the government of China led to the exercise of considerable control in the cultural realm through patronage, monopoly, and licensing. As Manchus, the Kangxi, Yongzheng, and Qianlong emperors strove to validate their reigns by being patrons of the arts and aspiring to high levels of connoisseurship and cultivation of the best of the literati. As in the other absolutist realms, they not only set the tone in matters of aesthetics

Observatory in Beijing. One of the ways the Jesuits were able to gain favor at the imperial courts of two successive dynasties was through the new science of the West. Jesuit mathematicians, technical advisors, mapmakers, and astronomers found an eager reception among their Chinese counterparts, the fruits of which included armillary spheres pictured on the left and right foreground and the celestial globe in the center. The instruments were cast by Chinese artisans to the specifications of the Jesuit court mathematician Ferdinand Verbiest in the 1680s.

but also used mammoth cultural projects to direct the energies of scholars and officials into approved areas. At the same time, they sought to quash unorthodox views through lack of support and, more directly, through literary inquisitions. Kangxi, for example, sponsored the compilation of a huge dictionary of approved definitions of Chinese characters—still considered a primary reference work today. Under his direction, the commentaries and interpretations of Neo-Confucianism championed by the Song philosopher Zhu Xi became the approved versions. Kangxi's 13 sacred edicts, embodying maxims distilled in part from Zhu Xi's thought, became the official Qing creed from 1670 on. Anxious to legitimize themselves as culturally "Chinese," Kangxi and Qianlong sponsored huge encyclopedia projects. Qianlong's effort, at 36,000 volumes, was perhaps the most ambitious undertaking of its kind ever attempted.

Neo-Confucian Philosophy   While the urge to orthodoxy pervaded both dynasties, considerable intellectual ferment was also brewing beneath the surface of the official world. As we saw in Chapter 12, in the sixteenth century the first major new directions in Neo-Confucianism were being explored by Wang Yangming (1472–1529). While Wang's school remained a popular one, his emphasis on intuition, on a kind of enlightenment open to all, and, more and more, on a unity of opposites embracing different religious and philosophical traditions placed his more radical followers increasingly on the fringes of intellectual life. In addition, the Qing victory ushered in an era of soul-searching among Chinese literati and a wholesale questioning of the systems that had failed in the face of foreign conquest.

Two of the most important later figures in Qing philosophy were Huang Zongxi [Hwang Zung-SHEE] (1610–1695) and Gu Yanwu [Goo Yen-WOO] (1613–1682). Both men's lives spanned the Qing conquest, and like many of their fellow officials, both men concluded that the collapse of the old order was in part due to a retreat from practical politics and too much indulgence in the excesses of the radicals of the Wang Yangming school. With a group of like-minded scholars, they based themselves at the Donglin Academy, founded

---

Toward Proper Behavior: The Sacred Edict of Kangxi

1. Esteem most highly filial piety and brotherly submission, in order to give due importance to the social relations.
2. Behave with generosity toward your relatives, in order to illustrate harmony and benignity.
3. Cultivate peace and concord in your neighborhoods, in order to prevent quarrels and litigations.
4. Recognize the importance of husbandry and the culture of the mulberry tree (i.e., as food for silkworms), in order to ensure sufficient food and clothing.
5. Show that you prize moderation and economy, in order to prevent the lavish waste of your means.
6. Give weight to colleges and schools, in order to make correct the practice of the scholar.
7. Banish strange principles, in order to exalt the correct doctrine.
8. Lecture on the laws, in order to warn the ignorant and obstinate.
9. Demonstrate ceremony and deference in order to improve popular customs.
10. Labor diligently at your proper callings, in order to stabilize the will of the people.
11. Instruct sons and younger brothers, in order to prevent them from doing wrong.
12. Put a stop to false accusations, in order to preserve the honest and good.
13. Warn against sheltering deserters, in order to avoid being involved in their punishment.
14. Fully remit your taxes, in order to avoid being pressed for payment.
15. Unite in hundreds and tens [i.e., the baojia system] in order to end thefts and robbery.
16. Remove enmity and anger, in order to show the importance due to the person and life.

—Translated by Victor Mair, "Language and Ideology in the Written Popularizations of the Sacred Edict." In: *Popular Culture in Late Imperial China.* Edited by David Johnson, Andrew J. Nathan, and Evelyn S. Rawski, pp. 325–359. Berkeley: University of California Press, 1985.

Qianlong Emperor (1736–1795).
One of the more interesting
cross-cultural interactions
during the early Qing period
was that inspired by the
Jesuit missionary, Giuseppe
Castiglione (1688–1766). Trained
as an architect and painter,
Castiglione (Chinese name Lang
Shining), arrived in Beijing in
1715 and served as court painter
to emperors Kangxi, Yongzheng,
and Qianlong. He influenced
Chinese painters in the use of
Western perspective and also
absorbed Chinese techniques
of portraiture and landscape
painting. Here, the young
Qianlong emperor is shown in
his imperial regalia—including
his robes of imperial yellow
with dragon motifs—but with
an authentically detailed face
looking confidently full on
toward the viewer.

in 1604. There, they devoted themselves to reconstituting an activist Confucianism based on rigorous self-cultivation and on remonstrating with officials and even the court. One outgrowth of this development, which shares interesting parallels with the critical textual scholarship of the European Renaissance, was the so-called Han learning movement. Convinced that centuries of Buddhism, religious Daoism, and Confucian commentaries of questionable value had diverted Confucianism from the intent of the sages, Han learning sought to recover the original meaning of classic Confucian works through exacting textual scholarship and systematic philology, or historical linguistics. The movement, though always on the fringe of approved official activities, peaked in the eighteenth century and successfully uncovered a number of fraudulent texts, while setting the tone for critical textual analysis during the remainder of the imperial era.

The Arts and Popular Culture   Although China's artists and writers clung to an amateur ideal of the "three excellences" of poetry, painting, and calligraphy, increasing official patronage ensured that approved schools and genres of art would be maintained at a consistent, if not inspired, level of quality. Here, the Qianlong emperor was perhaps the most influential force. Motivated in part by a lifelong quest to master the fine arts, he collected thousands of paintings—to which he added, in the tradition of Chinese connoisseurs, his own colophons—rare manuscripts, jade, porcelain, lacquerware, and other objets d'art. Because the force of imperial patronage was directed at conserving past models rather than creating new ones, the period is not noteworthy for stylistic innovation. One interesting exception to this, however, was the work of the Jesuit painter Giuseppe Castiglione (1688–1766). Castiglione's access to Qianlong resulted in a number of portraits of the emperor and court in a style that merged traditional Chinese subjects and media with Western perspective and technique. Evidence of this synthesis can also be seen in the Italianate and Versailles-inspired architecture at the emperor's Summer Palace just outside of Beijing.

Local Custom and Religion   Urban and village China were populated by storytellers, corner poets, spirit mediums, diviners, and a variety of other sorts of entertainers. While village social life revolved principally around clan and family functions, popular culture was also dominated by Daoism, Buddhism, and older traditions of local worship, all with their own temples, shrines, and festivals. The oldest beliefs of the countryside involving ancestral spirits, "hungry ghosts" (roaming spirits of those not properly cared for in death), fairies, and demons were enhanced over the centuries by a rich infusion of tales of Daoist adepts and "immortals," *yijing* diviners, Buddhist bodhisattvas, and underworld demons. Popular stories incorporating all of these, like *A Journey to the West* continued to be popular fare for the literate as well as for storytellers and street performers.

One of the richest glimpses into local society comes from Pu Songling's (1640–1715) *Strange Tales from the "Make-Do" Studio*, sometimes translated in English as *Strange Tales from a Chinese Studio*. Though considered a master stylist among his circle of friends, Pu never progressed beyond the provincial-level examinations and spent most of his life in genteel poverty. He traveled extensively, collecting folktales, accounts of local curiosities, and especially stories of the supernatural. Considered an unparalleled interpreter of the *pinghua* style of literary versions of popular tales, which had originated during the Song period, his stories are available to us today thanks to the foresight of his grandson, who published them in 1740. In Pu's world, "fox-fairies" appear as beautiful women, men are transformed into tigers, the young are duped into degenerate behavior—with predictable consequences—and crooked mediums and storytellers take advantage of the unwary.

The slow movement of popular literature away from the classical and toward more current, colloquial language would grow during the nineteenth century. Later, with an infusion of literature from the West and the westernizing Meiji culture of Japan, it would burst forth during the so-called literary renaissance at Peking University, from 1915 to 1921. This increasing emphasis on *baihua*, or "plain speech," would ultimately force the classical language aside. For most of the twentieth century, the great stylists of Chinese literature would be masters of the expressive power of colloquial language.

Ming and Qing China in Global Context   The trend we have noted among the Ming and Qing toward greater regulation and centralism in politics and diplomacy, economics, social institutions, and even literary pursuits may be seen more generally as part of a regional—even a global—trend during the seventeenth and eighteenth centuries. In the case of east and southeast Asia, governments emerging from internal or external conflict naturally sought to emphasize stability—even to the point of severely limiting foreign contact, banning foreign religions, and imposing new regulations aimed at limiting social mobility. As we saw in Chapter 17, many European governments, led by France under Louis XIV, came to adopt a governmental system of *absolutism*, in which the state attempts to eliminate disruptive tendencies among the nobility by creating professional armies and centralized bureaucracies as well as pursuing mercantilist economics. We have also seen this in the form of the fiscal–military state we noted among the Ottomans and Mughals. Now, however, we will examine one of the most extreme cases of these trends toward stabilizing the state, eliminating subversive influences and **hothousing** cultural traditions: that of Tokugawa Japan.

Hothousing: Carefully protecting and cultivating cultural traditions as one does with plants in a hothouse or greenhouse.

The Long War and Longer Peace: Japan, 1450–1750

As we recall from Chapter 13, the struggles by court factions in Japan's capital of Heian-Kyo (Kyoto) had ultimately resulted in the creation of the office of the *shogun*, the chief military officer of the realm, in 1185. Actual executive power gradually receded from the emperor's hands, however, into the shogun's; and by the fourteenth century the emperor had become in reality the puppet of his first officer. As we also saw, a fundamental shift occurred with the attempt by Emperor Go-Daigo to reassert his prerogatives in 1333. When his one-time supporter Ashikaga Takauji expelled him and set up his headquarters in the capital, power and prestige were pressed together once again, with profound political and cultural consequences for Japan. Courtly elegance insinuated itself into the brutal world of the warrior, while power, intrigue, and ultimately a prolonged and debilitating civil war would ravage the capital until it ended with Japan's unification.

The price for unification, however, was high. As we saw in the opening vignette of this chapter, the first of Japan's unifiers, Oda Nobunaga, was assassinated for his efforts; the invasions of Korea undertaken by his successor Hideyoshi resulted in the loss of hundreds of thousands of lives. The final custodians of Japanese unification, the Tokugawa family, created a system over several generations that they hoped would freeze Japan forever in a state of unity and seclusion. Yet over the two and a half centuries of the Tokugawa peace, forces were building that would allow Japan to vault into the modern world with unprecedented speed in the late nineteenth century.

The Struggle for Unification

As we have seen, the fundamental instability of the Ashikaga regime abetted continual contesting for the shogun's office among the more powerful *daimyo*, or regional warlords. In 1467, these factional battles finally erupted into a devastating civil war that would last off and on for more than a century. The opening phase of this struggle, the Onin War, lasted 10 years and devastated the city of Kyoto, while leaving the imperial court barely functional and the shogunate in tatters. With no real center of power, a bitter struggle of all against all among the daimyos continued into the 1570s.

Oda Nobunaga and Toyotomi Hideyoshi   For the Japanese, the period was called *Gekokujo*, or "those below toppling those above." By the mid-sixteenth century, a handful of daimyo began the painful process of consolidating their power and securing allies. One important factor in deciding the outcome of these wars was the result of intrusion from the outside. By the 1540s, the first Portuguese and Spanish merchants and missionaries had arrived in southern Japan. One daimyo who was quick to use the newcomers and their improved small arms to his advantage was Oda Nobunaga, the son of a small landholder who had risen through the ranks to command. Oda employed newly converted Christian musketeers to secure the area around Kyoto and had largely succeeded in unifying the country when he was assassinated in 1582. His second in command, Hideyoshi, whom we met in the opening of this chapter, was another commoner who had risen through the ranks. Now he assumed Oda's mantle and systematically brought the remaining daimyo under his sway over the next nine years.

Toyotomi Hideyoshi (1536–1598). Portraits of Japanese daimyo and shoguns tend to position them in similar ways, looking to the front left, with stiff, heavily starched official robes to reflect their austerity and dignity. In this 1601 portrait, done several years after his death, Hideyoshi is shown in a typical pose, with the signs of his adopted family and imperial crests around the canopy to denote his role of imperial guardian.

Hideyoshi viewed a foreign adventure at this point as an excellent way to cement the loyalties of the newly subdued daimyo. In addition, the army he had put together—battle-hardened, well trained, with perhaps the largest number of guns of any force in the world at the time—might prove dangerous to disband. Hence, as early as 1586 he announced his grandiose plans to conquer China itself. Thus, in 1592 he set out with a massive expeditionary force, which at its peak numbered over 200,000 men. Though his supply lines were harassed unmercifully by the Korean naval forces in their well-armored "turtle ships," the Japanese made good progress up the peninsula until massive Chinese counterattacks slowly eroded their gains and decimated large stretches of Korea.

Hideyoshi's adventure ended when he turned homeward to Japan with the remnants of his army in 1596. His stature as a commander and force of personality kept

MAP **21.5** The Campaigns of Hideyoshi.

his coalition of daimyo together until his death during his second Korean campaign in 1598. The coalition then broke in two, and a civil war began between Tokugawa Ieyasu, charismatic leader of the eastern coalition of daimyos, and their western counterparts. In the fall of 1600, the back of the western coalition was broken by the Tokugawa victory at the Battle of Sekigahara, near Kyoto. Ieyasu, who claimed to be a descendant of the Minamoto clan, the original shoguns, laid claim to the office and was officially invested with it in 1603. His accession marked the beginning of Japan's most peaceful, most secluded, and perhaps most thoroughly regulated and policed interval in its long history. Breaking precedent, the Tokugawas would create a hereditary shogunate, organized along Chinese Neo-Confucian models of morality and government, that would last until 1867 (see Map 21.5).

The Tokugawa *Bakufu* to 1750

The realm that Tokugawa Ieyasu (1542–1616) had won at the Battle of Sekigahara was one that had been scarred by seemingly endless warfare and social disruption.

The daimyo and samurai, their armies as large as hundreds of thousands of soldiers in some cases, employed some of the most advanced military technology in the world; but their depredations had broken old loyalties and alliances. The intrusion of European missionaries and merchants, along with their converts and agents, contributed to the social ferment. The brief interlude of unity that had supported Hideyoshi's continental adventures had thoroughly unraveled and, indeed, had been a contributing cause of the civil war that had brought Ieyasu to power.

Ieyasu's assumption of the shogunate in 1603 thus began a process of unparalleled centralization and stabilization in Japan that would last until 1867. Initially, however, seclusion did not figure among its principles. In fact, under the direction of European advisors, Ieyasu and his son Hidetada (1579–1632) laid plans to build a powerful naval and merchant fleet during their first decade of rule. The most pressing order of business, however, was to erect a system within which to place all the daimyo that would at once reward the loyal and keep a watchful eye on the defeated.

"Tent Government"   The system devised under the Tokugawa *bakufu* ("tent government," referring to the shogun's official status as the emperor's mobile deputy) was called *sankin kotai*, the "rule of alternate attendance." An inner ring of daimyo holdings was annexed by the Tokugawa family and administered by their retainers. All daimyo were then given either *fudai*, or "inner" domains, if they had been allies of the Tokugawa or *tozama*, "outer" domains, if they had ultimately surrendered to Ieyasu's eastern coalition. The shogunate placed its new headquarters in the Tokugawa castle in Edo, the future city of Tokyo. In order to ensure their loyalty, all outer daimyo were required to reside in the capital in alternate years and return to their domains during the off years. Members of their families were required to stay as permanent hostages in Edo. Daimyo were also required to bring their most important retainers and their households with them during their stays. Almost from the beginning, therefore, the main roads to Edo, most famously the Tokaido, were the scene of constant daimyo processions. Like the great pilgrimage routes of Islam, Buddhism, and Christianity, these roads spurred enormous commerce and the creation of an array of services to meet the needs of the constant traffic. (And

The Tokaido Road. This scroll map, from about 1700 and painted in watercolor, shows an aerial view of the country along the route of the most famous highway in Japan—the Tokaido. Fishing villages dot the coast and Mt. Fuji looms in the background.

like the French nobility a few decades later at Versailles, the daimyo found both their power and their purses increasingly depleted).

Freezing Society In turning the office of shogun over to his son Hidetada in 1605, Ieyasu made it legally hereditary for the first time. With the possibility of revolt always just under the surface, Ieyasu stayed on as regent and pursued further measures to enhance the stability of the regime. Under his grandson, Ie-mitsu (1604–1651), most of the characteristic Tokugawa policies in this regard became insti-tutionalized. The shogunate declared that, like the jati system in India, the members of the of-ficially recognized classes in Japan—daimyo, samurai, peasants, artisans, merchants—and their descendants would be required to stay in those classes forever. The Tokugawa adopted Neo-Confucianism as the governing ideology, thus joining the commonwealth of Confucian "religious civilizations" in the region; and its long-established precepts of filial piety, mod-els of ethical behavior, and unswerving loyalty to the government were incorporated into the new law codes.

Significant differences, however, separated the practice of this system in Japan from simi-lar, concurrent systems in China, Korea, and Vietnam. In China and Vietnam, a civil service had long been in place, complete with a graded system of examinations from which the best candidates would be drawn for duty. The situ-ation in Japan was closer to that of Korea, in which the *Yangban* were already a hereditary aristocracy in the countryside and so mo-nopolized the official classes. Japan, though, differed even further because the samurai and daimyo were now not just a hereditary class of officials but a military aristocracy as well. Not only was the low position traditionally given the military in Chinese Confucianism totally reversed, but the daimyo and samurai had ab-solute, unquestioned power of life and death over all commoners. Like their counterparts in China, they were expected to have mastered the classics and the refined arts of painting, poetry, and calligraphy. But official reports

---

A Code for Samurai Behavior: The Laws Governing Military Houses, 1618

1. The arts of peace and war, including archery and horse-manship, should be pursued single-mindedly.
2. Drinking parties and wanton revelry should be avoided.
3. Offenders against the law should not be harbored or hidden in any domain.
4. Great Lords [daimyo], the lesser lords, and officials should immediately expel from their domains any among their retainers or henchmen who have been charged with treason or murder.
5. Henceforth no outsider, none but the inhabitants of a particular domain, shall be permitted to reside in that domain.
6. Whenever it is intended to make repairs on a castle of one of the feudal domains, the [shogunate] authorities should be notified. The construction of any new castles is to be halted and stringently prohibited.
7. Immediate report should be made of innovations which are being planned or of factional conspiracies being formed in neighboring domains.
8. Do not enter into marriage privately [i.e., without noti-fying the shogunate authorities].
9. Visits of the daimyo to the capital are to be in accordance with regulations.... Daimyo should not be accompanied by a large number of soldiers. Twenty horsemen shall be the maximum escort of daimyo with an income of from one million to two hundred thousand *koku* of rice. For those with an income of one hundred thousand *koku* or less, the escort should be proportionate to their income. On official missions, however, they may be accompanied by an escort proportionate to their rank.
10. Restrictions on the type and quality of dress to be worn should not be transgressed.
11. Persons without rank shall not ride in palanquins [sedan chairs].
12. The samurai of the various domains shall lead a frugal and simple life.
13. The lords of the domains should select officials with a capacity for public administration.

The purport of the foregoing should be conscientiously observed.

—adapted from *Bukke Shohatto (Laws Governing Military Households). Dai Nihon shiryo (Chronological Sourcebooks of Japanese History)*, vol. 12, pt. 22, pp. 19–20. In: William T. DeBary, et al., *Sources of Japanese Tradition*, vol. 1, pp. 327–329. New York: Columbia University Press, 1964.

and popular literature are full of accounts of samurai cutting down hapless peasants who failed to bow quickly enough to daimyo processions or who committed other infractions, no matter how trivial.

Giving Up the Gun   In order to ensure that the samurai class would be free from any serious challenge, the government required them to practice the time-honored skills of swordsmanship, archery, and other forms of individual martial arts. But the rapid development of firearms and their pervasive presence in the realm remained a threat to any class whose skills were built entirely around hand-to-hand combat. Thus, in a way perhaps unique among the world's nations, the Tokugawa literally "gave up the gun." Tokugawa police conducted searches for forbidden weapons among commoners and destroyed almost the entire nation's stock of firearms. A few museum pieces were kept as curiosities, as were the bronze cannon in some of the Tokugawa seaside forts. Thus, weapons that had been among the most advanced in the world when they were cast in the 1600s were the ones that confronted the first foreign ships nearly 250 years later in 1853.

As the shogunate strove to impose peace on the daimyo and bring stability to the populace, it became increasingly anxious to weed out disruptive influences. In addition to the unsettling potential of the country's guns, therefore, they began to restrict the movements of foreigners, particularly missionaries. From the earliest days of European arrivals in Japan, subjects of competing countries and religions had brought their quarrels with them, often involving Japanese as allies or objects of intrigue. The influence of the missionaries on the growing numbers of Japanese Christians—perhaps 200,000 by the 1630s—was especially worrisome to those intent on firmly establishing Neo-Confucian beliefs and rituals among the commoners. Moreover, the bitter duel between Catholic and Protestant missionaries and merchants carried its own set of problems for social stability, especially in the ports, where the majority of such activities tended to take place.

Christian Martyrs. Beginning in 1617, and culminating in the suppression of a rebellion by impoverished Christian peasants in 1637–1638, missionaries and their converts to the foreign faith were brutally persecuted by the Tokugawa. Wholesale massacres and even crucifixions along the main roads were not uncommon, or as in this engraving, hanging criminals—in this case, Jesuits—upside down and setting them on fire.

Tokugawa Seclusion   Ultimately, therefore, missionaries were ordered to leave the country, followed by their merchants. The English and Spanish withdrew in the 1620s, while the Portuguese stayed until 1639. Ultimately, only the Dutch, Koreans, and Chinese were allowed to remain, in small, controlled numbers and subject to the pleasure of the shogunate. Further, in 1635 it was ruled that Japanese would be forbidden to leave the islands and that no oceangoing ships were to be built. Any Japanese who left would be considered traitors and executed upon return. Like the Canton system later in Qing China, foreign merchants would be permitted only in designated areas in port cities and could not bring their families with them. As the only Europeans permitted to stay, the Dutch were chosen because they appeared to be the least affected by the religious bickering that characterized their European counterparts. They were, however, restricted to a tiny island called Dejima (also known as Deshima) built on a landfill in Nagasaki harbor. In return for the privilege, they were required to make yearly reports in person to the shogun's ministers on world events. Over time, the collections of these reports found a small but willing readership among educated and cultured Japanese. This "Dutch learning" and the accounts of Chinese and Korean observers formed the basis of the Japanese view of the outside

Dutch Ships in Nagasaki Harbor, 1764. This detail from a 1764 map shows Dutch and Japanese ships in Nagasaki harbor. The Japanese ships are dwarfed by the much larger Dutch sailing vessels. The small fan-shaped area connected to the town of Nagasaki was the only place where the Dutch were allowed to disembark and trade. They were forbidden to cross the causeway into the city itself.

world for over two centuries. Like European learning in Korea and Vietnam, it also provided useful examples for reformers to use in critiquing Neo-Confucian society.

Trampling the Crucifix   Much less tolerance was meted out to Japan's Christian community. Dissatisfaction with the new Tokugawa strictures provoked a rebellion at Shimabara just outside Nagasaki in 1637 by Christian converts and disaffected samurai. As the revolt was suppressed, many of those facing the prospect of capture and execution by the Tokugawa flung themselves into the volcanic hot springs nearby. Those who were captured were subjected to what their captors understood to be appropriate European-style punishment: Instead of being burned at the stake, they were clustered together and roasted to death inside a wide ring of fire. Subsequently, remaining missionaries were sometimes crucified upside down, while suspected converts were given an opportunity to "trample the crucifix" to show they had discarded the new faith. Those who refused to convert back to approved faiths were imprisoned or executed. In the end, perhaps 37,000 people were killed. For all their attempts at suppressing the religion, however, tens of thousands continued to practice in secret until Christianity was declared legal again during the reign of Emperor Meiji (r. 1867–1912). Though foreign ships would occasionally attempt to call at Japanese ports, by the eighteenth century Europeans generally steered clear of the islands. As we will see in Chapter 24, however, by the middle decade of the nineteenth century the opening of more ports in China for trade, the growth of the whaling industry, and the quest for gold in California would all conspire to change this situation forever.

Growth and Stagnation: Economy and Society

While a number of the processes begun under earlier shogunates continued during the seventeenth and eighteenth centuries, their pace quickened immensely. Perhaps most dramatically, by 1750, Japan had become the most urbanized society on earth.

Edo itself reached a million people, making it arguably the world's largest city. Osaka and Kyoto were both approaching 400,000, and perhaps as much as 10 percent of Japan's population lived in cities with populations above 10,000 (see Map 21.6). In a way, such explosive growth is even more remarkable given that the Tokugawa placed strict curbs on travel within their realms. Commoners, for example, were not to leave their home districts without permission from the local authorities. On the other hand, as we have seen, the law of alternate attendance ensured an immense and growing traffic in and out of the major cities along the major routes into Edo. The vast array of services required to support that traffic aided urban and suburban growth and had the effect of spreading the wealth down to the urban merchants, artisans, entertainers, bathhouse proprietors, and even refuse collectors.

Population, Food, and Commerce   Perhaps a more direct cause of this urbanization may be found in the growth of the population as a whole. By various estimates, Japan may have had as many as 33 million people in 1720. The efficiency of small-scale, intensive rice and vegetable farming, aided by easy-to-operate, simple machines such as the Chinese-style "climbing stair" or "dragon chain" pump made

MAP 21.6 Urban Population and Road Major Transport Routes in Japan, ca. 1800.

Japanese agriculture the most efficient in the preindustrial world. Such efficiencies would create one of the most densely populated rural landscapes in the world even into the twentieth century.

As we have noted, various Tokugawa policies aimed at stabilizing the country politically and socially had the unanticipated effect of spurring the economy. A number of factors contributed to this in addition to the forced movement of the daimyo and their retinues in alternate years. The Tokugawa tax structure set quotas in rice for each village, rather than for individuals and left the individual daimyos responsible for remitting these to the capital. Thus, an immense traffic in bulk rice further spurred the carrying trade along the roads and in the coastal waters. In addition to guaranteeing provisions for the cities, the need to convert rice to cash for the treasury contributed greatly to building a banking and credit infrastructure. Indeed, the practice of merchant bankers advancing credit to wholesalers against anticipated rice crops created what some scholars have called an early kind of futures market. The progress of the famous Mitsui *zaibatsu*, or cartel, of the nineteenth and twentieth centuries followed such a route, starting in 1670 as dry goods merchants and gradually moving into the position of bankers for the shogunate.

The tastes of the three largest cities—Edo, with its high concentration of the wealthy and well-connected; Kyoto, with its large retinue of the imperial household; and Osaka, the chief port—created a huge demand for ever more sophisticated consumer goods and services. Such enterprises as sake brewing, wholesaling dried and prepared foods, running bathhouses, and managing large studios of artisans all became booming businesses. Even the import and export trades, slowed to a relative trickle by government regulations, proved quite lucrative for the few engaged in them. Books, porcelains, lacquerware, and objets d'art were exchanged for Japanese hard currency. Indeed, the vibrancy of Japanese urban life and a burgeoning middle class created what scholars have sometimes called the "democratization of taste." That is, what was once the strict province of the court, daimyo, and samurai was now widely available to anyone who had the money and interest to afford it. Moreover, the new moneyed classes were also creating new directions in the arts and entertainment.

Woodblock Print of the Fish Market at the East Side of Nihonbashi (The Bridge of Japan). The Tokugawa period, with its long interlude of peace and prosperity, was Japan's first great age of urban life. The constant traffic of daimyo progressions along the main roads and the large coasting trade along the Inland Sea ensured a growing middle class of artisans, tradespeople, and merchants. The capital, Edo, had ballooned to over a million people on the eve of the American intrusion; and the bustle of the capital is illustrated in this panel depicting a famous fish market.

Rural Transformations   Life in rural areas underwent certain changes as well. As they had with the military houses, the Tokugawa promulgated Neo-Confucian rules for the comportment of families and their individual members. Like parish churches in Europe, each local Buddhist temple was to keep the registers of the villagers in its district. Weddings, funerals, travel, rents, taxes, and so forth were subject to official permission through either the village headman or the samurai holding a position equivalent to a magistrate. Within these strictures, however, and subject to the hereditary occupation laws, families, clans, and villages were relatively autonomous.

This was especially true within rural families, where men, women, and children commonly worked together on their plots. While the "inner domain," so central to Neo-Confucian thought as the strict province of women, retained a good deal of that character, there were also any number of areas that served to mitigate it. Men, for example, routinely helped in the everyday tasks of childrearing. As late as the 1860s, foreign observers reported watching rural groups of men minding infants while their wives were engaged in some collective task. Women in cities and larger villages routinely ran businesses, especially those involved in entertainment. Indeed, the women of the famous geisha houses, owned and run by women, were renowned for their skills, education, wit, and refinement. Even on a more humble level, women ran bathhouses, taverns, restaurants, and retail establishments of all sorts. Interestingly, by the eighteenth century, merchants increasingly utilized the spinning and weaving talents of rural and semirural women in parceling out the various steps in textile manufacturing to them—a Japanese version of the English "putting out system" (Chapter 23).

The Samurai in Peacetime   As time went by, the position of the samurai in rural society changed as well. Though expected to hone his military skills, his role as an official and Neo-Confucian role model gradually became paramount. Samurai existed on stipends, either directly from the Tokugawa or from their local daimyo. These, however, were no guarantee of prosperity and by the later eighteenth century the samurai living in genteel poverty had become something of a popular stereotype. In many areas, they functioned as schoolmasters and founded village academies in the local temples for the teaching of practical literacy and correct moral behavior. By the mid-nineteenth century Japan may have had the world's highest level of functional literacy. As in Korea, this proved important in popularizing new crops or agricultural techniques.

By the middle of the eighteenth century there were signs of tension among the aims of the government in ensuring peace and stability, the dynamism of the internal economy, and the boom in population. Like China a century later, some scholars contend that Japan had approached the limit of the ability of the land to support its people. In fact, Japan's population remained remarkably steady from the middle of the eighteenth century to the latter nineteenth. Repeated signs of creeping rural impoverishment and social unrest manifested themselves, however, and were often noted by commentators. Inflation in commodity prices ran ahead of efforts to increase domain revenues, squeezing those on fixed incomes and stipends. Efforts to keep rural families small enough to subsist on their plots led to an increasing frequency of infanticide. Compounding such problems were large-scale famines in 1782 and 1830. By the early nineteenth century, there was an increasing perception that the government was gradually losing its ability to care for the populace.

Hothousing "Japaneseness": Culture, Science, and Intellectual Life

As with so many elements of Japanese cultural history, existing genres of art—major styles of painting, poetry, and calligraphy—continued to flourish among the daimyo and samurai, while exerting an increasing pull on the tastes of the new middle classes. Indeed, Zen-influenced **monochrome** painting, the ideals of the tea ceremony championed by Sen Rikyu, the austere Noh theater, and the abstract principles of interior design and landscape gardening were carefully preserved and popularized until they became universally recognized as "Japanese."

Monochrome: Single color; in east Asian painting, a very austere style popular in the fourteenth and fifteenth centuries, particularly among Zen-influenced artists.

New Theater Traditions   Traditional cultural elements coexisted with new forms, with some adapting aspects of these earlier arts and others conceived as mass entertainment. Among the former was the development of *bunraku*, the elaborate puppet theater still popular in Japan today. Bunraku puppets, perhaps one-third life size, generally took three puppeteers to manipulate. Their highly facile movements and facial expressions staged against a black backdrop to conceal the actions of their handlers readily allowed the audience to suspend disbelief and proved a highly effective way to popularize the older Noh plays. But renowned playwrights soon wrote special works for these theaters as well. The most revered was Chikamatsu Monzaemon [Chick-ah-MAT-soo Mon-ZAE-mon] (1653–1724), who skillfully transferred the tragically noble sentiments of the best Noh works into contemporary themes. The fatal tension between love and social obligation, for example, made his *Love Suicide at Sonezaki* wildly popular with Edo audiences. His most famous work *The Forty-Seven Ronin*, written in 1706, is based on a 1703 incident in which the daimyo of 47 samurai was killed by a political opponent, leaving them as *ronin*—masterless. Out of loyalty to their dead daimyo the ronin kill his assassin in full knowledge that their lives will then be forfeit to the authorities, a price they then stoically go on to pay.

> **Emotional Release Through Poetry: "Old Battlefield"**
>
> Old battlefield, fresh with spring flowers again
> All that is left of the dream
> Of twice ten-thousand warriors slain.
>
> —Translated by C. H. Page in *Classic Haiku: An Anthology of Poems by Basho and His Followers*. Asataro Miyamori, ed. and trans. (Tokyo: Maruzen Co. Ltd., 1932) Dover reprint p. 80

Originally written for bunraku, *The Forty-Seven Ronin* was adapted a few decades later as a work for *kabuki*, the other great mass entertainment art of Tokugawa Japan. Originally a satirical and explicitly bawdy form of theater, the government banned women from appearing in kabuki, hoping to sever its association with prostitution. Female impersonators as actors continued its risqué reputation, however, while more serious works also drew immense crowds to the pleasure districts, to which the theaters were by law segregated. Kabuki remained by far the most popular Japanese mass entertainment, and interestingly, given the medium's off-color reputation, *The Forty-Seven Ronin* remained the most frequently performed play throughout the Tokugawa period.

The era also marked the golden age of the powerfully brief poetic form of *haiku*, the most famous practitioner of which was the renowned Matsuo Basho (1644–1694). As a poet he used a dozen pen names; he took "Basho" from the banana plant he especially liked in his yard. In poems like "Old Battlefield" the 17-syllable couplets compressed unbearable emotion and release in a way that has made them a treasured form in Japan and, more recently, in much of the world.

Two Courtesans. During the late seventeenth century, the new genre of *ukiyo-e*, "pictures of the floating world," developed and remained popular through the nineteenth century. Finely wrought woodblock prints in both monochrome and color, their name comes from the pleasure districts whose people and scenes were favorite subjects. This work is from a series by the noted artist Kitagawa Utamaro (ca. 1753–1806) on famous courtesans of "the Southern District," part of the Shinagawa section of Edo.

The visual arts found new forms of expression through the widespread use of fine woodblock printing, which allowed popular works to be widely duplicated. The new genre was called *ukiyo-e*, "pictures of the floating world," a reference to the pleasure quarters on the edge of the cities that furnished many of its subjects. Though largely scorned by the upper classes, it remained the most popular form of advertising, portraiture, and news distribution until the end of the nineteenth century, when it began to be supplanted by photography. During Tokugawa times, one of the most famous practitioners of the art was Kitagawa Utamaro (1753–1806), whose studies of women became forever associated with Japanese perceptions of female beauty. In the works of Katsushika Hokusai (1760–1849) and Ando Hiroshige (1797–1858) scenes like Hokusai's *Thirty-Six Views of Mt. Fuji*, or, like Utamaro's work, gentle snowfalls on temples, formed many of the first popular images that nineteenth-century Westerners had of Japan.

While Neo-Confucianism occupied a central place as the Tokugawa's governing orthodoxy, the eighteenth and nineteenth centuries proved to be a fertile time for critical thought both within and without the approved avenues of discussion. On the one hand, scholars such as Hirata Atsutane (1776–1843) and Honda Toshiaki (1744–1821) managed to convey their admiration for "Dutch learning," the information about the events in the outside world contained in reports to the shogun made by the representatives of the Dutch East India Company, while still managing to acknowledge the primacy of Japan. Honda, in particular, advocated Japanese expansion along the lines of what he understood to be the policies of the European countries with regard to mercantilism, colonial possessions, and the pursuit of science in his "Secret Plan for Managing the Country." His late eighteenth-century colleague, Sato Nobuhiro (1769–1850), expressed similar sentiments in his "Confidential Memoir on Social Control."

On the other hand, some writers felt that Japan's problems lay in the stifling of its true national character by the Chinese-influenced Neo-Confucian institutions of the Tokugawa. Starting as early as the late seventeenth century, this "national learning" movement, whose most famous exponent was Motoori Norinaga (1730–1801), emphasized Japan's unique governmental tradition of a single imperial line—later an important part of the Meiji-era concept of *kokutai*, or "national polity"—and advocated a return to the earliest Japanese histories, the *Kojiki* and *Nihongi*.

Perhaps most influential of all was the outwardly mainstream Mito school. Formed by a branch of the Tokugawa family and hewing to the Neo-Confucian orthodoxy of the shogunate, writers like Aizawa Seishisai (1782–1863) demanded that the government take a firm stand against any foreign intrusion. Failure to do so would be to surrender the mandate of the shogunate as the emperor's military and political arm. In the turmoil following the American Commodore Matthew Perry's visits in the nineteenth century and the opening of the first treaty ports, the Mito scholars would be at the forefront of advocating the immediate expulsion of the foreigners by any means necessary.

Putting It All Together

During the late Ming and early Qing periods, imperial China achieved social and political stability and developed the world's largest economy. Yet, by the second part of the eighteenth century, internal problems were already germinating that would come to the surface in succeeding decades. In the following century, these initial cracks in the empire's structure would continue to grow and have a profound impact on China's fortunes.

The arrival of large numbers of foreign traders who brought with them the new technologies of the first scientific–industrial societies, combined with China's profound self-confidence in its own culture and institutions, added more pressure to an already volatile internal situation and ultimately created an unprecedented challenge for China. Over the coming decades, Chinese expectations of being able to civilize and assimilate all comers would dissolve, along with the hope that a renewed faithfulness to Confucian fundamentals would produce the leaders necessary to navigate such perilous times. But at the halfway mark of the eighteenth century, the Chinese still expected that they would successfully regulate the "inner" and "outer" domains of their empire and keep pernicious foreign influences at arm's length.

Ravaged by a century of warfare and foreign intrusion, Japan also sought to regulate its inner and outer domains and minimize outside influences. As with China, however, the stability perfected by the Tokugawa shogunate in the seventeenth and eighteenth centuries would be increasingly threatened in the nineteenth by the growing commercial power of the Europeans and Americans. Before the nineteenth

CHAPTER 21 CONCEPT MAP

Regulating the "Inner" and "Outer" Domains in China and Japan, 1600-1800

Inner Domain

CHINA

Outer Domain

Inner Domain

JAPAN

Outer Domain

century was finished, China would be rent by the bloodiest civil war in human history, while Japan would experience its own civil war and, in its aftermath, install a unified government under an emperor for the first time since the twelfth century. In the final years of the nineteenth century, Japan would once again invade Korea to attack China—this time with very different results. In the process, the relationship of more than two millennia between the two countries would be altered forever (see Concept Map).

Review and Respond

1. What innovations did the Qing bring to the governance of China?

2. What advantages did the late Ming "single-whip" tax system bring to those who had to pay it? What disadvantages did it bring?

3. Why were the Qing able to subdue the Ming in the 1640s?

4. What reasons best explain the actions of the Tokugawa in establishing a policy of seclusion?

5. Were the policies of the Qing and Tokugawa successful in keeping their realms safe and stable?

For additional resources, including maps, primary sources, visuals, and quizzes, please go to www.oup.com/us/vonsivers. Please see the Further Resources section at the back of the book for additional readings and suggested websites.

Thinking Through Patterns

▶ **Why did late Ming and early Qing China look inward after such a successful period of overseas exploration?**

In some respects the problem is similar to that faced by planners for defense spending in nations today: Why maintain huge, expensive systems when there are no enemies against which to use them? While the commercial prospects for China's fleets grew in prominence, maritime trade was simply not essential to the Chinese economy at that point. Moreover, urgent defense preparations were needed in the overland north against the resurgent Mongols. It is important to remember that the discontinuing of the fleets seems like a mistake in hindsight because of what happened to China hundreds of years later due to a lack of adequate naval defenses. At the time, however, these measures seemed both rational and appropriate to the Chinese and outside observers.

One almost universal pattern of world history among agrarian states is that their governments adopt policies aimed at promoting social stability. The reason for this is that, in short, nearly everything depends on having reliable harvests. Given the agricultural techniques and technology of preindustrial societies, the majority of the population must be engaged in food production to ensure sufficient surpluses to feed the nonproducing classes. If such a society places a premium on change and social mobility, it risks chronic manpower shortages and insufficient harvests. Thus, social classes—whether in feudal Europe, India, China, or Japan—are carefully delineated and the state directs its policies toward eliminating social upheaval.

▶ **How do the goals of social stability drive the policies of agrarian states? How does the history of China and Japan in this period show these policies in action?**

▶ **In what ways did contact with the maritime states of Europe alter the patterns of trade and politics in east Asia?**

In both China and Japan, these connections resulted in severe restrictions regarding the regulation of maritime trade: the Canton system in China and the seclusion policies of the Tokugawa in Japan. Earlier, the Chinese emperor had welcomed Jesuit missionaries for their expertise in mathematics and science and even considered conversion to Catholicism. But the backlash against "subversive" influence induced the Qing to drive Christianity underground. In Japan such contact had earlier injected European influences into Japan's civil wars, and the reaction against this was Tokugawa seclusion.

The fundamental difference was that Japan was a military society, which adopted the forms and structures of Neo-Confucianism to make daimyo and samurai into officials. They therefore were expected to maintain this civil role as bureaucrats but also stand ready to fight if need be. The low esteem in which the military was held in China was just the opposite of that of the martial elites of Japan. Another key difference was that officials in China were selected on the basis of competitive examinations, thus creating some social mobility. In Japan, the social classes were frozen and no exams were offered for potential officials.

▶ **How did Neo-Confucianism in China differ from that of Tokugawa Japan?**

PART FIVE

The Origins of Modernity

1750–1900

What we have termed "modernity" in this section may be said to have begun roughly around 1800 in western Europe and may be characterized as the product of what historian Eric Hobsbawm (b. 1917) called "the twin revolutions" of the late eighteenth century. One of these was the new political landscape brought into being by the trio of constitutional revolutions in North America, France, and Haiti, which dealt a telling blow to the concept of traditional monarchial rule by divine right and introduced popular sovereignty as the new justification for political power. The other was the Industrial Revolution, which began in England with the introduction of steam-driven, machine-produced textiles and other goods. Scientific–industrial modernity, with its developing constellation of values marked by experimentation, political, social, and technological progress, social mobility, and secularism, was thus set on a path to displace the older agrarian–urban order of religious civilizations that had been characterized by hierarchy, natural order, and divinely ordained law and morality. This transition is, in fact, still ongoing. Although the old agrarian–urban *political* order has been almost universally superseded, its values still contend with those of modernity in many parts of the world today.

The Origins of Modernity

The political and industrial revolutions that define modernity have intellectual roots reaching back to the 1500s. As scholars increasingly recognize, the discovery of the Americas, as well as the Copernican revolution in astronomy, provided powerful incentives for the introduction of new patterns of science and political philosophy. For more than two centuries, however, these ideas remained the province of only a small intellectual elite.

Political and Industrial Revolutions

By the 1700s, however, adherents of the new science and philosophy among urban, educated administrators and professionals in northwestern Europe had grown in numbers and began to become influential in society. In Britain, the *theory* of the social contract entered into the *practice* of constitutionalism following the Glorious Revolution of 1688. Both were vastly expanded by thinkers during the

1765
James Watt Perfects the Steam Engine

1776–1804
American, French, and Haitian Revolutions

1798–1801
Napoleon's Occupation of Egypt

1815
Congress of Vienna

1832
Greece Wins Independence from the Ottomans

1839–1876
Tanzimat Reforms in the Ottoman Empire

1848
Karl Marx and Friedrich Engels Publish *The Communist Manifesto*

1853–1854
Commodore Perry Opens Trade and Diplomatic Relations with Japan

eighteenth-century Enlightenment and helped to inspire the American, French, and Haitian Revolutions. These were narrow revolutions in the sense of ending monarchial–aristocratic rule—courageous revolts during still deeply religious times. Nonetheless, this era set human emancipation from the confining traditions of the past as a goal to be achieved. And in the case of Haiti, the idea that "all men are created equal" emblazoned earlier in the American Declaration of Independence and the French Declaration of the Rights of Man, formed the basis of a successful slave rebellion against revolutionary France itself.

The Industrial Revolution, beginning around 1800 in Great Britain, was a socially transformative and self-sustaining sequence of technical inventions and commercial applications. Britain industrialized during the first half of the 1800s through steam-driven iron foundries, textile factories, overland transportation, and ocean travel. In a second wave, Germany and the United States industrialized, with the introduction of chemicals, electricity, and motorcars into the factory system. The two waves of industrialization created an unequal class system, with a citizenry composed of both landed aristocrats—fading in power as the old agrarian–urban order decayed—and a new, dynamic urban middle class amassing political and economic power. But the equally new phenomenon of the industrial working class, bidding for political, social, and economic equality, added a volatile social factor to the mix as its members sought to make good on the promises of the constitutional revolutions.

Resistance and Adaptation to the Western Challenge

The twin political–industrial revolutions in Europe were a major factor in the mid-nineteenth-century expansion of the existing seaborne European empires in Asia and Africa. Postrevolutionary France renewed its competition with Britain, and both later used "gunboat diplomacy" to establish favorable commercial conditions and trade outposts. From here, these two and other European nations proceeded to compete in imperial conquests for what they now considered to be strategically important territories across the globe.

The traditional agrarian and religious empires and states of Asia and Africa responded to the increasingly superior military power of the European maritime empires and the United States during the 1800s with both resistance and adaptation. Resisting with traditional armies and weapons, however, became more difficult as the 1800s unfolded and the industrial development of the West spawned new and sophisticated weaponry. "Adaptation," as it occurred under the duress of imperialism, was a creative process in which the states under challenge selected generic elements from the constitutional and industrial revolutions that had made the West powerful and attempted to harmonize them with their inherited traditions.

Thinking Like a World Historian

▶ What were the origins of the "twin revolutions" of the late eighteenth century? How did they combine to create what we call "modernity"?

▶ Why were the values of scientific–industrial society opposed to the older agrarian–urban order? Why does this conflict still persist in many parts of the world today?

▶ What patterns of resistance and adaptation characterized the responses of traditional agrarian and religious empires to European military power and expansion?

1857
Sepoy Mutiny, India

1868–1912
Reign of Emperor Meiji, Japan

1878–1885
Independence of Serbia, Montenegro, Rumania, and Bulgaria

1888
End of Slavery, Brazil

1894–1895
Sino-Japanese War

1904–1905
Russo-Japanese War

1861
Emancipation of Serfs in Russian Empire

1869
Opening of Suez Canal

1884
Hiram Maxim Invents the First Fully Automatic Machine Gun

1900
Boxer Rebellion and Anti-Foreign War

1905
Albert Einstein Publishes Theory of Relativity

1908
Young Turks Rise to Power in Ottoman Empire

Chapter 22

1750-1871

Nation-States and Patterns of Culture in Europe and North America

THE NORTH ATLANTIC, 1750-1900

In a diary entry dated June 4, 1785, George Washington, the hero of the American War for Independence and future first president of the United States, noted that "the celebrated Mrs. Macauly [sic] Graham & Mr. Graham her Husband . . . arrived here." Washington seems to have thoroughly enjoyed the visit, for after their departure he wrote to his friend Richard Henry Lee to express his appreciation for his letter of introduction to this distinguished

▶ How did the pattern of constitutional nationalism, emerging from the American and French Revolutions, affect the course of events in the Western world during the first half of the nineteenth century?

▶ In what ways did ethnolinguistic nationalism differ from constitutional nationalism, and what was its influence on the formation of nation-states in the second half of the nineteenth century?

▶ What were the reactions among thinkers and artists to the developing pattern of nation-state formation? How did they define the intellectual–artistic movements of romanticism and realism?

Constitutional Nationalism in Action, London 1831. This colored lithograph, entitled *Staunch Reformers*, captures the way in which many ordinary Europeans and Americans, such as the rag-tag crew depicted here on a London street corner, saw themselves as part of a wider political reform movement. The drawing makes references to many important political developments and symbols of the era—one man holds a placard that reads, "Tom Paine's *Rights of Man*—one penny!' topped by a red liberty cap, symbol of revolutionary France." In the left background, a sign outside a doorway reads "Support The Crown"—a reminder that in Britain at least, political reform went hand in hand with loyalty to the King.

visitor from England, "whose principles are so much, & so justly admired by the friends of liberty and of Mankind."

Who was this "celebrated" woman, and what had she done to earn the abiding respect of George Washington? Biographical dictionaries of her day called Catharine Macaulay Graham (1731–1791) "the patroness of liberty," for her staunch views on constitutional liberties and rights, including women's rights. But British contemporaries also considered her an eccentric for her flamboyant personal lifestyle: After the death of her husband in 1785, she married William Graham, a medical apprentice—she was 47 and he was 21. Her star dimmed somewhat thereafter in Great Britain, but North Americans continued to admire her, as evidenced by the eager invitation to Washington's Mt. Vernon.

She published her political views on British constitutionalism and the American and French Revolutions in a number of widely read essays and books. For example, in a pamphlet of 1775, Graham expressed her support for the North American colonists, who "year by year [have been] stripped of the most valuable of their rights" and who have suffered under "oppressive taxes," particularly the Stamp Act, "by which they were to be taxed in an arbitrary manner." In 1783 she published the eight-volume *History of England*, which reflected many ideals of the Enlightenment, particularly antimonarchical sentiments, and support for the concept of natural rights and the sovereignty of the people. And in 1791, shortly before her death, she wrote a review of Edmund Burke's *Reflections on the Revolution in France* (1790), in which she issued a strongly worded rebuke of Burke's castigation of the French Revolution. Among other things, she observed "[t]hat the people have often abused their power, it must be granted . . . but *no abuse* of their power *can take away their right*, because their rights exists [sic] *in the very constitution of things.*"

Graham's writings fell into oblivion during the 1800s and through much of the 1900s when the defense of constitutional nationalism no longer aroused the passions of citizens in many nation-states. Indeed, the very fact that such debate no longer seemed fashionable is testimony to the ultimate success of her cause. But like her more famous contemporary, Mary Wollstonecraft, her early advocacy of feminism and views on education attracted attention again during the second half of the twentieth century; and today she is increasingly recognized as a pioneer of gender equality.

The first half of this chapter focuses on this new pattern of state formation that the American and French Revolutions of 1776–1789 introduced into world history—and that was so passionately espoused by Catharine Graham in its time. The revolutionaries in North America and France, and the many other places that followed in their wake, renounced or overthrew traditional divine-right kingdoms and empires and replaced them with the *constitutional nation-state*, that is, a state where all people were citizens with the same constitutional rights and duties and where the borders of the political state corresponded more or less to territories where people had developed a sense of collective identity: the *nation*. The ideology of constitutional nationalism became a powerful driving force in state formation during the 1800s and 1900s.

The constitutional nation-states that emerged after these initial revolutions, however, fell short of the lofty ideals above; and, in a backlash, monarchical and imperial regimes making minimal concessions to constitutional nationalism survived in Europe. Toward the middle of the 1800s, the new ideology of *ethnolinguistic nationalism* arose: the nation consists of people with strong ethnic ties and often sharing a common language, religion, and historical experience. It followed that such nations should also have their own states.

The movement toward ethnolinguistic nationalism was especially strong in central and eastern Europe, which had not had constitutional movements. It also developed in western Europe, where it grew to rival constitutional nationalism as a force within the pattern of nation-state formation. In some cases it led to the unification of ethnically related peoples who lived in smaller states into one large state, as with Italy and Germany. More frequently, it led people who saw themselves as nations governed by large empires to agitate for autonomy or independence in order to form their own ethnic nation-states—as with the many Balkan peoples under control of the Ottomans (see Chapter 25).

To complicate matters further, many people did not draw sharp distinctions between the two nation-state ideologies, especially in the realm of culture, on which the second half of this chapter concentrates. Indeed, ethnolinguistic nation-states that adopted constitutions embodied both trends, though sometimes rather uncomfortably. Moreover, these new patterns of state formation stimulated competition and disputes over national boundaries, which were now more intense because of the ethnic component. All of this would play a large role in the events leading up to World War I. Thus, the new culture of modernity that emerged in the nation-states during the nineteenth century was a complex and often volatile mixture of these two sometimes competing forms of nationalism. But as these forms evolved in the twentieth century, they became the pattern to which more and more states ultimately adhered. Today, the nation-state is not only the dominant form of polity but virtually the only one.

Origins of the Nation-State, 1750–1815

The subject of our vignette, Catharine Macaulay Graham, wrote many of her essays within the tradition of the rights and liberties obtained through the Glorious Revolution of 1688 in England. She was steeped, therefore, in not only the ideas but also the practices of constitutional nationalism that the Glorious Revolution pioneered. In this revolution, for the first time in Europe, the traditional divine rights of a monarch had been curbed through a set of constitutional rights and duties granted to the subjects of the kingdom. The innovative ideas of *subjects* becoming *citizens* with constitutionally guaranteed rights and duties and of the Parliament representing the nation—the people living in England—also became central in the American Revolution and developed close parallels during the French Revolution. Beyond the Glorious Revolution, however, the American and French Revolutions were more radical in the sense that they ended the British compromise of royal and parliamentary power and resulted in republican, middle-class nation-states without traditional divine-right monarchies.

| 1750-1800 | 1775-1783 | 1799-1815 | 1815 | 1870 |
| Later Enlightenment | American Revolution | Napoleonic Era | Congress of Vienna | Unification of Italy |

| 1756-1763 | 1789-1799 | 1804 | 1848 | 1871 |
| Seven Years' War | French Revolution | Beethoven's *Eroica* | Political and Economic Revolts in Europe | Unification of Germany |

The American and French Revolutions

The two revolutions were outgrowths of the Seven Years' War, in which Great Britain and France fought for the dominance of their respective seaborne empires in the world. The governments of both kingdoms went deeply into debt to win the war. They owed this debt to their wealthy subjects, many of whom were landowners and administrators forming the ruling class. To pay back the debt, however, the kings had to go to their subjects at large and raise their taxes. The incongruence of monarchs holding the mass of their subjects responsible for their debts to a few wealthy subjects was apparent to a large number of people, who had found the intellectual movement of the Enlightenment congenial and formulated political principles of reform, if not revolution.

Conditions for Revolution in North America
When Britain won the Seven Years' War, it acquired France's trade forts in India as well as French possessions in Canada and the Ohio–Mississippi River valley. France turned Louisiana over to its ally Spain (which had lost Florida to Britain) and retreated entirely from North America. But the British territorial gains came at the price of a huge debt: The payment of the interest alone devoured most of the country's regular annual budget. Taxes had to be raised domestically as well as overseas, and in order to do so the government had to strengthen its administrative hand in an empire that had grown haphazardly and—in North America—without much oversight.

By 1763, the 13 North American colonies had experienced both rapid demographic and powerful economic growth. Opening lands beyond the Appalachian Mountains into the Ohio valley would relieve a growing population pressure on the strip of land along the Atlantic coast that the colonies occupied. Environmental degradation, through overplanting and deforestation, had increased the landless population and contributed to the presence of growing numbers of poor people in the burgeoning cities of Philadelphia, Boston, and New York. The occupation of new land across the Appalachians, on the other hand, increased the administrative challenges for the British. They had to employ large numbers of standing troops to protect not only the settlers from the hostility of the Native Americans but also the native peoples from aggression by settlers. Grain, timber, and tobacco exports from the colonies had made the colonies rich immediately before 1763, but the war boom inevitably gave way to a postwar bust. While new land created new opportunities, the economic slump created hardships (see Map 22.1).

As the government faced the task of strengthening the British administration of the colonies, a young and inexperienced monarch, George III (r. 1760–1820), was determined to increase the influence of the Crown on British politics. Unfortunately, he was not terribly adept at surrounding himself with capable advisors. Furthermore, instead of conceiving a systematic plan for governing the colonies, British politics lurched from one measure to another. The Proclamation of 1763, for example, limited the expansion of settlement to lands east of the Appalachians, to forestall difficulties with England's recent Iroquois allies. In addition to protests from those hoping to open up the new lands acquired from France, it resulted in expanded migrations to the cities and towns.

Settlers could simply ignore the proclamation if they chose to take their chances in the wilderness. The Stamp Act of 1765, however, was much harder to evade. Suddenly, everyone had to pay a tax on the use of paper, whether for legal documents,

MAP **22.1** **British North America in 1763.**

newspapers, or even playing cards. The tax was to be used for the upkeep of the standing troops, many of which were withdrawn from the Ohio valley, ordered to be quartered in the colonies, and intended to be used for the enforcement of increased taxes.

A firestorm of protest against the Stamp Act broke out among the urban lower middle ranks of shopkeepers, small merchants, mechanics, and printers, who organized themselves in groups such as the "Daughters" or "Sons of Liberty." The Daughters declared a highly successful boycott of British goods and promoted the production of homespun textiles. Parliament withdrew the Stamp Act when British exports fell, but the efforts by British troops to suppress the urban riots that continued even after the act's withdrawal only inflamed an increasingly volatile situation. In Boston, one of the flashpoints of unrest, the British administration also managed to offend colonists of the upper urban classes when it dissolved the Massachusetts Assembly.

Two of its members were Samuel Adams and John Hancock, the one a repentant tax collector and son of a brewer-merchant and the other a nephew of a merchant and successful shipping entrepreneur. They became prominent organizers of the opposition to new and less visible indirect taxes, which the British sought to collect in

The Boston Tea Party. This print from the late 1700s is one of dozens of depictions of this famous incident during which a group of Bostonians dumped some 300 chests of tea shipped by the East India Company into the harbor.

place of the direct Stamp Tax. The Parliament in Britain, well aware that the taxes yielded only a fraction of colonial expenditures in North America, canceled all taxes in 1770 except for the tea duty. But since this decision came at the same time as the "Boston Massacre," a particularly incendiary killing by British troops of five Bostonians during a riot, this cancelation turned out to be too little too late: Principles came into play that now hardened the positions of both sides.

Sovereignty versus Independence   Britain retained the tea tax to assert a basic right of sovereignty. This elevation of the tea tax to a matter of principle was particularly galling to the Americans since it was actually a subsidy to keep the near bankrupt East India Company afloat and had nothing to do with America. On the other side, Adams and many others were openly propagating the principle of independence from about 1769 onward: "No Taxation Without Representation" had become one of the main rallying cries of the protestors. The governmental tax subsidy for a private company in India quickly became fodder for a vociferous propaganda campaign against an allegedly arbitrary, corrupt, and tyrannical George III who dared to rule North America from afar. The colonists' propaganda culminated with the symbolic—and rather expensive—dumping of a cargo of tea into Boston Harbor in 1773. In response to this "Boston Tea Party," Britain closed the harbor, demanded restitution, and passed the so-called Coercive Acts (called the "Intolerable Acts" in the colonies), which put Massachusetts into effective bankruptcy. Both sides now moved inexorably toward a showdown in which Thomas Hobbes's principle of indivisible sovereignty and John Locke's principle of equal representation would become locked in a bloody struggle for supremacy.

The War for Independence   Two Continental Congresses of the colonies in 1774–1775 failed to resolve this clash of principles. The colonial assemblies elevated themselves into the Continental Association, which claimed to speak for all the people. But the debate about representation—with one-third of the North American population not sufficiently propertied to have the right to vote for the assemblies—reverberated into the colonial assemblies themselves. Demands for expanded voting rights confronted complaints about "low" people like cobblers, caulkers, blacksmiths, religious dissenters, and non-Christians participating in the debate for independence. As with the French Revolution later on, the leaders needed the masses to support them in their bid for independence but were afraid of the potential violence and momentum of these masses, which might at any time overwhelm them.

While this coalition of leaders and the masses was coming together, Britain seized the initiative. In an effort to isolate the revolutionary hotbed of Massachusetts from the rest of the colonies, British troops ventured out in April 1775 to seize a suspected cache of arms and ammunition in Concord. The silversmith Paul Revere, son of a French Huguenot immigrant, in the midnight ride of later fame, warned Adams and Hancock of the British plans to arrest them and roused a militia of farmers—the famous "Minute Men"—near Concord to arms. War broke out in earnest, and the Second Continental Congress appointed George Washington, a former officer from a wealthy Virginian family of tobacco planters, as commander of the colonists' troops.

Feelings on both sides now ran at a fever pitch, as exemplified by Thomas Paine's widely read pamphlet *Common Sense*. Paine had been a corset maker and tax officer in Britain before emigrating to Pennsylvania in 1774. His plainspoken prose style powerfully appealed to craftspeople and laborers, as did his use of well-known biblical examples and avoidance of high-toned Latin quotes. By contrast, when the Second Continental Congress voted to separate the colonies from Britain on July 4, 1776, the resulting Declaration of Independence was a highly literate document steeped in Enlightenment thought. Its author was Thomas Jefferson, like Washington the son of a Virginian planter with an advanced university education that included the New Sciences. The great majority of the signers were also educated men of means—planters, landowners, merchants, and lawyers. Thus, the American and earlier English Revolutions shared a certain similarity in their leadership.

Although the revolution affirmed the Enlightenment idea that the equality of all "men" was "self-evident," it tacitly excluded the one-fifth of all Americans who were black slaves and the roughly half who were women, not to mention the Native Americans. On the other hand, the signers also excluded Locke's property ownership from what they considered to be the most valuable rights of citizens and rendered these rights as "life, liberty, and the pursuit of happiness." When the colonists eventually won the war of independence in 1783, the founders created a revolutionary federal republic with a Congress that was far more representative of its citizens than the Parliament in Great Britain.

The new republic's initial years, however, were fraught with organizational difficulties. The governing document, the Articles of Confederation, granted so much power to the individual states that the latter operated in effect like separate countries. In 1787 a constitutional convention was called in Philadelphia and a far more effective federal system created. Careful to add checks and balances in the form of a bicameral legislature and separation of powers into legislative, executive, and judicial branches, the new constitution seemed to embody many of the ideals of the Enlightenment—including a set of 10 initial amendments: the Bill of Rights. Though still imperfect—particularly in sidestepping the contentious issue of slavery—it provided a model for nearly all the world's constitutions that followed. A later commentator praised it as "a machine that would go of itself"; another, more critical one called its checks and balances "a harmonious system of mutual frustration." In 1789, under the new system, George Washington was elected the first president of the United States.

Though the new republic fell far short of what we would consider today to be "representative," its abolition of the divine right of monarchial rule and its replacement by the sovereignty of the people was for most people a previously unimaginable reversal of the natural order of things. In this respect, the American and French Revolutions signaled the inauguration of a new pattern of state formation and the advent of modernity.

The French Revolution   King Louis XVI (r. 1774–1792) and the French government had watched the American War for Independence with great sympathy, hoping for an opportunity to avenge the kingdom's defeat in the Seven Years' War. It supplied the Americans with money, arms, and officers and in 1778–1779, in alliance with Spain, declared war on Great Britain. The French–Spanish entry into the war forced Britain into an impossible defense of its entire colonial empire. Although

Reddition de L'Armée Angloises Commandeé par Mylord Comte de Cornwallis aux Armees Combineés des Etats unis de L'Amerique et de France aux ordres des Generaux Washington et de Rochambeau à Yorck town et Glocester dans la Virginie. le 19 Octobre 1781. Il s'est trouveé dans ces deux postes 6000 hommes de troupes regleés Angloises ou Hessoires et 22 Drapeaux 1500 Matelots 160 Canons de tout Calibre dont 75 de Fonte 8 Mortiers 40 Batimens dont un Vaisseau de 50 Canons qui a eté Brulé 20 Coulez Bas . Ce jour a jamais memorables pour les Etats unis ou ce qui assura definitivement leurs independances

The Battle of Yorktown, 1781. This French engraving emphasizes the key role they played in this decisive battle of the war. A large French army assisted in the siege of Yorktown, visible in the background, while the French fleet cut off British attempts to escape, forcing them to surrender.

mounting a creditable military effort, Britain conceded defeat in 1783 in the hope of escaping with minimal territorial losses, apart from the North American colonies. Indeed, in the peace negotiations France and Spain made few territorial gains. The French government furthermore had to begin exorbitant payments—much higher than what Britain faced after the Seven Years' War—on the interest for the loans to carry out the war. Crippling debt, which the French government was ultimately unable to pay, played a large role in establishing the preconditions underlying the outbreak of the French Revolution.

The Crises of the 1780s

As in America, the French population had increased sharply during the 1700s. Food production could barely keep up, and inflation increased. As recent scholarship has shown, the rural economy responded to the rising demand, though with difficulty; and in the region of Paris, production for the market was highly profitable. Furthermore, colonial trade with the Caribbean colonies boomed. Had it not been for the debt, the government would have been well-financed: It collected direct taxes as well as monies from compulsory loans and the sale of titles and offices to a large upper stratum of ordinary people of means—merchants, lawyers, and administrators. These people were deeply invested in the regime, buying themselves into the ranks of the aristocracy and benefiting from administrative offices handling the kingdom's tax revenue. Although claiming to be absolute, the king in reality shared power and wealth with a large ruling class of old and new aristocrats as well as aspiring ordinary urban people of wealth.

In 1781, suspicions arose about the solvency of the regime when the finance minister, who had kept the extent of the subsidies for the American revolutionaries a secret, quit. But the government continued to borrow, even though bad weather leading to two poor harvests in 1786–1787 diminished tax revenues. The hardship caused by these 2 years became crucial for the eventual revolution in 1789: Without reserves in grain and animals, the peasants suffered severe famine and grew increasingly angry when government imports intended to help ended up in the hands of profiteers and hoarders.

By 1788, the government was unable to make payments on short-term loans and had to hand out promissory notes, with bankruptcy looming in the background. As in Britain in the 1760s, a reform of the tax system became unavoidable. At first, the king sought to initiate this reform with the help of a council of appointed notables. When this failed, he held general elections for a popular assembly to meet in Versailles (called the "Estates-General," last convened in 1614). Voters, defined as males over 25 who were French and paid taxes, met in constituent meetings in their districts across France, according to their "estate" as clergy, aristocrats, or commoners. Peasants met in large numbers in the "Third Estate," or commoner meetings; but the deputies they elected to meet in Paris were overwhelmingly administrators, lawyers, doctors, academics, businessmen, and debt holders. At the request of the king, the deputies composed petitions in which they listed their grievances about taxes, waste, luxury at court, and ministerial "despotism" to form the basis for the reform legislation.

The most famous among the petitions was the pamphlet of the priest (*abbé*) Emmanuel-Joseph Sieyès [See-YES], entitled *What Is the Third Estate?* Sieyès was elected as a commoner from Paris and became one of the leading intellectual figures in the revolution. In his pamphlet he put forward the revolutionary idea that the French nation of 25 million *was* the Third Estate, while the other two estates, totaling 200,000 members, were no more than a tiny fraction. The Third Estate, embodying Rousseau's idea of the "general will" of the nation, should alone form the "National Assembly" and translate this general will into a constitution, fiscal reform, and the abolition of aristocratic privileges.

Outbreak of the Revolution   Amid widespread unrest and rioting among peasants in many places in France and workers in Paris, the Third Estate now outmaneuvered the other estates and the king. In June 1789 they seceded from the Estates-General and relocated to a local tennis court where they swore an oath not to disband until they had formed a constitution. Following this Tennis Court Oath, they declared themselves a National Assembly. Louis XVI had initially been favorably inclined toward the Third Estate since the other two estates had rejected the government's reform plans. But he changed his mind after the Third Estate's declaration. Pressured by the pro-aristocracy faction at court, he issued a veiled threat that if it would not support his reforms, "I alone should consider myself their [the people's] representative." The king then reinforced his troops in and around Paris and Versailles and dismissed his popular finance minister, Jacques Necker (1732–1804), who had brought some famine relief in spring. Parisians, afraid of an imminent military occupation of the city, swarmed through the streets on July 14, 1789, and provisioned themselves with arms and gunpowder from arsenals, gunsmith shops, and the Bastille, the royal fortress and prison inside Paris, which they stormed. Thus,

The French Revolution. The French Revolution began with the storming of the Bastille for weapons and gunpowder on July 14, 1789 (top left). It gained momentum when Parisian women marched to Versailles, demanding that the king reside in Paris and end the famine there (top right). The inevitability of a republic became clear when the king and queen were captured after they attempted to flee (bottom left).

by his vacillation—first inclining to accept the role as a constitutional monarch, then switching to a reassertion of absolutism—Louis XVI lost the initiative.

Three Phases of Revolution   The French Revolution, unfolding from 1789 to 1799, went through three phases: constitutional monarchy (1789–1792), radical republicanism (1792–1795), and military consolidation (1795–1799). The first phase began with the "great fear" of near anarchy, which reigned during July and August 1789. People in the provinces, mostly peasants, chased their aristocratic and commoner landlords from their estates. Paris, too, remained in an uproar since food supplies, in spite of a good harvest, remained spotty. Agitation climaxed in October when thousands of working women, many with arms, marched from Paris to Versailles, forcing the king to move to Paris and concern himself directly with their plight.

No longer threatened by the king, the National Assembly issued the Declaration of the Rights of Man and of the Citizen (1789), subjected the Catholic Church to French civil law (1790), established a constitutional monarchy (1791), and issued laws ending the unequal taxes of the Old Regime (1792). The principal author of the Declaration of the Rights of Man and of the Citizen was Marie-Joseph Gilbert du Motier, Marquis de Lafayette (1757–1834), descendant of an old French aristocratic family but an early joiner of the Third Estate Assembly. Earlier, Lafayette had made major contributions to the American War for Independence as a military officer, and during the French Revolution he was the commander of the fledgling French National Guard, engaged in efforts to protect what was at this point a constitutional revolution favoring an emerging propertied and urban middle class.

The second phase of the revolution, the period of radical republicanism (1792–1795), began when the revolutionaries found themselves unable to establish a stable constitutional regime. After the king tried unsuccessfully to flee with his unpopular Austrian-born, Habsburg wife Marie-Antoinette from Paris to a monarchist stronghold in eastern France in the summer of 1791, Austria and Prussia threatened to intervene if the king and queen were harmed. The idea of preventive war now gained adherents across the political spectrum as patriotic feelings were invoked: Many aristocratic families had fled to their relatives in Austria and Prussia. In April 1792 the prowar party declared war on its eastern neighbors. Then, in September, republicans seized the government, deposed the king, and held elections for a new assembly to draw up a republican constitution. They separately executed the king and queen in 1793, while the huge *levée en masse*, or conscript army, of the republic regained control of the French borders in 1794 after a lengthy and difficult war against its European neighbors.

In the meantime, a Committee of Public Safety had assumed power and launched the "Reign of Terror," in which perhaps 30,000 citizens were executed. One of its leaders was Maximilien Robespierre (1758–1794), a well-educated lawyer from an old administrative family in northern France who prided himself on his alliance with the laborers and craftspeople of Paris. Because they wore no middle-class silk breeches, they were called *sans-culottes* [san-coo-LOTT] and had become the shock troops of the revolution, particularly in Paris. Robespierre's theory of terror held that France needed to be cleansed of "counter-revolutionaries" and that by surmounting this last difficulty, all the benefits of the revolution would then take effect. Thus, he insisted, "there is only one crime, treason; and one punishment, death." At the same time, the new government was enacting laws designed to remake society along Enlightenment ideology in an astonishingly ambitious fashion. Robespierre, for example, promoted the new state Cult of the Supreme Being, a variation on the idea of deism. The Supreme Being was to be celebrated every tenth day of the new 10-day week in the new "rational" republican calendar that was dated to January 2, 1792. 1792 was now to be Year I of the Republic. The names of months were changed to match the seasons: Germinal for March, Floreal for April, Thermidor for July/August. New systems of measurement that culminated in the metric system were also developed. Egalitarianism in everyday life, such as addressing everyone as "Citizen" or "Citizeness," was pressed; and schemes were even proposed to eliminate private property. But such wholesale changes also alienated increasing numbers of people; and thus, the ranks of "counter-revolutionaries" multiplied as the revolution became more and more radical.

The Directory   With the foreign wars ended and the danger of a monarchist counterrevolution diminished, many revolutionaries grew fearful of Robespierre's dictatorial powers and use of terror. Plotters arrested him and had him and many supporters guillotined in July 1794. Since this coincided with the new French month of Thermidor, scholars of revolution sometimes refer to such a retreat from radicalism as a "Thermidorean reaction." With a new constitution and bicameral legislature, the revolution entered its third and final phase (1795–1799) under the so-called Directory. But political and financial stability remained elusive, and the Directory increasingly depended on an army that had become professionalized during the defense of the revolution against Austria and Prussia in 1792–1794. Within the army, a brash young brigadier general named Napoleon Bonaparte (1769–1821), of minor aristocratic Corsican descent, was the most promising person to continue the foreign wars successfully. From 1796 to 1798 Napoleon scored major victories against the Austrians in northern Italy and invaded Egypt, which he occupied in

> ### From Declaration of the Rights of Man and of the Citizen
>
> "Article 1. Men are born and remain free and equal in rights. Social distinctions can be based only on public utility.
>
> Article 2. The aim of every political association is the preservation of the natural and imprescriptible rights of man. These rights are liberty, property, security, and resistance to oppression.
>
> Article 3. The source of all sovereignty resides essentially in the nation. No body, no individual can exercise authority that does not explicitly proceed from it."
>
> —Primary Sources of the French Revolution, http://www.thecaveonline.com/APEH/frrevdocuments.html

Patterns Up Close | The Guillotine

It is estimated that during the period of the Terror (June 1793–July 1794) the guillotine was responsible for around 1,000 executions in Paris alone and for perhaps as many as 15,000–30,000 throughout France. This iconic symbol of grisly public executions is attended by many myths. Among these is the idea that the guillotine was invented by—and took its name from—one Dr. Guillotin solely for the purpose of speeding up executions of perceived enemies of the republic during the infamous Reign of Terror. Neither of these notions is true however. Indeed, the actual train of events is far more compelling—and ironic.

Far from appearing for the first time during the French Revolution, the first known model of a "decapitation machine" is probably the "Halifax Gibbet," in use in England from around 1300 until 1650. Another model, the "Scottish Maiden," was derived from the Halifax Gibbet and used in 150 executions from 1565 until 1708. It was subsequently turned over to a museum in Edinburgh in 1797 and may have earlier served as a model for the French machine.

The Execution of Marie-Antoinette. During the radical republican period of the French Revolution, the Committee of Public Safety had Queen Marie-Antoinette condemned to death for treason after a sham trial. She was executed on October 16, 1793, 9 months after the execution of her husband, Louis XVI.

When and how did the instrument first appear in France? Ironically, it came as an indirect result of efforts to end the death penalty. During the early days of the revolution the National Assembly pondered the abolition of the death penalty in France altogether. On October 10, 1789, the Assembly was addressed by Dr. Joseph Ignace Guillotin (1738–1814), founder of the French Academy of Medicine and a staunch opponent of capital punishment, who urged the assembly to at the very least find "a machine that beheads painlessly," if they could not ultimately agree to stop executions altogether. Toward this end Guillotin presented sketches of the kind of machine

preparation for an invasion of British India. But thwarted by a pursuing British fleet, he returned to France. There, the Abbé Sieyès, resurgent as a constitutionalist and worried about continued plots against the government, encouraged Napoleon to take over the weak Directory. But Napoleon outfoxed Sieyès and overthrew the Directory altogether in November 1799, thus ending the revolution.

Revival of Empire Napoleon embarked on sweeping domestic reforms that taken together curtailed much of the revolutionary fervor but restored order and stability in France. His crowning achievement was the reform of the French legal system, promulgated in the Civil Code of 1804, which in theory established the equality of all male citizens before the law but in reality imposed restrictions on many revolutionary freedoms. In 1804 Napoleon sealed his power and cloaked he had in mind, but his initial design was rejected, followed by a second rejection on December 1 of the same year. In 1791 the Assembly finally agreed to retain the death penalty, noting that "every person condemned to the death penalty shall have his head severed." But instead of adopting Dr. Guillotin's design, the Assembly accepted a model designed by Dr. Antoine Louis, secretary of the Academy of Surgery; Dr. Louis then turned to a German engineer, Tobias Schmidt, who constructed the first version of the "painless" decapitation machine. It was not until April 25, 1792, that the guillotine, nicknamed "Louisette" after Dr. Louis, claimed its first victim. It is not clear when the name was changed to "Guillotine" (the final "e" was added later),

but historians speculate that Dr. Guillotin's early advocacy of quick and painless executions was a major factor. As for Dr. Guillotin himself, the crowning irony was that after fighting a losing battle with the government to change the name of the machine because of embarrassment to his family, he changed his own name and retreated to the obscurity he now craved.

Execution by Guillotine in France, 1929. An Enlightenment innovation, the guillotine was intended to execute humans swiftly and humanely. But the mass executions of the French Revolution turned the guillotine into a symbol of barbarism. It was not until 1977 that France executed its last criminal by guillotine. Today, most countries subscribe to the belief that even criminals have inalienable human rights, the most basic being the right to live.

Questions

- Can the guillotine be viewed as a practical adaptation of Enlightenment ideas? If so, how?

- Why do societies, like France in the late eighteenth century, debate the forms of punishment they use to execute prisoners? What are the criteria by which one type of punishment is considered more humane than others?

himself in legitimacy by crowning himself emperor of the French. Secure in his authority at home, he now struck out on a lengthy campaign of conquest in Europe. Victory followed upon victory from 1805 to 1810, resulting in the French domination of most of continental Europe. The goal was the construction of a European empire, by necessity land-based and in the tradition of the Habsburgs, Ottomans, and Russians. With this empire, he planned to challenge the maritime British Empire that had thwarted the French ambitions in the Seven Years' War. As justification for his empire, ironically, he used the constitutional ideas of the French Revolution, allegedly destined to replace the old absolutist regimes of Europe (see Map 22.2).

The failure of Napoleon's Russian campaign in 1812, however, marked the beginning of the end of Napoleon's grand scheme. Sensing his weakness, Great Britain, Austria, Prussia, and Russia formed an alliance that brought about Napoleon's defeat

MAP 22.2 Napoleonic Europe, 1796–1815.

at Waterloo in Belgium on June 18, 1815. In exile on the British-controlled island of St. Helena off the west coast of Africa, Napoleon lived until 1821, composing his memoirs. His legacy was equivocal. On the one hand, his revival of traditional imperialism, under the pretense of creating republican nations, only to turn them into vassals of France, discredited constitutionalism. On the other hand, what now could be called a middle class of urban professionals, property owners, and entrepreneurs, liberated by the Napoleonic conquests, was in the process of emerging, which—through the pursuit of constitutional nationalism—began to implement the pattern of modernity that is still with us today.

Enlightenment Culture: Radicalism and Moderation

Enlightenment:
European intellectual movement (1650–1800) growing out of the New Science and based on the ideology of materialism in which matter is considered the basic constituent of reality and mind or reason is a derivative.

The American and French Revolutions flowed out of the culture of the later **Enlightenment** (ca. 1750–1800). This culture both influenced the revolutions and, in turn, was influenced by them. The political heritage of the early Enlightenment (1650–1750), whose twin poles were represented by Thomas Hobbes (1588–1679) and John Locke (1632–1704), had witnessed a new, narrow definition of reality modeled after the New Science (see Chapter 17). The primacy of mathematics as the means to understand nature pioneered by Galileo and the thinkers who championed the New Science had a profound effect on these men—as they did on many of the later Enlightenment *philosophes*. For Hobbes and Locke, reality consisted only of matter detectable by the senses, and mind or reason existed only insofar as it was embodied in matter in the form of consciousness. Hobbes, the more radical thinker and a mathematician himself, viewed consciousness as a kind of bundle in which the passions held reason hostage; Locke, in most ways a more moderate thinker, assumed that reason could dominate the passions. But both radical and moderate strains of these ideas, though undergoing considerable transformation, continued into the later Enlightenment.

Early and Late Enlightenment

The early Enlightenment, of course, embodied modes of thought shared by many other thinkers besides Hobbes and Locke, who are usually categorized as part of a distinct "English Enlightenment." Outstanding figures whose works are still read today include Baruch Spinoza (1632–1677), Gottfried-Wilhelm Leibniz (1646–1716), George Berkeley (1685–1753), and Charles-Louis de Secondat, Baron de Montesquieu (1689–1755), to name just a few. Taken together, the representatives of the early Enlightenment came close to forming a movement in the loose sense of the word: People read each other's works, often corresponded with each other, and sometimes engaged in protracted criticisms of and polemics against each other. What changed in the period after 1750 was not so much the culture; Enlightenment thinkers continued to adhere to the idea of reason or consciousness embedded in the material world as the basic constitution of reality. What gradually grew was the social dimension of the Enlightenment: Thanks to a number of energetic writers popularizing the new ideas, the later eighteenth century saw thousands subscribing to Enlightenment-themed books, pamphlets, and newspapers or attending academies, salons, and lectures. They still were a minority even among the growing middle class of urban administrators, professionals, merchants, and landowners, not to mention the 80 percent of the population engaged in the crafts and in farming. But their voices as radical or moderate "progressives" opposing tradition-bound ministers, aristocrats, or clergy became measurably louder.

It was the late eighteenth-century generation of this vociferous minority that was central to the revolutions in America and France and—a minority within the minority—in the French slave colony Haiti (see Chapter 27). They translated their materialist conception of reality into such "self-evident" ideals as life, liberty, equality, social contract, property, representation, nation, popular sovereignty, and constitution. In the wider, more broadly conceived culture of the Enlightenment, they translated the materialist approach into the creation of new scholarly disciplines and new forms of artistic expression.

Napoleon. This dazzling portrait of Napoleon by the French painter Jean Ingres (1780–1867) shows the glitzy majesty of the "Little Corporal" who crowned himself emperor in 1804.

Voltaire and Social Criticism   Perhaps the most famous champion of Enlightenment ideas and an accomplished writer, social critic, and *philosophe*, as the French thinkers were known, was François-Marie Arouet, better known by his pen name of Voltaire (1694–1778). He was also the most prolific of the Enlightenment writers, producing more than 2,000 books, articles, and pamphlets during his career. As a young man Voltaire experienced the arbitrary justice of France's absolute monarchy when he was imprisoned in the famous Bastille without trial for insulting a well-connected aristocrat. He managed to have his open-ended sentence commuted to exile in England, where he came away impressed with the balance of the English constitutional monarchy and the findings of the New Science as codified by Isaac Newton. On his return to France he formed a long and fruitful relationship with the Marquise Gabrielle-Emilie du Châtelet (1706–1749), who not only gave him emotional support but was a considerable scholar in her own right. They assembled a library of over 20,000 volumes and produced a formidable array of historical, political, philosophical, and scientific works. Following the death of the marquise, Voltaire accepted an invitation from the "enlightened despot" Frederick the Great of Prussia and moved to his court for a time. His quick temper and outspokenness again landed him in trouble however, and he left Prussia for Geneva and, finally, an estate just inside the French border at Ferney.

The most quotable of the *philosophes*, Voltaire is still remembered today for such sayings as "history is a pack of lies we play on the dead" and "if God did not exist it would be necessary to invent Him." He signed many of the thousands of letters he wrote with the injunction to "crush the infamous thing," by which he meant the Catholic Church. He is also reputed to have come up with the story of Isaac Newton grasping the nature of gravity when an apple fell on his head. But his most famous work was the savagely satirical, picaresque tale *Candide* (1759). As the hero, Candide, lurches from tragic–comic misadventure to misadventure, his experiences lay bare all the venality, corruption, and absurdity of government, religion, and even some Enlightenment ideas themselves. Indeed, Candide's mentor, the thinly disguised figure of Leibniz in the person of Dr. Pangloss, constantly informs anyone who will listen that "all is for the best in this best of all possible worlds"—this while he suffers misfortunes ranging from being hanged to contracting syphilis. Such sunny optimism outraged Voltaire, who wrote the book against the backdrop of the Lisbon earthquake of 1755, which killed perhaps 50,000 people.

Denis Diderot and the *Encyclopédie*

Denis Diderot and the *Encyclopédie*   The most visible manifestation of the social broadening of the Enlightenment in 1750–1800 was the differentiation of an autonomous, secular realm of material nature into a multiplicity of self-contained scientific and artistic branches. In the following sections we will look at representative figures in the fields of philosophy, economics, literature, and music. Here, Denis Diderot (1713–1784) will be the focus of attention as a man of many philosophical and literary talents whose most important contribution to the Enlightenment proliferation of secular scholarly and artistic knowledge was the assembly of this knowledge into an encyclopedia.

Diderot was a precocious son of a knife maker in northeast France, who had received his education at a religious school. But he abandoned the study first of theology and then of law in favor of becoming an independent writer, a new occupation in the urban world of later Enlightenment modernity. During his early years he was penniless and came into a modest income only when he sold his library to Empress Catherine the Great of Russia, who also gave him a regular stipend. In the course of a long life, he composed a great variety of works, from philosophy to literature and art criticism. As an ardent materialist, he became an atheist and spent time in prison for his radical views, unable to publish many of his writings.

The *Encyclopédie*, originally conceived as the translation of an earlier (1728) English encyclopedia, began as an independent work when the publisher hired Diderot. Under the editorship of Diderot, the first volume appeared in 1751 as a work that would encompass not only the fields covered by the academic disciplines but all fields of knowledge. Not only that, it was also to have the power "to change men's common way of thinking." For the next quarter of a century, Diderot poured all his energy into writing entries and soliciting contributions from the "republic of letters," as the French Enlightenment thinkers were called. Many entries dealt with delicate subjects, such as science, industry, commerce, freedom of thought, slavery, and religious tolerance, sometimes edited by the cautious publisher without Diderot's knowledge. Publication itself was not easy since the Catholic Church and the French crown banned the project for several years and forced its continuation in secret. But the roughly 4,000 subscribers received their twenty-eighth and last volume in 1772, ready and able to assimilate everything modern, urbane gentlemen and gentlewomen should know.

Philosophy: Rousseau and Kant Diderot and his radical friends contributing to the *Encyclopédie* believed in the primacy of freedom and equality of individuals in their natural state. Political and social institutions, they concluded, should be shaped in such a way that they would guarantee a maximum of freedom and equality for every person. What they brushed aside, however, was the problem that this maximum freedom and its justification could not be inherent in matter; therefore, consciousness would have to come from outside, for example, in the form of morality.

The *Encyclopédie*. Denis Diderot's massive work promoted practical, applied science, such as this illustration showing glass-making.

It was this unwillingness of the radicals to admit the necessity of this external or transcendent morality that was the point of departure for the philosopher Jean-Jacques Rousseau (1712–1778). Rousseau, in contrast to his atheist Enlightenment colleagues, was a firm believer in the existing Protestant and Catholic morality. The son of a cultivated and music-loving Geneva watchmaker, Rousseau was a philosophical moderate. To the consternation of the radicals in France, he espoused in his *Social Contract* (1762) the notion that humans had suffered a steady decline from their "natural" state ever since civilization began and imposed its own external authority on them. The radicals held that even though humans had lost their natural state of freedom and equality and had come under arbitrary authority, they were experiencing a steady progress of civilization toward ever improving degrees of freedom and equality. Rousseau did share with his former friends a low opinion of the absolutist French regime, of which he ran afoul just as much as they did. But he had little faith in such concepts as popular sovereignty, elections, and electoral reforms that they propagated. Instead, he believed that people, rallying in a nation, should express their unity directly through a "general will," a sort of direct democracy—more applicable to his native Geneva than a large nation like France.

Immanuel Kant (1724–1804) lived far away from France in Königsberg, East Prussia, which he never left and from which he was an observer of postrevolutionary France. A much more disciplined philosopher than Rousseau, he was nevertheless also a believer in the progress of civilization and history, as expressed in his *Perpetual Peace* (1795). In fact, he quite immodestly thought of himself as having performed a second "Copernican turn" in modernity with his two main books, *Critique of Pure Reason* (1781, second revised edition 1787) and *Critique of Practical Reason* (1787). As a moderate Enlightenment thinker he made the crucial contribution, through a systematic study of the "antinomies" (internal contradictions) of reason. Pure reason, said Kant, does not reside in material nature and is transcendent; practical reason, which does reside in nature and is immanent, has to be carefully distinguished from pure reason. In contrast to Rousseau, however, with his traditional Christian ethics, Kant sought to build morality on transcendent reason and came to the conclusion that this morality had to be erected on the basis of the *categorical imperative*: Act in such a way that the principle of your action can be a principle for anyone's action. This highly abstract principle entered modern thought as the basis for human rights, with their claim to transcendence or universality, as in the Charter of the United Nations (1945).

Economics   The late Enlightenment saw the birth of the academic discipline of economics. French and British thinkers who were appalled by the inefficient admin-istration of finances, taxes, and trade by the regimes in their countries found the official pursuit of mercantilism wanting. As discussed in previous chapters, mercan-tilism was the effort to import as little as possible, except from the colonies, and develop domestic crafts so as to export manufactured goods in exchange for the warm-weather commodities of the colonies. Building on the philosophical assump-tion of the material state of nature, the so-called Physiocrats, most notably François Quesnay (1694–1774) and Anne-Robert-Jacques Turgot (1727–1781), argued that freedom and equality should be the principles of the economy. The state should re-duce taxes and other means of control to a minimum so that entrepreneurism in the general population could flourish. It should adopt a policy of *laissez-faire* [les-say-FAIR], that is, "hands-off." The Scottish economist Adam Smith (1723–1790), who spent some time in Paris and was familiar with many of the Physiocrats, developed a British version of laissez-faire economics. In his *Inquiry into the Nature and Causes of the Wealth of Nations* (1776) Smith argued that if the market were largely left to its own devices, without many state regulations and restrictions, it would regulate itself through the forces of supply and demand, appropriate prices, and so forth. It would then move in the direction of increasing efficiency as if guided by "an unseen hand." Like Kant in philosophy, Smith became the founding father of modern economics, whose ideas are still regularly invoked today.

Literature and Music   As in the other fields of modern cultural expression, the Enlightenment also inspired writers, poets, and composers. Noteworthy among the writers and poets were Johann Wolfgang von Goethe (1749–1832) and Friedrich Schiller (1759–1805), sons of a lawyer and a military doctor, respectively. Goethe, a moderate Enlightenment thinker, had a low opinion of his native Lutheranism. He trained as a lawyer but, on the strength of his early writings, found employment under the duke of Weimar in central Germany. Among his numerous poems, nov-els, plays, and even scientific works (on color), his drama *Faust*, about an ambitious experimenter who sells his soul to the devil to acquire mastery of nature, became a metaphor of modernity—of the technicians and engineers whose dominance of natural forces ran roughshod over environmental concerns.

Schiller, Goethe's younger contemporary, was a trained doctor and later professor of history and philosophy. A moderate Enlightenment thinker, he was greatly disap-pointed by the violence of the French Revolution. Feeling drawn to Kant's thinking, he strove to harmonize the "sensual passions" and the "formal passions" with which Enlightenment thinkers reflecting on the natural state of humans were wrestling.

Schiller composed major, mostly historical, dramas; and his poem "Ode to Joy" (1785), celebrating the brotherhood and unity of humanity and set to music by Ludwig van Beethoven (1770–1827) in his Ninth Symphony (1824), can be considered the hymn of Enlightenment. As such, it became the anthem of the European Union in 1993.

Wolfgang Amadeus Mozart (1756–1791), son of the music director of the archbishop of Salzburg, was a child prodigy who, as an adult, spent his most productive years at the Habsburg imperial court in Vienna. There, he joined the local lodge of the Freemasons. During the early Enlightenment, Freemasonry had grown from Scottish masonry guilds into one of the many fraternal organizations, friendship circles, salons, and other associations that celebrated sociability. The Freemason slogan was "liberty, fraternity, and equality"— evidently a precursor to the similar slogan of the French Revolution. Toward the end of the 1700s Freemasonry was a substantial organization all across Europe, without, however, being involved in politics. It included many French thinkers, as well as Goethe, the composer Haydn, Benjamin Franklin, and George Washington. Mozart wrote half a dozen pieces for Washington's Masonic lodge, and his opera *The Magic Flute* (1791) is strongly influenced by Masonic concepts and ideas. Together with his older contemporary Franz Joseph Haydn (1732–1809), Mozart was the creator of the classical style, which succeeded the highly complex music of the baroque and was more suited, especially through the new genres of trios and quartets with independent voices, to the cultural sensibilities of the rising urban, educated classes.

Ludwig van Beethoven, from a family of royal court musicians in Cologne, Germany, was likely also a mason during his time in Vienna. (The Austrian emperor ordered the Vienna lodge to be closed down after the restoration of the monarchy, and the records were destroyed.) Beethoven was perhaps the most revolutionary composer of these revolutionary times: Full of admiration for the French Revolution in 1804, he composed his third symphony, the *Eroica* ("Heroic") for Napoleon, a work in which he broke—or departed—from the Classical style. But when Napoleon crowned himself emperor, Beethoven was so deeply disappointed that he is reported to have exploded in anger, ripping the name "Buonaparte" from the title page.

The imperial turn of the French Revolution may be said to have effectively ended the Enlightenment. A few years later, with the fall of Napoleon and the restoration of monarchies, the European kings actively worked on rescinding its effects; and in the face of overwhelming power, the constitutionalists went either silent or underground.

Last Movement of Beethoven's Piano Sonata no. 30 in E Major. Composed in 1820 or 1821, this is one of Beethoven's last piano sonatas.

The Other Enlightenment: The Ideology of Ethnic Nationalism

Most adherents of the Enlightenment in the German-speaking parts of Europe were moderate constitutionalists similar to Rousseau. Like the latter, they sought to combine reason and the "good" passions with tradition. Accordingly, they were constitutionalists but, for the most part, not republicans. In their view, monarchies were part and parcel of a heritage of ethnic, linguistic, and even religious traditions peculiar to a specific nation. They sought to combine the universalism of constitutional nationalism with the ethnic specificity of a people: a *nation*.

Ethnic and Linguistic Traditions

Ethnic and linguistic traditions had existed in Germany for centuries before they became a nationalist ideology. It was not easy to identify these traditions, however, given their great diversity. German thinkers frequently invented traditions and imagined earlier communities, as modern scholars have often charged. But while these charges are often justified, it would be wrong to characterize these traditions as simply fictitious. Aware of the general reality of so many of these traditions, therefore, historians have postulated a "protonationalism," which the German Enlightenment thinkers allegedly turned into an actual **nationalism**. At present, however, both the "imagination" and "protonationalism" interpretations are considered problematic, so historians are again going to the sources in search of more viable interpretations.

In the case of language barriers to unity we can say that when the revolutions of 1776–1789 occurred in America and France, the constitutional nationalists aspired to universal human rights against a background of monarchical states that had existed for centuries within broadly defined borders. The court and administration in the capital had fostered a culture centered on the specific dialect of English or French spoken and written in London or Paris. But the grammatically complex High French which the revolutionary leaders spoke, for example, was manifestly not shared with the rest of the people living within the borders of the French kingdom. Nearly half of the French spoke dialects; the other half, in the northwest and southwest, spoke no French at all. There is evidence that the French revolutionaries expected everyone to learn "good" French, the "male and sublime" language of French culture. But in 1789 it was clear that plurality was a reality, and uniformity was—at best—a dream.

A similar situation existed concerning ethnicity. The constitutional nationalists took it for granted that there had been kings in the past who represented a population that had a common origin, distinguished between themselves and foreigners, had won and lost battles together, shared the same legal tradition, possessed a central administration, sang the same songs and hymns, and so forth. That all this constituted "Frenchness" was quite clear to the revolutionaries, as is evident in many documents; but it formed the background for, not the conscious content of, a revolution that declared universal human rights. In the American colonies, the "Britishness" of the revolution was more complex since, in pursuit of their struggle for independence, the revolutionaries had to pick and choose what they wanted to retain and what to reject. Here, too, the British character of the United States remained largely unexpressed except for what was to be rejected, as enumerated in the Declaration of Independence. Whatever specific ethnolinguistic character appeared in the two revolutions was not overly emphasized.

Germany displayed ethnolinguistic characteristics very similar to those of Britain and France but, of course, was politically fragmented. Even though it had always possessed a central ruling institution, its imperial, rather than royal, constitution made for a much higher degree of decentralization than in the English and French kingdoms. In addition, many Germans in eastern Europe were widely dispersed among peoples with different ethnic–linguistic–religious heritages, such as Czechs, Slovaks, Hungarians, and Poles, to name only the largest ones. In the west, the Alsatians were ethnolinguistically German but under French royal authority. When the

Nationalism: Belief that people who share the same language, history, and sense of identity make up a nation and that every nation has the right to pursue its own destiny.

(a)

(b)

Mapping a Nation. Evidence for the emergence of a French national identity can be found by examining two maps that were drawn for the French monarchy at different periods in its history. Commissioned by Louis XIV in 1669, four succeeding generations of the Cassini family produced the first multisheet, topographic map series of an entire country (*a*). Over 100 years later, in 1789, the Geometric Map of France was finally completed on the eve of the revolution, consisting of 182 sheets that form a 36-foot square when assembled. Shown here is a detail of Paris and its environs. With its recognizable topography and realistic symbols, the map profoundly contributed to the idea of a French nation by articulating a vision of a country whose land was owned by all French citizens. By comparison, a map of France commissioned by King Henry IV in 1594, during a time when France was riven by political and religious strife, shows a completely different spatial geography (*b*). In contrast to the social patterns of life that can be discerned in the Cassini map, the General Map of France simply concerns itself with depicting the dynastic claims of the monarch. Towns are clearly labeled, but no information is conveyed about the land itself. In the 200 years that separate the two maps, the way the French viewed their land had changed.

In Praise of Language and Heritage

"What a treasure language is when kinship groups grow into tribes and nations! Even the smallest of nations . . . cherishes in and through its language the history, the poetry, and songs about the great deeds of its forefathers. The language is its collective treasure, the source of its social wisdom and communal self-respect. Instruction, games, and dances are connected with it."

—F. M. Barnard, trans. *Johann Gottfried Herder on Social and Political Culture*, p. 165. Cambridge: Cambridge University Press, 1969.

Grimm's Fairy Tales. Perhaps the most famous collection of folktales in the Western tradition, *Children's and Household Stories* (1812) was assembled by Wilhelm and Jakob Grimm as a way to preserve their country's national spirit and to rekindle in their countrymen an appreciation for their Germanic roots. The stories they collected, such as this illustration from *Rapunzel*, were brought together through fieldwork and by peasant women who would visit the brothers and recite stories that awoke "thoughts of the heart."

Enlightenment spread in educated circles, there was clearly an ethnolinguistic background; but in the absence of a central state, the educated urban professionals, administrators, and educators professed a constitutional nationalism tinged with ethnic and linguistic elements.

Herder's Ethnic German Nationalism A central figure in articulating these ethnolinguistic elements in Germany into what was later to become a German nationalist ideology was Johann Gottfried Herder (1744–1803). Herder's father was an elementary school teacher and Lutheran church warden in eastern Germany. At university, Herder studied with Kant but also with others under whose influence he became familiar with Pietism, a Lutheran version of the medieval Catholic mystical tradition. Employed first as a preacher and then as an administrator at assorted courts in central Germany, he published widely as a literary critic and was on close terms with Goethe and other German Enlightenment figures. Like Locke, he distinguished between negative and positive passions; and like Rousseau, he subverted the exaggerated emphasis on reason by an exploration of aesthetic and emotional "sentiments," as the positive passions were called. When, toward the end of his life, the French Revolution broke out, however, he gave it his full support, to the consternation of the German monarch as well as many of his Enlightenment colleagues who decried the republicanism in the revolution.

In his writings, Herder sought to meld a highly diffuse ethnic heritage into a more or less coherent set of ideas to be preached not only to the educated but to the people in general through school curricula, history, and the arts. His major work, *On the Origin of Language* (1772), contains the core concepts of his new ideology of ethnolinguistic nationalism.

Herder not only focused on the traditions of high culture but also encouraged the collection of folk stories and fairy tales, even though he realized that peasants and laborers were completely outside the nationalism he projected. Similarly, given his interests in mysticism, his extensive references to religion were reflective more of the enlightened but moderate urban, educated population than either the clergy or the Catholic and Lutheran peasants. In principle, however, ethnolinguistic nationalism was open to an incorporation of religion; and thus, this nationalism may be defined as "religio-ethnolinguistic." Finally, while the ethnolinguistic nationalism of Herder's writings centered on "Germanness," it did not exclude pluralism. Far from elevating German culture to the pinnacle of all culture, Herder recognized that other peoples, notably the Slavs, had their own traditions and were therefore entitled to their own nation-states.

Germany's ethnolinguistic version of the Enlightenment received a major boost during the transition from the French Revolution to the Napoleonic wars. The turning point was Napoleon's self-elevation as emperor, as we have already seen in the case of Beethoven. Another influential figure was Johann Gottlieb Fichte

(1762–1814), a student of Kant. In 1806, when the French had defeated Prussia, Fichte turned from his highly abstract Enlightenment thought in the tradition of Kant to flaming patriotic appeals for the liberation from French imperialism.

By this time, a German middle class of urban professionals, administrators, and educators was emerging whose members met at student fraternities, public lectures, salons, musical evenings, and gymnastics clubs. Aroused for the patriotic liberation of their states and political unification into a single Germany, they were deeply disappointed by the restoration of the pre-1789 regional monarchies, which made minimal concessions to constitutionalism. Superior force for the moment cowed them into reluctant acceptance or underground agitation.

The Growth of the Nation-State, 1815–1871

Napoleon's defeat in Russia in 1812 and the Congress in Vienna of 1815 were major turning points in the political development of Europe. Monarchies and aristocracies reappeared throughout the continent, and the restored kings allowed only for the barest minimum of popular representation in parliaments, if at all. In France, where republicans were the most numerous, monarchists and republicans went through several further rounds of revolution before the republican nation-state emerged supreme. The other countries of continental Europe did not go that far; here, constitutional monarchies survived, in spite of a major challenge in 1848. By contrast, in Anglo-America, the supremacy of constitutionalism was unchallenged during the 1800s. Here, the nation-state grew with no disruptions, gradually incorporating more citizens into the constitutional process. The exception in the United States, however, was the Civil War, over the question of slavery and the incorporation of African-Americans into full citizenship. The victory of the Union, however, guaranteed and even strengthened the continuation of the pattern of modern nation-state formation.

Restoration Monarchies, 1815–1848

For a full generation, monarchists in Europe sought to return to the politics of absolutism. This return required repression and elaborate political manipulation to keep the now identifiable middle class of public employees, professionals, schoolteachers, and early factory entrepreneurs away from meaningful political participation. A "Concert of Europe" emerged in which rulers avoided intervention in the domestic politics of fellow monarchs, except in cases of internal unrest when they appealed to their neighbors for support. This was especially the case in Italy, where Austria intervened in several places and at several occasions to suppress nationalist agitation.

The Congress of Vienna   European leaders met in 1815 at Vienna after the fall of Napoleon in an effort to restore order to a war-torn continent. The driving principle at the session was monarchical conservatism, articulated mainly by Prince Klemens von Metternich (1773–1859), Austria's prime minister. An opponent of

---

Germanness

"Thus was the German nation [**Volk**] placed—sufficiently united within itself by a common language and a common way of thinking, and sharply enough severed from the other peoples—in the middle of Europe, as a wall to divide races not akin.... Only when each people, left to itself, develops and forms itself in accordance with its own peculiar quality ... does the manifestation of divinity appear in its true mirror as it ought to be."

—Johann Gottlieb Fichte. *Thirteenth Address, Addresses to the German Nation*. Edited by George A. Kelly, p. 190. New York: Harper Torch Books, 1968.

Contempt for Constitutionalism

"We see this intermediary class abandon itself with a blind fury and animosity ... to all the means which seem proper to assuage its thirst for power, applying itself to the task of persuading kings that their rights are confined to sitting upon a throne, while those of the people are to govern, and to attack all that centuries have bequeathed as holy and worthy of man's respect."

—"Confession of Faith, Metternich's Secret Memorandum to the Emperor Alexander," in Clemens Wenzel Lothar Metternich (Fürst von), *Memoirs of Prince Metternich, 1773–1829*, ed. Prince Richard Metternich and trans. Mrs. Alexander Napier, vol. 3, p. 468 (New York: Charles Scribner's Sons, 1881).

constitutional nationalism, now called "republicanism," Metternich was determined to resist the aspirations of the still struggling middle classes outside France, whose members, as he saw it, were driven by the "evil" of "presumption." Metternich depicted this presumption as a "moral gangrene."

To accomplish his objective of reinstituting kings and emperors ruling by divine grace, Metternich had the congress hammer out two principles: legitimacy and balance of power. The principle of legitimacy was conceived as a way to both recognize exclusive monarchial rule in Europe and to reestablish the borders of France as they were in 1789. The principle of the balance of power involved a basic policy of preventing any one state from rising to dominance over any other. In the case of internal uprisings, member states promised to come to each other's aid. Members agreed to convene at regular intervals in the future in what they called the "Concert," so as to ensure peace and tranquility in Europe. What is remarkable about this is that with only minor exceptions this policy of the balance of power remained intact down to 1914 (see Map 22.3).

As successful as the implementation of these two principles was, the solution devised for the German territories—now no longer with an overall ruler since the Holy Roman Empire was dissolved in 1806—was less satisfactory. The Congress of Vienna created an unwieldy and weak confederation of 39

MAP **22.3** **Europe After the Congress of Vienna.**

Europe After the Congress of Vienna

——— Border of German Confederation

German states, including the empire of Austria and the kingdoms of Prussia, Denmark, and the Netherlands. Prussia and Austria promptly embarked on a collision course over dominance in the confederation, with Prussia keeping the initiative and creating a customs union in 1834. Prussia's main purpose in this was to find outlets for its rising industrial and commercial interests in the northern German Ruhr region. Constitutionalist and republican Germans disliked the confederation as well since they had no meaningful voice in it. Thus, by resolving the overall issue of coexistence among the German states, but not of their fragmentation, the Congress was only partially successful.

Further Revolutions in France   In keeping with the principle of legitimacy, the Congress restored the French Bourbon monarchy with the coronation of King Louis XVIII (r. 1814–1824), a brother of Louis XVI. Louis, even though determined to restore full absolutist powers, was indecisive as to which republican institutions to abolish first. Playing for time, he tolerated the "White Terror," during which the returning aristocracy and other royalists pursued revenge for their sufferings during the revolution. When Louis died in 1824 the conservatives succeeded in putting Charles X (1824–1830), a second brother of Louis XVI, on the throne. Charles took the extreme course of restoring the property of the aristocracy lost during the revolution and reestablishing the crown's ties to the Catholic Church.

Republican reaction to Charles's restoration policy was swift. In two elections, the republicans won a majority and overthrew the king in the 1830 election. But they stopped short of abolishing the monarchy and elevated Louis-Philippe (1830–1848), son of a pro-republican duke who had been guillotined and had fought in the republican guards during 1789–1792, to the throne. Under this "bourgeois king," as he was sometimes caricatured, however, rising income gaps in the middle class as well as difficult living conditions among the nascent industrial working class led to new tensions. In the ensuing revolution of 1848, in which thousands of workers perished, the adherents of restoration and republicanism attempted another compromise: Louis-Philippe went into exile, and the parliament elected Louis-Napoleon Bonaparte (r. 1848–1852; self-declared emperor 1852–1870), a nephew of the former emperor, as president.

Uprisings Across Europe   After the revolution in Paris, uprisings occurred in the spring of 1848 in cities such as Berlin, Vienna, Prague, Budapest, Palermo, and Milan, as well as in three Irish counties. In Prussia the king seemingly bowed to pressure from revolutionaries and promised constitutional reforms. In Austria, hit by uprisings in multiple cities and by multiple nationalities, both the emperor and Metternich, the driving forces of 1815, resigned. The successor

Rebellion. Following the successful revolution of 1848 that ended the monarchy of Louis-Philippe in France, similar uprisings broke out across Europe. This image shows the Berlin Alexander Square barricades of March 1848.

with Russian help slowly regained military control over the Italians, Czechs, and Hungarians, as well as his own Austrians.

In the German Confederation, also hit by uprisings, moderate and republican delegates convened a constitutional assembly in Frankfurt in May 1848. This assembly elaborated the basic law for a new, unified state for German speakers and elected a provisional government. The new hard-line Austrian emperor, however, refused to let go of his non-German subjects. Therefore, the constitution joined only the German Federation and Prussia (also with non-German minorities) into a unitary state, with the provision for a future addition of German-speaking Austria. Against strong resistance by republicans, the delegates offered the Prussian king a new hereditary imperial crown in the name of the German people. But the king, unwilling to accept the principle of popular sovereignty, refused the crown "of clay." This refusal turned the tide against this Frankfurt Assembly. Moderate delegates departed, and radical ones instigated revolts. Prussian troops stepped in and relieved a group of grateful regional monarchs of their insurrectionists. By July 1849, the provisional Frankfurt government had come to an end and Germany's constitutional experiment had ended.

Irish Nationalism

In Ireland, ethnolinguistic nationalism found adherents among groups of urban professionals and educators in the early 1800s. Since they were acutely aware that Ireland did not possess much in terms of a literary-artistic tradition, they sought to position the Catholic tradition as a nationalizing element, around which to center nationalism, while others were more firmly wedded to secularism. In the uprising of 1848 the secularists won out. But the example of Catholicism in Ireland demonstrates that ethnolinguistic nationalism could easily be extended into the religious heritage if desired, foreshadowing trends of the twentieth century.

The events of 1848 had their origins in the Young Irelander opposition movement against the British Union Act of 1800. Through newspapers, lectures, and election campaigns this movement demanded a repeal of the act, frequently invoking Catholic "Irishness." When in 1845 a potato blight broke out on the island (which probably arrived through guano fertilizer imports mined in potato-growing Peru) causing a severe famine, perhaps one-fifth of the population perished. Only mass emigration to the United States alleviated further suffering. The Young Irelanders vehemently (and justifiably) accused the British government of inaction. Groups of Young Irelanders, tenant farmers, and even a few landlords rose in insurrection and battled police forces in three counties. But they were no match for the police, and the revolt quickly collapsed. Ethnolinguistic nationalism with elements of Catholicism had not yet coalesced into a full nationalist ideology.

Ethnolinguistic Nationalism in Italy

Italy was as fragmented politically as Germany, but unlike Germany it was also largely under foreign domination. Austria controlled the north directly and the center indirectly through relatives from the house of Habsburg. The monarchy of Piedmont in the northwest, the Papal States in the center, and the kingdom of Naples and Sicily (the "Two Sicilies") were independent but administratively and financially weak. After the Metternich restoration, the Italian dynasties had made concessions to constitutionalists; but Austria repressed uprisings in 1820–1821 and 1831–1832 without granting liberties. The republican Carbonari inspired both uprisings; they were members of the crafts guild of "charcoal burners" who had formed fraternities similar to the Freemasons during the eighteenth century. After their decisive defeat in 1831, the remnants formed the "Young Italy" movement.

Realistic second-generation politicians of the Restoration recognized that the middle-class ethnolinguistic nationalism coming to the fore in 1848 was a potent force that could be dipped into. By remobilizing this force in the 1860s, they would be able to end state fragmentation and make Italy and Germany serious players in the European Concert. These politicians were more sympathetic toward French-style constitutionalism than the Restoration politicians but still opposed to republicanism. Their pursuit of "Realpolitik"—exploitation of political opportunities—resulted in 1870–1871 in the transformations of the Italian kingdom of Piedmont and the German Empire of Prussia into the nation-states of Italy and Germany.

The Italian politician who did the most to realize Italy's unification was the prime minister of Piedmont-Sardinia, Count Camillo di Cavour (1810–1861). Cavour was the scion of an old aristocratic family in northwestern Italy with training as a military officer. While in the army, he read widely among French and British political philosophers and became a constitutional nationalist. A supporter of Adam Smith's liberal trade economics, he imported guano fertilizer and grew cash crops, like sugar beets, on his estate. As prime minister he was the driving force behind the development of railroads, first in Piedmont and later in Italy. With the backing of his similarly liberal-minded king, Victor Emanuel II (r. 1849–1878), he engineered the unification of most of Italy under decidedly trying circumstances.

Cavour began the unification process in 1858 with lukewarm support from Louis Napoleon of France for Piedmontese military action against Austria. When Cavour was victorious, however, France withdrew its support (fearing a powerful Piedmont) and Austria did not budge from its fortifications in northern Italy. Through adroit maneuvering, Cavour was able to arrange for a favorable plebiscite in north-central Tuscany and Emilia in 1859, gaining these two regions from Austria for Piedmont. A year later Cavour occupied the Papal States and accepted the offer of Giuseppe Garibaldi (1807–1882) to add adjoining Naples and Sicily to a now nearly unified Italy.

Garibaldi, a mariner from Nice in the northwest (present-day France), was a Carbonari and Young Italy republican nationalist with a colorful career as a freedom fighter not only in Italy but also in Brazil and Uruguay. Dressed in his trademark red gaucho shirt with poncho and sombrero, the inspiring Garibaldi attracted large numbers of volunteers wherever he went to fight. Despairing of any republican future for Italy, he threw in his lot with Piedmont and, after invading Naples and Sicily and deposing its monarch in 1860, delivered these two regions to Cavour. Cavour died shortly afterward and, thus, did not live to see Piedmont transform itself into Italy in 1870, when it gained Venice from Austria and Rome from France in the wake of the Prussian–Austrian war of 1870–1871. But he clearly was the power politician who laid the decisive groundwork.

Giuseppe Garibaldi. Garibaldi was an Italian nationalist who, in collaboration with Count Cavour, prime minister of the kingdom of Piedmont, contributed decisively to the unification of Italy. Garibaldi and his "Red Shirts" were able to seize Sicily and Naples from its Bourbon-descended monarch in 1860. He then unified his conquests with the constitutional kingdom of Piedmont to form the nucleus of Italy, which was fully unified a decade later.

Bismarck and Germany

In contrast to Italy, neither King Wilhelm I (r. 1861–1888) nor his chancellor (prime minister) Otto von Bismarck (in office 1862–1890) had deep sympathies for constitutionalism. By combining their antipathies and forming a coalition of convenience, they succeeded in keeping the constitutionalists in the Prussian parliament in check. But they realized they could dip into the ethnolinguistic nationalism that had poured forth in 1848, using it for power politics: Realpolitik.

Bismarck was a Prussian aristocrat with a legal education rather than a military career. He was multilingual, widely read, and experienced in the diplomacy of the European Concert. He realized that Prussia, a weak player in the Concert, had a chance for greater influence only if the kingdom could absorb the German Federation. For Prussia to do so, Bismarck argued, it had to progress from the talk about unification, as in Frankfurt, to military action, using "blood and iron." From the time of his appointment to 1871, he systematically maneuvered Prussia into an internationally favorable position for the coup that would eventually bring unification: war with France.

First, he exploited a succession crisis in Denmark for a combined Prussian–Austrian campaign to annex Denmark's southern province of Schleswig-Holstein in 1865. Then, when Austria objected to the terms of annexation, he declared war on Austria. After Prussia succeeded in defeating Austria, Bismarck dissolved the German Confederation and annexed several German principalities. In France, Louis-Napoleon Bonaparte was greatly concerned about the rising power of Prussia. He had carried out a coup d'état in 1852, ending the Second Republic and declaring himself emperor—an act that prompted the always quotable Karl Marx to claim that "history always repeats itself, the first time as tragedy, the second time as farce." A distraction on his eastern flank was not at all what Emperor Napoleon III desired.

But he carelessly undermined his precarious strength. First, he prevented a relative of King Wilhelm from succeeding to the throne of Spain when it fell vacant. But when he demanded through his minister, then meeting with Wilhelm at the spa in Bad Ems, additional assurances that Prussia would not put forward candidates

Prussian Victory. After Napoleon III's defeat and surrender in the Franco–Prussian War of 1870–1871, French republican politicians declared the Third Republic and continued the war. But in spite of heroic defensive efforts, Prussian troops occupied Paris in January 1871 (the photo shows the victory parade on the Champs-Elysées) and in Versailles declared the unification of Germany and the foundation of the Second German Empire.

MAP 22.4 Europe in 1871.

for any thrones in the future, the canny Bismarck outmaneuvered him. When King Wilhelm politely refused the demand, the chancellor edited the refusal in such a way as to make it insulting to the French. France then declared war on Prussia and was defeated in the crucial battle of Sedan in 1870. Now Bismarck had the upper hand for which he had been diligently working. He used it to annex Alsace-Lorraine from the French, carried out the final unification of Germany, and elevated the new state to the status of an empire in 1871 (see Map 22.4).

Nation-State Building in Anglo-America, 1783–1865

After the independence of the United States in 1783, both the United States and Great Britain were free to pursue their versions of constitutional nation-state development. In the United States, the revolutionaries, as well as subsequent generations, remained faithful to the idea of a republican nation. The restoration of monarchies and ethnolinguistic nationalism that complicated nation-state formation in Europe did not affect the United States and gave rise to a long tradition among American historians of claiming American "exceptionalism." While it is indeed true that the growth of the United States in the 1800s followed its own trajectory, there is also no question that the underlying pattern of modern nation-state formation was very similar to that of Europe. The same conclusion can be drawn concerning Great Britain, which was exceptional in that it became the dominant seaborne world empire but similarly came together as a nation on Atlantic islands subordinating English, Scottish, and Welsh ethnolinguistic traditions to a national constitutionalism.

The United States   During the first half of the nineteenth century the newly independent American states not only prospered but also began a rapid westward expansion. As this process unfolded toward 1850 it became increasingly apparent that sectional differences were developing in the process. Whereas the North developed an industrial and market-driven agricultural economy, the South remained primarily agrarian, relying heavily upon the production of cotton for its economic vitality. Even more, the South relied upon vast numbers of slaves to work the cotton fields of plantations. Cotton was the main fiber for the industrial production of textiles, and it not only defined the wealth of the plantation owners but led them to see chattel slavery as the only viable means to keep the "cotton kingdom" prosperous. In defense of its stance, the South increasingly relied upon the notion of states' rights in opposition to federal control. With the acquisition of new territory extending to the Pacific coast after the war with Mexico from 1846 to 1848 and the constant push of settlement beyond the Mississippi, the vital question of which of the new territories would become "free states" and "slave states" resulted in increasing tensions between North and South.

The result was an attempt by a number of southern states to secede and form a new government, the Confederate States of America. When the new administration of President Abraham Lincoln attempted to suppress this movement, the disastrous American Civil War (1861–1865) began. Resulting in an enormous loss of life—more than 600,000 combatants on both sides were killed—the Civil War finally ended with a northern victory in 1865. There were several major results of the conflict, not least of which was an enhanced unification of the country during the occupation of the southern states by federal troops enforcing the policies of the Reconstruction (1865–1877). First, Lincoln's concept of the primacy of national government over individual assertions of states' rights was now guaranteed. Second, slavery was abolished and slaves were granted full citizenship. Third, rebuilding of the country and opening of the west resulted in a remarkable period of growth, facilitated especially by the expansion of a national network of railroads. By 1900, about 200,000 miles of uniform-gauge track crisscrossed the country and the United States was on its way to becoming the world's predominant industrial power (see Map 22.5). Moreover, there emerged a growing consensus that the American nation had come together after a divisive war, and this was aided by the adoption of signs like the Pledge of Allegiance to the national flag, along with a national anthem, "The Star-Spangled Banner." As a subtle testament to this national unification, historians have noted that before the war people said "the United States *are* . . .; after the war, it became "the United States *is*. . . ."

Despite the new bonds of national unification, the price of reintegrating the old South into the new order was the end of Reconstruction and the reversion over the course of two generations to an imposition of a de facto peonage on its black citizens. Indeed, between 1877 and 1914 state legislatures in the South systematically stripped African Americans of voting rights by means of poll taxes and literacy tests and imposed formal and informal segregation in social and public accommodations. These were enforced by law and all too often by lynchings and other forms of violence. In order to accommodate the sensibilities of white southerners regarding race, most northern policy and opinion makers gradually backed away from the views espoused by the champions of racial equality during Reconstruction and gave tacit acquiescence to southern efforts to retain white hegemony. The drive for full

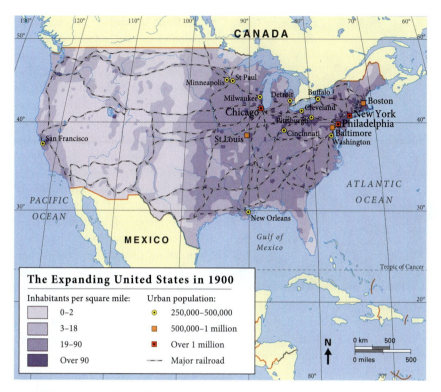

MAP **22.5** The Expanding United States in 1900.

civil rights would thus occupy a sizeable share of American domestic policy debates throughout the twentieth century.

Reform Measures   As in other Western nation-states, rapid industrialization produced social and labor unrest, resulting in the reforming initiatives of the Progressive era, which extended from 1890 to 1914. Although the later nineteenth century is referred to as the Gilded Age, epitomized by the staggering wealth of industrial tycoons like Andrew Carnegie (1835–1919) and John D. Rockefeller (1839–1937), all was not well beneath the surface. Big business had grown to such an extent that in the early 1900s a few hundred firms controlled two-fifths of all American manufacturing. The "trust buster" president, Theodore Roosevelt (r. 1901–1909), and Congress ended the monopolies of many firms, Rockefeller's Standard Oil among them, which had to cut itself up into 30 smaller companies. A new Department of Commerce and Labor (1903) and the Pure Food and Drug and Meat Inspection Acts (1906) helped the hard-pressed workers and consumers. With the Federal Reserve Act (1913) and the Federal Trade Commission Act (1914) Congress created an overall framework for the supervision of the financial and business sectors. As many contemporaries realized, a free market prospered only with at least a minimum of regulations.

Great Britain   The pattern of constitutional nation-state construction that Britain pursued in the eighteenth and nineteenth centuries was somewhat steadier. It remained more or less uninterrupted even during the Napoleonic wars, during

Evicted. Demolishing the houses of evicted tenants was ruthlessly practiced by British authorities in Ireland, particularly during the famine years of 1847–50. The wholesale destruction of homes—and livelihoods—horrified many contemporary observers, so much so that when Queen Victoria visited Ireland in 1849 she was publicly rebuked: "Thy royal name must be connected in future history with the astounding record of extermination of our unhappy race." This 1890 painting by Elizabeth Thompson, Lady Butler (1846–1933), one of the most accomplished English women artists of the time, is all the more striking because most of her other works portray the heroism and valor of British soldiers.

which Great Britain was the one enemy Napoleon was unable to harm. As was the Ile de France around Paris during the revolution and throughout the nineteenth century, England remained the core of the nation, to which the other British nationalities had to acculturate culturally if not ethnically. Scotland, traditionally divided between the highlands and lowlands, developed a greater sense of its own identity only slowly. The development began on the level of folklore, with the revival of Scottish dress and music (clan tartans, kilts, and bagpipes). More serious constitutional issues came to the fore in 1853 when the Scots, upset by what they thought was more attention paid by the government to Ireland, founded an association for the vindication of Scottish rights. The Scottish demand for home rule found sympathetic ears in the Liberal Party but not among the Conservatives. In 1885, the government established the position of secretary for Scotland. But home rule would come only after World War I.

The Welsh were even less satisfied with being ruled by London. In part this was due to the relatively early industrialization in Wales and the development of a Welsh working class, which had organized uprisings in the 1830s. Religious issues, mostly related to opposition to the Church of England among nonconformists (e.g., Methodists, Quakers, and Presbyterians), and education issues surrounding the so-called Treachery of the Blue Books added to the unrest. A governmental report of 1847, bound in blue covers, found that education in Wales was substandard: Sunday schools were the only schools offering education in Welsh, while regular schools were based on English for children who spoke only Welsh. Throughout the report ethnic stereotypes proliferated, documenting the fissures in the English-dominated acculturation process. As in Scotland, home rule came only after the Great War.

In Ireland, after the Great Famine of 1845–1849 already discussed in this chapter, rural production and land issues remained the main points of contention around which Irish demands for home rule and independence crystallized. A Protestant Irish landlord class still controlled most of the land in the second half of the nineteenth century. During the worldwide Long Depression of 1873–1896 Irish tenant farmers received low prices for their crops but no reductions in rent. Land reform became a large issue, woven closely into the politics of self-determination. A "land war" ensued between organized tenants and nationalists, on the one hand, and the British Army, on the other. It eventually led in 1898 to local self-rule for the Irish and in 1903–1909 to land reform. Home rule also did not come before World War I.

Apart from the issue of the constitutional nation-state, Britain's Parliament took cognizance of the growing middle class and the need to enact reforms for the working class. A contest between Liberal and Conservative governments ensued over the enactment of increasingly inclusive reforms. For example, the Great Reform Bill of 1832 shifted seats from southern districts to the more industrialized center and north. The result is often called the "victory of the middle classes" because industrial interests now took control of Parliament away from the propertied aristocracy. Further reforms followed: The repeal of the Corn Laws in 1846 liberated imports and made grain cheaper, and the Second Reform Act of 1867 extended the franchise to larger numbers of working-class voters. The end result was not only that Britain escaped the revolutions of 1848 but also that the British electorate was largely united during the Victorian period in its support for British imperialism around the globe.

Romanticism and Realism: Philosophical and Artistic Expression to 1850

The Victorian period, named after the long reign of Queen Victoria of Britain (r. 1837–1901), was a time in which Europeans and Americans alike celebrated the sobriety, frugality, and discipline of the emancipated urban middle class. While the perception of the superficial, extravagant, and dissolute aristocracy had now lost some of its power, the working classes—with their allegedly coarse, violent, and gullible ways—were increasingly seen as a threat to the social stability and moral fiber of the nation. This new "realist" middle class aesthetic at the end of the century was in many ways the opposite of the earlier "romantic" one, which had emerged from the Enlightenment at the beginning of the century. Early on, the liberation from political and artistic absolutism was exhilarating; as time wore on, however, the grim realities of the industrial transformation made this liberty considerably less exciting and more disturbing.

Romanticism: Intellectual and artistic movement that emphasized emotion and imagination over reason and sought the sublime in nature.

Romanticism

As we have seen, Rousseau and Kant had demonstrated the limitations of Enlightenment materialist thought in which *embodied reason*, surrounded by the senses and passions, constituted reality. Kant, therefore, proposed that reason, or mind, is in part independent or transcendent, containing the categories without which any talk about senses and passions would not even be possible. Philosophers, writers, composers, and painters of the period of **romanticism** drew the conclusion that the mind was entirely independent, creating aesthetic categories out of its own powers.

Dialectic: The investigation of truth by discussion; in the context here, dialectic refers to Hegel's belief that a higher truth is comprehended by a continuous unification of opposites.

Not all romantic thinkers and artists went this far, but for romantics creativity became absolute. Indeed, the stereotype of the creative "genius" heroically attempting to cross imaginative thresholds to grasp at transcendence became firmly implanted in the public imagination during this time.

Philosophers and Poets   The one philosopher who, building on Kant, postulated the complete freedom of mind or spirit was Georg Wilhelm Friedrich Hegel (1770–1831). The most systematic of the so-called idealist philosophers in Germany, Hegel asserted that all thought proceeded dialectically from the "transcendental ego" to its opposite, matter, and from there to the spiritualized synthesis of nature. This **dialectic** permeates his entire "system" of philosophy.

Nature as Teacher

One impulse from a vernal wood
May teach you more of man,
Of moral evil and of good,
Than all the sages can.

"The Tables Turned; An Evening Scene on the Same Subject," (1798). William Wordsworth, *The Complete Poetical Works*, ed. Henry Reed, p. 393 (Philadelphia: Trautmann & Hayes, 1854).

A parallel "ego-"centered creative poetry burst forth, with William Wordsworth (1770–1850), Samuel Taylor Coleridge (1772–1834), and Percy Bysshe Shelley (1792–1822) in Britain. In America, the "transcendentalist" Ralph Waldo Emerson (1803–1882) was the self-declared prophet of the absolute, imaginative self. Under Emerson's influence, the American Emily Dickinson (1830–1886) wrote poetry welling up "from the interior drama" of imagination. An afterglow of this imaginative absolute was still present in the later French symbolist Arthur Rimbaud (1854–1891), who sought ineffable beauty and pure feeling in the mere evocation by words, rather than formal rhyme.

Composers   While the romantics were struggling to express the sublime, ephemeral evocation of beauty with words that were at least in part concrete, the romantic composers had no such problems. The transitional figure of the German Ludwig van Beethoven, already discussed above, and the Frenchman Hector Berlioz (1803–1869) pioneered the new genre of program music, with the *Pastoral Symphony* (Symphony #6) and the *Symphonie phantastique*, respectively, emphasizing passion and emotional intensity and the freedom of the musical spirit over traditional form. From among the emerging middle class, eager to develop their romantic sensibilities and play music at home, a veritable explosion of composers erupted during the first half of the 1800s, such as Nicolò Paganini (1782–1840), Franz Schubert (1797–1828), Felix Mendelssohn (1809–1847), Frédéric Chopin (1810–1849), Robert Schumann (1810–1856), and Johannes Brahms (1833–1897). Often composing at a furious rate, these musicians were also virtuosi on the violin or piano, playing their own new musical forms and traveling on concert circuits all across Europe.

Painters   Similar to music, the medium of painting also lent itself to the expression of romantic feelings of passion and the mind's overflowing imaginative aesthetics. Not surprisingly, the proliferation of romantic painters numbered in the hundreds, and a small handful will have to suffice for discussion here. The common feature of these painters is that they departed from the established academic practices and styles. They either let nature dictate the direction and extent of their absorption into it or expressed their personal impressions forcefully with new, dramatic topics.

A follower of the first direction was Caspar David Friedrich (1774–1840) in Germany, who drew solitary figures absorbed by and absorbing an all-encompassing nature. Similarly, John Constable (1776–1837) was a British painter of superficially conventional landscapes that dramatically expressed the shapes and forces of nature. The French Théodore Géricault [Ge-ree-CO] (1791–1824) and Eugène Delacroix (1798–1863) followed the second direction and depicted dramatic or unusual scenes, as well as revolutionary gestures. Géricault caused a scandal when he exhibited *Raft of the Medusa* (1819), a float packed with sailors but without a captain: The conventions of traditional society demanded an orderly social hierarchy, even if in distress. Delacroix sought to express the drama of the French revolution of 1830 as well as Orientalist themes, for example, in *The Women of Algiers in Their Apartment* (1834), showing three women in languid poses with a black slave girl. While holding still firmly to the Renaissance style of perspective, light, and shadow, the turn to romantic freedom in these painters is unmistakable.

(a)

(b)

Romantic Art. Romantic painters expressed an absorbing, encompassing nature in their art. Note the barely recognizable steam-powered train in this painting (*a*) by J. M. W. Turner, *Rain, Steam, and Speed: The Great Western Railway* (1844). Romantic painters also depicted dramatic or exotic scenes relating to revolutions or foreign lands, such as the languid, bored harem scene in *The Women of Algiers in Their Apartment* (1834) by Delacroix (*b*).

Novels and Stories   As in the other art forms, romanticism in literature appears in heroines or heroes and their passions and sentiments. In the still strongly late Enlightenment-informed prose of the British author Jane Austen (1775–1817), witty and educated urbane society shapes the character and sensibilities of young women and prepares them for their reward, that is, love of the proper gentleman and marriage to him. These plots are developed with great intricacy in, for example, *Pride and Prejudice* (1813) and *Emma* (1816). A generation later, also in Britain, the three Brontë sisters, Charlotte (1816–1855), Emily (1818–1848), and Anne (1820–1849), published novels with equally complex plots but much greater emphasis on romantic passion, on the one hand, and character flaws or social ills, on the other. Charlotte's *Jane Eyre* (1847) and Emily's *Wuthering Heights* (1847) are two examples. Anne's *The Tenant of Wildfell Hall* (1848) goes a step further by including taboo topics such as a sensitive and suffering woman leaving her alcoholic and abusive husband with her son to live in hiding as an artist. The novels also contain mysterious, seemingly inexplicable happenings—artistic devices which the American Edgar Allan Poe (1809–1849) used more explicitly in his thematic Gothic stories and tales, such as "The Fall of the House of Usher" (1839).

Realism

Toward the middle of the 1800s, many artists and writers shifted their focus from the romanticism of the self and its aesthetic or moral sentiments to the **realism** of the middle classes, arraning this new group in an industrializing world. In philosophy, thinkers identified stages leading progressively to the rise of middle classes and industrialism. And in literature, the complex and tangled relationships that characterized the plots of the romantics continued, but now in the more prosaic urban world of factories and working classes.

Realism: The belief that material reality exists independently of the people who observe it.

Histories of Philosophy   One of the works in Hegel's system was *Lectures on the Philosophy of History* (1822–1830). In this work, the philosopher sketches the dialectical progression of the spirit to a progressively more differentiated

Realism. The documentary power of photography spurred the new impulses of realism that emerged around 1850. The photograph here shows the execution of hostages in the Commune of Paris in the spring of 1871 shortly before its final defeat by troops of the provisional French national government. One of the executed hostages was Georges Darboy, archbishop of Paris, a critic of the pope and strong patriot who cared for the wounded of the war against Prussia in 1870.

self-consciousness, until it culminates in his own time with the transcendental ego. The progression was also one from east to west, from India and China via the Middle East to Europe, culminating with the new revolutionary nations of 1776–1789. The French thinker Auguste Comte (1798–1857) composed a six-volume study entitled *The Positive Philosophy* (1830–1842), in which he arranged world history into the three successive stages of the theological, metaphysical, and scientific. In his view, the scientific advances of the sciences had all but phased out the metaphysical stage and had ushered in the last, scientific era. For Comte this was a sign of Europe's progress and a "positive" stage; his philosophy is therefore labeled "positivism." Comte further argued that the only sure way of arriving at truth was based on scientific facts and knowledge of the world acquired through the senses. Since in Comte's view the laws governing human behavior could be ascertained with the same degree of precision as the laws of nature, he became the founder of the science of sociology. Karl Marx (1818–1883), as we will see in more detail in Chapter 23, equally convinced of the scientific character of his philosophy of history, proposed the stages of slavery, feudalism, capitalism, world revolution, and socialism or communism. Today, these Eurocentric assumptions about Western triumphalism are no longer supportable, given that Enlightenment materialism, constitutionalism, nationalism, and industrialization have become the common, generic property of the contemporary world.

Prose Literature   Prose writers, of course, were for the most part unconcerned about the allegedly scientific character of their writings. On the other hand, as writers of fiction, the move away from sentiments to realistic scenes as they were encountered in middle-class society required new aesthetic experimentation so that the ordinary could be a heightened reflection of the new "reality" of life in the industrial age. William Makepeace Thackeray (1811–1863) in England, for example, was a supreme satirist, as displayed in *Vanity Fair*, a book on human foibles and peccadilloes. His compatriot Charles Dickens (1812–1870) had a similar focus but used working- and lower middle-class characters in his many novels. The English-woman George Eliot, born Mary Ann Evans, (1819–1880) was politically oriented, placing small-town social relations into sets of concrete political events in Great Britain, as in *Middlemarch* (1874). Gustave Flaubert (1821–1880) in France experimented with a variety of styles, among which extremely precise and unadorned description of objects and situations is perhaps the most important, for example, in *Madame Bovary* (1857). Henry James (1843–1916), an American living in Britain, in his self-declared masterpiece, *The Ambassadors* (1903), explored the psychological complexities of individuals whose entwined lives crossed both sides of the Atlantic. In the end, realism, with its individuals firmly anchored in the new class society of the 1800s, had moved far from the freedom and equality celebrated by the romantics.

Putting It All Together

Though the pattern of nation-state building in Europe and North America was relatively slow and, in places, painful, it has become the dominant mode of political organization in the world today. As we will see in subsequent chapters, the aftermath of World War I and the decolonization movement following World War II gave a tremendous boost to the process of nation-state formation around the world. Here, the legacy of European colonialism both planted these ideas among the colonized and, by supplying the Enlightenment ideas of revolution and the radical remaking of society, provided the ideological means of achieving their own liberation from foreign rule. In both cases, the aspirations of peoples to "nationhood" followed older European models as the colonies were either granted independence or fought to gain it from declining empires. But, in many respects, their efforts mirrored the difficulties of the first constitutional nationalist states and, more commonly, the initial ethnolinguistic ones.

Take the example of the United States. Though it achieved world economic leadership by 1914, it had faced an early constitutional crisis, endured a prolonged sectional struggle in which slavery marred the constitutional order for almost three-quarters of a century, fought a bloody civil war for national unification that very nearly destroyed it, and remained united in part by acquiescing in practices of overt segregation and discrimination against the 10 percent of its population that was of African descent. Or take the case of France. Its people adopted constitutional nationalism in 1789, but the monarchy it seemingly replaced bounced back three times. Thus, even in the later nineteenth century, Abraham Lincoln's hope that "government of the people, by the people, for the people shall not perish from the earth" was still very much open to question.

Yet another example is the case of Germany, where ethnolinguistic nationalism diluted the straightforward enthusiasm for the constitution and the symbols accompanying it. Historians continue to argue over whether Germany, and by extension other central and eastern European nations, took a special route (*Sonderweg*) to constitutional normality or whether the path was the same except that the pace slowed at critical times. In retrospect, it is impossible to say which of the speed bumps on the way toward the nation-state—slavery/racism, residual monarchism, or the

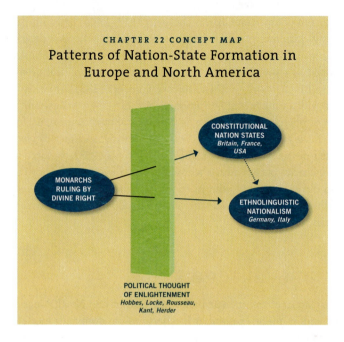

twentieth-century experiments of communism and supremacist nationalism—were responsible for the longest delay. In Part 6 we will consider all of these developments in more detail (see Concept Map).

Review and Respond

1. What were the origins and outcomes of the American Revolution? Of the French Revolution?

2. Why was there a period of monarchical restoration, in Europe in the first half of the nineteenth century?

3. What motivated the successful/abortive revolutions of 1848? Discuss their spread across Europe.

4. Which factors contributed to the unification of Italy and Germany?

5. Which parts of human nature did the romantics glorify and why? With what results?

6. How did realism differ from romanticism?

Thinking Through Patterns

▶ **How did the pattern of constitutional nationalism, emerging from the American and French Revolutions, affect the course of events in the Western world during the first half of the nineteenth century?**

Constitutional nationalism emerged as a result of the American and French revolutionaries succeeding in overthrowing absolute rule. The constitutional revolutionaries replaced the loyalty of subjects to a monarch with that of free and equal citizens to the national constitution. This form of nationalism called for unity among the citizens regardless of ethnic, linguistic, or religious identity. In the United States, this nationalism had to overcome a conservative adherence to slavery in the South before it gained general recognition after the end of the Civil War. In France, republican nationalists battled conservative monarchists for nearly a century before they were able to finally defeat them in the Third Republic.

Constitutional nationalists emphasized the principles of freedom, equality, constitution, rule of law, elections, and representative assembly regardless of ethnicity, language, or religion. However, nationalists in areas of Europe lacking centralized monarchies sought to first unify what they identified as dispersed members of their nation through ideologies that emphasized common origin, centuries of collective history, and shared literary, artistic, and religious traditions. In these ethnolinguistic (and sometimes religious) ideologies constitutional principles were secondary. Only once unification in a nation-state was achieved, the form of government—monarchist, constitutional-monarchist, republican—would then be chosen.

▶ **In what ways did ethnolinguistic nationalism differ from constitutional nationalism, and what was its influence on the formation of nation-states in the second half of the nineteenth century?**

▶ **What were the reactions among thinkers and artists to the developing pattern of nation-state formation? How did they define the intellectual-artistic movements of romanticism and realism?**

Philosophers and artists in the romantic period put a strong emphasis on individual creativity. They either viewed this creativity as an upwelling of impulses and sentiments pouring forth with little intellectual control or, conversely, considered their creativity as the result of an absolute or transcendent mind working through them as individuals. As middle classes emerged toward the mid-1800s, individual creativity gave way to a greater awareness, called "realism," of the social environment with its class structure and industrial characteristics.

Chapter 23

1750–1914

Industrialization and Its Discontents

THE INDUSTRIALIZING
WEST,
1750–1914

In the late summer of 1845, Mary Paul, age 15, came to a decision that would alter her life forever. Already at this tender age she had begun to realize just how limited her prospects were in the hardscrabble farm country of rural Vermont, so she decided to head for Massachusetts and stake her future on finding a job in the newly expanding textile industry.

Exactly how that future would unfold can be seen in numerous letters she wrote to her widowed father, Bela, over the coming years. As her correspondence reveals, the primary reason behind her dramatic decision to uproot herself was simply to make steady wages, rather than rely on the uncertainties and drudgery of farm work. On September 13, 1845, Mary

Seeing
Patterns

▶ Where and when did the Industrial Revolution originate?

▶ What were some effects of industrialization on Western society? How did social patterns change?

▶ In what ways did industrialization contribute to innovations in technology? How did these technological advances contribute to Western imperialism in the late nineteenth century?

▶ What new directions in science, philosophy, religion, and the arts did industrialism generate? What kind of responses did it provoke?

wrote for her father's consent to leave her nearby domestic job and seek employment in the booming mill town of Lowell, Massachusetts. On November 20, Mary wrote that she had already "found a place in a spinning room and the next morning I went to work." She continued, "I like very well have [sic] 50cts first payment increasing every payment as I get along in work. [I] have a first rate overseer and a very good boarding place." Shortly before Christmas, Mary reported that her wages had increased: "Last Tuesday we were paid. In all I had six dollars and sixty cents paid $4.68 for board. With the rest I got me a pair of rubbers and a pair of 50.cts shoes. Next payment I am to have a dollar a week beside my board." She then went on to offer her father some insights into her daily routine in the mill, one with which millions of workers around the world would soon grow quite familiar: "At 5 o'clock in the morning the bell rings for the folks to get up and get breakfast. At half past six it rings for the girls to get up and at seven they are called into the mill. At half past 12 we have dinner are called back again at one and stay till half past seven." Mary closes by pointing out that "I think that the factory is the best place for me and if any girl wants employment I advise them to come to Lowell."

Child Workers, North Carolina, 1910. The American photojournalist, sociologist, and reformer Lewis Hine (1874–1940) was hired by The National Child Labor Committee in 1908 to document the prevalence of underage boys and girls working in mills and factories throughout the rapidly industrializing United States. The young "spinners" in this North Carolina textile mill smile shyly, even proudly, but they cannot hide their disheveled appearance, visible signs of fatigue, and the psychological stress they endured working long hours for little pay in dangerous conditions.

After working for 4 years in the mill at Lowell, Mary moved to Claremont, New Hampshire, to be with her aging father. Two years later, however, she relocated to Brattleboro, Vermont, where she and another woman started a coat-making business. On November 27, 1853, Mary's letter to her father reveals her guilt about a conflict that would become all too familiar to workers in this new age: how to balance the need to earn a living with the obligation to take care of one's family: "It troubles me very much, the thought of your being lame so much and alone too. If there were any way that I could make it expedient I would go back to Claremont myself and I sometimes think I ought to do so but the chance for one there is so *small* [sic]."

Things apparently did not work out in Brattleboro, and 2 years later Mary's search for better employment led her to one of the many experimental communities that had sprung up in the United States during the first half of the nineteenth century. In this case it was the North American Phalanx, a utopian agricultural community in Red Bank, New Jersey, based on the socialist ideas of the Frenchman Charles Fourier. A little over a year later, however, the Phalanx dissolved, forcing Mary to move back to New Hampshire, where she found work as a housekeeper. Finally, at the age of 27, Mary married and moved to Lynn, Massachusetts, where she and her husband settled down to raise a family.

Mary Paul's experiences, reflecting those of thousands of other young, single women in rural farming regions, signaled a momentous change in the patterns of American and world history. Like Great Britain and areas throughout northern Europe, the northeastern United States was now in the initial stages of what we have termed "scientific–industrial society." The agrarian–urban model, which had lasted for millennia on every inhabited continent except Australia, was now slowly giving way to a society based on machine-made goods, large-scale factories, regimented work hours, and wage labor. Moreover, the economies of the industrializing states would increasingly be dominated by the developing practices of capitalism. An ideology of progress, backed by the acceleration of technology and science, along with the legacy of the Enlightenment, would constitute an important step toward creating what we term in this section "the challenge of modernity." That challenge was already being spread throughout the world, backed by the revolutions in transportation, communications, and weaponry produced by this Industrial Revolution.

For Mary Paul and her fellow mill hands, however, their primary concerns were much closer to home. They saw clearly that the rapid growth of textile factories rendered obsolete the home spinning and weaving of cloth and cottage occupations of farming communities. By migrating to industrial centers in New England like Lowell, where textile mills offered employment opportunities, they could attain economic independence by working for cash wages. In many cases, however, they also witnessed epic and sometimes bloody struggles between management and labor as the laws, institutions, and social norms of this new society were being painfully worked out. And amid the countless interactions and adaptations in which Mary and her fellow workers engaged, the modern world we live in today began to take shape.

Origins and Growth of Industrialism, 1750–1914

Like the agricultural revolution of the Neolithic age, which resulted in humankind's transition from foragers to food producers and made possible urbanization, the Industrial Revolution forever altered the lives of tens of millions around the globe. Whether or not this movement was in fact a "revolution," however, is a matter of some debate. It is perhaps more accurate to say that the process of industrialization evolved over time, originating in Britain in the eighteenth century, then spreading to the European continent and North America in the nineteenth century and subsequently around the globe, interacting with and adapting to local circumstances and cultures along the way. But there is no question that the transition from manual labor and natural sources of power to the implementation of mechanical forms of power and machine-driven production resulted in a vast increase in the production of goods and new modes of transportation, as well as new economic policies and business procedures. In the process the lives of untold numbers of people were forever transformed.

Early Industrialism, 1750–1870

The industrialization of western Europe began in Britain. As with all transformative events in history, however, a number of important questions arise. Why did the industrial movement begin in Britain? Why not, say, in China in the Song or Ming period? Why in the eighteenth century? Why in such areas as textiles, iron, mining, and transport? How did these changes become not only self-sustaining but also able to transform so many other manufacturing processes? And was this process "inevitable," as some have claimed, or was it contingent on a myriad of complex interactions that we are still struggling to comprehend?

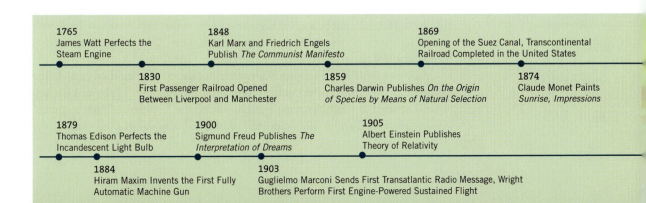

1765
James Watt Perfects the Steam Engine

1830
First Passenger Railroad Opened Between Liverpool and Manchester

1848
Karl Marx and Friedrich Engels Publish *The Communist Manifesto*

1859
Charles Darwin Publishes *On the Origin of Species by Means of Natural Selection*

1869
Opening of the Suez Canal, Transcontinental Railroad Completed in the United States

1874
Claude Monet Paints *Sunrise, Impressions*

1879
Thomas Edison Perfects the Incandescent Light Bulb

1884
Hiram Maxim Invents the First Fully Automatic Machine Gun

1900
Sigmund Freud Publishes *The Interpretation of Dreams*

1903
Guglielmo Marconi Sends First Transatlantic Radio Message, Wright Brothers Perform First Engine-Powered Sustained Flight

1905
Albert Einstein Publishes Theory of Relativity

Preconditions   Although there are no simple answers to these questions, it is possible to cite several conditions enjoyed by the British Isles that rendered them especially suitable for launching the industrial movement. Among other things, Britain benefited from what historians sometimes refer to as the "coal and colonies" theory. Britain has been described as "an island floating on a sea of coal." Large reserves of coal and iron ore, combined with the establishment of overseas colonies and subsequent global trading networks, provided a foundation for commercial expansion, which in turn would help provide capital to fund the new enterprises. In addition, a thriving merchant class, empowered by the Glorious Revolution of 1688, grew in significance in the House of Commons of the British Parliament and supported legislation aimed at economic development. At the same time, Britain developed a flourishing banking system; the Bank of England (1694) provided needed funds to entrepreneurs willing to make risky investments in new ventures.

Thanks to agricultural improvements, due in part to the introduction of new crops from the Americas such as potatoes and new fodder crops for livestock such as clover and turnips, Britain experienced a surge in population. Whereas in 1600 Britain's population amounted to no more than around 5 million, by 1700 it had nearly doubled to around 9 million. At the same time there was a demographic shift, in which displaced tenant farmers migrated to towns and cities, causing a rapid increase in urban growth and creating greater demand for food and consumer goods. In addition, urban dwellers began to crave more exotic consumer products now available from Britain's warm-weather colonies.

One of the first areas in which we see the effects of these changes was the textile industry. Although woolen cloth had long been the staple of the British textile industry, the introduction of new fabrics from Asia, such as silk and cotton, began to gain in popularity among consumers. Cotton's advantages of light weight and ease of cleaning resulted in a growing demand for the domestic production of affordable cotton clothing, or "calicoes." At first, the demand for finished cloth goods was satisfied by weavers working in the older, domestic cottage industries, a system known as "proto-industrialism." Due in large part to concerns for the woolen industry, however, Parliament enacted the protectionist Calico Acts of 1700 and 1720, which prohibited the importation of cotton goods from India. But this legislation had the unintended consequence of increasing domestic demand for English-made cotton textiles, which quickly outstripped available supplies. Given soaring demand, it was apparent that some sort of means was needed to speed up production.

British Resources   The impasse was resolved by a combination of factors peculiar to Britain at this time, which taken together made the use of machines more practical and cost-efficient than it might have been somewhere else. Since wages for workers in rural industries were high, the use of labor-saving machinery was increasingly seen as a means to help firms be profitable. By contrast, wages were relatively low in the Dutch Republic and France, with the result that there was no felt urgency in developing more cost-effective means of production. At the same time, Britain's vast reserves of coal resulted in cheap energy.

Moreover, Britain was singularly fortunate in its social and cultural capital. The composition of British society in the seventeenth and eighteenth centuries was unusually attuned to what historians sometimes call the "Industrial Enlightenment." As discussed in Chapter 17, eighteenth-century Britain was at the center of the

European scientific revolution. From Bacon to Boyle and from Harvey to Newton, the scientific revolution—particularly in its practical and empirical areas—was realized in a more widespread fashion in Britain than elsewhere. Here, too, was a flourishing group of scientific societies—for example, the Lunar Society in Birmingham and the Royal Society, founded in 1660—and the majority of British inventors had interests in and ties to societies aligned with scientific aspects of the Enlightenment. These groups served as centers of discourse and exchange between leading scientists and more down-to-earth men of a practical bent, including inventors, experimenters, and mechanics, who were not only often highly literate but also frequently educated in mathematics.

New Technologies and Sources of Power   These factors produced an explosion of technological innovation in Britain. From 1700 to 1800 over 1,000 inventions were developed, most of which were related to the textile industry. Among the most prominent were the flying shuttle (1733), the spinning jenny (1764), the water frame (1769), and the spinning mule (1779). Each of these devices greatly increased the speed and quality of spinning or weaving; the mule combined both operations into one machine. The power loom (1787) then set the technological stage for full-scale machine production of textiles.

Even these improvements were not enough, however, to supply both domestic and colonial markets with sufficient quantities of textiles. What was needed in order to speed up production was some sort of reliable mechanical power, instead of human, animal, wind, or water to drive the looms. The solution was provided by the development of the steam engine, easily the most important—and iconic—innovation produced during the industrial era.

The Factory System   The growing dependence on large machinery, the necessity of transporting fuel and raw materials to centers of production, and the increased efficiency of housing a multitude of machines under one roof necessitated the construction of large manufacturing buildings. These facilities were initially located near sources of running water in order to provide the necessary power to run mechanical looms. The implementation of steam power to drive machinery allowed entrepreneurs to move mills and production centers away from water sources in rural areas to urban settings, where there were large pools of cheap labor. Another attraction of urban areas was their greater accessibility to roads, canals, and, later, railroads. Once established, these factories in their turn drew larger and larger numbers of workers, contributing to population surges, particularly in the cities of the north and Midlands of England. Manchester, for instance, the leading textile manufacturing center, grew nearly 10-fold from 1750 to 1830. By the 1830s over 1 million people drew wages from textile factories and close to 25 percent of Britain's industrial production came from factories (see Map 23.1).

Railroads   While steam-powered factories provided much of the muscle of the Industrial Revolution, it was the steam railroad that captivated the imagination of the public. The spectacle of great locomotives pulling long trains of cars at previously unheard-of speeds, their pistons panting like the breath of giants, their plaintive whistles haunting the night, all became fixtures of the romance of rail travel. Their origins, like those of the earlier stationary pumping engines, began at the

"The Age of Steam"

More than any other innovation of the industrial age, the advent of practical steam power revolutionized manufacturing, transportation, communications, economics, and even politics and military matters. Indeed, at the height of steam's dominance, many people saw its ability to move freight and people and to run myriad kinds of machines as close to divine. As Frederic A. Bartholdi, builder of the Statue of Liberty, rhapsodized at the American Centennial Exhibition in 1876, the mammoth Corliss steam engine dominating the Machinery Hall there had "the beauty, and almost the grace of human form" in its operation. Even today, one sees a particular kind of avant-garde science fiction based on fanciful nineteenth-century contraptions labeled as "steam-punk."

The origins of the steam age lie in an environmental crisis. A growing shortage of wood for fuel and charcoal making in Britain in the early 1700s forced manufacturers to turn to another fuel source: coal. As we have seen, Britain was blessed with vast amounts of coal, but getting to it was difficult because of a high water table: Mineshafts often flooded after only a few feet and had to be abandoned. Early methods of water extraction featured pumps operated by either human or animal power; but these were inefficient, expensive, and limited in power.

The first steam-driven piston engine based on experimentation with vacuum chambers and condensing steam came from the French Huguenot Denis Papin (1647–ca. 1712), who spent his later career in England. Thomas Savery (ca. 1650–1715), also taking up the idea of condensing steam and vacuum power, built a system of pipes employing the suction produced by this process dubbed the "Miner's Friend" that was able to extract water from shallow shafts but was useless for the deeper mines that were more common in rural Britain.

This drawback was partially addressed by Thomas Newcomen (1663–1729). In 1712 Newcomen took Papin's piston-and-cylinder design and vastly improved its practicality. Newcomen's model featured a large wooden rocking beam, weighted on one end, to operate the pump. When the weighted beam was pulled down by the force of gravity, steam was drawn into a cylinder and then condensed by a spray of cold water. The resulting partial vacuum below the piston, augmented by atmospheric pressure above, pulled it downward, forcing the weighted end of the beam upward. The beam was in turn connected to another piston in the mineshaft, which sucked water in and drew it up a pipe.

Though over 100 Newcomen engines were in place throughout Britain and Europe at the time of Newcomen's death in 1729, a number of flaws still rendered them very slow and energy-inefficient, suitable only for places like coal mines, where abundant fuel was available. It remained for James Watt (1736–1819), a Scottish engineer, to make the final changes needed to create the prototype for fast engines sufficiently efficient and versatile to drive factory machinery. Watt had been engaged in repairing Newcomen engines and quickly realized their limitations. To

Corliss Steam Engine. A tribute to the new power of the steam engine was this huge power plant in the Machinery Hall of the American Centennial Exposition in 1876. The Corliss engine pictured here developed over 1,400 horsepower and drove nearly all the machines in the exhibition hall—with the distinct exception of those in the British display. Along with the arm of the Statue of Liberty, also on exhibition there, it became the most recognized symbol of America's first world's fair.

correct them he developed a separate condensing chamber, which allowed the piston cylinder to remain constantly hot; he also added a valve to eliminate the condensed steam after the piston stroke. The newly refined model, completed in 1765 and patented in 1769, was five times as efficient as Newcomen's engine and used 75 percent less coal.

After making several refinements Watt introduced a further improved model in 1783 that incorporated more advances. First, by injecting steam into both the top and bottom of the piston cylinder, its motion was converted to double action, making it more powerful and efficient. Second, through a system of "planetary gearing"—in which the piston shaft was connected by a circular gear to the hub of a flywheel—the back-and-forth rhythm of the piston was converted to smooth, rotary motion, suitable for driving machines in factories and mills. Watt's steam engines proved so popular that by 1790 they had replaced all of the Newcomen engines and by 1800 nearly 500 Watt engines were in operation in mines and factories.

Within a few decades, adaptations of this design were being used not just for stationary engines to run machinery but also to move vehicles along tracks and turn paddle wheels and screw propellers on boats—the first railroad engines and steamships. Both of these innovations soon provided the muscle and sinew of enhanced commerce and empire building among the newly industrializing nations. They were also among the most attractive as well as troublesome innovations for other countries around the globe to adopt. The Japanese fascination with the railroad can be said to date from its first demonstration by Commodore Perry's men in 1853 (see Chapter 24). Settlement of the United States was enormously accelerated by the advent of the railroad and river steamer. Indeed, by 1914, there was scarcely a place on the globe not accessible by either railroad or steamship. Yet, for societies seeking to protect themselves from outside influence, the railroad and steamer were seen as forces of chaos. The first railroad built in China, for example, was purchased by Qing officials and destroyed lest it upset the local economy and facilitate further foreign penetration of the empire. Nevertheless, as the web of railroad lines grew denser on every inhabited continent and the continents themselves were connected by the tissue of shipping lines, steam may indeed be said to be the power behind the creation of modern global society.

The Tools of Empire. Steam power allowed European colonizers and explorers to penetrate into the heart of hitherto inaccessible regions, such as this paddle steamer, the *Ma Roberts*, chugging up the Lower Zambezi in southern Africa in 1859. The bull elephant in the foreground roars in defiance, and while it appears the shooters on deck have missed their mark, the mood of the painting suggests that time is on their side.

Questions

• How does the innovation of steam power show the culmination of a pattern that began with the rise of the New Science in western Europe in the sixteenth and seventeenth centuries?

• Does Frederic A. Bartholdi's statement in 1876 that the Corliss steam engine "had the beauty and almost the grace of the human form" reflect a romantic outlook? If so, how?

mines. For more than a century, miners had used track-mounted cars to pull loads of coal and iron out of mines. By the 1820s experiments were already under way to attach Watt-type engines to moving carriages. In 1825, under the guidance of British engineer and inventor George Stephenson (1781–1848), the first freight line, the Darlington–Stockton, and in 1829–1830 the first passenger line, the Manchester–Liverpool, were opened; and travelers thrilled to the astonishing speeds of 15–20 miles per hour. This newfound speed, efficiency, and capability of moving passengers and freight resulted in a British railroad boom. Whereas in 1840 Great Britain counted only 1,800 miles of rail, by 1870 the figure had jumped nearly ninefold to 15,600 miles. Railroads not only vastly improved the shipping of coal and other bulk commodities but also greatly enhanced the sale and distribution of manufactures of all kinds. The railroad itself developed into a self-sustaining industry, employing thousands in all sorts of related jobs and spurring further investment by wealthy entrepreneurs.

Steamships   Although their impact was realized somewhat later, the application of steam to ships had far-reaching ramifications, especially in the second half of the nineteenth century. Credit for the first practical steam-powered riverboat goes to the American engineer and inventor Robert Fulton (1765–1815). Fulton's *Clermont*, constructed in 1807, plied the Hudson River from New York to Albany. English engineers were quick to copy Fulton's lead; by 1815 there were 10 steamboats busy hauling coal across the Clyde River in Scotland. In 1816 a steamship sailed from Liverpool to Boston in 17 days, cutting the transatlantic journey to one-half the time taken by sailing ships. In 1838 the *Great Western* began regular transatlantic service; its initial crossing from Bristol to New York took only 19 days. During the 1820s and 1830s steamboats were in regular use on Europe's principal rivers: the Rhine, the Danube, the Rhône, the Seine, and others. During the same time they played a vital role in opening up the Great Lakes and the Ohio and Mississippi Rivers to commerce in the United States. The year 1839 saw the inauguration of regular transatlantic steamship service from England to New York; 2 years later the famous Cunard line was founded. Then, during the 1830s and 1840s the British East India Company used iron-hulled steamers to facilitate maritime trade with its markets in India. Military uses soon presented themselves as well: as we will see in Chapter 24, the innovative iron-clad steam gunboat *Nemesis* shocked its opponents with its durability, mobility, and firepower during the Anglo–Chinese Opium War of 1839–1842.

An important innovation in maritime steam navigation was the development of the screw propeller in the late 1830s. Paddle-wheeled oceangoing ships tended to be top-heavy, and their "walking-beam" drive mechanisms and the paddle wheels themselves were vulnerable to damage in bad weather or, in the case of warships, to hits from enemy fire. The fast-turning screw propeller, in line with the ship's keel and rudder below the water line, proved far less troublesome and allowed all the moving parts of the engine and power train to be enclosed and protected. Still, paddle steamers remained in wide use until the latter part of the century and were the preferred system in shallow-draft river steamers.

The Spread of Early Industrialism

By the 1830s, in Belgium, northern France, and the northern German states—all of which had coal reserves—conditions had grown more suitable for industrialization than earlier when wages were low. More settled political conditions after the Napoleonic Wars led to population increases, contributing to higher consumer demand. At the same time, larger urban areas provided greater pools of available workers for factories. Moreover, within these regions improved networks of roads, canals, and now railways facilitated the movement of both raw materials to industrial centers and manufactured goods to markets. For example, in 1840 only 400 miles of rail were in existence in German territories, but that figure soared to 3,500 in 1850 and then to 11,150 in 1870. In addition, governmental involvement greatly enhanced the investment climate; protective tariffs for manufactures and the gradual removal of internal toll restrictions, particularly in the northern German states, opened up the trading industry.

The United States   Industrialism was imported to the United States toward the end of the eighteenth century by Samuel Slater (1768–1835), a British engineer. Known as the "father of the American Industrial Revolution," Slater established the first water-powered textile factory, in Rhode Island in 1793. By 1825 factories in the northeastern section of the country were producing vast quantities of textile goods on mechanically powered looms.

After a brief interruption during the American Civil War—during which the majority of factories on both sides were engaged in producing munitions and war materiel—industrialization in America resumed at a greatly accelerated pace. As production data indicate, by 1870 America was producing far more spindles of cotton than Great Britain, and its production of iron ingots was swiftly catching up to that of British and European producers. By 1914 the United States had become the world's single largest industrial economy.

In addition to manufacturing, trade and commerce across the vast span of the American continent were facilitated by a national network of railroads, which swiftly took over the carrying trade from the canal networks created in the early nineteenth century. Data for US rail construction show this astonishing growth: only 2,800 miles of rail in 1840 but 9,000 in 1850. At the conclusion of the Civil War there were already about 35,000 miles of railroads in the country—more than the rest of the world combined—though many were still of different gauges. By 1869 the first transcontinental single-gauge railroad was joined with a final golden spike at Promontory Point, Utah, resulting in an astonishing total of 53,000 rail miles by 1870.

Later Industrialism, 1871–1914

In many ways the next stage of industrialism, often referred to as "the second Industrial Revolution," grew out of the first phase. Perhaps the best measure of the difference in the two periods, however, is that while the first stage relied upon steam power, the second introduced several high-technology innovations that taken together altered the course not only of the Industrial Revolution but also of world history. Among the most significant of these were three major innovations: steel, electricity, and chemicals (see Map 23.2).

New Materials: Steel   A significant element in the second Industrial Revolution was the increasing use of steel instead of iron. Refined techniques of making steel had existed for many hundreds of years in different parts of the world but were largely the province of highly skilled craftspeople such as swordsmiths. New

The Industrialization of Europe by 1914

Major railway lines, 1914

Industry in 1870:
- Coal mining
- Iron working
- Textile production

Industry in 1914:
- Steel
- Shipbuilding
- Chemicals
- Electrical industry

MAP **23.2** **The Industrialization of Europe by 1914.**

technical advances, however, now made it possible to produce large quantities of high-grade *cheap* steel. The first of these was made in Britain by Henry Bessemer (1813–1898) in 1856, who devised a way to increase its carbon content in his "Bessemer Converter." Subsequent improvements in production soon followed in the 1860s and 1870s with the advent of the blast furnace and the open-hearth smelting method.

Following the conclusion of the Franco–Prussian war, Germany's annexation of the ore-rich regions of Alsace-Lorraine led to a dramatic increase in industrial production. Starting with almost no measurable steel production in the 1870s, Germany managed to catch up to British annual steel production in 1893 and then went on to surge far ahead: By 1914 its annual tonnage of steel was more than twice that of Britain. One advantage enjoyed by Germany was that it was able to model its new industrial facilities on those of its most modern competitors, saving substantial time and investment capital and resulting in newer and more efficient equipment and business methods. Yet another advantage was Germany's development of sophisticated research capabilities at universities, particularly in the sciences.

The advantages of steel over iron were that it was lighter, harder, and more durable. Thus, it provided better rails for railroads and, increasingly, girders for the construction of high-rise buildings. Indeed, structural steel and steel-reinforced concrete made possible the construction of high-rise "skyscrapers," which by the turn of the century were soaring past the tallest masonry buildings. The switch from iron to steel construction of ships also marked a significant advance in steamship technology during the third quarter of the nineteenth century. Steel ships greatly improved the travel time between far-flung continents. By 1900, 95 percent of all commercial ocean liners were being constructed of steel. Steel made possible stronger, faster, and roomier ships, while steel warships also proved far more durable in battle and set the tone for naval construction to this day.

Chemicals   Advances were also made in the use of chemicals. Here, the most significant developments were initiated by academic scientists, whose work resulted in later advances in the chemical industry. In 1856 the first synthetic dye, mauveine, was created, which initiated the synthetic dyestuffs industry. The result was not only a wider array of textiles but also new chemical compounds important in the refinement of wood pulp products, ranging from cheaper paper in the 1870s to artificial silk, referred to as "rayon." Later discoveries, such as the synthesizing of ammonia and its conversion to nitrates for use in fertilizers and explosives, were to have far-reaching effects during World War I. Associated with advances in chemical experimentation was the invention of dynamite by the Swedish chemist and engineer Alfred Bernhard Nobel (1833–1896). This powerful new explosive provided the means to blast through rock formations, resulting in great tunnels and massive excavation projects like the Panama Canal (1914). In yet another chemical advance, Charles Goodyear (1800-1860) invented a process in 1839 that produced vulcanized rubber; and celluloid—the first synthetic plastic—was developed in 1869. Additional offshoots, ranging from pharmaceuticals and drugs like aspirin to soap products, contributed to healthier lifestyles. By the early part of the twentieth century, these developments had led to a "hygiene revolution" among the industrialized countries.

New Energies: Electricity   Although electricity had been in use during the first period of industrialization, its development and application were greatly advanced after 1850, especially in the generation of electrical power. The first step came with Michael Faraday (1791–1867) patenting the electromagnetic generator in 1861. But large-scale electrical generation would require a number of other innovations before it became a reality. Perhaps the most important devices in this regard were developed by a relatively obscure engineer, Nikola Tesla (1856–1943). Among Tesla's inventions were alternating current (AC), the Tesla Coil (1891) for the more efficient transmission of electricity, and a host of generators, motors, and transformers. In 1888 the introduction of Tesla's "electric induction engine" led to the widespread adoption of electricity-generating power plants throughout industrialized Europe.

The first widespread use of electricity, however, had come earlier, in the realm of communications. Although electric telegraph messages were transmitted as early as the 1840s with the advent of Samuel F. B. Morse's (1791-1872) devices and code, it was only in the 1860s and 1870s that major continental landmasses were linked by submarine transoceanic cables. The first successful link from Britain to India was installed in 1865. The first transatlantic cable from Britain to America was laid as early as 1858, though it was only in 1866 that the cable was deemed operationally successful. By the latter part of the nineteenth century, telegraphic communication was a worldwide phenomenon, which has been likened to the Internet in its impact on human contact. This was vastly augmented with Alexander Graham Bell's (1847–1922) telephone in 1876, which made voice contact possible by wire.

But perhaps most revolutionary of all was the advent of wireless communication. The theoretical groundwork for this had been laid by James Clerk Maxwell (1831–1879), a Scottish physicist researching the theoretical properties of electromagnetism, and Heinrich Rudolf Hertz (1857–1894). In 1885 Hertz—whose name was later given to the units of measurement for radio wave cycles—discovered that electromagnetic radiation actually produces unseen waves that emanate through the universe. In the later 1890s, Guglielmo Marconi (1874–1937) developed a device using these radio waves generated by electric sparks controlled by a telegraph key to send and receive messages over several miles. By 1903 Marconi had enhanced the power and range of the device enough to send the first transatlantic radio message from Cape Cod in the United States to Cornwall in England. The "wireless telegraph" was quickly adopted by ships for reliable communication at sea. Subsequent improvements, such as the development of the vacuum tube amplifier and oscillator, resulted in greater power and reliability and, within a few years, the ability to transmit sound wirelessly.

New Energies: The Internal Combustion Engine

When oil, or liquid petroleum, was commercially developed in the 1860s and 1870s, it was at first refined into kerosene and used for illumination. One of the by-products of this process, gasoline, however, soon revealed its potential as a new fuel source. The first experimental internal combustion engines utilizing the new fuel appeared in the 1860s. Their light weight relative to their power was superior to steam engines of comparable size, and the first practical attempts to use them in powering vehicles came along in the next decade.

Who invented the automobile? Although it is usual to credit two Germans, Gottlieb Daimler (1834-1900) and Karl Benz (1844-1929), with the invention, the first true automobile was invented by an unheralded Austrian mechanic and inventor named Siegfried Marcus (1831–1898). As early as 1864 Marcus harnessed his own experimental internal combustion engine to a cart, which moved under its own power for over 200 yards. Over the next several years Marcus tinkered with several gadgets and devices in order to perfect his self-propelled contraption. Among these were the carburetor, the magneto ignition, various gears, the clutch, a steering mechanism, and a braking system. All of these inventions were incorporated in the first real combustion-engine automobile, which Marcus drove through the streets of Vienna in 1874.

Hiram Maxim. In this photo, taken in 1900, the proud inventor of the machine gun looks on with self-satisfied pride as Albert Edward, prince of Wales (the future King Edward VII), experiences for himself the awesome firepower of Maxim's "little daisy of a gun." In 1885 Maxim put on a similar demonstration for Lord Wolseley, commander-in-chief of the British Army. The British War Office adopted the gun 3 years later. The lethal power of the machine was first put to use in Africa at the Battle of Omdurman in 1898, where 20,000 Sudanese cavalrymen were slaughtered in fruitless charges against a line of 20 Maxim guns.

Internal combustion engines were also applied to early attempts at sustained flight. In 1900 Ferdinand von Zeppelin (1838–1917) constructed a rigid airship—a *dirigible*—consisting of a fabric-covered aluminum frame that was kept aloft by the incorporation of bags filled with hydrogen gas and powered by two 16-horsepower engines. Zeppelin's airships thus became the ancestors of the blimps that even today still ply the airways. Perhaps more momentous was the marriage of the gasoline engine to the glider, thus creating the first airplanes. Though there were several claimants to this honor, the Wright brothers in Kitty Hawk, North Carolina, on December 17, 1903, are usually credited with the first sustained engine-powered flight. By 1909, the first flight across the English Channel had been completed; in 1911 the first transcontinental airplane flight across the United States took place, though by taking 82 hours of flight time within a span of 2 months it could scarcely compete with railroad travel. Still, the potential of both the automobile and the airplane were to be starkly revealed within a few years during the Great War.

The Weapons Revolution   The advances in chemistry and explosives, metallurgy, and machine tooling during the second half of the nineteenth century also contributed to a vastly enhanced lethality among weapons. The earlier advances from the 1830s to the early 1860s that had included the percussion cap, the conical bullet, the revolver, and the rifled musket—all of which had made the American Civil War so deadly—now provided the base for the next generation of ever more sophisticated firearms. Breech-loading weapons, in their infancy during the early 1860s, rapidly came of age with the advent of the brass cartridge. By 1865, a number of manufacturers were marketing repeating rifles, some of whose designs, like the famous Winchester lever-action models, are still popular today. Rifles designed by the German firms of Krupp and Mauser pioneered the bolt-action, magazine, and clip-fed rifles that remained the staple of infantry weapons through two world wars.

Artillery went through a similar transformation. Breech-loading artillery, made possible by precision machining of breech-locks and the introduction of metallic cartridges for artillery shells, made loading and firing large guns far easier, faster, and more efficient. By the early 1880s the invention of the recoil cylinder—a spring or hydraulic device like an automobile shock absorber—to cushion the force of the gun's recoil eliminated the necessity of reaiming the piece after every shot. Field artillery could now be anchored, aimed, and fired continuously with enhanced accuracy: It had become "rapid-fire artillery." Its effectiveness was enhanced further by the new explosives like guncotton, dynamite, and later TNT, available for use in its shells. Another innovation in this regard was the development of smokeless powder, or *cordite*, which, in addition to eliminating much of the battlefield smoke generated by black powder, was three times more powerful as a propellant. Thus, the range and accuracy of small arms and artillery were pushed even further.

By far, the most significant—and lethal—advance in weaponry during the later nineteenth century, however, was the invention of the machine gun, the deadliest weapon ever developed, responsible for more deaths than any other device in history. Though many quick-firing weapons had been developed with varying degrees of success during these years—the most famous being the Gatling Gun (1861)—the first fully automatic machine gun was conceived by Hiram Maxim (1840–1916), an American inventor and dabbler in electricity. How he designed and manufactured the gun, first fired in 1884, along with how it was received and adopted by European states is recounted in Maxim's autobiography, *My Life* (1915), from which the accompanying excerpt is taken. Near the end of his memoir Maxim also recounts, somewhat ruefully, that he was applauded more highly for inventing his "killing machine" than for inventing a steam inhaler for those suffering from bronchitis.

By the outbreak of World War I, every major army in the world was equipping itself with Maxim's guns, now manufactured in licensed factories in Europe and the United States. Perhaps more than any other single weapon, the machine gun made the western front in Europe from 1914 to 1918 the most devastating killing field in human history.

> **Hiram Maxim on the Mechanics of His Machine Gun**
>
> "I first made an apparatus that enabled me to determine the force and character of the recoil, and find out the distance that the barrel ought to be allowed to recoil in order to do the necessary work. All the parts were adjustable, and when I had moved everything about so as to produce the maximum result, I placed six cartridges in the apparatus, pulled the trigger, and they all went off in about half a second. I was delighted.... I had made an automatic machine gun with a single barrel, using service cartridges, that would load and fire itself by energy derived from the recoil over six hundred rounds in a minute."
>
> —Hiram Maxim. *My Life* (London: Methuen, 1915), p. 170.

The Social and Economic Impact of Industrialism, 1750–1914

All of these changes in modes of production, particularly the emergence of the factory system, resulted in wholesale transformations in the daily lives of millions around the globe. Along with new networks of transportation, new materials, and new sources of energy, the industrialized nations underwent significant changes in the way they viewed politics, social institutions, and economic relationships across the period of industrialization.

Demographic Changes

Changes in the demographics of industrialized nations followed the development of new industries and consequent transformations in the lives of millions. Perhaps most significantly, the populations of these countries grew at unprecedented rates and became increasingly urbanized. Indeed, Great Britain became by the latter half of the nineteenth century the first country to have more urban dwellers than rural inhabitants. This trend would continue among the industrialized nations through the twentieth century.

Population Surge and Urbanization   As data from 1700 to around 1914 reveal, the industrialized nations experienced a significant population explosion (see Map 23.3). Advances in industrial production, expansion of factories, and improved agriculture during the first industrial revolution combined to produce increasing

MAP **23.3** **World Population Growth, 1700–1900.**

opportunities for jobs as well as more plentiful and nutritious food in order to sustain a larger population. In the second Industrial Revolution scientific advances in medicine, including medications and vaccinations, and notions of sanitation contributed to a declining mortality rate. For example, the population of Britain grew from around 9 million in 1700 to around 20 million in 1850. Then from 1871 to 1914 Britain's population soared from 31 million to nearly 50 million. Other industrialized states experienced similar population increases. In Germany much the same occurred: around 41 million in 1871 versus 58 million in 1914.

More revealing than overall population figures is the shift of populations away from rural areas and into urban areas. For example, in Great Britain in 1800 around 60 percent of the population lived in rural areas. By 1850, however, about

50 percent of the population lived in cities. In numerical terms, the population of London amounted to around 1 million in 1800, but by 1850 that figure had more than doubled to around 2.5 million. Moreover, in 1801 only 21 cities in Europe (including London) could boast of populations over 100,000. By 1850, this had more than doubled to 42. Significant in this respect were the appearance of new industrial and commercial centers such as Manchester, Liverpool, Birmingham, and Glasgow, as well as vast increases in the size of older capital cities such as Paris, Berlin, and St. Petersburg.

European Migrations   Another social change during the industrial era concerns emigrations of Europeans to foreign lands. In part, this movement was sparked

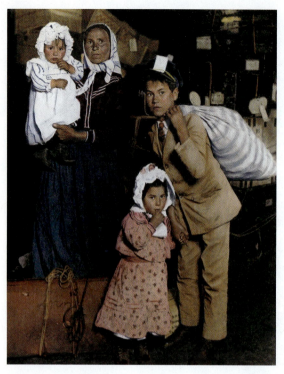

Italian Family at Ellis Island, New York, ca. 1905. This iconic photo of an Italian mother and her three children, taken by the photojournalist Lewis Hine and later hand colored, has come to portray the dreams of peace and prosperity that millions of immigrants to America brought with them in the late nineteenth and early twentieth centuries. The mother and her girls stare at the camera with dazed looks, but with a sack thrown jauntily on his back, the boy looks ready to explore his new world.

by the dramatic rise in population figures in industrialized areas of Europe. Another contributing factor, however, was the desire to escape the grinding poverty of underdeveloped regions of the West—particularly Ireland and southeast Europe—in order to seek better opportunities in developing industrial parts of the West. It should also be noted that advances in transportation, such as railroads and steamships, made it easier for Europeans to emigrate to foreign lands. In all, some 60 million Europeans left for other parts of the world (North and South America, Australia, and Asiatic Russia) between 1800 and 1914. Of these, the majority emigrated to the United States and Canada (see Map 23.4).

Industrial Society

Significant changes in the lower levels of society also occurred as a result of industrialization. Although the landed elites continued to enjoy their privileged status, they nevertheless began to lose ground to the rising middle classes. The principal alteration in social classes, however, was the appearance of a new class: the working class.

The Middle Classes   The prosperous middle classes, which included those in professional, administrative, educational, and commercial jobs, rose to prominence in the new age, thanks largely to their acquisition of liquid wealth. Distinguished from the landed aristocracy above them and from the working classes below, the middle classes themselves were divided into an upper class of wealthy industrialists, bankers, lawyers, and doctors at the top and tradespeople and handcrafters below.

These middle classes constituted around 15 percent of Europe's total population. It was this class that set the cultural and moral tone for most of the second half of the nineteenth century. What counted most in their eyes was "respectability"; not a hint of impropriety or sexual scandal was to be tolerated. As a measure of this, in 1867 the English Parliament passed the Obscene Publications Bill in an attempt to crack down on pornographic literature. The middle classes set themselves apart from the elites above and especially from those below by emphasizing what they considered their respectability, frugality, and industry. Indeed, with their emphasis on family and respectability, the morality of the middle classes during the reign of Britain's Queen Victoria inspired the adjective "Victorian" to describe a particular kind of prudish, self-disciplined—"earnest"—code of behavior. Determined to succeed at all costs, the middle classes eagerly consumed numerous self-improvement books, of which the most famous was Samuel Smiles's *Self Help* (1859). The book went through multiple editions in succeeding years and emerged as the most popular work on self-improvement in the Victorian era.

The Working Class   Urban factory workers were distinguished from farmers and workers in rural areas by their daily routine of regulation by the factory time clock and by selling their labor in return for cash wages. Among the working classes,

MAP **23.4** European Population Movements, 1750–1914.

divisions applied between skilled and unskilled workers, largely determined by familiarity with the intricacies of industrial machinery and its maintenance.

What were typical working conditions in British textile mills in the early 1800s? In a word, deplorable. In a new age when there were no traditional protective guilds or associations, workers were at the mercy of factory owners. The factory clock and the pace of factory machinery determined the day's work; the work was repetitive, dirty, and dangerous, not to mention dehumanizing. This was especially the case with young children—some as young 7 years—who either worked in factories alongside their parents as family units or had been orphaned or turned over to local parishes by parents who could no longer provide for their care. Working long hours—12- to 14-hour days were common in the early 1800s—children were constantly urged to speed up production and severely disciplined for "idling." Indeed, they were commonly beaten for falling asleep and to keep them from falling into the machinery, which, because of the lack of protection from its moving parts, could easily maim or kill them. In fact, until the 1840s in Britain, the majority of "hands," or factory workers, were women and children, who, by virtue of their inexperience and expendability, could be paid less than their male counterparts.

Conditions were often even worse in the mines. Children frequently began work in mines as early as age 6 or 7, most often as "trappers," responsible for opening and shutting ventilation doors in mineshafts. As they continued, they often moved up to "hurrying," or lugging newly dug coal along long, low underground passageways for conveyance to the surface. Girls were especially victimized in underground mines, where they not only had to drag heavy coal-filled carts by chains fixed to leather belts around their waists but also were frequently sexually abused by their supervisors.

Factory Towns Because industrial cities expanded close to factories and mills, conditions there generally mirrored those of the factories themselves. Clouds of coal smoke tended to hang over them, blackening buildings, acidifying the rain and soil, and often causing respiratory ailments among the citizens—prompting William

Working-Class Tenements in English Industrial Cities. In this engraving, entitled *Over London by Rail*, the celebrated engraver Gustave Doré (1832–1883) depicts the overcrowded and squalid living conditions in working-class tenements during the early years of the Industrial Revolution. Notice the long rows of houses separated by walls and arranged in back-to-back fashion. Notice also the stretched lines for drying clothes, as well as the large number of occupants in each outdoor area.

Blake's famous allusion to "dark Satanic Mills." In addition to the acrid smell of coal, there were usually a variety of other stenches assaulting the nostrils of the inhabitants. Piles of coal ash and clinkers, pungent waste materials from coking or from gas works, and vile outpourings from tanneries and dye-works all lent their smells to the more prosaic ones of household waste, sewage, and horse manure. With the population exploding and only rudimentary waste disposal and access to clean water, it was little wonder that diseases like cholera, typhus, and tuberculosis were rampant.

Adding to the miseries of the inhabitants were their wretched living conditions. The working classes lived in crowded tenements consisting of row after row of shoddily built houses packed together in narrow, dark streets. One social activist, Friedrich Engels (1820–1895), the son of a wealthy mill owner and later collaborator with Karl Marx, was determined to call attention to such abysmal conditions. As a young man Engels was sent to his father's cotton-producing factory in Manchester, England, to learn the factory system. What Engels observed there compelled him to write a scathing attack on the industrial movement, *The Condition of the Working-Class in England in 1844* (1845), in which he described what he perceived as the horrors of workers' lives.

Critics of Industrialism

It was not long before the criticisms of Engels and other socially conscious observers began to draw attention to the obvious abuses of the industrial movement and to stimulate reform of working conditions. Efforts to improve these sordid conditions were launched in Great Britain in the 1820s and 1830s and carried over into the 1870s.

The Laboring Quarters

"[R]ight and left a multitude of covered passages lead from the street into numerous courts, and he who turns in thither gets into a filth and disgusting grime.... In one of these courts there stands directly at the entrance, at the end of the covered passage, a privy without a door, so dirty that the inhabitants can pass into and out of the court only by passing through foul pools of stagnant urine and excrement."

—Friedrich Engels. *The Condition of the Working-Class in England in 1844* (London: Allen Unwin, 1943) p. 37

Socialists   The plight of the working classes caught the attention of a variety of social activists who determined to take up the fight for reform. Into the fray stepped several French and English "utopian socialists"—a term originally used derisively to describe the presumed impracticality of their schemes. One of the earliest of these activists was Henri de Saint-Simon (1760–1825), who presented a view of humanity that flew in the face of industrial society's competition for individual wealth. In Saint-Simon's view, private property should be more equally distributed, according to the notion that "from each according to his abilities, to each according to his works." Louis Blanc (1811-1882) criticized the capitalist system in his *The Organization of Work* (1839). In the book Blanc urged workers to agitate for voting rights, called for radical ideas like the right to work, and reconfigured Saint-Simon's memorable phrase to read "from each according to his abilities, to each according to his needs." Charles Fourier (1772–1837) advocated the founding of self-sustaining model communities in which jobs were apportioned according to ability and interest, with a sliding scale of wages tailored to highly compensate those doing the most dangerous or unattractive jobs. Fourier's concept of such "phalanxes" was the one adopted by the North American Phalanx, in which Mary Paul spent time (see the vignette to this chapter).

Robert Owen (1771–1858), a factory owner in the north of England, led a movement to establish the Grand National Consolidated Trades Union. Its objective was to call for a national strike of all trade unions, but owing to a lack of participation among workers, the movement was disbanded. Owen had previously established a model community in Scotland called "New Lanark," where more humane living and working conditions for workers resulted in greater profits. After campaigning for the formation of workers' unions, Owen left for America, where he set up a model socialist community in Indiana called "New Harmony," which eventually dissolved amid internal quarrels when he returned to England.

Chartism was another organized labor movement in Britain. Taking its name from the Peoples Charter (1838), chartism was formed by the London Working Men's Association; and its purpose was, among other issues, to call for universal male suffrage. Millions of workers signed petitions, which were presented to Parliament in 1839 and 1842; both were rejected. Nevertheless, the chartist movement galvanized for the first time workers' sentiments and aspirations, and it served as a model for future attempts at labor reform.

Karl Marx   By far the most famous of the social reformers was Karl Marx (1818–1883). The son of a prosperous German attorney, Marx proved a brilliant student, eventually earning a PhD in philosophy from the University of Berlin. Marx's activities, however, resulted in his being exiled from Germany and then from France. During a visit to the industrial center of Manchester, where he met and befriended Friedrich Engels, Marx observed both the miserable lives of factory workers and the patent inequities of industrialism. From this, Marx developed his theory, which he termed "scientific socialism," that all of history involved class struggles. Borrowing the dialectical schema of the German philosopher Georg Wilhelm Friedrich Hegel (1770–1831), Marx replaced its idealism with his own materialist concept based on economic class struggle: *dialectical materialism*. Moreover, Marx saw revolution as the means by which the industrial working classes will ultimately topple the capitalist order: Just as the Third Estate and bourgeoisie had overthrown the aristocracy during the French Revolution, the current struggle between the working classes and the capitalist entrepreneurs would ultimately result in the demise of capitalism.

Convinced of the need for the overthrow of the capitalist system, Marx and Engels joined the nascent Communist Party in London. In preparation for a meeting in 1848, the two collaborators dashed off a pamphlet entitled *The Communist Manifesto* (1848), a book that later on emerged as the bible for worldwide communism. The slender work is really a propaganda piece designed to rally support among the working classes, or *proletariat*, and to encourage them to rise up and overthrow the capitalist factory owners, or *bourgeoisie*. Compiled from a variety of

Karl Marx. In this photo, taken in London in 1875, Marx displays many of the character traits for which he is best known. Following the publication of his *Das Kapital* in 1871, Marx had established his reputation as a scholar of economic theory. Notice his self-satisfied and confident demeanor as he stares at the camera in an almost defiant manner. Notice as well his attire, ironically suggestive of a successful member of the bourgeoisie. After Marx's death, his longtime friend Friedrich Engels distributed 1,200 copies of this photo to communists around the world.

French socialist, German philosophical, and personal interpretations of past history, the *Manifesto* reflects Marx's vision that "the history of all hitherto existing society is the history of class struggle" and that the time had come for the working classes to follow earlier examples and to overthrow the capitalists: "The proletarians have nothing to lose but their chains. They have a world to win. WORKING MEN OF ALL COUNTRIES, UNITE!"

Inquiries and Reforms   As critics of industrialism began to cry out against obvious abuses of the industrial movement, many called for government efforts and programs for the reform of working conditions. Efforts to improve these horrid conditions were launched in Great Britain in the 1820s and 1830s. In 1832 Parliament launched an inquiry into abuses within factories. In 1833 the Factory Act was passed, which set a minimum age of 9 for child employees and limited the workday to 8 hours for children between the ages of 9 and 13 and to 12 hours for those aged 13–18. Similar inquiries were conducted concerning working conditions within mines. As a result, the Mines Act of 1842 forbade the underground employment of all girls and women and set a minimum age of 10 for child laborers.

Improved Standards of Living

Although still a matter of debate among historians, contemporary data suggest that in overall terms living and working conditions began to improve in Britain from around the 1830s to the end of the century. Thanks to the series of reforms already mentioned, conditions in factories and mines were substantially better than at the beginning of the century. Textile factories were now located in urban areas, and housing conditions for workers were more amenable. Most important, wage levels increased across the nineteenth century for industrial workers. For example, from 1850 to 1875 wages of British workers increased by around one-third and by nearly one-half by 1900.

New Jobs for Women   As a result of the second Industrial Revolution, many women fared far better in terms of employment. In overall terms, women represented around one-third of the workers in later nineteenth-century industrial jobs. Mary Paul's experience, discussed in the vignette at the beginning of this chapter, is one example of opportunities for women. Again, the data from these textile mills offer supporting evidence. While fewer than 2,000 women were employed in the mills in 1837, that figure nearly doubled by 1865; and by around 1900 the number of female textile workers had increased to nearly 6,000. But factory work in textile mills was not the only avenue opened to women as the industrial era unfolded in the later years of the nineteenth century.

When new technologies and social trends created new employment possibilities, women constituted a readily available pool of workers. Inventions like the typewriter (perfected in the 1870s), the telephone (invented by Alexander Graham Bell in 1876), and calculating machines (in use in the 1890s), for instance, required workers to handle related jobs, the majority of which went mostly to single women and widows. As a result, women became particularly prominent in secretarial office jobs. In addition, the explosion of business firms created countless jobs for secretaries, while department stores opened up jobs for women as clerks.

Women Working as Telephone Operators. The first telephone exchange appeared in 1879. In this image from 1881, women operators are shown at work at an early pyramidal switchboard. Women were selected as operators because their voices were considered pleasing to the ear and because they were considered more polite than men.

Women's Suffrage Movement   Although many women were afforded new opportunities in business and in professions like nursing and education after 1871, in many other areas women remained second-class citizens. Women in both the United States and Europe did not begin to gain the right to own property or to sue for divorce until the third quarter of the nineteenth century, as exemplified by the passage of the English Married Woman's Property Act in 1882.

More pressing in the eyes of many female reformers was the right to vote. Throughout Europe during the late nineteenth and early twentieth centuries, women formed political activist groups to press for the vote. The most active of these groups was in Britain, where in 1867 the National Society for Women's Suffrage was founded. The most famous—and most radical—of British political feminists was Emmeline Pankhurst (1858–1928), who together with her daughters formed the Women's Social and Political Union in 1903. They and their supporters, known as *suffragettes*, resorted to public acts of protest and civil disobedience in order to call attention to their cause. Although these tactics were of no avail prior to 1914, the right to vote was extended to some British women after the war (taken over from the British colony of New Zealand, which granted the right in 1893).

Political feminists were also active on the Continent. The French League of Women's Rights was founded in the 1870s, and the Union of German Women's Organizations was formed in 1894; in neither country was the right to vote granted women until after World War I. Women in the United States pursued a parallel course with similar results: After decades of lobbying before the war, women's suffrage was finally granted by constitutional amendment in 1920.

Emmeline Pankhurst. Pankhurst was arrested numerous times for her militancy and aggressive actions against the British government and its refusal to extend the suffrage to women. In this photo, taken on May 21, 1914, Pankhurst is shown being arrested outside Buckingham Palace after attempting to present a petition to King George V.

Improved Urban Living

Living conditions within the major urban areas in industrialized nations underwent significant improvements during the late nineteenth and early twentieth centuries. Largely the result of the application of new technologies emerging from the industrial movement, there is no question that the lives of urban dwellers were improved in the second half of the nineteenth century.

Sanitation and Electricity   One measure of improved living conditions was in the provision of better sanitation. A first of its kind was the Public Health Bill (1848) in Britain, followed by a further measure in 1875. Beginning in the 1860s and 1870s large cities in Britain and Europe established public water services and began to construct underground sewage systems to carry waste from houses, outfitted with running water, to rivers and other locations beyond urban areas. By the latter part of the nineteenth century, the widespread use of gas lighting gradually began to give way to electrical varieties. Thomas Edison (1847–1931) perfected the incandescent lightbulb in 1879, making the lighting of homes and business interiors more affordable and practical and gradually replacing gas lighting.

Paris represents a good example of the implementation of these reforms. In the 1850s and 1860s Napoleon III (r. 1852–1870) appointed the urban planner Georges Haussmann (1809–1891) to begin a massive reconstruction of the city. Haussmann tore down close-packed tenements in order to provide modernized buildings for residential and commercial use and to construct wide boulevards. This was in part driven by a desire to beautify the city, but it was also driven by the necessity of providing better access for government troops in the event of public demonstrations; barricaded streets, a feature of the revolutions of 1830 and 1848, thus became a thing of the past. And, like most cities of the industrialized West by the turn of the

The Great Stink. In the summer of 1858 the combination of a heat wave and unusually slow flow in the Thames resulted in one of London's worst modern health threats. The smell was so vile that shades treated with carbolic acid had to be mounted in the Houses of Parliament. The situation was also fair game for cartoonists, as depicted here. Beyond this, the incidence of waterborne diseases skyrocketed. The result was the building of a new citywide sewer and treatment system that vastly reduced the amount of raw sewage in the river.

PUNCH, OR THE LONDON CHARIVARI.—July 3, 1858.

DIPHTHERIA.   SCROFULA.   CHOLERA.

FATHER THAMES INTRODUCING HIS OFFSPRING TO THE FAIR CITY OF LONDON.
(A Design for a Fresco in the New Houses of Parliament.)

twentieth century, Paris featured lighted and paved streets, public water systems, parks, hospitals, and police.

A dramatic symbol of both the newly redesigned city of Paris and the triumph of industry and science during the second Industrial Revolution was the Eiffel Tower, designed and erected by Alexandre Gustave Eiffel (1832–1923). Constructed for the Paris Exposition of 1889, the tower took years to construct and, at nearly 1,000 feet in height, was the tallest structure in the world until the construction of the Empire State Building in New York in 1931.

Big Business

As the scale of urban planning and renewal increased toward the end of the nineteenth century, together with the size of buildings and other constructions, so did business. As manufacturing, transportation, and financing matured, entrepreneurs and businessmen became concerned about competition and falling profit rates. Since governments generally pursued hands-off liberalism (*laissez-faire*, see Chapter 22) in the economy, except for protective tariffs, entrepreneurs sought to establish cartels and monopolies, creating big business enterprises in the process.

Eiffel Tower and Paris Exposition, 1900. Although it was reviled as an eyesore by many when it was first constructed, the Eiffel Tower emerged as one of the world's great symbols of industrial elegance. It was the centerpiece—along with the great globe next to it and the Palace of Electricity—of the Great Exhibition in Paris in 1900, pictured above.

Large Firms   When Britain industrialized, it gradually shifted from a closed mercantilist economy to the liberal free-trade policy Adam Smith advocated (see Chapter 22). Britain's competitors, especially Germany and the United States, by contrast, erected high tariff walls around their borders in order to help their fledgling industries. After the second wave of steel, chemical, and electricity industrialization in the second half of the nineteenth century, the scale of industrial investments rose exponentially. On domestic markets, governments did not interfere with business organization and practice, except for labor protection in Europe. As a result, in several branches of the economy, big businesses emerged during the second half of the nineteenth century that protected their profit rates through *cartels* (market-sharing agreements) or strove altogether for monopolies.

Large firms typically developed in Germany and the United States, the leaders of the second wave of industrialization. Corporations like the Krupp steelworks in Germany and Standard Oil Company in the United States had evolved by the 1890s, controlling large shares of their markets. Standard Oil at its height, for example, produced over 90 percent of the country's petroleum. Another example is the United States Steel Company, founded in 1901 by Andrew Carnegie (1835–1919), which dominated the production of American steel. Carnegie himself amassed a huge personal fortune of almost $250 million, making him the richest man in the world.

New Management Styles   In addition, new technologies in all industrial sectors offered more efficient means of production; the result was a series of significant changes in production processes during the second phase of European industrialism. One example is the implementation of the so-called American System, incorporating the use of interchangeable parts, which greatly enhanced mass production. A related development was the appearance of "continuous-flow production," wherein workers

The Assembly Line. The American System of interchangeable parts for muskets of the early nineteenth century had evolved into the assembly line by the early twentieth. Here, Ford Model T automobiles are moved along a conveyor to different stations, where workers assemble them in simple, repetitive steps, resulting in production efficiency and low prices for the cars.

performed specialized tasks at stationary positions along an assembly line. In addition, new "scientific management" tactics were employed in mass-production assembly plants. Since no more than basic skills were required on many assembly lines, labor costs could be kept low.

The best known of the new management systems was "Taylorism," named after Frederick W. Taylor (1856–1915), an American engineer. The objective was to measure each factory worker's production based on how many units were completed in an hour's time. The result was that workers were not only more carefully managed by their superiors but also paid in accordance with their productivity. The combined result was a rapid escalation in the speed of production, which in turn contributed to a marked increase in the production of goods for daily consumption and, therefore, in the development of a consumer market at the turn of the twentieth century.

Intellectual and Cultural Responses to Industrialism

The new society that industrialism was creating not surprisingly spawned entirely new directions in science, philosophy, religion, and the creative fields such as literature and art. It generated new kinds of popular expression, from dime novels to photography. The advent of *mass society* also led to the beginnings of a mass culture, in which widespread literacy and public education allowed a far greater percentage of the populace access to what had largely been the province of elites. It allowed artists, writers, composers, and musicians to have mass followings for the first time. Men and women like Charles Dickens, Harriet Beecher Stowe, and Richard Wagner, to name only three, were the popular equivalent of today's "superstars" in their own time. Yet, there was also a profound disquiet among scientists, intellectuals, and artists. With so many of the old standards falling by the wayside, tremendous uncertainty was present just underneath the surface of material progress. This disquiet would come to the surface with a vengeance in the immediate years after World War I.

Scientific and Intellectual Developments

The latter half of the nineteenth century saw advances in both theoretical and empirical sciences that laid the basis for many of the staples of the twentieth century. Among the most far-reaching were atomic physics and relativity theory, Darwinism and evolution, and the foundations of modern psychology. Scientists also laid the foundations for medicine, although here the most important breakthroughs had to await the twentieth century.

New Theories of Matter   Quests for understanding the nature of matter, under way since Galileo (see Chapter 17), became systematic with the foundation of technical universities and science faculties in existing universities in the second half of the 1800s. Researchers carried out extensive experiments and made important discoveries in the 1890s that would have far-reaching consequences in defining atomic physics and theories of relativity. In 1892 the Dutch physicist Hendrik Lorentz (1853–1928) demonstrated that the atom, far from being a solid billiard ball, actually contained smaller particles, which he named "corpuscles"; these were later renamed "electrons." A few years later, Wilhelm Roentgen (1845–1923) discovered a mysterious form of emission he called "X-rays." The ability to generate these rays would shortly lead to using them in medical diagnoses and creating the modern X-ray machine. The following year, 1896, saw the first experiments in assessing radioactivity in uranium and radium by Antoine Becquerel (1852–1908) and Marie Curie (1867–1934).

As a result of these experimental findings, theoretical physics advanced new theories on the nature of light and energy. In 1900 Max Planck (1858–1947) proposed that instead of the accepted notion that energy is emitted in steady streams or waves, it is issued in bursts, or what he termed "quanta." This idea, later developed into quantum theory, suggested that matter and energy might be interchangeable. Ernest Rutherford (1871–1937), interested in this interchangeability, demonstrated in 1911 that radioactive atoms release a form of energy in the process of their disintegration. Thus, nearly three centuries of speculation about atoms as the building blocks of nature led to experimentally verified theories of subatomic particles.

Albert Einstein   These discoveries in the physical sciences set the stage for the appearance of perhaps the most sensational of the turn-of-the-century scientific theories: Albert Einstein's (1879–1955) theory of relativity. In 1905 and then again in 1915 Einstein published papers in which he destroyed the Newtonian notion of a certain, absolute, and mechanistic universe that obeys unvarying and objectively verifiable laws. Instead, Einstein argued that there are no absolutes of time, space, and motion; rather, these are relative to each other and depend on the position of the observer.

Moreover, Einstein demonstrated that Newton was incorrect in thinking that matter and energy were separate entities; they were, in fact, equivalent and he developed the corresponding mathematical formula. In his equation $E = mc^2$, Einstein theorized that the atom contains an amount of energy equal to its mass multiplied by the square of the speed of light. In other words, relatively small amounts of matter could convert into massive amounts of energy. This discovery, developed further in the twentieth century, provided the foundation for a full understanding of the forces among subatomic particles and the construction of nuclear weapons.

Charles Darwin   The basis of modern theories of evolution was laid by Charles Darwin (1809–1882). Darwin's *On the Origin of Species by Means of Natural Selection* (1859) argued that in nature species gradually evolved from lower to higher forms. As a young man Darwin sailed on an exploratory mission on the H.M.S. *Beagle* from 1831 to 1836 to the waters off the South American coast in the Pacific. Observing the tremendous variability of species in the string of the isolated Galapagos Islands, he found himself at a loss to explain why so many different species cohabited within such close geographical areas.

It occurred to Darwin—and independently to another English naturalist, Alfred Russell Wallace (1823–1913)—that an explanation for the appearance of new

Charles Darwin as Ape.
Darwin's theories about the
evolution of humankind
aroused enormous scorn. In this
scathing 1861 cartoon, Darwin,
with the body of a monkey,
holds a mirror to a simian-
looking creature. The original
caption quoted a line from
Shakespeare's *Love's Labor Lost*:
"This is the ape of form."

species in nature might lie in the struggle for food: Only those species equipped with the tools to survive in their environments would win out; those without these characteristics would become extinct.

In its essence, therefore, the Darwinian theory of evolution as spelled out in the *Origin* boils down to three main elements: (1) in nature more species appear than can be supported by existing food supplies, (2) there is a resultant struggle among species to survive, and (3) through inheritance subtle mutations within species are transmitted that render some more able than others to survive in the struggle for food. The most controversial part of this theory rests in the notion that characteristics are passed on by means of "natural selection." In other words, there is no intelligence or plan in the universe—only random chance and haphazard process, resulting in a pessimistic view of "nature red in tooth and claw."

Although the *Origin* said nothing about the theory of evolution as applied to humankind—this appeared later in the *Descent of Man* (1871)—there were those who quickly applied it to society and nations. As noted in other chapters in this section, the work of Herbert Spencer (1820–1903) was instrumental in proposing a theory that came to be called "social Darwinism," which sought to apply ideas of natural selection to races, ethnicities, and peoples. Spencer's ideas were frequently used to support imperial ventures aimed at the conquest and sometimes the "uplift" of non-European or American peoples as well as to justify increasingly virulent nationalism in the years leading to World War I.

Developments in Psychology   The first scientist to separate psychology from philosophy and to make it a serious scientific discipline was Wilhelm Wundt (1832–1920). A German physiologist and student of human behavior, Wundt established the first psychology laboratory in 1879, where he conducted early experiments on aspects of human behavior.

Increasingly important among psychologists was the topic of insanity. What especially concerned Victorians were apparently unconscious impulses for actions not subject to human will. The best known of the early psychologists was Sigmund Freud (1856–1939), an Austrian physician. After obtaining a degree in medicine in Vienna, Freud studied cases of emotionally disturbed patients in Paris, and then in 1886 he set up his own practice in Vienna. Freud specialized in treating patients suffering from what was then called "hysteria," which he treated using a technique he labeled "psychoanalysis." In 1900 Freud published his highly influential *The Interpretation of Dreams*, in which he drew connections between dreams and the unconscious in humans. Although controversial, and today largely discarded, Freud's theories stressed the dominance of unconscious urges and motivations—mostly sexual in nature—in determining human behavior. The sum total of Freudian psychological theories is that humans, so far from being rational creatures, are in fact irrational creatures, driven by subconscious, and not conscious, urges. Today, it no longer enjoys the unquestioned dominance it once did in the field and has largely become a branch of medicine and, in particular, the study of brain chemicals. But it still survives on the practical level in the form of lifestyle counseling and behavior modification.

The Meaning of the New Scientific Discoveries   Physics, biology, and psychology were not the only sciences contributing fundamentally to the emergence of scientific–industrial society at the end of the nineteenth century. Medicine began to acquire a scientific character, for example, with the discoveries of vaccines by Louis Pasteur (1822–1895). But it had to await the twentieth century before it reached maturity. With the arrival of the theories of relativity, Darwinian selection, and the psychological unconscious, however, enough of a transition toward the scientific–industrial age had occurred to throw people into deep philosophical and religious confusion.

In a sense, the path of reductionism begun in the seventeenth century and discussed in Chapter 17 was being reached. In previous centuries, the Hobbesian embodied mind, fear of death,"war of all against all," and the religious skepticism, secularism, and atheism of the Enlightenment were merely speculations that remained ultimately unproved. Now, the specter of a meaningless universe inhabited by beings devoid of free will and driven by biological forces over which they have no control seemed to many to be inescapable. Thus, the new era seemed to usher in a profoundly disturbing devil's bargain: The sciences had created so many useful things to ease the burdens of human life but had taken away the sense of purpose that made that life worth living. It was left to philosophers, religious leaders, intellectuals, and artists to wrestle with the implications of this central problem of scientific–industrial society.

Toward Modernity in Philosophy and Religion

Despite the impressive achievements of Western industrialized society during the late nineteenth century, there were many who felt uneasy about the results. Scores of detractors—mostly in the intellectual community of western Europe—decried the boastful claims of a "superior" scientific civilization. These voices ridiculed Western bourgeois values and advocated alternative approaches to personal fulfillment.

Friedrich Nietzsche   Easily the most celebrated of these detractors was the German philosopher Friedrich Nietzsche (1844–1900). A brilliant, but increasingly mentally unstable, professor at the University of Basel, Nietzsche railed against the conventions of Western civilization and criticized the perceived decadence of modern culture. Nietzsche represents a growing trend toward pessimism and doubt about the progress of Western culture near the end of the nineteenth century.

Nietzsche began his assault on Western culture in 1872 with the publication of *The Birth of Tragedy*, which was followed in later years by works like *Beyond Good and Evil* (1886) and *On the Genealogy of Morals* (1887). One object of derision for Nietzsche was the entire notion of scientific, rational thought as the best path toward intellectual truth. For Nietzsche, and for others of like mind, rational thought will not improve either the individual or the welfare of humankind; only recourse to "will" instead of intellect—what Nietzsche called the "will to power"—will suffice.

The individual who follows this path will become a "Superman" and will lead others toward truth.

Another target of Nietzsche's wrath was Christianity, which in his eyes led its believers into a "slave morality"; and in a famous quote, he declared that "God is dead."

Roman Catholicism

As might be expected, the various religious establishments of the West were forced into a defensive position by the growing prestige and influence of the sciences. Although mainstream Protestant leaders tended to urge accommodation with scientific progress—though they struggled considerably with the implications of Darwinism—the Catholic Church was more inclined to resist both the allure of science and the appeal of materialism and capitalism. Pope Pius IX for example, staunchly resisted the drift toward modernism by issuing the encyclical entitled "Syllabus of Errors" in 1864 and by convening the First Vatican Council in 1871.

With the death of Pius IX in 1878, however, the church adopted a new position under the leadership of Pope Leo XIII (r. 1878–1903). On the one hand, Leo mounted a full-scale offensive against what he considered an alarming trend toward secular materialism by urging Catholic workers to form socialist unions and workers' parties. In 1891 Leo XIII issued "De Rerum Novarum" ("On Modern Things"), in which he criticized capitalism for widening the gulf between the haves and the have-nots in the age of industrialism. On the other hand, Leo made slight concessions to science and the study of the sciences by Catholics and by establishing a Vatican office to look into scientific advances. Leo XIII's successor, Pope Pius X (r. 1903–1914), reversed these moves of moderation and criticized those who supported the church's reconciliation with science.

Toward Modernity in Literature and the Arts

As we have seen throughout this chapter, the creation of scientific–industrial society—modernity—was a slow and excruciatingly traumatic process. The social

A Blemish on Mankind

"I call Christianity the one great curse, the one enormous and innermost perversion, the one great instinct of revenge, for which no means are too venomous, too underhanded, too underground and too petty—I call it the one immortal blemish of mankind."

—Friedrich Nietzsche. *The Antichrist* (1888). Trans. with introduction by H. L. Mencken (New York: Knopf, 1918), p. 62.

Kulturkampf. The "conflict of cultures" between church and state in Germany reached its peak in the 1870s. In this cartoon from the period, the German chancellor Otto von Bismarck appears to have the upper hand in a game of political chess against Pope Pius IX.

realities of interacting and adapting to the new order were already on painful display in the post-romantic period of realism in the arts and literature that marked the second third of the nineteenth century (see Chapter 22). The succeeding decades were to yield what in many ways was an even grimmer and more disjointed view of the new scientific–industrial society. On the one hand, many artists sought to combat what they perceived as the ugliness and shoddiness of the machine age by returning to handcrafting furniture and decorative items. In this arts and crafts movement, which thrived from the 1880s until the outbreak of World War I, William Morris (1834–1896) and John Ruskin (1819–1900) championed an idealized nostalgia for medieval motifs and techniques as the high point of European art. But a much darker and more despairing critique of the period was also present among writers and artists, which set the foundation for many of the movements that would emerge in the 1910s and 1920s.

Literature   Literary expression was generally negative toward the popularization of "soulless" science and the materialism of the second half of the industrial revolution. Thomas Hardy (1840–1928), for example, in his *Far from the Madding Crowd* (1874) emphasized the despair resulting from the futility of fighting against the grinding forces of modernity. The plays of George Bernard Shaw (1856–1950) reflect the influence of Darwin, Nietzsche, and others and mock the shallowness and pretension of urban, bourgeois *fin de siècle* ("end of the century") society. Around the mid-1880s two new genres in literature, decadence and symbolism, made their appearance. The decadents registered disgust with prevailing bourgeois conventions and pretensions. A good example is the French novelist J. K. Huysmans (1848-1907), whose *A Rebours* (*Against the Grain*, 1884) shocked the literary world with its unsettling, bizarre allusions to the weird and mysterious. Huysmans himself had flirted with Satanism before taking up Catholicism. For their part, symbolists preferred to revert to a form of the earlier romantic era and in the process to emphasize the ideal, the aesthetic, and the beautiful side of life. Symbolist poets of note are the Irishman William Butler Yeats (1865–1939) and the American T. S. Eliot (1888–1965), whose early works capture the essence of symbolist representation.

Modernism in Art   Like their counterparts in literature, artists in the period 1871–1914 were similarly confronted by the sweeping changes in life brought on by industrialism and science. Artists during the latter part of the nineteenth and early twentieth centuries were seldom content with the world around them and sought novel ways to express their often hostile attitudes. The world of artistic expression in this period, often grouped together under the heading "modernism," in fact consisted of a great variety of successive movements, all of them skeptical of accepted middle-class conventions and truths; and they became more and more abstract and "avant-garde" as the Great War approached.

The first group of painters was known as the "impressionists," and their style dominated from the 1870s until around 1890. The movement takes it name from a painting by Claude Monet (1840–1926) entitled *Impression, Sunrise* (1874). By around 1890 the impressionist school had been superseded by a more freewheeling style known as postimpressionism, which ran into the new century. The driving force of the new school of artists was to depict particularly subjective interpretations of things from the mind's eye of the artist. Perhaps the most famous of the postimpressionists was the

(b)

Modernism in Art. Perhaps the most iconic artwork of the new age of anxiety at the end of the nineteenth century is the painting by Norwegian artist Edvard Munch, *The Scream* (1893). Munch himself described it as deriving from an incident in which he was walking with friends when the sky turned "blood red" and he was overcome with feelings of exhaustion and "sensed an infinite scream passing through nature." It has come to represent everything from mental illness to the unbearable crises of meaning in the industrial age (*a*). Fourteen years later, Pablo Picasso's *Les Demoiselles d'Avignon* generated similar anxieties when it was unveiled in Paris in 1907 (*b*). Its distorted and broken forms of expression set in a fractured and flattened space mark a conscious break with the Western artistic tradition. The painting's borrowing from "primitivist" African and ancient Iberian sources, and its forceful and unsettling depiction of *demoiselles*, a euphemism for prostitutes, unsettle the viewer.

(a)

Dutch painter Vincent Van Gogh (1853–1890), whose lurid anti-realist colors and twisted forms were intended as expressions of his mind. His life, ending in suicide, reflects the often tormented sensibilities of the modernists' reaction to scientific–industrial modernity.

The period of art history from 1905 to 1914 saw numerous offshoots of the postimpressionists, each one more revolutionary and experimental than the last. These various artistic "schools" truly represent the beginnings of twentieth-century avant-garde art. Perhaps the best known of these, cubism, is represented in the works of Pablo Picasso (1881–1973). Picasso stretched fascination with geometrical forms to their limits to deliberately fly in the face of accepted artistic conventions. In such works as *Les Demoiselles d'Avignon* (1907), for example, often considered the first of the cubist paintings, Picasso reveals his interest in African masks as an alternative to conventional European motifs.

Modernism in Music

The musical arts departed from other forms of expression in their development during the second half of the nineteenth century. The compositions of Liszt, Brahms, and Wagner were in many respects extensions of the early romantics and adhered to classical forms. During the 1870s, however, and especially after the death of Wagner in 1883, musical expression followed two separate tracks until 1914. One of these tracks is known as "modernism," which was more attuned to cultural developments evolving in other fields during the waning years of the nineteenth century and early years of the twentieth. Some musicians fell in line with the experiments of the impressionists. As might be expected, many of these were Frenchmen, including Claude Debussy (1862–1918) and Maurice Ravel (1875–1937). Debussy, for example, sought to establish a misty mood and dreamy atmosphere in his compositions.

More in line with emerging modernist trends in the period 1905–1914 was a movement in music often labeled "primitivism." Here, a series of composers set out to abandon the constraints of formal structure and convention and to express their personal musical perceptions. Perhaps best known of this school is the Russian composer Igor Stravinsky (1882–1971). Stravinsky's most famous—if not notorious—work was *Le Sacre du printemps* (*The Rite of Spring*), first performed in Paris on May 29, 1913. The work was so unconventional and dissonant that its first performance in Paris touched off 3 days of rioting in the streets.

Other musicians were even more outrageous and unconventional—and more typical of avant-garde rejections of Western musical conventions. In 1908 the Austrian composer and theoretician Arnold Schoenberg (1874–1951) deliberately began to compose pieces that abandoned the traditional tonal system of Western music in favor of atonality. In his *Theory of Harmony* (1911), Schoenberg proudly announced the inauguration of a new, modern style of musical composition, in which themes reflecting Freudian theories of the unconscious along with the noises and dissonances of engines, machines, and urban life would now dominate musical composition.

Putting It All Together

The series of dramatic and sweeping changes associated with the Industrial Revolution had profound implications for both the industrializing countries and the nonindustrialized world. Thanks in large part to new technologies and facilitated by advances in transportation and communication, the period from 1871 to 1914 saw world trade networks and empires dominated by the newly industrialized nations.

The Industrial Revolution began in Britain in the early eighteenth century and eventually spread to Europe and North America during the nineteenth century. Britain began the revolution when it harnessed steam engines to the rapid production of textiles. The subsequent development of the factory system along with more efficient transportation systems facilitated by railroads greatly expanded British manufacturing. Not everyone benefited, however, from the emergence of the factory system; capitalist entrepreneurs were reluctant to share with workers their slice of the economic pie, which in turn led to social unrest and calls for reform.

During the second Industrial Revolution in the later nineteenth century, advanced technologies led to the development of steel, electricity, and chemicals, which in turn greatly expanded the industrial economies of highly industrialized countries beyond Britain, including those of America and Germany. The daily lives of most citizens in industrialized nations were also improved by the application of industrial technologies to advances in transportation, communication, and even safety and sanitation.

These same advances also contributed to a new and greatly expanded surge of European imperialism. The explosive growth of industry and commerce, aided and abetted by new technologies and inventions, resulted in a quest among highly industrialized nations for raw materials, cheap labor, and new markets in order to sustain and expand their developing industries (see Concept Map). Moreover, Western industrial nations soon discovered that new needs forced the importation of not only raw materials but also foodstuffs. It is important to point out that nineteenth-century imperialism was made possible in the first place by technological innovations associated with advances in science and industrialism. Quinine prophylaxis, steam-powered gunboats, rapid-firing breechloaders, and the machine gun provided the overwhelming firepower to subdue nonindustrial societies and to open up interior regions of continents to Western colonialism. By the 1880s sailing ships were eclipsed by faster oceangoing ships powered by much more efficient compound engines and submarine cables provided for more efficient overseas communications and for the setting of more exact timetables. After 1871, the world's economy was increasingly divided into those who produced the world's manufactured products and those who both supplied the requisite raw materials and made up the growing pool of consumers.

Amid this process the basis for many of the patterns of twentieth-century modernity was being laid, as well as the foundations of its opposition. With the coming of World War I, and its aftermath, many of the cleavages created by modernity and its scientific–technological underpinnings were laid bare. Yet, as a new form of society,

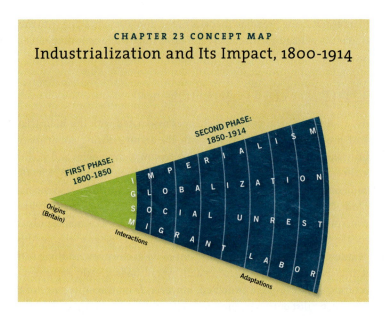

its interaction and adaptation with older forms continued unabated. Today, the two places that contain the largest number of "Mary Pauls" in world history—young women migrating from their farms to find work in urban factories—are the successors to the agrarian–urban religious civilizations that held out against the new order most tenaciously: India and China, both of whose economies now increasingly set the pace for twenty-first century industrial development. It is the story of the impact of modernity on these societies and others around the globe to which we now turn (see Concept Map).

Review and Respond

1. How was the steam engine originally used in the Industrial Revolution, and with what results?

2. How did industrialization improve daily life in Europe and the United States during the nineteenth century? What were the negative effects of industrialization?

3. Discuss the origin and development of negative reactions to the industrial movement.

4. Do you agree or disagree with the following statement: The expansion of Western imperialism in the nineteenth century reflects the positive contributions of inventions and technological advances emanating from industrialism.

5. Discuss and analyze ways in which the steady advance of industrialism during the second Industrial Revolution provoked responses from the scientific, intellectual, and cultural communities toward the turn of the twentieth century.

▶ For additional resources, including maps, primary sources, visuals, and quizzes, please go to www.oup.com/us/vonsivers. Please see the Further Resources section at the back of the book for additional readings and suggested websites.

Thinking Through Patterns

▶ **Where and when did the Industrial Revolution originate?**

Because of several advantageous factors, the Industrial Revolution began in Britain in the early eighteenth century. Among these were an earlier political revolution that empowered the merchant classes over the landed aristocracy, along with a prior agricultural revolution, and abundance of raw materials like coal.

Industrialization resulted in several social changes and adjustments. The capitalist middle classes were enriched and empowered by the growth of industrialism, as were the working classes, which did not exist as a group prior to industrialism. The benefits of industrialism were not evenly distributed across social strata; factory and mine workers were frequently exploited by the entrepreneurial and prosperous middle classes.

▶ **What were some effects of industrialization on Western society? How did social patterns change?**

▶ **In what ways did industrialization contribute to innovations in technology? How did these technological advances contribute to Western imperialism in the late nineteenth century?**

With the invention and perfection of the steam engine, capitalist entrepreneurs were able to substitute mechanical power for natural power and, thus, to develop the factory system. The factory system spread to the Continent and America as middle-class capitalism eclipsed mercantilism. Further advances contributed to a second Industrial Revolution after ca. 1850 that emphasized steel, chemistry, and electricity.

Progress in industrial technology during the second Industrial Revolution led to innovations ranging from practical inventions like the lightbulb to advances in communication and transportation. Inventions developed from industrial advances included the machine gun, new medicines, and startling developments in communications, to name a few. These tools facilitated the expansion of Western imperialism in Africa and Asia during the closing years of the nineteenth century

The new society that industrialism was creating not surprisingly spawned entirely new directions in science, philosophy, religion, and the creative fields such as literature and art. It generated new kinds of popular expression, from dime novels to photography. The advent of *mass society* also led to the beginnings of a mass culture, in which widespread literacy and public education allowed a far greater percentage of the populace access to what had largely been the province of elites. Yet, there was also a profound disquiet among scientists, intellectuals, and artists. With so many of the old standards falling by the wayside, tremendous uncertainty was present just underneath the surface of material progress. This disquiet would come to the surface with a vengeance in the immediate years after World War I.

▶ **What new directions in science, philosophy, religion, and the arts did industrialism generate? What kind of responses did it provoke?**

Chapter 24

1750-1910

The Challenge of Modernity

EAST ASIA

> In Asia, our two countries, China and Japan, are the closest neighbors, and moreover have the same [written] language. How could we be enemies? Now for the time being we are fighting each other, but eventually we should work for permanent friendship . . . so that our Asiatic yellow race will not be encroached upon by the white race of Europe.

EAST ASIA 1750–1900

So commented Chinese statesman Li Hongzhang to his Japanese counterpart, Ito Hirobumi, as they discussed terms to end the Sino–Japanese War at the Japanese town of Shimonoseki in the spring of 1895. For Li it was the culmination of more than three decades of frustration as China's most powerful advocate of *self-strengthening*—using new foreign

Seeing Patterns

▶ What was the impact of Western imperialism on the "regulated societies" of China and Japan?

▶ Why did European empire building in Asia have such dramatically different effects on China and Japan?

▶ How have historians seen the nature of these outside forces and their influences in east Asia?

technologies and concepts to preserve China's Confucian society in the face of European and American intrusion. During Li's lifetime such intrusions had come with alarming frequency. Now, at 71, he was forced to go to Japan to sue for peace as Japanese troops occupied Korea and southern Manchuria. To add injury to insult, he had just narrowly survived being shot in the face by a Japanese fanatic while en route to the peace talks.

For Ito, one of the architects of Japan's astonishing rise to power, the victory over China was tinged with sadness and puzzlement as he responded: "Ten years ago when I was at Tientsin (Tianjin), I talked about reform with [you]. . . . Why is it that up to now not a single thing has been changed or reformed? This I deeply regret." As did Li, whose reply betrays a weary bitterness at China's deteriorating position: "At that time when I heard you . . . I was overcome with admiration . . . [at] your having vigorously changed your customs in Japan so as to reach the present stage. Affairs in my country have been so confined by tradition that I could not accomplish what I desired . . . I am ashamed of having excessive wishes and lacking the power to fulfill them."

The significance of this rueful exchange was not lost on the other countries with interests in east Asia, who viewed the war's outcome with a

Li Hongzhang and Ito at Shimonoseki. In this ukiyo-e print of the peace negotiations held in the Shunpanro Restaurant in the Japanese town of Shimonoseki in early 1895, Li Hongzhang, the chief Chinese diplomat is dressed in the reddish brown gown at the right side of the table. His Japanese counterpart, Ito Hirobumi, sits opposite him and wears a sash; to his left is the Japanese foreign minister Mutsu Munemitsu, also wearing a sash. John W. Foster, former U.S. Secretary of State and advisor to the Chinese during the negotiations, stands at the head of the table close to Li. Interestingly, the negotiations were conducted in English through interpreters.

mixture of fascination and alarm. Japan's surprisingly complete victory over China was cited as proof that it was now ready to join the ranks of the great powers. It also upset a shaky balance of power that required China's feeble Qing dynasty to not collapse altogether. Now Japan had dramatically raised the stakes. In addition to imposing a crippling indemnity on the Qing, reducing Korea to a client state, and annexing the island of Taiwan, the new Treaty of Shimonoseki called for the occupation by Japan of Manchuria's Liaodong Peninsula, which guarded the approaches to Beijing.

For Russia, France, and Germany, who saw their own interests threatened by this move, it was time to act. In what became known as the Triple Intervention, they threatened Japan with joint action if it did not abandon its claims to Liaodong. Unable to take on all three powers, the Japanese bitterly acquiesced. They grew more bitter the following year when the Qing secretly leased the territory to Russia in a desperate attempt to counter Japanese expansion. For the Japanese, this began a decade-long state of tension with Russia that would culminate in the Russo–Japanese War of 1904–1905. For the other powers in east Asia, it began a "race for concessions" in China that stopped just short of dismembering the empire.

For the Chinese, however, it marked the most dramatic and humiliating role reversal of the past 1,500 years. China had always viewed Japan in Confucian terms as a "younger brother." Like Korea and Vietnam, Japan was considered to be on the cultural periphery of the Chinese world, acculturating to Chinese institutions and following Chinese examples in those things considered "civilized." Now, after barely a generation of exposure to Euro-American influence, Japan had eclipsed China as a military power and threatened to extend its sway throughout the region.

This new east Asian order also pointed up the larger effects of one of the most momentous patterns of world history: the phenomenon of imperialism growing from the innovations that created scientific–industrial society—one of the foundations of modernity that we have examined in this part of the text. As we began to see in the previous two chapters, in less than a century, European countries and their offshoots—and now Japan—expanded their power so rapidly and completely that on the eve of World War I in 1914 more than 85 percent of the world's people were under their control or influence. How were a very few countries like Japan able to resist and adapt to the broad forces of modernity, while China struggled to cope with its effects through most of the nineteenth and twentieth centuries?

China and Japan in the Age of Imperialism

As we saw in Chapter 21, the reign of the Qing emperor Qianlong (r. 1736–1795) marked perhaps the high point of China's power in the early modern world and the period in which the first hints began to appear of trouble to come. Some of the problems facing the Qing began to emerge within a year after Qianlong stepped down from the throne in 1795. A Buddhist sect with secret-society connections called the White Lotus sparked a smoldering rebellion, which took years to suppress, while at the same time highlighting the limitations of the Manchu bannermen as a military force. Less obvious, but perhaps more debilitating for the agrarian imperial order as a whole, were the new directions in economics. China was steadily drawn into the emerging European global commercial system, but the increasing forces of free trade were eroding its tried and true systems of exchange control. Specifically, China's efforts to retain close control over its export trade in tea, porcelain, silk, and other luxury goods coupled with action to stamp out the new, lucrative, and illegal opium trade created a crisis with Great Britain in the summer of 1839, which led to the First Opium War, China's first military encounter with the industrializing West.

China and Maritime Trade, 1750–1839

By the 1790s, with the China trade at record levels and the French Revolution making European trade increasingly problematic, the British government sought to establish diplomatic relations with the Qing. In the summer of 1793, they dispatched Lord George Macartney, an experienced diplomat and colonial governor, to Beijing with a sizeable entourage and boatloads of presents. His mission was to persuade the Qianlong emperor to allow the stationing of diplomatic personnel in the Chinese capital and the creation of a system for the separate handling of ordinary commercial matters and diplomacy along the lines of European practices. Qianlong, however, politely but firmly rebuffed Macartney's attempts to establish a British embassy. In addition to observing that China really had "no need of your country's ingenious manufactures," Qianlong stated bluntly that permanent foreign embassies were contrary to the tradition of tribute missions and would "most definitely not be permitted." A second British mission in 1816 met with similar results.

> ### Possessing All Things
>
> "As your Ambassador can see for himself we possess all things … this then is my answer to your request to appoint a representative at my Court; a request that is contrary to our dynastic usage, which would only result in inconvenience to yourself. I have expounded my wishes in detail and have commanded your tribute Envoys to leave in peace on their homeward journey …"
>
> —The Qianlong emperor's rebuff of the Macartney Mission, *in* H.F. MacNair, *Modern Chinese History, Selected Readings*, Shanghai: Commercial Press, 1923, p. 2.

China timeline:
- 1736-1795 Reign of Qianlong Emperor
- 1793 Macartney Mission to Beijing
- 1839-1842 First Opium War with Great Britain
- 1851-1864 Taiping Rebellion
- 1860-1895 Self-Strengthening Era
- 1894-1895 Sino–Japanese War
- 1898 Hundred Days of Reform, Emperor Placed Under House Arrest
- 1900 Boxer Rebellion and Anti-Foreign War

Japan timeline:
- 1853-1854 Perry Mission Opens Trade and Diplomatic Relations with Japan
- 1863-1867 Restoration War
- 1868-1912 Reign of Emperor Meiji
- 1900 Seiyukai (Constitutional Government Party) Founded
- 1899-1902 Japan Abrogates Unequal Treaties and Negotiates Alliance with Great Britain

The Imbalance of Trade?   One important reason that Europeans and Americans were anxious to bring the Chinese into their diplomatic system was the widespread perception that China was benefiting from a huge trade imbalance. Though recent scholarship has shown that China's economy actually supported much of the interconnected Eurasian commercial system, contemporary merchants and political economists were convinced that China's control of trade functioned in the same way as did European mercantilism. Thus, they believed that the money paid to Chinese merchants essentially stayed in the "closed" economy of the Qing Empire, draining the West of its stocks of silver. However, as Qianlong's reply to Macartney noted, European merchants offered little that the Chinese needed or wanted.

Thus, by the end of the eighteenth century, European and American traders had become increasingly anxious to find something that Chinese merchants would buy in sufficient quantities to stem the flow of Western silver into China. By the beginning of the nineteenth century, a growing number of merchants were clandestinely turning to a lucrative new commodity, with tragic consequences. When tobacco was introduced into China from the Americas, the innovation of smoking quickly spread. In southwestern China, tribesmen living in remote mountain villages began combining small quantities of powdered opium with tobacco. The Dutch, who briefly maintained bases on Taiwan, also introduced the practice there, from which it spread gradually to the maritime provinces of south China. Disturbed by the growing use of opium beyond normal medicinal practice in the area, the Qing banned the smoking of the substance as early as 1729. For the rest of the century opium use remained a strictly local problem in China's south.

Smugglers, Pirates, and "Foreign Mud"   By the end of the eighteenth century, the British East India Company's territory in Bengal had come to include the area around Patna, historically a center of medicinal opium production. While company traders were strictly prohibited from carrying opium to China as contraband, an increasing number of noncompany merchants willing to take the risk discovered that they could circumvent Chinese regulations and sell small quantities of the drug for a tidy profit. Initially, their customers were the wealthy of Canton society; and the exotic "foreign mud," as opium was nicknamed, soon became a favorite local diversion. With success came increased demand, and by the early decades of the nineteenth century, an elaborate illicit system of delivery had been set up along the south China coast. Heavily armed ships unloaded their cargo of opium on small, sparsely inhabited offshore islands, from which Chinese middlemen picked up the drug and made their rounds on the mainland (see Map 24.1). The ever-rising profits from this illegal enterprise encouraged piracy and lawlessness along the coast, and the opium trade soon became a major irritant in relations between China and the West.

The relationship that the British East India Company and the government-licensed Chinese merchant guild, or *Cohong* had so carefully developed over the previous century was now being rapidly undermined by the new commerce. Moreover, growing free trade agitation in England put an end to the East India Company's monopoly on the China trade in 1833. With the monopoly lifted, the number of entrepreneurs seeking quick riches in the opium trade exploded. With wealth came power, and in the foreign trading "factories" in Canton, newcomers engaged in the opium trade vied for prestige with older firms involved in legitimate goods.

The Opium Trade: Origins, Interactions, and Adaptations

MAP **24.1** **The Opium Trade: Origins, Interactions, Adaptations.**

The push for legitimacy among the opium merchants coincided with an aggressive attempt by Westerners to force China to open additional trading ports for legal items. Chinese authorities, however, viewed this Western assertiveness as driven primarily by opium and Christian evangelism. The East India Company itself was now fatally compromised as well since an estimated one-quarter of its revenues in India were directly tied to opium production.

Far worse, however, were the effects on the ordinary inhabitants of south China. The huge rise in availability and consequent plunge in prices increased opium usage to catastrophic levels. Its power to suppress pain and hunger made it attractive to the

Commissioner Lin Destroys the Opium. This drawing depicts Lin Zexu burning 20,000 chests of opium surrendered by the foreign merchants. Because of the potency of the drug, Lin not only burned it but mixed the ashes with lime and flushed them in sluiceways out to sea. He then offered prayers to the spirits of the sea asking forgiveness for burdening them with this noxious poison.

Chinese Opium Smoker. This photograph, taken in the early 1870s, shows the pervasiveness of the opium habit among ordinary Chinese. These men are smoking in the back room of a restaurant, a common practice, even here in British-controlled Hong Kong.

poor engaged in physical labor, though the dream-like state it induced often made it dangerous to work under its influence. Its addictive properties led people to seek it even at the expense of food, thus creating a health crisis for tens of thousands, made infinitely worse by the drug's notoriously difficult withdrawal symptoms.

Commissioner Lin Zexu   Matters came to a head in the spring of 1839. The Daoguang emperor sent Lin Zexu (1785–1850), a widely respected official with a reputation for courage and honesty, to Canton as an imperial commissioner. Lin's task was to cut off the opium trade at its source, and he was given wide-ranging powers to deal with both Chinese and foreign traffickers. In addition to setting up facilities for the recovery of addicts, he demanded that all foreign merchants surrender their opium stocks and sign an agreement that they would not, under penalty of death, deal in the drug anymore. When the foreign community balked at surrendering the goods, Lin blockaded the port and withdrew all Chinese personnel from Western firms. His determined stance finally cracked the stalemate, and the dealers eventually surrendered 20,000 chests of opium, with most also signing the pledge. Lin then publicly burned the surrendered opium and flushed the ashes into the sea. Following Lin's actions, however, the dealers appealed to the British government for compensation.

The British government decided to use the incident to settle the long-standing diplomatic impasse with the Qing over foreign representation and open ports. In a show of force, the British sent a fleet of warships to Canton to demand reparations for the burned opium, pressure the Qing to establish diplomatic relations, and open more ports. In sad contrast to the days four centuries earlier when Zheng He commanded his great fleets, the Chinese now had no real naval forces to contest the British. What vessels they had were modestly armed with seventeenth-century cannon and used for customs collection. The British fleet, on the other hand, was the most powerful in the world and in a high state of readiness. When negotiations broke down, a small Chinese squadron sailed out to confront the British men-o'-war. By an incredible chance, a rocket from a British ship hit the Chinese flagship in its powder magazine and blew it up. Such inauspicious circumstances marked the beginning of the First Opium War (1839–1842) and, with it, a long, painful century of foreign intrusion, domination, and ultimately revolution for China.

The Opium Wars and the Treaty Port Era

The hostilities that began in the fall of 1839 between China and Great Britain exposed the growing gap between the military capabilities of industrializing countries and those, like China, whose armed forces had fallen into disuse. The military had never been an honored profession in China, and the consequences of maintaining scattered Manchu banner garrisons, discouraging militia recruiting, and underfunding the Chinese regular forces (Armies of the Green Standard) were immediately put on painful display. The massive English ships of the line, mounting as many as 128 guns, moved with impunity among the small Chinese fleets of coastal vessels frantically sent to oppose them. The armored steam gunboat *Nemesis*, whose heavy pivot gun allowed it to dominate riverside batteries, landed the British expeditionary forces wherever they pleased.

Over the next 2 years, with a brief truce called in 1841, the British methodically attacked and occupied ports along the Chinese coast from Canton (Guangzhou)

Extraterritoriality: The immunity of a country's nationals from the laws of their host country.

Steam Power Comes to China. The new technologies of the Industrial Revolution were on painful display in China in 1840 as the British gunboat H.M.S. *Nemesis* took on provincial warships down the river from Guangzhou (Canton). The *Nemesis* featured an armored hull put together in detachable sections, shallow draft and steam–powered paddle wheel propulsion for river fighting, and a large pivot gun to take on shore batteries. Its power and versatility convinced Lin Zexu and a growing number of Chinese officials over the coming decades that China needed, at the very least, the same kinds of "strong ships and effective cannon" if they were to defend their coasts and rivers. By the 1860s the first attempts at such craft were finally under way.

to Shanghai at the mouth of the Yangzi River, for the most part without serious opposition. As the British planned to move north to put pressure on Beijing, Chinese officials opened negotiations in August 1842. The resulting Treaty of Nanjing (Nanking) marked the first of the century's "unequal treaties" that would be imposed throughout east Asia by European powers.

The Treaty of Nanjing   Curiously, the treaty ending the First Opium War did not mention opium. In the final agreement, the British claimed the island of Hong Kong, with its excellent deep-water harbor; levied an indemnity on the Chinese to pay the costs of the war; and forced the Chinese to open the ports of Shanghai, Ningbo, Fuzhou, and Xiamen (Amoy), in addition to Guangzhou (Canton). The Chinese were also confronted with British insistence on **non-tariff autonomy**: By treaty they could now charge no more than a 5 percent tariff on British goods. Taking a page from arrangements in the Ottoman Empire, whereby merchants of particular countries were the responsibility of their respective consuls, the British also imposed the policy of **extraterritoriality** in the newly open ports: British subjects who violated Chinese laws would be tried and punished by British consuls.

Over the next several years, the Chinese signed similar treaties with France and the United States. An important addition in these later treaties was the *most-favored nation* clause: Any new concessions granted to one country automatically reverted to those who by treaty were "most-favored nations." Thus, the time-honored Chinese diplomatic strategy of "using barbarians to check barbarians" was dealt a near fatal blow (see Map 24.2).

Non-tariff autonomy: The loss by a country of its right to set its own tariffs.

Treaty Ports and Foreign Spheres of Influence in China, 1842–1907

Spheres of influence:
- British
- French
- German
- Japanese
- Russian
- British territory
- Portuguese territory

Treaty port opened with:
- Britain
- France
- Germany
- Japan
- Portugal
- United States
- (1897) Date of opening by treaty

MAP **24.2** Treaty Ports and Foreign Spheres of Influence in China, 1842–1907.

The Taiping Movement, 1851–1864   In addition to the spread of the opium trade to the newly opened ports, long-established trade routes for more legitimate items swiftly shifted from Guangzhou to more convenient outlets. The growth of Shanghai was especially important in this regard because it served the Yangzi River, the greatest highway through China's heartland. Coastal trade also increased, while Hong Kong grew as the primary point of opium transfer to small smuggling vessels. The swiftness of all of these changes and their accompanying economic dislocation, along with smoldering discontent at the inability of the Qing government to resist foreign demands, made south China particularly volatile. In 1851 the region exploded in rebellion. Before it was over, this largest civil war in world history and its related conflicts would claim as many as 30 million lives.

The catalyst for revolt was in many ways symbolic of the diverse cultural influences penetrating the area. Though Christian proselytizing had been banned by the Qing since the early eighteenth century, missionary activity was protected in the foreign enclaves and now increased dramatically with the enactment of the new treaties. A candidate for the local Confucian examinations, Hong Xiuquan [HUNG SHIOO-chwahn] (1813–1864), had come upon some Christian missionary tracts passed on by a colleague. Not long after, he failed the examination for the third time and lapsed into a nervous breakdown. When he eventually recovered, Hong gradually came to believe that the Christian God had taken him up to heaven and informed him that he was in fact Christ's younger brother. Hong told his startled listeners that it had been revealed to him that he must now work to bring about the Heavenly Kingdom of Great Peace (*taiping tianguo*) on earth. The movement became known as the "Taiping Rebellion" and lasted from 1851 until 1864.

Hounded from their community, Hong and his group moved into a mountain stronghold and began to gather followers from the disillusioned and unemployed, anti-Manchu elements, religious dissidents, secret societies, and fellow members of south China's Hakka minority. By 1851 they had created a society based on Protestant Christian theology, Chinese traditions, and a vision of equality in which all goods were held in common; women worked, fought, and prayed alongside men; and foot binding, opium smoking, and gambling were forbidden. As a sign that they were no longer loyal to the Qing, the men cut their queues and let the hair grow in on their foreheads, prompting the Qing to refer to them as "the long-haired rebels." Repudiating Confucian tradition, the rebels targeted the scholar-gentry in their land seizures and executions.

By late 1851, the movement had gathered enough strength to stand against local government forces and began an advance to the north. By 1853 they had captured the city of Nanjing and made it their capital. That winter they were narrowly thwarted from driving the Qing from Beijing and pushed back to central China. For the next decade they would remain in control of the Chinese heartland, and the long, bloody contest to subdue them would leave thousands of towns and villages devastated for decades to come.

For the foreigners in China, the prospect of a Christian movement taking power seemed like a cherished dream about to come true. As time went on, however, missionaries and diplomats became less sure of where the movement was heading. On the one hand, Hong and his advisors talked about instituting Western-style administrative reforms and building a modern industrial base—something Western well-wishers had continually urged on Chinese officials. On the other hand, a powerful Taiping China might repudiate the unequal treaties and throw the new trade arrangements into disarray. Thus, the foreign powers in the end grudgingly elected to continue recognizing the Qing as China's legitimate rulers (see Map 24.3).

The Second Opium War, 1856–1860

At the height of the rebellion in 1856, a new dispute arose between the Qing and the British and French. After 4 years of intermittent fighting, it produced the next round of "unequal treaties" that greatly expanded foreign interests and control in the empire. Britain, France, and the United

The Taiping Rebellion, 1851–1864

Area controlled by rebels, ca.1861

Nanjing
Wuhan
Shanghai
Hangzhou
Nanchang
Wenzhou
GUANGXI PROVINCE
Xiamen (Amoy)
TAIWAN
Guangzhou
Hong Kong

0 km 200
0 miles 200
N

MAP **24.3** The Taiping Rebellion 1851–1864.

States all felt by the mid-1850s that the vastly expanded trade in China—and now Japan—called for the opening of still more ports, an end to Qing prohibitions on missionary activity, and diplomatic relations along Western lines.

The catalyst came in late 1856. A Chinese customs patrol in Canton hauled down the British flag on the *Arrow*, a Chinese vessel whose registry had been falsified to take advantage of British trading privileges. The British seized upon this purported insult to their flag as an opportunity to force treaty revision. The French, who considered themselves the protectors of Catholic missionaries and their converts, saw an excellent opening to pressure China on the missionary issue and so joined the British.

The war itself was fought intermittently in a highly localized fashion. The British seized the walled city of Canton, captured the governor-general of the region's two provinces, and sent him into exile in India. As the conflict moved into 1857, however, the Great Rebellion in India consumed British attention through much of the year, while in China negotiations dragged on intermittently and the Qing remained preoccupied with the Taipings. In 1858, a draft treaty was worked out, but the Qing court refused it. Returning in 1860 with a large expeditionary force, British and French troops advanced to Beijing, drove the emperor from the city, and burned and looted his summer palace. The final treaty stipulated that a dozen ports be opened to foreign trade, that opium be recognized as a legal commodity, that extraterritoriality be expanded, and that foreign embassies be set up in the capital. A newly created Chinese board, the Zongli Yamen, was to handle Qing foreign relations; and the Chinese were invited to send their own ambassadors abroad.

Self-Strengthening The end of the Second Opium War began a period lasting through the early 1870s sometimes referred to by historians as the "cooperative era." There were few major disputes between the foreign powers and the Qing; indeed, in several instances, foreigners worked closely with Chinese officials to help them in assessing ways to upgrade their defenses, lay the foundations of modern industrial concerns, and start programs that signaled institutional change. The motives of these men ranged from simple altruism to missionary devotion to what might be called "enlightened self-interest": the belief that a strong, modern China would be a more stable trade and diplomatic partner.

For their part, Chinese officials, desperate to roll back the foreign threat and suppress the Taipings, favored a diverse array of strategies. Few advocated simply fighting the foreigners with whatever means were at hand. Most, like the emperor's brother, Prince Gong, felt that over time these new peoples would be assimilated to Chinese norms, like invaders and border peoples of the past. In the meantime, however, they should be "soothed and pacified" but not unconditionally. As the prince later remarked to the British Ambassador, "Take away your opium and your missionaries and you will be welcome."

In order to do this, however, China needed to be able to halt further encroachments by the powers. Toward this end, a growing number of prominent officials advocated a policy that came to be called "self-strengthening." During the 1860s, the two most prominent were Li Hongzhang (1823–1901) and his senior colleague Zeng Guofan (1811–1872). Both men had distinguished themselves as Confucian scholars and as leaders of militia armies during the Taiping years. In 1864, their combined forces finally captured the Taiping capital at Nanjing and forced the suicide of Hong Xiuquan, bringing the movement to an end.

Like a number of leaders during these desperate times, Li and Zeng were also distinguished by the flexibility of their thinking and, increasingly, by their growing familiarity with the new weapons and techniques brought to China by foreign forces. By the end of the rebellion, they had begun to move toward a strategy of what a later slogan called "Chinese studies for the essence; Western studies for practical application." They sponsored an impressive array of projects in the 1860s and early 1870s: a foreign language and technical school, modern arsenals and factories at Nanjing and Jiangnan (Kiangnan), a modern navy yard at Fuzhou, initiatives to send Chinese students to the United States and Europe, a modern shipping concern (The China Merchants' Steam Navigation Company), and the first moves toward sending representatives abroad.

Opposition to such programs also mounted during the period and continued throughout the century. These were the people Li Hongzhang had cited as being "confined by tradition" in the vignette beginning this chapter. Often highly placed—including, ultimately, the Empress Dowager Cixi [SIH-shee] (1835–1908) herself—these opponents felt that any and all reforms of the kind advocated by Li and Zeng would bring down China's Confucian society. For them, the kind of change necessary to create an industrial base in China would erode the social, cultural, and economic ties that held that society together. In the end, they said, the people would cease to be Chinese in any meaningful sense and become like Europeans and Americans. As much as anything else, the lack of a clear strategy at the top and the ferocity of these debates among Chinese officials worked to frustrate the hopes of the "self-strengtheners" through the turn of the century.

Self-Straighteners. Two of the key figures in China's Self-Strengthening Movement were Zeng Guofan (top) and Li Hongzhang (bottom). The two men began working together during the last years of the Taiping Rebellion, both having formed and led militia armies in their home provinces of Hunan (Zeng) and Anhui (Li). Both men also pioneered the use of modern weapons by their troops. After Zeng's death in 1872, Li emerged as the most active proponent of self-strengthening and China's most powerful official.

Toward Revolution: Reform and Reaction to 1900

While China's efforts at self-strengthening seemed promising to contemporaries during the 1870s, the signs of their underlying weakness were already present for those who cared to look. As we have seen, the architect of many of these efforts, Li Hongzhang, was all too aware of the political constraints he faced. With the ascension of the infant Guangxu as emperor in 1874 came the regency of the Empress Dowager Cixi. Desperate to preserve Manchu power, Cixi constantly manipulated factions at court and among the high officials to avoid concentration of power in any particular area. Such maneuverings, sometimes favoring Li's colleagues and as often opposing them, severely hampered the long-term health of many self-strengthening

Interaction and Adaptation: "Self-Strengthening" and "Western Science and Eastern Ethics"

Most of the important technical innovations taking place in China and Japan during the late eighteenth and early nineteenth centuries came from outside east Asia. This, of course, is not surprising since the Scientific and Industrial Revolutions were largely focused on developing labor-saving machinery, weaponry, and improving the speed and efficiency of transportation—things of lesser priority in these labor-rich societies. Confronted by the expansive, newly industrialized countries of Europe and America, their possible responses were largely confined to what might be called the "three R's"—Reaction, Reform, and Revolution. Perhaps most interesting in this regard is the middle path of reform taken by both countries in attempting to create a synthesis of tried and true Confucian social structures and what were considered to be the best of the new technologies and institutions.

As we have seen in past chapters, Chinese philosophical concepts tended toward the desire for correlation and the reconciliation of opposites. In this tradition, *ti* and *yong*, or "essence" and "function/application," became the two key terms in the popular self-strengthening formulation, *Zhongxue wei ti; Xixue wei yong* ("Chinese

Interaction and Adaptation in China and Japan Weapons on display at the Nanjing Arsenal in 1868 include an early Gatling-type rotary machine gun, a Congreve rocket, and a pyramid of round explosive shells. (*a*), while an 1890 lithograph of a Japanese seamstress (*b*) shows the delicate balance between "essence" and "function" that Japan has tried to maintain since the middle of the nineteenth century. The woman is attired in Western dress and she works a Western-style sewing machine. Has the "function" degraded the essence of what she is doing? It is a question that many in Japan still ask today.

studies for the essence; Western studies for the practical application"). Thus, Chinese thinkers were able to accommodate the need for new foreign technologies within historically and philosophically acceptable terminology. Similarly, the Japanese, also schooled in Neo-Confucianism, were able to justify an even more thoroughgoing transformation of society by means of the balanced formula they called "Western science and Eastern ethics."

(b)

However, the two sides of the concept were not equally balanced. As with many Neo-Confucian formulae, the "essence" and "ethics" elements were considered to be primary and the method of implementation—"function"—secondary. Thus, their proponents could argue that their chief aim was the preservation of the fundamentals of Confucian society, while being flexible about the appropriate means of attaining their goals. Opponents, however, argued that the formula could—and eventually would—be reversed: that "function" would eventually degrade the "essence." Here, they pointed to the alleged Westernization of students sent abroad and the wearing of Western clothes in Japan as examples of the dangers of this approach.

Yet, in both countries, one can argue that this has remained a favored approach, even through war and revolution. Though societal and generational tensions over "tradition" and "modernity" have been present for nearly a century and a half in Japan, the Japanese have made foreign technologies and institutions their own, while retaining some of their most cherished Shinto and Buddhist practices alongside social customs still tinged with Neo-Confucianism. Similarly, in China, since the beginning of the Four Modernizations in 1978, coupling technological and institutional modernization with an effort to rediscover and preserve what is considered to be the best of traditional Chinese civilization has been the dominant approach. Thus, the present regime pursues a policy of "socialism with Chinese characteristics" and supports the founding of Confucian institutes alongside computer factories—all in the service of creating what the Communist Party calls "the harmonious society."

Questions

- How were the Chinese and Japanese adaptations to Western innovations similar? How were they different? What do these similarities and differences say about the cultures of these two countries?

- Do you believe that, over the course of time, the "function" of foreign innovations has degraded the "essence" in China and Japan?

measures. In addition, the new programs were costly, usually requiring foreign experts, and China's finances were continually strained by the artificially low treaty tariffs and the obligation to pay old indemnities.

China and Imperialism in Southeast Asia and Korea
By the 1880s foreign tensions exposed more problems. France had been steadily encroaching upon southeast Asia since the late 1850s. By the early 1880s, however, Vietnamese resistance led by a force called the Black Flags was on the verge of rolling back the French. Li Hongzhang supported the Black Flags, and in order to preempt outright Chinese intervention, the French launched a surprise attack on the modern Chinese naval facilities at Fuzhou, sinking the cream of China's steam fleet. Though Chinese forces gave a better account of themselves in other engagements, the French emerged from this conflict with control of the whole of Vietnam, which they promptly combined with Cambodia and Laos into the colony of French Indochina in 1885.

In 1885, as China was still involved with France, tensions with Japan over Korea threatened to dislodge that kingdom as a Qing client state. Japanese diplomats had exerted influence over the Korean court as it sought to deal with the smoldering Tonghak Rebellion (see later, "Creating an Empire"). China sent its own team of officials to keep watch on Qing interests, and both sides quickly threatened to send troops. In the agreement between Li Hongzhang and Ito Hirobumi at Tianjin (Tientsin) that year, both sides agreed not to take any action in the future without informing the other.

By the early 1890s, however, rising tensions surrounding the Korean court and intrigues by Japanese and Chinese agents involving various factions threatened war once again. Japan sent a force which was claimed to be diplomatic; troops of a Chinese counterforce were killed when a Japanese warship sunk their transport. By the fall of 1894, both sides were sending troops and naval forces to Korea and a full-scale war over the fate of Korea and northeast Asia was under way.

The Sino–Japanese War
As we noted at the beginning of this chapter, the war between China and Japan over control of Korea graphically exposed the problems of China's "self-strengthening" efforts. China's arms procurement, for example, was not carried out under a centralized program, as was Japan's. The result was that different Chinese military units were armed with a wide variety of noninterchangeable weapons and ammunition, making it difficult for them to support each other. China's rebuilt fleet, though impressive in size and armament, faced similar problems. Unlike the Japanese ships, China's largest warships had their components separately built at various shipyards in Europe. In one memorable incident during the Battle of the Yellow Sea in 1894, the recoil from the mismatched, oversized guns aboard the Chinese flagship destroyed its own captain's bridge. Worse still, Chinese gunners found to their dismay that many of the shells they were firing were filled with sand rather than explosive—the result of the empress dowager's diversion of naval funds to rebuild the summer palace destroyed in 1860.

While many of the land battles were hotly contested, superior Japanese organization and morale enabled them to drive steadily through Korea. A second force landed in southern Manchuria to secure the territory around the approaches to Beijing, while Japanese naval forces reduced the fortress across from it at Weihaiwei. By spring 1895, after some preliminary negotiations, Li made his humiliating trip to

(a)

(b)

Scenes from the Sino–Japanese War. News accounts of the Sino–Japanese War aroused great interest and an unprecedented wave of nationalism in Japan. They also marked the last extensive use of ukiyo-e woodblock printing in the news media as the technology of reproducing photos in newspapers was introduced to Japan shortly after the conflict. Because few of the artists actually traveled with the troops, the great majority of these works came from reporters' dispatches and the artists' imaginations. In these representative samples from the assault on Pyongyang and the use of the new technology of the electric searchlight to illuminate an enemy fort (*a*), the pride in Japan's modernization and the disdain for China's "backwardness" are all too evident. Note the almost demon-like faces and garish uniforms of the Chinese as they are invariably depicted as being killed or cowering before the Japanese; note, too, the modern, Western uniforms and beards and mustaches of the Japanese (*b*).

Shimonoseki and was forced to agree to Japan's terms. The severity of the provisions, especially the annexation of Taiwan, the control of Korea, and, temporarily at least, the seizure of Liaodong, signaled to the Western powers in east Asia that China was now weak enough to have massive economic and territorial demands forced on it.

Thus, a "race for concessions" began in which France demanded economic and territorial rights in south China adjacent to Indochina; Great Britain did the same in the Yangzi River valley; Russia and Japan made demands in the north for rights in Manchuria; and a newcomer, Germany, demanded naval bases and rights at Qingdao [Ching-DOW] (Tsingtao) on the Shandong Peninsula. China's total dismemberment was avoided in 1899 when John Hay, the US secretary of state, circulated a note with British backing suggesting that all powers refrain from securing exclusive concessions and instead maintain an "open door" for all to trade in China.

The Hundred Days of Reform
Amid this growing foreign crisis, the aftermath of the war produced a domestic crisis as well. The terms of the Shimonoseki treaty had prompted patriotic demonstrations in Beijing and raised levels of discussion about reform to new levels of urgency. A group of younger officials headed by Kang Youwei (1858–1927) petitioned Emperor Guangxu, now ruling in his own right, to implement a list of widespread reforms, many modeled on those recently enacted in Japan. Guangxu issued a flurry of edicts from June through September 1898, attempting to completely revamp China's government and many of its leading institutions. Resistance to this "hundred days' reform" program, however, was

EN CHINE
Le gâteau des Rois et... des Empereurs

Dismembering China. The weakness of the Qing during the final years of the nineteenth century prompted the so-called Race for Concessions among the imperial powers in east Asia. In this French cartoon, China is depicted as a flatbread or pizza around which caricatures of the monarchs and national symbols of the various powers sit with their knives poised arguing over who should get the best pieces. A desperate Chinese official—perhaps Li Hongzhang himself—with his long fingernails and flapping queue, holds up his hands imploring them to stop. The French caption says roughly, "In China: The cake of kings and emperors."

extensive, and much of it was centered on the emperor's aunt, the empress dowager. With support from her inner circle at court, she had the young emperor placed under house arrest and rounded up and executed those of Kang's supporters who could be found. Kang and his junior colleague, the writer and political theorist Liang Qichao [LEEAHNG chee-CHOW] (1873–1929) managed to escape to the treaty ports. For the next decade they traveled to overseas Chinese communities attempting to gather support for their Constitutional Monarchy Party.

The Boxer Rebellion and War   The turmoil set off by the "race for concessions" among the imperial powers was particularly intense in north China, where the ambitions of Russia, Japan, and Germany clashed. With the stepped-up activity of German missionaries on the Shandong Peninsula came a new wave of antiforeign sentiment, increasingly centered on a group called the Society of the Harmonious Fists. Anti-Qing as well as antiforeign, the members' ritual exercises and name prompted the foreign community to refer to them as the "Boxers." By late 1899 the Boxers were regularly provoking the foreign and Christian communities with the aim of pushing their governments to pressure the Qing to suppress the movement, by which they hoped to stir up rebellion against them.

In the spring of 1900 matters came to a head. Boxers assassinated the German ambassador, and the Germans demanded that the Qing crush the movement once and for all, pay a huge indemnity, and erect a statue to their ambassador as a public apology. In the midst of this crisis, the empress dowager, who had been negotiating in secret with the Boxers, declared war on all the foreign powers in China and openly threw the court's support behind the movement. The result was civil war across northern China as Boxer units hunted down missionaries and Chinese Christians, many Chinese army units aided the Boxers in attacking foreigners, and the foreign diplomatic quarter in Beijing was besieged from June until August.

The foreign governments quickly put together a multinational relief force led by the Germans and British and largely manned by the Japanese but including units of nearly all the countries with interests in China. By August they had fought their way to the capital and chased the imperial court nearly to Xi'an. Amid considerable carnage in the mopping up of Boxer sympathizers, Li Hongzhang, in his last official duty before his death, was commissioned to negotiate the end of the conflict for the court. With Qing power utterly routed, the foreign governments were able to impose the most severe "unequal treaty" yet: They extracted the right to post troops in major Chinese cities, they demanded the total suppression of any antiforeign movements, and they received such a huge indemnity that China had to borrow money from foreign banks in order to service the interest on the payments. The only bright point in the Boxer Protocols of 1901 was that the United States agreed to return its share of the indemnity money to China on the condition that it would be used to send Chinese students to study in American institutions.

Toward Revolution   With the return of the imperial court to Beijing and the enhanced foreign presence in the capital, the Qing finally turned to institutional reform. During the first decade of the twentieth century, the old Confucian examination system was abolished and new curricula—including science and technology—were created. Similarly, the army was overhauled and modernized. Perhaps most dramatically, the government itself was to be restructured more or less along the lines envisioned by Kang Youwei and Emperor Guangxu—who was still under house arrest. An imperial commission was sent abroad to study the constitutional systems of the great powers, and upon its return a plan to turn the Qing into a constitutional monarchy was created. By 1910, 2 years after the deaths of both the empress dowager and Guangxu, the first limited elections were being held for a planned legislative body.

The Empress Dowager Cixi. Following the rout of the Qing and Boxer forces in the fall of 1900, the empress dowager made herself more accessible to Western diplomats and photographers. There are numerous pictures of her in various royal poses; here, she sits with her court ladies-in-waiting. The legend above her throne reads from right to left: "The reigning Saintly Mother, Empress Dowager of the Great Qing, (may she rule) 10,000 years! 10,000 years! 10,000, 10,000 years!"—the last exhortation (*wan sui, wan sui, wan wan sui*) the Chinese rendering of the more familiar Japanese "Banzai."

While Qing reform efforts were proceeding apace, however, the plans of revolutionaries were moving even more rapidly. As we will see in Chapter 28, the central figure in this regard was Sun Yat-sen (1866–1925), a man in many ways emblematic of the changes in China during the nineteenth century. Born near Canton, Sun received the fundamentals of classical education but then undertook Western training in medicine in Hong Kong and developed a thriving medical practice in Canton. A student of European and American history, his political ideas were already germinating by the time of the Sino–Japanese War. Like growing numbers of Chinese, the war convinced Sun that the feeble and increasingly corrupt Manchu government was the biggest obstacle to China's regeneration. In the end, his movement would play the leading role in forcing it out.

In Search of Security Through Empire:
Japan in the Meiji Era

As we have just seen, the close of the nineteenth century saw Japan looming larger and larger as China's chief threat. Yet, they both faced similar pressures and, as Li Hongzhang observed, shared a common culture and in many ways a common cause. How, then, was Japan, with only a fraction of China's population and resources, able to not only survive in the face of foreign pressure but join the imperial powers itself?

The Decline of Tokugawa Seclusion   Though the eighteenth century saw occasional attempts by foreign ships to put in at Japanese ports, Europeans generally honored Japan's seclusion policies. Moreover, since all maritime trade with China took ships along a southerly route to Canton, the opportunity to go to Japan seldom presented itself. By the first decades of the nineteenth century, however, the situation was changing. The vastly expanded legitimate trade with China and the development of the opium trade increased the volume of shipping closer to Japanese waters. Moreover, the rapid growth of the whaling industry in the northern Pacific increasingly brought European and American ships into waters adjacent to

Japan. From their perspective, the need for establishing relations for the disposition of shipwreck survivors and perhaps trade was therefore becoming ever more urgent.

By the 1840s the pressure to establish relations with the Tokugawa shogunate became even more intense for the Western powers with interests in China. The treaty ports created in the wake of the First Opium War included Shanghai, which was rapidly becoming east Asia's chief commercial enclave. Because of its geographical position, major shipping routes to Shanghai now ran directly adjacent to southern Japan. Moreover, the Mexican War (1846–1848) brought the Pacific coast of North America under the control of the United States. At the same time, the discovery of gold in California made boomtown San Francisco the premier port for all American transpacific trade. In addition, increasing numbers of Chinese sought passage to the gold fields and the promise of employment in the American West, while the infamous "**coolie** trade" continually increased human traffic to Cuba and Peru. Plans to open steamship service along the great circle route from San Francisco to Shanghai, and the need for coaling stations to supply it, now threatened to place Japan squarely across the path of maritime traffic (see Map 24.4).

Coolies: Poor migrant laborers from China and India who performed menial work in other parts of the world in the nineteenth century.

The Coming of the "Black Ships"

The Tokugawa were well aware of the humiliation of the Qing at the hands of the British in 1842 and watched nervously as foreign commerce mounted in the Chinese treaty ports. As pressure increased on Japan to open its ports, divided counsels plagued the shogunate. The influential Mito School, long exposed to "Dutch learning" (see Chapter 21), feared the growing military and technological power of the Europeans and Americans and advocated a military response to any attempt at opening the country. Others looking at the situation in China felt that negotiation was the only possible way for Japan to avoid invasion.

MAP **24.4** Steamship Routes and Underwater Telegraph Cables, ca. 1880.

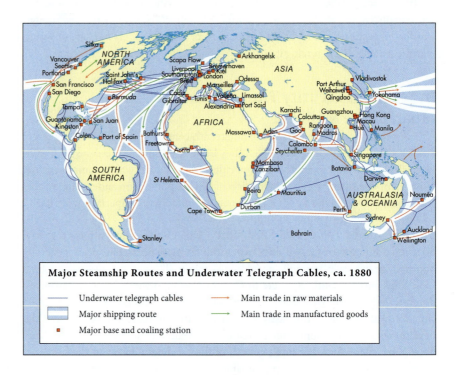

Major Steamship Routes and Underwater Telegraph Cables, ca. 1880

— Underwater telegraph cables
—▶ Main trade in raw materials
▭ Major shipping route
—▶ Main trade in manufactured goods
▪ Major base and coaling station

The Americans, taking the lead in seeking diplomatic and commercial relations, put together a fleet of their newest and most powerful warships in arriving in July, 1853. Their commander, Matthew C. Perry, assembled multiracial and -ethnic crews for them in order to impress his Japanese hosts with the reach and power of the United States. Anxious to awe them as well with the new technologies available, he brought along as presents a telegraph set and a model railroad, both of which proved immediately popular. When negotiations flagged, the shogun's men gleefully amused themselves aboard the miniature train, smacking the engine and its operator with their fans to make it go faster.

On Perry's return trip in 1854 with even more of the "black ships," as the Japanese dubbed them, the Treaty of Kanagawa was signed, Japan's first with an outside power. Like China, Japan had now entered the treaty port era.

"Honor the Emperor and Expel the Barbarian!"

The widely differing attitudes toward foreign contact expressed within the shogunate were reflected among the daimyo and samurai as well. The treaty with the Americans, and the rapid conclusion of treaties with other foreigners, tended to reinforce antiforeignism among many of the warrior elite, while emphasizing the weakness of the Tokugawa to resist further demands. Moreover, the new cultural contacts taking place in treaty ports like Yokohama and Nagasaki hardened positions and raised tensions further. Many samurai felt that dramatic gestures were called for to rouse the country to action. Hence, as with the Boxers later in China, they attacked foreigners and even assassinated Tokugawa officials in an effort to precipitate antiforeign conflict. By 1863, a movement aimed at driving out the Tokugawa and restoring imperial rule had coalesced around the samurai of two southern domains, Satsuma and Choshu. Taking the slogan *sonno joi* ("Honor the emperor, expel the barbarian!") members of this "Satcho" (*Sat*suma and *Cho*shu) clique challenged the shogunate and fought the smoldering Restoration War, which by the end of 1867 forced the Tokugawa to capitulate. In short order, the new regime moved to the Tokugawa capital of Edo and renamed it "Tokyo" (Eastern Capital).

The new emperor, 15-year-old Mutsuhito, took the reign name of Meiji (Enlightened Rule) and quickly moved to make good on its promise. As proof that the new regime would adopt progressive measures, the throne issued a charter oath in April 1868. A constitution was also promulgated, which spelled out in more detail how the new government was to be set up.

"Blue-eyed Barbarians." Japanese commonly referred to Westerners as "blue-eyed barbarians." In these sketches, part of a long series that artists made after Commodore Perry's four heavily-armed steamships sailed into Tokyo Bay in July 1853, Perry's son Oliver, who served as his father's personal secretary, is portrayed as jowly and slightly demonic looking *(a)*, while a group of US Marines are portrayed as both menacing and ridiculous at the same time *(b)*.

Emperor Meiji. A number of portraits and photographs of Emperor Meiji were done during his lifetime, particularly in his twenties and thirties. Here, in a portrait probably done in the late 1870s or early 1880s, he is shown as a vigorous and decisive man at the height of his powers. Note the European-style military uniform and Van Dyke beard of the kind frequently sported by Western monarchs and leaders.

Creating a Nation-State   While the Tokugawa had created an efficient warrior bureaucracy based on Neo-Confucianism, Japan was still dominated by regional loyalties and fealty to the daimyo of one's *han*, or feudal domain. The foreign threat and restoration of the emperor provided the opportunity as well as the necessity to forge a more thoroughgoing national unification. Thus, the new government quickly set about dismantling the feudal han and replacing them with a centralized provincial structure; the daimyo were replaced by governors, and the samurai were disbanded, given stipends, and encouraged to form business enterprises or to teach. In their place, a new conscript army modeled after that of Germany was created and a navy modeled on Great Britain's was established. In addition, the new order was to be held together by a national system of compulsory education in which loyalty to the emperor and state was carefully nurtured at every level.

The 1870s also marked the flourishing of government-managed social experimentation. Like the Chinese "self-strengtheners," Japanese senior advisors, or *genro* [hard "g": GEN-row], to the emperor sought to use new foreign technologies and institutions to strengthen the state against further foreign intrusion. Japan's planners, however, proved more systematic and determined in their efforts and, unlike their Chinese counterparts, had the full backing of the imperial court. Thus, Japan's proclaimed goals of using "Western science and Eastern ethics" in the service of "civilization and enlightenment" were seen as the primary tools in asserting eventual equality with the Western imperial powers and rolling back Japan's unequal treaties.

Adventures Abroad and Revolt at Home   Amid these dizzying changes, some senior advisors advocated an aggressive foreign policy in order to create a buffer zone around Japan. For these men, most prominently former samurai Saigo Takamori (1827–1877), Korea, which so far had resisted Western attempts to end its seclusion, was the obvious place to start. Saigo offered to sacrifice himself in order to create an incident in Korea that would justify Japanese action to "open" the so-called Hermit Kingdom. The Meiji court and inner circle, however, favored restraint. Instead, Japan contented itself with the expedition against Taiwan in 1874 and the purchase of the Ryukyu Islands in 1879.

The social turmoil at home and the tempering of Japan's ambitions abroad stirred discontent among many former samurai. In their view, Japan had abandoned its true character and was rapidly becoming a second-rate copy of the Western countries, fueled by greed, lack of honor, and international cowardice. In 1876, such sentiments helped spark a revolt among dissident samurai. Saigo, an imposing giant of a man much admired by the samurai, was persuaded to join them. Their movement, however, was crushed with brutal efficiency by the modern conscript army of Yamagata Aritomo (1838–1922), and Saigo himself committed suicide in April 1877. Though discontent at the direction of Japanese modernization continued to fester throughout the nineteenth century, it never again reached the level of open rebellion.

Creating an Empire   As we saw earlier in this chapter, rising tensions between Japan and China over the disposition of Korea ultimately led to the Sino–Japanese War of 1894–1895. The issue was temporarily held in abeyance by the Treaty of Tianjin of 1885, but continuing difficulties arising from the instability of the Korean government, feuding pro-Chinese and pro-Japanese factions within it, and the *Tonghak*, or "Eastern learning," movement, kept the region a volatile one. Combining elements of Confucianism, Buddhism, and a pronounced strain of antiforeignism, Tonghak-led peasant rebellions had erupted in 1810 and 1860. Though the rebellion had been suppressed in the 1860s, the forced opening of Korea to trade in the following decade and the constant intrigues of the Qing and the Japanese surrounding the Yi court in succeeding decades brought about the movement's revival in the 1890s.

As we have seen, Japan's successful showing in the war surprised and alarmed the Western powers in the region. The Triple Intervention, in which Russia, Germany, and France forced Japan to return the Liaodong Peninsula to China, only to have them lease it to Russia the following year, put that empire on a collision course with Japanese aspirations on the Asian mainland. Japan's control of Korea made it intensely interested in acquiring concessions in Manchuria. For Russia, it was vital to build rail links from the Trans-Siberian Railway to their new outposts of Port Arthur and Dairen (Dalian) in Liaodong and to extend the line across Manchuria to Vladivostok on the Pacific. As the twentieth century began, they pressured the Chinese into allowing them the rights to build the Chinese Eastern Railway across Manchuria and the South Manchurian Railway to Port Arthur, with a vital junction at Mukden, known today as Shenyang. Japan and Russia would shortly fight a war that would secure Japan's dominant position in northeast Asia and begin a long train of events that would end in revolution for Russia (see Map 24.5).

> ### Enlightened Rule
>
> "All matters [would be] decided by public discussion . . . evil customs of the past shall be broken off . . . [and] knowledge shall be sought throughout the world so as to strengthen the foundations of imperial rule."
>
> —From *Meiji boshin*, pp. 81–82. Quoted in Ryusaku Tsunoda, William T. De Bary, and Donald Keene, eds. *Sources of Japanese Tradition*, vol. 2, p. 137. New York: Columbia University Press, 1964.

Economics and Society in Late Qing China

The century and a half from 1750 to 1900 marked the structural, cultural, and economic decline of the great agrarian empires. Nowhere was this more evident than in Qing China. By 1900, China's treasury was bankrupt; its finances increasingly were controlled by foreign concerns; its export trade was outstripped by European and Japanese competitors; its domestic markets turned to factory-produced foreign commodities; and its land, ravaged by war, eroded by declining productivity, and squeezed by the world's largest population, grew less and less capable of sustaining its society.

The Seeds of Modernity and the New Economic Order

As we have seen a number of times in this chapter, the economic policies of late imperial China were increasingly at odds with those of the industrializing and

Japanese Territorial Expansion, 1870–1905

🟩	Japanese Empire, 1870
🟨	Territory acquired, 1874–1895
⬜	Japanese sphere of influence from 1905

MAP **24.5** Japanese Territorial Expansion, 1870–1905.

commercially expanding West. For Chinese thinkers, this was considered sound in both ideological and economic terms. Confucianism held that agriculture was China's primary concern; that the values of humanity, loyalty, and filial piety were tied to agrarian society; and that the values of the merchant—particularly the drive for profit—were in direct opposition to these agrarian values. As the nineteenth century advanced, the opium trade provided ample evidence to Confucian officials of the correctness of this stance.

While opium was the great entering wedge, the building pressures on China and other regulated societies to lower their barriers to legitimate trade and the steps taken by those countries exerting the pressure to safeguard their own markets had equally severe long-term effects. Briefly, China was squeezed both ways in terms of trade. That is, the unequal treaties imposed artificially low tariff rates on the empire, making it increasingly difficult to protect its markets; at the same time, trading nations in the West increased tariffs on their own imports and, in some cases, developed their own substitutes for Chinese products.

Self-Strengthening and Economics

The programs to improve China's economics and trade were set up as "government-sponsored/merchant-operated" enterprises. One of the most initially promising of these was the China Merchants Steam Navigation Company, founded in 1873. The company's purpose was to recapture the carrying trade on China's rivers from foreign operators. With key purchases of foreign steamers and dock facilities during the early and mid-1870s, the company had gone far toward reclaiming a significant percentage of China's river traffic by 1880. However, renewed foreign competition, lackluster governmental support, and traditional avenues of graft eroded the company's position until it folded later in the decade. In many respects, the company's experience marked a crucial tension between the entrepreneurial instincts of the merchants and the expectations of officials in regulation and receiving regular payoff income. The government itself and officials critical of self-strengthening were quick to point out the high cost of such programs, their potential for corruption, and the futility of attempting to beat the Westerners at their own game.

Amid the halting attempts at government-sponsored innovation, however, other economic forces at work would also have a profound effect on China's later economic development. The first is that in the treaty ports themselves the economic climate created by the Western powers for their own benefit exposed much of China's urban population to aspects of modern industrial and commercial society. A substantial class of Chinese people who made a living mediating between Westerners and Chinese interests had developed by the end of the nineteenth century.

The other long-term process at work was the growing influx and popularity of European, Japanese, and American consumer goods diffused from the treaty ports to the interior. While foreign curiosities had been popular with Chinese elites since the eighteenth century, Qing efforts to safeguard domestic markets through the Canton system and internal transit taxes had been steadily beaten down. By the end of the nineteenth century, foreign machine-made cotton cloth dominated the Chinese interior, John D. Rockefeller's Standard Oil Company was giving away kerosene lamps to market their fuel, the British–American Tobacco Company had established its products in the empire, and even the Japanese invention of the rickshaw had become a popular mode of transport in China's cities. With the Qing finally committed to railroad and telegraph construction and modern deep mining and with China's commercial ports resembling more and more their foreign counterparts, the seeds of economic modernity had been at least fitfully planted.

Rural Economics and Society

While about 80–85 percent of China's population remained rural, the old structures of the empire's peasant-based society were slowly beginning to crumble. As we saw during the Taiping era, tensions among peasants, village headmen, scholar-gentry, and local officials were never far from the surface. Landlordism, especially the growing incidence of absentee landlordism, tended to stretch these tensions further. As some controversial economic studies of rural Qing society have suggested, even with the most advanced intensive farming techniques available and the introduction of better crops for marginal areas like corn, peanuts, and potatoes, the land was approaching the limits of its ability to support the population without the widespread introduction of power-driven machinery. Living on the edge of poverty in many areas, with old trade routes and handicrafts disrupted by the treaty ports, many peasants saw in the Taipings, the Nian, and other local rebellions a desperate way to change their situations. But in the end, the radical ideologies and ruthlessness of the rebels disillusioned the peasantry, while in many places their poverty increased due to the immense destruction caused by rebel clashes and the flight of many wealthy scholar-gentry to the treaty ports. As a result, by the beginning of the twentieth century, absentee landlordism had become an increasingly acute problem. As some scholars have noted, the land problems of China—and their parallels in India and the Ottoman Empire—were an important impediment to an effective response to the scientific–industrial challenge of Europe and America.

Chinese Family, ca. 1873. While the later nineteenth century marked changes on a number of fronts, the centrality of the family and its Confucian hierarchy remained largely intact. In the portrait here of the Yang family of Beijing, the father and eldest son occupy the places of honor under the central window of the ground floor, while the wives, concubines, infants, and servants are arrayed on the upper veranda. In most cases, the seclusion of such wealthy women was nearly complete. The photographer reported, however, that these women frequently moistened their fingertips and rubbed them on the paper windowpanes to make them transparent so they could secretly watch events outside.

Social Trends   While changes were certainly noticeable in the family, in relationships between men and women, and in the confidence the Chinese displayed in the Confucian system—particularly among urban Chinese—the durability of long-standing traditions is probably far more striking. As we have seen in every chapter on China, the family remained the central Chinese institution. Within it, the father continued to be the most powerful figure and the Confucian ideal of hierarchical relationships between husband and wife, father and son, and elder brother and younger brother remained in force. Daughters, though most often treated with affection, were also considered a net drain on family resources because they would marry outside the family. Thus, the education they received was generally aimed at fostering the skills the family of their husbands-to-be would consider valuable—cooking, sewing, running a household, and perhaps singing and poetry. Enough literacy was also desirable for girls to read such classics as "Admonitions for Women," the "Classic of Filial Piety," and other guides to proper behavior. But the proverbial wisdom remained that "a woman with talent is without virtue." Hence, the daughters of the wealthy were kept secluded in the home, and most—with the exception of certain minorities like south China's Hakkas—continued the practice of foot binding.

The disruptions of the nineteenth century began to have some effect on this situation. Though there had been a slow trickle of foreign influence into China, particularly in the treaty ports, for much of the nineteenth century, the decade following the Sino–Japanese War saw an upsurge in it, particularly as the Qing moved belatedly toward reform and underground revolutionary movements began to gain adherents. Women in Taiping areas had had a brief taste of equality, though it had been undermined by Taiping excesses and the Confucian revival afterward. With wealthier Chinese beginning to send daughters abroad to be educated, the impressions they returned with began to erode some Chinese customs, though the full impact of this would not be felt until the 1920s and 1930s. Meanwhile, such customs as the selling of young girls and female infanticide continued to be common, particularly in economically hard-pressed areas.

Culture, Arts, and Science

Though the late Qing period is often seen by scholars as one more concerned with cataloging and preserving older literary works than innovation, there was nevertheless considerable invigoration due to foreign influences toward the end of the dynasty. Indeed, one could say that the era begins with one of China's great literary masterpieces and ends with China's first modern writers pointing toward a vernacular-language "literary renaissance" starting around 1915. Reversing the trend of thousands of years, the most significant Chinese developments in science and technology were those arriving from the West as products of the Industrial Revolution and the new kind of society emerging there.

The Dream of the Red Chamber   Though the novel during Ming and Qing times was not considered high literary work by Chinese scholars, the form, as with Europeans in the eighteenth and nineteenth centuries, proved immensely popular. During the mid-eighteenth century, what many consider to be China's greatest novel, *Hong Lou Meng* (*The Dream of the Red Chamber*) was written by the shadowy Cao Xueqin [SOW shway-CHIN] (ca. 1715–ca. 1764). Almost nothing is known of Cao, including exactly when he was born and who his actual father was. The novel itself chronicles the decline and fall of a powerful family over 120 chapters. Some scholars see in it a loose autobiography of Cao's own family and a thinly veiled account of events in the early days of the Qing. In fact, the novel has been so closely studied and analyzed that there is an entire field called "red studies" or "redology" (*hong xue*) devoted to examination of the work.

Poetry, Travel Accounts, and Newspapers   While the form of the interlocking "three excellences"—painting, poetry, and calligraphy—remained largely unchanged, their content increasingly treated subjects related to China's new position in the age of imperialism. Though sometimes confining himself to more traditional fare, Huang Zunxian (1848–1905), for example, wrote many poems based on his experience as a diplomat in Japan and the United States.

China's increasing need to understand the nature of the threat confronting it prompted a greater number of atlases, gazetteers of foreign lands, and by the 1860s the first eyewitness travel accounts. Many of the early attempts at compiling information about foreign countries were copies of Western works, whose sophistication gradually increased as the century wore on. The most significant of these were Wei Yuan's (1794–1856) *Illustrated Gazetteer of the Maritime Countries* of 1844 and Xu Jiyu's (1795–1873) *Record of the World* of 1848. These accounts, especially Xu's, formed the backbone of what Chinese officials knew about the outside world until the first eyewitness accounts of travelers and diplomats began to arrive in the late 1860s.

Though hundreds of thousands of Chinese had emigrated to various parts of the world by the mid-1860s, it was only in 1866 that the first authorized officials began to visit foreign countries and not until 1876 that diplomats began to take up their posts in foreign capitals and ports. All of these men, however, were required to keep

Li Gui (1842–1903) on the Philadelphia Exposition in 1876

"Considering that the intent of countries in holding expositions is primarily to display friendship and extend human talent, particular emphasis is placed on the four words 'expand and strengthen commerce.' For the most part, though, we Chinese have not seen this as advantageous nor, since so few of us have gone abroad, have we fully grasped its implications. Still, can it be the case that others do their utmost to understand the precise thoughts of foreigners and eagerly spend hundreds, thousands, tens, or even hundreds of thousands of dollars of their capital competing in enterprises that are not advantageous? We Chinese alone seem capable of thinking that the intent of the Westerners in undertaking these exhibitions rests on principles against which we should guard at any cost. Yet as a means of enriching the country on the one hand, and benefiting the people on the other, how could this . . . exposition attendance be considered wasteful?"

—Li Gui, *Huan you diqiu xin lu*, 10a; translated by Charles Desnoyers, in *A Journey to the East*. Ann Arbor: University of Michigan Press, 2004, p. 100.

journals of their experiences, and by the later part of the century China began to acquire a far more complete sense of what the outside world was like. The diaries of the diplomats Zhang Deyi (1847–1919) and Guo Songtao (1818–1891) were particularly significant in this regard.

A new popular medium also emerged in the treaty ports and eventually in most Chinese cities as well—the newspaper. For centuries newsletters tracking official doings at the capital had been circulated among the elites. However, the 1860s saw the first popular Chinese-language papers, the most prominent of which was *Shenbao*. By the turn of the century, Liang Qichao had emerged as China's most influential journalist and scholar, having started and edited five newspapers, each heavily influenced by his views on reform. Such publications and the growing numbers of journals and popular magazines, many started by missionaries anxious to use science and Western material culture as a vehicle for their work, were vitally important in the transfer of ideas between Chinese and foreigners.

Science and Technology   As we have seen, the most pressing need for China during the early nineteenth century was considered to be military technology. During the period between the Opium Wars, Chinese officials attempted with some success to purchase guns and cannon from European and American manufacturers to bolster their coastal defenses. It was quickly apparent to the self-strengtheners, however, that China must understand the basic principles behind these revolutionary weapons and begin to manufacture them on their own. Moreover, this would be impossible to do unless the infrastructure was in place and such supporting industries as mining, railroads, and telegraphy were also established.

One early move in this regard was the founding of the All-Languages Institute (*Tongwen Guan*) in 1861. Founded to provide interpreters for the newly arriving diplomats in Beijing, the foreign experts employed soon allowed the school to become a kind of all-purpose science and technology academy as well. With the founding of arsenals and dockyards and their supporting infrastructures, the need for technical knowledge accelerated. Here, the Chinese Education Mission to the United States, as well as later student missions to England and Germany, was meant to create a nucleus of trained personnel to modernize Chinese industry and defense.

Despite the general animosity directed against them by Chinese officials, missionaries ironically were key players in science and technology transfers. Unlike the Jesuit missionaries of the seventeenth century, Protestant missionaries in the nineteenth century directed their efforts at ordinary Chinese but often did so by attracting them with the new advantages of science. Central to their efforts was the role of medical missionaries in setting up clinics and using their presence in the community to foster conversion. The missionary community was also active in popularizing developments in Western science and technology through journals like *The Globe Magazine*.

By the latter part of the century, increasing numbers of Chinese scholars were becoming involved in the study of foreign subjects, going abroad for education, and in the translation of Western works into Chinese. The Chinese mathematician Li Shanlan (1810–1882), for example, collaborated with Shanghai missionaries in translating works on algebra, calculus, and analytical geometry. Later, Liang Qichao and Yan Fu (1854–1921) studied and translated a wide range of foreign scientific and social science works by John Stuart Mill, Thomas Huxley, Herbert Spencer, and Charles Darwin, as well as such Enlightenment authors as Hobbes, Locke, Hume, Rousseau, and Bentham.

Thus, while China had not yet completed its move to the new scientific–industrial society, the momentum had already begun among the empire's intellectual leaders. Even so, nearly all agreed that the future would not lie in slavish imitation of the West. In the meantime, however, the example of Japan confronted them only a short distance away.

Zaibatsu and Political Parties: Economics and Society in Meiji Japan

Scholars of Japan's economic history have often pointed out that the commercial environment developing through the Tokugawa period was well suited to the nurturing of capitalism and industrialism in the nineteenth century. As we saw in Chapter 21, for example, the imposition of the law of "alternate attendance" created a great deal of traffic to and from Edo as daimyo processions made their biannual trips to the capital. This guaranteed traffic supported numerous hostels, restaurants, stables, supply stores, theaters, and all the other commercial establishments necessary to maintain the travelers in safety and comfort. The infrastructure of the major roads also required constant tending and improvement, as did the port facilities for coastal shipping and fishing industries. Towns and cities along the routes also grew, as did the regionally specialized crafts and industries they supported. By 1850, for example, Edo had well over 1 million inhabitants, while Osaka and Kyoto both had about 375,000. Finally, commercial credit establishments, craft guilds, and large-scale industries in ceramics, sake brewing, fine arts, fishing, and coastal shipping—all intensified by being compressed into a relatively small area—had already regularized many of the institutions characteristic of the development of a modern economy.

Commerce and Cartels

Perhaps because of the urgency of their situation following Perry's visits, the Japanese were quicker to go abroad to study the industrially advanced countries of Europe and the United States. In 1860, for example, they sent an embassy to America in which the participants—including the future journalist Fukuzawa Yukichi (1835–1901)—were expected to keep diaries of everything they saw. Even during the last days of the Tokugawa regime, Japanese entrepreneurs were already experimenting with Western steamships and production techniques.

Cooperation and Capitalism   When the Meiji government began its economic reforms, its overall strategy combined elements that still mark Japanese policy today. The first was to make sure that ownership, insofar as possible, would

MAP **24.6** **The Modernization of Japan to 1910.**

remain in Japanese hands. The second was that, taking its cue from the success of the leading commercial nations of the West, Japan would develop its exports to the utmost while attempting to keep imports to a minimum. Japanese entrepreneurship also received an enormous boost from the cashing out of the samurai. While many of the former warriors found anything to do with commerce distasteful, some took to heart the government's injunction that starting economic enterprises was a patriotic duty. By the end of the century, Japan's industrial statistics were impressive by any standards: Coal production had increased to six times its 1860 base, and iron, copper, and other mining industries expanded at a similar rate—but still could not keep pace with Japan's industrial needs. By the turn of the century Japan needed to import much of its raw material, a situation that has continued to this day.

Not surprisingly, families with long-standing connections to capital swiftly moved to unite their enterprises to gain market share. The Mitsui Company, for example, used its extensive brewing profits to fund a host of other enterprises, soon becoming one of Japan's largest industrial concerns. Similarly, the Mitsubishi Company expanded from coastal shipping to manufacturing—later creating military vehicles and famous aircraft during World War II as well as popular cars today. The encouragement of the government and the cooperation of social networks among elites in finance and industry led to the creation of a number of **cartels** called *zaibatsu*. By the end of the nineteenth century, the zaibatsu would control nearly all major Japanese industries.

Cartel: A group of domestic or international businesses that form a group to control or monopolize an industry.

The Transportation and Communications Revolutions

The rapid development of railroads and telegraphs was one of the most stunning transformations of the Meiji era. The Japanese pursued these devices with an enthusiasm scarcely paralleled anywhere else in the world. Even today, Japan's fabled "Bullet Train" remains the standard for high-speed ground transportation, while companies such as Sony and Motorola continue to dominate electronic communications markets. By the mid-1870s Japan had in place a trunk railroad line paralleling the main coastal road and several branches to major cities in the interior. Though Westerners found Japanese trains quaint—along with the custom of leaving one's clogs on the platform before boarding the cars—they were efficient and marked a trend for railroad building wherever the Japanese went. Similarly, telegraph—and, by the end of the century, telephone—lines were swiftly strung between the major cities and towns, followed by undersea cables to the Asian mainland and North America. By 1895, Japan was estimated to have over 2,000 miles of private and government railroads in operation and over 4,000 miles of telegraph wires in place (see Map 24.6).

The Meiji Constitution and Political Life
While the Charter Oath and Constitution of 1868 were instituted with considerable success, a debate had already begun among the genro concerning the liberalization of representative government in Japan. In 1881 the emperor approved a plan whereby Ito Hirobumi (1841–1909) and several senior colleagues would launch a painstaking study of the constitutional governments of the United States, Great Britain, France, Germany, and other countries, to see what aspects of them might be suitable for Japan's needs. The Meiji Constitution, as it came to be called, was promulgated in 1889 and remained in force until it was supplanted by the constitution composed during the Allied occupation of Japan after World War II.

While borrowing elements from the US and British models, Ito's constitution drew most heavily from that of Germany. Much of it was also aimed at preserving the traditions of Japan's Confucian society that Ito and the genro most valued. Chief among these was the concept of *kokutai*, the "national polity." In this view, Japan was unique among nations because of its unbroken line of emperors and the singular familial and spiritual relationship between the emperor and his people. Thus, the Meiji Constitution is presented, in Ito's words, as "the gift of a benevolent and charitable emperor to the people of his country." The sovereignty of the country is placed in the person of the emperor as the embodiment of kokutai; the emperor's Privy Council, the army and navy, and the ministers of state are answerable directly to him. There is also a bicameral parliamentary body called the

Visions of the New Railroads. The marvels of the new systems of railroads and telegraphs springing up in Japan provided practitioners of ukiyo-e woodblock art a host of new subjects to depict in the 1870s and 1880s. Here is one of a number of views of new stations, in this case, Ueno on the Ueno–Nakasendo–Tokyo Railway, with small commuter trains arriving and departing.

Diet, with an upper House of Peers and a lower House of Representatives. Like the House of Lords in Great Britain, Japan's House of Peers consisted of members of the nobility; the representatives were elected by the people. The primary purpose of the Diet in this arrangement is to vote on financing, deliberate on the everyday items of governance, and provide advice and consent to the Privy Council, Ministry of State, and Imperial Court.

As for the people themselves, 15 articles spell out "The Rights and Duties of Subjects." Duties include liability for taxes and service in the military, while the rights enumerated are similar to those found in European and American constitutions: the right to hold office, guarantees against search and seizure, the right to trial, the right to property, and freedoms of religion, speech, and petition. All of these, however, are qualified by such phrases as "unless provided by law," leaving the door open for the government to invoke extraordinary powers during national emergencies.

Political Parties   As constitutional government began to be enacted in the 1890s, the factional debates among senior advisors naturally began to attract followers among the Diet members and their supporters. In the preceding decades there had been political parties; but their membership was limited, and they were seen by many as illegitimate because of their potential opposition to the government. Now, two major parties came to the fore by the turn of the century. The Kenseito [KEN-say-toe], or Liberal, Party had its roots in the work of Itagaki Taisuke (1837–1919) and his political opponent, Okuma Shigenobu [OH-ku-ma SHIH-geh-no-bu]. The two merged their followers but later split into factions at the turn of the century. It later was reestablished as the Minseito.

The more powerful party during this time was the Seiyukai, or Constitutional Government Party, founded by Ito and his followers in 1900. Generally associated with the government and the zaibatsu, the Seiyukai dominated Japanese politics in the era before World War I; after World War II, its adherents coalesced into Japan's present Liberal Democratic Party.

Social Experiments   In addition to creating an industrial base and a constitutional government, Japan's rulers attempted to curb practices in Japan that were believed to offend foreign sensibilities as part of its program of "civilization and enlightenment." Bathhouses, for example, were now required to have separate entrances for men and women, and pleasure quarters were restricted in areas near foreign enclaves; meat eating was even encouraged in largely Buddhist Japan, resulting in the new dish *sukiyaki*. In the boldest experiment of all, the government mandated the use of Western dress for men and women, accompanied by a propaganda campaign depicting the advantages of this "modern" and "civilized" clothing. Criticism from a variety of quarters, however, including many Westerners, ultimately forced the government to relent and make the new dress optional.

In the same vein, traditional restrictions on women were altered. Though the home remained the primary domain for women, as it does even today, women were far more often seen in public. Concubines were now accorded the same rights as wives. Courtesans and prostitutes were no longer legally considered servants. Among elites, the fad of following all things Western established to some degree Victorian European standards of family decorum. More far-reaching, however, was the role of the new education system. Even before the Meiji Restoration, Japan had one of the highest levels of preindustrial literacy in the world—40 percent for males and 15 percent for females. With the introduction of compulsory public education, literacy would become nearly universal; and the upsurge in specialized women's education created entire new avenues of employment for women.

This same trend toward emancipation was evident among the rural population. The formal class barriers between peasants and samurai were eliminated, though informal deference to elites continued. In addition, some barriers between ordinary Japanese and outcast groups, such as the Eta, were also reduced. During the latter part of the nineteenth century, aided by better transportation, improved crops, maximum utilization of marginal lands, and the opening up of Hokkaido for development, Japan became the most intensely farmed nation in the world. Japan's already well-developed fishing industry contributed mightily by introducing commercial fish-based fertilizers that boosted yields enormously. The result was that although Japan's population increased to 40 million by 1890, it was a net exporter of food until the turn of the century.

NEW YEAR'S DAY IN JAPAN

New Year's Day in Japan, ca. 1905. An important part of Japan's strategy to roll back its unequal treaties with the West was the campaign of *bunmei kaika*, or "civilization and enlightenment." The idea of this policy was to show Western observers in concrete terms that Japan accepted Western notions of what it meant to be a "civilized" nation. In this cartoon the contrast between the old Japan of the Tokugawa days and the new Japan of the "enlightenment and civilization" is graphically depicted. The upper panel, labeled "Old Style" shows two samurai bowing in greeting in a traditional room replete with screens and scrolls marking the occasion, and the wife of the host entertains the men. The lower panel shows the "new style," in which men and women wear Western fashions, with families greeting each other together on the street in front a Western house surrounded by a picket fence, while a pet dog romps nearby.

"Enlightenment and Progress": Science, Culture, and the Arts

As we saw in Chapter 21, while the Tokugawa sought seclusion, they were by no means cut off entirely from developments in other nations. Of particular importance in this regard was the requirement imposed on the Dutch merchants at Deshima to make their annual reports to the Shogun on the state of the world. By the time of Commodore Perry's visit the accumulated amount of "Dutch learning" was impressive. Much of it consisted of notes on scientific and technical developments.

Engaging "Western Science"   Nevertheless, at the time of their initial contact with the Western powers, the Tokugawa were stunned at the degree to which the accelerating technologies of the Industrial Revolution had armed their adversaries. During Perry's visits Japanese sketch artists frantically sought to capture the details of the ships' gun ports and cannon and the outward signs of their steam power. As we have seen, the Japanese were immediately engaged with the notion of the railroad; just as quickly they sought to create oceangoing steamships. By 1860, they had built and manned steamers and insisted that their embassy to the United States travel aboard one the Japanese had built themselves.

Western Science. The Japanese were fascinated by the new and strange technology they found on Perry's ships, including the paddle wheel from one of his steamships, which they drew with scientific precision.

Journalism in Modern Society

"In editing the paper [*Jiji-shimpo*] I encouraged the reporters to write bravely and freely. I have no objection to any severe criticism or extreme statements, but I warned them that they must limit their statements to what they would be willing to say to the victim face to face. Otherwise, they are what I would call *kage-benkei* [shadow fighters] attacking from the security of their columns. It is very easy for *kage-benkei* to fall into mean abuses and irresponsible invectives which are the eternal shame of the writer's profession."

—Fukuzawa Yukichi. *The Autobiography of Fukuzawa Yukichi*, Kiyooka Eikichi, trans., Tokyo, 1934. Quoted in Tsunoda, DeBary, Keene, *Sources of Japanese Tradition*, p. 129.

The demand for industrial and military technology required large numbers of Japanese to seek technical education. During the initial stages of the Meiji era, thousands of Japanese students studied in Europe and the United States, and the Japanese government and private concerns hired hundreds of foreign advisors to aid in science and technical training. By the 1880s a university system anchored by Tokyo Imperial University and including Keio, Waseda, and Doshisha was offering courses in medicine, physics, chemistry, engineering, and geology, among other advanced disciplines. By the turn of the century, Japan's Institute for Infectious Diseases had become world famous for its pathbreaking work in microbiology. On the whole, however, the bulk of the nation's efforts went into the practical application of science to technology and agriculture in order to support the government's modernization efforts.

Culture and the Arts   As was the case a decade later in China, Japanese intellectuals eagerly absorbed copies of Western Enlightenment, philosophical, and social science works in translation—including Locke, Hobbes, Spencer, Darwin, and Comte, to name but a few. As was also true in China, journalism played a dominant role as a disseminator of information to the public. Here, Fukuzawa Yukichi, like Liang Qichao in China, held a central place both in fostering the growth of newspapers and in articulating the role of journalists in a modern society.

As were nearly all the arts in late nineteenth-century Japan, the novel was also heavily influenced by Western examples. In some respects, the culmination of this trend was *Kokoro*, by Natsume Soseki, (1867–1916) published in 1914. Soseki utilizes the wrenching changes in Meiji Japan set against traditional and generational values to create the tension and ultimate tragic end of the central character in his work.

More traditional arts such as Noh and kabuki theater and ukiyo-e printing survived but often in a somewhat altered state. Updated kabuki variations now featured contemporary themes and often had female actors playing female parts.

In addition, European plays such as Ibsen's *A Doll's House* enjoyed considerable vogue. As for ukiyo-e, it remained the cheapest and most popular outlet for depictions of contemporary events until the development of newspaper photography. Especially telling in this regard are ukiyo-e artist's interpretations of the Sino–Japanese War.

Putting It All Together

Scholars of China and Japan have long debated the reasons for the apparent success of Japan and failure of China. One school of thought sees the fundamental reasons growing from the cultural outlooks of the two countries. China, it is argued, assumed that outsiders would simply be won over to Confucian norms and modes of behavior because this is what China's historical experience had been for the last 2,000 years. When it became apparent that defensive measures were necessary, it was still assumed that China's superior culture would win out. Japan, on the other hand, because of its long history of cultural borrowing and its much smaller size, assumed a more urgent defensive posture. In addition, the Japanese had the advantage of watching events unfold in China before the threat reached their own shores. This allowed them to act in a more united and pragmatic fashion when resisting the Western threat.

Some historians, however, disagree with this approach. They argue instead that the cultural differences between China and Japan were secondary in the face of the foreign threat. According to this school of thought, the primary cause of the radically different outcomes for China and Japan was that China was victimized by foreign imperialism much earlier and much more thoroughly than Japan. Once Japanese modernization efforts were under way, they won for themselves a breathing spell with which to keep imperialism at bay and ultimately fought their way into the great power club themselves (see Concept Map).

Both China and Japan were to continue their relative trajectories for decades to come. Japan would achieve its ultimate military power in early 1942. At that point, during World War II, the Japanese Empire encompassed Korea, Manchuria, much of China, the Philippines, Indonesia, most of southeast Asia, and hundreds of Pacific Islands. In a little over 3 years, however, the empire was gone, the home islands were in ruins, and for the first time in its history Japan was under occupation. Since that time, however, its economic development has resumed with even more vigor, and is today the third largest economy in the world.

China's troubles would, despite a few bright points along the way, multiply. Throwing off the Qing, the Chinese republic would be plagued by warlordism, civil war, and invasion, until the triumph of the Communist Party and founding of the People's Republic of China in 1949. Yet, it is only since 1978 that its most significant progress in industrial and economic development has taken place. Ironically, much of China's newfound economic might was inspired by the approaches employed in Japan's postwar recovery. In the long sweep of China's history, however, this resurgence is seen with growing confidence by the Chinese as marking a return to their accustomed place and in 2010 it passed Japan to become the world's second largest economy.

Review and Respond

1. How would you characterize the Western maritime countries' economic relationship with China during this period?

2. How did opium become such a problem between Britain and China? Was opium the real cause of the First Opium War? Why or why not?

3. Why did "self-strengthening" produce China and "Western science and Eastern ethics" in Japan as adaptations to modernity have such different results?

4. What do you see as the major strengths and weaknesses of the Meiji response to Western imperialism?

5. Why did Japan become an imperial power instead of simply strengthening its home islands?

▶ For additional resources, including maps, primary sources, visuals, and quizzes, please go to www.oup.com/us/vonsivers. Please see the Further Resources section at the back of the book for additional readings and suggested websites.

Thinking Through Patterns

▶ **What was the impact of Western imperialism on the "regulated societies" of China and Japan?**

The impact of the intrusion of Great Britain, France, the United States, and later Germany and Russia forced both China and Japan into defensive postures. Both countries had sought to keep out what they considered subversive foreign influences after an earlier period of exposure to Western traders and missionaries. China had created a tightly controlled system of overseas trade based in Guangzhou (Canton); Japan allowed only the Dutch to trade with them. But the expansion of trade in both legitimate goods and opium and the need of the British for regularization of diplomatic practices pushed Britain and China into a cycle of war and "unequal treaties" under which China was at an increasing disadvantage. Japan, suddenly thrust into international commerce and diplomacy by the young United States, now sought to protect its borders without pushing the Western powers into seizing any of its territory.

China's long history of absorbing and acculturating outside invaders to Confucian norms encouraged its leaders to assume that the Westerners would be no different. Though many officials realized the qualitative difference between the industrializing Euro-American countries and invaders from the Chinese past, they were of divided opinion about what to do. Thus, attempts at reform were often undercut by political infighting at court and in the bureaucracy. The Taiping Rebellion also played a central role in further depleting China's strength and resources. As time went on, increasing Western control of China's ports and tariffs, absentee landlordism, and declining agricultural productivity also played a role.

▶ **Why did European empire building in Asia have such dramatically different effects on China and Japan?**

For Japan, after a decade of indecision about how to handle the foreign intrusion, a civil war ended in the dismantling of the shogunate and the unification of the country under Emperor Meiji. With remarkable unity born of a deep sense of urgency, Japan embarked upon a thoroughgoing reform program aimed at remaking the country along avowedly Western lines. The focus and consistency displayed by Meiji and his advisors avoided many of the problems China experienced, and Japan's late Tokugawa economics to some degree had predisposed the country toward a smoother transition into that of scientific–industrial society.

▶ **How have historians seen the nature of these outside forces and their influences in east Asia?**

Historians have long debated the relative weight that should be assigned to cultural and material reasons for the differing paths of China and Japan. China's long history as the region's cultural leader, some have argued, made it difficult for the empire to remake itself to face the Western challenge; Japan, on the other hand, has a long history of cultural borrowing and, thus, found it easier to borrow from the Euro-American world. Some historians have argued that China's earlier experience with imperialism stunted the modernizing tendencies within the empire and kept it from responding; they argue that Japan had the advantage of being "opened" later and so could respond more effectively. Others have argued that Japan's tradition of military prowess played a role, still others that China's more complete incorporation into the modern "world system" crippled its ability to respond more independently.

Chapter 25

1683-1908

Adaptation and Resistance

THE OTTOMAN AND RUSSIAN EMPIRES

RUSSIAN AND OTTOMAN EMPIRES, 1683-1908

October 13, 1824, marked a most unusual event in Russia. On this date, Aleksander Nikitenko, born into serfdom, received his freedom at the young age of 20 from his lord, a fabulously wealthy landowning count. Even more remarkable is the subsequent course of Nikitenko's life and career. After earning a university degree, he went on to become a professor of literature at St. Petersburg University, a member of the distinguished Academy of Sciences, and a censor in the Ministry of Education.

▶ Which new models did the Ottomans adopt during the nineteenth century to adapt themselves to the Western challenge?

▶ Why did the tsars and landholding aristocracy fear Western constitutionalism? Why did the Russian constitutionalists eventually lose out to the revolutionaries?

▶ How did the agrarian Ottoman and Russian Empires, both with large landholding ruling classes, respond to the western European industrial challenge during the 1800s?

▶ Why did large, well-established empires like the Russian and the Ottoman struggle with the forces of modernity, while a small, secluded island nation like Japan seemed to adapt so quickly and successfully?

Auction of Serfs. In this painting, *Auction of Serfs* (1910), the well-known Russian realist painter Klavdiy Vasilievich Lebedev (1852–1916) depicted the room of a Russian aristocratic landowning family as it auctioned off valuables as well as serfs (standing on the right). The 1861 decree ending serfdom in Russia was far less than what its name suggested since the peasants had to buy their land from the nonfarming landowners.

Beginning in 1818 at the age of 14, the bright and precocious Nikitenko kept a diary. The account of events from this date until his emancipation in 1824 at the age of 20 was written as a retrospective memoir. The most important entries refer to the role of the European Enlightenment thinkers in shaping changing intellectual attitudes in Russia. For example, Nikitenko makes repeated reference to the works of Montesquieu, particularly *The Spirit of Laws*, which inspired the so-called Decembrists, leaders of an abortive proconstitutional uprising in 1825, with whom Nikitenko was in touch.

Nikitenko's diary provides deep insights into the role of **serfdom** in the Russian Empire. We are told that "when the inevitable happened," the errant serfs were turned over to a lackey in charge of meting out punishment in the form of flogging with birch rods: "Woe to the unfortunates who fell into [his] hands! He was a master and enthusiast of flogging, especially of girls, and they were terrified by the mere sight of him." Nikitenko also tells of his sadness when he had to part with his classmates upon graduating at age 13 from his country school: "But more painful than anything else was the knowledge that I would not be allowed to join the boys who were preparing to enter high school. For me its doors were inexorably closed.

Serfdom: Legal and cultural institution in which peasants are bound to the land.

Here, for the first time, I had to face the terrible curse that hung over me because of my social status, which later caused me so much suffering and almost drove me to suicide." Nikitenko's curse, Russian serfdom, was scarcely different from plantation slavery in the Americas or from the status of untouchables in India. Slavery was also the common lot of many in the neighboring Ottoman Empire and, though limited to households, was no less demeaning. The end of serfdom in Russia would not come until 1861 and that of slavery in the Ottoman Empire not until 1890.

Serfdom and slavery were dramatic examples of the kinds of practices that the new Enlightenment constitutionalism, in theory at least, stood firmly against. As such, they were among the first of many challenges the world outside western Europe and North America faced from the West in the nineteenth century. Russia was an empire that had inherited Byzantine Christian civilization but had not adopted the New Science and its offspring, the twin revolutions of the Enlightenment and Industrial Revolution. For its part, the Ottoman Empire was heir to both Islamic and Byzantine traditions but had also not participated in the transition to the New Science, Enlightenment, and industrialization. Even though Enlightenment thought had produced and elaborated the political theories of the social contract and popular sovereignty, which were realized in the American, French, and Haitian Revolutions, shortly before the onset of the Industrial Revolution in Great Britain, it would be the campaigns of Napoleon in the early nineteenth century that sowed these ideas throughout Europe.

They also would fling these seeds at the initially unpromising soil of the Russian and Ottoman Empires. Napoleon's invasions of Ottoman Egypt in 1798 and Russia in 1812 drove home to their rulers that his new armies of mass conscripts, equipped with flintlock muskets and light, mobile artillery and drilled to fight in flexible formations, were superior to their own military forces. It became inevitable for the Ottomans and Russians, short of losing their independence, to update their armies and training and to respond somehow to the constitutional nationalism arising from the French Revolution and carried by Napoleon's armies, which now attracted rising numbers of adherents among their subjects.

At the same time, the two empires became mortal enemies: An expanding eastern [Orthodox] Christian Russia declared its goal to be conquest of the former eastern Christian capital Istanbul (Constantinople) and to drive a shrinking Ottoman Empire from Europe back into "Asia" (Asia Minor or Anatolia). Since both empires were members of the Concert of Europe, their profound conflict involved the other European powers as well. These powers found themselves increasingly drawn into a conflict, culminating in the Crimean War of 1853–1856, that was only partially European and increasingly involved Russia and the Ottomans in Asia. For the monarchs, politicians, and diplomats focused after 1815 on the balance of power in western and central Europe, such a power struggle between the Russians and Ottomans held little interest: For them, this contest was "Oriental" and therefore alien.

It is important that we keep this partially non-Western identity of the Russian and Ottoman Empires in mind for this chapter: As forcefully as Russia asserted itself in the European Concert in the early years after 1815 and again at the end of the nineteenth century, it was in reality—despite its Christian character—not any more or less "European" than the increasingly harried Muslim Ottoman Empire. Indeed, as we will see, both empires had far more in common with each other, and to some degree with the empire of the Qing in China, than they did with the evolving nation-states of western Europe. Furthermore, their reactions to the challenges posed by the new nation-states paralleled each other to a degree not often appreciated by students and scholars studying them outside of a world context. Therefore, we consider them together here as their own case studies in the overall patterns of constitutionalism, nation-state formation, and the challenge of modernity.

Decentralization and Reforms in the Ottoman Empire

Prior to the Russian–Ottoman rivalry in the 1800s, the traditional enemies of the Ottomans were the Austrian Habsburgs. This enmity had reached its climax in the second half of the 1600s. The Habsburgs ultimately won but in the course of the 1700s were increasingly sidelined by the rise of Russia as a new, Orthodox Christian empire, whose rulers, the tsars, saw themselves as representatives of the "third Rome," that is, Moscow as the successor of Rome and Constantinople. After consolidating itself on the fertile northeast European plains, Russia expanded eastward and southward, clashing with the Muslim Ottomans, conquerors of Constantinople. Because the Russians adapted themselves earlier than the Ottomans to new western European military tactics, the Ottomans found it increasingly difficult to defend themselves in the later 1700s. They

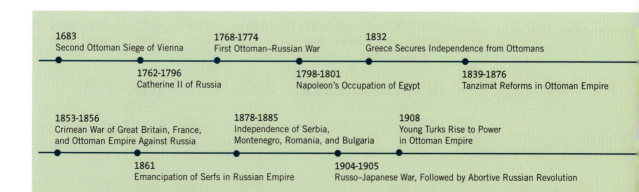

1683 Second Ottoman Siege of Vienna	**1768-1774** First Ottoman–Russian War	**1832** Greece Secures Independence from Ottomans	
1762-1796 Catherine II of Russia	**1798-1801** Napoleon's Occupation of Egypt	**1839-1876** Tanzimat Reforms in Ottoman Empire	
1853-1856 Crimean War of Great Britain, France, and Ottoman Empire Against Russia	**1878-1885** Independence of Serbia, Montenegro, Romania, and Bulgaria	**1908** Young Turks Rise to Power in Ottoman Empire	
1861 Emancipation of Serfs in Russian Empire	**1904-1905** Russo–Japanese War, Followed by Abortive Russian Revolution		

The Decline of the Ottoman Empire, 1683–1923

	Losses, 1683–99 (Treaty of Karlowitz)		Losses, 1879–1915 (Treaties of London and Bucharest)
	Losses, 1700–18 (Treaty of Passarowitz)		Losses, 1916–23 (Treaty of Lausanne)
	Losses, 1719–74 (Treaty of Küçük-Kaynarca)		Turkey in 1923
	Losses, 1775–1812 (Treaty of Bucharest)		Dependent state
	Losses, 1813–29/30 (Treaty of Adrianople)	1913	Date or period of autonomy
	Temporary loss to Austria, 1718–39	**1832**	Date of independence
	Losses, 1830–78 (Treaty of Berlin)		

MAP 25.1 The Decline of the Ottoman Empire, 1683–1923.

sought to improve their defenses through military and constitutional–nationalist reforms in the mid-1800s but were only half successful. Russia became the patron of nationalist movements among the Slavic populations in the European provinces of the Ottoman Empire. Although they strengthened themselves through reforms, the Ottomans were no match for the combined Russian–southern Slavic aggression. At the end of the Second Balkan War of 1913, they had lost nearly the entire European part of their empire to ethnic–nationalist liberation movements and were barely able to hang on to Istanbul (see Map 25.1).

Ottoman Imperialism in the 1600s and 1700s

In the period from 1500 to 1700 the Ottoman Empire was the dominant political power in the Middle East and North Africa, flanked by the two lesser realms of Persia in the east and Morocco in the west. At that time, as we noted, the main enemy of the Ottomans was not yet Russia but the Habsburg Empire in Spain, Germany, and Austria. The two were fighting each other on dual fronts, the Balkans in the east and North Africa in the western Mediterranean, each gaining and losing in the process and eventually establishing a more or less stable disengagement. It was during this disengagement period that Russia began its expansion southward at the increasing expense of the Ottomans.

Demographic Considerations   As with the other agrarian–urban regions of Asia and Europe, the Middle East had experienced a sustained recovery of population figures after the Black Death of the mid-1400s. This recovery came to an end around 1600, with 25 million inhabitants, though with slow increases to 27 million by 1700 and to about 30 million by 1800. The population figures were thus smaller than those of the Habsburg countries, with 37 million in 1700 and 42 million in 1800. If one takes into consideration, however, that the Spanish Habsburg line died out in Spain in 1700 and the Austrian Habsburgs governed only indirectly in Germany, the resulting figure for the smaller territory in 1800 is a comparable 25 million. Russia, for its part, had population figures roughly comparable to those of the Ottoman Empire. As the Ottomans approached the era of the challenge of modernity, they formed part of a relatively sparsely populated eastern Europe and Middle East.

From Conquests to Retreats   At the end of the 1500s, after a long period of military showdowns, the Ottomans and Habsburgs were beset by problems of military overextension. Therefore, in 1606 they concluded a peace to gain time for recovery, during which the Ottomans recognized the Habsburgs for the first time as a de facto Christian power on the border of the Ottoman province of Hungary. The peace lasted until the end of the 1600s when both were sufficiently recovered to renew their competition. The main administrators responsible for the Ottoman recovery were the viziers of the Köprülü family, from an Albanian line of Janissaries. They transformed many military assignments of the cavalry into tax farms, to increase the flow of revenue, and broadened the recruitment of the Janissary infantry from exclusively rural Christian boys to young, mostly urban Muslims. By shifting from the increasingly less important cavalry to their firearm-equipped infantry and artillery, the Ottoman army regained its edge.

In 1683 the Ottomans renewed their competition with the Habsburgs and marched with a giant force to their northwestern border. For a second time in their history, they laid siege to Vienna (the first siege was in 1529), the capital of the Austrian Habsburgs. But even though sappers and siege cannons succeeded in breaching the walls in several places, a Polish relief army arrived just in time to drive the besiegers, who had neglected to fortify their camp, into a retreat. The Habsburgs followed up on this retreat by seizing Hungary, Transylvania, and northern Serbia, thus making a third siege of Vienna impossible. In the peace of 1699, the Ottomans and Habsburgs finally agreed to recognize each other fully in the territories they possessed.

Renewed Reforms   During the war years of the later 1600s, the Janissary force had swelled to some 70,000 soldiers. In the end, however, only about 10,000 were on active duty. Since they were all on the payroll and given renewed fiscal shortfalls, the money was often debased or in arrears, forcing them to earn a living as craftspeople. A brisk trade developed in which Janissaries and non-Janissaries alike exchanged pay tickets that entitled the holders not only to wages but also to fiscal and juridical exemptions. Coffeehouses near Janissary barracks became flourishing trade centers for pay tickets, food rations, and military supplies. In short, the Janissary force was in the process of becoming a collection of crafts guilds on a kind of government welfare.

New reforms were clearly necessary. In the early 1700s the sultan's government cut the Janissary rolls by half and enlisted Anatolian farmers to supplement the active Janissaries. In order to improve revenues with which to pay the Janissaries, the reformers introduced the new institution of the lifetime tax farm, or **life lease**, for agricultural rents from village farmers. As in France, which developed a similar tax farm regime at the time, the idea was to diminish the temptation—endemic among

Life lease: Lifelong tax farm, awarded to a wealthy member of the ruling class, in return for advances to the central imperial treasury on the taxes to be collected from village farmers.

the annual tax farmers—to squeeze farmers dry so that they would flee from the countryside to the cities. Wealthy and high-ranking courtiers, officers, administrators, and Islamic clerics in Istanbul bought these life leases. They numbered about 2,000, shifting the weight in the ruling class increasingly from the military to civilians. The large cash outlays necessary for the purchase of these life leases required access to liquid capital, which Armenian merchants with European connections provided. Thus, here in the early 1700s was the beginning of a development parallel to similar developments in France and England, with efforts to organize a kind of capital market. As a result of the reforms, in 1720, for the first time in a century and a half, the central budget was balanced again.

(a)

The Tulip Era   The new ruling class, holding life leases, was less connected to the Topkapı, the sultan's palace, and its administrative quarters and invested its wealth in new constructions. A building boom ensued in the early 1700s, expressing itself in the erection of numerous office buildings and mansions in town as well as palaces and gardens along Istanbul's waterfront. Other construction included renovations, aqueducts, mosques, colleges, libraries, public baths, and fountains. In addition, villages in the provinces benefited from construction projects. Ruling-class members who remembered their modest rural origins competed in the capital and countryside for philanthropic recognition.

The new palaces and mansions were architecturally inspired by the long tradition of pre-Islamic Middle Eastern royal residences and parks, especially in Iran. In the salons of these residences, poets and musicians presented their compositions. Books, for the first time printed in Ottoman Turkish, became available: One of these books contained a summary of Copernicus's New Science, although there is no evidence of any intellectual impact made by heliocentrism in the empire. The gardens of the residences featured hundreds of varieties of flowers, plants, shrubs, and trees. (Many of these varieties, including tulips, had made their way earlier to Europe; and ever since the mid-1600s the Dutch have been *the* tulip specialists of the world.) Modern Turkish writers dubbed the time of cultural efflorescence in the first half of the 1700s the Ottoman "Tulip period."

(b)

The Tulip Period. During the "Tulip period," the Ottoman ruling class not only prided itself on its ability to breed ever new varieties of tulips, hyacinths, and roses (a) but also frequented coffeehouses and public parks for picnics (b).

Decentralization   During the Tulip period, an accelerating transformation of cavalry-held lands into tax farms started a pattern of political decentralization in the Ottoman Empire. Agents responsible for the collection of taxes for their superiors succeeded in withholding increasing amounts from the treasury in Istanbul. By the mid-1700s, these agents were in positions of considerable provincial power as "notables" (*ayan*) in the Balkans or "valley lords" (*derebeys*) in western Anatolia. Starved for funds, the sultan and central administration were no longer able to support a large standing army of infantry and cavalry in the capital.

In 1768–1774 the notables and valley lords played a crucial role not only in financing a major war against Russia but also in recruiting troops—untrained and underarmed peasants—since the numbers of government forces in fighting order had shrunk to minimal levels. The war was the first in which the Russian tsars exploited Ottoman decentralization for a systematic expansion southward. When the sultan promptly lost the war, he was more or less at the mercy of these notables and lords in the provinces.

The Western Challenge and Ottoman Responses

Soon after this Ottoman–Russian war, the Ottoman Empire began to face the challenge of Western modernity. As with China and Japan, the increasing military, political, and economic strength of the West allowed it to force the traditional Asian empires to adapt to its challenges. This adaptation was extremely difficult and entailed severe territorial losses for the Ottoman Empire. But after initial humiliations, the ruling class was able to develop a pattern of responses to the Western challenge, by reducing the power of the provincial magnates, modernizing the army, introducing constitutional reforms, and eventually transforming its manufacturing sector.

External and Internal Blows During the period 1774–1808, the Ottoman central government suffered a series of humiliations which were comparable in their destabilizing effects to those in the later Opium Wars and the Taiping and Boxer Rebellions in China. Russia gained the north coast of the Black Sea and Georgia in the Caucasus. Napoleon invaded Egypt and destroyed the local regime of Ottoman Mamluk vassals in 1798. But a British fleet sent after him succeeded in destroying his navy, and a subsequent land campaign forced him to return to France in 1801. As he was victimizing the Ottoman Empire, Napoleon apparently wanted to demonstrate the ineffectiveness of Great Britain's European continental blockade and teach it a lesson about the vulnerability of its control of India. Napoleon's sudden imperialist venture produced a deep shock in the Middle East: For the first time a Western ruler had penetrated deeply into the Ottoman Empire, cutting it effectively in half.

Internally, the lessening of central control in the second half of the 1700s left the provinces in virtual independence. Most notables and lords were satisfied with local autonomy, but a few became warlords, engaging in campaigns to become regional leaders. In other cases, especially in Egypt, Syria, and Iraq, *Mamluks*, that is, military slaves from the northern Caucasus whom Ottoman governors had previously employed as auxiliaries in the military, seized power. In eastern Arabia, a local Sunni cleric, Muhammad Ibn Abd al-Wahhab [Wah-HAHB], exploited Ottoman decentralization to ally himself with the head of a powerful family in command of a number of oases, Ibn Saud [Sa-OOD], to establish an autonomous polity in the desert, which today is the most powerful oil state in the world—Saudi Arabia. None of these ambitious leaders, however, renounced allegiance to the sultan, who at least remained a figurehead.

To take power back, the sultan and his viziers once more sought for ways to reform the empire. In 1792, they proclaimed a "new order" (*Nizam-i Cedid* [Nee-ZAHM-ee Jay-DEED]), defined as a reorganization of the army with the creation of a new, separate artillery and flintlock musket corps of some 22,000 soldiers alongside the Janissaries. The new corps was recruited from among Anatolian farmers, with the help of willing notables and lords, and financed through ad hoc measures, such as property confiscations, currency debasements, and tax increases. European officers trained these soldiers in drills, line fighting, bayonet combat, and formation marching. Officers received their education at the newly founded Land Engineering School. The corps underwent its baptism by fire when it defended Acre in Syria successfully against Napoleon.

The ad hoc financing of the new order, however, came to haunt the reformers. During a severe fiscal crisis in 1807, auxiliary Janissaries, refusing to wear new uniforms, assassinated a new order officer. Inept handling of this incident resulted in a quickly mushrooming, full-scale revolt of Janissaries as well as religious scholars and students, costing the sultan his life and ushering in the dissolution of the new troops. In a counterrevolt, thanks to the timely arrival of a Ukrainian-born notable from northern Bulgaria with his private army, a new sultan came to power in 1808. As a price for his accession, the sultan had to agree to power sharing with the provincial lords.

Renewed Difficulties

After a dozen years of careful maneuvering, during which the sultan reconstituted the nucleus for another new army and neutralized many notables and valley lords, he was able to crush the Janissaries in a bloody massacre (1826). But the new corps was in no shape yet to provide the backbone for a sustained recentralization of the empire. New internal enemies arose, in the form of Greek ethnic nationalists, whom the Ottomans would have defeated had it not been for the military intervention of the European powers. As a result, Greece became independent in a war of liberation (1821–1832). It was the first country, prior to Italy and Germany, in which ethnic nationalism was central to its foundation.

Russia, providing support for its fellow Orthodox Christian Greeks, acquired new territories from the Ottomans around the Black Sea. Several Balkan provinces achieved administrative autonomy. Algiers in North Africa was lost in 1830, falling to an invading French force. Worst of all, in 1831, the new Ottoman vassal in Egypt, the Albanian-born officer Muhammad Ali (r. 1805–1848), seeking greater influence within the empire, rose in rebellion. After occupying Syria (1831–1840), he would have conquered Istanbul had he not been stopped by Russian, British, and French intervention. Without the diplomacy of Great Britain, which carefully sought to balance the European powers after the end of the Napoleonic empire, the Ottoman Empire would not have survived the 1830s.

Life, Honor, and Property

The cumulative effect of these setbacks was a realization among Ottoman administrators that only a serious effort at recentralization would save the empire. In 1839, with a change of sultans, the government issued the Rose Garden Edict, the first of three reform edicts, plus more specific additional ones in between, which are collectively known as

Muhammad Ali. Muhammad Ali transformed Egypt during the first half of the nineteenth century more thoroughly than the Ottoman overlord sultan could in his far-flung empire. He astutely realized that long-staple cotton, bred first in Egypt, could make Egypt a wealthy state in the beginning industrial transformation of the world.

Tanzimat: Ottoman reforms inspired by constitutional nationalism in Europe, covering the adoption of basic rights, a legal reform, and a land code.

Tanzimat ("Reorganizations"). In the Rose Garden Edict, the government bound itself to three basic principles: the guarantee of life, honor, and property of all subjects regardless of religion; the replacement of tax farms and life leases with an equitable tax system; and the introduction of a military conscription system, all in accordance with the Shari`a, the compendium of Islamic morality and law. The edict carefully avoided a definition of the position of the Christians and Jews in the empire before the law, offering them the rights of life, honor, and property while maintaining their inequality vis-à-vis the Muslims proclaimed in Islamic law.

The edict addressed the two fundamental problems of the empire, that is, taxes and the military, carefully emphasizing the Islamic justification. It also enumerated basic human rights, inspired by the American Declaration of Independence and the French Rights of Man. Here, we can see a first adaptation of the Ottoman Empire to the Western challenge: The Ottoman Empire adapted, at least in an initial and partial way, to constitutional nationalism, the outgrowth of Enlightenment thought.

Further Reforms   As these reforms were being implemented, a new European political initiative challenged the Ottoman Empire. The aggressively imperialistic Napoleon III (1848-1852 president, 1852-1870 emperor), self-declared emperor of France, challenged the Russian tsar's claim to be the protector of the Christian holy places in Palestine, a claim which the Ottoman sultan had granted after his defeat in 1774. As we saw in Chapter 24, the French joined the British during the Second Opium War for much the same reason: protection of Catholics and French missionaries in China. While the French and Russian diplomats sought to pull a vacillating sultan back and forth toward their respective claims, the political situation turned increasingly tense. Through careful maneuvering, Ottoman diplomats were able to strengthen themselves in a coalition with Great Britain and France. In the Crimean War of 1853–1856 this coalition was victorious against an isolated Russia. It forced Russia in the subsequent peace to recognize the Ottoman Empire's right to full integrity, provided the latter would continue the reforms announced in 1839.

Accordingly, the sultan promulgated the "Fortunate Edict" of 1856, in which he clarified the question of equality left open in the earlier edict: Regardless of religion, all subjects had the right to education, employment, and administration of justice. A number of subsequent measures spelled out this right and the earlier edicts in greater detail. To begin with, the reformers reorganized the judiciary by establishing law courts for the application of newly introduced commercial, maritime, and criminal legal codes, based on European models. Muslim law was collected in the 16 volumes of the *Mecelle* (Arabic "Code"), containing the Hanafi Islamic legal tradition that was constitutive for the empire since its foundation in 1300. Family law remained in the hands of the traditional Islamic judges as well as the heads of the Christian and Jewish communities (called *millets*). Since Muslims were obliged to a 5-year military service in the new army, the edict extended this obligation to Christians and Jews as well. Ironically, however, this extension was subsequently undercut by a regulation which exempted Christians and Jews from the service with the payment of a fee. Hence, de facto equality remained an ambiguous concept in the empire.

A further reform measure was the introduction of a system of secular schools, initially for males, beginning with age 10 and culminating with high schools. But a lack of funds delayed building this system, which at the end of the 1800s still lagged far behind the traditional religious primary schools (*mekteps*) and colleges (*medreses*) as well as the more rapidly expanding Christian, Jewish, and foreign missionary schools. Literacy in the general population hovered around 10 percent in 1900, and thus, the edict had little to show even after half a century of efforts.

A measure that worked out quite differently from what was intended was the Land Code of 1858. The code reaffirmed the sultan as the owner of all land unless subjects or religious foundations possessed title to specific parcels of private property, such as urban real estate, suburban gardens, and endowments. But it also confirmed all users of the sultan's land, that is, farmers who produced harvests on family plots as well landowners collecting rents from the farmers of entire villages. Theoretically, the code subjected all users, family farmers as well as landowners, to taxation. But in practice the central administration had no money to appoint tax collectors (or even establish a land registry prior to 1908). It could not do without tax farmers, who still collected what they could get and transmitted to the government as little as they were able to get away with.

Highly uneven forms of landownership thus developed. In central and coastal Anatolia, as well as in the hill country of Palestine, family farmers received title to their individual plots. In Anatolian swamplands, tribal Kurdish steppe ranges, and Palestinian coastal strips large absentee landownership appeared. Syrian life leaseholders bribed officials to acquire a title to entire village districts. Similarly, Iraqi sheikhs succeeded in registering tribal lands in their name. Overall, tax yields remained as low as ever, improving only toward the end of the nineteenth century, long after the introduction of the Tanzimat. The much needed land reform remained incomplete.

Prohibition of Owning an Entire Village and Exemptions

"The land of an inhabited village cannot be given to one person independently in order to make a *çiftlik* [family plot]; but, as stated in Art. 72, if all the inhabitants of a village are scattered, and the *Tapu* [sovereign as supreme landowner] has acquired the right to its lands, if it is not possible to bring back that village to its original state by bringing fresh agriculturists to live there, and conferring on them the land separately, the land can be given in lots to one, two, or three persons ..."

—F. Ongley, trans., with revisions by Horace E. Miller. *The Ottoman Land Code.* London: William Clowes and Sons, 1892. Article 130, Internet Archive, http://www.archive.org/details/ottomanlandcodeooturkuoft.

Constitution and War
Seen in the context of the centralization reforms in previous centuries, the Tanzimat decrees of 1839 and 1856 were little more than enactments of traditional policies. In the context of nineteenth-century constitutional nationalism, however, they appeared like autocratic dictates from above, lacking popular approval. In the 1860s, younger Tanzimat bureaucrats and journalists working for the first Ottoman newspapers, meeting in loose circles in Istanbul and Paris under the name of "Young Ottomans," became advocates for the introduction of a constitution as the crowning element of the Tanzimat, to end the autocracy of the sultan.

The idea of a constitution became reality in the midst of a deep crisis in which the empire found itself embroiled from 1873 to 1878. The crisis began when the Ottoman government defaulted on its foreign loans. In order to service the renegotiated loans, it had to increase taxes.

Ottoman Parliament. The constitutional reforms (Tanzimat) of the Ottoman Empire culminated in elections for a parliament and two sessions, uniting deputies from a multiplicity of ethnic backgrounds (1876–1878). It met during the Russian–Ottoman War of 1877–1878, which the Ottomans lost. The newly installed Sultan Abdülhamit used the war as an excuse for ending constitutional rule and governing by decree.

Patterns Up Close | From Constitutional to Ethnic Nationalism

Visions of a New Order. The stirring events of 1848 produced visions of a new political order in which the peoples of Europe would form a "holy alliance" and a new "universal and social democratic republic," as shown in this lithograph where representatives from each nation march in solidarity with flags aloft past the rubble of toppled monarchs. In reality, the impulses of ethnic-linguistic nationalism sowed deep divisions among the very people depicted here.

The constitutional revolutions in the United States, France, and Haiti from 1776 to 1804 helped usher in the modern period of world history. They were rooted in two crucial developments in the preceding two centuries.

First, they were intellectually based on the concept of a fictive original state of individuals in nature giving up their independence in return for the establishment of a civilized state with a constitution. According to this constitution, individuals had rights and obligations resulting in elections of deputies, representation in a parliament, and an elected ruler under popular sovereignty.

Second, this intellectual constitutionalism did not remain on paper. It became a revolutionary reality thanks to the existing constitutional practice of England (later Great Britain), which in the Glorious Revolution of 1688 formalized the earlier constitutional practices of shared sovereignty between king and Parliament. In other words, because constitutionalism was functional in England/Great Britain, it became *the* aspirational model in the American colonies of Britain and later France.

As we saw in Chapter 22, however, in the course of the nineteenth century many constitutional nationalists began to add embellishments to the fundamental ideas of liberty, equality, and fraternity that had inspired the revolutions. Romantic thinkers in Germany, such as Johann Gottfried Herder (1744-1803), had already written voluminously on the concept of the "people" (*Volk*) prior to the revolutions. In their writings, the romantics assumed that there were ethnic, linguistic, literary, historical, and religious bonds that predated the formation of constitutional nations.

Byron Dressed as an Albanian. The famous Romantic English poet, George Gordon, Lord Byron (1788–1824) was one of many European intellectuals who came to the assistance of Greece and other Balkan countries in their liberation movements against the perceived tyranny of the Ottoman Empire. In this painting, Byron appears dressed as an Albanian—a backward corner of the Balkans that was then under Ottoman rule. His exotic dress shows his support for the ethnic-nationalist movements that were then bubbling up across the Balkans. Byron, in fact, died in Greece of 1824 of a fever, just a few years before Greece formally achieved independence.

This romantic thinking was highly speculative and largely undocumented. Above all, the requirement that a people—often dispersed and living among other peoples—should become a nation (requiring borders for the constitution) was often highly unrealistic. Ethnic–linguistic–religious nationalism was just as fictional as the assumption of an original state of individuals in nature.

As vague as it was, ethnic nationalism attracted groups of followers among many Europeans on the continent during the nineteenth century. They were typically students at the premier universities, graduating as lawyers, journalists, doctors, pharmacists, and other professionals. Much of the scholarship that university professors produced concerned the historical origins of European "peoples," their heroes, literary creations, and enemies against which they had to prevail. Many students, especially from eastern Europe, engaged in highly imaginative ethnic–linguistic–religious identity creation and, in the process, became nationalists who literally created the peoples whom they then wished to liberate from the yoke of their alien monarchs. Not surprisingly, the forces of ethnic-linguistic-religious nationalism would be particularly active within the large, multi-ethnic, multi-linguistic, and multi-religious empires of the Habsburgs, Ottomans, and Russia (see Map 25.2).

The first to proclaim a people entitled to become a nation under a constitution were the Greeks, who in 1821–1833 waged a war of liberation against the Ottoman sultan. They invoked a "Greekness" that was rooted in the assumption of a common Greek language, the history of the Greek city-states, Alexander the Great, the intellectual achievements of Plato and Aristotle,

MAP **25.2** **Ethnolinguistic Composition of Central Europe, ca. 1900.**

and a host of other real or imagined precedents. When it came to adopting constitutions, however, the liberators did not aim to create of republics, as the Americans and French had done. They opted for constitutional monarchies, thereby revealing what subsequently became a trademark of ethnic–linguistic–religious nationalism (or, for short, "ethnolinguistic nationalism"): that culture, including that of kings, was more important than the principle of popular sovereignty.

This remains true today. "Peoples" who are supposed to be or become "nations" often seem to tolerate autocrats or dictators who hold constitutions in low regard. Conversely, constitutionally unified "nation-states" encompass ethnic groups which are unwilling to curb their identities and strive for secession. In short, many people in the world have yet to find a balance between the two types of constitutional and ethnic nationalism. Yet, the nation-state, as we have seen, has become nearly the only form of political organization in the world today.

Questions

- How do the origins of ethnic nationalism show the power of an imagined past in shaping people's group identity?

- In which places in the world today is this process still a force in shaping people's national consciousness?

This increase triggered ethnic–nationalist uprisings in Montenegro, Serbia, and Romania in the Balkans in 1875. The heavy-handed repression of these uprisings resulted in a political crisis, with a palace coup d'état by the Young Ottomans, during which a new sultan, Abdülhamit II (r. 1876–1909), ascended the throne and a constitution was adopted. Finally, in this sequence of events, the Russians exploited the perceived political weakness of the new constitutional Ottoman regime for a new Russo–Ottoman war in support of the Balkan nationalist uprisings.

Amid a rapid advance of Russian troops against a crumbling Ottoman army, the Ottomans held elections for the constitutionally decreed parliament between December 1876 and January 1877. Provincial and county councils elected 130 deputies to meet for two sessions in Istanbul. With the invading Russian forces practically at the gates of Istanbul in February 1878, the deputies engaged in a spirited criticism of the government. Irritated, the sultan dismissed the parliament and ruled by decree.

A few months later, at the Congress of Berlin, the sultan had to accept the loss of two-thirds of the empire's European provinces. Montenegro, Serbia, Romania, and (after a delay of 7 years) Bulgaria gained their independence. Bosnia-Herzegovina and Cyprus, although still Ottoman, received an Austrian administration and a British administration, respectively. Sultan Abdülhamit never reconvened the parliament, and the empire reverted back to autocratic rule.

Autocracy   Sultan Abdülhamit surrounded himself with capable second-generation Tanzimat bureaucrats who did not have the constitutionalist leanings of the Young Ottomans. He had very little financial leeway since the Public Debt Administration, imposed by the European powers in 1881, collected about one-third of the empire's income to pay for its accumulated foreign debt. Furthermore, the European price depression in the second half of the nineteenth century (1873–1896) was not favorable to foreign investments in the empire. Nevertheless, a few short-distance railroads connecting the fertile Anatolian valleys and their agricultural exports with Mediterranean ports were built thanks to French capital. A postal service and telegraph system connected all provinces, and steamship lines connected the ports. Once the depression was over, foreign investors enabled the government to build long-distance railroads across Anatolia (see Map 25.3). By the early 1900s, a basic communication infrastructure was in place in the Ottoman Empire.

MAP **25.3** Railways in the Ottoman Empire, 1914.

Given his fiscal limits, the sultan was all the more active as a propagandist, burnishing his credentials as the pan-Islamic caliph of Muslims in Eurasia, from Austrian Bosnia and Russian Asia to British India. He astutely sensed that the Balkan events of 1878 and subsequent Congress of Berlin had been a watershed in European politics. The Concert of Europe, with its Britain-supported concept of a balance of power, was no more. It was being replaced by the beginning of an imperial rivalry between Germany and Great Britain. France, Austria-Hungary, and Russia played their own subsidiary imperial roles. Since France and Great Britain, furthermore, carried out their imperialism against the Ottoman

Empire, with the conquests of Tunisia in 1881 and Egypt in 1882, respectively, Abdül-hamit was particularly affected. His pan-Islamism was therefore a carefully executed effort to instill the fear of jihad in the European politicians and their publics.

Although most of the Ottoman Balkan provinces had become independent nations by 1878, three ethnic–nationalist movements were still left inside the empire. Abdülhamit met them with an iron fist. The first movement consisted of Serb, Bulgarian, Vlah, and Greek nationalists agitating in Macedonia during 1893–1895. Without outside support, none of these feuding groups could impose itself on the province; and Ottoman troops were therefore able to repress them.

The next were the Armenians, who formed sizeable minorities in the six eastern provinces of Anatolia. Most Armenian farmers and craftspeople in these provinces were politically quiet, but urban-based and secularized Armenian ethnic nationalists organized terrorist incidents. In reaction, the sultan armed Kurdish tribal units, which massacred thousands of Anatolian Armenian villagers from 1894 to 1896. Finally, the Ottomans met a revolt in Crete in 1897, in favor of union with Greece, with an invasion and defeat of Greece itself, which had to pay an indemnity. Europe, busy with its imperialist competition in Africa and Asia, had no time to help the remaining ethnic–nationalist stirrings of the Macedonians and Armenians in the Ottoman Empire.

In the later years of his rule, Abdülhamit increasingly failed to suppress dissatisfaction with the lack of political freedom among the graduates from the elite administrative and military academies. As so often prior to revolts or revolutions, improved economic conditions—as they materialized after the end of the worldwide recession of 1893—stoked political ambitions to create a condition social scientists sometimes call a "revolution of rising expectations." In a pattern similar to that unfolding in Qing China at the same time, oppositional circles among Ottoman intellectuals abroad merged with secret junior officer groups in Macedonia and Thrace in 1907. Barely one step ahead of the sultan's secret service, the officers launched a coup d'état in 1908, which urban Ottomans generally received with great relief. The officers forced the sultan to reinstate the constitution of 1878 and, after elections, accept a new parliament.

The Young Turks The officers, organized as the Committee of Union and Progress (CUP) and colloquially referred to as "Young Turks," did not initially force Abdülhamit from office. They did so in part because the wily sultan presented himself to the public as having engineered the reinstatement of the constitution, blaming his bureaucrats for not having done so earlier. Behind the scene, he did everything to get rid of the Young Turks. He had his courtiers arouse military and government employees, religious students, and religious brotherhood leaders into a countercoup in April 1909. The rebels demanded the reinstatement of the Sharia, which actually had never been suspended, as mentioned earlier. The government gave in to the demand, and the CUP leaders, unsure of army support in the capital, headed for the provinces to find more reliable troops. In short order, they returned at the head of trustworthy soldiers and this time deposed Abdülhamit, enthroning one of his brothers as his successor.

As the CUP consolidated its power against the conservative religious opposition, a weak imperial government fell into disarray. Members of the increasingly marginal (even if CUP-dominated) parliament as well as an array of provincial notables exploited the deposition of Abdülhamit for their own gains. Austria-Hungary and Bulgaria formally annexed Bosnia-Herzegovina and northern Rumelia, respectively, in 1908. Albania revolted in 1910 and Italy invaded Tripolitania in 1911, triggering a nearly 20-year guerilla war of resistance by members of the Sanusiyya brotherhood against the invaders. The CUP found itself in a near desperate position.

Even worse, the newly independent Balkan states of Serbia, Montenegro, Greece, and Bulgaria unified behind the Russian imperial idea of driving the Ottomans once and for all out of Europe. In 1912, they demanded sweeping reforms in Macedonia (where uprisings had been suppressed in 1895). When the Ottoman government rejected these demands, the four countries declared war against the empire. In response, the Ottoman general staff made the mistake of attacking the Balkan states on several fronts, instead of fighting a defensive war. Bulgarian troops broke through the Ottoman defenses, occupied Macedonia and Thrace, and advanced dangerously close to Istanbul. Once more, the survival of the empire hung in the balance.

In this extremely critical situation, the government was willing to give up on besieged Edirne, the second capital of the empire. Infuriated by this defeatism, a triumvirate of CUP officers staged another coup and assumed direct ruling responsibilities. Step by step, power had been narrowed, from the broad parliamentary coalition that had reinstated the constitution in 1908 to the CUP operating behind the scenes in 1909 to now three powerful men within the CUP supported by a cast of about 50 officers. Try as it might, however, the triumvirate was unable to prevent the fall of Edirne. At the subsequent conference in London, it had no choice but to accept the independence of Albania, the loss of Macedonia (with the city of Salonica, the birthplace of the CUP), Thrace, and nearly all of southern Rumelia, including Edirne.

Fortunately for the CUP, the four victorious Balkan states were unable to agree on the division of the spoils. The Ottomans exploited the disagreements and retook Edirne, succeeding in a new peace settlement to push the imperial border westward into Thrace. Nevertheless, the overall losses were horrendous: Except for a rump Rumelia, the Ottoman Empire had now been driven out of Europe, ending more than half a millennium of rule in the Balkans.

Economic Development   While the empire was disintegrating politically, the economic situation improved. The main factor was the end of the depression of 1873–1896 and a renewed interest among European investors in creating industrial enterprises in the agrarian but export-oriented independent and colonial countries of the Middle East, Asia, and South America. When Abdülhamit II was at the peak of his power in the 1890s and early 1900s, investors perceived the Ottoman Empire as sufficiently stable for the creation of industrial enterprises.

New research since the 1980s has considerably refined the concepts of less developed agriculture-based economies and industrialization during the 1800s. Prior to that time, scholars often compared the Ottoman Empire unfavorably to Japan, the only non-Western country that was successful in adopting the British model of industrialization. By 1900, Japan was essentially industrialized, producing its own iron and steel, heavy machinery, and machine-produced textiles. Historians had to free themselves from the fixation on the British and Japanese models and concede that more circuitous paths toward industrialization merited the same serious attention. For example, the Netherlands did not industrialize until the 1890s, and France continued to industrialize slowly from industrial "islands" in certain urban areas out

Silk Manufacture, Turkey, ca. 1892. Small textile factories were able to flourish in the nineteenth century, in spite of cheap English cotton goods. They did so on the basis of lowly paid workers and relatively coarse, low-quality goods affordable to the poor in cities, towns, and villages. Industrialization expanded in the 1890s with the foundation of textile factories, such as the silk manufacture in Bursa depicted here.

into the surrounding countryside and provincial centers until well into the twentieth century. Until the 1890s Latin American countries achieved high economic growth rates through commodity exports, without its leaders feeling a strong urge to industrialize. Thus, these countries all possessed viable economies in the second half of the nineteenth century even though their industries were still comparatively light.

With this notion of viable nonindustrial economies in the 1800s in mind, the Ottoman Empire in the 1800s can be described as a state in which the traditional crafts-based textile industry initially suffered under the invasion of cheap industrially produced English cottons in the period 1820–1850. But a recovery took place in the second half of the 1800s, both in the crafts sector and in a newly mechanized small factory sector of textile manufacturing, producing cottons, woolens, silks, and rugs. This recovery was driven largely by domestic demand and investments because the European price depression of 1873–1896 was not conducive to much foreign capital inflow. Operating with low wages and even more lowly paid female labor, domestic small-scale manufacturing was able to hold foreign factory–produced goods at bay.

Throughout the 1800s, the empire was also an exporter of agricultural commodities, particularly cotton, dried fruit, and nuts. But the recovery of the domestic textile production demonstrates that the Ottomans did not succumb completely to the British free market system. When foreign investments resumed in the 1890s and early 1900s, there was a base for industrialization to build on, similar to what people in the Netherlands, France, and Latin America had when they industrialized.

Iran's Effort to Cope with the Western Challenge

Iran (also called "Persia," in recognition of its long heritage) had risen in the 1500s as the Shiite alternative to the Sunni Ottomans. The two dynasties of kings (*shahs*) who ruled Iran, the Safavids (1501–1722) and Qajars (1795–1925), nurtured a hierarchy of Shiite clerics who formed an autonomous religious institution in their state. While

Isfahan, Ali Qapu (High Gate).
Entrance to the Qajar palace (*a*)
from a large rectangular square
around which major mosques
and bazaars are also located
(*b*). The palace contains rooms
on several floors with richly
plastered and decorated walls
and ceilings such as the music
room, with instrument motifs
set in the plaster (*c*).

the Ottoman sultans always kept their leading Sunni religious leaders under firm control, the Iranian rulers had to respect a careful balance of power with their Shiite leaders. Therefore, when Iran in the 1800s faced the Western challenges, reformers had to establish an alliance with the Shiite clerics to bring about constitutional reforms.

Safavid and Qajar Kings   The Safavid Empire was a less powerful state than that of the Ottomans. It comprised Shiite Iran, the Caucasus, Sunni Afghanistan, and parts of Sunni central Asia. The Safavid kings, whose lands were limited in most provinces to oasis agriculture, were not wealthy enough to recruit a large firearm infantry to match the Janissaries. As a result, for most of the time the Ottomans were able to keep the Safavid rivalry within manageable proportions, especially from the mid-1600s onward.

At this time, the Safavids ruled Iran from their newly founded capital of Isfahan in the center of the country, which they embellished with palaces and mosques. One of its suburbs was inhabited by a group of Armenian merchants who controlled silk production along the warm and humid Black Sea coast. Safavid Iran was a major exporter of silk yarn and clothes, second in quality only to Chinese wares, and thus supplemented its limited agrarian revenues with an international trade of silk.

The Safavids were vulnerable not only to the military challenges of their Ottoman neighbors to the west but also to those of tribal federations in the Sunni provinces to the east. In Afghanistan, one of the two major Pashtu tribal federations revolted repeatedly against the efforts of the Safavids to convert them to Shiite Islam. Eventually, in 1722, this federation succeeded in conquering Iran and ending Safavid rule, at a time of advanced decentralization in the empire. The Afghanis, however, were unable to establish a stable new regime. Instead, provincial Iranian rulers reunified and even expanded the empire for short periods during the 1700s. Stabilization finally occurred in 1796, with the accession of the new Qajar dynasty.

The Qajars had been among the founding Shiite Turkic tribal federation of the Safavids, but in contrast to their brethren, they had no Shiite aspirations of their own. Instead, they paid respect to the clerical hierarchy that had become powerful in the aftermath of the Afghani conquest in the 1700s. The clerics supported themselves through their own independent revenues from landholdings in the vicinity of their mosques and colleges, and the Qajars were not powerful enough to interfere.

During the 1800s, two developments dominated Iran's historical evolution. First, like the Ottoman Empire, primarily agrarian Iran was subject to oscillating periods of decentralization and recentralization, following the decline or rise of tax revenues from the countryside. Second, the increasingly hierarchical and theologically rigid Shiite clerics were challenged by the popular, theologically less tradition-bound Babi movement. This movement, begun in 1844, rallied around a figure who claimed to be the promised returned Twelfth Imam or Mahdi (Messiah) with a new law superseding the body of legal interpretations of the Shiite clergy. A combination of Qajar troops and clerically organized mobs succeeded in suppressing this widespread movement, which subsequently evolved into the Baha'i faith.

The Qajars not only faced an unstable internal situation but also suffered from Russian imperialism. The declared Russian goal of liberating Constantinople implied the conquest of the central Asian Turkic sultanates as well as the north face of the Caucasus Mountains astride the land bridge between the Black and Caspian Seas. Accordingly, Russian armies sought to drive the Qajars from their Caucasus provinces. In response, the Qajar kings embarked on centralizing military and

In the Gardens of the Caucasus. Tiflis (modern-day Tbilisi), the capital of Georgia, was the crossroads of the contested and strategically vital Caucasus region that Persia, the Ottomans, and Russia all fought over incessantly for centuries. Though today we tend to think of Georgia as a "post-Soviet" state and part of Russia's "near abroad," for millennia Georgia and its neighboring countries of Armenia and Azerbaijan looked southward toward the Middle East, as reflected in the dress of the Georgian ladies and the musical instruments seen in this lithograph from 1847. But while the Georgian language contains many loan words from Persian, Arabic, and Turkish that reflect this long association with the Middle East, it has always retained deep and ancient Christian roots, as evidenced by the thirteenth-century church perched on a high cliff in the background.

administrative reforms, which were similar to those of the Ottomans though less pervasive. In the absence of sizeable groups of reformers of their own and bowing to Russian pressures, they hired Russian officers to train a small corps of new troops, the Cossack Brigade. (The tsar, although bent on expanding into the Caucasus, did not want Iran to collapse as a counterweight to the Ottomans.) Swedish advisors trained the police force, in an effort to improve civil peace. British subjects acquired economic concessions, such as monopolies for minerals and telegraph connections or the manufacture of tobacco. The increasing foreign influence in Iran aroused the ire of the conservative clerical hierarchy, and the kings had to withdraw the concessions. The Qajar ruling class was acutely aware of the Western challenge, but its reformist power vis-à-vis the clerical establishment was limited.

Perceptive Iranian constitutional nationalists from among the educated younger ruling class were less numerous than their Young Ottoman colleagues. They therefore founded a tactical alliance toward the end of the 1800s with conservative clerics and merchants. In 1906, after widespread revolts against tax increases to cover a lavish European trip by the shah, this alliance mounted a successful constitutional revolution, imposing parliamentary limits on the Qajar regime. The constitutional-nationalist alliance with the clerics was, however, inherently unstable and parliamentary rule failed to become a reality. As World War I drew near, Iran reverted to autocratic rule by the shahs. Nevertheless, the memory of the abortive Constitutional Revolution of 1906 lived on, becoming decisive in the later twentieth century with the formation of the Islamic Republic in 1979 and the enactment of a hybrid Islamic–democratic constitution.

Westernization, Reforms, and Industrialization in Russia

The Russian Empire that expanded during the 1800s southward at the expense of the Qajar and Ottoman Empires had arisen in 1547 as a tsardom in Moscow, succeeding the Byzantine eastern Christian "caesars" (from which the Russian term "tsar" or "czar" is derived). It was a relatively late empire, succeeding that of the Mongols; and it spanned eastern Europe as well as Asia. Given this geographical location at the eastern edge of Europe and outside western Christian civilization, Russia developed along an uneven pattern of relations with western Europe. The western European Renaissance and Enlightenment did not spread to Russia. Western culture became a force only around 1700 when the tsar Peter the Great (r. 1682–1725) became its advocate. The idea of constitutionalism arrived in the wake of the French Revolution and Napoleon's failed invasion of Russia (1812). But it remained weak and was diluted by pan-Slavic ethnic nationalism, an ideology whereby Russians sought unification with the Slavic peoples of the Balkans. Multiple small political groups competed with each other, with no single united reformist force emerging. These groups rose amid the social dislocations that followed the Russian industrialization effort at the end of the nineteenth century, but none was able to take over leadership in the abortive revolution following the disastrous defeat at the hands of a modernizing Japan in 1905. Although this uprising produced a weak Russian parliament, the Duma, the autocratic tsarist regime tottered on until collapsing under the unbearable strain of World War I.

Russia and Westernization

In 1768 George Macartney, British envoy to Russia (whom we met as the leader of Britain's attempted diplomatic overture to Qing China in Chapter 24 and the man generally credited with saying that Britain had an empire on which "the sun never sets"), observed that Russia was "a great planet that has obtruded itself into our system, whose place is yet undetermined, but whose motions most powerfully affect those of every other orb." The states of western Europe were, of course, aware of a large empire on their eastern flank but did not consider it fully European. Indeed, at a time when feudal practices were dying in western Europe, Russia under the Romanov dynasty *institutionalized* serfdom. Half a century earlier, Tsar Peter the Great, attempting to travel incognito—despite his six-foot eight-inch frame—went on a mission of investigation to western Europe and began a reform and urbanization process from the top, against an often fierce resistance in both the ruling class and the population at large, to bring Russia closer to the western European norms. His legacy was the new capital of St. Petersburg, extensive military reorganization, and concerted attempts to reign in the power of Russia's high nobility, the *boyars*—including physically cutting off their beards so that they would be clean-shaven like their Western counterparts. But another legacy was a deep-set resistance on a political and cultural level to any such measures coming from outside Russia, not unlike the cultural resistance that would plague Chinese reformers in the nineteenth century.

The German-born "enlightened despot" Tsarina Catherine II, the Great (r. 1762–1796), continued the reform process from the top, which by its very nature, however, was slow to trickle down. When the constitutional-nationalist revolutions broke out in the United States, France, and Haiti, the Russian Empire was an autocratic, fiscal–military state that had expanded in all directions. And its expansion did, indeed, affect many other "orbs."

Aristocratic Charter. The charter that Empress Catherine II of Russia granted to the Russian nobility in 1785 consolidated the Russian aristocracy as a class with its own set of rights and privileges. The charter also contained ideas of liberty that later were interpreted as extending to the other ranks of society as well. Shown here is frontispiece, with the coats of arms of the various provinces of the Russian Empire extending along the edge of the document, while the empress's official title is handwritten in gold in the center.

Catherine II's Reforms

Catherine the Great was the dominant figure of tsarist Russia during the eighteenth century. By origin, she was the princess of a minor German family in the service of Prussia. Early on she learned the art of aristocratic discretion and later in life set a record with her string of lovers in the recesses of her palace in St. Petersburg. Also early in life she developed an abiding intellectual engagement with the Enlightenment trends that proliferated not only in academies and salons but also among the European courts. According to the courtly version of this thought, called "the royal thesis (*thèse*)," rulers were to remain firmly committed to absolute rule but should also pursue administrative, judicial, and educational reforms in order to increase the welfare of their subjects. Catherine subscribed to a digest reporting on the latest trends in Parisian Enlightenment thought. In correspondence with Voltaire, a supporter of the royal thesis, and even Diderot, whom she subsidized (ignoring his atheism and antimonarchical impulses), she kept abreast of who was in and who was out of fashion among the leading *philosophes*. With her Enlightenment engagement,

Catherine was far ahead of the Russian aristocracy, not to mention the small urban educated upper strata, both of which were still much beholden to eastern Christian traditions.

As much an activist as Peter the Great but more subtle, the energetic Catherine pushed through a number of major reforms. Urban manufactures, especially of linen and woolen cloth, had greatly expanded in the early 1700s; and Catherine strengthened urban development with a provincial reform in 1775 and a town reform in 1785 that allowed local nonaristocratic participation. But in 1785 she also strengthened the aristocracy with a charter that exempted its members from the poll tax and increased their property rights, including the purchase of serfs. This was largely a measure to head off a repetition of the terrible peasant rebellions of 1762–1775, which had culminated with Pugachev's Cossack revolt. In a reform of the educational system (1782), the government set up a free, mostly clergy-staffed educational system, from urban primary schools to high schools. Catherine's legal reform project, however, apart from a police ordinance issued in 1782, remained incomplete; and the codification and humanization of Russia's laws had to wait for another 80 years.

In foreign affairs, Catherine was determined to revive Peter the Great's expansionism. She first undertook the dismemberment of the kingdom of Poland, accomplished together with Prussia and the Austrian Habsburgs in three stages, from 1772 to 1795. Then, in two wars with the Ottoman Empire (1768–1792), Catherine waged a successful campaign to end the Ottoman alliance with the Tatars, a Turkic-speaking population of mixed ethnic descent that had succeeded the Mongols of the Golden Horde (ca. 1240–1502) in Crimea and adjacent northern Black Sea lands. Catherine's modernized infantry forces were successful in humbling the considerably larger but disorganized Ottoman army and navy. In the first war, Russia gained access to the Black Sea, ending the Tatar–Ottoman alliance and gaining free access for Russian ships to the Mediterranean. In the second war, Russia absorbed the Tatars within its imperial borders, which now advanced to the northern coast of the Black Sea.

Russia in the Early Nineteenth Century

The ideas of the French Revolution made their first fleeting mark on Russia in the form of the Decembrist Revolt in 1825, several decades before they did in the Ottoman Empire. But since in the pattern of traditional empire formation the personality of the ruler still counted more than the continuity of the administration, the reign of the deeply monarchical Nicholas I for a generation in mid-1800 Russia meant that whatever the Decembrists had set in motion could only spread under the surface. Above the ground, Nicholas pursued an aggressive foreign policy of expansion, in the tradition of Catherine the Great (see Map 25.4).

Russia and the French Revolution   In her old age, Catherine was aghast at the monarchical constitutionalism of the French Revolution, not to mention its republicanism and radicalism. In an abrupt about-face, her government had Voltaire's books burned and other Enlightenment books banned. Alexander Radishchev (1749–1802), a Russian landed aristocrat and prominent author with sympathies for the revolution, was forced into exile in Siberia. The situation eased under Catherine's grandson, Alexander I (r. 1801–1825), who was educated in Enlightenment ideas. He initially showed inclinations toward constitutionalism, coaxed by his

The Territorial Expansion of the Russian Empire, 1795–1914

Russian Empire, 1795	Russian sphere of influence	Coal mining
Russian acquisitions, 1796–1855	1824 Date of acquisition	Gold mining
Russian acquisitions, 1855–1914	*Kazakhs* People	Copper mining

MAP 25.4 **The Territorial Expansion of the Russian Empire, 1795–1914.**

discreetly constitutionalist minister Mikhail Speranskii (1772–1839); but Napoleon's imperial designs interrupted any idea of implementation.

Russia emerged as a key power in efforts to prevent Napoleon's takeover of Europe. In 1805 Russia joined Britain and Austria in the Third Coalition against France; but Napoleon's smashing victory at Austerlitz in December 1805—where Alexander personally commanded the Russian troops—doomed the coalition. Napoleon followed up on his victorious campaigns by defeating Russian forces in June 1807. This was followed by a dramatic meeting between Napoleon and Alexander on a raft anchored in the River Niemen on July 27, 1807. Napoleon forced

Alexander into an agreement of mutual aid and the recognition of French conquests on the European continent.

However, after the defeat of Napoleon during his disastrous Russian campaign of 1812, Alexander rebounded. At the Congress of Vienna in 1815 he assumed a prominent role in the negotiations for the territorial settlements and reestablishment of peace, advocating a "holy alliance" of monarchs to be its guarantors. As a result, Napoleon's duchy of Warsaw became the kingdom of Poland, with the Russian tsar as its king. In contrast to his monarchical colleagues in Europe, however, Alexander remained open to Enlightenment reforms, initiating the liberation of serfs in Russia's Baltic provinces, pursuing constitutional reform in Finland and Poland, and mapping out a new status for eastern Christianity. But Russia also experienced unrest, so Alexander gradually lost interest in the continuation of his reforms.

Orthodoxy, Autocracy, and Nationality

No sooner did Nicholas I (1825–1855) ascend the throne in 1825 than a bloody revolt broke out, led by a small number of Russian officers exposed to the ideas of constitutional nationalism. Known as the Decembrist Revolt, the uprising was quickly suppressed and its leaders were hanged. The revolt had few connections with civilians and was furthermore intellectually divided between federalists and unionists. The former serf Nikitenko, introduced at the beginning of this chapter, was fortunate to escape with his life from his contacts with Decembrists. Despite this relative lack of impact, the revolt represented the first anti-tsarist, constitutional-revolutionary movement and, thus, became a harbinger of things to come.

Determined to preclude any future constitutional revolts, in 1833 Nicholas implemented the doctrine known as "official nationality," aimed particularly at the suppression of constitutional movements sweeping the European continent in the early 1830s. According to this new formulation of tsarist policy, three fundamental theories would in future guide the government: *orthodoxy*, reaffirming the adherence to eastern Christianity and rejection of secularist notions originating in the Enlightenment; *autocracy*, meaning the absolute authority of the tsar; and *nationality*, or the equivalent of something like the "spirit" of Russian identity. In order to enforce these directives, Nicholas created a secret police agency known as the "Third Section," which vigorously suppressed dissidence against the government in any form.

Nicholas also carried through on his conservative policies by joining other conservative European rulers in suppressing constitutional revolts. When a revolt in Poland in 1830 threatened to topple the viceroy (meaning ultimately the tsar himself as overlord), Nicholas intervened by suppressing it and abolishing the country's autonomy. Then, during the widespread agitation of revolutionary constitutional movements across Europe in 1848, Nicholas supported the Austrian emperor in suppressing the Hungarian nationalists. The failure of the attempted constitutional revolutions of 1848 was largely attributable to Nicholas's determined intervention.

In larger terms, Nicholas was determined to continue Russia's drive toward Constantinople (Istanbul). In the Russo–Ottoman War of 1828–1829 Russia succeeded in helping the Greeks achieve independence. With Russian help Serbia attained autonomy, while Moldavia and Wallachia—technically still within the Ottoman Empire—became protectorates of Russia. However, when Napoleon III of France in 1853 demanded recognition as protector of the Christians in Palestine under Ottoman rule, Russia did not fare as well. After Nicholas responded by insisting that the Ottomans honor their agreement with the Russian tsars as the actual protectors, the ensuing diplomatic wrangling ended in the outbreak of the Crimean War between Britain, France, and the Ottoman Empire, on one side, and Russia, on the other.

Poor planning, missed opportunities, language barriers, and a lack of coordination between soldiers and officers plagued both sides in the Crimean War. One of the first products of the mid-nineteenth century industrial weapons

Hospital Ward, Scutari, Ottoman Empire, 1856. This airy, uncluttered, warm hospital room shows injured and recovering soldiers. Florence Nightingale is depicted in the middle ground, in conversation with an officer.

revolution, the French Minié ball, whose hollow expanding base allowed for ease of ramming in muzzle-loading rifles, quadrupled the effective range of infantry weapons and vastly increased their accuracy. As they would a few years later during the American Civil War, armies fighting with increasingly obsolescent tactics would suffer fearful losses from these new weapons. French steam-powered and iron-hulled floating batteries inaugurated the age of ironclad navies. Telegraph lines permitted correspondents to send frontline reports to their London newspapers. And the nascent technology of photography was there to document the conflict. To lessen the sufferings of the wounded, doctors and nurses on both sides staffed field hospitals—including the English nurse Florence Nightingale (1820–1910), the founder of modern medical care on battlefields and the first prominent advocate of nursing as a profession for women. The new scientific–industrial age had manifested itself for the first time in war.

The Ottomans, still in the initial stages of their military reform, did not acquit themselves well, suffering from a weak officer corps and the absence of noncommissioned officers. They would have been defeated, had it not been for allied participation. The Russians did not perform well either, except for their navy with its superior shells. The Russian army suffered from overextending its battle lines on too many fronts, from the Danube and Crimea to the Caucasus. Thus, as far as the two imperial foes, the Russian and Ottoman Empires, were concerned, the war was a setback for both in their effort to meet the challenges of the West. Like their counterparts in China during the Second Opium War, also fought in the mid-1850s, however, they did receive a renewed taste of the state of the art in military technology and usage. This would mark many of the reform efforts of all three empires in the coming decades.

The Golden Age   During the period 1810–1853, in spite of times of censorship and repression, Russia enjoyed an outburst of intellectual and cultural activity. Taken as a whole, this period was considered the golden age of Russian culture. Inspired by European romantics, a Russian *intelligentsia*—Western-educated intellectuals predominantly from the ranks of the landowner nobility—met in the salons of Moscow and St. Petersburg, where they considered and debated issues related to religion and philosophy, as well as Russian history. A significant development was the appearance of literary journals, which spread the ideas and appeal of new literary forms as well as new ideas. Many of these ideas were potentially seditious since they concerned ways to end the autocracy of the tsars and to reform serfdom. More importantly, the first stirrings of reform movements emanated from these circles.

Alexander Sergeyevich Pushkin (1799–1837) stood at the forefront of the new intellectual movement. His lineage included old aristocratic forebears and an African-descended servant of Peter the Great, and he committed himself early on to the cause of reform with his poems, novels, as well as political activism, which brought him into conflict with the authorities. Best known among his works are his fairy tale poem "Ruslan and Lyudmila" (1820), the historical drama *Boris Godunov* (1825), and the novel in verse *Eugene Onegin* (1837) about a St. Petersburg dandy. Another prominent figure was Pyotr Chaadayev (1794–1856), also of aristocratic parentage. His sharply critical *Philosophical Letters* (1836) began the debate between constitutionalist "Westernizers" and conservative "Slavophiles." Westernizers considered Western models of governance, exemplified by constitutional government, along with industrial development and urbanism, as good models for progress in Russia. Slavophiles, by contrast, clung to traditional Russian institutions like the eastern Christian Church and the village commune. Nikolai Gogol (1809–1852), of Ukrainian Cossack descent, for example, felt that the distinguishing feature of Russia was its devotion to the Russian Orthodox Church, which served as the focal point of existence for the peasantry. With their determined opposition to Westernization, Slavophiles developed an early form of Russian ethnic nationalism that later evolved into the movement of pan-Slavism.

The Great Reforms

The Russian defeat in the Crimean War convinced the newly enthroned Alexander II (r. 1855–1881) of the need for reforms. Russia, so he believed, lost the war because of a technologically inferior army, a lack of infrastructure, and the unwillingness of the serf-owning aristocracy to shift from subsistence to market agriculture. He implemented major reforms, which, however, took time to produce the intended effects. Many Russians did not want to wait, and the empire entered a time of social destabilization, balanced abroad to a degree by successes against the Ottoman Empire.

The Emancipation of Serfs   Nicholas tackled serfdom first. In 1861, Alexander (the "tsar liberator") issued the Emancipation Edict, in which peasants were ostensibly freed from their bondage to their villages and their dues and labor services to the Russian landowning aristocracy. The traditionally unfree status of the serfs is usually explained on the one hand by the sparse population of the empire, with few cities and poor communication, and on the other hand by the relatively high level of fertility of Russia's humus-rich "black soil" (*chernozem*). On the face of it, the edict ended the centuries-old system of serfdom, affecting some 50 million serfs. But the edict fell far short of liberating the peasantry and satisfying critics. For one thing the decree of emancipation did not go into effect immediately but took 2 years to be fully enacted. For another, peasants were not given land titles per se; the land was turned over to the control of local communities (*mirs*), which then in turn allocated parcels to individual serfs. Finally, serfs had to redeem their new holdings by making annual payments to the state in the form of long-term government loans, the proceeds from which were then used to compensate the landowning nobility. Even worse, these payments were often higher than the former dues which serfs had owed the aristocracy. In effect, then, tens of millions of farmers remained mired in poverty-stricken agricultural self-sufficiency.

Following Western models, Alexander enacted further reforms. For example, in 1864 the administration of government at the local level was reorganized by the establishment of regional councils known as *zemstva*. Each zemstvo was in reality controlled by the local aristocracy, although peasants had a say in their election. Whatever their drawbacks, it must be said that zemstva achieved advances in education, health, and the maintenance of roads within their regions. Legal reforms were enacted shortly afterward; these provided all Russians access to courts, trial by jury, and especially the concept of equality before the law. Then, in 1874, a series of reforms aimed at modernizing the military and bringing it closer to Western standards was enacted. Among these was the reduction of active duty service in the military from 25 to 6 years, followed by several years of service in the reserves, along with an overall improvement in the quality of life in the ranks. Planned infrastructural reforms, however, remained limited for lack of funds. As in the Ottoman Empire, the reforms brought important changes to Russia; but in many cases, their effects would not be known until years later. Yet, just as the Ottoman Empire was increasingly called, after the example of Nicholas, the "Sick Man of Europe," it remained an article of faith among many in the West that, despite its reforms, "Russia could always be beaten for her backwardness."

Radicalization Among Intellectuals   The incompleteness of the reforms and the glaring absence of constitutionalism among what reforms did come expressed itself in a transition from peaceful demands to radicalism. Many Russians perceived this transition as a generational change. The aristocrat turned liberal Ivan Turgenev (1818–1883) observed this transition most astutely. In his aptly named *Fathers and Sons* (1862), a novel still widely read today, he declared that the new generation was dominated by "nihilists" (from the Latin *nihil*, meaning "noth-

ing"). The term **nihilism**, coined in Germany a century earlier and popularized by Turgenev, was meant to signify the inevitable end result of Enlightenment thought, if driven to its extremes. Nihilists, forming small underground circles, were devoted to individual freedom above all else, rejecting society's institutions and morality.

Other circles of radical intellectuals espoused *populism*, an ideology that romanticized rural peasant communities and their allegedly thriving autonomy. Members of these circles demanded that intellectuals go to the villages and stir them up into a socialist revolution from which the empire would be overthrown. In reality, however, the years after 1861 saw tensions arising between more well-to-do villagers able to buy their lands (called *kulaks*) and poor villagers unable to do so. The urban populists, unable to relate to these tensions, found few followers in the countryside, from either the kulaks or the poor.

Nihilism: Intellectual and political movement of the late nineteenth century that rejected the institutions and morality of society.

The New Generation of Nihilists

"Well," replied Pavel Petrovich, "very well. You have discovered all that and you are not less decided not to undertake anything seriously."

"Yes, we have decided not to undertake anything seriously," replied Bazarov in a brusque tone. He reproached himself all at once for having said so much before that gentleman.

"And you confine yourself to insult."

"We insult at need."

"And this is called nihilism."

"This is what is called nihilism," repeated Bazarov, but this time in a tone peculiarly provoking.

Pavel Petrovich winced a little.

"Very well!" he said with a forced calm that was rather strange.

—Ivan Sergheïevich Turgenev. *Fathers and Sons: A Novel*, trans. Eugene Schuyler, p. 61. New York: Leypoldt & Holt, 1867.

Later groups, inspired by the writings of the aristocrat turned anarchist Mikhail Bakunin (1814–1876) and seeking to learn from the failures of the populists, sought to bring together the urban and rural poor for the organization of small, self-administering communities without the need for a state with a central government and bureaucracy. Action-oriented splinter groups among these anarchists devoted themselves to bringing the state down through terrorism, trying to assassinate Alexander II seven times before finally succeeding in 1881. No spontaneous revolutions from below, however, materialized; and the tsar's secret service found it relatively easy to keep the small revolutionary circles under surveillance, except for its final fatal lapse.

Pan-Slavism   Concurrently with the appearance of radical ideologies on the left, a new right-wing ideology known as **pan-Slavism** emerged in the 1870s. Pan-Slavism proclaimed the brotherhood of all Slavic peoples and gave Russia the mission to aid Slavs in the Balkan territories who were suffering from alleged Ottoman misrule. Pan-Slavism took on a religious identity, that is, a commitment to Russian eastern Christianity. One of the best-known proponents of this ideology was the novelist Fyodor Dostoyevsky (1821–1881), son of a military surgeon. Dostoyevsky advocated the idea of a Russian "spiritual community" (*sobornost*), whose members would devote themselves to bringing about the unity of all humankind in the name of Christianity. As a writer, he transcended his Russian environment and became one of the most outstanding nineteenth-century authors on the Eurasian continent, with such psychologically refined novels as *Crime and Punishment* (1866) and *The Brothers Karamazov* (1879–1880).

Pan-Slavism: Ideology that espoused the brotherhood of all Slavic peoples and gave Russia the mission to aid Slavs in the Balkans suffering from alleged Ottoman misrule.

Balkan Affairs   Two issues contributed to mounting Russian pan-Slavic engagement in the Balkans. First, across the nineteenth century the Ottomans had been forced to relinquish control of large areas of their empire in the Balkans, and an end was not in sight. Second, the increasingly popular appeal of ethnolinguistic nationalism in Europe—Italian unification in 1870, followed by German unification in 1871—strengthened the assertiveness of the Balkan nationalities. In 1875 Bosnia-Herzegovina revolted against the Ottomans, and the rebellion then spread to Bulgaria, Serbia, and Montenegro. What would happen if these provinces did in fact break away from the Ottoman Empire? Which of the European powers might then take them over and, thus, increase its presence in this vital region? Thus, the Balkans became an area of increasing attention for the leading powers, while at the same time representing a powder keg ready to ignite.

The Russo–Ottoman War   Encouraged by Russian popular pan-Slavic support and sensing an opportunity to exploit rising anti-Ottoman sentiments among ethnic national movements in the Balkans, the tsar reopened the war front against the Ottomans in July 1877. The pretext was the Ottoman repression of tax revolts in Bosnia-Herzegovina and Bulgaria, which had led to a declaration of war by neighboring Montenegro and Serbia in June 1876 and a call for Russian military aid. The Russians invaded across the Danube and by December had advanced as far as Rumelia. Serbia, claiming complete independence, and Bulgaria, under Russian tutelage, were now poised to gain control of Istanbul. The other European powers stood by, anxiously waiting to see whether Russia would advance on the Ottoman capital.

In 1878, alarmed over what appeared to be an imminent Russian occupation of Istanbul, Austria and Britain persuaded Germany to convene the Congress of Berlin. In order to preserve peace among the great powers and to diffuse rising tensions over this "eastern question," the Congress decided to amputate from the Ottoman Empire most of its European provinces. For its part, Russia agreed to give up its designs on Istanbul in return for maintaining control over lands it had secured in the Caucasus Mountains. Serbia, Romania, and Montenegro became independent states. Austria acquired the right to "occupy and administer" the provinces of Bosnia and Herzegovina. There things stood for the rest of the nineteenth century, as the European powers began their imperial scramble; and Russia, forced to deal with renewed internal unrest, turned its attention away from the Balkans.

Russian Industrialization

Following the assassination of Alexander II in 1881, the next Romanov tsars reaffirmed autocratic authority and exercised tight political control, harkening back to the policies of Nicholas I. They surrounded themselves with conservative advisors and buttressed their hold on absolute rule by connecting loyalty to the state with adherence to eastern Christianity. These tsarist policies provoked renewed calls for constitutional reforms and generated new movements opposed to the autocracy of the regime. At the same time, when the depression of 1873–1896 began to ease in the 1890s, the country enjoyed a surge in industrialization, aggravating the political and social contradictions in Russia.

The Reassertion of Tsarist Authority　In the face of increasing demands by constitutionalists and social reformers, Alexander III (r. 1881–1894) unleashed a broad program of "counterreforms" in order to shore up autocratic control over the country. These actions turned Russia into a police state, in which political trials

Aristocratic Splendor. This oil painting of the wedding of Nicholas II in 1894, by the Danish painter Laurits Regner Tuxen (1853–1927), completed in 1898, shows the rich glory of the eastern Christian Church and the empire in ascendancy, with their iconic art, ermine furs, veiled ladies in waiting, and decorated officers.

before military courts were commonplace. Anyone who opposed Alexander's policies was subjected to intimidation at best, exile or death at worst; revolutionaries, terrorists, and opponents among the intelligentsia were especially targeted. Outside Russia, Alexander insisted on a program of *Russification*, or forced assimilation to Russian culture, especially language, by Poles, Ukrainians, and the Muslim populations of central Asia. For the time being, the regime maintained its grip on power.

Nicholas II (r. 1894–1917), a narrow-minded, unimaginative, and ultimately tragic figure, followed in his father's footsteps. Nicholas's paramount concern was loyalty not only to the state but also to the church. Any deviations were considered treasonous. He held a special contempt for revolutionary groups and individuals, who therefore retaliated with increasingly strident demands for the overthrow of the tsarist government. In addition to continuing the repressive policies of his father, Nicholas held an enduring distrust of Russian Jews as unpatriotic, which climaxed in the pogroms of 1903–1906. These pogroms, a repetition of earlier ones in 1881–1884 following the assassination of Alexander II, triggered mass emigrations to the United States and smaller ones to Britain, South America, South Africa, and Palestine as Russian Jews sought to escape persecution (see Map 25.5).

Industrialization   Industrial development was as slow in Russia as in the Ottoman Empire and for many of the same reasons. For one thing, the empire suffered from a poor transportation infrastructure. Although canal construction had started under Peter the Great, road construction did not follow until the early 1800s. Railroad construction was even slower, owing to the great distances in the empire which made large capital investments from abroad necessary. The first line, from St. Petersburg to Moscow, opened in 1851; but only a few thousand miles of track were laid until 1890 when the European depression of the previous three decades lifted. A major reason for the defeat in the Crimean War was the absence of railroad connections from Moscow

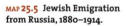

MAP **25.5** Jewish Emigration from Russia, 1880–1914.

Jewish Emigration from Russia, 1880–1914

Arrow	
→	65,000
→	200,000
→	Over 2 million
→	127,000
→	43,000
▨	Main area of Jewish settlement in Russian Empire

to the Black Sea, forcing the army to rely on water transport and horse-drawn carts. Moreover, even into the twentieth century, Russian railroads never adopted the standard gauge of their Western counterparts, necessitating costly and time-consuming changes of carriages and rolling stock at border crossings.

Still, in the 1890s, British, French, and Belgian capital poured into the empire and helped in building railroads, mining ventures, iron smelters, and textile factories. It is estimated that during this decade Russia's industrial output increased at an annual rate of nearly 8 percent. Among other factors driving the push toward accelerated industrialization was the dawning recognition of the regime that Russia was falling behind the industrialized nations of Europe in the race for economic—and thus political—global political influence.

The driving force in Russia's push for industrialization in the 1890s was the minister of finance, Sergei Witte (1849–1915, in office 1892–1903). Of German–Baltic descent from the Russian province of Estonia, Witte held a degree in mathematics and was a railroad official before becoming responsible for the Russian finances. His "Witte system" included an acceleration of heavy industrial output, the erection of import tariffs, increased taxes on the peasantry, and conversion to the gold standard in order to stabilize the currency. Although historians debate the overall success of Witte's reforms, there is no question that Russia made tremendous progress in heavy industrialization during the late nineteenth century. Dramatic increases in the miles of rail laid, tons of coal and steel produced, and square yards of textiles woven attest to Witte's vigor.

Witte's crowning achievement was the Trans-Siberian Railroad, built during 1891–1905 and connecting Moscow with Vladivostok on the Pacific coast. During Catherine's time, it took 3 years for communications to be sent to and from Vladivostok; now, the distance was covered in 8 days. Witte's objective was not only to make Russia more competitive but also to extend Russia's reach into the rich agricultural and mineral resources of Siberia, while at the same time extending Russia's influence in east Asia. Russia's policy of opening east Asia was the equivalent of Western imperialism in Asia and Africa and designed to ensure that Russia enjoyed a share of the global race for empire.

The Russo–Japanese War   The dramatic surge in industrialization, in conjunction with imperial ambitions in east Asia, brought Russia into conflict with Japan. As we saw in Chapter 24, with the Meiji Restoration in 1867–8, Japan had embarked on a concerted and systematic program of modernization and industrialization. Like western Europe and Russia, it developed imperial ambitions in the 1890s, seeking to replace China as the dominant power in east Asia. To this end Japan provoked war with China and in the Sino–Japanese War (1894–1895) occupied Taiwan and the Liaodong Peninsula of Manchuria. Although successful in defeating China and replacing it as the protector of Korea, the European powers forced Japan to give up the Liaodong Peninsula in the Triple Intervention (1895), which was in turn leased to Russia the following year. Determined to continue Russian expansion in east Asia, Witte completed the construction of a railway spur from the Trans-Siberian Railroad through Manchuria to the warm-water fortress city of Port Arthur on the southern tip of Liaodong.

The construction of this spur was the final straw for Japan, whose imperial goals seemed suddenly threatened by Russian expansion. Already smarting from what they considered Russia's double-dealing in helping to engineer the Triple Intervention and leasing the naval base at Port Arthur from the Qing, in early 1904 Japanese naval forces suddenly attacked the Russian fleet moored at Port Arthur, destroying several of its ships and laying siege to the fortress. The Japanese had had the foresight several years before of signing a treaty with Great Britain of "benign neutrality" in which the British agreed passively to help Japan in the event of war with a third party. They thus refused the Russian Baltic fleet passage through the Suez Canal on its voyage to raise the Japanese siege of Port Arthur. Following a decisive Japanese victory over Russian forces at Mukden in March 1905, Japanese forces finally cracked the stalemate at Port Arthur just as the Russian fleet, forced to sail around South Africa and across the Indian Ocean, attempted to run the narrow Straits of Tsushima. Here, the Japanese fleet was waiting for them and annihilated them in one of the most lopsided naval victories of the modern era. In the peace settlement, Japan gained control of the Liaodong Peninsula and southern Manchuria, as well as increased influence over Korea, which it finally annexed in 1910.

The Abortive Russian Revolution of 1905

In addition to Russia's mauling by the Japanese in the war of 1904–1905, a variety of factors coalesced in the early 1900s that sparked the first revolution against tsarist rule. One of these was a rising discontent among the peasantry, who continued to chafe under injustices such as the redemption payments for landownership. Another was the demand from factory workers for reform of working conditions: The workday ran to 11.5 hours and wages were pitifully low. Although the government had allowed for the formation of labor unions, their grievances fell on deaf ears. In response, workers in major manufacturing centers across the country, especially in St. Petersburg, mounted massive protests and occasional strikes.

Revolutionary Parties   The discontent among workers and peasants pumped new life into calls for reforms, resulting in the creation of two new political parties. One of these was the Social Democratic Labor Party, formed in 1898 by Vladimir Ilyich Lenin (1870–1924), a staunch adherent of Marxism (discussed in Chapter 23). This group sought support from workers, whom they urged to stage a socialist revolution by rising up and overthrowing the bourgeois capitalist tsarist government. The other group, the Social Revolutionary Party, was formed in 1901. Comprised mostly of liberal reformers among the intelligentsia, the Social Revolutionary Party advocated populism as a way to energize the peasantry, upon which they counted to lead the revolutionary effort.

During its meeting in London in 1903 the Social Democratic Labor Party split into two competing factions. The more moderate group, the Mensheviks ("minority," though they were actually numerically in the majority), was willing to follow classical Marxism, which allowed for an evolutionary process from fully evolved capitalism to social revolution and then on to the eventual overthrow of capitalism and tsarist rule. The more radical faction, known as Bolsheviks ("majority"), led by Lenin, was unwilling to wait for the evolutionary process to unfold and instead called for revolution in the near term. In 1902 Lenin had sketched out his agenda in *What Is to Be Done?* which laid out the principal Bolshevik aims. Foremost among these was a demand for the overthrow of the tsar, which could be accomplished only by relying on a highly disciplined core of dedicated revolutionaries leading the masses, whom Lenin distrusted as unwieldy and potentially unreliable. Even after the split in the Social Democratic Labor Party, however, the Bolsheviks were still a long way away from the kind of elite "vanguard of the revolution" party Lenin envisaged.

The Revolution of 1905 Events moved toward a violent climax in the Revolution of 1905. Amid mounting calls for political and economic reforms during the early 1900s, two concurrent events in 1904 shook the government to its foundations. First, reports of the humiliating defeats during the ongoing Russo–Japanese War began to filter to the home front. These made apparent the government's mismanagement of the war. Second, in January 1905, 100,000 workers went on strike in St. Petersburg, resulting in massive disruptions and loss of life commemorated later by Lenin.

The events of Bloody Sunday triggered further protests across the country during the spring and summer of 1905 (see Map 25.6). Then, from September to October, workers in all the major industrial centers staged a general strike, which brought the country to a standstill. Finally forced to make concessions, Nicholas issued the "October Manifesto," in which he promised to establish a constitutional government. Among other things, the Manifesto guaranteed individual civil liberties, universal suffrage, and the creation of a representative assembly, the Duma. During 1905–1907, however, Nicholas repudiated the concessions granted in the Manifesto, especially an independent Duma, which remained a rubber stamp parliament until Nicholas abdicated in 1917. Its momentum sapped, the revolution petered out.

What factors account for this deflation of revolutionary fervor? One event that enabled Nicholas to renege on his earlier promises was disagreement among the opposition parties; each had its own goals and ambitions, resulting in disagreement on how to bring down the tsarist government. More than that, each of the major political factions was unable to convince its followers among the workers and the peasants that its plans would in the end really address their specific concerns. Nicholas was therefore able to play off one group against the other and to reverse the reforms.

The revolution showed that the generational shift from constitutionalists to revolutionaries seeking to overturn the existing social order, which Turgenev had observed in the 1860s, was nearly complete. This shift made the formation of broader reformist coalitions, perhaps even with military participation, as in the Ottoman Empire, impossible. The tsarist regime, though humbled by Japan, still had enough military resources to wear down the combination of small groups of Marxist revolutionaries and street demonstrators. Without sympathizers in the army, a determined tsarist regime was impossible to bring down. But like Qing China during these years, whatever belated

---

Lenin on Bloody Sunday

"Today is the twelfth anniversary of 'Bloody Sunday,' [January 9 or 22, 1905, depending on different calendars] which is rightly regarded as the beginning of the Russian revolution.

"Thousands of workers—not Social-Democrats, but loyal God-fearing subjects—led by the priest Gapon, streamed from all parts of the capital to its centre, to the square in front of the Winter Palace, to submit a petition to the tsar. The workers carried icons. In a letter to the tsar their then leader, Gapon, had guaranteed his personal safety and had asked him to appear before the people.

"Troops were called out. Uhlans [Polish light cavalry] and Cossacks [southern Russian regiments] attacked the crowd with drawn swords. They fired on the unarmed workers, who on their bended knees implored the Cossacks to allow them to go to the tsar. The indignation of the workers was indescribable ..."

—Vladimir I. Lenin. *Collected Works*, vol. 23, p. 236. Moscow: Progress Publishers, 1964. Accessible through http://www.marxists.org/archive/lenin/works/1917/jan/09.htm.

Revolution in the Russian Empire, 1905–1907

- Peasant revolt in 50-75% of area
- Peasant revolt in over 75% of area
- Strike in urban area, 1905 / 1906 / 1907
- Armed uprising in urban area December, 1905
- Military mutiny, 1905 / 1906 / 1907

MAP **25.6** Revolution in the Russian Empire, 1905–1907.

reforms were initiated by the government would increasingly be seen as irrelevant. It was now perceived that nothing short of changing the system would be effective. For both empires, the revolutionaries would now dominate the scene.

Putting It All Together

Both the Ottoman and Russian Empires faced the initial Western military and constitutional challenges directly on their doorsteps, not from across the ocean, as China and Japan did. Of course, once military technology had undergone its own industrial transformation in Europe during the first half of the 1800s, China was no longer too far away for British steam-powered gunboats and rifled breech-loading weapons. The Ottoman Empire, as a mature empire struggling to regain its traditional centralism, fought largely defensive wars. Russia, still a young empire, expanded aggressively against the defensive Ottomans and its weaker Asian neighbors (except Japan), all the while suffering occasional military and diplomatic setbacks. India failed to master the Western military challenge altogether. China, the Ottoman Empire, and Qajar Iran survived it at the price of diminished territories. The Western challenge was pervasive across the world.

Western constitutional nationalism was another powerful and corrosive pattern. The transformation of kingdoms or colonies into nations in which subjects would become citizens,
regardless of language or dialect, social rank, or religion, was difficult enough in Europe. France, with its uneasy shift between monarchy and republic during the 1800s, demonstrated this difficulty. In the Ottoman Empire, a wide gap existed between constitutional theory and practice, especially as far as religion was concerned. Russia, plagued by the reluctance of its aristocracy to give up serfdom even after emancipation, left its constitutionalists out in the cold. Japan created a constitutional state but, like Germany, left the great majority of real power in the hands of its emperor and advisors. China's bid for a constitutional monarchy died once in 1898 and was never fully reborn before its revolution in 1911. Sultans, emperors, and kings knew well that none of their constitutions would fully satisfy the demands for liberty, equality, and fraternity.

To complicate matters for both the Ottoman and Russian Empires, in the second half of the 1800s, many members of the rising educated urban middle class deserted constitutional nationalism and turned to ethnic nationalism (in the Ottoman Empire) or to pan-Slavism, revolutionary socialism, and Marxism (in the Russian Empire). Marxism would eventually carry the day in Russia in the course of World War I. By contrast, both the Ottoman and Russian Empires met the Western *industrial* challenge—cheap, factory-produced cotton textiles—without completely surrendering their markets. Once they were able to attract foreign capital for the construction of expensive railroads and factories at the end of the 1800s, they even started on their own paths to industrialization—the seemingly stable Russia faster than the apparently sick Ottoman Empire. In spite of wrenching transformations, the two were still empires in control of themselves when World War I broke out. Neither would survive the war. Instead, they would be transformed by the forces that had beset them throughout the nineteenth century: Turkey would become a modern, secular nation-state, though always running somewhat behind its European contemporaries in economic development. Russia would be transformed into the world's first Marxist state, pursue breakneck industrial and economic development at a tragic cost, and emerge after World War II as one of two "superpowers" with the United States (see Concept Map).

Vladimir Egorovic Makovsky (1846–1920), *Death in the Snow* **(1905).** This dramatic oil painting of the crowd protesting against the tsarist regime during the abortive revolution of 1905 is one of the greatest realist paintings. Makovsky was one of the founders of the Moscow Art School and continued to paint after the Russian Revolution of 1917.

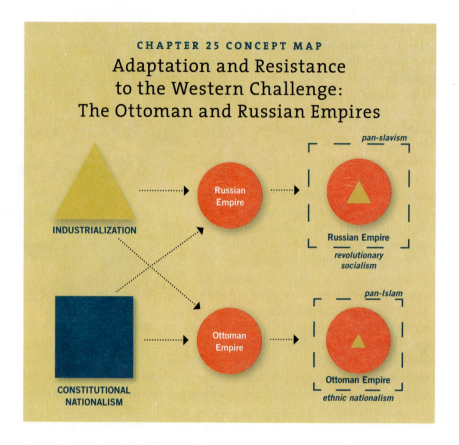

CHAPTER 25 CONCEPT MAP
Adaptation and Resistance to the Western Challenge: The Ottoman and Russian Empires

Review and Respond

1. What was the significance of Napoleon's invasion of Egypt in 1798?

2. How would you summarize the Tanzimat decrees in the Ottoman Empire.

3. What did the Committee of Union and Progress in the Ottoman Empire stand for, and what did it accomplish between 1908 and 1914?

4. Which features characterized Iran in this period, and how did the country adapt to the Western challenge?

5. What were the patterns of agrarian life in Russia during the nineteenth century?

6. Why did the tsars in Russia face a fractured opposition to their autocratic rule?

> For additional resources, including maps, primary sources, visuals, and quizzes, please go to www.oup.com/us/vonsivers. Please see the Further Resources section at the back of the book for additional readings and suggested websites.

Thinking Through Patterns

▶ **Which new models did the Ottomans adopt during the nineteenth century to adapt themselves to the Western challenge?**

The traditional model for reform in the Ottoman Empire was based on the Islamic concept of the divinely sanctioned, absolute authority of the sultan: Officials could be appointed or dismissed at will. The later history of the Ottoman Empire is significant in world history because it shows the *adaptation pattern* to the Western challenge, in this case, the borrowing of constitutional nationalism and modern military technology from Europe.

As agrarian polities with large landowning classes collecting rents from tenant farmers or serfs, the Ottoman and Russian Empires found it difficult to respond to the European industrial challenge. Large foreign investments were necessary for the building of steelworks, factories, and railroads. Given the long economic recession of the last quarter of the 1800s, these investments—coming from France and Germany—went to expanding Russia, more than the shrinking Ottoman Empire, as the safer bet.

▶ **How did the agrarian Ottoman and Russian Empires, both with large landholding ruling classes, respond to the western European industrial challenge during the 1800s?**

▶ **Why did large, well-established empires like the Russian and the Ottoman Empires struggle with the forces of modernity, while a small, secluded island nation like Japan seemed to adapt so quickly and successfully to them?**

This is in many respects a tantalizing question for world historians. Aside from philosophical debates about what actually constitutes "success," one avenue of inquiry is cultural: How receptive were the Russians and Ottomans—or the Qing, for that matter—toward the ideas of the Enlightenment? The short answer must be, "not very." Even the most willing leaders in these empires risked alienating a host of entrenched interests by attempting the most modest reforms. They therefore walked a very fine political line in what they attempted and often found that the reforms disrupted traditional routines but left little or nothing to replace them effectively. In addition, such large multiethnic empires as those of Russia and the Ottomans found it difficult to rally subjects around a distinct "nationality" since they encompassed so many divergent ones. In contrast, the Meiji reformers had the advantage of a unity derived from outside pressures. With the old shogunate gone, the emperor could formulate completely new institutions and count on the loyalty of subjects who had seen him as a semidivine figure. Moreover, the new regime commenced immediately in creating an ideology of Japaneseness—a form of ethnic nationalism—and institutionalized it in education and national policy. There was, to be sure, opposition; but it was scattered, class-based, and not effective against the modern army and industrial power the new regime created. Japan's legacy of cultural borrowing may also have been an advantage, as well as a nascent capitalist system developing in the late Tokugawa era. Finally, the goal of using its progress toward "enlightenment and civilization" according to Western standards could be measured along the way, as were the power and prestige of its new programs.

Riz: Mise en terre des plantes

Riz: Fleur et fruit

Riz:

Tabac: Mise en terre

Tabac: Plante de tabac

Taba

Middle East — India — China
Africa
INDIAN OCEAN — Southeast Asia
Australia

THE NEW IMPERIALISM

Chapter 26 | The New Imperialism in the Nineteenth Century

1750-1914

At the end of the Muslim month-long observance of Ramadan in 1827, Hussein (1815–1830), the ruler (*dey*) of the autonomous Ottoman province of Algeria in North Africa, held a celebratory reception for the diplomatic corps of consuls at his palace in the capital, the port city of Algiers. When he saw the French consul, Pierre Deval, Hussein signaled him to come up to the throne. In a quite undiplomatic harangue, the dey accused the consul of deliberately defrauding him of a large sum of money owed him by France for wheat deliveries between 1793 and 1798. He then demanded immediate payment of this long overdue debt. To emphasize his demand, the dey struck the consul with his fan and declared him *persona*

The British Colonies of India, Australia, and New Zealand

The transition in India from European trade-fort activities to governmental colonialism coincided with the decline of the Mughal dynasty (see Chapter 20). The British East India Company exploited the Mughal decline to evolve into a government in all but name. Its notorious corruption and ultimate inability to conduct military affairs, however, forced the British government to assume direct control. As a result, Britain became a colonial power in the Eastern Hemisphere, making India its center for the delivery of the cotton on which early British industrialization depended. Later on, sparsely inhabited Australia and New Zealand began as small British settler colonies, the former as a penal colony and the latter against fierce indigenous resistance.

The British East India Company

As with so many developments that helped to shape the later eighteenth century and its legacy, an important factor in the rise of British power in India was the Seven Years' War. As we have seen, the Seven Years' War resembled in many respects a kind of "first" world war in that fighting took place in Europe, in the Americas, on the high seas, and in India. It was the result of the war in India, along with the deepening political difficulties of the Mughals, that enabled the rise of the British to supremacy not only on the subcontinent but later in Burma and Malaya as well.

The Seven Years' War   The seeds had long been planted for a vibrant British commercial community among the European trading companies by the early eighteenth century. As we saw in Chapter 20, the British had joined forces at Surat on the west coast of India with the Dutch in the lucrative spice trade. But they had also established their own posts in provincial cities that would over time be transformed into India's greatest metropolises: Madras (Chennai), Bombay (Mumbai), and one created from scratch: Calcutta (Kolkata). By 1750 their chief commercial competitors were the French, who were aggressively building up both trade and political power from a base in Pondicherry in the southern part of peninsular India.

For the British East India Company, its evolution into a kind of shadow government in the area around Calcutta in Bengal on the northeast coast would now bear dividends. The decline of Mughal central power meant that regional leaders were being enlisted as French or British allies. If they were more powerful, they sought to use the Sepoy (from Persian *sipahi* [see-pa-HEE], "soldier") armies of the European companies as support in their own struggles. Out of this confused political and volatile military situation, the East India Company leader, Robert Clive (1725–1774), who

1600 Founding of (English, Later British) East India Company	**1757** Battle of Plassey	**1788-1840** 50,000 British Colonists Shipped to Australia
1602 Founding of Dutch East India Company	**1763** Opening of British Colonialism in India	**1830** Dutch Introduce Cultivation System in Indonesia
1830-1847 French Conquest of Algeria	**1857** Great Rebellion, or Sepoy Mutiny, India **1884-1885** Berlin Conference	**1899-1913** US Conquest of Philippines
1852-1885 French Conquest of Vietnam	**1882** British Expeditionary Force Occupies Egypt	**1893** New Zealand Grants Women Right to Vote

Nabob: A person who acquired a large fortune in India during the period of British rule.

was ambitious, ruthless, and finely attuned to the vagaries of the shifting political landscape, won a signal victory over the Indian French allies at Plassey in 1757 and soon eliminated the French from power in the subcontinent. By the terms of the treaty ending the war in 1763, the East India Company ended up as the sole European power of consequence in India; and Clive set about consolidating his position from Calcutta.

Perceptions of Empire. The British East India Company's real ascent to power in India began with Robert Clive's victory at Plassey in 1757, the symbolism of which is depicted here. Note the deference with which the assorted Indian princes treat the conqueror (*a*). Below, the second from last Mughal emperor, Akbar Shah II (r. 1806–1837), receives the British resident, ca. 1815 (*b*). Despite the fact that the British East India Company had extended its sway over much of northern India by this time, the Indian artist depicts the British government official in a pose of supplication to Akbar Shah—in almost a mirror image of the imagined Indian princes in the painting of Clive.

Going Native—the Nabobs Clive's aggressive style of economic aggrandizement set the style for what Indian scholars have often called "the Rape of Bengal" in the latter eighteenth century. The East India Company set about expanding its holdings across northern India, dealing, plundering, and extorting funds from pliant local princes. The company men had no interest in changing India or reforming Indian institutions. Indeed, many, inspired by Enlightenment ideals of cosmopolitanism, became great admirers of Indian culture. Some took this to the point of what became known as "going native": After gathering their fortunes, they took Indian wives, dressed as Indian princes, and on occasion wielded power as local magnates or **nabobs** (from Urdu *nawwab* [naw-WAHB], "deputy," "viceroy").

The period of the nabobs perhaps reached its height under the company directorship of Warren Hastings (1732-1818), Clive's successor. Where Clive was brutal and aggressive, Hastings, though acquiring immense wealth, developed an intense scholarly interest in Indian culture. The first translations into English of many of the classics of Indian literature took place during his governor-generalship from 1773 to 1785. Moreover, the first exposure of the Vedas to European scholars yielded the earliest hints that Sanskrit was a branch of the family of languages that came to be called "Indo-European." Over the coming decades additional scholarship on the Vedas contributed mightily to the first linguistic theories on the origins of some of Eurasia's earliest peoples—work that continues today.

The vast distances separating the company's London directors from operations in India, southeast Asia, and China tended to make its local activities more or less autonomous. Its power, organization, and, most importantly, army increasingly became the determining factors in local disputes across northern India, while its attractiveness to ambitious young men on the margins of British society—particularly among the Scots and Irish—wishing to "make their pile" in a few short years, left it vulnerable to corruption on a grand scale. This was particularly true because of the company's policy of paying low wages but winking at employees trading locally on their own behalf. Thus, Hastings was called back to London and subjected to a lengthy trial on a variety of charges of corruption, abuse of power, and abuse of Indians under company rule.

His replacement, in 1785, was a man most famous for ignominious defeat: Lord Charles Cornwallis (1738–1805), who had turned his sword over to George Washington in Britain's humiliating surrender to the American Revolutionaries at Yorktown. Cornwallis did considerably better as a reformer of the company. The British Parliament, appalled at company corruption, had set up a system of "indirect rule" by which the company's actions were to be supervised by a governor-general selected by the British government, rather than by the East India Company directors in London. Cornwallis labored to curb the worst excesses of private trading by increasing salaries and attempted to unify and rationalize the tax structure of the company's holdings.

By 1800, through the company's efforts to pacify turbulent territories adjacent to its holdings, British possessions extended across most of northern India (see Map 26.1). The irregular manner in which this was accomplished prompted many to say that the British Indian empire was created "in a fit of absence of mind." This extension also prompted a shift in the variety of trading goods as the eighteenth century wore on and as the new century dawned. Spices had been replaced by cotton goods as the most lucrative commodity and increasingly by raw cotton to be processed in Britain's mechanized textile revolution. Indian cotton would later be supplemented and eventually supplanted by cotton from the American South, Egypt, and Sudan.

The Perils of Reform
While we have become accustomed to seeing the nineteenth century as the period marking the beginning of Western supremacy, it is well

MAP 26.1 **The Expansion of British Power in India, 1756–1805.**

to remember—as we have noted in previous chapters—that even at this late date India and China were still the primary economic engines of Eurasia. As late as 1800, for example, Indian goods and services (what we call today the "GDP" or gross domestic product) accounted for perhaps 20 percent of the world's output, while Britain's came to only 3 percent. As the Industrial Revolution kicked into high gear by the mid-1800s, however, these numbers began to reverse (see Figure 26.1). As Britain's share of India's economy grew, moreover, the British increasingly sought to create markets for their own goods there and to shunt Indian exports toward the exclusive use of the British domestic market. As we saw in Chapter 24, the early acquisition of Patna by the British enabled the creation of the Chinese opium trade, which by 1830 accounted for nearly one-quarter of company revenues in India. In addition, the officials of "John Company," as the East India Company was nicknamed, were busily arbitrating disputes among Indian rulers, taking over their lands as payment for loans, and strong-arming many into becoming wards of the British. Because of this continuous attrition, by the end of the Napoleonic Wars, the Mughal emperor's lands had been reduced to the region immediately surrounding Delhi and Agra.

India's history, however, had long been marked by outsiders conquering large parts of the subcontinent, and while many chafed at company rule, its policy of non-interference with Indian customs and institutions softened the conquest somewhat. The period following the Napoleonic Wars, however, saw changes in this regard that had far-reaching consequences, by bringing the British government into a more direct role.

The economic slowdown, clashes between factory owners and labor, and drive for political reform in Britain during the period following the Napoleonic Wars found echoes in policy toward India. From the opening decades of the century, increasing numbers of Protestant missionaries, especially those of the new Evangelical denominations, saw India as promising missionary ground. As was the case in China, many missionaries brought with them practical skills, particularly in medicine, education, and engineering. Many of those active in mission-based reform in India had also been involved with the abolition of slavery, industrial workers' rights, and electoral reform movements in Britain. By 1830 many of these individuals were driving the agenda on British policy in India, which increasingly asserted that India should be reformed along the lines they envisioned for Britain: better working conditions for the poor, free trade, the abolition of "barbaric" customs, and a vigorous Christian missionary effort.

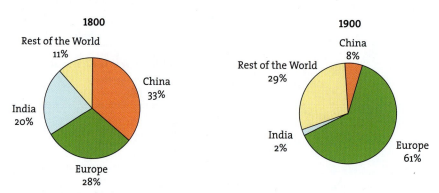

Figure 26.1 Share of World Manufacturing Output, 1800 and 1900.

Their opponents, many of them longtime company veterans, saw the pushing of such policies in India as unwarranted interference in their territory and largely unneeded as far as the Indians themselves were concerned. Nonetheless, missionaries mounted successful campaigns against female infanticide; against *sati*, the self-immolation of widows on their husbands' funeral pyres; and *thugee*, real or (many suggested) imagined ritual murders of travelers on Indian roads. Missionary efforts also increasingly used medicine and education as wedges for the introduction of Christianity to the Indian populace.

Christian Missionary. The diverse crowd gathered around the young Christian preacher, who is most likely a Methodist, includes Muslims, Hindus, women, a mendicant, and at least one child. But the spectators all share one thing in common: they regard the preacher with a mixture of curiosity and amazement.

In addition, the company reformed the tax system into a money-based land fee for greater efficiency of collection. At the same time, new industrial enterprises and transport and communication advances—steamboats, railroads, and telegraph lines—were being constructed, benefiting the economy at large but also disrupting the livelihoods of many. Coupled with these changes was a perception on the part of opponents, and even some supporters, of these efforts in both India and England as characterized by smug righteousness—the clichéd and often caricatured middle-class "earnestness"—and arrogance of the English toward Indian society. Perhaps the most famous expression of this was found in the parliamentary reformer and historian Thomas B. Macaulay's 1835 "Minute on Education in India," where he asserted that "a single shelf of European books is worth more than all the literatures of Asia and Arabia."

The Great Mutiny   The grim result of several decades of such wholesale change exploded in northern India in 1857. General disillusionment with the pace of change and the fear that British missionaries were, with government connivance, attempting to Christianize India came to a head among the company's Sepoy troops. With the introduction of the new Enfield rifle, which required its operator to bite the end off of a greased paper cartridge to pour the powder down its muzzle and ram the new conical bullet home, a rumor started that the grease had been concocted of cow and pig fat. Since this would violate the food restrictions of both Hindus and Muslims, the troops saw this as a plot to leave the followers of both religions ritually unclean and thus open to conversion to Christianity. Though the rumors proved untrue, a revolt raced through many of the Sepoy barracks and in short order became a wholesale rebellion aimed at throwing the British out of India and restoring the aged Mughal emperor, Bahadur Shah Zafar (r. 1837–1857), to full power. The accumulated rage against the perceived insults to Indian religions and culture pushed the troops and their allies to frightful atrocities, with even more that were rumored but never substantiated.

Execution of Indian Rebels. After British troops and loyalist Indian Sepoys had restored order in northern India, retribution was unleashed on the rebels. Here, the most spectacular mode of execution is being carried out. Mutineers are tied across the mouths of cannons and blown to pieces while the troops stand in formation and are forced to watch.

The Great Mutiny (also known by the British as the Sepoy Mutiny and by the Indians as the Great Rebellion, or First War of Independence) swiftly turned into a civil war as pro- and anti-British Indian forces clashed. The British frantically shipped troops just sent to China for the Second Opium War back to India in a desperate attempt to crush the insurgency. Through a number of hard-fought engagements they were ultimately able to reassert control but not without conducting frightful atrocities of their own in retribution for the rebels' excesses. The occupation of many towns was accompanied by mass hangings and indiscriminate shootings of suspected rebels and collaborators. In other areas, British commanders revived the old Mughal punishment of tying the victims to cannons and blowing them to bits in front of the assembled troops. Since this was thought to scatter the karmic "soul" of the victim as well as his body, it was meant to deprive the offender of his next life as well as his present one.

Direct British Rule

After assuming direct rule (Hindi *raj,* hence the term "Raj" for the colonial government), the British were crucially concerned to keep their apparatus of civilian administrators as small as possible but maintain an army large enough to avoid a repeat of 1857. These administrators made use of Indian administrators who, however, did not have any real decision-making powers. The raj functioned because of a "divide and rule" policy that exploited the many divisions existing in Indian society, which prevented the Indians from making common cause and challenging British rule.

Creation of the Civil Service Even as the pacification was winding down, the British government, stunned by the course of events, conducted an investigation which led to sweeping reforms in 1858. The East India Company was dismantled, and the British government itself took up the task of governing India. In a proclamation to England and India, Queen Victoria announced that British policy would no longer attempt to "impose Our convictions on any of Our subjects." An Indian civil service was created and made open to British and Indians alike to administer the subcontinent's affairs. The incorporation of India as the linchpin of the British Empire was completed when Queen Victoria assumed, among her many titles, that of "Empress of India" in 1877. India had now become, it was said, "the jewel in the crown" of the empire (see Map 26.2).

Less than a decade later, the fruits of the new civil service and the Indian schools feeding it were already evident, though perhaps not in the way its creators envisioned or desired. In 1885, Indians first convened the National Congress, the ancestor of India's present Congress Party. The Congress's ongoing mission was to win greater autonomy for India within the structure of the British Empire and, by the opening decades of the twentieth century, to push for Indian independence.

MAP **26.2** The British Empire in India, 1858–1914.

Already by the early 1890s, a young British-trained lawyer named Mohandas K. Gandhi (1869–1948) was actively campaigning for the rights of Indians in British-controlled South Africa. There, he honed the skills and developed the techniques that would make him among the most recognized world figures of the twentieth century as he pursued his quest to oust the British from India through nonviolence and noncooperation.

The Civil Service Caste   In the final decades of the nineteenth century the British community in India, rarely more than about 100,000 at any given time (in a population of some 270 million in 1900), increasingly set itself up as a caste and race apart. During the heyday of company rule, few wives and families moved from England to what was considered a hardship post. India's unrelenting summer heat and constant rain during the monsoon season took a considerable toll on those not fully acclimated, as did its array of tropical diseases, particularly malaria. One of the

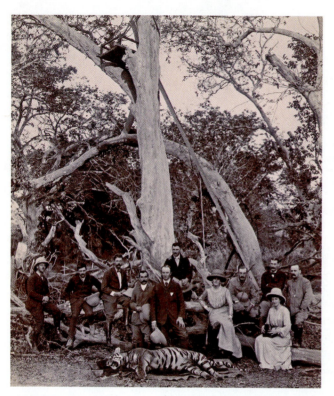

Lord Curzon. Following the Great Rebellion, the British government dissolved the East India Company and inaugurated direct rule of the subcontinent through a civil service. Here, Lord Curzon, the British resident, or governor-general, and Lady Curzon preside over a tiger they bagged during a hunting trip. Curzon was famous for mounting flamboyant spectacles to enhance British prestige during government-sponsored durbars and was responsible for building the modern Indian capital of New Delhi.

reasons young company men were so eager to "make their pile" in a hurry was the knowledge that their life expectancy in India was rather low.

With the coming of reformers and missionaries in the 1820s and 1830s, the number of English families and dependents grew rapidly, and this increased further with the assumption of direct British rule at the end of the 1850s. The older practice of company men marrying Indian women and leaving them and their children behind when they left for home was now replaced by the professional bureaucrat or businessman and his proper Victorian family living in India for long stretches of time. This was made less physically arduous by the widespread use of quinine to treat the fevers of malaria—and popularizing the famous drink gin and tonic (the "tonic" including quinine water). In places where there were concentrations of Europeans, they tended increasingly to mingle almost exclusively among themselves, setting up their own social circuits, clubs, literary and theatrical societies, and other activities and groups. Many vacationed together during the hot months at the "hill stations" in the cooler upland areas. Thus, with the exception of their servants and civil service subordinates, European families had little contact with ordinary Indians.

"Never the Twain Shall Meet"   This, of course, was by now a familiar pattern at other outposts in European colonial empires. But this social segregation also coincided with the rise of social Darwinism and pseudoscientific theories of race that increasingly encouraged the British to see the Indians as inferior and became an additional inducement toward segregation. These attitudes can be seen in bold relief in much of Rudyard Kipling's literary work, in which, although there is much he finds admirable about things Indian, in the end concedes that "East is East and West is West and never the twain shall meet." For Kipling, the inability of these two peoples to connect suggests the superiority of the white Europeans over their Indian "charges."

Divide and Rule   The Indian civil service, among the most difficult bureaucracies in the world in which to gain admission, seldom had more than 1,000 "Anglo-Indian" (ethnically British subjects who were either born in India or longtime residents there) and Indian officials to govern a quarter of a billion people. The civil service was intended as a showpiece of British incorruptibility and professionalism, in stark contrast to the perception of endemic graft and petty bribery customary among the Indian princes. Some of the ablest men in the British Empire, particularly those whose class or ethnic background might have proven a hindrance at home, passed the grueling examinations and entered the service as "readers." With so few officials, the workload was very heavy and demanded a sophisticated understanding of local conditions part-time and lowly paid Janissaries resisted all efforts at drills. Lack of finances caused these military reforms to grind to a halt. The Russian military, by contrast, learned much from the Seven Years' War (1756–1763), in which it was allied with Austria and France against Prussia and Great Britain. Its sizeable line infantries were of great importance during the war of 1768–1774 against the Ottomans. The victory was not easy, given the long supply lines south to the Black Sea and Danube. But in the end the sizeable Russian line infantry regiments prevailed over the un-coordinated and untrained Ottoman foot soldiers. Similarly, Napoleon successfully employed his small, highly mobile, and flexible units (composed of mixed infantry, cavalry, and artillery) in his victory against the lopsidedly cavalry-dominated Egyp-tian Mamluks in 1798.

The Mughals in India and the Qing in China did not have to worry about flintlock, bayonet, and line infantry attacks in the eighteenth century, either from their neigh-bors or from the far-away Europeans. Like the Ottomans, who continued to maintain large cavalry forces against their nomadic neighbors in the Middle East and central Asia, the Mughals and Qing privileged their cavalries and treated their ethnically indigenous and not very mobile firearm-equipped infantries as secondary. However, once British East India Company officers elevated indigenous infantry soldiers to the privileged ranks of the Sepoy regiments, as Karl Marx astutely observed, their discipline ultimately created such problems for the company that the British Crown had to take over the governance of India in 1858.

When European innovators introduced workable breech-loading rifles and artil-lery in the late 1850s, the technological balance shifted decisively toward Europe. The addition of rapid-firing mechanisms in the second half of the 1800s to these improved weapons further cemented Europe's technological superiority. They am-plified western Europe's ability to subdue and colonize all but the largest states of the Middle East, Africa, and Asia by World War I. In addition to infantries, cavalries could be equipped with rapid-fire rifles and pistols, enabling detachments to land on Middle Eastern, African, and Asian coasts and quickly sweep through the inte-rior. The French in particular made use of this improved cavalry capability in their conquests of Africa south of the Sahara.

Thus, in this shift from an initially slight to an eventually pronounced superiority of European arms during this period, the new imperialism and the Industrial Revolu-tion were parallel developments engendered by the same modernity that also saw the rise of constitutional nationalism and the formation of a new type of polity, the nation-state. Certainly, industrially produced weapons in the later nineteenth century greatly enhanced Europe's ability to dominate much of the Middle East, Africa, and Asia. But modernity is a complex bundle of many different interacting elements. In short, there is—if you will excuse the pun—no "smoking gun."

Questions

- Examine the photo showing French forces defeating the Mamluk cavalry. Are the military advantages of the line drill evident? If so, what are they?

- Does the photo of Ethiopian forces defeating an Italian army in 1896 show that indigenous peoples could adapt Western innovations to their own purposes? If so, how?

Subaltern: A person or thing considered subordinate to another.

with India's historic past, it was hoped that the perception of strength and legitimacy would be enhanced. This effort to co-opt local rulers into upholding the British government as the historically destined status quo is sometimes called by historians a **subaltern** relationship. Yet, a small but growing elite of Western-educated, often accomplished, Indian leaders began to use the arguments of empire against their occupiers. By the 1920s many of these people would make up the burgeoning national movement associated with Gandhi's strategy of noncooperation and the Indian National Congress's outlines for government when Britain was finally forced to "quit India."

The British Settler Colonies of Australia and New Zealand

India was merely one area in Asia and the Pacific where the British advanced from exploration and trade forts to imperial expansion and colonial settlement. In the continent of Australia and on the islands of New Zealand they colonized indigenous forager and agrarian populations as well as—in contrast to India—encouraged large-scale immigration of European settlers.

White Settlement in Australia and New Zealand

Dutch navigators, blown off course on their way to Indonesia, initially discovered the western coast of Australia in 1606; but when profitable trade opportunities with the forager Aborigines (the name given to the indigenous Australians) failed to materialize, they did not pursue any further contacts. The British navigator James Cook (1728–1779), during one of his many exploratory journeys in the Pacific, landed in 1770 on the Australian east coast and claimed it for Great Britain. After the United States wrested its independence from Britain in 1783, the British government looked to Australia as a place where it could ship convicts. Between 1788 and 1840, some 50,000 British convicts were shipped to the penal colony.

The Making of Australia. British Army redcoats register convicts disembarking in Australia at Sydney Cove. As a result of poverty and crime accompanying the early industrialization in Britain, prisons were so overcrowded that the authorities sought relief by sending prisoners to penal colonies overseas. About 25 percent of the prisoners were Irish, mostly arrested on political charges.

Immigration by free British subjects, begun a decade before the end of convict shipments, led to a pastoral and agricultural boom. Settlers pioneered agriculture in south Australia where rainfall, fluctuating according to dry and wet *El Niño/La Niña* cycles, was relatively reliable and provided the population with most of its cereal needs. Sugar and rice cultivation, introduced to the tropical northeast in the 1860s, was performed with indentured labor recruited from Pacific islands. Even during penal colony times, sheep ranching in the east and the exportation of wool developed into an early thriving business, with half of the wool needed by the British textile industry being supplied from Australia. Even more important for the evolution of the Australian colony was the mining of gold and silver, beginning in the east in 1851 and continuing thereafter in nearly all parts of the continent. Although a colony, Australia was very similar to independent Latin America (see Chapter 27) in that it was a labor-poor but commodity-rich region, seeking its wealth through export-led growth (see Map 26.3).

Mining generated several gold rush immigration waves, not only from Britain but also from China, as well as internal migrations from mining towns to cities when the gold rushes ended. Cities like Sydney and Melbourne expanded continuously during the 1800s and encompassed more than two-thirds of the total white population of about 5 million by 1914. The indigenous population of Aborigines, who had inhabited the continent since 65,000 BCE, shrank during the same time from several hundred thousand to 67,000, mostly as a result of diseases but also after confrontations with

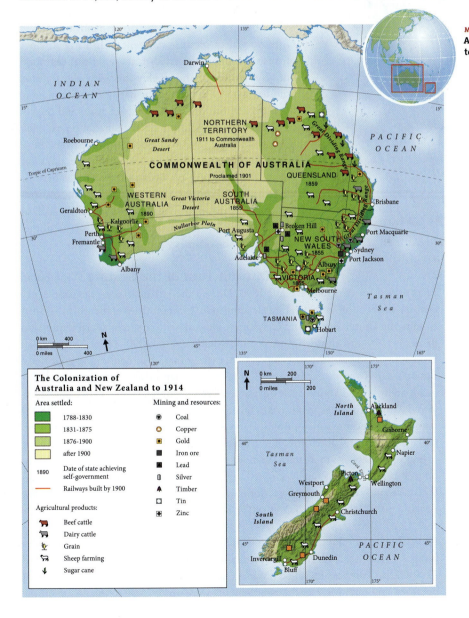

MAP **26.3** The Colonization of Australia and New Zealand to 1914.

The Colonization of Australia and New Zealand to 1914

Area settled:

- 1788–1830
- 1831–1875
- 1876–1900
- after 1900

1890   Date of state achieving self-government

— Railways built by 1900

Agricultural products:

- Beef cattle
- Dairy cattle
- Grain
- Sheep farming
- Sugar cane

Mining and resources:

- Coal
- Copper
- Gold
- Iron ore
- Lead
- Silver
- Timber
- Tin
- Zinc

**COVERNOR DAVEY'S
PROCLAMATION
TO THE ABORIGINES
1816**

"*Why Massa Gobernor, and Black Jack.. You Proklamation all gammon.. how*
"*Blackfellor read him? eh! He no learn him read Book!*'
'*Read that then, said the Gobernor pointing to a Picter*'

Racial Harmony in Australia.
The government's attempts to encourage cooperation between natives and settlers found little success, as shown in this 1816 oil painting. At top, whites and Aborigines, dressed in European clothing, mingle harmoniously. Harmony prevails in the second panel from the top, in which uniformed soldiers and a government official greet the Aborigines courteously. Things begin to deteriorate in the third panel, however, as an Aborigine spears a white man and is hung for his infraction. A cycle of violence takes over in the bottom panel as a white man shoots an Aborigine and is in turn hung by soldiers.

ranchers intruding on their hunting and gathering lands. As in North America, whites were relentless in taking an allegedly empty—or expected soon to be empty—continent into their possession.

The Long Boom As it did in Latin America, a long boom favored Australia in the second half of the nineteenth century, up until the 1880s. A wet La Niña cycle, strong wool and gold exports, and the inflow of investments for the construction of railroads supported growth. An Australian-born generation of whites came into its own during this boom, which, on the one hand, was still strongly colonial in outlook, cherishing the metropolitan ties, but, on the other hand, was proud of its Australian pioneer differences. In early stirrings of Australian literature and art, these differences stood out. The writers of the weekly magazine the *Bulletin*, founded in 1880, discussed the harshness of farming in the bush and the virtues of republicanism; and the so-called Heidelberg painters (after their camp near Melbourne) in the 1880s developed their own version of impressionism, emphasizing shades of ochre and olive green. The legislative councils of the colonies became veritable battlegrounds between native white Australians and the colonial government over issues such as "free selection" (the Australian equivalent of homesteading), land-squatting, and tariffs.

The Difficult Turn of the Century The boom years ended for Australia around 1890. During the last quarter of the nineteenth century, the economies of the three leading industrial countries of the world—Great Britain, the United States, and Germany—slowed, with first a financial depression in 1873–1879 and another more economy-wide one in 1890–1896. Australia had been able to ride out the first depression, mainly thanks to continuing gold finds. But in the 1890s, construction as well as banking collapsed and factories closed. Coincidentally, a dry El Niño cycle devastated free selection farming. Labor unrest followed: Although widespread strikes failed, the newly founded Labor Party (1891) immediately became a major political force. The country adopted labor reforms, an old-age pension, fiscal reforms, and a white-only immigration policy. The discovery of huge gold deposits in western Australia in 1892–1894 helped to redress the economy. In 1900, Australia finally adopted a federal constitution, which made the country the second fully autonomous "dominion," after Canada (1867) but before New Zealand (1907), Newfoundland (1907), South Africa (1910), and Ireland (1922).

New Zealand Fourteen hundred miles southeast of Australia lies the archipelago of New Zealand. Both the north and south islands had been settled around 1200 CE by Polynesians called "Maori," farmers who brought along yams, sweet potatoes, and taro. Most of their settlements were on or close to the coasts on the northern island, where agriculture was most productive. After initial hostile and even bloody encounters between Maoris, numbering about 100,000, and Europeans, the British negotiated a controversial treaty in 1840, which entitled the Maoris to their land and status as British subjects. The governor, however, disregarded the treaty; and white settlements proceeded apace, with Maoris pushed off their land. In a series of clashes from 1860 to 1872, a number of Maori groups retaliated with violence, slowing down white settlement severely but also eventually ending Maori independence. Disease reduced Maori numbers to a low of 40,000 in the 1890s.

Large-scale immigration began only in 1870, and within a decade the white population doubled to 200,000. As in Australia, wheat farming made New Zealand self-sufficient and wool and gold sustained export-led growth. High-quality coal, mined from 1873, added to the exports. Refrigeration (introduced in 1882) initiated New Zealand's specialization in lamb meat and butter production for export. In the wake of rapid urbanization and the rise of a textile industry, far-reaching social legislation was set in motion, which culminated in 1893 with New Zealand becoming the first country in the world to grant voting rights to women. Thus, a small British settler colony far away from either Europe or the United States set the pace for women's emancipation at the end of the nineteenth century.

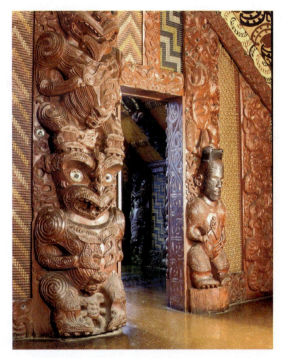

Maori Meeting House. Shown here is the entrance, made of carved wood, to the oldest tribal meeting house of the Maori, built in 1842. The chief carver, Raharuhi Rukupo, portrayed himself on the right. When the British colonial government proceeded with its land confiscations in 1860–1872, it transferred the house from the tribe to what is today the Museum of New Zealand. After lengthy litigations by the Maori, the government admitted in the 1990s to the illegality of the seizure.

European Imperialism in the Middle East and Africa

The British role in the Middle East during the eighteenth and early nineteenth centuries was much more modest, as was that of Europeans in general. Their function was limited to that of merchants, diplomats, or military advisors in an Ottoman Empire with a long tradition of conquering European lands. The situation changed at the end of the eighteenth century when Russia adopted a plan of southern expansion designed to drive the Ottomans back into Asia, take Istanbul, and convert it back into an eastern Christian capital. The other European powers sought to slow the Russian advances, with Great Britain assuming the lead role in protecting the Ottomans. In the long run, this policy of containment failed. Under Russian pressure, Ottoman territory shrank, the Europeans joined Russia in dismembering the Ottoman Empire, and a general imperialist competition for carving up other parts of the world—notably south and east Asia as well as Africa—ensued.

The Rising Appeal of Imperialism in the West

Empires (multiethnic, multi-linguistic, and multi-religious polities) were, as we have repeatedly seen in this book, of old lineage in world history. Their current embodiments were the Ottoman, Habsburg, and Russian Empires. The Russian Empire, a latecomer, saw its mission as replacing the Ottoman Empire as the dominant eastern

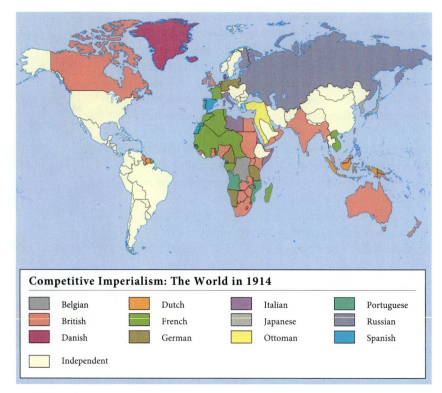

Competitive Imperialism: The World in 1914

Belgian		Dutch		Italian		Portuguese
British		French		Japanese		Russian
Danish		German		Ottoman		Spanish
Independent						

MAP **26.4** **Competitive Imperialism: The World in 1914.**

European power and, by expanding eastward across the steppe, the leading Asian power. Its ambition became the catalyst for France, Great Britain, Belgium, Germany, and even late-industrializing Italy to embark on competitive imperialism in other parts of the world (see Map 26.4).

The Ottoman, Russian, and British Empires

After the failure in 1815 of Napoleon's imperial schemes in both Egypt and Europe, Great Britain was the undisputed leading empire in the world. No country had a navy that could rival it, British trade posts and colonies were widely distributed over the world, and British colonialism in India was geared toward growing and exporting Indian cotton to fuel British industrialization. On the European continent, Britain worked to restore the monarchies of France, Austria, Prussia, and Russia so that they would balance each other as "great powers" in a **Concert of Europe**. Under no circumstances would Britain tolerate any renewed European imperialism of the kind that Napoleon had pursued. Meeting more or less regularly in congresses, the great powers were actually remarkably successful at maintaining peace in Europe. For an entire century not a single war engulfed the continent as a whole, throwing Europe into turmoil as had happened during the Napoleonic era.

The Concert of Europe, however, was less successful with curbing the imperial ambitions of its members reaching for lands outside the western European core. Russia did not hide its goal of throwing the Ottoman Empire (admitted to the Concert

Concert of Europe: International political system that dominated Europe from 1815 to 1914 and which advocated a balance of power among states.

for better protection of its integrity in 1856) back into "Asia," that is, Asia Minor or Anatolia. Great Britain, although it made itself the protector of the integrity of the Ottoman Empire, could at best only slow the ambitions of Russia. The movement to secure the independence of Greece (1821–1832) is a good example of this pattern. Russia, as the Greeks' coreligionist and protector, was centrally involved in initiating a pattern of ethno-linguistic nationalism that replaced constitutional nationalism as the organizing ideology for many Europeans in the nineteenth century.

The French Conquest of Algeria   Britain, unable to prevent an early spark of renewed French imperialism, directed outside Europe against Ottoman Algiers. The French naval expedition—the circumstances of which were described at the beginning of this chapter—conveniently took place in 1830 while British attention was still focused on the negotiations for Greece's independence. In its North African expedition, France followed an earlier short-lived blueprint of Napoleon's, which envisaged the creation of a Mediterranean empire encompassing Algeria and/or Egypt, prior to his lightning imperialism in Europe, possibly to signal to Britain the ease of reaching India via the Mediterranean.

Algeria was the crucial first step of a European power toward seizing provinces of the Ottoman Empire in competition with the Russians, while officially protecting its integrity. This first step was still full of hesitations and counter maneuvers. At first, the French stayed on a small coastal strip around Algiers and other places, encouraging the rise of indigenous leaders to take over from the Ottoman corsairs and Janissaries and share the country with the French. The British discreetly supported Algerian leaders with weapons to be used against the French.

In the longer run, however, coexistence proved impossible and the French military—against strong Algerian resistance—undertook an all-out conquest. The civilian colonial administration after 1870 encouraged large-scale immigration of French and Spanish farmers, who settled on small plots, as well as French corporate investments in vineyards and citrus plantations on the coast. The indigenous population of Arabs and Berbers, decimated by cholera epidemics in the 1860s, found itself largely reduced to less fertile lands in the interior.

The Conquest of Algiers.
Algiers fell to France in 1830, a development driven in part by the efforts of King Charles X (1824–1830) to salvage his regime. Charles, a younger brother of Louis XVI (executed in the French Revolution), had sought a restoration of absolutist rule. Although Napoleon had fleetingly thought of conquering Algeria, Charles had no plans beyond the defeat of the Algerian dey. In spite of the French victory, republican revolutionaries overthrew Charles and established the constitutional monarchy of Louis-Philippe (r. 1830–1848).

The Great Game:
Competition between
Great Britain and Russia
for conquest or control of
Asian countries north of
India and south of Russia,
principally Afghanistan.

Britain's Containment Policy

Great Britain adhered longer to the policy of protecting what remained of the Ottoman Empire. It also opposed Russia in its own backyard of central Asia, inaugurating what was called the **Great Game** against Russia in Asia with the first Anglo–Afghan war in 1838. Although Great Britain failed to occupy Afghanistan and make it an advance protectorate against the approaching Russians, it eventually succeeded in turning Afghanistan into a buffer state, keeping Russia one country away from India. A little later, in 1853–1856, Britain and France teamed up in the Crimean War to stop Russia from renewing its drive for Istanbul. This defeat, demonstrating the superiority of industrially produced new rifles and breech-loading artillery, chastened Russia for the next two decades.

In the second half of the nineteenth century, however, the ethnic–nationalist unification of Germany in 1870–1871, engineered by Prussia through a successful war against France (the Franco–Prussian War), destroyed the balance of the European Concert. Germany, much larger than Prussia and strengthened further through the annexation of the French industrializing region of Alsace-Lorraine, was now the dominant power in western Europe. Russia promptly exploited the new imbalance in Europe during anti-Ottoman uprisings in the Balkans in 1876. Leaving the humiliation of the Crimean War behind, Russian troops broke through Ottoman lines of defense and marched within a few miles of Istanbul. However, Great Britain, although no longer the arbiter of the European Concert, still had enough clout to force Russia into retreating.

British Imperialism in Egypt and Sudan

To prevent a repeat of the Russian invasion, Britain and the Ottomans agreed in 1878 to turn the island of Cyprus (off the Syrian coast) over to the British as a protectorate. This protectorate would have British advisors and troops, ready to defend Istanbul against a renewed Russian invasion. Thus, in the name of curbing Russian imperialism, Great Britain became an imperial power itself in the Mediterranean.

Events after the occupation of Cyprus, however, followed a dramatically different course. Instead of watching Russia, the commanders of the British navy squadron in Cyprus had to turn their attention to Egypt. This province was the wealthiest part of the Ottoman Empire. It was governed by a dynasty of autonomous rulers, beginning with Muhammad Ali (r. 1805–1848), an Albanian officer in the Ottoman army who assumed political control after Napoleon's troops had evacuated Egypt. An energetic statesman, Muhammad Ali reorganized the Nile-irrigated agricultural lands into large estates, producing Egyptian-bred long-staple cotton, and created his own independent army of conscripted Egyptians. Efforts to create a textile industry failed because he was unable (as an Ottoman governor) to establish high tariff barriers against British imports. Similarly, efforts to use his new army for a conquest of Istanbul and take over the Ottoman Empire were thwarted by a Great Britain anxious to protect the sultans. Even in failure, however, Muhammad Ali had a huge impact on Egypt. In a major cultural renewal, similar to the Tanzimat constitutional reforms in Istanbul, Cairo and Alexandria became centers of adaptation to European arts and letters as well as a reformed Islam.

Muhammad Ali's successors were less able rulers who incurred considerable debts, in part for the French-led construction of the Suez Canal in 1869. Britain took over a large part of the canal shares from the debt-ridden Egyptian ruler in 1857. A year later, Britain and France imposed a joint debt commission that garnished a portion of Egyptian tax revenue. Opposition in Egypt to this foreign interference grew in the following years, both inside and outside the Egyptian government. It culminated in 1881 with a revolt in the Egyptian army, endangering the continuation of the debt repayments.

British-initiated negotiations between the Ottoman sultan and the leader of the army revolt, Col. Ahmad Urabi (1841–1911, an early Egyptian—as opposed to foreign-descended—officer), over the issue of the debt collapsed after riots in Alexandria and a careless British bombardment of the port in response to Egyptian fortification efforts. Interventionists in London, fearing for their bonds and eager for more cotton imports from Egypt for the British textile industry, gained the upper hand. Overcoming the fiercely resisting Egyptian army, a British expeditionary force occupied Egypt in 1882.

The Ottoman sultan acquiesced to the occupation because the appointment of a British-appointed high commissioner, charged with the reorganization of the Egyptian finances, was announced to be only temporary. Costly campaigns by British-led Egyptian troops in Sudan during 1883–1885, however, derailed any early departure plans. Egypt had occupied Sudan in the 1820s and, as in Egypt, had made cotton a major export crop for the British textile industry. Sudanese resentment over the occupation and anxiety over the accompanying social changes became focused when Britain occupied Egypt and were expressed in a religiously inspired uprising in Khartoum in 1883.

> ### Strengthening the Empire
>
> "I have always, and do now recommend it [the purchase of the Suez Canal shares] to the country as a political transaction, and one which I believe is calculated to strengthen the Empire. That is the spirit in which it has been accepted by the country, which understands it though the two right honourable critics may not."
>
> —Benjamin Disraeli, Prime Minister of Britain (in office 1874–1880) addressing Parliament. In *The Nation. A Weekly Journal Devoted to Politics, Literature, Science and the Arts*, 22 (1876), p. 193.

Scottish Troops at the Sphinx, 1882. The British occupied Egypt as a means to secure the Suez Canal and guarantee the repayment of Egyptian debts. Subsequent negotiations with the Ottoman sultan for the status of Egypt failed, and the province became an unofficial protectorate of Britain. Although granted internal independence in 1922, Egypt remained in a semi-colonial relationship with Britain until 1956.

The leader of the uprising was Muhammad Ahmad Ibn Abdallah (1844–1885), head of an Islamic Sufi brotherhood and self-styled Mahdi ("rightly guided" or "Messiah"), sent to establish a realm of justice. After the Mahdi succeeded in driving the British–Egyptian forces from Sudan and establishing an independent state, he was left alone for the next decade.

Until the British slaughtered his forces at the Battle of Omdurman in 1898, Egypt's finances, aggravated by problems in Sudan, were sufficiently in disarray to keep the British focused on Egypt. On the one hand, the British wanted to put the Egyptian finances on a sound footing again, but, on the other hand, they wanted out so as to not be responsible for the country's governance. They had no plans yet for a full-fledged Mediterranean imperialism. As a compromise, they conceived of a conditional departure, with the right of return at times of internal unrest or external danger. The Ottoman sultan, however, refused to sign this compromise. He was grateful to Britain for recognizing Ottoman sovereignty but sought to avoid the responsibility of governance. A veritable dance around the question of governance developed. The two sides exchanged notes concerning the issue no fewer than 66 times, with neither side budging. In the end, Britain stayed for almost three-quarters of a century, running Egypt as an undeclared colony for the first 40 years. Without a clear plan, Britain had nonetheless transplanted the pattern of imperialism–colonialism it had first experimented with in India.

France's Tunisian Protectorate   The quid pro quo for Britain's acquisition of Cyprus in 1878 was for France to gain title to Tunisia. Similar to Algeria and Egypt, Tunisia was an autonomous Ottoman province, ruled by its own dynasty of *beys*. The dynasty had been founded by a Janissary officer in 1705 when the military ruling class began to shift from corsair raids against Christian shipping to the fiscal exploitation of the villages and nomadic tribes of the interior. Fertile northern Tunisia provided limited but fairly reliable tax revenues from olive oil, barley, wheat, fruits, and nuts. Annual tax expeditions to the south among the semi-nomadic sheep and camel tribes usually yielded few taxes and served mostly to demonstrate the dynasty's sovereignty.

The beys responded to the Western challenge early, being the first in the Muslim Middle East and North Africa to modernize their military and adopt a constitution (1857). With their more limited revenues, they hit the debt ceiling already in 1869, much earlier than the Ottomans and Egyptians, and had to accept a British–French–Italian debt commission for the reorganization of the country's revenues. When the French took over in 1881, they began with the same thankless task of balancing the budget as the British had in Egypt. Only later did they benefit from the French and Italian settlers they called in to the protectorate to intensify agriculture.

The Scramble for Africa

Competitive European imperialism exploded beyond the Mediterranean in early 1884 as Germany claimed its first protectorates in Africa. Conveniently, after having secured lands for his country, the German chancellor Otto von Bismarck (in various offices 1862–1890) called a conference in Berlin, which met from late 1884 to early 1885. The main agenda of the Berlin conference was a discussion on how the 14 invited European countries and the United States should "define the conditions under which future territorial annexations in Africa might be recognized." Bismarck's proposal of the main condition was "effective occupation," with the creation of "spheres of influence" around the occupied places. The first "protectorates," confirmed at the conference, were Cameroon in west central Africa for Germany and Congo as a private possession of King Leopold II of Belgium. The **scramble for Africa** was on (see Map 26.5).

Explorers, Missionaries, and the Civilizing Mission Sub-Saharan Africa was still little known in Europe and poorly misunderstood to most Europeans in 1880. The Enlightenment had instilled curiosity about the geography, flora, fauna, and ethnology of Africa among the European reading public. But to endure the hardships of traveling in the savanna, rain forest, and desert required strong commitment. David

Scramble for Africa: Competition among European powers from 1884 to 1912 to acquire African colonies.

MAP **26.5** The Scramble for Africa.

The Spread of Islam and Christianity in Africa, 1860–1900

- **Muslim areas, 1860**
- **Christian areas, 1860**
- **African religions**
- → **Muslim missionary activity**
- → **Christian missionary activity**

MAP **26.6 The Spread of Islam and Christianity in Africa, 1860–1900.**

Civilizing mission:
Belief that European colonizers had a duty to extend the benefits of European civilization to "backward" peoples.

Livingstone (1813–1873), a tireless missionary and passionate opponent of slavery, was the best known among the pioneers who explored much of south central Africa. The European middle class was fascinated with the early explorers' tales of exotic and mysterious lands and peoples.

The generation of explorers after Livingstone was better equipped, led larger expeditions, and composed more precise accounts. Here, the outstanding figure was Henry Morton Stanley (1841–1904), a Welsh journalist who worked in the United States and became famous for his encounter with Livingstone ("Dr. Livingstone, I presume?") at Lake Tanganyika in east central Africa. Still, in spite of extensive explorations, European politicians at the end of the century had only the vaguest idea of the geography of the "dark continent."

Christian missionaries contributed little to the knowledge of Africa but through their preaching shaped a sense of both responsibility for and superiority to the Africans in the European public. They were at the forefront of the **civilizing mission**, the belief prevalent in the West in the nineteenth century that colonists had a duty to extend the benefits of civilization, that is, European civilization, to the "backward" people they ruled. In the earlier 1800s, the danger of malaria and yellow fever still confined missionaries to the coasts of Africa. Supported by missionary societies in Europe, they trained indigenous missionaries to translate tracts and scriptures for the conversion of Africans in the interior. When quinine (made from the bark of a Brazilian tree) became available in the middle of the 1800s, allowing for treatment of malaria, missionaries were able to follow their indigenous colleagues into the interior (see Map 26.6). At that time, tensions often arose between the two groups. African converts preached the gospel in the spirit of Christian equality, as did the former slave and later Anglican bishop Samuel Adjai Crowther (ca. 1809–1891); but many Western missionaries considered African Christianity to be contaminated by animist "superstitions" and did not accept Africans as equal. Malaria was one infectious disease that could be overcome, but the rising racism of the Victorian period went largely unchecked.

Conquest and Resistance in West Africa   Colonialism on the coast of West Africa after 1885 was an outgrowth of the traditional trade-fort system. By the 1800s, the British had ousted the Dutch and the French from most of the trading forts and had become the dominant European presence in the region. Ghana is a particularly instructive example of the pattern of conquest and resistance. Ghana, previously known as the Gold Coast, was the land of the Ashante kingdom. The Ashante had emerged back in the time of the empire of Songhay, when they mined the gold of the Alkan fields that caravans carried across the Sahara. When gold declined in importance, the kingdom turned to the Atlantic slave trade and benefited handsomely from it. After the 1807 British prohibition of slavery, Ashante merchants switched to commodities, especially palm oil, used for the greasing of machinery and for making soap, that were in great demand in industrializing Europe.

But the Ashante and British traders were in constant conflict over the terms of trade in the forts. Disciplined and well-armed Ashante troops defeated the British repeatedly. Only in 1896, when the British sent regular troops with breech-loader rifles and machine guns to put down the Ashante with their now antiquated muskets, was Ghana finally turned into a protectorate. Later on, after well over a half-century of colonialism, the memory of Ashante nineteenth-century prowess was an important factor in the Ghanaian struggle for independence.

France lost its West African trade forts after the Seven Years' War (1756–1763) to Britain but later received one of them back, a fortified island at the mouth of the River Senegal. It was from this base that career-hungry French officers after 1850 carried out expeditions into the interior of the river rain forest, for alliances and trade purposes. In 1857 they came into conflict with Al-Hajj Umar (ca. 1791–1864), an Islamic reformer in the interior savanna who was in the process of building a state in what are today Guinea, Senegal, and Mali. The French barely survived a siege in a border fort and for decades were in no state to advance any further. Once the scramble was on, however, the West African Islamic state was doomed. In 1891, in the teeth of stiff resistance from the Islamists, the French began to carve out their huge colony in the steppe and savanna of West Africa that formed the core of their colonial empire.

Al-Hajj Umar was one of several West African Muslim religious scholars who became holy warriors (jihadists). Like other Middle Eastern and North African reformers, Umar was dismayed by the decline of Ottoman power. The reformers sought to rejuvenate Islam through a return to the study of the original Islamic sources. In the footsteps of what they perceived as the Prophet Muhammad's original state in Mecca, rising among the defeated unbelievers, the West African reformers forcibly converted black animists to Islam. In contrast to the Islamic kings and emperors of the previous centuries who made no efforts to convert their subjects, the jihadists of the 1800s succeeded in making Islam the dominant religion of West Africa.

A Slave Who Became Bishop. The remarkable life of Samuel Adjai Crowther (ca. 1809–1891) shows that Africans and Asians also participated in the "civilizing mission." Born in Yorubaland in present-day West Africa, Crowther was enslaved as a young man but was rescued by the British navy and freed in 1821. He then converted to Christianity, and after training in London he was ordained an Anglican priest in 1841. He was appointed the first African Anglican bishop in 1864 and went on to produce Yoruba translations of the Bible and the Book of Common Prayer.

Conquest and Resistance in East Africa   The arrival of colonialism in East Africa differed from the pattern in West Africa. Here, as early as the sixteenth century, the Portuguese had established trade forts in the south to acquire gold and ivory for their spice purchases in India. When Swahili patricians in the city-states

Ivory Merchants. Besides slaves, Zanzibar imported elephant tusks from the interior to be marketed for the carving of ivory jewelry and art objects. Principal buyers of the tusks were British, German, and Arab traders.

farther north resisted this intrusion into their traditional Indian Ocean trade, the Portuguese responded with piracy and the construction of coastal forts in their midst. But the arrival of the Dutch with more powerful and numerous ships in the 1630s to take over the spice trade forced the Portuguese to curtail their East African engagement. An Omani Arab expeditionary force exploited the reduced Portuguese presence in 1698 by conquering the Swahili city-state of Mombasa after a 2-year siege. Oman had long-standing trade relations with East Africa and seized its opportunity to expand its limited domestic agricultural base on the Arabian peninsula. Once in control, the Omanis developed a flourishing plantation system for sugar, rice, grain, and cotton on the coastal islands, along with slaves imported from the African interior. In the 1820s, the Omanis—by now under their separate sultan residing on the island of Zanzibar—began to specialize in cloves, becoming the main exporters of this precious spice on the world market. Thanks to the Omanis, the Swahili coast was prosperous again.

Zanzibar was the staging ground for adventurers, explorers, and missionaries in the nineteenth century to enter the African interior. It was here that they vied for places to occupy and spheres of influence to declare. Accordingly, in 1886 Germany received the lion's share on the coast and in the interior, Belgium gave up its claims in return for being recognized in the Congo, and Zanzibar somewhat later became a British protectorate. In its colony of Tanganyika (in current Tanzania), Germany used forced labor for the growing of cotton, provoking the fierce but in the end brutally suppressed Maji Maji rebellion of 1905–1907.

Atrocities and Genocides   Similar atrocities stalked the European civilizing mission. As Germany was quelling rebellion in Tanganyika, it led a ferocious campaign on the other side of the continent against the Herero and Nama people of southwest Africa (modern Namibia). In their determination to establish colonial rule in the region, the German general staff ordered the extermination of the Herero in terms that can be described only as genocide: "I believe that the nation as such must be destroyed," commented General Lothar von Trotha (1848–1920 [TROW-tah]). From 1904 to 1908 the war on the Herero resulted in 80,000 deaths. North of Namibia, King Leopold II (r. 1865–1909) of Belgium turned his personal colony of the Congo into a vast forced-labor camp for the production of rubber. The rubber tree, native to South America, gained great importance in Europe for a variety of industrial applications. Leopold was particularly sadistic in his exploitation of the native workforce, using beatings and mutilations if collection quotas were not filled. An astonishing 3,000,000 Congolese were either killed or starved to death. The horror of the Belgian Congo was the setting for Joseph Conrad's *Heart of Darkness* (1902), perhaps the most powerful anti-imperialist novel of the time and still widely read today. It was also the catalyst for Mark Twain's virulently satirical attack on the Belgian exploitation of the Congolese, *King Leopold's Soliloquy* (1905).

Colonial Atrocities. The German garrison at Windhoek, in present-day Namibia, was besieged by the native Herero people in 1904. Retaliation was swift and violent, with the colonial authorities encaging prisoners in concentration camps, which in turn led to reprisals, such as the massacre of railroad workers shown here.

The scramble finally ended in 1912 with the French declaration of a protectorate over Morocco. By this time, the political competition in Europe had narrowed to the struggle between Germany and Great Britain for political predominance in western Europe. Italy's imperialist dreams were stymied by its crushing defeat at the battle of Adowa in 1896, in which one-third of its army was killed by Ethiopian forces (see Patterns Up Close). Ethiopia emerged from the scramble as the only non-colonized state in Africa. French and British rivalry in Africa, which had cropped up during the scramble and had even led to a confrontation at Fashoda over the control of Sudan in 1898, ended between 1905 and 1911, when Britain allied with France to counter-balance Germany. As a result of this alliance, Britain recognized France's interests in Morocco, adjacent to the two French territories of Algeria and Tunisia, over protests by Germany.

Western Imperialism and Colonialism in Southeast Asia

Parallel to developments in Africa, the new imperialism made its appearance also in southeast Asia, specifically Indonesia, the Philippines, Vietnam, Cambodia, and Laos. While the new imperialism in southeast Asia was an outgrowth of the earlier trade-fort presence of Portugal, Spain, and the Netherlands, it also included the return of France to imperial glory.

The Dutch in Indonesia

The Dutch were heirs of the Portuguese, who had set up forts that traded for spices in Indonesia during the sixteenth century. For 100 years, they were the middlemen for the distribution of spices from Portugal to northern Europe. But after liberating themselves from Habsburg–Spanish rule, the Netherlands displaced Portugal from its dominant position as a spice importer to Europe. From 1650 to 1750, the Netherlands was the leading naval power in the world. After 1750, they shifted from the trade of spices in their trade forts in Indonesia to the planting of cash crops, such as sugar, cacao, coffee, and tobacco—the mild warm weather commodities to which Europeans were addicted and which they consumed in ever larger quantities. The aim of the full colonization of Indonesia during the nineteenth century was to profit from European industrial demand for agricultural and mineral commodities.

Early Indonesia   The western part of southeast Asia, comprising today's Indonesia, is a complex of well over 17,000 islands, fewer than half of which are inhabited. The term "Indonesia" dates to the eighteenth century, denoting sparsely inhabited large and small tropical islands to the southeast of India. The five largest and today most densely populated islands are, from west to east, Sumatra, Java, Borneo, Sulawesi (Celebes), and New Guinea. The earliest inhabitants were prehistoric foragers; the first agrarian–urban settlers were speakers of Austronesian languages. The Austronesians were intrepid sailors across the Pacific and Indian Oceans who settled islands as far away as Hawaii off the Americas and Madagascar off of Africa.

In Sumatra and the Malay Peninsula, chieftainships gave way to a first kingdom around 700 CE, organized around Buddhist religion and law. The kingdom was mostly coastal and commercial, trading pepper, nutmeg, cinnamon, cardamom, cloves, ivory, gold, and tin to the Middle East and China. In the following centuries, it extended its influence to islands as far as the Philippines in the east and the mainland in the north.

Islam gained converts in Indonesia only slowly in the face of stiff Buddhist opposition, but from about 1300, indigenous Indonesian rulers began to convert to Islam. The leading Islamic sultanate was Aceh [AT-shay] (1496–1903) on the western island of Sumatra, a major producer of pepper. In the sixteenth century, when the Portuguese rose to dominance in the Indian Ocean, the Ottomans supported it with firearms.

Portuguese and Dutch Trade Forts   Portuguese sailors arrived in the strategic Strait of Malacca (separating Sumatra from the Malay Peninsula and dividing the Indian Ocean from the Chinese Sea) in 1511, defeating the local sultanate and establishing a fort in the Malaysian capital, Malacca. Their main interest, however, given the power of Aceh on Sumatra, was to push onward to the spice islands of Maluku (today the Maluccas) in eastern Indonesia (between Sulawesi and New Guinea), where they established a trade fort in 1522, amid several Islamic island lords. From there, the Portuguese pushed on to China and Japan, where they arrived in the mid-1500s. Overall, their role in the Indonesian spice trade remained small, and indigenous Islamic merchants maintained their dominance.

After declaring their independence from Spain in 1581, the northern provinces of the Netherlands formed the Republic of the United Netherlands and pushed for their own overseas network of trade forts. In 1602, the Dutch government chartered the Dutch United East India Company (VOC), which spearheaded the expansion of Dutch possessions in India and southeast Asia. After a slow start, the company erected outposts on many Indonesian islands and in the mid-1600s founded Batavia (today Jakarta) on the island of Java as its main southeast Asian center. The VOC was by far the largest and wealthiest commercial company in the world during the seventeenth century, with a fleet consisting of nearly 5,000 merchant ships supported by large naval and land forces.

When the Dutch *stadhouder* (ruler) of the Netherlands, William of Orange (1650–1702), became king of England after the English Glorious Revolution of 1688 that imposed constitutional limits on monarchical rule, the Dutch and English overseas trade interests were pooled. Great Britain (as the country was known after

England's union with Scotland in 1707) deepened its Indian interests through the English East India Company, and the Dutch pursued their engagements in Indonesia. Like the British Company in India, the VOC was increasingly drawn during the early 1700s into dynastic wars. Supported by some 1,000 Dutch soldiers and 3,000 indigenous auxiliaries, the VOC established peace in 1755 in the fragmenting Islamic sultanate of Banten (1527–1808). Thereafter, it became the de facto government on the island of Java over a set of pacified Islamic protectorates.

Several decades earlier than its British counterpart in India, the VOC fell on hard times. Governing and maintaining troops was expensive. VOC employees often paid their expenses out of their own pockets since contact with the Netherlands in pre-telegraph times was slow and sporadic. In the late eighteenth century, trade shifted from spices to bulk commodities, such as sugar, cacao, coffee, tobacco, indigo, and cotton. The inability of the VOC to shift from spices to commodities, requiring investments in plantations and accompanying transportation infrastructures, was the decisive factor which led, in 1799, to the liquidation of the VOC. Similar to the British experience in India, the government of the Netherlands then became the ruler of Indonesian possessions that had grown from trade forts into small colonies, surrounded by dependent indigenous principalities as well as independent sultanates.

Dutch Colonialism

The Dutch government took the decisive step toward investments in 1830 when Belgium separated from the large Dutch kingdom created after the Napoleonic Wars to form an independent Catholic monarchy. Faced with severe budgetary constraints and cut off from industrializing Belgium, the Dutch government adopted the **cultivation system** in Indonesia. According to this system, indigenous Indonesian subsistence farmers were forced into compulsory planting and labor schemes which required them to either grow government crops on

Cultivation system: Dutch colonial scheme of compulsory labor and plantation of crops imposed on indigenous Indonesian self-sufficiency farmers.

Indonesia in the Nineteenth Century. A traditional house in north Sumatra, with animal stables in the bottom and human living quarters on top. (*a*) Dutch judges meting out harsh sentences, including death by hanging, against Indonesians. (*b*) Workers in Batavia (today Jakarta), ca. 1830, stacking tropical wood for export in the harbor. (*c*)

20 percent of their land or work for 60 days on Dutch plantations. Overnight, the Dutch and collaborating Indonesian ruling classes turned into landowners. They reaped huge profits while Indonesian subsistence farmers, having to replace many of their rice paddies with commercial crops, suffered in many places from famines. In the course of the nineteenth century, Indonesia became a major or even the largest exporter of sugar, tea, coffee, palm oil, coconut products, tropical hardwoods, rubber, quinine, and pepper to the industrial nations.

To keep pace with demand, the Dutch pursued a program of systematic conquest and colonization. In a half-dozen campaigns, they conquered the Indonesian archipelago, finally subduing the most stubborn opponents, the Muslim guerillas of Aceh, in 1903 (see Map 26.7). Even then, the conquest was incomplete and inland rain forests remained outside Dutch government control. Conquered lands were turned over to private investors who established plantations. To deflect criticism at home and abroad, the Dutch government also introduced some reform measures. In 1870 they liberated farmers from the compulsory planting of government crops, and in 1901 they issued an "ethical policy," announcing measures such as land distribution, irrigation, and education. Severe underfunding, however, kept these measures largely on paper; and it was clear that the profits from colonialism were more important than investment for indigenous people.

Spain in the Philippines

Adjacent to the Indonesian islands in the northeast were the Philippines. Here, the Spanish had built their first trade fort of Manila shortly after conquering Mexico from the Aztecs. Manila served as a port from which to trade with China. Using

MAP **26.7** Western Imperialism in Southeast Asia, 1870–1914.

Mexican silver, Spanish merchants bought Chinese luxury manufactures. Manila expanded only slowly, suffering from constant raids by indigenous highlanders from the interior, Islamic rulers from the southern islands, and Dutch interlopers. Imperial conquest had to await the later eighteenth century, and colonization followed in the middle of the nineteenth century with the introduction of sugarcane.

Galleons and Trade with China   Spain expanded early on from the Americas farther west in order to prevent Portugal from claiming all the lucrative spice islands of Indonesia. A Portuguese explorer in Spanish service, Ferdinand Magellan (d. ca. 1480–1521), successfully crossed the sea channels at the southern tip of South America in 1520 and, on a journey that took his fleet eventually around the entire globe, discovered what later became known as the "Philippines," in honor of King Phillip II of Spain. It took another half-century, however, before Spain could spare ships and men for the implantation of a first trade fort and small colony. This fort, Manila, became the base for subsequent biannual silver fleets from Mexico. Spanish merchants based in Mexico, from where Manila was administered, benefited greatly from the trade of silver for Chinese silk, porcelain, and lacquerware. Thus, Manila began as a small sub-colony of the large Spanish colony of Mexico or New Spain.

The Philippines are a collection of some 7,000 islands, with the four largest, from north to south, being Luzon, Visaya, Mindanao, and Sulu. The earliest inhabitants were prehistoric islanders, followed ca. 2000 BCE by Austronesians who settled mostly on the coasts, growing rice and exploiting maritime resources. Similar to the inhabitants of the Indonesian islands, the Filipinos were animists influenced to varying degrees by Indian and Chinese cultures. As the Spanish gradually expanded their hold on the coastal lowlands outside Manila on Luzon and Visaya (where the local king had converted to Christianity), they established estates, thus advancing from trade-fort imperialism to the beginnings of territorial expansion.

Incipient Colonialism   The indigenous farmers on the Philippine estates were obliged to deliver rents, paid in kind, in the form of rice and animals, to ensure the food supply for some 30,000 inhabitants of Manila, mostly merchants of Spanish, Chinese, and Japanese origin. Warrior chieftains outside Spanish lands who converted were confirmed as owners on their lands and transformed themselves into a Hispanicized landowner class. By the early eighteenth century, the Spanish controlled enough of a critical mass on the two islands of Luzon and Visaya that they were able to establish a regular administration for fiscal and juridical matters. The beginnings of colonialism in the Philippines had emerged.

The balance sheet for the colonial administration was always in the red, however, since the fiscal revenue did not yield surpluses and villagers produced only small quantities of exportable ginger, cinnamon, and gold. Much money had to be invested in defending the Spanish-controlled territory from attacks by independent Filipinos in the mountainous upland interiors of Luzon and Visaya who resisted conquest and conversion. Even more vexing were raids supported by Islamic sultanates which had formed in the south on the basis of trading hardwoods for luxuries with China.

To make matters worse, a brief British occupation of Manila during the Seven Years' War (1756–1763) demonstrated that Spain lacked the means to protect itself against the rising naval and merchant power of Great Britain in the China trade.

On Filipino Ethnic Nationalism

"Does your Excellency know the spirit of (my) country? If you did, you would not say that I am 'a spirit twisted by a German education,' for the spirit that animates me I already had since childhood, before I learned a word of German. My spirit is 'twisted' because I have been reared among injustices and abuses which I saw everywhere, because since a child I have seen many suffer stupidly and because I also have suffered. . . . And 'twisted' like my spirit is that of hundreds of thousands of Filipinos who have not yet left their miserable homes, who speak no other language except their own, and who, if they could write or express their thoughts, would make my *Noli me tangere* [one of Rizal's novels] very tiny indeed, and with their volumes there would be enough to build pyramids for the corpses of all the tyrants . . ."

—José Rizal. *La Solidaridad*, a newsletter published by the Propaganda Movement, February 15, 1890. In Diosdado G. Capino, Minerva A. Gonzalez, and Filipinas A. Piñeda, *Rizal's Life, Works and Writings: Their Impact on Our National Identity*, p. 104. Quezon City, Philippines: Publisher's Association of the Philippines, 1977.

Using Indian cottons and Chinese middlemen, the British diverted much of the American silver trade to India, calling into question the entire rationale for Spanish trade-fort commerce and limited colonialism in the Philippines. The last galleon bringing silver from Mexico sailed in 1815.

Full Colonialism   Major reforms, shifting the economy from silver to commodity exports, began at the same time, motivated by the Spanish loss of Mexico to independence. These reforms resulted in the liberalization of trade and the beginnings of commercial agriculture for export. Ports were opened to ships from all countries, discrimination against Chinese settlements ended, and Spanish administrators and churchmen lost their trade privileges. Foreign entrepreneurs cleared rain forests and exported hardwoods. On the new land they grew cash crops, such as sugar, tobacco, hemp (for ropes and sacks), indigo (as a dye), coffee, and cotton. Large-scale rice farms replaced a great number of small-scale village self-sufficiency plots, and thus, commercialization even invaded subsistence agriculture.

Strong resistance by landowners against a reform of the land regime and tax system until the very end of the nineteenth century, however, assured that Spain did not benefit much from the liberalization of trade. Additionally, Philippine society stratified rapidly into a wealthy minority and a large mass of landless rural workers and urban day laborers. Manila had over 100,000 inhabitants in the early nineteenth century. This stratification, however, was very different from that in the Americas. There was no real Creole class, that is, a Spanish–Philippine upper stratum of landowners and urban people. Although the French Revolution and subsequent Napoleonic upheavals in Spain had their impact on the islands, agitation for independence and constitutionalism was largely limited to urban intellectuals. The Philippines remained a colony, producing no revenue and still demanding costly administrative—especially fiscal—reforms and infrastructural investments, both of which Spain was unable to afford.

The first stirrings of Filipino nationalism, primarily among Hispanicized Filipinos of mixed Spanish and indigenous or Chinese descent, made themselves felt in the second half of the nineteenth century. The principal spokesman was José Rizal (1861–1896), whose subversive novels were a response to the Spanish justification of continued colonialism.

Colonial authorities promptly arrested Rizal for his activities, banishing him to Hong Kong; but he returned to Manila in 1892, inspiring both overt and underground resistance groups. One of these groups, Katipunan, operated in secret, advocating Filipino independence through armed struggle. In 1896 the government discovered the existence of the organization in Manila and executed hundreds of revolutionaries, including Rizal, before firing squads. But it was unable to destroy Katipunan in the provinces, and the two sides agreed in 1897 to a truce which included the end of armed revolt in return for exile of the leadership in Hong Kong.

Philippine–American War

Although it appeared that the colonial government was successful in suppressing the Filipino revolt for independence, events took a dramatic turn when the Spanish–American War broke out in 1898. A mysterious explosion of an American warship in Cuba—newly autonomous under Spanish suzerainty—had led to mutual declarations of war. The two sides fought their first battle in Manila Bay, where the United States routed a Spanish squadron. An American ship fetched the exiled Filipino rebel Emilio Aguinaldo (1869–1964) from Hong Kong, and he quickly defeated the Spanish and declared independence. Over four centuries of Spanish colonialism in the Pacific had come to an end.

After 4 months of fighting, Spain was defeated not only in Cuba, Puerto Rico, and Guam but also in the Philippines. The United States and Spain made peace at the end of 1898, ignoring the independent Philippine government in their agreement. Accordingly, US forces took possession of Manila in 1899 and within a year defeated the troops of the protesting Filipino government under the elected president, Emilio Aguinaldo. The Filipinos shifted to guerilla war, but US troops were able to capture Aguinaldo in 1901. The United States declared the war over in 1902 but had to fight remnants of the guerillas as well as southern rebels until 1913. Thus, the United States had joined the European race for imperial and colonial control of the non-Western world.

American Soldiers in the Philippines. The victory of the United States over Spain in 1898 and its decision to annex the Philippines created for the first time an American overseas empire. Resistance was immediate, and a brutal war against Philippine fighters lasted from 1902 until 1913, with isolated outbreaks continuing until Philippine independence in 1946. Here, American troops dig in and fortify an outpost in Luzon.

The French in Vietnam

North of Indonesia and west of the Philippines is Vietnam. Indochina, the peninsula on which Vietnam is located, also includes Cambodia, Laos, and Thailand. Portuguese monks were the first western Europeans to go to Indochina in the sixteenth century, seeking converts among the Buddhist, neo-Confucian, and animist indigenous inhabitants. French imperial and colonial involvement began in 1858, a time when Europe was industrializing and competition in the Concert of Europe was beginning to spill over from the Balkans and Middle East into Africa. At first focusing on the south of Indochina, France gradually expanded northward, establishing protectorates over the Nguyen royal dynasty, which was the last of a succession of kingdoms that had begun in the third century CE.

French Interests in Vietnam

As discussed in earlier chapters, in the later first and early second millennia CE Vietnam was intermittently part of China, from where the country received strong Buddhist, Confucian, and Daoist cultural impulses. Independent dynasties reemerged after 1400, and by the later eighteenth century a royally sponsored Vietnamese culture developed, replacing the original

Saigon Street Scene, 1915.
As they did in other areas in their empire, the French pursued what they termed their "civilizing mission." What this meant in practical terms was the importation of French culture, and urban planning including architecture as well as language, education, and literature. The French increasingly looked at their empire as "overseas France" and took it for granted that their subjects would want to adopt French culture and practices.

Chinese script with its own reformed script. French royal efforts in the seventeenth and early eighteenth centuries to sponsor Catholic missions and trading companies were largely unsuccessful and ended altogether after the lost Seven Years' War (1756–1763). When France renewed these efforts after the French Revolution and Napoleon, it was rebuffed by the Vietnamese kings, who shared Chinese concerns about the Western challenge. Both China and Vietnam adopted a policy of isolationism as their first answer to Western patterns of challenge.

The French, however, were not deterred. Napoleon had toyed with the idea of a Mediterranean empire that included either Algeria or Egypt before embarking on his campaign of European imperialism. The French then actually conquered Algeria in 1830–1847, as we have seen earlier in this chapter. The ruler who was subsequently most active in pushing for the renewal of Napoleon's imperialism outside Europe was his nephew, Napoleon III (r. 1848–1870). This self-styled emperor involved himself in a variety of short-lived ventures in Mexico, China, and Japan. His one enduring conquest was that of "Cochinchina," that is, southern Vietnam, in 1858–1862. Taking as a pretext the renewed torture and execution of French missionaries and Vietnamese converts, the French dispatched a squadron that occupied the sparsely inhabited Mekong River delta in 1858–1862, annexing it as a protectorate.

Conquest and Colonialism   Serious colonization efforts by the French had to await the scramble for the division of Africa and what remained of Asia in the mid-1880s. After Napoleon III's fall from power as a result of the lost war against Prussia and the establishment of the Third Republic, opinions among politicians about the wisdom of a French empire were divided. But when pro-imperialists came to power in 1883, the French challenged China a year later in a successful war for the control of northern Vietnam. In contrast to the thinly settled south, the Red River estuary with the capital of the kingdom, Hanoi, in the north was densely populated. When the imperialist frenzy was at its peak during the Berlin conference of 1884–1885 for the partition of Africa, the French conquerors united southern and northern Vietnam into the French colony of Indochina. Two members of the deposed Vietnamese dynasty took to the mountains and waged a guerilla war against the occupation, called the Black Flag Revolt. But by the early twentieth century the French had captured both and were in full control.

The French government and French entrepreneurs invested substantial sums in the Mekong delta. They established plantations for the production of coffee, tea, and rubber. Indigenous rice farmers had to deliver 40 percent of their crops to the colonial government. Hanoi was made the seat of the colonial administration in 1902 and was enlarged as an architecturally French city. The port of Haiphong, downriver from Hanoi, became the main entry point for ships to load agricultural commodities for export. The commodities for the world market, which French West Africa largely lacked, existed in Vietnam, Cambodia, and Laos (the latter two added in 1893–1904).

Early Nationalism Given Vietnam's long tradition of Confucian scholar-administrators, it was only a question of time before the pre-1858 spirit of anti-foreign Vietnamese patriotism reasserted itself. The driving force in this reassertion was Phan Boi Chau (1867–1940), trained by his father and other scholars and an eyewitness of the crushing by the French of a protest by scholars in 1885. Initially a royalist harking back to the glory of the last dynasty, in 1904 Phan Boi Chau founded the first of a number of small groups, mostly abroad, devoted to driving out the French. He spent some time in Japan, where he was active among Vietnamese students for a number of years, buoyed by the Japanese victory over Russia in 1904–1905 and seeking support from Japanese politicians.

Phan Boi Chau's activities and writings inspired antitax demonstrations and a provincial uprising in Vietnam in 1908–1909, which the French suppressed harshly. Under French pressure, the Japanese expelled Phan Boi Chau from Japan in 1909. By 1912, he had given up his royalism, and from then on a newly formed nationalist grouping favored the expulsion of the French and the formation of a Vietnamese democratic republic.

> **Creating a Revolutionary Party**
>
> "Inukai [Inukai Tsuyoshi, leader of the Progressive Party in Japan] went on to ask me: 'Have you organized a revolutionary party?' At that moment I felt so ashamed I wished to die, knowing that there was not yet any real revolutionary party in our country. Reluctantly, however, I replied: 'An organization there is, but its influence is negligible, as if it did not exist.'"
>
> —Phan Boi Chau. *Overturned Chariot: The Autobiography of Phan-Boi-Chau.* Translated by Vinh Sinh and Nicholas Wickenden, SHAPS Library of Translations, p. 89. Honolulu: University of Hawaii Press, 1999.

Putting It All Together

Ever since Vladimir Lenin, the founder of the Soviet Union, declared in his famous 1916 work that imperialism was "the highest stage of capitalism" (adopting a similar thesis first suggested by the English historian John A. Hobson in 1902), scholars have hotly debated the topic of whether or not the capitalist industrialization process in Europe, North America, and Japan needed colonies to sustain its growth. Most recent historians, beginning with David K. Fieldhouse in 1984, have come to the conclusion that imperialism and colonialism were not needed and that all the mineral and agrarian commodities crucial for industrialization during the first and second Industrial Revolutions could have been bought from independent countries on the world market. It so happened, of course, that Great Britain had transformed India from trade-fort imperialism to territorial imperialism just prior to its industrialization and used Indian cotton as raw material for its textile factories. But this raises the reverse question: Would industrialization have happened had Great Britain not conquered India? This counterfactual question has no easy answer.

Perhaps a better approach to finding an answer is to think of trade-fort and territorial imperialism as world-historical patterns of long standing. By contrast, industrialization was a much later phenomenon that arose out of the application of the New Science to practical mechanical uses, of which steam engines and textile factories were the first examples, appearing around 1800. Thus, old patterns of imperialism continued to exist during the rise of the new pattern of industrialization. These old patterns received a tremendous amplification as a result of the new power that industrialization bestowed on the European countries. Therefore, the new imperialism of

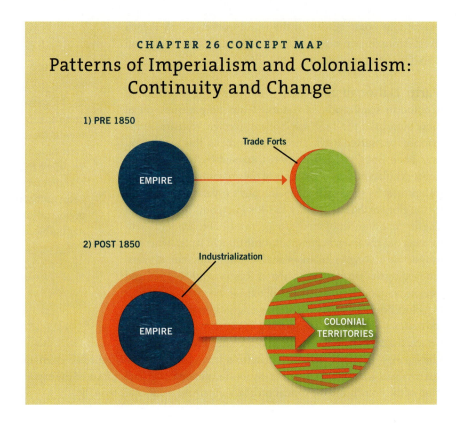

CHAPTER 26 CONCEPT MAP

Patterns of Imperialism and Colonialism: Continuity and Change

1) PRE 1850

EMPIRE

Trade Forts

2) POST 1850

Industrialization

EMPIRE

COLONIAL TERRITORIES

the nineteenth century and the colonialism which followed in its wake can be seen as phenomena in which old patterns continued but were superimposed on and enlarged by the patterns of industrial power (see Concept Map).

Review and Respond

1. What were the role and activities of the British East India Company, and why was this company important in the rise of British imperialism?

2. How did Australia and New Zealand evolve as British settler colonies?

3. What was the European Concert, and how did it affect the new imperialism?

4. How did the "scramble for Africa" originate, how did it evolve, and what were its results?

5. Compare and contrast Dutch, Spanish, and French imperialism and colonialism in southeast Asia.

For additional resources, including maps, primary sources, visuals, and quizzes, please go to www.oup.com/us/vonsivers. Please see the Further Resources section at the back of the book for additional readings and suggested websites.

Thinking Through Patterns

▶ **What new patterns emerged in the transition from trade-fort imperialism to the new imperialism?**

During the early modern period, European monarchs commissioned merchant marine companies, such as the British East India Company and the Dutch United East India Company (VOC), to avoid military expeditions of their own but still receive a share of the profits of trade. The mariner-merchants built coastal forts for storage and protection, granted to them by the local rulers with whom they traded. In the seventeenth and eighteenth centuries, much larger trading companies were formed, in which investors pooled their resources and large numbers of mariner-merchants now served in dozens of trade forts overseas. In India and Indonesia, these companies became too big to fail and resorted to their governments in England and the Netherlands to rescue them. Thus, through the back door, governments found themselves forced to conquer and to colonize—they had become imperialist-colonizers.

Great Britain was the pioneer in the development of exportable agricultural and mineral commodities in its colonies for the support of its expanding industries. By the middle of the nineteenth century, other industrializing countries either embarked on imperial conquests or shifted to full colonialism in order to obtain necessary commodities. As a rule, labor for the production of these commodities was scarce. Workers had to be recruited forcibly and were routinely paid low wages.

▶ **How did European colonizers develop their colonies economically, given that they were industrializing themselves at the same time?**

▶ **What were the experiences of the indigenous people under the new imperialism? How did they adapt to colonialism? How did they resist?**

Many imperial conquests involved protracted campaigns that claimed many indigenous victims. If one of the goals of the ensuing colonization was commodity production, the indigenous population was recruited, often forcibly and with low wages. Resistance to European colonialism manifested itself in ethnic nationalism, as demonstrated by the examples of José Rizal, Phan Boi Chau, and Emilio Aguinaldo discussed in this chapter. In Australia and New Zealand and other colonies where European settlement was encouraged, colonial governments or settlers ousted the indigenous population from the most fertile lands, often in the face of fierce resistance.

Chapter 27 | Creoles and Caudillos

1790-1917 | LATIN AMERICA AND THE CARIBBEAN IN THE NINETEENTH CENTURY

When the French Revolution broke out in 1789 a young Caribbean mulatto named Vincent Ogé (ca. 1755–1791) was on business in France. His extended family of free *Creoles*—inhabitants born in the Caribbean or Louisiana—owned a coffee plantation and a commercial business with slaves on Saint-Domingue [SAN-dow-MANG] (later Haiti). Caught up in the excitement of 1789, Ogé embraced the French revolutionary principles of liberty, equality, and fraternity with great enthusiasm and quickly became an adherent of French constitutional nationalism: As we saw in Chapter 22, the former absolute monarchy in France was swiftly

Seeing Patterns

▶ Which factors in the complex ethnic and social structures of Latin America were responsible for the emergence of authoritarian politicians or caudillos?

▶ Why did Latin American countries, after achieving independence, opt for a continuation of mineral and agricultural commodity exports?

▶ How do the social and economic structures of this period continue to affect the course of Latin America today?

reorganized to incorporate a written constitution and an elected National Assembly. As part of the general atmosphere of emancipation so prevalent during the early part of the revolution, he joined the antislavery Society of the Friends of Blacks in Paris and demanded that French constitutionalism be extended to Saint-Domingue.

In a short time the society's efforts appeared to bear fruit. In March 1790, the National Assembly granted self-administration to the colonies, and Ogé returned to Saint-Domingue full of hope that he would be able to participate as a free citizen in the island's governance. But the governor stubbornly refused to admit mulattoes as citizens of the new order. Ogé and a group of friends therefore joined a band of 250–300 freedmen and took up arms to carve out a stronghold for themselves in the north of the island by arresting plantation owners and occupying their properties. One plantation owner later testified that the rebels looted and killed during their uprising but that Ogé himself was a man of honor who treated his prisoners fairly and even left him in the possession of his personal arms.

After only a few weeks of fighting, however, government troops pushed the rebels into the Spanish part of the island. Ogé and his followers

To Preserve Their Freedom. The great African American painter Jacob Lawrence (1917–2000) depicted the Haitian Revolution in a series of 41 paintings between 1937–1938. The painting here shows the defeat of Napoleon's efforts to restore slavery by force in 1802.

surrendered after being guaranteed their safety. But the Spanish governor, washing his hands of his prisoners, turned them over to the French. After a trial for insurrection in February 1791, Ogé and 19 followers were condemned to death. Ogé suffered particularly barbaric tortures before expiring: He was condemned to perhaps the old French regime's most painful mode of public execution: being broken on the wheel. Executioners strapped him spread-eagle on a wagon wheel and systematically broke his bones with an iron bar until he was dead.

The Ogé insurrection was the opening chapter of the Haitian Revolution, which began in August 1791 and culminated with the achievement of independence under a black government in 1804. It was the third of the great constitutional-nationalist revolutions—after the American and French Revolutions—that inaugurated, with the Industrial Revolution, the modern period of world history. While the other two revolutions were events in which aristocratic rule ended and the middle classes assumed power, the Haitian Revolution was a much more radical movement in which the underclass of slaves liberated itself from both aristocratic and middle-class control. Indeed, the presence of a free, black republic in the New World both haunted slave owners in the Americas and lent itself to strengthening abolitionist sentiment. Thus, it presaged the eventual arrival of full emancipation of blacks in the United States and other states in the region.

After Haiti, Latin America followed with its own wars of independence, which took place during and immediately after the Napoleonic era and also produced constitutional revolutions. In some Spanish colonies Creoles and mulattoes collaborated, but in most colonies the Creoles—like the white colonists in the North American colonies—were by far the chief beneficiaries of the fruits of independence. Given their European cultural and intellectual connections, many Creoles found it relatively easy to adapt to the new challenges of modernity. After independence, wealthy Creoles often traveled to Europe, sent their children to France or England for education, and imported industrial consumer goods from Great Britain. Moreover, most of the Latin American regimes—with the prominent exception of Brazil—abolished slavery before mid-century. As in the United States, however, the lower classes of *mestizos* (mixed Native Americans and Europeans) and mulattoes and the underclasses of Native Americans and blacks were for the most part excluded from the benefits of modernization. For much of the nineteenth century, too, authoritarian **caudillo** regimes allied with landowners and army generals governed under the pretense of constitutional nationalism.

In the economy, the Creole landowners themselves had little interest in industrialization, which would have meant a shifting of scarce labor from

Caudillo: Latin American strongman or dictator.

the estates to factories in cities. They found it much more profitable instead to adopt the role of suppliers to the industrial states through mineral and agricultural exports until the very end of the nineteenth century. Latin America thus took a path of development that diverged substantially from that of Europe and most of North America after the initial constitutional-nationalist revolutions.

Independence, Authoritarianism, and Political Instability

As in the United States and France, the growth pattern of constitutional nationalism in Latin America was slow, full of reverses, and uneven. Historians now give greater weight to the participation of urban craftspeople, of both Iberian and African descent, in the independence movements; but it is generally agreed that the leadership was for the most part in the hands of the Creole landowning class. The revolutionary potential of urban mass participation, so visible in the United States and France, was relatively weak in Latin America. No changes in social structures occurred except in Haiti, from which the white Creole settlers had largely fled after the revolution. The outcome of the independence movements in Latin America was not a single federal or central, constitutionally defined *nation* but a multiplicity of states defined by more or less the same constitutional nationalism of the Creoles, unwilling to share power very broadly.

Independence and Political Development in the North: Haiti and Mexico

The French Revolution in 1789 had two very different consequences for Latin America. In Saint-Domingue, or Haiti, the revolution triggered a direct and immediate adaptation process among the large majority of slaves, who quickly embraced the radical concept of *égalité* for acquiring their freedom. They eliminated their competitors, the white Creoles, and pushed the adaptation process to its ultimate conclusion, independence and constitutionalism for what was now fundamentally a nation of blacks. By contrast, in Mexico, the adaptation to the French Revolution was indirect, limited largely to the Creoles, and never broadened to include much of the non-Creole population prior to the twentieth century. It was indirect insofar as it came only by way of Napoleon's invasion of Iberia and its consequences. And it

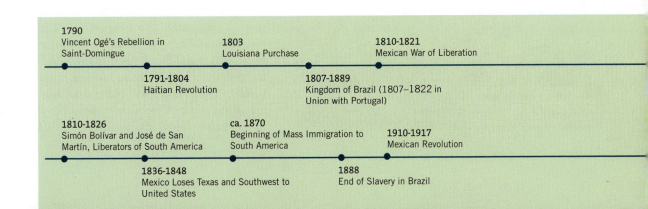

1790
Vincent Ogé's Rebellion in Saint-Domingue

1803
Louisiana Purchase

1810-1821
Mexican War of Liberation

1791-1804
Haitian Revolution

1807-1889
Kingdom of Brazil (1807–1822 in Union with Portugal)

1810-1826
Simón Bolívar and José de San Martín, Liberators of South America

ca. 1870
Beginning of Mass Immigration to South America

1910-1917
Mexican Revolution

1836-1848
Mexico Loses Texas and Southwest to United States

1888
End of Slavery in Brazil

Death Is Preferable to Slavery

"All men are born free and equal; any man born into arbitrary servitude has the right to kill his oppressor. The slave's insurrection against his master is a natural right; death is preferable to slavery."

—A black protagonist in a play written by an anonymous white author during the Haitian Revolution. In Jeremy D. Popkin, trans., *Facing Racial Revolution: Eyewitness Accounts of the Haitian Insurrection*, p. 248. Chicago: University of Chicago Press, 2007.

remained a stunted revolution, in part because the urban, small-propertied, entrepreneurial, and professional classes that provided so much of the momentum of the American and French Revolutions were much smaller than in the United States and France. Thus, the impulse toward radicalism and social leveling characteristic of France in early 1790 never really took deep roots during the independence movement in Mexico.

Sugar and Coffee in Haiti   The Caribbean island of Hispaniola, today Haiti and Santo Domingo, was one of the earliest and richest European colonies, based on plantations that produced vast amounts of sugar, coffee, and cotton for export to the Old World from the 1700s onward. At the time of the French Revolution, the French part of the island produced half of the world's sugar and coffee. Originally, the entire island had been a Spanish colony. But as Spain's power slipped during the seventeenth and eighteenth centuries, France took advantage of the situation and assumed control of the western end of the island in 1697. In the following century, settlers enjoyed French mercantilist protectionism for splendid profits from their slave plantations. By 1789, some 30,000 white settlers, 28,000 mulattoes (holding about one-third of the slaves), and about 500,000 black plantation and household slaves formed an extremely unequal colonial society in which fear and violence reigned supreme.

Revolt of the Slaves   After the failure of Ogé's uprising, discussed in the vignette that opens this chapter, resentment continued to simmer among the mulattoes and blacks in the north of Saint-Domingue. Resentment turned into fury, however, when the French revolutionary Constitutive Assembly in May 1791 began to debate the issue of citizen rights for propertied mulattoes (for which Ogé had been fighting), while the settlers in Saint-Domingue continued to refuse any debate. Plantation slaves chafing under a dehumanizing regime of exploitative owners and managers exploded in August 1791 with a collective rage not previously seen in an American colony. Within weeks, the slave rebellion numbered 100,000 followers and encompassed the entire northern province of the island. The settlers were well-armed but suffered heavy casualties under the onslaught of overwhelming numbers.

With the rebellion taking an increasingly severe toll on the economy, the Legislative Assembly of the new French Republic sent commissioners and troops in 1792 to reestablish order. But when war broke out between France and its neighbors in the following year, the possibility of an invasion of the island by Britain and Spain, and of their forming an alliance with the slave leaders, caused the commissioners to abolish slavery. This act

MAP **27.1** The Haitian Revolution.

The Haitian Revolution

→ Spread of slave revolt, 1791

of abolition, confirmed in France by February 1794, enabled the most powerful slave leader, François-Dominique Toussaint Louverture (ca. 1743–1803), to end foreign interference and make peace with the few thousand remaining French forces and settlers (see Map 27.1).

Nation-State Building To repair the plantation economy—sugar production, for example, had fallen by 75 percent—Louverture dispatched his officers, who forced former slaves to resume production. In 1801, Louverture was sufficiently strong to assume the governorship of Saint-Domingue and proclaim a constitution that incorporated the basic principles of French-inspired constitutional nationalism. Napoleon Bonaparte, in control of France since 1799, however, was determined to rebuild the French overseas empire and now revoked the abolition of slavery. He dispatched a military force to the island, which succeeded in capturing Louverture in 1802. Louverture died shortly thereafter in 1803.

His deputy, the former slave Jean-Jacques Dessalines (r. 1802–1806), was able to defeat Napoleon's troops and in 1804 declared the colony an independent nation. Subsequently, Dessalines made himself emperor and renamed the country "Haiti," its supposed original Native American name. When he changed the constitution in favor of autocratic rule, he provoked a conspiracy against him, which culminated in his assassination in 1806. In the aftermath, the state split into an autocratically ruled north with a state-run plantation economy and a democratic south with a small-farm privatized economy (1806–1821).

A subsequently reunified state annexed neighboring Spanish Santo Domingo for a short time (1822–1842) before losing it again. This loss touched off a period of political instability in the middle of the century before constitutional rule and the agricultural commodity economy were stabilized (1874–1911). Despite all its difficulties, Haiti entered the twentieth century as the first successful black constitutional state—and one with nearly one hundred years of independence behind it. Together with the United States and France, Haiti created the pattern of constitutional nationalism in the nineteenth century, which became part of the modern challenge to the traditional kingdoms and empires of the world.

Defending the Revolution. When Poland ceased to exist after the Third Partition of the Polish Commonwealth (1795) between Russia and Prussia, thousands of Polish soldiers joined Napoleon's forces. Napoleon sent some of the Polish soldiers to Haiti in 1802 to reconquer it; but even though the soldiers fought bravely, as depicted in *Battle on Santo Domingo* by the Polish painter January Sucholdoski (1797–1875), the Haitian Republic defeated Napoleon's troops and gained full independence in 1804.

Napoleon's Conquest of Iberia and Its Impact on the Americas

Napoleon's defeat in Haiti ended France's efforts to rebuild its overseas empire. Instead, the French embarked on the conquest of Europe for the end of absolutism and a new revolutionary empire from Portugal to Russia. The effect of this policy of European conquest, however, was a decisive weakening of Iberian colonialism in the Americas. Ironically, the first step in this weakening was unintended. In the Battle of Trafalgar off the southwestern coast of Spain in 1805 France and Spain lost a substantial part of their combined sea power. Great Britain, the victor, entered the nineteenth century as the unchallenged maritime power in the world.

Then, during the Peninsular War in 1807–1808, Napoleon Bonaparte conquered Portugal and Spain in a bid to put his brother on the Spanish throne. The Portuguese

Land and Liberty. This enormous mural by Diego Rivera (1886–1957), in the National Palace in Mexico City, shows Father Hidalgo above the Mexican eagle, flanked by other independence fighters. Above them are Emiliano Zapata and Pancho Villa, the heroes of the Revolution of 1910, holding a banner, "Tierra y Libertad." The other parts of the mural show historical scenes from the Spanish conquest to the twentieth century.

heir apparent, Prince Joâo (later Joâo VI of Brazil and Portugal, r. 1816–1826), and his family fled to Brazil; and the French ruled by military decree. In Spain, Napoleon forced the king, Fernando VII (r. 1808 and 1813–1829), to abdicate and placed his own brother, Joseph Bonaparte (r. 1808–1813), on the throne. Joseph ruled tenuously, dependent on generals under his brother's command as the Spanish mounted a determined guerilla campaign against their occupiers, and eventually abdicated with alacrity. An interesting legacy of this struggle is that the Spanish term *guerilla* for this kind of irregular warfare stuck and is the name we still use today for popular insurgencies against larger conventional forces.

As a consequence of Napoleon's conquest of Iberia, the Creoles of the Spanish colonies rejected Joseph Bonaparte's rule and declared their loyalty to the deposed king Fernando. But since Napoleon held the king captive in France, this declaration meant for all practical purposes independence for the American colonies. Once the Spanish had chased the French army out of Iberia and King Fernando returned to his throne in 1813, however, the American colonies had to fight in order to remain independent.

Mexican Independence

In New Spain (modern Mexico), Miguel Hidalgo y Costilla (1753–1811), son of a Creole hacienda estate administrator, launched his movement for independence from Bonapartist Spain in 1810. A churchman since his youth, Hidalgo was broadly educated, well versed in Enlightenment literature, and on the margins of strict Catholicism. Later in his life he became a parish priest and devoted himself to creating employment opportunities for native Americans or Amerindians in a province southeast of Mexico City. He had earlier participated in a conspiracy of Creoles, some of them members of the military, to overthrow a group of Spanish colonial military officers who had staged a successful coup d'état against the civilian colonial administration in 1808. On the point of being discovered, the conspiracy launched a popular rebellion in 1810, declaring itself in favor of Fernando VII, whom they considered to be Spain's legitimate ruler, as opposed to Joseph Bonaparte.

Under the leadership of Hidalgo, tens of thousands of poor Creoles, mestizos, and Amerindians who had suffered in a drought marched on Guanajuato, looting and killing *peninsulares* (Spaniards from Europe) and Creoles without distinction. They were initially successful in defeating the Spanish troops marching against them. When Hidalgo, shocked by the violence, avoided an attack on Mexico City, however, the rebellion began to sputter and was eventually defeated in 1811. Spanish forces ultimately captured and executed Hidalgo.

Under militarily experienced mestizo and Creole leaders, the war of independence continued in several southwestern provinces of Mexico but failed to make a comeback in the heartland around Mexico City. Here, monarchists intent on retaining the union between Spain and Mexico appeared to retain the upper hand. But during a constitutionalist uprising in Spain (1820–1823) King Fernando VII came close to defeat. The Mexican Creole monarchists, not wishing to submit to a Spanish republic, made the colony a regency ready to receive Fernando in order for him to continue Spanish colonial rule. Fernando, however, overcame the uprising in Spain. When he then declined to take up his American regency, the Creoles made Mexico an independent empire of its own in 1821, thereby provoking declarations of independence from Mexico in the southern provinces of El Salvador, Nicaragua, Costa Rica, and Honduras. Mestizo and Creole independence fighters in Mexico redoubled their efforts for an independent republic as well. In 1824, they succeeded with the declaration of the Republic of Mexico and a constitution broadly following the US and French models (see Map 27.2).

Early Independence   Initially, Mexico had a number of advantages as an independent nation. It had abundant natural resources, and its northern territories—Texas, Colorado, and California—contained much valuable pasture and agricultural

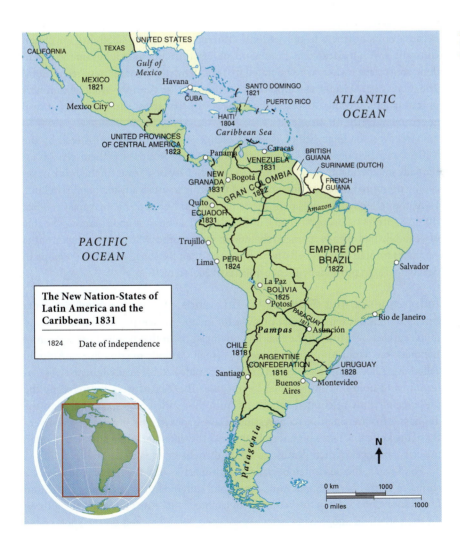

MAP **27.2 The New Nation-States of Latin America and the Caribbean, 1831.**

land. The great dying of the indigenous population of Amerindians from European mass diseases in the sixteenth and early seventeenth centuries, however, had radically depopulated much of the land. Thus, while Mexico's territory was vast, it was doomed to stay largely undeveloped unless a policy of open immigration was encouraged.

From the early 1820s, Mexico therefore encouraged immigration, gave generous terms for the purchase of land to settlers, and allowed them to be largely self-governing as long as taxes were duly paid. At the same time, Mexico's rapidly expanding northern neighbor, the United States, went through a protracted period of growth. Settlement of the rich agricultural areas of the formerly French Ohio and Mississippi valleys moved with astonishing speed. The new demand for American cotton in British and American factories drove a frenetic expansion into Alabama, Mississippi, Louisiana, and Arkansas. Cotton exhausted the soil quickly, and the availability of cheap land made it more efficient to abandon the depleted lands and keep pushing the realm of "King Cotton" ever westward.

As North American settlement drew closer to Mexico's territories, many North Americans emigrated to Mexico to take advantage of its land policies and autonomy. The Mexican province of Texas was particularly attractive, especially to southerners, because of its nearness to the settled southern states and its suitability for cotton cultivation. While Mexico had outlawed slavery from the time it became independent, most slave owners who migrated to Texas tended to ignore these restrictions. The increasingly blatant violation of the antislavery laws and the swelling numbers of immigrants seeking opportunity in Texas came to alarm the Mexican national government by the 1830s.

Moreover, the huge size of Texas, the habit of local autonomy fostered by the settlers, and their ties to the United States made many Texans view themselves as essentially independent. The perception in Mexico City of a Texas on the brink of seceding prompted the government to send the army to crush any incipient rebellion. Here, the actions of the president, General Antonio López de Santa Anna (in office from 1833, off and on, until 1855), in dissolving the congress and assuming the role of a caudillo had already sparked rebellion in several other Mexican provinces. Santa Anna confronted these rebellions in turn, and then personally led 4,000 troops to deal with Texan pro-independence militias in March of 1836.

Independence and Growing US Influence

For the Texan militias Santa Anna's actions became the cause of a war for independence, particularly as the caudillo's ruthlessness toward the militias convinced them that negotiation was out of the question. Santa Anna's men besieged a small Catholic mission in San Antonio called the "Alamo" in which several hundred Texans had barricaded themselves, determined to hold out until a relief force came. The Texans were bolstered by the presence of some celebrated volunteers from the United States, among them the Tennessee frontiersman and congressman Davy Crockett, and Jim Bowie, the inventor of the knife that bears his name. In the end, the defenders were all killed, though the circumstances of their deaths are still hotly debated today.

For Texans, the dead men became instant martyrs and the Alamo became "the shrine of Texas liberty." Santa Anna's army had suffered heavy casualties, and Texan forces soon defeated it in the battle of San Jacinto. Santa Anna himself was captured on the battlefield and, having narrowly escaped being lynched on the spot, ceded

Texas to the insurgents. Mexico's largest province now became an independent state. Santa Anna, after being taken to the United States and meeting with President Andrew Jackson (in office 1829–1837), was repatriated to Mexico and served as president six more times in his long career as that nation's most famous caudillo.

Mexico's Dismemberment   After some 30 years of not doing much with its right to govern Louisiana—the huge land on both sides of the Mississippi in the center of today's United States—Spain had returned its territorial rights there to France. Napoleon, for his part, sold the rights to the United States in 1803, in the hope of strengthening the latter against Great Britain, his main opponent in his European imperial conquests. By the early 1840s, American settlement of the territory of this so-called Louisiana Purchase on both sides of the Mississippi was proceeding rapidly. Settlers bought some land from the indigenous Amerindians, whose opinions had not been consulted during the purchase, and gained even more land from wars against them. Moving farther west, American settlers made claims on the Oregon Territory along the northern Pacific Coast. These claims now meant that the young US republic's ambitions were swiftly making it a continental power.

During the administration of President James K. Polk (1845–1849), the idea of "Manifest Destiny"—that it was the evident fate of the United States to be the dominant power of the North American continent, with territory stretching from the Atlantic to the Pacific—was becoming an article of faith. Both the British in Canada and the Mexican government were increasingly alarmed by this new aggressive US posture. Moreover, Texas, insecure as an independent republic between the United States and Mexico and dominated by Americans, now applied for annexation to the United States.

For Santa Anna, president once again of Mexico, such a move meant a war for survival; for Polk and many Americans, it meant a potential opportunity to expand the republic's borders directly to the Pacific. When Texas was admitted to the union, therefore, the United States and Mexico went to war. Despite vigorous protests against this war as one of conquest—including a spirited condemnation by a young Illinois congressman named Abraham Lincoln—the war was prosecuted by the United States with vigor. A small but well-trained expeditionary force, launching a seaborne invasion of central Mexico, fought its way to Mexico City. Other American troops fought in what were to become New Mexico and California. By 1848 Mexico sued for peace and gave up most of what is now the southwestern and western United States: Texas, New Mexico, Arizona, Colorado, Nevada, and California (see Map 27.3).

To make the territorial losses even harder to swallow for Mexico, the richest gold strike in the continent's history began almost immediately in California. The boomtown of San Francisco

MAP **27.3** Mexico's Loss of Territory to the United States, 1824–1854.

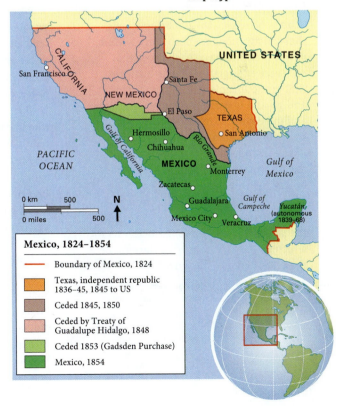

attracted tens of thousands of newcomers—"Forty-Niners"—seeking riches, and California entered the union as a state in 1850. Santa Anna stayed on in Mexico as caudillo until 1855. Then, even his supporters could no longer take his lavish crony-ism and payoffs to the military and deposed him. In a strange historical footnote, Santa Anna spent his last years of exile in the United States, where his efforts at im-porting *chicle*, the base for modern chewing gum, ultimately led to one of his associ-ates starting the Chiclets Chewing Gum company. In 1876, under a general amnesty, Santa Anna went back to Mexico and soon after passed away.

The French Interlude in Mexico

The Latin American independence move-ments had inspired the declaration of the US Monroe Doctrine in 1823. According to this policy, the US government would not tolerate European attempts to recolo-nize the new republics of the Western Hemisphere. For four decades the doctrine had been remarkably successful at deterring the European powers, largely because it suited British policy as well. Mexico easily beat back two attempts by small ex-peditionary forces at invasion, one from Spain in 1829 and another from France in 1838. With the American Civil War raging in the mid-1860s, however, the tempta-tion to create an empire in Mexico proved too much for Louis-Napoleon Bonaparte (in office 1848–1852 as president; r. 1852–1870 as emperor) of France to resist. As a nephew of Napoleon, he yearned to return France to imperial glory.

After staging a coup d'état in 1852 and becoming Emperor Napoleon III, he pursued imperial campaigns in North Africa, West Africa (Senegal), and In-dochina (Vietnam), apart from flexing France's military muscle in Russia, Italy, China, and Korea. His opportunity to intervene in Mexican affairs came after the downfall of Santa Anna in 1855 and the subsequent uprising of con-servatives against the liberal constitution of 1857, with its separation of church and state. The liberals under the lead-ership of Benito Juárez, the first Amerindian to become president (1861–1864, 1867–1872), thus defeated the conservatives.

But the state that Juárez inherited was bankrupt, and when he found himself forced to suspend payments on the state debt, the international repercussions were disastrous for Mexico. Napoleon III seized on the payment issue and, with an eye on the Mexican silver mines, set into motion an ambitious plan of imposing a pliable ruler from the outside. In 1862, he provided military backing to the Austrian prince Maximilian, well liked by Mexican conservatives, to install himself as the emperor of Mexico (1864–1867).

With the defeat of the Confederate states in April 1865, however, and the Union army ballooning to over a million men, many of whom had just been sent to Texas to suppress the last Confederate holdouts, Maximilian's position was suddenly in grave danger. In the following year, after some discreet aid from the US government under the aegis of the Monroe Doctrine, an uprising broke out in Mexico. Cut off from any hope of effective support from France, Mexican

---

Birth and Death of Constitutions

"With good reason the public now feels that constitutions are born and die, that governments succeed each other, that codes are enlarged and made intricate, that pronouncements and plans come and go, and that after so many mutations and upheavals, so much inquietude and so many sacrifices, nothing positive has been done for the people, nothing advantageous for these unhappy classes, from which always emerge those who shed their blood in civil wars, those who give their quota for armies, who populate the jails and labor in public works, and for which were made, finally, all the evils of society, and none of its goods."

— Special vote (report) of Ponciano Arriaga in the Mexican Assembly, June 23, 1856. In Kenneth L. Karst and Keith S. Rosenn. *Law and Development in Latin America: A Case Book*. UCLA Latin American Studies Series, vol. 28, p. 275. Berkeley: University of California Press, 1975.

liberal forces defeated Maximilian, captured him, and executed him by firing squad in 1867.

Porfirio Díaz's Long Peace

With the withdrawal of most US government troops from Texas at the end of Reconstruction—ending the potential threat of invasion or border incursions—and the rise of Mexico's next conservative caudillo, Porfirio Díaz (in office 1876–1880 and 1884–1911), a period of relative peace came at last. Díaz's lengthy hold on power allowed a degree of conservative stability to settle in on Mexico's turbulent politics. Moreover, the period also coincided with the defeat of

The Execution of Emperor Maximilian of Mexico, June 19, 1867. Édouard Manet has been characterized as the "inventor of modernity" not only for his technique, but for the way he portrayed events, even significant political events, in a calm and composed manner. The soldiers who dispatch the hapless Emperor come across as cool and professional—what they are doing is all in a day's work.

the last Amerindians north of the border and the settlement and development of the American West. In addition, Díaz, like his contemporary, President José Balmaceda (1886–1891) of Chile, favored some initial industrial and infrastructural development in Mexico. The basic lines of Mexico's major rail, telegraph, and telephone systems were laid during this time; textile factories and some basic heavy industry were set up; and modest agricultural improvements were made.

Most of this investment, however, came from British and American firms in return for Mexican mineral, precious metal, and fruit and vegetable exports. Toward the end of Díaz's dictatorship, the first petroleum drilling enterprises were set up, an industry that, although nationalized today, still has proved disappointing at consistently generating revenue. In assessing Mexico's relative lack of economic development since the late 1800s, poverty, and ongoing tensions with the industrial colossus to the north, it is no wonder that he once exclaimed so poignantly, "Alas, poor Mexico! So far from God, so close to the United States!"

The Mexican Revolution

Díaz's long presidency and Mexico's halting development tended to foster discontent, particularly among the poor urban workers and *peons*—agricultural laborers on large estates, who were held in conditions of virtual serfdom. In 1910, half of the Mexican population worked on estates and 20 percent of the farmland was foreign-owned. The reform-minded Francisco Madero, from a wealthy northern family, drove Díaz from power and through elections legitimized his own presidency (1911–1913); but he was unable to gain control over the country. Two additional movements now vied for power in different parts of Mexico: Emiliano Zapata (1879–1919) advocated for plantation land reform in the south and Pancho Villa (José Doroteo Arango Arámbula, 1878–1923) for hacienda land reform in the north. In addition, a seesaw struggle for the presidency erupted between reformers from wealthy backgrounds and conservative pro-Díaz officers, each seeking to gain a grip on the movements by Zapata and Villa as well as other provincial rebels.

During a short-lived interval in the middle of this struggle, a group of reformers were able to convene a constitutional congress, which passed a new, revolutionary

Mexican Oil Boom. After drilling at El Baño in 1904, the pressure of the gas and petroleum in the ground resulted in a blowout (a). The blowout was easily plugged. This was not the case at the Dos Bocas well in 1911, which resulted in an environmental disaster, producing a lake 1,000 feet in diameter, dead vegetation, and hot gases and water seeping to the surface (b). Apart from producing environmental problems, oil in Mexico during the Díaz regime benefited only the US investors and the Mexican oligarchy.

constitution with paragraphs establishing land reform, limits to foreign ownership of resources, a labor code, and a secular, compulsory educational system (1917). It took altogether at least 2 million and possibly in the vicinity of 3.5 million victims in the struggle for and against the revolution, as well as one more military coup, before a moderate general, Álvaro Obregón (in office 1920–1924), was able to stabilize the presidency and begin the implementation of the constitution. In contrast to the 1824 and 1857 constitutions, the new one of 1917 stood out for its socialist programs, creating greater equality in the distribution of farmland and ending the grip of the Catholic Church on land as well as education.

Independence and Development in Northern South America

The viceroyalty of New Granada in northern South America, with today's countries of Venezuela, Colombia, Ecuador, and Panama, had far fewer Creoles than that of New Spain, from which independent Mexico issued. For its struggle for independence to succeed, leaders had to seek support from the *pardos*, as the majority population of free black and mulatto craftspeople in the cities was called. Independence eventually came through the building of strong armies from these diverse elements, mostly by Simón Bolívar, the liberator of northern South America from renewed Spanish colonialism. After independence, however, the Creoles quickly moved to dissolve their coalitions with the lower classes and embraced the same conservative caudillo politics that Mexico practiced for most of the nineteenth century.

Comuneros and Pardos   In contrast to New Spain, with its relatively large Creole and mestizo populations in the cities and countryside, New Granada's Creole population was small in relation to mestizos and pardos. The latter constituted over half of the urban and two-thirds of the rural people. Unrest began early, expressing itself in loyalty to the Spanish king but also in fury against the high taxes collected by the peninsular administrators: The *comunero* revolt of 1781–1782—together with the Túpac Amaru revolt of 1780–1781 in Peru—was a harbinger of things to come during the independence struggle a generation later. The comuneros were urban and

Revolutionary Women.
Women, such as these
soldaderas taking rifle practice,
played many significant roles
in the Mexican Revolution,
1910–1920.

rural Creoles and mestizos whom the hard-pressed authorities placated with promises, only to renege once their assemblies dissipated.

In 1810, the battle cry was again loyalty to the Spanish king, the deposed Fernando VII, and outrage against the peninsulars, although this time it was more massive, bringing together Creoles and pardos. In 1810 they created *juntas*, or committees, among which the junta of Cartagena in what was to become Colombia was the most important, and drove the peninsulars from their administrative positions. Initially, they agreed on the equality of all ethnicities and worked on constitutions that provided for elections by all free men. But they were also suspicious of each other, denouncing their allegedly aristocratic versus democratic aspirations.

In 1811, cooperation broke down and the pardos assumed power in a coup. The Creoles struck back a year later when they declared the First Republic of Cartagena. Their power was limited by the pardo-dominated militias however, and in a compromise they agreed on the continuation of full voting rights. In the long run, during the 1800s, this revolutionary achievement did not last and the Creoles established oligarchic rule. But Cartagena, together with Mexico under Hidalgo, proved that Latin American independence was not exclusively the work of a conservative Creole class consolidating its privileges.

Bolívar the Liberator   The junta of Cartagena, together with other juntas, formed the federation of the United Provinces of New Granada in 1811, with a weak executive unable to prevent squabbling among the juntas. Fernando VII, after returning to Spain in 1813, was determined to reestablish colonial control by dispatching armies to Latin America. The largest forces, comprising some 10,000 troops, landed in the United Provinces in 1814, taking Cartagena after a siege, and resurrected the viceroyalty of New Granada.

The eventual liberator of northern South America from renewed Spanish rule in 1819 was Simón Bolívar (1783–1830). Bolívar was born in Venezuela, into a wealthy Creole background; his family owned cacao plantations worked by slaves and was engaged in colonial trade. Venezuela, like Colombia, was a part of New Granada. Although lacking a formal education, thanks to his tutor Bolívar was familiar with Enlightenment literature. In 1799, he visited Spain, where he met his future wife; and he later returned to Europe after her death. In 1804, he was deeply impressed when he watched Napoleon's lavish spectacle of crowning himself emperor in Paris. These European visits instilled in Bolívar a lasting admiration for European ideals of liberty and popular sovereignty, and he longed to create a constitutional republic in his homeland.

In 1810, as in Cartagena, Venezuelan cities formed Creole-led juntas with pardo participation. A young Bolívar participated in the congress of juntas that declared outright independence for Venezuela in 1812, against the resistance of royalists who remained faithful to Fernando VII. A civil war ensued, which made Bolívar's tenure in Venezuela insecure and, after the arrival of the Spanish expeditionary force of 1815, impossible. He went into exile first to British Jamaica and then to revolutionary Haiti. In 1816 Bolívar returned from exile to Venezuela with a military force, partly supplied by Haiti. After some initial difficulties, he succeeded in defeating the Spanish troops. In 1822, he assumed the presidency of "Gran Colombia," an independent republic comprising the later states of Colombia, Venezuela, Ecuador, and Panama.

The Bolívar–San Martín Encounter   After their defeat in Gran Colombia, Spanish troops continued to occupy Peru in the Andes, where an independence movement supported by Argentina was active but made little progress against Spanish and royalist Creole troops. In the face of this situation, the Argentinian general and liberator José de San Martín (ca. 1778–1850) and Bolívar met in 1822 to deliberate on how to get rid of the Spanish and to shape the future of an independent Latin America. As for fighting Spain, they agreed that Bolívar was in a better geographical position than San Martín to send military forces to Peru. But even for Bolívar that task was daunting. His troops were unaccustomed to high-altitude fighting and were hindered as much by mountain sickness as by enemy resistance. One of Bolívar's lieutenants finally got the better of the fiercely resisting Spanish in 1824. Two years later, Spanish colonialism in Latin America finally ended when the last troops surrendered on the Peruvian coast.

The content of the discussion for the future of Latin America between San Martín and Bolívar never became public and has remained a bone of contention among historians. San Martín, bitterly disappointed by endless disputes among liberal constitutionalists and royalists, federalists and centralists, as well as Creole elitists and mestizo and mulatto populists, favored monarchical rule to bring stability to Latin America. Bolívar preferred republicanism and Creole oligarchical rule, although he always sought limited pardo and mestizo collaboration, especially in his armies. Clearly, there was not much common ground between the two independence leaders.

San Martín's sudden withdrawal from the Andes after the meeting and his subsequent resignation from politics, however, can be taken as an indication of his realization that the chances for a South American monarchy were small indeed. Bolívar, also acutely aware of the multiple cleavages in Latin American politics, more realistically envisioned the future of Latin America as that of relatively small independent republics, held together by strong, lifelong presidencies and hereditary senates. He actually implemented this vision in the 1825 constitution of independent upper Peru, renamed after him "Bolivia." Ironically, in his own country Bolívar was denied the role of strong president. Although he made himself a caudillo, he was unable to coax his recalcitrant politicians into an agreement on a constitution for Gran Colombia similar to that of Bolivia. Eventually, in 1830 Bolívar resigned, dying shortly after of tuberculosis. In 1831 Gran Colombia fell apart into its component parts of Colombia, Venezuela, Ecuador, and (later) Panama.

Revolving-Door Caudillos Independent Venezuela, as perhaps the poorest and most underpopulated of northern South America's newly independent countries, acquired the dubious distinction of being among its most politically turbulent. In Carácas, the capital, caudillos displaced each other at an astonishing rate. By one estimate, there were 41 presidencies and 30 insurrections in the period 1830–1899. Although many of these presidents sought foreign financial support for development, little was accomplished and much of the money went into the private coffers of the leaders. The main issue that kept rival factions at odds was federalism versus tighter central control, with at least one all-out war being fought over the issue during the 1860s. Following this so-called War of the Caudillos, the official name of the country was changed from the "Republic of Venezuela" to the "United States of Venezuela," a name which it retained into the middle of the twentieth century.

Venezuela's neighboring countries traversed a similar pattern of caudillo politics. Though enjoying longer periods of stability, Colombia—the name adopted in 1861 to replace that of New Granada—also saw a continuing struggle between federalists and centralizers, liberals and conservatives, with each party seeking the support of the Catholic Church. From 1899 until 1902, the "War of a Thousand Days" was conducted, leaving the country sufficiently weak for Panamanian rebels to establish an independent state of Panama, supported by the United States. After independence, the administration of Theodore Roosevelt (1901–1909) swiftly concluded a treaty with the new country to control a 10-mile-wide strip bisecting the narrow isthmus and began the construction of the Panama Canal, completed in 1914.

Machines in the Garden. The first railroads in Latin America were constructed in Mexico in 1836. Initially, construction was supported by state funds, with private and foreign participation. A railway bridge spans the Rio Grande River in Costa Rica, 1902 (*a*). In the 1870s and 1880s, once profitable railroads were privatized and expanded. The United States built the 51-mile Panama Canal in 1904–1914 with Treasury bonds, after encouraging Panama to secede from Colombia and appropriating the land for construction (*b*).

Independence and Development in Southern and Western South America

Independence movements also began in 1810 farther south in South America. Under the guise of remaining loyal to the deposed Fernando VII of Spain, Creoles in Buenos Aires seized the initiative to establish a junta rejecting the viceregal peninsular authorities. By contrast, Creoles along the Andes similarly avoided declarations of loyalty to Napoleon but supported the existing colonial administration, even after 1814 when fresh Spanish troops arrived. The figure who eventually broke the logjam between the two sides of pro- and antipeninsular Creole parties in 1816–1822 was José de San Martín.

Independence in Argentina

Independence in Argentina   The viceroyalty of La Plata, comprising the modern countries of Argentina, Uruguay, Paraguay, and Bolivia, was the youngest of Spain's colonial units. In the course of the Bourbon reforms, Spain decided in 1776 to separate it from the viceroyalty of Peru, where declining silver exports diminished the importance of the port of Lima. La Plata, with the rising port of Buenos Aires, had grown through contraband trade with Great Britain; and the Bourbon reformers wanted to redirect its trade more firmly back to Spain. Buenos Aires was so important to the British even after the reform of 1776, however, that a naval commander and British merchants exploited the destruction of the Spanish navy by Britain in the battle off Trafalgar in southwestern Spain (1805) to occupy Buenos Aires in 1806–1807, until they were driven out by Spanish colonial forces.

Creoles in La Plata had far fewer Amerindians, African slaves, mestizos, and mulattoes to deal with—or fear—than in any of the other viceroyalties. But in 1810, when the first independence movements formed, there was a clear distinction between the proindependence Creoles of Buenos Aires, or *porteños*, and the Creoles of the *pampas*, or grasslands of the temperate interior of Argentina and Uruguay, and the subtropical plains and hills of Paraguay favoring continued colonialism. The latter either were royalists or strove for separate independence. Uruguay, furthermore, was initially claimed by Brazil and eventually achieved its own independence only in 1828. Upper Peru, or modern Bolivia, with its high-elevation plains, lowland Amazon basin rain forest, large Amerindian population, and Potosí silver mines, was heavily defended by colonial and peninsular Spanish troops. Given these various urban–rural and geographical circumstances, the porteño independence movement fought to no more than a standstill during the initial period 1810–1816.

As in the northern tier, the breakthrough eventually came via an experienced military figure, the highly popular José de San Martín. San Martín was a Creole from northeastern Argentina. His father, an immigrant from Spain, was a military officer and administrator of a Jesuit-founded Amerindian mission district. The son, educated from an early age in a Spanish military academy, began service in the porteño independence movement in 1812, where he distinguished himself in the Argentinian independence struggle.

During his service, San Martín realized that the final success for independence in the south also required the liberation of the Andes provinces. Accordingly, he trained the Army of the Andes, which included mulatto and black volunteers, with which he crossed the mountains to Chile in 1818, liberating the country from royalist forces. With the help of a newly established navy composed of ships acquired from the United States and Britain, he conquered Lima in Peru but was defied by the local Creoles when he sought to introduce social reforms, such as an end to the Amerindian tribute system, the *mit'a*, and the emancipation of the children of black slaves. When he was also unable to dislodge Spanish troops near the city, he traveled north for his meeting with Bolívar. As discussed, it was Bolívar who completed the liberation of the Andes lands and, thereby, also helped Argentina to defeat the peninsulars and royalist Creoles in the south.

Independent Peru   Peru's independence came following the defeat of Spanish forces in 1824–1826. As with the other new states in South America, it took decades for Peru, Chile, and Bolivia to work out territorial disputes. The most serious of these by far was the War of the Pacific from 1879 to 1884, resulting in a victorious Chile annexing Peruvian and Bolivian lands. Most devastating for Peru was the destruction that Chilean troops wrought in southern Peru. The economy, which had made modest progress by using nitrate exports in the form of guano to fund railroad building and mining, was only painfully rebuilt after the destruction of war. Political stability for several decades returned under the presidency of Nicolás de Piérola, who introduced a number of belated reforms during his terms (1879–1881 and 1895–1899). As the presidency from this time until the 1920s was held by men from the upper landowning Creole class, it is sometimes called the period of the "Aristocratic Republic."

Caudillos and Oligarchic Rule   During the later 1820s the independence junta in Buenos Aires solidified into an oligarchy of the city's wealthy Creole elite, but the vast, largely undeveloped areas of the pampas with their small floating population of Amerindian peoples and Creole *gauchos*, or cowboys, remained largely outside the new state. A war with Brazil drained the country of much of its manpower and resources. The political circles in Buenos Aires began to solidify around those favoring a strong central government to conduct a strong foreign policy and exercise control over the provinces, which advocated a looser federal system. By the 1830s these unsettled conditions gave rise to the first of many Argentine caudillos, Juán Manuel de Rosas (in office 1829–1852).

De Rosas was descended from a wealthy ranching family and tended to identify with the gauchos. But he saw himself as a champion of national unity rather than one who sought to limit the role of the government in regional affairs. After becoming governor of Buenos Aires in 1829, he systematically extended his personal influence (*personalismo*) over his fellow governors until he was named caudillo in 1835, imposing a severe and fundamentally conservative brand of autocratic rule on the country.

Ultimately, his centralism and appetite for expansion helped in his downfall. Fierce in his opposition to British annexation of the Malvinas Islands—or Falklands, as the British called them—though frustrated by not being able to reverse it, he unwisely intervened in a civil war in Uruguay in 1843. His popularity flagged as the war dragged on for 9 years. Finally, the unsuccessful war, coupled with his unwillingness to lend his support to a constitution favorable to the provinces, led to his ouster in 1852.

The Settling of the Pampas   The victor was a provincial governor named Justo José de Urquisa, who became the new caudillo. Urquisa swiftly extricated Argentina from Uruguay, defeated an army of de Rosas loyalists, and successfully sponsored a constitutional convention in 1853, lessening political centralism. In 1854 he

---

"In My Country I Am Like a Princess"

"Marriages were made among a small number of families, endogamously. Their children's education began in exclusive schools. Playmates continued as schoolmates and as classmates in the universities. . . . Families were generally large with an abundance of servants, who were sometimes treated as if they belonged to the same family circle. There were drawing rooms where only those with certain surnames could enter and which were closed to those who had only the power of money; there were families before which one knelt with respect, awe, and adulation. The daughter of one of these once said in Europe, 'In my country I am like a princess.'"

—Peter F. Klarén, trans. "The Origins of Modern Peru, 1880–1930." In *The Cambridge History of Latin America*, vol. 5, c. 1870 to 1930. Edited by Leslie Bethell, p. 613. Cambridge: Cambridge University Press, 1986.

Endogamy: Custom of restricting marriage to a local community, clan, or tribe.

was elected president, and it seemed for the moment that Argentina was on the road to a more open, representative government. But the presidency remained the property of a small Creole oligarchy from the provincial elite. Not surprisingly, renewed conflict broke out with Buenos Aires over the issue of a strong centralized regime versus a projected new federal arrangement. In 1861, the forces of Buenos Aires defeated Urquisa's provincial forces and the country was reintegrated, with Buenos Aires as the national capital.

In the following years, many of the same forces that were shaping the North American West were also actively transforming the pampas. The land was opened to settlement, driving the gauchos from their independent existence into becoming hired hands. The railroad was spurring settlement, and the remaining Amerindians were driven south to Patagonia or exterminated. In contrast to the homesteading policies in the United States, however, the pampas were divided up into huge *estancias*, or estates, of tens of thousands of acres, aided by the introduction of barbed wire to fence in the ranges. Thus, the old system of rounding up essentially wild livestock and driving it to market now gave way to the ranching of cattle, sheep, and goats. As in other areas of South America, the new landed Creole elites dominated politics and economics long into the twentieth century.

Toward Party Politics   Despite the cozy arrangement of nineteenth-century Argentine politics, the growing urban center of Buenos Aires and the waves of Spanish and Italian immigrants grew restless under the rotating presidency that characterized the period 1880–1900. Spurred by the development of radical politics in Europe, especially those adopting versions of Marxism and socialism, two major urban opposition parties took shape in the 1890s: the Radical Party and the Socialists. As the influence of these parties grew, electoral reforms were forced on an unwilling landed oligarchy. In 1912, universal male suffrage was passed, and voting would take place by secret ballot. By 1916, the closed oligarchy was at last cracked open by the arrival of a new president, Hipólito Yrigoyen (1916–1922, 1928–1930). He relied for support mostly on an urban constituency, which dominated politics in the early twentieth century.

Brazil: From Kingdom to Republic

During the late colonial period, Brazil underwent the same centralizing administrative, fiscal, and trade reforms as the Spanish possessions. These reforms were resented as much by the Brazilian planter and urban Creoles as by their Spanish counterparts, but their fear of rebellion among the huge population of black slaves held them back from openly demanding independence. As it happened, independence arrived without bloody internecine wars, through the relocation of the monarchy from Portugal to Brazil in the wake of Napoleon's invasion of Iberia in 1807. Brazil had since become an empire and when the second emperor, Dom Pedro II (r. 1831–1889), under pressure from Britain, finally abolished slavery in 1888, the politically abandoned plantation oligarchy avenged itself by deposing him and switching to a republican regime under the military in 1889. Given the enormous size of the country, as well as the split of the Creole oligarchy into mining, sugar, and coffee interests, the regime became solidly federal, making it difficult for caudillos to succeed and allowing eventually for the rise of civilian presidents.

Transfer of the Crown from Portugal to Brazil   Portugal's royal family fled the country in advance of Napoleon's armies in 1807. Escorted by British ships, it took refuge in Brazil and elevated the colony to the status of a coequal kingdom in union with Portugal but governed from Brazil after Napoleon's defeat in 1815. The arrival of some 15,000 Portuguese together with the dynasty, however, created resentment among the Brazilian Creoles, sharpening the traditional tension between Creoles and Portuguese-born reformers. A crisis point was reached in 1820 when rebels in Portugal adopted a liberal constitution, which demanded the return of Brazil to colonial status as well as the transfer of the dynasty back to Portugal. The reigning king returned but left his son, Pedro I (r. 1822–1831), behind in Brazil. On the advice of both his father and courtiers, Pedro uttered in 1822 his famous "*fico*" ("I remain"), and proclaimed "Independence or Death!" thereby making Brazil an independent kingdom.

Pedro I's Authoritarianism   On acceding to the throne, Pedro declared Brazil an empire because of its size and diversity. His rule, however, embodied many of the same characteristics as that of the caudillos in the Spanish-speaking South American countries. In addition, like the restoration monarchs of Europe in the early 1800s, he firmly adhered to his belief in divine right, which was incompatible with more than token constitutionalism. Consequently, he rejected an attempt by the landed Creole oligarchy to introduce limited monarchical rule. Instead, he issued his own constitution in 1823 that concentrated most powers in his hands as well as a council of state, with a weak lifetime senate and a legislative chamber based on severely limited voting rights. Since he also reserved to himself the nomination and dismissal of ministers, the dissolution of the chamber, and, above all, the appointment of provincial governors, his rule was far too authoritarian even for the conservative planter elite.

In reaction, in 1824 six northeastern provinces attempted to secede. They proclaimed the republican Federation of the Equator and, somewhat illogically, demanded more central government support for the traditional northern sugar and cotton plantations, neglected by a rising emphasis on south-central coffee plantations. Increased British patrols in the Atlantic to suppress the slave trade had increased the price for slaves. The sugar planters could ill afford the increased prices, but the expanding coffee market enabled its planters to pay (see "Patterns Up Close").

Given the close ties between Britain and Brazil, Pedro found it difficult to resist mounting British demands for the abolition of slavery. As a result, early signs of alienation between the crown and the Creole planter elite crept in. It also did not help that Pedro supported the open immigration to Brazil of skilled foreigners, as well as foreign loans and investments for development. Like their counterparts in the American South, the plantation elites sought to limit immigration except for servile labor and control the courts to assure severe punishments for infractions by slaves; and they voiced their opposition to internal improvements like railroads, for fear of disrupting the stability of the plantation system. Ultimately, a succession crisis in Portugal in 1830 led to a conservative revolt against Pedro. In 1831, he lost his nerve and abdicated, sailing back to Portugal. He left the throne for his 5-year-old son, Pedro II (r. 1831–1889), who required a regent. Given a temporarily weak monarchy, the plantation oligarchy exploited the situation by renewing its demands for federalism.

Slave Rebellions in Cuba and Brazil

The successful slave revolt in Haiti was the most inspiring event for blacks in the first half of the nineteenth century. Blacks had gained little from the American and French Revolutions, and the pattern of brutal exploitation continued in many parts of the Americas. Not surprisingly, therefore, blacks sought to emulate the example of Haiti during the first half of the 1800s. Through careful and systematic preparation, they sought to tap into the repressed fury of the plantation slaves. However, none of the subsequent Haiti-inspired revolts was any more successful against the well-prepared authorities than previous revolts had been in the 1700s, as a look at rebellions in Cuba and Brazil during the first half of the nineteenth century shows.

In Cuba, the decline of sugar production in Haiti during the revolution encouraged a rapid expansion of plantations and the importation of African slaves. As previously in Haiti, a relatively diversified eighteenth-century society of whites, free mulattoes, and blacks, as well as urban and rural black slaves, was transformed into a heavily African-born plantation slave society, forming a large majority in many rural districts. The black freedman José Antonio Aponte (ca. 1756–1812), militiaman and head of the Yoruba confraternity (*cabilde*) in Havana, led an abortive revolt in 1812 that drew support from both sectors. In the subsequent revolts of 1825, 1835, and 1843, the urban element was less evident. Authorities and planters, invested heavily in new industrial equipment for sugar production and railroads, and exhausted by the unending sequence of uprisings, unleashed a campaign of sweeping arrests of free blacks and mulattoes that cut the urban–rural link once and for all.

Brazil, like Cuba, also benefited from the collapse of sugar production on Haiti in the 1790s and the first half of the 1800s. It expanded its plantation sector,

Slave Revolt Aboard Ship. Rebellions aboard ship, such as the famous 1839 mutiny aboard the *Amistad* shown here, were common occurrences. The *Amistad* was engaged in intra-American slave trafficking, and the slaves overpowered the crew shortly after embarkation in Cuba. After protracted legal negotiations, the slaves were eventually freed and retuned to Africa.

particularly in the province of Bahia, and imported large numbers of slaves from Africa. But here distrust divided African-born from Brazilian slaves, freedmen, and mulattoes. Many freedmen and mulattoes served in the militias that the authorities used to suppress the revolts. Furthermore, in contrast to the narrow island of Cuba, plantation slaves could run away more easily to independent settlements (called *quilombos*) in the wide-open Brazilian interior, from where revolts were more easily organized than either in cities or on plantations. In fact, no fewer than a dozen quilombo revolts extending into plantations occurred in Bahia during 1807–1828, revolts which the militias found difficult to crush, having to march into often remote areas.

Two urban revolts of the period were remarkable for their exceptional mix of insurgents, unparalleled in Cuba or elsewhere in Latin America. The first was the Tailor's Rebellion of 1798 in Salvador, Bahia's capital. Freedmen, mulattoes, and white craftspeople cooperated in the name of freedom and equality against the Creole oligarchy. The second was the Muslim uprising of 1835, also in Bahia, organized by African-born freedmen as well as slaves with Islamic clerical educations that they had received in West Africa before their enslavement.

The impact of Islam on African American slave societies has not been sufficiently studied. West African Muslims, including clerics, were frequently enslaved in the early 1800s during the many conflicts and the civil wars in what is today coastal Nigeria. These clerics represented an African strand of Islam that was tolerant of West African animism, to which the majority of slaves in Salvador adhered. Distinguished by their knowledge of Arabic, white gowns, and protective amulet necklaces, the clerics converted slaves in Salvador and surrounding areas to Islam and took up arms as freedom fighters during the short-lived rebellion in 1835. The role of Islam as an alternate ideology to that of constitutionalism, as symbolized by the Haitian Revolution, is an important reminder that American slaves, far from being culturally dependent, had the freedom to carve out their own unique identities.

Man of Many Worlds. The life of Mahommah G. Baquaqua demonstrates the way in which some enslaved Africans could forge their own identities in the New World despite the daunting obstacles they faced. Captured and enslaved in West Africa in 1845 at about the age of 20, Baquaqua was taken to Pernambuco, Brazil, and then later to Rio de Janeiro, where a ship's captain bought him. He eventually escaped, made his way to New York City and then Haiti and then back to New York and finally on to Canada where he wrote his autobiography, the cover of which is shown here. He last shows up in the historical record in Britain, where seems to have lived out his remaining days.

Questions

- Do the slave rebellions in Cuba and Brazil in the early nineteenth century confirm or complicate the pattern of slave revolution that was first manifested first in Haiti?

- Why would Islam be attractive to many slaves in the Americas?

The Federalist Interlude   After lengthy debates, in 1834 the government granted the provinces their own legislative assemblies with strong tax and budget powers, effectively strengthening the provincial landholding elites with their various regional interests. It also abolished the council of state but created a national guard to suppress slave revolts and urban mobs. This mixed bag of reforms was not enough for some provinces. The most dangerous one was that of 1835 in Rio Grande do Sul, a southern province led by cattle owners who commanded military forces composed of gauchos. These owners established an independent republic that attracted many domestic and foreign radicals opposed to slavery, including Giuseppe Garibaldi, the Italian nationalist who played a crucial role in the unification of Italy. In reaction to the coexistence of a now weak and decentralized monarchy with an antislavery republic offering a refuge to runaways on Brazilian soil, the centralists reasserted themselves. In 1840 they proclaimed the 14-year-old Pedro II king and curbed the powers of the provincial assemblies, and in 1845 they negotiated a return of Rio Grande do Sul to Brazil.

The End of Slavery   The 1830s and 1840s coincided with a transition in Brazil from sugar to coffee as a major export commodity on the world market. The old sugar plantation elite lost clout, and a newer coffee planter oligarchy ascended to prominence. Both needed slaves, and as long as the crown did not seriously fulfill its promises of 1831 to the British to curb the importation of slaves, there was no more than unease about the mutual dependence of the king and the oligarchy on the continued existence of slave labor. But when the British in 1849 authorized warships to enter Brazilian waters to intercept slave ships, the importation of slaves virtually ceased. A serious labor shortage ensued, leading to a movement of slaves from the north to the center. For different reasons, sugar, cotton, and coffee plantation owners began to think of ridding themselves of a monarchy that was unable to maintain the flow of slaves from overseas.

In the 1860s and 1870s, anti-monarchy agitation gathered speed. Brazilians, especially professionals and intellectuals in the cities, became sensitive to their country being isolated in the world on the issue of slavery. After the United States, the Spanish colonies of Puerto Rico and Cuba ended slavery for all aged slaves and newborn children. Brazil was now left as the only unreformed slave-holding country in the Western Hemisphere. In the following decade and a half, as the antislavery chorus increased in volume, the government introduced a few cosmetic changes and it fell on the provinces to take more serious steps. Planters began to see the demise of the system on the horizon and encouraged their provinces to increase the flow of foreign immigrants, to be employed as wage labor on the coffee plantations. The political situation neared the point of anarchy in 1885, with mass flights of slaves from plantations and armed clashes to keep them there. Only then, in 1888, did the central government finally end slavery.

The Coffee Boom   Predictably, given the grip of the planter oligarchy on the labor force, little changed in social relations after the abolition of slavery. The coffee growers, enjoying high international coffee prices and the benefits of infrastructure improvements, through railroads and telegraph lines since the 1850s, could afford low-wage hired labor. The now free blacks received no land, education, or urban jobs, scraping by with low wages on the coffee and sugar plantations. Economically, however, after freeing itself from the burdens of slavery, Brazil expanded its economy in the 5 years following 1888 as much as in the 70 years of slavery since independence.

The monarchy, having dragged its feet for half a century on the slavery issue, was thoroughly discredited among the plantation elite and its offshoot, the officer corps in the military. By the 1880s, officers were also drawn from professional and intellectual urban circles. Increasingly, they subscribed to the ideology of *positivism* coming from France, which celebrated secular scientific and technological progress (see Chapter 22). Positivists, almost by definition, were liberal and republican in political orientation. In 1889, a revolt in the military supported by the Creole plantation oligarchy resulted in the abolition of the monarchy and proclamation of a republic, with practically no resistance from any quarter.

Two political tendencies emerged in the constituent assembly 2 years after the proclamation of the republic. The coffee interests of the south-central states favored federalism, with the right of the provinces to collect export taxes and maintain militias. The urban professional and intellectual interests, especially lawyers, supported a strong presidency with control over tariffs and import taxes as well as powers to use the federal military against provinces in cases of national emergency. The two tendencies were embodied in a compromise with a tilt toward federalism, which produced provincial caudillos, on the one hand, but regularly elected presidents, on the other.

Following this tilt, in the 1890s the government was strongly supportive of agricultural commodity exports. Coffee, rubber, and sugar exports yielded high profits and taxes until 1896, when overproduction of coffee resulted in diminishing returns. The State of São Paulo then regulated the sale of coffee on the world market through a state purchase scheme, which brought some stabilization to coffee production. At the same time and continuing into the early twentieth century (and without much state or central government support), immigrants and foreign investors laid the foundation for **import-substitution industrialization**, beginning with textile and food-processing factories. The comparative advantage from commodity exports had run its course by the late 1800s and early 1900s and now had to be supplemented with industrialization.

Children Picking Coffee in Brazil, ca. 1900. The first coffee bush was planted in Brazil in 1727. With the decline of the slave trade in the late nineteenth century, Brazil increasingly had to rely on immigrants—such as the children shown here—to provide labor for its booming coffee industry, which was centered in the hilly region near Rio de Janeiro and in the Paraíba Valley in the state of São Paulo.

Import-substitution industrialization: The practice by which countries protect their economies by setting high tariffs, and construct factories for the production of consumer goods (textiles, furniture, shoes; followed later by appliances, automobiles, electronics), and/or capital goods (steel, chemicals, machinery).

Latin American Society and Economy in the Nineteenth Century

Independence brought both disruptions and continuities in the economy as well as in politics. In Spanish America, four colonial regions broke apart into eventually 21 independent republics, organized around the pattern of constitutional nationalism. Trade with Europe was thus radically altered. What continued were deep divisions between the small landowning elites and the urban masses of officials, professionals, craftspeople, and laborers. Although many members of the elites and urban lower classes had collaborated in the drive for independence, afterward they broke apart into conservative and liberal wings, unable to establish a consensus and stable state institutions. When trade with Europe resumed, a lowest-denominator pattern of export-led growth based on mineral and agricultural commodities evolved (see Map 27.4).

MAP **27.4** The Economy of Latin America and the Caribbean, ca. 1900.

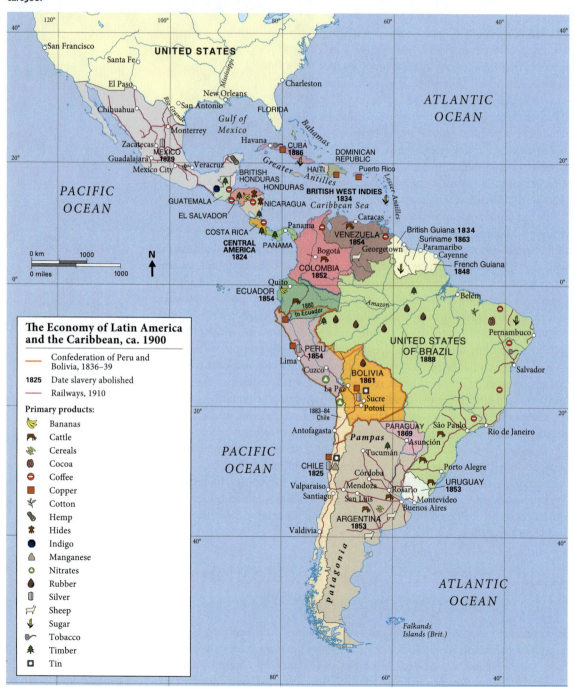

The Economy of Latin America and the Caribbean, ca. 1900

— Confederation of Peru and Bolivia, 1836–39
1825 Date slavery abolished
— Railways, 1910

Primary products:
- Bananas
- Cattle
- Cereals
- Cocoa
- Coffee
- Copper
- Cotton
- Hemp
- Hides
- Indigo
- Manganese
- Nitrates
- Rubber
- Silver
- Sheep
- Sugar
- Tobacco
- Timber
- Tin

Rebuilding Societies and Economies

Reconstruction in the independent republics and the Brazilian monarchy took several decades. Mercantilist trade was gone, and in its place, free trade had to be built. Social structures changed little, and constitutional disagreements took some time to be settled. Production in the mines and on the estates had to be restarted with fresh capital. All this took time, and it was only by mid-century that Latin America had overcome the aftereffects of the wars of independence.

On the Eve of Independence   During the colonial period, the economies of Spain and Portugal in the Americas followed a pattern of mercantilism. In mercantilist theory, as we have seen a number of times, the Spanish and Portuguese colonies could purchase only goods manufactured in Iberia and had to pay with gold, silver, sugar, cocoa, indigo, or other goods from the colonies. In practice, as Spain and Portugal reformed colonial administration and trade in the 1700s, it became easier for the colonies to buy from European countries via transit through Iberia. Contraband trade similarly mitigated and undercut Iberian mercantilism. Interregional trade increased during the reform period, especially for foodstuffs and cattle, Mexican and Ecuadorian textiles, and Argentinean and Chilean wine. Overall, however, interregional trade remained a poor cousin of the export trade.

Taxes were considerably higher in the Americas than in Iberia, with estimates of a 40–70 percent differential. But since tax surpluses from rich regions, such as Mexico, had to subsidize poor regions for administrative, judicial, and military costs, Spain did not earn much from its American colonies. Portugal was luckier with its colony of Brazil, which more or less consistently yielded a tribute. But, in contrast to earlier centuries, during the 1700s Iberia as a whole did not earn much from its American conquests.

After Independence   The achievement of independence in the 1820s, after lengthy struggles with Spain and local and internal conflicts, had a number of far-reaching consequences. The most important result was the end of Spain's mercantilist monopoly. The Latin American republics were free to buy or sell and to borrow money anywhere in the world. Among trading partners, this freedom benefited Great Britain most directly. Its merchants had already established themselves in several Latin American cities during the continental boycott of Napoleon, which had shut out Great Britain from trade with the European continent.

Initially, however, for Latin Americans the freedom to trade was more hope than reality. Dislocations from the struggle of independence were considerable. Capital had fled the continent and left behind uncultivated estates and flooded mines. The Catholic Church held huge, uncollectable debts. In many areas taxes could not be collected. Troops helped themselves to payment through plunder. In Mexico, where the struggle between republicans and royalists was the fiercest, the disruptions were worst and reconstruction took longest. Chile also experienced violent struggles but stabilized itself relatively quickly. On average, though, it took until about 1850 for Latin America to fully recover.

Constitutional Nationalism and Society   The Creoles were everywhere the winners in the wars of independence. Many were ardent constitutional nationalists, finding it easy to adapt to conservative versions of this form of the Western challenge of modernity. The most powerful among them were large landowners, that is, owners of grain-farming self-sufficiency estates, cattle ranches, and sugar, indigo, cacao, coffee, or cotton plantations. Independence did not produce much change in agrarian relations: Landowners of self-sufficient estates and plantations in many parts of Latin America continued to employ tenant farmers and slaves.

The large majority of the Creoles were urban administrators, professionals, craftspeople, and laborers. Their leaders, ardent constitutional nationalists, tended toward political and economic liberalism. In many areas they were joined by mestizos, mulattoes, and black freedmen, also largely craftspeople and laborers. The main issue dividing the liberals and conservatives, as in the French Revolution, was the extent of voting rights: Liberals wanted to extend it to all males, while conservatives sought to limit it through literacy and property requirements to a minority of males. No influential group at this point considered extending voting rights to women.

Deep Political Divisions   Once independence was won, distrust between the two groups with very different property interests set in and the political consensus fell apart. Accordingly, landed constitutional conservatives restricted voting rights, to the detriment of the urban constitutional liberals. The exceptions were Argentina and, for a time during the mid-century, Peru: The one had few mestizos and mulattoes but a relatively large urban Creole population that gained the upper hand, and the other had large numbers of urban mestizos and Amerindians who could not be ignored. Nevertheless, even if constitutionalism was submerged for periods of time under caudillo authoritarianism, as we have seen, adaptation to constitutionalism, in its conservative or liberal variation, remained a permanent fixture. It was this early adoption of constitutionalism which distinguished Latin America from the Ottoman Empire, Russia, China, and Japan.

Split Over State–Church Relations   Among the many issues over which conservatives and liberals split, the relationship between state and church was the deepest. Initially, given the more or less close collaboration between republicans and conservatives during the struggle for independence, Catholicism remained the national religion for all. Accordingly, education and much property remained under church control.

But the new republics ended the powers of the Inquisition and claimed the right of *patronato*, that is, of naming bishops. At the behest of Spain, however, the pope left bishoprics empty rather than agree to this new form of lay investiture. In fact, Rome would not even recognize the independence of the Latin American nations until the mid-1830s. The conflict was aggravated by the church's focus on its institutional rather than pastoral role. The Catholic clergy provided little guidance at a time when industrial modernity, even if only indirectly via urbanization, was crying out for spiritual reorientation. At the same time, papal pronouncements made plain the church's hostility toward the developing capitalist industrial order.

This hostility of the church was thus one of the factors that in the mid-1800s contributed to a swing back to liberalism, beginning with Colombia in 1849. Many countries adopted a formal separation between church and state and introduced secular educational systems. But the state–church issue remained bitter, especially in Mexico, Guatemala, Ecuador, and Venezuela, where it was often at the center of political shifts between liberals and conservatives. In Colombia, for example, it even led to a complete reversal of liberal trends in the mid-1880s, with the reintroduction of Catholicism as the state religion.

Economic Weakness   Given the difficulties of arriving at a political and cultural consensus during the period of recovery after independence (ca. 1820–1850), the reconstruction of a fiscal system to support the governments remained contradictory and problematic. For example, governments resorted to taxation of trade, even if this interfered with declared policies of free trade. The yields on tariffs and export taxes, however, were inevitably low and made the financing of strong central governments difficult. Consequently, maneuvering for the most productive mix of the two taxes trumped official pronouncements in favor of free trade and often eroded confidence among trade partners.

This maneuvering had little effect on the domestic economy—self-sufficiency agriculture and urban crafts production—which represented the great bulk of economic activities in Latin America. Grain production on large estates and small farms, especially in Brazil where gold production declined in late colonial times, had escaped the turbulence of the independence war and recovery periods relatively unscathed. Land remained plentiful, and the main bottleneck continued to be labor. The distribution of marketable surpluses declined, however, given the new internal borders in Latin America with their accompanying tariffs and export taxes. Self-sufficiency agriculture and local economies relying on it thus remained largely unchanged throughout the 1800s.

The crafts workshops, especially for textiles, suffered from the arrival of cheap British factory-produced cottons, which represented the majority of imports by the mid-1800s. Their impact, however, remained relatively limited, mostly to the coasts, since in the absence of railroads transportation costs to the interior were prohibitively expensive. Only Mexico encouraged the financing of machine-driven textile factories, but the failure of its state bank in 1842—from issuing too many loans—ended this policy for a number of decades. On the one hand, there was a definite awareness in most countries of the benefits of factories, using domestic resources, and linking the self-sufficiency agricultural sector to modern industrial development. On the other hand, its necessity in the face of traditional opposition was not demonstrated until later in the nineteenth century.

Export-Led Growth

The pursuit of a policy of commodity exports—export-led growth—from about 1850 led to expanding rates in the standard of living for many Latin Americans. The industrializing countries in Europe and North America were voracious consumers of the minerals and materials that Latin America had in abundance and of its tropical agricultural products. More could have been sold, had there not been a chronic labor shortage.

Raw Materials and Cash Crops   Mining and agricultural cash crop production recovered gradually so that by the 1850s, nearly all Latin American governments had adopted export-led economic growth as their basic policy. This was about

Loading Nitrate into Rail Cars, Chile, 1915. In the 1830s, farmers realized the value of nitrate as a fertilizer and an export boom to industrializing Europe ensued. Most of the deposits were located in what were then coastal lands of Peru and Bolivia. In 1879, Bolivia raised its taxes on nitrate mining, and in response Chile declared war on Bolivia. Chile won the war against Bolivia (and Peru, which sided with the latter) in 1884; as a result, Bolivia became landlocked. The nitrate boom eventually collapsed in World War I when Germany began making synthetic fertilizer.

all the conservatives and liberals were able to agree on since land distribution to poor farmers and a system of income taxes were beyond any consensus. Mexican and Peruvian silver production, the mainstay of the colonial mercantilist economy, became strong again, although the British adoption of the gold standard in 1821 imposed limits on silver exports. Peru found a partial replacement for silver with guano mining. Guano, seabird excrement accumulated over the millennia and fossilized, was mined by laborers using simple implements, such as pickaxes and shovels. It was exported for use as an organic fertilizer and as a source of nitrates for explosives. Chile hit the jackpot with guano, nitrate, and copper exports, of crucial importance during the chemical- and electricity-driven second Industrial Revolution.

In other Latin American countries, tropical and subtropical cash crops defined export-led economic growth during the mid-1800s. In Brazil, Colombia, and Costa Rica, labor-intensive coffee growing redefined the agricultural sector. In Argentina, the production of jerked (dried) beef, similarly labor-intensive, refashioned the ranching economy. The main importers of this beef were regions in the Americas where plantation slavery continued into the second half of the 1800s, especially the United States, Brazil, and Cuba. The latter, which remained a Spanish colony until 1895, profited from the relocation of sugarcane plantations from the mainland and a number of Caribbean islands after the British outlawing of the slave trade (1807) and slavery itself (1834) and the Latin American wars of independence (1810–1826).

In the long run, however, like silver, cane sugar had a limited future, given the rise of beet sugar production in Europe. Minerals and cash crops were excellent for export-led economic growth, especially if they required secondary activities such as the processing of meat or the use of mining machinery. But competition on the world market increased during the 1800s, and thus, there was ultimately a ceiling, reached in the 1890s.

Broadening of Exports   With their eyes increasingly focused on exports, Latin American governments responded quickly to the increased market opportunities resulting from the Industrial Revolution in Great Britain, the European continent, and the United States. Peru broadened its mineral exports with copper, Bolivia with tin, and Chile with nitrates. Brazil and Peru added rubber, Argentina and Uruguay wool, and Mexico *henequen* (a fiber for ropes and sacks) to its traditional exports. Luxuries from tropical Latin America, like coffee, cacao (for chocolate bars, invented in 1847), vanilla, and bananas, joined sugar after 1850 in becoming affordable mass consumer items in the industrialized countries. Argentina, with investments in refrigeration made by Britain, added frozen meat to this list in 1883. This commodity diversification met not only the broadened demand of the second Industrial Revolution, with its demand for chemicals and electricity, but also the demand for consumer goods among the newly affluent middle classes.

Since the choice among minerals and crops was limited, however, most nations remained wedded to one commodity only (50 percent of exports or more). Only two, Argentina and Peru, were able to diversify (exports of less than 25 percent for the leading commodity). They were more successful at distributing their exports over the four main industrial markets of Great Britain, Germany, France, and the United States. On the eve of World War I the United States had grown to be the most important trading partner in 11 of the 21 Latin American countries. Given its own endowments and under the conditions of world trade in the second half of the nineteenth century, the continent's trade was relatively well diversified.

The prices of all Latin American commodities gyrated substantially up and down during the second half of the nineteenth century. This fluctuation was in contrast to the imported manufactured goods, primarily textiles, metal utensils, and implements, which became cheaper over time. In fact, Brazil's government was so concerned about fluctuating coffee prices in the 1890s that it introduced the Taubaté coffee valorization scheme in 1906. As the largest producer, it regulated the amount of coffee offered on the world market, carefully adjusting production to keep market prices relatively stable in much the same way that oil-producing countries would later do with petroleum. Since coffee trees need 5 years to mature, Brazil was largely successful with its scheme until World War I, when worldwide conditions changed. An American oligopoly (the United and Standard Fruit Companies) in control of banana production in Central America from the 1890s similarly controlled prices. A careful investigation of commodity prices by economic historians has resulted in the conclusion that in spite of all fluctuations commodity prices rose overall during 1850–1914.

Rising Living Standards   From all evidence, in the period from the middle of the 1800s to the eve of World War I, the governments can be judged as having been successful with their choice of export-led growth as their consensus policy. Living standards rose, as measured in gross domestic product (GDP). At various times during 1850–1900, between five and eight Latin American countries kept pace with the living standards in the industrialized countries. Argentina and Chile were the most consistent leaders throughout the period. Thus, although many politicians were aware that at some point their countries would have to industrialize in addition to relying on commodity export growth, they can perhaps be forgiven for keeping their faith in exports as the engine for improved living standards right up to World War I.

Labor and Immigrants   As in the industrialized countries, the profitable exports were achieved through low wages. Together with the rest of the world, Latin America experienced high population increases during the 1800s. The population grew sevenfold, to 74 million, although it remained small in comparison to the populations of Europe, which doubled to 408 million, and Africa and Asia, which each grew by one-third to 113 and 947 million, respectively. The increases were not large enough to dent the favorable land–person ratio, so it is not surprising that the high demand for labor continued during the 1800s. This demand, of course, was the reason the institution of forced labor—revolving labor duties (mit'a) among Amerindians in the Andes and slavery—had come into existence in the first place.

Not surprisingly, mit'a and slavery continued during the 1800s, liberal constitutionalism notwithstanding, in a number of countries. Even where forced labor was abolished early, however, low wages continued. One would have expected wages to rise rapidly, given the continuing conditions of labor shortage and land availability. Mine operators and landowners, however, were reluctant to raise wages because they feared for the competitiveness of their commodities on the world market. Governments, doing their bidding, preferred to resort to selective and mass immigration from overseas to enlarge the labor pool.

Typical selective immigration examples were *coolies* (from Urdu *kuli*, hireling), that is, "indentured" laborers recruited from India and China on 5- or 10-year contracts and working off the costs of their transportation. During 1847–1874, nearly half a million East Indians traveled to various European colonies in the Caribbean. Similarly, 235,000 Chinese came to Peru, Cuba, and Costa Rica, working in guano pits and silver mines, on sugar and cotton plantations, and later on railroads. If the experience of five Caribbean islands can be taken as a guide, only about 10 percent of the coolies returned home. Coolie migration to Latin America, therefore, can be described as a major part of the pattern of massive migration streams across the world that typified the nineteenth century (see Map 27.5).

Immigration to Latin America from Europe was on an even bigger scale. In Argentina, Uruguay, Brazil, and Chile, Italians and Spaniards settled in large numbers from around 1870 on. In Argentina, nearly one-third of the population consisted of immigrants, a share much higher than at any time in the United States. The Italian population of Argentina numbered close to 1 million by the turn of the century. Most immigrants settled in cities, and Buenos Aires became the first city on the continent with more than a million people. Only here did a semi-regular labor market develop, with rising urban and rural wages prior to World War I. Elsewhere in Latin America, governments, beholden to large landowners, feared the rise of cities with immigrant laborers who did not share their interests. They, therefore, opposed mass immigration.

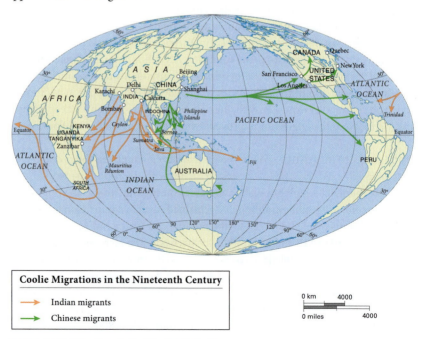

Coolie Migrations in the Nineteenth Century

→ Indian migrants

→ Chinese migrants

MAP **27.5** **Coolie Migrations in the Nineteenth Century.**

Dining Hall for Recently Arrived Immigrants, Buenos Aires. Immigrants, all male, and more than likely all Italian, rub shoulders sometime around 1900 in a dining hall in Buenos Aires set up for newly arrived immigrants. By 1914, 2 percent of the population of Buenos Aires—about 300,000 people—had been born in Italy, most from the poor southern regions of Campania, Calabria, and Sicily.

Self-Sufficiency Agriculture   Except for Argentina, Chile, and Uruguay, the levels of commodity exports did not rise sufficiently to reduce the size of the rural labor force not working for exports, a major condition for improved living standards across the board. On the eve of World War I, two-thirds to half of the laborers in most Latin American countries were still employed as tenant farmers or farmhands on large estates. In much smaller numbers, they were indigenous villagers who owned their small farmsteads. Their contribution to the national GDP, for example, in Brazil and Mexico was less than one-quarter. Toward the end of the century, observers began to realize that export-led growth—even though it looked like an effective economic driver—did not have much of a transformative effect on the rural masses in most countries.

The absence of such transformative effects was visible, for example, in the high levels of illiteracy among rural inhabitants. Adult illiteracy rates of up to 80 percent were not uncommon, even in relatively diversified countries, such as Brazil and Mexico. Only Argentina and Chile after 1860 invested heavily in primary education, on levels similar to the United States and Britain, followed by Costa Rica in the 1890s. Literate self-sufficiency farmers, knowledgeable in plant and animal selection as well as fertilizers, were practically nonexistent north of the southern end of Latin America.

Governments paid greater attention to the improvement of rural infrastructures from about 1870 onward, with the development of railroads. Almost everywhere, they looked to direct foreign investment, given the low-yielding and highly regressive trade taxes on which the relatively slim central domestic revenues depended. The foreign investors or consortiums built these railroads primarily for the transportation of commodities to ports. Many self-sufficiency farmers or even landlords, therefore, received little encouragement to produce more food staples for urban markets. Argentina and Chile, followed by Costa Rica and Uruguay, built the most railroads, with between 2.8 and 1.5 miles per 1,000 heads of population. Correspondingly, with fertilizers and better implements available via railroads, corn yields quintupled

Mexican Textile Factory.
Cocolapam in the state of Veracruz was the site of the first Mexican cotton textile factory, founded in 1836 by Lucas Alamán, a Mexican government minister and investment banker. Its machinery, imported from Great Britain, was water-driven. The textiles it produced remained inferior to imports, but they were cheap and satisfied the needs of most Mexicans.

in Argentina. Conversely, these yields changed little in Mexico, which had only 1.2 miles per 1,000 heads. Overall, the Latin American railroad network represented only about one-fifth to one-third of that in other Western developing settler countries, such as Australia, Canada, and New Zealand.

Factories   Until about 1870, the handicrafts sector met the demands of the rural as well as low-earning urban population. It produced cheap, low-quality textiles, shoes, soap, candles, tools, implements, cutlery, and horse tack. As is well known, this sector failed in most parts of the world during the 1800s or 1900s to mechanize itself and establish a modern factory system. Latin America was no exception. Most crafts shops were based on family labor, with a high degree of self-exploitation, unconnected to the landowning elite and deemed too small by lending banks. There was no path from workshops to factories.

However, even entrepreneurial investors interested in building factories for the manufacture of yarn or textiles were hampered in their efforts. They had little chance for success prior to the appearance of public utilities in the 1880s, providing water during the dry season and electricity as an energy source, in the absence of high-quality coal in most parts of Latin America. Even then, the risk of engaging in manufacturing, requiring long-term strategies with no or low profits, was so great that the typical founders of factories were not Creoles but European immigrants.

In Argentina and Chile these immigrants labored hard during their first years after arrival and saved the start-up capital necessary to launch small but modern textile, food-processing, and beverage factories. Argentina, Chile, Mexico, and Peru made the greatest advances toward factory industrialization, producing import-substituting consumer goods to the tune of 50–80 percent. Prior to World War I, the only country that took the step from consumer goods to capital goods (goods for factories) was Mexico, with the foundation of the Fundidora Iron and Steel Mill in 1910 in Monterrey, which, however, was unprofitable for a long time. Full capital goods industrialization had to await the postwar period.

Culture, Family, and the Status of Women

Economic growth and urbanization added considerably to the growth of constitutional-nationalist modernity in Latin America. But the absence of industrialization until the end of the nineteenth century impeded the transformation of society and its cultural institutions. The law and custom represented by the Catholic Church remained pervasive. In the second half of the nineteenth century, however, the idea of separating church and state gained adherents, with some major legal consequences for social institutions.

Legal Changes   In most countries, repeated attempts by governments after independence to reduce the role of the Catholic church in society remained unsuccessful. The church resisted the efforts of the constitutional nationalists to carry out land expropriations and to separate state and church in social legislation. In a number of civil codes women's rights in inheritance and property control improved, but overall husbands retained their patriarchal rights over their families. Typically, they were entitled to the control over the family budget, contractual engagements, choice of husbands for their daughters (up to age 25 in some countries), or residence of unmarried daughters (at home, up to age 30). Only from the middle of the nineteenth century did the influence of the Catholic Church diminish sufficiently to allow legislation for secular marriages and divorce in a number of countries. Catholicism remained doctrinally unchanged.

"Men in the Street and Women at Home"　As it also developed in the Euro-American Victorian world, on the cultural level there was a popular ideal in nineteenth-century Latin America of nuclear family domesticity. But, as research has also shown, in both places this was often honored more in the breach than in the observance. That is to say, in Mexico and South America, despite the long-standing proverb *El hombre en la calle, la mujer en la casa* ("Men in the street, women in the home"), it was often the case that the two roles were intermingled. In urban areas, women frequently ran shops, managed markets, were proprietors of *cantinas*, and performed a host of skilled and unskilled jobs, particularly in the textile and food trades. In rural areas, farm work on small holdings and peonages was often shared by men and women, though a number of individual tasks—plowing, for example— were most frequently done by men.

As in Europe and North America, too, there was a remarkably high level of widowhood and spinsterhood. In areas where the predominant form of employment was dangerous—mining, for example—the incidence of widowhood was very high. Widows often could not or chose not to remarry, especially if they had relatives to fall back on or were left an income. The stereotype of the stern patriarchal husband was also pervasive enough so that many middle-class women, often to the consternation of their families, chose not to marry at all. Both of these conditions were common enough so that by one estimate one-third of all the households in Mexico City in the early nineteenth century were headed by women. Widows were entitled to their dowries and half of the community property, while boys and girls received equal portions of the inheritance. Thus, despite society's pressures to marry and raise children, many women did not marry or, after becoming widowed, remained single. In this sense, they achieved a considerable degree of autonomy in a male-dominated society. Thus social realities and legal rights diverged in early independent Latin America, even before legal reform.

The Visual and Literary Arts　To try to encapsulate the culture and arts of more than a continent—and one so vast and diverse as Latin America—is far beyond the scope of this textbook. In general terms, the legacy of European baroque and romantic-era paintings remained alive throughout the nineteenth century as a background current until giving way to the influences of European impressionists and painters.

The trend in all of Latin America colonial-era high culture under the aegis of Spanish and Portuguese influences after independence was toward "indigenization": Much like the way the United States attempted during this time to break away from European art and literary influences, a similar movement pervaded the Latin American world. Along with attempts to form national and regional styles of their own, many countries also engaged in art as a nation-building exercise—artistic and literary celebrations of new national heroes or famous historic instances through portraiture and landscape painting. Finally, there were also periodic engagements with the popular or folk arts of Amerindian peoples, mulattoes, mestizos, and Africans in celebration of regional uniqueness.

Literature to some extent paralleled the trajectory of the other arts. In the latter eighteenth and early nineteenth centuries, a style had developed called *criollo* (Creole), for its inception and popularity among that class. The most famous of work in this style was José Joaquin Fernández Lizardi's *The Mangy Parrot* (*El Periquillo Samiento*), published in 1816. Though ostensibly a tale of children's stories, it is more in the vein of Voltaire's *Candide* in lampooning the venality, corruption, and incompetence of the late colonial world. Initially, there was little nostalgia for the pre-independence years.

Following independence, as in painting, literature often turned to themes befitting countries trying to establish themselves as nations with distinct historic pasts and great future potential. In some cases, as with sometime newspaper crusader and later Argentine president Domingo Faustino Sarmiento (in office 1868–1874), critique of the present was the order of the day. Sarmiento relentlessly criticized the authoritarian rule and arbitrary ways of the caudillo Juán Manuel de Rosas in his book *Facundo: Civilization and Barbarism*. The book, written while Sarmiento had been forced into exile by Rosas in 1845, is an indictment of Rosas thinly disguised as a biography of the brutal gaucho leader Juán Facundo Quiroga. It is also, however, a meditation on the meaning of "civilization" and "barbarism" as exemplified by Europe, Asia, Africa, and Latin America. As such, it has been called by some the most important book to be published in the nineteenth century in Latin America.

> ### Civilization and Barbarism
>
> "No, we are not the lowest among Americans. Something is to result from this chaos; either something surpassing the government of the United States of North America, or something a thousand times worse than that of Russia—the Dark Ages returned, or political institutions, superior to any yet known."
>
> —Domingo F. Sarmiento. *Life in the Argentine Republic in the Days of the Tyrants: Or Civilization and Barbarism*, p. 247. New York: Hurd and Houghton, 1868.

The themes of the social sciences and reportage merged in much of the work of the Brazilian writer Euclides da Cunha (1866–1909). In his most famous work, *Os Sertões* (*The Rebellion in the Backlands*, 1902), he examines with a critical eye the social demography of Brazil, its racial composition and conflicts, and weighs them against the claims of the new Brazilian Republic. The vehicle for this is the attempt by the government to crush a rebellion of isolated settler outcasts in Bahia, during the 1890s, who, despite the odds against them, repeatedly defeat the government forces and become regional heroes. The book acquired considerable popularity in Brazil and was also championed by a number of leading writers in Europe and the United States. In Brazil as in the Spanish-speaking Americas, authors in the nineteenth century had a keen eye for society caught between tradition and modernity.

Putting It All Together

The term "banana republic" appeared for the first time in 1904. The American humorist O. Henry (1862–1910) coined it to represent politically unstable and economically poor Latin American countries, governed by small elites and relying on tropical exports, such as bananas. O. Henry had spent several years at the end of the nineteenth century in Honduras, hiding from US authorities. Thus he knew whereof he spoke.

Today, political stability is much greater; but many parts of Latin America are still poor and underindustrialized. Consequently, banana republics still resonates. Were Latin American elites, therefore, wrong to engage in a pattern of export-led growth, and did they collude with elites in the industrial countries to maneuver the continent into permanent dependence on the latter? Indeed, an entire generation of scholars in the second half of the twentieth century answered the question in the affirmative and wrote the history of the 1800s in gloomy and condemnatory tones. They called their analysis "dependency theory."

Contemporary historians are less certain about many of these conclusions. They compare Latin America not with the United States or western Europe but with the settler colonies of South Africa, Australia, and New Zealand or the old empires of the Middle East and Asia. In these comparisons, Latin America did very well and was not any more dependent on the industrializing countries than the latter were on Latin America.

Dependence increased only at the very end of the 1800s when industrial countries like the United States and Britain began to make significant capital investments. It was then that foreign companies, such as those that owned railroads in Nicaragua and Honduras, succeeded in exploiting and controlling production and export. The question we may need to ask then is not why Latin America failed to industrialize in the 1800s but, rather, did Latin America, choosing from the available choices, make

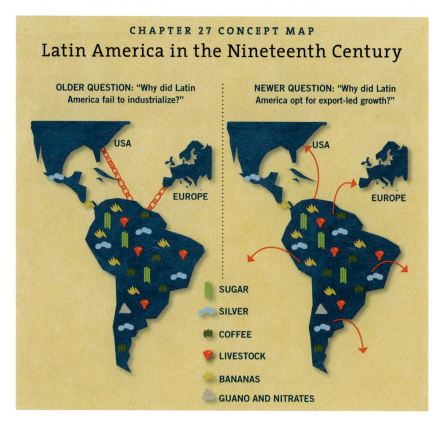

CHAPTER 27 CONCEPT MAP
Latin America in the Nineteenth Century

OLDER QUESTION: "Why did Latin America fail to industrialize?"

NEWER QUESTION: "Why did Latin America opt for export-led growth?"

USA

EUROPE

USA

EUROPE

- SUGAR
- SILVER
- COFFEE
- LIVESTOCK
- BANANAS
- GUANO AND NITRATES

the right decision when it opted for export-led growth up to about 1890? Did such a choice represent a "third way" toward economic growth, separate from industrial capitalism and tenacious attempts to keep economies closed off from the vagaries of world trade? Perhaps it did (see Concept Map).

Review and Respond

1. Define the concept of constitutional nationalism, and explain how and why it became a pattern of state formation in Latin America in the nineteenth century.

2. Compare Vincent Ogé and Toussaint Louverture. How are these two revolutionaries similar? How are they different?

3. Compare the political development of Haiti and Mexico in the early nineteenth century.

4. Why did the Creoles not become radical constitutional nationalists? Which kind of constitutionalism did they espouse?

5. Why did slavery persist for so long in Brazil? How is Brazilian slavery an example of the origins-interactions-adaptations model that informs this book?

6. Who were Simón Bolívar and José de San Martín, and what brought them together?

7. What distinguished the political development of Brazil from a colony to an independent country in Latin America?

8. Compare and contrast the dependency theory model and the export-led growth model for understanding patterns of development in Latin America in the nineteenth century.

> For additional resources, including maps, primary sources, visuals, and quizzes, please go to www.oup.com/us/vonsivers. Please see the Further Resources section at the back of the book for additional readings and suggested websites.

Thinking Through Patterns

▶ **Which factors in the complex ethnic and social structures of Latin America were responsible for the emergence of authoritarian politicians or caudillos?**

Similar to the United States and France, which also underwent revolutions in the late 1700s and early 1800s, Latin America's independence movements (1810–1824) did not extend the constitutional revolution beyond a small number of property owners who inhabited the highest levels of the social strata. The dominant class of large landlords and plantation owners was conservative and did not favor land reform for the benefit of small farmers. Urban professionals and craftspeople, divided in many places by ethnicity, did not share common interests that allowed them to provide an effective opposition to the landed class. Landowning and plantation interests thus protected themselves through authoritarian caudillo politics and sought to keep the opposition weak.

In colonial times, Latin America was the warm-weather extension of Europe, sending its mineral and agricultural commodities to Europe. When it acquired its independence and Europe industrialized during the 1800s, these commodities became even more important and the continent opted for a pattern of export-led development. This meant the systematic increase of mineral and agricultural commodity exports, with rising living standards not only for those who profited directly from the exports but also for many in the urban centers. Even with rising living standards it became clear by the turn of the century that a supplementary policy of industrialization had to be pursued.

▶ **Why did Latin American countries, after achieving independence, opt for a continuation of mineral and agricultural commodity exports?**

▶ **How do the social and economic structures of this period continue to affect the course of Latin America today?**

Many countries in Latin America are barely richer than they were in the 1800s. Even though industry, mineral, and commodity exports, as well as services, expanded in urban centers in the early part of the twentieth century, poor farmers with low incomes continued to be a drag on development. This phenomenon still characterizes many parts of Latin America today.

PART SIX

From Three Modernities to One

1914–PRESENT

World War I and the Interwar Period

The first great crisis in the evolution of modern scientific–industrial society was World War I (1914–1918). Although imperial competition in the Balkans indirectly triggered the war, there were even stronger forces playing their part in the background, together with other reasons still hotly contested by historians today.

For our purposes, the most dramatic effect of the war was that the single nineteenth-century pattern of modernity—constitutional and ethnic–linguistic nationalism and scientific–industrial society—splintered into the three subpatterns: capitalism–democracy, socialism–communism, and supremacist nationalism. The countries representing these subpatterns of modernity formed camps that were bitterly hostile to each other:

- Capitalist democracy (most notably the United States, Britain, France, and parts of Latin America): support for the concepts of freedom (especially the free market), capitalism, and international institutions for maintaining peace.

- Communism–socialism (the Soviet Union): professed support for equality over freedom and a command economy originating from the top.

- Supremacist nationalism (Italy, Germany, and Japan): contempt for both democracy and communism, the celebration of racial supremacy and authoritarian/dictatorial rule, a state-controlled economy, and territorial expansion through military conquest.

In the period after World War I, the countries representing these three modernities moved in very different directions:

- The democratic victors, Great Britain and France, expanded their colonial empires by acquiring, under the rubric of "mandates," new territories taken from the liquidated Ottoman Empire in the Middle East and German possessions in Africa. Since a variety of ethno–linguistic nationalisms in these territories were forming at the same time, future conflicts were inevitable.

1908
Oil Discovered in the Middle East

1911–1912
Revolution in China, Fall of Qing Dynasty

1914–1918
World War I

1917
Bolshevik Revolution

1919
Versailles Treaty, Founding of League of Nations

1929–1933
Stock Market Crash and Great Depression

1937–1945
World War II in China and the Pacific

1942
Nazis Implement the Final Solution

1947
Indian and Pakistani Independence

1948
State of Israel Founded, First Arab–Israeli War

1950–1953
Korean War

1957
Soviet Union's Launch of Sputnik Satellite, Decolonization Begins in Africa

1958
Great Leap Forward in China

1962
Cuban Missile Crisi

- In Russia, a small but highly disciplined communist party managed to engineer a political takeover, withdraw from the war, and build a communist state: the Union of Socialist Soviet Republics (USSR or Soviet Union). The Soviet Union acquired full industrial strength in the 1930s.

- The loser of World War I, Germany, together with Italy and Japan (both of which had joined the Allies in hopes of territorial gains), turned toward supremacist nationalism.

World War II and the Rise of New Nations

In contrast to World War I, the Second World War was actively planned by the supremacist nationalists and was far less avoidable. Both World War I and the Great Depression effectively ended the global free trade that had characterized the nineteenth century. All countries, including the capitalist democracies, now subscribed to the idea that the future of industry lay in economic "spheres" each dominated by one *autarkic*—that is, self-sufficient—industrial power. With the victory of the Allies, the United States and Soviet Union emerged after World War II as the leading examples of the two surviving patterns of modernity: capitalist democracy and socialism–communism. The proponents of each of these patterns competed with the other during the Cold War (1945–1991):

- The first, or "hot," phase, 1945–1962: The United States and Soviet Union surrounded themselves with allies in Europe and Asia and fought one another militarily through proxies, that is, smaller allied states. They also sought to align the new nations, emerging in the wake of decolonization, into their respective camps. The Cold War climaxed during the Cuban Missile Crisis of 1962.

- The second, "cooling" phase, 1962–1991: During this time, the two nuclear powers reduced tensions ("détente") and agreed on a mechanism to limit, and then to reduce, their nuclear arsenals. But they continued their proxy wars, in particular in Vietnam and Afghanistan.

Capitalist-Democratic Modernity

Perhaps the most significant event that put the United States on course for eventual victory over the Soviet Union in 1991 was the computer revolution—the third industrial revolution after the steam engine (ca. 1800) and steel, electricity, and chemicals (ca. 1865). After fully adapting itself to this revolution, the United States became the unrivaled superpower, deriving its strength from its advanced computer technology, powerful financial services, and unmatched military strength.

Thinking Like a World Historian

▶ How are the three patterns that emerged after World War I different adaptations to modernity? Despite their marked differences, what common features do they share?

▶ Why, after World War II, was socialism–communism in many ways a more attractive pattern to decolonizing countries than capitalism–democracy?

▶ Why was the United States better able to adapt to technological innovation than the Soviet Union?

▶ How do consumerism and the widespread use of social networking show the emergence of a global culture in the twenty-first century? Can we predict what future patterns will look like?

1963
Nuclear Test Ban Treaty

1966–1969
Cultural Revolution in China

1968–Present
Rise of "Women's Liberation" and Modern Feminism

1979
Shah of Iran Overthrown, Soviet Union Invades Afghanistan

1989
Tiananmen Square Demonstrations in China, Berlin Wall Torn Down, and German Unification

1989–1991
Collapse of Communism in Soviet Bloc

1965–1973
Vietnam War

1968
Massive Student Demonstrations in Europe, the United States, and Mexico

1978
Deng Xiaoping Announces "Four Modernizations" in China

1985–1989
Perestroika and Glasnost in the Soviet Union

1991
Collapse of the Soviet Union and End of the Cold War

1990–2000
Civil War and Ethnic Cleansing in Former Yugoslavia

1994
End of Apartheid and Election of Nelson Mandela as President in South Africa, Hutu Genocide Against Tutsis in Rwanda

2001
Al-Qaeda Attack on United States

2007-2011
Global Financial Crisis and Economic Recession

2010
Number of Cell Phones Reaches 5 Billion Worldwide

2011
"Arab Spring," Nuclear Crisis in Japan, World Population 7 Billion

Chapter 28

1900-1945

World War and Competing Visions of Modernity

A WORLD AT WAR, 1900–1945

Professor Minobe seemed clearly rattled. For 30 years he had been Japan's leading jurist and constitutional theorist. His decades of work in the law school of Japan's leading academic institution, Tokyo Imperial University, were celebrated not just in Japan but among scholars throughout the world. Indeed, such was his prestige that he had received a noble rank and occupied an honored place in Japan's House of Peers, the upper chamber of its Diet, or

Seeing Patterns

▶ Which three patterns of modernity emerged after World War I? How and why did these patterns form?

▶ What were the strengths and flaws of each of the three visions of modernity?

▶ Why did supremacist nationalism disappear in the ashes of World War II?

parliament. A self-confident, even combative, man, he was not ordinarily given to suffering fools or meekly taking a dressing down.

But today was different, and only later would Minobe Tatsukichi (1873–1948) realize what a dramatic turning point it was for him and for the direction of Japanese law and politics. On this bleak February day in 1934, his fellow peer, Baron Takeo Kikuchi, had taken the floor and publicly denounced Minobe's most famous legal theory. Decades earlier, Minobe had posited that the relationship of the emperor to the constitution was one in which the emperor was an "organ" of the state. More than a generation of Japanese lawyers and scholars had internalized and practiced law according to this "organ theory." But now, the baron had accused Minobe of belittling the emperor's role in Japan's unique *kokutai*, or "national polity/ essence." This concept, as we shall see, played a key role in Japanese supremacist nationalism during the 1930s.

Though Minobe defended his position skillfully, reminding his colleagues that to say the emperor was an organ of the state simply means that he rules for the state and not for himself, the damage had been done.

Tracing Modernity's Path. Members of the People's Liberation Army undergo artillery training during the civil war between the Nationalists and Communists, which ended with Communist victory in 1949.

975

Following more attacks in the Diet, Minobe resigned from his position, narrowly escaped being tried for his views, and was nearly assassinated in 1936. Already, however, in their drive to "clarify" the meaning of the "national essence," the cabinet had eliminated all of Minobe's writings and banned his works from study or circulation.

Minobe's experience personalizes a struggle to come to grips with new visions of modernity not only in Japan but in much of the world as well. By the 1930s, the liberal principles of modernity—constitutionalism, capitalism, science, and industry—were being tested in the crucible of the Great Depression and increasingly found wanting. In Japan, these values were already giving way to what we call "supremacist nationalism," offering close parallels to the ideologies of Nazism in Germany and fascism in Italy. In Russia, Communism represented another new subpattern of modernity. Other nations—Spain, Portugal, and China, for example—struggled with variations of one or more these competing ideologies.

In this chapter we will explore how the conflicts of spreading modernity spawned these new visions and how each fared through two world wars and the largest economic depression in history. We will also see how the supremacist nationalism that haunted Minobe, as embodied in the Axis powers, was utterly destroyed by the alliance of Communism and capitalist democracy. Their interlude of victory, however, was destined to be short-lived. Within a few years the remaining two divisions of modernity renewed the struggle for supremacy against each other under the shadow of potential nuclear annihilation.

The Great War and Its Aftermath

On July 27, 1914, the nations about to plunge into the abyss of total war the following day represented a host of different conditions with regard to modernity. As we saw in the preceding chapters, some, like Great Britain, Germany, and France, were, along with the United States, among the world leaders in the development of what we call "scientific–industrial society." Others, like Austria-Hungary, Ottoman Turkey, the newly independent Balkan nations, Russia, and even Japan, were at various stages of industrialization, more or less along the lines of the leading powers. In most cases, this latter group had come to this condition somewhat reluctantly, often after violent interactions with the new industrial powers. In terms of political modernity, all of these initial members of what would shortly be known as the Allies and Central powers—with the exception of France—were monarchies, though a number had become modified over the course of the nineteenth century with the addition of constitutions and legislative assemblies. The larger powers were also imperial powers which, collectively, had reduced much of Asia and effectively the entire continent of Africa to the status of colonies. Over the next 4 years, this picture would change so completely that the old order would be dimly glimpsed only through the fog of memory of the diminished numbers who could recall it.

Once the war was on, science and industry made it far more lethal than any previous conflict had ever been; and when it ended, peace turned out to be elusive. Though the old empires of Germany, Austria-Hungary, and Ottoman Turkey were broken up, the new nations that arose from their wreckage emerged with their own sets of problems. Moreover, the new international order embodied by the League of Nations lacked the power to resolve conflicts and enforce its sanctions. Finally, the contradictions inherent in modernity between constitutionalism, imperialism, and emancipation were powerfully brought home to inhabitants of the colonial empires of the victors. For many, it meant using the ideas of nationalism—both ethnolinguistic and constitutional—and those of the new subpattern of communism as tools to achieve autonomy or independence.

Total War. By 1918, large swaths of northern France and Belgium resembled moonscapes from four years of destruction and carnage. One of the unluckiest places was the Belgian city of Ypres, which suffered three battles and was all but completely obliterated by war's end.

1908		1915-1916	1919	1929
Oil Discovered in Middle East (Iran)	1914-1918 World War I	Destruction of Armenians in Ottoman Empire	Versailles Treaty, Founding of League of Nations	Stock Market Crash and Beginning of Great Depression

1911-1912	1917	1917	1922
Revolution in China, Fall of Qing Dynasty	Balfour Declaration Promises Jews a Homeland in Palestine	Bolshevik Revolution	Mussolini's March on Rome

1931	1932-1945	1936-1939	1937	1942
Japanese Annexation of Manchuria	New Deal in United States	Spanish Civil War	Rape of Nanjing	Hitler Implements the Final Solution—Genocide of European Jews

1929-1932	1933	1937-1945	1939-1945
Collectivization of Agriculture in Soviet Union	Hitler Becomes Chancellor in Germany	World War II in China and the Pacific	World War II in Europe, the Mediterranean, and North Africa

A Savage War and a Flawed Peace

Time-honored imperial politics, tempered by the need for a balance of power among the major states, dominated Europe during the century following the Napoleonic Wars. This intersected with the two trends of nineteenth-century modernity we have identified in the last several chapters: the political patterns of constitutional nationalism and ethnolinguistic nationalism and the pattern of industrialization. The rise of the new imperialism in the nineteenth century, itself part of the growth of nationalism and industrialism accompanying modernity, carried a logic of its own that seemed destined to disrupt the ongoing efforts of statesmen to adjust the balance of power to ever-shifting political conditions. Here was the desire for naked conquest for a variety of reasons: markets, raw materials, strategic advantage, and national prestige, to name only the most prominent. For the moment, the victims of these conquests were the peoples of Africa, Asia, and Oceania, though the lesser European powers saw that they could be victims as well. Hence, as nationalism, imperialism, and industrialization moved forward, powers great and small sought alliances for protection and maintenance of the balance of power.

Empires and Nations in the Balkans   The causes of World War I have been endlessly debated from the moment the first shot was fired. Indeed, the role of Germany, rightly or wrongly, was enshrined in the Versailles Treaty ending the war as the famous "war guilt" clause. After decades of consensus and revision, modern scholars have begun to emphasize German aspirations for expansion into Eastern Europe as one of the prime catalysts for its support of Austria against Serbia in 1914. For its part, France had sought at various times *revanche*—revenge—for Germany's annexing of its "amputated provinces" of Alsace and Lorraine in 1870, though this was tempered by the painful awareness of Germany's superior might. In the first decade of the twentieth century, however, the key to the preservation of peace in Europe was seen as maintaining the balance among the three unequal empires that met in the Balkans.

The shrinking Ottoman Empire, beset by continuing demands from ethnic-nationalist minorities for independence, struggled to survive. The expanding Russian Empire, despite having suffered a defeat at the hands of Japan and an abortive revolution in 1904–1905, was rapidly recovering its aggressiveness, if not its military strength. For its part, the opportunistic Habsburg Empire of Austria-Hungary opposed Russian expansionism but also sought to benefit from Ottoman weakness. Germany had largely replaced Great Britain as the protector of the Ottomans and assisted the latter in strengthening their army. Though it had taken Mediterranean territories from the Ottomans, Britain still had a stake in keeping the rest of the Ottoman Empire in existence, as did the other powers, all of whom feared the results of a territorial scramble if the Ottoman Empire collapsed altogether. Hence, as there had been in China during the scramble for concessions of the late 1890s, there was also a rough community of interest aimed at strengthening the Ottoman Empire, whose leaders were themselves seeking to improve their military posture.

One unresolved ethnic-nationalist issue of concern to the three empires was Bosnia-Herzegovina. After the Balkan war of 1878, Austria-Hungary had become the territory's administrator—but not sovereign—as a compromise with the Ottomans, who were unable to keep Serbs, Croats, and Muslims apart. When Russia renewed its support for Serb ethnic nationalism in the Balkans after 1905, Austria-Hungary felt compelled to assume sovereignty of Bosnia-Herzegovina in a protective move in 1908. This in return offered Russia support for its demand for open shipping through the Bosporus. Britain and Germany, however, forced Russia to withdraw this demand. Russia, committed to a policy of pan-Slavism—support for the aspirations of Slavs everywhere—avenged itself by stirring up Serb nationalists. On June 28, 1914, members of a Bosnian Serb nationalist group assassinated the Austrian heir to the throne, Franz Ferdinand, and his wife while they toured the Bosnian city of Sarajevo. This assassination began the tragic slide of the two rival alliances that maintained the balance of power into the cataclysm of World War I. Yet even this occurred only after a month of intense diplomacy and increasing desperation among most of the politicians involved. In the end, each country's perceived military necessities were invoked to trump any diplomatic solution to the crisis.

Total war: A type of warfare in which all the resources of the nation—including all or most of the civilian population—are marshaled for the war effort. As total war became elaborated, all segments of society were increasingly seen as legitimate targets for the combatants.

The Early Course of the War   In contrast with past conflicts, this war was no longer limited and localized but comprehensive from the start: **total war**. In addition, the contingency plans of the combatants' general staffs in many cases relied on precise timing and speedy mobilization of their forces. Here, the most dramatic example was that of Germany. In order to avoid a two-front war, Germany, with its allies Austria-Hungary and the Ottoman Empire (the Central powers), had to defeat France before Russia's massive army was fully mobilized. The German Schlieffen Plan therefore called for a massive assault on northern France through Belgium that would take Paris in 6 weeks, while trapping and isolating the Allied armies aimed at invading Alsace and Lorraine, taken by Germany after the Franco–Prussian War of 1870.

Though the German plan came close to succeeding, it ultimately failed after the desperate French–British victory in the first Battle of the Marne in early September 1914, a more rapid Russian mobilization than expected, and a poor showing of the Austrians against Russia. After several months of seesaw fighting along the lines of the initial German advance into France, the Germans and the French and British dug in. By 1915 the two sides were forced to conduct grinding trench warfare in northeastern France and an inconclusive war in the east. The Germans, with superior firepower and mobility, were able to keep the Russians at bay and inflicted heavy losses on their troops—many of whom marched into battle without weapons, being expected to pick them up off their dead comrades. For its part, the Ottoman Empire suffered a crushing Russian invasion in the Caucasus, prompting it to carry out a wholesale massacre of its Armenian minority, which was alleged to have helped in the invasion. From official Turkish documents published in 2005 it can be concluded that the number of Armenians killed was close to 1 million. This planned

War of Annihilation

"I got to my position and looked over the top. The first thing I saw in the space of a tennis court in front of me was the bodies of 100 dead or severely wounded men lying there in our own wire . . . I sent my runner 200 yards on my right to get into touch with our right company, who should have been close beside me. He came back and reported he could find nothing of them. It subsequently transpired that they never reached the front line as their communication trenches had caught it so much worse than mine, and the communication trench was so full of dead and dying, that they could not get over them. . . . Those three battalions [2,500 men] who went over were practically annihilated. Every man went to his death or got wounded without flinching. Yet in this war, nothing will be heard about it, the papers have glowing accounts of great British success . . . 60 officers went out, lots of whom I knew. I believe 2 got back without being wounded . . ."

—Quoted in Michael Kernan. "Day of Slaughter on the Somme." *Washington Post*, June 27, 1976. From the diary of Captain Reginald Leetham, a British soldier who fought in the Battle of the Somme, July–November 1916. Nearly 60,000 British soldiers were killed in the first day of battle.

massacre, the one large-scale atrocity of the war, still requires a full accounting today and is hotly debated by scholars, lawyers, and politicians.

As the war dragged on, both camps sought to recruit new countries to their sides. Italy, Greece, and Romania entered on the Allied side with the hope of gaining territory from Austria-Hungary and the Ottomans; Bulgaria joined the Central powers in the service of its own territorial ambitions. Japan declared war on Germany in 1914 as part of a previous alliance with Britain but used its occupation of German territories in the Pacific and China as a step toward expanding its own empire. The Allies also recruited volunteers from among their dominions and colonies in considerable numbers, some 800,000 from India alone. Thus, with soldiers from the mostly white dominions of Australia and New Zealand, as well as the African and Asian colonies of Britain and France fighting and dying in the trenches, the war became a true world war. With the token entrance of China in 1917 and the pivotal entrance of the United States that same year the war now involved every major state in the world.

The Turning Point: 1917

By early 1917 the ever-intensifying slaughter took its first toll. In March 1917, tsarist Russia collapsed in the face of horrendous casualties, crippled industry, extensive labor unrest, government ineptitude, and general internal weakness. This February Revolution (actually in March, so called because it took place during February in the old-style Julian calendar still in use in Russia at the time) forced Tsar Nicholas II to abdicate and created a provisional government. The new social-democratic government committed itself to carrying on the war, which now grew even more unpopular and untenable for Russia to manage. The communist Bolshevik Party of Vladimir Lenin (1870–1924), now liberated from persecution by the provisional government, steadily campaigned against continuing the war and in early November (October in the Julian calendar) launched a takeover of the government in the capital of Petrograd—as St. Petersburg had been renamed

Supporting the Empire. The colonies were drawn into the conflicts of their rulers. One million Indian troops, such as the ones shown here, fought with the British during World War I.

at the beginning of the war. Capturing the reins of government, the Bolsheviks began tortuous negotiations with the Germans, which resulted in the disastrous Treaty of Brest-Litovsk in March 1918. Roughly one-third of the Russian Empire's population, territory, and resources were handed over to the Germans in return for Russia's peaceful withdrawal from the conflict. They had now come close to what the Supreme Army Command (*Oberste Heeresleitung*, OHL) had secretly declared as its war goal: the creation of *Lebensraum* (living space) for Germany in the industrialized European part of Russia.

The United States had declared neutrality at the outset of the war, but despite President Woodrow Wilson's plea to Americans to stay "neutral in thought" as well as action, the course of the war had shifted US opinion decidedly toward the Allied side. The German violation of Belgian neutrality in the opening days of the war and extensive German use of the new technology of the submarine swung Americans toward a profound distaste for German actions. The German torpedoing and sinking of the British liner *Lusitania* on May 7, 1915, cost the lives of more than 100 Americans and brought the United States to the brink of war. German guarantees to abandon their policy of "unrestricted" submarine warfare contained the crisis for the time being. Still, the ties of American banks and industries to France and Britain continued to tilt the United States increasingly toward the Allies.

Several key decisions prompted the Germans to risk and ultimately bring on war with the United States. With each side increasingly desperate to gain a decisive advantage over the other and the British naval blockade of Germany wreaking increasing hardships on their economy and populace, the German naval staff calculated that they could starve England into submission with an all-out campaign of submarine warfare. Knowing this would bring the United States into the war, they concluded that they could accomplish their task before the Americans could draft and train a large army. They also felt that their submarines could sink many American troop ships and stifle any US efforts to bolster the Allies. However, they then made a singularly clumsy diplomatic overture to Mexico to join the Central powers if the United States declared war on Germany. The British intercepted this so-called Zimmerman note and gleefully passed it on to the Americans. When Germany announced resumption of unrestricted submarine warfare, Wilson had no choice but to ask Congress to declare war, which it did on April 6, 1917.

The entrance of the United States added the critical resources needed by the Allies to ultimately win the war. More importantly, Wilson's war aims, embodied in his Fourteen Points, sought to transform the conflict from one of failed diplomacy and territorial gain to a war "to make the world safe for democracy." He called for freedom of the seas, the rights of neutral powers, self-determination for all peoples, and peace "without annexations or indemnities." These new causes represented not only American war aims but now were presented as the Allies' war aims as well. For peoples in all the world's empires yearning for independence and self-determination, it appeared, briefly at least, that one side decisively championed their desires.

It was not until early 1918, however, that American troops began to land in France in appreciable numbers. This coincided with the last spring offensive mounted by Germany. Bolstered by the addition of troops from the now peaceful Russian front, the Germans threw everything they had at the Allies and once again came close to seizing Paris. But the new American troops in France gave the Allies the advantage they needed to stop the German effort, and it soon collapsed. By June, more than 1 million Americans had arrived; by September, nearly 2 million; by the end of fighting in November, 4 million more Americans were in various stages of progress to the western front. Faced with these new conditions and reeling from the Allies' September counteroffensive that now threatened to advance into Germany, the Germans agreed to an armistice on November 11, 1918.

The Versailles Peace   As the staggering war toll sank in, the Allies settled down to make peace. About 20 million soldiers and civilians were dead, and 21 million were wounded. Military deaths were 5 million for the Allies and 4 million for the Central powers. Many more millions perished in the world's worst influenza pandemic, abetted by the massive transportation of goods and soldiers at war's end. The settlement, signed at Versailles on June 28, 1919—the fifth anniversary of the assassination of Franz Ferdinand—has been described unflatteringly as a "victor's peace."

In the peace treaty, the German, Austro-Hungarian, and Ottoman Empires were all dismantled and new nation-states were created in their stead. Germany lost its overseas colonies, Alsace-Lorraine, and East Prussia. The Allies declared Germany responsible for the war and condemned it to substantial military restrictions and huge reparation payments. France did not prevail with plans to divide Germany again into its pre-1871 components but succeeded in acquiring temporary custody of the Saar province with its coal reserves and steel factories as a guarantee for the payment of war reparations. For a long time, historians considered the Allied-imposed reparations excessive but more recent research has come to the conclusion that Germany, not destroyed by war, had the industrial-financial capacity to pay. A new supranational **League of Nations** was entrusted with the maintenance of peace. But since one of its clauses required collective military action in case of aggression, the US Senate refused ratification, rejecting this infringement on American sovereignty. Altogether, the Versailles peace was deeply flawed. Instead of binding a Germany that could not be diminished economically into a common western European framework, the Allies actually encouraged it to go it alone by flanking it in the east with small and weak countries that could be dominated in the future (see Map 28.1).

America First: The Beginnings of a Consumer Culture and the Great Depression

The United States emerged from the war as by far the strongest among the Allied democracies. From a debtor country, it had turned into a creditor country; a majority of Americans now lived in nonrural environments; and the war economy shifted relatively easily into a sustained peacetime expansion. Far less hampered by old traditions than its European counterparts, it espoused modernity with a brusque enthusiasm, although its writers and intellectuals were often all too aware of modernity's contradictions.

Modernity Unfolding in the United States   Increased mechanization in industries such as construction materials, automobile assembly lines, and electrical appliance manufacturing spurred the economic expansion. A new dream arose among Americans: to move from countryside to city and to own a house (with running water and sewage), car, refrigerator, radio, and telephone. Once in the city, during the "Roaring Twenties," as the decade came to be called, Americans wanted

League of Nations:
An international body ultimately numbering 58 states created as part of the Versailles Treaty and functioning between 1919 and 1946 that sought to ensure world peace by curbing secret diplomacy, settling international disputes through negotiation, supervising colonial dependencies under a mandate system, and punishing aggressor nations through the practice of "collective security."

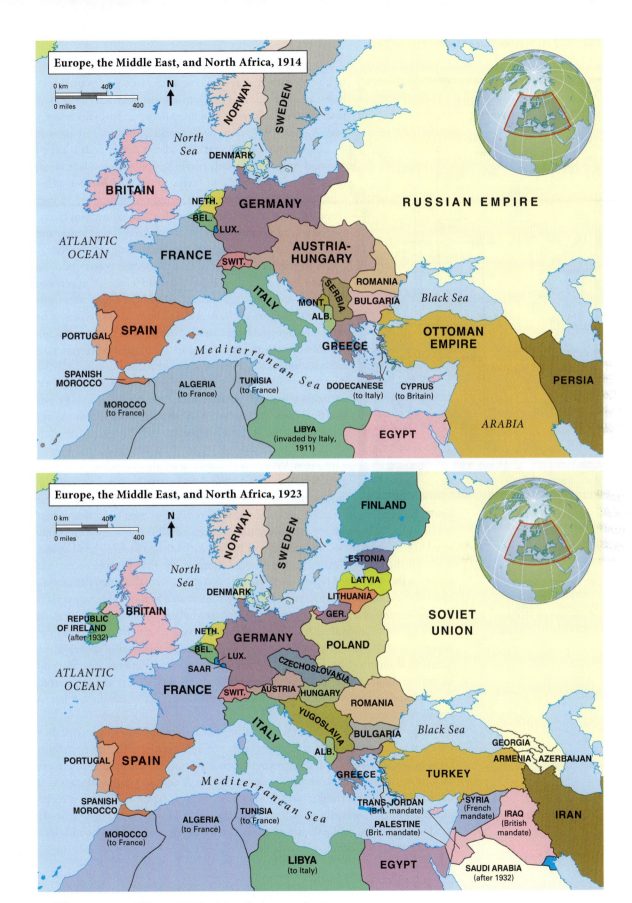

Europe, the Middle East, and North Africa, 1914

0 km 400
0 miles 400

N

NORWAY
SWEDEN
North Sea
DENMARK
BRITAIN
NETH.
BEL.
LUX.
GERMANY
ATLANTIC OCEAN
FRANCE
SWIT.
AUSTRIA-HUNGARY
ITALY
MONT.
SERBIA
ALB.
ROMANIA
BULGARIA
Black Sea
GREECE
RUSSIAN EMPIRE
OTTOMAN EMPIRE
PORTUGAL
SPAIN
Mediterranean Sea
DODECANESE (to Italy)
CYPRUS (to Britain)
PERSIA
SPANISH MOROCCO
ALGERIA (to France)
TUNISIA (to France)
MOROCCO (to France)
LIBYA (invaded by Italy, 1911)
EGYPT
ARABIA

Europe, the Middle East, and North Africa, 1923

0 km 400
0 miles 400

N

NORWAY
SWEDEN
FINLAND
North Sea
DENMARK
ESTONIA
LATVIA
LITHUANIA
BRITAIN
REPUBLIC OF IRELAND (after 1932)
NETH.
BEL.
LUX.
SAAR
GER.
GERMANY
POLAND
SOVIET UNION
ATLANTIC OCEAN
FRANCE
SWIT.
AUSTRIA
CZECHOSLOVAKIA
HUNGARY
ROMANIA
ITALY
YUGOSLAVIA
ALB.
BULGARIA
Black Sea
GEORGIA
ARMENIA
AZERBAIJAN
PORTUGAL
SPAIN
Mediterranean Sea
GREECE
TURKEY
TRANS-JORDAN (Brit. mandate)
SYRIA (French mandate)
IRAQ (British mandate)
IRAN
SPANISH MOROCCO
ALGERIA (to France)
TUNISIA (to France)
PALESTINE (Brit. mandate)
MOROCCO (to France)
LIBYA (to Italy)
EGYPT
SAUDI ARABIA (after 1932)

MAP **28.1** Europe, the Middle East, and North America in 1914 and 1923.

A Vision of American Modernity. This detail from a ca. 1930 Gulf Gasoline "Florida Info Map" vividly captures the American pattern of modernity—miles of roads and highways stretching in all directions, ample leisure opportunities, and a natural environment where the sun always shines.

to be entertained. A remarkable efflorescence of popular culture accompanied the rising urban prosperity. City and small-town dwellers alike were caught up in the mania of the movies, which, after 1927, came with sound. Americans frequented ballrooms to experiment with a large variety of dance steps and to listen to bands playing popular tunes. Jazz music with a large variety of styles found avid listeners. One could now listen to recorded sound on convenient 78-rpm records played on gramophones. The film industry of Hollywood and a recording industry came into being, churning out "hit" after "hit" as their popular products came to be called.

As far-reaching as both of these were, the growth of radio went one step further. From a primitive system of sending Morse-code messages via electrical "spark–gap" transmissions at the turn of the century, radio received vacuum tube amplification and by the time of the war was capable of sending sound and voice messages. In 1919, the first commercial radio station in the United States began broadcasting; by 1930, the number of radios was in the tens of millions. Moreover, experimental work on an even more advanced technology was also under way during the 1920s, though its impact would not come for nearly 30 years: television.

The New Woman   The Nineteenth Amendment of 1920 gave American women the right to vote, enormously expanding the promise of constitutional nationalism by half the population. In addition to winning political rights, American women heightened their social profile. Many colleges and universities went co-ed, although women often majored in education to become teachers, or home economics to become good housewives for the husbands they met at school. Alternatively, they became secretaries skilled in shorthand and typing or nurses in hospitals. Indeed, the typewriter, developed in the latter nineteenth century, directly contributed to the shift from employing mostly men as secretaries to making it an overwhelmingly female profession. Its ease of operation and speed of copying and reproduction (through the use of carbon paper) was ideally suited to what were perceived to be "women's skills" and abilities. Similarly, women swiftly dominated the new occupations of telephone operator and switchboard operator as the new century advanced. By the 1920s it was rare indeed if one picked up the telephone to make a call in the United States and did not hear a female voice ask, "Number please?"

For people of color, however, the situation was far different. Black women, if they were not agricultural laborers, rarely were able to become more than domestic servants or laundry workers in the growing urban economy. In larger segregated areas with more diversified economies, however, African American women often found similar kinds of opportunities as white women, though far more limited in scope and availability. Hence, although emancipation was real for white women, it clearly remained gendered, while the situation for black women continued to be additionally hampered by racism.

Nevertheless, women on the whole became consumers and participants in pop culture in their own right. The new female ideal—or troubling stereotype, depending on your perspective—for many young women was the "flapper." Wearing lipstick and other cosmetics (which were no longer considered signs of being "of ill repute"), having her hair "bobbed" under her cloche hat, wearing dresses above the knee, and throwing away her corset, she drank and smoked cigarettes—and might even drive her own car. She might go to jazz clubs and indulge in such daring dances as the Charleston or the Black Bottom. Sex was also becoming something that she might openly talk about in public, and sexual satisfaction was no longer an emotion to be suppressed. One can still see this contemporary vision of the flapper and her successors in the cartoon series *Betty Boop* from the early 1930s. Liberal social values, as they were called, including premarital sex, divorce, and tolerance for homosexuality, made inroads, although mostly among the relatively small number of white-collar, educated people in the cities.

Inevitably, there was also a conservative backlash, expressing itself most directly in the ratification of the Eighteenth Amendment. From 1920 to 1933, the commercial production of alcohol was prohibited in the United States, primarily for the purpose of reducing public drunkenness among the largely immigrant working classes. Since it did not outlaw noncommercial home brewing or bars, however, widespread production of "moonshine," "bathtub gin" and other "bootleg liquor" and discreet sale of liquor in "speakeasies" (bars where one spoke softly so as not to draw attention) made Prohibition the subject of ridicule and impossible to enforce effectively. The rise of organized crime in America was greatly abetted by its domination of the illegal alcohol industry in the 1920s and 1930s.

High Artistic Creativity   American intellectuals, writers, and artists viewed consumer and pop culture modernity with mixed feelings. On the one hand, they hailed what they viewed as the progress of liberal values. But, on the other hand, they were often uneasy about what they perceived as an increasing superficiality and materialism in modernity, furthered by ads, fashions, and fads. Prior to World War I, Europeans continued to consider themselves culturally superior, as reflected in a quip from Oscar Wilde's play *A Woman of No Importance*, where one character remarks that when good Americans die they go to Paris and another character replies that when bad Americans die they go to America. But after World War I, the ambiguities of modernity engendered a veritable explosion of creativity in American culture.

The shattered illusions of the pre–world war era and search for a new beginning in modernity fueled much of this creativity. An entire cohort of artists and intellectuals viewed themselves as belonging to a "lost generation," a term referring to the generation that had lost its best years of life, or even life altogether, to a senseless world war. Such figures as Gertrude Stein (1874–1946), a writer and poet who coined the term, and Wallace Stevens (1879–1955), Sinclair Lewis (1885–1951), Ezra Pound (1885–1972), T. S. Eliot (1888–1965), Eugene O'Neill (1888–1953), F. Scott Fitzgerald (1896–1940), Thornton Wilder (1897–1975), William Faulkner (1897–1962), and Ernest Hemingway (1899–1961)—five among them recipients of the Nobel Prize in Literature—defined the new American style of "modernism" and are still widely read and taught today. For African Americans, a new cultural touchstone was the Harlem Renaissance, featuring the leading innovators in jazz and the writers Claude McKay (1889–1948), Langston Hughes (1902–1967), James Weldon Johnson (1871–1938), and Zora Neale Hurston (1891–1960).

Few later authors plumbed modernity with the breadth of education as these "modernists" did, analyzing its contradictions, exposing its follies, articulating its inner emotional tensions in a "stream of consciousness," or offering countermodels of spirituality, naturalness, Greek classicism, or Chinese monism. Not only did the United States give mass culture to the world; it also provided many of the literary tools to grapple with modernity and attempt to understand it, either by loathing it or by living with it critically.

Business and Labor   Just as much energy characterized American business. Business tycoons and probusiness politicians were integral parts of the Roaring Twenties. Presidents Harding, Coolidge, and Hoover along with the Congress exercised a minimum of political control, illustrated by the slogan "Less government in business and more business in government." President Calvin Coolidge (in office 1923–1929), legendary as "Silent Cal" for his taciturn manner—when the famous wit Dorothy Parker (1893-1967) told him of a bet she had made that she could make him say more than two words, his reply was "You lose"—expressed the spirit of the day with characteristic succinctness: "The business of America is business."

While business boomed, trade and industrial unions stagnated. The American Federation of Labor (AFL), founded in 1886, was the largest trade union pushing for improved labor conditions. But, in contrast to European labor unions, it was always hampered by the problem that its members were unskilled workers of many ethnic, linguistic, and religious backgrounds and, therefore, difficult to organize. Business easily squashed widespread strikes for the right to unionize in 1919. An anti-immigration hysteria followed, with laws that cut immigration by half. The hysteria, mixed with anticommunism, climaxed in 1927 with the trial of Ferdinando

A Klan Lynching. Outside the South, Indiana was the state that experienced the greatest surge in Klan activities in the period immediately after World War I. In 1925, the governor and half the state assembly were Klansmen and about 30 percent of the state's white population were members. In this photo from August 1930, a crowd gathers to gawk at Tom Shipp and Abram Smith, two African American men who were lynched by a mob for allegedly committing robbery and rape.

Nicola Sacco and Bartolomeo Vanzetti, two Italian anarchist immigrants who were convicted and executed for murder on contradictory evidence.

The Backlash   The antiforeigner and anticommunist hysteria was part of a larger unease with modernism. Fundamentalist religion, intolerance toward Catholics and Jews, and fear and violence directed at African Americans rose visibly. The revival of the Ku Klux Klan was at the center of repeated waves of lynchings in the South and attempts to control the local politics of a number of states, most prominently Indiana. The Klan remained a powerful force in the South and Midwest until World War II.

The most startling offenses against the modern principles of liberty and equality, however, came from ideologues wrapping themselves in the mantle of modern science. Researchers at the leading private universities lent respectability to the pseudoscience of **eugenics**, conceptualizing an ideal of a "Nordic" race and searching for ways to produce more athletic, blond, and blue-eyed Americans. Foundations such as the Carnegie Endowment and businessmen such as Henry Ford financed research on how to prevent the reproduction of genetically "inferior" races. California and other states passed laws that allowed for the sterilization of nearly 10,000 patients—mostly women (black and white)—in state mental hospitals, and the Supreme Court in 1927 upheld these laws. Ironically, some of the practices that would inspire Hitler and the Nazis were already quietly in place during the 1920s in the United States and actually seen by many as progressive.

Eugenics: The supposed study of hereditary breeding of better human beings by genetic control. Beginning in the 1920s, a well-financed social movement in the US succeeded in sterilizing thousands of women considered to be mentally and/or racially inferior.

The Great Depression   The Roaring Twenties came to a screeching halt in 1929, when saturation of the market for consumer goods behind high tariff walls during the later 1920s led to falling profit rates. Many of the wealthy had begun to shift their money from investments in manufacturing to speculation on the stock market. In addition, stocks began to be seen as a viable outlet for ordinary investors due to widespread margin borrowing with little money down. As long as the market boomed, investors made money; but if stocks went down, the margin calls went out, and investors could be wiped out. By the late 1920s, a general slowdown in production shifted attention to unsustainable debt levels. Farmers were particularly deep in debt, having borrowed to mechanize while speculating wrongly on a continuation of high prices for commodities. In October 1929, the speculators panicked, selling their stock for pennies on the dollar. The panic rippled through both the finance and manufacturing sectors until it burst into a full-blown cascade. As banks began calling in loans at home and abroad, the panic swiftly became a worldwide crisis: the Great Depression of 1929–1933. Harrowing scenes of unemployment and poverty put the American system of capitalist democratic modernity to a severe test.

Americans largely blamed their probusiness president, Herbert Hoover (in office 1929–1933), for failing to manage the crisis and in 1932 elected Franklin D. Roosevelt (in office 1933–1945). Hoover's approach had been one that previous administrations had turned to in times of economic crisis: cut government spending, raise tariffs to protect US industries, and let market forces correct themselves. But such measures seemed only to make things worse, while the Smoot-Hawley Tariff of 1930—with the highest tariff rates in American history—encouraged retaliatory tariffs in other countries and discouraged world commerce, thus contributing to a world-wide economic collapse. Under Roosevelt's prodding, Congress immediately enacted what he called the "New Deal," in which the government engaged in deficit spending to enact measures designed to help the unemployed and revive business and agriculture. Among the most ambitious of these were the National Recovery Act (1933) aimed at fostering competition, safeguarding the rights of labor, and discouraging monopoly practices; and the Agricultural Adjustment Act (1933), which began the use of subsidies to stabilize the prices of farm commodities Other notable programs included the Civilian Conservation Corps (CCC) in 1933, which enlisted large numbers of the unemployed to conduct improvements in the country's national parks and nature preserves; and the Works Progress Administration (WPA) in 1935, which utilized the talents of the nation's creative community by subsidizing the arts and literature.

One showpiece of the New Deal was the Tennessee Valley Authority, a government-owned corporation for the economic development of large parts of the southeastern United States particularly hard hit by the Depression. In addition, a social safety net was created for the first time, with unemployment benefits and the Social Security Act. Finally, a Securities and Exchange Commission (SEC) was created in 1934 to supervise and enforce regulations governing the stock market in order to prevent a number of the practices that had led to the collapse of 1929.

To finance the New Deal, Roosevelt took the United States off the gold standard, a monetary system that linked currencies to the value of gold, and went deep into deficit spending. In 1937, however, a Congress frightened by the deficit slackened efforts to reduce unemployment, while the Supreme Court declared several of the new programs unconstitutional. The result was a new slump, from which the economy finally recovered only with America's entry into World War II.

Great Britain and France: Slow Recovery and Troubled Empires

While the impact of World War I on the United States was relatively slight, Britain and France suffered severely (see Map 28.2). A lack of finances hampered the recovery, as did the enormous debt both countries contracted during the war. Conservative politicians relinquished the state capitalism of the war period and returned to politics favorable to private investors, without, however, allowing for the same uncontrolled speculations as in the United States. Although socialist politicians gained in importance, they did not succeed in improving working-class conditions or the safety net. Britain benefited from the discovery of oil in its mandates in the Middle East, and the demands of the League of Nations mandate system, in which the colonies were to be prepared for future independence, were not pursued vigorously by either France or Britain.

Weak British Recovery   As the economy shifted from state control during the war back to free enterprise, industry was still in a leading role; but Britain was also heavily dependent on world trade, carried by its merchant fleet. Unfortunately for Britain, world trade declined dramatically after the war. In addition, the country owed a war debt of $4.3 billion to the United States for war materiel, which the United States insisted on receiving back (relenting only during the Depression). Since much of Britain's ability to repay these debts rested upon Germany's ability to pay its reparations, the entire European economic system remained problematic throughout the 1920s.

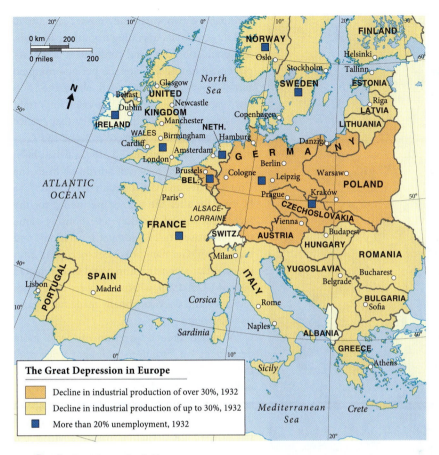

MAP **28.2** **The Great Depression in Europe.**

With the restructuring of Germany's debts under the Dawes Plan in 1924, some stability finally came to the international capital markets. Still, close to half of the annual British budgets in the interwar period went into paying off the war debt. In this situation, industrial investments were low and unemployment was high, dipping below 10 percent of the workforce only once during the 1920s. In addition, business lowered wages, causing labor to respond with a massive general strike in 1926. The strike collapsed after only 9 days, but business, without capital to make industry competitive again, did not benefit either. The British economy remained stagnant.

The dominant conservatives in the government could not bring themselves in the 1930s to accept deficit spending. At a minimum, however, they went off the gold standard and devalued the currency to make exports competitive again. World trade, of course, had declined; but by lowering tariffs within the empire, Britain created the equivalent of the **autarky** that Nazi Germany and militaristic Japan were dreaming of with their planned conquests. A semblance of prosperity returned to the country in the 1930s.

Autarky: The maintenance of a self-supporting state economic system.

France: Moderate Recovery
Together with Russia, France suffered devastating human losses and destruction of property during the war. For every 10 men of

Down and Out in Wales. The 1930s' prosperity was largely limited to southern England. Most of the rest of the British Isles, such as this unemployed miner in Wales, who totters from either drink or depression and is consoled by his two children, were largely left out. George Orwell (1903–1950) published his investigations of British poverty in *The Road to Wigan Pier* (1937), a widely read essay in which he castigated the Conservatives for their lack of a job-creating policy. A strong advocate for social democracy, he became well known after World War II for his opposition to antidemocratic regimes, expressed in his novels *Animal Farm* (1945) and *Nineteen Eighty-Four* (1949).

working age, two were dead, one was an invalid, and three were recuperating from their wounds. The population drop and consequent lack of replacement during the interwar period prompted some French observers to talk about the "hollow years." Alsace-Lorraine, the most important industrial region and the territory that France desperately wanted to recover from the Germans, was now a wasteland. The war had been fought with war materiel borrowed from the United States and Great Britain ($5 billion), to be paid for after the war. Some money for the reconstruction of industry and housing came from increased taxes, German reparations, and taxes from German provinces occupied after the war. But reconstruction could be completed only in 1926–1929, when taxes were once more increased and Germany finally made full reparation payments.

Although French governments were more dependent on coalitions among parties and, therefore, less stable, labor was more often than not represented in the governments. France did not suffer a traumatic general strike like England did, and even though it also returned to the gold standard (1928–1936), it wisely avoided the prewar parity, thereby making the low wages for its workers a bit more bearable. Since it had to reconstruct so much from the ground up, France modernized more successfully in many ways than Britain in the interwar period.

Thanks to its successful reconstruction, France weathered the Depression until 1931. Even then, conservative politicians found the idea of deficit spending as a way to get out of the Depression too counterintuitive. Instead, like the Hoover administration in America, they slashed government spending and refused to devalue the currency. Unrest in the population and rapidly changing governments were the consequences which, in 1933–1934, made supremacist-nationalism an attractive model, especially for business, which was afraid of labor strife. When fascist–communist street fighting broke out in Paris, the Communist Party initiated the formation of a Popular Front coalition with the Socialist Party and others (1936–1938). Although this coalition prevented a further slide into supremacist nationalism, it was too short-lived to allow for the centrist middle-class core to broaden, with disastrous consequences for France's ability to resist Hitler in World War II.

"The Crazy Years"   American pop culture, with its music, dance, movies, and fashions, swept both Britain and France during the 1920s. As in the United States, the ambiguities of modernity also provoked a burst of artistic creativity. The *années folles* ("crazy years") produced in Britain the Bloomsbury Group (after a district in London), a loose collection of modernist writers, such as Virginia Woolf (1882–1941) and E. M. Forster (1879–1970), intellectuals, philosophers, and the economist John Maynard Keynes (1883–1946). Woolf is remembered for her interests in the literary tool of inner monologue, parallel to Faulkner. In addition, the Irishman James Joyce (1882–1941) and D. H. Lawrence (1885–1930) left their permanent imprint on modernity. Joyce employed the stream-of-consciousness approach with extreme formal variations and precision of description. Lawrence became notorious among conservatives for his modernist interests in human intimacy while endearing himself to them with his doubts about the blessings of democracy. A majority of these modernists, reflective of the contradictions of modernity, practiced liberal ethics and expressed socialist leanings.

In France, the 1920s produced *surrealism*, an artistic movement that took its inspiration from the theory of the subconscious popularized by the contemporary Austrian psychiatrist Sigmund Freud. Prominent surrealist painters in Paris were the German Max Ernst (1891–1976) and the Spanish Salvador Dalí (1904–1989). Surrealist poets were André Breton (1896–1966) and Louis Aragon (1897–1982). Ernst famously declared himself dead in 1914 and resuscitated in 1918, a declaration reminiscent of Gertrude Stein's

Surrealism. Surrealist painters allowed their Freudian subconscious to flow into their creations. (*a*) Marcel Duchamp, *Fresh Window* (1920). (*b*) Max Ernst, *Two Children Are Threatened by a Nightingale* (1924). (*c*) Salvador Dalí, *Ghost of Two Automobiles* (1929).

term the "lost generation." Both followed Freud's assertion that the unconscious dominates the artist's creativity: Dreams and myths are stronger influences than reality. Many members, coming originally from the earlier movement of Dadaism in Zurich, also celebrated accident and coincidence as elements in their work, especially in poetry. *An Andalusian Dog* (*Un chien andalou*, 1929) by the Spanish director Luis Buñuel (1900–1983) was a stunning short movie, a visual companion to the surrealist game of "exquisite corpse," the sequential utterance of sentences in free association. In the view of surrealists, the Freudian subconscious typically produced spontaneous, uncontrolled creations. With their playful and often ironic stances, often disdainful of the modernists' adherence to "rational" form, the surrealists anticipated postmodernism, which dominated the arts and humanities during the last quarter of the century.

Colonies and Mandates   The carefree consumer modernity in France and Britain during the 1920s contrasted sharply with the harsh reality of sustaining expensive colonial empires covering much of the world's land mass. After World War I, the British Empire grew by 2 million square miles to 14 million, or one-quarter of the earth's surface, adding 13 million to its 458 million subjects, or one-quarter of the world population. The French Empire at the same time measured 5 million square miles, with a population of 113 million. Although the wisdom of maintaining empires was widely debated in the interwar period, in view of increased subsidies that had to be given many of the colonies, conservatives held fast to the prestige that square mileage was presumed to bestow on their holders. Defense of these far-flung empires, interpreted as the "strategic interest" of the colonial powers, dominated the policies of Britain and France toward their dependencies and mandates during the interwar period (see Map 28.3).

The most important area strategically for both the British and the French after World War I was the Middle East. Under the postwar peace terms, the British and

MAP **28.3** European Empires, 1936.

French had received the Arab provinces of the former Ottoman Empire (other than Egypt and Sudan, acquired in 1881) as *mandates*—that is, as territories to be prepared for independence. Since a British geologist had in 1908 discovered oil in southwestern Iran, however, Britain and France put a high premium on their new Middle Eastern imperial possessions. Neither was in a hurry to guide its mandates to independent nationhood.

Twice-Promised Lands As would be expected, Arab leaders were strongly opposed to the British and French mandates. Nationalism was on the rise, ironically encouraged by the British during the war as they were searching for regional allies against the Ottomans. Their agent, T. E. Lawrence (1888–1935), the famous "Lawrence of Arabia," fluent in Arabic and Islamic customs, helped the members of a prominent family, the Hashemites from Mecca in western Arabia, to assume leadership of the Arabs for a promised national kingdom in Syria and Palestine in the so-called McMahon–Sharif Hussein correspondence of 1915–1916.

Since the British, to rally support among Jews in Britain as well as Germany, Poland, and Russia, also promised the Jews a "national home" in Palestine in the Balfour Declaration of 1917, Arab nationalism was stymied even before it could unfold. The French ended a short-lived Arab-declared kingdom in 1920 in Damascus, and the British moved the Hashemites into their mandates of Iraq and Transjordan in 1921, in accordance with the Sykes–Picot agreement (1916) concerning the imperial division of the Middle East between the Allies. As Iraq was divided by majority Shiites and minority Sunnis, the British inaugurated a policy of divide and rule in their Middle Eastern mandates, while dangling the prospect of eventual independence in front of their populations.

In Palestine, the contradiction between the promises to Arabs and Jews during the war forced Britain to build an expensive direct administration under a high commissioner. In 1920, Palestine was inhabited by nearly 670,000 Arabs and 65,000 Jews. Many religious Jews had arrived as refugees from anti-Semitic riots or pogroms in Russia in the early 1880s and 1890s and the difficult postwar years in eastern Europe. When the Austrian Jewish journalist Theodor Herzl (1860–1904) made ethnic nationalism the ideology of secular Jews, early pioneers of **Zionism**, as secular Jewish nationalism was called, began to arrive as well. A Jewish National Fund collected money from Jews worldwide to buy land from willing Palestinian absentee landlords residing in Beirut and Jerusalem. As a consequence, Jewish settlers evicted the landlords' Palestinian tenant farmers. These evictions were the root cause of two Palestinian–Arab nationalist uprisings, in 1929 and 1936–1939, for which the British had no real answer except force and belated efforts in 1939 to limit Jewish immigration.

> **The Balfour Declaration**
>
> Foreign Office
> November 2nd, 1917
>
> Dear Lord Rothschild:
>
> I have much pleasure in conveying to you, on behalf of His Majesty's Government, the following declaration of sympathy with Jewish Zionist aspirations which has been submitted to, and approved by, the Cabinet:
>
> His Majesty's Government view with favor the establishment in Palestine of a national home for the Jewish people, and will use their best endeavors to facilitate the achievement of this object, it being clearly understood that nothing shall be done which may prejudice the civil and religious rights of existing non-Jewish communities in Palestine, or the rights and political status enjoyed by Jews in any other country.
>
> I should be grateful if you would bring this declaration to the knowledge of the Zionist Federation.
>
> Yours,
> Arthur James Balfour
>
> —*The Times* (London), November 9, 1917. Arthur James Balfour was the British foreign secretary; Lionel Walter de Rothschild (1868–1937) was the leader of the Jewish community in Britain.

Zionism: The belief, based on the writings of Theodor Herzl, that European Jews—and by extension all Jews everywhere—were entitled to a national homeland corresponding to the territory of Biblical Israel. It grew into a form of ethnolinguistic-religious nationalism and ultimately led to the formation of the state of Israel in 1948.

Arab–Jewish Violence. British police step in to separate Palestinians and Jewish immigrants fighting each other in November 1933 in Jaffa. Continued unrest led to the Palestinian Arab Revolt of 1936–1939, a nationalist uprising confined initially to urban areas and later spreading to the countryside. The British authorities suppressed the revolt brutally, by most estimates killing perhaps as many as 5,000 Arab Palestinians. Jews aided the British through self-defense forces, both the official Haganah and the clandestine Irgun. In 1939 the British issued a white paper that deplored the hostilities between the two national communities and restricted Jewish immigration.

Egypt and Turkey After 1882, the Suez Canal acquired vital importance for the British in India and relinquishing it was unthinkable. They rejected a demand in 1919 by a delegation of Egyptian nationalists for independence out of hand and exiled its leader, Saad Zaghlul (ca. 1859–1927). After deadly riots and strikes, the British relented and invited Zaghlul to the peace negotiations in Paris. But the independence the British granted in 1923 was of modest proportions: Both military defense and control of the Suez Canal were withheld from Egypt. A year later, Zaghlul and the Wafd Party won the first independent elections with 90 percent of the vote. The ruling class, as in Iraq, was composed of landlords and urban professionals and, with few exceptions, was uninterested in industrial development. Thus, at the onset of World War II, Egypt was still entirely dependent on agricultural production and exports, though its strategic position was absolutely vital to the British Empire.

The severe punishment meted out to the Ottoman Empire by the Allies provoked the rise of local grassroots resistance groups in Anatolia. These groups merged under the leadership of General Mustafa Kemal "Atatürk" ("Father of the Turks," 1881–1938) into a national liberation movement, driving out the Greeks from western Anatolia, occupying one-half of Armenia (the other half was taken by the new Soviet Union), and ending the Ottoman sultanate (1921–1923) altogether. Atatürk, son of an Ottoman customs official in Salonika, was among the few militarily successful officers in World War I, most notably in his defense of Gallipoli against the British. Atatürk was the driving force behind the creation of a modern, secular Turkey that was able to stand up against the European powers.

Although he was authoritarian, Atatürk saw to it that the new Turkish parliament remained open to pluralism. Parliament adopted the French model of *laicism* (separation of state and religion), European family law, the Latin alphabet, the Western calendar, metric weights and measures, modern clothing, and women's suffrage. During the Depression, Atatürk's economic advisors launched *étatism*, the Turkish version of deficit spending. State capitalism, rather than private domestic or foreign capital, provided for the construction of steel and consumer good factories, including textile plants. Both modernism and étatism showed only modest successes by 1939, and the rural masses in Anatolia remained mired in small-scale self-sufficiency farming and wedded to religious tradition. But the foundation was laid in Turkey not only for a Westernized ruling class but also for a much larger urbanized middle class.

Indian Demands for Independence

The compromises negotiated during the Versailles Peace Conference, as we have seen, had a profound effect on the colonial world. Nowhere was this truer than in India. In April 1919, frustrated by a British crackdown on political protest, a large crowd gathered in a walled square in the Sikhs' sacred city of Amritsar. The British responded with a wholesale slaughter of the assembled men, women, and children by an elite unit of Gurkha troops. As the international furor over this "Amritsar Massacre" raged, the British, giving in to the inevitable, reformed the Indian Legislative Assembly by enlarging the portion of elected members to nearly three-quarters and the property-based franchise to 5 million, out of a population of 250 million. The Indian National Congress was infuriated by this minimal improvement and called for full self-rule (Hindi **swaraj**), urging nonviolent noncooperation, which, among other measures, called for a refusal to pay the land tax, for a boycott of British goods, and for people to spin and weave textiles at home.

Inevitably, civil disturbances accompanied the congress' push for self-rule. Mohandas Gandhi (1869–1948), a trained lawyer and the most prominent advocate of nonviolence, suspended the push in 1921. The leaders—lawyers, doctors, journalists, and teachers—exited the cities and, with the help of a large influx of party workers, scoured the countryside preaching renunciation. It was during the 1920s and 1930s that the National Congress transformed itself from a small Westernized elite into a broad urban as well as rural mass party.

In Britain, the Labour Party attained a majority of seats in Parliament for the first time in 1929. The Labour government explored the possibility of changing India to dominion status, but there was strong opposition from the other parties. When Labour could not deliver, Gandhi responded with the demand for complete independence and, on March 12, 1930, embarked on his famous 24-day Salt March to the sea in order for his followers to pan their own salt, which the government refused to free from taxation. Crowds in other places also marched to the sea. Disturbances accompanied the marches, and in a massive crackdown, with 100,000 arrests, the government succeeded in repressing the National Congress.

Nevertheless, after lengthy discussions in three roundtables during the following years—accompanied by much unrest, many jailings (including that of Gandhi), and a rising split with unsupportive Muslims—the British government in 1935 passed the Government of India Act, which devolved all political functions except defense

Secularizing Turkey. Atatürk was a committed educational reformer who sought to create a "public culture," and he was advised by the famous American philosopher of education, John Dewey (1859–1952). Here, in 1928, dressed in a Western-style suit and necktie he gives a lesson on the new Turkish alphabet, a variant of the Latin alphabet, whose use was mandated throughout the Republic.

Swaraj: Literally, "self-rule" (*swa-raj*). Gandhi interpreted this term as meaning "direct democracy" while the Congress Party identified it with complete independence from Great Britain.

Gandhi Leading the Salt March.
Perhaps the most famous act of civil disobedience in Gandhi's career was the Salt March in 1930 to protest the British salt monopoly in India. It was a perfect embodiment of Gandhi's belief in nonviolent civil disobedience, which he called *satyagraha*, "soul-" or "truth-force." Though it failed to win major concessions from the British, it focused worldwide attention on the Indian independence movement.

and foreign affairs to India. The members of the National Congress were unhappy, however, because of the decentralized structure of the reformed Indian government and particularly because the act recognized the Muslim League of Muhammad Ali Jinnah (1876–1948), not the congress, as the representative of the Muslims. The British viceroy further inflamed matters in 1939 when he declared India in support of the British World War II effort, without even asking the congress. As in Egypt and Iraq, with their similar forms of "independence," there was a profound reluctance by the Western colonial powers to relinquish colonialism. The legacy of this unwillingness would haunt the capitalist democracies well into the later twentieth century.

Latin America: Independent Democracies and Authoritarian Regimes

Like Britain and France, Latin America remained faithful to its constitutional-nationalist heritage throughout the nineteenth century, though with a preference for strong authoritarian rule. In addition, a pattern of narrow elite rule had evolved in which large estate owners controlled the elections and politics of their countries and, through the military, kept rural black and indigenous Amerindian peoples, as well as the mixed urban populations, in check. Politicians in some countries realized the voting potential of the urban populations after World War I and pursued a new type of autocratic politics, called "populism," in conjunction with more or less extensive industrialization programs. Estate owner politics and populism, together with industrialization programs, characterized Latin America during the later interwar period.

Postwar Recovery   At the beginning of the 1900s, Mexico had enjoyed a long period of political stability and economic growth. It had a relatively diversified array of mineral and agricultural export commodities and began to exploit its mineral wealth in the early 1900s to set up an iron and steel industry. But no change had taken place in agriculture, where the traditional oligarchy of rich ranching and plantation landowners continued to keep wages low. Thanks to American investments, railroad construction had progressed but more to support mining interests than agriculture as there was no desire to improve the mobility of either the landless workers on landlord properties or the indigenous Native American population engaged in subsistence farming.

Latin America During the Depression   In Mexico, a rapid urbanization process, begun in the late 1800s, continued during the interwar period. Immigration from overseas, mostly southern and eastern Europe, as well as rural–urban migration fueled this process. In 1929 the newly created Institutional Revolutionary Party (Partido Revolucionario Institucional, PRI) brought the revolution of 1910–1917 to an end. A sufficiently strong government was in place again to complete land distribution to poor farmers, expand education, and begin social legislation. The PRI weathered the Depression with some difficulty, but thanks to increased state control of economic investments, it was able to maintain its footing until European and east Asian war preparations increased demand for commodities again.

Like Mexico, the countries with the largest internal markets, such as Argentina and Brazil, rode out the Depression more successfully than others. Nevertheless, overall the impact was substantial, with a reduction of commodity exports by over 50 percent (see Map 28.4). Luckily, the countries which were unable to pay back their foreign loans no longer had to fear gunboats and debt commissions but could make more equitable arrangements. Still, the Depression resulted in urban unrest, especially in countries with newly expanded mines or oil wells, such as Chile, Peru, and Venezuela, or expanded administrative bureaucracies, as in Brazil. At no time except the period of independence were there more coups, attempted coups, and uprisings than during 1930–1933.

Thereafter, the political situation remained unstable, except for Argentina and Uruguay under a tenuous constitutionalism. But an important shift away from landed oligarchies began to appear in the ruling classes. Millions of people now lived in urban environments, although in the absence of sizeable import-substitution industries, they did not have the clearly delineated social classes of workers and the nonindustrial lower classes that could be organized by communists, socialists, fascists, and militarists. Instead, a new generation of military officers, with urban backgrounds and no longer tied to the traditional oligarchy, appeared. They offered populist authoritarian programs that mixed elements from the prevailing European ideologies.

Decline in Commodity Exports Worldwide, 1929–1933

Decline in exports of primary goods by:

- Over 80%
- 70%–80%
- 60%–70%
- 50%–60%
- 30%–50%

MAP **28.4** Decline in Commodity Exports Worldwide, 1929–1933.

New Variations on Modernity I: The Soviet Union and Communism

After capitalist democracy, communism was the second pattern of modernity that arose out of the ashes of World War I. Following their communist coup in November 1917, the Bolsheviks under Lenin overcame a debilitating civil war and established the Union of Soviet Socialist Republics. Lenin's successor, Joseph Stalin (1879–1953), built the Communist Party into an all-powerful apparatus that violently shifted resources from agriculture into industry and dealt ruthlessly with opposition to its policies. By World War II, Stalin's brutal policies had lifted the Soviet Union into the ranks of the industrialized powers.

The Communist Party and Regime in the Soviet Union

As we saw in Chapter 23, Karl Marx (1818–1883), the leading ideologue of communism—which he also referred to as "scientific socialism" or simply "socialism"—believed that capitalist democracy would ultimately be overthrown by an ever-expanding working class—the **proletariat**. For this to happen, however, countries had to be in an advanced stage of industrialization. He did not think that the underdeveloped Russian Empire, with its large majority of peasants, would be ready for a communist revolution for a long time to come. It was the achievement of Vladimir Lenin, however, as the leader of the Bolsheviks, the Russian Communist Party, to adapt communism to his circumstances. For him, the party was the disciplined, militarily armed vanguard that ruled with monopoly power and instilled the ideology of communism in a gradually expanding working class.

Proletariat: A term for the industrial working classes popularized by Marx and Engels in the *Communist Manifesto* and other works.

The Bolshevik Regime

Lenin was from a well-educated middle-class family with Swedish, German, Russian, and Jewish ancestry. Both of his parents were teachers, and his father had been given a patent of nobility; Lenin himself had a degree in law. The execution of his brother by the tsarist government for alleged complicity in the assassination of Tsar Alexander II (1881) imbued him with an implacable hatred for Russian autocracy. At the same time, he became steeped in the writings of Marx and radical thinkers across the political spectrum then circulating around Russia's intellectual underground. Contemplating the revolutionary potential of a communist party in Russia, he published a pamphlet in 1903, called *What Is To Be Done?* Here, he articulated for the first time the idea of professional revolutionaries forming an elite strike force. By eliminating the tsar and seizing control of the government, he argued, Russia's highly centralized political structure would make it possible for an ideologically trained mass communist party to implement its program of equality and industrialization from the top down.

The fall of the tsar's government in the spring of 1917 allowed Lenin and his fellow Bolsheviks to return from political exile, including Leon Trotsky (1879–1940), the well-educated son of an affluent Ukrainian Jewish family, and Joseph Stalin, the hardnosed son of an impoverished Georgian cobbler who had escaped exile in Siberia seven times before the outbreak of World War I. Well aware of Lenin's subversive potential, the German government provided Lenin safe passage from Switzerland to Petrograd. In the words of Winston Churchill, Lenin emerged "like a bacillus" from his special passenger car. By the summer of 1917, the Bolsheviks were mounting massive demonstrations with the slogans "Land, Peace, Bread" and "All Power to the Soviets" (councils of workers and soldiers that helped maintain order as the nation struggled to create a constitution). The collapse of a disastrous Russian summer offensive emboldened the Bolsheviks, who controlled the Petrograd Soviet, which included a "Red Guard" that consisted of some 20,000 armed factory workers in the capital, to make a bid for power. In early November 1917, the Bolsheviks staged a successful coup d'état in Petrograd.

Civil War and Reconstruction   The takeover of Russia by a tiny radical minority unleashed a storm of competing factions all across the political spectrum. For the Bolsheviks the first necessity became building an army from scratch. Here, Trotsky proved a genius at inspiration and ruthless organization. From his armored train flying the new "hammer and sickle" red flag, he continually rallied his forces against the far more numerous but utterly disunited "White" armies arrayed against his "Red" forces. From 1918 to 1921, the Ukraine, Georgia, Armenia, and Azerbaijan were each forced back into the new Bolshevik state. The price for communist victory in the civil war was a complete collapse of the economy, amid a coincidental harvest failure. Lenin had initiated a policy of "war communism"—sending the Red Army into the countryside to requisition food, often with unrestrained brutality. Peasants fought back, and by 1922 a second civil war threatened. Only then did Lenin relent by inaugurating the temporary New Economic Policy (NEP), with a mixture of private and state investment in factories and small-scale food marketing by peasants. At the same time, however, the party—now several hundred thousand members strong—established an iron grip, with no deviation allowed. By 1928, a successful NEP had helped the Soviet Union to return to prewar levels of industrial production.

The Collectivization of Agriculture and Industrialization

Lenin suffered a stroke in 1922 and recovered only for short periods before he died in 1924. His successor was Joseph Stalin, who had garnered the key position of general secretary of the Communist Party in 1922. He had to fight a long struggle, from 1924 to 1930, to overcome potential or imagined rivals, a struggle which left him with a deep reservoir of permanent suspicion. His chief victim was Trotsky, whom he outmaneuvered, forced into exile, and removed altogether by ordering hitmen to assassinate him in Mexico in 1940.

"Liquidation of the Kulaks as a Class"   When Stalin finally felt more secure, he decided that industrialization through the NEP was advancing too slowly. The most valuable source of funds to finance industrialization came from the sale of grain on the world market. But farmers had lost all trust in the communist regime after the forcible requisitions during the civil war and hoarded their grain. Grain production had fallen off from predictions and created a so-called "Crisis of 1928." In November, 1929, therefore, the party Central Committee officially decreed the collectivization of agriculture as the necessary step for an accelerated industrialization. Over the next two years , in a carefully laid out plan, 3–5 percent of the "wealthiest" farmers on grain-producing lands, called *kulaks* (Russian for "fist," meaning tightfistedness of wealthier farmers vis-à-vis poor indebted ones) were "liquidated"—selected for

Marching for Modernity. Farmers of a *kolkhoz* behind their party boss prepare to march with their rakes to their fields in May 1931, under a banner propagandizing their success. In reality, Russian peasants experienced the collectivization program of 1929–1940 as a second serfdom, especially in the Ukraine, where private rather than collective village farming was widespread. They resisted it both passively and actively, through arson, theft, and especially the slaughtering of livestock.

execution, removal to labor camps, or resettlement on inferior soils. Their properties were confiscated and the remaining peasant masses were regrouped as employees either of state farms (*sovkhozy*) or of poorer collective farms (*kolkhozy*). Animals were declared collective property, with the result that farmers slaughtered their cherished livestock rather than turn them over to the collectives. Altogether, it is estimated, that between 6 and 14 million farmers were forcibly removed, with the majority killed outright or worked and starved to death.

Stalinism   The impact on agriculture was appalling. Grain, meat, and dairy production plummeted and failed to regain 1927 levels during the remainder of the interwar period. Food requisitions had to be resumed, bread had to be rationed on farms as well as in cities, and real wages on farms and in factories sank. On the other hand, the one-time transfer of confiscated wealth from the kulaks to industry was substantial. Income from accelerated oil exports and renewed grain exports from state farms in the 1930s was similarly plowed into factory construction. By 1939, the rural population was down from 85 to 52 percent and, for all practical purposes, industrialization had been accomplished, though at an unparalleled human cost (see Map 28.5).

The industrial and urban modernity which the Soviet Union reached was one of enforced solidarity without private enterprises and markets. The communist prestige objects were huge plant complexes producing the industrial basics of oil, coal, steel, cement, fertilizer, tractors, and farm combines (see Patterns Up Close). Little investment was left over for textiles, shoes, furniture, and household articles, not to mention cars, radios, and appliances. Consumers had to make do with shoddy goods, delivered irregularly to government outlets and requiring patient waiting in long lines.

The disaster of collectivization had made Stalin even more concerned about any hidden pockets of potential resistance in the country. Regular party and army purges decimated the top echelons of the communist ruling apparatus. In 1937

MAP 28.5 Industrialization and Collectivization in the Soviet Union, 1928–1939.

alone, Stalin had 35,000 high-ranking officers shot, with disastrous effects for the conduct of World War II a few years later. Thus, in view of the enormity of Stalin's policies, scholars have since wondered about the viability of this attempt at accelerated modernity.

New Variations on Modernity II: Supremacist Nationalism in Italy, Germany, and Japan

The third vision of modernity, underlying the development of the three countries of Italy, Germany, and Japan, was an ideology of nationalist supremacism. In contrast to communism, which was a relatively coherent ideology, the systems of fascism,

Patterns Up Close | Mapping Utopia in Soviet Georgia

When most of us think of "utopias" we tend to imagine far-off or fictional places, such as Thomas More's sixteenth-century island community for which he first invented the word (from the Greek for "not place"). Or we may think of social or religious communities whose members seek to seclude themselves from the corrupting influences of the outside world: the Shakers, who flourished in New England in the early part of the nineteenth century, may immediately come to mind.

Utopian Paradise. The Georgian city of Batumi, located on the Black Sea, was developed by the Soviets into a subtropical vacation resort, famed for its tea, citrus, and pleasure beaches.

Few of us probably consider the Soviet state during the late 1920s and 1930s as sharing anything remotely similar to the impulses guiding nineteenth-century utopias (including Marx's own original utopia of a proletarian revolution ushering in a state-less and class-less society). Stalin's ruthless drive to industrialize was accompanied by extreme violence. Millions perished from hunger, and thousands lost their lives in the political purges of the "Great Terror." Certainly, the upheavals associated with Stalinism make it difficult for us today to view them as part of a utopian enterprise.

However, if we shift our perspective and transport ourselves back in time, we can begin to see how Soviet policymakers regarded their mission as the creation of a type of utopia. Central to this "revolution from above" was the transformation of space. The vast expanses of the Soviet Union were to be improved, civilized, and, above all, industrialized. "We conquer space and time/We are young masters of the land" was a popular refrain from the 1930s. On the right, a map of the Soviet republic of Georgia, from *The Great Soviet*

MAP 28.6 **Georgia and the Caucasus Region, ca. 1935.**

The civilizing effects of socialism are brought to the Georgian people by the Georgian-Military Highway, which runs through the Caucasus Mountains and connects the country with Russia.

Georgia's strides toward utopia are charted by the number of automobiles it produces each year, as well as the level of production of its petroleum, timber, manganese, cement, and silk and wool industries.

Energy production is a key metric for determining conformity with the socialist pattern of modernity. The colored stars stand for different types of energy sources.

The design of the map is highly original, laying out industrial production in giant circles, subdivided by color according to the type of industry, with the size indicating the amount of output. For the power needed to run various industries, the map designers employed a six-sided star whose size corresponded to an exact amount of output. Different color stars correspond to the type of energy--coal, petroleum, or hydroelectric.

The map celebrates Soviet agricultural and industrial successes through a "Growth Chart." Each row of graphs is devoted to an area of success: The top row shows increased agricultural output, the second and third improved industrial production, and the fourth and fifth rows the increase in the number of people attending school as well as the growing number of books printed. Just like agriculture or industry, the progress of human culture can be scientifically and precisely graphed.

World Atlas of 1937–1939, provides a vivid demonstration of this utopian impetus. Through its innovative use of symbols, the map shows how Soviet technocrats visualized their socialist utopia—literally, on paper.

Questions

- Does the map above confirm or alter the way you think about the goals that animated the socialist–communist pattern of modernity? Do you believe that the term "utopian" can also be applied to those who strove to implement the democratic-capitalist and nationalist-supremacist patterns of modernity? If so, why?

- What does this map say about the Soviet Union as an empire? What dynamics between the center (Russia) and the periphery (Georgia) can you see revealed in this map?

Nazism, and Japanese militarism were far more diffuse, and cobbled together from a wide variety of nineteenth-century intellectual sources. Fascism became a persuasive alternative to democracy and communism in Italy right after World War I. The much more brutal German Nazi and Japanese militarist ideologies became acceptable only once the Depression hit and discredited capitalist democracy as being capable of weathering the crisis.

From Fascism in Italy to Nazism in the Third Reich

Benito Mussolini (1883–1945), son of a blacksmith with anarchist leanings and a teacher, was well read in nineteenth-century philosophy and held positions as a journalist at various socialist newspapers. His support for the war as an instrument of radical change brought him into conflict with the majority of socialists, who bitterly opposed the war. As a result, he grew disillusioned with Marxism and founded the "Italian Combat Squad" (*Fasci italiani di combattimento*). War veterans, dressed in black shirts and organized in paramilitary units, roamed the streets and broke up communist labor rallies and strikes. The symbol of the movement was the *fasces* [FAS-sees]—derived from the old Roman emblem of authority with a bundle of sticks and an ax, tied with a ribbon.

With their street brawls, the fascist "Blackshirts" contributed mightily to the impression of a breakdown of law and order, which the democratic government allegedly was unable to control. Anticommunism thus was accompanied by denunciations of democracy as a chaotic form of government incapable of decisive action. Although Mussolini's party was still woefully behind the Socialist, Christian Democrat, and Conservative Parties in the parliament, he demanded and received the premiership by threatening a march on Rome by 10,000 Blackshirts. This turned into a victory parade, with the king acquiescing to the fascists' "third way" between democracy and socialism.

Mussolini's Dictatorship   Once given his chance, Mussolini transformed the Blackshirts into a militia for national security, paid for by the state. In 1923 he used the threat of their violence again when he led his coalition government in the passing of a law that gave two-thirds of the seats in parliament to the party that garnered the most votes (at least 25 percent). A year later, "Il Duce" ("The Leader"), as he now styled himself, won his two-thirds and began to implement his fascist **corporate state**.

By 1926, elections were abolished, strict censorship of the press was in place, and the secret police kept a close eye on the population. Fascist party officials, provincial governorships, and mayors were appointed from above and labor unions closed down. In the Ministry of Corporations, industrialists and bureaucrats, representing labor, met and sharply curtailed wages and labor conditions. The Lateran Accords of 1926–1929 made Catholicism the Italian state religion in return for full support by the Vatican. Youth and women's organizations instilled authoritarian behavior. The new vision of Italian efficiency prompted observers to say admiringly of Mussolini that "he made the trains run on time." In architecture and art, as well as the new technologies of automobiles and aircraft, Italy, long seen as backward, now became a world pacesetter.

Depression and Conquests   Italy weathered the Depression through deficit spending and state investments. In 1933, Mussolini formed the Industrial

Reconstruction Institute, which took over the industrial and commercial holdings of the banks that had failed earlier. This institute was crucial in efforts to revive the Italian industrial sector, which was still much smaller than elsewhere in Europe. Only in the mid-1930s did the urban population, concentrated mostly in the north, acquire majority status. In spite of a few swamp-reclamation and grain-procurement reforms, the fascists had no answer for the endemic underdevelopment of southern Italy, which remained profoundly rural and poor.

Nevertheless, Italy's military industry was sufficiently advanced for Mussolini to proclaim a policy of autarky with the help of overseas territories. First, the conquest of formerly Ottoman Libya was completed with utmost brutality in 1931. Declaring Libya to be the "Fourth Shore," the fascists encouraged emigration into the largely infertile Sahara colony, which eventually numbered some 100,000 settlers. The other major colony was the proud Christian kingdom of Ethiopia, conquered by Italy in 1935–1936 and merged thereafter with the earlier territories of Italian Eritrea and Somalia into Italian East Africa. Eager to avenge Italy's defeat by the Ethiopians forty years before, Mussolini's forces invaded with airplanes, tanks, and poison gas and, after crushing Ethiopian resistance, pacified the new colony with the settlement of 200,000 Italians.

The Ethiopian conquest prompted protests by the League of Nations. Although these were ineffective, Mussolini felt sufficiently isolated to seek closer relations with Adolf Hitler and the Nazis. He had formerly treated Hitler as a junior colleague but now found him to be a useful counterweight against international isolation. An increasingly close cooperation began between the two dictators, who formed the nucleus of the later Axis powers, joined in 1941 by Japan.

The Foundation of the Weimar Republic   In September 1918, the German Supreme Army Command came to the conclusion that Germany had lost World War I. In the subsequent 2 months unrest broke out in the navy and among workers. German soldiers melted away from the western front, and communist worker councils formed in a number of major cities. Alarmed civilian politicians in Berlin did everything in their power to bring about a peaceful transition from empire to republic. When the emperor eventually abdicated, his last chancellor (head of the government) appointed Friedrich Ebert (1871–1925), a prominent member of the German Social Democratic Party, on November 9, 1918, as his successor. This appointment was not quite legal, but Ebert immediately contacted the OHL for armed support; and in the following months the two cooperated in crushing well-organized and armed communist workers' councils.

The first test for the new republic (founded in nearby Weimar during the height of communist unrest in Berlin) came in the summer of 1919 when the Allies presented their peace settlement. The French, concerned about both their military security and the future economic power of their more populous and industrially advanced German neighbor, would have liked to have Germany divided again, as it was before 1871. The British and Americans, however, were opposed to such a drastic settlement. Germany was let off with what historians now see in retrospect as relatively moderate reparations for civilian casualties and the loss of two western provinces, although it was also forced to accept responsibility for the beginning of the war. The compromise settlement was satisfactory to no one: France's security remained unresolved, German conservatives and nationalists screamed defiance, and

Corporate state: Sometimes called an "organic state"; a philosophy of government that sees all sectors of society contributing in a systematic, orderly, and hierarchical fashion to the health of the state, the way that the parts of the body do to a human being. In practice, it was a polity in which a dictator or an authoritarian leader orchestrated the single state party and all ministries, business corporations, associations, and clubs, while other parties and organizations such as labor unions were outlawed.

Play Money. German children in 1923 playing with bundles of money in the streets. Hyperinflation had made money in the Weimar Republic worthless: Printed overnight, it was practically worthless before it even hit the market in the morning. At the height of inflation, $1 US was worth 4.2 million reichsmark.

the democrats of Weimar who accepted the settlement were embittered by its immediate consequence: inflation.

Asked to begin the payments immediately, Germany was unable to correct the general inflation which also occurred in other countries in 1918–1919, when pent-up consumer demand exploded with the onset of peace. Instead, the inflation accelerated to a hyperinflation in which the German mark became virtually worthless and Germany had to suspend payments. France and Belgium responded by occupying the industrial Ruhr province in 1923. German workers in the Ruhr retaliated with passive resistance, and a deadlock was the result.

Faced with this crisis, the new Weimar Republic made peace with the French by recognizing the new borders. Recognizing, too, the dire financial implications of an economically crippled Germany, the American-crafted Dawes Plan of 1924 had US banks advance credits to European banks to refinance the now considerably reduced German reparation payments. France and Belgium withdrew from the Ruhr, inflation was curtailed, and the currency stabilized. The newly solvent Weimar Republic then experienced a considerable economic and cultural efflorescence during the rest of the decade.

The Golden Twenties   In these years, Germany produced more movies than the rest of Europe combined, with such classics as *Metropolis*, by the director Fritz Lang (1890–1976). Sports fans followed the career of the boxer Max Schmeling (1905-2005), world champion in 1930, and watched car races on the Avus in Berlin, the first freeway (*Autobahn*). The *Kabarett* ("cabaret"), with its biting political satire, attracted major literary figures who wrote sketches for this new popular art form. Playwrights probed the conflicts of social class, which were more pronounced in Germany than elsewhere. Perhaps best known was *The Threepenny Opera* of 1928, with lyrics by Bertolt Brecht (1898–1956) and music by Kurt Weill (1900–1950).

Painters and architects probed the geometrical and detached style they assumed was the essence of modernity at the Bauhaus school in Weimar, which became an international trendsetter for art, architecture, and design. The Russian Wassily Kandinsky (1866–1944) and the Swiss Paul Klee (1879–1940) taught the new style of abstract painting, which they had pioneered at the school. Similarly, the pioneer of modern glass, steel, and concrete architecture, Ludwig Mies van der Rohe (1886–1969), began his career at the Bauhaus, before he designed some of the best-known skyscrapers of the Chicago cityscape.

The Rise of the Nazis   The Golden Twenties disintegrated quickly in the months after the US stock market crash of 1929. American banks, desperate for cash, began to recall their loans made to Europe. Beginning in 1931 in Austria, European banks began to fail; and in the following 2 years world trade shrank by two-thirds, hitting an exporting nation like Germany particularly hard. Unemployment soared at the same time to 30 percent of the workforce. Once more, as during the hyperinflation of 1923, millions of Germans were cast into misery. The number of people voting for extremist opponents of democracy—communists and nationalist supremacists—rose from marginal to more than half of the electorate by July 1932. Among them, the National Socialist German Workers' Party (NSDAP), or Nazi Party, achieved 38 percent, becoming the largest party in parliament.

In early 1933, the Nazi leader, Adolf Hitler (1889–1945), a failed artist and son of an Austrian customs official, could look back on a checkered postwar political career. He had led a failed uprising in 1923, done time in prison, and in *Mein Kampf* (*My Struggle*), a book published in 1925, openly announced a frightening political program. Hitler advocated ridding Germany of its Jews, whom he blamed for World War I, and communists, whom he blamed for losing the war, and sought to punish the Allies for the peace settlement they had imposed on Germany. In its most grandiose sections he supported the German conquest of a "living space" (*Lebensraum*) in Russia and eastern Europe for the superior "Aryan" (German) race, with the "inferior" Slavs reduced to forced labor. No one who followed politics in Germany during the 1920s could be in doubt about Hitler's unrestrained and violent supremacist nationalism. Throughout the decade, however, he remained marginalized and ridiculed for his extreme views.

Function and Simplicity. The architect Walter Gropius (1883–1969) founded the Bauhaus movement. Its emphasis on function and simplicity still exerts great influence.

The Nazis in Power   When the Nazis won a plurality in parliament, however, not only in spring 1932 but again in the fall (albeit with a loss of 4 percent, while the communists gained nearly 3 for a total of nearly 17 percent), Hitler demanded the chancellorship. Upon the advice of his counselors, President Paul von Hindenburg (in office 1925–1934), one of Germany's heroes as a leading general during World War I, nominated Hitler to the post on January 30, 1933, in an effort to neutralize Nazism and keep Hitler under control. Hitler, however, wasted no time in escaping all restraints. Following a major fire in the Reichstag (German parliament) building in February 1933, the causes of which have never been fully explained, but which Hitler blamed on the communists, the president allowed his new chancellor the right to declare martial law for a limited time. Two months later, the Nazi Party in parliament passed the Enabling Act with the votes of the mostly Catholic Centrist Party: Its leaders calculated that they could control Hitler while receiving a much desired agreement between the Vatican and Germany parallel to the one of Mussolini. According to the constitution, Hitler now had the power to rule by emergency decree for 4 years.

Taking their cue from Mussolini's policies, the Nazis abolished the federalist structure of the Weimar Republic, purged the civil service of Jews, closed down all parties except the NSDAP, enacted censorship laws, and sent communists to newly constructed concentration camps. Other inmates of these camps were Roma (Gypsies), homosexuals, and religious minorities. In order to gain the support of Germany's professional army, Hitler replaced his *Sturmabteilung* (SA) militias of thugs with the smartly outfitted *Schutzstaffel* (SS). A new secret police force (abbreviated *Gestapo*) established a pervasive surveillance system in what was now called the Third Empire (*Drittes Reich*), following that of the Holy Roman Empire and Germany after its unification in 1871.

At the same time, Hitler succeeded in gaining enthusiastic support from among the population. Aided by a general recovery of the economy, within 1 year of coming to power he lowered unemployment to 10 percent. He had the support of able economists who advised him to reduce unemployment through deficit spending and build a mixed economy of state-subsidized private industrial cartels. Enthusiastic Germans built freeways, cleared slums, constructed housing, and, above all, made arms, for minimal wages. A once mediocre artist and aspiring architect, Hitler also pronounced upon the "decadence" of modern art and pushed his planners to create monumental buildings in older neoclassical or art-deco styles. In all of these endeavors he advocated a personal vision of a stridently "nationalist" German art. In his appeal to the patriotic and economic aspirations of so many Germans, Hitler thus succeeded in making himself a genuinely popular leader (*Führer*) among the great majority of Germans.

German rearmament was initially secret but, after 1935, public knowledge, with the introduction of the draft and the repudiation of the peace settlement cap on troop numbers. During 1935–1939, the army grew from 100,000 to 950,000 men, warships from 30 to 95, and, most startling of all, the air force from 36 to over 8,000 planes. France, realizing the danger this rearmament signified for its security, signed a treaty of mutual military assistance with the Soviet Union, which Hitler took as a pretext for the remilitarization of the Rhineland (one of the German provinces temporarily occupied by France after World War I) in 1936.

This first step of German military assertion was followed with the unofficial air force support of General Francisco Franco (1892-1975) who rose against the legitimate Republican government in the Spanish Civil War (1936–1939) and incorporation of Austria in 1938. Now alarmed at Germany's growing appetite for expansion and committed by treaty to defend the eastern European states created after the war, the heads of state of Britain and France met with Hitler and Mussolini in Munich in the summer of 1938 to hammer out a general agreement on German and Italian territorial claims. In the Munich Agreement, Hitler was allowed to occupy the Sudetenland, an area largely inhabited by ethnic Germans in Czechoslovakia, with the understanding that it represented his final territorial demand. The British prime minister, Neville Chamberlain, (in office 1937–1940) seeking to mediate between the less compromising France and Hitler, claimed that this appeasement of Germany represented "peace in our time." Hitler went to war, however, in little more than a year.

World War II in Poland and France

In 1939 Hitler decided that the German armed forces were ready to begin the quest for Lebensraum in eastern Europe. In a first step, Poland needed to be taken; and in order to do so, Stalin had to be led to believe that it was in the best interest of the Soviet Union and Germany to share in the division of eastern Europe. Stalin, of course, was under no illusions about Hitler's plans but needed time to rebuild his army after the purges of 1937 and found the idea of a Russian-dominated Polish buffer against Germany appealing. Accordingly, the two signed a nonaggression pact on August 23, 1939; and German troops invaded Poland on September 1, triggering declarations of war by Poland's allies Britain and France 2 days later. World War II had begun in Europe.

Having removed the two-front problem that had plagued Germany in World War I, Hitler had to eliminate Britain and France before turning to the next phase in the east. This he did by attacking France on May 10, 1940. The German army in Poland had pioneered a new kind of warfare: "lightning war," or *Blitzkrieg*. Using aircraft to cripple rear area defenses and harass enemy troops, while smashing enemy lines

---

A Fatal Error

"I really thought that it was [Hitler's] earnest desire to comply in matters of religion. In his speeches in the Reichstag to March 1933, he said that he respected Christian fundamentals and would do everything to uphold them. It was I who asked Hitler to include this point in his speeches."

—Franz von Papen, interviewed by Leon Goldensohn, *Nuremberg Interviews: A Psychiatrist's Conversations with the Defendants and Witnesses*, p. 180. New York: Vintage, 2004. Papen was a Centrist deputy, former chancellor, and one of the advisors of Hindenburg urging the appointment of Hitler.

with tanks and motorized infantry, the Germans turned warfare from the stagnant defensive posture of World War I into a fast, highly mobile form of conflict. The French, bled dry of manpower in the previous war, had since relied largely on the highly elaborate but fixed defenses of their Maginot Line. Now, the German troops simply went around these fortifications on a broad front, from the Netherlands and Belgium to Luxemburg. After breaking through the thick unprotected Ardennes Forest in southern Belgium, to the great surprise of the French and British, the German troops turned northward, driving the Allies toward the Atlantic coast. Establishing a desperate defensive perimeter at Dunkirk, the encircled French and British troops used every available vessel to escape across the English Channel to Britain as the Germans regrouped for their final thrust.

France had no choice but to agree to an armistice. Hitler divided the country into a German-occupied part, consisting of Paris and the Atlantic coast, and a small unoccupied territory under German control, with its capital in Vichy. The German follow-up effort of an invasion of Britain failed when the air force, having suffered more losses than anticipated in the invasion of France, was unable to deliver the final blow. During the worst air raids the conservative politician Winston Churchill (in office 1940–1945) replaced Neville Chamberlain as prime minister. Churchill's inspirational and unbending will during the aerial Battle of Britain proved to be a turning point in rallying the Allied cause.

The Eastern Front   A year after finishing with France, and with Britain only desperately hanging on, Hitler launched an invasion of the Soviet Union on June 22, 1941, to the surprise of an unprepared Stalin. Although the Soviet forces were initially severely beaten, they did not disintegrate, thanks in part to a force of new T-34 tanks that proved superior to German models and were four times more numerous than the Germans expected. The Soviets held out against the German attacks on Leningrad (the renamed St. Petersburg/Petrograd), Moscow, and the Ukraine. Neither side made much progress in 1942, until the Soviets succeeded in trapping a large force of Germans in Stalingrad on the lower Volga, near the vital Caspian oil fields. The Soviet victory on February 2, 1943, became the turning point in the European war. Thereafter, it was an almost relentless and increasingly desperate retreat for the Germans, particularly after the western Allies invaded the continent in Italy and France.

The Final Solution   As Hitler's *Mein Kampf* foretold, the war in the east became an ideological war of annihilation: Either the supremacist or the communist vision of modernity would prevail. The Soviets began early with their killings, when they massacred nearly 22,000 Polish prisoners of war in the forest of Katyn and sent hundreds of thousands of eastern Europeans to their eventual deaths in labor camps. The German SS and army, driven by their racism against Slavs, murdered soldiers and civilians alike; and German business tycoons worked their Slavic slave laborers to death. The so-called **Final Solution** (*Endlösung*), the genocide of the European Jews, was the horrendous culmination of this struggle. After Poland and the western Soviet Union were conquered, the number of Jews under

Genocide. The specters of the Holocaust that haunt us usually involve the infamous extermination camps—Auschwitz, Treblinka, Majdanek, Sobibor—but millions of Jews and other "undesirables"—Slavs, gypsies (Roma), and homosexuals—were shot, such as this man calmly waiting for the bullet to penetrate his brain while SS stooges accomplices look blithely on.

Final Solution: German nationalist-supremacist plan formulated in 1942 by Adolf Hitler and leading Nazis to annihilate Jews through factory-style mass extermination in concentration camps; resulting in the death of about 6 million Jews or roughly two-thirds of European Jewry.

German authority increased by several million. The Final Solution, set in motion in January 1942, entailed transporting Jews to eight extermination camps, the most infamous of which was at Auschwitz, in Poland, to be gassed in simulated shower stalls and their corpses burned in specially constructed ovens. In its technological sophistication in creating a kind of assembly line of death and the calm, bureaucratic efficiency with which its operators went about their business, the Holocaust (Hebrew *Shoa*) marks a milestone in twentieth-century inhumanity. It has since become the standard of genocide against which other planned mass murders are measured.

The Turn of the Tide in the West   The first counteroffensives of the Allies in the west after their defeat in 1940 came in November 1942. After fighting a desperate rearguard action against the German general Erwin Rommel (1891–1944), "The Desert Fox," British forces in Egypt and American forces landing in occupied French North Africa launched a combined offensive, capturing Rommel's forces in a pincer movement and driving them to capitulate 6 months later. But it took another 2.5 years of long campaigning to grind down the forces of the Axis powers. Here, the industrial capacity of the United States proved to be the determining factor. For example, between 1942 and 1945 American factories produced 41,000 Sherman M4 tanks alone, which was more than the production of all German tank types taken together. German aircraft production peaked in 1944 at 44,000 planes; US manufacturers produced more than 100,000 the same year. The United States enjoyed similar advantages in manpower. By war's end, over 16 million American men and women, or 10 percent of the entire population, had served in the armed forces. Finally, the natural barriers of the Atlantic and Pacific Oceans and American naval power ensured against invasion, while the lack of a long-range strategic bombing force prevented Axis air attacks on North America.

Furthermore, starting in 1943, the US Army Air Force and Britain's Royal Air Force began a furious campaign of "around-the-clock" bombing of military and civilian targets in Germany. Despite heavy Allied losses in planes and men, by war's end, there was scarcely a German city of any size or industrial center that had not been reduced to rubble by air attack—quite a contrast to World War I, when Germany's interior was unscathed. With the landing of troops in Sicily in July 1943 and Normandy in June 1944, combined with the steady advance of Soviet forces in the east, the eventual unconditional German surrender on May 8, 1945 ("Victory in Europe," or "VE," Day) was inevitable (see Map 28.7).

Japan's "Greater East Asia Co-Prosperity Sphere" and China's Struggle for Unity

The Japanese ruling class that implemented the Meiji industrialization consisted for the most part of lower-ranking samurai "oligarchs." After World War I, this generation retired and for the first time commoners entered politics. These commoners formed two unstable conservative party coalitions, representing small-business and landowner interests, but were financed by big-business cartels, the zaibatsus (see Chapter 24) By the mid-1920s Japan's interwar liberalizing era had reached perhaps its high point, with universal male suffrage for all over the age of 25. Thereafter, however, and at an accelerated pace during the Depression of 1929–1933, the military increased its power and ended the liberalizing era.

MAP **28.7** World War II in Europe, 1939–1945.

Liberalism and Military Assertion

In the midst of the middle-class ferment of "Taisho Democracy," as Japan's politics during the reign of Emperor Taisho (r. 1912–1926) was known, the government not only broadened the suffrage but also enacted the first of what would be a long line of security laws. Worried about communist influence, the Peace Preservation Law of 1925 drew a line against frequent labor strikes and general leftist agitation. Anyone violating the "national essence" (*kokutai*) not only through action but also thought could be arrested. A branch of the secret services, the *Tokko*, made widespread use of this law, with some 70,000 mostly arbitrary arrests during 1925–1945. The law was a turning point as Western-inspired liberalism began to swing toward militarism. Nowhere was this more dramatically on display than in the saga of Professor Minobe, described at the beginning of this chapter, who would go in a few short years from being Japan's leading legal theorist to being denounced as a traitor.

Supremacist Nationalism   Military officers of modest rural origin, trained prior to World War I and without much general education, were unable or unwilling to comprehend the democracy, cultural transformation, and labor strikes of the 1920s. They intoxicated themselves with the staples of supremacist nationalism, such as

- the superiority of the Yamato "race" of Japan and the inferiority of all other "races" in Asia;
- the supremacy of the "national essence" over the individual;
- the depravity of communism and democracy;
- the establishment of a "Greater East Asia Co-Prosperity Sphere" (*Dai-to-a Kyoeiken*) to be established in the Pacific by conquest;
- the abolition of class divisions in favor of social corporatism;
- the absolutism of the emperor, above law and parliament;
- and the right of junior officers to refuse to execute parliamentary laws.

The latter two points were decisive for actions through which the military achieved dominance over parliament in the 1930s.

Militaristic Expansion   The early 1930s saw the end of a period of diplomacy by which Japan sought to consolidate its gains in international prestige from the Washington Naval Treaty and subsequent treaties stabilizing Japan's position in China. The growth of the power of the Chinese Nationalist Party (Guomindang, GMD) and its creation of a relatively stable regime in China after 1927 altered the fragile balance of power among the contending warlord regimes that Japan had exploited for over a decade for expanding its influence. The generation of rural junior officers who frowned on the liberalization of Japan and hearkened back to samurai values also found a home and opportunity in the colonial armies of Manchuria. In addition, nationalist radicals like Kita Ikki (1883–1937) expounded a complete reorganization of Japan based on a stricter interpretation of the kokutai. Finally, the long-standing maneuverings of semimilitary groups advocating further expansion in the Asian heartland, such as the Black Dragon Society, kept the situation in Japan's Asian possessions in turmoil.

The first step in this new direction was taken in 1928 when the Japanese Kwantung Army (the name for Japan's force in Manchuria) blew up the train of Chinese warlord Zhang Zuolin because of his leanings toward the GMD. This was followed by the Mukden Incident of 1931, in which the Japanese military engineered another railroad bombing, which was blamed on local warlords and used as the pretext for the annexation of Manchuria. Politicians in Tokyo, cowed by the aggressiveness of supremacist nationalist ideologues, and by the select assassinations of political opponents of Japan's expansion, acquiesced. By way of making it a puppet state, they installed the last Manchu Qing Chinese emperor (Henry) Pu-Yi (r. 1908–1912; 1932–45), deposed in the Chinese Republican Revolution of 1911–1912. Over the next several years, the Japanese army in Manchuria systematically moved into northern China. In July 1937, after a clash between Chinese and Japanese forces near the Marco Polo Bridge outside Beijing, Japan launched a full-scale invasion of China.

The Republican Revolution in China   The Qing dynasty had failed to develop a sustained effort at reform in response to the Western challenge during the

1800s. Following belated attempts at institutional reform in the wake of the Boxer uprising in 1900, a variety of radical groups, aided by the growing numbers of overseas Chinese, began to work for the overthrow of the Qing. The most important figure among these groups was Sun Yat-sen (1866–1925), a medical doctor and son of peasants in south China, with his Revolutionary Alliance of 1905. Making common cause with a number of local revolutionary groups and Chinese secret societies, Sun's group formed an umbrella organization for a wide array of political ideas. Sun's core ideas, however, were relatively straightforward and given as the Three Principles of the People (*san min zhuyi*):

- Nationalism: Expulsion of the Manchus and later all Western interests.
- Democracy: Representative institutions based on a constitution. One-party tutelage until the Chinese people grow used to the new forms of democratic institutions.
- "People's livelihood": Sometimes rendered as "socialism," this principle called for comprehensive land reform and a government commitment to safeguard the economic well-being of the people.

On October 10, 1911, an explosion in a Wuhan barracks signaled a takeover of the base. The movement quickly spread, and by the end of the year three groups of Qing opponents—provincial warlords, scholar-gentry, and nationalists—staged separate uprisings which reduced the Qing to a small territory in the north. The Qing commander, Yuan Shikai (1859–1916), struck a deal with the insurgents whereby he came over to them in return for the presidency of the new republic, formed upon the abdication of the Qing in February 1912. Sun was thus elbowed aside by the revolution he had done so much to begin. With Yuan's death in 1916, the remaining warlords feuded with each other for control of the country for the next decade.

Reemergence of Nationalism   Sun Yat-sen, however, was not quite finished. With the republic in shambles and the provinces hijacked by the warlords, Sun remained a profoundly inspirational figure for Chinese nationalists, mostly through his numerous publications issued from exile in the Western treaty port of Canton (Guangzhou). Meanwhile, the decision announced on May 4, 1919, by the Allies at Versailles to allow Japan to keep the German territory in China it had seized at the beginning of the war set off mass demonstrations and a boycott of foreign businesses. This May Fourth Movement, as it came to be called, is often cited as the modern beginning of Chinese nationalism. Shortly thereafter, inspired by the Bolshevik Revolution in Russia, the Chinese Communist Party (CCP) was founded in 1921.

By 1923, encouraged by support from the Third Communist International (Comintern), Sun's Nationalist Party was being reorganized and supplied with Russian help, in return for which the party agreed to allow members of the CCP to join with them to form what became known as the First United Front (1924–1927). The Nationalist Party organized the National Revolutionary Army in the south, and the CCP fomented communist-inspired strikes in the industrial cities of the Yangtze delta, including Shanghai. Sun died in 1925, and a year later Chiang K'ai-shek (1887–1975) ascended to the leadership of the army. Chiang came from a wealthy salt merchant family and was a military officer trained in the Nationalist Party academy and in Moscow. The most pressing objective in 1926 was the unification of China. The two parties mobilized an army of some 85,000 men, and the so-called

Mao. The images of Mao that dominate our consciousness are usually the old Mao, when his health was failing, his youthful vigor was long gone, and his political power diminished. But it is in the young Mao, such as this photo from 1938, that we can best see his leadership skills in action. As Mao's longtime associate Zhou Enlai (1898–1976) observed in 1943, "The Comrade's style of work incorporates the modesty and pragmatism of the Chinese people; the simplicity and diligence of the Chinese peasants; the love of study and profound thinking of an intellectual; the efficiency and steadfastness of a revolutionary soldier; and the persistence and indomitability of a Bolshevik."

Northern Expedition of 1926–1927 became a remarkably successful effort which brought about the unification of southern China as far north as the Yangzi River.

In the middle of the campaign, however, the bonds between the GMD and CCP ruptured. The socialist wing of the GMD and the CCP had taken the important industrial centers of Wuhan and Shanghai in the Yangtze delta from warlords, setting the stage for a showdown with the nationalist wing. Though he had been trained in Moscow, Chiang had grown intensely suspicious of Comintern and CCP motives and, thus launched a preemptive purge of communists in nationalist-held areas. Though much of the leftist opposition was eliminated, a remnant under Mao Zedong (1893–1976) fled to the remote province of Jiangxi in the south to regroup and create their own socialist state. Mao, a librarian by training from a wealthy peasant family, was an inspiring rural organizer; and he set about developing his ideas of Marxist revolution with the heretical idea of having peasants in the vanguard.

By the early 1930s Mao's Chinese communists had developed this crucial variant of rural communism, which Marx and Lenin had found impossible to envisage. Mao replaced the capitalists with the landlords as the class enemy and promised a much needed land reform to the downtrodden peasants. Moreover, the peasants would be the leading participants in the "People's War"—a three-stage guerilla conflict involving the entire populace and borrowing from sources as diverse as Sun Zi's *Art of War* and American tactics against the British in the War for Independence.

Believing the communist threat to be effectively eliminated, Chiang resumed his Northern Expedition in 1928, submitting Beijing to his control but failing to eliminate the strongest northern warlords. Nevertheless, China was now at least nominally unified, with the capital in Nanjing, the National Party Congress functioning as a parliament, and Chiang as president. Chiang made substantial progress with railroad and road construction as well as cotton and silk textile exports. Thanks to the silver standard of its money, rather than the fatal gold standard of most other countries, the financial consequences of the Depression of 1929–1933 remained relatively mild. Chiang made little headway, however, with land reform. Furthermore, the volatile relations with the remaining warlords made the government vulnerable to border violence and corruption. Hovering above all after 1931 was the Japanese annexation of Manchuria and creeping encroachment on northern China.

The Long March and the Rape of Nanjing   In the early 1930s, Chiang knew that Japan was the enemy to watch, but he was painfully aware of the need to completely eliminate his internal opponents. Following the old proverbial advice of "disorder within, disaster without" he resolved to eliminate the remaining threat from Mao's "Jiangxi Soviet." He mounted increasingly massive "bandit extermination" campaigns from 1931 to 1934, but each one was defeated by the superior mobility, local loyalty, and guerilla tactics of Mao's growing People's Liberation Army. With the help of German advisors, Chiang turned to encircling the CCP areas with a ring of trenches and blockhouses to eliminate the mobility of his opponents. By the fall of 1934 he had tightened the noose around the communists and almost succeeded in destroying their army.

But Mao and about 100,000 soldiers broke out in October 1934, thanks to the negligence of one of the warlords entrusted with the encirclement. Once free, the majority of the Red Army embarked on its epic Long March of 6,000 miles, describing a semicircle from the south through the far west and then northeast toward Beijing. Along the way harassment by nationalist troops, warlords, and local people as well as hunger, famine, heat, swamps, bridgeless rivers, and desertion decimated the bedraggled marchers. In the fall of 1935 some 10,000 communists eventually straggled into the small enclave of Yan'an (Yenan), out of Chiang's reach. Living in caves cut into the loess soil, they set up communes and concentrated on agricultural production and reconstituting their forces.

The communists had seized upon Japan's aggression as a valuable propaganda tool and declared war against Japan in 1932. Chiang's obsession with eliminating his internal enemies increasingly made him subject to criticism of appeasement toward Japan. By 1936, a group of warlords and dissident nationalist generals arrested Chiang outside the city of Xi'an and spirited him off to CCP headquarters at Yan'an. After weeks of fraught negotiations, Chiang was released as the leader of a China now brought together under a Second United Front, this time against Japan.

The Rape of Nanjing. Of the many horrors of the twentieth century, few can match the Rape of Nanjing for its sadistic brutality, in which perhaps as many as 300,000 people lost their lives in a killing orgy.

Seeing their prospects for gradual encroachment quickly fading, Japan seized on the so-called Marco Polo Bridge Incident and launched an all-out assault on China. The bridge was a key point along the frontier between Japanese and Chinese forces just outside Beijing, and on the night of July 7, 1937, a brief exchange of fire accidentally took place between the two sides. When a Japanese soldier seeking to relieve himself during the exchange did not return to post, the Japanese used this as a pretext to move against the Chinese. Though Chinese resistance was stiff in the opening months, the Japanese were able to use their superior mobility and airpower to flank the Chinese forces and take the capital of Nanjing (Nanking) by December 1937. Realizing the need to defeat China as quickly as possible in order to avoid a war of attrition, they subjected the capital to the first major atrocity of World War II: "the Rape of Nanjing." Though scholars are still debating the exact number of casualties, it is estimated that between 200,000 and 300,000 people were slaughtered in deliberately gruesome ways: hacked to death, burned alive, buried alive, and beheaded. Over and above this brutality, however, rape was systematically used as a means of terror and subjugation.

The direct message of all of this was that other Chinese cities could expect similar treatment if surrender was not swiftly forthcoming. Like the British and Germans under aerial bombardment a few years later, however, the destruction only stiffened the will to resist of the Chinese. Continually harassed as they retreated from Nanjing, the Chinese adopted the strategy of trading space for time to regroup, as did the Soviets a few years later. In an epic mass migration, Chinese soldiers and civilians stripped every usable article possible and moved it to the region of the remote city of Chongqing (Chungking), which became the wartime capital of China until 1945. Thereafter, both nationalists and communists used the vast interior for hit-and-run tactics, effectively limiting Japan to the northeast and coastal urban centers but themselves incapable of mounting large offensives.

World War II in the Pacific While Japan had used its control of Manchuria, Korea, and Taiwan in its support of autarky and economic stability in the 1930s, its bid for empire in the Pacific was portrayed as the construction of "The Greater East Asia Co-Prosperity Sphere." This expansion was considered essential because oil, metals, rubber, and other raw materials were still imported in large quantities from the United States and the Dutch and British possessions in southeast Asia. After Hitler invaded the Netherlands and France in 1940, the moment arrived when the Japanese could plan for extending their power and removing the United States from the Pacific. Moreover, the stalemate in China was increasingly bleeding Japan of vital resources, while mounting tensions with the United States over China were already resulting in economic sanctions. Accordingly, in the summer of 1941, the Japanese government decided on the extension of the empire into the Dutch East Indies and southeast Asia, even if this meant war with the United States. Under the premiership of General Tojo Hideki (in office 1941–1944), Japan attacked Pearl Harbor, Hawaii; the Philippines; and Dutch and British territories on December 7–8, 1941. Within a few months, the Japanese completed the occupation of all the important southeast Asian and Pacific territories they had sought (see Map 28.8).

Japan's newfound autarky did not last long however. Within 6 months, in the naval and air battle of Midway, American forces regained the initiative. The Japanese now

MAP **28.8** **World War II in the Pacific, 1937–1945.**

exploited the populations of their new territories for their raw materials with increasing urgency. As the American forces slowly deprived the Japanese of these resources through their highly effective "island-hopping" strategy, they came within bombing range of the Japanese home islands by late 1944. Starting in March 1945, they subjected Japan to the most devastating firebomb attacks ever mounted. Finally, President Harry S Truman (in office 1945–1953) made the fateful decision to have two experimental atomic bombs dropped on Hiroshima and Nagasaki (August 6 and 9, 1945), effectively obliterating both cities. With the Soviets declaring war against Japan on August 8 and advancing into Manchuria, the Japanese were finally convinced that the war was lost and surrendered on August 14, 1945, with the final ceremony taking place aboard the US battleship *Missouri* on September 2, 1945.

Putting It All Together

As discussed in previous chapters, the patterns of constitutional nationalism and industrialization in the late eighteenth and early nineteenth centuries were most visibly manifested in Great Britain, the United States, and France. Subsequently, two further patterns complicated the evolution of nations joining in the pursuit of modernity: ethnolinguistic nationalism and the rise of the industrial working class. Abetted by the imperialistic tendencies inherited from before 1800, all of these patterns collided in the First World War. After the war, they recombined into the three ideologies of modernity analyzed in this chapter: capitalist democracy, communism, and supremacist nationalism (see Concept Map).

For the most part, only democracy and communism are considered to be genuine ideologies of modernity, in the sense of being based on relatively coherent programs. More recent historians, however, have come to the conclusion that nationalist supremacism was a genuine variety of modernity as well, though one defined more by what it opposed than by what it supported. The adherents of the three modernities bitterly denounced the ideologies of their rivals. All three considered themselves to be genuinely "progressive" or modern.

What is very difficult to understand in a country like the United States, still deeply loyal to its foundational national constitutionalism, is that someone could be an ardent ethnic nationalist, have little faith in constitutional liberties, find the conquest of a large and completely self-sufficient empire perfectly logical, and think of all this as the wave of a future modernity. Indeed, historians have customarily thought of these views as revolts *against* modernity. Yet, as we have seen so often, innovations frequently create a "gelling" effect in which opposition to the new clarifies and solidifies, often in unexpected ways. The "modern" notion of ethnolinguistic nationalism thus created

> **Emperor Hirohito's (r. 1926–1989) Surrender Message to the Japanese People, August 14, 1945**
>
> "We declared war on America and Britain out of Our sincere desire to ensure Japan's self-preservation and the stabilization of East Asia, it being far from Our thought either to infringe upon the sovereignty of other nations or to embark upon territorial aggrandisement. But now the war has lasted for nearly four years. Despite the best that has been done by everyone—the gallant fighting of the military and naval forces, the diligence and assiduity of Our servants of the State and the devoted service of Our one hundred million people, the war situation has developed not necessarily to Japan's advantage, while the general trends of the world have all turned against her interest. Moreover, the enemy has begun to employ a new and most cruel bomb, the power of which to damage is indeed incalculable, taking the toll of many innocent lives. Should We continue to fight, it would not only result in an ultimate collapse and obliteration of the Japanese nation, but also it would lead to the total extinction of human civilization. Such being the case, how are We to save the millions of Our subjects; or to atone Ourselves before the hallowed spirits of Our Imperial Ancestors? This is the reason why We have ordered the Acceptance of the provisions of the Joint Declaration of the Powers."
>
> —Transmitted by Domei Tsushinsha (Japanese Federated News Agency) and recorded by the US Federal Communications Commission, August 14, 1945

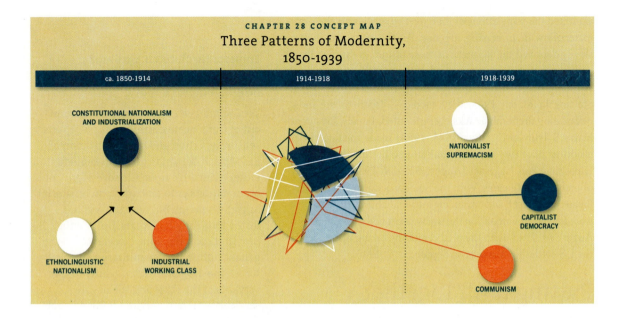

ways of opposing other modern innovations such as constitutionalism and industrialism—with their messy uncertainties and feelings of rootlessness—by insisting on a purer, more mystical bond for the modern nation-state that, ironically, hearkened back to a simpler, reimagined past. But Mussolini, Hitler, and the Japanese generals all aspired to the same scientific–industrial future as Roosevelt, Churchill, Stalin, Chiang K'ai-shek, and Mao Zedong.

Review and Respond

1. How did the Allies deal with Germany after its defeat in 1918, and how did it recover?

2. Explain the shift from capital goods to consumer goods investment in the capitalist economies after World War I. How did this shift express itself?

3. Which factors contributed to the Great Depression of 1929–1933?

4. What role did the protagonist play in the communist vision of modernity? Why was industrialization central to the Soviet communist pattern of modernity?

5. Trace the steps through which Hitler advanced from prisoner to dictator.

6. How did a version of constitutionalist modernity arrive in Japan, and which factors limited its impact?

7. What reasons limited constitutional nationalism in China after the creation of the republic in 1912?

8. What were some of the artistic responses to modernity? How did they reflect the anxiety of the period?

> For additional resources, including maps, primary sources, visuals, and quizzes, please go to www.oup.com/us/vonsivers. Please see the Further Resources section at the back of the book for additional readings and suggested websites.

Thinking Through Patterns

▶ **Which three patterns of modernity emerged after World War I? How and why did these patterns form?**

Ethnic nationalism was difficult to accommodate in the nineteenth century, which began with the more inclusive constitutional nationalism of Great Britain, the United States, and France. New nations like Italy, Germany, and Japan were formed on the basis of an ethnic nationalism that in a sense created nations but not necessarily ones with the ideals of equality embodied in constitutional nation-states. World War I set back Germany, Italy, and Japan, but afterward they inflated their ethnic nationalism into supremacist nationalism and adopted imperialism, all under the banner of modernity. In Russia, communists seized the opportunity offered by the turmoil of World War I to turn a constitutionally as well as industrially underdeveloped empire into a communist one-party, industrial empire. The United States, Britain, and France, each based on variations of constitutionalism, industry, and smaller or larger empires, became advocates of a capitalist democratic modernity.

Capitalist democracy was a modernity that upheld free enterprise, the market, and consumerism. It succeeded in providing the modern items of daily life, but it suffered a major setback in the Depression and had to be reined in through tightened political controls. It also withheld freedom, equality, and the staples of daily life from minorities and the colonized. Communism succeeded in industrializing an underdeveloped empire and providing the bare necessities for modern life; it did so with untold human sacrifices. Supremacist nationalism was attractive to nationalists who were not workers and therefore afraid of communism. Supremacist nationalists held democracies in disdain because they considered constitutions meaningless pieces of paper.

▶ **What were the strengths and flaws of each of the three visions of modernity?**

▶ **Why did supremacist nationalism disappear in the ashes of World War II?**

Supremacist nationalism was a modernity that failed because the conquest of new, self-sufficient empires proved to be an impossible goal. The advocates of democratic capitalist and communist modernity—most notably the United States, Great Britain, France, and the Soviet Union—were dangerously threatened by Germany, Italy, and Japan and came together to destroy these supremacist national countries.

Chapter 29

1945-1962

Reconstruction, Cold War, and Decolonization

By any standard the event seemed symbolic of a new world order, one in which the emerging nonaligned nations would set the pace of innovation. Appropriately enough, it also marked the beginning of a new decade, one that would begin full of promise and peril and end in conflict and confusion for much of the world. The event was the 1960 election of the world's first female prime minister, Sirimavo Bandaranaike (1916–2000), of what was then called Ceylon (renamed Sri Lanka in 1972), a large island off the southeastern coast of India.

Her country had achieved independence from Great Britain only a dozen years before and had maintained close ties to its former colonial

THE COLD WAR AND DECOLONIZATION

Seeing Patterns

▶ Why did the pattern of unfolding modernity, which offered three choices after World War I, shrink to just capitalist democracy and socialism–communism in 1945? How did each of these two patterns evolve between 1945 and 1962?

▶ What are the cultural premises of modernity?

▶ How did the newly independent countries of the Middle East, Asia, and Africa adapt to the divided world of the Cold War?

overlord. In 1956, however, Bandaranaike's husband Solomon was elected prime minister with a pronounced nationalist and socialist platform, in the newly assertive spirit of the nonaligned nations reflected in the Bandung Conference the year before. As prime minister, he replaced English with Sinhalese as the country's language and evicted the British military from its bases. When a Buddhist monk opposed to Western medicine assassinated him in 1959, she succeeded her husband, winning an election in 1960, becoming prime minister in her own right, and serving her first term from 1960 to 1965.

Coming from a prominent Buddhist family, she held the same deep political convictions as her husband, believing in a strong national foundation for her country as an independent nation beholden to neither West nor East. As a socialist, she continued the nationalization of the banking, insurance, and petroleum sectors begun by her husband; ordered the state to take over all Catholic schools; and joined the Nonalignment Movement in 1961. The movement sought to bring India, Egypt, Yugoslavia, Indonesia, and a number of other states together as a bloc to retain their independence from the pressures of the Cold War between the two superpowers of the United

Democracy in Action. One important element in the spread of representative government in Asia was the right of women to vote and hold office. Here, in a remote village on the island of Ceylon (now Sri Lanka) men and women line up separately to cast their votes in the general election of March 22, 1960. The victor in the race for prime minister, Sirimavo Bandaranaike, became the world's first woman prime minister.

United Nations: Successor of the League of Nations, founded in 1945 and comprising today about 200 countries; with a Secretary General, a General Assembly meeting annually, and a standing Security Council composed of permanent members (United States, China, Russia, Great Britain, and France) as well as 5 rotating temporary members.

States and the Soviet Union and their allies. Her strong commitment to a Sinhalese-only language policy, however, aroused considerable resistance in the country, especially from the Tamil minority in the north. The Theraveda Buddhist Sinhalese comprise about 74 percent and the Hindu Tamils 17 percent of the population. Only 2 years into Bandaranaike's tenure, the country was gripped by a Tamil civil disobedience campaign and it rapidly became apparent that Ceylon was entering a time of political turbulence. Ultimately, anti-Tamil discrimination led to the abortive Tamil Tiger liberation war (1976–2009), pursued on both sides with the utmost brutality.

During her four terms as prime minister (1960–1965, 1970–1972, 1972–1977, and 1994–2000), Bandaranaike was a prominent leader on the world stage. Like her fellow female prime ministers Benazir Bhutto in Pakistan and Indira Gandhi in India and first-generation nonaligned leaders like Jawaharlal Nehru of India, Sukarno of Indonesia, and Gamal Abdel Nasser of Egypt—Bandaranaike spent much of her time and scarce resources trying to navigate the turbulent waters of ethnic and religious conflict, superpower pressure, and nation-building in an increasingly competitive economic arena. The backdrop against which all these nonaligned nations acted was woven from two main developments in the unfolding pattern of scientific–industrial modernity: the Cold War and decolonization. The capitalist–democratic and the socialist–communist spheres competed with each other for political, military, and economic dominance; at the same time, the West rid itself of what was now seen as its biggest curse—colonialism—which bedeviled it and had severely detracted from its appeal during the interwar and early postwar periods.

The early Cold War, discussed in the first half of this chapter, dominated world politics during this time because the contest between the two superpowers allowed practically no escape. The one partial exception was China, which presented itself as a nonaligned country as it distanced itself from the Soviet Union but was viewed with ambivalence by its nonaligned colleagues. Decolonization, discussed in the second half of this chapter, was a subsidiary political process; but it nevertheless played a major role in the dynamics of the Cold War because it created many of the new nations over which both superpower blocs sought influence and so many tried to escape. By the 1962 Cuban Missile Crisis, during which the superpower confrontation reached its climax, the configuration of the two superpower blocs and the camp of the nonaligned nations was still in flux. Over the coming years, the tilting to one camp or another of India, Pakistan, Indonesia, and ultimately China, to name only a few, would loom large in the superpower struggle. And the role of Bandaranaike and other nonaligned leaders as spoilers between the superpowers, for a time at least, was secure.

Superpower Confrontation: Capitalist Democracy and Communism

World War II was the most destructive war in human history. Nearly 6 years of fighting in Europe and 9 years in Asia resulted in casualties on a scale scarcely conceivable in the past. The total loss of life, including combatants, civilians, and victims of the Holocaust, is estimated at over 50 million, three times as many as in World War I. With the exception of the continental United States, which was unreachable by enemy aircraft, all combatant countries in World War II suffered widespread destruction. Most ominous was that the final days of the war also ushered in the nuclear age. The use of the first atomic weapons by the United States against Japan meant that future general wars would almost certainly be nuclear ones. Yet, while the war was still on, the foundations of a new world organization to replace and fix the shortcomings of the old League of Nations—the **United Nations**, whose charter was later signed by 51 nations in October 1945—were being laid in San Francisco. Thus, the year 1945 was simultaneously one of hope that the war's end might result in a better world and one of grim assessment as the full extent of the global damage began to be understood. Remarkably, within a few years, out of the ruins, the world's remaining strains of modernity—capitalism–democracy and socialism–communism—would reemerge stronger than ever, each according to its own vision.

Destruction and Despair in the Nuclear Age. World War II was the most destructive human conflict in history, far exceeding the damage of what had only a short time before been considered to be "the war to end all wars"--World War I. Nowhere was the damage more complete than in Japan, where an aerial campaign of firebombing Japanese cities by American B-29s had destroyed nearly every major Japanese center. The culmination of this campaign was the first—and to date, last—use of nuclear weapons in warfare on the Japanese cities of Hiroshima and Nagasaki in August, 1945. Here, a mother and child who survived the nuclear destruction of Hiroshima sit plaintively amid the utter devastation of their city in December, 1945.

The Cold War Era, 1945–1962

As the world rebuilt, the United States and the Soviet Union promoted their contrasting visions of modernity—capitalist-democratic and communist—with deep missionary fervor. For the next 45 years the two powers were locked in a prolonged struggle to determine which approach would eventually prevail in the world. While each on occasion engaged in brinkmanship—pushing crises to the edge of nuclear war—as a rule both sought to avoid direct confrontation. Instead, they pursued their aims of expanding and consolidating their respective systems, dubbed the "Cold War," through ideological struggle and proxy states (that is, states acting as substitutes against each other). Two phases can be discerned in the early Cold War. The first lasted from 1945 to 1956, when the Soviet Union continued to pursue Stalin's prewar policy of "socialism in one country," which was now extended to include Eastern Europe. The second comprised the years 1956–1962, when Stalin's

1945	1947	1949	1952
Yalta and Potsdam Conferences	Indian and Pakistani Independence	People's Republic of China, Formation of NATO	Nasser Assumes Power in Egypt

1946	1948	1950-1953	1953
Churchill's "Iron Curtain" Speech	State of Israel Founded, First Arab–Israeli War	Korean War	CIA-Inspired Coup d'Etat in Iran

1955-1956	1957	1958	1961
Morocco, Tunisia Independent	Soviet Union's Launch of Sputnik Satellite	Great Leap Forward in China	First Space Orbit by Yuri Gagarin, Erection of Berlin Wall

1956	1957-1962	1959	1962
Suez War of Great Britain, France, and Israel against Egypt	Independence for Most African Colonies	Castro Assumes Power in Cuba	Cuban Missile Crisis

Cold War: Ideological struggle between the United States and its allies and the Soviet Union and its allies that lasted from 1945 to 1989.

Containment: U.S. foreign policy doctrine formulated in 1946 to limit as much as possible the spread of communism.

successor Nikita Khrushchev (1894–1971, in office 1953–1964) reformulated the policy to include spreading aid and influence to new nationalist regimes in Asia and Africa that had won their independence from Western colonialism, even if these regimes were not (yet) communist. This new policy, applied to Cuba, produced the near disaster of the Cuban Missile Crisis in 1962 during which the United States and the Soviet Union almost came to blows (see Map 29.1).

Cold War Origins   The origins of the **Cold War** have been bitterly debated and minutely studied since the 1940s, with apologists for each side tending to see its inception in the actions of the other. While it may not be possible at this point to establish an exact time or event for the beginning of the Cold War, we can point to certain mileposts in its development. One such milepost that most scholars point to came in the spring of 1945, when the Soviet Red Army occupied German-held territories in Eastern Europe and communist guerillas made rapid advances in the Balkans. In a secret deal between British Prime Minister Churchill and Soviet leader Josef Stalin in May 1944, Greece became part of the British sphere, in return for Romania and Bulgaria being apportioned to the Soviet sphere of responsibility for occupation at war's end.

Later, at the Yalta Conference in February 1945, Churchill, Stalin, and a haggard and ill American president Franklin Roosevelt agreed that the armies of the Allies would each undertake the occupation of the territories they held at war's end and hold free elections in those areas as soon as possible. Stalin also agreed that the Soviet Union would enter the war with Japan after the surrender of Germany. At the Potsdam Conference in July 1945, American interests were represented by Roosevelt's former vice president, Harry S Truman, who had assumed the office of president following Roosevelt's death in April.

Truman (in office 1945–1953) was more openly skeptical of Stalin's motives than Roosevelt, and he now had an edge that his predecessor lacked: On July 16, scientists at the "Manhattan Project," the US effort to develop an atomic weapon, had succeeded in detonating a plutonium test device in New Mexico. Armed with the astonishing results of the device's power and the knowledge that bombs were already being constructed for use against Japan, Truman felt confident he could deal firmly with Stalin's demands. His assessment of Stalin's motives was not reassuring; he felt the Russians had no intention of either withdrawing from Eastern Europe or allowing for democratic elections. By early 1946, Churchill, in a speech at Fulton, Missouri, coined the phrase that would define the communist sphere for decades to come in the West: the "Iron Curtain."

Accordingly, the United States formulated a policy designed to thwart Soviet expansion known as "**containment**." First spelled out in 1946 by George F. Kennan, a diplomat in the State Department, the proposed policy served as the foundation for the administration's determination to confront communist expansion.

Containing the Soviet Threat

"It is clear that the main element of any United States policy toward the Soviet Union must be that of long-term, patient but firm and vigilant containment of Russian expansive tendencies.... It is clear that the United States cannot expect in the foreseeable future to enjoy political intimacy with the Soviet regime. It must continue to regard the Soviet Union as a rival, not a partner, in the political arena. It must continue to expect that Soviet policies will reflect no abstract love of peace and stability, no real faith in the possibility of a permanent happy coexistence of the Socialist and capitalist worlds, but rather a cautious, persistent pressure toward the disruption and weakening of all rival influence and rival power."

—George F. Kennan. "The Sources of Soviet Conduct." *Foreign Affairs* 24, no. 4 (1947): 566–582. www .historyguide.org/europe/kennan.html.

The Cold War, 1947-1991

![blue]	Countries in North Atlantic Treaty Organization (NATO)) (1949–)
![pink]	Countries ruled by communist regimes for all or part of Cold War
![green]	Nonaligned countries, 1961
➘	Country with nuclear capability by 1987
☭	Direct military action by USSR and/or allies
★	Direct military action by USA and/or allies
☭	Economic and political intervention by USSR and/or allies
☆	Economic and political intervention by USA and/or allies
—	Iron Curtain

MAP **29.1** The Cold War, 1947–1991.

Confrontations, 1947–1949   Several confrontations between the Soviet Union and the United States followed. The first occurred in the Balkans. In Yugoslavia, the anti-Nazi resistance hero Josip Broz Tito (1892–1980) took over the government in November 1945 with the help of Soviet advisors. He then provided Greek communists with aid, to overthrow the royal government that had returned to rule with British support in 1946. The United States stepped in with supplies in 1947, assuming that Stalin was orchestrating aid from Yugoslavia, Bulgaria, and Romania. Under the **Truman Doctrine**, proclaimed in a speech of the same year, the United States announced its support of all "free peoples who are resisting attempted subjugation by armed minorities or by outside pressures."

What appeared like a proxy civil war between East and West raged for 2 years in Greece until it ended in the aftermath of the split between Tito and Stalin. In 1948, Tito claimed his right to regional communism, against Stalin's insistence on unity in the Communist Bloc. Although Stalin had never supported the Greek communists directly, given his agreement with Churchill, a surprising majority of the latter opted for Stalin. Tito withdrew his support for the pro-Stalin Greek communists, and the bid for communism in Greece was doomed to collapse in 1949.

Following up on his doctrine, Truman announced the **Marshall Plan** of aid to Europe, for the recovery of the continent from the ruins of the war, named after its architect, the secretary of state George C. Marshall (1880–1959). Although invited to take part, Stalin flatly rejected American aid and forbade Hungary, Czechoslovakia, and Poland to ask for it. In addition to the political reasons behind Stalin's injunction, the Marshall Plan's requirement of free markets and convertible currencies contradicted the communist ideology of a central command economy. Stalin was in the midst of engineering his fledgling communist governments in Eastern Europe and the Balkans, transforming them into the Communist Bloc, and integrating their economies with that of the Soviet Union. This was formalized in 1949 as the Council for Mutual Economic Assistance (COMECON).

The success of the Marshall Plan, with its billions of American dollars poured into relief and reconstruction in Western Europe, further irritated Stalin because it made the Western sectors of Germany and Berlin magnets for Eastern Europeans fleeing to the West. In 1948, therefore, the Soviets took the provocative step of setting up a highway and rail blockade of food and supplies to Berlin. The United States and Britain responded with a demonstration of technological prowess by mounting the "Berlin Airlift." For nearly a year, food, fuel, and other supplies required by this large city were flown in until Stalin finally gave up the blockade.

So far, the Cold War in Europe had been confined to diplomatic maneuvering between Washington and Moscow. During the Berlin crisis, however, the confrontation assumed military dimensions. Thanks in part to an elaborate espionage network embedded inside the nuclear programs of Britain and the United States, the Soviets had been able to accelerate their efforts to build a nuclear bomb. In 1949, they detonated their first device 4 years earlier than anticipated. Now, with its advantage in nuclear weapons eliminated and concern increasing over the possibility of a communist takeover in Western Europe, the United States formed a defensive alliance known as the North Atlantic Treaty Organization (NATO) in 1949. In response, the Soviet Union later formed the Warsaw Pact in 1955 among the states of the Eastern Bloc.

Truman Doctrine:
Policy formulated in 1947, initially to outline steps directed at preventing Greece and Turkey from becoming communist, mostly through military and economic aid.

Marshall Plan:
Financial program of $13 billion to support the reconstruction of the economies of 17 European countries during 1948–1952, with most of the aid going to France, Germany, Italy, and the Netherlands.

The Berlin Airlift. During nearly 1 year from June 1948 to May 1949 US, British, and British Commonwealth airplanes delivered more than 2 million tons of food and supplies to Berlin after Stalin had blocked all land access to the city. Berlin children eagerly await the next delivery of supplies.

Hot War in Korea   Emboldened by the development of the nuclear bomb and the victory of the Chinese communists over the nationalists in October 1949, Stalin ratcheted up the Cold War. After a series of raids and counterraids between communist North Korea and nationalist South Korea and Stalin's blessing for an invasion by the north, the Cold War turned hot. In June 1950, large numbers of communist troops crossed over into South Korea in an attempt at forcible unification. South Korean troops fought a desperate rearguard action at the southern end of the peninsula. Under US pressure and despite a Soviet boycott, the United Nations (UN) Security Council branded North Korea as the aggressor, entitling South Korea to UN intervention. At first, in July 1950, the North Korean invaders trapped US troops arriving from Japan and what remained of the South Korean defense forces in the southeast. But by October US troops, augmented by troops from a number of UN members, had mounted a surprise amphibious invasion and fought their way into North Korea, occupied the capital (Pyongyang), and advanced to the Chinese border.

In the meantime, the United States had sent a fleet to the remnant of the Chinese nationalists who had formed the Republic of China on the southern island of Taiwan, to protect it from a threatened invasion by a newly communist China. Thwarted in the south at Taiwan, Mao Zedong took the pronouncements of General Douglas MacArthur, the commander of the UN forces in Korea, about raiding Chinese supply bases on the North Korean border seriously. Stalin, on the other hand, opposed an escalation and gave Mao only token support.

Secretly marching to the border in October 1950, communist Chinese troops launched a massive surprise offensive into the peninsula, pushing the UN forces back deep into South Korea. Over the next 3 years, the war seesawed back and forth over the old border of the 38th parallel, while negotiations dragged on. Unwilling to expand the war further or use nuclear weapons, the new Eisenhower administration and the North Koreans agreed to an armistice in 1953. The armistice has endured from that date, and no official peace treaty was ever signed. For more than half a century, the border between the two Koreas has remained a volatile flashpoint, with provocative incidents repeatedly threatening to reopen the conflict.

McCarthyism in the United States   The strains of a "hot war" in Korea produced troubling domestic fallout in the United States as well. Amid the general atmosphere of anticommunism, Joseph McCarthy (1908–1957), a Republican senator from Wisconsin, rose to prominence almost overnight when he revealed in a 1950 speech that he had a lengthy list of members of the Communist Party employed by the State Department. Though he never produced the list, his smear tactics, together with denunciations made by the House Committee on Un-American Activities, ruined the careers of hundreds of government employees, movie actors and writers, and private persons in many walks of life. McCarthy went as far as accusing Presidents Truman and Eisenhower of tolerating communist "fellow travelers" in their administrations. For 4 years hysteria reigned until finally enough voices of reason arose in the Senate to censure McCarthy and relegate him to obscurity in 1954. The legacy of bitterness engendered by the "McCarthy era" remained for decades and generated abundant political accusations on both sides.

Revolt in East Germany   As the McCarthy drama unfolded in the United States and the frustrating Korean armistice negotiations at Panmunjom dragged on, Stalin died of a stroke in April 1953. The death of this all-powerful, inscrutable, and paranoid dictator was profoundly unsettling for the governments of the Eastern Bloc. This was especially the case in the German Democratic Republic (East Germany), where the government was nervously watching the rising wave of defections to the Federal Republic (West Germany)—nearly a million persons during 1949–1953. It had sealed off the border through a system of fences and watchtowers, but Berlin—also divided into East and West sectors—was still a gaping hole. The population was seething over rising production quotas, shortages resulting from the shipment of industrial goods to the Soviet Union (in the name of reparations), and the beginnings of a West German economic boom in which it could not share.

In June 1953, a strike among East Berlin workers quickly grew into a general uprising, encompassing some 500 cities and towns. East German police and Soviet troops, stunned at first, quickly moved to suppress the revolt. The Politburo (the Communist Party's Central Committee Political Bureau) in Moscow, still trying to determine Stalin's succession, refused any concessions, except for a few cosmetic changes in the reparations. The German Stalinist government obediently went along.

Stalin's eventual successor in the fall of 1953 was Nikita Khrushchev, a metalworker from a poor farmer's family on the Russian–Ukrainian border who had worked his way up through the party hierarchy during the war years. It took Khrushchev a year and a half to consolidate his power as party secretary and premier, during which he made substantial investments in agriculture, housing, and consumer goods. In February 1956 he gave a much-noted speech in which he denounced Stalin's "excesses" during collectivization and the purges of the 1930s. Thousands were released from prisons and the labor camps in Siberia (*gulags*) and other remote areas. In the Communist Bloc Khrushchev pushed for the removal of Stalinist hard-liners and the arrival of new faces willing to improve general living conditions for the population. To balance the new flexibility within the Soviet Bloc, Khrushchev was careful to maintain toughness toward the West. He alarmed leaders of the West when he announced that he was abandoning Stalin's doctrine of socialism in one country for a new policy that supported anticolonial nationalist independence movements around the globe even if the movements were not communist. The policy sent shivers down the spines of the cold warriors in the West.

Revolt in Poland and Hungary   Khrushchev's speech and reforms awakened hopes in Eastern Europe that new leaders would bring change there as well. In Poland, where collectivization and the command economy had progressed only slowly and the Catholic Church could not be intimidated, Khrushchev's speech resulted in workers' unrest similar to East Germany 3 years earlier. Nationalist reformists gained the upper hand over Stalinists in the Polish Politburo, and Khrushchev realized that he had to avoid another Tito-style secession at all costs. After a few tense days in mid-October, pitting Soviet troops and an angry population against each other, Poland received its limited autonomy.

In Hungary, the Politburo was similarly divided between reformers and Stalinists. People in Budapest and other cities, watching events in Poland with intense interest, took to the streets. The Politburo lost control and the man appointed to lead the country to a national communist solution similar to that of Poland, Imre Nagy [Noj] (1896–1958), felt emboldened by popular support to go further by announcing a multiparty system and the withdrawal of Hungary from the Warsaw Pact. These announcements were too much for Khrushchev, who unleashed the Soviet troops stationed in Hungary to repress the by now fully blossoming grassroots revolution.

Aware of British, French, and American preoccupation with the Suez Crisis, the Soviets crushed the uprising in November 1956. Nagy, finding sanctuary in the Yugoslav Embassy and promised safe conduct out of the country, was duped and found

Unrest in the Soviet Bloc. In the Hungarian uprising from October to November 1956, some 2.500 Hungarians and 700 Soviet troops were killed, while 200,000 fled to neighboring Austria and the West. Here, a young boy and older man watch with a surprising degree of nonchalance while a Soviet tank rumbles through an intersection with barricades set up by Hungarian "freedom fighters."

Aiming for the Stars. New scholarship sheds light on Sputnik's role in Russian cultural history. As this commemorative postcard from 1958 reveals, the connection between the technological achievement of Sputnik and popular interest in space travel was strong. The legend reads in Russian: "4 October, the USSR launched Earth's first artificial satellite; 3 November, the USSR launched Earth's second artificial satellite."

himself arrested. The new pro-Moscow government executed him in 1958. During the brief uprising, perhaps a quarter of a million Hungarian citizens escaped to the West. For those who stayed, in the hopes of experiencing greater freedom, the events were a crushing blow.

ICBMs and Sputniks   The suppression of anticommunist unrest in the Eastern Bloc decreased the appeal of communism among many Marxists and revolutionary socialists in the West. But steady advancement in weapons technologies and by extension in missiles and space flight, revealed that there was a powerful military punch behind Soviet repression. In 1957 the Soviet Union announced the development of the world's first intercontinental ballistic missile (ICBM), with a range of around 3,500 miles, making it capable of reaching America's East Coast. In the same year, the Soviet Union launched the world's first orbiting satellite, named "Sputnik," into space. Then, in 1961, Russian scientists sent the world's first cosmonaut, Yuri Gagarin (1934–1968), into space, followed 2 years later by Valentina Tereshkova (b. 1937), the world's first female cosmonaut.

These Soviet achievements duly frightened the Eisenhower administration and Congress as the implications of nuclear weapons falling from space with no practicable defense against them began to set in. Politicians played up the apparent technological leadership of the Soviet Union to goad Congress into accelerating the US missile and space program even at the risk of reheating the Cold War with the Soviet Union. Thus, in 1958 the United States successfully launched its first satellite, Explorer I, and the following year its first ICBM, the Atlas. The space and missile races were now fully under way.

Communism in Cuba   In 1959, Fidel Castro (b. 1926), a nationalist guerilla fighter opposed to the influence of American companies over a government generally perceived as corrupt, succeeded in seizing power in Cuba. A trained lawyer, Castro was the son of a Spanish immigrant who had become a wealthy planter. About 6 months after the coup, Cuba was the new symbol of the Khrushchev government's widely hailed openness toward national liberation movements worthy of communist largesse. The Soviet Union lavished huge sums on the development of the economy of the island. Khrushchev's instincts were proven right when Castro openly embraced communism in 1960.

To counter Khrushchev's overtures to national liberation movements, President Eisenhower and the head of the American Central Intelligence Agency (CIA), Allen Dulles (1893–1969), secretly supported and trained anticommunist dissidents in the Middle East, Africa, and Latin America. In the case of Latin America, a group of Cuban anticommunists trained in Guatemala with CIA support for an invasion and overthrow of Castro in Cuba. President John F. Kennedy (in office 1961–1963) inherited the initiative and, against his better judgment, decided to steer a middle course, sanctioning an invasion of Cuba by seemingly independent freedom fighters with no direct US armed forces support. The so-called Bay of Pigs invasion in April

1961 (named for the small bay in southern Cuba where the anticommunist invasion began) was promptly intercepted and easily defeated by Castro's forces, to the great embarrassment of Kennedy.

The Berlin Wall   Fortunately for the United States, Khrushchev suffered a severe embarrassment of his own. East Germany, which retained its Stalinist leadership, pressured Khrushchev to close the last loophole in Berlin through which its citizens could escape to West Germany. Between 1953 and 1961, the East German "brain drain" reached 3 million defectors or nearly one-fifth of the population, most of them young and ambitious people whose talent and skills the regime coveted. The East German Stalinists, allied with a few remaining Stalinists in the Politburo, prevailed over Khrushchev's opposition and built the Berlin Wall in 1961, effectively turning the German Democratic Republic into a prison.

The playing field between East and West was now level, with setbacks on both sides, when the two reached the climax of the Cold War: the first direct confrontation between the Soviet Union and the United States nearly two decades after the end of World War II. In October 1962 US spy planes discovered the presence of missile launching pads in Cuba. In October 1962 President Kennedy demanded their immediate destruction and then followed up with a naval blockade of the island to prevent the arrival of Russian missiles. In defiance, Khrushchev dispatched Russian ships to Cuba; when it was discovered that they were bearing missiles, President Kennedy demanded that Khrushchev recall the ships. The world held its breath for several days as the ships headed steadily for Cuba, raising the very real possibility of a nuclear exchange between the world's superpowers (see Map 29.2).

In the face of American determination, Khrushchev recalled the ships at the last minute. Kennedy, for his part, agreed to remove American missiles from Turkey. Realizing just how close the world had come to World War III, Kennedy and Khrushchev signed the Nuclear Test Ban Treaty in 1963, an agreement banning the aboveground testing and development of nuclear weapons. The treaty also sought to prevent the spread of these technologies to other countries. After this dramatic climax in the Cold War, relations gradually thawed.

MAP 29.2 The Cuban Missile Crisis.

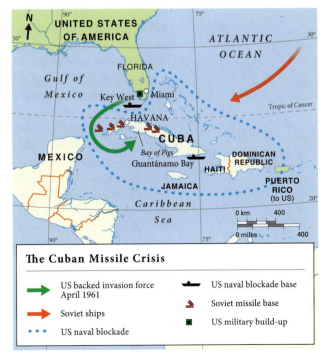

Society and Culture in Postwar North America, Europe, and Japan

As in many other wars, World War II was followed by years of conservatism during which the generation of war veterans, deprived of some of their best years because of military service, sought to pursue civilian lives of normalcy and comfort. Intellectuals and artists again cast a critical eye on the modernity that was relentlessly evolving around them, not unlike the previous generation had after World War I. Now, however,

The G.I. Bill for African Americans. Staff Sergeant Herbert Ellison explains the G.I. Bill to members of his company. The bill, enacted in 1944, provided soldiers returning from the war with support for training and education as well as subsidized home loans. Some 7.8 million veterans benefited from the training and education it provided.

the political and ideological options were narrower. Supremacist nationalism in the form of fascism, Nazism, or militarism had been thoroughly bankrupted; and choices had shrunk to communism and capitalist democracy. Still, among the emerging nations, artists and intellectuals struggled to forge new paths, often with attempts at synthesis among indigenous culture and socialist and democratic ideas.

Mass Consumption Culture As discharged American soldiers returned to civilian life, they married and had children. The "baby-boomer" generation appeared on the scene between 1945 and 1961. Families with four to six children were almost the norm. Medical advances and improved diet and nutrition helped in the health and survival of parents and children. The growing population triggered increased consumer demand, not only for the basics of living, such as food, clothes, shoes, and shelter, but also for consumer durables which increased the comfort of living, such as refrigerators, dishwashers, vacuum cleaners, radios, televisions, telephones, and cars. In the United States, the G.I. Bill supported not only the middle-class lifestyle but also university studies for better-paying jobs. In Europe, the Marshall Plan helped to provide Europeans with similar, if still somewhat lower, living standards. Americans increasingly took on credit to move into their middle-class lives, while Europeans tended to save first before spending their money on consumer goods.

One convenience symbolic of the new era was the innovative plastic container with a tight-fitting lid to keep food fresh in the refrigerator. Earl Tupper (1907–1983), a subcontractor of the chemicals conglomerate DuPont during the war, experimented with the plastic compound polyethylene and in 1947 launched his line of Tupperware, inexpensive containers of all sizes and shapes. Sales began to pick up, however, only after the Tupperware company hired Brownie Wise (1913–1992), an eighth-grade dropout from Georgia who sold household products through a home party plan which she had developed. This plan provided suburban housewives with the motivation to organize neighbors at parties where they could demonstrate and sell Tupperware. Successful housewives rose in the sales-force hierarchy, and annual jubilees celebrated the champion saleswomen of the year at the "Tupperware College of Knowledge" in Kissimmee, Florida. Tupperware sales took off, and a highly accomplished Wise went on to become vice president and the first female entrepreneur featured on the cover of *Business Weekly*. Wise and a half-dozen other women were the first executives to break into the male-dominated corporate structure of American business, pioneers of a trend that is only now becoming more commonplace.

In addition to the Tupperware parties, the Avon lady and the encyclopedia man were fixtures of American suburban life. In the idealized family of the 1950s and early 1960s, husbands worked downtown from 9:00 to 5:00, while mothers and grandmothers were responsible for the household and children. Shopping was done in the new suburban mall, and everybody went to church or synagogue on weekends

Suburban Convenience. Three suburban housewives examine the latest in food container design and utility at what had become a fixture in the postwar landscape—the Tupperware party. Tupperware sparked and reinivigorated a host of other women-dominated, door-to-door businesses like Avon, Amway, Herbalife, and Mary Kay Cosmetics. Note that while middle-class hair styles and clothing have undergone fashion cycles over the intervening decades, the differences between the styles of these women from the early 1960s is not dramatically different from styles of the early 2000s.

and occasionally treated themselves with a trip to the downtown department store and movie theater. This gendered and spatially segregated life was highly structured, corresponding to the yearning of the expanding middle classes for regularity and order after the years of economic depression and war. In Europe and Japan, with variations due to cultural differences and a later suburbanization process, similar changes in consumer culture took place. An important minority of baby boomers found this middle-class life eventually so stultifying that they revolted in the 1960s, as we will see in Chapter 30.

American Popular Culture Dominates the World   Thanks to US leadership in the entertainment industry first established during the Roaring Twenties, American pop culture spread again across the world. American shows produced for television in the 1950s were wildly popular and constituted over one-half of televised shows played in British and Western European homes. Westerns were exemplified by the long-running success of *The Lone Ranger*, which was broadcast from 1949 to 1957. Some of the most successful film directors were John Ford (1894–1973), Alfred Hitchcock (1899–1980), and Joseph Losey (1909–1984), who recruited internationally known stars such as Marlene Dietrich (1901–1992), Clark Gable (1901–1960), James Stewart (1908–1997), Marilyn Monroe (1926–1962), and Elizabeth Taylor (1932–2011) to their productions. American music had a similar influence in shaping the development of popular culture on both sides of the Atlantic. Blues and, especially, jazz resumed their pre-1930s dominance of

Patterns Up Close | Popular Culture and Rock and Roll

Perhaps the most successful musical genre and export of twentieth-century popular culture was rock and roll. Today, rock and roll and its descendents—disco, rap, and hip-hop, among many—are all-pervasive on the world scene, appearing in tiny cafes in Congo and remote villages in South America and spawning a host of local artists and imitators worldwide. As part of an identifiable global youth culture, it has also inspired most of the fashions associated with youth and rebellion since the mid-1950s.

Music scholars avidly debate who actually "created" the music, and a host of pioneers have been cited. The origins of the music may be found in blues, rhythm and blues, and jazz. By the late 1940s many African American musicians were performing in small groups featuring combinations of recently developed electrically amplified guitars and basses, drums, horns, and keyboard instruments. This kind of group allowed for a loud, hard-driving music with a more economical configuration than the large jazz groups that dominated the war years. Some scholars have cited Ike Turner's 1951 "Rocket 88" as the first rock and roll record; more conventionally, Bill Haley and the Comets' "Rock Around the Clock" (1954) is considered to be the breakout song that took African American musical forms and made them accepted by a larger—and mostly white—teenage audience.

Rock Around the Clock. The breakthrough success of the new form of popular music called "Rock and Roll" by the mid-1950s was unmistakable, though its origins in African American music forms led many conservative white parents to view it as dangerous and subversive—while their sons and daughters took to it with enthusiasm. Here, the first rock-and-roll group with cross-over success, Bill Haley and the Comets, wails away with exuberance.

Within short order, Elvis Presley, Buddy Holly, Little Richard, Jerry Lee Lewis, and a host of other performers also came to dominate the charts; their recordings sold in the millions from the mid-1950s onward. By the early 1960s the influence of this music in Great Britain led to the famous "British Invasion" of the United States by such groups as the Beatles, the Rolling Stones, the Yardbirds, the Kinks, the Who, and others. By the late 1960s the international appeal of what was now being called "rock music" or simply "rock" and its successful transplantation far and wide had created rock culture throughout Europe, Latin America, and Asia. Despite vigorous efforts to ban it or create substitutes for it in Soviet-Bloc nations, it also achieved major cult status as underground music for a variety of political and lifestyle dissidents. Since the 1950s, each successive generation has sought to use a variation of the music to push its own ideas of rebellion and outrageousness in distancing itself from its predecessors. But in the end, they all seem to agree with the Rolling Stones, who sang "It's only rock and roll but I like it!"

Questions

- How is rock and roll a cultural expression of the capitalist-democratic pattern of modernity?

- Does rock's global impact show that cultural forms of expression are in many ways more enduring than political ones?

Rock Around the World. Over the succeeding decades, rock-and-roll—later shortened to simply "rock"—became a kind of world music, with local variants. By the end of the twentieth century there was probably no place on earth where the music had not become established. In this startling scene an image of the wildly successful performer Madonna graces a van door window in the city of Jenné-Jeno, in Mali in West Africa.

European popular music. A new musical form, rock and roll, arose from the older musical forms and appealed to the baby-boom generation as it entered its teenage years in the later 1950s. Parents were generally aghast at this "noise," but the teenagers prevailed—and rock and roll conquered the world (see "Patterns Up Close").

Existentialism   Consumerism was a central element in the capitalist-democratic order and was based on the belief in the autonomous individual as the basic component of society. The Enlightenment ideas of materialism and the social contract continued to dominate the Anglo-American cultural sphere, but their reductionist vision, which diminished everything to nature and atoms, had prompted Kant and Hegel to reintroduce the transcendence of mind into continental European thought in the early nineteenth century.

The effect of these different orientations was that when the broad nineteenth-century movements of early modernity—first romanticism and then realism—gave way to the twentieth-century **modernism**, the great majority of Anglo-American thinkers and artists continued their broad modernist approaches. By contrast, European thinkers and artists, dissatisfied with the nineteenth-century solutions to modernity's materialist shortcomings, remained more strongly committed to finding new ideological solutions to materialism. In philosophy, the most important modernist thinker was Martin Heidegger (1889–1976), who saw himself as a prophet offering a non-materialist future in his work *Being and Time* (1927). His ideas became constitutive not only for the ideology of existentialism, which swept continental Europe in the 1950s and early 1960s, but also for the ideologies of poststructuralism and postmodernism which became dominant in the world after the mid-1970s.

In Germany, Heidegger was tainted by his support for the Nazis. But in France, his castigation of what he viewed as a modernity of meaningless materialism exerted a powerful attraction on intellectuals, such as Jean-Paul Sartre (1905–1980) and Albert Camus (1913–1960). Sartre was a communist enthralled by the egalitarian core of socialism; Camus was an anticommunist who was appalled at the barbarity of Stalin as revealed by Khrushchev after Stalin's death in 1953. Sartre, in *Being and Nothingness* (1943) and other essays and plays, described life as a material existence without God amid the horrors of a gaping nothingness in space and time. For him, the only way of living in such a bleak reality was to espouse the absurdity of existence in the here and now as intensively as possible, choosing whatever would give one authenticity from among equally relative possibilities.

For Camus, who rejected the label of **existentialism**, the absurdity of life in a purely material universe without God was nevertheless also a point of departure. He pinned his hope not on socialist egalitarianism but on rebellion against the denial of human rights in any form of mass politics. His novel *The Stranger*, essay *The Rebel* (1951), and other essays and plays were pleas for a spirited engagement of the individual in an existence of honesty and justice as a way out of modernity's materialist absurdity. The Irish playwright Samuel Beckett (1906–1989) and the Romanian playwright Eugène Ionesco (1909–1994), both writing in French, were less optimistic about humanity's ability to escape absurdity. For them, even more than Sartre and Camus, the only point of one's existence was to uncover modern life's abundant moments of pointlessness, often presented in a hilarious way in their scripts, so as to make existence less hypocritical and more honest.

Modernism: Any of various movements in philosophy and the arts characterized by a deliberate break with classical or traditional forms of thought or expression.

Existentialism: A form of thought built on the assumption that the scientific–industrial society of modernity is without intrinsic meaning unless an answer to the question of what constitutes authentic existence is found; in the later 1970s this question was renewed in the intellectual movement known as postmodernism.

Poetry and Literature   Not surprisingly, the basic materialist problem of modernity was fertile ground not only for existentialists in philosophy and the theater but in a more generalized form also for writers and film directors, the two often collaborating. With cultural variations, typically modern themes (individualism, loneliness, and alienation; conformism, freedom, and personal fulfillment; family bonds and parental relations; class, race, and gender sensibilities; political persecution, torture, and mass murder), all provided fodder for rich national literary and cinematographic post–World War II cultures in Western countries. As culture-specific as many authors and filmmakers were, by not merely dwelling on the reductionism of modernity but rather confronting it with their rich inherited premodern traditions, they created works that could be understood across cultures. In many cases, they created classics that are today as fresh and relevant as they were then.

A few representative examples illustrate the breadth of global culture in 1945–1962. In the United States it was the rich premodern culture of the South which produced figures such as William Faulkner (1897–1962) and Tennessee Williams (1911–1983), who explored in different ways the complexities of southern family life. The influential southern journal *New Criticism* revolutionized the understanding of literary works on their own formal and substantive merits, without recourse to biography and social environment. The poets Wallace Stevens (1879–1955) and Elizabeth Bishop (1911–1979) emerged from interwar modernism with fresh approaches. Stevens focused his attention on the autonomy and depth of modern imagination, while Bishop wrote a carefully crafted formal poetry that obscured more than it revealed about her search for belonging in the modern world.

Poetry in Great Britain was similarly oriented toward personal struggles with the emotional effects of modernity, as in the work of the Englishman (later American citizen) W. H. Auden (1907–1973) and the Welshman Dylan Thomas (1914–1953). By contrast, German-language authors, such as the Swiss playwright Max Frisch (1911–1991), the Romanian-born Jewish poet–essayist Paul Celan (1920–1970), the Austrian Ingeborg Bachmann (1926–1973), and the German Günter Grass (b. 1927)—albeit in their own different ways—focused on social themes such as identity, suffering, guilt, and the truth of language. Similar social themes within different cultural contexts are found in the works of the Italian Alberto Moravia (1907–1990), the Japanese Shohei Ooka [OH-kah] (1909–1988), the Russian Aleksandr Solzhenitsyn (1918–2008), and the Spaniard Jorge Semprún (1923–2011). Latin America was a microcosm of the varieties of modernism, coming to the fore in such different authors as the Argentine Jorge Luís Borges (1899–1986), the Chilean Pablo Neruda (1904–1973), and the Mexican Octavio Paz (1914–1998). Strikingly, in all of these authors the ebullient and often strident modernism of the early twentieth century gives way to a more reflective, sometimes distant, and always more personal encounter with the ambiguities and contradictions of modernity.

Sartre on Consciousness

"Thus it amounts to the same thing whether one gets drunk alone or is a leader of nations. If one of these activities takes precedence over the other, this will not be because of its real goal but because of the degree of consciousness which it possesses of its real goal; and in this case it will be the quietism of the solitary drunkard which will take precedence over the vain agitation of the leader of nations."

—Jean-Paul Sartre. *Being and Nothingness*. Translated by Hazel E. Barnes, p. 797. New York: Philosophical Library, 1956.

Abstract Expressionism. (*a*) Hans Hofmann (1880–1966), *Delight*, 1947. (*b*) Willem de Kooning (1904–1997), *Montauk Highway*, 1958. Abstract expressionism was a New York–centered artistic movement that combined the strong colors of World War I German expressionism with the abstract art pioneered by the Russian-born Wassiliy Kandinsky and the artists of the Bauhaus school. Before and during the Nazi period, many European artists had flocked to New York, including Hofmann and de Kooning. The movement caught the public eye when Jackson Pollock, following the surrealists, made the creation of a work of art—painting a large canvas on the floor through the dripping of paint—an art in itself.

Film, Painting, and Music   Many literary works, including some by the afore-mentioned authors, made their way into film, in the hands of directors who elevated the pop-culture entertainment movie into an art that sought to visualize the multi-faceted literary modernity of 1945–1962. The pioneers of the "art flick" were Erich von Stroheim (1885–1957) and Jean Renoir (1894–1979, son of the impression-ist painter Pierre-Auguste Renoir), who made their main contributions during the modernist interwar period. After World War II, two broad movements emerged: the neorealist school of Italian filmmakers that dealt with the harsh life in post–World War II Italy and the related New Wave (*Nouvelle vague*) in France, beginning in the late 1950s, that featured free-wheeling baby boomers breaking loose from the regi-mented post-war life.

Similar to the movements in film, two artistic developments swept through painting and music in the post–World War II period: abstract expressionism and serialism. The proponents of these two movements presented their works as existen-tialist reflections of conflicted emotions, expressed in art as pure color without form and in music as sound without harmony or traditional form. Abstract expressionism began in the United States with Mark Rothko (1903–1970) and Jackson Pollock (1912–1956) and swiftly spread across the world.

Latin America, by contrast, continued to follow social realism, a version of early twentieth-century modernism which, especially in Mexico, fit well within the cul-tural approach of the dominant revolutionary party. Here, the outstanding represen-tatives were the Mexican husband and wife team Diego Rivera (1889–1957) and Frida Kahlo (1907–1954). Rivera executed many commissioned murals celebrat-ing important historical episodes from the Aztec and early independence periods. Kahlo's folk art approach masks a deep and often troubled self-exploration, which has had a strong impact both in Mexico and the world.

Serialism, based on the pioneering "atonal" music of the Austrian American composer Arnold Schoenberg (1874–1951), was international from the start, with such representatives as the Italian Luigi Nono (1924–1990), the French Pierre Boulez [Boo-LEZ] (b. 1925), and the Germans Werner Henze (b. 1926) and Karlheinz Stockhausen (1928–2007). The 12–tone octave allows for 66 pitches, or sound frequencies, and is no longer organized around a key, or central tone, characteristic of all music from the Renaissance to Romanticism. Compositions after the middle of the twentieth century were, typically, mathematically related series of pitches (hence "serialism"). The works of both abstract expressionism and serialism require considerable understanding to be enjoyable, and for many people they remain unknown cultural territory.

Populism and Industrialization in Latin America

Given its large Creole and European immigrant populations, Latin America's dominant social classes had participated since the time of the constitutionalist revolutions in the pattern of unfolding cultural modernity. But Latin America also had a large population of Amerindians and blacks, who participated only marginally in this modernity and large majorities of whom were mired in rural subsistence. Since these populations increased rapidly after World War II, the region faced problems that did not exist in North America or Europe, where industry and its related service sector employed an overwhelmingly urban society. Latin America began to resemble Asia and Africa, which also had massive rural populations, small middle classes, and limited industrial sectors. Populist leaders relying on the urban poor thus sought to steer their countries toward greater industrialization, although with limited success.

Slow Social Change

Latin America had stayed out of World War II. The postwar aftermath therefore neither disrupted nor offered new opportunities to the pattern of social and economic development. The region had suffered from the disappearance of commodity export markets during the Depression of the 1930s, and politicians realized that import-substitution industrialization, replacing imported manufactures with domestically produced ones, had to be seriously taken up as a postwar policy. Tackling industrialization, however, was not easy since landowners opposed it and the great majority of rural and urban Latin Americans were too poor to become consumers.

Rural and Urban Society
Prior to 1945, the rural population had been decreasing, though very slowly. It still comprised about two-thirds of the total population. But during 1945–1962, the pace of urbanization picked up, with the proportions nearly reversed (see Map 29.3). Overall population growth during this period accelerated, but the poverty rates remained the same or even increased, making Latin America the one world region with the greatest income disparities. The inequalities were exacerbated by the continuation of sizeable indigenous Amerindian farming populations in Guatemala, Ecuador, Peru, Bolivia, and parts of Mexico, as well as blacks in Brazil. Landowners continued to thwart efforts at land reform: Except for Mexico (in spurts after 1915) and Bolivia (1952) no country abolished landlordism

Urbanization and Population Growth in Latin America and the Caribbean, 1950

Urban population as percentage of total in 1950:

- Below 30%
- 30%–50%
- 50%–70%
- Over 70%

Approximate population of the five largest cities (in thousands)

- ca. 1920
- 1950

Cities with population in 1950 of:

- ■ 250,000–500,000 (and capital cities below 250,000)
- ● 500,000–1,000,000
- ○ Over 1,000,000

MAP **29.3** Urbanization and Population Growth in Latin America and the Caribbean, ca. 1950.

prior to 1962. Cuba's land reform (1959) and the threat of local peasant revolutions made the issue urgent again, but agrarian reforms picked up only in the 1960s.

Much of the landless population migrated to the cities, making up nearly half of the arrivals. They settled in sprawling shantytowns with no urban services. Some migrants found employment in the expanding industrial sector, but more often than not they survived through occasional labor in the so-called informal sector, a new phenomenon of peddling, repairing, and recycling which comprised about one-third of the urban population. In contrast to the villages, rural–urban migrants benefited at least marginally from the health and education benefits which populist politicians introduced. The industrial labor force grew to about one-quarter of the total labor force, a growth that was far behind that of the East Asian "Tigers" or "Little Dragons" of Korea, Taiwan, and Hong Kong in the 1950s and reflected the hesitant attitude of the politicians toward industrialization in view of rebounding commodity exports in the 1950s.

At the end of World War II, industrialism was still confined mainly to food-processing and textile manufacturing; only Mexico and Brazil had moved into basic goods, such as steel and chemicals. In the later 1940s and early 1950s, the larger Latin American countries moved to capital goods and consumer durables, such as machinery, tools, cars, and refrigerators. Smaller countries, like Bolivia, Peru, and Paraguay, overextended themselves with industrial import substitution and, after a few years of trying, had to return in the early 1950s to a primacy of commodity exports. Very little private capital was available on the domestic market for risky industrialization ventures, and therefore, the state jumped into the fray to allocate the necessary funds.

Populist Guided Democracy

As we have seen, the period 1945–1962 was the time when the siren songs of fascism and Nazism faded and only democracy and communism remained as political and ideological choices. The attraction of democracy in its constitutional-nationalist North American and European forms, however, was limited since the United States, in the grip of the Cold War, was primarily interested in the professed loyalty of autocratic rulers in its Latin American backyard. Communism was initially also of limited appeal, given Stalin's preference for large, obedient communist parties that toed his line, and flourished only once Khrushchev supported national liberation movements, as in Cuba. **Populism** was an intermediate form of governance that found strong, albeit brief, support in Latin America from 1945–1962.

The Populist Wave   Democracy in Latin America during this time was represented by the three countries of Venezuela (1958), Colombia (1953–1964), and Costa Rica (1953–). Democratic politicians, however, were unable to put Venezuela's oil to productive use or bring about land reform in Colombia, resulting eventually in the formation of a communist guerilla underground in the latter country in 1964. Eight Latin American countries had populist regimes for varying periods from the mid-1940s onward: Guatemala (1944–1954), Argentina (1946–1955), Brazil (1946–1954), Venezuela (1945–1948), Peru (1945–1948), Chile (1946–1952), Costa Rica (1948–1953), and Ecuador (1948–1961). In Guatemala, the Cold War and the banana plantation interests of the United Fruit Company formed the background for a CIA-fomented military coup d'état which ended the rule of the elected populist Jacobo Arbenz and was the prelude to a vicious civil war (1960–1996). The

Populism: Type of governance in which rulers seek support directly from the population, through organizing mass rallies, manipulating elections, and intimidating or bypassing parliament.

remaining countries similarly moved in and out of coups d'état and authoritarian or dictatorial regimes from 1945 to 1962.

Peronism is the best-known form of the populist interlude in Latin America that characterized the period of 1945–1962. Colonel Juan Perón (1895–1974), of modest rural background, was a member of a group of officers who staged a coup in 1943 against the traditional landowners and their conservative military allies. They sympathized with the urban population of workers in the nascent food-processing industries as well as the poor in the traditional crafts, service employments, and the informal sector of street vending, repairing, mending, and trash collecting. Perón became minister of labor in the junta. In this position, he entered into an alliance with labor unions and improved wages, set a minimum wage, and increased pensions. After an earthquake, as the junta solicited donations from celebrities, Perón met Eva Duarte (1919–1952), a movie actress. An attractive, popular person in her own right, she headed a variety of social organizations and charities; and the two together became the symbol of Peronism. In elections in 1946, at the head of a fractious coalition of nationalists, socialists, and communists, Perón gained a legitimate mandate as president.

After the elections he started a 5-year plan of nationalization and industrialization—the characteristic state socialism pursued also in Asia and Africa. Banks, phone companies, railroads, and streetcars, mostly in the hands of British and French capital, were nationalized, as was the entire export of agricultural commodities. A year later, construction of plants for the production of primary and intermediate industrial goods, such as iron, steel, farm machinery, ships, and airplanes, got under way. Interestingly, Perón's state socialism stopped short of the automobile sector in order to avoid a confrontation with US investors. During Perón's tenure, the economy expanded by 40 percent.

To get the national factories going, however, they had to be equipped with imported machinery. Initially, Perón paid for these imports with reserves accumulated from commodity exports during World War II. But soon the costs for the imported machinery exceeded the internal reserves and revenues of Argentina. Inflation and strikes plagued the country. What eventually derailed Perón, however, was the Cold War. President Truman refused to include Argentina in the list of recipients for Marshall Plan aid. He disliked a populist regime in his own hemisphere that strove to leap into full industrialization through state socialism. Plagued by chronic deficits and unable to pay its foreign debts, Perón was overthrown by a conservative-led coup against him in 1955. Thus, Argentina, instead of leaping into industrialization, stumbled—not unlike China in the later 1950s.

The End of Colonialism and the Rise of New Nations

Like Latin America, Asia and Africa also experienced rapid population growth and urbanization in the period 1945–1962. But in contrast to the politically independent American continent, colonialism was still dominant in Asia and Africa at the end of World War II. The governments of Great Britain and France had no inclination to relinquish their empires at this point, but both were too exhausted by the war to hold them completely. Thus, in a first wave after the end of war, a few independence movements succeeded in more or less forcibly prying themselves loose, notably in the Middle East and Asia. A major shift in the perception of the benefits of colonialism during the mid-1950s, however, had to take place before Britain and France were willing to relinquish their colonial grip in Africa.

"China Has Stood Up"

Japan maintained a short and brutal colonial regime from 1937 to 1945 in China. Given Japan's defeat in World War II by the Allies, the Chinese did not have to fight for their independence; but they were not spared conflict. In 1949 the communists finally prevailed over the nationalists after 4 more years of a civil war that had begun over a decade earlier. China was still fundamentally a peasant-based economy with scant industrial resources. Mao's theories of revolution had adopted Marxist principles to put peasants instead of industrial workers at the forefront of the movement toward socialism. For Mao, this reinterpretation of Marxism opened up fresh possibilities of development, with the expropriation of landlords, the construction of communal farms, and the eventual leap into decentralized village industrialization. During the Stalin years, China depended heavily on Soviet material aid and advisors. After Khrushchev introduced his consumer-oriented reforms in the mid-1950s and refused to share nuclear and space technology, estrangement set in, culminating in the Soviet Union's withdrawal of all advisors from China in 1960.

Victory of the Communists China emerged from World War II on the winning side but was severely battered militarily, economically, and politically. The brutal war with Japan had taken 10–20 million lives, according to various estimates. Moreover, the shaky wartime alliance between the communists under Mao Zedong and the nationalists under Chiang K'ai-shek unraveled in the later civil war. The communists, who had entrenched themselves deeply in the countryside, were at a strategic advantage in China's overwhelmingly rural society. Despite the nationalists' superiority, resulting from modern arms and American support, the communists were able to systematically choke the cities, causing hyperinflation in Shanghai and other urban centers in 1947.

By 1948 the size of the two armies had reached parity; but Mao's People's Liberation Army had unstoppable popular momentum, and the United States cut back on its aid to Chiang as he faced imminent defeat. By 1949, Chiang and most of his forces had fled to Taiwan, Mao's forces took Beijing, and the new People's Republic of China set about reshaping the country according to the Maoist vision of the communist pattern of collectivist modernity. For millions of Chinese Mao's pronouncement on October 1, 1949, from atop the Gate of Heavenly Peace in Beijing that "China has stood up" and would never be a victim of imperialism again was a source of enormous pride. What would follow in the next decade, however, would be welcomed with more selective enthusiasm.

Land Reform During the 1950s, a central aspect of Mao's thinking was the idea that Chinese peasants were the only reliable resource the country possessed. Lacking a workable industrial and transportation base, the early Maoist years thus were

Land Reform with a Vengeance, 1952. A Chinese farmer kneels at gunpoint before a Communist court enforcing land redistribution policies. Like thousands of others, the landowner was convicted of being a "class enemy" and was executed.

marked by repeated mass mobilization campaigns. Aside from the "Resist America/ Aid Korea" campaign in support of Chinese intervention in Korea, the most important of these was the national effort at land reform. Party cadres moved into the remaining untouched rural areas and proceeded to expropriate land and divide it among the local peasants. Landlords who resisted were "struggled"—abused by tenants who were egged on by party cadres—and often lynched. By some estimates, land reform between 1950 and 1955 took as many as 2 million lives. As hoped for, peasant landownership caused agricultural productivity to increase.

Several years into the land reform program, party leaders decided it was time to take the next step toward socialized agriculture. Mao desperately wanted to avoid the mass chaos and bloodletting that had accompanied Soviet collectivization of agriculture in 1930–1932. The party leadership felt that by going slowly they could greatly ease the transition. Thus, in 1953 peasants were encouraged to form "agricultural producers' cooperatives" in which villages would share scarce tools and machinery. Those who joined were given incentives in the form of better prices and tax breaks. By 1956, agricultural production had recovered to pre–World War II levels and was registering impressive gains.

"Let a Hundred Flowers Bloom"   By 1957, Mao was ready to take the temperature of the nation's intellectuals. Many had been initially enthusiastic about the reforms, but Mao was not sure whether these people were really behind the programs or simply being circumspect. The party therefore invited intellectuals to submit their criticisms and suggestions. Adopting a slogan from China's philosophically rich late Zhou period, "Let a hundred flowers bloom, let a hundred schools of thought contend," officials threw open the door to public criticism of the party's record, assuring the intellectuals that offering their critique was patriotic.

By mid-1957 the trickle of criticisms had become a torrent, but when some critics suggested forming an opposition party, Mao acted swiftly. The "Hundred Flowers" campaign was terminated and the "Anti-Rightist" campaign was launched. Calls for an opposition party were denounced as the worst kind of right-wing thinking—as opposed to the "correct" left-wing thinking of the monopoly Communist Party. Those accused of "rightism" were rounded up and subjected to "reeducation." Even Deng Xiaoping (1904–1997), an old companion of Mao's and later the architect of China's present market economy, was forced to endure 5 years on a hog farm. In addition to being imprisoned and made to endure endless "self-criticism" sessions, many intellectuals were sentenced to long stretches of "reform through labor" in remote peasant villages.

The Great Leap Forward   At about the same time, Mao was growing impatient with the pace of Chinese agricultural collectivization. If production could be ramped up sufficiently, the surplus agricultural funds could then be used to fund 5-year plans for industrial development along the lines of those in the Soviet Union. Moreover, China had been borrowing heavily from the Soviet Union through the 1950s and had availed itself of Soviet technicians and engineers. All of the progress of the decade might be radically slowed or halted if agricultural revenues could not keep pace.

Mao therefore prodded the Communist Party into its most colossal mass mobilization project yet: the Great Leap Forward (1958–1961). The entire population of the country was to be pushed into a campaign to communalize agriculture into self-sustaining units that would function like factories in the fields. Men and women would work in shifts and live in barracks on enormous collective farms. Peasants were to surrender all their iron implements to be melted down and made into steel to build the new infrastructure of these "communes." The most recognizable symbol of the campaign was the backyard steel furnace, which commune members were to build and run for their own needs. Technical problems were to be solved by the "wisdom of the masses" through politically correct "red" (revolutionary) thinking. The entire country would therefore modernize its rural areas and infrastructure in one grand campaign.

Predictably, the Great Leap was the most catastrophic policy failure in the history of the People's Republic. Knowledgeable critics had been cowed into silence

Great Leap Backward. Workers at the Shin Chiao (Xin Jiao) Hotel in Beijing, in the process of constructing a small steel furnace in October 1958, during the Great Leap Forward. Mao Zedong's plan was to transform China within 15 years and 600,000 furnaces from an agrarian–urban into a scientific–industrial country. Instead, the policy became a total disaster, costing China some 30 million deaths.

by the anti-rightist campaign, and the initial wave of enthusiasm that greeted the mobilization swiftly ground to a halt as peasants began to actively resist the seizure of their land and implements. So many were forced into building the communal structures and making useless steel that by 1959 agricultural production in China had plummeted and the country experienced its worst famine in modern times over the next several years. By 1962 an estimated 30 million people had died in its wake.

Conditions became so bleak that Mao stepped down from his party chairmanship in favor of "expert" Liu Shaoqi (1898–1969) and retreated into semiretirement. Liu, from a well-off peasant background in south-central China, and the rehabilitated Deng Xiaoping were now reinstated. Together they tackled the task of rebuilding the shattered economy and political structures, made worse by the Soviet withdrawal of its advisors, who had become useless during the Great Leap. The next 5 years saw impressive gains in China's technical, health, and education sectors as the country returned to something like normalcy. But Mao was soon plotting his return.

Decolonization, Israel, and Arab Nationalism in the Middle East

Parallel to China ridding itself of Japanese colonialism after World War II, independence movements arose in the Middle East and North Africa against the British and French colonial regimes. Here, countries achieved their independence in two waves, the first following World War II and the second during 1956–1970 (see Map 29.4).

MAP **29.4** Decolonization in Africa, the Middle East, and Asia Since 1945.

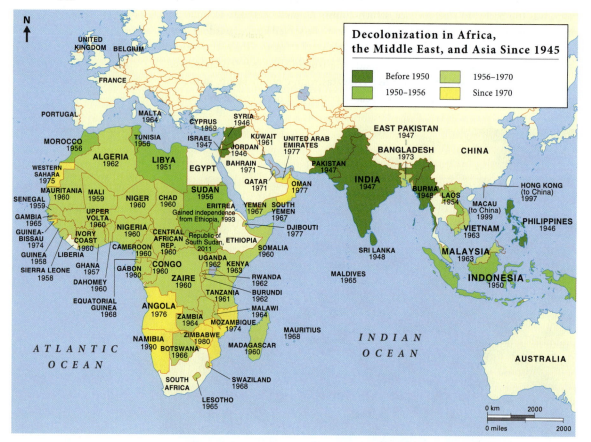

The first wave was the result of local pressures, which colonial authorities found too costly to resist, as in the cases of Syria, Lebanon, Iraq, Jordan, and Israel. The second wave had to await the realization of the British and French governments that they were no longer powerful enough in a world dominated by the United States and the Soviet Union to maintain their empires.

Palestine and Israel   As World War II ended, Britain found itself in a tight spot in Palestine. After the suppression of the uprising of 1936–1939, the Arab Palestinians were relatively quiet; but Zionist guerilla action protesting the restrictions on Jewish immigration and land acquisitions had begun in the middle of the war. Sooner or later some form of transition to self-rule had to be offered, but British politicians and the top military were determined to hold on to the empire's strategic interests (oil and the Suez Canal), especially once the Cold War heated up in 1946.

When it became impossible to find a formula for a transition acceptable to the Arabs,

The Palestine Conflict, 1947-1949

Proposed by UN, 1947:

▨ Jewish state

▨ Arab state

▨ International zone

— Boundary of Israel, 1949

MAP **29.5** **The Palestine Conflict, 1947–1949.**

in February 1947 Britain turned the question of Palestinian independence over to the United Nations. After the collapse of the Soviet Union in 1991, documents surfaced showing that—interestingly, given the Soviet Union's later animosity toward the Jewish state and support of the Arabs—during the 1940s Stalin had used the United Nations to push for a weakening of the British imperial position in the Middle East by favoring the creation of the state of Israel. Accordingly, the United Nations adopted a partition plan worked out with American assistance in November and Israel declared its independence on May 14, 1947 (see Map 29.5).

The Soviet Union backed up its tactical, Cold War–motivated support for Israel to release 200,000 Jewish emigrants from the Soviet Bloc and have Czechoslovakia deliver rifles, machine guns, and World War II vintage planes to Israel. Israel was victorious against the Arab armies that invaded from surrounding countries, which, although determined to contest the new state, were unable to obtain weapons as the result of British and American embargoes. Only Jordan was successful, conquering the West Bank and Old Jerusalem. Between November 1947 and the end of fighting in January 1949, the territory in and around the new state experienced, albeit on a smaller scale, the same kind of tragic and chaotic population shift that took place at about the same time in India and Pakistan. Some three-quarters of a million Palestinians were either forced from their villages or fled, leaving only 150,000 in an Israeli territory now substantially larger than that of the original partition plan. In response, the Arab countries expelled about half a million Jews during the next decade from their countries. In the end, Stalin's early Cold War tactics were a grave miscalculation: Israel became a staunch Western ally. But the Western camp did not fare much better: The Arab "catastrophe" (Arabic *nakba*), as it was called, led to the replacement of liberal, landowning Arab nationalists by ardent military hard-liners of refugee background determined to end what remained of Western colonialism—which now, in their eyes, included the state of Israel.

The Officer Coup in Egypt   One Egyptian officer serving with distinction in the war against Israel was Colonel Gamal Abdel Nasser (1918–1970), eldest son of a postal clerk from southern Egypt. Nasser had benefited from the opening of the officer corps from the landowner elite to commoners. He was bitter toward the Egyptian royalty—supported by landowners who had done little to support the country with arms and supplies in the war. In the middle of a declining internal security situation—massive British retaliation against acts of sabotage in the Suez Canal Zone—the secret "Free Officers," with Nasser at their head, assumed power in a coup in July 1952. They closed down parliament and sent the king into exile on his private luxury yacht. The coup was bloodless, and there was little reaction in the streets.

Within a short period of time, Nasser tightened the rule of his military regime. To break the power of the landowners, the Free Officers in 1952 initiated the first round of a land reform that eventually eliminated large estates. A rival for power was the Muslim Brotherhood, a militant organization founded in 1928 by the preacher Hasan al-Banna (1906–1949), who propagated a reformed Islam in place of the traditional Sufi Islam to poor and rural–urban migrants in the cities with some success and advocated the establishment of an Islamic regime. Accusing the Brotherhood of an assassination attempt, Nasser outlawed it in 1954, driving it underground. In a plebiscite in 1956, Nasser made himself president, with a largely rubber-stamp parliament.

Once firmly in power, Nasser espoused the Arab nationalist cause. Palestinian Arab "freedom fighters" carried out raids against Israel from refugee camps in the Arab countries, which inevitably provoked Israeli reprisals. After the first raid and reprisal involving Egypt in February 1955, Nasser realized that the Egyptian military needed urgent improvements. When the United States would not sell weapons readily, Khrushchev jumped in 6 months later, based on his new Soviet strategy of supporting anticolonial nationalists. Where Stalin had failed, Khrushchev succeeded: After its failure in Israel, the Soviet Union was in the Middle Eastern Cold War struggle again.

At the same time, Nasser laid early plans for infrastructural improvements in advance of a later state-industrialization plan: He asked the World Bank for a loan to finance the Aswan High Dam. Initially, the United States and Britain, main underwriters of the World Bank, were in support. But they withdrew this support in spring 1956 when Nasser pressured his neighbor, Jordan, into dismissing the British commander of its crack troops, the Arab Legion. Now the gloves were off: Nasser responded with the nationalization of the Suez Canal (but with compensation of the shareholders) and closure of the Strait of Tiran (used by Israel for Indian Ocean shipping) in July 1956. Without the necessary loans, Nasser had to put the construction of the High Dam on hold.

Israel considered the closure of the Strait of Tiran an act of war and, with French participation, prepared for a campaign to reopen the straits. France, anxious to punish Nasser for weapons deliveries to the Algerian war of liberation that had begun in 1954, persuaded Britain to join in a plan that would be initiated with an attack on Egypt by Israel. If Nasser would close the Suez Canal, France and Britain would occupy it, ostensibly to separate the combatants but actually to reestablish Western control. The plan was hatched in secret because of US opposition to the use of force against Nasser. It unraveled badly when Israel ended its canal campaign victoriously on November 2 but the British and French troops were unable to complete the occupation of the Canal Zone before November 4, the day of the ceasefire called by the UN General Assembly and the United States. Although defeated militarily, Nasser scored a resounding diplomatic victory, effectively ending the last remnants of British and French imperialism in the Middle East.

After the Suez War, Nasser rode high on waves of pan-Arabism, nonalignment, and Arab socialism. The monarchical regimes in Arabia were on the defensive and maintained themselves only thanks to the United States, heir of the strategic oil interests of Britain after the demise of the latter's empire. Although unification with Syria as the United Arab Republic (1958–1961) did not work out, Egypt succeeded in establishing a cultural hegemony from North Africa to Yemen based on propaganda, movies, and music. The relationship with the Soviet Union

Contrasting British and US Votes in the UN Security Council on the Suez Crisis. Although the Western powers agreed to keep the Soviet Union out of the Middle East, the United States viewed a Suez Canal under Egyptian control as the lesser evil. In spite of having been defeated in the war, Nasser emerged as the diplomatic victor. He kept his distance from the United States and became a leader of the Nonalignment Movement. This photo starkly contrasts the different votes of the British and American ambassadors during the UN Security Council session on the crisis.

deepened: Thanks to the Soviets, the Aswan Dam was completed, Soviet military and technical support grew, and Egyptian students received advanced educations in the Eastern Bloc. In 1961, the regime cofounded the **Non-Alignment Movement**, together with Indonesia's Sukarno, India's Nehru, Yugoslavia's Tito, and Ceylon's Bandaranaike. In the same year, Nasser announced his first 5-year plan, which included the nationalization of all large businesses and the construction of heavy steel, aluminum, cement, and chemical plants. Egypt espoused industrial modernity but under the aegis of state investments similar to what Stalin had originally pioneered in 1930. Nasser called this "Arab socialism."

Non-alignment movement: An international, anti-colonialist movement of state leaders that promoted the interests of countries not aligned with the superpowers.

Decolonization and the Cold War in Asia

Nationalist forces similar to those in the Middle East arose also in south and east Asia as a consequence of World War II. The war had either thoroughly destroyed or considerably diminished the colonial holdings of Great Britain, France, the Netherlands, and Japan in Asia. With the destruction of Japan, the Greater East Asia Co-Prosperity Sphere around the Pacific Rim and its islands dissolved. In several colonies, existing independence movements established nationalist governments or fought against the attempted reimposition of European rule. In quick succession India and Pakistan (1947), Burma (1948), Malaysia (1948), Ceylon (1948), Indonesia (1950), and Vietnam (1954) achieved independence from the British and French. India and Vietnam merit a closer look as countries that played important roles during the Cold War competition between the two modernities of communism and capitalist democracy on which this chapter focuses.

Independence and Partition on the Subcontinent   India, Pakistan, and Bangladesh form a prime example of the trials and tribulations encountered by the newly independent ethnic–religious nations in Asia. As the Indian crown colony emerged from the war, to which it had once again contributed huge numbers of volunteer soldiers, nationalists demanded nothing less than full independence. Gandhi, Nehru, and the majority of the Indian National Congress envisaged an Indian nation on the entire subcontinent in which a constitution, patterned after that of Britain, would trump any ethnic, linguistic, and/or religious identities, of which there were literally hundreds. For the congress, to be an Indian meant adherence to the constitutional principles of equality before the law, due process, and freedom from oppression.

The Muslim minority, however, beginning in the 1930s, had drifted increasingly toward religious nationalism, demanding a separate state for themselves in regions where they formed a majority. The main advocate for this separatism was the Muslim League, led by Muhammad Ali Jinnah (1876–1948). Not surprisingly, there was also a small minority of Hindu religious nationalists who had already in the 1920s published pamphlets advocating independence under the banner of "Hindu-ness" (*hindutva*). To the dismay of the Indian National Congress, the British negotiators lent an ear to the demands of the Islamic religious nationalists and prevailed on Gandhi and Nehru to accept independence with partition—and the possibility of widespread disruption, given that even the northwest and northeast, with their Muslim majorities, were home to sizeable minorities of millions of Hindus.

When, on August 15, 1947, the two nations of India and Pakistan ("Land of the Pure") became independent, the jubilation for being free at last was immediately mixed with the horrors of a population exchange on a scale never seen before. Desperate to save themselves and a few belongings, more than 2 million panicked people fled hundreds of miles on foot, by cart, or by railroad to settle in their respective countries. More than 100,000 Indians died in the accompanying communal violence. Gandhi himself fell victim 5 months later to an assassin from the hindutva supremacist-nationalist minority who was enraged by both the partition and Gandhi's principled adherence to constitutional nationalism, to which Hindu nationalism was to be subordinated.

Predictably, while India settled into a freewheeling, boisterous, and rough-edged federal parliamentary democracy, Pakistan's constitution became disposable and the regime authoritarian. From the start, it was clear that religious nationalism was insufficient to define the identity of Pakistanis, distributed over two physically separated regions of the nation, Punjab in the west and East Bengal in the east. The capital, Islamabad, was in the west and Urdu became the national language, relegating Bengali in the east to secondary status (to the dismay of its speakers, who eventually seceded in a bloody civil war and formed the nation of Bangladesh in 1971).

A decade into independence, a military officer, Field Marshal Ayub Khan (1907–1974) from the Pashtu minority in Waziristan on the western border, assumed power in a bloodless coup. Subsequently, he abrogated the 1948 British-style constitution and in 1962 imposed a new constitution, providing for a "guided democracy" of elected village councilors who voted for the president and the members of the national assembly. The constitution's definition of Islam as a national identity and its relationship to subsidiary ethnic and linguistic identities in the country, however, were so contentious that they remained unresolved in the constitution.

Worst of all, given the role of Islam as the religious–nationalist foundation principle, Pakistan was in conflict with India over Kashmir, a province lying in the north between India and Pakistan. In 1947, its Hindu prince hesitated to join Pakistan, while its majority Muslim population demanded incorporation. In the ensuing first war between Indian and Pakistan, India succeeded in conquering most of the province, with Pakistan holding on to only a small sliver, but Kashmiri Muslims remained restive. As in so many other postcolonial territorial disputes, clashes between constitutional and ethnic–linguistic–religious nationalism became irresolvable.

Independent India

As a newly independent India embraced its "tryst with destiny," as its first prime minister, Jawaharlal Nehru (in office 1947–1964), called it, his powers of negotiation and firmness served him well. Tying the subcontinent's disparate constituencies together into a united government was a formidable task. Within the British system, perhaps one-quarter of the territory had remained under the nominal rule of local princes, who now had to surrender their realms to the national government. The bewildering array of castes and the social inequalities built into the system also posed a powerful obstacle, especially since the British had, in many cases, played upon these inequalities to divide and rule. The new government

Srinagar. This 1948 color photo shows Srinagar on the Jelhum River in Kashmir, a northern province disputed between Pakistan and India. The river, flowing in and out of a chain of lakes, is surrounded by the Himalayas and empties into the Indus. The majority population of Kashmir is Muslim, but its former Hindu prince inclined in 1947 toward Indian sovereignty, thereby touching off a conflict that has yet to be resolved.

was itself in the uncomfortable situation of constitutionally mandating equality for women and outlawing caste discrimination, while being forced to acquiesce to the de facto absence of the former and continuation of the latter. In the end, the British parliamentary and court systems were adopted and the old civil service was retained, while the economy of the new government would officially be a modified, nonrevolutionary kind of socialism. Nehru's admiration for Soviet successes persuaded him to adopt the 5-year plan system of development. Not surprisingly, India's first 5-year plan (1951–1955), like the early efforts in the Soviet Union and China, was geared toward raising agricultural productivity as a precondition for industrial development.

The most formidable problem was poverty. Though the cities were rapidly expanding beyond the ability of their local governments to keep pace with services, India, like China at the same time, was still fundamentally rural. The new nation's village population was second only to China's in size. The strains upon the land and reliance on the monsoon cycle could spell famine at any time. In the 1950s, India launched a family planning program, to encourage a slowing of the demographic expansion. As a democratic country, however, India had to rely on the voluntary cooperation of the villagers, a cooperation which was difficult to achieve as long as urbanization and industrialization were in their initial stages. For poor families, children were either important laborers in agriculture or, among the landless and the poor in city slums, crucial additional breadwinners as soon as they were old enough to work.

Political and Economic Nonalignment   Similar to the governments of the Soviet Union, China, and Egypt, Nehru and the Congress Party argued that the pressing rural poverty could be overcome only through rapid industrialization undertaken by the state. A hybrid regime of capitalist-democratic constitutionalism with private property (on a small scale) and guided "socialist" state investments came into being, which was officially aligned with neither the West nor the East. This nonalignment (Nehru coined this term in 1954) became the official policy of India and under its initiative also the founding principle of an entire organization, the Non-Alignment Movement, informally established in Bandung, Indonesia, in 1955, and formally inaugurated in 1961. The Nonaligned Movement, still in existence today, sought to maintain neutrality in the Cold War. It predictably incurred the wrath of Western Cold War warriors but was generally successful in maintaining its own course independent from the Western and Soviet Blocs.

Indian state socialism began with the state's second 5-year plan (1956–1961), which focused on state investments in heavy industry. Existing private enterprises were nationalized, and an immense hydroelectric complex and five steel plants were built, along with numerous cement works and an ambitious expansion of coal mines and railroads. In 1958, the Atomic Energy Commission was formed, to pursue both peaceful and military applications of nuclear fission. With the iron, aluminum, cement, and chemicals from heavy industry, so the planners

The Strains of Nonalignment. India's determined stance to navigate its own course between the superpowers was a difficult one, especially during the height of the Cold War. Here, however, a degree of diplomatic warmth appears to pervade the proceedings in Geneva, Switzerland, as People's Republic of China Foreign Minister Chen Yi (left) toasts his Indian colleague, Defense Minister V.K. Krishna Menon (right), and Soviet Foreign Minister Andrei Gromyko (center background) smiles on them both. The date of this conference, however, formally convened to discuss issues between the Soviet and American sides over influence in the Southeast Asian nation of Laos in July, 1962, also coincided with rising border tensions between India and China. This photo was specifically released to show that both sides were still on friendly terms. Within a few months, however, they were shooting at each other.

hoped, private Indian investors, still minute in number but recipients of compensation for factories lost to nationalization, would buy the heavy industrial goods—iron, aluminum, and chemicals—to construct housing and build factories for the production of basic consumer goods, such as textiles, shoes, soap, and toothpaste. The giant domestic market of India was to become fully self-sufficient and independent of imports.

Though begun with much hope at a time of prosperity, the second plan failed to reach its goals. The government debt, owed both to domestic banks and to foreign lending institutions, grew astronomically. Tax collection was notoriously difficult and unproductive, and chronic national and federal budget deficits drove up inflation. Bad monsoon seasons caused food shortages. In democratic India it was not possible to use the draconian dictatorial powers a Stalin had employed. India ran into difficulties that were experienced time and again in other countries after independence.

Southeast Asia   In contrast to India, where the postwar British imperialists gave in to the inevitable, the French under Charles de Gaulle (1890–1970) in 1944–1946 were determined to reconstitute their empire. De Gaulle and a majority of French politicians found it inconceivable that this new republic would be anything less than the imperially glorious Third Republic. To de Gaulle's chagrin, military efforts to hold on to Lebanon and Syria failed against discreet British support for independence and the unilateral establishment of national governments by the Lebanese and Syrians in 1943–1944. After these losses, the politicians of the Fourth Republic were determined not to lose more colonies.

Unfortunately for the French, however, when they returned to Indochina (composed of Vietnam, Laos, and Cambodia) in the fall of 1945, the prewar independence communist movement had already taken over. With covert American assistance, the communists had fought the Japanese occupiers in a guerilla war; and on September 2, 1945, the day of Japan's surrender to the United States, Ho Chi Minh, the leader, read a Vietnamese declaration of independence to half a million people in Hanoi.

Following protracted negotiations in early 1946 between Ho and the French, a stalemate ensued. Ho did not budge from independence, while the French insisted on returning to their "colony." The Vietminh promptly relaunched their guerilla war. Because of the rapid escalation of the Cold War, particularly the communist victory in China, the Soviet atomic bomb, and the Korean War, the French were successful at persuading the American administration that a victory of the Vietminh was tantamount to an expansion of communism in the world. By the early 1950s, the United States was providing much of the funding and the French and allied Vietnamese troops did the actual fighting.

In May 1954, however, the Vietminh defeated the French decisively. Having created an isolated base at Dien Bien Phu in the northwest, the French allowed Vietminh forces to encircle them and pound them with heavy artillery from surrounding hills in their now indefensible

Undeniable Truths

"The Declaration of the French Revolution made in 1791 on the Rights of Man and the Citizen also states: 'All men are born free and with equal rights, and must always remain free and have equal rights.' Those are undeniable truths. Nevertheless, for more than eighty years, the French imperialists, abusing the standard of Liberty, Equality, and Fraternity, have violated our Fatherland and oppressed our fellow citizens. They have acted contrary to the ideals of humanity and justice . . ."

—Ho Chi Minh. *On Revolution: Selected Writings, 1920–1966.* Translated by Bernard B. Fall, p. 143. New York: Praeger, 1967.

camp beneath. Resupply through airdrops eventually became impossible. During the Geneva negotiations carried out later that year, the French surrender resulted in a division of Vietnam into north and south along the 17th parallel, pending national elections, and the creation of the new nations of Laos and Cambodia.

The elections, however, never took place and instead Ngo Dinh Diem [No Deen Jem, in office 1955–1963], an authoritarian politician with a limited power base primarily composed of Catholics, emerged in the south. He legitimized his rule in 1955 through a fraudulent plebiscite. Although the new Kennedy administration (1961) was well aware of Diem's shaky and unscrupulous rule, concerns about military successes being achieved by Laotian and South Vietnamese communists receiving North Vietnamese support, led to the fateful American decision to carry the Western Cold War into Indochina. President Eisenhower had already sent several hundred military advisors to Diem but President Kennedy, faced with the Bay of Pigs disaster in Cuba (April 1961) and the East German wall in Berlin (August 1961), increased the military to 16,000 personnel by 1963. Since Diem was corrupt and unwilling to carry out much-needed land reforms, the United States engineered a coup in November 1963 that put a military government in place. This proxy regime was soon propped up by a growing American military presence that would reach a half-million men by 1967.

Decolonization and Cold War in Africa

Only 7 months after their defeat at Dien Bien Phu, the French had to face the declaration of a war of independence by the Algerian Front of National Liberation (November 1, 1954). Algeria, a French colony of 10 million Muslim Arabs and Berbers, had a European settler population of nearly 1 million. The French army was determined to prevent a repeat of the humiliation it had suffered in Indochina. But that is precisely what happened only 2 years later in the Suez war of 1956, and British and French politicians began to realize that the maintenance of colonies was becoming too costly. France hung on to Algeria and was even able to largely repress the liberation war by the later 1950s. But in the long run, Algerian independence (in 1962) could not be prevented, even though French military elements and settlers did everything (including two revolts in 1958 and 1961 against Paris) to keep the country French. France's colonial interests were too costly to be maintained and the United States took over the West's strategic interests in the world. Since the colonies required immense expenditures to support newly burgeoning populations, and the reconstruction of Europe was still far from complete, both Britain and France were forced to rethink the idea of colonialism.

Amid much soul-searching, European governments began to liquidate their empires, beginning in 1957. Only Portugal and Spain continued to maintain their colonies of Angola, Mozambique, and Rio de Oro. South Africa introduced its apartheid regime (1948–1994), designed to segregate the white Afrikaaner (Dutch-descended) ruling class from the black majority. As the British, French, and Belgians decolonized, however, they ensured that the governments of the newly independent African countries would remain their loyal subalterns. For them, African independence would be an exchange for support in the Cold War and continued economic dependence.

The Legacy of Colonialism   Between 1918 and 1957, even though the governments of Britain, France, Belgium, and Portugal had invested little state money in their colonies, vast changes had occurred in sub-Saharan Africa. For one thing, the

population had more than doubled from 142 to 300 million, mostly as a result of the reduction of tropical diseases through better medicine. Urbanization was accelerating, reliance on commodity exports alone was becoming too narrow, and an emerging small middle class of merchants, lawyers, doctors, pharmacists, and journalists was becoming restless. Heavy investments were required, not merely in mining and agriculture but also in social services to improve the lot of the growing African population. Faced with this financial burden, most of the colonial powers decided to grant independence rather than divert investments badly needed at home.

Ghana, the African Pioneer

Once Britain had decided to decolonize, the governmental strategy toward African independence was to support nationalist groups or parties that adopted British-inspired constitutions and the rule of law, guaranteed existing British economic interests, and abided by the rules of the British Commonwealth of Nations. The first of these to fit the criteria was Ghana in 1957. Its leader was Kwame Nkrumah (1909–1972), a graduate with a master's degree in education from the University of Pennsylvania who appeared to be a sound choice.

Ghana made an initial bid to be the pioneer of sub-Saharan independence and development. It had a healthy economy based on cocoa production as well as some mineral wealth. Its middle class was perhaps the most vital of any African colony. Nkrumah had had a long career as an activist for African independence and a leading advocate of pan-African unity. Jailed during the 1950s for his activism in the Convention People's Party and therefore viewed with some concern, the British nevertheless also realized that Nkrumah wielded genuine authority among a majority of politically inexperienced Ghanaians.

Only 2 years into his rule, however, Nkrumah discarded the independence constitution. Exploiting ethnic tensions among Ashante groups, where an emerging opposition to his rule was concentrated, he promulgated a new republican constitution, removing the country from the British Commonwealth. A year later, he turned to socialist state planning, similar to that of Egypt and India.

The construction of a massive hydroelectric dam on the Volta River, begun in 1961, was supposed to be the starting point of a heavy industrialization program, including aluminum, steel, glass, and consumer goods factories. But the country soon ran into financing problems since cocoa, the main export commodity, was fetching declining prices on the world market and large foreign loans were required to continue the program. On the political front, Nkrumah in 1964 amended the already once-changed constitution by making Ghana a one-party state with himself as leader for life. An unmanageable foreign debt eventually stalled development, and an army coup, supported by the CIA in the name of Cold War anticommunism, ousted Nkrumah in 1966.

> **True Freedom**
>
> "Capitalism is too complicated a system for a newly independent nation. Hence the need for a socialistic society. But even a system based on social justice and a democratic constitution may need backing up, during the period of independence, by emergency measures of a totalitarian kind. Without discipline true freedom cannot survive."
>
> —Kwame Nkrumah. *Ghana: The Autobiography of Kwame Nkrumah*, p. XVI. London: Panaf Books, 2002.

The Struggle for the Congo's Independence

Among the large group of sub-Saharan colonies achieving independence between 1957 and 1960, the Belgian Congo is an important case study because, like Vietnam, it became a battleground of the Cold War. The Belgian Congo had been under the authority of the Belgian government since the beginning of the century, when it took over from the king, who had exploited the colony as his personal property with scandalous brutality. During the interwar period, concession companies invested in mining, especially in the southern and central provinces of Katanga and Kisaï, where huge deposits of copper, cobalt, iron, uranium, and diamonds were discovered. Little money went into human development until after World War II when Catholic mission schools, with state support, expanded the health and the primary school systems. The urban and mine worker populations expanded considerably, but no commercial or professional middle classes to speak of existed.

Serious demands for independence arose in the Congo only after Ghana became independent in 1957. Several groups of nationalists, some advocating a federation and others a centralized state, competed with each other. The urban and mine worker–based National Congolese Movement (*Mouvement National Congolais*, MNC), founded in 1958 by the former postal clerk and salesman Patrice Lumumba (1925–1961), was the most popular group, favoring a centralized constitutional nationalism that transcended ethnicity, language, and religion. After riots in 1959 and the arrest of Lumumba, accused of stirring up the riots, Belgian authorities decided to act quickly so as not to lose control over events: They needed compliant nationalists who would continue existing economic arrangements. A Brussels conference with all nationalists—including Lumumba, freed from prison—decided to hold local and national elections in early 1960. To the dismay of Belgium, the centralists led by the gifted firebrand orator Lumumba won. On June 30, 1960, the Congo became independent, with Lumumba as prime minister and the federalist Joseph Kasa-Vubu (ca. 1910–1969) from Katanga as president.

Lumumba's first political act was the announcement of a general pay raise for state employees, which the Belgian army commander countermanded by spreading the rumor that the Congolese foot soldiers would be left out. Outraged, the soldiers mutinied; and amid a general breakdown of public order, Katanga declared its independence. Lumumba fired the Belgian officers, but for the restoration of order he had to ask for help from the United Nations. Order was indeed restored by the United Nations, but Belgium made sure that Katanga did not rejoin the Congo. To force Katanga, Lumumba turned for support to the Soviet Union, which airlifted advisors and equipment into the country. The Cold War had arrived in Africa.

Kasa-Vubu and Lumumba dismissed each other from the government on September 5, giving the new Congolese army chief, Mobutu Sese Seko (1930–1997), the opportunity to seize power on September 14. Mobutu was a soldier turned journalist and member of the MNC whom Lumumba had appointed as army chief, even though it was general knowledge that he was in the pay of the Belgians and the CIA. (Mobutu went on to become the dictator of the Congo, renamed "Zaire," and was a close ally of the United States during the period he held power, 1965–1996.) He promptly had Lumumba arrested. Eventually, Belgian agents took Lumumba to Katanga, where they executed him on January 17, 1961.

At the time, as it is now known from documents studied in the 1990s, the Belgian government and the Eisenhower White House were deeply convinced that Lumumba was another Castro in the making, a nationalist who would soon become a communist, falling prey to Khrushchev's charm offensive among the African nationalists about to achieve independence. In the Cold War between the United

States and the Soviet Union the fierce but inexperienced Lumumba was given no chance by the Belgian and American governments acting with mutual consultation. At all costs, the Congo had to remain in the Western camp as a strategic, mineral-rich linchpin in central Africa.

Putting It All Together

Rapid, dizzying change characterized the pattern of modernity as it unfolded in the middle of the twentieth century. After only 150 years of constitutionalism and industry, 75 years of worldwide imperialism, and 15 years of a three-sided competition among the modernist ideologies of capitalist democracy, communism, and supremacist nationalism, the world changed drastically once more. An intense Cold War competition between the proponents of the ideologies of capitalist democracy and communism ensued. Imperialism and colonialism collapsed within a mere 17 years. And nearly 200 nations came to share the globe in the United Nations. Compared to the slow pace of the agrarian–urban period of world history for 5,300 years, the speed of development during a mere 145 years of scientific–industrial modernity was dizzying (see Concept Map).

Perhaps the most noteworthy series of events characterizing the 17 years of the early and intense Cold War between capitalist democracy and communism in 1945–1962 was the sad fate of many countries as they emerged into independence or as they struggled to accommodate themselves as best they could in the Western camp, Eastern Bloc, or Non-Aligned Movement. As we have seen in this chapter, US and Soviet leaders were ruthless wherever they perceived communists, communist fellow travelers, or heretics of the Communist Party line in their ranks. But even when new nations could not easily be brought into line and instead pursued a policy of nonalignment, there were subtler ways through which both West and East could apply financial pressures with devastating consequences: Egypt lost its finances for the Aswan Dam, and China lost its Soviet advisors during the Great Leap Forward.

Not that capitalist democracy and communism were on the same plane: The former, even if it did not readily offer meaning or equality to its adherents, provided greater political participation than the latter, which paid only lip service to its notions of equality, as became obvious by 1991. But the period of the early, active Cold War and decolonization from 1945 to 1962 was far less brutal than the preceding interwar period. Although several confrontations between East and West were hot, and nuclear war on one occasion posed a serious threat, humanity was spared the cataclysms of World War II. Change was rapid but less horrific.

Review and Respond

1. What was the Cold War? Sketch the salient moments in its evolution.

2. Describe the differences in Stalin's and Khrushchev's approaches to communism.

3. Why did the United States issue the Marshall Plan, who benefited, and what were the results?

4. Why was the Cuban Missile Crisis the major turning point in world history during the second half of the twentieth century?

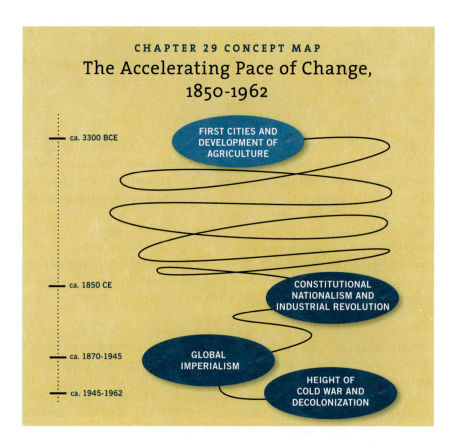

CHAPTER 29 CONCEPT MAP

The Accelerating Pace of Change, 1850-1962

- ca. 3300 BCE
- ca. 1850 CE
- ca. 1870-1945
- ca. 1945-1962

FIRST CITIES AND DEVELOPMENT OF AGRICULTURE

CONSTITUTIONAL NATIONALISM AND INDUSTRIAL REVOLUTION

GLOBAL IMPERIALISM

HEIGHT OF COLD WAR AND DECOLONIZATION

5. Discuss the basic tenets of existentialism, and explain why understanding this philosophy is important for modernity during the middle of the twentieth century.

6. Explain the different paths of evolution between India and Pakistan after independence in 1947.

7. Why was populism such an attractive mode of governance in Latin America after 1945?

8. Outline the sequence of policies which Mao Zedong pursued in communist China after 1949.

9. Discuss the significance of Ghana and the Congo for understanding decolonization in Africa.

> For additional resources, including maps, primary sources, visuals, and quizzes, please go to www.oup.com/us/vonsivers. Please see the Further Resources section at the back of the book for additional readings and suggested websites.

Thinking Through Patterns

▶ **Why did the pattern of unfolding modernity, which offered three choices in 1918 after World War I, shrink to just capitalist democracy and communism in 1945? How did each of these two patterns evolve between 1945 and 1962?**

The pattern of modernity evolved in the nineteenth century with four major ingredients: constitutional nationalism, ethnic–linguistic–religious nationalism, industrialism, and communism. However, traditional institutions such as monarchies and empires from times prior to 1800 continued to flourish. World War I wiped out most monarchies, but capitalist democracy continued, communism came into its own in the Soviet Union, imperialism and colonialism survived, and supremacist nationalism attracted all those who found democracy and communism wanting. World War II eliminated supremacist nationalism and, after a delay of 17 years, also imperialism and colonialism. The remaining choices of capitalist democracy and communism were divided between two power blocs, which during the early Cold War period of 1945–1962 almost evenly shared the world among themselves.

Modernity grew out of the philosophy of the New Science in the 1600s, with its assumptions of materialism and the social contract. After acquiring mass support, modernity with its twin ideologies of constitutional nationalism and industrialism evolved into scientific–industrial modernity with profound cultural consequences. On the one hand, wave after wave of ever more modern ideologies and artistic movements appeared, from early nineteenth-century romanticism to mid-twentieth-century existentialism. On the other hand, these consecutive waves of newness could at best only paper over the basic materialist flaw of modernity, which in each generation gave rise to the question of the meaning of it all. Did a modern world without transcendence, rampant consumer choices, and gaping social inequities have intrinsic meaning even if people continued to find ever new and thrilling possibilities in material and intellectual–artistic life? The question still haunts us today.

▶ **What are the cultural premises of modernity?**

▶ **How did the newly independent countries of the Middle East, Asia, and Africa adapt to the divided world of the Cold War?**

During 1945–1962 the number of nations on earth quadrupled to eventually (in 2011) comprise about 200. The new nations, emerging from colonialism, were in theory, like the older nations of early modernity in the nineteenth century, countries with ethnic–linguistic–religious cores and functioning constitutional institutions. In fact, many were not. Since most, furthermore, were still overwhelmingly agrarian, industrialism was beyond reach. With great hope, the ruling elites in a number of large new nations embraced a mixed capitalist-democratic and socialist regime, with heavy state investments in basic industries, such as textiles, steel, chemicals, cement, and fertilizer. However, in contrast to Stalin, who first introduced these type of investments under the label of state-guided socialism, none of the elites in the new nations had the will to collect the money for these investments from their rural population. Instead, they borrowed heavily from the capitalist-democratic countries. True independence remained an elusive goal.

Chapter 30

1963-1991

The End of the Cold War, Western Social Transformation, and the Developing World

THE WORLD, 1963–1991

North America

Europe

Asia

Africa

South America

Australia

The machine made an aggressive, rapid thudding sound as it slowly worked its way through the air by the dun-colored, snow-capped mountain. The fighter recognized it immediately, and his stomach tightened on seeing what it was: *Shaitan Arba*—"Satan's Chariot," the Soviet MI-5 "Hind" attack helicopter. This new, heavily

Seeing Patterns

▶ How did the political landscape of the Cold War change from 1963 to 1991?

▶ Why did such radically different lifestyles emerge in the United States and the West during the 1960s and 1970s? What is their legacy today?

▶ Why did some nations that had emerged from colonialism and war make great strides in their development while others seemed to stagnate?

armed, and armored helicopter gunship was more like a flying tank and had proven largely impervious to the rifle and small arms fire the fighter and his *mujahideen* Afghan warriors had used in their usually vain attempts to down it. Worse still, it carried a devastating array of rockets and machine cannon; the fighter had seen these gunships wipe out entire squads of his comrades. In this desperate fight in the Afghan high country, the Soviets, it appeared, had acquired a decisive technological edge as they sought to eliminate resistance to the client regime they had installed in the capital of Kabul nearly 8 years before, in 1979.

Just as he took a last look before seeking cover, he heard a peculiar sound, a kind of *whoosh*. He raised his eyes just in time to see the machine explode into a lurid red and orange fireball and plummet swiftly into the mountainside, its rotor blades windmilling helplessly without lift. A rapidly dissolving vapor trail marked a spot about 200 meters away from where it appeared a rocket had been fired. A small group of men shouted "God is great!" and cheered lustily at their victory.

This scene was to be repeated more than 300 times during the coming years. The weapon that had downed the helicopter was a new American

Mujahideen Soldiers Standing on a Destroyed Soviet Helicopter. The determination of Afghan resistance to secularism and Soviet-style communism is vividly portrayed in this photograph of the momentary triumph of a small unit of fighters celebrating the downing of a Russian helicopter. The technological disparity between the sides is clear as well: Note that all of the Afghan fighters hold long-obsolescent bolt-action rifles, many of them British models dating from before World War I. The arrival and capture of large quantities of automatic weapons and the secret supplying of American shoulder fired antiaircraft missiles would soon decisively change this situation.

"Stinger" shoulder-fired missile, which the United States was now clandestinely supplying to the Afghan Muslim fighters attempting to expel the Soviet forces occupying their country. Perhaps more than any other weapon, the Stinger neutralized the Soviet technological advantage in airpower and enabled an international force of mujahideen to ultimately push the Soviets out of Afghanistan in this last contest of the Cold War, in much the same way that the United States had been forced from South Vietnam. In fact, as we will see in more detail in this chapter, the immense cost of the Soviet–Afghan War, added to the even higher price of trying to match the American effort to create a missile defense system against intercontinental ballistic missiles (ICBMs), helped to grind the Soviet economy into a state of collapse by the end of the 1980s and led to the end of the Eastern Bloc and the Soviet Union itself. It thus appeared that the West and its version of modernity—capitalist democracy—had convincingly won both the physical and ideological contests of the Cold War.

In this chapter we will trace the progress of this struggle and the immense social changes associated with the period from 1963 to 1991 in the West and the progress of the struggle in the developing world. Although the end result was an apparent victory for democracy and capitalism—both of which were to be introduced into the successor states of the Soviet Union in the 1990s—the contest in the developing world was still active even beyond this time. From the seedbed of Muslim resistance to the secular communist vision of modernity in Afghanistan would sprout a new worldwide movement of resistance to the secular West, democratic capitalism, and the sole remaining vision of modernity itself: al-Qaeda and its affiliates.

The Climax of the Cold War

The Cold War continued through several phases into the 1980s when the power of the Soviet Union began to markedly ebb. During the 1960s, despite the progress of the Nuclear Test Ban Treaty, the United States and the Soviet Union remained bitter ideological enemies and both the Soviet Union and the People's Republic of China sent aid to Ho Chi Minh's forces fighting the Americans in Vietnam. The Soviets also supported the Arab efforts against United States–backed Israel in 1967 and 1973. Moreover, both sides continually upgraded and expanded their nuclear arsenals. Despite this continuing hostility, the late 1960s and early 1970s also witnessed the era of *détente*: a downplaying of overt aggression toward one another and the pursuit of competition through diplomatic, social, and cultural means. The Soviet invasion of Afghanistan in 1979, however, ushered in a final phase of openly hostile competition and covert warfare. In the end, the Soviet Union's resources were simply not sufficient to outlast those of the West in the struggle.

The Soviet Superpower in Slow Decline

In 1963, only a few months after the Cuban Missile Crisis, it still appeared that the Soviet Union was an adversary more or less equal to the United States. In fact, in many respects, it seemed to have the momentum of history on its side. Marxism and socialism more broadly were gaining popularity in the world as means of rapid development; the United States did not seem particularly successful at stopping the expansion of Soviet influence in Southeast Asia, Latin America, or Africa; and the Soviet Union still seemed to be setting the technological pace in the "space race." Yet, in less than 30 years the Soviet Union would fall apart, to be replaced by its core political unit of Russia and a host of newly independent former Soviet republics. What forces were at work in setting this unexpected course of events in motion?

From the Brink of War to Détente   While Nikita S. Khrushchev had developed an earthy, peasant-flavored popularity in the Soviet Union and, to some extent, on the international stage, his initial success in rolling back some of the worst abuses of Stalinism had been overshadowed by two signal failures during the early 1960s. The first was allowing the Sino–Soviet split of 1960 to become a complete break. By 1963, the Soviet response to Chinese displeasure with Khrushchev's lack of notice prior to his denunciation of Stalin and Chinese criticism of Khrushchev's more temperate approach toward the United States and the West were met by the wholesale withdrawal of Soviet advisors from China. Moreover, Khrushchev's building of the Berlin Wall, though largely effective in its immediate objective of stopping the flood of refugees from East Berlin, had been a propaganda failure. His American

1963
Nuclear Test Ban Treaty

1964
Soviet Premier Khrushchev Steps Down

1965-1973
Vietnam War

1966-1969
Cultural Revolution in China

1967
Arab–Israeli War ("Six-Day War")

1968
Assassination of Martin Luther King Jr., Massive Student Demonstrations in Europe, United States, and Mexico

1968-1973
Era of Détente Between United States and Soviet Union

1973
Arab–Israeli War ("Yom Kippur/Ramadan" War)

1968-Present
Rise of "Women's Liberation" and Modern Feminism

1978
Deng Xiaoping Announces "Four Modernizations" in China

1979
Shah of Iran Overthrown, Soviet Union Invades Afghanistan

1985-1989
Perestroika and *Glasnost* in Soviet Union

1989
Tiananmen Square Demonstrations in China, Berlin Wall Torn Down and German Unification

1991
Collapse of Soviet Union and End of Cold War

Soviet N-1 Being Rolled Out to Its Launching Pad. The power of Soviet rocket boosters and ICBMs was a source of great anxiety to American military planners and those in NASA involved in US space initiatives. In this rare photograph, a Soviet booster developed specifically for the Russian manned lunar program is wheeled out to its launching area in the 1960s.

counterpart, the youthful, charismatic President John F. Kennedy (in office 1961–1963), had rallied world support against the wall when he proclaimed before it, "Ich bin ein Berliner" ("I am a Berliner")!

But Khrushchev's key blunder had been in appearing to back down during the Cuban Missile Crisis in October 1962. Seeking to test the resolve of the young American president by installing nuclear missiles on America's doorstep, the premier instead was forced to dismantle their bases in Cuba. Though the United States also agreed to the face-saving gesture of dismantling its own medium-range missiles in Turkey, the Soviet Politburo shortly acted to oust Khrushchev, who duly resigned in October 1964. The succession was remarkably smooth for the Soviet system, which tended toward intrigue and occasional violence when leaders left. Into the position of power stepped Leonid Brezhnev (in office 1960–1964, 1977–1982), who would preside over the Soviet Union as first secretary of the Communist Party until 1982, with Aleksey Kosygin (1964–1980) as premier.

The Brezhnev years were noteworthy in a number of areas. Both the United States and the Soviet Union had been shaken by how close they had come to all-out nuclear war in October 1962. One way that this danger had been partially defused was by the Nuclear Test Ban Treaty, signed in October 1963. Alert to the toxic effects of nuclear fallout and the possibility that tests may raise false alarms about attacks, the signatories agreed to abandon all aboveground nuclear testing. Nonnuclear nations were severely discouraged from developing their own weapons in subsequent "nonproliferation" treaties. Additional safeguards were built into the detection and early warning systems both sides used as part of missile defense. The last, and most famous, link in this chain was the installation of the Hot Line—a direct telephone link between the White House and the Kremlin—for American and Soviet leaders to alert each other if an accident or false attack signal had been issued. Nonetheless, the mood of the 1960s remained one of nuclear tension on both sides, and American popular culture was rife with doomsday fantasies of the catastrophic effects of nuclear war. Moreover, new types of weapons systems, such as submarine-based ICBMs that could be launched close to enemy shores and independently guided multiwarhead ICBMs (multiple independent reentry vehicles, or MIRVs) that could hit several targets simultaneously, raised tensions on both sides. Not surprisingly, from the early 1970s on, the two sides engaged in a series of Strategic Arms Limitation Treaty (SALT) talks.

By the late 1960s, the United States and the Soviet Union had entered into a period of relatively tranquil relations often referred to by historians as "détente," from the French term for "release of tension." Because a principal goal of the administration of President Richard M. Nixon (in office 1969–1974) was to achieve "peace with honor"—that is, a viable way for the United States to withdraw its forces while somehow avoiding the stigma of defeat—in Vietnam, the Americans sought Russian support for peace talks with North Vietnam. For the Soviets, tensions were

Détente. Following closer diplomatic contact between the United States and the Soviet Union in the wake of the Arab–Israeli War in the beginning of June 1967, President Lyndon Johnson and Soviet Premier Aleksey Kosygin met at Glassboro State College (now Rowan University). The talks centered around the US position in Vietnam and the possibility of opening talks on lessening nuclear tensions. Here, President Johnson and Soviet foreign minister Andrei Gromyko are engaged in a frank discussion.

swiftly mounting with the People's Republic of China over disputed borders along the Amur River and the rising chaos of the Cultural Revolution. At several points, military engagements took place; and at least once, the Americans were approached by the Soviets about the possibility of a preemptive nuclear strike against China.

The era of détente abruptly ended in the fall of 1973, however, with the Egyptian and Syrian surprise attack on Israel, which coincided with both the Jewish holy day of Yom Kippur and the Muslim month of Ramadan and sparked the largest Arab–Israeli conflict to date. While the Soviets had been supplying equipment and advisors to Arab countries during the earlier "Six-Day War" in 1967, that conflict had ended too quickly for either the US or USSR to contemplate intervention. The more protracted fighting of the 1973 war and the support of the United States for Israel, which finally defeated its opponents, raised superpower tensions for the next several years. The Soviets actively supported the largely Arab Organization of Petroleum Exporting Countries (OPEC) boycott of oil shipments to the United States during the mid-1970s and resumed support for North Vietnam's final drive to conquer South Vietnam after the American withdrawal in 1973.

"Prague Spring" and "Solidarity" in Poland

The Brezhnev years were also marked by a growing incidence of dissent, both in the Soviet Union and, even more markedly, in its Eastern European client states (see Map 30.1). Since the uprising in Hungary in 1956, for example, the government efforts to stifle dissent and reform had been increasingly difficult and threatened to stir up latent nationalistic feeling. One result was the evolution under János Kádár (in office 1956–1988), Hungarian party secretary, of what came to be called "goulash communism": a relatively relaxed attitude toward criticism of the regime, the introduction of limited market reforms, some attention to consumer demands, and limited trade with the West.

In 1968, dissent took a more direct course in Czechoslovakia, in what came to be called the "Prague Spring." With the rise to power of Alexander Dubček (in office

MAP 30.1 Communist Eastern Europe, 1945–1989.

1968–1969) in January 1968, a sweeping set of reforms, more extensive than those by Kádár in Hungary, was introduced. Calls for a new decentralized administrative structure, relaxation of censorship, free speech, and opposition political parties were voiced; and an atmosphere of excitement and expectation prevailed in the capital of Prague. Brezhnev's government, however, saw this as evidence of the Czech Communist Party slipping in power and entered into negotiations in order to bring the country back into line. By August, as the push for reform became more and more persistent, the Soviets sent Warsaw Pact forces into Czechoslovakia, where they ousted Dubček, installed Gustáv Husák (1913–1991), and promptly dismantled the reforms of the previous 7 months. The Soviet move became known as the "Brezhnev Doctrine"—the right of the Soviets and Warsaw Pact to forcibly hold in line any member country attempting to abandon socialism and the alliance with the Soviet Union.

With the shadow cast by the Brezhnev Doctrine, dissent once again went underground. In 1980, however, it reemerged in Poland, this time with more lasting results. Several factors were at work. One of these was the still prominent position of the Roman Catholic Church in Poland, which the local Communist Party was never able to totally suppress. The election of a Polish pope, John Paul II, in 1978 galvanized Polish Catholics even further. In addition, Poland had been undergoing a long economic crisis in the late 1970s, with consumer goods reduced to a minimum and many workers laid off. In 1980, a strike by electrical workers at the Lenin Shipyard in Gdansk was called, which quickly spread to other port cities. A labor union was formed called "Solidarity," led by an electrician named Lech Walesa (b. 1943), which called for an end to censorship, the lifting of economic restrictions, and the right of workers to organize outside of the Communist Party. Despite numerous arrests and government threats, by the end of 1980 one-fourth of Poland's population had joined the movement, including 80 percent of the country's workers.

The Polish government declared martial law in an attempt to stave off Soviet invocation of the Brezhnev Doctrine. Still, a massive general strike crippled the country, while international sympathy for the movement increased. This became even more intense after a visit by the pope and Walesa's selection for the Nobel Peace Prize in 1983. With the installation of Mikhail Gorbachev as the new Soviet leader in 1985, and his liberalizing policies of *glasnost* and *perestroika* in the Soviet Union, the future of Solidarity as a political movement became more assured. In 1989 Solidarity was finally relegalized, and it became the largest political party in Poland during the 1990s. Not surprisingly, Walesa was elected president of Poland, serving from 1991 to 1995.

Lech Walesa and Solidarity. The strike at the Gdansk shipyard in Poland in 1980 brought to the fore an obscure electrician but able leader named Lech Walesa. Here, he is shown at a 1981 meeting of the organization he helped found, Solidarity, which ultimately helped topple Poland's communist government. Walesa himself went on to win the Nobel Peace Prize and was elected president of Poland in 1991.

The 1980s: Afghanistan and "Star Wars"

Despite the tensions following the collapse of détente and the Brezhnev Doctrine, some genuine progress on strategic arms limitation was achieved between the superpowers. During the late 1970s, the

United States sought to counter the overwhelming conventional power of the Soviet ground forces in Europe with medium-range ballistic missiles armed with the new technology of the "neutron bomb"—a nuclear weapon designed for minimal blast damage but maximal radiation lethality. The idea was that such weapons would leave many structures intact but devastate the personnel of an invading army. During the ongoing SALT II talks from 1977 to 1979, a historic agreement was reached in 1979 that would, for the first time, require the United States and the Soviet Union to limit certain types of nuclear weapons and begin a process of actually reducing them—a process that would later be known as START (Strategic Arms Reduction Talks/Treaty).

Much of the feeling of progress achieved by this breakthrough was checked, however, by the Soviet invasion of Afghanistan in December 1979. The Egyptian–Israeli treaty of 1979, the tilting of Saudi Arabia and Iraq toward the United States, and the Iranian Revolution had altered the Middle Eastern landscape radically in favor of the West. Fearful of having a weak, nominally communist Afghan government on its flank, adjacent to pro-American Pakistan and a China that appeared to have shifted toward the United States, the Soviets launched a swift coup in Afghanistan and installed a strong communist leader with a massive military force to back him up. The Soviets were immediately subjected to international condemnation, and the United States announced that it would boycott the 1980 Summer Olympics, scheduled to take place in Moscow.

More concretely, the resistance to Afghan communism, led chiefly by idealistic Afghan Muslims and an increasingly large volunteer force of mujahideen, armed with small arms funneled through North Atlantic Treaty Organization (NATO) countries, battled the Soviets for a decade. As the fight wore on, Soviet morale deteriorated, especially with the introduction of more sophisticated weapons capable of countering the immense Russian advantage in armor and airpower. The key weapon is this regard was the shoulder-fired antiaircraft missile we encountered in the vignette at the beginning of this chapter.

At the same time, the new administration of President Ronald Reagan (in office 1981–1989) in the United States sought to adopt a more assertive policy toward the Soviet Union. The administration felt that the previous president, Jimmy Carter (in office 1977–1981), had been somewhat soft toward both the Iranian taking of American hostages and the Soviet invasion of Afghanistan. At the same time, breakthrough technologies in computers and satellite communications made it theoretically possible for the United States to create an antiballistic missile system in outer space. Such a system was in violation of the antiballistic missile provisions of the 1969 SALT I accords, but the advantages of having a reliable missile defense hundreds of miles in space—while at the same time retaining "first strike capability"—were overwhelming to American defense planners. Thus, over Soviet protests, the United States began to develop its Strategic Defense Initiative (SDI), nicknamed "Star Wars" from the popular movie of the same name.

From the mid-1980s, both superpowers thus began an enormously expensive strategic arms development race. For the Soviets, however, the drain of this new arms race, combined with the increasingly expensive and unpopular war in Afghanistan, was simply unsustainable for very long. As we will also see in the next chapter, the Soviet Union's increasing inability to reap the advantages of the computer revolution, and American economic dominance of the world economy through the "dollar regime" proved to be central factors in the decline of the USSR. By 1985, moreover, a new factor was also at work to undermine the old order.

Glasnost and Perestroika

The death of Leonid Brezhnev in 1982 ushered in two short-lived successors before the relatively young Mikhail Gorbachev (b. 1931) took office as first secretary in the Politburo in 1985. Faced with growing dissent in Poland and other Eastern Bloc countries, an increasingly inefficient economy (the problems of which seemed highlighted by successful Chinese experiments with market economics), the endless war in Afghanistan, and now the expensive arms race with the United States, Gorbachev called for large-scale structural reforms in the Soviet system.

What's for Dinner? Not much, if you are one of the miserable-looking shoppers eyeing the meager selection of meat at a Moscow market in early December 1991, just a few weeks before the dissolution of the Soviet Union. By the final days of the Soviet Union, consumer goods and food had become so scarce that many items had to be imported from abroad.

Up until the 1980s, the Soviet economy had functioned as a giant command economic pyramid. Some 100 ministries in Moscow and 800 in the provinces oversaw some 50,000 enterprises, which produced some 24 million individual products. At that time, the Soviet Union had some 200,000 computers compared to the United States with 25 million. With entire roomfuls of computers, the army of ministerial bureaucrats crunched every figure connected with the production and distribution process, figured out prices and wages, and saw to it that the books were balanced at the end of the budget year. The bureaucrats could never count on accurate figures, however, since both workers and managers had every incentive to overreport production figures and produce shoddy consumer goods manufactured as cheaply as possible. Periodic shortages were inevitable, and at any given time a percentage of workers were out in the streets with shopping bags, searching for stores where rumor had it that a fresh consignment of goods had arrived. As the saying on factory floors went, "They pretend to pay us and we pretend to work."

By the mid-1980s, however, Soviet planners had realized that their command system was delivering diminishing returns. Overall growth rates—in the 1950s and 1960s ranging around an impressive 10 percent—had declined to 3 percent. Several factors were responsible for the decline: fewer people were migrating to the factories, lack of investment in new technologies and labor-saving machinery meant that factories were becoming less productive, and the percentage of people over 60 years of age had doubled between World War II and the mid-1980s, requiring the increasingly unproductive labor force to support more and more retirees. In addition, raw materials were less abundant and had to be shipped in from farther away, on top of which bad weather in the later 1970s and early 1980s kept agricultural production low and required large purchases, with dollars, of foodstuffs on the world market. Soviet economic planners therefore asked themselves with increasing urgency how they could return to high growth rates and find the finances to do so.

Two years after becoming secretary of the Politburo in 1985, Gorbachev launched his two trademark economic and political programs, "restructuring" (**perestroika**)

Perestroika: "Restructuring" of the Soviet bureaucracy and economic structure in an attempt to make it more efficient and responsive to market demand.

Glasnost: "Openness"; an attempt to loosen restrictions on media in the Soviet Union with an aim at more accurate reporting of events and the creation of "socialist pluralism."

and "openness" (**glasnost**), which were intended to revitalize communism. Restructuring entailed the partial dismantling of the command economy. Gorbachev drastically reduced the Politburo's oversight function. He slashed the planning bureaucracy by nearly half. Partially freed from the planners' oversight, managers could sell up to one-third of what their factories produced on the market, instead of delivering everything to the state. Citizens were free to establish "cooperatives," the communist euphemism for private business enterprises. By the end of the 1980s, the law permitted co-ops in practically all branches of the economy, including agriculture. Gorbachev sold the new mixed command and market economy as a "socialist" or "regulated" system, advertising it as the same order once pursued by Lenin (then called the New Economic Policy, or NEP).

In practice, perestroika did not work out as intended. Market production rose to a meager 5 percent of total production. Many managers were stuck with the manufacture of unprofitable goods, such as soap, toothpaste, matches, and children's clothes. Consumers complained about continued or even worse shortages in the stores. Other managers, eager to increase production, granted irresponsible wage increases to their workers as incentives. People of modest means founded stores, restaurants, repair shops, construction firms, and software and engineering offices. They charged outrageous prices and did everything to evade paying taxes. Support structures for the co-ops, such as credit, banking, contract law, wholesale distribution centers, and wage bargaining mechanisms, were lacking. Gorbachev's measures, therefore, did little to get the state factories out of stagnation and encouraged the rise of wild "carpetbagger" capitalism.

Parallel to economic restructuring, Gorbachev introduced political "openness," or glasnost. The catalyst for glasnost was the nuclear accident at Chernobyl in the Ukraine in April 1986. When it became impossible to conceal the magnitude of the disaster, reporting in the media became remarkably frank, quickly turning to other hitherto suppressed topics. Journalists, writers, filmmakers, historians, and social scientists proceeded to unmask the taboos and hypocrisies of the previous decades. Gorbachev's glasnost was supposed to produce a "socialist pluralism," but the unintended result was a more genuine pluralism, reducing communism to just one of many competing ideologies in the rapidly evolving Soviet political scene.

Transformations in the Soviet Bloc   The countries of the Soviet Bloc, which were not oil producers, had borrowed heavily from the West in the 1970s and early 1980s for their costly oil imports and the renewal of their industrial base at the beginning of the electronic revolution. Others borrowed to build oil and gas pipelines from Russia via their territories to Western Europe. But the oil price collapse of 1985–1986 forced all Soviet Bloc countries to reschedule their debts and cut their budgets, especially expenditures for their social safety nets and subsidies for basic consumer goods. Popular protests against these cuts rose up from the grass roots in 1989 and 1990 in Poland, Hungary, and Czechoslovakia, accompanied by demands for power sharing.

In the German Democratic Republic (GDR, East Germany), a particularly dramatic shift occurred. Germans, at the end of their summer vacations at the Black Sea in 1989, refused to return home. They massed at the Hungarian border with Austria in hopes of being permitted to leave. Hungary, at that moment in search of its own reforms, including the introduction of democracy, let the vacationers cross the border. Back in the GDR, massive demonstrations led to the fall first of the communist government and then of the infamous Berlin Wall on the night of November 9, 1989. A year later, with Gorbachev's blessing, the two Germanys united, ending nearly a half-century of division.

Communist governments now fell in other Soviet Bloc countries as well (see Map 30.2). Before too much pressure built up from below, the governments of the Baltic states of Estonia, Latvia, and Lithuania, as well as that of Bulgaria, gave way

MAP 30.2 The Fall of Communism in Eastern Europe and the Soviet Union.

The Fall of Communism in Eastern Europe and the Soviet Union

Former republics of the Soviet Union gaining independence in 1991	Independence from Soviet Union declared 1991; at war with Russia, 1994-2000	Boundary of the former Soviet Union to 1991
Boundary of Russian Federation after December 1991	Former Warsaw Pact country holding free elections, 1990-1992	Violent ethnic conflicts

more or less voluntarily to democracy. Albania followed suit in 1992. The only exception was Romania, where Nicolae Ceaușescu [Chow-CHESS-coo] (in office 1974–1989) had built a strong personality cult and had put family members into key party and government offices. The botched eviction by the police of a protestant Hungarian minority pastor from his parish in western Romania in November 1989 resulted in scores of deaths. Following a mass demonstration in Bucharest protesting the deaths, portions of the army defected and arrested the fleeing Ceaușescu and his wife Elena. Army elements assembled a tribunal, sentenced the two to death, and summarily executed them on December 25, 1989. Subsequently, however, the army and the Communist Party reconciled and the country returned to a dictatorship. It was not until 1996 that Romania adopted a democratic system.

The dissolution of communism in the Eastern Bloc eventually caught up with the 15 states making up the Soviet Union. Most of these states declared their sovereignty or even independence in the course of 1990. Gorbachev alienated his supporters by allowing the Soviet army to harass or even kill demonstrators in Georgia and Lithuania, in a vain attempt to salvage the Soviet Union. Meanwhile, elections in several Soviet states brought legitimate presidents to power. One of the presidents was Boris Yeltsin (in office 1991–1999), who was elected in Russia, the largest of the union states. As the president elected by a newly created but feeble Soviet Union parliament, Gorbachev did not have the popular mandate Yeltsin had within Russia and he resented the latter's grassroots support.

After arduous negotiations, Gorbachev agreed with Yeltsin and the other state presidents to a new federal union treaty for the Soviet Union in spring 1991, to be signed in August. This treaty triggered an abortive plot by eight communist hardliners who briefly succeeded in arresting Gorbachev as he was vacationing for a few days in his dacha on the Black Sea. The conspirators, however, showed thier ineptitude by failing to arrest Yeltsin. In a tense showdown with troops sent to occupy the Russian parliament, Yeltsin and a large crowd of Muscovites forced the hardliners to blink. Officially, the Soviet Union ended on Christmas Day, 1991, replaced by the Commonwealth of Independent States with a democratic Russia under Yeltsin at its center.

With the establishment of the new commonwealth, the Cold War and the epic struggle of competing modernities that had colored so much of the twentieth century quickly and quietly faded away. Russia's transformation to capitalism and democracy, however, was destined to be fraught with corruption, false starts, tension with former enemies, and pressure to return to a more authoritarian ethnolinguistic nationalist system.

Transforming the West

While North America and Western Europe certainly enjoyed an era of impressive growth and social change from the late 1940s through the early 1960s, scholars of popular culture have singled out the period from 1963 through the early 1970s as particularly intensive. Social movements that had long been germinating, such as the African American civil rights movement in the United States, moved to the center of the national agenda; the long-term drive for equal rights for women similarly moved into prominence, as did those of other historically marginalized groups such as the disabled, gays and lesbians, and a host of ethnic groups. Nearly all of these movements borrowed strategies and tactics from the movement for African American civil rights. Most of them also involved peaceful protests and civil disobedience, some borrowing directly from the strategies and philosophy of Gandhi. Some, however, advocated violent confrontation.

Civil Rights Movements

As we saw in Chapters 22 and 29, the story of African Americans since the end of the American Civil War had been one of emancipation from slavery and acquisition of the formal rights of citizenship in the constitutional order, but considerable opposition to their social integration, especially in the southern states. Indeed, by the time of World War II, all of the southern states had laws mandating segregation, and even some northern states and cities had formal and informal restrictions on such things as where African Americans could live and work. The "great migration" of blacks from the rural south to the industrial north during this time and the lobbying by such organizations as the National Association for the Advancement of Colored People (NAACP; founded 1909) increased the pressure for more civil rights for black people. In this respect, the war proved a decisive turning point in their struggle.

The Postwar Drive for Civil Rights   The massive mobilization during World War II began the process of greatly accelerating civil rights efforts on a number of fronts. The vast numbers of African Americans serving in the armed forces, along with professed US and Allied war aims regarding Nazi racial policies, made segregation in the military increasingly untenable. In 1947, therefore, President Truman signed an executive order desegregating the American armed forces. Repeated anti-lynching and civil rights bills now began to appear before Congress. In 1954, the Supreme Court reversed its earlier stand on segregation in education in the momentous *Brown v. Board of Education* ruling. Overturning the 1896 *Plessey v. Fergusson* decision that "separate but equal" facilities were constitutional, the court now ruled that the "separate" facilities were by definition not equal. Schools were therefore ordered to desegregate "with all deliberate speed." This met with determined resistance in many communities; in 1957, President Dwight D. Eisenhower (in office 1953–1961) was compelled to send in the military to Little Rock, Arkansas, to enforce the ruling. Still, by the early 1960s there was a dramatic movement under way for civil rights and equal treatment for African Americans in the American south.

In addition to the new domestic sense of urgency that desegregation was long overdue, international conditions played a role in pushing it forward. One of these conditions was postwar anticolonialism, particularly in Africa, where former European colonies (e.g., Ghana in 1957) secured their independence. The Cold War also played a vital role. Soviet propaganda had long played up the discrepancies between American claims of freedom and equality and its treatment of black people. Thus, the argument was increasingly made that desegregation and civil rights would give the lie to Soviet claims and thus be patriotic. When the accelerating pressure of civil rights marches and protests resulted in violence against the protesters in the early 1960s, President John F. Kennedy sponsored civil rights legislation to end discrimination.

A high point occurred in August of 1963 when the Reverend Martin Luther King Jr. (1929–1968) delivered his electrifying "I Have a Dream" speech before a huge crowd at the Lincoln Memorial in Washington, D.C. After the assassination of Kennedy that November, his successor, Lyndon B. Johnson (in office 1963–1969),

(a)

(b)

(c)

The Civil Rights Struggle. One of the first major contests for desegregation of public transportation in the American South was the Montgomery, Alabama, bus boycott of 1955. Here, Rosa Parks, by refusing to sit in the back of the bus in the area reserved for African Americans, sparked the boycott of Montgomery's bus lines by people of color (a). As the 1960s began the further desegregation of public areas, in this case, lunch counters were taken over by students "sitting in" and refusing to leave. (b) The career of the charismatic minister Dr. Martin Luther King Jr. was launched during the Montgomery bus boycott. By the early 1960s he had emerged as America's preeminent civil rights leader. Here, he is shown at the peak of his influence, delivering his famous "I Have a Dream" speech on the Capital Mall in Washington, D.C., in August 1963 (c).

secured the passage of the Civil Rights Act of 1964, which provided significant protections for African Americans, not least of which was the prohibition of segregation in public places. This was followed by the 1965 Voting Rights Act, aimed at outlawing the poll taxes, literacy tests, and other means by which states attempted to limit their citizens' ability to vote.

With many legal remedies now in place for past discrimination, civil rights leaders increasingly turned their attention to economic and social justice. The Johnson administration had created a comprehensive program, called "The Great Society," aimed at eliminating poverty in America. Civil rights advocates lobbied vigorously to make sure the proper proportion of jobs and poverty-relief programs were aimed at their constituents. Since that time, the emphasis has been largely on job equity, affirmative action (weighing one's minority status in hiring to make up for past group injustices), and ongoing efforts to improve education in largely African American or minority inner-city areas.

While the drive for African American civil rights was perhaps the most sweeping movement of the 1960s and early 1970s, it also generated many others. Taking their cue from the prominence and media attention of African American efforts, a host of ethnic groups facing discrimination of various kinds mounted their own drives for recognition and rights. Mexican Americans, Asian Americans, Puerto Ricans, the disabled, and gays and lesbians all borrowed heavily from the methods of the African American and the women's movements. In all of these cases, their drives resulted in legislation and social changes aimed at making up for past discrimination and protection from future reversals.

The Antiwar Movement   For many of the thousands of idealistic students who had taken part in civil rights demonstrations and programs to register African American voters in southern states in the early 1960s, it seemed to be a natural transition from political activism in favor of civil rights to activism for other causes. By 1965, the building American military effort in Vietnam began to attract protests

By the 1970s the women's liberation movement had become firmly anchored in the national consciousness and had inspired similar movements in Europe and many other areas around the world. A new, more radical edge within the movement began to advocate increasingly extreme positions. For example, some argued that marriage itself was essentially sexist and should not be pursued by women; others went so far as to characterize all heterosexual activity as rape under a different name; still others argued for "cultural lesbianism" for women—proposing that women form a distinct community from men and pursue activities within that culture as exclusively as possible.

Although a "third wave" of feminism has taken hold from the 1990s in coexistence with the older ones and often projects a less restrictive attitude toward sexuality of all types than much second-wave feminism, all three waves have become part of the ordinary political landscape of many countries. Indeed, "feminism" has completely supplanted "women's liberation" as the term for a constellation of values and causes that includes equal pay in the workplace, free and full reproductive rights, greater sexual freedom for women, and a thoroughgoing lack of discrimination in society on the basis of gender. In many places, there are still quite specific causes that women seek to champion: an end to female genital mutilation, the abolition of "honor killings" of rape victims, an end to the total domination of males in marriages and arranged marriages, the elimination of female bond slavery, outlawing selective abortion of female fetuses, ending female infanticide, greater emphasis on the prevention of HIV/AIDS transmission, and so on. During the 1980s an evolving movement among scholars from India, Africa, and Southeast Asia (including Gayatri Spivak, Gloria Anzaldua, Chandra Talpade Mohanty, and Trinh Minh-ha), called "postcolonial feminism," explicitly linked sexism and patriarchy to latent colonial racism and its effects among its indigenous "subalterns." During this period, too, there was much theoretical groundwork laid for the problem of the "feminization of poverty" in the developing world: According to a recent United Nations report, women do 66 percent of the world's work, produce at least half of the food, but make only 10 percent of the income and own a scant 1 percent of the property. Thus, female poverty is intricately linked with the patriarchy embedded in long-standing cultural practices.

Women's Liberation in the US and India. Taking a page from the success of demonstrations for African American civil rights and the anti–Vietnam War movements, various women's activist organizations mounted their own marches to protest discrimination based on patriarchy and male domination. In this demonstration from 1968 the focus is on eliminating gender discrimination and artificial, male-dictated standards of beauty (*top*). Post-colonial feminism in action: members of the National Federation of Dalit Women demonstrate in support of rights for women of the Dalit ("untouchables") caste in New Delhi, India in 2008 (*bottom*). While discrimination against Dalit is proscribed by law in India, bias against Dalit women is still widespread.

As the 1990s dawned and the Soviet Bloc collapsed, the problems of women in those countries were also brought to the fore. Thus, feminism as a worldwide movement, despite the many institutional, cultural, and religious obstacles facing it, has grown into perhaps the world's most widespread and influential phenomenon. It promises to be the great emancipation movement of the twenty-first century.

Questions

- How does the women's liberation movement demonstrate many of the characteristics of evolving modernity?

- Why does feminism promise to be the great emancipation movement of the twenty-first century?

Woodstock. The iconic event of the "hippie" or "counterculture" era of the late 1960s was the Woodstock music and art festival held in August 1969 in upstate New York. It was a massive event, attended by perhaps as many as 400,000 people—as this aerial photo dramatically shows (a). Of the dozens of performers playing over the 3 days of the event, one of the most electrifying was the guitarist Jimi Hendrix. Hendrix pioneered a wild, free-form, jazz-inflected style that is still widely admired and imitated today (b).

increased emphasis on sex and eroticism, also played a part in new attitudes toward female sexuality. By the late 1960s, a "women's liberation" movement aimed at such things as equal pay for equal work, more social freedom for women to pursue careers outside the home, and, among the most radical, the pursuit of woman-centered values had come to the fore.

"Tune In, Turn On, Drop Out"   At the same time as this political transformation was taking place, students were increasingly engaged in protest against what they perceived as the excessive materialism, conformism, and sexual prudishness of the previous generation. Many of this "permissive generation" of "baby boomers" (those born during the postwar "baby boom" between 1945 and 1961) repudiated the rigidity of their parents by growing their hair long—in imitation of the Beatles and other rock bands—wearing jeans, T-shirts, and "workers'" clothing; dabbling in Asian philosophies; taking drugs and engaging in a variety of forms of sexual experimentation.

The early center for this movement of "hippies" was San Francisco, in which 1967 was proclaimed the "summer of love." The growing popularity of drugs like marijuana and the hallucinogenic compound lysergic acid diethylamide (LSD) encouraged many to experiment with mind-altering substances. Perhaps the most famous advocate of these allegedly "mind-expanding" drugs was Timothy Leary (1920–1996), a former Harvard University psychologist who advised people to "tune in, turn on [i.e., take LSD], and drop out [of society]." Musical groups espousing hippie values—often crudely summed up as "sex, drugs, and rock and roll"—also arose and dominated much of the popular music scene during this time. Among the most influential were The Grateful Dead, Jefferson Airplane, and, from England, Pink Floyd. Perhaps the peak of this movement came in August 1969, when the Woodstock Festival in New York State drew an estimated 300,000–500,000 attendees and sparked a decade of giant music and culture festivals attempting to capture the spirit of what became known as the "Woodstock generation." Though the hippie movement as a force for "liberation" from mainstream values had largely spent itself by the early 1970s, its influence in fashion, sexual attitudes, music, and drug use continues to some extent even today.

The Oil Crisis of 1973-1974

Major exporters of oil 1973 (in million tonnes):

- 10-100
- 100–200
- 200–300
- 300–400

Major importers of oil 1973 (in million tonnes):

- 0–50
- 50–150
- 150–300
- **IRAN** Member of OPEC, 1973

MAP **30.4** **The Oil Crisis of 1973–1974.**

Economics and Politics in the 1970s and 1980s   Whereas the 1950s and 1960s represented unprecedented growth and prosperity, a sudden economic downturn in the early 1970s initiated a prolonged period of economic stagnation. Several factors were at work here. One cause was the ramping down of the Vietnam War effort, which had driven the US defense industry. Another cause stemmed from renewed hostilities between Arab and Israeli factions in 1973. In retaliation against American support of Israel, the newly formed OPEC, led by Arab states, dramatically increased the price of oil for export to America. The price per barrel of oil rose dramatically from $1.73 in 1973 to nearly $35 in 1981 (see Map 30.4). The consequences of these economic downturns were at first inflation and then by the late 1970s **stagflation**. The emergence of developing economies in Asia and South America also began to lure American manufacturers to relocate to these countries in order to take advantage of lower labor costs, resulting in the decline of major industries in the United States.

The combined effect of these economic fluctuations and restrictions caused corresponding realignments in politics in the 1970s and 1980s. In many Western countries—the United States, Britain, and Germany—the trend shifted toward the adoption of more conservative policies. The most notable examples of what has been termed the "New Conservatism" were the policies of the American president Ronald Reagan and Britain's prime minister Margaret Thatcher (in office 1979–1990). Reagan's fiscal policies, by way of example (sometimes termed "Reaganomics") featured lower taxes as a way to increase jobs, lower interest rates, and offset deficit spending. Although the subject of considerable debate, these policies have been credited with producing a sustained period of economic growth during his presidency. Both leaders orchestrated cutbacks in governmental spending for

Stagflation: Increased prices and record high interest rates but a stagnant economy overall.

social services and welfare programs, and in both countries industrial strikes and the power of labor unions were restricted and the nationalization of major industries was replaced by privatization.

Other countries, like France, took an opposite approach. They rejected conservatism as a way to solve economic problems. The election of François Mitterand (in office 1981–1995) resulted in the adoption of socialist policies like nationalization of banks and industries, increases in wages, and increased spending on social welfare programs. Instead of improving the French economy, however, Mitterand's policies created an economic downturn, resulting in the election of a more conservative leader, Jacques Chirac (in office 1995–2007) at the end of his term.

From "Underdeveloped" to "Developing" World, 1963–1991

As the Cold War reached it peak in the 1960s, the drive for independence in Africa also crested, with the last colonies finally achieving nationhood in the 1970s. At the same time the drive for economic development, national prestige, and national power continued to grow among all of the newly independent nations everywhere. The 1960s through the 1980s marked in many ways the height of the contest among the nonaligned nations for preeminence between our two competing modernisms: market capitalism with democratic governments and variants of communism, based on the Soviet or Chinese model. Some newly independent governments attempted assorted combinations of both forms of modernity as paths to development. Although many countries remained in dire poverty and scarred by internal and external wars, the period also witnessed many more moving from the catchall category of "underdeveloped" to the more optimistic one of "developing."

While the unsurpassed prosperity of the West in this period mightily impressed leaders in the developing world, many, if not most, continued to question whether capitalism was appropriate for their nations as an economic basis. There were several reasons for this, both practical and historical. On a practical level it was considered that capitalism had developed in the West over a long time and with great suffering among the working classes. Putting a newly independent nation into competition with developed nations thus placed the latter at an unfair advantage. Additionally, capitalism encouraged continued economic dominance of the former colonial powers and thus skewed the economies of developing nations toward supporting the economies of their former occupiers. Moreover, the perceived connection between capitalism and imperialism was distasteful to many who had fought to rid their countries of colonialism. Finally, for decades after the end of imperial rule, the legacy of imperialism was blamed for many of the remaining problems of struggling developing countries.

As we saw in Chapter 29, the socialist road for many of these same reasons had a powerful theoretical appeal to many leaders in these emerging nations. The examples of the Soviet Union and China, and implicitly the "Communist Bloc" countries, appeared to show that formerly poor countries could become rich and powerful— even to the point of being superpowers. Moreover, they appeared to be able to do it far more quickly than capitalist countries. Finally, they were without the fatal stain of having been colonialists—at least in the sense that they had not created overseas empires—and thus could be perceived to be without a long-standing ulterior motive.

One key development that is worth considering in this regard revolves around the ideological approaches of the rival camps. Marxist theorists had long argued that underdevelopment was *caused* by capitalism and imperialism. That is, by taking control of the economy of a new colony, imperialism plugged it into the world capitalist system and shunted its products into areas useful to the mother country rather than the people of the colony. This disturbed the natural balance of the colony's economic life and retarded its further development according to its own needs. When the colony becomes independent, therefore, it remains at a disadvantage because its economy still depends on that of the mother country and has no way of breaking away cleanly and reestablishing an independent economy. The only way this can be done, said the theorists, was through a thoroughgoing political and social revolution.

Economists and political thinkers in the West eager to combat this Marxist view asserted that underdevelopment was caused by a lack of modern institutions, basic industries, and infrastructure that would support a market economy. Their *modernization theory* argued that, although the modern elements in the former colonies had certainly not been set up for the benefit of the colonized, they were precisely those needed for survival in the modern world and should therefore be used as the modern base upon which new nations should build. Thus, instead of imperialism being seen as creating underdevelopment, it was viewed as the force that, however grudgingly, created the basis for modern development.

> ### Germs of Rot
>
> "Violence is man re-creating himself.... Imperialism leaves behind germs of rot, which we must clinically detect and remove from our land, but from our minds as well.... The starving peasant ... is the first among the exploited to discover that only violence pays. For him there is no compromise, no possible coming to terms; colonization and decolonization are simply a question of relative strength."
>
> —Frantz Fanon. *The Wretched of the Earth*, p. 71. New York: Grove Press, 1961.

China: Cultural Revolution to Four Modernizations

Of all the major world powers, the People's Republic of China experienced perhaps the most wrenching policy changes during the period 1963–1991. Having just emerged from the first Maoist era of the 1950s, it entered into a less frenetic few years of more Soviet-style socialist development, only to be catapulted into the frenzy of the Cultural Revolution in the late 1960s. The death of Mao in 1976, however, ushered in a complete reversal of economic course. In 1978, the Four Modernizations of Deng Xiaoping called for opening the country to foreign experts, aid and investment, and creating a market economy—that is, to introduce capitalism. To this day, China's economic policy is officially called "Socialism with Chinese characteristics."

China's "Thermidorean Reaction," 1960–1966

The turbulence of the first round of the Maoist years ebbed considerably under the leadership of Liu Shaoqi. The decade began, however, with the "Sino–Soviet split," in which Soviet apprehensiveness about China's radical programs and Mao's distrust of Soviet policy changes under Khrushchev led to a complete withdrawal of Soviet aid and advisors in 1960. For Western observers accustomed to seeing the communist world as a "monolith," this was the first real divide among ideological allies since Tito's independent stance in Yugoslavia in 1948. By the end of the decade, Chinese and Soviet forces would be exchanging fire along several disputed border crossings.

Nonetheless, the early 1960s saw a reassertion of the need for education and technical training in China under Liu, and China made several important technological advances. Chief among these was the detonation of China's first nuclear device in October 1964. This was quickly followed by the testing of a thermonuclear (hydrogen) device in 1966. Chinese scientists also synthesized insulin and made advances in missile technology that would yield the first Chinese satellites in the following decade. Extensive studies of China's natural resources also disclosed large coal deposits and led to the discovery of oil fields at Daqing and in the extreme west. In addition, Liu's regime engaged in a more assertive policy of border rectification. Chinese forces had entered Tibet in 1959 to suppress an independence movement, resulting in the flight of the Dalai Lama to India. In securing Tibet, however, disputes arose regarding the actual border with India. In 1962, Chinese forces moved into the disputed regions and fought a brief undeclared war until withdrawing and submitting the issue to negotiation. This kind of display of force in order to make a point would be seen again in China's attack on Vietnam in 1979, though with far less effectiveness.

The Cultural Revolution   As China's Communist Party and government assumed a more Soviet-style approach to running the People's Republic, Mao Zedong grew increasingly uneasy about the direction of policy. For Mao, the party was reverting to a bureaucracy, increasingly unresponsive to the needs of pushing the revolution forward toward a pure communism. Mao's position of politics taking command was in direct opposition to the increasingly technocratic stance he saw in Liu Shaoqi's policies. Thus, Mao spent several years writing widely circulated essays extolling the virtues of devoted communists and plotting his comeback. An important step along the way was the publication of his famous "little red book," *Quotations from Chairman Mao Zedong*, in 1964. His ideological ally, Lin Biao (in office 1954–1971), as Vice-Premier and head of the People's Liberation Army, made it required reading for the troops and helped Mao establish an important power base.

In the spring of 1966, Mao launched a violent critique of the new direction of the party and called on the nation's youth to rededicate themselves to "continuous revolution." They were encouraged to criticize their elders and form their own pure "red" ideological path to socialism. Mao announced the launching of the Great Proletarian Cultural Revolution, the purpose of which was to stamp out the last vestiges of "bourgeois" and "feudal" Chinese society. Students formed themselves into squads of "Red Guards" with red armbands and attacked their teachers and elders. By August, millions of Red Guards converged on Beijing, where Mao addressed over 1 million of them in Tiananmen Square and symbolically donned their red armband as a show of solidarity.

From 1966 until 1969, when the Cultural Revolution was officially declared over, millions of people were hounded, tortured, killed, or driven to suicide by Red Guards and

---

A Revolution Is Not a Dinner Party

"People of the world unite and defeat the U.S. aggressors and their running dogs!"

"Every Communist must grasp the truth, 'Political power grows out of the barrel of a gun...'"

"A revolution is not a dinner party, or writing an essay, or painting a picture, or doing embroidery; it cannot be so refined, so leisurely and gentle, so temperate, so kind, courteous, restrained and magnanimous. A revolution is an insurrection, an act of violence by which one class overthrows another..."

—Mao Zedong. *Quotations from Chairman Mao Zedong. Mao zhuxi yulu*, 1964. English language version by Foreign Languages Press, Quotations from Chairman Mao Tsetung (Peking: 1972), pp. 82,11, 59.

Red Guards on the March.
Mao Zedong's injunction to the youth of China to question the authority of party bureaucrats had swift effects on everything from the school system to factory production. The students banded together into Red Guard units and challenged their elders, often violently, on their adherence to Mao's thought as expressed in the famous "little red book," *Quotations from Chairman Mao Zedong.* In this photo from 1967, Red Guards parade with a portrait of Mao, while many carry the red book in their hands.

their allies. The "little red book" became the talisman of the movement, with people struggling to interpret it correctly to prove their ideological fitness. China's official ideology was now listed as "Marxism–Leninism–Mao Zedong Thought." A cult of personality surrounding Mao and the book sprang up as people waved it at mass rallies and even attributed magical powers to it. By 1968 the country was in complete chaos as pro- and anti–Cultural Revolution factions battled each other in several regions. It was chiefly to end this endemic civil war that Mao declared the Cultural Revolution over in 1969. Its aftermath, however, continued until Mao's death in 1976.

"To Get Rich Is Glorious": China's Four Modernizations The final years of Mao's tenure as party chair saw at least one important change in policy. Despite the Sino–Soviet split, the People's Republic had maintained a strong anti-American posture in its domestic and foreign policy. This was matched by American Cold War antipathy toward "Red China" as a linchpin of the communist bloc. By the early 1970s, however, with the Vietnam War winding down and Soviet–Chinese tensions still high, President Nixon made a bold visit to the People's Republic, which resulted in the Shanghai communiqué of 1972. In this document, the United States and the People's Republic of China announced plans to begin formal diplomatic and cultural relations (which went into effect in 1979), the United States pledged to no

longer block the People's Republic's bid for a seat in the United Nations, and the United States agreed to downgrade its diplomatic presence in Taiwan.

The death of Mao Zedong in September 1976 opened the way for a new generation of Communist Party leadership in China. The end result was a repudiation of the Cultural Revolution and those who promoted it and an entirely different direction in strategy for building a new China. After some jostling among the party factions, the hardy Deng Xiaoping (in office 1978–1992) emerged on the scene in 1978 with the title of "vice premier" but, in fact, held the real power in the regime. The ascendancy of the pragmatic Deng, whose motto was "It doesn't matter whether the cat is black or white, as long as it catches mice," swiftly led to the unveiling of the fundamental policies that remain in force in China to the present: the Four Modernizations.

Painfully aware of the difficulties of pursuing socialism in a country with little wealth to share, Deng's strategy was bent on upgrading the quality of agriculture, industry, science, technology, and the military. China would pursue a new "open-door" policy with regard to foreign expertise from the West; it would allow its own students to study abroad and, most tellingly, allow the market forces of capitalism to

MAP **30.5** Open Cities and Special Economic Zones in China, 1980–2000.

Open Cities and Special Economic Zones in China, 1980-2000

- ● City opened to foreign trade in 1980s
- ● City opened to foreign trade in 1990s
- ○ Other city
- ■ Special Economic Zone

create incentives for innovation in all sectors of the economy. The new motto thus became "To get rich is glorious!"

The "responsibility system," as it was called, was introduced in a special economic zone set up in south China at Shenzhen to take advantage of capital and expertise from Hong Kong. The experiments in capitalism would then be expanded to the country at large once the flaws had been worked out. Peasants were among the first beneficiaries as the communes were disbanded, individual plots assigned, and market incentives introduced. By the mid-1980s China, which had long been a byword in the West for hunger, was rapidly approaching self-sufficiency in food production and, by the 1990s, would register surpluses (see Map 30.5). Through the 1980s and 1990s China's gross domestic product (GDP) would grow at an astonishing double-digit rate. In 2010 it surpassed Japan as the second largest economy in the world, after the United States.

Another more controversial innovation was the "one-child policy." Mao felt that China's huge and growing population was an advantage because of its potential manpower and as a hedge against catastrophic losses from nuclear war. But population pressures were also a powerful brake on China's development. Thus, a policy was inaugurated in 1979 mandating that families (excluding those of most minorities) were to have only one child. A second child would result in loss of subsidies for childrearing; a third pregnancy would result in mandatory abortion. Despite the many problems in enforcing such a policy, and its severe cultural impact on the male-centered traditional Chinese family structure, China's population has remained remarkably stable since the 1980s at around 1.3–1.5 billion. It has, however, abetted problems of selective female abortion, giving up girl babies for adoption, and even, in extreme cases, female infanticide. Moreover, all of these conditions have lent themselves to a large and growing gender imbalance: China currently has 117 male births for every 100 female births.

The "Fifth Modernization" and Tiananmen Square
The heady atmosphere of the early days of these sweeping changes brought political reformers temporarily out of hiding. In the so-called Peking Spring of 1979, thousands of demonstrators called for a wide array of democratic reforms by hanging "big-character" posters on the walls near Tiananmen Square, the site of China's most important government buildings and Mao's mausoleum. This "democracy" movement calling for a "fifth modernization: democracy" was shortly suppressed, but political agitation calling for a more open society, crackdowns on corruption, and even a multiparty system continued in muted form throughout the decade.

For its part, the government managed a delicate balance between allowing foreign technology to come into China while preventing cultural items "injurious to public morals" to enter. Hence, IBM computers were welcome, but MTV was not. Repeated campaigns against such "spiritual pollution" were conducted throughout the 1980s, though with less and less effect. Prodemocracy protests again took place in Beijing following the death of the popular moderate leader Hu Yaobang in 1989. The gatherings grew in size and force as the seventieth anniversary of the May Fourth nationalist movement grew closer. At one point students even constructed a large statue they called "the Goddess of Democracy," which dominated the center of the square near the Monument to the People's Revolutionary Martyrs. By the beginning of June the movement had turned into generalized protest of workers and

Tiananmen Square Demonstrations. At their peak in May 1989, the demonstrations by students seeking greater government accountability and a more open political system were joined by workers and people from all walks of life. Here are two memorable images from this event: (*a*) the "goddess of democracy," taken from behind in a pose that seems to confront the portrait of Mao Zedong on the Gate of Heavenly Peace, and (*b*) the suppression of the demonstration—a lone man confronting a tank. The driver of the tank tried to get around the man and eventually stopped, together with the other tanks. At that point, demonstrators pulled the man back to safety. His subsequent fate is unknown. Both images were widely broadcast throughout the world.

ordinary citizens in addition to students. When they refused to disperse, the government sent in the army on June 4 to crush what to many in the party had become incipient rebellion. One arresting image was flashed in various media around the world and became an instant icon of the movement: television footage of a lone man attempting to stare down an approaching tank. To this day, the number of killed and injured is unknown.

Vietnam: War and Unification

As we noted in Chapter 29, by the early 1960s Vietnam, having finally thrown off French colonialism in the 1950s, had failed to achieve final unification because of Cold War politics and remained divided into North and South Vietnam. The development of communist guerrilla fighters, the Vietcong, in South Vietnam and similar guerrilla threats in Laos had prompted the United States to send aid and military advisors to the shaky government of the Republic of Vietnam (South Vietnam) through the late 1950s. Rocked by clashes between Catholics and Buddhists, the government of South Vietnam was ousted in a coup with help from the American Central Intelligence Agency (CIA) in late 1963. Several weak governments took its place until a more stable one under Nguyen Van Thieu emerged and lasted from 1965 to 1975.

The American War   In the summer of 1964 several alleged attacks on American ships in the Gulf of Tonkin (the authenticity of these allegations is still murky today) resulted in the United States radically ramping up its presence in Southeast Asia, effectively beginning what became known in Vietnam as the American War and in the United States as the Vietnam War. In retaliation for the attacks, American planes bombed sites in North Vietnam. By 1965 tens of thousands of American combat troops were being sent to support the South Vietnamese against the Vietcong. But, as in Korea, the Americans and their allies were plagued by unclear goals and the impatience of a public hoping for quick, decisive results. The task of "winning the hearts and minds of the people," as the slogan went, however, was a long and torturous one at best and always vulnerable to the problem of being a foreign presence in someone else's land. Thus, American forces were increased until they reached a high of over a half-million by 1967. Despite official optimism, there was little evidence that the war was being won (see Map 30.6).

In February 1968, during the Vietnamese lunar new year (*Tet*), the Vietcong, supported by North Vietnamese forces, launched an all-out assault on the South Vietnamese capital of Saigon and a number of other cities. American and Army of the Republic of Vietnam (South Vietnam) forces reeled for several days but launched a successful counterattack, finally destroying the Vietcong as an effective fighting force. In the United States, however, the "Tet Offensive," as it came to be called, was seen as an American defeat. In the wake of massive protests against the war, President Johnson announced he would not seek reelection; and the way was clear for the United States to begin negotiations to end the war by political means. With the election of Richard Nixon in 1968, a combination of massive bombings of North Vietnam and Cambodian supply lines for North Vietnamese forces and peace talks in Paris over the next 5 years finally brought the war to an end.

Though South Vietnam survived the peace treaty in 1973, the American withdrawal spelled its demise within 2 years. Though the country was now finally united, much of Vietnam, Cambodia, and Laos lay devastated from fighting and bombing. Over the next 2 years a Cambodian revolutionary group, the Khmer Rouge (Red Khmers), launched a radical program of depopulating the cities, forced labor, and genocide against religious and political opponents that killed perhaps one-third of the country's population. The ideas and practices of the Khmer Rouge leader Pol Pot (1925–1998) were so radical and brutal that in 1977 Vietnam invaded the state and initiated his overthrow in favor of a more moderate and pliable candidate. In response, China briefly invaded northern Vietnam in 1979 but was soon repulsed by Vietnamese forces, the last and least successful of the many Chinese invasion attempts launched over two millennia.

MAP 30.6 **The Vietnam War.**

(a)

(b)

The Arab-Israeli War of June 1967. The stunning victory of Israel over the combined armies of Syria and Egypt generated both admiration in the West and consternation in the Arab world and the Soviet Bloc. The Israelis' preemptive use of air power against Egyptian and Syrian tank and troop concentrations and their expert use of armor proved the deciding factors in the conflict. Here, Egyptian prisoners (in white underclothes in the truck to the right) are being transferred to holding camps (a). The war also led to a dramatic rise in the popularity of the Palestinian cause in the Arab and communist spheres. Here, Yassir Arafat marches with members of Al Fatah in 1970 (b).

The Middle East

One of the most troubled areas of the world during the twentieth century was also one that, as we have seen over the course of this book, has been perhaps the most prolific producer of influential religions: the Middle East. Since 1945, the area encompassing the Arabian Peninsula, Iran, Iraq, and the eastern shores of the Mediterranean has seen a number of major wars and minor conflicts; innumerable guerilla raids and assaults; and attacks directed against the religious symbols of Judaism, Christianity, and Islam. As of this writing, despite peace talks that have been conducted over the course of decades, no comprehensive settlement has been reached.

Israeli and Arab Conflict   In addition to competition arising from the increasing demand for petroleum as a strategic commodity, and Shia–Sunni conflict within the context of Persian–Arab competition, by far the most contentious issue in the Middle East has been the presence of the Jewish state of Israel. Israel during the 1950s and 1960s was largely seen in the West as a plucky young country fighting democracy's battles against a vast array of Arab states supported by the Soviet Union. The number of highly educated immigrants in the postwar decades helped the new state immensely in building an efficient agriculture—often through the socialist device of the communal farm, or *kibbutz*—and an increasingly sophisticated manufacturing sector. Mandatory military service and generous American support also contributed to the creation of top-notch armed forces equipped with the latest military technology.

The "Six-Day War"   For the Palestinian Arabs and their allies, however, the perspective was very different. For them it was "the disaster." Hundreds of thousands displaced since 1948 awaited their return in surrounding countries—often in camps—for decades, a situation that grew worse when new refugees arrived after every Arab–Israeli conflict. In the polarized Cold War climate, the Arab states viewed Israel as simply a new Western imperial outpost in what was rightfully Arab territory. Consequently, many subsequent attempts at Arab unity were premised on war with Israel. While Arab nationalism was largely secular, and often socialist-leaning with Soviet support, Muslim fundamentalist groups such as Egypt's Muslim Brotherhood gained adherence, despite government repression, as Western secular values came to be seen as causes of Muslim difficulties.

In 1964, Yassir Arafat (1929–2004) and other like-minded Palestinian nationalists formed the Palestinian Liberation Organization (PLO), whose militant wing, Al Fatah, began a guerilla war against Israel and its backers. Matters soon came to a head in June 1967. Following an Egyptian military buildup along the Sinai border and the expulsion of UN forces there, Iraq sent troops to Jordan at its invitation and local Muslim leaders began to call for holy war against Israel. The Israelis launched a massive preemptive air assault to neutralize the Egyptian and Syrian air forces. With an overwhelming advantage in number and quality of aircraft, Israel took out the Arab armor and ground troops with astonishing skill. The Six-Day War, as it came to be called, established Israel's reputation for military prowess and enlarged the state by the annexing of territories on the eastern side of the Jordan River, known since that time as the Occupied Territories. For many observers, Israel had now moved from a state simply fighting for its existence to one bent on expansion.

The Yom Kippur/Ramadan War

For the two superpowers, the Arab–Israeli conflict provided valuable data on the performance of the weapons systems they supplied to their respective allies. Thus far in these "proxy wars" (as they were sometimes called), American and European weapons—and increasingly, Israeli-made arms like the famous Uzi submachine gun—had tended to outperform the Soviet ordnance supplied to the Arab states. This was almost reversed in 1973 however. In early October

The Arab-Israeli Wars of 1967 and 1973

- Israel, before 1967 war
- Territory occupied by Israel, June 1967
- Territory occupied by Israel, Oct 1973
- Territory occupied by Egypt, Oct 1973

MAP **30.7** The Arab–Israeli Wars, 1967 and 1973.

1973, Egypt, Syria, and a coalition of Arab states, stung by their defeat in 1967, launched a massive attack during the Jewish holy day of Yom Kippur, which in 1973 coincided with the Muslim holy month of Ramadan. This time, with Israel, the United States, and the Soviet Union caught unawares, Egyptian tanks crossed the Suez Canal on pontoon bridges and attacked Israel (see Map 30.7). Syria attacked the Golan Heights and put pressure on Israeli forces at the other end of the state. After taking severe losses and giving ground for a week, Israeli forces managed to take the initiative and ultimately defeat the combined Arab armies once again. Having trapped Egyptian forces along the Suez Canal, Israeli units occupied the west bank of the Canal, pushing within 63 miles of Cairo. Other units drove 25 miles into Syria. A ceasefire was brokered by the United Nations, but the intensity of the fighting and the resupply efforts by the United States and Soviet Union moved both countries dangerously close to direct confrontation. For their part, the Arab oil producers and Iran immediately launched an oil boycott of the United States. Stringent measures and a degree of rationing and vastly higher gasoline prices drove home to Americans how dependent they had now become on foreign oil. (Much of the interest in solar and other alternative energy thus stems from this period.)

For Egypt, the defeat resulted in a transformation of policy toward Israel. Under President Anwar el-Sadat (in office 1970–1981), Egypt took the initiative in undertaking peace talks by visiting Israel in 1977. The following year, the two sides reached an understanding about a basic framework for peace; and with the backing of the American president Jimmy Carter, Egypt and Israel signed the first treaty between an Arab country and the Jewish state at Camp David, Maryland, in 1979. Egypt and Jordan are the only Arab states to date to maintain diplomatic and cultural relations with Israel. While Egyptian–Israeli relations remained relatively cordial on the surface, no other Arab countries followed suit. Syria remained hostile, having lost the Golan Heights, while the PLO stepped up its efforts throughout the 1980s. Profound resentment against Sadat for signing the treaty festered among many Egyptians. Despite some concessions to increasingly vocal fundamentalist Muslim groups—for example, agreeing to base Egyptian legislation on Islamic Shari`a law—Sadat was killed by assassins in 1981.

Africa: From Independence to Development

During the period 1963–1991, the main struggles in Africa moved from those mainly concerned with independence to those revolving around development. As with other parts of the postcolonial world, vigorous internal debates were conducted about strategies for economic development, how best to deploy scarce resources, and the relative merits of a planned economy versus one centered on market forces. But in nearly all cases, the economies of the newly independent states, regardless of which economic system they favored, were problematic. In most cases they were tied to their former colonial regimes by means of the same raw materials—minerals, petroleum, agricultural or forest products—that had been exploitatively extracted during their colonial days. Moreover, they were more frequently than not competing in these products with other former colonies. Thus, they were at the mercy of world commodity prices but not insulated from the worst ups and downs by their former colonial regimes.

In addition, the newly independent states now had to use the revenues generated to support governmental, transport, and military infrastructures, whose costs had formerly been underwritten by the colonial governments. Since many of the new countries, acculturating to the norms of ethnolinguistic nationalism, also wanted to rectify border problems or expand their borders to include ethnic regions ignored by the colonists, their militaries often consumed substantial portions of their budgets. In many cases, too, the first and second generations of government officials and business leaders, smarting from decades of colonial exploitation, felt entitled to reap the benefits of their new status and simply skim the profits from their new positions. Such regimes were often derisively referred to as "kleptocracies." As some scholars have also pointed out, instead of fostering an entrepreneurial middle class, opening up new and innovative areas of investment, all too many members of this "caretaker bourgeoisie" were simply content to milk the enterprises they had to their maximum capacity. Hence, they became far more reliant on foreign aid and investment, which all too often the volatile political environments of their countries made unattractive. For those countries trying to mount socialist policies of land reform and nationalization of businesses, corruption of this type was also an ongoing problem, coupled with little real wealth to share among their growing populations.

As in Chapter 29, far too many new nations emerged in Africa during this period for this chapter to cover them all. Therefore, we will center our examination on Nigeria, Zimbabwe, and South Africa as representative of the problems and prospects of the era.

Nigeria: Civil War and Troubled Legacies

While in the Congo the Cold War played out in fairly dramatic fashion with the United States supporting the overthrow of Patrice Lumumba in favor of Mobutu Sese Seko in the early 1960s, Nigeria's independence started in more promising fashion. With a large and fairly prosperous population, sound agriculture, and abundant resources, it started its postcolonial era as a

Nigerian Civil War. The attempt by the region of Biafra to secede from Nigeria resulted in one of the bloodiest and most desperate confrontations of the 1960s. In its attempt to starve the Biafrans into surrender, Nigeria blockaded food supplies to the breakaway region with the result of mass malnutrition, starvation, and, ultimately, a sizeable UN relief effort. In this picture relief workers dish out scarce rations to Biafran women and children.

republic with a British parliamentary system, commonwealth membership, and a federal-style constitution. Like many former African colonies, however, it soon became apparent that Nigeria was also saddled with ethnic and religious conflicts that were its legacy from the old colonial divisions in the continent. Thus, its growing pains were marked by clashes between its established system of constitutional nationalism and the desires of its major constituent groups for their own nation-states more reflective of Nigeria's ethnic, linguistic, and religious makeup.

The new nation brought together three major antagonistic groups, the Yoruba, Igbo, and Hausa, divided by history, culture, religion, and language. The largest, the Yoruba, who controlled most of the national offices, were predominantly Muslim. The Igbo, mostly living in the eastern region where valuable oil deposits had been recently discovered, were predominantly Christian or animist. Starting in 1966, the central government under strongman Yakubu Gowon (in office 1966–1975) had authorized raids to bring Igbo areas under greater control. In 1967, the eastern Igbo region declared itself independent as the state of Biafra under Colonel Chukwuemeka Odumegwu Ojukwu (b. 1933). What followed was perhaps the bloodiest civil war of the era. Both sides fought determinedly, and when a military stalemate was reached the Nigerian forces attempted to starve Biafra into submission. More than 1 million Biafrans died, mostly of starvation and malnutrition, before Biafra surrendered in early 1970. In the remainder of the period to 1991, Nigeria was ruled by a series of military strongmen, each in turn attempting to stabilize the volatile political situation of the central government. By 1991, the prosperity that seemed so promising in 1960 had vanished as a probability to all but the most optimistic observers.

Zimbabwe: The Revolution Continued

Some of the former European colonies in Africa came to independence with substantial populations of white settlers, some of whose families had been there for several generations. Accustomed to a life of relative privilege, they had, in many cases, opposed independence; and when it came, they sought guarantees from the new governments against expropriation of land, discrimination, and reprisals. In 1964 the old colony of Northern Rhodesia gained independence as Zambia, breaking up a federation of the two colonies and Nyasaland, which subsequently became independent as Malawi.

Threatened by the independence of nearby black African nations and confident of support from apartheid-based South Africa, the white leaders of what now called itself simply "Rhodesia" declared unilateral independence in 1965 and set up a government in the colonial capital of Salisbury under Ian Smith (in office 1965–1970). Distressed at this move, Britain refused to recognize the new government and expelled Rhodesia from the commonwealth. Few countries outside of South Africa recognized the regime, which now faced international sanctions and a guerilla movement from within.

Two rival groups, the Zimbabwe African National Union (ZANU) under Robert Mugabe (b. 1924) and the Zimbabwe African People's Union (ZAPU) led by Joshua Nkomo (1917–1999) struggled to bring Smith's regime down and create a majority rule state. The war was a long and bitter one, lasting throughout the 1960s and 1970s, until Mugabe and ZANU finally triumphed and created a new state called "Zimbabwe" in 1980. Mugabe's regime pledged fairness to the remaining white settlers and, after changing the name of the capital to Harare, set about creating a socialist state. In this sense, despite constant condemnation of Africa's imperial legacy, Mugabe has been in constant need of the economic power of the country's white minority and, thus, initially trod fairly lightly on their rights. By the 1990s, however, vigilante seizures of white lands by "revolutionary veterans" became a regular occurrence. By the early-2000s, the chaotic agricultural sector combined with repression of challenges to ZANU one-party rule had plunged the country into a serious economic crisis.

South Africa: From Apartheid to "Rainbow Nation"

South Africa, the richest of the continent's countries, was also the one with the most complex and restrictive racial relations. From the seventeenth century, first Dutch, then English, settlers came to service the maritime traffic around the Cape of Good Hope. By the nineteenth century, the Dutch-descended *boers* had moved inland from Cape Town and begun setting up farms, ranches, and vineyards, pushing the local people before them. The expansion of Zulu power at roughly the same time forced the British

Black Commuters in South Africa. The regime of apartheid (the strict separation of the races) that had been inaugurated by the white minority government in South Africa in 1948 obliged all black citizens, such as these workers congregating in a Johannesburg train station in the late 1950s, to carry "passbooks" that specified what areas they were permitted to enter. Resentment at the passbook requirement prompted mass demonstrations that resulted in the Sharpeville Massacre of March 21, 1960, which in turn sparked widespread protests against the apartheid system.

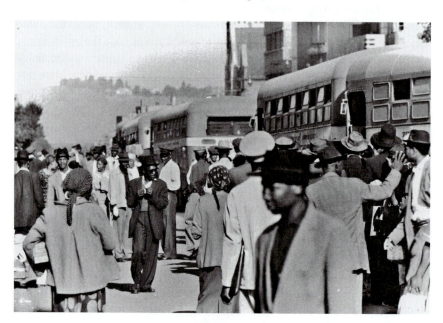

rulers and Dutch settlers into protracted Zulu wars that, climaxing in 1879, broke the last black empire in the region. By the end of the nineteenth century, the discovery of vast mineral wealth in gold and diamonds led to both the expansion of the colony's holdings and an influx of immigrants, including Chinese and Indians.

By the early twentieth century, the social divisions among whites, Africans, and "coloreds"—south and east Asians and peoples of mixed descent—were hardening into legal classifications. The Indian nationalist leader Mohandas Gandhi, for example, developed his successful nonviolent strategies leading protests in South Africa for Indian rights. After 1910, immigration restrictions on Asians went into effect along with ever more restrictive laws governing relations between whites and Africans. The climax of this trend was the creation of the institution of **apartheid** (Afrikaans, "apartness") in 1948. Africans were relegated to a legal second-class status, they were to live in designated "townships" and tribal "homelands" or "Bantustans," they were required to carry passes when traveling, those commuting to work in white urban areas had to leave by sunset, and even in the townships they were subject to curfew regulations.

> **Apartheid:** System of social and legal segregation by race enforced by the government of South Africa from 1948 until 1994.

Through the 1950s South Africa faced international criticism for its policies, which the white government justified as necessary to maintain its rule, since whites made up less than one-sixth of the population. Moreover, as newly independent black majority countries came into being, the white government felt itself increasingly besieged. It pointed with some justification to a number of these emerging states as Marxist and, thus, claimed that it was fighting the free world's battle against the expansion of the Soviet Bloc in Africa. Nonetheless, it withdrew from the British Commonwealth in 1961, and a number of black political organizations—most prominently the African National Congress (ANC)—campaigned for the dismantling of apartheid. The brutality of the white armed forces and police and the constant harassment of dissenters, both white and black, added to the oppressive atmosphere.

By the 1980s it was clear that events on the continent would sooner or later force the breaking up of apartheid. International boycotts of South Africa had gained momentum, particularly after the public calling for sanctions by the African Episcopal bishop Desmond Tutu (b. 1931), who was awarded the Nobel Peace Prize in 1984. In the townships, the ANC, through a political and guerilla campaign, was making gradual gains. Massive strikes by black workers in 1987 and 1988 also led to increasing paralysis of the government. Finally, in 1990, the newly elected president, F. W. de Klerk (b. 1936), began a sweeping set of reforms aimed ultimately at dismantling apartheid. In quick succession, the ANC was legalized and became South Africa's largest political party; its leader—soon to be the country's president—Nelson Mandela (b. 1918) was released from prison; in 1991 all of the apartheid laws were repealed; and finally, in 1992 white voters elected to amend the constitution to mandate racial equality among all citizens. By 1994, the first multiracial elections were held, and Mandela became the first president of the new South Africa, which Archbishop Tutu dubbed the "Rainbow Nation" in its newly recognized diversity.

Latin America: Proxy Wars

The 1960s in Latin American politics were marked in many ways by the forces contending for dominance against the backdrop of the Cold War. Here, however, because the countries in question had long since achieved their independence—if not yet long-term stability in government—the issues guiding the respective sides were largely ideological and economic, as well as centering around revolutionary politics. This was particularly true for the rural poor, who in many cases continued to live in virtual peonage on large estates, with little hope for economic advancement and little effort on the part of their landlords to improve their lot. In this respect, the appeal of a Marxist movement drawing on such diverse sources as Maoism—with its emphasis on peasants as a revolutionary force—and the recent example of Cuba standing up to the United States and pursuing its own brand of land reforms were often attractive. Cuba, particularly its most visible and charismatic exponent of Latin American revolution Che Guevara, was active throughout this era, though Guevara's execution in Bolivia set the Cuban efforts back somewhat.

By the 1970s, dissatisfaction with the authoritarian regimes of the region, particularly in Central America, resulted in several revolutionary efforts, the most notable being in Nicaragua and El Salvador. Since the mid-1930s, the United States had supported the family of the authoritarian strongman Anastasio Somoza Garcia (collectively in office from 1936–1979). Landlordism and rural poverty had been particularly acute problems in Nicaragua, and from the early 1960s a guerilla insurgency called the Sandinista National Liberation Front (FSLN) had sought to overthrow the Somozas and mount a socialist land-reform scheme. The Somoza regime fell in 1979, and a new government under the Sandinistas (so-called to invoke the name of Emilio Sandino, one of the original Somoza opponents) was formed led by Daniel Ortega (in office 1979–1990; 2007–). The socialist direction of the new regime prompted the American administration of President Ronald Reagan to cut off aid to Nicaragua, begin a covert operation to destabilize Ortega through funding and arming of opposition groups know collectively as the "Contras," and boycott trade with the regime. With US support and fading aid from Cuba and the Soviet Bloc in the late 1980s, the two sides agreed to elections in 1990. These resulted in the presidency of the conservative opposition candidate, Violeta Barrios de Chamorro (in office 1990–1997). In similar fashion, guerilla groups in El Salvador fought United States–backed government forces, whose actions were sometimes directed against Catholic clergy believed to support the insurgents, in a bloody conflict throughout the 1980s, until elections were finally held in 1992. The death toll in this tiny country is estimated to be as high as 75,000. By the early 1990s, however, the two sides, as in Nicaragua, had resolved to work within the new political system.

The commitment of the United States to oppose any groups espousing Marxist or communist aims in Latin America also revealed itself in covert policy toward governments recognized as legitimate. As we saw in Chapter 29, for example, the CIA helped engineer a coup against Guatemalan leader Jacobo Arbenz (in office 1951–1954) in 1954 because he allowed a communist labor union to exist in his country. The most spectacular instance of American Cold War covert action, however, was directed at Chilean President Salvador Allende (in office 1970–1973) in 1973. Allende had led a coalition of socialists, communists, and liberal Christian Democrats to a plurality win in 1970. Many of his policies met opposition within Chile, while his ideology and nationalization of American interests in Chile's mines pushed the Nixon administration to back his opposition. With American blessings and CIA help, Allende was overthrown and the repressive but friendlier regime of General Augusto Pinochet (in office 1973–1990) installed. After Pinochet's term of 16 years in power, his rule remained repressive; but Chile also became increasingly economically vibrant and slowly began to move toward a more open and democratic government. In 1998 Pinochet was arrested in London on charges of human rights violations and torture. After a lengthy court battle, he was ultimately released and returned to Chile, where he died in 2006.

Liberation Theology   In addition to the Marxist-inspired revolutionary movements in Latin America during this period, there were religiously based, activist ideologies animating a host of issues from land reform to protest against human rights violations. These are usually lumped under the heading of "liberation theology." The idea itself is an old one dating back to the Catholic Church's frequent role as champion of the Amerindians and the poor during the colonial and national periods. The calls during the Vatican II Council for a more activist and relevant place for the church resonated with many clergy—Catholic and Protestant—who had formed a vision of Christ's historical and religious role as one of social change. Though particularly active in Latin America, by the early 1970s it had become a worldwide movement within Catholicism and received cautious endorsement of the papacy, though with the caveat that the liberation of the poor and oppressed should not be seen as an endorsement of Marxism. Still, as the decade wore on, increasing numbers of clergy became involved in grassroots organizing, in preaching and pastoral care aimed at propagating a socially active Christianity, and in denouncing the inequities of the economics and politics of authoritarian regimes. The line between such activism and revolutionary work could be thin indeed—Daniel Ortega and his wife, for example, were married by a priest who had become a Sandinista guerilla. The regimes and local elites that were the targets of liberation theology advocates thus often struck back with violence against outspoken priests and nuns. But with the demise of many of these regimes in the 1980s and 1990s and the end of the Cold War, much of the momentum ebbed from the movement, though it is still directed against inequity and poverty among the rural poor even today.

Liberation Theology Service.
The historical role of the Catholic Church at various times as advocate for the poor and oppressed in Latin America reemerged with vigor in the 1960s and 1970s against the backdrop of revolutionary turmoil and a new emphasis emanating from the Vatican on social activism. In the accompanying photo, a Mass is being celebrated in Brazil in the 1970s with a distinct message embodying themes associated with Liberation Theology: The banner reads in Portuguese, "The Church of Maranhao prays and fasts for peace and justice in the countryside."

"The Dirty War" and the "Disappeared"   As we have seen in this section, the damage inflicted by the Cold War and the actions of its combatants, real and proxy, upon Latin America was considerable. One of the most tragic and internationally condemned episodes of this struggle was the "Dirty War" (*Guerra Sucia*) carried out in Argentina from 1976 to 1983. The tangled politics of the post-Perón era resulted in a series of guerilla groups ranging from Peronists to radical communists conducting a smoldering guerilla war against various regimes from the 1960s onward. By the early 1970s, many of these groups had coalesced into the Peronist Montoneros and the Marxist People's Revolutionary Army (ERP). While the Montoneros were essentially crushed in 1977, the ERP remained active; and under the cover of "Operation Condor" pursued by the juntas of Jorge Raphael Videla, Roberto Viola, and Leopoldo Galtieri, tens of thousands of Argentinians were kidnapped, imprisoned, and killed. Many, if not most, of these men and women were not guerillas but writers, editors, labor organizers, teachers, and others suspected of having left-wing leanings or whom the government sought to eliminate for other reasons.

These victims became know as the "disappeared." Their plight is still poignantly brought to light by the Mothers of Plaza de Mayo, a group of women who have kept vigil for lost friends and relatives in that plaza in Buenos Aires since 1977 and whose movement has grown into an internationally recognized human rights organization. Already by 1979 the wholesale imprisonments prompted US President Carter to offer asylum to those languishing in Argentine jails.

In 1983, having deeply miscalculated in provoking and losing the Falklands War with Great Britain, the junta stepped down, elections were held, and a National Commission of the Disappearance of Persons (CONADEP) was established in December. While the figures vary greatly, from 15,000 to perhaps 30,000 "disappeared," the progress of the commission and its findings of torture, killing, and indefinite incarceration caused an international sensation. Today, most of the surviving military and political leaders held responsible are in prison themselves or have already served lengthy terms. As with so many other aspects of the Cold War era, the consequences for those involved have far outlived the conflict itself.

Putting It All Together

During the years 1962 to 1991, from the Cuban Missile Crisis to the dissolution of the Soviet Union, the Cold War contest between the two remaining twentieth-century versions of modernity—capitalist democracy and the different varieties of communism-socialism—reached its climax. At the beginning of the period it seemed at the very least that communism was competing evenly, perhaps even winning, in its appeal to so many developing nations and their leaders. But in the end, the wealth and power of the West, particularly the United States, ultimately wore the Soviet Bloc down. Along the way, the most populous communist state, China, abruptly changed from extreme radical leftist programs during its Cultural Revolution to a very capitalist style of market economics by 1991. Many other countries were now looking for some mixture of the two systems or a third way between the two for their own development. As the period drew to a close, it was, ironically, the two iconic communist regimes, the Soviet Union and the People's Republic of China, that were pioneering the way *out* of Marxist socialism. The Chinese sought to do this by retaining a powerful authoritarian government while embracing market economics.

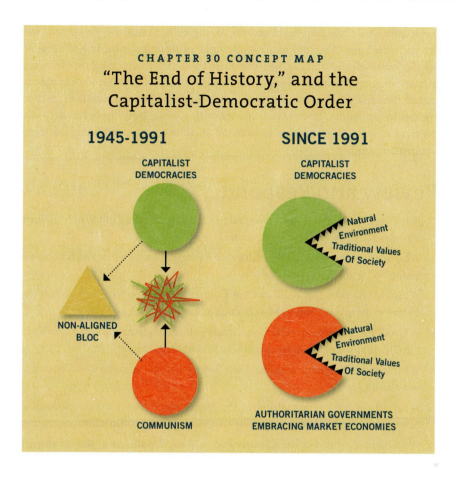

The former Soviet Union adopted democratic political values and guardedly introduced capitalism.

For the people of the world observing these changes it might indeed have seemed as if the triumphant words of Francis Fukuyama's 1989 essay "The End of History?" actually did sum up the age:

> a remarkable consensus concerning the legitimacy of liberal democracy as a system of government had emerged throughout the world over the past few years, as it conquered rival ideologies like hereditary monarchy, fascism, and most recently communism. More than that, however . . . liberal democracy may constitute the "end point of mankind's ideological evolution" . . . and as such . . . the end of history.

The next two decades, however, would see the emergence of new and unanticipated challenges to the domination of the capitalist-democratic order. For many, its secular character and its breaking down of traditional norms of family, gender, and sexuality in the West convinced them that the evolving culture of this surviving version of modernity would undermine the core values of their own societies. Hence, like the reformers in many of the old empires of the nineteenth century, they engaged in an erratic struggle to acquire the material advantages of modernity while isolating themselves from the cultural threat it presented. Still others in both the West and various other places around the world had come to see the forces of modernity as breaking down the delicate natural balance between human beings and the environment (see Concept Map). They therefore sought to curtail the rapacity of capitalist-democratic countries and corporations in their contest for resources. In the final chapter of this book, both these trends—and the devil's bargain they present to so many—will occupy a considerable amount of our attention.

Review and Respond

1. What were some of the most important turning points of the Cold War? Why have historians designated these as important?

2. What factors ushered in the era of *détente* between the United States and the Soviet Union? Why did this period end?

3. What are the principal causes of the Cultural Revolution in China during the 1960s? What was the role of Mao Zedong in inaugurating it and ending it?

4. Why did the Soviet leadership launch their policies of glasnost and perestroika in the mid-1980s? Did these programs help or hurt the USSR?

5. What is meant by feminism? How do we distinguish among first, second, and third wave feminism?

6. What causes led to the collapse of the Soviet bloc? How did the relationship between the Soviet Union and its allies contribute to this collapse?

7. What were the main political, economic, and social patterns in the developing world from 1963 to 1991? How does the Marxist theory of underdevelopment differ from the modernization theory?

8. Some have claimed that the end of the Cold War spelled the end of ideological struggle—even the "end of history." Do you think this argument has merit on its own terms? Why or why not?

> For additional resources, including maps, primary sources, visuals, and quizzes, please go to www.oup.com/us/vonsivers. Please see the Further Resources section at the back of the book for additional readings and suggested websites.

Thinking Through Patterns

▶ **How did the political landscape of the Cold War change from 1963 to 1991?**

Perhaps the biggest changes came in the 1980s. Though the United States had been defeated politically in Vietnam and was facing a recession at home, it still was the world's largest economy and could weather a protracted arms race. Though it was not fully perceived at the time, the Soviet Union was far more economically fragile—which ultimately made it ideologically fragile as well. The strains of Polish dissent, the Afghan War, and a renewed arms race with the United States simply wore the Soviet state down.

The unprecedented prosperity of the United States and the West more generally allowed younger people to attend universities in record numbers, experiment with new ideas of living, and simply indulge their desires for fun and new experiences. The idealism of the era also played a role, as did the threat of the draft and the larger threat of nuclear war. For many, the materialism of the age repelled them and made them long for a simpler, more "authentic" existence. Thus, a popular motto from the time was "turn on, tune in, drop out."

▶ **Why did such radically different lifestyles emerge in the United States and the West during the 1960s and 1970s? What is their legacy today?**

▶ **Why did some nations that had emerged from colonialism and war make great strides in their development while others seemed to stagnate?**

By and large, the nations that prospered were the ones that had already achieved self-sufficiency in agriculture, had at least the basic of a transportation and communications infrastructure, and were resourceful in adopting policies that maximized their labor force. Taiwan, South Korea, and Singapore are good examples of countries that made great strides in their development during this period. China, under Deng Xiaoping, followed a modified version of this strategy and was already growing at record levels by 1991. In the following decades, nearly all Asian countries (an exception being North Korea) would follow suit, with India moving into the top ranks of development and growth. Many Latin American countries—in particular, Brazil—also make great strides, and the drive to follow the example of using cheap labor to create a successful export manufacturing base was also took hold in Africa.

In all cases, culture and ideology could and did play a powerful role in setting the psychological conditions for citizens to believe that progress was possible. Peace and stability also played, for obvious reasons, an important role. he many internal conflicts that pockmarked Latin America and Africa held back development during this period.

Chapter 31
1991-2011

A Fragile Capitalist-Democratic World Order

I t was a scene that had been repeated hundreds of times across North Africa and the Middle East during the winter of 2010 and the early spring of 2011. First in Tunisia in December, then with daily regularity in Egypt, Libya, Bahrain, Yemen, and Syria, growing crowds gathered to remonstrate with authoritarian governments over a wide range of issues that had marked the process of modernity for two centuries: the constitutional rights of life, liberty, security, economic opportunity, emancipation of minorities and women, and freedom of expression; the rights of ethnic and religious groups to nationhood, autonomy, or even mere existence.

Population increase, 1950–2010
Country where population increased by:
☐ 0–100%   ☐ 200–300%
☐ 100–200%   ☐ over 300%

Seeing Patterns

▶ How did the United States acquire its dominant economic position toward the end of the twentieth century? How did it accelerate the process of globalization?

▶ What made capitalist democracy so attractive toward the end of the twentieth century that it became a generic model for many countries around the world to strive for?

▶ Which policies did China and India pursue so that they became the fastest industrializing countries in the early twenty-first century?

▶ How have information technology and social networking altered cultural, political, and economic interactions around the world?

▶ What is global warming, and why is it a source of grave concern for the future?

The governments challenged by these movements had long been entrenched behind brutal and repressive security services. Unable or unwilling to broaden political participation, aging authoritarian rulers had groomed their sons or favorites to succeed them. The rulers pretended to have liberalized the economies of their countries, but instead "crony capitalism" benefited their relatives and followers and discouraged entrepreneurial innovation. Chronic unemployment and underemployment left both the poor and the middle class in despair over their future. For many years, the unemployed youth of the Middle East had found solace in an Islamism whose preachers promised it would be the solution for all ills. But the ability of these preachers to deliver had turned out not to be any better than that of the increasingly despised rulers. A general stagnation had set in throughout the region.

By mid-spring 2011 the relentlessly repeated, massive, and unarmed street protests had toppled the governments of Tunisia and Egypt. Crowds massed as well in Syria, Bahrain, Libya, and Yemen. Syria and Bahrain sought to suppress the democracy movements while in Libya and Yemen civil wars tore the populations apart. More remarkably, however, was that

The Arab Spring. Tawakkol Karman, a religiously conservative journalist and mother of three, received the 2011 Nobel Peace Prize for her nonviolent struggle for democracy and the safety of women. Throughout the year, she remained steadfastly devoted to a democratic future for Yemen even as the country descended into civil war. Here she leads a rally in Sana, the capital.

here in this male-dominated bastion of conservative Islam, the movement was being led by that most "modern" of world personalities, a charismatic female journalist and grassroots organizer. Armed with computers, smart cell phones burgeoning with apps, Twitter, Facebook, and all the latest tools of social networking, Tawakkol Karman, 32, leader of "Women Journalists Without Chains" and mother of three, harangued mostly male crowds of thousands with calls for revolution. "We will make our revolution or we will die trying," she thundered, her words echoing those of so many insurgents of the recent past. "We are in need of heroes," said one Yemeni observer. "She manages to do what most men cannot do in a society that is highly prejudiced against women." But with her personal role models including Nelson Mandela of South Africa, Mohandas Gandhi of India, and Martin Luther King Jr. and Hillary Clinton of the United States, Karman as much as any woman of her time embodied the choices and challenges marking the patterns of world history in the rapidly globalizing early twenty-first century.

Many of the challenges faced by Yemen today are shared by many small, poor, largely traditional societies confronting the growing momentum of capitalist-democratic modernity. Its authoritarian government, for all its faults, has maintained a fragile balance among Yemen's many feuding tribes and religious groups; if and when it falls, what will take its place? Will its tribal groups unite or "balkanize?" As the war on terror continues, will the United States and the West risk chaos in the region as a magnet for such opponents of secular culture as al-Qaeda? What prospects are there for emancipation of women in such a traditional society, especially if economic development in this harsh land stays problematic? How will the continued progress of environmental degradation affect a new regime's approach to economic modernization? Little grows in many parts in the best of times; moreover, like many peoples in the region, Yemenis have traditionally enjoyed chewing *qat*, a mildly narcotic shrub leaf. But the plants themselves and the water needed to process them take up precious resources. Will a future government act to curtail the practice? At what cost? And perhaps the most immediate question: Will political empowerment along constitutional lines resulting from a revolution be sufficient to satisfy the aspirations of the Yemenis who took to the streets?

In the largest sense, then, achieving modernity through the surviving route of urbanization, science, industrialization, the accumulation of capital, and grassroots participation in political pluralism has become close to a universal goal in the world. Where it will lead is anyone's guess. But the story of how this pattern of modernity has grown to become nearly universal—and the old and new forces that oppose it—is the focus of this final chapter in our survey of world history.

Capitalist Democracy: The Dominant Pattern of Modernity

With the demise of communism, the struggle among the three ideologies of modernity that had characterized much of the twentieth century now was over. In the first flush of enthusiasm, some Western observers declared history to have ended, henceforth to be written merely as a series of footnotes to the triumph of capitalism and democracy in the world. Others prophesized soon after that culture would replace ideology as the basis for world competition. More sober observers expressed the hope that capitalist modernity in the coming decades would become an increasingly generic pattern, adoptable in non-Western cultures. But they also realized that democracy would not spread rapidly as long as countries remained poor and stuck in inherited forms of authoritarianism or even autocracy. History continued, the nation-state (as problematic as it was in many parts of Africa and Asia) became standard across the world, and its citizens strove for adaptation to the now dominant pattern of modernity: capitalism, democracy, and consumerism.

A Decade of Global Expansion: The United States and the World in the 1990s

In the aftermath of the oil crisis of 1985–1986, and with even greater vigor after the collapse of communism in 1991, the United States advocated free trade, fiscal discipline, and transnational economic integration as the proper course for world development. It did so as the most economically and politically powerful country. Two characteristics made the United States the sole superpower it currently is. First, the United States dominated the so-called dollar regime—that is, dollars functioned as the currency for all oil sales and purchases. In fact, despite the growth in popularity of the European Union's euro, and other major currencies like the English pound, Swiss franc, and Japanese yen, the dollar remained in a very real sense the world's currency. Second, with its giant consumer economy, the United States functioned as the world's favored destination for manufactured goods, particularly from East Asia. The leverage which the United States gained from these two economic functions was bolstered by overwhelming military force, which made the United States the principal enforcer of peace in the world.

A Hierarchy of Nations   During the 1990s, there were some 190 sovereign countries in the world, forming a three-tier hierarchy. At the top of the first tier, almost in a category of its own, was the United States. It was the richest, most evolved constitutional nation-state, based on a mature scientific–industrial society,

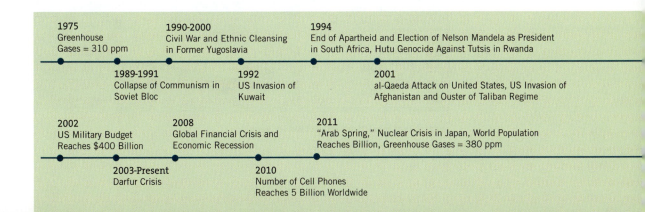

1975 Greenhouse Gases = 310 ppm	1990-2000 Civil War and Ethnic Cleansing in Former Yugoslavia	1994 End of Apartheid and Election of Nelson Mandela as President in South Africa, Hutu Genocide Against Tutsis in Rwanda

1989-1991 Collapse of Communism in Soviet Bloc

1992 US Invasion of Kuwait

2001 al-Qaeda Attack on United States, US Invasion of Afghanistan and Ouster of Taliban Regime

2002 US Military Budget Reaches $400 Billion

2008 Global Financial Crisis and Economic Recession

2011 "Arab Spring," Nuclear Crisis in Japan, World Population Reaches Billion, Greenhouse Gases = 380 ppm

2003-Present Darfur Crisis

2010 Number of Cell Phones Reaches 5 Billion Worldwide

sophisticated financial institutions, and by far the most powerful military. In addition, it could boast the densest infrastructure of universities, colleges, public libraries, museums, theaters, and other cultural institutions. Below the United States, the fully industrialized democracies in Europe, North America, and Australia occupied the rest of the first tier. In the course of the 1990s, four "newly industrialized countries" joined this tier, the Asian "Tigers" or "Dragons:" Taiwan, South Korea, Hong Kong, and Singapore. Such was the economic power of the 30 fully industrialized and largely democratic countries in the top tier that they alone conducted nearly three-quarters of all world trade in goods and services.

In the second tier of the world hierarchy were 88 "middle-income countries," according to the United Nations' definition. These were developing countries in economic and democratic "transition." They were either industrializing states in the Middle East, South Asia, East Asia, and Latin America or reindustrializing states located in the former Communist Bloc. The reindustrializing states were replacing their obsolete communist-era manufacturing infrastructures with modern systems. In the broad bottom tier were 66 countries defined as "low-income" or "poor," located for the most part in sub-Saharan Africa and Southeast Asia. Many of these countries were in early stages of economic development, with little or no democratization (see Map 31.1).

In 2000, about one-fifth of the world's population of 6 billion lived in fully industrialized countries, two-thirds in middle-income countries, and 15 percent in poor countries. The world population was still expanding, but the pace of the expansion was slowing, largely as a result of improved female education and contraceptives. The dominance of scientific–industrial society was such that only two centuries after

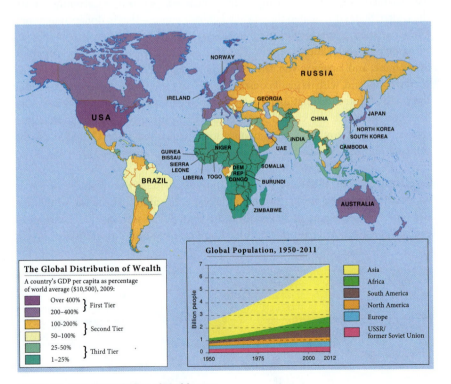

MAP **31.1** The Global Distribution of Wealth, 2009.

its beginnings 90 percent of the world population was more or less integrated into the pattern of capitalist modernity characterized by market exchange and consumerism and no longer by traditional agrarian–urban subsistence agriculture.

The Dollar Regime   The United States stood at the top of the world hierarchy thanks largely to the power of its financial system. The beginnings of this system date back to the years following 1971 when President Richard Nixon took the dollar off the gold standard. At that time, in a period of war expenditures in Vietnam and high inflation, the United States was running out of gold payable for dollars at the internationally agreed price of $35 an ounce. Two years later, Nixon persuaded the Middle East–dominated Organization of Oil-Producing Export Countries (OPEC) to accept only dollars as means of payment for oil. In support of Egypt and Syria against Israel in the October War of 1973, OPEC had just quadrupled oil prices. Despite American support for Israel, however, OPEC was anxious to remain in the good graces of the United States as its largest buyer. As a result of the Nixon–OPEC deal, the dollar took over from gold as the acknowledged international standard of exchange.

Under the **dollar regime**, all oil-importing countries, except for the United States, had to manage two currencies. One, denominated in dollars, was for energy purchases; the other, in domestic currencies, was for the internal market of oil consumption. Countries had to carefully look after the strength of their domestic currency as rising dollar prices could lead to severe crises in efforts to control inflationary domestic prices and pay back foreign, dollar-denominated loans. OPEC countries on their part invested their "petrodollars" in US Treasury bills ("T-bills"), as well as in American stocks and bonds. There were repeated grumblings among the non-oil producers of the world, both developed and developing, about being cheated by the dollar regime. But the US–OPEC deal did endure, backed up by a gigantic American financial system that emerged as a result of the dollar regime.

Dollar regime: A system maintained by the United States whereby dollars are the sole currency in which the price of oil and most other commodities and goods in the world are denominated; the regime forces most countries to maintain two currencies, with consequent financial constraints.

The United States as an Import Sinkhole   In a parallel development, the United States tied the industrial countries of the world to itself by becoming the country to which everyone wanted to export. Building these ties was particularly important in East Asia. During the Cold War, the United States had encouraged import substitution industrialization along the lines of Japan in Korea, Taiwan, Hong Kong, Thailand, and Southeast Asian countries. By becoming prosperous, so it was assumed, these countries would be less susceptible to the expansion of communism. Although uneven, the industrialization process advanced apace in most East Asian countries. In the 1990s, it reached levels where the United States began to pressure the Asia Tigers to reduce import substitution protectionism and replace it with free trade. In return for the United States buying their industrial goods, the countries of East Asia agreed to give free access to American financial institutions, such as banks and hedge funds.

In the meantime, communism collapsed and China, pushing its own import substitution industrialization, began to export cheap industrial goods as well to the United States. In the 1990s, aided by abundant cheap labor, these goods undercut those produced by the Asian Tigers and the United States became an even deeper "sinkhole," this time for textiles, toys, and simple electrical and electronic devices made in the People's Republic of China. The United States in effect underwrote China's industrialization, binding the country's economic interests closely to its own financial interests within the dollar regime (see Map 31.2).

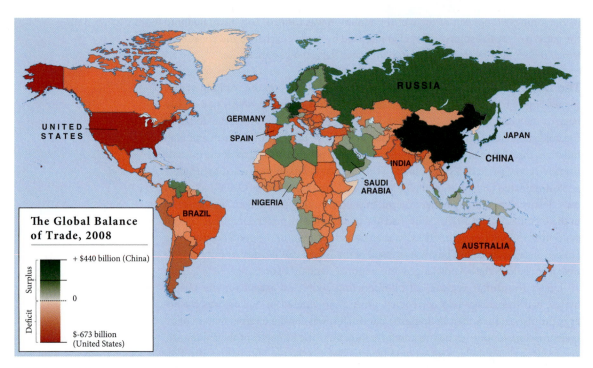

The Global Balance
of Trade, 2008

Surplus

+ $440 billion (China)

0

Deficit

$-673 billion
(United States)

MAP **31.2** The Global Blance of Trade, 2008.

US Technological Renewal and Globalization   Communism had collapsed in part because the Soviet Union had been unwilling or unable to leap into the new industrial age of consumer electronics. The United States, by contrast, transformed itself thoroughly in the 1990s. Electronics was one of those periodic new technologies with which capitalism, always threatened by falling profit rates in maturing industries, became more profitable again. By computerizing industrial processes, businesses saved on labor. Personal computers in offices made bureaucratic procedures more efficient. A fledgling Internet speeded up communication. An entirely new branch of industry, **information technology** (**IT**), put cell phones, online delivery of music and entertainment, and a vast array of other services into the hands of consumers. In the phrase of the Nobel Prize Laureate in economics, Joseph Stiglitz, the United States had entered the "roaring nineties."

Information technology: The array of computers, information, electronic services, entertainment, and storage available to business and consumers; with information increasingly stored in "the cloud," that is, storage centers rather than individual computer hard drives.

During this decade, the national budget was balanced; America became the leader in what was now called the "high-tech industry" of electronics, microbiology, and pharmacology; unemployment shrank; inflation remained low; and the foreign debt was moderate. Worldwide, the volume of trade goods doubled and the volume of capital flows quadrupled. The US Federal Reserve kept up with demand and printed more than half as many dollars in the course of the 1990s as were already in circulation. The domestic economy was humming, and the dollar was literally as good as gold even in remote corners of the world.

The only blemish in the **globalization** process, from an American perspective, was continued protectionism and low consumption in many Asian countries. President Bill Clinton's (in office 1993–2000) closest economic advisors were bankers and investors who had greatly expanded the size and influence of the financial services sector since the Nixon years. This sector handled the spectacularly enlarged volume of dollars floating around in the world. Alongside the traditional means of investment—stocks and bonds—new, more speculative instruments called "derivatives" gained in popularity. Derivatives were complex bets on higher or lower future prices of stocks, bonds, commodities, currencies, or anything else traded on the world market. The US globalization offensive in the 1990s was thus in large part an effort to open protected foreign markets to American financial institutions.

Globalization and Its Critics

In many ways, the dollar and sinkhole regimes were so complex that they attracted critics from the entire political spectrum dissatisfied with one or another specific aspect of the evolving system. Conservative critics were appalled that the United States no longer adhered to the gold standard and sacrificed its sovereignty to oil sheikhs trading oil for dollars. They furthermore bemoaned the disappearance of the traditional manufacturing sector and its replacement by financial institutions and Internet start-ups that produced nothing tangible. In their judgment, the United States could be held hostage to policy dictates by the foreign holders of T-bills.

Progressive critics accused the United States of using its arrangements with OPEC and the East Asian countries to exclude the poorer countries in the world that had little to offer. In their opinion, the United States pursued the establishment of an imperialist capitalist system that limited wealth to a minority of industrialized and industrializing countries and refused to share it with the have-nots. Progressive criticisms were expressed in vociferous protests and occasionally even riots, accompanying meetings among the leaders of the industrial nations, usually in posh resorts around the world. Overall, however, both conservative and progressive criticisms remained marginal during the 1990s, given the general prosperity of the industrial countries.

US Military Dominance

Parallel to pursuing global economic integration, the United States emphasized a number of basic political principles in the 1990s. A first principle was that America was and must continue to be the unchallenged military power in all regions of the world. It defined itself as the guarantor of last resort for the maintenance of world peace. Accordingly, in the year 2002, the US military budget amounted to $400 billion. This astronomical sum was considerably smaller than during the Cold War but still larger than the defense budgets of the next eight countries combined. On the basis of this military machine, President Bill Clinton operated from a position of de facto world dominance. His successor, George W. Bush (in office 2001–2009), articulated this dominance in an official doctrine, the "national security strategy" of 2002. American might was highly visible in all parts of the world, generating considerable resentment among those for whom the combined economic–military power of the United States amounted to a new kind of world dominance (see Map 31.3)

Intervention in Iraq

The national security strategy elevated two policies already in practice into doctrine: prevent countries from establishing dominance in a region and destroy terror organizations bent on destruction in the United States. The first policy was enacted after Saddam Hussein (1937–2006) and his Baath regime occupied Kuwait (1990–1991). President George H. W. Bush (in office 1989–1993) intervened when it became clear that Saddam Hussein, by invading

Globalization: The ongoing process of integrating the norms of market economies throughout the world and binding the economies of the world into a single uniform system.

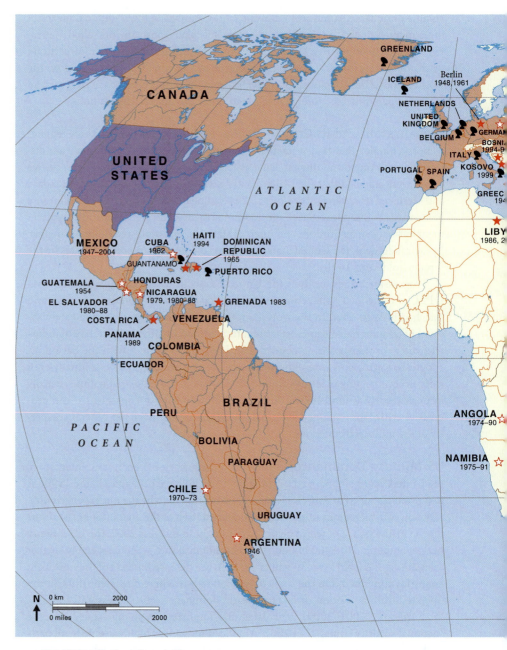

MAP **31.3** **US Security Commitments Since 1945.**

Kuwait, wanted dominance over Middle Eastern oil exports from Saudi Arabia and the region was unable or unwilling to prevent him from achieving it. At the head of a coalition force and with UN backing, in 1992 Bush ordered US troops to evict the Iraqis from Kuwait in Operation Desert Storm. In a devastating combined air and ground war of 6 weeks the coalition force drove the Iraqi occupiers from Kuwait.

In the following decade, the United States and United Nations subjected Iraq to a stringent military inspection regimen to end Saddam Hussein's ambitions for acquiring nuclear and chemical weapons. The inspectors discovered large quantities

US Security Commitments Since 1945

Countries with defense treaties with US

★ US military intervention, with date

☆ US economic/political intervention

♟ US military bases overseas, 2011

of weapons and supervised their destruction. But in the face of massive Iraqi efforts at obstruction, the inspectors eventually left. Their departure was followed by a re-taliatory US bombardment of Baghdad in 1998. After the US invasion of Afghani-stan in 2001, a chastened Saddam Hussein readmitted the inspectors. Their inability to find anything significant touched off an intense debate among the members of the UN Security Council. The United States and Great Britain considered further inspections worthless, while France, Russia, and China argued that these inspec-tions should be given more time. A stalemate ensued, and in an extraordinarily

Day of Infamy. Smoke billowing from the north tower of the World Trade Center in New York on September 11, 2001. The south tower had already collapsed. Nearly 3,000 people died in the inferno, in which the heat of the exploding commercial airplanes in the interior of the high rises melted the steel girders supporting the buildings.

passionate worldwide discussion the multilateralists who advocated continued United Nations–led sanctions squared off against the unilateralists favoring a preemptive United States–led invasion of Iraq.

In the end, in March 2003, President George W. Bush espoused the unilateralist cause and ordered a preemptive invasion without Security Council backing, arguing that Iraq had once more become a regional threat. To the surprise of many, Saddam Hussein's regime put up little resistance and fell after just 3 weeks to the vastly superior US armed forces. Afterward, no weapons of mass destruction were discovered, in spite of an intense scouring of every corner of the country.

Intervention in Afghanistan The second US principle announced in President Bush's national security strategy was swift retaliation, prevention, and even preemption against nonstate challengers of American supremacy. This doctrine was a response to the rise of Islamic terrorism. In 1992, al-Qaeda ("the base") under the leadership of Osama bin Laden (1957–2011) had emerged as the principal terrorist organization operating on an international scale. Bin Laden, multimillionaire son of a wealthy Yemen-born Saudi Arabian contractor, won his spurs as a holy warrior (*mujahid*) for Islam against the Soviet occupation forces in Afghanistan (1979–1989). After the Soviet retreat from Afghanistan, he turned against the United States. In his eyes, America was a godless country without moral principles, bent on a Western crusade to destroy Muslim independence.

Al-Qaeda's campaign of terrorism climaxed on September 11, 2001. Suicide commandos, in an operation beyond anyone's imagination, hijacked four commercial airliners in the northeastern United States and crashed them into the World Trade Center's Twin Towers in New York City, the Pentagon outside Washington, D.C., and (after passengers on the plane disrupted the attempted hijacking) a field near Shanksville, Pennsylvania. Nearly 3,000 people died in the disasters. In response, US troops invaded Afghanistan on October 7, 2001, in an effort to eliminate bin Laden, who was protected by the regime in power. They destroyed the pro-al-Qaeda government of the Taliban, receiving support from anti-Taliban Afghans, and drove the al-Qaeda terrorists to western Pakistan. It took another decade for the United States to track down and assassinate bin Laden (May 2011) and several of his close collaborators and to come to grips with the resurgent Taliban terrorists in its ongoing war in Afghanistan.

The United Nations and Regional Peace Even though it was the United States and sometimes the North Atlantic Treaty Organization (NATO) that guaranteed peace in the 1990s and early 2000s and not the United Nations, the UN nevertheless fulfilled vital, if not always successful, peace missions in regional conflicts.

An important example of a failure in this regard was the Rwandan civil war of 1994, in which mostly French peacekeeping troops serving under UN auspices looked the other way as the Hutu ethnic majority massacred the Tutsi ethnic minority by the hundreds of thousands. On the other hand, despite the bloodshed on both sides, the crisis in the Sudan saw the United Nations fare somewhat better. Two vicious civil wars raged between Arab Muslim northern Sudan, on the one hand, and Christian and animist southern Sudan (1983–2005) and the African Muslim region of Darfur in western Sudan (2003–present), on the other. After lengthy efforts under UN mediation, the two sides in the first conflict agreed to the secession of South Sudan as an independent country in 2011. The second conflict continued to smolder, with the United Nations pursuing criminal charges against the president of Sudan and an African Union force seeking to protect the refugees from Arab-inspired attacks. First steps toward settling the ethnic–religious conflicts in Sudan were taken, but much more needed to follow.

American Finances Go Global: Crisis and Recovery

Under the umbrella of world peace maintained by the United States and United Nations, the world economy dominated by the dollar regime expanded during the early 2000s. In the so-called Washington Consensus, lasting a little more than a decade (1989–2002), Western economists and foreign aid officers preached "stabilize, privatize, and liberalize" to the governments of the emerging nations. To receive investments, foreign aid, or emergency loans to overcome recurrent economic crises, recipient countries had to submit to stringent rules concerning balanced budgets, the privatization of state firms, and the opening of protected branches of the economy. Submission to the Washington consensus, however, in many cases had unforeseen consequences.

Spurred by the consensus in the 1990s, private US investors had nearly tripled the value of their assets abroad, to a total of over $6.5 trillion. On the other hand, the now more accessible public and private financial systems in many newly industrialized and developing countries were often not sufficiently robust to respond adequately. In a first crisis, the Mexican government—pressured in 1994 by inflation, budget deficits, and political instability—could not avoid devaluing the peso. It promptly ran out of pesos to service its short-term, dollar-denominated debt. Fortunately, President Clinton was at that time anxious to complete the North American Free Trade Agreement (NAFTA) with Canada and Mexico. He had Congress and the International Monetary Fund (IMF) bail out Mexico with a massive infusion of loans. (The IMF is an international bank, with the US government as the largest shareholder, that provides emergency loans to countries in sudden financial distress.) With the help of this loan, the Mexican government paid off the foreign lenders and steadied its financial system.

The next crisis began in 1997 in Thailand. Here, the state finances were more solid than in Mexico. The liberalized private banking sector was still in its infancy however, with huge unpaid loans on its books. When many private banks could not pay back their American creditors, the latter began withdrawing what they could from Thailand. American funds for derivatives moved in to speculate on the distress. Derivative managers specializing in currency bets sensed an imminent devaluation of the Thai currency, the *baht*. Since they bet with hundreds of billions of dollars, their speculation became a self-fulfilling prophecy. Accordingly, when the devaluation of the baht finally happened, it stripped Thailand of its currency reserves.

Thailand—in good times one of the world's leading tourist destinations—scraped along the edge of bankruptcy, recovered in 1999, but was thrown again into turmoil in 2010–2011 in a near-civil war over allegations of corruption in the government.

From Thailand the crisis expanded in 1998 quickly to Malaysia, Indonesia, and finally even the newly industrialized Korea, Singapore, and Taiwan. These countries suffered from variations of the same problem of overcommitted banks with nonperforming portfolios. They thereby made themselves also vulnerable to American derivatives speculators invading their financial markets. The IMF had to move in with massive loans to the Southeast and East Asian countries. In return, these countries had to tighten credit, close unprofitable banks and factories, tolerate higher unemployment, and promote increased exporting.

Newly industrialized South Korea was relatively successful with its reforms and quickly cranked up its exports again. Less developed Indonesia, however, was singularly unsuccessful. Large-scale demonstrations forced President Mohammed Suharto (in office 1967–1998) from office. Under weak successors and a slow recovery beginning in 2000, enraged Indonesian Muslims turned to militant Islamism or even terrorism as their solution for the country's persistent poverty. Thanks to the majority of moderate Muslims firmly opposed to terrorism and supportive of the new democratic process, however, an Islamic war of secession in Aceh ended in 2005 and politics entered regular democratic channels.

Russia's Crisis and Recovery   Russia defaulted in 1998 on its internal bonds and from 1999 to 2001 on several of its external loans. These defaults were a culmination of the disastrous postcommunist economic free fall. In the decade after 1991, Russia's gross domestic product (GDP) dropped by nearly half, a decline far worse than that experienced by the United States during the Great Depression of the 1930s. Ordinary Russians had to reduce their already minimal consumption by half of what they had been used to under communism. Moreover, the government had yet to dismantle the system of unproductive former state enterprises financing themselves through local tax collection. Consequently, the state was periodically starved of funds needed for the repayment of its external loans. Fortunately, higher oil prices after 2001 eased the debt situation of Russia somewhat.

The oil and gas revenues from state firms available directly to the government, however, strengthened its autocratic tendencies. The former KGB officer Vladimir Putin, president of Russia 2000–2008, was the principal engineer of this autocracy. He eliminated independent television and had state prosecutors go after potential political rivals. Pervasive corruption and obedience to state directives undermined the rule of law so severely that it was no longer possible to speak of the rule of law in Russia. Politically motivated assassinations of journalists, carried out by secret operatives suspected of enjoying government protection, went unpunished. Rival political parties were intimidated and elections manipulated. An obedient parliament changed the federal constitution so that presidents in the republics of the Russian Union were no longer elected but appointed. Given the small size of the private sector in the early 2000s, the country was still years away from subjecting its state enterprises to market rules and creating a comprehensive market economy.

After the Mexican, Asian, and Russian debt crises, private investors began to lose interest in the emerging markets of developing countries. With funds drying up, debt-ridden Latin American states became vulnerable. Thanks to an emergency IMF loan in 1999, Brazil narrowly avoided a financial meltdown. Argentina, however, in 2002 was less fortunate. Here, the government imprudently prolonged a recession with a tax hike. A yawning budget deficit remained unbalanced, high foreign debts were unpaid, and the peso had to be devalued. This time, however, the IMF did not bail out the government with an emergency loan, arguing that Argentina had been reckless with its finances. Without a loan, the government fell, the middle class was virtually wiped out, and the country—like Russia—limped in the next few years from one loan default to another. Recovery set in only toward the end of the decade.

Globalization and Poor Countries   The mixed record of development in the middle-income countries was mirrored in the bottom tier of poor countries. Even the World Bank had to admit in a 2000 report that the 1990s expansion with its freewheeling financial sector had brought little improvement to many countries in the bottom tier. Since these countries still had weak manufacturing bases, their governments relied on the export of mineral or agricultural commodities to finance development. Apart from the oil-rich desert states of the Middle East, some 50 poor states depended on three or fewer commodities for over half of their export earnings. In about 20 of these states, these commodities even made up over 90 percent of export earnings. As a result of overproduction on the world market, commodity prices were depressed through most of the 1990s. The price depression imposed severe budget cutbacks on many poor countries, with consequent unemployment, middle-class shrinkage, reduction in education, and a rise in AIDS cases.

In a global view, however, the developing world benefited from the globalization of the 1990s. Poverty declined up until the recession of 2007, although this decline was unevenly distributed among the regions of the world. The World Bank defines as "absolutely poor" a man or woman who has to live on less than $1.25 a day. According to statistics compiled during 1990–2000, the total number of the poor went down from 29 to 24 percent, even though the world population grew by nearly 1 billion. As encouraging as this figure was, the gains were concentrated almost exclusively in East and South Asia, particularly China, Vietnam, and India. The number of the absolute poor actually increased in sub-Saharan Africa, Southeast Asia (except Vietnam), Russia and central Asia, and Latin America. Thus, while globalization benefited an absolute majority of humans, its uneven geographical distribution made the benefits look substantially smaller in many regions.

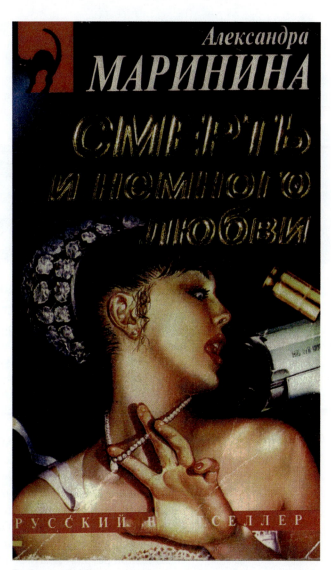

Sex and Violence in the New Russia. An often lurid mixture of sex and violence has been a defining feature of post-Soviet popular culture and a source of much public concern. The illustration above shows the cover of a popular detective novel by Alexandra Marinina, *Death and a Little Love*, in 1995. Note the provocative positioning of the automatic pistol jutting at the face of the women in a way both startling and demeaning.

Contrasting Worlds. A quiet street early in the morning in Havana, with an old American car parked on the curb. The American embargo, together with a still dominant command economy prohibiting imports, forces most car owners in Cuba to hold on to their clunkers, repairing them over and over (*a*). A Vietnamese woman in a traditional straw hat and with two baskets, balanced on a pole, passing by a French luxury goods store in Hanoi, the capital of Vietnam. The country enjoyed near double-digit growth rates in its economy during the first decade of the 2000s (*b*).

The Communist Holdouts: North Korea, Cuba, China, and Vietnam

Communism as an official ideology survived in North Korea, Cuba, China, and Vietnam. North Korea and Cuba stubbornly continued to cling to both the command system and party control. China and Vietnam opened their command economies to the market but maintained single-party control and some large state firms. In both cases, the parties remained communist in name but became in fact ordinary autocracies presiding over capitalist economies.

North Korea and Cuba   After the death of North Korea's founding leader, Kim Il-Sung (b. 1912), in 1994, his son Kim Jong-il (b. 1941) became the Communist Party secretary and, thereby, the head of North Korea's government. He inherited a command economy in free fall, with Soviet subsidies having ended and strained relations with China after that country's normalization of relations with South Korea. Several years of floods and drought in the 1990s had accelerated the economic breakdown, culminating with a colossal famine, which killed some 2.5 million people—nearly one-fifth of the population. A moderate turnaround finally began in 1998 with the inauguration of an industrial zone with foreign investments and a limited free market. Kim Jong-il, the army, and the party remained unified during the catastrophic 1990s and continued their iron grip even through 2008 when the leader allegedly suffered a stroke. Since North Korea was a highly armed nuclear country asserting itself regularly through military provocations against South Korea, the political situation on the Korean peninsula continued to be unstable.

Cuba, too, suffered a severe setback when Soviet communism collapsed. Without Soviet subsidies and the ability to continue its sugar exports, the Cuban GDP shrank by one-third, imposing severe hardship on the population. President Fidel Castro (b. 1926) and the Communist Party were forced to reduce their reliance on the command economy. They allowed farmers to exceed their state quotas and grow fruits and vegetables for the open market, and a limited number of urban workers were allowed to open their own shops. Tourism was opened up, catering mostly to Europeans and East Asians since the long-standing US embargo continued almost unchanged. Thanks to a highly developed health sector, Cuba also built export-oriented pharmaceutical and biotechnological industries. During the early 2000s, the government was able to turn the economy around and achieve high growth rates. The hope of discovering substantial offshore oil fields even injected excitement into the country. Castro's resignation from the presidency for health reasons in 2008, however, raised questions of transitional politics similar to those concerning North Korea. In both countries communism remained outwardly as unreconstructed as ever.

The Chinese New Middle Class   After the crushing experience of Tiananmen Square, the new Chinese middle class benefiting from the economic reforms of the Open Door and Four Modernizations had to accommodate itself as best it could to a repressive top layer and a corrosively corrupt bottom layer of a monopoly party that was communist in name but autocratic in practice. The basic characteristics of the middle class were remarkably similar to those of India and Turkey, discussed later in this chapter. Socially conservative migrants from the provinces to the cities found unskilled jobs in the early 1980s. They acquired skills and earned enough to send their children to school. From around 2005, the children, now with college degrees, took jobs as managers, technicians, professionals, and entrepreneurs in state companies, private firms, and Chinese branches of foreign firms. They began to flex their muscles as consumers.

Two Views of China Today.
Despite recent attempts to regulate its pace, China's economic acceleration continues at or near double digits. In 2010, its GDP surpassed that of Japan to become second only to that of the United States. The new prosperity has created startling contrasts and a growing diversity of lifestyles in the PRC. In the image above, young Chinese hipsters sport T-shirts harkening back with purposeful irony to revolutionary leaders Mao Zedong and Cuba's romantic figure of Che Guevara. In the lower panel, China's current leadership—smartly decked out in Western suits and "power ties"—strive to steer the country toward continued growth as the means to preserve the ascendancy of the Chinese Communist Party.

The social conservatism of the middle class was rooted in rural popular religious practices, such as ancestral offerings and funeral rituals, blessings, or birthday festivals of gods that involved processions and pilgrimages to and from temples under the leadership of local Daoist priests. During the Maoist period, many temples were destroyed and practices outlawed, disrupting for nearly a generation the transmission of traditional customs. Since the mid-1990s, however, the government authorized or tolerated the reconstruction of temples and resumption of practices, while at the same time regulating the training and accreditation of Daoist and Buddhist ritual specialists. In villages, retired folk who remembered the customs participated in the reconstitution of temple committees, the collection of funds, and the staging of operas, marionette and puppet shows, or movies. In cities, the merged rural and urban scriptural traditions expressed themselves in a standardized Confucianism–Daoism–Buddhism under government control.

To keep the middle class from demanding political participation outside the Communist Party, the government pursued accelerated annual GDP growth, which in some years went into double digits. Wages rose beyond those paid in Vietnam,

Disharmonious Society

"On the other hand . . . there now are so many acutely 'unharmonious' factors in Chinese society that the party policymakers have to spend their annual gathering to ponder possible solutions. For if society were quite harmonious, the party elite would devote their precious time to other more urgent issues.

"Indeed, social problems, such as the widening wealth gap and social injustices, have piled up to such an extent that if the CCP [Communist Party] were to fail to address them properly, its very legitimacy would be questioned and challenged . . .

"And there are good reasons for the CCP elite to be deeply concerned. The wealth gap has caused increasingly serious social differentiation, threatening social stability . . .

"One of the major causes for rapidly expanding wealth disparity is social injustice, which is also a major source of growing public discontent. Many people have gained their wealth not through their own enterprise but through their connections with officialdom . . ."

—Wu Zhong. "China Yearns for Hu's 'Harmonious Society.'" *Asia Times*, October 11, 2006, http://www.atimes.com/atimes/China/HJ11Ad01.html.

Bangladesh, India, and Pakistan. Instead of spending its earnings, however, the middle class saved at rates double those in Japan or Europe prior to the recession of 2007. The only partially subsidized new health-care and education systems consumed much of those savings, even though the payments were bearable under the continued conditions of the one-child law. In addition, urban real estate and rental apartments became increasingly unaffordable in many Chinese cities during the early 2000s. Under the slogan of the "harmonious society"—in which all segments of the populace worked together with no toleration for "disruptive elements," or those advocating independence for Tibet or Uighur regions in Xinjiang—the government and party staked its continued legitimacy on ongoing economic progress.

The Chinese Countryside   This high-wire act was even more pronounced in the countryside. The government maintained the Maoist-era *hukou* registration system, which did not allow farmers to move to cities and find work without a permit, even though this system was largely ignored. The government reformed the system marginally but still refused to grant amnesty to some 100 million migrants working illegally in cities or allow their children access to urban schools. An equal number of farmers were pushed off their lands by authorities eager to make room for businesses, roads, and railroads. Since land continued to be state-owned and farmers were merely leaseholders, corrupt local authorities found it easy to cheat the farmers out of their land. The value of *guanxi* ("connections") thus continued more or less unabated. Tens of thousands of local protests annually in the early 2000s attested to a smoldering resentment in the villages, no matter how loudly the government touted its success in reducing the poverty rate.

The Transformation of Vietnam   As a country that looked to the Soviet Union for leadership, Vietnam was as surprised as Cuba when Soviet-style communism collapsed in 1991. Like the Soviet Union, Vietnam had begun economic liberalization reforms in 1986, especially in agriculture where farmers were permitted to sell above-quota harvests on the open market. Vietnam quickly became the world's third largest rice exporter, after the United States and Thailand, and reduced its poverty rate as drastically as China. But vehement ideological struggles over political liberalization did not end until a decade later with the decision to avoid a multiparty system, as did China a little later. Now the path to a full commitment to economic liberalization was open. In 1995–1996 Vietnam normalized relations with the United States, took out a large World Bank loan, revitalized foreign investment, and began reforming its unprofitable state firms by encouraging the participation of private domestic capital.

With stellar double-digit growth rates in the 1990s, Vietnam outpaced other poor Asian neighbors, such as Cambodia and Bangladesh, diversifying its manufacturing sector from textiles to footwear and electronics. Hong Kong, Taiwanese, and Korean companies, the principal foreign investors, showed a strong preference for Vietnam, on account of its advanced literacy rate and lower wages compared to China. A major new export sector from the later 1990s onward was *aquaculture*, the farming of shrimp, catfish, and tilapia. Vietnam was poised at the beginning of the second decade of the 2000s to move from the poor to the intermediate countries on the world list of nations moving to modernity.

A Decade of Global Shifts: Twenty-First Century Currents and Cross-Currents

In the first decade of the 2000s, there was a palpable swing toward pessimism in the West. Two recessions framed the decade, the Washington consensus fell apart over protests from borrower countries, and the problematic postwar settlement in Iraq demonstrated the limits of US power. The Middle East fared even worse, with terrorism, suicide bombings, no Arab–Israeli peace, and a potential Iranian nuclear bomb. By contrast, China and India, with strong economic growth rates, expanded their educated and entrepreneurial middle classes. Africa and Latin America, benefiting from the voracious demand for oil and minerals in China and India, experienced similarly strong growth. By the second decade of the 2000s, it was clear that, while there might be doubts about the course of modernity in the West, the commitment to it was growing everywhere else.

Unease in the West   Two recessions in the first decade of the 2000s in the United States sapped much of the enthusiasm about the future of modernity that had begun so optimistically after the fall of communism. The first recession, of 2001–2003, was the so-called dot.com crisis, which had its origins in uncontrolled speculation about the expansion of the new medium of the Internet and the World Wide Web. The second recession, of 2007–2011, was rooted in private and public overspending (housing and credit). By 2011, US debts reached the astronomical sum of nearly $14.6 trillion (for comparison, the US GDP was $14.5 trillion).

The recession of 2001–2003 hit the African American and Hispanic working class particularly hard; in the following recession of 2007–2011 many white workers lost their jobs. An unraveling of the credit markets built on speculation on financial derivatives and "credit default swaps" in the mortgage sector spurred a cascade of financial failures in 2008. Only massive intervention by the federal government prevented a general financial panic. As anger over corporate greed, government bailouts, massive federal economic stimulus packages, and health-care reform grew among largely white, middle-class, older, and evangelical voters, a new "Tea Party" movement ("Taxed Enough Already") introduced radically populist antiestablishment and antiforeigner agendas into the political debate. The largely conservative middle classes of self-employed small businesspeople and professionals found themselves squeezed between unskilled and low-earning workers on the bottom and an expanding, increasingly rich upper middle class of corporate officers and Internet entrepreneurs on top, causing no small amount of unease.

The campaign and eventual election of Barack Obama (b. 1961, in office beginning 2009), a law professor and the first African American president of the nation, provided much optimism to a majority of Americans. At first, it appeared that the president's deficit-spending helped in steadying the recession of 2007–2011. But

Edge People

"Being 'Danish' or 'Italian,' 'American' or 'European' won't just be an identity; it will be a rebuff and a reproof to those whom it excludes. The state, far from disappearing, may be about to come into its own: the privileges of citizenship, the protections of card-holding residency rights, will be wielded as political trumps. Intolerant demagogues in established democracies will demand 'tests'—of knowledge, of language, of attitude—to determine whether desperate newcomers are deserving of British or Dutch or French 'identity.' They are already doing so. In this brave new century we shall miss the tolerant, the marginals: the edge people."

—Tony Judt. "Edge People." *The New York Review of Books*, March 25, 2010. Judt, who died in 2010, was one of the leading critics of capitalist democracy.

soon this spending turned out to be insufficient, and the grind of the 2007–2011 recession soon dragged the ebullient mood down again. Meanwhile, conservatives and Tea Party activists relentlessly targeted government spending, health-care reform, illegal immigrants, and especially the slow economic recovery. In the 2010 elections, the Republicans regained the House and rejected tax increases to offset budget deficits out of hand.

A year later the Tea Party wing of the Republican Party held the nation hostage in the negotiations for an increase of the national debt ceiling. It nearly drove the country into default and the credit worthiness of the United States was damaged. Given the unwillingness of lawmakers to reform the tax code, the gap between the wealthy and poor—beginning with the electronic revolution and apparent opportunities for new wealth—continued to widen. This gap increasingly threatened the ability of middle-class Americans to consume and thereby sustain the capitalist system, given that 45–70 percent (depending on conservative or liberal calculations) of the GDP was consumer-generated.

Europe saw a similar trend of rising income disparities, although it was mitigated by a stronger manufacturing sector (around 20 percent of GDP vs. 11 percent in the United States in 2010) and a more generous social safety net. But the costs of this net weighed heavily on the budgets of many countries, seriously imperiling the future not only of, for example, Greece, Portugal, and Ireland (which fell into near bankruptcy in 2008–2011) but also of the European Union (1992) itself, as well as the euro, which was launched with great fanfare in 1999. Since the unemployed were entitled to long-term support in most European countries, the angry populist debate was more muted. Nevertheless, the rise of anti-Muslim immigrant political parties in Scandinavia and the Netherlands and the spectacle of unemployed youth in Portugal and Spain (up to 40 percent) setting up makeshift camps in major cities were stark reminders of the lack of confidence in the future of many young Europeans. As in the United States, optimism about the future of modernity was at a low ebb by the start of the new decade.

On the other hand, given the still comparatively strong, export-oriented manufacturing sector, Europe was years ahead of the United States in industrial innovation. In the first decade of the 2000s, European countries became the leading producers of renewable energy technologies, such as wind turbines, solar cells, and batteries. A study, carried out in Germany in 2010, suggested that it would be feasible for the country to shift entirely from fossil fuels to green energy by 2050. Europe also had an edge in the manufacture of fuel-efficient or electric cars and the exploration of hydrogen propulsion. Though nuclear energy was widely used, particularly in France, its future was open to question after the earthquake, tsunami, and partial nuclear power plant meltdown in Sendai, Japan, in the spring of 2011. The commitment to environmentalism in the early 2000s was much stronger in Europe than in the United States and in this sector at least, gloom is tempered with considerable hope.

A Bloody Civil War in Yugoslavia Eastern Europe and the Balkans went through an economic collapse and political restructuring similar to Russia, Ukraine, Belarus, and the other republics after the end of communism in 1991. This collapse and restructuring was mostly peaceful except for Yugoslavia, where a civil war raged from 1990 to 1995. Until the 1980s, communism was the main ideology in Yugoslavia through which the country's ethnic nationalisms of the Orthodox Christian Serbs (one-third of the population), Catholic Croats (20 percent), Muslim Bosnians (9 percent), Catholic Slovenes (8 percent), and mostly Muslim Kosovo Albanians (8 percent) were kept under the mantle of a federal constitution granting these ethnic groups a degree of autonomy. The main enforcer of communist unity, through carrot and stick, was President Josip Tito (1892–1980), a Croat whose authority—based on his legitimacy as an underground fighter against the Nazi occupation during World War II—was unimpeachable. After his death, however, the Serb president Slobodan Milošević (1941–2006) exploited the demographic superiority of his ethnic community for the establishment of political dominance while holding on to communism as the pro forma ideology.

Yugoslavia, like many Eastern European communist states, had borrowed heavily from Western countries to keep its industries from collapsing during the oil price slump of 1985–1986. At the end of the 1980s it was practically bankrupt, with hundreds of thousands of unemployed workers carrying their dashed hopes for the good life of consumerism in the city back to their native villages. This disappointment exploded in 1990 with extraordinary fury into deadly religious–nationalist hatred, led by the smaller ethnic groups against Serbs on their territories. The Serb supremacist-nationalist backlash, with an effort to "cleanse" minorities from their "greater Serbian" territory, was no less explosive. It took more than a decade for the European Union and the United States to stop the Serbs from murdering Bosnians and Albanians and enforce a semblance of peace in the Balkans.

Since then, the five successor states of Yugoslavia have struggled to adapt to capitalism and democracy. Slovenia did so quite successfully, while others like

Ethnic Cleansing. The upheavals in the wake of the breakup of the former Yugoslavia brought long simmering ethnic and religious tensions to the surface, particularly in the struggles between the Orthodox Serbs seeking to create a "greater Serbia" in Bosnia and Herzegovina and Bosnia's Muslims. In the accompanying photo, a woman, Hajra Eatiae--the president of the Association of Women of Srebenica--takes a poignant private moment in front of a wall of photographs of the 8,000 Bosnian victims of the massacre in the city of Srebenica at the hands of Serbs. Eatiae herself lost her husband and son in this largest European mass murder since World War II.

Bosnia-Herzegovina, Serb-controlled Bosnia, and Kosovo have not yet at all. Serb supremacist nationalism survived the longest and only gradually died down when the democratically elected pro-European government decided to arrest the main perpetrators of ethnic cleansing, Radovan Karadžić (b. 1945) and Ratko Mladić (b. 1943) in 2008 and 2011, respectively. The two had lived more or less openly in Serbia for years, protected by diehard followers. With these arrests and much relief, the Serbian government opened the way toward joining the European Union.

The Middle East: Paralysis, Islamism, and Liberation

As in the United States and Europe, the momentum that was generated after the collapse of communism had largely expired in the Middle East and North Africa by the early 2000s. In fact, with the exception of Turkey, a pall of economic and political paralysis hung over the region. The republics in the 1990s and early 2000s (e.g., Egypt, Syria, Algeria, Tunisia, and Yemen) inched intermittently toward privatization of state-run businesses but not at all toward democratization. Monarchies (Saudi Arabia, Jordan, Oman, and the Gulf sheikhdoms) actively encouraged private investment, especially in the oil sector, but were extremely cautious, if not altogether hostile, toward democratic reforms. Under the impact of the Arab Spring, in 2011 the kingdom of Morocco adopted constitutional reforms allowing for greater democracy. The "rejection front" of autocratic regimes in Iran and Syria, as well as the guerilla terrorist organizations Hezbollah in southern Lebanon and Hamas in the Gaza Strip, opposed Washington and globalization out of hand. Syria did, however, open state-controlled economy ever so cautiously to privatization in the early 2000s.

Islamism: Religious-nationalist ideology in which the reformed Sunni or Shiite Islam of the twentieth century is used to support the institutions of the state.

Islamism was a major factor accounting for the immobility of "republican autocrats" as well as monarchs. Western secular observers often expressed their surprise at the strength of the religious resurgence in the Middle East after watching its apparent demise with the rise of secular Arab nationalism and Arab socialism. In this case, however, while Islam was less visible in the region in the twentieth century when the political elites consisted of secular liberals and nationalists, it had not receded at all from the villages and poor city quarters, where it remained as vital as ever (see Map 31.4).

The key to understanding the rise of Islamism lay in the acceleration of rural–urban migration in the Middle East in the late 1990s and early 2000s. Ever since the 1960s, when Middle Eastern and North African governments built the first large state-run manufacturing plants in their cities, the workers were largely peasants arriving from villages with highly localized cultures of saintly Sufi or mystical Islam. They encountered militant preachers in the cities who—representing a unified, standard, urban Sunni Islam—were appalled by the "un-Islamic" saint cults among the workers. The children of these workers learned a similar standardized Islam in the schools, intended to buttress Arab nationalism, in which the Prophet Muhammad was the first nationalist. Standard Islam and militant urban Islamism gradually crowded out the rural saintly Islam and eventually produced small but potent offshoots of Islamist terrorism, such as al-Qaeda and the Taliban.

In the 1990s and early 2000s Middle Eastern governments essentially barricaded themselves behind their secret services and armies against the onslaughts of these Islamists. Terrorists attacked tourists, as happened periodically in Egypt, seeking to bring down a government that relied heavily on Western tourism. Sometimes they picked weak states such as Yemen, which, relying on dwindling oil revenues began

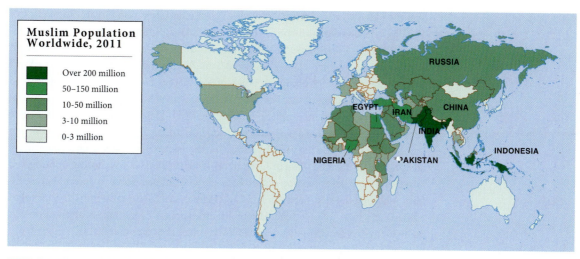

MAP **31.4** **Muslim Population Worldwide, 2011.**

to lose control of its nomadic tribes in the east, agricultural minorities in the north, and urban secessionists in the south, became a haven for al-Qaeda terrorists. Even a stronger state, Algeria, suffered a devastating civil war that claimed 150,000 victims from 1992 to 2002. Under the threat of Islamist terrorism, Middle Eastern and North African governments found it impossible to proclaim bold new initiatives of the kind that China or India advanced (see Map 31.4).

Islamic Terrorism and Israel   Two areas where Islamists achieved breakthroughs of sorts were Lebanon and the Gaza Strip. Hezbollah ("Party of God"), an Islamist guerilla organization with attendant social services and recruits from among the Shiite majority of Lebanese Muslims, waged an underground war against Israel and Westerners in Lebanon and abroad. Hezbollah was accused of bombing the US embassy in Beirut in 1983, hijacking an American airliner in 1985, and two bombings against Jews in Argentina in 1992 and 1994. Thereafter, the party changed its tactics, focusing its forces entirely on driving Israel out of southern Lebanon, which it achieved in 2000. Since then, it has steadily increased its role in the Lebanese government and in the Arab–Israeli conflict, regularly firing rockets into northern Israel. After a retaliatory Israeli invasion in 2006, Hezbollah and Israel, kept apart by a contingent of UN soldiers, returned to an uneasy standoff.

Israel successfully transformed itself during the globalization of the 1990s into an advanced economy specializing in high-tech software and microbiology. In 1994, it was officially at peace with two Arab neighbors, Egypt and Jordan. But it continued to face a hostile Arab Middle East and North Africa, in general, and restless Palestinians in the occupied territories on the West Bank and in Gaza, in particular. To protect its citizens from guerilla attacks, the Israeli government began building a border fence in 2002, supplemented in places by a wall of concrete slabs, inside the entire length of the occupied West Bank. In a parallel move it withdrew from the fenced-in Gaza Strip in 2005. Suicide attacks were fewer, but cross-border rocket attacks (from Gaza) increased, trapping Israel in a cat-and-mouse game of low-level cross-border warfare.

After 2006, Israel slid into an even worse trap. The first ever Palestinian elections gave the victory in Gaza to the Islamic guerilla organization Hamas, founded in 1988, over the older, secular, ethnic-nationalist Palestinian Liberation Organization (PLO). The PLO, deprived of its inspiring leader Yasser Arafat (1929–2004), was able to prevail only in the West Bank. The PLO refused to recognize the elections, and a civil war broke out, in which Hamas was victorious, forcing the PLO to retreat to the West Bank. Israel imposed a complete embargo on Hamas-ruled Gaza, in an attempt to bring the organization down. For those in Israel who wished to renew the Camp David peace process, left incomplete in 2000, the PLO–Hamas split was a disaster since it threw the entire idea of a two-state solution into doubt. Hamas was happy to deepen this doubt in the following years by launching thousands of rockets against Israel. In retaliation, Israel invaded Gaza in December–January 2008–2009, causing unmitigated misery for the Palestinian population of Gaza, without being able to defeat Hamas. Efforts at healing the split between PLO and Hamas, crucial for salvaging the concept of a Palestinian state, followed thereafter with little success. Nonetheless, application was made to the UN for recognition of a Palestine state in September 2011.

Israel's Predicament and the Iranian Bomb

Predictably, the failure of the invasion brought a conservative government into power in Israel. The government renewed the open pursuit of Israeli settlement construction on the West Bank while tightening the embargo on Gaza. But neither more Jewish settlements on the West Bank (making the two-state solution illusory) nor punishing Israel's neighbors Hezbollah and Hamas with invasions and/or embargoes brought the country closer to peace. Israel's long dominance over its neighbors, gradually acquired in the last half of the twentieth century, appeared to have reached its limits in the early years of the twenty-first.

Hezbollah and Hamas were able to assert themselves against Israel thanks to Iran, which supplied them with rockets. Iran, a leader of the rejection front against Israel, had experienced a "pragmatic" period after the death of its spiritual guide, Ruhollah Khomeini, in 1989. This pragmatism had raised the hope that the Shiite Islamist regime was lessening its policy of eradicating what it viewed as the "satanic" Western culture of secularism, liberalism, and pop culture. But the reformers were timid, and the still powerful clerics systematically undermined attempts at democratic and cultural reforms.

Any remaining hopes for reform were dashed when Mahmoud Ahmadinejad (b. 1956) [Ah-ma-DEE-nay-jahd], an engineer from a modest rural background, was elected president. He renewed the anti-Western crusade and adopted a policy of populism, with subsidies for food and gas as well as cash distributed by the suitcase on his cross-country trips. Most importantly, under his leadership, the Revolutionary Guard became not only the most effective military organization but, by investing in a wide variety of businesses, also a huge patronage machine. The precipitous decline of revenues from oil exports during the recession of 2008–2011, however, seriously reduced Ahmadinejad's populist largesse. Hence, he needed the Revolutionary Guard commanders to falsify the elections of 2009 to stay in power. Food and gasoline subsidies were cut substantially, but a nuclear program begun three decades earlier continued unabated. Suspected Iranian ambitions for acquiring a nuclear bomb, coupled with North Korea's already existing nuclear arsenal, created recurrent nightmares in the world about nuclear proliferation, "dirty" nuclear material in the hands of terrorists, and the possibility of nuclear war by "rogue" nations.

Guardians of the Revolution.
Female Iranian members of parliament listening to Iranian President Mahmoud Ahmadinejad as he presents his annual budget bill in February 2011. Iran follows strict gender segregation, with women required to wear the *chador*, a black cloak that covers the full body, and the *hijab*, a white headdress. Women have, however, full access to education and at present number about 60 percent of all university students.

The Ascent of Turkey   Turkey was the one Middle Eastern country to have largely escaped Islamist militancy and become one of the most dynamic newly industrialized countries in the world. It became the top producer of TV sets in Europe and began the construction of high-speed rail links as well as the world's deepest prefabricated tunnel, under the Bosporus. In contrast to other regimes in the Middle East, Turkish Muslims found access to the political process, thanks to a well established and functioning multiparty system. After many false starts and interruptions by military coups d'état, an Islamic party in 1983 not only captured the premiership of the country but simultaneously implemented bold new initiatives of economic privatization and industrial export orientation. Benefiting from these initiatives, an entire new middle class of socially conservative but economically liberal entrepreneurial businesspeople arose. In an even more effective second wave of middle-class expansion after 2003 under Prime Minister Recep Erdogan [RAY-jep Er-dow-AHN] (b. 1954), Turkey's GDP climbed to become the world's fifteenth largest. Elections in June 2011 enabled Erdogan's party to garner slightly more than half of the vote and, on the basis of this vote, begin constitutional reforms which will rescind the military's role in politics. Thus, Turkey largely completed its arrival in capitalist-democratic modernity.

The Arab Spring of 2011   Turkey was a model example for the compatibility of Islam and democracy. But in spring 2011 Tunisia and Egypt each saw constitutional-nationalist revolutions, which demonstrated that democracy can sprout in Arab countries as well. On December 17, 2010, 26-year-old Mohamed Bouazizi set himself ablaze in a last spectacular act of despair brought about by the humiliations he had suffered at the hands of a Tunisian policewoman. For months she had sought to drive him and his illegal produce cart from the streets of Sidi Bouzid in central Tunisia. In a region plagued by 30 percent unemployment, Bouazizi had become moderately successful selling his produce, which earned him enough to support the university studies of one of his sisters. But on this day he had finally had enough.

Democracy's Martyr. A refashioned monument in the city of Sidi Bouzid, Tunisia, in honor of Mohamed Bouazizi, whose portrait is visible on top of the monument. Bouazizi was a street vendor, selling fruits and vegetables without a license. After months of harassment by the police, he set himself afire in despair. His example galvanized young, educated, and social network–savvy Tunisians into their peaceful Arab Spring revolution.

Bouazizi's heartbreaking death touched off the mostly peaceful democratic revolutions dubbed the "Arab Spring," on which we centered this chapter's opening vignette. Beginning in Tunisia, they snowballed into Egypt, Libya, Bahrain, Yemen, and Syria in the course of early 2011. In Tunisia and Egypt they ousted longtime and aging autocrats, Tunisia's Zine El Abidine Ben Ali (r. 1987–2011) and Egypt's Hosni Mubarak (r. 1981–2011). After months of fighting, Libya's Muammar el-Qaddafi (r. 1969–Sep. 2011; killed October 20) was finally toppled. Autocratic rulers in countries seeing similar protests held on with iron nerves and unrestrained brutality. Central to the nonviolent daily rallies in Tunisia and Egypt, continuing for days and weeks, were demands for freedom, equality, fair elections, the end of corruption (especially crony capitalism), new democratic constitutions, the rule of law, and, last but not least, jobs.

The demonstrators, for the most part young, Internet-savvy, educated, and fully conversant with international youth culture, documented the events through pictures, videos, and blogs and revealed police violence for the world to instantly see. Social connectedness and the direct transmission of facts on the ground gave these constitutional revolutions a new character. Now a world public watching these events could declare solidarity with the demonstrators and demand action from its own politicians. As these democratic revolutions were beginning to be implemented, they raised the question of how closely the young demonstrators were integrated with the rest of the population—Islamists as well as the poor urban and rural traditional Muslims—to make constitutional and economic reforms meaningful for them as well (see Map 31.5).

The New Middle Class in India
The rise of a conservative Islamic middle class in Turkey had its parallel in India in the rise of a religiously conservative Hindu middle class of shopkeepers, traders, merchants, and small manufacturers who had chafed under the tyranny of the petty socialist bureaucrats from the Congress Party in the 1980s. The leading businesspeople in this middle class came from the relatively privileged commercial occupations within the Vaishya stratum of the caste system and were represented by the Indian People's Party (Bharatiya Janata Party, BJP). They demanded the dismantling of the Soviet-style state socialist system,

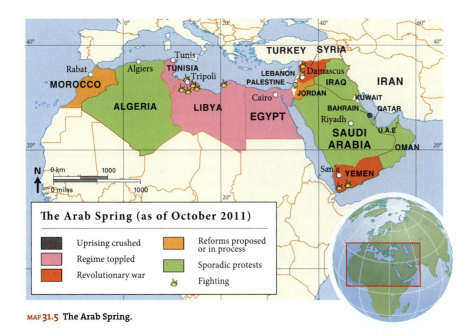

MAP 31.5 The Arab Spring.

which had dominated India since the 1950s and had run into the same financial difficulties as the Soviet Union in the 1970s. Not surprisingly, the BJP won the 1991 elections on a platform of economic reform and globalization.

The BJP government, however, did not accomplish much. Once in power, it succumbed to its traditional supremacist-nationalist ideology of "Hinduness" (*hindutva*), which the business leaders had sought to tone down. In 1992, the BJP protected radical local hindutva organizations that whipped up a crowd of 150,000 Hindus to raze the Babri Mosque (allegedly founded in the place of a Hindu temple) in the northern Indian state of Uttar Pradesh, home to 31 million Muslims. In the predictable Muslim backlash, some 2,000 Indians died. In the elections of 1998, the BJP played down its hindutva tradition and won again, but its involvement in renewed incidents of communal violence contribtued to an alienation of the voters in 2004. The Congress Party, now also enthusiastically in favor of economic liberalization, returned to power.

The new Indian middle class—defined by a cell phone, motorized transportation, and a color TV—included anywhere between 60 and 300 million Indians, in a population of 1.2 billion in 2010. The most dynamic members of this class lived and worked in the southern heavy industry and high-tech hub of Bangalore. Because the city is 12.5 hours ahead of California, it is perfect for effecting linkages to maintain around-the-clock computing with Silicon Valley. By the second decade of the 2000s, these two leading world centers of information technology on opposite sides of the globe had become closely integrated.

The rapid expansion of urban centers, such as Bangalore, greatly contributed to the decline of the traditional caste divisions in Hinduism within the urban and even, to some degree, rural context. Since descent could be hidden in the cities, even the untouchable caste (*dalit*) began to enter the new middle class. Widespread protests in 2006 against the complex affirmative action system introduced in the 1990s in favor of less privileged social groups indicated the beginning of a dissolution of the caste divisions in the urban environment.

Social Networking

As we have seen, the Tunisian revolution sparked a wave of revolts across Africa and the Middle East in what has come to be called the "Arab Spring." What makes these movements unique, however, is that they were organized and carried out by means of *social networking sites* (SNSs) like Twitter, Facebook, and YouTube, supported by cell phones and other modern communication technologies. But what are the origins of these devices and how have they developed into such important tools of political and social revolution?

SNSs can ultimately be traced back to the origins of the Internet and the World Wide Web. The Internet is a product of the Cold War. Stunned by the Soviet launch of Sputnik the previous year, in 1958 President Eisenhower called for the creation of a national electronic communication network to help protect the United States from a nuclear attack launched from space. In 1969 the US government initiated the Advanced Research Projects Agency (ARPA), which created a system inking computers at major universities into a network that allowed them to share vital information. From this small, highly classified step the Internet expanded during the 1990s into a global computer network. The World Wide Web (or www) was conceived in 1989 and launched two years later as a part of the Internet. Simply put, the "web" uses the Internet to gain access to categories of data, documents, and other resources found within the larger network.

SNSs sprang up in the 1990s when it was recognized that the Internet and the World Wide Web provided social groups the means to easily communicate with each other and to share information. Among the earliest of these were Classmates. com (1995) and SixDegrees (1997), which enabled users to "network" with each other by means of shared e-mail addresses. The next step allowed users to develop personal sites from which to share information with like-minded readers. The first of these was Friendster in 2002, followed by Linked In and MySpace in 2003, YouTube in 2004, and Facebook and Twitter by 2006. Along with a welter of personal "blogs" (from "web-logs") these sites represented a global explosion of instantaneously distributed information that revolutionized the nature of communication.

Easily the most recognizable use of SNSs to effect change relates to the recent wave of uprisings in North Africa and the Middle East. An early example of this came in Iran in 2009. Called the "Twitter Revolution," anti-government activists used the full range of SNSs while engaged in an ultimately futile effort to overthrow the Iranian regime. Following the success of the Tunisian revolution, however, an even more spectacular display of the power of SNSs erupted in Egypt on January 25, 2011, when thousands of protesters took to the streets to demand the ouster of

The Face of Revolution. Perhaps the most novel aspect of the ongoing "Arab Spring" has been the widespread use of electronic media and Social Networking Sites (SNSs) in recruiting, organizing, and popularizing the efforts of activists in various countries. The inventiveness of the participants in avoiding government scrutiny and bypassing restrictions on SNSs by means of proxy servers and third-party connections to outside sites has become legendary. In Syria, the government lifted a ban on these sites in an attempt to stave off unrest in the wake of the successful uprisings in Tunisia and Egypt. Here a Syrian man logs into his Facebook account "legally" for perhaps the first time in February, 2011. Most observers agree, however, that such restrictions have had little effect in blocking access to the most popular SNSs.

authoritarian President Hosni Mubarak. This "Facebook Revolution," was launched by the April 6 Youth Movement, a Facebook group comprised of social and political activists. In 2011 the movement was propelled forward by Wael Ghonim, a young Google marketing executive, who set up a Facebook site to mobilize participants for a rally against harsh governmental policies. Ghonim hoped for a gathering of 50,000 protesters. When, however, over 100,000 showed up, he observed, awe-struck, that "I have never seen a revolution that was preannounced before" [NY Times, February 14, 2011]. Moreover, the Egyptian success was made possible in part by valuable lessons gleaned from SNS exchanges with anti-government coun-terparts in Tunisia. One message, for example, read: "Advice to the youth of Egypt: Put vinegar or onion under your scarf for tear gas" [Ibid.].

For all their success in facilitating uprisings against authoritarian governments, however, SNSs are used with equal effectiveness by extremist terrorist groups. Al Quaeda and the Taliban have learned to take advantage of Facebook and Twitter to broadcast their calls for global *jihad*. SNSs are also used to solicit financial sup-port and share information concerning plans for forthcoming attacks. Moreover, SNS—particularly Facebook—serve as effective recruitment tools. The recent death of Anwar al-Awlaki, known popularly as "the bin Laden of the Internet," especially brought into the open the effectiveness of YouTube to inspire *jihad*. The Taliban, too, has established an effective network of sites to get out its propaganda and re-cruitment messages to a global audience. As its "Voice of Jihad" proclaims, "Wars today cannot be won without media. Media aims at the heart rather than the body, [and]if the heart is defeated, the battle is won" [blog posted by Stephanie Maier, May 15, 2011]. There is even an American website, "Jihadology," which recently lamented the death of Al Quaeda leader Osama Bin Laden: "Goodbye, Oh Honor-able Shaykh," "You Lived Benevolent and Died a Martyr. . . " [Ibid.].

In the origin and evolution of social networking sites we are afforded yet another example of how the power of modern technologies has altered the course of world history. How ironic that Internet websites originally intended for exchanges among friends have been transformed into to tools to spread revolution, violence, and ter-rorism. Indeed, the wave of protests and revolutionary fervor initiated in Tunisia and Egypt represent only the beginning of uprisings in the modern Middle East; on-going revolts have spread to Libya—where strongman Muammar Gaddafi was overthrown and executed—as well Syria, Bahrain, Jordan, and Yemen. As one of the organizers of the Egyptian revolution so presciently predicted: "Tunis is the force that pushed Egypt, but what Egypt did will be the force that will push the world" [NY Times, February 14, 2011]. And the sinews binding this force are now electronic.

Questions

- How do SNSs show how an innovation can be adapted for purposes wholly differ-ent from the original purposes for which they were intended?

- Do you believe SNSs have allowed young people around the world to make their wishes and aspirations more powerfully felt? If so, what does this say about the connection between technology and youth?

Driving Toward Prosperity.
The Bajaj scooter was the early status symbol of the emerging Indian middle class. On account of their size, the Indian and Chinese middle classes, numbering perhaps in the hundreds of millions, are a powerful group, representing a huge reservoir of ever more demanding consumers. This picture is from 2010, when the Indian middle class had come of age.

The success of the middle class in India, impressive as it is, must also be measured against conditions in the countryside, much of which is still largely outside the market economy. Almost three-quarters of the population lived in villages with poor water, electricity, and roads during the beginning of the twenty-first century. An overwhelming majority of villagers lived in extreme poverty (less than $1.25 per day), existing completely outside the market circuit and depending on handouts. Although this majority in 2010 was somewhat smaller, perhaps by one-quarter, a birth rate that refused to decline below 2.8 percent did not help much in poverty reduction. A major factor in the persistence of poverty was incomplete land reform. Landlordism and tenancy continued to encompass nearly half of the rural population. Large landholdings had been abolished after independence, but medium and small landlordism persisted undiminished. As a major voting bloc in the Congress Party, the landlords were successful in resisting further land reform.

The unproductive landlord system, providing India with little more than wheat and rice, required enormous state subsidies in seed, fertilizer, and irrigation infrastructures to keep going. These subsidies discouraged investments in a much needed agricultural diversification. The e-Choupal system by the Indian conglomerate ITC was a remarkable exception. ITC developed the system in 2000, about a decade after India had opened its borders to the world market, and used it in its strategy to counter the invading American, European, and Japanese multinationals with competitive Indian exports. Through e-Choupal, Indian soybean farmers were equipped with computers (hooked up to solar panels), through which they could follow soybean prices on the Chicago futures market as well as their nearby ITC station, selling their harvests at the latter instead of in the traditional markets, where brokers collected high fees. A decade later, e-Choupal was a highly successful venture and attracted other private firms. Collectively, its impact was still slight, but every initiative that empowers local farmers to link up with larger markets signifies a gradual improvement.

African Transformations   The half-decade between the oil price slump, debt crisis, and disappearance of communism (1985–1991) was as challenging for sub-Saharan Africa as for India. The continent's GDP in the early 1990s was down by almost half from what it was in 1975 when all main social and economic indicators were at their peak. The decline of living conditions was particularly devastating in the health services, cut back by half in almost all countries, in spite of a steady increase in HIV/AIDS. Many countries expended more hard currency on their debt services than on education. With a doubling of the population at the absolute poverty level ($1.25 per day), sub-Saharan Africa became by far the poorest region in the world.

During this time, the urban population of sub-Saharan Africa increased to almost one-third of the total population, making it more numerous than in India but still smaller than in China, where nearly half of the population was urban. This urbanization process was an important factor in the political consequences of the crisis: Students, civil servants, and journalists became restless and demanded political reforms. Up until the early 1990s, almost everywhere state structures were patronage hierarchies: the civilian or military rulers in power provided cushy government jobs for the ethnic groups from which they hailed. Although all 54 African countries were officially "nations" with seats in the United Nations, none (except South Africa) was either a functionally constitutional or ethnically uniform nation. Urban dwellers, however, were less tied to ethnicity and more committed to constitutionalism. They felt little sympathy for autocratic rulers and their kin running the states into financial ruin and pushed for democratic reforms in the late 1990s and early 2000s.

Freedom, Justice, and Dignity. The end of apartheid in 1994 and the election of Nelson Mandela, seen here visiting his former prison cell, was an inspiring event in Africa and the world. South Africa is the richest and most industrialized country of Africa, with large mineral and agricultural resources. Nearly 80 percent of the population is black, speaking its own languages isiZulu and isiKhosa, but Afrikaans (a Dutch-originated language) remained the dominant media language, with English being only the fifth most spoken language. In spite of South Africa's relative wealth, years of apartheid have resulted in vast income disparities.

Unfortunately, the push for reforms had mixed results. On the one hand, while a majority of rulers in power prior to 1991 had exited office as a result of coups or assassinations, after 1991 they either resigned voluntarily or stepped down after losing elections. On the other hand, incumbents still won more often than not and honest elections were rare. Some regime changes were truly thrilling, notably the end of apartheid and the election of Nelson Mandela (b. 1918, president 1994–1999) in the Republic of South Africa; two cycles (2004 and 2008) of clean multiparty elections in Ghana; the first election of a female president, the Harvard-trained economist Ellen Johnson Sirleaf (b. 1938, in office beginning 2006) in Liberia; and the relatively clean Nigerian presidential elections of 2007 and 2011. African adherence to constitutional politics so painfully fraught in the past was now definitely coming of age.

Ethnic and Constitutional Nationalism   Unfortunately, the beginning of movement away from ethnic nationalism to broader constitutional nationalism was offset by plenty of violence and state instability. The Rwandan Tutsi genocide of 1994 continued on a lower but equally vicious scale in the neighboring Democratic Republic of Congo. This country suffered not only a new military revolution in 1997 but unending military challenges and lootings of mineral resources ever since. Successful coups d'état occurred in no less than eight African countries during the two decades between 1991 and 2010.

A particularly sad case was the political and economic implosion of Zimbabwe, following the expropriation of white farmers in 2000. Here, President Robert Mugabe (b. 1924), in power since overthrowing the white minority regime of Rhodesia (1980), became impatient with the slow process of legal land reform. Mugabe inherited a state whose tiny minority of white farmers controlled 70 percent of all farmland and whose highly productive, modern farms grew most of Zimbabwe's agricultural exports of coffee, tea, and tobacco. In 2000 Mugabe encouraged

A Black American Confronts Africa

"How can anyone talk about democracy
and constitutions and the rule of law
in places where paramilitary security
forces firebomb the offices of opposition
newspapers? Where entire villages get
burned down and thousands of people
are made homeless by competing political
loyalties? Where whole chunks of countries
are under the sway of armed guerrillas?
And where traditional belief runs so deep
that a politician can be arrested and
charged with casting magic spells over
poor villagers to force them to vote for
him?"

—Keith B. Richburg. *Out of America: A Black Man
Confronts Africa*, pp. 226–227. New York: Basic Books, 1997.

his followers to seize the vast majority of white farms in a violent occupation movement, with the effect that commercial agriculture broke down, the economy collapsed, and hyperinflation ravaged the country. The overall situation in Zimbabwe became so desperate that Mugabe was forced to accept his despised rival Morgan Tsvangirai (b. 1952) as prime minister in 2009 and return to a semblance of constitutionalism. Since then, the economy has begun to improve, with small-plot farmers producing beyond self-sufficiency again, even if overall production was still only one-third of what it was in 2000.

Another example was the corrupt election of 2007 in Kenya, resulting in 1,000 deaths during riots among ethnic groups. When order was reestablished, the two top opponents, incumbent President Mwai Kibaki (b. 1931) and challenger Raila Odinga (b. 1945), came together in a grudging compromise of shared power between them, the former filling the position as president and the latter in the newly created but constitutionally unsanctioned position of prime minister. Odinga, successful in transcending ethnic affiliation for a constitutionalist-nationalist presidential bid, had been widely seen as the winner; and the unrest after the fraud-ridden elections was a regrettable relapse into ethnic nationalism. To repair constitutionalism, it was necessary to make the prime-ministerial arrangement legal, a necessity which was incorporated into a wider constitutional reform. Accordingly, Kenyans adopted a new constitution in 2010, which created a senate in addition to the existing parliament and devolved power from the center to the counties while reverting to a pure presidential system. Endemic corruption, however, continued to accompany the efforts to return to stability (see Map 31.6).

In Ivory Coast, elections in 2010 similarly ended initially in an impasse. President-elect Alassane Ouattara (b. 1942) was able to take office only after a 5-month hiatus (November 2010–April 2011), during which his supporters attempted to depose his defeated predecessor, Laurent Gbagbo (b. 1945) [BAG-bow]. Gbagbo had refused to step down even though the electoral commission had declared Ouattara the winner. The one encouraging note in this continuing cycle of power grabs in the first decade of the 2000s was that there were "only" half as many illegal office seizures in Africa as in 1970–1991. Still, authoritarianism and military rule continued to endure.

Economic Recovery   Similarly spotty was the economic recovery, although it picked up in the early 2000s, mostly because of rising commodity prices. The main oil exporters (Nigeria, Angola, Chad, Sudan, Gabon, Cameroon, Equatorial New Guinea, and the two Republics of Congo) benefited from higher oil prices, as did the mining countries of South Africa, Zambia, both Congos, and Malawi with their diamonds, gold, copper, silver, zinc, lead, and rare metals. In a United Nations–sponsored scheme in 1998, "blood diamonds" mined to finance civil wars, as in Angola, Sierra Leone, Liberia, Ivory Coast, and both Congos, were subjected to certification so as to prevent future wars. (Diamonds mined in Zimbabwe were exempted since Zimbabwe's disintegration into a failed state was not considered to be the effect of a civil

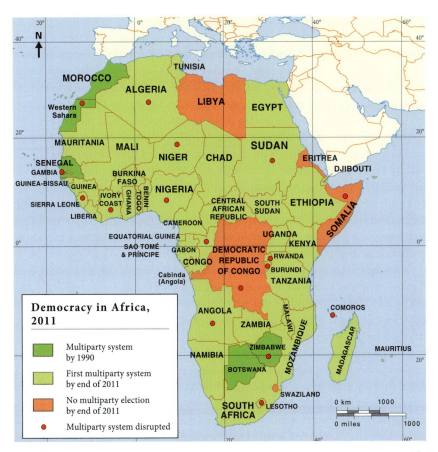

MAP **31.6 Democracy in Africa, 2011.**

war.) Apart from minerals, agricultural products, such as coffee, cotton, and fresh flowers for the European market, also regained significance in the early 2000s. The recession of 1990–2011 did not have a major impact, largely because of the arrival of China on the scene as a major buyer and investor. Optimism about a sustained recovery and modernity within reach was clearly visible on the continent.

Latin American Expansion   Elections after the scare of the financial meltdowns in the freewheeling 1990s produced more fiscally restrained, socially engaged governments in the large Latin American countries during the early 2000s. Orderly democratic transitions in Mexico, Brazil, Argentina, and Chile (the latter three with socially oriented governments) demonstrated that the unhappy years of military dictatorships in the 1980s had been left behind. In Mexico the long rule of the Institutional Revolutionary Party came to an end in 2000, with an orderly transition to less socially engaged Christian Democratic presidents in the following two elections. Either way, however, the continent enjoyed a sustained economic recovery.

Two extraconstitutional events in smaller Latin American countries, however, demonstrated that authoritarian temptations still survived. The first was an abortive uprising in 2002 of army units in Paraguay, allegedly instigated by a former commander outside the country and wanted for an earlier coup attempt. The second, in Honduras in 2009, was the forcible removal of the president, who intended to hold a referendum on his unconstitutional plan for reelection, even though forbidden by the Honduran constitutional court. More disruptive were continued efforts by revolutionary Marxists in Colombia to overthrow the government, even though their liberation movement, founded in 1964, declined in the early 2000s. In neighboring Venezuela, President Hugo Chávez (b. 1954), a former officer from a working-class background, was alone in mainland Latin America in his adherence to state socialism, encountering periodic middle-class resistance. Mexico, by contrast, deepened its democratic commitment but was severely tested by drug traffickers, organized as cartels for the shipping of drugs to markets in the United States. These cartels became increasingly violent in the course of the first decade of the 2000s, to the point where they infiltrated the police as well as the army and even interfered with elections. Central and South American governments, still reeling from the population explosion of the second half of the 1900s, were not yet rich enough to pay their civil servants well so that the latter could resist the narco-traffickers' bribes.

Although the business of drugs was a blight in Colombia, Mexico, and several Central American countries, the mainstream economy recovered impressively after the financial meltdowns of the 1990s. The countries continued to rely on exports of oil, minerals, and tropical agricultural goods. But industrialization, until the 1990s largely through foreign investments, stimulated state-run firms to become competitive and even private. In some cases, as with Brazilian Embraer commercial airplanes or the electronics and information technology industry of Guadalajara in Mexico, Latin American countries have become world competitors. All four large economies—Brazil, Mexico, Argentina, and Chile—exported more manufactured goods than commodities by 2008. Brazil, in fact, is a member of the "BRIC"—which also includes Russia, India, and China—countries that have attained advanced economic development since the 1990s. As increasingly important trade partners with China and India, these countries clearly demonstrated the features of scientific–industrial modernity by the second decade of the 2000s.

The Environmental Limits of Modernity

What we have defined in the last two parts of this book as *modernity*—the political systems marked by constitutional nationalism and ethnic nationalism and the economic systems propelled by science and industrialism—has now become not simply a regional or "Western" phenomenon but a global one. In the absence of the competing subpatterns of modernity—communism and supremacist nationalism—the systems of capitalism, consumerism, and democracy characterized by the United States, Canada, and Western Europe have increasingly become the ones to emulate. All new nations in the world either are industrializing or want to do so if they have the financial means. The principal obstacle for these nations is the debilitating poverty of the great majority of their inhabitants, who are still mired in either subsistence farming or marginal work in the shantytowns of sprawling cities. The poorest are unskilled and uneducated and, because of high infant mortality rates and the need for farm labor, still view large families as a necessity. Improved public health care is helping to raise life spans for the poorest people, but the combination of modern medicine and the desire for large families has caused a startling increase in the world population since the middle of the twentieth century (see Map 31.7).

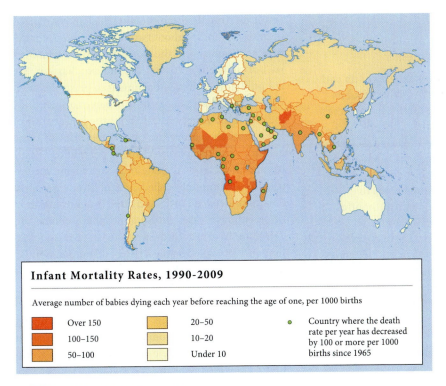

Infant Mortality Rates, 1990-2009

Average number of babies dying each year before reaching the age of one, per 1000 births

- Over 150
- 100–150
- 50–100
- 20–50
- 10–20
- Under 10
- Country where the death rate per year has decreased by 100 or more per 1000 births since 1965

MAP **31.7** Infant Mortality Rates, 1990–2009.

Demography and Job Creation   Even though the demographic increase is beginning to slow, there is no question that for the foreseeable future the manufacturing and service sectors of modern industry will not be able to offer enough employment to increase the affluence of the poor and significantly raise their rates of consumption. **Consumerism**, however, is what drives the economics of scientific–industrial modernity; thus, we are dealing with a vicious circle: Without consumers, industry cannot offer sufficient numbers of jobs and the poor cannot become consumers because they are jobless.

As with all vicious circles, this can be overcome only through gradual transformation on both sides of the equation: Scientists, industrialists, and businesspeople have to be innovative and offer new consumer products requiring new jobs; and the poor, through enhanced access to education, need to acquire the resources to motivate them to find their way into modernity. So far, this gradualism appears to be working, albeit slowly. Perhaps the most striking example is the victorious march of the cell phone across the world. In 2010 the world population reached 6.9 billion, the number of cell phones was 5 billion, and the number of computers was close to 1 billion. The e-Choupal example in India is still a drop in the bucket, but it demonstrates how electronics, the most recent industrial innovation, are beginning to make a difference.

Sustainability and Global Warming   The critical factor in this gradualism is modernity's long-term environmental sustainability. In 1800, there was only one country (Great Britain) embarking on industrialization; by 1918, there were about a dozen countries (Europe and Japan); and by 1945, about three dozen

Consumerism: The acquired habit to shop for goods and gadgets (often with built-in obsolescence) beyond the basic needs of food and shelter.

Pope John Paul II on Consumerism

"The historical experience of the West, for its part, shows that even if the Marxist analysis and its foundation of alienation are false, nevertheless alienation—and the loss of the authentic meaning of life—is a reality in Western societies too. This happens in consumerism, when people are ensnared in a web of false and superficial gratifications rather than being helped to experience their personhood in an authentic and concrete way. Alienation is found also in work, when it is organized so as to ensure maximum returns and profits with no concern whether the worker, through his own labor, grows or diminishes as a person, either through increased sharing in a genuinely supportive community or through increased isolation in a maze of relationships marked by destructive competitiveness and estrangement, in which he is considered only a means and not an end."

—Pope John Paul II. "On the Hundredth Anniversary of Rerum Novarum: Centesimus Annus." Encyclical letter of May 1, 1991. Washington, DC: Office for Publishing and Promotion Services, United States Catholic Conference, 1991.

countries (on three continents) had industrialized themselves. Today, about two-thirds of the 194 independent countries of the world are either industrialized or on the way toward full industrialization. We are only now, however, beginning to grasp the environmental consequences of this move to scientific–industrial modernity. Until about the last quarter of the twentieth century the carbon footprint of these countries had risen from 280 parts per million (ppm) of volume of carbon dioxide and other chemical compounds—commonly called "greenhouse gases"—to 330 ppm. Between 1975 and 2010 the concentration of greenhouse gases in the atmosphere climbed to 380 ppm. In other words, what had been a rise of 50 ppm in 175 years became a rise of 70 ppm in only 35 years (see Figure 31.1).

While there has been considerable debate over the last several decades on the nature and degree of global warming—whether it is a natural cyclical phenomenon or human-produced or even if it exists at all—there is a general scientific consensus that greenhouse gases are the main contributors to temperature increases on earth. Scientists generally assume that at current rates of greenhouse gas production the earth will reach a "tipping point" of 450 ppm that will have catastrophic consequences for the planet's climate before the middle of this century.

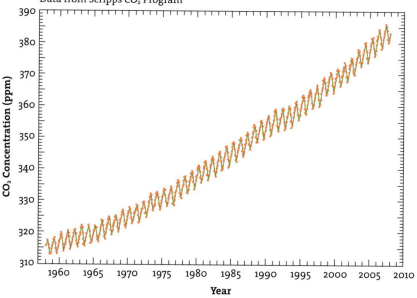

**Mauna Loa Observatory, Hawaii
Monthly Average Carbon Dioxide Concentration**
Data from Scripps CO_2 Program

Figure 31.1 Greenhouse Gas Emissions Since 1950.

What will happen when this tipping point is reached? If projections hold true, the polar ice caps and high mountain glaciers will have melted. Ocean levels, rising from the melted ice, will have submerged many islands and made inroads on the coasts of all continents. Widespread droughts and violent storms will regularly pound various parts of the earth, eroding by wind and flood what in many places had shortly before been fertile land. The world's tropical forests, already considerably reduced from timber harvesting and agricultural expansion, may well be wiped out, removing the most important agents for cleaning the atmosphere of greenhouse gases. Pollution and overfishing threaten the world's oceans and marine life. The consequence of these grim developments will likely be a severe reduction of the earth's arable land and fisheries needed for the production of food. In addition, biodiversity will be dramatically reduced, further decreasing food supplies (see Map 31.8).

The ultimate outcome of this prospective climate transformation will be much worse for the new countries with less wealth to cushion them than for the older ones that industrialized early and have the resources to adjust. The crushing irony of such projections, therefore, is that the nations which viewed their adaptation to modernity as their salvation may well find themselves among the condemned.

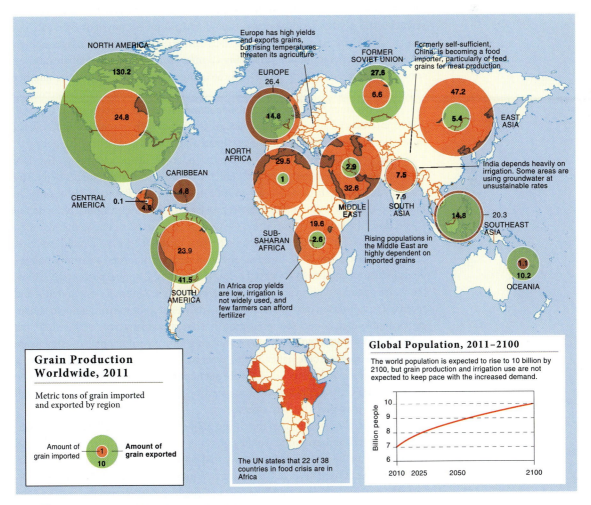

MAP **31.8** Grain Production and Irrigation Use Worldwide, 2011.

A Smoggy Future. China, the world's worst emitter of greenhouse gases, has large numbers of coal-fed power plants and factories which continue to belch carbon dioxide as well as toxic substances into the air, with little scrubbing or other devices to clean the emissions before they reach the atmosphere. Here, a power plant on the outskirts of Linfen in Shanxi Province southwest of Beijing fouls the environment in 2009.

Scientific and Political Debate   There is a general consensus among scientists that the warming trend in the world from greenhouse gases is real. Very few scientists still hold a skeptical view—though the prominent physicist Freeman Dyson (b. 1923), for example, remains a trenchant critic and advocate of technological fixes. The general public is gradually coming around to taking global warming seriously, though in Europe more than the United States. To judge by the number of people who watched the 2006 documentary *An Inconvenient Truth*, based on the book by the former American vice president and presidential candidate Al Gore (b. 1948), interest and agreement may have reached their own tipping point. But vocal minorities still vociferously denounce climate warming as a hoax or conspiracy.

So far, political response has been tepid and largely divided. Although two UN conferences have convened since 1992 and the environmental agreements of the 169 participating nations became binding in 2005 in the so-called Kyoto Protocol, only the European Union was on track to meet its provision mandating an annual reduction of 5.2 percent. The United States, during the George W. Bush presidency, refused to sign on to Kyoto and increased its emissions every year by about 1.5 percent until the onset of the recession in late 2007. Sweden, on the other hand, imposed a hefty carbon tax on its industries and has so far stayed below the critical 5.2 annual percentage. China, the worst offender with over half of all the world's greenhouse gases emitted—and seven of the world's ten most polluted cities—refuses to comply in order not to endanger its double-digit annual economic growth. Here, as in many parts of the world, the political risks of curtailing growth in favor of long-term environmental investment are seen as increasingly problematic. But the environmental risks associated with staying the course—such as drilling for oil—were put into stark relief in 2010 when a massive oil spill in the Gulf of Mexico wreaked catastrophic environmental damage, the full effects which have yet to be fully ascertained.

At present, the consensus is that if the 5.2 percent reduction rate were to continue after 2012 and everyone would sign on to reduction, the eventual decline in temperature by the middle of the twenty-first century would be 0.2 degree Fahrenheit below the current average temperature. Whether this would be sufficient to reverse the melting of polar ice and the onset of irregular weather patterns is debatable.

But if present trends continue, the projected temperature increase in 2050 will be more likely in the range of 3–4 degrees Fahrenheit—enough for the projections to indicate the catastrophic consequences we have mentioned, which are widely agreed to be irreversible.

Thus, global warming and its relationship to greenhouse gas emissions remains at present a problem in which some agreement has been achieved as to ends but very little as to means. Its relative imperceptibility makes it difficult to stir people to decisive action on a mass scale. Recessions and economic vitality, the demands of growth, and, at the most basic level, whether one has a job or not—these are all much more immediate problems than small temperature increases or even a few more droughts, storms, and floods, which always seem to hit others and not ourselves. It does seem safe to say, however, that the relationship of all aspects of the patterns of modernity to the environment will be a central problem of the coming decades.

Putting It All Together

The first decade of the twenty-first century witnessed the final transformation of the world from a centuries-old agrarian–urban pattern of life to a new scientific–industrial pattern. All of this was accomplished in the breathtakingly short span of 200 years. What had begun as a culturally specific, western European–pioneered transition, first from descriptive to mathematical science and then from agriculture to industry, had become ubiquitous. Everywhere in the world people have been adapting to a new role as individuals with well-defined "human rights," who aspire to be educated, find fulfilling jobs, become consumers, and achieve a materially secure life—in short, they are becoming *modern*.

The twentieth century also saw the original pattern of modernity split into three. World War I was a cataclysm that produced proponents of a first modernity, who sought to create competitive, capitalist, democratic societies; a second modernity, which sought to collapse power hierarchies and differences of wealth through equality in socialist-communist societies; and a third modernity, in which supremacist-nationalist societies sought to impose the will of allegedly superior races or ethnic groups through conquest (if not complete elimination) of inferior ones. Tremendous suffering and destruction accompanied the struggle among the proponents of these visions of modernity, and in a gradual process of elimination, it was the messiest and most unruly of the three forms of modernity—capitalist democracy—that survived.

Today, the faith in democracy that marked the exuberant beginnings of modernity at the end of the eighteenth century appears to be just as vigorous and unbounded in places far outside its birthplace. People—young, poor, educated, ambitious—continued to be its martyrs (Tiananmen Square, 1989; Tehran, 2009; Arab, Spring 2011) as well as its proud and triumphant flag bearers (Tunisia and Egypt, 2011).

Faith in the future of the environment at this point is a good deal more subdued, however. Here, the devil's bargain of materialism that accompanied the evolution of

Rooted in the Earth

"Yes, the only real hope of people today is probably a renewal of our certainty that we are rooted in the earth and, at the same time, the cosmos. This awareness endows us with the capacity for self-transcendence. Politicians at international forums may reiterate a thousand times that the basis of the new world order must be universal respect for human rights, but it will mean nothing as long as this imperative does not derive from the respect of the miracle of Being, the miracle of the universe, the miracle of nature, the miracle of our own existence. Only someone who submits to the authority of the universal order and of creation, who values the right to be a part of it and a participant in it, can genuinely value himself and his neighbors, and thus honor their rights as well."

—Vaclav Havel. "The Need for Transcendence in the Postmodern World." *The Futurist*, July–August 1995.

CHAPTER 31 CONCEPT MAP
The Human Impact on the Planet

1950

$ $ $
AFFLUENCE
World GDP 5.3 Trillion Dollars

POPULATION
2.5 Billion

TECHNOLOGY
412,000 Patents Per Year

2011

$ € ¥
AFFLUENCE
World GDP 55 Trillion Dollars

POPULATION
7 Billion

TECHNOLOGY
1.9 Million Patents Per Year

modernity continues to haunt us: On the one hand, it gave us the human right to a decent existence in material security; on the other hand, the means of achieving that security through exploitation of the earth's material resources has given us the nightmare prospect of an irreversibly changed nature that may allow for fewer and fewer of the comforts we currently enjoy (see Concept Map). The pattern of modernity and the scientific–industrial society that supports it will no doubt continue, but its future shape will be just as unknowable to us as the patterns of society in the past were to those living through them.

Review and Respond

1. What is the dollar regime? Explain its function in the world.

2. Discuss the two basic principles of the American military posture in the world since 1992.

3. What is IT? How has it transformed cultural interactions? Economic activity?

4. Which countries remained communist after 1991 and in which form?

5. What is globalization? Do the benefits of globalization outweigh its drawbacks? Are the effects of globalization the same throughout the world?

6. Explain the connection in the pattern of modernity between industrialization and consumerism.

7. Is the future of the world environment a grave problem, and if yes, why? Can a balance between the desire to preserve the environment and the need to save jobs be achieved?

▶ For additional resources, including maps, primary sources, visuals, and quizzes, please go to www.oup.com/us/vonsivers. Please see the Further Resources section at the back of the book for additional readings and suggested websites.

Thinking Through Patterns

▶ **How did the United States acquire its dominant economic position toward the end of the twentieth century? How did it accelerate the process of globalization?**

The United States acquired its dominant economic position through the dollar regime and by becoming the sinkhole for industrial exports from developing countries. In compensation for the latter, it expanded the reach of its financial system worldwide. The result was the globalization of the world economy.

Capitalist democracy became the universal model of modernity in part because growing middle classes in cities demanded liberalized markets where they could develop personal initiative and accumulate capital for business ventures. Socially conservative new middle classes became the engines that powered more than half a dozen successful industrialization processes throughout Asia, Latin America, and Africa.

▶ **What made capitalist democracy so attractive toward the end of the twentieth century that it became a generic model for many governments around the world to strive for?**

▶ **Which policies did China and India pursue so that they became the fastest industrializing countries in the early twenty-first century?**

China and India accelerated their industrialization by systematically encouraging the expansion of their middle classes as the engines of investment and innovation. China, however, did not allow the development of a multiparty system, fearing the chaos of popular agitation. India, by contrast, possessed constitutional-nationalist traditions reaching back to the nineteenth century that contained constraints against populism and allowed for peaceful democratic competition.

Perhaps more than any other innovation in the last 20 years, or even the last 200 years, the communications revolution has reshaped the way humans interact with each other. The exponential growth of networking boggles the mind. In 2006, 50 billion e-mails were sent. Just 4 years later, that number had risen to 300 billion. Because of this connectedness, politics, culture, and economic activity now mutate more rapidly--and with more volatility--than ever before.

▶ **How have information technology and social networking altered cultural, political, and economic interactions around the world?**

▶ **What is global warming, and why is it a source of grave concern for the future?**

Global warming is caused by the increase of carbon dioxide and other gases that accumulate in the upper atmosphere and trap the sun's heat in the lower atmosphere. Warming and cooling trends have occurred periodically since the end of the last Ice Age, and for a long time scientists labored to distinguish clearly between a temporary trend toward warmer temperatures and a permanent, greenhouse gas–caused trend toward a catastrophic tipping point that will permanently alter nature as we know it. Today, there is an overwhelming scientific consensus concerning the reality of global warming. But politicians and the general public are not yet entirely convinced that the efforts begun with the Kyoto Protocol of 2005 should be decisively intensified.

Further Resources

Chapter 1

Burroughs, William J. *Climate Change in Prehistory: The End of the Reign of Chaos*. Cambridge: Cambridge University Press, 2005. Very well-researched and up-to-date discussion of climate and human evolution.

Conard, Nicholas J. "Cultural Modernity: Consensus or Conundrum?" *Proceedings of the National Academy of Sciences of the United States of America* 107, no. 17 (2010): 6721–6722, http://www.pnas.org/content/107/17/7621.full. Thoughtful critique, with references, of the out-of-Africa hypothesis of anatomically and culturally modern humans by the archaeologist of Vogelherd in southwestern Germany.

Flood, Josephine. *Archaeology of the Dreamtime: The Story of Prehistoric Australia and Its People*. New Haven, CT: Yale University Press, 1989. Overview of the Australian archaeological record; short on discussion of Aboriginal Dreamtime and myths.

Johanson, Donald, and Kate Wong. *Lucy: The Quest for Human Origins*. New York: Three Rivers, 2009.

McBrearty, Sally, and Allison S. Brooks. "The Revolution that Wasn't: A New Interpretation of the Origin of Modern Human Behavior." *Journal of Human Evolution* 39 (2000): 453–463. Crucial, pioneering article in which the authors grounded anatomically and intellectually fully evolved H. sapiens in Africa.

Stringer, Chris, and Peter Andrews. *The Complete World of Human Evolution*. London: Thames and Hudson, 2005. Clearly organized and richly illustrated summary.

WEBSITES

http://iho.asu.edu/. Arizona State University, Institute of Human Origins, runs the popular but scholarly well-founded website Becoming Human (http://www.becominghuman.org/).

http://www.bradshawfoundation.com/. The Bradshaw Foundation has a large website on human evolution and rock art, with many images, and a link to Stephen Oppenheimer's, The Journey of Mankind—The Peopling of the World, an important overview of *Homo sapiens'* migrations.

Chapter 2

Assmann, Jan. *The Search for God in Ancient Egypt*. Ithaca, NY: Cornell University Press, 2001. Reflective investigation of the dimensions of Egyptian polytheism by a leading Egyptologist.

Bottéro, Jean. *Mesopotamia: Writing, Reasoning, and the Gods*. Chicago: University of Chicago Press, 1992. Classic intellectual history of ancient Mesopotamia.

Drews, Robert. *The End of the Bronze Age: Changes in Warfare and the Catastrophe ca. 1200 B.C.* Princeton, NJ: Princeton University Press, 1993. Closely argued essay on the destruction of Mycenaean culture and its consequences for the eastern Mediterranean.

Finkelstein, Israel. *The Archaeology of the Israelite Settlement*. Jerusalem: Israel Exploration Society, 1988. Authoritative presentation of the archaeology of the earliest period of Israelite social formation.

Kuhrt, Amélie. *The Ancient Near East, c. 3000–330 BCE*, 2 vols. London: Routledge, 1994. Comprehensive handbook surveying all regions of the Middle East.

Mithen, Steven. *After the Ice: A Global Human History, 20,000–5000 B.C.* Cambridge, MA: Harvard University Press, 2003. Engagingly written story of humans settling, becoming farmers, and founding villages and towns, as seen through the eyes of a modern time traveler.

Van de Mieroop, Marc. *The Ancient Mesopotamian City*. Oxford: Clarendon Press, 1997. Full examination of Mesopotamian urban institutions, including city assemblies.

WEBSITES

http://mesopotamia.lib.uchicago.edu/. "Ancient Mesopotamia," Website of the Oriental Institute, University of Chicago. A user-friendly portal to the world-renowned Mesopotamia collection of the Oriental Institute.

http://www.ancientegypt.co.uk/menu.html. "Ancient Egypt," website of the British Museum. Pictorial introduction, with short texts.

http://www.livius.org/babylonia.html. "Livius, Articles on Ancient History." A large collection of translated texts and references to philological articles, with portals on Mesopotamia, Egypt, Anatolia, and Greece.

Chapter 3

Bryant, Edwin. *The Quest for the Origins of Vedic Culture: The Indo-Aryan Migration Debate*. Oxford: Oxford University Press, 2001. A scholarly yet readable attempt to address the linguistic and archaeological evidence surrounding the thesis of Aryan migration versus the more recent theory of indigenous Vedic development.

Embree, Ainslee T., ed. *Sources of Indian Tradition*, vol. 1, 2nd ed. New York: Columbia University Press, 1988. Though the language is dated in places, this is still the most comprehensive sourcebook of Indian thought available. Recent additions on women and gender make it even more so. Sophisticated yet readable introductions, glosses, and commentary.

Eraly, Abraham. *Gem in the Lotus: The Seeding of Indian Civilization*. London: Weidenfeld & Nicholson, 2004. Readable, comprehensive survey of recent scholarship from prehistory to the reign of Ashoka during the Mauryan dynasty of the fourth and third centuries BCE. Emphasis on transitional period of sixth-century religious innovations, particularly Buddhism.

Fairservis, Walter A. *The Roots of Ancient India. The Archaeology of Early Indian Civilization*. New York: Macmillan, 1971. Classic, well-detailed, and well-documented treatment of Indian archaeology and history to 500 BCE. Particularly well done on the so-called Vedic dark ages to 800 BCE. More useful in general for experienced students.

Kenoyer, Jonathan Mark. *Ancient Cities of the Indus Valley Civilization*. New York: Oxford University Press, 1998. Comprehensive work by team leader of Harappan Research Project. Particularly good on Lothal.

Kinsley, David R. *Hinduism. A Cultural Perspective*. Englewood Cliffs, NJ: Prentice Hall, 1993. Short, highly accessible overview of the major traditions within the constellation of belief systems called by outsiders "Hinduism." Sound treatment of the formative Vedic and Upanishadic periods.

Possehl, Gregory L., ed. *Harappan Civilization: A Recent Perspective*, 2nd ed. New Delhi: Oxford University Press, 1993. Sound and extensive treatment of recent work and issues in Indus valley archaeology by one of the leading on-site researchers and a former student of Fairservis. Used to best advantage by experienced students.

Trautmann, Thomas. *India: Brief History of a Civilization*. New York: Oxford University Press, 2011. A succinct and lucid account of 4,000 years of Indian history, with particular emphasis on early developments.

Wolpert, Stanley. *A New History of India*, 5th ed. New York: Oxford University Press, 2004. Another extremely useful, readable, one-volume history from Neolithic times to the present. Excellent first work for serious students.

WEBSITES

www.columbia.edu/cu/lweb/indiv/southasia/cuvl/history.html. Run by Columbia University, this site contains links to "WWW.Virtual Library: Indian History"; "Regnal Chronologies"; "Internet Indian History Sourcebook"; and "Medical History of British India."

http://www.harappa.com. Contains a wealth of images of artifacts and other archaeological treasures from the Indus Valley.

Chapter 4

Chang, Kwang-chih. *The Archaeology of Ancient China*, 4th ed. New Haven, CT: Yale University Press, 1986. Sophisticated treatment of archaeology of Shang China. Prime exponent of the view of overlapping periods and territories for the Sandai period. Erudite, yet accessible for experienced students.

Ebrey, Patricia Buckley, ed. *Chinese Civilization: A Sourcebook*, 2nd ed. New York: Free Press, 1993. Wonderful supplement to the preceding volume. Some different classical sources and considerable material on women and social history. Time frame of this work extends to the modern era.

Keightly, David N., ed. *The Origins of Chinese Civilization*. Berkeley: University of California Press, 1983. Symposium volume on a variety of Sandai topics by leading scholars. Some exposure to early Chinese history and archaeology is necessary in order to best appreciate these essays.

Keightly, David N., ed. *Sources of Shang History: The Oracle-Bone Inscriptions of Bronze Age China*. Berkeley: University of California Press, 1978 (2nd ed. 1985). Benchmark in the authoritative interpretation and contextualization of ritual inscriptions. Some grounding in ancient Chinese history helpful.

Lowe, Michael, and Edward L. Shaughnessy, eds. *The Cambridge History of Ancient China. From the Origins of Civilization to 221 B.C.* Cambridge: Cambridge University Press, 1999. The opening volume of the Cambridge History of China series, this is the most complete multiessay volume on all aspects of recent Chinese ancient historical and archaeological work. The place to start for the serious student contemplating in-depth research.

Schirokauer, Conrad. *A Brief History of Chinese Civilization*. New York: Harcourt, Brace Jovanovich, 1991. Readable one-volume text on Chinese history up to the present. More thorough treatment of Sandai period than is generally the case with other one-volume texts.

Thorp, Robert L. *China in the Early Bronze Age: Shang Civilization*. Philadelphia: University of Pennsylvania Press, 2006. Comprehensive yet accessible survey of recent archaeological work on the period 2070–1046 BCE, including traditional Xia and Shang periods under the heading of China's "bronze age."

Wang, Aihe. *Cosmology and Political Culture in Early China*. Cambridge: Cambridge University Press, 2000. Part of the Cambridge Studies in Chinese History, Literature, and Institutions series. Wang argues that control of *cosmology*—how the world and universe operate—was a vital key to the wielding of power among the Shang and Zhou rulers. Recommended for serious students.

Watson, Burton, trans. *The Tso Chuan. Selections from China's Oldest Narrative History*. New York: Columbia University Press, 1989. Elegant translation by one of the most prolific of scholars working today. Excellent introduction to Zhou period and politics. Appropriate for beginning students, though more useful for those with some prior introduction to the period.

WEBSITES

http://lucian.uchicago.edu/blogs/earlychina/ssec/. This is the site of the Society for the Study of Early China. The site is for scholars, and the organization also publishes its own journal, *Early China*, as well as scholarly books.

www.ancientchina.co.uk. This site provides access to the British Museum's ancient Chinese collections and is highly useful for students seeking illustrations of assorted artifacts in a user-friendly environment.

Chapter 5

The Americas

Benson, Sonia, and Deborah J. Baker. *Early Civilizations in the Americas Reference Library*. Farmington Hills, MI: Gale UXL, 2009. Extensive three-volume encyclopedia available as a download or in hard copy. Contains an almanac of historical information and one of biographies and primary sources. Recommended for beginning and experienced students.

Bruhns, Karen Olsen, and Karen E. Stothert. *Women in Ancient America*. Norman: University of Oklahoma Press, 1999. A comprehensive account of women's roles in daily life, religion, politics, and war in foraging and farming as well as urban societies in the Americas.

Burger, Richard L. *Chavín and the Origins of Andean Civilization*. London: Thames and

Hudson, 1992. Though somewhat outdated with the work being done on Caral-Supé, this richly illustrated discussion of Andean civilization still has considerable import.

Fiedel, Stuart J., *Prehistory of the Americas*, 2nd ed. Cambridge: Cambridge University Press, 1992. Accessible, detailed survey of the archaeology of the Americas by a leading American scholar.

Thomas, David Hurst. *Exploring Native North America*. Oxford: Oxford University Press, 2000. Selected chapters are useful on the major early North American sites, particularly Adena and Hopewell.

Trigger, Bruce G., Wilcomb E. Washburn, Richard E. W. Adams, Murdo J. MacLeod, Frank Salomon, and Stuart B. Schwartz, eds. *Cambridge History of the Native Peoples of the Americas*, 3 vols. Cambridge: Cambridge University Press, 1996–2000. As with all of the Cambridge histories this is a highly useful set for beginner and accomplished scholar alike. Useful bibliographies with the article entries.

von Hagen, Adriana, and Craig Morris. *The Cities of the Ancient Andes*. Thames and Hudson, 1999. While more geared to later periods, still a useful overview, with illustrations, by specialists on Andean cultures.

Oceania

Bellwood, Peter S. *Man's Conquest of the Pacific: The Prehistory of Southeast Asia and Oceania*. New York: Oxford University Press, 1979. Along with Bellwood's later volume, *The Polynesians*, traces the migrations of succeeding groups through the archipelagoes of the Pacific. Balanced treatment of controversies over gradual versus episodic migrations of Lapita cultures. For advanced students.

Fagan, Brian M., ed. *The Oxford Companion to Archaeology*. New York: Oxford University Press, 1996. Perhaps the best place to start for students interested in archaeological and historical overviews of the peopling of the Pacific. Extensive coverage of Lapita culture and expansion into Micronesia and Polynesia.

Kirch, Patrick V., *The Lapita Peoples: Ancestors of the Oceanic World*. Cambridge, MA.: Blackwell, 1997. Basic introduction by one of the pioneers of Polynesian research.

WEBSITES

http://novaonline.nvcc.edu. Reputable site containing links to online lectures on subjects including "Civilizations in America," "History of the American Indians," "Mesoamerican Civilization," and "Ancient Meso-American Civilizations."

http://www.pbs.org/wayfinders/polynesian2.html. PBS series that examines the Polynesians and their migrations.

Chapter 6

Sub-Saharan Africa

Collins, Robert O., and James M. Burns. *A History of Sub-Saharan Africa*. Cambridge: Cambridge University Press, 2007. Balanced, well-informed textbook with nearly half of its pages on the pre-1450 period.

McIntosh, Roderick J. *Ancient Middle Niger: Urbanism and the Self-Organizing Landscape*. Cambridge: Cambridge University Press, 2005. Important revisionist work on the origins of urbanism and kingship in West Africa.

Vansina, Jan. *Paths in the Rainforests: Toward a History of Political Tradition in Equatorial Africa*. Madison: University of Wisconsin Press, 1990.

Magisterial presentation of the Bantu dispersal and village life in the rain forest.

Mesoamerica and the Andes

Aveni, Anthony F. *Skywatchers*, rev. ed. Austin: University of Texas Press, 2001. Classic study on astronomy and calendars of pre-Columbian Americans, including a discussion of the Nazca lines.

Evans, Susan Tobey. *Ancient Mexico and Central America: Archaeology and Culture History*. London: Thames and Hudson, 2004. Densely but clearly written and detailed, with many sidebars on special topics.

Grube, Nikolai, ed. *Maya: Divine Kings of the Rain Forest*. Cologne, Germany: Könemann, 2001. Lavishly illustrated book with short contributions by many hands.

Schele, Linda, and David Freidel. *A Forest of Kings: The Untold Story of the Ancient Maya*. New York: Quill-William Morrow, 1990. Classic study summarizing the results of the Maya glyph decipherment, by two pioneers.

WEBSITES

http://www-sul.stanford.edu/depts/ssrg/africa/history.html. Africa south of the Sahara: A large, resource-filled website based at Stanford University.

http://www.allempires.com/article/index.php?q=americas_history. Americas: World-historical site with interesting overviews of Pre-Columbian History.

http://www.wsu.edu/~dee/CIVAMRCA/MAYAS.HTM. Washington State University's comprehensive webpage for its studies on Civilizations in America, includes images and information about the Mayans, the Olmecs, the Aztecs, the Incas, and Chavin under headings such as religion, writings, economy, and society.

Chapter 7

Boatwright, Mary, Daniel J. Gargola, and Richard J. A. Talbert. *The Romans: From Village to Empire*. New York: Oxford University Press, 2004. Clearly written, comprehensive introduction to Roman history.

Boyce, Mary. *A History of Zoroastrianism*, vol. 1. *The Early Period*. Handbuch der Orientalistik, second impression, with corrections. Leiden, the Netherlands: E. J. Brill, 1989. Standard work by the leading scholar on the subject.

Briant, Pierre. *From Cyrus to Alexander: A History of the Persian Empire*. Warsaw, Poland: Eisenbrauns, 2000. Monumental work, the most detailed and authoritative study of the topic to date.

Burstein, Stanley M. "The Hellenistic Period in World History." American Historical Association Pamphlets, August 1997, http://www.historians.org/pubs/Free/BURSTEIN.HTM. Comprehensive overview of recent scholarship in Hellenistic studies.

Cameron, Averil. *The Mediterranean World in Late Antiquity, AD 395–600*. London: Routledge, 1993. New perspective on the strengths and weaknesses of the late empire.

Dignas, Beate, and Engelbert Winter. *Rome and Persia in Late Antiquity: Neighbours and Rivals*. Cambridge: Cambridge University Press, 2007. Detailed historical investigation of the rivalry between Rome and Persia.

Shaked, Shaul. *Dualism in Transformation: Varieties of Religion in Sasanian Iran*. London: School of Oriental and African Studies, 1994. Short history of the different religions in Sasanid Persia.

Smith, Mark S. *The Early History of God: Yahweh and the Other Deities in Ancient Israel*. San Francisco: Harper & Row, 1990. Very readable introduction to the problem of early monotheism among Israelites.

WEBSITES

http://www.perseus.tufts.edu/hopper/. Perseus Digital Library, probably the largest website on Greece and Rome, with immense resources, located at Tufts University.

http://darmc.harvard.edu/icb/icb.do?keyword=k40248&pageid=icb.page188868. The University of Harvard allows students to tailor searches in order to access specific geo-political and spatial cartographical representations of the Roman and medieval worlds.

http://www.ancientgreece.co.uk/menu.html. Open the door to the compelling world of Ancient Greece. The British Museum has compiled a collection of images and information on various aspects of Greek History such as the Acropolis, Athens, daily life, festivals and games, Sparta, war, and gods.

Chapter 8

Auboyer, Jeannine. *Daily Life in Ancient India*. London: Phoenix Press, 2002. Overview consisting of sections on social structures/religious principles; individual/collective existence; and royal and administrative existence. Multidisciplinary approach appropriate for most undergraduates.

Chakravarti, Uma. *The Social Dimensions of Early Buddhism*. New Delhi: Oxford University Press, 1987. Thorough analysis, with extensive glossary, of the influence of the north Indian economic transition to peasant market farming on the social milieu of early Buddhism.

Embree, Ainslee T. *Sources of Indian Tradition*, 2nd ed., 2 vols. New York: Columbia University Press, 1988. The latest edition contains a number of new selections useful for the study of social relations in addition to the older religious material. As with all of the works in this series, the level of writing is sophisticated, though accessible; the overviews are masterly; and the works are ably translated.

Keay, John. *India. A History*. New York: Grove Press, 2000. Lively, highly detailed narrative history, with a number of highly useful charts and genealogies of ruling houses. Sympathetic treatment of controversial matters.

Knott, Kim. *Hinduism: A Very Short Introduction*. New York: Oxford University Press, 1998. Sound, brief discussion of modern Hinduism and its formative influences. Asks provocative questions such as "What is a religion?" and "Is Hinduism something more than the Western conception of religion?"

Nikam, N. A., and Richard McKeon, eds. and trans. *The Edicts of Asoka*. Chicago: University of Chicago Press, 1959. Slim but useful volume for those interested in reading the entire collection of Ashoka's Pillar, Cave, and Rock Edicts. Short, accessible introduction.

Pelikan, Jaroslav, ed. *Buddhism: The Dhammapada*. Translated by John Ross Carter and Mahinda Palihawadana. Sacred Writings, vol. 6. New York: Quality Paperback Book Club, 1992. Erudite but accessible translation of one of the key texts in the Buddhist corpus. Students with some exposure to the introductory ideas of Buddhism will find it very useful in its step-by-step elucidation of a number of central concepts.

Willis, Michael. *The Archaeology of Hindu Ritual*. Cambridge: Cambridge University Press, 2009. Best utilized by experienced students, this book uses site archaeology, Sanskrit documents, and studies of ancient astronomy to plot the development of Hinduism under the Guptas and their use of it in statecraft as they created their vision of a universal empire.

Wolpert, Stanley. *A New History of India*, 6th ed. Oxford, New York: Oxford University Press, 2000. The standard introductory work to the long sweep of Indian history. Evenly divided between the period up to and including the Mughals and the modern era. Good coverage of geography, environment, as well as social and gender issues. Good select bibliography arranged by chapter; highly useful glossary of Indian terms.

WEBSITES

www.dli.ernet.in. Digital Library of India. This online resource, hosted by the Indian Institute of Science at Bangalore, contains primary and secondary sources for not only history but also culture, economics, literature, and a host of other subjects.

http://www.pbs.org/thestoryofindia/timeline/1/. Based on P.B.S.'s six part series on the history of India, this colorful website allows you to navigate your way along Ancient India's timeline.

Chapter 9

Ebrey, Patricia Buckley, ed. *Chinese Civilization: A Sourcebook,* 2nd ed. New York: Free Press, 1993. Varied primary sources with an accent on social history material: letters, diary excerpts, etc. Particularly strong on women's history sources.

Hinsch, Bret. *Women in Early Imperial China.* Lanham, MD: Rowman and Littlefield, 2002. Broad examination of the place and transition of the place of women during the crucial early Chinese dynasties.

Huang, Ray. *China: A Macro History.* Armonk, NY: M.E. Sharpe, 1997. Readable, entertaining, and highly useful one-volume history. Particularly good on the complex politics of the post-Han and Song-Yuan periods.

Lewis, Mark Edward. *The Early Chinese Empires: Qin and Han.* Cambridge, MA: Harvard University Press, 2007. Detailed exploration of the rise and adaptations of China's initial empires. Better for advanced students.

Loewe, Michael. *Everyday Life in Early Imperial China During the Han Period, 202 B.C.–A.D. 220.* New York: Harper and Row, 1968. Short, highly useful one-volume survey of Han social history by a preeminent scholar. Especially good on details of peasant and elite daily existence.

Snow, Philip. *The Star Raft: China's Encounter with Africa.* Ithaca, NY: Cornell University Press, 1988. Important, accessible study of the little known area of China's maritime trade with Africa from Han times to the epic fifteenth-century voyages of Zheng He and beyond.

WEBSITES

http://afe.easia.columbia.edu/cosmos/ort/daoism.htm. Defining "Daoism": A Complex History, looks at Daoism as a term, it's use and its practice in terms of morality, society, nature and the self.

http://www.metmuseum.org/explore/china_dawn/index.html. The journey begins with the end of the Han Empire and the arrival of the Xianbei and other Nomads. Packed with interactive features, this site has a fully indexed catalogue of artifacts, maps of historical China and the Silk Road, a chronology and glossary, and even allows you to explore ancient tombs.

http://newton.uor.edu/departments&programs/asianstudiesdept/. *East and Southeast Asia: An Annotated Directory of Internet Resources.* "China," "History." One of the most complete guides to web sites dealing with all manner of Chinese history and society.

Chapter 10

al-Khalili, Jim. *The House of Wisdom.* New York: Penguin, 2010. Elegant and accessible introduction to the golden age of Arabic science.

The Arabian Nights. Translated by Husain Haddawy. New York: Norton, 1990. Translation of the new edition by Muhsin Mahdi, which reconstitutes the original, thirteenth-century text.

Chaudhuri, K. N. *Trade and Civilization in the Indian Ocean.* Cambridge: Cambridge University Press, 1985. Discusses the historical evolution of the trade and its various aspects (sea route, ships, commodities, and capital investments).

Fryde, Edmund. *The Early Palaeologan Renaissance (1261–c. 1360).* Leiden, the Netherlands: Brill, 2000. Detailed presentation of the main philosophical and scientific figures of Byzantium after the recovery from the Latin interruption.

Laiou, Angeliki E., and Cécile Morrisson. *The Byzantine Economy.* Cambridge: Cambridge University Press, 2007. Comprehensive and well-researched study of ups and downs in the demography, productive capacity, and long-distance trade of Byzantium.

Lapidus, Ira. *Muslim Cities in the Later Middle Ages.* Cambridge: Cambridge University Press, 1984. Seminal work and still the only study of Muslim urban society, although it should be supplemented by Shlomo D. Goitein's monumental study of Jews, *A Mediterranean Society* (1967–1988).

Rippin, Andrew. *Muslims: Their Religious Beliefs and Practices,* 2nd ed. London: Routledge, 2001. One of the best and most accessible introductions to the basic beliefs and practices in Islam, based on the reevaluation of Islamic origins also presented in this chapter.

Tyerman, Christopher. *God's War: A New History of the Crusades.* Cambridge, MA: Belknap Press, 2006. Persuasive revisionist history by a leading Crusade historian.

Whittow, Mark. *The Making of Byzantium, 600–1025.* Berkeley: California University Press, 1996. Revisionist study of the Byzantine struggle for survival in the early years.

WEBSITES

Applied History Research Group, University of Calgary. *The Islamic World to 1600,* http://www.ucalgary.ca/applied_history/tutor/islam/. A multimedia tutorial by a university research group.

University Libraries, University of Washington. "History: Middle East." http://guides.lib.washington.edu/content.php?pid=63215&sid=466019. This website is a comprehensive research guide to primary and secondary sources for Middle Eastern history.

Asia Topics in World History. http://afe.easia.columbia.edu/mongols/. With a timeline spanning 1000-1500 C.E., The Mongols in World History delivers a concise and colorful history of the Mongol's impact on global history.

Chapter 11

Bartlett, Robert. *The Making of Europe: Conquest, Colonization and Cultural Change, 950–1350.* Princeton, NJ: Princeton University Press, 1993. Analyzes the expansion of Europe from a cultural perspective.

Brown, Peter. *The Rise of Western Christendom: Triumph and Diversity, A.D. 200–1000,* 2nd ed. Oxford: Wiley-Blackwell, 2003. Traces the development of Christian Europe from the perspective of the Church.

Grant, Edward. *The Foundation of Modern Science in the Middle Ages.* Cambridge: Cambridge University Press, 1996. Seminal study of the contributions of medieval science to the scientific revolution of the seventeenth century.

Lawrence, C. H. *Medieval Monasticism: Forms of Religious Life in Western Europe in the Middle Ages,* 2nd ed. New York: Longman, 1984. Thorough survey of the development of the Western monastic tradition.

McKitterick, Rosamond. *Charlemagne: The Formation of a European Identity.* Cambridge: Cambridge University Press, 2008. An examination of how Charlemagne's policies contributed to the idea of Europe.

Platt, Colin. *King Death: The Black Death and Its Aftermath in Late-Medieval England.* Toronto: University of Toronto Press, 1997. Riveting analysis of the effects of the Black Death on all aspects of society.

Reynolds, Susan. *Fiefs and Vassals: The Medieval Evidence Reinterpreted.* Oxford: Oxford University Press, 1994. Important revisionist study of medieval feudal institutions.

Riley-Smith, Jonathan, ed. *The Oxford Illustrated History of the Crusades.* New York: Oxford University Press, 1995. A very useful and readable history of the crusading movement.

WEBSITES

http://www.bc.edu/bc_org/avp/cas/fnart/arch/gothic_arch.html. Boston College's Digital Archive of Architecture has a quick index reference guide, which opens up links to images from both early and high Gothic architecture.

http://www.bl.uk/treasures/magnacarta/virtual_curator/vc9.html. An excellent website that makes available a digitized version of the Magna Carta. Audio files answer many FAQ's about the manuscript and its significance.

Chapter 12

DeBary, William T., ed. *Sources of Chinese Tradition*, vol. 1. New York: Columbia University Press, 1960. Excellent introduction to major Chinese philosophical schools. Extensive coverage of Buddhism and Neo-Confucianism with accessible, highly informative introductions to the documents themselves.

Ebrey, Patricia Buckley, ed. *Chinese Civilization: A Sourcebook*, 2nd ed. New York: Free Press, 1993. More varied than DeBary with more social history material: letters, diary excerpts, etc. Particularly strong on women's history sources.

Ebrey, Patricia Buckley, ed. *The Inner Quarters*. Berkeley and Los Angeles: University of California Press, 1993. Perhaps the best scholarly exploration of the roles of women in Song China.

Hansen, Valerie. *The Open Empire: A History of China to 1600*. New York: W. W. Norton, 2000. A fresh and accessible synthesis of pre-modern Chinese history.

Levathes, Louise. *When China Ruled the Seas*. London: Oxford University Press, 1994. Delightful coverage of the voyages of Zheng He from 1405 to 1433. Particularly good on the aftermath of the voyages.

Mujeeb, M. *The Indian Muslims*. London: Allen Unwin, 1967. Thorough historical overview from the eighth century to the twentieth. Especially useful on political and administrative systems of the early and middle periods of Muslim hegemony in north India.

Singh, Patwant. *The Sikhs*. London: John Murray, 1999. Readable popular history of the Sikh experience to the present by an adherent. Especially useful on the years from Guru Nanak to the changes of the early eighteenth century and the transition to a more militant faith.

WEBSITES

http://ngm.nationalgeographic.com/ngm/data/2001/07/01/sights_n_sounds/media.2.2.html. National Geographic traces the journey of Marco Polo from Venice to China to the court of Kublai Khan and back home to his arrest in Genoa.

www.afe.eastasia.columbia.edu. Part of Columbia University's websites on Asia for educators, this segment deals with basic information on China's golden age, 600–1600. Helpful to beginning students and teachers.

Chapter 13

General

Mann, Susan. *East Asia (China, Korea, Japan)*. Washington, DC: American Historical Association, 1999. The second volume in the Women's and Gender History in Global Perspective series. Short, informative volume with historiographic overviews and cross-cultural comparisons among the three title countries. Critical annotated bibliographies on the use of standard texts in integrating women and gender into Asian studies.

Murphey, Rhoads. *East Asia. A New History*. New York: Longman, 1997. One of the few one-volume histories that includes material on China, Japan, Korea, Vietnam, and southeast Asia. Written by a leading scholar of modern China and east Asia. Appropriate for beginning students but more useful for those with some background on the area.

Ramusack, Barbara N., and Sharon Sievers. *Women in Asia*. Bloomington: Indiana University Press, 1999. Part of the series Restoring Women to History. Far-ranging book divided into parts on "Women in South and Southeast Asia" and "Women in East Asia." Coverage of individual countries, extensive chronologies, valuable bibliographies. Most useful for advanced undergraduates.

Korea

DeBary, William T., ed. *Sources of Korean Tradition*, vol. 1. New York: Columbia University Press, 1997. The latest in the renowned Columbia series on the great traditions of east Asia. Perhaps the most complete body of accessible sources for undergraduates.

Korean Overseas Information Service. *A Handbook of Korea*. Seoul: KOIS, 1993. Wonderfully complete history, geography, guidebook, and sociology text. Excellent source, but students should keep in mind its provenance and treat some of its historical claims to uniqueness accordingly.

Japan

DeBary, William T., ed. *Sources of Japanese Tradition*, vol. 1. New York: Columbia University Press, 2002. Like the volume above on Korea, and the others of this series on India and China, the sources are well selected, the glossaries are sound, and the overviews of the material are masterful. As with the other east Asia volumes, the complexities of the various Buddhist schools are especially well drawn. As with the others in the series, students with some previous experience will derive the most benefit from this volume.

Reischauer, Edwin O., and Albert Craig. *Japan. Tradition and Transformation*. Boston: Houghton Mifflin, 1989, and subsequent editions. The companion volume to J. K. Fairbank's *China*, by the leading American scholar of and former US ambassador to Japan. A one-volume history but more emphasis on the modern than ancient periods.

Totman, Conrad. *A History of Japan*. Oxford: Blackwell, 2000. One of Blackwell's History of the World series. A larger, more balanced, and comprehensive history than the Reischauer volume. More than half of the material is on the pre-1867 period, with extensive coverage of social history and demographics.

Vietnam

Steinberg, Joel David, ed. *In Search of Southeast Asia*, rev. ed. Honolulu: University of Hawaii Press, 1987. Extensive coverage of Vietnam within the context of an area study of southeast Asia. Though weighted toward the modern period, very good coverage of agricultural and religious life in the opening chapters.

Taylor, Keith W. *The Birth of Vietnam*. Berkeley: University of California Press, 1983. Comprehensive, magisterial volume on early Vietnamese history and historical identity amid the long Chinese occupation. Best for students with some background in southeast Asian and Chinese history.

WEBSITES

http://www.britishmuseum.org/the_museum/departments/prints_and_drawings.aspx. Department of Prints and Drawings, British Museum. A comprehensive source for all manner of interests related to Asian studies.

http://digicol.library.wisc.edu/PAIR. Portal to Asian Internet Resources. Extensive list of Internet sources for Asian studies.

Chapter 14

Birmingham, David, and Phyllis M. Martin, eds. *History of Central Africa*, vol. 1. London: Longman, 1983. The first chapter, by Birmingham, provides an excellent summary of the history of Luba prior to 1450.

Crummey, David. *Land and Society in the Christian Kingdom of Ethiopia: From the Thirteenth to the Twentieth Century*. Urbana: University of Illinois Press, 2000. The first book in which the rich land records of the church have been used for a reconstruction of agriculture and land tenure.

Horton, Mark, and John Middleton. *The Swahili: The Social Landscape of a Mercantile Society*. Oxford: Blackwell, 2000. A study that gives full attention to the larger context of East Africa, in which the Swahilis flourished. Middleton is the author of another important study, *The World of the Swahili: An African Mercantile Civilization* (1992, Yale University Press).

Huffman, Thomas N. *Mapungubwe: Ancient African Civilization on the Limpopo*. Johannesburg, South Africa: Witwatersrand University

Press, 2005. Short but illuminating summary of the archaeological record by a leading South African expert, although his interpretation of Zimbabwe in an earlier work (*Snakes and Crocodiles*, 1996, Witwatersrand University Press) is controversial.

Levtzion, Nehemia. *Ancient Ghana and Mali*. New York: Africana Publishing, 1980. Originally published London: Methuen, 1973. Standard history of ancient Ghana, Mali, and Songhay based on a thorough knowledge of the Arabic sources; a revision by David Conrad, Paulo Farias, Roderick J. McIntosh, and Susan McIntosh has been announced but has yet to appear.

Robinson, David. *Muslim Societies in African History*. Cambridge: Cambridge University Press, 2004. Advertised as part of a series of new approaches, this book, nevertheless, presents a conventional view of Islam, albeit in its African context.

Trigger, Bruce. *History and Settlement in Lower Nubia*. Yale University Publications in Anthropology 69. New Haven, CT: Yale University Press, 1965. Chapter 9 is still the best overview of Nubian history, by a scholar with a broad understanding of early civilizations.

WEBSITES

http://www.metmuseum.org/toah/hd/ife/hd_ife.htm. "Heilbrunn Timeline of Art History," "Ife (from ca. 350 B.C.)." An excellent introductory we site can be found at the Metropolitan Museum of Art. It contains many links and presents clear overviews.

Hhttp://apollo5.bournemouth.ac.uk/africanlegacy/index.htm. "Recording West Africa's Visible Archaeology," "Sungbo's Eredu."

For a website by Patrick Darling, the principal archaeological investigator of the Nigerian earthworks see http://cohesion.rice.edu/Centers AndInst/SAFA/emplibrary/49_ch09.pdf for a copy of a 1998 article.

Chapter 15

Bruhns, Karen Olsen, and Karen E. Stothert. *Women in Ancient America*. Norman: University of Oklahoma Press, 1999. Comprehensive account of women's role in the daily life, religion, politics, and war in hunter–gatherer and agrarian–urban societies.

Brumfield, Elizabeth M., and Gary F. Feinman, eds. *The Aztec World*. New York: Abrams, 2008. Collection of expert short chapters on a variety of topics, richly illustrated.

Carrasco, Davíd. *Daily Life of the Aztecs: People of the Sun and Earth*. With Scott Sessions. Westport, CT: Greenwood Press, 1998. Clear, straightforward account by a specialist.

D'Altroy, Terence. *The Incas*. Malden, MA: Blackwell, 2002. Well-organized, comprehensive, and up to date overview.

Hassig, Ross. *War and Society in Ancient Mesoamerica*. Berkeley: University of California Press, 1992. Best study of the rising importance of militarism in Mesoamerican city-states, up to the Aztec Empire.

Malpass, Michael A. *Daily Life in the Inca Empire*, 2nd ed. Westport, CT: Greenwood Press, 2009. Clear, straightforward, and readable account of ordinary people's lives by a specialist.

WEBSITES

http://www.aztec-history.com/. Aztec-History.com. Introductory website, easily maneuverable, with links.

http://www.discover-peru.org/category/history/history-inca-culture-civilization/. Discover Peru. This website, by the Peru Cultural Society, provides basic articles on aspects of Inca culture.

Chapter 16

Agoston, Gábor. *Guns for the Sultan: Military Power and the Weapons Industry in the Ottoman Empire*. Cambridge: Cambridge University Press, 2005. Thorough study, which is based on newly accessible Ottoman archival materials and emphasizes the technological prowess of Ottoman gunsmiths.

Casale, Giancarlo. *The Ottoman Age of Exploration*. New York: Oxford University Press, 2010. Detailed correction, based on Ottoman and Portuguese archives, of the traditional characterization of the Ottoman Empire as a land-oriented power.

Casey, James. *Early Modern Spain: A Social History*. London: Routledge, 1999. Detailed, well-documented analysis of rural–urban and royal–nobility tensions.

Elliott, John Huxtable. *Spain, Europe, and the Wider World: 1500–1800*. New Haven, CT: Yale University Press, 2009. A comprehensive overview, particularly strong on culture during the 1500s.

Glete, Jan. *War and the State in Early Modern Europe: Spain, the Dutch Republic, and Sweden as Fiscal–Military States, 1500–1660*. London: Routledge, 2002. A complex but persuasive construction of the forerunner model to the absolute state. Unfortunately leaves out the Ottoman Empire.

Murphy, Rhoads. *Ottoman Warfare, 1500–1700*. New Brunswick, NJ: Rutgers University Press, 1999. Author presents a vivid picture of the Janissaries, their discipline, organization, campaigns, and voracious demands for salary increases.

Pamuk, Sevket. *A Monetary History of the Ottoman Empire*. Cambridge: Cambridge University Press, 2000. Superb analysis of Ottoman archival resources on the role and function of American silver in the money economy of the Ottomans.

Ruiz, Teofilo R. *Spanish Society, 1400–1600*. London: Longman, 2001. Richly detailed social studies rewarding anyone interested in changing class structures, rural–urban movement, and extension of the money market into the countryside.

Subrahmanyam, Sanjay. *The Career and Legend of Vasco da Gama*. Cambridge: Cambridge University Press, 1997. Focuses on the religious motivations in Vasco da Gama and the commercial impact of his journey to India.

WEBSITES

http://www.pbs.org/wgbh/pages/frontline/shows/apocalypse/. *Frontline*, "Apocalypse! The Evolution of Apocalyptic Belief and How It Shaped the Western World," PBS, 1995. The contribution by Bernard McGinn, University of Chicago, under the heading of "Apocalypticism," is of particular relevance for the understanding of Christopher Columbus viewing himself as a precursor of Christ's Second Coming.

http://www.pbs.org/empires/islam/timeline.html. Comprehensive and informative, PBS website on the Ottoman Empire examines the various facets of this Islamic culture such as scientific innovations, faith and its leaders.

Chapter 17

Black, Jeremy. *Kings, Nobles, and Commoners: States and Societies in Early Modern Europe—A Revisionist History*. London: Tauris, 2004. Available also electronically on ebrary; persuasive thesis, largely accepted by scholars, of a continuity of institutional practices in Europe across the sixteenth and seventeenth centuries, casting doubt on absolutism as being more than a theory.

Geanakoplos, Deno John. *Constantinople and the West: Essays on the Late Byzantine (Paleologan) and Italian Renaissances and the Byzantine and Roman Churches*. Madison: University of Wisconsin Press, 1989. Fundamental discussion of the extensive transfer of texts and scholars during the 1400s.

Jacob, Margaret C. *Scientific Culture and the Making of the Industrial West*. Oxford: Oxford University Press, 1997. Widely cited short book emphasizing the connections between New Science, scientific societies, and the steam engine.

Margolis, Howard. *It Started with Copernicus: How Turning the World Inside Out Led to the Scientific Revolution*. New York: McGraw-Hill, 2002. Important scholarly study of the connection between the discovery of the Americas and Copernicus' formulation of a sun-centered planetary system.

Nexon, Daniel H. *The Struggle for Power in Early Modern Europe: Religious Conflict, Dynastic Empires & International Change*. Princeton, NJ: Princeton University Press, 2009. Charles Tilly–inspired reevaluation of the changes occurring in sixteenth- and seventeenth-century Europe.

Rublack, Ulinka. *Reformation Europe*. Cambridge: Cambridge University Press, 2006. Cultural history approach to the effects of Luther and Calvin on western Christians.

Schiebinger, Londa. *The Mind Has No Sex? Women in the Origins of Modern Science*. Cambridge, MA: Harvard University Press, 1989. A pioneering study presenting biographies and summaries of scientific contributions. Discusses the importance of Marie Cunitz.

WEBSITES

http://www.earlymodernweb.org.uk/emr/ (http://sharonhoward.org/). "Early Modern Resources." Website with many links on the full range of institutional and cultural change.

http://galileo.rice.edu/index.html. Spanning every facet of the scientist's life, The Galileo Project is both informative and concise in its assessment of Galileo's life work and contribution to modernity and science.

http://kepler.nasa.gov/Mission/JohannesKepler/. NASA's website looks at the life and views of Johannes Kepler. It examines his discoveries, contemporaries and the events that shaped modern science.

Chapter 18

Alchon, Suzanne A. *A Pest in the Land: New World Epidemics in a Global Perspective*. Albuquerque: University of New Mexico Press, 2003. A broad overview, making medical history comprehensible.

Behringer, Wolfgang. *Witches and Witch-Hunts: A Global History*. Cambridge: Polity Press, 2004. A well-grounded overview of the phenomenon of the fear of witches, summarizing the scholarship of the past decades.

Bulmer-Thomas, Victor, John S. Coatsworth, and Roberto Cortés Conde, eds. *The Cambridge Economic History of Latin America*. Vol. 1, *The Colonial Era and the Short Nineteenth Century*. Cambridge: Cambridge University Press, 2006. Collection of specialized summary articles on aspects of Iberian colonialism.

Burkholder, Mark A., and Lyman L. Johnson. *Colonial Latin America*, 6th ed. Oxford: Oxford University Press, 2008. A well-established text, updated multiple times.

Ekberg, Carl J. *French Roots in the Illinois Country: The Mississippi Frontier in Colonial Times*. Urbana: University of Illinois Press, 1998. Detailed, deeply researched historical account.

Socolow, Susan M. *The Women of Latin America*. Cambridge: Cambridge University Press, 2000. Surveys the patriarchal order and the function of women within it.

Stein, Stanley J., and Barbara H. Stein. *Silver, Trade and War: Spain and America in the Making of Early Modern Europe*. Baltimore: Johns Hopkins University Press, 2000. Covers the significance of American silver reaching as far as China.

Taylor, Alan. *American Colonies*. London: Penguin, 2001. History of the English colonies in New England, written from a broad Atlantic perspective.

Wood, Michael. *Conquistadors*. Berkeley: University of California Press, 2000. Accessible, richly illustrated history of the conquest period.

WEBSITES

http://www.pbs.org/conquistadors/. Wonderful interactive website that allows you to track the journey's made by the Conquistadors such as Cortés, Pizzaro, Orellana, and Cabeza De Vaca. Learn more about their conquests in the Americas and the legacy they left behind them.

Chapter 19

Carney, Judith A. *Black Rice: The African Origins of Rice Cultivation in the Americas*. Cambridge, MA: Harvard University Press, 2001. Study which goes a long way toward correcting the stereotype that black slaves were unskilled laborers and carefully documents the transfer of rice-growing culture from West Africa to the Americas.

Dubois, Laurent, and Julius S. Scott. *Origins of the Black Atlantic: Rewriting Histories*. New York: Routledge, 2009. Book that focuses on Afri-

can slaves in the Americas as they had to arrange themselves in their new lives.

Gray, Richard, and David Birmingham, eds. *Pre-Colonial African Trade*. London: Oxford University Press, 1970. Collective work in which contributors emphasize the growth and intensification of trade in the centuries of 1500–1800.

Hall, Gwendolyn Midlo. *Slavery and African Ethnicities in the Americas: Restoring the Links*. Chapel Hill: University of North Carolina Press, 2005. Study that focuses on slaves in the Americas according to their regions of origin in Africa.

Heywood, Linda M., and John K. Thornton. *Central Africans, Atlantic Creoles, and the Foundation of the Americas*. Cambridge: Cambridge University Press, 2007. Pathbreaking investigation of the creation and role of Creole culture in Africa and the Americas.

Iliffe, John. *Africans: The History of a Continent*. Cambridge: Cambridge University Press, 1995. Standard historical summary by an established African historian.

Kriger, Colleen E. *Cloth in West African History*. Lanham, MD: Altamira, 2006. Detailed investigation of the sophisticated indigenous West African cloth industry.

Oliver, Roland, and Anthony Atmore. *Medieval Africa, 1250–1800*. Cambridge: Cambridge University Press, 2001. Revised and updated historical overview, divided into regions and providing detailed regional histories on the emerging kingdoms.

Thornton, John. *The Kongolese Saint Anthony: Dona Beatriz Kimpa Vita and the Antonian Movement, 1684–1706*. Cambridge: Cambridge University Press, 1998. Detailed biography of Dona Beatriz, from which the vignette at the beginning of the chapter is borrowed; includes a general overview of the history of Kongo during the civil war.

WEBSITES

http://www.slavevoyages.org/tast/index.faces. Atlantic Slave Trade Database. A large electronic website based at Emory University and sponsored by a number of American universities, presenting up-to-date demographic tables.

http://hitchcock.itc.virginia.edu/Slavery/index.php. Described as a visual record, the University of Virginia's website on the Atlantic Slave trade has an extensive collection of images relating to every aspect of slavery from maps of pre and post-colonial Africa, to the slave ships, life in colonies, punishments and emancipation.'

http://www.liverpoolmuseums.org.uk/ism/slavery/americas/abolition_americas.aspx. An amazing and well-planned website that offers students a comprehensive overview of the Atlantic Slave trade from life in Africa before slavery, to the horrific conditions on slave ships, right through to abolition. Students can also listen to extracts depicting the experiences of the enslaved, such as Olaudah Equiano.

www.britishmuseum.org/PDF/british_museum_benin_art.pdf. In addition to offering a brief historical backdrop to the art of the Benin Kingdom, The British Museum's PDF also depicts various artifacts taken by the British from the Royal Palace.

Chapter 20

Bernier, Francois. *Travels in the Mogul Empire, A.D. 1656–1668*. Translated by Archibald Constable. Delhi: S. Chand, 1968. One of many fascinating travel accounts by European diplomats, merchants, and missionaries.

Eaton, Richard M. *Essays on Islam and Indian History*. New York: Oxford University Press, 2002. A compendium of the new scholarly consensus on, among other things, the differences between the clerical view of Islamic observance and its actual impact in rural India. Contains both historiography and material on civilizational and cultural issues.

Nizami, Khaliq A. *Akbar and Religion*. Delhi: IAD, 1989. Extensive treatment of Akbar's evolving move toward devising his Din-i-Ilahi movement, by leading scholar of Indian religious and intellectual history.

Richards, John F. *The Mughal Empire*. Cambridge: Cambridge University Press, 1993.Comprehensive volume in the New Cambridge History of India. Sophisticated treatment; best suited to advanced students. Extensive glossary and useful bibliographic essay.

Schimmel, Annemarie. *The Empire of the Great Mughals: History, Art, and Culture*. London: Reaktion Books, 2004. Revised edition of a volume published in German in 2000. Lavish illustrations, wonderfully drawn portraits of key individuals, and extensive treatment of social, family, and gender relations at the Mughal court.

WEBSITES

http://www.aasianist.org/EAA and http://www.aasianist.org/links/index.htm. As with other Asian topics, two of the most reliable websites are sponsored by the Association for Asian Studies.

http://www.bbc.co.uk/religion/religions/islam/history/mughalempire_1.shtml. The Mughal Empire ruled most of India and Pakistan in the 16th and 17th centuries. Learn more about the religious divides and governance of Muslim Mughals in a country with a majority of Hindi populace.

http://www.pbs.org/treasuresoftheworld/taj_mahal/tlevel_1/t1_mughal.html. PBS's Treasure's of the World series looks at the Mughal dynasty and the art and architecture that flourished under the reign of Babur, Akbar and Shah Jahan. Links allow students to tour the Taj Mahal and Mughal gardens.

Chapter 21
China

DeBary, William T., and Irene Bloom. *Sources of Chinese Tradition*, vols. 1 and 2, 2nd ed. New York: Columbia University Press, 1999. Thoroughgoing update of classic sourcebook for Chinese literature and philosophy, with a considerable amount of social, family, and women's works now included.

Fairbank, John K., and Edwin O. Reischauer. *China: Tradition and Transformation*. Boston: Houghton Mifflin, 1989. A complete textbook on Chinese history, with the majority of the material geared toward the modern era. Emphasis on the "change within tradition" model of Chinese history.

Pomeranz, Kenneth. *The Great Divergence. China, Europe, and the Making of the Modern World Economy*. Princeton, NJ: Princeton University Press, 2001. Pathbreaking work mounting the strongest argument yet in favor of the balance of economic power remaining in east Asia until the Industrial Revolution was well under way.

Spence, Jonathan. *The Memory Palace of Matteo Ricci*. New York: Penguin, 1984. Highly original treatment of Ricci and the beginning of the Jesuit interlude in late Ming and early Qing China. Attempts to penetrate Ricci's world through the missionary's own memory techniques.

Japan

DeBary, William T., ed. *Sources of Japanese Tradition*, vols. 1 and 2. New York: Columbia University Press, 1964. The Tokugawa era spans volumes 1 and 2, with its inception and political and philosophical foundations thoroughly covered in volume 1, while the Shinto revival of national learning, the later Mito school, and various partisans of national unity in the face of foreign intrusion covered in the beginning of volume 2.

Duus, Peter. *Feudalism in Japan*, 3rd ed. New York: McGraw-Hill, 1993. Updated version of short, handy volume spanning all of Japanese history to 1867, with special emphasis on the shogunates. Good introduction on the uses and limitations of the term "feudalism" with reference to Japan within a comparative framework.

Gordon, Andrew. *A Modern History of Japan from Tokugawa Times to the Present*. New York: Oxford University Press, 2009. One of the few treatments of Japanese history that spans both the Tokugawa and the modern eras, rather than making the usual break in either 1853 or 1867/68. Both

the continuity of the past and the novelty of the new era are therefore juxtaposed and highlighted. Most useful for students with a background at least equivalent to that supplied by this text.

WEBSITES

http://ngm.nationalgeographic.com/ngm/0507/feature2/map.html. Track the voyages made by Zheng He to Southeast Asia, India, Arabia and Africa.

http://www.chinaculture.org/library/2008-02/09/content_22914.htm. With some illustrations, ChinaCulture.org offers a short biographical account of the reign of Kangxi, the fourth emperor of the Qing dynasty.

Chapter 22

Israel, Jonathan I. *A Revolution of the Mind: Radical Enlightenment and the Origins of Modern Democracy*. Princeton, NJ: Princeton University Press, 2010. Israel is a pioneer of the contemporary renewal of intellectual history, and his investigations of the Enlightenment tradition are pathbreaking.

Kaiser, Thomas E., and Dale K. Van Kley, eds. *From Deficit to Deluge: The Origins of the French Revolution*. Stanford, CA: Stanford University Press, 2011. Thoughtful reevaluation of the scholarly field that takes into account the latest interpretations.

Kitchen, Martin. *A History of Modern Germany: 1800 to the Present*. Hoboken, NJ: Wiley-Blackwell, 2011. A broadly conceived historical overview, ranging from politics and economics to culture.

Rakove, Jack. *Revolutionaries: A New History of the Invention of America*. Boston: Houghton Mifflin, 2010. A new narrative history focusing on the principal figures in the revolution.

Riall, Lucy. *Risorgimento: The History of Italy from Napoleon to Nation-State*. New York: Palgrave Macmillan, 2009. Historical summary, incorporating the research of the past half-century, presented in a clear overview.

Wood, Gordon S. *The American Revolution: A History*. New York: Modern Library, 2002. A short, readable summary reflective of many decades of revisionism in the discussion of the American Revolution.

WEBSITES

http://www.nationalismproject.org/what.htm. Nationalism Project. A large Website with links to bibliographies, essays, new books, and book reviews.

http://chnm.gmu.edu/revolution/. This website boasts 250 images, 350 text documents, 13 songs, 13 maps and a timeline all focused on the French Revolution.

Chapter 23

Allen, Robert C. *The British Industrial Revolution in Global Perspective*. Cambridge: Cambridge University Press, 2009. An in-depth analysis, well supported by economic data, of not only why the Industrial Revolution occurred first in Britain but also how new British technologies carried industrialism around the world.

Dublin, Thomas, ed. *Farm to Factory: Women's Letters, 1830–1860*. New York: Columbia University Press, 1981. A fascinating collection of correspondence written by women who describe their experiences in moving from rural areas of New England to urban centers in search of work in textile factories.

Headrick, Daniel R. *The Tools of Empire: Technology and European Imperialism in the Nineteenth Century*. Oxford: Oxford University Press, 1981. A fascinating and clearly written analysis of the connections between the development of new technologies and their role in European imperialism.

Hobsbawm, Eric. *The Age of Revolution: 1789–1848*. London: Vintage Books, 1996. A sophisticated analysis of the Industrial Revolution (one element of the "dual revolution," the other being the French Revolution) that examines the effects of industrialism on social and cultural developments from a Marxist perspective.

Mokyr, Joel. "Accounting for the Industrial Revolution." In *The Cambridge Economic History of Modern Britain*, vol. 1. Edited by Roderick Floud and Paul Johnson. Cambridge: Cambridge University Press, 2004. An analysis of the industrial movement that emphasizes its intellectual sources, embraced in the term "Industrial Enlightenment."

More, Charles. *Understanding the Industrial Revolution*. London: Routledge, 2000. A comprehensive explanation of how theories of economic growth account for the development of the industrial movement in Britain.

Stearns, Peter N. *The Industrial Revolution in World History*. Boulder: University of Colorado Press, 1993. A comprehensive study of the origin, spread, and influence of the European industrial revolution and its impact on globalization.

WEBSITES

http://www.thomasedison.org/. Remarkable website that explores Thomas Edison's impact on modernity through his innovations and inventions. This site also reproduces all of Edison's scientific sketches which are available to download as PDF files.

http://www.monetpainting.net/. A visually beautiful website which reproduces many of Monet's masterpieces, this site also includes an extensive biographical account of the famous painter's life and works. It also includes information about his wife Camille, his gardens at Giverny, and a chronology.

http://darwin-online.org.uk/. This website has reproduced, in full, the works of Charles Darwin. In addition to providing digitized facsimiles of his works, private papers and manuscripts it has also added a concise biographical account and numerous images of Darwin throughout his life.

http://www.alberteinstein.info/. Fantastic and informative website that houses digitized manuscripts of Einstein's work. Also includes a gallery of images.

Chapter 24

China

Cohen, Paul. *Discovering History in China*. New York: Columbia University Press, 1984.

Fairbank, John K., and Su-yu Teng. *China's Response to the West*. Cambridge, MA: Harvard University Press, 1954.

Kang, David C. *East Asia Before the West: Five Centuries of Trade and Tribute*. New York: Columbia University Press, 2010.

Spence, Jonathan D. *The Search for Modern China*. New York: Norton, 1990.

Spence, Jonathan D. *God's Chinese Son*. New York: Norton, 1996.

Japan

Beasley, W. G. *The Meiji Restoration*. Stanford, CA: Stanford University Press, 1972.

Reischauer, Edwin O., and Albert M. Craig. *Japan: Tradition and Transformation*. Boston: Houghton Mifflin, 1989.

Totman, Conrad. *Japan Before Perry*. Berkeley: University of California Press, 1981.

Totman, Conrad. *A History of Japan*. Oxford: Blackwell, 2000.

WEBSITES

http://www.asian-studies.org/eaa/. Education About Asia. This site provides the best online sources for modern Chinese and Japanese history.

http://www.asian-studies.org/. This is the site of the Association for Asian Studies, the home page of which has links to sources more suited to advanced term papers and seminar projects.

http://sinojapanesewar.com/. Packed with maps, photographs and movies depicting the conflict between Japan and China at the end of the 19th century, students can learn more about causes and consequences of the Sino-Japanese war.

Chapter 25

Gaudin, Corinne. *Ruling Peasants: Village and State in Later Imperial Russia*. DeKalb: Northern Illinois University Press, 2007. A close and sympathetic analysis of rural Russia.

Inalcik, Halil, and Donald Quataert, eds. *An Economic and Social History of the Ottoman Empire*. Vol. 2, *1600–1914*. Cambridge: Cambridge University Press, 1994. A pioneering work with contributions by leading Ottoman historians on rural structures, monetary developments, and industrialization efforts.

Kasaba, Resat, ed. *The Cambridge History of Turkey*. Vol. 5, *Turkey in the Modern World*. Cambridge: Cambridge University Press, 2008. An ambitious effort to assemble the leading authorities on the Ottoman Empire and provide a comprehensive overview.

Lieven, Dominic. *Empire: The Russian Empire and Its Rivals*. New Haven, CT: Yale University Press, 2002. Broad, comparative history of the Russian Empire, in the context of the Habsburg, Ottoman, and British Empires.

Nikitenko, Aleksandr. *Up from Serfdom: My Childhood and Youth in Russia, 1804–1824*. Translated by Helen Saltz Jacobson. New Haven, CT: Yale University Press, 2001. Touching autobiography summarized at the beginning of the chapter.

Poe, Marshall T. *Russia's Moment in World History*. Princeton, NJ: Princeton University Press, 2003. A superb scholarly overview of Russian history, written from a broad perspective and taking into account a good number of Western stereotypes about Russia, especially in the nineteenth century.

Quataert, Donald. *Manufacturing in the Ottoman Empire and Turkey, 1500–1950*. Albany: State University of New York Press, 1994. The author is still the leading American historian on workers and the early industrialization of the Ottoman Empire.

Riasanovsky, Nicholas, and Mark Steinberg. *A History of Russia*, 8th ed., 2 vols. New York: Oxford University Press, 2011. A comprehensive, fully revised history, ranging from politics and economics to literature and the arts.

Uyar, Mesut, and Edward J. Erickson. *A Military History of the Ottomans: From Osman to Atatürk*. Santa Barbara, CA: Praeger Security International, 2009. A detailed, well-documented history of the Ottoman Empire from the perspective of its imperial designs and military forces, by two military officers in academic positions.

WEBSITES

http://www.paradoxplace.com/Insights/Topkapi/Suleiman%20Topkapi%20Ottomans.htm. A basic web site on the Ottoman Empire at its height, with numerous illustrations.

http://www.russianlegacy.com/en/go_to/history/russian_empire.htm. Russian Legacy, a website devoted to the Russian Empire, organized as a timeline with links.

Chapter 26

Belich, James. *Replenishing the Earth: The Settler Revolution and the Rise of the Anglo-World, 1783–1939*. Oxford: Oxford University Press, 2009. Important study by an Australian historian, focusing on the British settler colonies.

Burbank, Jane, and Frederick Cooper. *Empires in World History: Power and Politics of Difference*. Princeton, NJ: Princeton University Press, 2010. Well-written and remarkably comprehensive comparative work.

Ferguson, Niall. *Empire: The Rise and Demise of the British World Order and the Lessons for Global Power*. New York: Perseus, 2002. Controversial but widely acknowledged analysis of the question of whether imperialism deserves its negative reputation.

Fieldhouse, David K. *Economics and Empire, 1830–1914*. New York: Macmillan, 1984. A classic, profoundly influential study of the economic costs of imperialism, coming to the conclusion that it was not cost-effective.

Hobsbawm, Eric. *The Age of Empire, 1875–1914*. New York: Vintage, 1989. Immensely well-informed investigation of the climactic period of the new imperialism at the end of the nineteenth century.

Jefferies, Matthew. *Contesting the German Empire, 1871–1918*. Malden, MA: Blackwell, 2008. Up-to-date summary of the German historical debate on the colonial period.

Ricklefs, Merle Calvin. *A History of Modern Indonesia Since c. 1200*, 3rd ed. Stanford, CA: Stanford University Press, 2001. Standard history with relevant chapters on Dutch imperialism and colonialism.

Singer, Barnett, John Langdon, and John W. Langdon. *Cultured Force: Makers and Defenders of the French Empire*. Madison: University of Wisconsin Press, 2004. Study of the principal (military) figures who helped create the French nineteenth-century empire.

WEBSITES

http://www.allempires.com/. All Empires Online History Community. Website dedicated to assembling materials on all historical empires, including those of the nineteenth century.

http://www.bbc.co.uk/history/british/empire_seapower/east_india_01.shtml. The BBC looks back at its colonial past and its presence in India. Topics include the East India Company, regional politics, company government and territorial expansion.

Chapter 27

Bulmer-Thomas, Victor. *The Economic History of Latin America Since Independence*, 2nd ed. Cambridge: Cambridge University Press, 2003. A highly analytical and sympathetic investigation of the Latin American export and self-sufficiency economies, calling into question the long dominant dependency theories of Latin America.

Burkholder, Mark, and Lyman Johnson. *Colonial Latin America*, 6th ed. New York: Oxford University Press, 2008. Overview, with focus on social and cultural history.

Dawson, Alexander. *Latin America Since Independence: A History with Primary Sources*. New York: Routledge, 2011. Selection of topics with documentary base; for the nineteenth century on the topics of the nation-state, caudillo politics, race, and the policy of growth through commodity exports.

Drake, Paul W. *Between Tyranny and Anarchy: A History of Democracy in Latin America*. Palo Alto, CA: Stanford University Press, 2009. The author traces the concepts of constitutionalism, autocracy, and voting rights since independence in clear and persuasive strokes.

Eakin, Marshall Craig. *The History of Latin America: Collision of Cultures*. New York: Palgrave Macmillan, 2007. A Brazilianist with a special eye on the ethnic and social class system of Latin America.

Meade, Teresa A. *A History of Modern Latin America: 1800 to the Present*. Chichester, UK: Wiley-Blackwell, 2010. The nineteenth-century portion of this study presents a comprehensive political, social, and economic survey, going more deeply into the details of many aspects discussed in this chapter.

Prados de la Escosura, Leandro. "The Economic Consequences of Independence in Latin America." In: *The Cambridge Economic History of Latin America*. Vol. 1, *The Colonial Era and the Short Nineteenth Century*. Edited by Victor Bulmer-Thomas, John H. Coatsworth, and Roberto Cortés Conde, pp. 463–504. Cambridge: Cambridge University Press, 2006. Superb analysis of the main factors characteristic for Latin America's special path toward economic development without industrialization.

Thurner, Mark, and Andrés Guerrero, eds. *After Spanish Rule: Postcolonial Predicaments of the Americas*. Durham, NC: Duke University Press, 2003. Collection of articles by different authors on the multiple cultural and social challenges which Latin Americans faced after independence.

Wasserman, Mark, and Cheryl English Martin. *Latin America and Its People*, 2nd ed. New York: Pearson Longman, 2007. Thematic approach, drawing general conclusions by comparing and contrasting the individual countries of Latin America.

WEBSITES

http://www.casahistoria.net/latin_american_history19.html. Casahistori.net. Website on nineteenth-century Latin America, for students.

http://www.suite101.com/latinamericanhistory. Suite101.com. A website featuring a long list of short essays on Latin American topics.

http://blpc.bl.uk/onlinegallery/features/spanishamericanind/homepage.html. The British Library looks back at the Spanish-American Independence from the movements origins and key figures to Bolívar's triumphant march. The site has also reproduced extracts from contemporary texts.

Chapter 28

Berend, Ivan T. *An Economic History of Twentieth-Century Europe: Economic Regimes from Laissez-Faire to Globalization*. Cambridge: Cambridge University Press, 2006. Includes Europe-wide, comparative chapters on laissez-faire and state-directed economies, including deficit spending.

Bose-Sugata, and Ayesha Jalal. *Modern South Asia: History, Culture, Political Economy*. New York: Routledge, 2004. Well-informed analyses by two of the foremost South Asia specialists.

Fritzsche, Peter. *Life and Death in the Third Reich*. Cambridge, MA: Harvard University Press, 2008. Book that seeks to understand the German nation's choice of arranging itself to Nazi rule.

Gelvin, James L. *The Modern Middle East: A History*, 3rd ed. Oxford: Oxford University Press, 2011. Contains chapters on Arab nationalism, British and French colonialism, as well as Turkey and Iran in the interwar period.

Gordon, Andrew. *A Modern History of Japan: From Tokugawa Times to the Present*, 2nd ed. Oxford: Oxford University Press, 2009. Detailed overview of Japan's interwar period in the middle chapters.

Grasso, June M., J. P. Corrin, and Michael Kort. *Modernization and Revolution in Modern China: From the Opium Wars to the Olympics*, 4th ed. Armonk, NY: M. E. Sharpe, 2009. General overview with a focus on modernization, in relation to the strong survival of tradition.

Lombardo, Paul A., ed. *A Century of Eugenics in America: From the Indiana Experiment to the Human Genome Era*. Bloomington: Indiana University Press, 2011. Study of a dark chapter in U.S. history.

Martel, Gordon, ed. *A Companion to Europe 1900–1945*. Malden, MA: Wiley-Blackwell, 2010. Collective work covering a large variety of cultural, social, and political European topics in the interwar period.

Meade, Teresa A. *A History of Modern Latin America: 1800 to the Present*. Malden, MA: Wiley-Routledge, 2010. Topical discussion of the major issues in Latin American history, with chapters on the first half of the twentieth century.

Snyder, Timothy. *Bloodlands: Europe Between Hitler and Stalin*. New York: Basic Books, 2010. Book that chronicles the horrific destruction left behind by these two dictators.

WEBSITES

http://www.ushistory.org/us/. Maintained by Independence Hall Association in Philadelphia, it contains many links to topics discussed in this chapter.

http://www.bbc.co.uk/history/worldwars/wwone/ and http://www.bbc.co.uk/history/worldwars/wwtwo/. The BBC's treatment of the causes, course and consequences for both WWI and WWII from an Allied position.

http://www.marxists.org/subject/bolsheviks/index.htm. A complete review of the Bolshevik party members including biographies and links to archives which contain their works.

http://www.ushmm.org/wlc/en/article.php?ModuleId=10005151. The U.S. Holocaust Memorial Museum looks back on one of the darkest times in western history. http://www.nanking-massacre.com/Home.html. A disturbing collection of pictures and articles tell the gruesome history of the Raping of Nanking.

Chapter 29

Baret, Roby Carol. *The Greater Middle East and the Cold War: US Foreign Policy Under Eisenhower and Kennedy*. London: Tauris, 2007. Thoroughly researched analysis of American policies in the Middle East, North Africa, and south Asia.

Birmingham, David. *Kwame Nkrumah: Father of African Nationalism*. Athens: University of Ohio Press, 1998. Short biography by a leading modern African historian.

Conniff, Michael L. *Populism in Latin America*. Tuscaloosa: University of Alabama Press, 1999. The author is a well-published scholar on modern Latin America.

Damrosch, David, David Lawrence Pike, Djelal Kadir, and Ursula K. Heise, eds. *The Longman Anthology of World Literature*. Vol. F, *The Twentieth Century*. New York: Longman/Pearson, 2008. A rich, diverse selection of texts. Alternatively, Norton published a similar, somewhat larger anthology of world literature in 2003.

De Witte, Ludo. *The Assassination of Lumumba*. Translated by Ann Wright and Renée Fenby. London: Verso, 2002. An admirably researched study of the machinations of the Belgian government in protecting its mining interests, with the connivance of CIA director Allen Dulles and President Dwight D. Eisenhower.

Goscha, Christopher E., and Christian F. Ostermann. *Connecting Histories: Decolonization and the Cold War in Southeast Asia, 1945–1962*. Stanford, CA: Stanford University Press, 2009.

Guha, Ramachandra. *India After Gandhi. A History of the World's Largest Democracy*. New York: Harper Collins, 2007. Highly readable, popular history with well-sketched biographical treatments of leading individuals, more obscure cultural figures, and ordinary people. Accessible to even beginning students.

Hasegawa, Tsuyoshi. *The Cold War in East Asia, 1945–1991*. Stanford, CA: Stanford University Press, 2011. A new summary, based on archival research by a leading Japanese historian teaching in the United States. New insights on the Soviet entry into WWII against Japan.

WEBSITES

http://www.economist.com/node/7218678. The Economist Magazine looks back on 'An Affair to Remember, the Suez Crisis and its implications.

http://www.nasa.gov/mission_pages/shuttle/sts1/gagarin_anniversary.html. In addition to providing information and video footage regarding Yuri Gagarin's orbit of the earth, students will also find information on America's space history.

http://www.newseum.org/berlinwall/. The Newseum's interactive website looks at what life was like on both sides of the Berlin Wall.

Chapter 30

Duara, Prasenjit. *Decolonization: Perspectives from Now and Then*. London: Routledge, 2004. A leading scholar of China and postcolonial studies edits essays in this offering in the Rewriting Histories series on the fall of the colonial empires by scholars such as Michael Adas and John Voll and activists and leaders such as Frantz Fanon and Kwame Nkrumah.

Fanon, Frantz. *The Wretched of the Earth*. New York: Grove Press, 1961. One of the most provocative and influential treatments of theoretical and practical issues surrounding decolonization. Fanon champions violence as an essential part of the decolonization process and advocates a modified Marxist approach that takes into consideration the nuances of race and the legacies of colonialism.

Frieden, Jeffrey. *Global Capitalism: Its Fall and Rise in the Twentieth Century*. New York: W. W. Norton, 2006. Despite the title, a comprehensive history of global networks from the days of mercantilism to the twenty-first century. Predominant emphasis on twentieth century; highly readable, though the material is best suited for the nonbeginning student.

Gaddis, John Lewis. *The Cold War: A New History*. New York: Penguin, 2005. Though criticized by some scholars for his pro-American positions, America's foremost historian of the Cold War produces here a vivid, at times counterintuitive, view of the Cold War and its global impact. Readable even for beginning students.

Gitlin, Todd. *The Sixties: Years of Hope, Days of Rage*, rev. ed. New York: Bantam, 1993. Lively, provocative account of this pivotal decade by the former radical, now sociologist. Especially effective at depicting the personalities of the pivotal period 1967–1969.

Liang Heng and Judith Shapiro. *After the Nightmare: A Survivor of the Cultural Revolution Reports on China Today*. New York: Knopf, 1986. Highly readable, poignant, first-person accounts of people's experiences during the trauma of China's Cultural Revolution by a former husband and wife team. Especially interesting because China was at the beginning of its Four Modernizations and the wounds of the Cultural Revolution were still fresh.

Smith, Bonnie. *Global Feminisms Since 1945*. London: Routledge, 2000. Part of the Rewriting Histories series, this work brings together under the editorship of Smith a host of essays by writers such as Sara Evans, Mary Ann Tetreault, and Miriam Ching Yoon Louie on feminism in Asia, Africa, Latin America, as well as Europe and the United States. Sections are thematically arranged under such topics as "Nation-building," "Sources of activism," "Women's liberation," and "New waves in the 1980s and 1990s." Comprehensive and readable, though some background in women's history is recommended.

WEBSITES

www.wilsoncenter.org/program/cold-war-international-history-project. Cold War International History Project of the Woodrow Wilson International Center for Scholars. Rich archival materials including collections on the end of the Cold War, Soviet invasion of Afghanistan, Cuban Missile Crisis, and Chinese foreign policy documents.

Codlibrary.org. College of DuPage Library. Typing in the "search" box "Research guide to 1960s websites" yields a wide-ranging set of relevant topics.

http://news.bbc.co.uk/onthisday/hi/dates/stories/june/4/newsid_2496000/2496277.stm. BBC's archive ON THIS DAY shows video footage from the Tiananmen Square massacre in 1989.

Chapter 31

Béja, Jean-Philippe, ed. *The Impact of China's 1989 Tiananmen Massacre*. New York: Routledge, 2011. Highly diverse contributions on this watershed event and the devastating effect it had on middle-class self-evaluation.

Chau, Adam Yuet, ed. *Religion in Contemporary China*. New York: Routledge, 2011. Collection of fascinating chapters on the revival of Daoist, Confucian, and Buddhist traditions and their adaption to middle-class modernity, with their proponents operating often in a gray zone between official recognition and suppression.

Daniels, Robert V. *The Rise and Fall of Communism in the Soviet Union*. New Haven, CT: Yale University Press, 2010. A magisterial summary of the communist period by a specialist.

Dillon, Michael. *Contemporary China: An Introduction*. New York: Routledge, 2009. Concise yet quite specific overview of the economy, society, and politics of the country.

Eichengreen, Barry. *Exorbitant Privilege: The Rise and Fall of the Dollar and the Future of the Monetary System*. New York: Oxford University Press, 2011. The author is an academic specialist on US monetary policies, writing in an accessible style and presenting a fascinating picture of the role of something as prosaic as greenbacks.

Meade, Teresa A. *A History of Modern Latin America: 1800 to the Present*. Malden, MA: Wiley-Blackwell, 2010. The book is an excellent, comprehensive analysis and has a strong final chapter on recent Latin America.

Saxonberg, Steven. *The Fall: A Comparative Study of the End of Communism in Czechoslovakia, East Germany, Hungary, and Poland*. Amsterdam: Harwood Academic, 2001. A well-informed overview of the different trajectories by an academic teaching in Prague.

Speth, James Gustav. *The Bridge at the Edge of the World: Capitalism, the Environment, and Crossing from Crisis to Sustainability*. New Haven, CT: Yale University Press, 2008. A strong plea to change our capitalist system.

Swanimathan, Jayshankar M. *Indian Economic Superpower: Fact or Fiction?* Singapore: World Scientific Publishing, 2009. A thoughtful evaluation of the pros and cons, in concise overviews.

Wapner, Kevin. *Living through the End of Nature: The Future of American Environmentalism*. Cambridge, MA: MIT Press, 2010. A specialist's look at the vast transformation of nature which is taking place according to the best evidence science can marshal.

WEBSITES

http://sierraclub.org/. Balanced and informative environmental websites.

http://www.bbc.co.uk/history/worldwars/wwone/yugoslavia_01.shtml#four. Tim Judah traces the destruction and violence which led to mass genocide in the conflict known as the Yugoslav Wars.

http://www.epa.gov/climatechange/. The U.S. Environmental Protection Agency's website reviews the threat to the world's climate and the implications of consistent abuse. The site also looks at various initiatives to help reverse some of the damage already done.

http://www.bbc.co.uk/news/world-africa-12305154. The BBC News looks back at the life and career of Nelson Mandela.

Credits and Notes

Credits

Chapter 1: pg. 4–5 © Christoph Hormann; pg. 8 Morton Beebe / Corbis; pg. 12 (top left) akg-images / CDA / Guillemot; pg. 12 (top right) akg-images / CDA / Guillemot; pg. 12 (bottom) National Museum of Tanzania, Dar es Salaam, (c) 1985 David L. Brill; pg. 16 © Kenneth Garrett Photography; pg. 20 Photograph by Chris O'Connell, Bradshaw Foundation, Geneva; pg. 22 (left) © ALEX GRIMM / Reuters / Corbis; pg. 22 (middle) Lion-man", statuette carved of mammouth-tusk, H 296 mm. Site: Hohlenstein-Stadel-cave, community. Asselfingen, Baden-Württemberg, Germany. Upper Paleolithic period (Aurignacien), approx. 32 000 BP. Inv. Ulmer Museum Prä Slg. Wetzel Ho-St. 39 / 88.1. Photo Thomas Stephan, © Ulmer Museum; pg. 22 (right) Foto: Hilde Jensen, copyright University Tübingen; pg. 23 (top) © Walter Geiersperger / Corbis; pg. 23 (bottom) © Charles and Josette Lenars / Corbis; pg. 24 Illustrations used with permission of Michel Lorblanchet and Éditions Sud Ouest; pg. 26 (top) Francesco d'Errico; pg. 26 (bottom) Photo Pierre-Jean Texier; pg. 31 AP Photo / Perfect Image, James Chatters, HO

Chapter 2: pg. 34–35 The Trustees of The British Museum / Art Resource, NY; pg. 39 Courtesy of the Peabody Museum of Archaeology and Ethnology, Harvard University, 61-23-60 / N10296.0 (digital file #98790058); pg. 43 adapted from Gianni Tortoli / Photo Researchers, Inc; pg. 45 Erich Lessing / Art Resource, N.Y.; pg. 48 Réunion des Musées Nationaux / Art Resource, NY; pg. 50 © Copyright Alfred Molon; pg. 52 Nimatallah / Art Resource, NY; pg 55. © Gérard Degeorge / CORBIS; pg. 56 Werner Forman / Art Resource, NY; pg. 59 Réunion des Musées Nationaux / Art Resource, NY; pg. 64 © Nathan Benn / Alamy; pg. 66 (left) akg-images / John Hios; pg. 66 (right) Marie Mauzy / Art Resource, NY.

Chapter 3: pg. 74–75 © DeA Picture Library / Art Resource, NY; pg. 77 (left) © Diego Lezama Orezzoli / CORBIS; pg. 77 (right) © Doranne Jacobson; pg. 78 Photo courtesy of National Museum of Pakistan, Karachi; pg. 79 © Harappa; pg.80© Harappa; pg. 84 V&A Images, London / Art Resource, NY; pg. 87 bpk, Berlin / Museum fuer Asiatische Kunst, Staatliche Museen / Iris Papadopoulos / Art Resource, NY; pg. 91 Firmin Didot, ~ 1810, Copyright: ImagesofAsia.com; pg. 93 (top left) © Doranne Jacobson; pg. 93 (top right) © Doranne Jacobson; pg. 93 (bottom) © Doranne Jacobson.

Chapter 4: pg. 98–99 © Xiaoyang Liu / Corbis; pg. 104 (top) Photo ChinaStock; pg. 104 (bottom) Photo ChinaStock; pg. 105 (top) Photo ChinaStock; pg. 105 (bottom) Photo ChinaStock; pg. 110 (top) V&A Images, London / Art Resource, NY; pg. 110 (bottom) photo by Gary Lee Todd; pg. 111 photo by Gary Lee Todd; pg. 118 Photo ChinaStock; pg. 120 Photo ChinaStock; pg. 121 (top) © Asian Art & Archaeology, Inc. / CORBIS; pg. 121 (bottom) The Art Archive / Museo Nazionale d'Arte Orientale Rome / Gianni Dagli Orti.

Chapter 5: pg. 128–129 ERNESTO BENAVIDES / AFP / Getty Images / Newscom; pg. 137 (top) © Ricardo Azoury; pg. 137 (bottom) © David Muench / CORBIS; pg. 139 National Geographic; pg. 140 © Sean Sprague / The Image Works; pg. 144 © Charles & Josette Lenars / CORBIS; pg. 145 The Metropolitan Museum of Art / Art Resource, NY; pg. 146 (top) © Charles & Josette Lenars / CORBIS; pg. 146 (bottom) akg-images / Bildarchiv Steffens; pg. 148 Science © 2006; pg. 152 © Caroline Penn / Impact / HIP / The Image Works; pg. 153 © ImageSpan.

Chapter 6: pg. 169 Werner Forman / Art Resource, NY; pg. 171 (top) Roderick J. McIntosh; pg. 171 (bottom) Courtesy Susan McIntosh; pg. 175 Werner Forman / Art Resource, NY; pg. 179 Richard Maschmeyer; pg. 182 bpk, Berlin / Ethnologisches Museum, Staatliche Museen / Art Resource, NY; pg. 184 Photograph K2803© Justin Kerr; pg. 185 Erich Lessing / Art Resource, NY; pg. 188 DEA / G. DAGLI ORTI; pg. 189 © Gianni Dagli Orti / CORBIS; pg. 191 (top) / akg / Bildarchiv Steffens; pg. 191 (bottom left) Bildarchiv Steffens. Henri Stierlin; pg. 191 (bottom right) © Keren Su / CORBIS.

Chapter 7: pg. 196–197 Vanni / Art Resource, NY; pg. 202 SEF / Art Resource, NY; pg. 205 Louis and Nancy Hatch Dupree Collection, Williams Afghan Media Project Archive; pg. 209 Vanni / Art Resource, NY; pg. 214 Scala / Art Resource, NY; pg. 220 © Wolfgang Kaehler / Corbis; pg. 224 (top) Photo © Zev Radovan; pg. 224 (middle) Photo © Zev Radovan; pg. 224 (bottom) Photo © Zev Radovan; pg. 228 akg-images / Gerard Degeorge; pg. 230 Image copyright © The Metropolitan Museum of Art / Art Resource, NY; pg. 232 (top) Erich Lessing / Art Resource, NY; pg. 232 (bottom) Scala / Art Resource, NY.

Chapter 8: pg. 236–237 Courtesy of the Library of Congress; pg. 243 Borromeo / Art Resource, NY; pg. 244 (top) Image copyright © The Metropolitan Museum of Art / Art Resource, NY; pg. 244 (bottom) © Clive Friend; pg. 247 © Lindsay Hebberd / CORBIS; pg. 249 R. u. S. / akg-images / A.F.Kersting / ; pg. 252 (top) akg-images / A.F.Kersting / ; pg. 252 (bottom) Borromeo / Art Resource, NY; pg. 255 Image copyright © The Metropolitan Museum of Art; pg. 258 (top) Bruno Morandi / Getty Images; pg. 258 (bottom) © The Trustees of the British Museum; pg. 263 (left) Image copyright © The Metropolitan Museum of Art / Art Resource, NY; pg. 263 (right) Image copyright © The Metropolitan Museum of Art / Art Resource, NY.

Chapter 9: pg. 268–269 © The Trustees of the British Museum; pg. 273 © Glow Asia RF / Alamy; pg. 288 akg-images / Laurent Lecat / ; pg. 279 HIP / Art Resource, NY; pg. 282 photo by Gary Lee Todd; pg. 285 Courtesy of ChinaStock; pg. 287 (all) Courtesy of ChinaStock; pg. 293 Courtesy of the Museum of Fine Arts, Boston. Francis Bartlett Donation of 1912; pg. 294 (top) Image copyright © The Metropolitan Museum of Art / Art Resource, NY; pg 294 (bottom) Marilyn Shea, Ph.D. University of Maine at Farmington.

Chapter 10: pg. 300–301 Library of Congress; pg. 305 © Kazuyoshi Nomachi / Corbis; pg. 307 The Trustees of the British Museum / Art Resource, NY; pg. 310 (right) ALIMDI.NET / Fabian von Poser; pg. 310 (left) bpk, Berlin / Art Resource, NY; pg. 314 (right) © Jon Hicks / Corbis; pg. 314 (left) © Bruno Morandi / SOPA / Corbis; pg. 316 © Steven Vidler / Eurasia Press / Corbis; pg. 321 (left) bpk, Berlin / Staatsbibliothek zu Berlin, Stiftung Preussischer Kulturbesitz, Berlin, Germany / Ruth Schacht / Art Resource, NY; pg. 321 (right) bpk, Berlin / Staatsbibliothek zu Berlin, Stiftung Preussischer Kulturbesitz, Berlin, Germany / Ruth Schacht / Art Resource, NY; pg. 322 © British Library Board. All Rights Reserved; pg. 323 Scala / White Images / Art Resource, NY; pg. 326 bpk, Berlin / Bibliotheque Nationale / Gérard Le Gall / Art Resource, NY; pg. 327 With kind permission of the University of Edinburgh; pg. 330 The Metropolitan Museum of Art / Art Resource, NY; pg. 331 The Metropolitan Museum of Art / Art Resource, NY; pg. 333 Giraudon; pg. 334 V&A Images, London / Art Resource, NY.

Chapter 11: pg. 338–339 Erich Lessing / Art Resource, NY; pg. 344 bpk, Berlin / Cathedral (Palatine Chapel), Aachen, Germany / Stefan

pg. 650 Werner Forman / Art Resource, NY; pg. 652 The Metropolitan Museum of Art / Art Resource, NY; pg. 653 Art Resource; pg. 657 HIP / Art Resource, NY; pg. 661 Art Resource; pg. 664 Bristol Docks and Quay, c.1760 (oil on canvas), English School, (18th century) / © Bristol City Museum and Art Gallery, UK / The Bridgeman Art Library International; pg. 665 © Michael Graham-Stewart; pg. 667 Abby Aldrich Rockefeller Fold Art Museum, The colonial Williamsburg Foundation, Williamsburg, Va; pg. 668 © Robert Holmes / CORBIS; pg. 669 Collection of Herbert M. and Shelley Cole. Photo by Don Cole; pg. 670 (top) Archives Charmet; pg. 670 (bottom) Courtesy of the Library of Congress.

Chapter 20: pg. 674–675 © dbimages / Alamy; pg. 678 (c) The British Library Board, J. 1,2; pg. 679 The Art Archive / Victoria and Albert Museum London / V&A Images; pg. 681 (top) Erich Lessing / Art Resource, NY; pg. 681 (bottom left) Werner Forman / Art Resource, NY; pg. 681 (bottom right) Image copyright © The Metropolitan Museum of Art / Art Resource, NY; pg. 683 (top) Getty Images; pg. 683 (bottom) © Arthur Thévenart / CORBIS; pg. 684 Courtesy of The Chester Beatty Library; pg. 685 The San Diego Museum of Art, Edwin Binney 3rd Collection. 1990.293; pg. 692 Rijksmuseum, Amsterdam; pg. 693 CBL In 03.54 Akbar (r.1556–1605) Receives Gifts from the Ambassadors of Badakhshan, from the 'Akbarnama', c.1605 (gouache on paper), Indian School, (17th century) / © The Trustees of the Chester Beatty Library, Dublin / The Bridgeman Art Library International; pg. 694 The Art Archive / Bodleian Library Oxford / shelf mark MS Pers d43 folio 89v; pg. 697 2009 Museum Associates / LACMA / Art Resource, NY; pg. 701 © Historical Picture Archive / CORBIS; pg. 704 Photograph © 2011 Museum of Fine Arts, Boston.

Chapter 21: pg. 708–709 John C Weber Collection. Photo: John Bigelow Taylor; pg. 714 The Metropolitan Museum of Art / Art Resource, NY; pg. 715 The Metropolitan Museum of Art / Art Resource, NY; pg. 716 Courtesy of the Library of Congress; pg. 717 © Hulton-Deutsch Collection / CORBIS; pg. 719 © CHINASTOCK / QI WEN; pg. 721 © Bettmann / CORBIS; pg. 723 Roy Miles Fine Paintings; pg. 726 Courtesy of the Library of Congress; pg. 728 Réunion des Musées Nationaux / Art Resource, NY; pg. 730 © The Granger Collection, New York; pg. 732 Courtesy of the Library of Congress; pg. 735 (top) University of British Columbia Library, Rare Books and Special Collections; pg. 735 (bottom) Courtesy of the Library of Congress; pg. 737 akg-images; pg. 740 V&A Images, London / Art Resource, NY.

Chapter 22: pg. 746–747 © Trustees of the British Museum; pg. 752 Stock Sales WGBH / Scala / Art Resource, NY; pg. 754 Courtesy of the Library of Congress; pg. 756 (top left) © Bettmann / CORBIS; pg. 756 (bottom left) © Gianni Dagli Orti / CORBIS; pg. 756 (right) © Gianni Dagli Orti / CORBIS; pg. 758 © Gianni Dagli Orti / CORBIS; pg. 759 Courtesy of the Library of Congress; pg. 760 Musée de l'Armée / Dist. Réunion des Musées Nationaux / Art Resource, NY; pg. 763 SSPL / Science Museum / Art Resource, NY; pg. 767 (top) Courtesy of the Library of Congress; pg. 767 (bottom) Courtesy of the Library of Congress; pg. 768 bpk, Berlin / Art Resource, N; pg. 771 © Lebrecht Music & Arts / Corbis; pg. 773 © The Print Collector / Corbis; pg. 774 © Hulton-Deutsch Collection / CORBIS; pg. 778 National Folklore Collection, University College Dublin; pg. 781 (top left) National Gallery, London / Art Resource, NY; pg. 781 (bottom left) Erich Lessing / Art Resource, NY; pg 781 (right) Saturn Devouring one of his Children, 1821–23 (oil on canvas), Goya y Lucientes, Francisco Jose de (1746–1828) / Prado, Madrid, Spain / The Bridgeman Art Library International; pg. 782 © Hulton-Deutsch Collection / CORBIS.

Chapter 23: pg. 786–787 Courtesy of the Library of Congress; pg. 792 SSPL via Getty Images; pg. 793 The 'Ma Roberts' and an Elephant in the Shallows, Lower Zambezi, 1859, Baines, Thomas (1820–75) / Royal Geographical Society, London, UK / The Bridgeman Art Library

International; pg. 800 Peter Newark Military Pictures; pg. 804 © Bettmann / CORBIS; pg. 806 The Stapleton Collection; pg. 807 © Bettmann / CORBIS; pg. 809 (top) Archives Charmet; pg. 809 (bottom) © Everett Collection Inc / Alamy; pg. 810 Photo: IAM / akg-images; pg. 811 Archives Charmet; pg. 812 Peter Newark Pictures; pg. 814 Professor Darwin, 'This is the ape of form' Love's Labour's Lost, Act V, scene II, Charles Darwin (1809–72) as an ape, 1861 (colour litho), English School, (19th century) / Natural History Museum, London, UK / The Bridgeman Art Library International; pg. 816 akg-images / ullstein bild; pg. 818 (left) The Scream, 1893 (oil, tempera & pastel on cardboard), Munch, Edvard (1863–1944) / Nasjonalgalleriet, Oslo, Norway / © DACS / The Bridgeman Art Library International; pg. 818 (right) Giraudon.

Chapter 24: pg. 822–823 © Philadelphia Museum of Art / CORBIS; pg. 827 (left) The Art Archive; pg. 827 (right) Courtesy of the Library of Congress; pg. 829 The Art Archive / Eileen Tweedy; pg. 833 (top) National Palace Museum; pg. 833 (bottom) © The Print Collector / Heritage / The Image Works; pg. 834 (left) akg-images / British Library; pg. 834 (right) Peter Newark Pictures; pg. 837 (top left) © Philadelphia Museum of Art / CORBIS; pg. 837 (top right) © Philadelphia Museum of Art / CORBIS; pg. 837 (bottom) © Mary Evans Picture Library / The Image Works; pg. 838 Tz'U-Hsi (1835–1908) Empress Dowager of China with ladies of the court, 1903 (b / w photo), Chinese School, (20th century) / Private Collection / The Bridgeman Art Library International; pg. 841 (top) Courtesy of the Library of Congress; pg. 841 (bottom) Courtesy of the Library of Congress; pg. 842 IAM / akg / NA; pg. 851 Courtesy of the Library of Congress; pg. 853 © Mary Evans Picture Library / The Image Works; pg. 854 Courtesy of the Library of Congress.

Chapter 25: pg. 858–859 Auction of Serfs, 1910 (w/c on paper), Lebedev, Klavdiy Vasilievich (1852–1916) / Arkhangelsk Museum, Russia / The Bridgeman Art Library International; pg. 865 (top) Bibliothèque nationale de France or BnF; pg. 865 (middle) Réunion des Musées Nationaux / Art Resource, NY; pg. 865 (bottom) akg-images / British Library; pg. 867 © Bettmann / CORBIS; pg. 869 © Bettmann / CORBIS; pg. 870 (top) Courtesy of the Library of Congress; pg. 870 (bottom) Portrait of George Gordon (1788–1824) 6th Baron Byron of Rochdale in Albanian Dress, 1813 (oil on canvas), Phillips, Thomas (1770–1845) / National Portrait Gallery, London, UK / The Bridgeman Art Library International; pg. 875 © Roger-Viollet / The Image Works; pg. 876 (left) © Diego Lezama Orezzoli / CORBIS; pg. 876 (top right) © Tibor Bognar / Corbis; pg. 876 (bottom right) © Paule Seux / Hemis / Corbis; pg. 877 Courtesy of the New York Public Library; pg. 879 Courtesy of the Library of Congress; pg. 883 © Heritage Images / Corbis; pg.887 © Reproduced by permission of The State Hermitage Museum, St. Petersburg, Russia / CORBIS; pg. 893 RIA Novosti.

Chapter 26: pg. 896–897 Kharbine Tapabor; pg. 900 (top) © National Portrait Gallery, London; pg. 900 (bottom) (c) The British Library Board, Add.Or.3079; pg. 903 (top) The Art Archive / United Society for Propagation of Gospel / Eileen Tweedy; pg. 903 (bottom) © CORBIS; pg. 906 / akg-images / British Library; pg. 908 (top) Réunion des Musées Nationaux / Art Resource, NY; pg. 908 (bottom) Archives Charmet; pg. 910 Dorling Kindersley; pg. 912 National Library of Australia; pg. 913 Werner Forman / Art Resource, NY; pg. 915 Snark / Art Resource, NY; pg. 917 © Hulton-Deutsch Collection / CORBIS; pg. 921 Getty Images; pg. 922 © Bojan Brecelj / CORBIS; pg. 923 ullstein bild / The Granger Collection , New York; pg. 926 (left) Werner Forman / Art Resource, NY; pg. 926 (top right) HIP / Art Resource, NY; pg. 926 (bottom right) © Stapleton Collection / Corbis; pg. 929 Courtesy of the Library of Congress; pg. 930 Courtesy of the Library of Congress.

Chapter 27: pg. 934–935 The Jacob and Gwendolyn Lawrence Foundation / Art Resource, NY; pg. 939 Battle on Santo Domingo, a painting by January Suchodolski; pg. 940 Schalkwijk / Art Resource, NY; pg. 945 Erich Lessing / Art Resource, NY; pg. 946 (left) Published by permission of the Archival Center, Archdiocese of Los Angeles; pg. 946 (right) Ralph Arnold Collection, Huntington Library, San Marino, California; pg. 947 © CORBIS; pg. 949 (top) Rebecca Emery / Getty Images; pg 949 (bottom) Win Initiative (Getty Images); pg. 954 The Granger Collection, New York; pg. 955 Schomburg Center for Research in Black Culture / Manuscripts, Archives and Rare Books Division / New York Public Library; pg. 957 Courtesy of the Library of Congress; pg. 962 © Bettmann / CORBIS; pg. 965 Courtesy of the Library of Congress; pg. 966 © akg-images / The Image Works.

Chapter 28: pg. 974–975 Courtesy of the Library of Congress; pg. 977 © Hulton-Deutsch Collection / CORBIS; pg. 980 Popperfoto / Getty Images; pg. 984 Courtesy of the Library of Congress; pg. 986 Getty Images; pg. 990 The Granger Collection, NYC—All rights reserved; pg. 991 (left) © The Museum of Modern Art / Licensed by SCALA / Art Resource, NY; pg. 991 (top right) © The Museum of Modern Art / Licensed by SCALA / Art Resource, NY; pg. 991 (bottom left) © 2007 Artists Rights Society (ARS), New York / VEGAP, Madrid; pg. 994 © Instructional Resources Corporation; pg. 995 Getty Images; pg. 996 Getty Images; pg. 1000 © Bettmann / CORBIS; pg. 1002 © K.J. Historical / CORBIS; pg. 1006 © Hulton-Deutsch Collection / CORBIS; pg. 1007 © Arcaid / Corbis; pg. 1010 Courtesy of the Library of Congress; pg. 1014 Getty Images; pg. 1016 © Bettmann / CORBIS.

Chapter 29: pg. 1020–1021 Getty Images; pg. 1023 Time & Life Pictures / Getty Images; pg. 1027 Associated Press; pg. 1029 © Bettmann / CORBIS; pg. 1030 © Rykoff Collection / CORBIS; pg. 1032 © CORBIS; pg. 1033 SSPL via Getty Images; pg. 1034 ABC via Getty Images; pg. 1035 Chris Brown; pg. 1038 (left) © The Museum of Modern Art / Licensed by SCALA / Art Resource, NY; pg. 1038 (right) © 2009 Museum Associates / LACMA / Art Resource, NY; pg. 1044 Courtesy of the Library of Congress; pg. 1045 AFP / Getty Images; pg. 1049 Courtesy of the Library of Congress; pg. 1051 © Volkmar K. Wentzel / National Geographic Society / Corbis; pg. 1052 Courtesy of the Library of Congress.

Chapter 30: pg. 1060–1061 © Alain DeJean / Sygma / CORBIS; pg. 1064 Courtesy of Spacephotos.ru; pg. 1065 © CORBIS; pg. 1067 © Robert Maass / CORBIS; pg. 1069 AP Photo / Yuri Romanov; pg. 1074 (top left) © Bettmann / CORBIS; pg 1074 (top right) © Jack Moebes / CORBIS; pg. 1074 (bottom) © Bettmann / CORBIS; pg. 1077 (top) © Bettmann / CORBIS; pg. 1077 (bottom) India Today Group / Getty Images; pg. 1078 (left) © Henry Diltz / CORBIS; pg. 1078 (right) © Bettmann / CORBIS; pg. 1083 © Bettmann / CORBIS; pg. 1086 (left) © Jacques Langevin / Sygma / Corbis; pg. 1086 (right) © Reuters / CORBIS; pg. 1088 (top) © Tim Page / CORBIS; pg. 1088 (bottom) © Bettmann / CORBIS; pg. 1091 © Bettmann / CORBIS; pg. 1092 Courtesy of the Library of Congress; pg. 1095 © Bernard Bisson / Sygma / Corbis.

Chapter 31: pg. 1100–1001 Getty Images Europe; pg. 1110 © Hubert Boesl / dpa / Corbis; pg. 1113 Courtesy of Eliot Borenstein; pg. 1114 (left) © Lee Frost / Robert Harding World Imagery / Corbis; pg. 1114 (right) Getty Images; pg. 1115 (top) ASSOCIATED PRESS; pg. 1115 (bottom) AP Images; pg. 1120 © Manca Juvan / In Pictures / Corbis; pg. 1123 AFP / Getty Images; pg. 1124 © Samuel Aranda / Corbis; pg. 1126 Associated Press; pg. 1128 Associated Press; pg. 1129 © Louise Gubb / CORBIS SABA; pg. 1136 AFP / Getty Images.

Notes

Chapter 3: p. 86 Translated by R. N. Dandekar, in Sources of Indian Tradition, Ainslie T. Emree, ed., 2nd Ed., Vol I (New York: Columbia University Press, 1988) p. 247; p. 88 Translated by Joel Brereton, in Sources [same ed. As above; p. 19; p. 89 Yajnavalkya Smirti, (Code of Vajnavalkya), R.N.Dandekar in Sources, p. 227–8]; p. 89 From Manu Smriti [The Code of Manu], Ibid. [same translator], pp. 228–9.

Chapter 5: p. 140 Greg Borzo, "Anthropologists Establish Date and Importance of the Americas' Oldest City," The Field Musueum, Chicago, Museum Notes, April 26, 2001; http://www.fmnh.org/museum_info/press/press_hass.htm.

Chapter 11: p. 367 Abbot Suger: On the Abbey Church of St.-Denis and Its Art Treasures, ed., trans., and annotated by Erwin Panofsky, (Princeton, 1946), pp. 100--01; 375–376 Dante, Monarchia, trans. and ed. By Prue Shaw (Cambridge: Cambridge University Press, 1995), Book One, ch. 5, part 3, p. 15.

Chapter 20: p 688–689 John F. Richards, The Mughal Empire, in The New Cambridge History of India (Cambridge: Cambridge University Press, 1995), p.105; p. 688–689 From Muhammad Sadiq, "Shahjahan-Nama," (The autobiography of Shah Jahan) quoted in Richards, The Mughal Empire, p. 135.

Chapter 21: p. 714–715 See Kenneth Pomeranz, The Great Divergence. China, Europe, and the Making of the Modern World Economy, (Princeton, NJ: Princeton University Press, 2001.)

Chapter 23: p 747 Mary Paul to Bela Paul, September 13, November 20, December 21, 1845, November 27, 1853, in Thomas Dublin, Farm to Factory: Women's Letters, 1830–1860, (New York: Columbia University Press, 1993), pp. 124–125, 128, 135; p. 808 Karl Marx, Friedrich Engels, The Communist Manifesto. A Modern Edition. With an introduction by Eric Hobsbawm, (London: Verso, 2001) p. 77.

Chapter 24: p. 822–824 All quotes in the vignette are from John K., and Su-yu Teng. China's Response to the West. Cambridge, MA: Harvard University Press, 1954. p. 126; p. 832 Prince Gong to Rutherford Alcock, 1869, quoted in Robert Hart, These From the Land of Sinim (London: Chapman and Hall,1901), p. 68

Chapter 31: p. 1102 Dexter Filkins, "After the Uprising," The New Yorker (online edition) (April, 11, 2011), pp. 5; Sudarsan Raghavan, "In Yemen, Female Activist Struggles for an Egypt-like Revolution," The Washington Post, February 15, 2011, Section A, p, 1; p. 1127 NY Times, February 14, 2011. Ibid. "explosives" quote from IPT News, December 10, 2010; p. 1130–1131 NY Times, February 14, 2011.

Index

The letter f following a page number denotes a figure or map.